Twentieth-Century Literary Criticism

Guide to Gale Literary Criticism Series

For criticism on	Consult these Gale series
Authors now living or who died after December 31, 1959	*CONTEMPORARY LITERARY CRITICISM (CLC)*
Authors who died between 1900 and 1959	*TWENTIETH-CENTURY LITERARY CRITICISM (TCLC)*
Authors who died between 1800 and 1899	*NINETEENTH-CENTURY LITERATURE CRITICISM (NCLC)*
Authors who died between 1400 and 1799	*LITERATURE CRITICISM FROM 1400 TO 1800 (LC)* *SHAKESPEAREAN CRITICISM (SC)*
Authors who died before 1400	*CLASSICAL AND MEDIEVAL LITERATURE CRITICISM (CMLC)*
Authors of books for children and young adults	*CHILDREN'S LITERATURE REVIEW (CLR)*
Dramatists	*DRAMA CRITICISM (DC)*
Poets	*POETRY CRITICISM (PC)*
Short story writers	*SHORT STORY CRITICISM (SSC)*
Black writers of the past two hundred years	*BLACK LITERATURE CRITICISM (BLC)*
Hispanic writers of the late nineteenth and twentieth centuries	*HISPANIC LITERATURE CRITICISM (HLC)*
Native North American writers and orators of the eighteenth, nineteenth, and twentieth centuries	*NATIVE NORTH AMERICAN LITERATURE (NNAL)*
Major authors from the Renaissance to the present	*WORLD LITERATURE CRITICISM, 1500 TO THE PRESENT (WLC)*

ISSN 0276-8178

R

Volume 92

Twentieth-Century Literary Criticism

**Criticism of the
Works of Novelists, Poets, Playwrights,
Short Story Writers, and Other Creative Writers
Who Lived between 1900 and 1960,
from the First Published Critical
Appraisals to Current Evaluations**

Jennifer Baise
Editor

Thomas Ligotti
Associate Editor

GALE GROUP

Detroit
New York
San Francisco
London
Boston
Woodbridge, CT

STAFF

Jennifer Baise, *Editor*

Thomas Ligotti, *Associate Editor*

Maria Franklin, *Permissions Manager*
Kimberly F. Smilay, *Permissions Specialist*
Kelly A. Quin, *Permissions Associates*
Sandy Gore, *Permissions Assistant*

Victoria B. Cariappa, *Research Manager*
Andrew Guy Malonis, Barbara McNeil, Gary J. Oudersluys, Maureen Richards, Cheryl L. Warnock, *Research Specialists*
Patricia T. Ballard, Tamara C. Nott, Tracie A. Richardson, *Research Associates*
Phyllis Blackman, Corrine Stocker, *Research Assistant*

Mary Beth Trimper, *Production Director*
Stacy L. Melson, *Buyer*

Gary Leach, *Graphic Artist*
Randy Bassett, *Image Database Supervisor*
Robert Duncan, Michael Logusz, *Imaging Specialists*
Pamela Reed, *Imaging Coordinator*

Library of Congress Catalog Card Number 76-46132
ISBN 0-7876-2749-6
ISSN 0276-8178

Printed in the United States of America
10 9 8 7 6 5 4 3 2 1

Contents

Preface   vii

Acknowledgments   xi

Preface

Since its inception more than fifteen years ago, *Twentieth-Century Literary Criticism* has been purchased and used by nearly 10,000 school, public, and college or university libraries. *TCLC* has covered more than 500 authors, representing 58 nationalities, and over 25,000 titles. No other reference source has surveyed the critical response to twentieth-century authors and literature as thoroughly as *TCLC*. In the words of one reviewer, "there is nothing comparable available." *TCLC* "is a gold mine of information—dates, pseudonyms, biographical information, and criticism from books and periodicals—which many libraries would have difficulty assembling on their own."

Scope of the Series

TCLC is designed to serve as an introduction to authors who died between 1900 and 1960 and to the most significant interpretations of these author's works. The great poets, novelists, short story writers, playwrights, and philosophers of this period are frequently studied in high school and college literature courses. In organizing and reprinting the vast amount of critical material written on these authors, *TCLC* helps students develop valuable insight into literary history, promotes a better understanding of the texts, and sparks ideas for papers and assignments. Each entry in *TCLC* presents a comprehensive survey of an author's career or an individual work of literature and provides the user with a multiplicity of interpretations and assessments. Such variety allows students to pursue their own interests; furthermore, it fosters an awareness that literature is dynamic and responsive to many different opinions.

Every fourth volume of *TCLC* is devoted to literary topics. These topic entries widen the focus of the series from individual authors to such broader subjects as literary movements, prominent themes in twentieth-century literature, literary reaction to political and historical events, significant eras in literary history, prominent literary anniversaries, and the literatures of cultures that are often overlooked by English-speaking readers.

TCLC is designed as a companion series to Gale's *Contemporary Literary Criticism,* which reprints commentary on authors now living or who have died since 1960. Because of the different periods under consideration, there is no duplication of material between *CLC* and *TCLC*. For additional information about *CLC* and Gale's other criticism titles, users should consult the Guide to Gale Literary Criticism Series preceding the title page in this volume.

Coverage

Each volume of *TCLC* is carefully compiled to present:

- criticism of authors, or literary topics, representing a variety of genres and nationalities

- both major and lesser-known writers and literary works of the period

- 6-12 authors or 3-6 topics per volume

- individual entries that survey critical response to each author's work or each topic in literary history, including early criticism to reflect initial reactions; later criticism to represent any rise or decline in reputation; and current retrospective analyses.

Organization of This Book

An author entry consists of the following elements: author heading, biographical and critical introduction, list of principal works, reprints of criticism (each preceded by an annotation and a bibliographic citation), and a bibliography of further reading.

- The **Author Heading** consists of the name under which the author most commonly wrote, followed by birth and death dates. If an author wrote consistently under a pseudonym, the pseudonym will be listed in the author heading and the real name given in parentheses on the first line of the biographical and critical introduction. Also located at the beginning of the introduction to the author entry are any name variations under which an author wrote, including transliterated forms for authors whose languages use nonroman alphabets.

- The **Biographical and Critical Introduction** outlines the author's life and career, as well as the critical issues surrounding his or her work. References to past volumes of *TCLC* are provided at the beginning of the introduction. Additional sources of information in other biographical and critical reference series published by Gale, including *Short Story Criticism, Children's Literature Review, Contemporary Authors, Dictionary of Literary Biography,* and *Something about the Author,* are listed in a box at the end of the entry.

- Some *TCLC* entries include **Portraits** of the author. Entries also may contain reproductions of materials pertinent to an author's career, including manuscript pages, title pages, dust jackets, letters, and drawings, as well as photographs of important people, places, and events in an author's life.

- The **List of Principal Works** is chronological by date of first book publication and identifies the genre of each work. In the case of foreign authors with both foreign-language publications and English translations, the title and date of the first English-language edition are given in brackets. Unless otherwise indicated, dramas are dated by first performance, not first publication.

- Critical essays are prefaced by **Annotations** providing the reader with information about both the critic and the criticism that follows. Included are the critic's reputation, individual approach to literary criticism, and particular expertise in an author's works. Also noted are the relative importance of a work of criticism, the scope of the essay, and the growth of critical controversy or changes in critical trends regarding an author. In some cases, these annotations cross-reference essays by critics who discuss each other's commentary.

- A complete **Bibliographic Citation** designed to facilitate location of the original essay or book precedes each piece of criticism.

- Criticism is arranged chronologically in each author entry to provide a perspective on changes in critical evaluation over the years. All titles of works by the author featured in the entry are printed in boldface type to enable the user to easily locate discussion of particular works. Also for purposes of easier identification, the critic's name and the publication date of the essay are given at the beginning of each piece of criticism. Unsigned criticism is preceded by the title of the journal in which it appeared. Some of the essays in *TCLC* also contain translated material. Unless otherwise noted, translations in brackets are by the editors; translations in parentheses or continuous with the text are by the critic. Publication information (such as footnotes or page and line references to specific editions of works) have been deleted at the editor's discretion to provide smoother reading of the text.

- An annotated list of **Further Reading** appearing at the end of each author entry suggests secondary sources on the author. In some cases it includes essays for which the editors could not obtain reprint rights.

Cumulative Indexes

- Each volume of *TCLC* contains a cumulative **Author Index** listing all authors who have appeared in Gale's Literary Criticism Series, along with cross references to such biographical series as *Contemporary Authors* and *Dictionary of Literary Biography*. For readers' convenience, a complete list of Gale titles included appears on the first page of the author index. Useful for locating authors within the various series, this index is particularly valuable for those authors who are identified by a certain period but who, because of their death dates, are placed in another, or for those authors whose careers span two periods. For example, F. Scott Fitzgerald is found in *TCLC,* yet a writer often associated with him, Ernest Hemingway, is found in *CLC.*

●Each *TCLC* volume includes a cumulative **Nationality Index** which lists all authors who have appeared in *TCLC* volumes, arranged alphabetically under their respective nationalities, as well as Topics volume entries devoted to particular national literatures.

●Each new volume in Gale's Literary Criticism Series includes a cumulative **Topic Index,** which lists all literary topics treated in *NCLC, TCLC, LC 1400-1800,* and the *CLC* yearbook.

●Each new volume of *TCLC*, with the exception of the Topics volumes, includes a **Title Index** listing the titles of all literary works discussed in the volume. In response to numerous suggestions from librarians, Gale has also produced a **Special Paperbound Edition** of the *TCLC* title index. This annual cumulation lists all titles discussed in the series since its inception and is issued with the first volume of *TCLC* published each year. Additional copies of the index are available on request. Librarians and patrons will welcome this separate index; it saves shelf space, is easy to use, and is recyclable upon receipt of the following year's cumulation. Titles discussed in the Topics volume entries are not included *TCLC* cumulative index.

Citing Twentieth-Century Literary Criticism

When writing papers, students who quote directly from any volume in Gale's literary Criticism Series may use the following general forms to footnote reprinted criticism. The first example pertains to materials drawn from periodicals, the second to material reprinted from books.

[1]William H. Slavick, "Going to School to DuBose Heyward," *The Harlem Renaissance Re-examined,* (AMS Press, 1987); reprinted in *Twentieth-Century Literary Criticism,* Vol. 59, ed. Jennifer Gariepy (Detroit: Gale Research, 1995), pp. 94-105.

[2]George Orwell, "Reflections on Gandhi," *Partisan Review,* 6 (Winter 1949), pp. 85-92; reprinted in *Twentieth-Century Literary Criticism,* Vol. 59, ed. Jennifer Gariepy (Detroit: Gale Research, 1995), pp. 40-3.

Suggestions Are Welcome

In response to suggestions, several features have been added to *TCLC* since the series began, including annotations to critical essays, a cumulative index to authors in all Gale literary criticism series, entries devoted to criticism on a single work by a major author, more extensive illustrations, and a title index listing all literary works discussed in the series since its inception.

Readers who wish to suggest authors or topics to appear in future volumes, or who have other suggestions, are cordially invited to write the editors.

Acknowledgments

The editors wish to thank the copyright holders of the criticism included in this volume and the permissions managers of many book and magazine publishing companies for assisting us in securing reproduction rights. We are also grateful to the staffs of the Detroit Public Library, the Library of Congress, the University of Detroit Mercy Library, Wayne State University Purdy/Kresge Library Complex, and the University of Michigan Libraries for making their resources available to us. Following is a list of the copyright holders who have granted us permission to reproduce material in this volume of *TCLC*. Every effort has been made to trace copyright, but if omissions have been made, please let us know.

COPYRIGHTED ESSAYS IN *TCLC*, VOLUME 92, WERE REPRODUCED FROM THE FOLLOWING PERIODICALS:

American Book Review, v. 5, January-February, 1983. © 1983 by The American Book Review. Reproduced by permission—*The American Historical Review,* v. 84, April, 1979. Reproduced by permission of the author.—*Art History,* v. 2, June, 1979; v. 17, June, 1994. © 1979, 1994 Reproduced by permission of Blackwell Publishers.—*Art in America,* December, 1982 for "Kandinsky's Book of Revelation" by Carter Ratcliff. Copyright © 1982 by the author. Reprinted by permission of the author.—*Art Journal,* v. 46, Spring, 1987. Reproduced by permission.—*Artforum,* v. XVII, November, 1978 for "Kandinsky and Problems of Abstraction" by Alwynne Mackie. Reproduced by permission of the publisher and author.—*Boundary 2,* v. 20, Spring, 1993. Copyright © 1993 by Duke University Press, Durham, NC. Reproduced by permission.—*Critical Inquiry,* v. 23, Summer, 1997. Copyright © 1997 University of Chicago. Reproduced by permission.—*Critical Quarterly,* v. 35, Spring, 1993. © Manchester University Press 1993. Reproduced by·permission.—*Encounter,* v. LVII, November, 1981 for "Was Stalin (the Terrible) Really a 'Great Man'?: A Conversation with W. Averell Harriman" by George Urban. © 1981 by the author. Reproduced by permission of the author.—*GQ,* v. 60, December, 1990. © 1990 by the author. All rights reserved. Reproduced by permission of the author.—*The Hudson Review,* v. XXVI, Spring, 1973. Copyright © 1973 by The Hudson Review, Inc. Reproduced by permission.—*Humanity and Society,* v. 9, February, 1985. Reproduced by permission of th author.—*Journal of Urban History,* v. 18, May, 1992. © 1992 Sage Publications, Inc. Reproduced by permission.—*Los Angeles Times Book Review,* August 22, 1982. Copyright, 1982, Los Angeles Times. Reproduced by permission.—*The Midwest Quarterly,* v. XXV, Summer, 1984. Copyright © 1984 by The Midwest Quarterly, Pittsburgh State University. Reproduced by permission.—*Mosaic: A Journal for the Interdisciplinary Study of Literature, v. XVII, Summer, 1985.* © Mosaic 1985. Acknowledgment of previous publication is herewith made.—*The Nation,* v. CXLV, December 11, 1937 for "Stalin, Trotsky, and Willi Schlamm" by Edmund Wilson. Copyright, 1937, 1965 by Edmund Wilson. Reprinted by permission of Farrar, Straus & Giroux, Inc. on behalf of the estate of Edmund Wilson.—*New England Review,* v. 18, Winter, 1997 for "Anna Akhmatova: The Stalin Years" by Roberta Reeder. Copyright © 1997 by Middlebury College. Reproduced by permission of the author.—*The New Republic,* v. 213, September 4, 1995. © 1995 The New Republic, Inc. Reproduced by permission of The New Republic.—*The New York Review of Books,* v. XXVIII, August 13, 1981. Copyright © 1981 Nyrev, Inc. Reproduced with permission from The New York Review of Books.—*The New Yorker,* v. XXII, May 4, 1946. © 1946 by The New Yorker Magazine, Inc. © 1973 by Edmund Wilson. All rights reserved. Reprinted by permission of Farrar, Straus & Giroux, Inc. on behalf of the estate of Edmund Wilson. *October,* Spring, 1977. © 1977 by MIT and IAUS. Reproduced by permission of the author.—*The Pacific Spectator,* v. VII, Spring, 1953. Reproduced by permission.—*Paideuma,* v. 21, Winter, 1992 for "The Third Dimension: Ezra Pound and Wassily Kandinsky" by Michael Faherty. Reproduced by permission of the publisher.—*Partisan Review,* v. LVIII, Winter, 1991 for "On the Crimes of Lenin, Stalin, and Hitler" by Lionel Abel. Copyright © 1991 by Partisan Review. Reproduced by permission.—*The Russian Review,* v. 41, October, 1982. Reproduced by permission *Slavic and East European Journal,* v. 23, Winter, 1979. © 1979 by AATSEEL of the U.S., Inc. Reproduced by permission.—*Slavic Review,* v. 50, Spring, 1991. Reproduced by permission.—*Social Forces* v. 37, March, 1959. Copyright © 1959, Social Forces. Renewed July 10, 1987 by University of North Carolina Press. Reprinted by permission of the publisher.—*Soviet Studies,* v. XXVIII, July, 1976. Reproduced by permission.—*The South Atlantic Quarterly,* v. LIX, Winter, 1960. Copyright © 1960, 1978 by Duke University Press, Durham, NC. Reproduced by permission.—*The Wallace Stevens Journal,* v. 16, Fall, 1992. © 1992 The Wallace Stevens Society, Inc. Reproduced by permission.—*The Western Political Quarterly,* v. XXI, September, 1968 for "Dismantling the Cults of Stalin and Khrushchev" by Thomas B. Larson. Reproduced by permission of the publisher and the author.—*Western Humanities Review,* v. XLV, Winter, 1991. Copyright, 1991, University of Utah. Reproduced by permission.—*Wide Angle,* v. 3, 1979. © 1979. Reproduced by permission of The Johns Hopkins University Press.

COPYRIGHTED ESSAYS IN *TCLC*, VOLUME 92, WERE REPRODUCED FROM THE FOLLOWING BOOKS:

Everdell, William R. From *The First Moderns: Profiles in the Origins of Twentieth-Century Thought.* University of Chicago Press, 1997. © 1997 by William Everdell. Reproduced by permission of the publisher and author.—Kester,

Marian. From *Passion and Rebellion: The Expressionist Heritage.* Edited by Stephen Eric Bronner and Douglas Kellner. J. F. Bergin Publishers, Inc., 1983. Copyright © 1983 by J. F. Bergin Publishers, Inc. Reproduced by permission of Greenwood Publishing Group, Inc., Westport, CT.—Lipsey, Roger. From *An Art of Our Own: The Spiritual in Twentieth-Century Art.* Shambhala Publications, Inc. 1988. © 1988 by Roger Lipsey. Reproduced by arrangement with Shambhala Publications, Inc.—Long, Rose-Carol Washton. From *The Life of Vasilii Kandinsky in Russian Art: A Study of On the Spiritual in Art.* Edited by John E. Bowlt and Rose-Carol Washton Long. Translated by John Bowlt. Oriental Research Partners, 1980. © Oriental Research Partners, 1980. Reproduced by permission.— Marsh, Rosalind. From *Images of Dictatorship: Portraits of Stalin in Literature.* Routledge, 1989. © 1989 Rosalind Marsh. Reproduced by permission.—Napier, Elizabeth R. From an introduction to *Wassily Kandinsky: Sounds.* Translated by Elizabeth R. Napier. Yale University Press, 1981. Copyright © 1981 by Yale University. Reproduced by permission.—Parry, Albert. From *Terrorism: From Robespierre to Arafat.* The Vanguard Press, Inc., 1976. Copyright © 1976 by Albert Parry. Reproduced by permission of Random House, Inc.—Read, Herbert. From *Art and Alienation: The Role of the Artist in Society.* Horizon Press, 1967. © Herbert Read Discretionary Trust 1967. Reproduced by permission.—Reiss, Albert J. Jr. From an introduction to *On Cities and Social Life* by Louis Wirth. The University of Chicago, 1964. © 1964 by The University of Chicago. Reproduced by permission of the publisher and the author.—Selz, Peter. From *German Expressionist Painting.* University of California Press, 1957. © 1957 by the Regents of the University of California. Renewed October 15, 1985 by Peter Selz. Reproduced by permission. Thiher, Allen. From *The Cinematic Muse: Critical Studies in the History of French Cinema.* University of Missouri Press, 1979. Copyright © 1979 by the Curators of the University of Missouri. Reproduced by permission.—White, E. B. From *Essays of E. B. White.* Harper & Row, Publishers, 1977. Copyright © 1934, 1939, 1941, 1947, 1949, 1954, 1955, 1956, 1957, 1958, 1960, 1961, 1963, 1966, 1971, 1975, 1977 by E. B. White. Reproduced by permission of HarperCollins Publishers, Inc.—Williams, Robert C. From *Russia Imagined: Art, Culture, and National Identity, 1840-1995.* Peter Lang, 1997. © 1997 Peter Lang Publishing, Inc., New York. Reproduced by permission.

PHOTOGRAPHS AND ILLUSTRATIONS APPEARING IN *TCLC*, VOLUME 92, WERE RECEIVED FROM THE FOLLOWING SOURCES:

Kandinsky, Vasili, photograph. The Bettmann Archive. Reproduced by permission.

Jean Epstein

1897–1953

French director, poet, and critic.

INTRODUCTION

One of the foremost directors of the French silent cinema, Epstein is also remembered as a cinematic theorist whose writings such as *Ecrits sur le cinema* examined the philosophical impact of film. Epstein's works, considered precursors of the avant-garde movement in film, are admired for their visual modernity and innovative techniques. His use of cinematic devices such as close ups, overlapping images, and non-sequential narrative foreshadowed techniques that would not be employed by other filmmakers for several decades. The creative nature of Epstein's best-known works, such as *La chute de la maison Usher* (*The Fall of the House of Usher*) and *Coeur fidèle,* offers a significant artistic transition between the experimental nature of silent films and the French *Nouvelle Vague* (New Wave) movement of the 1960s.

Biographical Information

Epstein was born in Warsaw into a Jewish family. When his father died in 1908, the family relocated to Switzerland, where he attended secondary school. He attended university in Lyon, France, and received a medical degree. At Lyon, he met the pioneer filmmaker Auguste Lumière. Influenced by the works of American directors Charlie Chaplin and D. W. Griffith, Epstein and Lumière founded a film journal, *Le promenoir,* in 1920. The next year, Epstein published *Bonjour cinema,* a treatise on poetry, photography and the nature of the relatively new artistic medium of film. The positive response to his early films such as *Pasteur,* the biography of scientist Louis Pasteur, allowed Epstein to set up his own production company, *Les Films Jean Epstein.* In a short time, he produced a number of diverse films, including *The Fall of the House of Usher* and *La glace à trois faces.* However, with the advent of sound technology, Epstein's experimental works fell out of favor, and he relocated to Brittany, where he made short films and documentaries. At the beginning of World War II, Epstein and his sister were captured by the Gestapo, but they were not deported. Unable to make films because of the German occupation in France, Epstein worked for the Red Cross and honed his writing skills. In 1947, he returned to Brittany, where he finished his career with several critically acclaimed films, most notably *Le tempestaire,* the tale of a French fisherman. Although Epstein continued to write, he ceased filmmaking shortly thereafter. In 1953, he died of a cerebral hemorrhage.

Major Works

Epstein's first film, *Pasteur,* was a biography that did not display the cinematic innovations of later films. *Coeur fidèle,* the story of a romantic triangle, however, utilized such innovative devices as non-sequential timelines and flashback sequences. Epstein strapped the camera to a merry-go-round at one point to provide images of increasing twirling and dizziness. The startlingly inventive and fantastic elements of Epstein's early works such as *Mauprat,* are considered a precursor of works of the Spanish filmmaker Luis Buñuel, who worked with Epstein on his early films. However, the frequently surreal and experimental content of these works hindered both their critical and popular success. One of Epstein's most highly regarded films, *La glace à trois faces* tells the story of a young man with three mistresses. When he suddenly dies, the women describe him in such diverse ways it appears that they know three different men. This film's visual inventiveness is displayed in overlapping images and use of the close-up, Epstein's favorite cinematic device. *The Fall of the House Of Usher,* based on Edgar Allan Poe's short story, is the tale of an artist who paints his wife's portrait. However, he finds that as he works, her health fails. Here, Epstein's cinematic devices that anticipate works of filmmakers several decades later include innovative lighting, flashbacks, and slow-motion photography. Epstein's first Breton film, *Finis terrae* is shot as a documentary but utilizes innovative camera styles. *Le tempestaire* is considered by many critics to be the culmination of his most experimental techniques, such as slowed sound and overlapping visual elements. In this film, Epstein rejected the romanticism and extravagance that typified Hollywood productions in favor of simplicity and realism, a philosophy mirrored in his life as well as his art.

Critical Reception

Although Epstein is not well known today, modern filmmakers' aesthetic and stylistic debt to him is apparent with the advent of the cinematic avant-garde movement. His films are rarely shown, but limited recent viewings have served to emphasize his modernity. Many of his techniques, in fact, were so advanced that they have only been recently been identified as foreshadowing contemporary cinematic devices. Today, Epstein is remembered as a filmmaker and theorist who sought to continuously examine the connection between the viewer and the screen.

PRINCIPAL WORKS

Bonjour cinema (essays and poetry) 1921
La poésie d'aujourd'hui (poetry) 1921
Pasteur (film) 1922
L'auberge rouge (film) 1923
La belle nivernaise (film) 1923
Coeur fidèle (film) 1923
La montagne infidèle (film) 1923
L'affiche (film) 1924
Le lion des mogols (film) 1924
Les aventures de Robert Macaire (film) 1925
Le double amour (film) 1925
Mauprat (film) 1926
La glace à trois faces (film) 1927
Six et demi onze (un kodak) (film) 1927
La chute de la maison Usher (film) 1928
Finis terrae (film) 1929
Sa tête (film) 1929
Le pas de la mule (film) 1930
Mor-Vran (film) 1931
L'homme à l'Hispano (film) 1932
L'or des mers (film) 1932
La chatelaine du Liban (film) 1933
Le cinema du diable (essays) 1947
L'intelligence d'une machine (essays) 1947
Le tempestaire (film) 1947
Les feux de la mer (film) 1948
Esprit du cinema (essays) 1955
Ecrits sur le cinema (essays) 1974

CRITICISM

Catherine Wunscher (essay date 1953)

SOURCE: "Jean Epstein," in *Sight and Sound,* Vol. 23, No. 2, October-December, 1953, p. 106.

[*In the following essay, Wunscher praises the magical elements of Epstein's work, noting that their lack of dialogue provides a more pure cinematic experience.*]

Being about the same age as the sound film myself, I am one of the generation that was astonished when the characters in *Modern Times* didn't talk. Of course, since that time, I have seen *Potemkin, Caligari, La Charrette Fantome, The Kid, Greed, Metropolis, Chapeau de Paille d'Italie,* etc., but I have never been as fascinated by silent images as I was by Jean Epstein's, whose shadows have outlived him. Again, I had never before realised how much the screen lost when it was allowed to talk. Living in a white frame, Epstein's phantoms take on an independent existence, a true gift of mystery and enchantment.

After having seen for the first time, at the rate of three a day, most of Jean Epstein's films, my judgment is somewhat paralysed. What can one say, except that they are beautiful, with the incontestable beauty of masterworks? Epstein gave me something I had been vainly searching for in contemporary production (and had failed to find except in Renoir and Ford): a purely cinematic emotion, a beauty based uniquely on rhythm and the plastic perfection of moving images.

While these memories are still fresh, I must try to analyse something of what I found.

Up to ***La Chute de la Maison Usher*** (1928), Epstein's films seem curiously *demodé*. Certainly, there are some remarkable moments—the night sequence and the execution in ***L'Auberge Rouge*** (1923), the two lovers meeting by the water's edge and the country fair in ***Coeur Fidèle*** (1923), the automobile death race in ***La Glace à Trois Faces*** (1927); but the "modernistic" and historical styles of decor appear restrictive now. When one remembers that he made these films between the ages of 25 and 29 (he was born in Warsaw, of a French father, in 1897), one is inclined to reconsider this verdict; yet the general impression persists.

La Chute de la Maison Usher stands a little apart from the rest of his work. (It is little known, incidentally, that Bunuel was the assistant director.) The film contains some unforgettable imagery: the vistas of corridors with a wind sweeping down them, the bizarre hangings, guttering candles, the supernatural features of Madame Gance, and the splendid, marvellous, strange and too brief sequence of the burial, in which four men, walking through a landscape stripped bare by autumn, carry a white coffin behind which floats a long white veil. Edgar Allan Poe was not betrayed.

But the real revelation comes with ***Finis Terrae*** (1929), and continues up to ***Le Tempestaire*** (1947), films with a love and understanding of the sea, of Brittany, and of simple, noble, hard-pressed people. Before writing of Rossellini and the birth of neo-realism, critics should look at these films by Epstein. All the beauty of the austere images in the final scene of *Paisa* is already there in 1929, in Epstein's figures stretched out on a white sandy beach, scarcely distinguishable from the surrounding rocks.

The actors in these films are not only Bretons and thickset Breton women, always in mourning for a loved one; they are, too, the unceasing wind, blowing salt water spray along with itself, flattening the drenched manes of horses, swallowing up candle flames, eddying peasant women's skirts already soaked by the rain and the sea, fluttering black veils against a grey sky—the wind that twists round trees, bends flimsy grasses, sharpens the sound of horses galloping on the little island of Bannec; and, above all, the sea, that Epstein never tires of photographing—calm, crowned with circlets of foam, swelling, breaking ceaselessly on the rocks, sending up its immaculate foam to fall again, slowly, on succeeding waves; the sea of great storms, sometimes throwing up an oar, sometimes a body, sometimes a necklace, sometimes a mysterious casket, containing, perhaps, *L'Or des Mers:* the sea by which these people are obliged to live, and by which they are punished. Unlike the Flaherty of *Man of Aran*, Epstein does not describe exceptional circumstances, but a people whom he watched living day by day, his eyes opened wide by love. Sometimes, unconsciously, one licks one's lips, astonished not to find the taste of salt on them.

Epstein's films are slow; when their narrative finally reaches its end, it seems to be because life has brought it there. He is never chary of lingering over a detail—on the contrary, his stories are often composed only of details, integrated into a complete fresco. He will dwell on the limbs, the walk of a character if the motion fascinates him, on shrivelled hands, a handkerchief being dropped, a single face. He will contemplate a pool of water with the rain driving into it (*L'Auberge Rouge*), a face reflected in a tarnished mirror (*Coeur Fidèle*), a bleeding hand (*Finis Terrae*), faces that exchange long and slow glances, an Ile de France landscape: or, simply, the sea whose last secret he seems determined to prise out.

His characters are never in a hurry. They live their daily lives under our eyes, performing the innumerable everyday acts and gestures that make up their "plot"; but one doesn't for a moment long for the feverish rhythm of most of today's films, in which nothing is allowed unless it advances the action; the montage of Epstein's films gives them a rhythm which is like the rhythm of breathing.

The term "magician of the screen" has been used and abused. Jean Epstein is one of the few who perhaps deserve it. The little girl in love in *Coeur Fidèle,* and her crippled friend, Lady Usher, the Breton fishermen and their families, the passionate poetic images of men and nature, these will live with the breath of love that Jean Epstein gave them.

Jean Epstein (essay date 1974)

SOURCE: "Magnification, and other Writings," in *October*, No. 3, Spring, 1977, pp. 9-25.

[*In the following excerpt, which was originally published in French in 1974 as part of* Ecrits sur le cinema, *Epstein expounds on the cinematic concepts of the close-up and the different means by which he conveys the passing of time in his films.*]

I will never find the way to say how I love American close-ups. Point blank. A head suddenly appears on screen and drama, now face to face, seems to address me personally and swells with an extraordinary intensity. I am hypnotized. Now the tragedy is anatomical. The decor of the fifth act is this corner of a cheek torn by a smile. Waiting for the moment when 1,000 meters of intrigue converge in a muscular *dénoument* satisfies me more than

the rest of the film. Muscular preambles ripple beneath the skin. Shadows shift, tremble, hesitate. Something is being decided. A breeze of emotion underlines the mouth with clouds. The orography of the face vacillates. Seismic shocks begin. Capillary wrinkles try to split the fault. A wave carries them away. Crescendo. A muscle bridles. The lip is laced with tics like a theater curtain. Everything is movement, imbalance, crisis. Crack. The mouth gives way, like a ripe fruit splitting open. As if slit by a scalpel, a keyboard-like smile cuts laterally into the corner of the lips.

The close-up is the soul of the cinema. It can be brief because the value of the photogenic is measured in seconds. If it is too long, I don't find continuous pleasure in it. Intermittent paroxysms affect me the way needles do. Until now, I have never seen an entire minute of pure photogeny. Therefore, one must admit that the photogenic is like a spark that appears in fits and starts. It imposes a *découpage* a thousand times more detailed than that of most films, even American ones. Mincemeat. Even more beautiful than a laugh is the face preparing for it. I must interrupt. I love the mouth which is about to speak and holds back, the gesture which hesitates between right and left, the recoil before the leap, and the moment before landing, the becoming, the hesitation, the taut spring, the prelude, and even more than all these, the piano being tuned before the overture. The photogenic is conjugated in the future and in the imperative. It does not allow for stasis.

I have never understood motionless close-ups. They sacrifice their essence, which is movement. Like the hands of a watch, one of which is on the hour and the other on the half hour, the legs of St. John the Baptist create a temporal dissonance. Rodin or someone else explained it: in order to create the impression of movement. A divine illusion? No, the gimmick for a toy presented at the *"concours Lépine,"*[1] and patented so that it can't be used to make lead soldiers. It seemed to Rodin that Watteau's *Cythera* could be animated by the movement of the eye from left to right over it. The motor-bikes posters race uphill by means of symbols: hatching, hyphens, blank spaces. Right or wrong, they thereby endeavor to conceal their ankylosis. The painter and the sculptor maul life, but this bitch has beautiful, real legs and escapes from under the nose of the artist crippled by inertia. Sculpture and painting, paralyzed in marble or tied to canvas, are reduced to pretence in order to capture movement, the indispensable. The ruses of reading. You must not maintain that art is created out of obstacles and limits. You, who are lame have made a cult of your crutch. The cinema demonstrates your error. Cinema is all movement without any need for stability or equilibrium. Of all the sensory logarithms of reality, the photogenic is based on movement. An exhibition of inventions held annually in Paris. Derived from time, it is acceleration. It opposes the event to stasis, relationship to dimension. Gearing up and gearing down. This new beauty is as sinuous as the curve of the stock market index. It is no longer the function of a variable but a variable itself.

The close-up, the keystone of the cinema, is the maximum expression of this photogeny of movement. When static, it verges on contradiction. The face alone doesn't unravel its expressions but the head and lens moving together or apart, to the left and right of each other. Sharp focus is avoided.

The landscape may represent a state of mind. It is above all a state. A state of rest. Even in those landscapes most often shown in documentaries of picturesque Brittany or of a trip to Japan are in serious error. But 'the landscape's dance' is photogenic. Through the window of a train or a ship's porthole, the world acquires a new, specifically cinematic vivacity. A road is a road but the ground which flees under the four beating hearts of an automobile's belly transports me. The Oberland and Semmering tunnels swallow me up, and my head, bursting through the roof, hits against their vaults. Seasickness is decidedly pleasant. I'm on board the falling airplane. My knees bend. This area remains to be exploited. I yearn for a drama aboard a merry-go-round, or more modern still, in airplanes. The fair below and its surroundings would be progressively confounded. Centrifuged in this way, and adding vertigo and rotation to it, the tragedy would increase its photogenic quality ten-fold. I would like to see a dance shot successively from the four cardinal directions. Then, with strokes of a pan shot or of a turning foot, the room as it is seen by the dancing couple. An intelligent *découpage* will reconstitute the double life of the dance by linking together the viewpoints of the spectator and the dancer, objective and subjective, if I may say so. When a character is going to meet another, I want to go along with him not behind or in front of him or by his side, but in him. I would like to look through his eyes and see his hand reach out from under me as if it were my own; interruptions of opaque film would imitate the blinking of our eyelids.

One need not exclude the landscape but adapt it. Such is the case with a film I've seen, *Souvenir d'été à Stockholm*. Stockholm didn't appear at all. Rather, male and female swimmers who had doubtlessly not even been asked for their permission to be filmed. People diving. There were kids and old people, men and women. No one gave a damn about the camera and had a great time. And so did I! A boat loaded with strollers and animation. Elsewhere people fished. A crowd watched. I don't remember what show the crowd was waiting for; it was difficult to move through these groups. There were Café terraces. Swings. Races on the grass and through the reeds. Everywhere, men, life, swarms, truth.

That's what must replace the Pathé color newsreel where I always search for the words "Bonnie Fête" written in golden letters at the corner of the screen.[2]

But the close-up must be introduced, or else one deliberately handicaps the style. Just as a stroller leans down to get a better look at a plant, an insect, or a pebble, the lens must include in a sequence describing a field, close-ups of a flower, a fruit, or an animal: living nature. I never

travel as solemnly as these cameramen. I look, I sniff at things, I touch. Close-up, close-up, close-up. Not the recommended points of view, the horizons of the Touring Club, but natural, indigenous, and photogenic details. Shop windows, cafés, quite wretched urchins, a cashier, ordinary gestures made with their full capacity for realization, a fair, the dust of automobiles, an atmosphere.

The landscape film is, for the moment, a big zero. People look for the picturesque in them. The picturesque in cinema is zero, nothing, negation. About the same as speaking of colors to a blind man. The film is susceptible only to photogeny. Picturesque and photogenic coincide only by chance. All the worthless films shot near the Promenade des Anglais proceed from this confusion; and their sunsets are further proof of this.

Possibilities are already appearing for the drama of the microscope, a hystophysiology of the passions, a classification of the amorous sentiments into those which do and those which do not need Gram's solution.[3] Young girls will consult them instead of the fortune teller. While we are waiting, we have an initial sketch in the close-up. It is nearly overlooked, not because it errs, but because it presents a ready-made style, a minute dramaturgy, flayed and vulnerable. The amplifying close-up demands underplaying. It's opposed to the theater where everything is loudly declaimed. A hurricane of murmurs. An interior conviction lifts the mask. It's not about interpreting a role; what's important is the actor's belief in his character, right up to the point where a character's absent-mindedness becomes that of the actor himself. The director suggests, then persuades, then hypnotizes. The film is nothing but a relay between this source of nervous energy and the auditorium which breathes its radiance. That is why the gestures which work best on screen are nervous gestures.

It is paradoxical, or rather extraordinary, that the nervousness which often exaggerates reactions should be photogenic when the screen deals mercilessly with the least forced gestures. Chaplin has created the overwrought hero. His entire performance consists of reflexes of a nervous, tired person. A bell or an automobile horn makes him jump, forces him to stand anxiously, his hand on his chest, because of the nervous palpitations of his heart. This isn't so much an example, but rather a synopsis of his photogenic neurasthenia. The first time that I saw Nazimova agitated and exothermic, living through an intense childhood, I guessed that she was Russian, that she came from one of the most nervous peoples on earth. And the little, short, rapid, spare, one might say involuntary, gestures of Lillian Gish who runs like the hand of a chronometer! The hands of Louise Glaum unceasingly drum a tune of anxiety. Mae Murray, Buster Keaton. *Etc.*

The close-up is drama in high gear. A man says, "I love the far-away princess." Here the verbal gearing down is suppressed. I can see love. It half lowers its eyelids, raises the arc of the eyebrows laterally, inscribes itself on the taut forehead, swells the massiters, hardens the tuft of the chin, flickers on the mouth and at the edge of the nostrils. Good lighting; how distant the far-away princess is. We're not so delicate that we must be presented with the sacrifice of Iphigenia recounted in alexandrins. We are different. We have replaced the fan by the ventilator and everything else accordingly. We demand to see because of our experimental mentality, because of our desire for a more exact poetry, because of our analytic propensity, because we need to make new mistakes.

The close-up is an intensifying agent because of its size alone. If the tenderness expressed by a face ten times as large is doubtlessly not ten times more moving, it is because in this case, ten, a thousand, or a hundred thousand would—erroneously—have a similar meaning. Merely being able to establish twice as much emotion would still have enormous consequences. But whatever its numerical value, this magnification acts on one's feelings more to transform than to confirm them, and personally, it makes me uneasy. Increasing or decreasing successions of events in the right proportions would obtain effects of an exceptional and fortunate elegance. The close-up modifies the drama by the impact of proximity. Pain is within reach. If I stretch out my arm I touch you, and that is intimacy. I can count the eyelashes of this suffering. I would be able to taste the tears. Never before has a face turned to mine in that way. Ever closer it presses against me, and I follow it face to face. It's not even true that there is air between us; I consume it. It is in me like a sacrament. Maximum visual acuity.

The close-up limits and directs the attention. As an emotional indicator, it overwhelms me. I have neither the right nor the ability to be distracted. It speaks the present imperative of the verb to understand. Just as petroleum potentially exists in the landscape that the engineer gropingly probes, the photogenic and a whole new rhetoric are similarly concealed in the close-up. I haven't the right to think of anything but this telephone. It is a monster, a tower and a character. The power and scope of its whispering. Destinies wheel about, enter, and leave from this pylon as if from an acoustical pigeon house. Through this nexus flows the illusion of my will, a laugh that I like or a number, an expectation or a silence. It is a sensory limit, a solid nucleus, a relay, a mysterious transformer from which everything good or bad may issue. It looks like an idea.

One can't evade an iris. Round about, blackness; nothing to attract one's attention.

This is a cyclopean art, a unisensual art, an iconoscopic retina. All life and attention are in the eye. The eye sees nothing but a face like a great sun. Hayakawa aims his incandescent mask like a revolver. Wrapped in darkness, ranged in the cell-like seats, directed toward the source of emotion by their softer side, the sensibilities of the entire auditorium converge, as if in a funnel, toward the film. Everything else is barred, excluded, no longer valid. Even the music to which one is accustomed is nothing but additional anesthesia for what is not visual. It takes away

our cars the way a Valda lozenge takes away our sense of taste. A cinema orchestra need not simulate sound effects. Let it supply a rhythm, preferably a monotonous one. One cannot listen and look at the same time. If there is a dispute, sight, as the most developed, the most specialized, and the most generally popular sense, always wins. Music which attracts attention or the imitation of noises is simply disturbing.

Although sight is already recognized by everyone as the most developed sense, and even though the viewpoint of our intellect and our mores are visual, nevertheless, there has never been an emotive process so homogeneously, so exclusively optical as the cinema. Truly, the cinema creates *a particular system of consciousness limited to a single sense.* And after one has grown used to using this new and extremely pleasant intellectual state, it becomes a sort of need, like tobacco or coffee. I have my dose or I don't. Hunger for a hypnosis far more violent than reading offers because reading modifies the functioning of the nervous system much less.

The cinematic feeling is therefore particularly intense. More than anything else, the close-up releases it. Although not dandies, all of us are or are becoming blasé. Art takes to the warpath. To attract customers, the circus showman must improve his acts and speed up his carousel from fair to fair. Being an artist means to astonish and excite. The habit of strong sensations which the cinema is essentially capable of producing, blunts theatrical sensations which are, moreover, of a lesser order. Theater, watch out!

If the cinema magnifies feeling, it magnifies it in every way. Pleasure in it is more pleasurable, but its defects are more defective.

TIMELESS TIME

LEARNING PERSPECTIVE

Every spectacle which is the imitation of a series of events creates, by the very fact of the succession contained within it, a time which is its own, a distortion of historical time. In primitive theatrical manifestations, this illusory time dared depart only a very little from the time in which the described action actually occurred. Similarly, the first designers and painters explored the illusion of relief timidly, hardly knowing how to represent the illusion of spatial depth; they remained attached to the reality of the flat surface on which they worked. Only gradually did man, developing as the imitative animal *par excellence,* become accustomed to providing himself with fictive spaces and times which, proceeding from imitations of nature to secondary and tertiary versions of these first imitations, progressively distanced themselves from their original models.

Thus, the length of mystery plays performed in the Middle Ages reflects the difficulty which minds of this epoch still experience in shifting temporal perspective. At that time, a drama which did not last almost as long on stage as the actual unfolding of the events would not have seemed believable and sustained the illusion. And the rule of the three unities which established 24 hours as the maximum of solar time which it was permitted to compress into three or four hours of performance time marks another stage of the advance toward the comprehension of chronological abridgement, that is, of temporal relativity. Today, this reduction of duration by one eighth which classical tragedy offered at best seems a very small endeavor compared to the compressions of 1/50,000 which the cinema achieves, though not without inducing slight dizziness.

THE MACHINE WHICH THINKS TEMPORALLY

Another astonishing quality of the cinematograph is its ability to multiply and make immensely more supple the play of temporal perspective, to train the intellect in an exercise which is always difficult: to move from established absolutes to unstable conditionals. Here again, this machine which extends or condenses duration, which demonstrates the variable nature of time, which preaches the relativity of all standards, seems endowed with a kind of psyche. Without it we would not see and therefore would understand nothing at all of a time which may physically be 50,000 times more rapid or four times slower than the one in which we live. It is a physical implement, certainly, whose functioning, however, provides an illusion so fully elaborated and ready for the mind's use that it can be considered as already half-thought, conceived according to the rules of an analysis and synthesis which man, without the cinematic instrument, had been unable to use.

DIMENSIONS OF SPACE

The respect with which the precious standard measures of irradiated platinum are conserved in armored and padlocked tabernacles at constant temperatures recalls the worship accorded to miraculous objects, materializations of revealed truths descended from the absolute in the heavens onto this world of errors. No one, however, considers the meter—a one ten-millionth part of a quarter of the terrestrial meridian line—as a sacred and essential truth. Many countries still use other measuring units. We have seen four millimeters become three and a half centimeters under a magnifying glass long ago. Travellers know that each kilometer has a different meaning depending upon whether it is traversed on foot, on horseback, on a bicycle, in a car, in a train or in a plane, according to the terrain, the climate and the season. Like the lunar, Martian and Venusian meters—one ten-millionth part of a quarter of the meridian lines of this satellite and these planets—the terrestrial meter possesses only a relative significance. And if these celestial bodies, as is believed, gradually contract into themselves, we must ask ourselves where our true meter can be found—whether in the less variable standards of the Bureau of Longitudes or in the subdivision of a meridian line in perpetual regression?

DIMENSIONS OF TIME

More mysteriously, the truth-value of the hour has proved less subject to caution. The hour is not merely the secret product of standard clocks that are also buried in deep crypts and venerated as religious objects. It is nothing but the result of a simple measurement of the globe's surface; it originates on sundials from the trace inscribed by the incomprehensible, divine movement which animates the whole celestial mechanism. While the meridian line can for better or worse be divided by the decimal system, the orbit's elliptical shape refuses to submit to the arbitrariness of this human convention; it imposes its own number of days and nights so tyrannically that even if the total were unsatisfactory, nothing could be done to change it and calendars would have to be readjusted constantly. Occasionally, no doubt, a boring hour seems to pass more slowly than a pleasant one, but these impressions, always confused and often inconsistent, are not sufficient to shake the faith in the inalterable stability of a universal rhythm. A belief also confirmed by the irreversibility of duration, invariably positive, an image of the constancy of astronomical movements, since in its length, breadth and depth, space may be crossed and measured in one way one time and in an opposite way at another. Thus, until the invention of accelerated and slow cinematic motion, it seemed impossible to see—and it was not even dreamed of—a year in the life of a plant condensed in ten minutes, or thirty seconds of an athlete's activity inflated and extended to ten minutes.

TIME IS A RELATION IN SPACE

Thus, an hour and the time it defines, produced and regulated by cosmic dynamism, appears to be of a very different reality than that of the meter and space: more mysterious and more exalted, intangible and immutable. But the cinematograph, by "laminating" time to demonstrate its extreme malleability, has caused it to fall from these heights and reduced it to a dimension analogous to those of space.

The fourth dimension has been discussed for a long time, misconstrued, all the while, as to its nature, its existence even subject to doubt. For certain mathematicians, it was an essentially geometric dimension similar to the three others, a fiction or reality of calculation, yet practically ungraspable because our senses provide us with no data about it. For numerous scholars and novelists, philosophers and poets, it was ether or the means to go to the stars, the habitat of pure spirits or the way to the square the circle. . . . Nevertheless, just as all things which preoccupy man sooner or later come true, the fourth dimension—like the unicorn that will eventually be captured in Nepal—appeared, endowed with probability in the relativists' space-time.

Time, understood as a scale of variables, as the fourth of a system of coordinates in which our representation of the universe is inscribed, would have merely remained for a long time to come a construct of the mind, satisfying only a restricted audience of scholars, if the cinematograph had not visualized and reinforced this concept by experimentally producing very ample variations, hitherto unknown, in temporal perspective. That our time is the frame of a variable dimension, just as our space is the locus of three kinds of relative distances, can now be understood by everyone because all can see the extension or abridgement of time on screen just as they see the elongation or shortening of a distance through one end or another of a pair of binoculars. If today, every modestly cultivated man can represent the universe as a four dimensional continuum in which all material accidents are situated by the interplay of four spatio-temporal variables; if this richer, more variable, perhaps truer figure is gradually supplanting the three dimensional image of the world just as it had substituted itself for primitive flat schematizations of the earth and heavens; if the indivisible unity of the four factors of space-time is slowly acquiring evidence which modifies the inseparability of the three dimensions of pure space, the cinema is responsible for the wide fame and popularity of the theory with which Einstein and Minkowski have principally associated their names.

FOURTH OR FIRST DIMENSION?

Nevertheless, while the three spatial dimensions merely offer by no means essential differences of position among themselves, the temporal dimension retains a particular character which is at first attributed to the irreversibility of the march of time. Movements within any spatial dimension are supposed, on the contrary, to be capable of being effected in a positive direction sometimes, in a negative direction at others. But since the four dimensions form inseparable covariants, it seems strange that one of them can be irreversible without requiring the three others to also become so. In fact, nothing that moves, whether living or inanimate, can ever erase the route it has travelled. The kilometer traversed while returning does not annul the kilometer traversed while going, but is added to it because it is a new kilometer, different from the first. The evening's route, even if it doesn't differ a millimeter, is always another route than that of the morning, bathed in another light, in another atmosphere, traversed in another frame of mind and with different feelings. The irrevocable march of time effectively imposes a unique, irrecuperable and indestructible, perpetually positive meaning on all the movements of the universe. The *sui-generis* quality of the temporal dimension has a power to orient geometric space in such a way that the successions in it can only be produced according to the direction of this polarization. It is only through the polarized movement which it brings to images that the cinema—when given stereoscopic capacities—will be able to create the perfect illusion of a four dimensional continuum, an alternative reality.

In order to take into consideration the chronological order in which man familiarizes himself with the measures of length, surface and duration, wouldn't it be better to call time the first and not the fourth dimension in recognition of the general orienting function that it exerts over space?

LOCAL AND INCOMMENSURABLE TIMES

Not only does the cinematograph show that time is a controlled dimension correlated with those of space, but that furthermore, all the valuations of this dimension merely have a local value. It is conceded that the astronomical conditions in which the earth is situated impose an aspect and a division of time very different from what they must be in the Andromeda nebula, whose heaven and movements are not the same; for those who have never seen cinematic fast or slow motion, however, it is difficult to imagine, viewing from outside, the appearance that a temporality other than ours could have. That is why a short documentary film which describes in a few minutes twelve months in the life of a plant from its germination through its maturity and withering to the formation of the seed of a new generation (in a few minutes) suffices to make the most extraordinary voyage, the most difficult flight that man has yet attempted, come true for us.

This film seems to free us from terrestrial—that is, solar—time, from whose rhythm, it seemed, nothing would ever dislodge us. We feel introduced to a new universe, to another continuum in which change in time occurs fifty thousand times more rapidly. In this little domain, a special time reigns, a local time which constitutes an enclave within earth time, which is itself merely a local time, though extending over a vaster zone, in its turn enclosed within other times, or juxtaposed and mingled with them. The temporality of the whole of our universe itself is but a specific time, valid for this aggregate but neither beyond it nor in all its interior sections.

By analogy, innumerable ultra-specific temporalities, organizers of atomic ultra-microcosms, are foreseen as probably incommensurable in terms of wave or quantum mechanics, guesses are they share no common measure with solar time.

TIME IS NOT MADE OF TIME

Sustained by the senses, the intellect separates itself with difficulty from its primary conception of a sensory continuum. Just as it had filled space with ether, it had endowed time with a sort of extremely thin consistency corresponding to the uncertain fluidity of ordinary perceptions of duration offered by synesthesia. This exquisite weft, this fine thread of fate, this veil of sorrow, this indefinite substance subtler than ether which even refused to accept the precision of a proper name nevertheless remained a physical reality.

The cinematograph destroyed this illusion; it demonstrates that time is only a perspective generated by the succession of phenomena just as space is only a perspective on the coexistence of objects. Time contains nothing that can be called time-in-itself any more than space is comprised of space-in-itself. They are only composed, one as much as the other, of relationships, variable in their essence, between appearances which are produced successively or simultaneously. That is why there can be thirty-six different times and twenty kinds of space just as there can be innumerable specific perspectives depending upon the infinitely diverse positions of objects and their observer.

Thus, the cinema, having shown the unreality of continuity and discontinuity alike, confronts us rather brutally with the unreality of space-time.

THE UNIVERSE HEAD OVER HEELS

Experience since time immemorial has created the dogma of life's irreversibility. The course of evolution in both the atom and the galaxy, in inorganic matter as in both animal and human forms, derives its irrevocably unique meaning from the loss of energy. The constant increase in entropy is the catch which stops the gears of the terrestrial and celestial machine from ever moving in reverse. Time cannot return to its origin; no effect can precede its cause. And a world which would claim to break with or modify this vectorial order seems both physically impossible and logically unimaginable.

Focus attention, however, on a scene in an old avant garde film or a slapstick comedy that has been filmed in reverse motion. Suddenly, with an undeniable precision, the cinema describes a world which moves from its end to its beginning, an anti-universe which until now man had hardly managed to picture for himself. Dead leaves take off from the ground to hang once again upon tree branches; rain drops spurt upwards from the earth to the clouds; a locomotive swallows its smoke and cinders, inhales its own steam; a machine uses the cold to produce heat and work. Bursting from a husk, a flower withers into a bud which retreats into the stem. As the stem ages, it withdraws into a seed. Life appears only through resurrection, crossing old age's decrepitude into the bloom of maturity, rolling through the course of youth, then of infancy, and finally dissolving in a prenatal limbo. Universal repulsion, the energy loss of entropy, the continual increase of energy constitute truth values contrary to Newton's law and the principles of Carnot and Calusius. Effect has become cause; cause, effect.

Could the structure of the universe be ambivalent? Might it permit both forward and backward movements? Does it admit of a double logic, two determinisms, two antithetical ends?

THE CINEMA AS THE INSTRUMENT OF A PHILOSOPHY AS WELL AS OF AN ART

For several hundred years, the microscope and the telescope have helped to intensify the acuteness of our dominant sense: vision, and reflection on the world's new aspect thereby obtained has prodigiously transformed and developed every philosophical and scientific system. In turn, the cinematograph, although hardly fifty years old, has to its credit some admittedly important revelations, notably in the analysis of movement. But for the general public, the machine which generated the "seventh art" chiefly represents a way of reviving and popularizing the theater, a machine for the fabrication of a type of spectacle accessible to the minds and purses of the largest possible international common denominator. A beneficent and prestigious function, certainly, whose only drawback lies in the stifling effect of its popularity upon those other possibilities of the same instrument which then pass almost unnoticed.

Thus, little or no attention has been paid until now to the many unique qualities film can give to the representation of things. Hardly anyone has realized that the cinematic image carries a warning of something monstrous, that it bears a subtle venom which could corrupt the entire rational order so painstakingly imagined in the destiny of the universe.

Discovery always means learning that objects are not as we had believed them to be; to know more, one must first abandon the most evident certainties of established knowledge. Although not certain, it is not inconceivable that what appears to us as a strange perversity, a surprising nonconformity, as a transgression and a defect of the screen's animated images might serve to advance another step into that "terrible underside of things" which terrified even Pasteur's pragmatism.

THE INTERCHANGEABILITY OF THE CONTINUOUS AND THE DISCONTINUOUS: A KIND OF MIRACLE

We know that a film is composed of a large number of images, discrete and slightly dissimilar according to the more or less modified position of the filmed subject, juxtaposed on the film strip. The projection at a certain speed of this series of figures, separated by short intervals of space and time, produces the appearance of uninterrupted movement. And this is the most striking and prodigious quality of the Lumière brothers' machine; it transforms discontinuity into continuity; it permits the synthesis of discontinuous and static elements into a continuous, mobile whole; it effects the transition between the two primordial aspects of nature which have always, ever since the constitution of a metaphysics of science, been opposed as mutually exclusive.

FIRST MANIFESTATION: THE PERCEPTIBLE CONTINUUM

At the level where it is directly or indirectly perceived by the senses, the world at first appears as a rigorously coherent assemblage of material parts between which the existence of a cavity of nothingness, a veritable discontinuity seems so impossible that whenever one is not sure what is there, a substance, baptised ether, has been imagined to fill it up. Indeed, Pascal showed that nature's supposed abhorrence of the void was purely imaginary, but he did not efface that abhorrence of the human intellect for a void inaccessible to sensory experience is available.

SECOND MANIFESTATION: THE DISCONTINUITY
OF THE PHYSICAL SCIENCES

Since Democritus, the atomic theory which takes matter to be constituted of corpuscles, indivisible and separated from each other, has emerged as the victor over the primitive conception of a universal continuum. Despite its supposed indivisibility, the atom has had to be subdivided into several kinds of electrons. Nevertheless, the hypothesis of a gaping, discontinuous—one might say gaseous—material structure of both the infinitely small and the infinitely large, in which solid elements occupy a very small volume in comparison to the immense voids through which they circulate, is still generally accepted today. Thus, a galaxy can be compared to a starry mist just as the atom recalls a miniature solar system.

Beneath the consistent world of our practical experience hide the surprises of a reality that is very diffuse, in which the proportion of what is to what is anything but definite, can be rendered by the image of a fly in flight in a space of some eight cubic kilometers cubed.

THIRD MANIFESTATION: THE MATHEMATICAL CONTINUITY

If material corpuscles can be conceived as separate, they cannot be thought to be independent of each other for they exert reciprocal influences upon each other which account for their behavior. The network of these innumerable interactions or force fields represents a mysterious weft which entirely fills the relativists' space-time. In this new four-dimensional continuity, the latent energy dispersed throughout condenses here and there in granules endowed with mass which are the constituents of matter.

Beneath the material discontinuity—molecular, atomic, intra-atomic—one can therefore imagine a deeper and even more hidden continuity which should be called pre-material because it facilitates and directs the measurable and probabilistic positions of mass, light and electricity.

THE TRANSMUTATION OF THE DISCONTINUOUS
INTO THE CONTINUOUS, NEGATED BY ZENO,
BUT ACCOMPLISHED BY THE CINEMATOGRAPH

The most obscure moments of this poetry occur during the transitions between or the superimpositions of superficial continuity over the intermediary discontinuous level, and of this intermediary level over the pre-material continuity whose existence is only mathematical. The fact that reality can encompass continuity and discontinuity, that an unbroken order can be a sum of interruptions, that the addition of static phases produces movement, has amazed the rational mind ever since the Eleatics.

Now, the cinematograph seems to be a mysterious mechanism intended to assess the false accuracy of Zeno's famous argument about the arrow, intended for the

analysis of the subtle metamorphosis of stasis into mobility, of emptiness into solid, of continuous into discontinuous, a transformation as stupefying as the generation of life from inanimate elements.

CONTINUITY, PRETENSE OF DISCONTINUITY

Is it the recording apparatus or the projector which creates this marvel? In fact, every part of each film image, successively projected on the screen, remains as perfectly still and separate as it had been since its appearance at the sensory level. The unity and animation of these forms are effected neither on the film strip, nor by the lens, but in man himself. The discontinuity becomes continuity only after it has made its way in the spectator. It is a purely internal phenomenon. Outside the spectator, there is no movement, no flux, no life in the mosaics of light and shadow which the screen always presents as fixed. Within, there is an impression which, like all other sensory data, is an interpretation of the object, that is, an illusion, a phantom.

BAD EYESIGHT, THE SOURCE OF THE METAPHYSICS
OF THE CONTINUOUS

The spectre of a non-existent continuity is known to be caused by a defect of sight. The eye's power to distinguish space and time is strictly limited. An alignment of points very close to each other is perceived as a line; it sustains the appearance of spatial continuity. And a sufficiently rapid succession of separate images, each slightly different, creates, due to the slowness and persistence of retinal sensations, another more complex spatio-temporal continuity which is also imaginary.

Every film thus provides us with a clear example of a mobile continuum formed by what might be called its somewhat deeper reality of discontinuous static elements. Zeno was therefore right to maintain that the analysis of movement yielded a collection of stops; his only error lay in denying the possibility of the irrational, absurd synthesis achieved by the cinema thanks to that weakness of our vision which effectively recomposes movement through the progressive addition of static moments. Faraday once observed that "The irrational is not impossible." The natural sequence of phenomena is not necessarily logical, as one also discovers, when light added to light produces darkness within the gaps between.

THE DISCONTINUOUS, REALITY OF AN UNREAL CONTINUITY?

The perceptual continuum whose existence outside ourselves is confirmed by daily experience, but denied in its reality by scientific research, is only a trap which has its source, like the misleading continuity of film, in the inadequate discrimination of our sight, as of all our senses. Thus, the charm of music, the perfectly smooth flux of harmony which we enjoy when hearing a symphony comes from the ear's inability to situate each vibration of each flow of sonic waves distinctly in space and time. Similarly, the relative crudeness of the multiple sensations to which we give the name of "touch" does not enable us to experience the extreme division nor the extraordinary agitation of the miniscule components of the objects we handle. From these perceptual deficiencies derive all the false notions of a matter without void, of a compact world, a solid universe.

The visible, palpable, audible, breathable continuum in every domain is only a very superficial semblance which is undoubtedly useful, that is to say, empirically true; it conceals, however, a basically discontinuous organization, the knowledge of which has proven to be still more useful and whose reality, therefore, can and should also be considered deeper.

DISCONTINUITY, THE PRETENSE OF A CONTINUUM

What is the source of this discontinuity considered more real? Where and how in the cinematic process, for example, are the discontinuous images with which the spectator forms the film's subjective continuity obtained? These images are taken from the perpetually moving spectacle of the world: a spectacle which is fragmented, cut into brief slices by a shutter which during each rotation uncovers the lens for a mere third or fourth of the necessary time. This fraction is brief enough so that the snapshots obtained can be as sharp as photographs of static subjects. Considered in themselves, the discontinuity and immobility of cinematic images are therefore created by the recording camera. They provide a very imprecise interpretation of that continuous and mobile aspect of nature which assumes the role of a fundamental reality.

IF A MAN IS ORGANIZED THROUGH HIS SENSES TO PERCEIVE THE DISCONTINUOUS AS A CONTINUUM, THE MACHINE 'IMAGINES' THE CONTINUOUS AS DISCONTINUOUS MORE EASILY

A mechanism proves, as it happens, to be endowed with its own subjectivity since it represents things not as they are perceived by human eyes but only according to the way it sees them itself, according to that particular structure which constitutes its personality. And the discontinuity of static images, (static at least for the time of their projection, in the intervals of their jerking passage through the projector) a discontinuity which functions as a material foundation for the continuity which man is capable of imagining in the projected film, turns out to be in turn a mere phantom, conceived, thought by a machine.

The cinematograph has first shown us a subjective transfiguration of a truer discontinuity within the continuous; this same cinematograph then shows us an arbitrary interpretation of a primordial continuity within the discontinuous. We realize then that cinematic continuity and discontinuity actually are equally non-existent, or, what is essentially the same thing: the continuous and the discontinuous act alternatively as object and as concept,

their reality being only a function in which one can be substituted for the other.

NOTES

[1] The *"concours Lépine":* an exhibition fair for inventors held in Paris.

[2] Epstein is evidently referring to the practice of early film companies who inscribed their trademarks emblem on the theatrical sets or inserted placards bearing such emblems into shots taken outdoors to prevent pirating of their prints. Epstein rejected such a declaration of artificiality as inappropriate for film.

[3] "Gram's solution": a solution used in the differential staining of bacteria.

Richard Abel (essay date 1979)

SOURCE: "Jean Epstein's 'La Chute de la Maison Usher': Reversal and Liberation," in *Wide Angle,* Vol. 3, No. 1, 1979, pp. 38-44.

[*In the following essay, Abel examines narrative progression in several segments of* The Fall of the House of Usher.]

Jean Epstein's *La Chute de la Maison Usher* (1928) interests me for several reasons. First of all, Epstein was one of the most important filmmakers (perhaps the most important) of what I would call the "narrative avantgarde" in the French cinema of the 1920s, and *La Chute de la Maison Usher* is the only example of his work currently available in the United States.[1] Second, although the film is mentioned often enough in studies of the Twenties, it probably has more detractors than advocates; and its advocates, even in France, tend to emphasize its exquisite atmosphere of gothic fantasy or its technical experimentation as "pure cinema" (the use of slow motion and extensive camera movement).[2] What I would like to suggest is that its value lies at least equally elsewhere.

In a remark since repeated by other cineastes of the period, Epstein once said that, in filmmaking, theory generally follows practice rather than precedes it.[3] The statement aptly fits Epstein's own theoretical writing and filmmaking practice in the final years of the French silent cinema. Specifically, although references to narrative are virtually absent in those writings, one of the most fascinating features of the films, especially those he made independently from 1926 to 1928, is precisely the way the discourse operates rhetorically, syntactically, structurally—as narrative.[4] I would argue that Epstein's filmmaking *"recherche"* clearly extends to film narrativity, and *La Chute de la Maison Usher* is a major work in sustaining that *"recherche."* Indeed, the *Usher* text may have added significance since it appears to mark a shift in Epstein's aesthetic from the films he had directed previously to the "documentary fiction" of *Finis terrae* (1929) and *L'Or des mers* (1932).

The following pages offer a preliminary study of narrativity in *Usher* by examining some (not all) of the ways the text organizes its discourse to produce narrative. For the sake of specificity, I have confined myself, not arbitrarily, I will admit, to two segments of the text: the initial appearance of Roderick and Madeleine in Usher and the burial of Madeleine's coffin in the grotto.[5] What I have tried to examine is the way these particular segments organize themselves in terms of similarity and difference, or more specifically, in terms of alternation, displacement or substitution, metonymy and metaphor.[6] Such an analysis will produce a provisional reading of the overall narrative structure of the film.

Our introduction to the interior of Usher and its two inhabitants is preceded by an intertitle: "Dans ce manoir menaçant ruine, Sir Roderick tenait ,dans une étrange réclusion sa femme Madeleine, la dominant par sa nervosité tyrannique."[7] Hero and heroine are joined in marriage, the one controlling, dominating the other through his nervous condition. Roderick, the dominant figure, first appears in a series of close-ups (CUs):

1) CU of two hands slightly outstretched, moving from right to left in conjunction with a revolving body.

2) CU of a painter's palette on a dimly lit table.

3) CU of the same two hands, now still, poised.

4) CU of Roderick's face, calm but slightly pained, with his eyes gazing off towards the left foreground.

5) FS (full shot) of a dark area or niche in which a painting stands obscurely (this shot exists in the Cinémathèque française print but is excised from the Museum of Modern Art print).

6) CU of Roderick's face which suddenly turns to the right—his eyes look off intently to the right (frame).

This fragmented, elliptical introduction is quite typical of Epstein, evidencing his belief that the close-up was the "soul" of cinema, the intensifying agent par excellence, the maximum expression of the *photogénie* of movement.[8] It occurs repeatedly in his earlier films: in *Coeur fidèle* (1923)—Gina Manès' hands collecting and moving wine bottles on a café bar top, in *L'Affiche* (1925)—Nathalie Lissenko's hands tying artificial flowers into a bouquet. In the earlier films the close-ups had been a means of defining character immediately in terms of occupation and milieu. Here in *Usher,* the close-ups imply something more, an associative chain—from hands to palette, from eyes to painted image. Two schema are being placed in paradigm. Succinctly, even abruptly, the text is defining Roderick as subject in terms of desire and potential action.[9] His sickness (mentioned earlier in a letter to his friend, the guest who is yet to arrive), his tyrannical dominance enunciated in the intertitle preced-

ing these shots, are both becoming manifest in the desire to paint, to transfer paint from palette to canvas. The next series of shots continues an alternation that has begun to appear in the text: in Roderick's looking towards the left foreground and his point-of-view shot of the painted image. Now he turns to the right, and his glance determines the appearance of a second object, displacing the first, his wife Madeleine. The look of the subject both creates a space and draws an opposition between painted image and wife. Two more schema are being placed in correlation: Roderick's look towards the painted image/Roderick's look towards his wife Madeleine. If desire (what kind of desire?) marks the relationship between Roderick and the painted image, what marks that between Madeleine and him? The alternation is disturbed in two ways that threaten Roderick's dominance as subject. Instead of cutting immediately from Roderick's gaze to a point-of-view shot of Madeleine, the text interjects a sudden extreme long shot of the vast interior space of Usher which has the effect of reducing or circumscribing that look as well as presenting its object with some degree of equality. Furthermore, the shots that follow emphasize the object Madeleine, at the expense of Roderick (two shots of her to one of him).

The next series of shots subdue this threat to Roderick's dominance through a double displacement, a double operation of metonymy. Roderick's look is displaced metonymically (through contiguity) by his hands in a shot which shows them clasped together and moving to the right. Then the palette, which initially had been correlated with the hands, is displaced metonymically by Madeleine. By replacing the look, the shot of the hands connotes a blindness in the subject (absence of sight). Through repeated alternation, the increasingly nervous clenching hands suggest a blind compulsion that seems to threaten the object Madeleine. When Roderick's hands pick up the palette at the conclusion of the series, the action latent in the opening shots of the sequence is on the verge of being realized. But the act of painting, of transferring paint from palette to canvas, is now charged metonymically—it involves a transfer, a threat to Madeleine.

In the next five shots, the alternation between subject and object, Roderick and Madeleine, is disturbed briefly once more, this time by opposing movements within the frame. Roderick moves left with the palette (towards the painting off-screen), while Madeleine turns to move away from him into the right background. He turns to follow her movement; she stops and turns back to face the left foreground again, her image caught within the frame of a harp (the metaphorical value of entrapment here will be transferred later to Roderick's guitar—its strings breaking when the climactic storm approaches Usher). In a near repetition of the first shot in this series, Roderick moves left again, his attention once more on the palette.

The next shots finally realize Roderick's desire in action; they complete the correlation of subject-object predications. A paintbrush metaphorically replaces both

Roderick's hands and look, so that the schema of hands/palette is condensed into a single shot of paintbrush touching palette, while the schema of look/painted image is condensed into a shot of brush touching canvas. The two acts of touching and painting, through metonymy and metaphor, articulate a transfer from one object to another: adding to the painted image subtracts from Madeleine. As the paintbrush strokes the canvas, Madeleine reacts as if struck, as if her face were being taken away. Roderick's desire is being defined as a compulsion to transfer life to the painted image—to give life to artifice, at the expense of life itself. The discourse seems to be asserting that, as an aesthetic, such a compulsion is blind, sick, and cruelly, deadly possessive: to enclose Madeleine living within the frame of the painting is to imprison her, to place her in a kind of coffin.

The "spell" Roderick holds over Madeleine—and which dominates him as well—is broken only by a change in his look. And the change is motivated by the arrival of his summoned friend from outside Usher. In this the text foreshadows the eventual breaking of the "spell"; it will come from the natural world outside Usher.

What strikes me about this initial sequence involving Roderick and Madeleine is how concisely, how sophisticatedly and yet how easily the text narrates, according to a visual syntax of paradigmatic and syntagmatic relations. Except for the opening intertitle, there is no recourse to verbal language at all. The sequence, in fact, constructs a paradigm of the narrative action for the first half of the film. Roderick transfers Madeleine (as the object of value) from reality to artifice, from a condition of "freedom" to one of imprisonment, from a condition of living to a condition of "life-in-death."[10] Though presented as subject, Roderick functions from the beginning as an unconscious villain.

The second half of the film involves a reversal of the narrative action in the first half, with an important difference. The transition from one to the other occurs in the sequence of Madeleine's burial, which Roderick at first resists. This sequence, like the introduction of Roderick and Madeleine, also organizes its discourse according to alternation, displacement, metonymy and metaphor.

The grotto in which Madeleine will be interred is at some distance from Usher. Thus the funeral procession of Roderick, his guest, the doctor and the butler, all bearing the coffin, becomes a kind of journey or voyage (across a river or tarn at one point); and certain connotations become attached to it. Madeleine's burial clothes are much like a bridal costume, and a long veil trails behind the coffin like the train of a wedding dress.[11] Superimposed over most shots of the journey are tall, thin flaming candles, creating a kind of path or aisle through which the funeral procession moves. Taken together, these images suggest that the journey is as much a wedding march as funeral—two actions are being conveyed metaphorically as one. When the procession reaches its destination, the grotto is depicted in a single establishing shot as a double chamber framed by obviously painted rocks and columns (in the manner of Méliès fantasy films).[12]

The grotto thus becomes analogous to the painting Roderick has done, and the placement of Madeleine's body there simply reenacts the earlier transfer of her from reality to artifice, from life to death, through painting. With the allusion to Méliès, the grotto also becomes the possible site of magic, of further mysterious doings or undoings.

The burial sequence itself is organized according to a simple alternation. The doctor and butler stay by the coffin on the left side of the grotto while the guest keeps Roderick away from it and tries to push him up the grotto stairs on the right. In the alternation between sets of characters/sides of the grotto, the spatial description repeats that of the opening sequence in Usher, but with an important reversal of positions. Madeleine's coffin takes the place of the painted canvas, while Roderick has replaced her and is now in a similarly powerless condition (no longer agent but object). The third shot of the sequence makes the metaphorical relationship between the sequences quite clear. Since the coffin has replaced the painted canvas, the close-up of the butler's hands holding the hammer becomes a replacement for Roderick's hands with the paintbrush. Thus when in close-up the butler begins driving nails into the coffin lid, the action stands in a metaphorical relation to Roderick's act of painting (so, too, are the later multiple-exposed shots of hammering paradigmatically connected to the earlier multiple-exposed shots of Madeleine in agony just before she collapses and dies). This enclosing, sealing, entombing, is at once the logical outcome of Roderick's compulsion and its reenactment. Only now it is Roderick who reacts to the hammer strokes much the way Madeleine reacted to the strokes of his paintbrush.

Midway through the sequence, just as Roderick is pushed out of the grotto altogether, an important change occurs in the alternating series. The shot outside the grotto already signals some kind of shift, but what happens is quite unexpected. Instead of cutting back to a close-up of the hammering inside the grotto, the discourse suddenly interjects a shot of a toad on wet stony ground (completely free of any character's point of view). A shot of the hammering reappears followed by another shot of the toad, only this time a second toad is on the first's back in mating position. Again two terms/images are being placed in association. Hammering nails into a coffin is being made visually equivalent to the mating of toads. But the visual metonymy produces a schema of metaphorical opposition: hammering nails into a coffin connotes entombing, death/mating toads connote impregnating, life.[13] Through displacement and metonymy, the discourse introduces an antidote to Roderick's compulsion. But how will it function?

The insertion of mating toads modifies the alternating series through displacement, but since a shot of Roderick and his guest at the grotto's entrance recurs, a triplet or triadic pattern begins to form: 1) hammering, 2) toads mating, 3) Roderick and guest. However, its repetition is disrupted immediately by a second unexpected displacement. Instead of Roderick and his guest, the discourse suddenly interjects a negative (or high contrast) image of an owl sitting motionless in a web of branches (that includes part of Madeleine's veil) against a black background. This new triplet pattern is then repeated a half dozen times (the shots of toads and owl lasting but two seconds each), and only in the final two repetitions does a further change occur. The close-up of hammering gives way to a shot of the sealed coffin lid and then to a shot of the doctor and butler ascending the grotto stairs. The whole sequence ends with a long shot of the two joining Roderick and his guest in the trees before the grotto entrance. The repetition and continued contiguity of toads and owl/veil suggest that these conjoined images are being placed in opposition to the nailing of the coffin. Fertility is being projected metonymically onto the owl, but what does the owl bring to the schema? Is it the wisdom of the "white goddess," confirming the grotto as the site of life-in-death and as the possible site of resurrection?[14] With the veil, is it a sign of "natural" wedding, union? Whatever the precise correlation of schema, Madeleine's burial functions simultaneously as an entombing, a withdrawal of life, and as an insemination, a seeding, a renewal of life.

The schema of metaphorical associations constructed in this sequence is crucial to the final sequences of the film. As the storm wind rises one night, blowing leaves and billowing curtains in Usher's interior, lightning begins to flash in exterior shots of the tower (and slowly tolling bell). As Roderick drags his guest to the window to see, the discourse inserts that same shot of the owl/veil in wind-whipped tree branches followed by a long shot of the exterior landscape as fire and smoke begin to appear around Usher. Through a simple instance of metonymy, the owl and storm are placed in conjunction. The schema of fertilizing, renewal, is equated with the storm, and its fire and smoke begin reversing the process of the first half of the film. Shots of the logs burning and smoking in Usher's huge fireplace alternate with Madeleine's coffin moving as if suspended in the dark and then falling off its support in the grotto. A shot of candle flames igniting a blowing curtain is intercut with Madeleine's veil beginning to unfurl from the grotto entrance. All these alternations are intercut with Roderick's guest reading the medieval tale of Ethelred who escapes his prison and slays the firebreathing dragon (a further metaphorical schema to Madeleine's future action). Madeleine's return in the storm thus coincides with/causes the destruction of Usher by wind and fire.

The reverse transfer of Madeleine from the grotto to Usher, mediated by the mating toads, the owl/veil and the storm, transforms her into the narrative agent of a final operation. When Roderick returned to Usher after the burial, he lived as one imprisoned, in silence and monotony, his senses intensified to the point of decadence.

His existence became a kind of death-in-life, the inverse to that of Madeleine in the coffin or in the painting. Metaphorically, the artifice of Usher as a whole came to equal the artifice of his painting, the walls around him analogous to the sealing frame of the coffin.[15] He, too, had become the victimized object of his own blind desire. Thus, while the storm destroys Usher (and the painting), Madeleine rescues Roderick from a living death. Whereas he had taken her from life by transferring her into a painted image, she reverses the process. Inverting the Orpheus-Eurydice myth, she restores him to life by plucking him from Usher and returning him to the natural world outside, to "reality." There, perhaps he will be free truly to *see*.

In conclusion, **La Chute de la Maison Usher** seems to establish a certain aesthetic as a destructive compulsion of decadent perception. Roderick's aesthetic (inherited, social) transfers value from the living or from "reality" to "fiction" or artifice. It is sick, blind and ultimately self-imprisoning. That compulsion is destroyed by "natural" forces which return the artist to the "real" world. Whatever aesthetic will be accepted now will be posited on the "natural." The change within the film announces the break that occurred in Epstein's own life[16] and a corresponding change in his aesthetic, articulated in the essays written after **Usher**'s production.[17] That aesthetic was to be embodied in the practice of his next three years of film-making. Rejecting the studios and the "ultra-modern" decor of his previous films, and impelled by a deep love for the sea, he ventured out to remote islands off the coast of Brittany and, in **Finis terrae** (1929), placed both his eyes and his *"machine de la cinématographe"* in the service of a people who enacted their own stories in the "real" world.

NOTES

[1] The Museum of Modern Art is in the process of acquiring several more of Epstein's silent films. Just recently, a print of *La Glace à trois faces* (1927) became available for study purposes at the University of Wisconsin-Madison.

[2] Henri Langlois, "Jean Epstein," *Cahiers du cinéma*, 24 (juin 1953), pp. 22-24; Pierre Leprohon and Marie Epstein, *Jean Epstein* (Paris: Seghers, 1964), pp. 83-85; Jean Mitry, *Histoire du cinéma muet*, III (Paris: Editions universitaires, 1973), pp. 381-382.

[3] For instance, René Clair, in an interview with Armand Panigel for the latter's "Histoire du cinéma français" (Antenne II, 1975). I would like to thank M. Panigel for permission to consult the transcripts of this interview made in 1973.

[4] See Epstein's own comments on *Usher* in Jean Epstein, *Ecrits sur le cinéma* I (Paris: Seghers, 1974), pp. 187-191. I have argued similarly on the subject of Louis Delluc's theory and practice in "Louis Delluc: the Critic as Cinéaste," *Quarterly Review of Film Studies*, I, No. 2 (May, 1976), pp. 205-244.

[5] This analysis is based on a study of the 35mm print at the Cinémathèque Française (courtesy of Mlle Marie Epstein) and the 16mm print (with French titles) at the Museum of Modern Art (courtesy of Charles Silver).

[6] The use of these concepts in film theory and criticism, in part, can be traced from Roman Jakobson's "Two Aspects of Language and Two Types of Aphasic Disturbances," *Fundamentals of Language* (The Hague: Mouton, 1956), pp. 76-82; through Raymond Bellour's *"Les Oiseaux," Cahiers du cinéma,* 216 (octobre 1969), pp. 24-38, and "Le Blocage symbolique," *Communication,* 23 (1975), pp. 235-350; Christian Metz' *Le Signifiant imaginaire,* (Paris: Editions 1080, 1977); and Linda Williams' "The Prologue to *Un Chien andalou:* a Surrealist Metaphor," *Screen,* XVII, 4 (Winter, 1976-1977), pp. 24-33.

[7] As is well known, Epstein's film synthesizes two Edgar Allan Poe stories, "The Fall of the House of Usher" and "The Oval Portrait." The incestuous brother-sister relationship of the first story is transformed into a husband-wife relationship in the film.

[8] Epstein, *Ecrits sur le cinéma,* pp. 93-99. Translated by Stuart Liebman as "Magnification," *October,* 3 (Spring, 1977), pp. 9-15. In one sense, Epstein's practice here can be seen as a deliberate inversion of the American convention of first establishing the space and then the character.

[9] The concept of narrative functions is drawn primarily from A. J. Greimas, "Elements of a Narrative Grammar," *diacritics,* 7 (March, 1977), especially pp. 30-33.

[10] Greimas, pp. 34-36.

[11] Phil Brown, Jr. first drew my attention to this association as well as that between the hammer driving nails into the coffin and Roderick's hands painting the canvas.

[12] The effect is created either by means of a "glass shot" (though I am not certain when that technique was first used by the French) or superimposition.

[13] Toads or frogs have been associated with sexuality in many myths and fairy tales. See Bruno Bettelheim, *The Uses of Enchantment* (New York: Random House, 1975), pp. 289-291.

[14] Robert Graves, *The White Goddess,* (2nd ed.; New York: Viking, 1958), pp. 92, 343.

[15] So the use of an obviously miniature set for the exterior of Usher, imposed presumably by budget limitations, is not inconsistent with the film's conceptual design.

[16] Marie Epstein was emphatic about this in an interview given to me in Paris, August 14, 1976.

[17] Epstein *Ecrits sur le cinéma,* pp. 191-200. This aesthetic has roots in Delluc's "neo-realist" pronouncements in 1919 and in the French documentary tradition that includes Jean Grémillon, André Sauvage, Alberto Cavalcanti, Dmitri Kirsanoff, Léon Poirier, Georges Lacombe, Jean Lods, Jean Vigo and even Epstein himself.

Allen Thiher (essay date 1979)

SOURCE: "The Impressionist Avant-Garde," in *The Cinematic Muse: Critical Studies in the History of French Cinema,* University of Missouri Press, 1979, pp. 16-23.

[In the following essay, Thiher acknowledges Epstein's work as a significant precursor of the cinematic avant-garde movement.]

It is surprising today to recall that French film producers once dominated the world film market; but this was during the period of primitive films before World War I. For the film historian it is a fascinating period. The diversity of these films is quite amazing, and they exercise an attraction on us that is undoubtedly out of proportion to their artistic worth (though Méliès, Durand, Feuillade, and others have their cults). As far as their influence on the elaboration of film discourse in France is concerned, they seem to belong to a remote epoch that has little in common with the silent films of the postwar period, not to mention with the classic narrative films of the thirties. World War I marked a rupture in French cinema, for during the war the French film industry nearly disappeared from the world market. It would appear that the early, primitive filmmakers were so nearly forgotten in the twenties that in 1924 René Clair could pay nostalgic homage to Méliès by putting the emblem of his Star Films on the rampaging hearse that stars in Clair's *Entr'acte.*

When companies like Pathé and Gaumont ceased to be the suppliers for the world's demand for film, Hollywood became the creator of the popular myths, of the vamps and sheiks, that soon became *the* modern form of popular myth. The disappearance of these companies' industrial power also meant, however, that in France it was possible for independent directors to step into the vacuum that the monopolies left behind them and to follow their individual creative bent. Thus a commercial avant-garde formed soon after the war in Paris. Influenced by the work of such theorists as Louis Delluc, this school, whose work should not be confused with surrealist, Dadaist, or cubist experiments in film, included such directors as Abel Gance, Germaine Dulac, Marcel L'Herbier, and the young Jean Epstein. Avant-garde in their zeal for experimentation and their desire to expand the mimetic range of cinema, these filmmakers were nonetheless also concerned with the commercial side of their work and wanted to reach a large audience, or at least the same public that serious literature spoke to. Cinema was no longer a product to be sent to circuses or music halls for a semiliterate, boisterous public of peasants, workers, and tipplers. For these directors, film was to become an art that could rival the stage and the printed page. Perhaps to differentiate them from the German expressionists of the early twenties, historians commonly call these filmmakers the Impressionist School, though there is nothing especially impressionistic about their work. In fact, one might even prefer *expressionist* as a more adequate term to describe their primary mimetic concerns, which went beyond the desire to explore the narrative techniques that American filmmakers such as Griffith and Von Stroheim were developing. Of course, the French Impressionists, like their Russian contemporaries, were quick to incorporate into their work the filmic conventions developed by the Americans that allowed filmmakers to transpose into film the narrative conventions of the Victorian and the naturalistic novel.

Griffith's role in developing narrative montage and the way in which this technique allowed him to represent the Victorian *Weltanschauung* in terms of a simplistic conflict of good and evil are well known. In Griffith's case, parallel montage is the structural principle that allows the episodic unfolding of ethical conflict. Equally interesting—though only belatedly recognized—is Von Stroheim's work in the transposition of naturalistic narrative structures. In his *Greed* (1923) it appeared that the logic of naturalistic narration could be completely transposed to the screen. The naturalistic novel's third-person point of view could be represented by the camera's exterior vision of the surface of objects and events. The seemingly objective nature of the photo-image could be accepted without question as a form of representation that was the equivalent of the naturalist's totally adequate descriptive language. For the naturalist, both image and word can exhaust, with often savage simplicity, the world through their expressivity. For this reason Von Stroheim had no need for the more complicated montage that Griffith developed. The image as Von Stroheim used it was adequate for mimesis, and the simple unfolding of episodic experience in terms of linear causality, with the sequence as the basic narrative unit, was adequate to express the relationships among events. Narrative structure and *Weltanschauung* again coincide, though here in the expression of a vision of man adrift in a world bereft of transcendental solace.

The French Impressionists quickly took over the American work on the development of narrative structures, but they were not as interested in the narration of episodic experience for its ethical or sentimental value. As might be expected of artists who were part of the generation that was reading symbolist poets, Bergson, and Gide while discovering Proust, Pirandello, and surrealism, these filmmakers were more interested in developing techniques that would allow film to explore more subjective modes of representation. By *subjective modes of representation,* one should understand a fairly wide scope of mimetic possibilities, including attempts to endow film with first-person narrative structures, the capacity to express what are generally called inner emotional states, and the attempt to represent hallucination and other idiosyncratically subjective images, as well as the effort to create poetic structures that could represent the director's emotional attitude toward the narrated experience (as in the case of Gance's experiments with rhythmic montage).

Exemplary in this respect (and important for an understanding of surrealist experimentation in film) was Pirandello's decision to allow Marcel L'Herbier to base a film on his *The Late Mattia Pascal.* L'Herbier's *Feu Mathias Pascal* (1926) is a key film for an understanding of the modes of mimesis that the Impressionist directors developed, for it attempts to combine linear narration of a naturalistic sort with exploration of subjective modes of representation. Pirandello's somewhat disjointed novel offered L'Herbier a first-person narration in which a middle-class protagonist has unintentionally and unhappily married a woman to whom he had proposed on the behalf of his best friend. He escapes from his prisonlike existence when he breaks the bank at Monte Carlo and then discovers that his friends and family erroneously believe he has committed suicide. Mathias has made a lifelong study of the nature of freedom. Suddenly rid of the burdensome identity that has denied him his own freedom, he goes to Rome, where he discovers that his lack of identity forces him to live outside civic norms. He is ensnared in a vacuous freedom that resembles a new form of imprisonment. It is worth noting that whereas Pirandello left his hero in his quandary, with no resolution at all, L'Herbier, perhaps for commercial reasons, appended a happy ending to his film by granting Mathias a new wife and a new identity.

This brief résumé indicates that such a film turns in large part on ideological and psychological questions such as the nature of freedom and identity. What is of interest, then, are the conventions L'Herbier used to represent the way in which his protagonist experiences the problems these questions pose. Though none of L'Herbier's choices are original, his work does bring together a series of solutions that are both typical of the Impressionist period and relatively successful within their own frame of reference. For instance, the sets that Cavalcanti designed for the film are initially its most striking feature. Using multiple framing devices within the image frame—windows and columns or multiple arches within a hallway—Cavalcanti created rigid patterns that suggest boxes within boxes, confining walls within confining walls, abstractions limited by other abstractions. Though not as extreme in effect as the decor of *The Cabinet of Dr. Caligari,* this is nonetheless an expressionist use of decor in the sense that the decor exists as an extension or a representation by analogy of a character's inner state. It is an objective correlative that relates both a psychological state and an ideological problem to an exterior manifestation or symbol. This type of mimesis is hardly unique to film, though in various guises it continues to attract filmmakers, for it is what we might call one aspect of purely plastic representation. . . .

The most interesting aspect of these mimetic devices, especially the ones using various sorts of trick photography, is how quickly their status changed from that of arbitrary inventions to that of a codified series of conventional signs that audiences quickly learned to "read" as a form of psychological representation. On the other hand, the Impressionists also sought to create more original devices for mimesis, and in this quest they often turned away from narrative structures borrowed from the novel and from the representation of psychological states that one could attribute to a single character. They then sought to develop purely cinematic devices for the representation of various poetic states. This search for mimetic devices of a poetic rather than a narrative sort seems in general to derive from the nature and the manipulation of the camera. Such work is typified by Jean Epstein's *Fall of the House of Usher* (1928)—a film, we might add, for which Buñuel was the assistant, immediately before making *Un Chien andalou.* This film is typical in that it too attempts to rival literature, although Epstein, perhaps more influenced by Baudelaire and Mallarmé than by novelists, was as much interested in creating a Poe-like atmosphere as in retelling a Poe short story by cinematic means. Borrowing motifs liberally from "Ligeia" and "The Oval Portrait," as well as "The Fall of the House of Usher," Epstein used narration only insofar as it gave him a framework in which he could create images expressing various poetic states. By *poetic states* one might understand emotional states that are dissociated from any specific protagonist and exist as a form of communication that has no narrative function. Rather, all narrative functions in the film are subordinated to the communication of these various states.

To borrow from Poe's symbolist doctrine as he expressed it in "Ligeia," we might say that Epstein seeks to render the viewer sensible to a "circle of analogies" that exist "in the commonest objects of the universe." Poetic communication is achieved when these analogies are made evident. The principle of analogy is especially noticeable in Epstein's montage, in which he often juxtaposes somewhat disparate images so that by a kind of visual metaphor based on contiguity he might communicate the irrational associations that obtain in the world of the film. Usher, for example, sits in his cavernous salon and plays his guitar. The following images show trees as the wind buffets them about, suggesting both affective turbulence and a world permeated with the passion of music. The outer world of nature and its violence are set in analogy to the inner world of creation and the demonic imagination (which, as in "The Oval Portrait," is destructive of life). The juxtaposition of the outer and inner worlds creates foreboding and dread, though . . . one should not necessarily attribute this state to any character within the film.

Another comparable example can be given: the scene in Epstein's version of "The Fall of the House of Usher" when Usher's wife dies (Epstein's changing the story's sister into a wife would appear to be his way of refusing the incest motif that fascinated Poe). Using a form of montage within the frame, Epstein superimposes rows of candles on the shot of the funeral procession as it proceeds slowly through a somber forest. Here the analogy is created by trick photography as Epstein, in an overly contrived bit of juxtaposition, uses his candles to suggest that grief permeates the world of nature. In the same sequence, however, Epstein reverts to the mimetic device of a supposedly subjective camera; the "subjective" camera represents the point of view of a character within the film. Epstein's creation of this type of subjective mimesis is ingenuous. As the bier is transported, he points his camera toward the sky, thus espousing the point of view of the corpse and at the same time representing her as a living being—which she is in one sense. Within a single sequence, then, Epstein runs the gamut from poetic analogy to subjective representation of a most peculiar sort.

Epstein also typifies development of the most varied use of camera movement and angles for types of mimesis that rely entirely on the mobile nature of the camera. In exploring the cursed house, for instance, the camera, shooting from an awkward, oblique angle, rushes down the hall of the mansion, skirting along the floor, as though fleeing some impending catastrophe. Here motion itself is a form of mimesis, and the camera's extremely rapid forward trajectory through space is an analogy for the fear-flight that permeates the film. This use of motion to create analogy is perhaps the film's most unique feature, and one that, after the Impressionists, does not appear to have been really exploited again until Resnais. Indeed, for many viewers the most memorable moment in the film is probably the sequence in which Usher, after he has killed his wife by incorporating her soul into his painting, is propelled across the room in another moment of anguish-flight. Here Epstein placed his actor on the camera dolly and sent it rolling across the floor. Usher's face thus remains at a fixed distance from the lens while the background flies by in a blurred rush. The effect of such a composition, as Usher's mad eyes remain fixed upon us, is not unlike Munch's *The Scream,* for the blurred background, isolating Usher's contorted face, acts again as an analogon to the dread that engulfs Usher's world.

The comparison with Munch, whose influence on expressionist painting can hardly be overestimated, is instructive, for it points to the affinities that the so-called Impressionists have with their German contemporaries. Perhaps this is one reason why French critics and historians have often been less than sympathetic to filmmakers like Epstein. Georges Sadoul, for example, considers the Impressionist School to be a deviation from the naturalist tradition that he sees as the most constant aspect of French cinema. This seems a rather strange way of viewing both Epstein and the Impressionists in general, for even if they were not entirely successful in their experimentation, they seem to us to be typical of an avant-garde tradition that is as constant an aspect of French cinema as naturalism. They were singularly important for making American and Russian developments known in France and for attempting to translate some of the narrative and poetic concerns of literary modernism into filmic expression. Moreover, they created the climate in which Dada and surrealism could come to grips with film. For example, it is only against the backdrop of the Impressionist School that one can fully understand Buñuel's first work in cinema.

Wassily Kandinsky

1866–1944

Russian painter, critic, and poet.

INTRODUCTION

Considered one of the most influential painters of the German Expressionist movement, Kandinsky is best known for his artistic and theoretical contributions to the development of nonrepresentational, or abstract, art. Using brilliant colors in compositions of geometric shapes and lines, he sought to communicate experiences and emotions through a purely visual language divested of all symbolic or narrative content. In doing so, Kandinsky redefined traditional concepts of the picture plane and provided the rationale for much of modern art.

Biographical Information

Kandinsky was born to an affluent family in Moscow and educated in Odessa, a port city in the southern Ukraine. In 1886 he enrolled in a program of law, economics, and politics at Moscow University, where, after graduating in 1893, he accepted a position on the Faculty of Law. During his years as a student and instructor, he became fascinated with art, and after viewing the paintings of the French Impressionists in 1895 he abandoned his teaching position to study painting. As a student at the Munich Academy of Art, he developed and interest in *Art Noveau* or *Jugendstil*, a movement whose adherents promoted decorative art. By 1901, Kandinsky had become a noteworthy figure in the art community in Munich. Critics generally refer to the years between 1908 and 1914—when Kandinsky first espoused abstractionism—as the period of his greatest achievements. According to an often-cited anecdote, Kandinsky's "discovery" of abstract art occurred in 1908 when, struck by the beauty and originality of one of his own paintings, he realized that the work had been turned upside-down; the figures he had found especially pleasing and communicative owed their advantage to their lack of conventional denotation.

In 1912 Kandinsky, along with his colleagues Gabriele Münter, Franz Marc, and August Macke, formed the Blaue Reiter (Blue Rider) group. Blue Rider offered a forum in its publication *Blaue Reiter Almanach* for the diverse viewpoints concerning art, music, and architecture found in the Expressionist movement. At the onset of World War I, he returned to Russia, where he remained for seven years, teaching art at the University of Moscow and serving as a consultant for the country's cultural education program. In 1922 Kandinsky accepted a teaching position on the staff of the Bauhaus, Germany's creative center for architecture and design. He remained as an instructor at the Bauhaus until 1933, when the

National Socialist Government forced the school to close. He then moved to Paris where he set up a studio and devoted his time to painting. He died in 1944.

Major Works

Kandinsky's early paintings were highly stylized and colorful landscapes that reflect the influence of the Fauvists, often containing figures reminiscent of fairy tale and Russian folklore characters, as in his *Couple Riding* of 1905. After his discovery of abstract art in 1908, his paintings became increasingly abstract, consisting of black lines and vividly colored arcs and triangles in compositions dominated by blue, purple, yellow, and red, colors that he believed representative of specific psychological states, In addition to painting, he documented the artistic principles upon which he based his use of color and form, publishing his theories as *Concerning the Spiritual in Art* in 1911. This essay proved to be one of the most influential treatises on art ever written. His later work is generally considered a culmination of his talents, and most critics note that the geometric and organic shapes in his later works are more precisely defined and more intricate in dimension, than those of his earlier works, creating an impression of energy and movement.

Critical Reception

While Kandinsky's delineation of the aims of abstract art is regarded as eloquent and important, many critics contend that his own work often failed to incorporate the principles he advanced. Such critics note in particular that his paintings do not achieve his goal of creating nonrepresentational works that would transcend mere decoration through their power to express ideas and emotions. However, Kandinsky's theories were successfully realized by subsequent artists and art movements, and he is therefore acknowledged as the primary theorist of modern abstractionism.

PRINCIPAL WORKS

Klänge [*Sounds*] (prose poems) 1912
Über das Geistige in der Kunst [*Concerning the Spiritual in Art*] (criticism) 1912
Punkt und Linie zu Flache: Beitrag zur Analyse der malerischen Elemente [*Point and Line to Plane: Contributions to the Analysis of the Pictorial Elements*] (criticism) 1926
Kandinsky: The Bauhaus Years (catalog) 1966
Ecrits Complets. 2 vols. [*Kandinsky: Complete Writings on Art*] (criticism) 1970
Arnold Schönberg, Wassily Kandinsky: Briefe, Bilder und Dokumente einer aussergewöhnlichen Begegnung [*Arnold Schoenberg, Wassily Kandinsky: Letters, Pictures, and Documents*] (letters) 1980
Kandinsky: Catalogue Raisonné of the Oil-Paintings. 2 vols. (catalog) 1982
Kandinsky: Watercolors and Drawings (catalog) 1992
Kandinsky (catalog) 1999

CRITICISM

Wassily Kandinsky (essay date 1899)

SOURCE: "Secession," in *Critical Inquiry,* Vol. 23, No. 4, Summer, 1997, p. 729.

[*In the following translation of an 1899 review, Kandinsky assesses the work shown at the 1899 Munich Secession's international exhibit.*]

Kandinsky's review of the 1899 Munich Secession's international exhibition is his first major art essay.[1] It appeared in *Novosti dnia* (News of the Day), 4 November 1899, a prominent Moscow daily newspaper covering local, national, and international events, with occasional features on literature and art. Its discovery revises the status given to Kandinsky's 1901 article **"Critique of Critics,"**[2] which has been credited by Western scholars as his first essay on art.[3] **"Secession"**'s publication thus gives us some of the earliest indications of Kandinsky's views on art, when he was a student in Munich. It was written only weeks before the approaching new century at a time when Kandinsky witnessed profound changes in art whose impact would be felt for years to come.

In **"Secession,"** Kandinsky recognized art's affinity with the momentum of the changing age and the promise it would bring for greater innovation and expertise. The essay was a response to debates within Russia's art community on the value of such progress to Russian culture and society. **"Secession"** follows a series of articles written in 1898 and 1899—among others, Igor Grabar's "Decline or Renaissance?" and Sergei Diaghilev's "Complicated Questions"[4]—that challenged Russian realism's dominance and resistance to artistic change. These authors sought legitimacy for "decadent" Western European art, such as impressionism, postimpressionism, and symbolism, as an arbiter of progress for contemporary art in Russia. Western European art, in all its innovation and potential as a salvation for Russia's stagnant art climate, offered Russian artists a means of expressing their individuality freely; they thus defied the dated and repressive policies promoted by the Russian realists and the tsarist art academy. Kandinsky's review of the Munich Secession exhibition provided him with a means of broadening the Russian public's awareness of a pervasive international phenomenon. Artists throughout Europe were progressing towards individual expression as an acceptable form of artistic behavior. Popular support for this movement gave it a level of credibility difficult for even its most ardent Russian opponents to challenge.

Kandinsky was already painting at the time he wrote his review and was attuned to the changes in techniques and materials impacting Europe's art world so deeply. In painting, artists' rediscovery of tempera provided them with the technical means of treating color differently. Tempera's properties as a stable, quick-drying pigment, whose colors produced a bright and intense richness, were conducive to the creation of paintings in which artists could assert themselves through color as an expression of their individuality. The significance of this development in painting was paralleled by the Arts and Crafts Movement, which had elevated goods from their merely functional value to a higher art form, as a source of spiritual enrichment. Beauty became a commodity available not only to the cultured elite but to the masses. Sold in the form of household items designed by artists, their sense of color, line, and materials brought the industry an aesthetic sensibility that had been heretofore unseen.

Kandinsky's message of progress and artistic reform and its power as an indicator of what art would become in the future century was tempered three years later, however, in his 1902 review of the Munich Secession and Artists' Association (Kunstlergenossenschaft) exhibitions, entitled **"Correspondence from Munich."**[5] As the new age failed to bring with it a consistent path of achievement, Kandinsky was unable to offer his Russian public the level of encouragement he had so willingly expressed in his earlier review. The work of many artists in both shows fell short of his expectations as artists' evolution towards mastering the synthesis of individual expression with technique and style either did not materialize in its own right or succumbed to faddish trends.

In one of my first accounts of Munich's art exhibits I spoke, by the way, of that strange and still-yielding impression, which turned up among spectators in the exhibition halls devoted to Scottish painting. I spoke of the tiresomeness and monotony of that foggy veil which covered these artists' paintings: fog in the morning, afternoon, evening, and night, with sun and in overcast weather; fog, appearing in landscape, genre, portrait, a beautiful fog, giving that fairy-tale and peculiarly poetic impression, but with too often recurring persistence as if by order of law, until exhausted. Arising now and then on its own but most of the time drifting over from Scotland, this foggy mood was cultivated in the painting of countries all over the world.

And it is just now, perhaps, that a reaction is beginning: pure and intense light, purity and brightness of colors are beginning to burn here and there with intense patches among many others, immersed as usual in a dull haze of paintings. I am not presuming to confirm with assurance that time will disintegrate these weakened colors sooner or later. But another tendency is already clearly emerging. In places, the bright sun shines, which is of a specific character; the mood of dusk that not too long ago took first place among motifs is now beginning to be interpreted differently—the purity and intensity of colors stare out shyly even in overcast weather. Munich's exhibit of innovators in art, this year's "Secession," will give a rough picture of these two trends in contemporary painting.

Whistler's brilliant words on the harmony of dusk flew all over the world with astonishing speed. It was also often reiterated by them that true beauty springs up with the death of day. "When the evening mist," said that great artist,

> clothes the riverside with poetry, as with a veil, and the poor buildings lose themselves in the dim sky, and the tall chimneys become campanili, and the warehouses are palaces in the night, and the whole city hangs in the heavens, and fairy-land is before us—then the wayfarer hastens home; the working man and the cultured one, the wise man and the one of pleasure, cease to understand, as they have ceased to see, and Nature, who, for once, has sung in tune, sings her exquisite song to the artist alone, her son and her master—her son in that he loves her, her master, in that he knows her.[6]

The matter has come to the point where some of the most exceptional artists have begun to look at the sun through the dusky prism. They go to extremes trying to soften tones and turn the sun's spot into an apparition. The famous Scotsman Brangwyn, whose influence spread all over Europe in its turn and found avid supporters in Munich, acts in this fashion. This year a decorative panel was presented to these supporters at the "Secession": a few nude male figures playing classical pipes in a mist-filled sunny glade amidst trees with translucent shadows. As usual, it is an extremely pretty and interesting piece. The young and talented Angello Jank of Munich exhibited several pieces, which bore extremely close resemblance in tones to those of the Scotsman. His knights are very beautiful in the gloomy evening hours. The well-known Englishman Greiffenhagen submitted *Annunciation,* in which, as always, he combined the same foggy color treatment with the composition of the true offshoots of the English Pre-Raphaelites. The Municher Pipho reflected the same colors in his own work as if in a mirror. The forefather of all of Munich's school and on the whole of most of Germany's landscapists, Dill, again submitted several ultrafoggy pictures. The prominent French artist Carriere exhibited fog in the form of a portrait. From Russia fog was sent by Levitan (*Silence*).

And here, in the midst of this international assembly of fogs, patches of the new light caught on fire in some places. While this new light is not very obvious, nor stands on its own, it is still anxiously and timidly forging a path. Among the forefathers of this trend we welcome with steadfast fondness Claude Monet and alongside him the great Bocklin who, almost at the same time, could both paint colorless tones of oleographic pigments and create colorist masterpieces. The tempera and oil paintings of other artists follow them, following the path of purity of tones and intensity of coloring. Of those who seek to resolve this problem with oil paints, there is not one who could sustain the purity of intense colors throughout the piece. Professor of the Munich Academy L. Herterich, in his *Ulrich von Hutten,* combined intense and pure tones on the armor with muddy and boring colors in a huge painting of a crucifixion and the head of a knight. Hierl-Deronco's huge painted canvas—*Garden of Love*—a row of female figures in a landscape—gave the most tasteless combination of intense strokes of color with the blackness and mud of mixed tones.

Pigments that are not ground in oil, but in various other binding materials, so-called tempera,[7] represent of themselves a more worthwhile remedy in these investigations. It is well known that, with Van Dyke's idea of grinding pigments in oil, old tempera paints were soon given up and the recipes for their preparation forgotten. Oil paints, which remained unchanged in tone upon drying, were appealing to artists because of their comparative technical ease. Many artists of late still were not aware of the existence of other paints, and known tempera recipes are used on a limited basis, albeit with ever-growing popularity. Now, when the time of the cult of the individual has come that one can call the coloristic, brightness, intensity, and especially the guaranteed stability of temperas should tend to draw our attention.[8] But the novelty and high level of difficulty of the tempera technique intimidate novices in this field. This technique requires a number of years of specialized study, which still does not yet guarantee mastery. Sometimes the artist, having painted in tempera for many years, is forced to return to oil since he still doesn't satisfactorily know the formula for preparing a painting with those alluring and mysterious colors. Franz Stuck continually gets his paintings back from galleries and private collectors because his tempera paint falls off the canvas. His practice of occasionally combining both processes is in his hands, at the very least, a coloristic nonsense. Take his *Sisyphus* of this year. A huge, struggling, naked man who, as usual, is talentedly executed in the exertion of his musculature, rolls an enormous stone upwards. The man and the landscape are a dirty greenish tone, which appears lackluster next to two red, clearly tempera'd areas in the sky.

Besides the difficulty of the technique, tempera often has the dangerous property of carrying artists to the extreme in their use of bright colors that only great talent and knowledge can combine into one whole. The novice artist Anetsberger fell into just this trap. Even if he had enough talent, his lack of experience prevented him from creating a coloristically unified work from his own interesting thought.

And that insufficient coherency of tone also magnifies another shortcoming in this painting. Captivating only for its colors (but not mastering them), the painting's composition has been entirely neglected, which one unwittingly expects from a painting entitled *The Legend*. On one side of a marble well stands a knight in full armor, on the other—a woman without any clothes, with a cup in her hands, and loose hair. In back are trees. The knight is looking in one direction, the woman—in the other, and they have nothing to do with one another. Of course, it would have been impossible to demand a tedious emphasis of the motif because the connection between the composition and the latter must not awaken an unsolvable riddle.[9]

Hetze better resolved the problem with tempera in his *Solitude*. His is a small, narrow, and long painting where the contemplative figure of an old monk slowly walks through the midst of the thick trunks of a gloomy forest. Here, though dull as they are, tones are tied together satisfactorily. The ultimate expert in this matter is the eminent old man, A. Bocklin, in a tempera that impresses artists. Two symbolic figures, *Troubles* and *Poverty,* are painted in soft, pure, and unusually beautiful colors, where the problem of coloring is resolved with inimitable ease and simplicity. His other painting, *War,* addresses another problem—mood. Four frightful figures (death, terror, murder, and fire) are galloping madly through the air; everything is burned and destroyed in their path; the only thing left behind them is a bright blazing legendary town.

Speaking particularly of portraits, I should carefully focus on the characteristics of the two tendencies manifested in this "Secession," but I fear tiring the reader with specialized details. I'll only say that the best and most interesting in this body of works are the portraits by Zorn, Serov, Samberger, and Habermann. The first two, with usual mastery, go into greater detail than the latter. Samberger and Habermann seek only an overall impression, painting the heads in large masses. (I beg specialists' pardon for the forced inaccuracy of my characterization.) From that perspective, both of them impress with enormous knowledge, and Habermann moreover in outlandish colors, which on the whole, he seems to totally disregard.[10] One finally must recognize the most beautiful portrait, which is without a doubt Serov's.

With regard to sculpture—the most interesting and skillful appear in the works of the new professors of Moscow's painting school, P. Trubetskoi and F. Stuck. The latter, it appears, is very talented, especially in this field of art. He's a born sculptor; already in his painting he works almost exclusively on bodily forms and increasingly disregards color. His small sculpture *Ballet Dancer* is a real *chef d'oeuvre.*

With the exception of drawings, where the outstanding Degas stands in first place, the "Secession" allotted its largest space to art industry that, according to the opinion of many, should rechristen it from "Kleine" to "Grosse Kunst." Almost half of the exhibition rooms are occupied with this again blossoming field of production. In Munich there is a special "school of art industry" (Kunstgewerbeschule), with a very serious seven-year course, from which emerge artists who have devoted the strengths of their talent and knowledge to the beauty of household articles. The most exceptional of them founded—it seems it hasn't even been a year—their own factory and store (called the Union of Art Workshops in Handicraft—Vereinigte Werkstatte fur Kunst in Handwerk), which is like an ongoing exhibit of artistic objects. Here you can find entire furnishings for a room, a kitchen, and hallways and a mass of decorative pieces: clocks, candlesticks, hooks for clothes, tables for the family, briefcases, frames, tea sets, ashtrays, gold and silver pieces, and so on and so on.

Admittance into this store is free. Having entered it, you can walk around, look at pieces, without planning to buy anything; a female assistant accompanying you gives you the names of the authors of the designs. Business for this new company is going very well, and its products are rapidly penetrating into life. Three of the most popular members of this company obtained four rooms at the "Secession," which they finished with their designs down to the last detail: walls, ceilings, windows—all transformed by them in those rooms, some of which have ovens and fireplaces; and every small little object is tied to the whole by design and color, even illustrated journals scattered here and there match in color the entire installation. The young artist F. Erler arranged two rooms, the first of which (the sitting room) was especially interesting with its bold combination of two colors—white and bright red (vermillion), in which are executed simple wall and fireplace decorations that were carried through on the objects and on which a female portrait and a decorative panel, painted by Erler, are constructed. Bruno Paul, excellent caricaturist, collaborator of *Simplicissimus*,[11] executed a dining room that was similarly consistent in tone. Its walls are covered with a plain thick fabric, like canvas, on top of which soft, flowing ornaments are painted. A tea arrangement is laid out on the dining room table, its legs matching in design and tone the entire installation. Beside this great master is, in this respect, B. Pankok, who decorated his room (like a receiving room) a light grey stained oak. There is a very interesting men's study room, made by the Belgian H. Van-de-Velde; it has an enormous writing table, a stool with it, a bookcase, secretary, a rug, and so on, characterized by those leisurely flowing-meandering lines, which are readily cultivated not only by this artist, but in general in the new contemporary style. In addition to those rooms, the great hall is filled with furniture and cases of objects for every kind of use and luxury: clocks, lamps, the finest women's adornments, statues—stuff from every rank of artists from every country. All that is in that section of the exhibition, entitled "Art in Handicraft," numbers over three hundred. Arising in its main form in England and having found fertile ground in all countries of Europe and in part in America, the new style of the coming century has made striking progress in a very short time. The words of one of the English artists, that beauty ought to enter into every detail of daily life, encountered sympathy and application. It can be said that, with every year, the style's character becomes more defined, and in its time the art historian clearly formulates that common spirit which serves as the sign of a great epoch in art. The bold negation of aged models, the cessation of those dull and feeble contours on the strength and flick of a line, and recently the development of some special kind of charming simplicity—there the character of this new phenomenon is superficially noted. We are experiencing a more interesting period, when art and especially painting is beginning to come out of the embryo of a new epoch, where everything bright is not just a premonition among a few specialists but a great renaissance, for which the approaching twentieth century is opening its doors. The striving for beauty genuinely seizes the hearts of people; self-satisfied, profane people, these days still throwing lumps of dirt at evolving art, are already beginning to feel embarrassed in some places; the number of talented people with a comprehension of beauty is growing, and already more than one of these artists-creators of that renaissance found for themselves sympathy and understanding among their own group. And it wasn't that long ago that the endlessly far, foggy, and that which is seen with especially sharp-sighted eyes—the light of the new age burns brighter from time to time and everything blazingly illuminates the way. Let those who are blinded by that light turn away and search for the past because the tarnished past brings peace to their weak eyes.

TRANSLATOR'S NOTE

This translation emerged through the course of research on my dissertation, begun at the University of Chicago in 1991. The citation for Kandinsky's article is found in V. P. Lapshin, "Iz istorii khudozhestvennykh sviazei Rossii i Germanii v kontse XIX-nachale XX veka" [From the History of Artistic Relations between Russia and Germany at the End of the Nineteenth-Beginning of the Twentieth Centuries], in *Vzaimosviazi russkogo i sovetskogo iskusstva i nemetskoi khudozhestvennoi kul'tury* [Interrelations between Russian and Soviet Art and German Artistic Culture], ed. Z. S. Pychnovskaia (Moscow, 1980), pp. 193-235, esp. p. 231. I am grateful to several people for their assistance during the course of this project. They include Yuri Tsivian and Cynthia A. Klima, who provided valuable editorial comments and criticism; Reinhold Heller, for his encouragement and support; and June Pachuta Farris, for her resourcefulness and persistence in helping me acquire a copy of the original article.

I have followed the Library of Congress's system of transliteration. Unless otherwise marked, footnotes within the translated text are Kandinsky's.

NOTES

[1] Kandinsky wrote several essays on other subjects prior to his Secession review. He was trained as a lawyer and had an avid interest in ethnography, resulting in a number of publications in 1889 and 1890. For a discussion of the relevance ethnography had for Kandinsky and his art, as well as references for these early writings, see Peg Weiss, *Kandinsky and Old Russia: The Artist as Ethnographer and Shaman* (New Haven, Conn., 1995), p. 261. See also Weiss, *Kandinsky in Munich: The Formative Jugendstil Years* (Princeton, N.J., 1979), in which she addresses Kandinsky's artistic development during his years in Munich, from 1896 until 1914.

[2] See Wassily Kandinsky, "Kritika kritikov" [Critique of Critics], *Novosti dnia* [News of the Day], nos. 6407 & 6409, 17 and 19 Apr. 1901. For an English translation, see *Kandinsky: Complete Writings on Art,* ed. Kenneth C. Lindsay and Peter Vergo, 2 vols. (Boston, 1982), 1:33-44.

[3] See *Kandinsky: Complete Writings on Art,* 1:33; Jelena Hahl-Koch, Kandinsky (New York, 1993), pp. 17, 413-15; Der fruhe Kandinsky, 1900-1910, ed. Magdalena M. Moeller (exhibition catalogue, Brucke Museum, Berlin, 1 Sept. 1994-27 Nov. 1994), pp. 317-19; and Weiss, *Kandinsky and Old Russia,* pp. 261-62.

[4] See Igor Grabar, "Upadok ili vozrozhdenie?" [Decline or Renaissance?], *Niva* [The Field], nos. 1-2 (1897): 38-74, 295-314, and Sergei Diaghilev, "Slozhnie voprosy: Nash mnimyi upadok" [Complicated Questions: Our Imaginary Decline], *Mir iskusstva* [World of Art] 1, nos. 1-2 (1898): 1-11; "Vechnaia bor'ba" [The Endless Fight], *Mir iskusstva* 1, nos. 1-2 (1898): 12-16; "Poiski krasoty" [In Search of Beauty], *Mir iskusstva* 1, nos. 3-4 (1899): 37-49; and "Osnovy khudozhestvennoi otsenki" [The Fundamentals of Artistic Creation], *Mir iskusstva* 1, nos. 3-4 (1899): 50-61.

[5] Kandinsky, "Korrespondentsiia iz Miunkhena" [Correspondence from Munich], *Mir iskusstva*, nos. 5-6 (1902): 96-98. For an English translation, see *Kandinsky: Complete Writings on Art*, 1:45-51.

[6] Kandinsky excerpted Whistler's passage from Grabar's essay, "Upadok ili vozrozhdenie?" The English original, as it appears here, is taken from James McNeill Whistler, "Mr. Whistler's 'Ten O'Clock,'" *The Gentle Art of Making Enemies* (London, 1890), p. 144. —TRANS.

[7] These pigments are made the same way by factories as by artists themselves, regarding the setting up of discovered ancient recipes and current-day experiments and trials.

[8] Numerous and quite serious investigations have shown that oil paints, by the very nature of their property, lose tone, darken, and deteriorate over the course of time. In the opinion of the chemist Professor Pettenkofer, pure oil paintings are doomed sooner or later from complete damage.

[9] I don't know why, but the colorists in today's "Secession" willingly unite purely mechanical knights with various painting titles, whose inner meaning is not always easy to discern. Perhaps it arises from the colorist seeking suitable material for the expression of his aspirations, and then as tradition dictates thinks himself obligated to christen it with whatever interesting name, in keeping with accidentally having found objects on the canvas which are united as a whole by their colors only.

[10] Meaning, Habermann's piece is successful even though he gives the impression of not working his colors very conscientiously. - TRANS.

[11] Still a young satirical journal, it is exceptional in this genre and in its use of artistic drawings.

Peter Selz (essay date 1957)

SOURCE: "Esthetic Theories of Wassily Kandinsky," in *German Expressionist Painting*, University of California Press, 1957, pp. 223-33.

[*In the following essay, Selz delineates the major themes of Kandinsky's theoretical writings, in particular his* Concerning the Spiritual in Art *and "Über die Formfrage."*]

The artistic purpose of the Blaue Reiter movement was most thoroughly articulated in Kandinsky's theoretical writings, especially the two essays, **Concerning the Spiritual in Art** and **"Über die Formfrage,"** published in *Der Blaue Reiter*. Although these essays, which both appeared in 1912,[1] are largely based on earlier esthetic theory, they constitute almost a programmatic manifesto for the expressionist generation:

> If *Der Blaue Reiter*, published by R. Piper, is taken together with Kandinsky's supplement, **Das Geistige in der Kunst**, as a unity, then this double volume is just as much *the* book of the pre-war years, as Hildebrand's *Problem der Form* was *the* book of the turn of the century. The separation of the two generations is already made clear in the title, which emphasizes form in the one and spirit in the other.[2]

Kandinsky's particular didactic style makes his writings difficult to read and analyze. Kenneth Lindsay, in his study of Kandinsky's theories, described Kandinsky's peculiar literary style as follows:

> Characteristic of Kandinsky's writing is the technique of breaking up the given topic into opposites or alternatives. These opposites or alternatives usually follow directly after the posing of the problem and are numbered. Often they suggest further sets of opposites and alternatives. The sequence of thought is flexible, sometimes abrupt and cross-tracking, and frequently associative. The dominating relativity of the thought process contrasts strongly with the conclusions, which are often positively stated.[3]

THE REJECTION OF MATERIAL REALITY

Kandinsky was always strongly predisposed toward sense impressions. In his autobiography he indicates that he experienced objects, events—even music—primarily in terms of color; he did not conceive of color in its physical and material aspects, but rather in its emotional effect. During his scientific studies he lost faith in the rational scientific method and felt that reality could be fully comprehended only by means of creative intuition.

Kandinsky was not alone in his rejection of positivism and pragmatism at the turn of the century. His doubt of the ultimate possibilities of quantitative analysis was shared by many philosophers, not only by neo-Hegelian idealists. His philosophy found perhaps its closest parallel in the thinking of Henri Bergson, who taught that true reality can be grasped only through artistic intuition, which he contrasted to intellectual conception. The intellect, according to Bergson, is man's tool for rational action, but "art, whether it be painting or sculpture, poetry or music, has no other object than to brush aside the utilitarian symbols, the conventional and socially accepted generalities, in short everything that veils reality from us, in order to bring us face to face with reality itself."[4]

"The twentieth century has in its first third taken up a position of reaction against classic rationalism and intellectualism."[5] Even in the pure sciences the value of the intuitive as against the purely experimental was stressed during the early part of the twentieth century, so that by 1925 Werner Heisenberg was able to formulate the "Principle of Uncertainty." According to this principle, there is a limit to the precision with which we can observe nature scientifically. This did not mean a return to metaphysics, but it indicated the inherent limitations of quantitative observation.

The concept that matter was not eternally fixed, but could be transmuted into energy, was also of great interest to the artists in their attempt to liberate themselves from servitude to the material world. Franz Marc, aware of the developments in scientific thought, hoped to find, behind the curtain of appearances, the "true reality":

> I am beginning more and more to see behind or, to put it better, through things, to see behind them something which they conceal, for the most part cunningly, with their outward appearance by hoodwinking man with a façade which is quite different from what it actually covers. Of course, from the point of view of physics this is an old story. . . . The scientific interpretation has powerfully transformed the human mind; it has caused the greatest type-change we have so far lived to see. Art is indisputably pursuing the same course, in its own way, certainly; and the problem, our problem, is to discover the way.[6]

Similarly, Kandinsky was "struck with terrific impact" by the discovery of the disintegration of the atom.[7] As early as his first encounter in Moscow with the paintings by Monet, he felt that the material object was not a necessary element in his painting: "I had the impression that here painting itself comes into the foreground; I wondered if it would not be possible to go further in this direction. From then on I looked at the art of ikons with different eyes; it meant that I had 'got eyes' for the abstract in art."[8] Later he wrote: "The impossibility and, in art, the purposelessness of copying an object, the desire to make the object express itself, are the beginnings of leading the artist away from 'literary' color to artistic, i.e. pictorial aims."[9]

Agreeing with earlier writers, such as the symbolists van de Velde and Endell, Kandinsky and Marc felt that art must express the spirit, but that in order to accomplish this task it must be dematerialized. Of necessity, this meant creating a new art form.

Kandinsky wished to forsake objective reality not only for philosophic reasons; psychological reasons, it seems, also played their part. Speaking about his period of study at the Munich Art Academy, Kandinsky wrote: "The naked body, its lines and movement, sometimes interested me, but often merely repelled me. Some poses in particular were repugnant to me, and I had to force myself to copy them. I could breathe freely only when I was out of the studio door and in the street once again."[19]

Franz Marc, when turning toward nonobjective painting shortly before his death, gave a similar reason: "Very early in life I found man ugly; the animal seemed to me more beautiful and cleaner, but even in it I discovered so much that was repelling and ugly that my art instinctively and by inner force became more schematic and abstract."[11]

Significantly, the human body, which is an almost universal motif in the art forms of most cultures, is here eschewed as subject matter. It is true that the art of the West emphasized the nonhuman aspects during the nineteenth century, when painters turned their attention to still life and landscape. The conscious rejection of the human form is, however, certainly fraught with significance. A psychological interpretation of the reasons for this response would be a highly rewarding task, especially as it might result in a more profound understanding of the nonobjective artist and his work. Such an analysis, however, goes beyond the framework of this [essay].

From the point of view of the history of esthetics it is also interesting that Kandinsky's rejection of the forms of nature occurred at approximately the same time as Worringer's publication *Abstraction and Empathy,* which advances the theory that the cause for abstraction is man's wish to withdraw from the world or his antagonism toward it.[12]

Kandinsky and Marc gave no further reasons for their retreat from natural and human forms.[13] Kandinsky said in his autobiography that he often preferred to leave the studio to follow his own dreams and visions. Returning from a walk one day, he had the experience of seeing one of his paintings in an unusual position, which made it clear to him that the representation of nature was superfluous in his art.[14] His experience shows the importance of the element of distance in the esthetic experience, as stated by Edward Bullough in 1912: "The sudden view of things from their reverse, usually unnoticed, side, comes upon us as a revelation, and such revelations are precisely those of art."[15]

Kandinsky felt, however, that he could not immediately turn to "concrete" or "absolute" painting. In a letter to Hilla Rebay[16] he said that at that time he was still alone in the realization that painting ultimately must discard the object. A long struggle for increasing abstraction from nature was still necessary. In 1910 he was still saying: "Today the artist cannot progress exclusively with purely abstract forms, as these forms are not sufficiently precise. Limiting oneself to the unprecise, it deprives one of possibilities, excluding the purely human and therefore, weakening the power of expression."[17]

But he was already pointing out at that time, that the abstract idea was constantly gaining ground, and Kandinsky predicted that the final predominance of the abstract would be inevitable. He said that the choice of subjects must originate from the inner necessity of the artist, and that material, or objective, form might be more or less superfluous. He insisted that the artist must be given complete freedom to express himself according to the "principle of inner necessity." He looked hopefully to the future: "When the possibility of speaking through artistic means will be developed, it will become superfluous to borrow from the exterior world for spiritual expression."[18]

In 1910 Kandinsky executed his first abstract work: a water color. The first large nonobjective oil dates from 1911; throughout 1912 he did both objective and "concrete" paintings. After 1912 there were very few objective works. His art had become completely free from nature; like music, its meaning was now meant to be inherent in the work itself and independent of external objects.

Kandinsky distinguished what he called "objective" art from "concrete" art by distinguishing between the means chosen by the artist. In objective art both artistic and natural elements are used, resulting in "mixed" art; in concrete art exclusively artistic means are used, resulting in "pure" art.[19] In a short article, published in 1935, he gave a lucid example of this distinction:

> There is an essential difference between a line and a fish. And that is that the fish can swim, can eat and be eaten. It has the capacities of which the line is deprived. These capacities of the fish are necessary extras for the fish itself and for the kitchen, but not for the painting. And so, not being necessary they are superfluous. That is why I like the line better than the fish—at least in my painting.[20]

The element of representation was thus rejected by Kandinsky for his art. He insisted that a picture's quality lay in what is usually called form—its lines, shapes, colors, planes—without reference to anything outside the canvas. But here was an apparent contradiction in Kandinsky's theory, because he—like expressionist theoreticians in general—did not believe that a picture must be evaluated from its formal aspects. Kandinsky and the expressionists did not agree with "formalists" like Roger Fry, who believed that the esthetic emotion was essentially an emotion about form. Seeing Kandinsky's first abstractions, Fry concerned himself only with their form: ". . . one finds that . . . the improvisations become more definite, more logical and more closely knit in structure, more surprisingly beautiful in their color oppositions, more exact in their equilibrium."[21]

Kandinsky took strong issue with this theory. In his esthetics the formal aspect of a work of art was as unimportant as its representational quality.

THE INSIGNIFICANCE OF FORM

Form, to Kandinsky, was nothing but the outward expression of the artist's inner needs. Form is matter, and the artist is involved in a constant struggle against materialism. Kandinsky's words are reminiscent of medieval thought: "It is the spirit that rules over matter, and not the other way around."[22]

The artist should not seek salvation in form, Kandinsky warned in his essay **"Über die Formfrage,"** because form is only an expression of content and is entirely dependent on the innermost spirit. It is this spirit that chooses form from the storehouse of matter, and it always chooses the form most expressive of itself. Content always creates its own appropriate form. Form may be chosen from anywhere between the two extreme poles: the great abstraction and the great realism. Kandinsky then proceeded to prove that these opposites, the abstract and the realistic,

are actually identical, and that form is therefore an insignificant concern to the artist: In the "great realism" (as exemplified in the art of Henri Rousseau) the external-artistic element of painting is discarded, and the content—the inner feeling of the object—is brought forth primitively and "purely" through the representation of the simple, rough object. Artistic purpose is expressed directly because the painting is not burdened with formal problems. The content is now strongest because it is divested of external and academic concepts of beauty. Kandinsky preferred this "great realism" (also found in children's drawings) to the use of distortion, which always aroused literary associations.[23]

Since the "great abstraction" excludes "real" objects, the content is embodied in nonobjective form. Thus the "inner sound" of the picture is most clearly manifest. The scaffolding of the object has been removed, as in realism the scaffolding of beauty has been discarded. In both cases the artist arrives at the spiritual content itself.

> The greatest external differentiation becomes the greatest internal identity:
>
> Realism = Abstraction
>
> Abstraction = Realism[24]

The hypothesis that the minimum of abstraction can have the most abstract effect—and vice versa—is based by Kandinsky on an esthetic law, which he postulates: A quantitative decrease can be equal to a qualitative increase—2 plus 1 can be less than 2 minus 1 in esthetics. A dot of color, for example, may lose in its *effect* of intensity if its *actual* intensity is increased.[25] The pragmatic function of a form and its sentient meaning are dissimilar, yet abstraction and realism are identical.

Kandinsky cited several examples to prove this thesis. A hyphen, for instance, is of practical value and significance in its context. If this hyphen is taken out of its practical-purposeful context and put on canvas, and if it is not used there to fulfill any practical purpose at all—such as the delineation of an object—it then becomes nothing but a line; it is completely liberated from signification and abstracted from all its meaning as a syntactical sign; it is the abstract line itself. At the same time, however, it has also become most real, because now it is no longer a sign but the real line—the object itself.

It may be argued that Kandinsky used a very narrow definition of both the abstract and the realistic, and that the line may be a great deal more realistic and more meaningful as a sign (such as a hyphen) in its context than it is as a line only. It is a valid objection to say that this identity of the abstract and the real holds true only in this verbal analogy, and that Kandinsky did not present logical proof. Kandinsky, however, was not concerned with the correctness of intellectual thought, or with the proof of his spiritual values. He admitted: "I have always turned to reason and intellect least of all."[26]

He concluded his analysis of form by saying: "In principle there is no problem of form."[27] The artist who expresses his "soul vibrations" can use any form he wants. Formal rules in esthetics are not only impossible but a great stumbling block to the free expression of spiritual value. It is the duty of the artist to fight against these rules to clear the way for free expression. In the history of art, artists were often bogged down by matter and could not see beyond the formal. The nineteenth century was such a period, in which men failed to see the spirit in art as they failed to see it in religion. But to seek art and yet be satisfied with form is equivalent to the contentment with the idol in the quest for God. Form is dead unless it is expressive of content. There cannot be a symbol without expressive value.

In his introduction to the second edition of *Der Blaue Reiter*, Kandinsky said that the aim of the book was "to show by means of examples, practical arrangement and theoretical proof, that the problem of form is secondary in art, that art is above all a matter of content."[28]

Kandinsky understood his own time as the beginning of a new spiritual age when the abstract spirit was taking possession of the human spirit.[29] Artists would increasingly recognize the insignificance of form per se and realize its relativity, its true meaning as nothing but "the outward expression of inner meaning."

ART THE AFFIRMATION OF THE SPIRIT

In Kandinsky's esthetics the form and representational aspects of art have no importance by themselves, but are meaningful only as they express the artist's innermost feelings. Only through the expression of the artist's inner emotion can he transmit understanding of true spiritual reality itself. The only "infallible guide" that can carry the artist to "great heights" is the *principle of internal necessity* (Kandinsky's italics). This concept of internal necessity is the core and the basis of Kandinsky's esthetic theory, and becomes a highly significant element in expressionist criticism in general.

Kandinsky believed that a period of spiritual revolution—which he called the "spiritual turning point"—was approaching. He perceived indications of this period of transition in many cultural manifestations. In the field of religion, for example, theosophy was attempting to counteract the materialist evil. In the Theosophical Society, "one of the most important spiritual movements,"[30] man was seeking to approach the problem of the spirit by the way of inner enlightenment. In the realm of literature, Kandinsky cited Maeterlinck as

> . . . perhaps one of the first prophets, one of the first reporters and clairvoyants of the *décadence* . . . Maeterlinck creates his atmosphere principally by artistic means. His material machinery . . . really plays a symbolic role and helps to give the inner note. . . . The apt use of a word (in its poetical sense), its repetition, twice, three times, or even more frequently, according to the need of

the poem, will not only tend to intensify the internal structure but also bring out unsuspected spiritual properties in the word itself.[31]

By using pure sound for the most immediate effect upon the reader or listener, the writer depends upon prelanguage signs—that is, sounds that, like music, do not depend upon language for their meaning. This level of signification was also the basis of Kandinsky's non-objective painting. In music, Kandinsky pointed to Schönberg's panchromatic scheme, which advocates the full renunciation of functional harmonious progression and traditional form and accepts only the means that lead the composer to the most uncompromising self-expression: "His music leads us to where musical experience is a matter not of the ear, but of the soul—and from this point begins the music of the future."[32] Kandinsky thought of music as an emancipated art; further, music had the quality of time extension, and was most effective in inspiring spiritual emotion in the listener. Painting, although still largely dependent upon natural form, was showing similar signs of emancipation. Picasso's breakdown of volumes and Matisse's free use of color for its own sake were manifestations of the turning point toward a spiritual art.[33]

How would the artist achieve full spiritual harmony in his composition? Kandinsky said that the painter had two basic means at his disposal—form and color—and that there was always an unavoidable mutual relationship between them.

In Kandinsky's prewar writings he did not come forth with a thorough analysis of forms as he did later in his systematic **Point and Line to Plane**, yet he was already saying: "Form alone, even though abstract and geometrical, has its internal resonance, a spiritual entity whose properties are identical with the form. A triangle . . . is such an entity, with its particular spiritual perfume."[34]

Color is the most powerful medium in the hand of the painter. It has a psychic as well as a physical effect upon the observer. It can influence his tactile, olfactory, and especially aural senses, as well as his visual sense; chromotherapy has shown that "red light stimulates and excites the heart, while blue light can cause temporary paralysis."[35] Color is the artist's means of influencing the human soul. Its meaning is expressed metaphorically by Kandinsky: "Color is the keyboard, the eyes are the hammers, the soul is the piano with many strings. The artist is the hand that plays, touching one key or another purposively, to cause vibrations of the soul."[36]

Kandinsky then proceeded to develop an elaborate explanation of the psychic effect of color. This contrasts to the more scientific color theories of Helmholtz, Rood, Chevreul, and Signac, and closely approaches the psychological color theory of Goethe and metaphysics of color of Philipp Otto Runge. Like his romanticist predecessor, Kandinsky believed that color could directly influence the human soul.[37]

Blue is the heavenly color. It retreats from the spectator, moving toward its own center; it beckons to the infinite, arousing a longing for purity and the super-sensuous. Light blue is like the sound of the flute; dark blue has the sound of the cello.

Yellow is the color of the earth. It has no profound meaning; it seems to spread out from its own center and to advance to the spectator from the canvas. It has the shrill sound of a canary or of a brass horn, and is often associated with the sour taste of lemon.

Green is the mixture of blue and yellow. The concentricity of blue nullifies the eccentricity of yellow. It is passive and static, and can be compared to the so-called "bourgeoisie"—self-satisfied, fat, and healthy. In music it is best represented by the placid, long-drawn middle tones of the violin.

White, which was not considered a color by the impressionists, has the spiritual meaning of a color. It is the symbol of a world void of all material quality and substance—it is the color of beginning. It is the "sound" of the earth during the white period of the Ice Age.

Black is like eternal silence. It is without hope. It signifies termination, and is therefore the color of mourning.

By the symbolic use of colors combined "according to their spiritual significance" the artist can finally achieve a great composition: "Color itself offers contrapuntal possibilities and, when combined with design, may lead to the great pictorial counterpoint, where also painting achieves composition, and where pure art is in the service of the divine."[38]

Kandinsky's color symbolism is in no way based upon physical laws of color or upon the psychology of color vision. "All these statements are the results of empirical feeling, and are not based on exact science."[39] This may even explain his own inconsistencies—such as his statement in *Concerning the Spiritual in Art* that "red light stimulates and excites the heart,"[40] contradicted by his assertion that "red . . . has brought about a state of partial paralysis."[41]

Specific colors call forth different associations in people as well as cultures. Specific reactions to specific colors have never been proved experimentally. Max Raphael, in his book *Von Monet bis Picasso,* said that colors have had altogether different meanings for those individuals most occupied with them. Yellow, for example, signified the earth for Leonardo; had gay, happy connotations for Goethe; meant friendliness to Kant, and heavenly splendor to van Gogh; suggested the night to Gauguin, and aggressiveness to Kandinsky.[42] Yellow symbolizes jealousy in German usage, an emotion associated with green in English idiom.

Kandinsky did not attempt to set down scientific rules for color associations. He merely indicated his own personal associations:

It is very clear that all I have said of these simple colors is very provisional and general, and so are the feelings (joy, grief, etc.) which have been quoted as parallels to the colors. For these feelings are only material expressions of the soul. Shades of color, like those of sound, are of a much finer texture and awaken in the soul emotions too fine to be expressed in prose.[43]

In his second significant book, *Point and Line to Plane: A Contribution to the Analysis of the Pictorial Elements,* Kandinsky presented his grammar of line, forms, and space, as he had done with his color theory in *Concerning the Spiritual in Art.*

The task of the painter, according to Kandinsky, is to achieve the maximum effect by bringing his media, color, and form into orderly and expressive composition. Each art has its own language, and each artist—painter, sculptor, architect, writer, or composer—must work in his specific medium and bring it to the expression of greatest inner significance. But once painting, for example, is divested of the crutch of natural form and becomes completely abstract, the pure law of pictorial construction can be discovered. Then it will be found that pure painting is closely related *internally* to pure music or pure poetry.

SYNTHESIS OF THE ARTS

Kandinsky pointed out that human beings, because of individual differences, differ in the type of art expression to which they are most receptive—for some it is musical form, for others painting or literature. The artist can also achieve esthetic effects in sensory fields not limited to his own medium. Kandinsky was much interested, for example, in Scriabin's experiments with sound-color combinations. The reënforcement of one art form with another by means of synesthesia greatly increases the final esthetic effect upon the receptor. The greatest effect can be obtained by the synthesis of all the arts in one "monumental art," which was the ultimate end of Kandinsky's esthetics.

Kandinsky here continued the nineteenth-century tradition—from Herder to Wagner—with its desire for a union of all arts. A synthesis of the arts is possible, because at a basic level all artistic means are identical in their inner meaning—ultimately the external differences will become insignificant, and the internal identity of all artistic expression will be disclosed. Each art form causes a certain "complex of soul vibrations." The aim of the synthesis of art forms is the refinement of the soul through the sum total of these complexes.

Kandinsky's **"Über Bühnenkomposition"**[44] and **"Schematic Plan of Studies and Work of the Institute of Art Culture"**[45] outlined the possible steps to be taken for the achievement of "monumental art." Present-day drama, opera, ballet are as criticized as the plastic arts. A greater internal unity can be achieved by discarding external factors in "stage composition"[46]—particularly plot, external relationship, and external unity. Kandinsky experimented with such a composition: *Der Gelbe Klang.*[47] He attempted to combine music, the movement of dancers and of objects, the sound of the human voice (without being confined by word or language meanings), and the effect of color tone (after experiments by Scriabin).

Kandinsky admitted that his "stage composition" was weak but believed the principle to be valid. It is necessary to remember that we are still at the very beginning of the great abstract period in art. Materialism still has its grasp on modern activity, and is not as yet completely vanquished. But the new, "the spiritual in art," already manifests itself in most fields of creativity.

Kandinsky made his first attempt at the realization of a synthesis of the arts when he founded the Institute of Art Culture in Moscow in 1920, a comprehensive institute for the study and development of the arts and sciences. Kandinsky was active in this organization as vice-president for about a year; then political pressure forced his resignation, and he found a similar field of activity in the Bauhaus in Weimar, which he joined in 1922.

THE DIRECT COMMUNICATION OF VISUAL ELEMENTS

Expressionism, which began by shifting emphasis from the object to be painted to the artist's own subjective interpretation, reached in Kandinsky the total negation of the object. In this respect he was of great inspiration to succeeding artists. The final phase of expressionism also became the beginning of an altogether new artistic concept: nonobjective painting. Kandinsky was heralded by the following generation as the innovator of nonobjective painting, even by painters whose own direction was completely different:

> I know of nothing more real than the painting of Kandinsky—nor anything more true and nothing more beautiful. A painting by Kandinsky gives no image of earthly life—it is life itself. If one painter deserves the name "creator," it is he. He organizes matter as matter was organized, otherwise the Universe would not exist. He opened a window to look inside the All. Some day Kandinsky will be the best known and best loved by men.[48]

In his rejection of the representational aspects of art, Kandinsky cleared the way for new values in art. By experimenting with the possibility of an expressive—rather than a formalistic—art in the nonobjective idiom, he threw out a challenge that performed a most valuable function in the history of modern art. Through his activity as an esthetician as well as a painter, he wrote a series of books that clearly articulated his ideas and became as influential in the history of modern painting as his paintings did.

Kandinsky's esthetic theory emphasized, among other things, the precept that the elements of painting—lines and colors and their combinations—evoke emotional associations in the observer. This precept was basic to expressionism, although not original with the expressionist movement. Much of this precept was implied in romanticist esthetics, and was clearly stated in the theory of empathy; it was expressed differently in Paul Signac's theory of neoimpressionism, and recurred in Bergson's *Essai sur les données immédiates de la conscience;*[49] it was a significant part of symbolism and its corollary Jugendstil, and was reiterated by such men as Gauguin, Denis, Sérusier, Walter Crane, and Endell.

Kandinsky's essays are exceedingly important because they were written by the man who was the innovator of nonobjective painting. In the total absence of representational objects, the plastic elements were to become sole carriers of the artist's message—which is probably why he felt called upon to express verbally what he had done in his painting through the intuition of "inner necessity."

In the analysis of Kandinsky's color theory it was pointed out that no direct parallels can be established between the artist's statement and the observer's response. Both projections rest on highly personal and subjective factors, and do not differ greatly from music. It has, for example, been shown that the major and minor modes are by no means endowed with characteristics that call forth identical reactions in different listeners[50]—much depends upon previous experience and training.

As Kandinsky indicated, prose cannot express the shades of emotion awakened by sound and color. Each person may verbalize differently about the experience of a work of art, and his verbalization may be at great variance with that of the artist. Yet direct communication can take place on a primary visual (preverbal) level before either spectator or artist articulates. It is toward this level of communication that the art of Kandinsky and other expressionists was directed. For in art, "things that cannot be stated may nonetheless be *shown*—understood, symbolized and presented to our direct apprehension."[51]

NOTES

[1] In 1926 Kandinsky published his most systematic treatise, *Punkt und Linie zur Fläche* as Bauhaus Book no. 9 (Munich, 1926). This book, translated as *Point and Line to Plane* by Howard Dearstyne and Hilla Rebay (New York, 1947), was written at the Bauhaus and elucidates most clearly Kandinsky's thinking during this later period. It falls, however, outside the realm of the present [essay].

[2] Hans Hildebrandt, *Die Kunst des 19. und 20. Jahrhunderts* (Potsdam, 1924), p. 382.

[3] Lindsay, "An Examination of the Fundamental Theories of Wassily Kandinsky," p. 40. Lindsay's dissertation is a considerably more complete and broader survey of Kandinsky's theories than I am attempting here. It raises many important issues; if Lindsay's interpretation seems at times too partial to the artist, its major importance rests in the incisive relationships he establishes between Kandinsky's theories and his paintings. While doing research in Kandinsky's studio in Neuilly-sur-Seine in the

spring of 1950 I had adequate opportunity to compare my interpretations with those of Lindsay. In many ways our interpretations differ, especially as to the placing of emphasis. I am also greatly indebted to Klaus Brisch for many provocative ideas during our discussions in Cologne in the summer of 1953. Unfortunately I have not been able to consult his doctoral dissertation, "Wassily Kandinsky: Untersuchung zur Entstehung der gegenstandslosen Malerei" (University of Bonn, 1955).

[4] Henri Bergson, *Laughter* (New York, 1911), p. 157.

[5] Thomas Mann (ed.), *The Living Thoughts of Schopenhauer* (New York, 1939), p. 29.

[6] Marc, diary entry, Christmas, 1914, in Thoene, *Modern German Art* (Harmondsworth, England, 1938), pp. 66-67.

[7] Wassily Kandinsky, *Wassily Kandinsky Memorial* (New York, 1945), p. 55.

[8] Kandinsky, *Notebooks,* quoted in Nina Kandinsky, "Some Notes on the Development of Kandinsky's Painting," in Kandinsky, *Concerning the Spiritual in Art* (New York, 1947), p. 10.

[9] Kandinsky, *Concerning the Spiritual in Art,* p. 48.

[10] Kandinsky, *Wassily Kandinsky Memorial,* p. 65.

[11] Marc, letter, April 12, 1915, in *Briefe, Aufzeichnungen . . . ,* II, 50. In this respect Kandinsky and the late Marc differed decidedly from Paul Klee, who was always concerned with creating symbols to interpret man and the forces of nature. "The naked body is an altogether suitable object. In art classes I have gradually learned something of it from every angle. But now I will no longer project some plan of it, but will proceed so that all its essentials, even those hidden by optical perspective, will appear upon the paper. And thus a little uncontested personal property has already been discovered, a style has been created." Paul Klee, June, 1902, "Extracts from the Journal of the Artist," in Margaret Miller (ed.), *Paul Klee* (New York, 1945), pp. 8-9.

[12] See chapter i.

[13] In his chapter "Reality and Art," Lindsay deals only with conscious aesthetic reasons for Kandinsky's absolute painting. He does not analyze the underlying causes for this retreat from physical reality, nor does he mention the important statement of repulsion to the naked body that appeared in the artist's autobiography.

[14] See chapter xiv.

[15] Edward Bullough, "Psychical Distance as a Factor in Art and in Aesthetic Principle," *British Journal of Psychology,* V (1912-1913), pp. 87-118.

[16] See chapter xiv.

[17] Kandinsky, *On the Spiritual in Art* (New York, 1946), p. 48. It is necessary to quote the Guggenheim edition of *Über das Geistige in der Kunst* for this passage as it approximates most clearly the original German version. Additions made by the artist in 1914 are incorporated in the Wittenborn edition. These changes imply Kandinsky's later, more hopeful attitude toward pure abstraction. Cf. *Concerning the Spiritual in Art,* p. 48.

[18] Kandinsky, *On the Spiritual in Art,* pp. 80-81.

[19] Kandinsky, "Abstrakte Kunst," *Cicerone,* XVII (1925), 639-647.

[20] Kandinsky, "Line and Fish," *Axis,* II (1935), 6.

[21] Roger Fry in the *Nation* (Aug. 2, 1913), quoted in Arthur J. Eddy, *Cubists and Post-Impressionism* (Chicago, 1914), p. 117.

[22] Kandinsky, *Wassily Kandinsky Memorial,* p. 64.

[23] Lindsay points out correctly that "these opinions of his must be taken into consideration when he is labeled an 'expressionist.'" Lindsay, "An Examination of the Fundamental Theories of Wassily Kandinsky," [University of Wisconsin, 1951], p. 59. On the other hand, expressionist painting may make use of distortion, but to consider expressionism an art of distortion is a frequently encountered misconception.

[24] Kandinsky, "Über die Formfrage," in Kandinsky and Marc, *Der Blaue Reiter* (Munich, 1912), p. 85.

[25] *Ibid.,* p. 84.

[26] Kandinsky, *Wassily Kandinsky Memorial,* p. 71.

[27] Kandinsky, "Über die Formfrage," p. 88.

[28] *Ibid.* [p. v].

[29] This idea is very similar to Herder's theory of Inspiration. J. G. Herder, *Ideen zur Philosophie der Geschichte der Menschheit* (Leipzig, 1821). Here Herder maintained that cultural articulations were human manifestations of the Spirit, which came to man to use him as its organ of expression.

[30] Kandinsky, *Concerning the Spiritual in Art,* p. 32. Kandinsky himself—as Lindsay has pointed out ("An Examination of the Fundamental Theories of Wassily Kandinsky," pp. 208-213)—was not a member of the Theosophical Society. He admired, however, the cosmology of Mme Blavatsky, which attempted to create a significant synthesis of Indian wisdom and Western civilization. The antimaterialistic concepts of the Theosophical movement attracted a good many artists and writers yearning for a new religious spirit in the early part of the century, including Piet Mondrian, Hans Arp, Hugo Ball, and William Butler Yeats.

[31] Kandinsky, *Concerning the Spiritual in Art*, pp. 33-34.

[32] *Ibid.*, p. 36.

[33] *Ibid.*, p. 39.

[34] *Ibid.*, p. 47.

[35] *Ibid.*, p. 45.

[36] *Ibid.*

[37] The remarks about color are taken from "The Language of Form and Color," *ibid.*, chap. vi, pp. 45-67.

[38] *Ibid.*, pp. 51-52.

[39] *Ibid.*, p. 57, *n.*

[40] See p. 229.

[41] Kandinsky, *Wassily Kandinsky Memorial*, p. 75.

[42] Max Raphael, *Von Monet bis Picasso* (Munich, 1919), p. 102.

[43] Kandinsky, *Concerning the Spiritual in Art*, p. 63.

[44] Kandinsky, "Über Bühnenkomposition," in Kandinsky and Marc, *op. cit.*, pp. 103-113.

[45] Kandinsky, *Wassily Kandinsky Memorial*, pp. 75-87.

[46] By "stage composition" ("Bühnenkomposition") Kandinsky referred to the totality of movement on the stage. The possibilities of a unity of the arts in the film were still far beyond consideration in 1912.

[47] Kandinsky, "Der Gelbe Klang," in Kandinsky and Marc, *op. cit.*, pp. 119-131.

[48] Diego Rivera, quoted in "Notes on the Life, Development and Last Years of Kandinsky," in Kandinsky, *Wassily Kandinsky Memorial*, p. 100.

[49] Bergson, *Essai sur les données immédiates de la conscience* (Paris, 1904).

[50] Christian P. Heinlein, "The Affective Characteristics of the Major and Minor Modes in Music" (dissertation, Johns Hopkins University, Baltimore, 1928); quoted in Lindsay, *op. cit.*, p. 104.

[51] Suzanne K. Langer, "Art: The Symbol of Sentience," *New World Writing*, IV (New York, 1953), 54. This concept of art is by no means unique to expressionism, but is shared by many twentieth-century movements, including constructivism. "The constructive artist . . . has found the means and methods to make new images and convey them as emotional manifestations in our everyday experience. This means that shapes, lines, colors, forms are not illusory nor are they abstractions, they are factual forces and their impact on our senses is as real as the impact on light or an electric shock." Naum Gabo, lecture at the Institute of Design, Chicago, March, 1948 (mimeographed).

Herbert Read (essay date 1967)

SOURCE: "The Lucid Order of Wassily Kandinsky," in *Art and Alienation: The Role of the Artist in Society*, Horizon Press, 1967, pp. 138-50.

[*In the following essay, Read traces the development of Kandinsky's painting and philosophy of art.*]

As a painter Kandinsky's achievement was coherent in development, original in style, and accumulative in force; but the painting was the direct expression of a slowly matured philosophy of art. It is possible that this philosophy of art has as much significance for the future as the paintings that were its outcome, but in this essay I shall try to show how the philosophy and the painting evolved, step by step in dialectical correspondence.

Wassily Kandinsky was born on 4 December 1866, in the city of Moscow. His father belonged to a family that had for many years lived as exiles in East Siberia, near the Mongolian frontier. There seems to have been some mingling of blood in the family history: one of Kandinsky's great grandmothers is said to have been a Mongolian princess, and there was a distinct Mongolian cast on Kandinsky's own features. His mother, however, was a true Moscovite, and the son was always sentimentally attached to the city of his birth. His maternal grandmother was German, and German was a language he spoke in his infancy; he was fascinated by German fairy-tales. The Kandinskys seem to have been fairly well-to-do; when Wassily was only three he travelled with his parents in Italy. Then in 1871 they all moved to Odessa, where Kandinsky began to learn music and where from 1876-85 he went to school. At the end of this period it was decided that he should study law, which meant a return to Moscow. These legal studies lasted until 1892, but during this period he paid his first visit to Paris (1889), an experience he repeated as soon as he had passed his final examinations (1892). These visits to Paris seem to have been for recreation only—Kandinsky does not record any artistic experiences at this time. More significant, from this point of view, was an exhibition of the French Impressionists which he saw in Moscow in 1895. A painting by Monet was a revelation to him, and made him aware of a nascent longing to paint. In 1896 he declined an offer of a post in the University of Dorpat and went instead to Munich, determined to test his now fully awakened desire to be an artist. In 1897 he became a pupil of Anton Azbé, but did not make much progress in the academic methods of his school. There, however, he met a fellow Russian student, two years older, Alexei von Jawlensky, from whom he first heard about Van Gogh and Cézanne. In 1900 he joined the Munich Academy where Franz von Stuck had been the master of painting since 1895, and had gained considerable fame as a teacher. Von Stuck was a romantic landscape painter of the school of Böcklin, but his influence on Kandinsky was not profound. Of more significance, probably, was the movement which, originating in England, Scotland and Belgium, swept over Europe in the last decade of the nineteenth century and was variously known as the Modern Movement, Art Nouveau and Jugendstil. In Germany, Munich became the centre of this movement, and *Jugend* and *Simplicissimus,* two illustrated magazines founded in 1896, represented its spirit and style. In painting the style was represented by Munch, Hodler and Klimt, and this is the style adopted by Kandinsky in his apprentice years.

Will Grohmann, in his monograph on the artist,[1] illustrates a poster which Kandinsky designed for the first exhibition of the Phalanx, a group he himself had founded in 1901. It is in the new style, and apart from the typography typical of the movement, represents two knights with shields and lances attacking an encampment in front of a castle. The stylization is already extreme, and from this design onwards we can trace a gradual evolution of form which ends in the first completely abstract paintings of nine years later. Other influences were to be superimposed, particularly that of the French Fauves; but the argument I shall put forward in this essay is that the continuity of Kandinsky's stylistic development is unbroken from this early Jugendstil phase until the end of his life. One must therefore begin with a consideration of the formal qualities of Jugendstil or Art Nouveau.

The formal characteristics of distinct periods in the history of art have often been described, especially since Wölfflin's invention of a useful terminology; but the psychological motives that determine these morphological peculiarities are still very obscure. Following Wölfflin we can speak of linear as opposed to painterly composition, and such a linear emphasis became apparent in the last quarter of the nineteenth century. We find it manifested not only as a renewed interest in drawing as such, and in the popularity of etching and engraving among amateurs of art, but as a quality in decorative motifs of every kind—in wrought ironwork and silverware, in furniture and above all in typography. Book design, including magazines and catalogues, provides a very good index to the whole development, and in this medium one can follow the gradual transition from the naturalistic fantasies of a Beardsley or a Crane to the linear abstractions of a Van Doesburg or a Mondrian. Kandinsky's designs for catalogues and posters, for the decoration of the two books he produced at this time (*Über das Geistige in der Kunst* and *Klänge*) illustrate this same gradual transition from naturalism to linear abstraction. Nevertheless, gradual as the transition was, there came a point when abstraction *as such* was deducible from the extremes of Jugendstil, and the discovery was Kandinsky's.

It is sometimes claimed that a painter in Lithuania (Ciurlionis) or Russia (Larionov or Malevich) was the first abstract painter; in Paris they would say Picabia or Delaunay. No doubt it has many times in the past

occurred to a painter that his colours might be composed like sounds in music, and many such harmonic elements exist even in classical painting. These questions of priority belong to the childish aspects of historiography; what is of serious interest is the conviction that carries a discovery through to a coherent style. Kandinsky himself was quite firm on the question of his 'priority'. In a letter to me dated 9 May 1938, describing the early days of his experiments in Munich, he wrote: 'C'était un temps vraiment héroïque! Mon Dieu, que c'était difficile et beau en même temps. On me tenait alors pour un "fou", des fois pour un "anarchiste russe qui pense que tout est permis", avec un mot pour un "cas très dangereux pour la jeunesse et pour la grande culture en général," etc., etc. J'ai pensé alors que j'étais le seul et le premier artiste qui avait le "courage" de rejeter non seulement le "sujet", mais même chaque "objet" dehors de la peinture. Et je crois vraiment que j'avais complètement raison—j'ai été le premier. Sans doute la question "qui était le premier tailleur" (comme disent les Allemands) n'est pas d'une importance extraordinaire. Mais le "fait historique" n'est pas à changer.'

One might say that once Jugendstil had reached its limit of development, the further step to abstraction was inevitable, and that no particular artist deserves the credit for a crystallization that was the impersonal outcome of the situation that existed in the first decade of the twentieth century. Kandinsky always believed that he had made an independent discovery, and he has related the circumstances. Coming home to his studio one day in 1908 he saw a painting on his easel and was thrilled by an unexpected beauty. Coming closer he saw that the painting was one he had left upside-down, and that its adventitious beauty was due to the non-representational function of the forms and colours in that position. He was already experimenting at the extreme limits of Fauvism, but he now suddenly realized that far more direct and powerful possibilities of communication were latent in form and in colour used symbolically, without any representational intention. He set about to explore these possibilities, working cautiously and testing his methods at every step. At the same time he began to elaborate a theory to justify his experiments, and this theory he set out in a thesis to which, when it was published in 1912, he gave the title *Über das Geistige in der Kunst* (Concerning the Spiritual in Art). A close study of this book is essential to any complete understanding of Kandinsky's art.

It is often objected that art needs no theoretical justification—that it is a sign of weakness in an artist to attempt any verbal exposition of his activity. If so it is a weakness many artists have felt, from Leonardo to Reynolds and Delacroix. Several modern artists, though not venturing to compose a formal treatise, have written statements or letters that give us necessary guidance as to their intentions—Van Gogh and Cézanne are examples. One of the greatest artists of our time, whom no one would accuse of intellectualism, has left us with perhaps the profoundest writings on art of all time—Paul Klee. Kandinsky did not have Klee's intensely introspective vision; nevertheless, **Concerning the Spiritual in Art** is a bold and original essay in aesthetics, written on the basis of general experience, and establishing for the first time a programme for an advance into what Kandinsky called 'an age of conscious creation'. We shall see in a moment what he meant by this phrase, but one should note that he makes very little use of the word 'abstraction', though he was familiar with Wilhelm Worringer's *Abstraction and Empathy*,[2] published by his own publisher two years before he began to write **Concerning the Spiritual in Art.** Worringer had shown that a tendency towards abstraction was one of the recurrent phenomena of the history of Northern art. Kandinsky realized that the spiritual condition of Europe was calling for another of these recurrent phases of abstraction, and more consciously, more deliberately than any other artist of the time, he decided to lead European art in this required direction.

The theory put forward by Kandinsky in his book may be summarized as follows: Art begins where nature leaves off (Oscar Wilde had said this). Art springs from an internal necessity, a need to communicate feeling in an objective form. (Nature interferes with the exactitude of such communication.) The work of art is a construction (not necessarily geometric) making use of all the potentialities of form and colour, not in an obvious way, for the most effective construction may be a hidden one, composed of seemingly fortuitous shapes—'somehow' related forms that are actually very precisely bound together. 'The final abstract expression of every art is number', but Kandinsky recognized that the artist might be dealing with irregular rather than regular elements, and that it would therefore be difficult to translate his structure into mathematical form. The motive is always psychological—Kandinsky did not hesitate to say 'spiritual', though the German word he used, 'geistig', has not quite the same superstitious overtones as the English word. But 'the artist must have something to communicate, for mastery over form is not his goal, but rather the adapting of the form to inner significance'. The test, the standard of judgement, is always subjective—in this Kandinsky identifies himself with the expressionist theory of art. 'That is beautiful which is produced by inner need, which springs from the soul.'

There is in this theory of art an Hegelian synthesis which must be appreciated: the eternal contradiction between inner and outer, between subjective and objective, between human consciousness and an indifferent world of fact (Nature), is resolved in the unity of the work of art. Kandinsky maintained that the supreme work of art is a highly conscious construction determined by the patient elaboration of plastic forms to correspond to a slowly 'realized' inner feeling. The forms might have an arbitrary beginning—a scribble, an improvisation of line and colour; but these forms are then modified or manipulated, teased and tested, until they correspond to an even more clearly realized inner feeling—the feeling is realized as the forms achieve a correspondence—can be realized only if the artist succeeds in so disposing the forms that they express the feeling.

The 'method' that Kandinsky now adopted has been described by Grohmann and others: what at first sight seems to be the most fortuitous kind of doodling was actually a careful disposition of irregular formal elements. The first composition relying entirely on such abstract elements is a water-colour of 1910 in the possession of the artist's widow. But Kandinsky did not immediately devote all his energies to abstraction. He felt his way slowly forwards, and between 1910 and 1914 there are many compositions that clearly have a basis in naturalistic elements (even much later, for example during the First World War when he returned to Moscow, he occasionally painted in a representational style). But there was no turning back, and after his return to Western Europe at the end of 1921 he never again returned to realism.

Kandinsky was alone at first, but he was soon to receive support from other and younger artists. During the course of 1911 he made the acquaintance of Paul Klee, Hans Arp, August Macke and Franz Marc. Of these Marc seems to have best understood Kandinsky's intentions, and together they decided to organize the group which they called 'Der Blaue Reiter' (The Blue Rider). They held their first exhibition in Munich in December of that year, and two months later, in February 1912, a second exhibition in Munich, followed later in the year by an exhibition in Berlin. This same year Klee, Marc and Macke visited Paris and made contact with Robert Delaunay, whose 'orphic' painting was also developing in the direction of abstraction. Delaunay was henceforth to keep in close touch with the Munich group, and there is no doubt that he had a considerable influence on Klee, Marc and Macke, and was perhaps in his turn influenced by the theories of Kandinsky.

The outbreak of the war brought to an end the activities of the Blaue Reiter. Kandinsky was displaced and returned to Russia via Switzerland and the Balkans. In Moscow he found two abstract movements already in existence—Suprematism under the direction of Malevich and Constructivism under the direction of Tatlin. The first two years of his residence in Moscow do not seem to have been very productive—very little work survives from this period of his life (Grohmann calls it an 'intermezzo'). In 1917 Gabo and Pevsner returned to Moscow and the next five years were devoted to politics and administration rather than to creative work. After the Revolution Kandinsky became a professor at the National Art School and in 1919 founded and directed a whole organization of central and provincial art galleries. In 1920 he was appointed Professor of Art at the University of Moscow; in 1921 he founded an Academy of Art. But the thermidorian reaction was already setting in and the official policy of 'socialist realism' was opposed to a revolutionary art. Kandinsky decided to leave Russia. By the end of the year he had reached Berlin, a city he did not find very congenial. The artistic scene was dominated by Dadaists and Expressionists, for whom Kandinsky had never much sympathy, and a spirit of desperate nihilism pervaded the intellectual life of the German capital. Luckily he received almost immediately an invitation from

Walter Gropius to join the staff of the Bauhaus, the school of basic design which Gropius had directed since 1919 in Weimar. There he found Klee and Lyonel Feininger, the architect Adolf Meyer, the designer Johannes Itten, and in general an atmosphere and a policy which were completely to his liking. Kandinsky was to remain at the Bauhaus until the tragic end in 1933—five years longer than Gropius himself, who resigned the directorship in 1928.

The Moscow 'intermezzo' and the closing of the Bauhaus by the Nazis are events that divide Kandinsky's abstract work into three distinctive periods—the Munich years (1908-14), a period of experiment and discovery; the Bauhaus years (1922-33), a period of definition and exposition; and the Paris years (1933-44), which were years of consolidation and elaboration. I have already described the formative period in Munich; I will now try to characterize the remaining periods.

Kandinsky ended his book of 1912 by announcing that 'we are fast approaching a time of reasoned and conscious composition, in which the painter will be proud to declare his work constructional', and this gives the clue to his own future development. The Constructivist movement which he encountered in Russia must have clarified his ideas and given him fresh confidence, though he seems at the time to have reacted against the severely geometrical forms of Malevich and Tatlin. The comparatively few pictures that have survived from the Moscow period, or of which photographic records exist, are continuous with the last paintings done in Europe—violently explosive forms often contained within an irregular oval outline. The shapes of the constituent elements are still vaguely suggestive of the features of a landscape, of the débris of an earthquake or a flood, but just at the end of the Moscow period a tendency towards geometric precision becomes evident—for example, the ***Bunter Kreis (Varicoloured Circle)*** of 1921 now in the Yale University Art Gallery. From 1921 onwards the geometricization proceeds apace, and by 1923, when Kandinsky was settled in the Bauhaus and fully productive once again, the process is complete. But if one examines a typical canvas of this period (***In the Black Square,*** 1923) one can still see the skeleton of a landscape. The circles do not represent the sun, nor the triangles mountains, nor the curves clouds, but they are the archetypal elements of a landscape and suggest a deliberate refinement of such elements. 'Step by step,' Grohmann suggests, 'Kandinsky in Moscow approached a new harder and more objective form of composition which came as a surprise to his acquaintances when it was first shown to them in Berlin. As in the case of Klee, any new departure was always regarded by his friends as a mistake.'

But Kandinsky was now sure of himself, and the Bauhaus period is to be regarded as a period of consolidation in which a new method and indeed a new form of art was for the first time perfected. It was a lonely path that Kandinsky had chosen. In so far as it was always based on fantasy—that is to say, on a free combination of

images—it had something in common with Klee's art. But Kandinsky did not possess Klee's sense of humour, nor Klee's essentially poetic imagination. Kandinsky's images were always *plastic,* that is to say, elements of form and colour that were completely divorced from sentimental associations (I use the word 'sentimental' in its precise and not in its derogatory meaning). This does not imply that the plastic forms have no symbolic function; on the contrary, a line, a circle, a triangle, or any other geometrical element, always has a reliable significance for Kandinsky. It is true that he would sometimes give a painting a sentimental title—***Obstinate,*** for example. But this is an exception: the usual titles (***Yellow Point, Sharp-calm Pink, Quiet Harmony, Calm Tension, Capricious Line, Contact, Bright Unity, Wavering, Counterweights, Upward,*** etc.) refer to physical forces or conditions. These physical elements constitute a language of forms, used to communicate a meaning, an inner 'necessity'. Kandinsky was not very precise in his definition of this inner necessity—he seems to have regarded it as an indefinite spiritual (or one can say psychological, or even neural) tension which was released in the act or process of composition. There is no doubt that he always had the analogy of musical composition in mind, and I know no better clue to Kandinsky's method of composition than the *Poetics of Music* by his compatriot and fellow exile, Igor Stravinsky.[3] (There is, I believe, a close similarity between the formal evolution of these two great contemporary artists.) In the first chapter of this book Stravinsky writes: 'We cannot observe the creative phenomenon independently of the form in which it is made manifest. Every formal process proceeds from a principle, and the study of this principle requires precisely what we call dogma. In other words, the need that we feel to bring order out of chaos, to extricate the straight line of our operation from the tangle of possibilities and from the indecision of vague thoughts, presupposes the necessity of some sort of dogmatism.' And Stravinsky proceeds to define dogmatism as a feeling or taste for order and discipline fed and informed by positive concepts.

When he comes to deal with the composition of music, Stravinsky defines music in its pure state as free speculation. 'It is through the unhampered play of its functions that a work is revealed and justified. We are free to accept or reject this play, but no one has the right to question the fact of its existence. To judge, dispute and criticize the principle of speculative volition which is at the origin of all creation is thus manifestly useless.' Stravinsky then proceeds to maintain that 'inspiration is in no way a prescribed condition of the creative act, but rather a manifestation that is chronologically secondary.'

'*Inspiration, art, artist*—so many words, hazy at least, that keep us from seeing clearly in a field where everything is balance and calculation through which the breath of the speculative system blows. It is afterwards, and only afterwards, that the emotive disturbance which is at the root of inspiration may arise—an emotive disturbance about which people talk so indelicately by conferring upon it a meaning that is shocking to us and that compromises the term itself. Is it not clear that this emotion is merely a reaction on the part of the creator grappling with that unknown entity which is still only the object of his creating and which is to become a work of art? Step by step, link by link, it will be granted him to discover the work. It is this chain of discoveries, as well as each individual discovery, that give rise to the emotion—an almost physiological reflex, like that of the appetite causing a flow of saliva—this emotion which follows closely the phases of the creative process.'

I have quoted this passage at length because it is an exact description and explanation of Kandinsky's method of composition and indeed of his whole philosophy of art. Stravinsky once described himself (to a gendarme) as an 'inventor of music'. Kandinsky was an inventor of paintings, and both artists maintained that 'invention presupposes imagination but should not be confused with it'. Kandinsky invented his formal elements; but his creative imagination enabled him to give expressive coherence and unity to these elements.

Every apparently casual scribble or brush-stroke in a composition by Kandinsky is deliberately invented: he would spend many hours drawing and redrawing these apparently informal details, and not until they had become accurately expressive signs would he transfer them to the composition. This is what Kandinsky meant by 'conscious creation': it is identical with Stravinsky's 'principle of speculative volition', and it should not be confused with the 'informal art' that has come into existence since Kandinsky's death. This informal art (tachism, action painting, etc.) can claim some relationship to the first phase of Kandinsky's abstract development, and even to the early stage of 'improvisation' in the composition of his later compositions. What separates Kandinsky from most of the later 'informalists' is his insistence on the conscious control of the constituent elements of form and colour. Compare the difference between the disciplined structure of the atonal music of Berg and Webern and the informal expressionism of 'musique concrète'.

During his Bauhaus period, in 1926, Kandinsky set down his principles of composition in a treatise which he called **Point and Line to Plane.** This carries the theoretical exposition that forms a part of **Concerning the Spiritual in Art** to a more thorough analytical stage. The earlier book had been concerned mainly with the effect of colour in relation to form; Kandinsky now explores the dynamism of line and plane, especially in relation to the techniques of etching, wood-engraving and lithography. Horizontal and vertical are interpreted not merely as opposed directions, but also as symbolic 'temperatures': horizontal as cold, vertical as warm. In fact, a temperature or a temperament is ascribed to all linear directions and spatial areas—the bottom of a composition is an area of constraint or heaviness, the top an area of lightness and liberation. A composition thus becomes an orchestration of vital forces expressed in plastic symbols. The musical analogy is always in the background, and the concepts of

time, rhythm, interval and metre hitherto reserved to music are freely introduced into the aesthetics of painting. Kandinsky's aesthetics (a total aesthetics covering all the arts) stands or falls by the justness of this analogy, and from the early days of the Blaue Reiter it was based on discussions with composers like Arnold Schönberg.

The Paris period does not differ fundamentally from the Bauhaus period, but Kandinsky was now free to develop his art in isolation, and with a self-confidence that had been proved in ten years of pedagogic activity. There is no decisive change in the character of his painting, though new motives are frequently invented and certain 'schema', such as a division of the picture-space into self-contrasted panels or architectural 'façades', are adopted. More remarkable, perhaps, is a certain barbaric richness of colour which seems to be a reminiscence of the indigenous art of Russia and Asia. Grohmann compares these late paintings with Mexican and Peruvian art, relying on the 'Amerasian' speculations of Strygowski for an historical link. Whether these and other similarities are due to an atavistic recollection on Kandinsky's part, or to his conscious knowledge of and sympathy for these exotic arts, is a question I would not like to decide.[4]

Since Kandinsky's death in 1944 the understanding and appreciation of his work has grown very considerably, but there is always a latent opposition to it. In so far as this opposition is part of a general failure to understand and appreciate abstract tendencies in art, it calls for no comment. But there are many sincere lovers of contemporary art, admirers say of Klee or Picasso, who are unmoved by Kandinsky's work. In the same way there are music lovers who admire Bartók or Prokofiev, but who remain unmoved by Alban Berg or Anton Webern. Perhaps the clue to this limitation lies in the word 'unmoved'.

In Kandinsky's work, as in the work of the composers I have mentioned, the emotion involved is Apollonian rather than Dionysian. 'What is important for the lucid ordering of the work—for its crystallization [I am quoting Stravinsky again]—is that all the Dionysian elements which set the imagination of the artist in motion and make the life-sap rise must be properly subjugated before they intoxicate us, and must finally be made to submit to the law: Apollo demands it.' Kandinsky's art is not for every taste; but for those who can appreciate the strength and beauty of an art that imposes the clearest intellectual unity on a chaos of Dionysian elements, his achievement will rank among the highest in the history of modern art.

NOTES

[1] (p. 139), Cologne, 1958; London, 1959

[2] (p. 142), First German edition, Munich, 1908. English translation by Michael Bullock, London, 1953

[3] (p. 146), London, 1947

[4] (p. 149), Cf. Jean Arp: "Kandinsky told me that his grandfather had come trotting into Russia on the back of a small charger that was spangled with bells, arriving from one of those enchanted Asiatic mountains all made of porcelain. There is no doubt that this grandfather had bequeathed deep secrets to Kandinsky.' *Wassily Kandinsky,* by Max Bill. Paris, 1951

Charles W. Millard (essay date 1973)

SOURCE: "The Kandinsky Paradox," in *The Hudson Review,* Vol. XXVI, No. 1, Spring, 1973, pp. 177-87.

[*In the following essay, Millard maintains that although Kandinsky was a great theoretician, he was not a great painter.*]

Because Kandinsky occupies a particularly prominent place in the development of twentieth-century painting there has been an unspoken tendency to assume that his is an art of the first quality. If not ranked with the work of masters such as Matisse, it is tacitly presumed to occupy a place among the output of the major painters not much below the top level. It is, therefore, something of a shock to review a sizable and representative selection of his work and to realize that if Kandinsky was perhaps the most powerful and daring intellect among the artists of the last seventy-five years he was far from being possessed of a strong pictorial sensibility. Put more simply, he was a great theoretician, and perhaps on that account a great artist, but by no means a great painter. Apart from more specific problems, which an investigation of his development will make apparent, Kandinsky's work suffers from a pervading dryness which consistently keeps it from being a rich visual experience however much it may offer to the analytical mind.

During the early years of his career, until about 1908, Kandinsky's work seems largely to have been composed of modest essays in painting and printmaking. The small oil sketches of these years are fresh and vigorous, executed in a variety of Impressionist technique that depends on high-keyed color broadly applied, sometimes over a neutral-colored support that is allowed to furnish broad background areas against which the lighter and darker paint tonalities stand out. The prints, largely woodcuts which enforce a certain breadth of touch, exploit an all-over patterning which depends on extreme value contrast and has affinities with a type of Art Nouveau decorative patterning. The discreteness of the elements in these prints, both the represented elements and the lines used to define them, parallels the discreteness of the strokes in the oil sketches. Paradigmatic of Kandinsky's technique during these early years, and a small masterpiece of the period, is the tempera *Market Place in Tunis* of 1904-05. The tempera is used in a granular, flat way like pastel and, like pastel, each stroke defines form not by outlining it but by creating or helping to create it. Starting with a deep-toned brown paper, Kandinsky works up to increasingly light tonalities,

carefully balancing colors and tones so that a brilliant overall pattern emerges, and leaving enough of his paper unworked to allow the composition to breathe. If the resulting statement is a modest one, it is both charming and without weakness, evidencing distinctly what were to remain the artist's principal abilities.

By 1908 Kandinsky, perhaps led on to larger scale by the overall effects with which he worked, was attempting more ambitious work. *Blue Mountain* of that year declares his interest in major painting, at once clearly demonstrating how thoroughly such an interest undermined his pictorial strengths. The most apparent of the picture's weaknesses is its coloristic vulgarity, a vulgarity not contributory to the artistic statement as with Fauve painting but detrimental to it. This vulgarity, and an inability to control his color and make it work for his compositions, was to plague Kandinsky all his life. In *Blue Mountain* one has only to consider how the mustard yellow sun at the center of the composition is modulated through sour green and blue to the pink sky and the dark blue mountain to understand with what little suavity Kandinsky approached his problem. To keep color from running away from him and to unify his composition, which tends toward large pictorial scale at the top and toward smaller figural scale at the bottom, the artist has resorted to black, partly as outlining but principally as overall stippling. The armature thus created does help hold things together, but there remains a slightly frantic quality about the effort to master complex painterly techniques that is made all the more poignant by the figure at the lower right, rapidly brushed in flat, distinct color areas in what is clearly a style more sympathetic to Kandinsky.

In the following year—1909—Kandinsky attempted a large French-type figure composition in the frieze-like *Crinolines.* Although its unsubtle color modulations work against it, as with *Blue Mountain,* the intensity of hue and obviousness of facture help hold it to the surface, an important strength of Kandinsky's since his first woodcut illustrations. In *Crinolines* black and its equivalent (dark blue and green) are relegated entirely to outline, containing some of the color areas and thereby strengthening the composition. In a not dissimilar picture of two years later, *Pastorale,* Kandinsky eliminated black altogether, a daring move which, however, weakened the total composition. Anti-atmospheric because of the density of its color, *Pastorale* is also anti-structural because of the suppression of outline and the simplification of value contrast. Nothing illustrates as well as the progression from *Crinolines* to *Pastorale* Kandinsky's basic artistic courage, not to say abandon, nor the difficulty he had manipulating and controlling the painterly means bodying forth that courage. On the one hand, he tried to create a major figure composition and to control its intense color with outline, while simultaneously modulating his color and dispersing his tonalities so as to work against the outline. On the other, he dispensed with outline altogether, letting his color float free but contradicting the implied opening of the composition with dense, saturated color and obvious facture. One almost feels that

Kandinsky's ambitions to be a painter (in the traditional sense) and to be an artist (in the modernist sense) worked directly against each other.

Between about 1910 and about 1920 Kandinsky created the abstract pictures on which his reputation has most securely rested—large, complex compositions which are at once his most famous and his least realized works. By freeing both color and line from their attachment to represented objects, as well as to each other, Kandinsky burst the bonds of traditional painting in one heroic effort. The pictorial solutions he thus envisaged were infinitely more advanced than those of Cubism, which was bridging the gap between representation and abstraction less chaotically and, perhaps for that reason, more productively in an historic sense. Kandinsky's production during this decade reached a frenzied peak about 1915 in paintings so intellectually complex that it is even now difficult to grasp them, paintings so visually out of control that they resist every effort at analysis. Black line, most often freed from its bounding functions, becomes increasingly irregular and fantastic. Color, always Kandinsky's weakest point, continues to fall into vulgarity or muddiness, and coloristic and tonal modulations often seem wholly capricious. Because Kandinsky had not developed a firmly-rooted sense of scale neither his color nor his line were sufficiently in control in these early abstractions to carry the pictorial burden placed upon them, and in some inexplicable way he used them both as if he were painting representational pictures, although all references to nature were swept away. The uncontrolled result is, to paraphrase Clement Greenberg, a kind of homeless non-representation, a series of pictorial elements apparently unable to coalesce into a harmonious and meaningful totality. The importance of these large canvases is almost entirely in what they stand for and not in what they are.

Great Fugue of 1914 is typical of both the achievements and failures of the pictures of this time. One glance is sufficient to show the number of elements Kandinsky was juggling and the difficulty he had in resolving them. The congestion at the top center shows both his problems in passing from figural scale to pictorial scale and the multiplicity of shapes and elements with which he was trying to cope. Although carefully organized, the picture is understructured, just as later pictures were to be overstructured. Neither color, line, nor scale provide a scaffolding on which it can hang and one senses the pictorial elements working against Kandinsky rather than with him. Spatially, the painting is particularly awkward. Although Kandinsky was always better using dense, nonspatial effects, he seems to have felt the need to "space-up" his pictures as they opened into broad, abstract compositions. He did this either with linear diagonals or, as in *Great Fugue,* by lightening and modulating his color (in this case, toward the bottom of the canvas). The result is a further sense of awkwardness and of devices working against their creator. Elements that could register more strongly, such as the ladder image at the lower left that was to come back in future works, are not

sufficiently isolated to have their full effect. What one notices most of all, however, is the growing sense of fantasy, a fantasy related to the handling of non-representational elements as if they were representational. Although line is no longer a boundary and color no longer an attribute, both continue to behave as if they were boundary and attribute respectively. One somehow expects a recognizable image to coalesce out of the chaos at any minute. Since Kandinsky's was a fantasy evidenced in a kind of overgrown doodling, one based on innerness, it was a fantasy that lent itself only with difficulty to a large pictorial conception, and the conflict between the size of pictures such as *Great Fugue* and their fussy execution merely adds to the confusion about their ultimate pictorial meaning.

By 1920 Kandinsky's awareness of Cubism seems to have helped him in finding a structural scaffolding and in controlling his pictorial space. In pictures such as *Red Oval* the represented elements are reduced in number, regularized in shape, and drawn toward the center of the composition. The background, in turn, is painted in—in this case in green—bringing it forward and thereby making the picture both denser and stronger. A rectangular yellow shape modulates between that background and the cluster of freer shapes seen against it. Spatially, the forms overlap in a combination of analytic and synthetic Cubist effects. In some places, Kandinsky has made his tendency to modulate color work for him by modulating only at the edge of forms in an analytical Cubist way, indicating shapes shading into one another or receding behind one another. In others, he has lapped solid forms so as to reduce them to thin planes lying on top of one another, and he holds the yellow plane down with the stippled rainbow-like shape at the right, which comes from behind the yellow shape to lie on top of it. In sum, by the early '20's he was beginning to create less adventurous, less important, and less chaotic canvases in favor of pictures that were more comprehensible, more thoroughly an expression of his own pictorial talents, and more successful within the terms they set for themselves.

If Cubism first suggested to Kandinsky a means of controlling his compositions, it was the Bauhaus and Constructivism that gave him an organizational method to make them fully comprehensible and Paul Klee who pointed the way toward a more meaningful scale and use of fantasy. Neither of these influences was able wholly to improve his color sense (see *Tempered Pink* of 1936), nor was the former able to ameliorate his enthusiastic tendency to push what he did beyond the limits within which he was able to do it meaningfully (his Constructivist pictures became rigidly over-geometricized as his earlier pictures had become over-chaotic), but both helped guide him toward a more realistic personal style. *On Gray* of 1923 is one of the early fruits of his study of Constructivism. In it, his earlier confused cosmogenies take on comprehensible shape. Color modulations are suppressed in favor of the clearly-defined shapes which Kandinsky always handled most easily. Although most of these shapes gather in toward the center, many are allowed to wander to the periphery of the canvas, re-establishing the kind of all-over patterning that was also apparently native and sympathetic to the artist. Color once again becomes associated with particular forms—becomes a meaningful attribute—and black again serves its linear function, sometimes thickening into more substantial shapes. The diagonals which earlier had suggested space now lie flat on the surface, the longer ones stretched like taut strings between the corners of the canvas, pulling the other elements up to them. During the '20's and '30's this tendency toward simplification of form continued, largely under Klee's influence, until there accumulated a group of small-scale works, looking very much like Klee's watercolors, in which Kandinsky was able to realize his pictorial talents as successfully as in the **Market Place in Tunis** of a quarter-century earlier. In these works, geometricized shapes—often denotative (figures, arrows, pyramids)—float free against a simplified background. Although this background is sometimes stippled it never becomes wholly atmospheric, to the ultimate benefit of the compositions concerned. Frequently, and happily, compositions are organized to reflect the format of the canvas or paper on which they are created—vertical arrangements on vertical supports, more spread-out compositions on horizontal supports. **Pronounced Rose** of 1932 is a paradigm of this kind of picture, and among the most successful of the works of the period. In it, the discrete and carefully-delineated shapes call contrapuntally to one another across the surface of the canvas in a lively, staccato rhythm. The background is, to all intents and purposes, a single color field and other colors are relegated to a few clearly-outlined shapes. All are flat and unmodulated. There is almost no attempt to create space, the slight halations surrounding each shape as modulating or atmosphere-creating devices being so close in hue and value to the background as hardly to be visible at all. This kind of pulsing pattern, which Mondrian was to attempt in different ways ten years later, finally delivered into Kandinsky's hands an instrument for combining the successful patterning of his early illustrations with wholly abstract configurations, and he continued to play variations on it until his death.

Kandinsky's late pictures, deeply indebted to Klee at a moment when Klee was moving away from the effects they employed toward a more monumental art, legitimized both his pictorial strengths and the increasingly strong strain of fantasy in his images. The intricacy and delicacy of their images demand that they be read rather than seen at once, and the small scale at which Kandinsky worked increases that necessity. Larger works now became simply smaller ones enlarged, rather than larger-scaled conceptions. Those pictures with the greatest value contrast between the forms and the ground, and the greatest discreteness of shape, were the best. Compositions in which shapes overlapped, ran off the canvas, or were entirely bounded by other shapes tended toward weakness. Kandinsky once again used toned papers to good effect, and sometimes refined the push-pull surface tension of his pictures by using a dark-valued image against a light-valued ground. This device made the ground seem visually on top of the image, and to suppress the resulting hole-like effect Kandinsky drew on top of the image in such a way as to bring it up to the surface. In general, he moved steadily toward a more modest art in which he could more fully realize his pictorial talents. If the dryness of his pictures persisted, it increasingly became a dryness that was used to positive effect, and if his art became less ambitious—less important—it became simultaneously more realized and truer to what seems the artist's own sensibility.

Reviewing Kandinsky's work, one is constantly made aware that his pictorial sensibilities were essentially those of an illustrator, most at home in small-scaled images created out of flat colors and shapes arranged as punctuation across a page. Informed with a quality of fantasy uniquely Kandinsky's, these images require careful reading—travelling through—to be fully comprehended. Ultimately the sensibility that created them undermined every effort on the artist's part to develop a major painterly statement. By contrast, one cannot but be awed by Kandinsky's tremendous intellectual stature. Precisely in his least successful pictures, those of 1910-1915, his grasp of where painting was going and his willingness to pursue the implications of that tendency to their limits become most apparent. It is ultimately upon the comprehensiveness of that grasp and the daring of that pursuit that Kandinsky's claims to greatness must rest.

Alwynne Mackie (essay date 1978)

SOURCE: "Kandinsky and Problems of Abstraction," in *Artforum,* Vol. XVII, No. 3, November, 1978, pp. 58-63.

[*In the following essay, Mackie explores the role of abstract form in Kandinsky's art and artistic philosophy.*]

In a very sympathetic article Hilton Kramer once voiced his misgivings (and disappointments) about Kandinsky, arriving at the view that he populated naturalistic (19th-century landscape) space with abstract forms and was unable to come to terms with the pictorial implications of the tendency of abstract forms to flatten space.[1] Implicit in this criticism, of course, is the assumption that abstract forms *demand* a certain kind of spatial treatment, and this assumption, in turn, is part of a view about the nature and purpose of abstraction itself. Kandinsky was well aware that abstract forms *suggest* a narrowing of spatial depth, but he obviously did not think that they demanded it, as at least two passages from **Concerning the Spiritual in Art** show. So the first question we should ask is, "To what end did Kandinsky introduce abstract forms into his art?"

The answer, I think, lies in his theoretical writings and the fact that they embody the fundamentals of theosophical thought. Such connections have been made before, notably by Sixten Ringbom, who transfers the metaphysics of auras and thought-forms to the works and reads them in a symbolic way.[2] That is a very literal approach, whereas all the evidence of Kandinsky's writings suggests that he did not have a very literal mind. It is true that such an interpretation must enter into one's account of **Woman in Moscow** (though not quite as literally as Ringbom suggests[3]), of the glass-painting **Cow in Moscow** and, to a lesser extent, of **Impression III (Concert)**.[4] But that is only a small part of the story, and such paintings are few. For the rest, such literal interpretations are strained; but more importantly, they tell us nothing of why the pictorial structure is the way it is.

The literalist interpretation also underestimates Kandinsky's intelligence, for it fails to appreciate that he was not so much interested in the trappings of theosophical theory as in the more fundamental issue of the relation between spiritual and material substance (of which auras and thought-forms are merely an outgrowth). The present-day mind tends to focus on these oddities rather than on the supporting thought, and recent interest in the occult has been attracted to these and other psychic phenomena out of a concern with knowledge and experience, or, more accurately, knowledge as experience. The early theosophists, on the other hand, wrote at a time when orthodox religion and its accompanying metaphysics had been eroded by Darwinism and other forces, and when philosophers and even physiologists had raised doubts about the existence of spiritual (or mental) substance by attempting to explain all mental and emotional activity in material—neural—terms. Physicists, on the other hand, had begun to undermine the comforting solidity of material substance by splitting the atom. As Kandinsky himself wrote in **"Reminiscences"**:

> The crumbling of the atom was to my soul like the crumbling of the whole world. Suddenly the heaviest walls toppled. Everything became uncertain, tottering and weak. I would not have been surprised if a stone had dissolved in the air in front of me and became invisible. Science seemed to me destroyed; its most important basis was only a delusion, an error of the learned, who did not build their godly structures stone by stone with a steady hand in transfigured light, but groped at random in the darkness for truth and blindly mistook one object for another.[5]

Although the theosophists and Kandinsky set the attainment of spiritual knowledge as their ideal, this did not involve a crude rejection of the material world and of material substance as unworthy of enlightened attention. Rather the emphasis was on seeing it the right way: material substance as just a "solid" manifestation of astral (or spiritual) substance, which, therefore has an "inner life"—the "inner necessity" that gives vitality to the external form. In the words of Madame Blavatsky, whom Kandinsky read a great deal:

> Matter is *Eternal*. It is the *Upadhi* (the physical basis) for the One infinite Universal Mind to build thereon its ideations. . . . Or: Spirit and Matter are the two states of the One. . . . Spirit is the just differentiation of (and in) Space: and Matter is the first differentiation of Spirit.[6]

Blavatsky herself, in more understandable terms, quoted from an Indian source: "Wherever there is an atom of matter, a particle or a molecule, even in its most gaseous condition, there is life in it, however latent and unconscious."[7]

Kandinsky's writings—particularly **Concerning the Spiritual in Art**—are full of remarks which echo these statements. Many of them, like the theosophical writings from which they derive, are cast in terms which translate the principle of latent life into terms of the "sounds," "resonances" or "vibrations" of the inner life of the material. Kandinsky frequently attributes the ultimate failure of a work to its failing to express the inner sound (see his remarks on Cubism)[8]. And of his own **Composition VI** he wrote:

> In several sketches I dissolved the objective forms and in others I tried to achieve the impression in a more abstract way. But this did not work either.
>
> The reason for it was, that myself while being forced to render the expression of the deluge, I did not listen to the expression of the word "deluge."
>
> Not the inner sound, but the exterior expression was dominating me.[9]

Theosophists are not dualists; they do not believe the world is sharply divided into two discrete kinds of substances, material and mental. This fact is central to Kandinsky's beliefs and to his art. Leadbetter, for example, divides substance into several planes—solid, liquid, gaseous, etheric, and astral—and then says that these planes

> . . . must not be imagined as lying above one another like the shelves of a book-case, but rather as filling the same space and interpenetrating one another. . . . Every physical atom is floating in an astral sea—a sea of astral matter which surrounds it and fills every interstice in this physical matter.[10]

Kandinsky puts the same point in a slightly different, perhaps more comprehensible, way when he says that all substance, whether material, spiritual or mental, is basically composed of the same thing:

> Frequent reference is made to "material" and "non-material," and to the intermediate phrases, "more" and "less material." Is everything material—or is *everything* spiritual? Can the distinctions we make between matter and spirit be nothing but relative modifications of one or the other? Thought, which although a product of the spirit can be defined with exact science, is matter, but of fine and not coarse substance. Is whatever cannot be *touched* spiritual? The discussion lies beyond the scope of this little book: all that matters here is that the boundaries drawn should not be too definite.[11]

Hence Kandinsky's remark on hearing of the splitting of the atom, that he would not have been surprised to see a stone dissolve before his eyes and become invisible.

This interpenetration of material substance and ethereal essence is the subject of Kandinsky's art from the first growing awareness around 1904 up to 1919-20. He himself articulates it in terms of expressing the "inner necessity" of external forms. But what we actually witness in his painting is the disintegration of the nexus between form and color, so that color is liberated to float free of form, while the discarded form itself is left, not like an emptied shell but with a substanceless life of its own. In the best of his oil paintings (*Black Lines, Composition V,* the Campbell panels, *Composition VII,* and *Improvisation Without Title,* 1914, for example),[12] and in his watercolors (which are in many ways more interesting and innovative than his oils), color and line interpenetrate/separate as they move across the canvas in a state of flux, always looking as if in some former existence they had been combined to present a solid object. A sense of movement expresses the flux and transition from material into etheric substance. And the impression that line had once belonged to colored form is achieved by placing a contour slightly out of register with a patch of color, as if it were sliding off, sometimes by opening the contour at one end and trailing the line off to melt into another shape, and by carefully controlling the spatial depth between color and line so that their connection, as well as their separation, is visually plausible. This is particularly true of *Composition V,* where the figure/ground distinction is muted by the uniform tonality of the colors, and where the vibrant black lines which swing across the erupting landscape seem to have been generated out of the black in the color patches themselves, looking *organically* connected with the substance of the color.

The beginnings of this kind of visual thinking can be seen in Kandinsky's early work from around 1904 onward. From 1904 through 1906 he defined form in his oil paintings by means of large blocks of color which, in some cases—notably *Beach Baskets in Holland,* 1904[13]—are so large as to suggest that the substance of the form is to be seen solely in terms of the colored pigment applied with all the evidence of the brushstroke (as de Kooning was to do). This attempt to present form as simply color has a parallel in the graphics of the same period, where line is used not to define form, but to break it up into counterpointed areas of black and white. The resulting color/line and space dichotomy makes the works difficult to read, as if Kandinsky *wanted* the dissolution of forms but had not yet been able to realize to what end. At the same time, many of his works are very romantic and mystical in theme and mood, a fact which suggests a striving after an unknown fantasy world (always bathed in color), an ethereal world which does not impinge on reality as we see it. Whether romantic riders of medieval chivalry or single figures in a soft and strangely colored landscape, these are images of people removed from our ken, figures of the same substance as the landscape. Frequently Kandinsky uses black to melt one form into another (as in *Die Nacht* of 1903), and in *Der Spiegel,* 1907, and the 1906-07 *Die Nacht* the flowers against black dresses merge almost imperceptibly with flowers on black grass.[14]

Kandinsky often depicts a world in cataclysm: sometimes this is literal, as in the "Deluge" and "Resurrection of the Dead" works, but frequently it is just compositional, as if by shaking the world he could free essence, color and line from their physical imprisonment. In two watercolors of 1913, for instance, he prises color and line apart, not so much to present "pure" color and line as entities in their own right (as some critics have felt he should have done), but so that the ghost of a form is retained—although a form from which material solidity has evaporated. In *Study for Painting with White Form,*[15] although the lines do establish the forms, many of them have become detached and wander freely around the landscape as objects of interest in themselves—very black, thick and vibrant. Although such forms inevitably establish some depth, the emphasis is not on spatial illusion, but on the quality of the lines themselves: in fact, they tend to negate the spatial effect by pulling together the various planes of black-outlined forms. The color is left floating behind the lines. In *Watercolor (No. 13),*[16] on the other hand, line is used mainly to define form and remains relatively stable; the deliberate indeterminacy of planes (for example, the intersecting sides of the mountains) and the unity of color tonality have the effect of freeing the patches of color to float forward toward the viewer, each one vying for attention. Also, the juxtaposition of nonoutlined, indeterminate shapes next to determinate, recognizable objects such as hills creates an ambiguity of substance that again tends to free the color.

The ancestor of this technique can be seen in *Church at Murnau,* 1909,[17] where large expanses of black or dark forms are lifted, with jewellike effect, by splotches of high-tone color, and unified through their uniformity of tone and saturation. Despite the representational subject matter, the patches of color establish their own existence, partly because they are difficult to read as *objects* (especially the color-patches on the path) and partly because of the counterpoint of lighter tones over dark, and darker over light, which makes one very aware of the brushstroke and of the color as pigment. On the roof a totally irrational black-green shadow falls across the large area of yellow-orange, breaking up the color and delocalizing it, making it seem that color capriciously inhabits the objects that it visits. Sometimes Kandinsky abandons actual forms and uses color so that it emanates from line alone, as if substance and form had disintegrated and been subsumed, as color, into the quality of the line. In an untitled watercolor of 1915 from the Rebay collection,[18] for instance, within a central ovoid "frame" of the work streaks of color overlap or abut onto black, energy-creating lines; rather than reading as adjacent but separate lines, however, their dark tone links them generically with the black lines, as if the "black" had begun to disintegrate into its own manifold color components: the color appears to burn through from the very center of the black.

From around 1909 to 1919 Kandinsky's best works succeed regardless of whether they are representational or abstract; in fact, whether they are representational or not seems to have very little to do with it. This may seem a strange observation to make of an artist who is often regarded as the father of abstract art (and whose work therefore has to be seen in terms of striving toward that end). But it raises certain crucial questions about the nature and purpose of abstraction. Although Kandinsky's theory of painting is embedded in theosophical metaphysics, basically he painted pictures about the way the world of nature looks—or would look, if only we attended to it a little more carefully. Given his views of the unity of all substance, and the interpenetration of its various solid, "etheric," and mental "manifestations," it is not surprising that many of his forms are, or are derived from, objects in the world: they are the source from which spring those images of color, line and vaporous form. Forms which did not originate in the visual experience of the world were impossible for Kandinsky. As he says:

> And the most important [question]: what should replace the missing object? The danger of ornamentation stood clearly before me, *the dead make-believe existence of schematical forms could only repulse me.*[19]

The important thing was, however, for the stimulus object to lose its identity as a concrete object having a certain material function in the world, so that a viewer might concentrate on the way it looks rather than on what it is. In Kandinsky's terms, this meant freeing the image from any connotations which might get in the way of seeing its "inner form".

> Here we find the same criterion and principle which thus far we have encountered everywhere as the only purely artistic one free from the unessential, *the principle of inner necessity.*
>
> If, for example, features of the face or parts of the body are changed or distorted for artistic reasons, one encounters not only the purely pictorial question, but also that of anatomy, which hampers the pictorial intention and imposes upon it the consideration of unimportant details.

He goes on to say,

> In our case, however, the unessential disappears automatically and only the essential remains, the artistic aim. These seemingly arbitrary but, in reality, well-reasoned alterations in form are one of the sources of an infinite number of artistic creations.[20]

What Kandinsky is pointing to here, apart from one of the limitations of representation, is a certain kind of abstractional thinking which puts an image through a sieve. Such an attitude toward the portrayal of forms invites the kind of abstraction which concentrates with great specificity on one aspect of a form while reducing and filtering out others. It has its forebears in the volumetric anatomical abstraction of Ingres, and is especially evident in the economy of the telling line in much of Matisse's work—in the *Dance,* 1909, in the Museum of Modern Art, for example. It is also the basic principle of

stylization in general (epitomized, perhaps, in Japanese Noh masks) and of caricature. But such abstraction can never be totally abstract; that is to say, it can never effect a total divorce between object and image. For no matter how much the viewer is urged to discard the question of representation, the artist never forgets the source of the image, for it is in this abstract image that he has sought to crystallize what he sees as the essentials of the stimulus-object. From this point of view, total abstraction is an impossibility, since there must always be something *to abstract from,* which precludes the severance of the umbilical cord connecting the abstraction with nature.

Given this essential connection with the real world, there is nothing intrinsic to this kind of abstraction which *demands* a particular (let's say flat, or shallow) use of space (though it may, of course, on occasions aid it):[21] since the forms are always ultimately connected with forms in the visible world, they do not have to strive to appear as if they were not. Since such forms are not necessarily bound to avoid looking as though they inhabit real space, criticism of Kandinsky's abstractions on the grounds that he employs naturalistic space is beside the point. If by naturalistic space one means deep space as opposed, say, to the shallow space of Cubism (and all such space is "illusionistic"), why should the latter be more appropriate to Kandinsky's particular illusion of the dismembering of line and color from the substance of forms? Indeed, that situation might well be more easily achieved within a not-too-shallow space, which is evidently what he had in mind when he wrote in *Concerning the Spiritual in Art*:

> One of the first steps away from representation and towards abstraction was, in the pictorial sense, the exclusion of the third dimension, i.e. the tendency to keep the picture on a single plane. Modeling was abandoned. In this way the concrete object was made more abstract, and an important step forward was achieved—this step forward has, however, had the effect of limiting the possibilities of painting to the actual surface of the canvas: and thus painting acquired another material limit.
>
> Any attempt to free painting from this material limitation, together with the striving after a new form of composition, must concern itself first of all with the destruction of the theory of one single surface. . . .
>
> There are other ways of using the concrete plane as a space of three dimensions in order to create an ideal plane: the thinness or thickness of a line, the placing of a form on the surface, the crossing of one form by another may be mentioned as examples of the extension of picture space in depth through drawing. Similar possibilities are offered by color, which, when rightly used, can advance or retreat, and can make the picture suspended, non-material form. The combination of both means of extension-in-depth in harmony or counterpoint is one of the richest and most powerful elements in pictorial structure.[22]

Clearly Kandinsky felt that the preservation of the flatness of the picture plane was incompatible with his desire to make line and color look as if they had once belonged to the same substantial form, although, at the same time, he was always careful to avoid a space which is so deep and coherent as to re-endow his forms with the solidity of material substance. Of his own *Composition VI* he wrote:

> Here the pink and white are mixed in a foam which gives the impression of neither laying on the canvas nor on any ideal plane. Rather it seems to hang in the air and appears to be surrounded by haze. Such an absence of plane and an uncertainty of distance may be observed for instance in Russian steambaths. A human figure standing amid the steam seems to be neither close nor far; it is 'somewhere'.[23]

There is, however, another kind of abstraction within which total abstraction is, in a sense, realizable, an abstraction whose image derives not from the visual world, but which is architectonically put together from ideas of the mind. That is, of course, an overstatement, for in a sense all ideas are ultimately derived from experience of the world. The painter of abstract images (as opposed to abstracted images) constantly treads a knife-edge from which he may slip into producing images which have a specificity of references to things or qualities in the real world, on the one hand, or else may lapse into incoherency and noncommunication, on the other. The problem of translation from nonmaterial idea to material visual image is an acute one—and ultimately an impossible one that necessarily involves compromise. Some of the artists of the Bauhaus and De Stijil resolved it, in theoretical terms at least, by invoking metaphysical "universals" which somehow expressed themselves in certain generalized forms such as triangles, squares and circles, or through other theoretical devices such as synaesthesia.

Whether or not the conviction of such paintings is attributable, at least in a major part, to the truth of the theories behind them is another question. For my part, I find it difficult to believe that they are, if only because such theories are essentially untestable. What is more likely, however, is that the theories have acquired some truth, not in absolute terms, but simply by virtue of constant repetition. In other words, even if the circle does not embody, in a real sense, perfection and eternal endurance, if we have been told so since early Greek times, we might well have come to accept the fiction (as a fiction) so that it indeed *symbolizes* those things. In the case of synaesthesia, it is hard to know whether we associate the color red with passion, intensity, danger and excitement because of the heightened physiological response we experience on seeing it, or whether the increased heart-beat, adrenalin flow and so on occur *because of* the associations it has; as with blue/depression and other correspondences, the hypothesis tends to become self-fulfilling after a while.

The other point—and pictorially a much more important one—is that the images of this kind of abstraction can never be completely generalized and must have some determinable qualities of form and color even to be perceivable. Then the struggle for the artist is to avoid that kind of specificity of qualities which will be *read* as having specificity of reference to some object or visual experience. The suspicion remains, however, that in such abstraction the art succeeds at least in part through a specificity of reference which is not explicitly recognized as such. In a sense, how could it be otherwise? How could an image ever be played with by the mind and the eye if it is so generalized as to have no connection with one's visual experience? My suspicions about this sort of hidden reference are strengthened by the fact that later abstract artists not concerned with eschewing the specificity of an image nevertheless took over the pictorial syntax of Mondrian and others and adapted it to their own ends without too much sense of strain.

Be that as it may, something can still be said about the limitations this kind of abstraction imposes. One very obvious point is that the forms it employs must divest themselves of any sense of being located in "real" space: hence the flatness of the picture-space and the "skin of paint" across the surface, which Hilton Kramer feels is so lacking in Kandinsky's work. Also, of course, there is danger in letting the figure/ground phenomenon have its way, for it has a tendency to suggest a specific object in a particular space, albeit a shallow or flat one. At the same time, abstract art took on that quality of tactility that almost inevitably comes with closeness of vision as well as the necessity of avoiding the discreteness of forms. Kandinsky's art is never concerned with tactility: his artistic vision was always completely visual, as both his works and his writings testify.

Since the abstract image must avoid *looking like* something else (being representational, that is, in the broad sense), and if a belief in metaphysical correspondence is no longer tenable, then the only viable option is for art to become self-reflexive, and for the image to look like nothing but itself, a painted image. That, too, is a chimera, of course, but the point is that we are prepared to overlook the gap between the intention and the realization, provided it is within acceptable limits, because we share the artist's impulse to perform these impossibilities.

That much is history, and Kandinsky's kind of abstraction did not prevail. He was never interested in painting ideas: "The dead make-believe existence of schematical forms could only repulse me." He always painted images from experience, and his art was always art at the service of a vision of the world. With historical hindsight, his art turned out not to be a principal resource (like Cubism), for all its quality and beauty. That, however, is quite another thing from saying that Kandinsky failed to appreciate or accept the implications implicit in abstract art. As I have tried to show, that is to confuse one kind of abstract intention with another.

The *fait accompli* of history conditions us to believe that the art development we have passed through was an inevitable one developing out of the intrinsic nature and problems of art. True, but that encourages a dangerously narrow view of historical evaluation. To measure all art at the crossroads of an artistic development against the aims and achievements of what finally developed out of the ferment—as if that were what it already should have been—seems to me misguided. Judged by those standards Kandinsky's work was a failure; judged by its own, it is not.

NOTES

[1] Hilton Kramer, "Kandinsky." *Artforum,* May 1963. He makes these criticisms of Kandinsky's best period, from 1907 to 1919 approximately.

[2] S. Ringbom. *The Sounding Cosmos: a study in the spiritualism of Kandinsky and the genesis of abstract painting.* Abo Akademi, Abo, Finland. 1970.

[3] Ringbom, pp. 94-99.

[4] *Woman in Moscow,* 1912, oil on canvas. Städtische Galerie im Lenbachhaus. Munich: *Cow in Moscow,* 1912, glass painting. Städtische Galerie im Lenbachhaus. Munich. *Impression III (Concert),* 1911, oil on canvas, Städtische Galerie im Lenbachhaus, Munich.

[5] W. Kandinsky. *Reminiscences* (1913), in R. Herbert, *Modern Artists on Art.* Englewood Cliffs, N.J., 1964, p. 27.

[6] H. P. Blavatsky. *The Secret Doctrine* (1877). Los Angeles, 1947, vol. 1. p. 280; vol. 1. p. 258.

[7] H. P. Blavatsky, *Isis Unveiled* (1877), Los Angeles, 1931, vol. 2. p. 263.

[8] W. Kandinsky, *Concerning the Spiritual in Art* (1912), New York, 1947, p. 67.

[9] Quoted (no source given) by Hilla von Rebay in *Kandinsky,* published on the occasion of the Kandinsky Memorial Exhibition, March-May, 1945. Museum of Non-Objective Paintings. Solomon R. Guggenheim Foundation. New York, 1945, p. 10.

[10] C. W. Leadbetter. *Man visible and invisible.* Wheaton. Ill. 1971, p. 9.

[11] Kandinsky. *Concerning the Spiritual in Art.* p. 29.

[12] *Black Lines,* 1913, oil on canvas. Solomon R. Guggenheim Museum, New York: *Composition V,* 1911, oil on canvas, private collection: wall panels for Edwin R. Campbell, 1914, oil on canvas. *Spring, Summer,* Museum of Modern Art, New York, *Autumn, Winter.* Solomon R. Guggenheim Museum, New York: *Improvisation without title.* 1914, oil on canvas. Städtische Galerie im Lenbachhaus, Munich.

[13] *Beach Baskets in Holland,* 1904. oil on canvas. Städtische Galerie im Lenbachhaus, Munich.

[14] Kandinsky, of course, did not invent the style as such, which is basically Jugendstil; what is distinctive about it, however, is the use to which it is put. Likewise other elements of style which I isolate do not take place in a vacuum: for instance in terms of sheer technique, the use of color that I describe in *Church at Murnau* (see page 9) has obvious connections with Fauvism and, to a lesser extent, with Neo-Impressionism: the centricality is also to be found in Cubism. However I am not concerned with tracing these roots here.

[15] *Study for Painting with White Form,* 1913, watercolor, Museum of Modern Art, New York.

[16] *Watercolor (No. 13),* 1913, Museum of Modern Art, New York.

[17] *Church at Murnau,* 1909, oil on cardboard, Museum of Modern Art, New York.

[18] *Untitled watercolor,* 1915, Rebay Foundation, No. R172, Solomon R. Guggenheim Museum, New York.

[19] *Kandinsky, Retrospects,* trans H. Rebay in *Kandinsky,* op. cit., p. 28; italics mine.

[20] Kandinsky, *Concerning the Spiritual in Art,* p. 51.

[21] This point needs some qualification. Every pictorial task will impose its own limitations, and it is not true to say that this kind of abstraction *always* allows the use of any kind of space. In Kandinsky's case his use of the image compels him to forsake volume and the easiest way to deny volume is to avoid deep space, though it is not the only way. In fact, Kandinsky's space is not as deep as Kramer and Greenberg (in "Kandinsky," *Art and Culture.* Beacon Press, Boston, 1961, pp. 111-114) seem to think, though it is never flat either; it is important to notice; however, that despite its depth, the ground is insubstantial and ambiguous as to location, and the image is constantly referred back to the surface. The point I am making is that he modifies the use of "naturalistic space in accordance with his pictorial aims; but this is different from saying (as Kramer and Greenberg imply) that abstract forms must be in flat or very shallow space in order to be abstract forms. The following discussion should elucidate this.

[22] Kandinsky, *Concerning the Spiritual in Art,* pp. 66-67.

[23] Quoted (no source given) in Rebay, *Kandinsky,* p. 11.

Jonathan Fineberg (essay date 1979)

SOURCE: "'Les Tendances Nouvelles', The Union Internationale Des Beaux-Arts, Des Lettres, Des Sciences et De L'Industrie and Kandinsky," in *Art History,* Vol. 2, No. 2, June, 1979, pp. 221-46.

[*In the following essay, Fineberg traces Kandinsky's relationship with the influential art journal* Les Tendances Nouvelles.]

1. THE HISTORY AND CHARACTER OF *LES TENDANCES NOUVELLES*

The Parisian *revue, Les Tendances Nouvelles,* emerged in May of 1904 as part of an ambitious enterprise, consisting not only of a periodical, but of a gallery, an exhibition society, and an international artists' co-operative with explicitly Utopian goals. This effort actually put into practice many of the characteristic ideals of Symbolism, which still held sway in the Paris art world during the first decade of this century and were passed on to the young Expressionists. Despite the broad variety of individual viewpoints published by the magazine, its Symbolist profile remained clear—in its social aspirations for art, its co-operative nature, its belief in the metaphysical unity of the various arts, its espousal of parallels between art and science, and its not infrequent forays into the mystic. Even the wide range of authors with different beliefs stems from a Symbolist appreciation for sincere individuality. Indeed, *Les Tendances Nouvelles* may be a more concrete and representative embodiment of this period ideology than any other known document of the time.

Beyond its usefulness as an example and as a lexicon (of sorts) for lesser known artists of the period, *Les Tendances Nouvelles* also made significant contributions to the evolution of early modern art. These are of three general kinds: First, it established a network of contacts between a wide international spectrum of vanguard—as well as not so vanguard—artists. This established links for artists like Kandinsky and Jawlensky with associates of the Fauves, Mondrian, the young Duchamp-Villon, and other important, chiefly French artists at a time when they had been thought (until now) to have known nothing of one another. Second, it provided a vehicle for such major artists as Kandinsky, Feininger, Le Corbusier (Jeanneret), the Futurists, and Rodin, as well as for provocative thoughts by lesser known figures who, in their own turn, affected the work of the more prominent personalities. Lastly, it served as a model for other similar ventures, not the least of which was Kandinsky's *Blaue Reiter*; but Kandinsky's very special relationship with *Les Tendances Nouvelles* will be taken up separately, in the second part of this essay.

The inaugural exhibition of this enterprise, the 'Groupe d'Art des *Tendances Nouvelles*' opened on 1 June 1904 bringing together an international cross-section of artists including French Symbolists, Fauves, German Expressionists, and individuals who a few years later developed strong allegiances to Cubism. As listed in the first issue of the magazine, the fifty-three members of this co-operative salon included J.-P. Dubray (the poet-painter who was a life-long friend of Jacques Villon), Pierre Girieud (who later showed with the *Blaue Reiter*), Alexei Jawlensky, Wassily Kandinsky (translated into French as 'Basile Kandinsky'), Kaethe Kollwitz, E. de Krouglicoff (who was active in the Union of Russian Artists in Paris, a frequent participant in Fauve exhibitions at the Galerie Berthe Weill, and an associate of the Abbaye de Créteil group), Georges Le Meilleur (a close friend of La Fresnaye and Le Fauconnier), A. Plehn (perhaps related to the German painter who in February 1906, in an article entitled 'The Struggle Against Pictorial Content', advocated the rejection of narrative representation and praised the spiritually enhancing value of art),[1] the later Cubist sculptor Raymond Duchamp-Villon, and others. This exhibition took place in its own 'Galerie des Tendances Nouvelles' at 20 rue Le Peletier, a little street that ran through the heart of the gallery district on the right bank.

As is explained in the second issue of *Les Tendances Nouvelles,*[2] the exhibition was intended to remain more or less permanent for a year—except as the participants wished to alter it. For each artist, the gallery kept nine works in storage to sell, in addition to the one on the wall, and took a ten per cent commission. The annual dues were 150 francs, with forty payable the first month and ten each following month. In addition, every member was entitled to a feature show of one week in the special display case. The membership shifted somewhat from month to month, but the major personalities remained.

The driving force behind all this activity was a part-Fauve, part-Symbolist painter named Alexis Mérodack-Jeaneau. Mérodack-Jeaneau conceived the idea of the periodical and exhibition society, and for most of its first year he ran it out of his studio at 9 rue du Val-de-Grâce, just south of the *quartier latin.*

Mérodack himself was born in Angers, 1 December 1873. He came from a well-off commercial and professional family and had studied at the École des Beaux-Arts in Angers. In 1890, he went off to Paris, where he studied for some time with Gustave Moreau and Luc Olivier-Merson. He exhibited regularly in the *Indépendants* (the so-called 'Neo-Impressionist salon') and from 1897 served as a member of its *comité,* where he became friendly with Toulouse-Lautrec, Henri Rousseau, and Manguin.[3] Among Mérodack's fellow students in Moreau's atelier from 1891-9 were Matisse, Rouault, Marquet, Manguin, Jules Flandrin, René Piot, Charles Guérin, Jacques Brissaud, Bernard Boutet de Monvel, Charles Milcendeau, and after 1897 Charles Camoin. Mérodack probably knew them all, but Milcendeau was the only one of the group to participate in the first *Tendances Nouvelles* showing in 1904.

In 1899, Mérodack had his first one man show (at the Bodinière) and it was warmly received by a number of critics. These critics included Gustave Geoffroy (whose writing appeared in the pages of *Les Tendances Nouvelles* from its inception), Arsène Alexandre, Louis Vauxcelles, Edouard Larradin, Léonce Bénédit, Pascal Tarthumy, Fontainas, Gustave Kahn, Gabriel Mourey, and Yvanhoë Rambosson. In 1902 Clovis Sagot gave him an exhibition which Gustave Coquiot reviewed for *Le Journal,* 14 May 1902. Mérodack showed regularly at the *Indépendants* from 1903, and although he did not usually exhibit in the *Salon d'Automne,* he showed three works there in 1904 (and in the catalogue listed his address as rue de Val-de-Grâce, 9).

Personally, Mérodack was highly unstable; hospitalized with emotional disorders on a few occasions, he suffered from a persecution complex centred on an abiding suspicion of plagiarism, which led later to some unnecessarily painful ruptures with friends and colleagues.[4] In 1905 he apparently began spending more time in Angers; in the *Indépendants* catalogue of that year he gave his address as '26 rue de la Chalonière, Angers'. But presumably this was partly because he needed to be there during the summer of 1905 to organize the first salon of the *Union Internationale des Beaux-Arts, des Lettres, des Sciences et de l'Industrie,* into which the group around *Les Tendances Nouvelles* had by that time grown. He may have been sick again in 1906, and there was no salon of the *Union* in that year. He organized a second salon of the *Union* held in Angers during May and June of 1907, and this one included an enormous display of works by Kandinsky. In 1909 he composed his manifesto 'Le Synthétisme', based on ideas that had been germinating since 1899; however, he did not finally publish the work until around 1912-14. Still more salons of the *Union* took place in Paris in the years following 1909. The organization finally disintegrated with the start of the war, and on 8 March of 1919 Mérodack died in Angers.

Mérodack-Jeaneau's manifesto of Synthetism, as well as his other writings (published in newspapers),[5] reflect all of the social idealism, the belief in the artist's prophetic role, and the rhetorical style of the other *Tendances Nouvelles* writers. Given his literary proficiency, the seemingly total absence of his prose from *Les Tendances Nouvelles* is conspicuous; notwithstanding Mérodack's almost exclusive responsibility for the administration of the organization and journal, his designs for its logo and the continued practice of his own art, it seems unlikely that he would never have found time to write for his own periodical. The motto added early in 1905 below Mérodack's design for the back cover was a slogan by the periodical's chief spokesman, Gerôme-Maësse: 'A renaissance can only come through a powerful and durable union.' The style and terminology of this motto—although generally consistent with most of what appeared in *Les Tendances Nouvelles*—sounds particularly like the writing of Mérodack himself. Gerôme-Maësse was the official critic of *Les Tendances Nouvelles* from its inception until the end; but he does not seem to have ever appeared in any other journal. In a review of the 1907 salon of the *Union,* Gerôme-Maësse referred to himself as the one who was responsible for the exhibition,[6] whereas Mérodack actually did the job. So close are the turns of phrase, as well as the viewpoint and style in the writings of Gerôme-Maësse and Mérodack-Jeaneau that it is probable Gerôme-Maësse was a pseudonym for Mérodack-Jeaneau.[7] One might even wonder if it is not a cryptic variant on 'Mérodack-Jeaneau', arrived at in emulation of Sâr Peladan, for whom Mérodack and his friends simultaneously felt admiration and rivalry.

Some of the articles by Gerôme-Maësse even seem to reflect Mérodack's personality traits. 'La Question Sociale en Art', for example, reveals a somewhat paranoid fantasy about the conspiracy of dealers and art critics. Gerôme-Maësse refers to the artist as the 'sad victim' who has been 'flayed' (*écorché*) by these oppressors.[8] This terminology in itself indicates the intensity with which he felt the persecution of 'the artist', and it closely parallels Mérodack's later fantasy of being plagiarized by other artists and unjustifiably ignored by the critics.

Whatever Mérodack's personal peculiarities, he was a successful editor. For about a decade, *Les Tendances Nouvelles* brought elder statesmen and young talent into contact with one another by seeking out the patronage of the former while open-mindedly presenting the new ideas of the latter. Despite his own inclination for Symbolism, Mérodack's artistic and intellectual contacts cut broadly across stylistic and national categories, as his *comité* of honorary directors demonstrates.

In the first issue of *Les Tendances Nouvelles,* the well-known Symbolist critic Gustave Geoffroy wrote an opening statement entitled 'Un groupe d'Artistes' to express the ambitions of the new organization. He described the association: 'A group of artists has united in order to put itself in direct contact with the public. It is a sort of co-operative society which has come into being and that fact is interesting enough to remark upon.'[9] They wanted to have their own gallery and magazine to promote young artists who might otherwise be suffocated by the salons, and as far as possible they tried to find art critics to write from within their own ranks. From the outset the journal manifested a broad interest in all the arts and attempted to chronicle theatrical events and concerts as well as the *beaux-arts.* The international scope and the idealistic notion of reaching (and even uplifting) 'the average man' with advanced art seem implicit from the first; and both ideas quickly evolved into strongly stated objectives.

With an article by Louis Leroy, 'L'Art et la Science', this first issue also expressed the poetic fascination with science and scientific means which recurred throughout the life of this association. Leroy lamented the past lack of complete co-operation between science and art, and indicated his belief in the usefulness of objective processes in art. He wrote that science should begin to consider art 'a materialization of thought, a tangible expression of human feelings',[10] implying that it could thus be measured and analysed with 'scientific' methods—an idea that the Neo-Impressionists shared. Meanwhile, he also implies a reciprocal influence. 'The artist seeds science',[11] as another *Tendances Nouvelles* author put it, expressing the belief in art as a means of acquiring knowledge of the Creation, as an enquiry that goes hand in hand with science.

The pervasive social idealism of *Les Tendances Nouvelles* emerged frequently in its pages. Explicitly it was stated by the writers in almost every issue. In March of 1905, Gustave Huë (one of the regular spokesmen) outlined a programme for the 'groupe idéa' as he called the artists of *Les Tendances Nouvelles.* He said,

The principal purpose of 'Idéa' will be to group them [the artists] around the ideas which are common to them and—while permitting them, because of the association, to know each other's reciprocal efforts and to obtain a maximum of practical results—to aid them to reach the public, to educate it, and to guide it by a reasoned, scientific orderly initiation; finally, to form a living and permanent seed of a next renaissance where *Art* will be regenerated by *Idea*.[12]

Many of the *Tendances Nouvelles* writers—notably Gustave Geoffroy and Paul Adam—had already manifested a strong interest in social issues before they joined this group, and these involvements continued naturally through their association with the journal. But various new activities initiated by *Les Tendances Nouvelles* also indicate its deep commitments in this area. The association's large salon of 1907 was called 'Le Musée du Peuple' and as Gerôme-Maësse proclaimed:

The doors of the Museum of the People will therefore open very wide before the intellectual elite at the same time as before the mass of manual labourers.[13]

Les Tendances Nouvelles attempted to make good art more available to the average man by operating a mail order service for paintings, graphics and sculpture. Beginning in 1907 the back pages started to carry a list of half a dozen or so works by a couple of artists—different artists in each issue—intended for sale by post. They encouraged the artists to make the prices especially low so that a working man could afford them. The artists listed were by no means all minor; Khnopff, Maurice Denis, Guillaumin, and Ensor appeared there, and in one issue Kandinsky offered a variety of work, ranging from woodcuts starting around 20 francs to paintings (about a dozen in number) priced between 70 and 2000 francs.[14]

But inevitably there was some disillusionment with the public response to this project and, in an article entitled 'Notre Command-Office' (our mail order office), Gerôme-Maësse later admitted that 'certain goals in our programme have frankly been difficult to fulfill';[15] mainly the hope of widely dispensing works of young unknown artists when the public just isn't used to things of good quality. The article laments the disappearance of the 'amateur' who paid little but bought regularly. Now, says the author, there is only the 'millionaire' who buys names; the 'command office' attempted to encourage the little collector again. The editor suggested—speaking in first person, probably Mérodack again—that only the best art be reproduced in the magazine so that the public would be properly educated. He proposed that he create a decorative stamp for works that he recommended for purchase (a sort of 'good housekeeping seal' to assure the average person of quality).

Les Tendances Nouvelles expressed its deep commitment to social causes, especially to public education, in many ways. The *Union* established a travelling scholarship for

artists and began publishing novels, poems, and portfolios of artists' prints.[16] In an article entitled 'L'Art populaire' Gustave Huë wrote,

if it is true that the public is unable to judge a work of art doesn't that come simply from a faulty education?[17]

And he goes on to say that it is the responsibility of artists to teach people. Accordingly, the *Tendances Nouvelles* group opened a school of applied art in the summer of 1905.

In addition, many *Tendances Nouvelles* articles discussed social issues such as the implications of private property (which must be maintained to preserve individuality in art without, however, abandoning responsibility to the masses, according to one writer),[18] the impact of science and the machine on culture, and the theories of Kropotkin. The concept of the artists' co-operative periodical and exhibition society in itself reflects a social idealism, and early in 1905 Mérodack extended this co-operative when he established the *Union Internationale des Beaux-Arts des Lettres, des Sciences, et de l'Industrie* as the central organization for all the various activities.

This social concern was not unique to *Les Tendances Nouvelles*. A number of journals and writings of the period manifested a general interest in the masses of the poor. Special salons dedicated themselves to designs for homes and furnishings within the price range of working-class people—in 1905 *L'Art Décoratif* carried an article on 'La maison ouvrière' ('the worker's house') shown at the Grand Palais exhibition of social economy and hygiene; in 1907 Yvanhoë Rambosson (an admirer of Mérodack) wrote an article in the same journal on inexpensive designs for modern furniture; essays appeared on the simple folk crafts of Marie Tenichev's Talashkino colony; and many other similarly oriented writings frequently made their way into the *revues* of the period.

In a more abstract, philosophical form, Kandinsky, Mérodack-Jeaneau, and many others associated with *Les Tendances Nouvelles* vehemently expressed the same kind of social idealism in their belief that the artist had special obligations as a spiritual leader, and that art should raise the moral level of society. Mérodack-Jeaneau's international ambitions for the *Union* revealed his idealistic belief in his mission to uplift the masses with art. He advertised at the back of the journal that manuscripts could be sent in French, Spanish, German, Italian, or English and he attempted to set up a network of collaborators all over Europe. In one issue he spelled out the 'missionary' obligations of *Union* members, addressing especially those who had been selected as *correspondants* (this included at least fifty members).[19] They were to consider themselves as the representative of the *Union* in their country or city and the house of the correspondent was therefore to be the gathering place where artists and literary people, 'irrespective of their religious or political orientation', could find support, particularly *Union* members holding the group's honorific distinction—the golden bee.[20] The correspondent 'must' do everything possible to promote a positive atmosphere for art in his area, rallying around himself artists, literati, and collectors to form a circle receptive to the aims of the *Union*. He is to keep the *Union* up to date on the developments in his area and to make himself known as a representative of the organization to city authorities, museum officials, directors of all public institutions, presidents of salons, etc., so that he may be invited to participate in their various activities and promote *Les Tendances Nouvelles*. 'The correspondent must, without hesitation report the abuses—from the artistic point of view—committed around him while endeavouring, however, to remedy them.' The correspondent was also instructed to go to certain conventions on behalf of the *Union* and to organize local events (especially for educating young people from 'different social classes'). How many correspondents actually fulfilled these obligations is uncertain but their involvement with the *Union* must have been extensive. Like the claim that *Les Tendances Nouvelles* could be found in 'all important libraries' everywhere (which seems unlikely since it cannot be found anywhere today), this conception of the *Union*'s great international activity and the extensive participation of all its members may contain an element of wishful thinking. Nevertheless, one newspaper reported that by 1912 the group had 2000 members.[21]

Exhibiting the work of its members became the most important task of the *Union*, apart from publishing *Les Tendances Nouvelles*. The first official salon of the *Union* opened 1 August 1905 in Angers, with three nights of lectures followed by a banquet attended by Henri Rousseau.[22]

In 1906, the *Union* did not hold an exhibition, but the manifestation of May 1907, called *Le Musée du Peuple*, was large; according to Gerôme-Maësse, the catalogue included 1244 entries![23] This show (probably the most ambitious one) aspired to open culture to the masses and involved the whole range of the arts, including concerts and theatrical performances every night. This salon took place in Angers. The 1910 salon was held in Paris; Mondrain, Kollwitz, and Christian Rohlfs all participated, as members of the *Union*.[24] Another Paris salon took place in 1911 and still another was planned for 1914. It is not certain whether salons were held in 1908 and 1909, 1912 and 1913, or after; verification of such occurrences does not appear in the magazine; probably no such shows materialized.

In an article anticipating the opening of the *Union*'s 1907 salon, Gerôme-Maësse outlined the utopian notions behind the planning.[25] He talked of how workers as well as intellectuals would flock to the show, he spoke of reviving the natural alliance between artists and artisans, and he attacked the tasteless bourgeois patronage which was 'contemptuous' of artists. At the same time he looked to science in a similarly idealized way, much as Seurat and Kandinsky had done. In addition, he

fantasized of ultimately building a permanent home for the *Musée du Peuple* in 'la grande Cité d'Art'.

The *Musée du Peuple* attracted considerable attention in Angers; the mayor gave a speech at the inauguration and at least three major regional newspapers covered the events of the Congress and salon. The specific contents of the exhibition—including Kandinsky's contribution—remain unclear since no copies of the catalogue appear to have survived, although one did exist; hence the newspaper accounts provide some of the most important information available. The articles in *Le Pays Bleu* indicate not only the local pride in this organization but the fact that a previous *congrès* of the *Union* had taken place there in 1905.

> This congress suddenly places our town on a level with art centres like Lyon and Nancy. Without fear, artists send their works to Angers to be judged by an audience already educated (by the previous congress of 1905).[26]

The review cites the side-by-side exhibition of paintings with applied art objects and the revival of wood engraving (a painstaking medium in danger of extinction), specifically mentioning that

> The prodigious Russian engraver Kandinsky, of whose works we reproduce here *The Lake* and *Siege*, will exhibit about a hundred works—paintings and prints—in the place where in 1905 there were the nineteen large canvases of the Lyonnais Jacques Martin.[27]

Other participants are also mentioned, sometimes with specific works; among them,

> the famous painter Henri Rousseau whose canvases captivate all Paris. He will probably exhibit the canvas which was acquired at the last *Salon d'Automne* by the dealer Vollard. It is well known that this year at the *Indépendants* the crowds were so large in front of Rousseau's works that in order to see them better a step-ladder was provided, of which not even a fragment survived after a few hours of use.

> Cézanne's canvases will be exhibited along with these works. We expect still other important entries.[28]

This review also reported that theatrical performances would be given by actors from the theatres Antoine, Palais Royal, Odéon, and Grand Guignol and that an orchestra would play during intermission while people go through the exhibition. In the next issue *Le Pays Bleu* listed more contributors. The most important were: André Lhôte, Auguste Chabaud (provincial landscapes), and Julio Gonzales (Spanish).[29] The next issue provided still more names, and remarked on the exhibit of 'the complete work of Kandinsky, his wonderful wood engravings and his little canvases bursting with colour and reality'.[30]

The works in *Le Musée du Peuple* were grouped by nationality and all the pictures by any one artist hung together, sectioned off, where possible, for greater intimacy in the display. The *Union* even encouraged artists to show photos of themselves or of their country to make their exhibit more personal. In addition, *Le Musée du Peuple* included a book fair, presentations of industrial arts and a special exhibition of small private art collections. Lectures or study groups discussed (1) the relation of artist and artisan, (2) 'the moral and material life of artists', (3) the creation of 'the city of art', including a free art school and artistic manufacturing, (4) 'the hygiene of intellectual work', and (5) scientific discoveries applicable to the arts.[31]

Having started out of Mérodack's own studio, the March 1905 issue of *Les Tendances Nouvelles* announced a new official address near the gallery district on the *rive droite,* 15 rue Rochechouart, where it remained until around 1910. At about the same time (March or April of 1905), Mérodack also founded *L'Union Internationale des Beaux-Arts, des Lettres, des Sciences, et de l'Industrie* under the official presidency of Paul Adam, Auguste Rodin and Vincent d'Indy.[32] The composer Vincent d'Indy (teacher of Debussy, Erik Satie, and Edgard Varèse, among others) had close ties to the Nabis artists;[33] Rodin, of course, was among the most prominent artists of this period; and Paul Adam had a considerable reputation as a novelist. The three thus gave status to the organization in its three foremost areas of interest—music, literature, and the *beaux-arts.*

At this time, Le Gendre mysteriously disappeared from the masthead as co-editor; the editors of *Les Tendances Nouvelles*—the 'official illustrated organ' of the *Union*—were then Alexis Mérodack-Jeaneau and Louis Leroy. Since the establishment of the *Union,* the inside cover of *Les Tendances Nouvelles* also began to carry a list of principal collaborators. In 1905, the list included *philosophie d'art:* Jules Breton, L.-M. Themanlys; *critique d'art:* Gùstave Geoffroy, Gerôme-Maësse, Gustave Huë, Frantz Jourdain, Louis Leroy, Jean Levallière, M.-L. Neau; 'correspondants à l'étranger': Belgique—G. Lemmen; Angleterre—Léon Morel. Beginning with the 15 April 1905 issue (no. 7), the inside cover carried a *comité d'honneur.* From then on a number of other important names began appearing, mostly as honorary directors rather than as correspondents. They included: Vibert, Albert Besnard, Eugène Carrière,[34] Georges Lecomte, Louis Majorelle, Roger-Marx, Comtesse de Noailles,[35] Émile Perrault, Paul Sebellieau, M. Goldberg, Louis Vauxelles; and in later years: Leo Tolstoy, Aimée Wilson (a correspondent from England who was involved in Theosophy and reviewed Kandinsky's 1907 *Musée du Peuple* show in the English press), Troubetzkoy, Monet, Renoir, Rudyard Kipling, Anatole France,[36] and others.

The tone of *Les Tendances Nouvelles* did not change after the formation of the *Union,* although it occasionally became even more explicit in its social idealism and in its desire to connect science with art. Its contributors' interest in Neo-Impressionism, for example, arose from their imputation of scientific method to this style of painting;[37] they understood it as a Symbolist interpretation of Impressionism. Despite the Symbolist character of *Les Tendances Nouvelles,* its critics reviewed all the major French salons and a variety of gallery exhibitions—Symbolist and otherwise. From the beginning, they followed a large sample of important avant-garde artists, ranging from Sâr Peladan to Julio Gonzales, Friesz, Matisse, Rouault, and André Lhôte. Kandinsky woodcuts illustrate certain articles, and somewhat later Feininger occupied practically a whole issue.

In a series of issues, dating from 1910 to 1913, *Les Tendances Nouvelles* devoted much attention to the Futurists, reproducing a number of their works, publishing Marinetti's 'Futurist Discourse to the Venetians', excerpts from the 'Technical Manifesto of Futurist Painting' and the introduction to the catalogue of the contemporaneous first Futurist Exhibition at Bernheim-Jeune (the essay was called 'The Exhibitors to the Public'), Boccioni's 'Technical Manifesto of Futurist Sculpture', and Valentine de Saint-Point's 'Futurist Manifesto of Lust'. The editorial spokesman, Henry Breuil (anticipating a number of enraged readers who wrote letters for the next issue), stated that he did not understand what the Futurists were doing. However, Breuil explained, *Les Tendances Nouvelles* attempted to be as open as possible to new ideas, and perhaps history might one day prove that the Futurists have something.[38] Works by Diego Rivera, Élie Nadelman, and Torres-Garcia appeared, the magazine carried original woodblocks and reproductions of paintings by Gabriele Münter, and Le Corbusier's article 'Étude sur le mouvement décoratif en Allemagne' (written under the name of Jeanneret) was serialized in the last issues.

Both the range of artists and writers and the variety of styles and theories represented in *Les Tendances Nouvelles* are striking. What becomes increasingly clear as one studies this document—and indeed the intellectual history of early twentieth-century Europe as a whole—is how much communication of ideas existed, and how freely individual artists cultivated and drew upon associations that cut across all national, stylistic, and philosophical boundaries.

Edgard Varèse, for example, studied at Vincent d'Indy's *Schola Cantorum* (like Debussy and Erik Satie); he came to know Rodin at about the same time and even lived with him briefly at Meudon. Varèse was an old family friend of Julio Gonzales (who came to Paris in 1900) and, through the sculptor, he met Picasso, Max Jacob and others. When Varèse conceived his revolutionary *Arcana* using a kind of immaterial leitmotif—an idea more abstract than conventional melody, a pure sound realized through effects of orchestration—he doubtless utilized a wide spectrum of sources not only from his own discipline (like the repeated sequence of sounds in Erik Satie's *Furniture Music*), but also from literature or art, such as the Symbolist poets' use of the repeated word as pure sound, or the neutralized object used 'in an analogous way in Maillol's sculpture or in Kandinsky's abstraction.[39]

Whether or not these specific extramusical sources shaped Varèse's *Arcana*, this example demonstrates the breadth and formal unpredictability of the intellectual sources on which the great individual talents of the twentieth century could have drawn. *Les Tendances Nouvelles* underscores the inadequacy of approaching modern art solely in terms of 'schools', 'isms', or other closed concepts, by documenting the extraordinarily fluid exchange of ideas that animated the intellectual life of this period.

2. KANDINSKY'S RELATION WITH *LES TENDANCES NOUVELLES* AND ITS IMPACT ON HIS ART THEORY

On 1 June 1904, a full two years before Kandinsky purportedly made his first contact with advanced French art circles, he participated in the founding exhibition of the Parisian 'Groupe d'Art des *Tendances Nouvelles*'. Kandinsky contributed several pieces to their next Paris show in 1905, and in 1907 the group's salon (this time in Angers) featured Kandinsky, showing 109 of his works! *Les Tendances Nouvelles* reviewed Kandinsky's entries in other Paris shows, discussed his work in feature articles, and published in its pages nearly forty original woodcuts by him. In 1909, *Les Tendances Nouvelles* produced a portfolio of six of Kandinsky's wood engravings—called *Xylographies*—with an essay on his art by their chief writer, Gerôme-Maësse.

The first critical notice of Kandinsky's work written in *Les Tendances Nouvelles* was Gerôme-Maësse's October 1906 review of the *Salon d'Automne*, in which he refers to the works of Kandinsky, Friesz and others as interesting and promising.[40] Kandinsky's woodcut of the *Russian Rider* appeared on the cover of the Christmas 1906 issue and inside, on pages illustrated with Kandinsky woodcuts, Gerôme-Maësse published a lengthy article on 'Kandinsky, La Gravure sur Bois, l'Illustration'.[41]

This article commends Kandinsky's skilful revival of the wood engraving despite the trend towards mechanical processes which do not directly show the artist's hand. The critic praises Kandinsky's richness of design, his facility, and his 'extreme originality', which leaves the viewer 'with the impression of things appearing in a dream'. 'The light which emanates [from Kandinsky's paintings] is of a bizarre radiance' and 'their author appears something of a magician'. The dark grounds on which Kandinsky painted gave the spots of bright tempera a mysterious dazzling luminescence so that they appeared like little lights hovering over the surface of the picture. Gerôme-Maësse sensitively picked out this quality in his article of 1906, making him perhaps the first critic to recognize the remarkable, original qualities of Kandinsky's tempera painting. The critic went on to remark on the richness of content with which Kandinsky invests his subjects and his use of minute details to evoke multiple emotions. According to Gerôme-Maësse, Kandinsky marvellously refuted the 'contemporary' notion that 'detail doesn't exist'. He even comprehended Kandinsky's intrinsically mystic spiritual intentions—perhaps because they resembled his own.

His language is that of an initiate. His formula, at first sight disconcerting, contains, for one who explores it, a very expressive scheme of innumerable material appearances. As he studies in it the least reflections, as he appreciates in it all the correspondences with the *higher self* of the beings, the images, which he opens up to us under an impulse from the external world, admirably sum up for us his most cherished internal visions.[42]

At the end of issue no. 26 (December 1906), the editor noted that the library of the *Union*[43] received five original woodcuts from Basile Kandinsky (as the French referred to him) and photographs of several other works. The next four issues (nos 27-30) also contained Kandinsky woodcuts, and in the last of these Gerôme-Maësse discussed at length Kandinsky's large display at the *Union*'s 1907 *Musée du Peuple* exhibition:

> . . . the numerous entries of the Russian Kandinsky . . . paintings, watercolours, and prints extend across a panel of a dozen metres in length . . . every exhibition of the Union permits two artists, new ones each time, to present their entire oeuvre to the public. . . . As varied as they are numerous, the works of Kandinsky unfailingly entice the spectator. They intrigue him, then they captivate him. If some derive from the school of Munich, they all, nevertheless, express the slavic soul and the least of them remains a delightful discovery. The artist who created his work of imagination is still more imaginative in technique. Do we know from what mysterious mixtures of pastes and copal-varnishes are born these unforgettable splendours of the orient? (fn. Unfortunately I must warn the artist against the temptation to continue in that manner, very beautiful but susceptible in a short time to making his painting crackle.) This very modern artist, couldn't he have been an ancient glass maker, an old ceramist, or tapestry weaver? Here the clocktowers of his 'town' appear to me like multi-coloured glass beads blown up in fusion! The blues, the yellows, and such strong yellows! Mixed with the lacquers. In the foreground, brick red cabarets, eastern prelates in violet, mujiks in strong green; the teeming crowd of likewise multi-coloured costumes; manifold colouration of the popular life. For we are far from the tedious and restrained painting behind which one always feels the rationality and the compass, which bores even the one who made it and which I will readily personify in the character of honest and rich bourgeois, certainly pretty, but of such limited spirit! The painting which occupies our attention [almost certainly Kandinsky's **Buntes Leben**] is expressive, seductive, aggressive and charming, sometimes exaggerated, volatile and often disquieting, but it absorbs us and stirs our emotions; it is the unfaithful mistress, it enchants us. One of the most remarkable aspects of the artist's talent is this: a wood engraver of incontestable quality, he is also a real painter of 'values'. And this breaks with custom. The whole world knows that the pictorial efforts of many of his most appreciated colleagues—I will only cite Vibert— are silently passed over. For even without counting

his important paintings of which I have already spoken and his great watercolours handled according to the formula of the wood; with characters whose clothing and flesh burst forth in a fanfare from a dark background, Kandinsky exhibits a series of little oil studies of an extraordinary accuracy of vision.[44]

No more Kandinsky woodcuts appeared in *Les Tendances Nouvelles* again until issue 34 (February 1908).[45] *Les Tendances Nouvelles* published Kandinsky's print **Belief** in issue 35 at the end of the first installment of an article which Kandinsky later cited in **Concerning the Spiritual in Art,** and in no. 36 two more prints appeared along with the second part of the article.[46]

Issue no. 36 also contained Henry Breuil's review of the 1908 *Salon des Indépendants* in which he praised 'The Russian Basile Kandinsky' as an 'alluring and captivating artist'. He went on:

> One has been able to evaluate a part of his oeuvre this year in *Les Tendances Nouvelles* where they have pleased us greatly. I am a great admirer of his **Promenade.**[47] Since then he has made an evolution towards the dream, the chimera. In his vignettes he seeks the abstract forms, the curious lines of bewildering newness. He varies and over-elaborates his arabesques in spirals or cuts them out in jagged blacks on the white horizons. It is rich with ancient symbols; a whole cabalistic world sleeps in Kandinsky. This beautiful artist has already given much but as a visionary he goes on dreaming a new concept.[48]

Breuil's description here and three issues later in his review of the 1908 *Salon d'Automne* displays a remarkable sensitivity to Kandinsky's intentions. His encouragement of the artist's 'search for the abstract' may even have spurred Kandinsky on in that direction. Yet perhaps Kandinsky also influenced Breuil. In the *Salon d'Automne* review Breuil describes

> Four graphics by the indefatigable Basile Kandinsky, who wants to join line and sound with darks and lights as part of the wonderful enchantments of the total art which combines itself in a single expression: a quest for the unity of artistic conception, an unexplored and desired domain.[49]

This terminology, the talk of total unity and the allusion to synaesthetic sound in the painting, resembles the words Kandinsky himself used to describe his goals:

> We should struggle for form only as long as it serves as a means of expression for the inner sound.[50]

In issue no. 40 of *Les Tendances Nouvelles* (February 1909) there were three Kandinsky woodcuts. Five photographic reproductions of paintings by Münter appeared in number 42 (probably June 1909) along with an article by Gerôme-Maësse which praises the charm of her work. This issue also announced a free weekly class in 'Rhythmic-gymnastics (method Jacques Dalcroze) aimed at the

development of the rhythmic, musical sensibilities and of the body . . .'.[51] Kandinsky's comrade from the Stuck studio, Alexander von Salzmann, went to work with Dalcroze at about this time (after several years at the Théâtre des Champs Elysées in Paris) and created a new mode of theatrical lighting which used the lights as an expressive medium in their own right[52] Salzmann's lighting probably influenced Kandinsky's abstract concepts of light in his **Gelbe Klang.** Kandinsky noted the name of Jacques Dalcroze in a sketch book of around 1908,[53] and his friend Michael Sadleir went to see Dalcroze immediately after visiting Kandinsky in 1911, possibly at Kandinsky's suggestion.[54] Another Kandinsky woodcut showed up in issue no. 46,[55] and the last one appeared in issue no. 49, probably from November 1910.[56]

The high point and most intriguing episode in Kandinsky's relations with *Les Tendances Nouvelles* was the featured exhibition of his works that the organization sponsored at its salon in the late spring of 1907. Nothing is known of what Kandinsky showed in the exhibition of May 1904 or at the salon in the summer of 1905. But we can reconstruct at least a partial list of his probable entries to the great exhibition of 1907, in Angers.

Le Journal de Maine et Loire carried notes on this exhibition, called the *Musée du Peuple,* in about half a dozen separate issues. It said little of Kandinsky, however, except to mention 'the curious notations of Kandinsky, the Russian with the mosaicist's vision, whose entries occupy a side of the hall'.[57] From this and the statement in *Le Pays Bleu* it seems that Kandinsky showed the full range of his work—the woodcuts the nature studies, and the mosaic-like temperas.

When the Angevine daily, *Le Patriote de l'Ouest,* reviewed this show, it mentioned Kandinsky only briefly; but it was more specific.

> The complete oeuvre of Basile Kandinsky (109 nos.). We note: *Esquisse, Au bord de l'eau, Promenade à cheval, La confusion des races, Jour de fête, Accident, Cavaliers, Vers le soir, Venise, Mardi Gras,* etc. The work of Kandinsky colourful and strong is one of the principal points of this congress.[58]

Without the exhibition catalogue it is impossible to identify securely all 109 works shown by Kandinsky, but these newspaper accounts and Kandinsky's personal house catalogue do help to pinpoint some works. The artist's house catalogue contains numbered, chronological lists of paintings, small oil studies, coloured drawings and prints. It contains only about 50 paintings, 130 coloured drawings, 100 little oil studies and around 30 woodcuts done before the middle of 1907. Although incomplete, the catalogue gives some basic idea of the size of Kandinsky's oeuvre by 1907 and indicates that an exhibition of 109 of his works at that time cannot have left very much out.

Kandinsky himself noted that certain works were shown at the Angers exhibition of May 1907:[59] 'paintings' (both of 1907)—no. 46 *Buntes Leben* and no. 47 *Esquisse*; 'woodcuts'—no. 21 *Der Speigel* (R49), no. 22 *Le Chasseur* (R50), no. 23 *Trompette* (R51), and no. 24 *Moine* (R52). On the list of small oil studies (dating from 1901 to 1907) the first ten are bracketed and marked with the initials 'T.N.' Next to these entries, as well as those of most of the other studies (nos 1-10, 19-75, 78-83, 100 and 101) on this list, are prices in French francs, ranging from 125 to 225 Fr. Presumably these first ten works were shown at the Angers exhibition, and perhaps also some of the later ones which have French rather than German prices. These first ten works are: no. 1 *Etudie*, no. 2 *Etudie*, no. 3 *Le parc d'Achtyrka,* nos 4-8 *Kochel,* nos 9-10 *Kallmunz.*

The pictures referred to in the newspaper review seem to have been: the oil painting *Esquisse* (house catalogue, 'paintings', no. 47); *Au bord de l'eau* is probably *Vers le Soir* (*Au bord de l'eau*) (house catalogue, 'coloured drawings', no. 61) which Kandinsky later listed for sale through the mail order office of *Les Tendances Nouvelles;*[60] *Promenade à cheval*—also listed for sale by order—may have been the tempera *Reitendes Paar* of 1903 (house catalogue, 'paintings', no. 20), which the artist noted as having been shown at 'Ste. Nat. B-A Ap. 1907', but as no Kandinskys were catalogued in the Paris *Salon National des Beaux-Arts* for 1907 this may have been a confusion of name, intending to indicate the salon of the *Union Internationale des Beaux-Arts; La confusion des races* is certainly the great tempera *Buntes Leben* (house catalogue, 'paintings', no. 46) which the artist clearly marked as having been at the Angers show; *Jour de fête* was probably the tempera picture *Feirtag* ('coloured drawings', no. 101); *Accident* was probably the 1906 painting *Ereignis* ('painting', no. 44, tempera); *Cavaliers* could be the Russian riders listed as 'coloured drawings', no. 85 in the house catalogue (the only picture titled *Cavaliers*), but as the critic of *Le Patriote* seems not to have been very exact about the titles (as with *Buntes Leben,* where the identification is relatively certain), this title could also have been a variation on *Cavaliers arabes* ('coloured drawings', no. 96); *Vers le soir* was almost certainly *Cegen Abend* ('coloured drawings', no. 98); *Venise* (probably 'coloured drawing', no. 119); and the house catalogue does not list anything under the title of *Mardi Gras* but the picture was probably *Bal Masqué* ('coloured drawing', no. 111) and this may have been the work reproduced in the *Der Sturm* album along with *Mosquée* ('coloured drawings', no. 71) and *Arabische Reiterei* ('coloured drawings', no. 96).[61]

Finally there is also a notation in the house catalogue, regarding a group of prints, which consist of a list of nine numbers and written beside it 'aus T. N. Paris'. The numbers clearly relate to the house catalogue numbers for the 'woodcuts'; they are 1, 2[b], 4, 6[b], 7[b], 8, 11, 12 and 14. Kandinsky used the small 'b' to indicate the coloured state of a print, hence this list consisted of *Promenade* (R1), the coloured state of *Abend* (also called *Dame mit Facher,* R2). *Sängerin, Die Nacht* (a colour state of the large version, R6), a colour state of the large version of *Abschied* (R7), *Einsame* (also called *Der*

Goldene Segel, R8), *Wintertag* (R34), *Mondaufgang* (R35), and *Abenddämmerung* (R37). This list does not correspond at all to the prints by Kandinsky which were published in *Les Tendances Nouvelles* (which also never printed any colour) and must have been designated this way in the house catalogue to signify that they had gone to the *Tendances Nouvelles* show. However, it may also be that these prints went to one of the earlier *Tendances Nouvelles* exhibitions of 1904 or 1905.

It seems likely that the original prints given to the library of *Les Tendances Nouvelles* at the end of 1906 and the works of which they received photographs at the same time must have figured in the show. Kandinsky may also have exhibited the prints published by *Les Tendances Nouvelles* up to that time, but as they were made (at least in one state) for publication in the review the artist considered them 'ex libris' rather than as 'woodcuts', and none of them appeared in his house catalogue. Lastly, there are also a few works in the house catalogue with exhibition notes that do *not* clearly indicate the Angers show but which—by the hurried inscription or minor confusion of names—could have been intended as such. *Der Blaue Reiter* ('paintings', no. 18) bears the inscription 'Paris mai, 1907'; this picture may well have been in the Angers exhibition. The catalogue of the *Paris Salon National des Beaux-Arts* has no indication of participation by Kandinsky at any time, however, the notation 'Ste. Nat. de B-A Av. 1907' follows the artist's entry for *Reitendes Paar* ('paintings', no. 20) and since the reviewer did cite a *Promenade à cheval* by Kandinsky which seems to have been this work, the annotation in the catalogue may have intended 'Internationale des B-A mai 1907', which would have designated the T.N. salon.[62] 'Coloured drawing', no. 63, *Der Fremde Stadt,* simply has the name 'Paris' written after it; perhaps this too went to the 'Union's' salon.

Bringing together all the evidence and speculation above, the following 72 objects may be suggested as a partial list of Kandinsky's 109 entries into the 1907 show at the *Musée du Peuple.* They are:

'paintings'

18 Der Blaue Reiter 1903
20 Reitendes Paar 1903
27 Sonntag (Altrussisch) 1904
40 Ankunft der Kaufleute 1905
44 Ereignis 1906
46 Buntes Leben 1907
47 Esquisse 1907

'small oil studies'

1 Étudie
2 Étudie
3 Le parc d'Achtyrka
4 Kochel
5 Kochel
6 Kochel
7 Kochel
8 Kochel

9 Kochel
10 Kochel

'coloured drawings'

7 Zwei Kampf
25 Gräner Vogel
29 Im Garten
31 Petite Ville Ancienne
37 Abschied
38 Am Strande
40 Sommertag
61 Gegen Abend
63 Der Fremde Stadt
68 Mühle (Holland)
79 Die Ammen
85 Cavaliers (Russe)
87 Une Rue de Tunis
96 Arabische Reiterei
98 Gegen Abend
101 Feiertag
111 Bal Masqué
119 Venedig

'woodcuts'

1 Promenade (R1)
2 Abend (Dame mit Facher, R2)
4 Sängerin (R4)
6 Die Nacht (R6)
7 Abschied (R7)
8 Einsame (Das goldene Segel, R8)
11 Wintertag (R34)
12 Mondaufgang (R35)
14 Abenddämmerung (R37)
17 Herbst (R40)
18 Parc St. Cloud (R41)
21 Der Spiegel (R49)
22 Le Chasseur (R50)
23 Trompette (R51)
24 Moine (R52)

'ex libris'[63]

R11 Schiffe
R12 Der Rhein
R13 Gegen Abend
R14 Rosen
R15 Gebirgsee
R16 Zuschauer
R17 Altes Stadtchen
R20 Abschied (small version)
R21 Die Nacht (small version)
R22 Zweikampf
R23 Die Jagd (small version)
R25 Ewigkeit
R26 Drei Köpfiger Drache
R28 Im Schlossgarten
R29 Der Reitende Ritter
R30 Belagerung
R31 Finsterer Abend
R44 Arabische Reiter
R45 Promenade Gracieuse
R46 Die Ammen
R48 Russische Reiter
R72 Springbrunnen

Kandinsky's participation in this exhibition and in the *Tendances Nouvelles* manifestations of 1904 and 1905 may account for the artist's entry of many pictures in his house catalogue with French rather than German titles.[64] Eight of them are already on the list above but there are nine coloured drawings and six prints which do not figure there: 'coloured drawings'—66. *Marseille*, 74. *Interieur*, 84. *Reiter (Cheveaux arabes)*, 88. *Fêtes des moutons*, 93. *Ruine*, 110. *Redoute*, 120. *Enterrement*, 121. *L'ours*, 122. *Scène*; and 'woodcuts'—19. *Printemps* (R42), 20. *Promenade Gracieuse* (R43), 26. subtitled *Noir et blanc no. 1* (R54), 27. subtitled *Noir et blanc no. 2* (R55), 31. subtitled *Noir et blanc no. 3* (R59), 32. subtitled *Noir et blanc no. 4* (R60).[65]

It may also be that the medals Kandinsky received at the 1904 'Exposition International de Paris' and the 'Grand Prix de l'Exposition Internationale de Paris'[66] were actually awarded by the 'Exposition' of the 'Union Internationale' (i.e. *Les Tendances Nouvelles*), held in Paris in 1904 and organized from the office of the magazine in Paris.

Les Tendances Nouvelles may also have provided an earlier and more influential source for Kandinsky's interest in the occult than his encounter with theosophy around 1908, although his Russian religious upbringing certainly disposed him towards mysticism long before. To cite one example, *Le Journal de Maine et Loire* reported that the *Musée du Peuple* sponsored two spiritualist lectures (excerpts from which were published in *Les Tendances Nouvelles*):

> The commandant Darget, who has been a long time specialist in the study of spiritism, will speak about vital rays: photographs of thought, of feeling, of anger, of illnesses, of animal and plant fluids (80 projections will be made in all).[67]

Kandinsky's involvement with *Les Tendances Nouvelles* was unquestionably deep, beginning 1904, peaking around May of 1907 and trailing off around 1909-10. No one knows how Kandinsky came into contact with Mérodack-Jeaneau; although they could have met via Sagot, who showed Mérodack's work in 1902 and Kandinsky's somewhat later. But the relationship between Mérodack and Kandinsky probably explains how Kandinsky found his way to a little, out-of-the-way hotel on the rue des Ursulines when he first arrived in Paris in May of 1906, since it stood just around the corner from Mérodack's studio. The connection to *Les Tendances Nouvelles* provided Kandinsky with substantial inroads into avant-garde French art circles—especially the Symbolist and Neo-Impressionist groups that spawned Fauvism. Like the Fauves, Kandinsky seems to have understood Neo-Impressionism as a visual embodiment of the Symbolist belief that colour and composition have laws of their own, independent of nature; thus he explored Neo-Impressionism as a vehicle for liberating colour.[68]

Even though the artists around *Les Tendances Nouvelles* indirectly made a great long-term contribution to

Kandinsky's development by opening his eyes to a more profound pictorial understanding of Neo-Impressionism (and Symbolism), *Les Tendances Nouvelles* influenced Kandinsky's art theory, in the most direct and specific sense, far more than his painting. Intellectually, *Les Tendances Nouvelles* shared and encouraged Kandinsky's Symbolist ambitions; it supplied specific vocabulary for his theories on artistic expression; and it provided the model for the application of his utopian ideas about the artist and society.

Symbolism nurtured Kandinsky's interest in the analysis and 'scientific' application of his expressive means; his art of 'conscious construction' discussed in **Concerning the Spiritual in Art** and his 'science of art' still present in **Point and Line to Plane** expressed this poetic infatuation with science. Similarly, Mérodack-Jeaneau advocated the use of science in art and asserted that artistic innovators were always linked with scientists.[69] Various aspects of science fascinated many Symbolists. Maurice Denis advised: 'to achieve the absolute, go back to the intimate secret of nature, the number'.[70] A renewed interest in the golden section, and an apocryphal notion that Leonardo based his theories on it, also gained popularity among some Symbolists, Cubists, and others in the decade before the Great War. In music, the period produced Schenker analysis, which postulated that the expressive continuity in all great music from Bach to Brahms could be reduced systematically to a single type of musical structure. The Russian poet André Bièly, in an article for *Zolotoe Runo* (*La Toison D'Or*), applied mathematical formulas to aesthetics.[71] Numerous other examples of this romanticized invocation of science might be cited.

In **Concerning the Spiritual in Art,** Kandinsky correlated specific colours with definite emotions.

> Blue is the typical heavenly colour; the ultimate feeling it creates is one of rest. (note: Supernatural rest, not the earthly contentment of green. The way to the supernatural lies through the natural. And we mortals passing from the earthly yellow to the heavenly blue must pass through green). When it sinks almost to black, it echoes a grief that is hardly human. It becomes an infinite engrossment in solemn moods.[72]

In the *Blue Rider Almanac,* Kandinsky discussed 'various specifically curved lines, which always make a certain internal impression; they too can be "happy", "sad", etc.'[73] These passages exemplify Kandinsky's systematic analysis, and they have a narrower genaeology passing from Symbolism and Neo-Impressionist theory to more specific ideas in *Les Tendances Nouvelles.*

Kandinsky's first theoretical writings appeared in 1911-12, but he had begun making his notes for **Concerning the Spiritual in Art** in 1906-7 at the height of his involvement with this French group. In the foreword to the first edition of **Concerning the Spiritual in Art** (December 1911), the artist explained, 'The thoughts which I set forth here are the results of observations and experiences of feelings which gradually collected themselves in the course of the last five or six years'[74] (i.e. approximately 1906-11).

One of the quasi-scientific credos of Mérodack-Jeaneau's 'École Synthétique' was that it 'follows the theories which tend to prove the fundamental unity of matter, infinitely variable in appearance'.[75] This has both transcendental and scientific inspiration and provided an appealing 'substantiation' of the idea of the unity of all the arts, particularly the parallels between music and painting which recurred so often in Kandinsky's writings and in *Tendances Nouvelles* articles, of which one of the most important is the 1907 essay, 'L'Audition colorée' by Gerôme-Maësse. In it the author coined the term 'a musician of painting' and discussed what he regarded as the inextricable intermingling of all the arts in that period. After passing through a literary stage, painting now, according to the author, encroaches on music. He cited scientific experiments and other evidence of correspondences between colours and pains, sounds, tastes, words and even numbers. He also correlated colours with specific musical instruments, as Kandinsky later did in **Concerning the Spiritual in Art**[76]—however, they are tentative and do not correspond exactly with Kandinsky's pairings. In addition, Gerôme-Maësse related the experience of a nineteenth-century pianist who experienced a constellation of colour and smell sensations while listening to a Schubert symphony:

> The *Aria in A-major,* in the scherzo, is of a heat so sundrenched and of a green so tender, that, in hearing it, it seems to me to breathe the scent of young pine shoots.[77]

This resembles Kandinsky's later account, in his 'Reminiscences', of a synaesthetic experience he had while listening to Lohengrin.[78] Gerôme-Maësse also assigned colours to certain geometric configurations—specific angles, arcs, rectangles, etc.—and to natural phenomena. However, Gerôme-Maësse concluded that even though the artist can get precious information from articles such as his or books like that of Chevreul, he does not advocate following external rules.

> The true artist is a medium endowed with special faculties, and this gift, which supplies everything, remains his guide and his internal beacon.[79]

Like some of the writers for *Les Tendances Nouvelles,* Kandinsky later expressed an idealistic sympathy for anarchy:

> [A]narchy is regularity and order created not by an external and ultimately powerless force, but by *the feeling for the good.* Limits are set up here, too, but they must be internal limits and must replace external ones.[80]

This coincides with the anti-materialism and the broadminded acceptance of a wide variety of styles strongly advocated both by *Les Tendances Nouvelles* and by Kandinsky. Kandinsky explained:

The absolute cannot be sought in the form (materialism). Form is temporal, i.e., relative. . . . Since form is only an expression of content, and content is different with different artists, it is clear that there may be many different forms at the same time that are equally good.[81]

In *Concerning the Spiritual in Art,* Kandinsky described the artist as a kind of prophet who

always comes to the rescue—someone like ourselves in everything but with a secretly implanted power of 'vision' he sees and points out. This high gift (often a heavy burden) at times he would gladly relinquish. But he cannot. Scorned and disliked, he drags the heavy weight of resisting humanity forward and upward.[82]

Three years earlier, in his speech at the opening of the *Musée du Peuple,* Mérodack-Jeaneau stated a similar view:

Disdainful of the mummified model as of a cumbersome fetish, artists assert their right finally to freely express their thoughts or their feelings and reclaim awareness of their true role, that of initiator of the masses of which they are the primordial force. For it is in effect—whether one likes it or not—under the sole direction of the artist that the industry of nations can efficiently and nobly develop itself.[83]

In a later chapter of *Concerning the Spiritual in Art,* Kandinsky expounded on the processes by which these elevating transcendental insights are communicated. He explained that each colour evokes certain emotions through sympathetic 'vibrations'.

If you let your eye stray over a palette of colours, you experience two things. In the first place you receive a purely physical effect, namely the eye itself is enchanted by the beauty and other qualities of colour. You experience satisfaction and delight, like a gourmet savouring a delicacy. . . . But to a more sensitive soul the effect of colours is deeper and intensely moving. And so we come to the second result of looking at colours: their psychic effect. They produce a corresponding spiritual vibration, and it is only as a step towards this spiritual vibration that the physical impression is of importance.[84]

This concept and terminology seem to have come out of an important article in *Les Tendances Nouvelles* by Henri Rovel, to which Kandinsky referred in a footnote in *Concerning the Spiritual in Art.*[85] Rovel's article, 'The Laws of Harmony for Painting and for Music are the Same', appeared in the spring of 1908, in issues 35 and 36 of *Les Tendances Nouvelles.* It argued, as the title implies, that aesthetic harmony has universal rules which do not vary from one art to another. He advanced the theory that perceptions result from 'vibrations'—as Kandinsky first stated some three years later in *Concerning the Spiritual in Art*—and Rovel hypothesized that sound and colour have different magnitudes of corresponding wave lengths and that the vibratory capacities of the human eye are sometimes so active that they 'tune-in' on sounds so as to produce synaesthesia. Rovel admitted—as did Kandinsky—that the scientific structuring of the visual arts had not as yet developed to the point where the rules of harmony can be as systematically applied as they can in music. Rovel explained:

The human being is one; all the sensations of harmony which he feels are the result of vibrations; consequently whether he perceives these sensations with his eyes or ears the laws which govern them are the same.

Now music is precise and the rules which permit the connection of sounds bringing them together in relationships to produce such and such a sensation, are perfectly understood. For painting, on the other hand, the apportionment of colour has no mathematic, . . . also he has never been able to establish the laws of harmony of colours which, however, I don't doubt are identical with those of sounds.[86]

He then reproduced a scale of colour wave lengths (based on O. N. Rood's *Modern Chromatics*) and compared it to a chart showing the relative wave lengths of musical chords, with the suggestion that the C major chord may correspond to the relation of the colour wave lengths in the spectrum. He reviewed the literature—including Chevreul, Rood, Maxwell, Helmholz, Young, Boll and Kuhne—but concluded that their explanations were too complex. Instead, he offered the idea that perception may be reduced simply to vibrations and a dilation or contraction of retinal nerve endings to correspond to wave lengths.

Life is characterized by vibration. Without vibration there is no life. The entire world is subject to that law. Individually we form a whole; our organism is activated by a single motor, and following the more or less great perfection of that organism we are more or less capable of vibration and hence of feeling.[87]

In the second instalment of his article, Rovel carried this concept even further. He stated that each individual has a personal 'coefficient' which codifies his personal 'vibrations' and that, in a given experience, if two people's vibration coefficients are multiples or in simple mathematical relation to one another—like 2/3, 3/4, 4/5, etc.—they will have a harmonious relation in their sensations. But if the ratios have numbers like '13' or '29' there will be discord. With numbers like '30' and '3' the relation would be very close but dominated by '30' and exhausting for '3.' This, he claimed, clarifies why so many marriages start off happily but end badly. He stated that happiness corresponds to long vibrations and that individuals with coefficients like 7, 13, 17 and 19 are probably those we think of as having bad luck. These vibrations explain telepathy and, indeed, Rovel also believed that eventually physiologists would be able to bring people back to life with vibrations—like starting the pendulum of a clock again.

Three years later, when Kandinsky wrote of 'vibrations', the theories of Rovel had made a deep impression (as indeed they must also have impressed Mondrian, who was a member of the *Union* and probably saw this article). In the *Blue Rider Almanac,* Kandinsky declared that

> When the artist finds the appropriate means, it is a material form of his soul's vibration, which he is forced to express. If the method is appropriate, it causes an almost identical vibration in the soul of the audience.[88]

In *Concerning the Spiritual in Art,* Kandinsky emphasized the paramount importance of the 'spiritual vibration' which colour produces,[89] and in another part of the *Blue Rider Almanac* he asserted, 'these vibrations and the plus arising from them will enrich his soul as no means other than art can do'.[90] Kandinsky also believed in the healing power of these vibrations and (like some writers in *Les Tendances Nouvelles*)[91] he even expressed an explicit interest in chromotherapy.[92]

Behind the aspirations for universality in *Les Tendances Nouvelles* lies a broad acceptance of many different approaches to making art. Similarly, Kandinsky also expressed the conviction that artists of many varied styles make a positive contribution in their own terms to the moral revaluation of society through art; and that they should join forces to show their work and to write their own theory and criticism for the purpose of furthering their common moral goal. Kandinsky advocated 'an intense co-operation among artists'[93] in *Concerning the Spiritual in Art,* and in his essay **'On the Question of Form'**, in the *Blue Rider Almanac,* he said that the critic should help further the spiritual goals of art by concentrating its expressive aspect and trying to communicate this subjective expression poetically to his reader.[94]

In many respects the *Blue Rider Almanac* fulfills the programme of *Les Tendances Nouvelles.* Kandinsky's earliest correspondence with Marc about his idea for the *Blue Rider Almanac* includes many of the basic tenets of *Les Tendances Nouvelles:* the notion of a periodical, written and edited by artists, with a chronicle of art events; articles concerning all the arts (including music and dance); the international scope; the interest in children's art and in the gifted amateur; the aspiration to make art directly available to the common man and through that to uplift society; and even the idea of the almanac as the official organ speaking for a world-wide 'Union' of artists with 'representatives' in other capitals. In his letter to Marc, 19 June 1911 Kandinsky announced:

> Well, I have a new idea. Piper must be the publisher and the two of us the editors. A kind of almanac (yearbook) with reproductions and articles . . . and a chronicle!! that is, reports on exhibitions reviewed by artists, and artists alone.[95]

Although the plan for the chronicle was eventually cancelled, they did invite a number of articles for it. On 1 September 1911 Kandinsky wrote to Marc making specific reference to ideas of a 'Union' with 'representatives':

> . . . I for my part wrote to Hartmann, told him about our union, and bestowed on him the title of 'Authorized Representative for Russia'.[96]

For Kandinsky, *Les Tendances Nouvelles* was the paradigm of an international periodical-exhibition society completely run by artists, and it appears to have been the direct inspiration for his concept of the **Blue Rider.** The Phalanx prefigured this aspiration, with its stylistically broad-minded exhibitions and school (which *Les Tendances Nouvelles* also had);[97] but it had nothing of the ambitious programme of publication and international dissemination of *Les Tendances Nouvelles,* nor the full participation of all branches of the arts, nor the more democratic quality of the French group's organization. The *Neue Kunstlervereinigung* had more feeling of the artists' co-operative, but, again, it was limited to fine art exhibitions. Certainly none of the major European salons or societies were at all similar to it; the *Salon d'Automne* was the closest, offering readings and concerts associated with the salons and establishing a kind of 'democratic' structure to its governance. Just as Neo-Impressionism (possibly via *Les Tendances Nouvelles* associates) provided Kandinsky with the stylistic direction for realizing his Symbolist expressive goals, *Les Tendances Nouvelles* gave him the model of a theoretical programme for carrying out his utopian ambitions, in which the artist stood at the centre of the regeneration of society.

NOTES

Note: An unabridged facsimile of *Les Tendances Nouvelles,* along with a complete index of names contained in it, is forthcoming from Da Capo Press in August of 1979. Footnotes for general references to individuals or articles in the magazine have therefore been eliminated from this article, since this information is readily available in that index. Other notes to *Les Tendances Nouvelles* have been abbreviated as much as possible. In the introduction to the 1979 edition, I have discussed the chronology of the journal in detail. Briefly, the schedule seems to have been as follows: numbers 1 (May 1904), 2 (July 1904), 3 (October 1904), 4 (December 1904), 4 (February 1905), 6-25 (monthly from March 1905 through October 1906), 26 (December 1906), 27 (February 1907), 28 (March 1907), 29-46 (bimonthly from April 1907 through February 1910), 47-51 (quarterly from May 1910 through May 1911), 52 (December 1911), 53-63 (quarterly from February 1912 through August 1914).

[1] A. Plehn, 'The Struggle Against Pictorial Content', *Die Kunst für Alle,* xxi (February 1906), 229 ff.

[2] *Les Tendances Nouvelles,* no. 2, 20-2.

[3] Musée de l'Athenée, *Mérodack-Jeaneau,* exposition catalogue (introduction by Jean-Luc Daval), Genève (October 1969), 9.

[4] He writes about such an incident with Marinetti in a letter to *Gil Blas*, entitled '*Chez les Artistes:* Bombe, Elephant, Carafe; manifeste de Mérodak-Jeaneau'. From an undated clipping found among Mérodack's papers—presumably around 1912.

[5] Mérodack-Jeaneau published statements in *Gil Blas* (23 June 1913), *L'Angevine de Paris* (28 April 1912) and elsewhere. The two most important were in the *Revue de l'Anjou* (Summer 1907, 510-13) and 'Le Synthétisme' (published privately in Paris, 11 January 1914, and also published in an unidentified newspaper clipping found among Mérodack's papers).

[6] *Les Tendances Nouvelles,* no. 29, 525 ff.; and nos 30, 557 ff.

[7] This speculation was confirmed by the second husband of Mérodack's wife. The only evidence to the contrary is a newspaper report (probably taken from a *Tendances Nouvelles* press release which Mérodack could have written) quoting from remarks of both Mérodack and Gerôme-Maësse supposedly delivered at the Congrès of 1905. See *Le Journal de Maine et Loire* (8 August 1905) and *Le Patriote de l'Ouest* (12 August 1905) reprinted in *Les Tendances Nouvelles,* no. 11, 165.

[8] *Les Tendances Nouvelles,* no. 17, 259-60.

[9] *Les Tendances Nouvelles,* no. 1, 2.

[10] *Les Tendances Nouvelles,* no. 1, 6.

[11] *Les Tendances Nouvelles,* no. 2, 15.

[12] *Les Tendances Nouvelles,* no. 6, 60.

[13] *Les Tendances Nouvelles,* no. 30, 557.

[14] *Les Tendances Nouvelles,* no. 40, 882. The woodcuts were R20, R1, and R52 (these numbers refer to the graphic raisonnée: Roethel, *Kandinsky, das graphische Werk,* Cologne 1970); the 'Études' were probably small oil nature studies; the two less expensive paintings were probably listed in Kandinsky's house catalogue as 'coloured drawings', perhaps the first is no. 61 *Vers le soir* (*au bordde la mer*); and two major works—probably *Reitendes Paar* of 1903 ('paintings' no. 20) and *Buntes Leben* (certainly 'paintings' no. 46).

[15] *Les Tendances Nouvelles,* no. 40, 863.

[16] *Les Tendances Nouvelles,* no. 22, 353.

[17] *Les Tendances Nouvelles,* no. 3, 26.

[18] *Les Tendances Nouvelles,* no. 44, 993.

[19] *Les Tendances Nouvelles,* no. 17, 265.

[20] The golden bee (*L'abeille d'or*) was the Napoleonic emblem of work. The writers of *Les Tendances Nouvelles* repeatedly spoke of a desire to strengthen the ties between artists and the craftsmen who are their natural co-workers.

[21] A newspaper clipping found among Mérodack's papers, source as yet unidentified.

[22] *Les Tendances Nouvelles,* no. 10, 146.

[23] *Les Tendances Nouvelles,* no. 30, 569.

[24] *Les Tendances Nouvelles,* no. 49, 1152-64.

[25] *Les Tendances Nouvelles,* no. 30, 525-7.

[26] *Le Pays Bleu,* 3e année, no. 16 (Angers, dimanche, 21 avril 1907), 1.

[27] *Le pays Bleu,* 3e année, no. 16 (Angers, dimanche, 21 avril 1907), 1. The two Kandinskys were *Gebirgsee* (R15) and *Belagerung* (R30), reproduced in *Les Tendances Nouvelles,* no. 7, 482 and 489. 'Le prodigieux graveur russe Kandinsky, dont nous reproduirons ici *Le Lac* et *Le Siege,* exposera une centaine d'oeuvres—pentres et gravures—à la place où etaient en 1905 les dix-neuf grandes toiles du Lyonnais Jacques Martin.'

[28] *Le Pays Bleu,* 3e année, no. 16 (Angers, dimanche, 21 avril 1907), 1. 'et le fameux peintre Henri Rousseau dont les toiles firent courir tout Paris. Il exposera probablement la toile qui fut acquise au dernier *Salon d'Automne* par le marchand Voland [*sic*]. On sait que cette année aux *Indépendants* le public etait tellement nombreux devant les oeuvres de Rousseau que pour mieux les voir il fut apporte des escabeaut dont il ne restait miette au bout de quelques heures.

'A côté de ces oeuvres seront exposes des toiles de Cézanne. On attend encore d'autre importants envois.'

[29] *Le Pays Bleu,* 3e année, no. 17 (Angers, dimanche, 28 avril 1907).

[30] *Le Pays Bleu,* 3e année, no. 18 (Angers, dimanche, 5 mai 1907). 'L'oeuvre entière de Kandinsky, ses prodigieuses gravures sur bois et ses petites toiles debordantes de couleur et de realité.'

[31] *Les Tendances Nouvelles,* no. 29, 553-4.

[32] Later issues state the founding date of the 'Union' as 26 April 1905; however, the 15 March 1905 issue is subtitled 'organe officiel illustré de l'Union des Beaux-Arts et des Lettres'. It may have come out of an existing organization with which Rodin and some others were already associated.

[33] See Agnès Humbert, *Les Nabis et leur époque* (Genève, 1954), 15.

[34] In *L'Angevin,* Neuvième année, no. 17, dimanche, 28 avril 1912, I; Mérodack-Jeaneau refers to his friendship and early encouragement by Carrière, Lautrec, and various critics.

[35] The Comtesse de Noailles was an extremely wealthy writer and patroness of the arts who lived part of the time at Fontainbleau.

[36] In *Les Tendances Nouvelles,* no. 31, 607-9; Anatole France published an article on art education for children.

[37] See for example the article by Milesi on Neo-Impressionism (*Tendances Nouvelles,* no. 29, 537-9) where the author discusses the book by Gaetano Previati, *Les principes scientifiques du divisionisme.*

[38] *Les Tendances Nouvelles,* no. 58, 1295.

[39] With Maillol this involves his repetition of a single subject—his female nude—until it loses its narrative quality and takes on an abstract, evocative power like a sound. Kandinsky removes an object-reference so completely from a narrative context and blends it in with abstract colours and shapes to such an extent that it loses its objective identity. For a more detailed discussion of Kandinsky's concept of the neutralized object see: Jonathan Fineberg, 'Kandinsky's Prints: Jugendstil to Bauhaus', *Art in America,* May-June 1974, 96-7.

[40] *Les Tendances Nouvelles,* no. 25, 402.

[41] *Les Tendances Nouvelles,* no. 26, 436-8. The Kandinsky woodcuts reproduced in this issue are: cover and page 436—*Chevalier russe* (*Russische Reiter,* R48), back cover and page 437—*Cavaliers arabes* (*Arabische Reiterei,* R44), p. 439—*La Promenade* (R1), p. 441—*Femme à l'eventail* (*Dame mit Facher,* R2), p. 444—*Promenade gracieuse* (R45), p. 445—*Paysage* (*Ewigkeit,* R24), p. 446—*Le Soir obscur* (*Finsterer Abend,* R31), p. 447—*Les Nounous* (*Die Ammen,* R46), listed in the table of contents but not actually reproduced—*Femme au manchon* (R3).

[42] *Les Tendances Nouvelles,* no. 26, 438.

[43] *Les Tendances Nouvelles,* was the journal of *L'Union Internationale des Beaux-Arts, des Lettres, de la Science, et de l'Industrie.* For further details see 'The History and Character of *Les Tendances Nouvelles',* above.

[44] *Les Tendances Nouvelles,* no. 30, 560-1.

[45] In his *raisonnée* entries for the prints published in issues 30 and 34, Roethel incorrectly dates issues 30 and 34 and hence incorrectly dates the states of the prints in question. The correct dates are issue 30—June 1907 (not March) and issue 34—February 1908 (not July 1907). For a complete history of all prints by Kandinsky in *Les Tendances Nouvelles* consult the index to the 1979 edition.

[46] W. Kandinsky, *Concerning the Spiritual in Art,* N.Y., 1947, 67, fn. 1. He cites Henri Rovel, 'Les lois d'harmonie',

which appeared in two parts in *Les Tendances Nouvelles,* no. 35, 721-3 and no. 36, 753-7. Roethel misdates both issues and hence this state of R27, R73 and R62.

[47] R1, Kandinsky's earliest print. It may or may not have been in the 1908 *Indépendants* but it was published in the February 1907 issue of *Les Tendances Nouvelles,* no. 27, 439.

[48] *Les Tendances Nouvelles,* no. 36, 747.

[49] *Les Tendances Nouvelles,* no. 39, 835. The four Kandinsky woodcuts were: (nos 1037-40) *Son des cordes* (R53) *Leier* (Kandinsky noted this—house catalogue no. 25—as having been in the *Automne* of 1908), *Grüne Frauen* (R57), *Zwei Mädchen* (R63), *Verfolgung* (R64). Breuil also praises Gabriele Münter's seven entries.

[50] Kandinsky, 'On the Question of Form', in *The Blue Rider Almanac,* English translation edited by Klaus Lankheit, Viking, N.Y., 1974, 149. The original German reads: 'Und man sollte nicht langer um die Form kampfen, als sie zum Ausdrucksmittel des inneren Klanges dienen kann.'

[51] *Les Tendances Nouvelles,* no. 42, 942.

[52] See *Franz von Stuck,* Katalog Stuck Villa, Munich, 1958, 114.

[53] Kandinsky, sketchbook GMS 328 (Stadtische Gal., Munich), 86. Erika Hanfstaengl dated this notebook 1908-10 in Erika Hanfstaengl, *Wassily Kandinsky Zeichnungen und Aquarelle im Lenbachhaus Munchen,* München, 1964, 148.

[54] The account is in Michael Sadleir, *Michael Ernest Sadler 1861-1943: A Memoir by his Son,* London, 1949, 243; cited in Peg Weiss, *Wassily Kandinsky: The Formative Years,* unpublished doctoral dissertation, Syracuse U., 1973, 323. Weiss suggested the idea that Kandinsky might be responsible and this evidence seems to strengthen her supposition.

[55] *Frauen im Wald* (R60) in *Les Tendances Nouvelles,* no. 46, 1048. Roethel incorrectly dated this issue to 1909; it probably dates from February 1910.

[56] *Vogel* (R65) in *Les Tendances Nouvelles,* no. 49, 1166. Roethel incorrectly dated this issue 1909.

[57] *Journal de Maine et Loire,* Angers, 10 mai 1907, 3; 'les curieuses notations de Kandinsky, le Russe a la vision mosaïste, dont les envois occupent un côte de la salle'.

[58] *Le Patriote de l'Ouest,* Angers, mercredi, 12 juin 1907, 2; 'Toute l'oeuvre de Basile Kandinsky (109 nos.). Notons: Esquisse, Au bord de l'eau, Promenades à cheval, La confusion des races, Jour de fête, Accident, Cavaliers, Vers le soir, Venise, Mardi gras, etc. L'Oeuvre de Kandinsky colorée et puissante est une des principales curiosites de ce congres.' The review also

mentioned the names of Tarkhoff and Princesse Annina Gagarine-Stourdza as fellow exhibitors.

[59] After the work's title in the house catalogue the artist usually noted a number of exhibitions. In this case he designated the pictures by 'Angers v. 07'.

[60] *Les Tendances Nouvelles,* no. 40, 882.

[61] *Kandinsky: 1901-1913,* Der Sturm, Berlin, 1913, 25.

[62] House catalogue, 'paintings', nos 41 (*Stilles Wasser*) and 42 (*Die Rivallen*), and 'coloured drawings', nos 11 (*Ausflug zu Pferde*), and 12 (*Alte Zeiten*) have the suffixed note 'Paris Exp. d B-A 15 xi. 05'. A similar circumstance may apply here; Kandinsky did not show in the *Nationale* but may have sent these to the 1905 salon of the 'Union Internationale des Beaux-Arts' in Angers, which may have occurred in the fall.

[63] The 'ex libris' prints published in *Tendances Nouvelles* after May 1907 have not been included on this list although they were done before the show and could have been included. They were: *Der Drache* (R18), *Katze* (R69), *Sterne* (R75), *Glaube* (R27), *Der Schleier* (R73), *Ohne Bewegung* (R62), *Kirche* (R55), *Sitzende Mädchen* (R67), *Reiterin und Kind* (R74), *Frauen im Wald* (R60), and *Vogel* (R65).

[64] Some of these may also have been in the 1907 exhibition. The list includes 'paintings', no. 47; 'coloured drawings', nos 66, 74, 79, 84, 85, 88, 93, 110, 111, 120, 121, 122; and 'woodcuts', nos 18, 19, 20, 22, 23, 24, 26, 27, 31, 32.

[65] 'Woodcuts', nos 26, 28, 31, and 32 appeared later in the *Tendances Nouvelles* Kandinsky portfolio 'Xylographies' but other prints (for example 34 (R62) *Ohne Bewegung*) which appeared there had no French subtitle in the house catalogue; *Ohne Bewegung* is captioned there as *Schwarzweiss No. 6.*

[66] These were noted by Nina Kandinsky in 'La Vie de Kandinsky', in Max Bill, *Wassily Kandinsky,* Maeght, Paris, 1951, 118.

[67] *Journal de Maine et Loire,* Angers, juin 5 1907. Excerpts from the speech reprinted in *Les Tendances Nouvelles,* no. 30, 575-6.

[68] I have discussed this at greater length in my unpublished doctoral dissertation, *Kandinsky in Paris 1906-7,* Harvard University, Cambridge, 1975.

[69] A. Mérodack-Jeaneau, 'L'Ecole Synthétique', *Angevin de Paris,* 28 April 1912, 1.

[70] Maurice Denis, *Théories,* Paris (4th edn), 1920, 32; ' . . . pour realiser l'absolu, reprend l'intime secret de la nature, le nombre'.

[71] Andre Biély, 'le principe dans l'ésthetique', *Zolotoë Runo* (*La Toison d'Or*), no. 11, November-December 1906, 88.

[72] W. Kandinsky, *Concerning the Spiritual in Art,* N.Y., 1947, 58-9. Geothe's colour theories probably had some influence on this formulation.

[73] Kandinsky, 'On the Question of Form', *Blue Rider Almanac,* N.Y., 1974, 165.

[74] Kandinsky, *Über das Geistige in der Kunst,* first edition, Munich 1911, Vorwort; 'Die Gedanken, die ich hier entwickle, sind Resultate von Beobachtungen und Gefuhlserfarungen, die sich allmählich im Laufe der Letzten funf bis sechs Jahre sammelten.'

[75] A. Mérodack-Jeaneau, 'L'École Synthétique', *Angevin de Paris,* 28 April 1912, 1. 'L'école synthétique suivra les théories qui tendent a prouver l'unité fondamentale de la matière, variable d'aspect à l'infini.'

[76] Kandinsky, *Concerning the Spiritual in Art,* N.Y., 1947, 71. Also, L. Sababiev in his article for the *Blue Rider Almanac,* 'Scriabin's "Prometheus" ' cited another article of 1911 in which Scriabin correlated colours and musical notes (*Blue Rider Almanac,* N.Y., 1974, 131).

[77] Louis Ehlert, *Lettres à une amie,* Berlin, 1859, cited in *Les Tendances Nouvelles,* no. 33, 658; 'L'Air en la majeur, dans le scherzo, est d'une chaleur si ensoleillée et d'un vert si tendre qu'il me semble, en l'entendant, respirer la senteur des jeunes pousses de sapin.'

[78] Kandinsky, 'Reminiscences', in R. Herbert, *Modern Artists on Art,* N.J., 1964, 26.

[79] *Les Tendances Nouvelles,* no. 33, 663.

[80] W. Kandinsky, 'On the Question of Form', *Blue Rider Almanac,* English translation, N.Y., 1974, 157.

[81] W. Kandinsky, 'On the Question of Form', *Blue Rider Almanac,* 1974, 149-50.

[82] Kandinsky, *Concerning the Spiritual in Art,* N.Y., 1947, 26.

[83] Speech by Mérodack-Jeaneau at the inaugural of the *Musée du Peuple* reported in *Revue de L'Anjou,* 1907, 510-14; 'Dedaigneux du modèle momifié comme d'un fetiche encombrant, des artistes, revendiquent leur droit d'exprimer enfin librement leurs pensées ou leurs sensations et reprennent conscience de leur role veritable, celui d'initiateur de la foule, dont ils sont la force primordiale. Car, c'est en effet—qu'on le veuille ou non—sous la seul direction de l'artiste que peut efficacement et noblement se developper l'industrie des nations.'

[84] W. Kandinsky, *Concerning the Spiritual in Art,* N.Y., 1947, 43-4. The text has been amended here, translating the German 'psychisch' as 'psychic' instead of 'psychological'.

[85] W. Kandinsky, *Concerning the Spiritual in Art*, N.Y., 1947, 67.

[86] *Les Tendances Nouvelles*, no. 35, 721.

[87] *Les Tendances Nouvelles*, no. 35, 727.

[88] Kandinsky, 'On Stage Composition', *Blue Rider Almanac*, N.Y., 1974, 191.

[89] Kandinsky, *Concerning the Spiritual in Art*, N.Y., 1947, 44.

[90] Kandinsky, 'On the Question of Form', *Blue Rider Almanac*, N.Y., 1974, 186. *Einfühlungstheorie* (Empathy theory) also emphasized an instantaneous projection of emotion and sensation but it did not offer this mystic explanation of vibrations nor was it overtly messianic and moralistic in its ambitions as Rovel and Kandinsky were.

[91] *Les Tendances Nouvelles*, no. 44, 1003-4.

[92] W. Kandinsky, *Concerning the Spiritual in Art*, N.Y., 1947, 45; 'Those who have heard of chromotherapy know that coloured light can influence the whole body. Attempts have been made with different colours to treat various nervous ailments. Red light stimulates and excites the heart, while blue light can cause temporary paralysis.'

[93] Kandinsky, *Concerning the Spiritual in Art*, N.Y., 1947, 26.

[94] Kandinsky, 'On the Question of Form', *Blue Rider Almanac*, N.Y., 1974, 171.

[95] K. Lankheit, 'A History of the Almanac', *Blue Rider Almanac*, N.Y., 1974, 15.

[96] K. Lankheit, 'A History of the Almanac', *Blue Rider Almanac*, 1974, 16: in the German letter he uses the word 'Union' and 'Bevollmachtigten Mitarbeiters für Russland'.

[97] The 'Union' may also have asked Kandinsky to teach at a school set up by *Les Tendances Nouvelles*. Johannes Eichner, *Wassily Kandinsky und Gabriele Münter*, Munich, 1957, 86; 'Die Tendances Nouvelles boten ihm 1907 "eine Klasse der Schule der Union" unter gunstigen Bedingungen an.'

Rose-Carol Washton Long (essay date 1980)

SOURCE: "Kandinsky's Vision," in *The Life of Vasilii Kandinsky in Russian Art: A Study of 'On the Spiritual in Art'*, edited by John E. Bowlt and Rose-Carol Washton Long, and translated by John Bowlt, Oriental Research Partners, 1980, pp. 43-61.

[*In the following essay, Long analyzes the purpose and meaning of Kandinsky's* On the Spiritual in Art, *maintaining that the artist "attempted to resolve the dilemma of how to effectively communicate a vision of man's spirituality while avoiding both materialistic representation on the one hand and decorative ornament on the other."*]

The publication of Kandinsky's **On the Spiritual in Art** in 1912[1] can be considered one of the catalytic forces which helped trigger an increasing number of experiments with abstraction before World War I. Although the idea of painting in an abstract style was not new, after **On the Spiritual in Art** reached the public, a number of artists such as Kupka, Mondrian, Delaunay, Picabia, Larionov, and Goncharova began to exhibit works which contained few if any remnants of imagistic references in their colorful surfaces. A direct connection between Kandinsky and each of these artists cannot always be substantiated, but by 1912 critics across Europe had begun to view Kandinsky's paintings and essays as an example of one of the most radical trends in contemporary art.

In Russia, soon after a version of **On the Spiritual in Art** was read to the All-Russian Congress of Artists late in 1911, one critic called Kandinsky "the preacher of the newest art" and concluded that he had renounced "all content" in his search "for new forms of expression—not borrowed from nature."[2] In his adopted country—Germany—to which he had moved in 1896, Kandinsky was called the "representative of a new idealism."[3] He was not only recognized for his paintings and writings, but for his work with Franz Marc in formulating the anthology, the *Blaue Reiter*,[4] which brought together examples of folk and primitive art with reproductions of the most recent developments in French, German, and Russian painting. In France, critics such as Guillaume Apollinaire reviewed his paintings,[5] and painters such as Robert Delaunay corresponded with him.[6] Kandinsky's reputation also extended into England. Painters such as Edward Wadsworth, writing in 1914 about Kandinsky's **On the Spiritual in Art,** proclaimed: "He writes of art . . . in its relation to the universe and the soul of man. He writes . . . as an artist to whom form and colour are as much the vital and integral parts of the cosmic organization as they are his means of expression."[7]

The messianic tone of **On the Spiritual in Art** appealed to a number of artists across Europe, and Kandinsky's belief that an abstract style of painting had great potential for the forceful expression of cosmic ideas helped to take the concept of abstraction out of the realm of decorative design. Since he equated representationalism with materialistic values, it followed that abstraction offered a way to express more powerfully the transcendental values of a spiritual vision. In **On the Spiritual in Art,** Kandinsky attempted to resolve the dilemma of how to effectively communicate a vision of man's spirituality while avoiding both materialistic representation on the one hand and decorative ornament on the other.

To understand the vision that moved Kandinsky to develop a new style of painting, it is necessary to examine the sources of his philosophical and aesthetic beliefs. The roots of Kandinsky's concept of abstraction lie within the international Symbolist movement, which first gained prominence as a literary force in France in the 1880s. The Symbolist emphasis on creating a new aesthetic which would be suggestive of the "higher realities"—the "cosmic order"—rather than descriptive of the mundane, physical world affected all of the arts as it spread from France into Germany and then into Russia. It remained the dominant aesthetic throughout Europe until a few years before World War I. Many of those involved with Symbolism were also involved with mysticism, occultism, and the numerous revivals of esoteric religions such as Rosicrucianism and Theosophy.[8] Occult ideas often reinforced Symbolist contentions. Both emphasized that the truths of the higher worlds were not easily understandable and could best be communicated by indirect and vague means.

Like many artists associated with the Symbolist movement, particularly those in Russia, Kandinsky viewed the artist as an elite figure who had a responsibility to transmit cosmic ideas to the ordinary individual. His belief in a forthcoming utopia underlay his commitment to an abstract style of painting. Kandinsky interpreted his age as one dominated by a struggle between the forces of good, or "the spiritual," and the forces of evil, or materialism. Even before *On the Spiritual in Art* was published, he expressed his anxiety about the state of the world in an article which he sent to a Russian periodical: "Our epoch is a time of tragic collision between matter and spirit and of the downfall of the purely material world view; for many, many people it is a time of terrible, inescapable vacuum, a time of enormous questions; but for a few people it is a time of presentiment or of precognition of the path to Truth."[9] Since he felt that abstraction had the least connection with the materialistic strivings of the world, he believed that abstract paintings might help to awaken the individual to the spiritual values necessary to bring about a utopian epoch.

Kandinsky ended *On the Spiritual in Art* with the optimistic statement that the type of painting he envisioned would advance "the reconstruction already begun, of the new spiritual realm . . . the epoch of great spirituality."[10] Kandinsky obviously believed that painting could be a powerful instrument for social change. He felt that painting had a specific purpose—to "serve the development and refinement of the human soul."[11] He added that "no other power"[12] could replace the power of art in assisting with this goal. Art, he explained, was "one of the most powerful agents of the spiritual life," a "complicated but definite movement forward and upward."[13] He called the artist a "prophet"[14] and an "invisible Moses."[15] Both Kandinsky and Marc spoke of the role that the artist would play in the "coming spiritual religion."[16] Both believed that a revolution in the arts could directly effect a change in the spiritual climate. But what influenced them to hope for a new age?

A reading of the 1912 German editions of *On the Spiritual in Art* suggests that Kandinsky's belief in a coming utopian epoch was influenced in part by Theosophical ideas.

In these 1912 editions, Kandinsky described. Theosophy as "one of the most important spiritual movements"[17] of his time and as a strong force in the "spiritual atmosphere, which offered redemption to many despairing hearts enveloped in gloom and darkness."[18] Although Kandinsky never called himself a Theosophist he was sympathetic toward the Theosophical search for universal hidden truths. He included in *On the Spiritual in Art* the conclusion from one of the books written by the founder of the Theosophical Society, H. P. Blavatsky, which proclaimed: "Earth will be a heaven in the twenty-first century in comparison with what it is at present."[19] In this German edition, Kandinsky also praised Rudolf Steiner,[20] the head of the German Theosophical Society, which was based in Munich. Steiner's physical presence during this period, his belief that artistic experiences were the strongest stimulants for the development of an understanding of the spiritual, plus his own artistic activities, undoubtedly contributed to Kandinsky's interest in this Theosophist. Moreover, Kandinsky, who often compared himself and his friends to the early Christians for trying to raise "the weakest to spiritual battle,"[21] and who frequently referred to his love for the Russian church, must have been attracted by Steiner's interpretation that Christianity incorporated the wisdom of all previous religions and cults and consequently offered the richest source for advancing the destiny of mankind. While Blavatsky emphasized the importance of Hinduism and Buddhism, Steiner used The Revelation to John as the major framework to express his belief in the inevitability of catastrophe before the emergence of a new epoch.

By 1908, several of Kandinsky's friends in Germany had become involved with Steiner. Maria Strakosch-Geisler, one of Kandinsky's earliest students, heard one of Steiner's lecture cycles in Berlin in March, 1908 and was very much impressed.[22] A schoolmate of Strakosch-Geisler, Emy Dresler, who exhibited with Kandinsky's Neue Künstlervereinigung in the winter of 1909-10, also had become involved with Steiner in 1908. She worked directly with the German Theosophist, painting stage scenery for several of his plays[23] which were performed in Munich from 1910 to 1913. Alexej Jawlensky and his companion Marianne von Werefkin, two of the Russian-German members of the Neue Künstlervereinigung who lived with Kandinsky in Murnau during the summers of 1909 and 1910, also seem to have had contact with Steiner. Von Werefkin, who was more deeply involved with Theosophical ideas, is reported to have transmitted Steiner's concepts directly to Kandinsky.[24] In the next few years, Kandinsky, his mistress Gabriele Münter, and their friends studied the writings of Steiner. Kandinsky and Münter owned a number of books and articles by Steiner, which they annotated.[25]

At the time when Kandinsky seemed to have become aware of Steiner, the German Theosophist was predicting that a period of regeneration was ahead. He felt that the time had arrived when the secret knowledge of Theosophy could be communicated to a larger audience than the limited circle of the initiated. Steiner's focus on The

Apocalypse as the significant document for modern times coincided with an idea many Russians thought of as peculiarly Russian. And his subsequent mention of Russia as a future leader of the world seemed to be a repetition of the centuries-old Russian belief that Russia itself would be the "Third Rome." Steiner had begun to emphasize that Russia would play a crucial role in bringing East and West together to create a universal brotherhood of man. It was this attitude that attracted the Russian Symbolist poet Andrei Belyi to Steiner. He saw Steiner's apocalyptic prophecies as a continuation of his own views and of those of the Russian philosopher Vladimir Soloviev. In a letter of 1912 to his friend and fellow poet Alexander Blok, Belyi wrote: "From the autumn of 1911, Steiner had begun to say the most amazing things about Russia, her future, the spirit of the people, and about Vladimir Soloviev. (In Russia he saw a great and singular future.)"[26] Belyi explained in the same letter that Steiner's ideas were particularly attractive to a number of his associates. "From 1910, Steiner entered into a special and rare contact with all of us. Some threw themselves at Steiner blindly like Ellis. Others not so blindly followed after him like Voloshina. A third group made a furtive pilgrimage to him [referring here to himself]."[27] Kandinsky would not have been unaware of the great interest in Steiner and in Theosophy among his Russian compatriots. Several months after making a trip to Russia in the fall of 1910, he wrote to his friend Franz Marc to say that the anthology they were working on had to include some mention of Theosophy and of the religious tendencies in Russia: "We will include some reports on the Russian religious movement in which *all* classes participate. For this I have engaged my former colleague Professor Bulgakov (Moscow, political economist, one of the greatest experts of religious life). Theosophy, must be mentioned briefly and powerfully (statistically, if possible). . . . "[28]

Despite Kandinsky's praise of Steiner and his interest in Theosophy, the Russian edition of *On the Spiritual in Art,* published in 1914, omits any direct references to either Blavatsky or Steiner. However, the 1914 edition, which was based on the 1911 reading at the All-Russian Congress, contains comments made by others after the reading which indicate that some reference to Theosophy may have been made during the reading after all. For example, a comment by Prince S. M. Volkonsky is quoted to the effect that he had been "won over by Kandinsky" because of the painter's Theosophical views. Volkonsky is reported to have remarked about Kandinsky's ideas: "In any case, when the theosophical principle is linked to something close to me, i.e., art, I'm always won over."[29] Why the references were left out in the Russian 1914 publication of the reading (if, of course, they had really been made) are not clear. It is possible that Kandinsky sent to the Congress an abridged version of *On the Spiritual in Art,* which eliminated most references to non-Russian sources so that his material would be more acceptable. But it is also possible that the transcription was abbreviated or altered in 1914. At that point, the omission of Steiner's name might have been due to the factionalization of the

Theosophical movement in Germany and the disillusionment with Steiner in Russia. A war-time censor may also have been responsible for the elimination of German sounding names such as Steiner.

But Kandinsky's connection of a new style in painting to the evolution of a new world order is evident in any edition of *On the Spiritual in Art.* He warned that the character of the age could no more be interpreted with direct representationalism than it could be reflected in precise geometric forms or ornamental design. He advised artists to strengthen their spirit "through exercise"[30] so that their experiments would not lead merely to "the beauty of color and form."[31] He insisted that the artist "have something to say"[32] and that forms serve an end beyond themselves. Although Kandinsky believed that ultimately a truly universal work with the strongest of spiritual vibrations would come from an abstract art,[33] he did not believe at this time that he or other artists should work completely with "purely emancipated color and form combinations."[34] He explained: "If we begin to sever our connection with 'nature' today, to force our way through to freedom and to confine ourselves exclusively to the combination of pure colors and independent forms, we would create works similar to geometric ornament, which, coarsely stated, would seem like a necktie or a carpet. The beauty of color and form, despite the assertion of purist aesthetes and naturalists in search of beauty for beauty's sake, is not an adequate goal for art. Because of our rudimentary development in painting, we are still little able to acquire inner experience from purely emancipated color and form combinations."[35]

Kandinsky's great fear that his work would be considered decorative and ornamental may stem in part from his close contact at the turn of century with a German variant of Symbolism, the arts and crafts movement, frequently referred to as the Jugendstil. Recent studies have pointed to the influence that the theoreticans of the Jugendstil had on Kandinsky's concept of abstraction.[36] Indeed, shortly after Kandinsky arrived in Munich in 1896 he became acquainted with a number of Jugendstil artists, particularly those interested in developing an abstracted ornamental design as the basis for a new style. Kandinsky was friendly with one of the founding fathers of the Munich Jugendstil, Hermann Obrist, who prophesied that forms derived from ornamental and decorative design could be applied to painting. But Münter commented that Obrist's designs were "always more decorative, in their intention, than Kandinsky's abstraction," and thus had less influence on him than one would imagine.[37]

In *On the Spiritual in Art,* perhaps in tribute to what he had learned from the Jugendstil artists, Kandinsky indicated that decorative designs were not lifeless, that they could even cause "vibrations" of the "soul."[38] However, he pointed out that repetitive patterns of decorative design were rarely effective because few people in this age were capable of deciphering the "inner worth" of decorative design.[39] He may, indeed, have been referring to

Jugendstil designs for tapestries and rugs when he stated he did not want his paintings to resemble "geometric ornament, which, coarsely stated, would seem like a necktie or a carpet."

Kandinsky's attack on geometric ornamental form may also have been in reaction to the analysis of abstract forms delineated by the German art historian Wilhelm Worringer in his book, *Abstraction and Empathy,* which was published in 1908. Worringer, who had himself been influenced by Jugendstil theories of the emotive power of line, stressed that abstraction represented man's transcendental impulse, while naturalism, which he connected with empathy, seemed to belong to a culture that was more at ease with itself and not in turmoil. Kandinsky most likely agreed with Worringer in general. Both he and Marc were interested in Worringer's writings and thought of asking Worringer to write an essay for a proposed second edition of the *Blaue Reiter* almanac.[40] However, Kandinsky might very well have been disturbed by Worringer's description of geometric abstraction as "lifeless," and may have felt, as a result, that his own development of abstraction had to be based on something other than geometric forms, or the flat rhythmic designs of the Jugendstil. But what would that be?

When Kandinsky proposed an alternative to geometric patterning in *On the Spiritual in Art,* he stated: "It is not obvious (geometrical) constructions that will be richest in possibilities for expression, but hidden ones, emerging unnoticed from the canvas and meant less for the eye than for the soul."[41] Kandinsky urged artists to lead the spectator into the abstract sphere step by step, balancing abstract forms with barely perceptible signs. He suggested that objects could be transformed into these hidden signs and could become an additional means of causing a vibration. *On the Spiritual in Art* contains an extensive discussion of how the object could have an evocative power similar to that of pure color and form. Kandinsky explained that a combination of veiling the object with ambiguous shapes and colors and also stripping the object into a skeletonlike outline or construction would create a "new possibility of leitmotivs for form composition."[42] Consequently, his paintings from this period are filled with hidden images. In his autobiography, dated June 1913, Kandinsky used the term *gegenstandslos* (objectless) to refer to some of his works, and he defined that term as meaning forms deriving mostly or exclusively "'from within the artist'"[43] as contrasted to forms derived from nature. But even at that point, he indicated that there was a tenuous separation between those of his works which he considered abstract and those which he felt to be only partially abstract. In this same autobiography, he warned the artist about the dangers of completely abandoning imagery: " . . . the removal of an object in art makes very great demands on the inner experience of the purely painterly form, that therefore an evolution of the observer in this direction is absolutely necessary and can in no way be lacking."[44] In all the editions—German, Russian, and English—of *On the Spiritual in Art* published before World War I,

Kandinsky insisted: "Today the artist cannot confine himself to completely abstract forms. They are still too indefinite for him. To confine oneself exclusively to the indefinite means depriving oneself of possibilities, of excluding the purely human element. This weakens one's means of expression."[45]

To exclude the human and to weaken expression were antithetical to Kandinsky's aim. Since he believed his painting could be a major weapon in the creation of a new utopian realm, he felt he needed the additional stimuli of hidden imagery to communicate his utopian visions. Kandinsky maintained in *On the Spiritual in Art* that the object, color and form each had its own psychic effects, its own spiritual possibilities. He stressed that if the object were used effectively, it could have extraordinary power in a painting. Rather than depict the object naturalistically, Kandinsky proposed to hide its physical aspects through the process of "veiling and "stripping."[46] The process of veiling involved placing the object where it would not be expected or blurring its outline with unrelated colors. The process of stripping involved simplifying the object to a partial outline. The union of these two methods produced what Kandinsky called the *versteckte Konstruction* (the hidden construction).[47] Kandinsky relied on these basic structural devices until he left Germany in 1914. Through the "hidden construction," Kandinsky hoped to avoid the materialism of representational art while still involving the spectator by providing familiar key motifs. Kandinsky felt the "hidden image" would lead the spectator to take part in the creation of the work almost as if he were taking part in a mystic ritual. By forcing the spectator to decipher mysterious ambiguous images, he would involve him in the process of replacing confusion with understanding. Kandinsky equated such participation in the creation of art with the creation of the world.[48]

Kandinsky looked to the Symbolist aesthetic for a theoretical basis for hiding and veiling the imagery in his paintings. The Symbolist interpretation of language, which had spread from France to Germany and then to Russia, emphasized that words could create a strong emotional impact if their literal meanings were disguised. Kandinsky's acceptance of synesthesia—the interrelationship of the arts—allowed him to transfer a theory formulated for poetry and drama to painting; it allowed him to believe that he could give to the visual object the evocative power the Symbolist poets and dramatists gave to words.

Although the Symbolist interpretation of language found coherent expression in many individuals, the Belgian dramatist Maurice Maeterlinck is the only Symbolist to be discussed at length in *On the Spiritual in Art.* In the Russian edition (where specific references to other artists are fewer than in the German version), Kandinsky praised Maeterlinck as "one of the first fighters, one of the first sincere composers of modern art."[49] In the German editions, Kandinsky referred specifically to three of Maeterlinck's plays and to one essay, and he applauded a Russian production of one of Maeterlinck's plays for the imaginative quality of its set designs, noting that the designers had used the simplest of backdrops to involve the spectator.[50] Kandinsky may have considered Maeterlinck as representative of the many diverse elements of Symbolism, especially since Maeterlinck was admired by a wide variety of intellectuals—from German Theosophists such as Steiner to Russian Symbolists such as Viacheslav Ivanov.[51] Excerpts from his plays and numerous articles about him appeared in many literary magazines devoted to Symbolism published during the first decade of the twentieth century. Kandinsky referred to Maeterlinck's use of words in the essay, **"Whither the 'New' Art,"** published in Russia early in 1911. In this essay, he praised Maeterlinck for listening to the "inner sounds" of words.[52] In *On the Spiritual in Art,* Kandinsky devoted considerable space to an analysis of Maeterlinck's use of words to manipulate moods "artistically." Kandinsky stressed that Maeterlinck removed the external reference from words by constant repetition and by dislocation from the narrative. Kandinsky translated Maeterlinck's suggestions for the dematerialization of words into his own proposal for the dematerialization of objects, writing: "Just as each spoken word (tree, sky, man) has an inner vibration, so does each represented object."[53]

Kandinsky not only wrote about objects in the same fashion that the Symbolists wrote about words, he also wrote about color as being equivalent to music and line as being equivalent to dance. Kandinsky's acceptance of the concept of synesthesia led him to believe that his paintings might stimulate multiple sensory responses in the viewer. His belief that his paintings contained multiple stimuli (form, color, line, images) lay behind his conviction that an abstract style could eventually have enormous evocative potential for communicating the spiritual. Kandinsky not only believed that one means of stimulating the senses would cause the other senses to respond, he also believed that one stimulus might be substituted for another to achieve a similar effect. He felt that sensory equivalents could be scientifically measured; he believed, for example, that exact equivalents could be found for individual musical notes within the color spectrum.[54] Once a system of identifying these equivalents was developed, Kandinsky felt equivalents could be combined or contrasted to intensify reactions. Unlike many Symbolists and those experimentors among his contemporaries like Skriabin who attempted to parallel a color with a sound— Kandinsky felt a stronger expression of his ideas could be achieved if the various arts were used to produce contrasting effects rather than corresponding ones. For Kandinsky, the use of repetitive or corresponding stimuli[55] was a nineteenth-century device and could not be as directly reflective of the conflict and disharmony which he felt were characteristic of his age.

Kandinsky's advocacy of contrasting stimuli was related to his conviction that a powerful work of art must reflect the characteristic tone of its time. For Kandinsky, "storm and tempest . . . broken chains . . . antithesis and contradictions,"[56] were the prime characteristics of his age. several contemporary composers—two Russians and one Austrian—Thomas von Hartmann, Nikolai Kulbin, and Arnold Schönberg, were exploring this same principle. In essays especially written for the *Blaue Reiter* almanac, these men associated dissonance in music with a more forceful means of expression. Schönberg for example explored principles of relating one medium to another, in this instance the problem of composing music for a text. The Austrian composer, who set a poem of Maeterlinck's to music for the almanac, called parallelism between text and music "the most banal of conceptions."[57] He even went so far as to equate the "external conformity of music to text" with the kind of "imitation of nature" that resulted from "the copying of a model."[58] He explained that the effect could be "more profound" if a "delicate thought" were expressed by a "fast and vigorous theme."[59] Kulbin, who had read Kandinsky's major essay to the All-Russian Congress, focused in his piece in the almanac on an exploration of new intervals in music, such as the use of quarter-tones and eighth-tones, and the incorporation of vibrations, which he called "close combinations" and characterized as providing excitable tones.[60] A variant of Kulbin's essay, "Free Music" appeared earlier in a collection entitled *Studio of the Impressionists* published in 1910, where he presented the idea that both harmony and dissonance were "the basic phenomena of the universe" and the "basis of art." He proclaimed that "complete harmony is death," and added that "discord" was the principle which excited and aroused mankind.[61] Kandinsky echoed these ideas when he wrote: "Our harmony rests primarily on the principle of antithesis."[62]

Kandinsky felt he expressed the "antithesis and contradictions" of his age through the contrasting colors he used in his paintings, the ambiguous and hidden imagery, and the spatial dislocations. He advised using colors, such as juxtapositions of red and blue, which for centuries had been considered "dissonant." He warned against the use of flat ornamental forms because they would produce, he felt, works which were merely decorative, and in no way reflective of the disharmony and anxiety of his age. Although he felt that the tendency to step away from traditional spatial concepts was a beginning in the movement away from naturalism and materialism, he also felt that the emphasis on the flat plane of the canvas reinforced its material effect. In the German edition, he expanded the section discussing the use of antithesis in painting. He wrote that the use of "the thinness or thickness of a line, or further the placing of the form on the surface, the crossing of one form through the other" could help to create an "ideal plane" which could suggest "three-dimensional space."[63]

Kandinsky's concept of antithesis and contradiction not only provides us with clues as to his use of strong color and to his interest in creating spatial effects but also it provides us with clues as to the meaning of the hidden imagery in the painting. His emphasis on his age as one of struggle, fraught with turmoil helps to explain why he chose imagery of storms, battles, floods, and Last Judgments in many of his paintings from 1910 through 1913. Many of these paintings have religious themes; a number have specific biblical titles such as *Horsemen of the Apocalypse, Deluge,* and *Last Judgment.*[64] Others have titles such as *Paradise* or *Garden of Love* which relate to his utopian vision of the "new spiritual realm," which he felt would emerge after the "'terrible struggle . . . going on in the spiritual atmosphere'."[65] Although after 1913 Kandinsky's oils do not have biblical titles and the imagery is much more diffuse, the eschatological nature of the imagery is usually still identifiable through one or more key images that are clearer than the others.[66] To give these images broad appeal, Kandinsky frequently based them on popular or folk depictions of Christian myths, many from The Revelation to John. He took as a starting point the stylized motifs found in folk art—Russian *lubki,* "Gothic" fifteenth-century woodcuts, and Bavarian glass paintings—but he then transformed these motifs by veiling and stripping them to hide the images.[67] In this way, he dematerialized the object and created a sense of mystery which not only mirrored the chaos of his age but also suggested the struggle involved in trying to understand hidden truths. If his paintings were too easily understood they would not be suitable equivalents for the intimation of the higher world.

Kandinsky emphasized the struggle involved in the attempt to reach a new "spiritual epoch." His paintings and writings were meant to reflect this struggle. He referred to his work as both "a child of its time" and "the mother of our emotions."[68] Consequently, he placed keys or clues to his intentions in his paintings and his writings. *On the Spiritual in Art* contains a number of verbal images which not only correspond to motifs in Kandinsky's paintings but also help to illuminate the themes which preoccupied him before World War I. For example, in his 1912 essay he described the anxiety and fear of his age as similar to the "sense of insecurity" of those at sea when the shore begins to disappear from view, "dark clouds gather, and the winds raise the water into black mountains."[69] In a number of paintings such as *Improvisation 7* or *Composition VI* a boat in a storm-tossed sea can be found. In *Improvisation 7* which was subtitled "Storm,"[70] several boats with prows sticking above high waves can be identified, especially when this oil of 1910 is examined next to its preparatory sketch and study.

Kandinsky characterized the dark forces threatening the spiritual life as a "great dead black spot"[71] in his major essay. He directly translated this verbal metaphor into a visual one in an oil of 1912, which he titled *Black Spot.* In the center of the painting is a large irregular shaped black oval. To its left is a blue-black oval-shaped cloud which arches over a mountain and the domed towers of a tiny walled city. This motif is most clearly visible in the lower left of an ink study for the oil. Kandinsky used the motif of the walled city in a number of his paintings, including the cover design for the German edition of *On the Spiritual in Art.* In the German edition, Kandinsky wrote a lengthy description of the walled city:

"Humanity . . . actually lives in a spiritual city, where suddenly such powers are at work, which the architects and the mathematicians of the spiritual did not expect. Here is a piece of the thick wall which has fallen as a house of cards. There a colossal tower lies in ruins, which once reached to the skies, built out of many-pointed but 'immortal' spiritual shafts. The old forgotten spirits rise up from them. The artfully constructed sun shows spots and darkens, and where is the surrogate in the struggle against darkness?"[72]

The cover of the German edition is an appropriate testament to the prophetic message implicit in the above quotation. Although the motifs on the cover are very simplified and "abstracted"—reduced to skeleton outline, they are purposively retained to reinforce Kandinsky's vision. When the cover itself is compared to the center of a sketch called *Sound of Trumpets,* a preparatory work for a glass painting of the Last Judgment,[73] the black lines on the cover can be seen to represent a mountain topped by a walled city with bent tower in front of which a horse with rider leaps. Kandinsky has placed his troubled "spiritual city" on the cover of his major essay and specifically depicted it high on a mountain as the spiritual city is so often depicted in Russian folk renditions.

Although the cover does not contain direct references to the angels of Judgment Day which are clearly apparent in *Sound of Trumpets,* it seems to contain a reference to the white horse described in The Revelation to John. The white shape of the horse motif on the cover is particularly striking, due to the contrasting dark wall behind it. By choosing a single white horse, Kandinsky may be referring to the white horse who appears when the heavens open at the end of The Revelation to John rather than to the four horsemen of doom described at the beginning of The Revelation. In so doing, Kandinsky may have wished to emphasize the regenerative aspects of The Apocalypse which the Christian Theosophist Rudolf Steiner was also doing at this time.[74] Kandinsky equated the horse and rider to the artist and his talent and believed that the artist was to lead the way to the future.[75] He also believed that "a new creation" would arise from the destruction of the old.[76] The horse and rider on the cover of *On the Spiritual in Art* may have dual implications. After all, Kandinsky explained in his autobiography of 1913 that his major essay of 1912 was conceived for the explicit purpose of awakening the "capacity, absolutely necessary in the future, for infinite experiences of the spiritual."[77]

One of the ironies of Kandinsky's vision of abstraction in *On the Spiritual in Art* was its possible contribution to the development of a geometric type of abstraction. A chart called "Elementary Life of the Primary Color and its Dependence on the Simplest Locale," which contained a yellow triangle, a blue circle, and a red square on a white and black ground, appeared in color only in the 1914 Russian transcription of *On the Spiritual in Art.* These geometric illustrations may have been an inspiration to Russian artists such as Malevich[78] as an example of how to channel the spiritual into the abstract, and they may have been another factor which helped to consolidate the development of geometric abstract painting in Russia in 1915. Interestingly, after Kandinsky returned to Russia in 1916, his style began to lose its soft flowing shapes and began to change toward harder edges, flatter planes, and less painterly qualities.

After World War II, two new English discussions of *On the Spiritual in Art* published in the United States made many of Kandinsky's ideas available to a generation of American painters, including those who were to become known as Abstract Expressionists. As painters like Jackson Pollock and Robert Motherwell began to move away from the geometric abstraction of the thirties and forties, they looked again at Kandinsky's pre-World War I ideas on color symbolism, movement and rhythm. Although their paintings are larger, more spontaneous, and more gestural than Kandinsky's they continue the painterly and expressive tradition emphasized in *On the Spiritual in Art.*

NOTES

[1] By the end of 1912, R. Piper had published three editions of *Über das Geistige in der Kunst* in Munich. The first edition went to press in mid-December, 1911, and the second edition was published in April, 1912; a third edition appeared in the Fall of that year. In this essay, reference will be to the seventh edition (Bern-Bümpliz: Bentelli, 1963), hereafter *UGK,* which follows the second edition of 1912. Throughout their book the Editors have retained the word "spiritual" as the closest counterpart to the German *geistige* and the ·Russian *dukhovnyi.* Although the word *geistige* can also denote "intellectual," "of the intellect," the content of Kandinsky's text and his use of the Russian word *dukhovnyi* (which does not pertain to the notion of "intellect") indicate that "spiritual" is the most suitable rendition in this context. In the Editors' essays quotations appear from both the German and the Russian editions of *On the Spiritual in Art.* Consequently, there are some divergences in translation, depending on the original language being used.

[2] N. R., "Khudozhestvennye vesti s zapada: Germaniia," *Apollon* (St. Petersburg), 3, No. 9 (1912), 56.

[3] Wilhelm Hausenstein, "Für Kandinsky," *Der Sturm* (Berlin), 3, No. 150-51 (1913), 277.

[4] *Der Blaue Reiter* was also published by R. Piper Verlag in 1912; a second edition of the almanac with a new preface was printed in 1914. Reference in this text will be to the reprinted documentary edition, hereafter *DBR,* ed. Klaus Lankheit (Munich: R. Piper, 1965).

[5] See, for example, his 25 March 1912 review of the Salon des Indépendants, first published in *L'Intransigeant;* reprinted in *Apollinaire on Art, Essays and Reviews, 1902-1918,* ed. LeRoy C. Breunig, trans. S. Suleiman (New York: The Viking Press, 1972), p. 214.

[6] See letters from Delaunay to Kandinsky, 1912, in R. Delaunay, *Du Cubisme à l'art abstrait,* ed. P. Francastel (Paris: S.E.V.P.E.N., 1957), pp. 178-79.

[7] Edward Wadsworth [Introduction to excerpts from *UGK*], *Blast* (London), No. 1, 20 June 1914, p. 119.

[8] For a general background explicating this relationship, see Alain Mercier, *Les Sources Esotériques et Occultes de la Poésie Symboliste (1870-1914),* 2 vols. (Paris: A.-G. Nizet, 1969, 1974). Also see John Senior, *The Way Down and Out: The Occult in Symbolist Literature* (Ithaca, N.Y.: Cornell Univ. Press, 1959), p. 36.

[9] Kandinsky, "Kuda idet 'novoe' iskusstvo," *Odesskie novosti* (Odessa) 9 Feb. 1911, p. 3.

[10] Kandinsky, *UGK,* p. 143.

[11] *Ibid.,* p. 134.

[12] *Ibid.*

[13] *Ibid.,* p. 26.

[14] *Ibid.,* p. 44.

[15] *Ibid.,* p. 33.

[16] Franz Marc, "Die 'Wilden' Deutschlands," *DBR,* p. 31.

[17] Kandinsky, *UGK,* p. 42.

[18] *Ibid.,* p. 43. For references to the literature on Kandinsky and Theosophy, see R.-C. Washton Long, "Kandinsky and Abstraction: The Role of the Hidden Image," *Artforum* (New York), 10, No. 10 (June 1972), 49, notes 10, 18.

[19] H. P. Blavatsky, *The Key to Theosophy,* 1st pub. 1889, as cited in *UGK,* p. 43. Kandinsky spelled her name "Blawatzky" and referred to the 1907 German edition published by Max Altmann in Leipzig. For centuries the word "theosophist" had been used as a synonym for those interested in uncovering "secret doctrines" and uniting or illuminating all religions. But by the time of the publication of *The Key to Theosophy,* the term "Theosophist" began to be specifically applied to those who followed Blavatsky's attempt to blend the hidden secrets of Eastern and Western religions and to explore such esoteric or occult practices as seances and mesmerism. By 1889 a number of branches of Blavatsky's Theosophical movement had been established across Europe and they united to form the International Theosophical Society.

[20] Kandinsky, *UGK,* p. 42. Kandinsky specifically cited Steiner's book *Theosophie* and his articles for the Theosophical journal *Lucifer-Gnosis.* Because of increasing differences with the International Theosophical Society, Steiner founded his own group, which he

called Anthroposophical, in the Winter of 1912-13; see R. Steiner, *The Story of My Life* (London: Anthroposophical Publishing Co., 1928), p. 300.

[21] Kandinsky, *UGK*, p. 107.

[22] Alexander Strakosch, *Lebenswege mit Rudolf Steiner* (Strasbourg: P. H. Heitz, 1947), pp. 22-24.

[23] *Der Blaue Reiter, Städtische Galerie im Lenbachhaus München*, collection catalogue 1, 2nd ed. (Munich, 1966), p. 12.

[24] Clemens Weiler, *Alexej Jawlensky* (Cologne: M. DuMont Schauberg, 1969), pp. 68, 70-73. Weiler has based his statements upon his readings of Von Werefkin's unpublished notebooks and diaries. For a discussion of other Russians living in Germany and their interest in Steiner, see R. C. Williams, "Concerning the German Spiritual in Russian Art: Vasilii Kandinskii," *Journal of European Studies* (London) 1, No. 4 (1971), 325ff.

[25] Kandinsky's notebooks are located in the archives of the Städtische Galerie, Munich. S. Ringbom in *The Sounding Cosmos* (Åbo: Åbo Akademi, 1970), pp. 62-64, discusses some of the annotations in the Theosophical books owned by Kandinsky. For reminiscences by Kandinsky's friends on Kandinsky's and their own interest in Theosophy, see R.-C. Washton, "Vasily Kandinsky 1909-1913: Painting and Theory," unpublished doctoral dissertation, Yale University, 1968, p. 139 ff.

[26] Letter from Andrei Belyi [pseudonym of Boris Bugaev] to Aleksandr Blok, 1/14 May 1912, in *Aleksandr Blok-Andrei Belyi. Perepiska* (Munich: Fink, 1969), p. 295. Samuel D. Cioran, in *The Apocalyptic Symbolism of Andrej Belyi* (The Hague: Mouton, 1973), discusses the influence of Steiner and Theosophy on Belyi's work; see p. 161ff.

[27] Letter from Belyi to Blok, 1/14 May 1912, *loc. cit.* Ellis is the pseudonym of a Symbolist poet and critic L. L. Kobylinsky. Voloshina, wife of the Symbolist poet and painter, later wrote a book in Germany about her experiences with Steiner; see M. Woloschin, *Die Grüne Schlange* (Stuttgart: Deutsche Verlags-Anstalt, 1956).

[28] Letter from Kandinsky to Marc, 1 Sept. 1911, as partly cited in Lankheit introduction, *DBR*, p. 261. Theosophy, however, was not discussed in the almanac.

[29] See "O dukhovnom v iskusstve," *Trudy Vserossiiskago sezda khudozhnikov v Petrograde, dekabr 1911-ianvar 1912gg.* (Petrograd: Golike and Vilborg, 1914), I, 74. See also Editors' Preface.

[30] Kandinsky, *UGK*, p. 86.

[31] *Ibid.*, p. 16.

[32] *Ibid.*, p. 135.

[33] *Ibid.*, p. 75.

[34] *Ibid.*, p. 115.

[35] *Ibid.*

[36] Peg Weiss, "Kandinsky and the 'Jugendstil' Arts and Crafts Movement," *The Burlington Magazine* (London), 117, No. 866 (May 1975), 270-79; also Weiss, "Wassily Kandinsky, The Formative Munich Years (1896-1914)—From Jugendstil to Abstraction," unpublished doctoral dissertation, Syracuse University, 1973.

[37] Edouard Roditi, "Interview with Gabriële Münter," *Arts* (New York), 34, No. 4 (Jan. 1960), 38.

[38] Kandinsky, *UGK*, p. 115.

[39] *Ibid.*, pp. 116-17.

[40] For a discussion of Kandinsky's and Marc's interest in Worringer, see K. Lankheit, "A History of the Almanac," *DBR*, pp. 261-62, 272, 277.

[41] Kandinsky, *UGK*, p. 129.

[42] *Ibid.*, p. 78.

[43] Kandinsky, "Rückblicke," *Kandinsky: 1901-1913* (Berlin: Der Sturm, [1913]), p. XXV. The word *gegenstandslos* has frequently been mistranslated as "non-objective," following the curious usage of that German word by Hilla Rebay in the first catalogue of the Guggenheim collection for the exhibition in 1936 at the Gibbs Memorial Art Gallery, Charleston, South Carolina. Rebay, who had come to the United States in 1926 from Germany and had helped Solomon R. Guggenheim assemble his famous collection, now the basis of The Solomon R. Guggenheim Museum, New York, had attempted, not only in the 1936 catalogue but in others that followed, to divide abstract painting in general and Kandinsky's paintings in particular into evolutionary stages of partly abstract-"objective abstraction"-and abstract-"non-objective"; see *Kandinsky* (New York: The Solomon R. Guggenheim Foundation, 1945), p. 15. In several letters to Rebay, particularly one from 16 December 1936, Kandinsky made references to her distinctions, indicating that some paintings in the Guggenheim collection such as *Black Lines* could be called paintings which did not utilize objects, or as she called them, "non-objective", (letters from Kandinsky to Rebay are now in the Rebay archive at the Guggenheim Museum). But the letters contain many indications of Kandinsky's dislike of this term; he primarily referred to his works as abstract. In an article entitled "Abstrakte Malerei" written for the *Kronick van Hedendaagse Kunst en Kultuur* in 1935, Kandinsky had commented on the negative connotations of the German term *gegenstandslose Kunst*: "Die Negationsteile dieser Worte ('non' und 'los') sind nicht geschicht: sie streichen den 'Gegenstand' und stellen nichts an seine Stelle. Schon seit längerer Zeit versuchte man (was auch

ich noch vor dem Krieg tat), das 'abstract' durch 'absolute' zu ersetzen." This article is reprinted in *Kandinsky, Essays über Kunst und Künstler,* ed. Max Bill, 2nd ed. (Bern-Bümpliz: Benteli, 1963), p. 182.

[44] Kandinsky, "Rückblicke," *loc. cit.,* p. XXXVI.

[45] Kandinsky, *UGK,* p. 71; also see the reprint of the 1914 English translation now entitled *Concerning the Spiritual in Art* (New York: Dover, 1977), p. 30.

[46] Kandinsky, *UGK,* p. 78. The German reads: "Das Kombinieren des Verschleierten und der Blossgelegten wird eine neue Möglichkeit der Leitmotive einer Formenkomposition bilden."

[47] *Ibid.,* p. 129.

[48] Kandinsky, "Rückblicke," *loc. cit.,* p. XIX.

[49] Kandinsky, "O dukhovnom v iskusstve," *loc. cit.,* p. 72.

[50] Kandinsky, *UGK,* p. 45.

[51] Steiner praised Maeterlinck's work as one of the most "distinguished experiences of the modern soul," in an article, "Maeterlinck, der 'Frei Geist'," first published 21 January 1899, reprinted in *Rudolf Steiner, Veröffentlichungen aus dem literarischen Frühwerk,* XXIV (Dornach: Rudolf Steiner Nachlassverwaltung, 1958), pp. 22-24. For an expression of Ivanov's interest in Maeterlinck, see "Predchuvstviia i predvestiia. Novaia organicheskaia epokha i teatr budushchago," *Po zvezdam* (St. Petersburg: Ory, 1909), p. 204ff. Other members of the *Blaue Reiter,* in addition to Kandinsky, revealed an interest in Maeterlinck. Schönberg set one of Maeterlinck's poems—"Herrgewächse"—to music for the almanac. August Macke wrote in an essay for the almanac that the works of Maeterlinck and Ibsen could be equated with medieval mystery plays, paintings by Van Gogh, Cézanne, and with Japanese masks; see *DBR,* pp. 53-54.

[52] Kandinsky, "Kuda idet 'novoe' iskusstvo," *loc. cit.,* p. 3.

[53] Kandinsky, *UGK,* p. 76.

[54] One is struck by the number of references Kandinsky made in *UGK* to color-musical equivalents; see p. 60ff, and p. 114. Among those whose work he cited for relating color and sound were Alexandra Vasilievna Zakharina-Unkovskaia, a St. Petersburg Theosophist, and Henri Rovel, a French writer for the periodical *Les Tendances Nouvelles.* See J. Bowlt's "Vasilii Kandinsky: The Russian Connection," p. 24, and J. Fineberg, "Kandinsky in Paris, 1906-07," unpublished doctoral dissertation, Harvard University, 1975, p. 131 ff.

[55] See Kandinsky, *UGK,* p. 126. In an essay in *Der Blaue Reiter* called "Über Bühnenkomposition," Kandinsky used the term "eine parallele Wiederholung"; *DBR,* pp. 193, 196.

[56] Kandinsky, *UGK,* pp. 108-09.

[57] Arnold Schönberg, "Das Verhältnis zum Text," *DBR,* p. 64.

[58] *Ibid.,* p. 75.

[59] *Ibid.,* p. 65.

[60] N. [Nikolai] Kulbin, "Die freie Musik," *DBR,* p. 128.

[61] Kulbin, "Svobodnoe iskusstvo, kak osnova zhizni. Garmoniia i dissonans. (O zhizni, smerti i prochem)," *Studiia impressionistov* (St. Petersburg: N. I. Butkovskaia, 1910), p. 3. For the English translation, see J. Bowlt, ed. and trans., *Russian Art of the Avant-Garde: Theory and Criticism, 1902-1934* (New York: The Viking Press, 1976), p. 13.

[62] Kandinsky, *UGK,* p. 109.

[63] *Ibid.,* p. 111.

[64] Many of the titles of Kandinsky's oils are recorded in Kandinsky's house catalogues, the year by year lists of most of his major paintings. The house lists are in the collection of his widow, Nina, in Neuilly-sur-Seine. Other titles can be found in exhibition catalogues from the period before World War I.

[65] Letter from Kandinsky to Michael Sadler, reprinted in M. Sadler, *Modern Art and Revolution* (London: Hogarth Press, 1932), pp. 18-19.

[66] Studies for Kandinsky's oils help to identify the motifs and themes in Kandinsky's paintings. E. Hanfstaengl's *Wassily Kandinsky, Zeichnungen und Aquarelle im Lenbachhaus München* (Munich: Prestel, 1974), is particularly helpful for the great number of reproductions of studies for oils of the period prior to World War I.

[67] For a more extensive discussion of Kandinsky's use of folk sources for his paintings with apocalyptic themes, see R.-C. Washton Long, "Kandinsky's Abstract Style: The Veiling of Apocalyptic Folk Imagery," *Art Journal,* 34, No. 3 (Spring 1975), 217-28.

[68] Kandinsky, *UGK,* p. 21.

[69] *Ibid.,* pp. 37-8.

[70] *Improvisation 7* was exhibited at the *Ausstellung des Sonderbundes West Deutscher Kunstfreunde und Künstler,* Dusseldorf, 1910, no. 101, with the title "Sturm." For a discussion of the painting and its studies, see Washton, "Vasily Kandinsky, 1909-1913: Painting and Theory," pp. 82-83.

[71] Kandinsky, *UGK,* p. 30.

[72] *Ibid.,* pp. 39-40.

[73] See Long, "Kandinsky's Abstract Style: The Veiling of Apocalyptic Folk Imagery," *loc. cit.,* for a fuller discussion of the imagery in *Sound of Trumpets.*

[74] See also Long, "Kandinsky and Abstraction: The Role of the Hidden Image," *loc. cit.,* pp. 47-48, for a discussion of the three horsemen in Kandinsky's depiction of the *Horsemen of the Apocalypse.*

[75] Kandinsky, "Rückblicke," *loc. cit.,* p. XVI.

[76] Kandinsky, "Notizen-Komposition 6," *Kandinsky, 1901-1913,* p. XXXVIII.

[77] Kandinsky, "Rückblicke," *loc. cit.,* p. XXVII.

[78] See J. Bowlt, "The Semaphors of Suprematism: Malevich's Journey into the Non-Objective World," *Art News* (New York), 72, No. 10 (Dec. 1973), 20ff.

Elizabeth R. Napier (essay date 1981)

SOURCE: An introduction to *Wassily Kandinsky: Sounds,* translated and with an introduction by Elizabeth R. Napier, Yale University Press, 1981, pp. 134-36.

[*In the following essay, Napier provides a stylistic and thematic overview of Kandinsky's poetry.*]

In 1938, recalling the publication of *Klänge,* Kandinsky spoke of it as "a small example of synthetic work":

> This is, for me, a "change of instrument"—the palette to one side and the typewriter in its place. I use the word "instrument" because the force which motivates my work remains unchanged, an "inner drive." And it is this very drive which calls for a frequent change of instrument.[2]

For Kandinsky, 1908-14 were crucial years of transition and experimentation. By 1909, he had begun the composition of *Klänge;* by summer of that year, he was exhibiting in his painting the first decisive signs of a turning away from objective representation and a growing interest in abstraction. As the orientation of Kandinsky's work shifted, a change occurred in his compositional procedure: the logical demands of an extrinsic subject matter gradually began to give way to an organizational theory founded upon inherent properties of color and form. In principle, the transition was from an "absolute" mode of composition that derived from sources outside the work to one that arose from the artistic materials themselves and the way these materials produced and modified their own terms of organization. Kandinsky expressed this theory succinctly in 1919:

> Every work chooses its own form and is subject to inner necessity alone. Every element of form has its absolute physical effect (= value); the construction chooses among these media in such a fashion as to turn absolute value to relative value, so that, for example, warm becomes cold and sharp dull.[3]

The poems of *Klänge,* written during the seminal years of Kandinsky's residence in Munich, attest to the growth of this transformational urge. On the levels of both form and theme, they afford insight into the artist's attitude toward abstraction and his commitment to the complex energies of redefinition and change.[4]

Jean Arp, who with Hugo Ball and the Zurich Dadaists recognized in Kandinsky one of the forebears of the new artistic movement,[5] proclaimed his indebtedness to *Klänge* in an essay of 1951. He called the work "one of the extraordinary, great books." He saw in the poetry compositions in perpetual motion, forms en route from an earthly to a spiritual realm:

> These works breathe the secrets of eternal and unexplored depths. Forms arise, as powerful as talking mountains. Sulphur and poppy stars blossom at the lips of the sky.[6]

The poems of *Klänge,* Arp noted, exhibit a recurrent concern with transformation; their design suggests a continual interchange of appearing and dissolution, a world in explicit transfiguration:

> Through the poetry of Kandinsky the readers witness to the eternal cycle, the becoming and the disappearing, the transformation of this world.[7]

The poems also reveal Kandinsky's formal means for the expression of this change: his experimentation with the construction of words and his attention to modes of repetition and variation in dialogues and chants. These lexical and compositional procedures are augmented by patterns of narrative in the poetry which move from situations of stasis to those of ongoing process. The result is a series of poems that suggest a world of multiple interpretative possibilities, and in which perception figures as the central, crucial form of engagement with the real.

Kandinsky's interest in types of patterning and variation is pervasive in *Klänge.* The simplest form of patterning, basic repetition recurs as a fundamental syntactical and metrical device in his poems. In *"Erde,"* syntactical repetition and assonance (of the key terms, "schwer" and "Erde") are utilized to slow the rhythm of the language and emphasize the gross, elemental quality of manual labor with the earth. The uncomplicated incantatory rhythms of a poem such as **"Tisch"** ("Es war ein langer Tisch. Oh, ein langer, langer Tisch") stress, in similar fashion Kandinsky's awareness of the primitive (and here notably childlike) attraction of pure reiteration.

Although in both **"Erde"** and **"Tisch"** repetition serves to stabilize and to simplify an already circumscribed universe, the reduplication of phrases and single words occasionally evokes resonances of a more complex nature. In **"Offen,"** the mysterious quality of the poem's landscape derives from heavily rhythmical cycles of sounds which, in imitation of the recurring seasons, approach and recede from the deep, central *o* of "Rohre."

Syntactical repetition in **"Hymnus,"** accentuated by strangely monotonous patterns of rhyme and meter, suggests an elemental process of a similarly enigmatic type. Here, as in the poem "Klänge," the appearance of opaque symbols creates the effect of an impenetrable surface of mystery. Often the device of repeating affords access into the realm of the alogical and the absurd. The struggle for precision reflected in the "etwas, etwas, etwas" ["a little, little, little"] refrain of **"Anders"** points to the limitations of a traditionally quantitative appraisal of reality. The frenzied incantations of the characters in **"Bunte Wiese,"** the verbal concatenation of **"Blick und Blitz,"** and the "deng, deng, deng, deng, deng" of the bell which concludes the poem **"Glocke"** encourage a similar escape from the convention of logical resolution.[8]

Within such highly iterative structures, the appearance of variation is attended with particular formal and thematic significance. As repetitive patterns typically increase the connotative capacity of language, so in the poems of **"Klänge"** complex iterative patterns with variation are often used to move language away from the denotative into the domain of the abstract and suggestive:

> Language no longer functions as a keyboard, the word frees itself from the stocktaking of reality, and a combination of words . . . materializes into a thing that approaches painting and thus returns to that material form with which the painter is familiar. In short: the object here is not the elementary red, but the result of the artistic act.[9]

A tendency to unstring and manipulate the elements of language shows itself frequently in Kandinsky's **"Klänge."** His poetry evinces a repeated interest in syntactical jokes, in the unravelling and reassembling of words and phrases. Such activity reaffirms Kandinsky's central concern with the relationship between a pattern and its variation. Thus, in the poem **"Vorhang,"** the dissection of the verb *hängen* produces the absurd litany, "Der Vorhang hing"; the cumulative rhythm of the "Ein Stein" chant in **"Bunte Wiese"** operates with similar ridiculous effect. It is significant throughout that occurrence of variation does not in a conventional sense "unlock" the meaning of the pattern that it modifies: the "tin-ten" of the clock in **"Unverändert"** throws no logical light on the "Tinten" with which the Turk waters his little tree. The isolation of the symbolic sword and rope in the poem **"Klänge"** fails similarly to resolve the meaning of the actions in which these emblems participate. In drawing repeated formal notice to pattern, Kandinsky has, in effect, transferred interpretative weight from a language system affording possible denotative solutions to an abstract complex in which design attains dominant thematic significance.

Much as the language of **"Klänge"** asserts the syntactical importance of pattern and variation, so, on the level of narrative structure, interplay between pattern and modifier functions as a central organizing device in the poetry. Within the longer narrative poems, action of "plot" typically moves from a point of stasis, where a pattern is established, to a point at which that pattern has become modified through interpolation of an often irrational or absurd event. In poems such as **"Hügel," "Hoboe," "Abenteuer,"** and **"Blätter,"** quiet landscapes are "invaded" by men (or beasts) behaving in highly enigmatic ways. In **"Hügel,"** the blackness of the drummer introduces a new dimension into a previously simple landscape: "Wie gründlich erschöpft liegt er da, der schwarze Mann, lang gestreckt auf dem weiâen Pfad, zwischen den Hügeln in allen Farben" ["As if utterly exhausted he lies there, the black man, all stretched out over the white path, among the hills of all colors"]. The blue man who rides his mysterious goat into the landscape of **"Blätter"** initiates a more radical revision of poetic scenery: the leaves fall from the tree and the flowers turn into red berries. Action, as in the poems **"Fagott," "Wasser,"** and **"Der Turm,"** attains here the qualities of pure design—it consists of an alien pattern manifesting itself in an established landscape.

In many of the poems, formal changes in setting may be traced to a specific object or event. In **"Fagott,"** a line of crows flying across the sky induces a stilling of all activity: the orange-cloud disappears, the sky and town change color. The poem **"Wasser"** portrays the alterations of land and seascape effected by the physical and mental progress of the little thin red man. In **"Der Turm,"** the appearance of the woman provokes a similar rearrangement of setting: "Sie setzte sich neben ihm und alle Pilze verschwanden" ["She sat down beside him and all the mushrooms disappeared"].

The verses of **"Klänge,"** as the poem **"Das Weiche"** attests, describe a world in constant formal tension. In nearly all the poems an act of transformation occurs or hovers in the background. Revolutionary or social transition is not the primary area of concern, although Kandinsky may move tentatively in that direction in poems such as **"Fagott," "Glocke,"** and **"Doch Noch?";** his interest resides, rather, in the more abstract context of formal relationships, in the manner in which a created artistic reality may be modified and transformed.

In a world in which change has become a factor of relevance, man's capacity to adjust to and understand his environment depends critically upon his ability to perceive. For Kandinsky, moments of impotence and confusion are typically moments of not seeing. The barrier in the poem **"Blick"** thus impedes not only vision but a potential moment of human contact. A similar dilemma is described in **"Käfig."** Here, the narrator's inability to apprehend his surroundings has been reified as an invisible cage which arrests his forward movement. The singing man of the poem **"Lied,"** deprived of both hearing and seeing, is surrounded in like fashion by a constricting "ring." Other impediments to communication recur intermittently throughout **"Klänge."** In **"Frühling"** and **"Doch Noch?"** silence becomes a pervasive metaphor for the alienation and despair of the speakers. In **"Frühling"** the air has explicitly ceased to carry sound; it no longer serves as a medium for communication. The result is a peculiar stasis of meaning, in which the poem's central symbols—the rotting cross and the lightning—remain uninterpreted and obscure.

Reality, as a line from the poem **"Anders"** admits, is not easy to see. Indeed, it is the central function of visual evidence in **"Klänge"** to bring into question what we regard as real. Throughout Kandinsky's poetry, unusual events or settings are treated as nothing out of the ordinary: the extinguished flash of lightning and the disappearing bench in **"Unverändert"** constitute the continually shifting categories of one speaker's existence, and "everybody" knows the giant cloud in **"Das"** that resembles a cauliflower. Objects of landscape may also take on troubling and indefinable symbolic resonances, as in **"Frühling"** and **"Ausgang,"** where the vision of the cross and the dry scrape of the stick deliberately begin to veer off into the realm of the surreal. The detachment of landscape elements in the poem **"Klänge"** operates in similar fashion to isolate and intensify symbolic possibilities at the expense of empirical probability.

Often the boundaries between what is perceived and what is not perceived tend to dissolve: "Der Fisch ging immer tiefer. Ich sah ihn aber noch. Ich sah ihn nicht mehr. Ich sah ihn noch, wenn ich ihn nicht sehen konnte" ["The fish went deeper and deeper. But I could still see it. I couldn't see it anymore. I could still see it, when I couldn't see it"] (**"Einiges"**); "Und die grünen Ohren! / Waren sie grün? Oder doch nicht? Oder doch?" ["And the green ears! / Were they green? Or weren't they? Or were they?"] (**"Kreide und Russ"**). In **"Klänge,"** Kandinsky toys with the notion of a reality which is purely speculative, in which, as in **"Kreide und Russ,"** one may choose whether one prefers to have seen a black face with white lips or a white face with black lips. The frequency of the conditional "perhaps" in his poetry suggests the complex potential of the sensory in Kandinsky's world. Is reality determined by the wishes of the observer (as is the shape of the hills in **"Hügel"** or the presence of fish in **"Einiges"**) or is it, in fact, as the poem **"Anders"** implies, merely an arbitrary way of ordering experience: "Es war vielleicht auch anders" ["But then again maybe it was different"]? The ability to respond to enigmatic or paradoxical settings (as the "little round flat hill" in **"Hoboe"** or the tree, in **"Fagott,"** that does not move with the wind) presupposes an expressly untraditional method of seeing. In constructing landscapes of "alternatives," Kandinsky hints at a reality which is unfixed, in which perception becomes of paramount importance. The poem **"Sehen"** pronounces the necessity of a shift in point of view, a radical commitment to "the art of seeing."[10] The issue here is not one of bringing a logical order to an illogical universe; indeed, the "white leaps" of **"Sehen"** and the unexpected symbol of the tree and apples that resolves the poem **"Käfig"** point directly away from conventional or static notions of interpretation. In **"Klänge,"** as well as in Kandinsky's paintings of the same period, form and content enforce a view of reality that places implicit faith in the activity of transformation, that entertains and participates in the crucial possibilities of change.[11]

It would be unwise and unfortunate to disregard certain facts (one might call them "events") which surround us and which push us toward the freedom that is synthesis. Too bad for those who wish to block the way.[12]

A NOTE ON KLÄNGE

A note by Kandinsky in the publisher's prospectus for *Klänge* indicates that Kandinsky began the composition of the prose-poems around 1909-10.[13] The woodcuts date from 1907. It is difficult to trace the beginnings of *Klänge* with more precision. In the Salon d'Automne in Paris in 1910, Kandinsky placed on exhibition four woodcuts "pour un album avec texte"; later that year, six woodcuts "zu einem Album mit Text" appeared in an exhibition of the Neue Künstlervereinigung in Munich; another reference to an album accompanied by text occurs in the catalogue of an exhibition in Berlin in March 1912. Letters to Gabriele Münter in the summer of 1911 indicate that Kandinsky was working assiduously on the woodcuts for *Klänge,* and by August he wrote that the work ("mein Album") was nearly complete.

The book was originally designed for publication in Moscow: a maquette for a Russian edition (which Kandinsky may have planned during his stay in Odessa in December of 1910) is in the Gabriele Münter Foundation in the Städtische Galerie, Munich.[14] This original version of *Klänge,* which contained seventeen poems in Russian, was to have been published in 1911 by Vladimir Izdebsky, a sculptor acquaintance of Kandinsky and organizer of two major international exhibitions of Western avant-garde art in Odessa in 1909-11. The book never materialized.

On September 12, 1912, Kandinsky signed the contract to publish with Piper Verlag of Munich. The book appeared in November in a single edition of three hundred signed and forty-five unsigned copies; the sale price was fixed at thirty marks. The agreement included mention of a possible second printing of *Klänge,* to be considered one or two years after the publication of the first edition. This version, with a price of approximately three marks, was to have been presented in a reduced format with a selection of the smaller woodcuts. It did not appear.

The original *Klänge* contains thirty-eight poems and fifty-six woodcuts, twelve of which are full-page color prints. The poems are set in bold type on handmade Dutch paper. The book measures 11¼ inches square. It is bound in a dark red pasteboard cover and has a spine of purple linen. On the front and back covers a small vignette by Kandinsky is impressed in gold.

Though there was some disagreement about its popular reception,[15] *Klänge* is now regarded as one of the most significant artist's books of the twentieth century. *Klänge* has its roots in a period of radical change: conceived during the period of Kandinsky's movement toward abstraction, it is a work which both verbally and visually insists on the energy of nonobjective form. The poems and woodcuts of *Klänge* exhibit a repeated experimentation with the limits of the conventional objective world: the poems are alternately narrative and expressive in quality; the woodcuts—which, as a medium, were of special importance in Kandinsky's emergence into abstraction[16]—range from early Jugendstil-inspired (and still highly representational) designs to vignettes that are purely abstract in form.

Because Kandinsky's *Klänge* is a rare example of a work in which text and illustrations have been executed by the same artist, it poses special questions to the literary critic concerned with the relationship of illustration to text. The case of *Klänge* is particularly interesting because, in the transposition of poems from the proposed Russian edition into the German edition, the original order of the woodcuts was not adhered to. How, then, should these works of visual art be viewed? Are they illustrations of the text in the conventional sense or do they in some way modify our definition of the word *illustration?* The relationship of prints to poems in *Klänge* is, perhaps, more fundamental than is usual in an illustrated book: it lies in the conceptual unity between visual art and text, in the peculiar tension between representation and abstraction that characterizes both artistic forms.

A NOTE ON THE TRANSLATION

Kandinsky's interest in the possibilities of synthesis between painting and the word poses special problems to the translator of *Klänge.* The poems are characterized by a deliberate simplification of vocabulary—Kandinsky's language tends to be general rather than highly specific—and he often refuses to adhere to an accepted grammatical code. His punctuation is irregular: in **"Hügel,"** he writes of a "langen schwarzen, faltenlosen Rock" ["a long smooth, black coat"].[17] He may (as he does in **"Fagott"**) change tense abruptly in midstream: "Da wusste man schon, dass durch die gänzlich leeren Strassen ein weisses Pferd ganz allein wandert" ["And they knew that through the totally empty streets a white horse is walking all alone"]. At other times, he may arbitrarily rearrange the order of words in a single sentence, as in **"Wurzel"**: "Das Licht des Abendsternes um die angegebene Stunde kommt" ["The light of the evening star at the appointed hour comes"]. Often, as in the poems **"Klänge"** and **"Wasser,"** he leaves sentences incomplete. In other poems (notably **"Fagott"** and **"Glocke"**), he extends them beyond the limits of rhetorical probability.

Because attention to form is an issue of central significance in *Klänge,* it is critical to attempt to reproduce that surface of artifice which the poems maintain. Throughout *Klänge,* language and poetic form remain curiously simple and precise. Kandinsky's interest in patterns of repetition, alliteration, and rhyme typically involves multiple variations on a small, often apparently insignificant, group of phrases or sounds. The introductory

fragments of the poem **"Im Wald"** or the hypnotic rhythms of the verse **"Hymnus"** embody a conscious playing with a minimum of poetic materials. Kandinsky will often devise more complex plays on individual words. This tendency is manifested most explicitly in **"UNVERÄNDERT,"** where three words are "redefined" through clever syntactical dismemberment. The fragmentation of "Banane" to "Bann! Ahne!," "furchtbar" to "Furcht bar," and "Tinten" to "tin-ten" (the last of which undergoes translator's metamorphosis to "tickling" and "ting-a-ling") has a less complicated counterpart in the dialogue which opens the poem **"Warum?":** "Keiner. / Einer? / Nein. / Ja!" ["No one. / One? / No. / Yes!"]. More conventional puns occur—on "fest" ["solid"] and "bange" ["alarmed"]—in the poems **"Das"** and **"Abenteuer."**

Like the play on "Tinten," some of Kandinsky's syntactical jokes resist literal translation and must be refashioned. The variation on *hängen* in the poem **"Vorhang"** ("Der Vorhang hing") consequently becomes "a certain curtain hung"; the "Ein Stein" chant in **"Bunte Wiese"** diminishes into "one stone."

To heighten the reader's consciousness of a formalized poetic universe, Kandinsky occasionally introduces words of his own. Generally, these words pertain to the domain of color and function on a principle of paradox rather than one of denotative specificity: "braunweiss" ["brownwhite"], "rotblau" ["redblue"], and "scharfrot" ["sharp-red"] are examples. The verbal pyrotechnics of **"Blick und Blitz"** are not characteristic of Kandinsky, though other Expressionist poets (notably August Stramm and Dadaists such as Jean Arp and Hugo Ball) exercised an active interest in word inventions and collages.

NOTES

[1] "Autrefois on regardait le peintre 'de travers', quand il écrivait—même si c'était des lettres. On voulait presque qu'il mange non pas à la fourchette, mais avec un pinceau." Wassily Kandinsky, "Mes gravures sur bois," *XXe Siècle* 1, no. 3 (1938): 31.

[2] "Ce qui est pour moi un 'changement d'instrument'—la palette de côté et à sa place la machine à écrire. Je dis 'instrument', parce que la force qui me pousse à mon travail reste toujours la même, c'est-à-dire une 'pression intérieure'. Et c'est elle qui me demande de changer souvent d'instrument." Kandinsky, "Mes gravures sur bois," p. 31.

[3] "Jedes Werk wählt sich seine Form und unterliegt nur der inneren Notwendigkeit. Jedes Formelement hat seine absolute physische Wirkung (= Wert); die Konstruktion wählt unter diesen Mitteln so, daâ sie den absoluten Wert zu einem relativen macht, so daâ zum Beispiel Warmes kalt wird und Spitziges stumpf." Wassily Kandinsky. "Selbstcharakteristik," *Das Kunstblatt* 3, no. 6 (1919): 174. Unless otherwise noted, translations from German to English are my own.

[4] That *Klänge* was regarded by Kandinsky himself as an expression of the artist's transitional years is suggested in a passage from "Mes gravures sur bois," p. 31.

> Dans ces bois comme dans le reste—bois et poèmes— on retrouve les traces de mon développement du "figuratif" à l' "abstrait" ("concret" d'après ma terminologie—plus exacte et plus expressive que l'habituelie—à mon avis du moins).

> [In these woodcuts, as in the rest—woodcuts and poems—can be found traces of my development from the "figurative" to the "abstract" (the "concrete" according to my terminology—which is, in my opinion at least, more precise and more expressive than the usual).]

Kandinsky executed his first abstract work around 1909; by 1914 the figurative element had virtually disappeared from his painting.

[5] Ball, in particular, was inspired by Kandinsky's example. "When we said Kandinsky and Picasso," he recalls, "we meant not painters but priests; not craftsmen, but creators of new worlds and new paradises." *Flight out of Time: A Dada Diary, 1910-21, 1924-,* ed. John Elderfield, trans. Ann Raimes (New York: Viking, 1974), p. 7 (originally published as *Die Flucht aus der Zeit* [Munich: Duncker & Humblot, 1927]). "There was no art form that he had tried," Ball wrote of Kandinsky, "without taking completely new paths, undeterred by derision and scorn. In him, word, color, and sound worked in rare harmony . . ." (p. 8); "in poetry too he is the first to present purely spiritual processes. . . . Nowhere else, even among the futurists, has anyone attempted such a daring purification of language" (p. 234). Kandinsky, though he did not become directly involved with the Dadaists, was a driving force behind the new group in Zurich. His paintings were included in Dadaist exhibitions and his poems recited at Dada soirées through 1919. Ball's diaries and his 1917 lecture on Kandinsky (trans. Christopher Middleton, in *Flight out of Time,* pp. 222-34) attested repeatedly to the strength of his influence.

[6] "Il passe dans ces morceaux un souffle venu de fonds éternel et inexplorés. Des formes se lèvent, puissantes comme des montagnes parlantes. Des étoiles de soufre et de coquelicot fleurissent aux lèvres du ciel." Jean Arp, "Kandinsky, le poète," in *Wassily Kandinsky,* ed. Max Bill (Paris: Maeght, 1951), pp. 89-93. According to Kandinsky, Arp valued his copy of *Klänge* so highly that he would lend it to no one and forbade even his wife to read it. See Hans Konrad Roethel. *Kandinsky: Das graphische Werk* (Cologne: M. DuMont Schauberg, 1970), p. 448.

[7] "Par la poésie de Kandinsky, nous assistons au cycle éternel au devenir et à la disparition, à la transformation de ce monde." Arp, p. 90.

[8] Kandinsky also explores this point in *Über das Geistige in der Kunst:* "repetition . . . will not only tend to intensify the inner harmony [of a word] but also bring to light unsuspected spiritual properties of the word itself. Further than that, frequent repetition of a word . . . deprives the word of its original external meaning." *Concerning the Spiritual in Art,* trans. M. T. H. Sadler (New York: Dover, 1977), p. 15 (originally published as *Über das Geistige in der Kunst* [Munich: Piper Veriag, 1912]).

[9] "Die Sprache hört auf, Tastatur zu sein, das Wort löst sich von der Bestandsaufnahme der Wirklichkeit, und eine Wortverbindung . . . materialisiert sich zu einem Ding, das dem Gemälde nahekommt und damit zu jener Stofflichkeit zurückkehrt, die dem Maler vertraut ist. Kurz: das Objekt ist hier nicht das elementare Rot, sondern Resultat der künstlerischen Handlung." Hans Platschek, *Dichtung moderner Maler* (Wiesbaden: Limes, 1956), p. 8.

[10] The expression is El Lissitzky's: "Das Sehen ist nämlich auch eine K[unst]." "K[unst] und Pangeometrie," in *Europa-Almanach,* vol. 1, ed. Carl Einstein and Paul Westheim (1925; reprint ed., Nendeln, Liechtenstein: Kraus, 1973), p. 103.

[11] It is interesting to note, for example, in many of Kandinsky's *Improvisations* of 1911-12, and in *Komposition V* (1911) and *Mit dem schwarzen Bogen* (1912) in particular, a frequent tendency to superscribe large formalized areas of landscape with winding or diagonal black lines. See Will Grohmann, *Wassily Kandinsky: Life and Work,* trans. Norbert Guterman (London: Thames & Hudson, 1959), pp. 103-59.

[12] "C'est imprudent et malheureux de fermer les yeux sur quelques faits (on pourrait dire 'événements') qui nous entourent et qui nous poussent vers la liberté de la synthèse. Tant pis pour ceux qui veulent barrer la route." Kandinsky, "Mes gravures sur bois," p. 31.

[13] "Alle 'Prosagedichte,'" wrote Kandinsky, "habe ich im Laufe der letzten drei Jahre geschrieben. Die Holzschnitte gehen bis in das Jahr 1907 hinauf." ["I wrote all of the prose-poems in the course of the last three years. The woodcuts go back to the year 1907."] See Roethel, p. 445. I am indebted throughout this section to Roethel's researches into the publishing background of *Klänge.*

Kandinsky's poetic activity dated from his childhood. "Like many children and young people," he recalled, "I attempted to write poetry which sooner or later I tore up." *Reminiscences,* trans. Mrs. Robert L. Herbert, in *Modern Artists on Art: Ten Unabridged Essays,* ed. Robert L. Herbert (Englewood Cliffs, N.J.: Prentice-Hall, 1964), pp. 19-44 (originally published as "Rückblicke," in *Kandinsky, 1901-1913* [Berlin: Der Sturm, 1913]). Drawing, Kandinsky maintained, eventually "released" him from this condition of personal doubt (p. 27). By the time of *Klänge,* he was to synthesize the two creative processes which he then regarded as separate and conflicting.

[14] A full comparison of the German and Russian editions of *Klänge* is currently being undertaken by Dr. Jelena

Hahl, who kindly provided me with detailed information on her research. Her study will be published in the Roethel/Hahl edition of Kandinsky's writings (in progress).

[15] The book, later lauded by Arp and the Zurich Dadaists, was unfavorably reviewed by Hans Tietze in *Die Graphischen Künste* 37 (1913): 15-16. In his article, Tietze commended the theoretical premises of *Klänge* but expressed serious reservations about the poetry and art, which he saw as unsuccessful embodiments of those theories. Piper and Kandinsky, too, held different views of the book's success. Piper wrote to Kandinsky in 1914 that fewer than one hundred copies of *Klänge* had been sold and for that reason, presumably, did not bring out a second edition. However, Kandinsky maintained in "Mes gravures sur bois" and elsewhere that the volume had been bought up quickly.

[16] See Kenneth Lindsay, "Graphic Art in Kandinsky's Oeuvre," in *Prints: Thirteen Illustrated Essays on the Art of the Print,* ed. Carl Zigrosser (London: Peter Owen, 1963), pp. 235-47; Peg Weiss, *Kandinsky in Munich: The Formative Jugendstil Years* (Princeton: Princeton University Press, 1979), pp. 127-32; Peter Vergo, "Kandinsky: Art Nouveau to Abstraction," in *Kandinsky: The Munich Years 1900-14: An Edinburgh International Festival Exhibition Organised by the Scottish Arts Council in Association with the Lenbachhaus* (Edinburgh: Edinburgh International Festival and Scottish Arts Council, 1979), pp. 4-10.

[17] The translator's specific problem here (as in many of the poems of *Klänge*) is to determine the relative importance of assonance and word order in the original verse. Literal translation of this phrase, of course, produces a "long black, smooth coat." The relationship of the adjectives in German is based upon repetition of three main sounds (the *I*, the *a*, and the ending, *-en*). The closer affinity (through assonance, syllabic count, and the lack of usual punctuation) of the first two words of the original series, and the variation in the final word, help to justify a syntactical rearrangement in the English.

Stephen Spender (essay date 1981)

SOURCE: "The Glow of Irreality," in *New York Review of Books,* Vol. XXVIII, No. 13, August 13, 1981, pp. 40-43.

[*In the following favorable review of* Sounds, *Spender considers the relationship between Kandinsky's poetry and his painting.*]

The coincidence of the exhibition "Kandinsky: The Improvisations" at the National Gallery of Art in Washington with the publication of Elizabeth Napier's translation of Kandinsky's book **Sounds (Klänge)** is happy. Both belong approximately to the second decade of the present century. Kandinsky painted the first Improvisation in 1909. In 1913 **Klänge,** a volume of thirty-eight prose poems and fifty-six woodcuts, twelve of them in color,

was published by Piper Verlag in Munich, in an edition of 345 copies. This edition, which did not sell well at the time, is one of the masterpieces of twentieth-century German book production. Five copies are on display in the present exhibition, though, as is inevitable, they are in a glass case, so that one can see only three poems and five woodcuts.

Nineteen of the original thirty-six Improvisations are here, together with drawings, watercolors, and prints. It is a small exhibition—about thirty items in all—the third in the excellent series of such exhibitions in the new building of the National Gallery, where the awed visitor searches for pictures among the overpowering architecture as for needles in a wonderfully constructed haystack. The previous exhibitions were of Mondrian's "The Diamond Compositions" and Picasso's "The Saltimbanques."

Beautifully hung and arranged, this exhibition communicates the excitement of the avant-garde of the Blaue Reiter artists in Munich before the First World War. In Germany at that time, with a rawness not Parisian, the twentieth century seemed the beginning of an era in which the arts—music, poetry, and architecture, as well as painting—would transform the world with a new style which would influence men and women to live lives of pleasure, candor, truth, love.

In 1909 Kandinsky, who had abandoned his legal career in Russia to move to Germany, lived with the painter Gabriele Münter in a house known as "Russenvilla" at Murnau. Its very name brings with it a whiff of discussion of the relation of the inner life to art, the different significances of red, blue, green, and yellow, the music of Wagner and of Schoenberg—and also Schoenberg's paintings—and of theories which are set forth didactically in Kandinsky's pamphlet—a central document of modernism—**Concerning the Spiritual in Art** (1911).

Apart from Gabriele Münter, the artist closest to Kandinsky was Franz Marc, painter of horses, deer, and other animals which, within brilliant, stylized landscapes, seem in their elegant, shimmering, rainbow-like luminosity to have been restored by the artist to some Garden of Eden. Franz Marc shared with Kandinsky visionary religious views.

Despite his intermittent association with this "movement" of painters—endlessly dissenting from one another, exhibiting and refusing to exhibit together—Kandinsky appears isolated in his highly cerebral intellectualism, his passion for theory, his mysticism. There is an enchanting and enchanted description of him in 1912 by Jean Arp in "Kandinsky the Poet." Arp promotes him from the Blaue Reiter to Dada:

> Kandinsky spoke to me with tenderness, richness, vivacity, and humor. In his studio, speech and form and color fused and were transmuted into fabulous, extraordinary worlds. Across the bellowing and tumult of these worlds, by listening attentively,

I could hear the tintinnabulation of the brilliant and gaudy mushroom cities of Russia. Kandinsky told me that his grandfather had come trotting into Russia on a small steed studded with bells, from one of those enchanted Asian mountains made of porcelain.

Kandinsky's grandfather certainly bequeathed profound secrets. *Anno dada,* poems of Kandinsky's, were recited for the first time in the Cabaret Voltaire in Zurich, and the audience received them with prehistoric howls. The dadaists were the combative and enthusiastic vanguard of concrete poetry. In 1916 Hugo Ball and Tristan Tzara were writing sound poetry that greatly helped to clarify the meaning of concrete poetry. My collection *The Cloud Pump* consists mainly of concrete poetry.

Kandinsky's intellect and art reached deeper and further than the Munich of his time. In *Concerning the Spiritual in Art,* he shows his awareness of everything happening then in all the arts—and fifty years before—from Moscow to Paris, which tended toward the modern. He refers to: Wagner (notably the Wagner of *Lohengrin*), Debussy, Moussorgsky, Scriabin, Schoenberg—among composers; Rossetti, Segantini; Böcklin, Hodler, Cézanne, Matisse, Picasso among painters. Maeterlinck especially appeals to him, on account of his use of symbolism both in language and in staging. One passage about Maeterlinck is particularly significant:

> [His] principal technical weapon is his use of words. The word may express an inner harmony. This inner harmony springs partly, perhaps principally, from the object which it names. But if the object is not itself seen, but only its name heard, the *mind* of the hearer receives an abstract expression only, that is to say as if the object dematerialized, and a corresponding vibration is immediately set up in the *heart.*

There is also mention of Rudolf Steiner and Madame Blavatsky. Some of these names today cause one to shudder. What all have in common is first the Wagnerian insistence on the interrelationship of the arts—music, painting, poetry, theater, ballet; and secondly, the idea that art should be about an inner vision, and should avoid imitating "nature." Kandinsky remarks of Matisse:

> He paints "pictures," and in these "pictures" endeavors to reproduce the divine. To attain this end he requires as a starting point nothing but the object to be painted . . . and then the methods that belong to painting alone. . . .

What we have here is a pre-two-world-wars internationalism in the art of this century that no longer exists in a period when air travel would seem to have abolished distances. Part of this internationalism is symbolism in all the arts connected with a mysticism which is present in Rilke, and also Yeats, and even with the apocalyptic vision of D. H. Lawrence, evident in the concluding pages of *The Rainbow.*

And, of course, also with Kandinsky there were Russian links, of suprematism and other movements in painting, as well as of his visions remembered from childhood of the towers of the Kremlin, and of Odessa.

Looking at the Improvisations elucidates Kandinsky's poetry, and reading the poems elucidates the paintings. This is not because the poems "explain" the pictures or that the pictures illustrate the poems, but because behind both we see the same religious-visionary and abstract-analytic, almost scientific, intelligence.

In the later Improvisations, as in the woodcuts accompanying the poems in *Sounds* (I do wish that Miss Napier had translated *Klänge* as *Resonances*—but doubtless she has excellent reasons for not doing so), objects are transformed into signs or indicators, like those arrows and exclamation marks which Kandinsky's friend—and, later, colleague at the Bauhaus—Paul Klee introduces sometimes into his work. E. A. Carmean Jr., in the notes provided for the guide to the Washington exhibition calls these "abstract signs." In the poems, names for things in nature are qualified by adjectives in such a way that they tend to become abstract symbols which the poet assumes to be present in the mind of the reader. For instance, in **"Hills,"** the opening poem of *Sounds,* Kandinsky assumes the existence in the reader's mind of a clearly visualized yet abstract concept of hills as *one mental or imagined hill,* different from particular hills:

> A mass of hills of all the colors you can imagine or care to imagine. All different sizes, but the shapes always alike, i.e., just one: Fat at the bottom, puffed out around the sides, flat-round up above. Just plain, ordinary hills, like the kind you always imagine and never see.

The poet-painter here assumes that the reader shares with him the universal inward image (like an archetype of the Jungian collective unconscious) "the hill you always imagine." This is in part surrealist play between poet and reader (before the word "surrealist" came into use). A good deal of the bright attractiveness of Kandinsky's poetry is that it can be surrealistic without being turgid.

Another characteristic that the poems have in common with the Improvisations is that every object seems to be moving on a trajectory in which it may evolve into something else. The external natural landscape is only a mask, a deception behind which the spirit that dwells within the inner landscape of the spiritual life is engaged in a perpetual task of transforming appearances.

In all this, study of what goes on in the poetry is, I think, helpful in understanding the paintings. Especially the later Improvisations, in which the transformation of external things into "abstract signs," or ideograms of the spiritual life, becomes complete.

In the earlier Improvisations this has not happened yet. In them, Moscow with the towers of the Kremlin, horse,

horse and rider, the Lohengrin-like figure of a knight, hieratical priestly figures, the walls of Tunis (as recollected from a journey there taken together with Gabriele Münter) are represented or illustrated, while at the same time being drawn into a pattern of which they become only the parts. For example, in *Improvisation 8* (1910) the upper third of the picture is a hallucinatory childhood memory of the Kremlin with its bulging towers, semi-haloed by a rainbow. This is divided by an irregular wall (somewhat like the upside-down figure of an animal) from the lower part of the picture, dominated by the figure of a crusader knight, extending his rigid arm toward an enormous sword, pointed against the earth. This sacred knight seems reminiscent of Lohengrin. Behind him, on the right, there are Oriental-seeming cloaked figures, or so they appear to me.

Moscow, the knight, the sword, the rainbow, etc., are not representational. Rather they are illustrational, impregnated with a glow of irreality partly derived from childhood memory, partly from children's books read, and pictures seen in them, partly from journeys made. They have the aura of Vaughan's lines:

When on some gilded cloud or flower
My gazing soul would dwell an hour,
And in those weaker glories spy
Some shadows of eternity. . . .

Behind all there is Holy Russia, the things seen there. Will Grohmann in *Wassily Kandinsky, Life and Work* writes of a visit which Kandinsky, then only twenty-three years old and a government official (he did not become an art student till he was thirty), made in 1889 to the northern province of Vologda, to make an anthropological report:

People in their local costumes moved about like pictures come to life: their houses were decorated with colorful carvings, and inside on the walls were hung popular prints and icons; furniture and other household objects were painted with large ornamental designs that almost dissolved them into color. Kandinsky had the impression of moving about inside of pictures—an experience of which he later became quite conscious when he invited the beholder to "take a walk" in his pictures and tried to forget himself, to dissolve himself in the picture.

This Russia was the ultimate of Kandinsky's world just as much as it was Chagall's.

This is still the world of the early Improvisations. Its images are not perhaps altogether representational, though too much so for anyone to call, say, *Improvisation 8* abstract. They are stereotypes, cut-outs from memory (Kandinsky had, rather to his distress, a photographic memory), illustrational, and with color which, as it were, floats off from the subject and creates a wash or veil of abstraction, and has the meanings, separate from it, which he attaches to colors. Intense yellow is aggressive, recalling the sound of a trumpet, green is the color

of compromise—bourgeois life, smug and passive—blue is the color of heaven, and corresponds in music to flute, cello, double bass. Such associations are of poetry and remind us of Rimbaud's sonnet on vowels, or Auden's,

Whose favourite colour is blue,
Colour of distant bells
And of boys' overalls.

In the early Improvisations, these stereotypes are collaged within a wider overall composition, like themes in a symphony:

Complex composition, consisting of various forms, subjected more or less completely to a principal form. Probably the principal form may be hard to grasp outwardly, and for that reason is possessed of a strong inner value. [*Concerning the Spiritual in Art*]

In the later Improvisations, what I call stereotypes of memory are replaced completely by abstract signs. The representational has been swallowed up within the ideo-grammic, like Chinese ideograms in which what originates from a thing soon becomes changed into a "character."

E. A. Carmean, Jr., has done very extensive research into the "abstract signs" in the Improvisations. Some of these are explained in the exhibition guide. Water is a wave, indicated by an outline like that of a gloved six-fingered hand. This refers to the power of water and thus to the destructive force of the Deluge. Signs for arisen soul, boats, horse and rider, towers, and troika are interpreted. The troika, a rake-shaped transverse line with behind it small, wiry lines indicating the manes of horses, followed by three trailing lines, derives from the familiar Russian team of three horses, and refers also to the horses of the Apocalypse. A childishly recognizable cannon with loop-shaped smoke coming out of the mouth denotes the end of the world. A chrysalis-shaped outline, often darkened in, indicates lovers. What looks like an inkblot, evil. The most frequent of the configurations appearing in the later Improvisations is that of ghosts: long lines moving diagonally across the canvas and linked up at the end by a crossing line like the top of an *n*.

The "abstract signs," thanks to Mr. Carmean, can now, most of them, be interpreted, but if the pictures separately or as a whole are meant as messages, these are concealed, mysteries spoken in mysterious language. Some pictures seem clearer than others, because we recognize what they are about, and tend to read our own fears or wishes into them. For instance, *Improvisation 27* (*Garden of Love*), with its sun at the center of the garden, clasping lovers, fence, serpent, etc., seems easy; as does *Improvisation 30*, with cannon-smoke ghosts of the dead rising toward heaven, the war we know so well.

The Apocalypse was an inspired subject for Kandinsky for several reasons. In it he was painting the subject matter of his esoteric religion. He was also painting the strange feeling of things coming to an end and at the same time of total renewal, which artists, in particular, had in the years preceding 1914. However, the important reason why the subject had a certain inevitability for him at this stage of his career is that the view of life contained in the book of Revelation corresponds not just to his religious mysticism, but to his view of art. It provided him with a subject that was also a style and also the proper use of "the methods that belong to painting alone."

It did so because the apocalyptic view of life reverses the whole order of appearances in the world and in history. What we call nature is only a deceptive covering; what we think of as history is only a procession of masks, historic figures, apocalyptic beasts, behind whose faces and actions the struggle between God and Satan, light and darkness, good and evil continues. There is a cast of God and Satan, angels and devils, the horses of the Apocalypse, acting out a play whose cataclysmic events—the Deluge, earthquakes, Armageddon, war, the end of the world, etc.—are only symbols of invisible events going on in the conflict of abstract divine and eternal forces.

In the late Improvisations, Kandinsky was "using the methods that belong to painting alone"—painting the invisible. This may seem a contradiction in terms until one reflects that a vision is precisely this—a vision of the invisible. The struggle between abstract forces of good and evil is what many painters throughout history have tried to depict. It is quintessential, basic painting. This is evident in primitive cultures where the artists who carve and paint totems, masks, gods, hunting scenes, are painting invisible magic. In doing so, the act of making art itself becomes magic. Kandinsky's Improvisations are the magical works of modernism in which the act of painting is itself a form of creating a book of Revelation.

The misunderstanding of European religious artists since the Renaissance and earlier has been to try to express the invisible through the literally rendered description of the human body, nude or clothed, at a time when artists were infatuated with the human body anyway. The result of this is that we have a tradition of religious art which moves us because we instinctively recognize in it a religion of art—and of the human figure, the artist's model. Kandinsky in these pictures reverses this process by making art into religion, not a religion of art but art as religious ritual sign language. The Improvisations resist being regarded as aesthetic secular objects. They are the documents of an intense spiritual struggle.

Their position in Kandinsky's own work is that in them all his affinities, influences, memories, theories, religious feelings, are in a fluid state. One has the impression when one looks at the later pictures in the series of witnessing an explosion. Apart from everything else there is here the joy of the paint itself, laid on with such different surfaces: sometimes as wash, sometimes as swift diagonal strokes of the brush in a parallel direction, sometimes as trailing lines, sometimes as the outlines of abstract signs, which are the heart's handwriting; and

always with patches of brilliant color forming abstract patterns that fly apart from the lines.

It is worth pointing out that these pictures do not at all strike the note of tragic pathos which we find in Picasso's Blue Period paintings. They are entirely exhilarating, Nietzschean in being beyond good and evil.

The temptation to read journalistic prophecy into certain of the Improvisations which are concerned with war is even stronger with some of the poems. It is difficult to read the opening lines of **"Bassoon"** without the feeling—"he must be talking about us":

> Very large houses suddenly collapsed. Small houses remained standing. A fat hard egg-shaped orange-cloud suddenly hung over the town. It seemed to hang on the pointed point of the steep spindly town hall tower and radiated violet. A dry, naked tree stretched its quaking and quivering long branches into the deep sky. It was very black, like a hole in white paper. Its four little leaves quivered for a long time. But there was no sign of wind.
>
> But when the storm came and buildings with thick walls fell down, the thin branches didn't move. The little leaves turned stiff: as if cast out of iron. A flock of crows flew through the air in a straight line over the town.
>
> And suddenly again everything was still.
>
> The orange-cloud disappeared. The sky turned piercing blue. The town yellow enough to make you cry.
>
> And through this silence a single sound rang: hoofbeats. And they knew that through the totally empty streets a white horse is walking all alone.
>
> The sound lasted for a long time, a very, very long time. So no one knew exactly when it disappeared. Who knows when silence begins?
>
> Through elongated, extended, somewhat expressionless, unsympathetic notes of a bassoon rolling far, far away deep in the distant emptiness, everything slowly turned green. First low and rather dirty. Then brighter and brighter, colder and colder, poisonous and more poisonous, even brighter, even colder, even more poisonous. . . .

These poems were written in German (Kandinsky also wrote some poems in Russian). They are concisely and clearly translated by Elizabeth Napier and are close to the original text (one hardly expects this from translators nowadays, and is grateful). In either language the poems read as though they were written in a kind of basic English (or German), like instructions on the box of a do-it-yourself kit. They often have humor, but underneath there is the tone of another kind of instruction, on how to live in an apocalyptic era.

It is difficult to write about these poems except in the language of surrealist hyperbole (as Arp does) or with extreme aridity. Elizabeth Napier writes rather surrealist things in a language of extreme aridity. Here is a passage:

> Although in both *Erde* and *Tisch* repetition serves to stabilize and to simplify an already circumscribed universe, the reduplication of phrases and single words occasionally evokes resonances of a more complex nature. In *Offen,* the mysterious quality of the poem's landscape derives from heavy rhythmical cycles of sounds which, in imitation of the recurring seasons, approach and recede from the deep, central *o* of "Rohre."

Even if, through repetition, one were able to stabilize "an already circumscribed universe" (what can that be?), how, after accomplishing this feat, could he possibly, through reduplication, be expected to evoke "more complex resonances"? I did, however, manage to gather from the above, after reduplication of my reading of it, that repetition of a word or phrase tends to hold up the forward movement of a sentence. It is true that since Kandinsky's language lacks a rich verbal texture of the kind one expects in poetry, one has to look for other qualities to explain its very real appeal. It combines sharpness, brightness, precision with an underlying ominousness, and this is due to the positioning of words so that they make one see beyond them into colors and sounds they represent. It is excellent painter's poetry or word-painting. Kandinsky can be surrealist without being verbose or turgid, as here in **"Early Spring"**:

> A man on the street took off his hat. I saw black-and-white hair stuck down to the right and left of his part with hair cream.
>
> Another man took off his hat. I saw a big pink, slightly greasy bald spot with a bluish highlight.
>
> The two men looked at one another, each showing the other crooked, greyish yellowish teeth with fillings.

This edition is printed clearly in very black typography on shiny paper. The woodcuts, although greatly reduced in size, come out black and strong. It is good that it should be widely accessible to readers. It is a pity, however, that there are not colored reproductions of the twelve original color blocks. It is greatly to be hoped that someone enterprising someone enterprising (if I may dare stabilize and simplify an already circumscribed universe by repetition of a phrase, for a moment) will publish a replica of the book as printed by Piper Verlag. Perhaps in Germany someone enterprising is already doing this.

Carter Radcliff (essay date 1982)

SOURCE: "Kandinsky's Book of Revelation," in *Art in America,* December, 1982, pp. 105-09, 157-59.

[*In the following essay, Radcliff examines the apocalyptic vision in Kandinsky's seminal essay,* Concerning the Spiritual in Art, *and compares it to the biblical book of Revelation.*]

I would like to propose that Expressionism enjoys a special relationship with apocalypse. This is not a new idea. The Expressionists themselves came up with it. Nor, I must admit, does this notion permit us to draw very clear lines. What modernist style has not served as a more or less sensitive seismograph of our century's millennial tremors? High modernism aside, every plateau of the culture offers a platform from which to broadcast the jitters endured awaiting the final demise of everything— or of everything deemed significant. "End of Consumer Culture?" asks an editorial in *ZG,* a London-based art magazine with an earnestly street-level view of our situation.

That end, foreshadowed for *ZG* in the work of Jack Goldstein and David Salle, would be liberation as well as cataclysm. Apocalypses always damn those who deserve it while preserving the elect, those who signal their state of grace with an ability to see doom far off, across the mirage-filled wasteland where the damned muddle through obliviously. Thus "the death-knell of a dying consumer culture" may well have the lilt of glad tidings, for "perhaps it heralds the beginnings of a new age of art" (*ZG,* issue 81/3). What we thought was art was only the image of art. Now the actuality will replace the image. The Futurists had similar thoughts about the contents of Italian museums. In fact, just about everyone who has given serious thought to art in our century has given in, now and then, to such expectations.

I believe nonetheless that the Expressionist version of apocalypse has particular importance. Among Expressionists, Wassily Kandinsky is St. John the Divine. His short book, ***Concerning the Spiritual in Art,*** 1911, serves the movement as its Book of Revelation. It serves all of us that way. Nowhere in the writing that surrounds modern art is there a clearer set of hints of what apocalypse is to the radical imagination, and how it differs from the Scriptural variety. I should point out here that biblical apocalypse is still very much with us, in the imaginations of those who sustain their faith in the New Testament. The biblical interpretations of believers may be metaphorical, literary; or they may be astonishingly literal, as in the fundamentalist exegeses that take the appearance of the numerals 666 in commercial packaging codes as the Mark of the Beast (Rev., 13, xviii), a sign that the machinery of the Last Judgment is already in gear. Radical art and literature substitute the self for God, Coleridge's "creative imagination" for the divinity of Genesis, so the primary difference between Kandinsky's writing and St. John the Divine's is in the use of the word "I."

Neither uses it very much, so the word has plenty of context in both books—a detailed backdrop against which to make the outlines of ego clear. That backdrop, the text itself, appears in each instance as a privileged emanation from the writer's "I." St. John is the conduit through which radiant images flood for the benefit of all those, including himself, who will be saved, absorbed into the godhead at the source of the vision. Scriptural apocalypse destroys the world from all individual points of view, recreating every atom as those granted grace are reborn into a state beyond selfhood. By contrast—a contrast that could not, so far as I can see, be any greater—Kandinsky's vision of the future, the time for building "the spiritual pyramid which will some day reach to heaven," is the product of his own "inner life." Further, the redeemed and redemptive artist never asks himself to give over his individuality. (For the "pyramid," see M.T.H. Sandler's 1914 translation of *Concerning the Spiritual in Art* (1911), Dover Publications. All further unattributed page citations refer to this text.) Still further, and this is what makes Kandinsky a modern artist instead of an occultist mystagogue like Mme. Blavatsky and others he so much admired, his inner life begets the forms of his paintings and drawings.

Kandinsky intended to create, not merely record, a vision of ultimate destinies—his own, first of all. This is clearest in his "Improvisations," a group of 31 paintings with variants that served as the subject of an exhibition in the spring and summer of 1981 at the National Gallery in Washington, D. C. E. A. Carmean, Jr. organized the show. He found it possible to assemble only about half of the entire series. Some of the "Improvisations" exist now only as studies. Others are in inaccessible collections. However, Carmean was able to hang a number of them side-by-side with their studies, and to show how motifs from the *Improvisations* migrated to the woodcuts for Kandinsky's book of poems, *Klänge (Sounds,* 1913). It was a small show with a dense texture.

His reading of the entire series, as set forth in the brochure accompanying the exhibition, is aggressively narrative. In *Improvisation 7* (1910), Carmean sees schematic waves threatening all other forms with a final inundation. Extrapolating from slightly earlier quasi-figurative images of the Blue Rider, Carmean interprets the elegantly squiggling lines of *Number 20* (1911) as the Horsemen of the Apocalypse. In *Number 27* and a study for *Number 25* (both 1912), rather larval forms signify lovers in the paradise that appears in the wake of apocalypse. A bit later in the series, paradise disappears. *Number 28a* (1912) shows tubes spouting loops—cannons belching smoke. Destruction continues. Or perhaps Kandinsky's disjunctive narrative suggests that ordinary time unravels under the pressures of prophecy fulfilled. Carmean carefully ties the artist's vision to the Book of Revelation, his main point being that Kandinsky's own comments make such interpretations possible, despite the long-nurtured supposition that the "Improvisations" from 1910 on show non-figurative art coming into being before one's eyes.

When Kandinsky talks of "the internal truth only art can divine, which only art can express by those means of expression which are hers alone" (*Concerning the Spiritual in Art*), one might insist on hearing a proclamation of autonomous—i.e., abstract—form. And when he discusses his rejection of academic modeling, a tactic designed to hasten art's exit from "the material realm," he uses the word "abstract" (at least in Sandler's translation). Yet Carmean convincingly insists that the "Improvisations" must be "decoded," and that the message thus revealed has a story line. After working one's way through Carmean's exhibition notes, it's hard to remember that these paintings ever counted as abstract. They crawl with emblematic presences.

Carmean has officially pulled the rug out from under those who rushed to judge the "Improvisations" non-figurative. And his presentation of studies and variants, all very close to the primary images, gives a disconcerting jolt to those who took the term "improvisation" literally and claimed Kandinsky as an ancestor figure for the Action Painters. For Kandinsky the issue was not facture but the nature of experience: his "Impressions" are "direct impression[s] of outward nature," while an "Improvisation" is a "largely unconscious, spontaneous expression of inner character" (*Concerning . . .*)—and thus easily reinscribed, once made manifest on paper or canvas. In other words, though dominant motifs of the "Improvisations" originate in unpremeditated gestures of the hand, they froze into reusable pictograms the moment they appeared.

Shuffled and reshuffled, these pictograms give the "Improvisations" a lively formal appeal. But if we find ourselves admiring only the formal qualities of the series, we overlook Kandinsky's purpose for what he called, in a disapproving echo of Walter Pater, "'art for art's sake'" (*Concerning . . .*). On the road to Kandinsky's apocalypse, the esthetic and the spiritual were to join as one prophetic power. That was his intention, and we shouldn't ignore it, because he means the forms of his art as forms of his "inner life." He put his will to redemption on such intimate terms with his imagination that he leaves the two indistinguishable. His is an art for prophecy's sake.

Concerning the Spiritual in Art describes the relationship of the artist and his times as a dialectic whose giddy ascension turns subjectivity objective. In this text, thanks to Kandinsky's lack of focus, one doesn't really know what he means by subjective and objective. This is not a problem, at least not for him. As he says, "It is impossible to theorize about this ideal of art" (*Concerning . . .*), but he makes his key point radiantly clear: in his universe, he is the creator. Perhaps he is only a demiurge in the period of the "Improvisations," but an apocalypse approaches that will raise him to the stature of a stand-in for Jehovah. Kandinsky quotes with horror the catch-phrase "God is dead," cliché already in 1911, then goes on to offer himself as a substitute, or at least one of those prophets, those "divine martyrs" (*Concerning . . .*), who prefigure God's resurrection as an artist. So the forms of his art are no less than the contents of a respiritualized world.

God was "dead" for Nietzsche because the self-created individual had replaced him as prime mover. Or it has become possible to imagine that had happened. God's death may have been in the works from the time of the High Renaissance, but only the Romantics dared offer the artist as a substitute. So it's interesting to look back from

J.M.W. Turner's apocalyptic imagery to that of the academic Benjamin West, who dutifully worked his way through six of the two dozen themes from Revelation that artists had taken up before him. The most fully finished of these works (several remained quick chalk drawings) show the frenzies of the sublime ruffling the feathers of Neoclassical decorum, as this is precisely what West's British classicizing required—see especially his *Death on a Pale Horse* (1817), at the Pennsylvania Academy. Disturbing no deeper niceties, the artist keeps his place in a scheme of things long-ordained by history, divine and secular. He touches Holy Scripture only to illustrate it. Turner is more audacious. Like his Parliaments burning or upland pastures strewn with, edelweiss, his themes from Revelation—*Angel Standing in the Sun* (1846), *Death on a Pale Horse* (ca. 1825-30)—give him occasion to assert the primacy of his own vision. We have shifted from the subject of apocalypse to the enactment of it, as the artist transforms agreed-upon appearances into colors and textures to be seen only in his art.

Many artists before Kandinsky enacted this drama, as did many after him. Few went about it as calmly as he. The script requires the leading (and, in a way, the only) actor in the scene to point forcibly at his own consciousness—the source, if not of a new heaven and earth, then of utterly original meanings for these things. This millennial gesture is so grand as to be laughable—or pathetic. To make it is to risk complete failure, and only a very partial success is possible in any case: the cultural margin on which even the most powerful intention can hold complete sway is very, very narrow. So artists in general try to avoid facing up to this inevitable failure. Irony is helpful here—that atmosphere of unmeaning, of desperate, ruinous play, that hangs over so many major revisions of self and world, from the late works of Byron to those of Robert Smithson. Kandinsky, by contrast, is appallingly sincere.

There is something archaic, half-conscious, about the confidence with which he spins out his revelations. The radical imagination, as Blake saw, is Luciferian, with origins in a gesture of disobedience to spiritual law and worldly usage. The artist recognizes no authority but that of his creative power, the generative energy whose proper work is to reveal itself as the source of all true meaning. When such ambitions make contact with mundane fact, the result is often a dismal spectacle—see Byron expiring of fever in Greece, having hoped to transfer his sense of poetic liberation to the political situation in the Ottoman Empire. He died, one might say, of the attempt to literalize the workings of his imagination. Most radical artists, no matter how ambitious, did not (and in our period, do not) make that mistake. The greater the claim an artist makes for his vision, the greater his need to protect it from the brutal unrolling of ordinary events. For all their distrust of traditional allegory, the Romantics became allegorists of a new (perhaps unconscious) kind: they taught themselves to read the banal texture of life for signs that the radical imagination was changing for the better the very

nature of existence. Hence Shelley's claim, simply silly from a certain point of view, that poets are the world's "secret legislators."

By 1825 or so, Shelleyan optimism was impossible. Yet ambitious painters and poets continued to make claims for the absolute powers of their creativity. As the 19th century ground on, writers began to say that such power could only make itself fully manifest in zones of mystical correspondence (Symbolism) or of "autonomous" formal development (Whistler). Among a hyper-conscious few—Baudelaire, Manet, Degas—the worldly limits on creative ambition produced bitterness, an anguish to be borne only in the dandy's detached condition. Yet such figures were no less Luciferian in their ambition than Shelley or Turner (himself a prey to Saturnine fits of spleen in his later years). Though artists began to hide away from the ordinary world in labyrinthine ironies, they still offered themselves as central to the universe of genuine meaning, and they still assumed that position with gestures of total disobedience to all external authority. They continued, in other words, to construct apocalyptic self-images, individualities which premise their mythic vitality on the death of God and the absence of all the claims made on ordinary people by ordinary life.

The radicality of most ambitious art is covert, so only initiated spirits sense the full force of its violence. As Barbey d'Aurevilley said, the dandy's joke is to behave so properly that his behavior becomes a critique of propriety. But even at its most slyly secretive, Romantic and modernist art is haunted by the ghosts of all the meanings, values and ordinary affections it must kill off in order to live. This encrusts our most serious imagery with the esthetic equivalent of blood-guilt.

Kandinsky takes no note of this. He moves with trancelike sureness toward the epiphany of his esthetic godhead, as if a numbness pervades his spirit as he nears the brink of apocalypse. He claims ultimate meanings for his art, yet remains innocent of the implications—all the deep changes in personal, social and political life that would occur if his vision were somehow to make its energies felt in the larger world. And he remains innocent of the knowledge that such success is doubtful. Kandinsky is a visionary in blinkers. His intimacy with apocalypse is intense but half-conscious. And this is remarkable, for the apocalypse in question is that of consciousness itself rendered nearly God-like in its reach and clarity.

Every artist in the Romantic-modernist tradition wears Kandinsky's blinkers on occasion. Finding that irony is of limited use in dealing with the ambiguities and absurdities—the failures—of radical art, artists must sometimes resort to the expedient of refusing to see. Expressionist blindness is thus emblematic, not a quirk of that style but an extreme instance of a trait seen in ambitious artists of all sorts. Yet Kandinsky seems permanently blinkered, eternally entranced, and this is what gives him his special relationship to apocalypse. He hovers on its brink for decades, incessantly purifying his vision, feeling neither doubt nor the need for those ironies with which other modernists deflect their sense of failure. We consider ourselves more sophisticated than he, more inveterately ironic, yet all of us are conscious, now and then, of blank spots in consciousness—vacuums created by those acts of censorship by which we suppress our questions about the futility of radical esthetics.

Kandinsky has the look of a heroic, unwanted *döppleganger* of us all, with his inability to see that he was overlooking something important: the procreative hubris that, once noted by Marcel Duchamp, for instance, drove him into the ironic labyrinth of his middle years. This hall of mirrors was the world perceived as the unconscious of radical esthetics, not the emanation of prophetic vision but a quirky, self-piloting urban landscape-machine around whose odd corners works of art popped up readymade. Duchamp was willing to tinker with a puzzle of form and meaning so long as its intricacies reassured the spectator that no millennial answers would be forthcoming, even if the puzzle let itself be solved. This citified, petit-bourgeois fastidiousness takes us a long way from Kandinsky's pastoral of primordial form.

I should point out that not all Expressionists were such Titans of serene unseeing as Kandinsky. Max Beckmann and George Grosz, for a major and a minor example, were as ironic as any Parisian (and far more sardonic). As for the *Brücke* and Blue Rider groups, nearly everyone on their rosters suffered an incessant, dithering anxiety. God the father is not all that easy to replace. Even estheticized, blood-guilt is a dreadful burden. Revved up to panic levels, Expressionist anxiety projected itself outward. Apocalyptic consciousness could carry on if the immanent crisis were imagined to be external, borne into view on the terrifying side of current events. And current events obliged in the early years of this century with rural dislocation, restive cities, the prospect of war. Frederick S. Levine quotes a prospectus Franz Marc wrote in 1912 for *The Blue Rider Almanac:* "Art today proceeds along paths which our fathers never imagined possible: one stands before the new work as in a dream and hears the apocalyptic riders in the air . . ." (*The Apocalyptic Vision*, 1975). The artist struggled to believe that politics, economics, the coming war—all the frightful portents and happenings outside himself—were the cause of his dread. Thus he avoided facing up to the immense (perhaps unfulfillable) responsibilities brought down on him by the project of pushing individuality to the edge of apocalypse, and over.

At present there are young artists who try to outsmart the pressures of their ambition by putting their imagery to work in the protest against nuclear war, as if *that* were the sole cause of their terror. Or they comment on social and political pathologies in a more or less Expressionist manner. This is to evade the burden of radical art while asking credit for struggling against the imperfections of life, much as the original Expressionists did. Like Franz Marc or Ludwig Kirchner, these artists of the present day flee

from a consciousness of the nature of modernist consciousness, its presumptuousness and guilt, its failures and consequent addiction to irony. Marc tried to remain primitive while attaining to radical sophistication, an impossible dream familiar in New York since the time of the studiously inarticulate Action Painter. In 1915 Marc wrote, from the front, of his "feeling for the animalistic, for the 'pure animals' . . ." (Levine). Kandinsky enjoyed without effort the innocence of the art-making animal, so he never felt the anxieties that might have driven him to claim that the cannons of his "Improvisations" were those of World War I. A collector asked him in 1914 if his images of apocalypse referred to the current conflict. Carmean's exhibition brochure quotes Kandinsky's answer: "'No, not this war,' the artist replied . . . the pictorial image recorded 'that a terrible struggle was going on in the spiritual sphere'"—the sphere delimited by the reach of Kandinsky's own creative powers, as they battled toward glory through "the soulless life of the present" (*Concerning . . .*).

Season after season throughout his life, Kandinsky's "inner need" returned him to that battlefield. One of his few concessions to the world and to others was to try to give universal import to the apocalyptic rebirth of his spirit. Thus he stuck it out at the Bauhaus until his esthetic, with its unshakable focus on himself, came into unbearable conflict with Hannes Meyer, the director of the Dessau Bauhaus, a leftist with no use for Kandinsky's "bourgeois" individuality. Earlier, in the days of the "Improvisations," Kandinsky had labored to invigorate a fast succession of artists' groups, of which the Blue Rider is the best known. This was Kandinsky's Munich period, the subject of an exhibition put on in early '82 at the Guggenheim Museum.

I have no hope of doing justice to this startling assemblage of paintings, illustrated books, stained glass windows, toys, clothes and much, much more. The show's curator, Peg Weiss, seemed to have tumbled the attic of Kandinsky's Munich out along the ramps of the Guggenheim. The Munich Academy and the Munich Secession, the Neue Kunstlervereiningung München, the Blue Rider and a group called Phalanx were all represented by work from dozens of hands. Marc, Auguste Macke, Paul Klee and Gabriele Münter are familiar figures, the Symbolist-academic Franz von Stuck and the Finnish artist-craftsman Akselli Gallen-Kallela far less so. There was a cluster of watercolors and studies Kandinsky did around the time of the "Improvisations," though Weiss included only one of the latter—*Number 6* (1909), whose motifs range from the funeral march to arisen souls and on to the waves of the deluge that destroys so that some may be reborn.

For the most part, woodcuts from 1903-07 represented Kandinsky here. Symbolist evocations of Russian folklore and fairy tale, they shimmer with the dark, remembered light of childhood, a fog of nostalgia that, lifting, leaves a modernist sensibility stranded in the harsh light of its yen for an apocalyptic tomorrow. The Guggenheim exhibition included some of Kandinsky's most cloying images, yet his Symbolist sentimentality never bogged down his inventiveness—his was clearly the motor that kept running when others' sputtered and stalled. One felt the artist's "inner need" pervading this assembly of works, yet the sheer weight of his colleagues' lesser art overpowered Kandinsky's, dragging his apocalypse down to well-kept regions where a genteel, dutifully liberal application of radical styles to everyday objects counted as radicality itself.

This is not Expressionism's worst fate. On the right, the style's decorative gentility gives way to violence. Emil Nolde, for a prime example, is always aggressive, never more than half-conscious. He acknowledges the blood-guilts of the radical self, but not for what they are. In his Expressionism, the apocalyptic self offers its aggression as a natural force, an instinctual hence innocent up-welling of primal energies. That way lies fascism, and Nolde tried to take it. The Nazis only let him go so far along that path, which leads to the Romantic artist-as-führer—or führer-as-Romantic-artist. Preserving his own ambitions in a form too grandiose, Nolde could not be directly useful to Hitler's regime, which expected its official art to send a haze of "classical" propriety through public spaces. They saved Expressionism for political rallies and wall posters.

In Kandinsky's Munich, painting is a decorative art unfortunately deprived of embroidery's tactile appeal. No wonder Kandinsky went back to Russia at the time of the Revolution. There, events proceeded at the scale of his own self-image. And there, for a time, he found it possible to mesh the workings of his personal epiphanies with those of Bolshevik politics. What happened later on the plane of Bauhaus ideology happened on the littered ground of Revolutionary fact: Kandinsky found that Marxism had no room for the singularity of his imagination, no tolerance for the imperatives of his "inner need." So he moved back to Germany, and then—after leaving the Bauhaus—to Paris, where he lived out his days in the revered isolation to which his esthetic had been trying to condemn him for three decades. The Bauhaus and Paris periods of Kandinsky's career are the subjects of exhibitions to come at the Guggenheim.

The color and line set forth with such clarity in St. John's Book of Revelation are, to my inward eye, far more splendid than Kandinsky's. The angels and beasts of Revelation, the tales of fire and frogs leaping from mouths, the city of "pure gold, like unto clear glass," form a spectacle surpassing anything in 20th-century art. Yet that spectacle appears across a vast, unbridgeable distance, and it is necessary to say why. St. John asks us to let ourselves be absorbed by the imagery of his vision. We who sustain, however ironically, the radical traditions in the art of the two last centuries will not do this. We refuse to be absorbed, defining ourselves by this refusal. In one of his prophetic books, *Jerusalem* (1804-20), Blake says, "I must create a system or be enslav'd by another man's" (plate 10, line 20). This is sheer imperative, the inner need felt by a kind of self that was new in those days. The imperative, like the self, is irrational, if you like: "I will not Reason & Compare: my business is to Create" (plate 10, line 21).

Beginning with Romanticism, even critics claim to be creators, and apocalyptic too: in the moment of critical vision, a work of art attains a redeeming radiance. Or that is the ambition. Irony usually tempers it. At any rate, art and criticism in radical traditions cannot *serve* apocalypse. They must be apocalyptic, at least in intent, or admit utter defeat. In Revelation, 10, x, St. John eats the angel's book. Painters usually show him kneeling and receiving the book into his hands, though Dürer has him tucking in at one corner of the object—ingesting imagery so that he may in turn be ingested by it. The play of color, shape and light in Revelation emanates from a god with the power to absorb the ineffabilities of the individual self. In Kandinsky's *Concerning the Spiritual in Art,* those ineffabilities of the self *are* the emanations of power, made manifest as the artist fulfills the need of color and form to reveal its "inner meaning" (1911). By this exceedingly vague process, art guides the world out of its materialist nightmare (*Concerning . . .*). Kandinsky looked forward to seeing all of existence newly spiritualized—redeemed through the medium of the artist's own being. "The artist," says Kandinsky, "must be blind to . . . conventions of form, deaf to the . . . demands of his particular age. He must watch only the trend of the inner need, and harken to its words alone" (*Concerning . . .*). He must, in other words, treat his own imagination as the regenerative center of the universe; further, he must remain deaf and blind to evidence that no one's imagination has the power to play this role.

This blindness and deafness appear in most of the artists we call Expressionist—in a form absolute in Kandinsky, wrenched by panic in Marc, by fascist ambition in Nolde. Even in the politically liberal images of Kandinsky's Munich circle, this handicap persists as a fixation on the nuances of individual consciousness. Reflexive focus is so steady in Romantic and modernist art as to count after all as a sort of unconsciousness: the artist dazzled into unseeing by reflections of himself, those idealized dreams of his own being from which he makes his art.

When world and self begin to feel interchangeable, it is doubt—not prophetic fervor—that redeems. Major art in our period courts those failures that force the imagination into contact with zones, comprising the vastly greater portion of the world, that resist its creative powers. Consciousness approaches completeness when it begins to see its limits, its necessary fragmentedness. But even with the benefit of this (seeming) paradox, radical sensibilities show some of the willful deafness and blindness of Kandinsky and his Expressionist crowd. We all share in some part their apocalyptic hubris. This doesn't make us tragic. It only ensures that Expressionism will always have for us the emblematic value of figuring forth the primitive desires and dangers at the heart of our sophistication.

Marian Pester (essay date 1983)

SOURCE: "Kandinsky: The Owl of Minerva," in *Passion and Rebellion: The Expressionist Heritage,* edited by Stephen Eric Bronner and Douglas Kellner, J. F. Bergin Publishers, Inc., 1983, pp. 250-75.

[*In the following essay, Pester deems Kandinsky and his work an embodiment of the revolutionary ideas spreading throughout Europe during the early twentieth century.*]

Kandinsky (1866-1944) was one of the foremost philosophers of the abstract expressionist movement in painting. He was an artist of unsurpassed lucidity who refused to choose for the "analytical" against the "mystical/lyrical," and successfully *materialized* his vision in oils, watercolor, and graphics. At once artist and intellectual, he was the common point of a number of creative vectors, among them Dada, Surrealism, German Expressionism, the Bauhaus, Constructivism, and the many other lively trends in early Soviet art. For example, as a poet, Kandinsky contributed to the Dada review *Cabaret Voltaire* in 1916; he was instrumental in introducing the *Neue Sezession* group of Berlin to the Munich *Neue Kunstlervereinigung* and to the Russian Suprematists and Rayonnists: his nephew was Kojeve, the professor of philosophy who introduced Hegel to the Generation of 1905 in Paris; he was a major figure in the Bauhaus and personally recruited a number of participants to that unique experiment. In effect Kandinsky formed an individual center of gravity around which the ideas of revolutionary art revolved in the 1910-1933 period, a living symbol of what those ideas sought to embody.

Kandinsky's background and character were very unlike those of most of the young artists involved in the new movement. He was born into a well-to-do Russian family which at one point had been transported to Siberia for anti-czarist activity. His father, after financing the son's lengthy course of study in political economy and law at the University of Moscow, still proved willing to support Kandinsky's belated decision (at age 30) to study painting in Munich.

In contrast to most of his younger, less disciplined colleagues, Kandinsky's relationship to art was always that of a scholar, experimenter, and publicist—almost a technician. His theoretical writings on the nature of painting and the meaning of abstractionism are among the most comprehensive and striking of any modern artist. Moreover, his work was never conducted in romantic isolation, but always in the full light of journalistic publicity, association, cultivation of a hoped-for mass "audience," and the sort of quasi-political organizing efforts typical among movements of the period (Futurism, Constructivism, Dada, and so on).

The year 1912 was the cutting edge: a new "spiritualism," like the social revolution, was springing to life simultaneously in different fields and cultures, and individuals embarked upon greatly varied projects were to recognize *affinities of spirit* with one another's efforts. In Russia the mass strikes were building like a wave, soon to topple centuries of stonelike social edifice. To Western Europe came the calm before the storm: not even the war proved able to consume the energies about to burst forth in this period.

The most sensitive gave voice to—or "mirrored"—the underlying longings for transcendence, immediate appropriation of technology's potential, the freeing of man from labor and squalor, the transformation of everyday life according to the laws of beauty and the "luxury" of art. This longing for *realization* was, paradoxically, the ideological motive for the turn toward nonobjective, nonrepresentational, abstract art—a turn led by Kandinsky.

Art had been steadily evolving, mediated by the capitalist market, into an existential racket, perpetrated in the self-interest of its practitioners and their speculator patrons. Perhaps the most piercing whistle blown on this "Art" was Dada, a revolt which ripened most fully in France and Germany, and culminated in the temporary entry of the Surrealist Group into the French Communist Party, and in the politicization of Expressionism in Berlin and Munich. With what savage joy Dada and its offspring attacked "art for art's sake," the "integrity" of the *objet d'art.* How little they cared for purity, for the confinement of art to the mirrored palace of contemplation. Escaping from Axel's Castle[1] only to be forced back into the hovel of Art, the European avant-garde carried out a series of artistic revolts, often with strong political overtones.

> Today, more than ever before, *the liberation of the mind,* the express aim of surrealism, demands as a primary condition, in the opinion of the surrealists, *the liberation of man,* which implies that we must struggle against our fetters with all the energy of despair. . . . Today more than ever before the surrealists entirely rely for the bringing about of the liberation of man upon the proletarian revolution.[2]

This spirit of revolt destroyed forever the possibility of good conscience in Art. What Hegel had foreseen— namely, *the end of representation* and the passage of Mind to increasingly direct knowledge of itself—had reached a point of no return, a point which coincided with the post-World War I social explosion against the outgrown forms of capitalist order: money, parliamentarism, laissez-faire market relations, the factory, and other alienating hierarchies of production for profit (all of these, too, being kinds of representation). "Representation," according to Hegel, was a product of the alienation of the Subject from its own content or powers, the historical emergence of the split between being and appearance. Speaking generally of Mind, he stated:

> In pressing forward to its true form of existence, consciousness will come to a point at which it lays aside its semblance of being hampered with what is foreign to it, with what is only for it and exists as an other; it will reach a position where appearance becomes identified with essence. . . .[3]

Relating this conception specifically to art, he wrote of its passage through the symbolic, classical, and romantic phases, culminating in

> the falling to pieces of Art, a process . . . which was due to an imitation of the objects of Nature in all the detail of their contingent appearance. . . . [4]

That is to say, Art-as-representation would come to an end when it had fully contemplated the world and made it a part of itself, when it was no longer seduced and "divided" (in Blake's sense) by appearance, but could penetrate the living mystery of its own experience. This demystification was, moreover, in Hegel's view, an ineluctable development.

How does one locate the work of Wassily Kandinsky within the general premise of the "end of representation"? It is our thesis here that Kandinsky may be said to have done for art (and oil painting in particular) what Hegel attributed to the great philosophical systems:

> When philosophy paints its gloomy picture, a form of life has grown old. Only when dusk starts to fall does the owl of Minerva spread its wings and fly. [5]

THE SIGNIFICANCE OF THE ABSTRACT

It is well known that photography provoked a severe crisis in easel painting. The effect was not instantaneous or total, but slowly, surely, the nature and aims of art had to be rediscovered and reconsidered. (A similar problem was faced by the theater with the advent of cinema). The camera simply caught more, from every angle; every pore and shadow, every cloud and wave could be eternalized. Thus the surface of things, whose reproduction had come to be seen as painting's *raison d'etre,* was looted once and for all by the mechanical competitor.

Notes for what was to become Kandinsky's abstractionist manifesto, *Concerning the Spiritual in Art,* as well as studies for what were to be the first purely nonobjective canvases ever produced, date back to 1901, although neither was to achieve full-fledged expression until 1910. Up to that point, Kandinsky had been obsessed with variations, increasingly free-form, on a horse-and-rider motif, a symbolic working-out of his personal struggle to resolve the reason/unconscious duality: "The horse bears the rider with strength and speed. But the rider guides the horse." [6]

In *Concerning the Spiritual in Art,* Kandinsky argued that abstraction was the necessary next step, the *revolutionizing perspective* which could free art of the false consciousness that had initially led to the crisis over photography's superior ability to represent reality. While recognizing that other artists would continue to fear "excluding the human" from their work, [7] since for them immateriality possessed as yet no "precise significance," Kandinsky considered abstraction to be the "left wing" of the new art movement, an "emergent great realism," a

departure more radical than any figurative mode, however "expressive." It is not hard to understand why he thought so: the entire tendency of post-Impressionism had been to abolish the primacy of the material object, the thing, in order to reveal that inner force which was the sole true "subject" of artistic knowing.

> The love visionaries, the hungry of soul, are ridiculed or considered mentally abnormal. . . . In such periods art ministers to lower needs and is used for material ends. . . . Objects remaining the same, their reproduction is thought to be the aim of art. [8]

Relinquishing the object offered the artist undreamed-of new freedom. *Concerning the Spiritual in Art* refers constantly to the image of a world choking on dead matter, on reifications which must be superseded in order to reverse the hardening process and release the dammed and vital flow of creative energies. Pure abstractionism for Kandinsky was primarily an intensification of man's struggle with matter. That this concern was not "escapist" is confirmed repeatedly in his own writings. The four chief works[9]—*Concerning the Spiritual in Art (Ueber das Geistige in der Kunst),* "On the Question of Form" ("Ueber die Formfrage"), "Reminiscences" ("Rückblicke"),* and *Point and Line to Plane (Punkt und Linie zur Fläche)*—radiate an ecstatic sense of history and a serene (if Manichean) confidence in the victory of "the white, fertilizing ray" of creativity over "the black, fatal hand" of blindness, hatred, fear of freedom, and insensate materialism. Whatanimates these writings is the desire that all evolving "new values" be *materialized,* and then—because "we should never make a god out of form"—that they should give way before still newer values.

It was also important to create an art freed of literary associations, of that oppressive narrative quality that stifled the potential development of visual language by tying it to readymade verbal categories. Painting was no longer to be a branch of conventional literature, telling a "story in pictures," but a world of its own.

Klee put it thus, writing of the tendency of modern art toward abstraction:

> [The artist] is, perhaps unintentionally, a philosopher, and if he does not, with the optimists, hold this world to be the best of all possible worlds, nor to be so bad that it is unfit to serve as a model, yet he says: "In its present shape, it is not the only possible world." [10]

Abstractionism was to enable the artist and audience to experience alternative realities, a different order of things, another possible cosmos. By stepping outside the given and offering an unanticipated perspective, nonobjective painting played its own role in the disintegration of old verities which characterized the death throes of the nineteenth century.

There can be no doubt that Kandinsky was conscious of this broader, world-historical significance of his abstract

Expressionism. He alluded repeatedly (as did his collaborators on the 1912 *Blaue Reiter Almanac*) to "a great awakening," a "new religion arising" as yet without prophet or leader:

> Today is one of freedom such as characterizes great germinative periods. . . . And sometimes when the human soul is gaining greater strength, art also grows in power, for the two are inextricably connected and complementary. Conversely, at those times when the soul tends to be choked by materialist lack of belief, art becomes purposeless, and it is said that art exists for art's sake alone. . . .
>
> The causes of the necessity to move forward and upward—through sweat and suffering, evil and torments—are obscure. . . . The path often seems blocked or destroyed. But someone always comes to the rescue—someone like ourselves in everything, but with a secretly implanted power of "vision."
>
> He sees and points out. This high gift (often a heavy burden) at times he would gladly relinquish. But he cannot. Scorned and disliked, he drags the heavy weight of resisting humanity forward and upward.[11]

To our ears these words perhaps sound archaic and naive. It is difficult to imagine the (relative) innocence and confident teleology of this former time, much less to tolerate the application of Christian imagery to the problems of art. Nonetheless, the content or spirit of such passages endures, if one is willing to look beyond their outmoded form.

As art is precisely the *sensuous* mediation of self-consciousness;[12] let us now turn to the paintings in which Kandinsky made his vision concrete.

THE WORK ITSELF: THEORY AND MATERIALIZATION

Kandinsky's work went through at least six distinct phases. First came canvases reminiscent of Russian folk and religious art, then impressionistic studies and landscapes, already notable for their fascination with color and disinterest in human subjects. Studying in Munich at this time, he recalled "wandering about with a paintbox, feeling in my heart like a hunter." Natural phenomena, which aroused in him strong emotions, communicated themselves as bright, inchoate, yet distinct visions: visual metaphors.

There followed a rather Fauvist period: brilliant-hued towns, animals, fairy-tale figures on horseback in transfigured night. But the practice of rendering particular objects in themselves began to strike him as absurd and pointless. What he wished to capture was the ontological ground in which these particularities participated and upon which they moved and reveled in their being. The last of Kandinsky's conventional works were done while he was already, with a mixture of patience and impatience, experimenting with creating his own autonomous forms in a series of "improvisations," first in pen and ink and aquarelle, and later in lithographs and oils. The "objects" they depicted, although obviously suggested by a richly *lived* and observant life, seemed increasingly to refer to nothing beyond themselves. From *Point and Line to Plane,* written in 1926 to serve as a Bauhaus educational text, it is clear that Kandinsky studied many varied forms—crystals, star clusters, architectural drawings, construction frameworks (e.g., the Eiffel Tower), flowers, microorganisms, alphabets. The new forms were meant to suggest the energy state of matter which, though just as real as mass, was rarely *seen* by man as he sleep-walked (or rather, did a forced march) through existence.

By 1910, Kandinsky felt himself "ready at last" to make a complete break with the final vestiges of representation in his work. The horse and its rider, the slant of a village roof, the curve of blue mountain in the distance—these forms freed themselves entirely from verisimilitude and took flight with visible joy. The ability to make this break he ascribed to a *maturation of the spirit of the age* within himself; indeed, that Kandinsky became the first pure abstractionist was a matter of chance, as others like Franz Kupka and even Arthur Dove were following closely upon the same path. Yet Kandinsky's work is especially revealing of this "dematerialization process": one can *see* the objects and their fixed associations twist and turn upon the canvas in convulsive beauty, seeking liberation.

Several works after the "spiritual turning point" of 1910 were entitled "Improvisation" and given a number. But Kandinsky's method remained constant throughout: before each completed composition came numerous preliminary sketches, "Impressions," in which each individual element of the whole was painstakingly arranged and rearranged until the proper harmony was achieved. *Point and Line to Plane* is a veritable encyclopedia of the various types of lines, forms, colors (by themselves or in combination), and other configurations which must be put into resonant relationship with one another on the canvas:

> Only by means of a microscopic analysis can the science of art lead to a comprehensive synthesis, which will extend far beyond the confines of art into the realm of the "oneness" of the "human" and the "divine."[13]

He begins by dissecting the Point, defined with a certain mathematical poetry as "the highest degree of restraint which, nevertheless, speaks, . . . the ultimate and most singular *union of silence and speech.*" Then he proceeds, uncannily like a natural scientist, "to determine wherein the living conforms to law" in painterly composition. Such a highly deliberate method of composition could not be more foreign to the romantic theory of "genius." Yet the finished works of this fourth period have about them a look of spontaneous and natural existence, of internal *necessity,* that makes their actual laboratory-style genesis seem implausible.

The fourth period in particular, longest of the six, saw the emergence of most of the typical and distinctive forms comprising Kandinsky's "language of the eye." They swim or float about some unseen center of gravity: powerful black lines and curves, translucent amoeba-like creatures, jagged rainbows of color, spheres (often deep blue), triangles, swirls reminiscent of gas clouds, targets, orbiting planets, arrows, chessboard grids. More metaphorically, they resemble the tracks of subatomic particles; power lines, cityscapes viewed from above, untranslatable hieroglyphs, engineering blueprints, and in particular the notational systems of certain modern composers.

Kandinsky may not have been aware that he had converged, from the opposite direction, upon the same symbols at which modern music had arrived as it distanced itself from the assumptions of classical tonality. In any event, Kandinsky, the voluptuary of color, was himself a frustrated musician; like Klee, he had first experienced his creativity as a musically-talented child, and ever afterward regretted that his own metier could only *suggest* the total immateriality of which music was capable. He often spoke of painting in musical terms, referring to "the inner sound" of a work:

> Color is the keyboard, the eyes are the hammers, the soul is the piano with many strings. The artist is the hand that plays, touching one key or another purposively, to cause vibrations in the soul.[14]

While at the Bauhaus he experimented with the *Gesamtkunstwerk*—for instance, **"The Yellow Sound,"** which was a kind of tone poem enacted within a three-dimensional painting, integrating color, words, music, and drama.

Colors, instead of music, turned out to be Kandinsky's medium as an artist, but he continued to hear as well as see them:

> Blue is the typical heavenly color; the ultimate feeling it creates is one of rest. When it sinks almost to black, it echoes a grief that is hardly human. It becomes an infinite engrossment in solemn moods. As it grows lighter it becomes more indifferent and affects us in a remote and neutral fashion, like a high, cerulean sky. The lighter it grows, the more it loses resonance, until it reaches complete quiescence, in other words, white. In music a light blue is like a flute, a darker blue a cello; a still darker blue the marvelous double bass; and the darkest blue of all, an organ.[15]

The serene blue sphere to be found in most of the "Improvisations" and "Compositions" represents a sort of celestial vantage-point from which the spectator gazes down at these systems of color and energy as upon an "ideal plane." The "subject" of each canvas is the universe itself viewed from a different angle and in a different energy state.

Kandinsky's search for the laws of the soul and senses culminated during the 30's in a cool geometric style, his "Bauhaus period"; the glowing radiation had lessened, like planets slowly crystalizing out of clouds of glittering dust. The compositions no longer appear to have been spontaneously improvised. This is considered by some to be the "reification phase" of Kandinsky's vision. In terms of the social reality to which that vision was hypersensitive, such crystalization mirrored the growing *stasis* of the postwar revolutionary movement, from Weimar Germany to the USSR. The new style further reflected, in its rigidity and almost excessive self-containment, the *implosion* of that movement. This fifth phase is severe, mechanical, inorganic. For his part, Kandinsky felt the "coldness" to be the coldness of *necessity,* a necessity which his undertaking was meant all along to unearth.[16]

But it would be unwise to make of Kandinsky's development a mere mirror of general events. His sixth and last period, arising out of Parisian exile, has been called a "great synthesis," and witnessed the reintroduction of motion, warmth, organicism, playfulness, and grace, while retaining the clarity and definition of form attained during the Bauhaus years. Such works as **Relations** and **Sky Blue** resemble delightful microscopic worlds where tiny beings sport in harmony, and this vision can hardly be said to "reflect" society during the Nazi occupation of France. At a certain point Kandinsky's project became transfixed, as it were, and it is at such points that the autonomous development of the individual can be said to overcome external determination.

SPIRITUALISM VS. TECHNOLOGY

Kandinsky and his collaborators may certainly be considered prophets and leaders of *art's* spiritual awakening, but what the *Blaue Reiter* seemed further to be pointing toward was an awakening of the entire social organism, hence toward some political manifestation as well. What sort of political movement did these prophecies presage? Did they, too, express the sort of vitalist, irrationalist revolt that led so many artists sickened by modernity to the dream of fascism? There are several ways of approaching this problem, but an analysis of the following quotation from Victor Aubertin, a typical prewar protofascist utterance, will help develop a "political" interpretation of where Kandinsky stood:

> Art is dying of the masses and of materialism. It dies because the land it needs is all built up, the land of naïvete and of illusions. . . . On each national holiday a joint toast to art and science is proposed; perhaps they mean one and the same to the idiot. But they are deadly enemies; where one of them exists, the other flees. . . . [17]

Perhaps a wiser formulation might be, "Where one advances, the other recedes." Wiser still, to point out that the knowns and unknowns of the universe are not finite, like a glass either half full or half empty, so that an activity does not have to be seen as *either* art *or* not-art, but as a process whereby both known and unknown develop and extend one another, ad infinitum. At any rate, it can be granted: art is not the same as science. And what of this? As though art does not act precisely to make the unknown *known,* conscious, "scientific"; as though there were no intimate historical relationship between the two. Or perhaps, as the quotation suggests, the role of art is to *keep* the unknown unknown, to make sure the stone of mystery remains unturned to light? If so, one can no longer speak of freedom as a property of art: rather, of willful blindness, the enforcement of mystification.

Such static notions as the art/science (technology) dualism derive in the end from what might be called the resentment of consciousness. Humans are conscious: this is the Fall, the human tragedy. The religious *Weltanschauung* gradually degenerated from a fertile sense of wonder to a stifling refusal to take responsibility ("usurp divine power") for the preeminent role of humanity within evolving nature. To recognize and affirm this role constitutes, for all mysticism, the sin of pride, the Original Sin. Hence the dark wish to keep things veiled: the mystic shuts his eyes to save his feckless innocence. What art (the creative process) has unearthed, he forcibly relegates to the superstitious backwaters of the brain. It is an act of bad faith.[18]

The core of Kandinsky's art and philosophy could not possess a nature more antithetical to the sentiments of a mystic like Aubertin. The evidence is everywhere in his writings and canvases; it is almost always "internal" evidence, however, as Kandinsky gave scarcely a thought in his life to politics as such. But a consideration of his itinerary suggests (at worst) a mere desire to work in peace, and a principled commitment to the free development of his ideas and their communication to others through active associations of like-minded artists.

On the relation of art to scientific knowledge or technology, Kandinsky was always crystal clear:

—The blind following of scientific precept is less blameworthy than its blind and purposeless rejection. At least the former produces an imitation of material objects which may have some use.

—Thought, which although a product of the spirit can be defined with exact science, is material, but of a fine and not a coarse substance.

—The ideal balance between the head (the conscious moment) and the heart (the unconscious moment, intuition) is a law of creation, a law as old as the human race.

—The final abstract expression of every art is *number*.

Such statements tend to cast doubt on the opinion held by some that in philosophy Kandinsky was a complete Bergsonian, for despite Bergson's attempts to integrate "the analytical" into his theory of creative evolution, he persisted in viewing intuition as the one true wellspring of creation.

In Kandinsky's earlier years he had feared, as had many of his contemporaries, that science would become wholly subservient to the dead bourgeois concept of matter, but in the 20's and 30's Kandinsky saw that science had moved away from positivism, its concerns were with synthesis and process, and had thus come closer to what artists since 1910 had been concerned with.[19]

He spoke in **"Reminiscences"** of the tremendous impact that the splitting of the atom had had upon him, how it confirmed his belief that "nothing is absolute," that all lies in the relations among dynamic forces. Writing in 1912, he noted that:

The theory of electrons, that is, of waves in motion, designed to replace matter completely, finds at this moment bold champions who overstep here and there the limits of caution and perish in the conquest of the new scientific fortress.

Whatever the allusion to "perishing" may mean here, it is clear Kandinsky felt he had allies in the new physics. Still later, writing for *Cahiers d'Art* in 1935, he stated that modern (relativistic) physics was seeking "to rediscover forgotten relationships between the smallest phenomena, and between these phenomena and first principles. . . . "

It was precisely the *relativity* of the new physics which the National Socialists found especially distasteful and "Jewish," and it is no accident that the Bauhaus—along with Jewish organizers, intellectuals, academics, and writers—was among the first to feel the wrath of "true German" restoration of the Absolute.[20] Kandinsky perfectly symbolized, in fact, the sort of "rootless cosmopolitan" and "restless element" the fascists feared. This passage from **Point and Line to Plane,** on the mission of the Bauhaus, reveals an attitude that was expelled from Germany in 1933:

It can be maintained altogether without exaggeration that a science of art erected on a broad foundation must be international in character: it is interesting, but certainly not sufficient, to create an exclusively European art theory.

Thus, whereas a central tenet of fascist ideology held that science and the scientific method, by their very nature, violated the necessarily irrational basis of life, Kandinsky's two-sided approach merely noted that "perpetual corrections are necessary from the angle of the irrational," lest perception become overdetermined and formalized. For him, art *conveyed thought to the senses.* "To speak of mystery in terms of mystery. Is this not content? . . . Man speaks to man of the superhuman—the *language* of art." On the pseudo-question of whether man is "permitted" to apprehend the universe, then, Kandinsky was quite sure that he is.

One further note: Kandinsky's passing interest in Theosophy has nourished the interpretation that his thought lies well within the mystic-spiritual tradition. Further definition is required here. First, there exists no hard and fast division between "materialism" and "spiritualism" when one is dealing with dialectical thought.[21] For this reason Hegel by no means needs to be "stood on his head" in order to deliver himself of profound insights into the material development of society. Dialectical thought entirely transcends such a dichotomy, which is then seen to be a derivative problem. It derives from the real distinction, that between dialectics and reification.

Second, Kandinsky's was not the only enthusiastic mind to have been seduced by the totalizing power of an essentially *static* dialectic. The static and dynamic dialectics in fact complement and even provide correctives to one another. Yeats, indeed, displayed a movement which is the reverse of Kandinsky's: drawn initially to the socialism of William Morris, he repudiated it as a vanity of vanities and embraced the timeless antagonism of what he termed the "primary" and "antithetical."

Finally, Kandinsky's involvement with Madame Blavatsky's Secret Doctrine was never thorough or long-lived. In his own writings we find scarce mention of it. Perhaps this hesitation was due to his characteristic mistrust of organized movements; at one point he refers to his skepticism regarding Theosophy's "excessive anticipation of definite answers in lieu of immense question marks."[22] Certainly the bitter infighting and mean-spirited squabbles over doctrine that plagued the Theosophical Society cannot have appealed to him. In any case, too much has been made of the connection.

INTERNAL NECESSITY

There is a further dimension to Kandinsky's itinerary: the backward Soviet Union demanded an art that was explicitly practical, a dynamic architectural and mechanical art which reflected the urgent need of the new state to industrialize before it was overcome by internal and external pressures. Kandinsky was a highly-educated middle-class man at the moment of the Revolution; he thought it "revolutionary," on the contrary, to be unconcerned with "practical-useful applications," and abhorred the tyrannical, technocratic implications of "production for use." The point, he felt, was not to subordinate creativity to utility, but to *gain control* over the creative process. Like the German Idealists, whose philosophical systems better reflected the achievements of the French Revolution than did the writings of their French contemporaries, Kandinsky had already gone beyond the aesthetic sensibility hegemonic in the young USSR.

This sensibility, in great part a breathlessly condensed and millenarian version of Renaissance-Industrial Revolution ideology, itself initially took the form of the strictest abstraction, but demanded a "constructive," task-oriented, utilitarian commitment from the artist. In *Isms of Art,* El Lissitzky declared:

> The Constructivists look at the world through the prism of technology. . . . The shortsighted see therein only the machine. Constructivism proves that the limits between mathematics and art, between the work of art and a technical invention, are not to be fixed.[23]

Although sympathetic to the abstract enthusiasms of the Constructivists, and indeed influenced by them, Kandinsky refused in the end to subordinate his project to that of Soviet urbanization, and it is not surprising that Lissitzky was his chief critic during Kandinsky's Soviet sojourn. Founded, however heroically, upon *scarcity,* the Soviet aesthetic already contained the seeds of that most virulent of isms, Socialist Realism. In the advanced industrial nation of Germany, on the other hand, a more immediate leap to the transcendence of oppressive materiality could be attempted, both in theory and practice.

Nevertheless, Kandinsky made a substantial contribution to the brief flowering of the Soviet cultural scene. Working directly under Lunacharsky, from 1918 to 1921 he was successively Professor at the Moscow Academy of Fine Arts, Director of the Museum of Pictorial Culture in Moscow, Professor at the University of Moscow, founder of the Institute of Art Culture (a "union of the arts" experiment which foreshadowed the Bauhaus), and founder of the Russian Academy of Artistic Sciences. As mentioned earlier, after a resignation forced by anti-Lunacharsky forces (forces which were soon to support the Trotskyist purges), Kandinsky moved on to the Bauhaus in Weimar, where his own ideas were being implemented. There he continued his second vocation, teaching, and made a tremendous impact, both as a man and an educator, upon the radical young artists drawn to that experiment.

In a rare moment of semipolitical enthusiasm, Kandinsky styled himself an anarchist, and wrote that "anarchy is regularity and order created not by an external and ultimately powerless force, but by *the feeling for the good.*"[24] In **"Reminiscences"** Kandinsky described his involvement in Russian student unrest over the oppressive University Law of 1885, during which he directly experienced the mass "spontaneity" that was to touch the lives of most Europeans in the course of that brief new world we call the mass-strike period. The experience moved him to the following observations on political organization:

> Every individual (corporative or personal) step is full of consequence because it shakes the rigidness of life—whether it aims at "practical results" or not. It creates an atmosphere critical of customary appearances, which through dull habit constantly deaden the soul and make it immovable. Thence the dullness of masses about which freer spirits have always had reason for bitter complaint. Corporative organizations should be so constituted that they have the most open form possible and incline more to adapt to new phenomena and to adhere less to "precedent" than has hitherto been the case. Each organization should be conceived only as a transition to freedom, as a necessary bond which is, however, as loose as possible and does not hinder great strides toward a higher evolution.[25]

However, for Kandinsky such an observation merely served as an extension of his critique of reification and formalism in the arts, and the passing mention ends with, "Luckily politics did not ensnare me." He did, however create a more elaborated "triangle" paradigm in *Concerning the Spiritual in Art*: this triangle, "the movement of cognition," depicts human society moving ahead

> slowly but surely, with irresistible strength moving ever forward and upward. . . . Where the apex was today, the second segment will be tomorrow; what today can be understood only by the apex, is tomorrow the thought and feeling of the second segment.

The key word in Kandinsky's rudimentary symbolic account of how "the abstract spirit" progresses, is *necessity*. For Kandinsky, who expressed his "basic principle" as "internal necessity," this concept bore several related meanings:

> —The effect of internal necessity and the development of art is an ever-advancing expression of the eternal and the objective in terms of the historical and subjective.

> —In real art, theory does not precede practice but follows it. Everything is at first a matter of feeling.

> —This absolute liberty [of abstractionism] must be based on internal necessity, which might be called honesty. . . .

And we have already quoted the passages where he implied that "the causes of the necessity to move forward and upward . . . are obscure," and where he spoke of "regularity and order created not by an external and ultimately powerless force, but by *the feeling for the good*." This "good" is defined in purely human terms: that which increases the freedom of humanity in its struggle against the entropic material world.

Thus internal necessity is an evolutionary principle whose content is "feeling," both objective and subjective. "New values," the subjective force as borne by the artist, are described thus: "This is the positive, the creative. This is goodness. The white, fertilizing ray." The objective "obstacles," which are described in an equally simple Manichean manner as "the black, fatal hand," try

> with every available means to slow down the evolution, the elevation . . . Obstacles are constantly created from new values that have pushed aside old obstacles.[26]

In other words, what initially sounds like a mystical force emanating from within is actually a progressive idea, not a demand for absolute order.

> The strife of colors, the sense of the balance we have lost, tottering principles, unexpected assaults, great questions, apparently useless striving, storm and tempest, broken chains, antitheses and contradictions—these make up our *harmony*.[27]

Kandinsky, unlike the growing fascist intelligentsia of his time,[28] *embraced* the transformations he could feel occurring around him, though he did not give them the standard political names. Like all original thinkers, he developed his own universe of discourse. He understood that the abstract spirit, the force of human creativity, took hold of a people irresistibly and gave birth to great social movements. In light of this, he observed that "One should not set up limits because they exist anyway"; the sole imperative he would admit was "Open feeling—to freedom."

This is a libertarian spirit, affirmative and anti-authoritarian. True, it partakes of a certain "vitalism" in the air of the period, but there is a difference between Kandinsky's faith in "the winding path of instinct" (Yeats) and Lawrence's hysterical condemnation of modernity or Eliot's dry dismissal of it. These latter two critics of modern capitalist society arrived at a one-sided refusal both of its achievements and of its crimes. Kandinsky, on the other hand, was acutely aware of the real progress which had prepared and which underlay the ongoing "advance" he allied with:

> True form is produced from the combination of feeling and science. . . . An important characteristic of our time is the increase of knowledge; aesthetics gradually assumes its proper place.

As for his own task, the attempt

> to banish external artistic elements [objects] from painting . . . is possible *because we can increasingly hear the whole world, not in a beautiful interpretation, but as it is.*[29]

In such passages throughout his writings, Kandinsky reproduced Hegel's prophetic notion of the end of representation.

Kandinsky was far from being the only artist to respond to the quickened atmosphere of the pre- and interwar world; many did. It may be argued that the major contributions to a great art of our time originated during the revolutionary process that brought much of the Northern hemisphere to the brink of socialism by 1919. The art schools of the present—op, pop, kineticism, luminism, Happenings, Environments, found-objects, assemblagism, mixed media, conceptual and minimal art, concrete poetry, serial music, modern Abstract Expressionism—represent little more than the cannibalization of this earlier period, banal exercises stumbling through absurdity and ending in silence. . . .

Modern art has been unable to consummate itself—although the material *basis* for transcendence, for the utter transformation of social identity, was and remains very palpably in existence—because the necessary social revolution has failed to materialize. The "surreality" and "immateriality" so passionately espoused by the movements of the early twentieth century were premised on the expectation of an imminent supersession of classes, wage labor, coercion—in short, all the evils born of scarcity.

THE CRITIQUE OF COMMODITY FETISHISM

The Expressionists in general and Kandinsky in particular viewed themselves as a vanguard—but advancing toward what? In **"On the Question of Form"** Kandinsky located the two aspects of "the modern movement" as:

> —Disintegration of the soulless, materialistic life of the 19th century . . . and

> —Construction of the spiritual and intellectual life of the 20th century that we experience and that is already manifested and embodied in strong, expressive, and distinct forms.

What characterized this modernism was its cultivated ability to hear "the inner sound" directly, as a child, unburdened by sad experience, is able to "ignore the external." There is no contradiction, Kandinsky asserted, between modern realism and modern abstractionism:

> The "representational" reduced to a minimum must in abstraction be regarded as the most intensely effective reality.

In other words, internal necessity is more "real" than external appearance or form: the emphasis is constantly on *content.*

What is this content? It is, once again, "the feeling for the good," the unfailing guide of emotional honesty. Only relearning how to "open feeling to freedom" (Blake's "organiz'd Innocence") permits the acquisition anew, by the overfamiliar, "disenchanted" world, of its lost *inner resonance.*

In condemning "the soulless, materialistic life of the 19th century," Kandinsky echoed a well-established rhetorical tradition. On this question, at least, sections of the left (the Frankfurt School, Tucholsky, Paul Nizan, Sartre, the Surrealists, the Philosophes, Sorel, de Man, etc.) and the right could unite: the positivistic, utilitarian concept of progress that accompanied the rise of a secular bourgeois economy had proven both empty and destructive. The most insightful spokesmen for this tradition, Kandinsky included, foresaw a great mechanized disaster as the only possible culmination of that rise—what was to be World War I. Some glorified in the "release" of warfare: Marinetti, Georg Heym, Gabriele D'Annunzio, Charles Maurras. But for Kandinsky the war was pure evil, "the black, fatal hand" in all its life-negating malevolence.

The socialist movement, in particular its communist wing, has historically called itself "materialist," and in many cases attacked any critique of materialism as at best antimarxist and at worst fascistic. But what Kandinsky clearly meant to criticize was crude, mechanistic materialism of the same variety refuted by Hegel and Marx themselves. While "spiritualism" meant, to a thinker like Mussolini, that man did not live by bread at all, Kandinsky was precisely concerned with the necessary moment of *materialization*—in beautiful forms corresponding to their internal necessity—of those realities which man could as yet barely experience, much less express, due to his dulled state of "incompletely developed feeling." The marxist art critic John Berger poses the problem very well in *Ways of Seeing:*

> Oil painting did to appearances what capital did to social relations. It reduced everything to the equality of objects. Everything became exchangeable because everything became a commodity. All reality was mechanically measured by its materiality. The soul, thanks to the Cartesian system, was saved in a category apart. A painting could speak to the soul—by way of what it referred to, but never by the way it envisaged. Oil painting conveyed a vision of total exteriority. . . .

> When [Blake] came to make paintings, he very seldom used oil paint and, although he still relied upon the traditional conventions of drawing, he did everything he could to make his figures lose substance, to become transparent and indeterminate one from the other, to defy gravity, to be present but intangible, to glow without a definable surface, not to be reducible to objects.

> This wish of Blake's to transcend the "substantiality" of oil paint derived from a deep insight into the meaning and limitations of the tradition.[30]

In his belief that abstraction was more real than representation, that the dream of the ideal is more real than what passes for real life, Kandinsky recreated the critique of commodity fetishism, that vise of ideology which Marx considered the *sine qua non* for reproducing the alienated "capitalist type" among individuals.[31]

For the person in bourgeois society, manipulated and ruled by appearances, separated from his own activity by the intervention of money and the labor market, the constant struggle is to *recover the content of existence.* This is exactly what Kandinsky proposed as the task of his art.

ARTIST AND AUDIENCE

A sober technical endeavor such as **Point and Line to Plane** demonstrates the difference between early Expressionism and the later, matured sensibility of the Bauhaus. The Bauhaus, committed to synaesthesia and an operative fusion of art and technology (form and function), appealed immediately to Kandinsky's deep-rooted purposiveness, his sense of art as "labor" which aimed to communicate the capacity "for infinite experiences of the spiritual in material and in abstract things."[32]

If art is not an arbitrary or superfluous luxury but a necessity, that fact must somehow be expressed in a social response: if art has no audience, then it is not art. The great trial of the modern artist has been staged by the indifference or ridicule of society in general vis-a-vis his vision of "necessity." In part, this gap has resulted from the failure of the social-revolutionary thrust mentioned earlier to do more than awake incredible, unquenchable desires in a handful of visionaries, but it also derives from the extreme difficulty inherent in trying to change, virtually overnight, the entire visual language of a society.

Very broadly speaking, two major strategies arose to deal with this disturbing rift: Socialist Realism, which proposed to deliver Art to the People in readily accessible—virtually predigested—forms; and a reincarnation of the old avant-gardist aestheticism, typified by the Second Vienna School, whose contempt for the masses was so striking.

Kandinsky's argument against Socialist Realism was rarely made explicitly, but his departure from the Soviet art scene expressed eloquently enough his feelings on the subject. It was not that he insisted, out of some dogmatic fervor of his own, that representation be banned from painting, or that figurative modes were completely impotent; he simply doubted their power to convey the real in all its revolutionized new possibilities:

> Since form is only an expression of content, and content is different with different artists, it is clear that there may be *many different forms at the same time* that are *equally good.* . . . One should discard nothing without making an extreme effort to discover its living qualities.[33]

In his flexibility and tolerance for ambiguity and diversity, Kandinsky exemplified the position of the Bauhaus on the question of "audience": a synthesis of *concern* for popular comprehension and participation, on the one hand, and principled *commitment to working from an advanced standpoint,* on the other, rather than capitulating to the prevailing "materialist" limits on the imagination. That is to say, the masses would not benefit from having artistic conceptions degraded to their existing level of comprehension; only the *exemplary* presentation of new and higher forms of consciousness could be either effective or honorable. Klee also struck his balance at the end of his statement "On Modern Art":

> We have found the parts but not the whole!
>
> We still lack the ultimate power, for: the masses are not with us.
>
> But we seek a people. We began over there in the Bauhaus.
>
> We began there with a community to which each one of us gave what we had. More we cannot do.[34]

It is ironic that although both during and after his *Blaue Reiter* collaboration, Arnold Schoenberg saw himself as wholly sharing Kandinsky's vantage-point, he actually misunderstood that vantage-point. For example, in his essay "The Relationship to the Text," Schoenberg debunked the notion that music deals with ideas; while poetic art may, he wrote, be "bound to matter" due to "the poverty of concepts," music deals purely with "the language of the world, which perhaps has to remain unintelligible. . . ." He dismissed as unprofound "the language of men, which is abstraction," and loftily declared:

> There are signs that even the other arts, which apparently are closer to the subject matter, have overcome the belief in the power of intellect and consciousness. . . . Kandinsky and Oskar Kokoschka paint pictures in which the external object is hardly more to them than a stimulus to improvise in color and form and to express themselves as only the composer expressed himself previously.[35]

The reference to Kandinsky's ability to compose with elements of his own choosing was essentially sound, but on the whole Schoenberg had missed the point. Not only did Kandinsky embrace "the power of intellect and consciousness," but his conception of internal necessity, the wisdom expressed by the artist-seer, was above all social. Abstractionism might signify that *man has soared beyond material necessity* (in consciousness, as well as potentially in social practice), but it still signifies *purposive* play, oriented toward the creation of higher orders of Freedom/Necessity. Kandinsky never let his dialectic collapse or lapse.

The early writings of Kandinsky's young collaborator Franz Marc evince similar confusion over this question, as well as a great deal of emotionalism of the sort often encountered in the imperious, passionately obscure, and vaguely threatening genre of the Manifesto. Both Marc and Schoenberg seemed at a loss as to how an audience for modern music and painting might be developed. Marc, whose notion of abstraction was that it slyly created "*symbols* . . . behind which the technical heritage cannot be seen," announced that "the artist can no longer create out of the now-lost artistic instinct of his people," thereby implying unintelligibility and isolation to be the artist's inescapable fate.[36] Schoenberg professed himself unperturbed by the problem, and refused to assume what he called "guilt" for the failure of the Second Vienna School to move any significant fraction of the masses.

Though neither resigned *nor* petulant, Kandinsky and the Bauhaus generally can themselves hardly be said to have resolved what Breton had called "the crucial misunderstanding which results from the apparently insurmountable difficulties in objectifying ideas." (see note 33.) The so-called audience problem is just another way of musing upon the fate of the social revolution—a fate which, while still unsealed, has yet to be satisfactorily addressed or explained.

THE END OF REPRESENTATION

Kandinsky called the final phase of the abstraction process "monumental," "absolute," or "concrete" art; it would be the point at which all of life was deliberately composed in a single language of beauty, continuously renewing itself at the call of internal necessity. Gropius himself expressed the same rather hazy idea:

> Our ultimate goal, which is still far off, is the unified work of art, the "great work" in which no distinction between monumental and decorative art will remain.[37]

Since Kandinsky's death in 1944, it seems the reverence—indeed, the love—he received while alive has only grown. He is constantly being "rediscovered" in his capacity as visionary, champion of articulate beauty, and creator of vividly beautiful images. Diego Rivera, who can scarcely be accused of harboring mystic impulses, wrote of him in 1931:

> I know of nothing more real than the painting of Kandinsky—nor anything more true and nothing more beautiful. A painting by Kandinsky gives no image of earthly life—it is life itself. . . . He organizes matter as matter was organized, otherwise the universe would not exist. . . . Some day Kandinsky will be the best known and best loved by men.[38]

Yet it is perhaps this beauty for which he is so beloved that poses the greatest problem: it too can get in the way of necessity, as Kandinsky well knew. Beauty is easily "recuperated": it would come as no surprise to see Kandinsky motifs turn up on frocks at the next Paris rag fair. There is no aspect of knowledge about how people perceive the world ("the laws of the soul and senses") that is immune to perversion in the service of the market. How color, line, and form affect the viewer emotionally, how they play in concert upon the piano of the soul—all this passionately interested Kandinsky with regard to his project of creating "a new humanism and a truly popular culture" (Marc). The same knowledge becomes just another technique of advertising and behavioral control in the hands of a society driven to turn every native impulse against itself as a means of self-preservation.

The road to the Absolute has turned out to be the road to the obsolete, after all. Kandinsky himself situated the dilemma as early as 1913: "The danger of ornamentation was clear, yet the dead make-believe of stylized forms could only frighten me away."[39] He rightly turned away from dead make-believe, but could do no more. Abstraction calls "painting" itself into question: the end of pictorial *representation* points past itself, perforce, toward the real thing: toward a resolution which lies well beyond the canvas and the colorful death agonies of art. Kandinsky either did not or could not realize this:

> The general viewpoint of our day, that it would be dangerous to "dissect" art since such dissection would inevitably lead to art's abolition, originated in an ignorant underevaluation of these [artistic] elements thus laid bare in their primary strength. . . . [The] "injurious" effects are nothing other than the fear which arises from ignorance.[40]

Kandinsky, born in the old world, maintained a delicate, immovable balance on the cutting edge of the new. At the precise moment that art could no longer resist pointing beyond itself, he turned its secrets inside out, revealed all its ruses, and located its demise within that vast sweep of history which was already putting a *practical* end to "representation." "We have before us," he wrote, "an age of *conscious* creation."

To revivify modern art actually presupposes a renewal of the social movement for mass democratic control of the means of life, which must now be conceived as a struggle for absolute control of "nature." But this is no more than a glib statement. For if Kandinsky's work is prophetic, it is also a warning: the right, too, opposes the status quo of modern capitalism; its populist and libertarian posturings must be taken at least as seriously as its nostalgic, Social Darwinian, and mystical aspects. What happens during the radicalization of a people in crisis periods to swing the balance in favor of the right's "alternative revolution" is, quite simply, *the fatal hesitation and abdication of the socialist vision.*

The distinction between left and right is quite real and must be preserved. Innumerable historical examples exist where the *style* of fascist and socialist formations—what Kandinsky would have termed their external form—proved so indistinguishable that youth in Italy, Germany, and France found themselves shifting with vertiginous frequency between the two. How, then, can one ascertain the *content* of a given "radicalism"? What in the end can be depended upon to pierce through the infinite rationalizations and grandiose verbiage to the objective inner meaning?

"The feeling for the good"; the spirit open fearlessly to all possibilities; the belief in the unfettered creative process and in the divinity of *man,* against all those, fascist and stalinist alike, who would force humanity back into "stale repetitions of a world already too well known"[41]—this vital spirit Kandinsky both expressed and embodied. It is the content of his work: *being,* generosity, transparency. It is what one can learn, or rather relearn, from that body of work. Only a genuine, active commitment to the development of free, purposive human creativity could have expressed itself in an aesthetic achievement of such value, such substance as Kandinsky's farewell to art as we have known it. Only of such achievements can no mistake be made.

NOTES

[1] See Edmund Wilson's treatment of the dilemma of aestheticism in *Axel's Castle* (New York: Scribner's Sons, 1969).

[2] Andre Breton, *What is Surrealism?* (London: Faber & Faber Ltd., 1936), p. 49.

[3] G.W.F. Hegel, *Phenomenology of Mind* (New York: Harper & Row, 1967), p. 145.

[4] "We have, however, no reason to regard this simply as a misfortune which the chance of events has made inevitable, one, that is to say, by which art has been overtaken through the pressure of the times, the prosaic outlook and the death of genuine interests. Rather it is the realization and progress of art itself, which, by envisaging for present life the material in which it actually dwells, itself materially assists on this very path . . . to make itself free of the content that is presented. . . . Spirit only concerns

itself actively with objects so long as there is still a mystery unsolved, a something unrevealed. . . . A time comes, however, when Art has displayed, in all their many aspects, these fundamental views of the world. . . . There is, in short, no material nowadays which we can place on its own independent merits as superior to this law of relativity; and even if there is one thus sublimely placed beyond it, there is at least no absolute necessity that it should be the object of *artistic* presentation. . . . In this passing away of Art beyond itself, however, Art is quite as truly the return of man upon himself. . . . by which process art strips off from itself every secure barrier set up by a determinate range of content and conception, and unfolds within our common humanity its new holy of holies, in other words, the depths and heights of the human soul simply, the universal share of all men in joy and suffering, in endeavor, action, and destiny." From G.W.F. Hegel, *Philosophy of Fine Art,* Vol. II (N.Y.: Hacker Art Books, 1975), see especially pp. 388-401.

[5] Hegel, Preface to *The Philosophy of Right* (London: Oxford University Press, 1975), p. 13.

[6] Wassily Kandinsky, "Reminiscences," *Modern Artists on Art* (New Jersey: Prentice Hall, 1964), p. 33.

[7] Kandinsky, *Concerning the Spiritual in Art* (New York: Wittenborn, Schultz, 1947), p. 48.

[8] *Ibid.,* p. 28.

[9] Kandinsky's writings are sufficiently brief and "of a piece" that particular ideas and even phrases need not be ascribed to a single source. Rather than litter this article with references, I will occasionally dispense with citation.

[10] From Paul Klee, "On Modern Art," *Modern Artists on Art,* p. 87.

[11] Kandinsky, *Concerning the Spiritual in Art,* pp. 72, 74, 26.

[12] For Hegel, all human activity is mediated: that is, Mind only acts on reality via some medium or mediator (Other). Art he defines as sensuous, while philosophy, for instance, is mediated through concepts.

[13] Kandinsky, *Point and Line to Plane,* (New York: Solomon R. Guggenheim Foundation for the Museum of Non-Objective Painting, 1947), p. 21.

[14] Kandinsky, *Concerning the Spiritual in Art,* p. 45.

[15] *Ibid.,* pp. 58-59.

[16] Exhaustive descriptions and reproductions (in quality ranging from completely distorted to dazzling) of Kandinsky's work are to be found in Paul Overy's *Kandinsky: The Language of the Eye,* Willi Grohmann's *Wassily Kandinsky, Life and Work,* the Guggenheim Foundation's several retrospective collections, and *Homage to Kandinsky,* an anthology of tributes to the artist.

[17] From "Introduction," *The Blaue Reiter Almanac,* edited by Kandinsky and Franz Marc (New York: Viking Press, 1974). Quoted from Victor Aubertin, "Die Kunst stirbt," 1911.

[18] Does the phenomenological symbolism of a Blake lose its charm when recognized for what it is—a clairvoyant contribution, predating Hegel, Marx, Nietzsche, and Freud alike, to the understanding of desire, repression, and society, the limits of formal logic and Newtonian physics, the fraud of Natural Religion, and other positivistic excesses of the Enlightenment? Is it a violation of the discoveries of Delacroix or the Impressionists concerning color's emotive properties when these discoveries are found to apply to the science of optics? Where, after all, lie the origins of science, if not in magic, art, religion, and early philosophy—all equally "scientific" endeavors in the context of their proper epochs? (See Paul Feyerabend, *Against Method,* London: NLB, 1975).

[19] Paul Overy, *Kandinsky, The Language of the Eye* (New York: Praeger, 1969), p. 31.

[20] See George Mosse, *Nazi Culture* (New York: Grosset & Dunlap, 1966), pp. 197-234.

[21] See Joseph Gabel, *False Consciousness: An Essay on Reification* (New York: Harper & Row, 1975).

[22] Kandinsky, *Concerning the Spiritual in Art,* p. 33.

[23] El Lissitzky, *The Isms of Art,* reprint (New York: Arno Press, 1968).

[24] Kandinsky, "On the Question of Form" in *The Blaue Reiter Almanac,* p. 157 (emphasis in original). His biographer Overy calls him a "Christian anarcho-syndicalist."

[25] Kandinsky, "Reminiscences," p. 24.

[26] This image is from Kandinsky, "On the Question of Form," pp. 149.

[27] Kandinsky, *Concerning the Spiritual in Art,* p. 66.

[28] Among the many sources on this subject: John R. Harrison's *The Reactionaries,* Peter Gay's *Weimar Culture,* William M. Chace's *The Political Identities of Ezra Pound and T. S. Eliot,* W. B. Yeats' *A Vision,* D. H. Lawrence's *Apocalypse,* Patrick Bridgewater's *Nietzsche in Anglosaxony,* Ezra Pound's *Jefferson and/or Mussolini,* and Alistair Hamilton's *The Appeal of Fascism.*

[29] Kandinsky, "On the Question of Form," pp. 161-162 (emphasis added).

[30] John Berger, *Ways of Seeing* (London: BBC & Penguin Books, 1977), pp. 87 and 93.

[31] See Marx, *Early Writings* (New York: McGraw-Hill, 1964), p. 189, pp. 193-194. See also Marx's 1843 letter to

Ruge: "The world has long possessed a dream of things which it need only possess in consciousness in order to possess them in reality."

[32] Kandinsky, "Reminiscences," p. 42.

[33] Kandinsky, "On the Question of Form," pp. 150 and 187 (emphasis in original), Andre Breton composed a masterful critique of Socialist Realism, a propos of abstraction in literature, in a broadside against the "childish, declamatory, unnecessarily *cretinizing*" style of *L'Humanite:*

> Nothing here seems to me to contribute to the desirable effect, neither in surface nor in depth. . . . I say that the revolutionary flame burns where it lists, and that it is not up to a small band of men, *in the period of transition we are living through,* to decree that it can burn only here or there . . . I have no leisure to publish "short works of fiction" even in *L'Humanite.* I have never written stories, having neither the time to waste nor to make others waste. The genre, I believe, is exhausted . . . Today, in order to write, or to read, a "story," one must be a poor wretch indeed. . . . For it is indeed *substance* that is involved, even in the philosophical sense of a fulfilled necessity. The fulfillment of necessity alone is of a revolutionary order. Hence we cannot say of a work that it is of a revolutionary essence unless . . . the "substance" in question is not entirely lacking. . . . What is thought (for the mere glory of thinking) has become incomprehensible to the mass of men, and is virtually untranslatable for them. . . . The whole meaning of my present critique is here. I do not know, I humbly repeat, how we can hope to reduce in our times the crucial misunderstanding which results from the apparently insurmountable difficulties in objectifying ideas.

(From Maurice Nadeau, *History of Surrealism* (New York: Macmillan, 1965), pp. 242-251.

[34] From *Modern Artists on Art,* p. 91.

[35] *The Blaue Reiter Almanac,* p. 102.

[36] Essays "The 'Savages' of Germany" and "Two Paintings" in *The Blaue Reiter Almanac,* pp. 64 and 68.

[37] Quoted in Marcel Brion, *Kandinsky* (New York: Harry N. Abrams, 1961), p. 57. Brion has observed that the "concrete," as Kandinsky preferred to call abstractionism, signified "primordial reality," out of which unprecedented beings were coaxed to the canvas as though ex nihilo.

[38] Quoted in Peter Selz, *German Expressionist Painting* (Berkeley: University of California Press, 1974), p. 232. And Andre Breton's accolade: "I know of no art since Seurat with more philosophical foundation than that of Kandinsky. . . . [His] is the eye of one of the first and one of the greatest revolutionaries of vision." (From the compendium *Homage to Kandinsky.*)

[39] Kandinsky, "Reminiscences," p. 32.

[40] Kandinsky, *Point and Line to Plane,* pp. 17-19.

[41] Brion, *Kandinsky,* p. 83.

Jed Rasula (essay date 1983)

SOURCE: A review of *Sounds,* in *American Book Review,* Vol. 5, No. 2, January-February, 1983, pp. 4-5.

[*In the following review, Rasula offers a positive assessment of Kandinsky's* Sounds, *deeming it "one of the essential books of poetry of the century, whatever one may think of Kandinsky's art."*]

One of the essential conjunctions between modernists that never came to pass was a meeting between Kandinsky and the London artists of the Wyndham Lewis/Ezra Pound circle. Not that any such meeting was ever a possibility, but the English translation of **Sounds** makes one wish it had come to pass, somehow, more for Pound's benefit than Kandinsky's, I should add. Lewis and Pound were well aware of Kandinsky, both through his painting and his book **On the Spiritual in Art.** Lewis' magazine *BLAST,* appearing in June 1914, contained a lengthy review of Kandinsky's book, recently translated by M.T.H. Sadler under the title **The Art of Spiritual Harmony.** The review was by Vorticist artist Edward Wadsworth, though "review" is not quite the term for a text that consists almost entirely of extracts from the book. The intent was clearly to expose readers to Kandinsky's treatise not obliquely by reference but, in the manner of *BLAST*'s overall substance, by direct impact. So extensive are the passages quoted from Kandinsky's book, in fact, that this crucial opening issue of *BLAST* was in effect grounded in the insights of the Russian artist and those of Wyndham Lewis.

Lewis, for his part, mentions Kandinsky only to the extent of pronouncing him "much more original and bitter" (better?) than Matisse. Pound, on the other hand, goes so far as to make Picasso and Kandinsky "father and mother" of the vorticist movement. In an article in *The Egoist* contemporaneous with *BLAST* Pound advised his readers to take half a year to get acquainted with the works of Lewis, Matisse, Cezanne, Picasso, Gauguin and Kandinsky. A few months later in the *Fortnightly Review* the actual impact of Kandinsky on Pound's work is autobiographically related. He is there described not so much as an influence as an affirmation of the directions Pound felt himself committed to: " . . . when I came to read Kandinsky's chapter on the language of form and colour, I found little that was new to me. I only felt that someone else understood what I understood, and had written it out very clearly." Repeating the principle, first articulated in *BLAST* a few months earlier, that "The image is the poet's pigment," Pound advises his readers to then look into Kandinsky's book and apply his observations on form and color to the writing of verse. It is tempting to think of Pound downplaying the artist's influence on him, but it becomes clear in the *Fortnightly* article that the formal principles set forth by Kandinsky had already been transmitted to Pound from Whistler, and that Kandinsky really was a later affirmation of the imagist and vorticist preoccupation with the materiality of the composition. "Whistler said somewhere in the *Gentle Art:* The picture is interesting not because it is Trotty Veg, but because it is an arrangement in colour.' The minute you have admitted that, you let in the jungle, you let in nature and truth and abundance and cubism and Kandinsky, and the lot of us." Pound sees Kandinsky's crucial role in "ousting literary values" from art, and the implication is clearly that Pound himself sought to eradicate extra-poetic considerations from the modern poem.

It is the presence in English now of Kandinsky's own book of poems and woodcuts, *Sounds,* that occasions these reflections, because however much Pound either learned or affirmed from reading Kandinsky's prose, the example Kandinsky set in the poems would undoubtedly have proven even more stimulating. For one thing, Kandinsky single-handedly anticipated and solved the actual obstacle to postimagist or vorticist poetry, which is precisely the "extraliterary" content. Even in his most purely imagistic poems, Pound never entered the realm of purely formal linguistic play that is so fully explored in *Sounds. Sounds* is, in short, everything that Pound recognized contemporary painting to be, *but in a fully literary mode.*

Short of a personal meeting between painter and poet, however, chances of Pound seeing *Sounds* were minimal. *Klange* was issued by Piper in Munich in 1912 in an edition of only 345 copies. This Yale translation is the first into English. Pound did not know German, nor did Kandinsky know English to my knowledge. Again: one of the great impossible conjunctions. But maybe it's just as well; Pound had enough trouble introducing even the modest reforms inherent in imagism, and working with Lewis to keep the monkey of futurism off their backs. It's hard to imagine the hostility that poetry like Kandinsky's *Sounds* might have aroused in England in 1914.

No more appropriate time could be imagined, however, for the appearance of *Sounds* in English, than 1982 America, for the work of such poets as Coolidge, Palmer, Silliman, Watten, Hejinian, Bernstein and others has many affinities with Kandinsky's book. (There has not been, to my knowledge, acquaintance with Kandinsky's book among these poets, though curiously a magazine that has been prominent in presenting their work is called *Hills,* the title of Kandinsky's opening poem.) The only one of the thirty-eight poems that bears some affinity with Pound's imagist practice is **"Early Spring"**:

A man on the street took off his hat. I
saw black-and-white hair stuck down to
the right and left of his part with hair cream.
Another man took off his hat. I saw a big
pink, slightly greasy bald spot with a bluish
· highlight.
The two men looked at one another,

each showing the other crooked, greyish
yellowish teeth with fillings.

In subtle ways this connects Kandinsky's Munich with the London of Pound's "Moeurs Contemporaines" and the vignettes of *Lustra.*

In the context of *Sounds,* however, **"Early Spring"** is atypical in that it is a straightforward scene one might easily encounter in a street. Some of the poems, like **"Water,"** appear as dream episodes. There, a red man travels through a landscape muttering "Water . . . Blue water." He encounters a green rider who shoots an arrow into his heart, but "at the last moment, the red man grasped it with his hand and threw it to one side." He is then struck by a boulder that a white man topples from a cliff: "And the block fell on the red man. He caught it on his left shoulder and tossed it behind him.—The white man up above smiled and nodded to him in a friendly fashion.—The red man grew even larger, i.e. taller.——'Water, water,' he said."

More of the episodes in the poems can be attributed to this dream-related inconsequentiality, but only **"Water"** seems dominated by the device. In actuality, dream and street-scene are extraliterary, and Kandinsky simply doesn't leave much room for materials that aren't strictly generated by the compositional matrix. Images are, in Pound's sense, the "pigment" of his poems, and time and again we read the first line less as a literary opening than as a daub of color and a shape: "Now disappearing slowly in green grass." "A mass of hills of all the colors you can imagine or care to imagine." "Once there was a big 3—white on dark brown." These are all first lines. Interestingly, Kandinsky displays little painterly bias (apart from the constant attribution of color to people and objects), and the poems open even more frequently with verbal action: "That as he (the man) sought nourishment, the dense white comb beat down the rosebird." "Oh, how slowly he goes." "The rope went down and a certain curtain went up." "The jumping man interested me a great deal."

Kandinsky's emphasis on the spiritual dimension of art gives us, in both the woodcuts and poems in *Sounds,* a double sight (literally, in text juxtaposed with illustration) which is continually a play between seeing and insight. **"A Thing Or Two"** is worth quoting in its entirety, both to indicate in a substantial way the full rotundity of these "sounds" and the questing impulse underlying the simplest perceptions:

A fish went deeper and deeper into the water. It was silver. The water blue. I followed it with my eyes. The fish went deeper and deeper. But I could still see it. I couldn't see it anymore. I could still see it, when I couldn't see it. Yes, yes I saw the fish. Yes, yes I saw it. I saw it. I saw it. I saw it. I saw it. I saw it. I saw it. A white horse on long legs stood quietly. The sky was blue. The legs were long. The horse was motionless. Its mane hung down and didn't move. The horse stood motionless on its long legs. But it was alive. Not a twitch of a muscle, not quivering skin. It was alive.

Yes, yes. It was alive.

In the wide meadow there grew a flower. The flower was blue. There was only one flower in the wide meadow.

Yes, yes, yes. It was there.

The exploratory resonance here faithfully remains within the materials at hand. The fish inseparable from the eye perceiving it, the horse whose whiteness instantly feeds the pallette of the contemplative eye: these are precisely the algebraic variables Pound insisted were at the heart of the modern poetic practice, in contradistinction to the fixed values in symbolism.

The texts seem possessed throughout of an extraordinary literary sophistication as well as a playfulness most literature avoids. The fifty-six woodcuts reinforce the text throughout, though an artistic eye might be disposed to put that the other way around. The titles often seem as relevant to the pictures as to the poem, and this striking ambiguity reminds the textually-biased reader that the woodcuts, too, are there to be *read*. The figures that emerge from the stark masses of black and white are, like the poems, spellbinding, awesome, and a little silly all at once. The frequent citation of colors in the text makes one wish the twelve colored woodcuts in the original were presented in color here, which they are not. But this Yale edition does faithfully enliven Kandinsky's book in its layout, with the bold nonserif typeface standing out well against the heavy clusters of woodcuts. The German texts are tucked away at the back of the book to ensure that the visual appearance of the volume is not upset by more text than the original displayed. A concise introduction unobtrusively services the reader.

The handsome presentation of the text is surely to be commended, yet Napier's wonder-working translation is the outstanding accomplishment here. I would venture to call this the finest translation from the German that I've read in many years. The book is not glibly named *Sounds*: Kandinsky explored the poetic format rigorously as a sonic dimension. It's important to understand the degree to which the images derive from the sounds. A poem like **"Table"** is really nothing but the fullest extension of the sound patterns: "Rechts und links an diesem Tische sassen viele, viele Menschen, Menschen, Menschen, Menschen." (Right and left at this table sat many, many, many people, people, people, people.)

In poem after poem Napier confronts the stylistic feature that demands most care and generally comes up with English versions that read effortlessly, but are full of ingenuities. She gives us a Kandinsky as simple and full of clarity as he is in German; but when he twists the language, plays with it, or lets it have its way with him, she somehow manages to achieve the same feel in English. The farthest she ever departs from the original is in the poem **"Curtain"** in the phrase (repeated over and over) "A certain curtain hung." The German reads: "Der Vorhang hing." There is no "certain"; but the German

"hang/hing" is literally the substance of Kandinsky's piece, and Napier draws that substance to our attention by rhyming curtain with certain. This is a liberal, permissive translation which I regard as a rather ingenious documentation of the inner motion of another language. Nowhere else does she take such liberty, because she simply doesn't need to: the clarity of the English matches the German point for point, and her choice of words and syntactic arrangements are meticulously assembled to duplicate the German rhythms and the force-fields of sound. So satisfying is Napier's translation, that in the end it's hard to decide whether she happened to come up with all the "right solutions" or whether *Sounds* is one of those very rare combinations of the right book in exactly the right translator's hands. Whichever it may be, we should be profoundly grateful to have an impeccable English edition of Kandinsky's *Sounds* available at last, for it is one of the essential books of poetry of the century, whatever one may think of Kandinsky's art.

Rose-Carol Washton Long (essay date 1987)

SOURCE: "Occultism, Anarchism, and Abstraction: Kandinsky's Art of the Future," in *Art Journal*, Vol. 46, No. 1, Spring, 1987, pp. 38-45.

[*In the following essay, Long determines the influence of occultism and anarchism on Kandinsky's writings and art.*]

As art historians in recent years have examined the development of modern art, it has become more and more apparent that the interest in occult and mystical knowledge evinced by many artists was often part of a search for alternatives to restrictive social and political attitudes and outworn conventions. For solutions to the problems created by an increasingly industrialized and commercialized society, many artists explored heretical metaphysical concepts, fringe political systems, and deviant sexual patterns and, in the process, discovered new artistic methods for themselves. Yet the varied anarchistic, socialistic, and sexual theories that engaged these artists in conjunction with occultism and mysticism have too often been neglected by scholars. Although the quests for a spiritual utopia and a secular one have often been closely related, many art historians have equated artists' interest in mysticism with hostile attitudes towards social and political change.

A few scholars have noted that both social concerns and mystical thought provided stimuli to modern artists interested in abstraction. Although Donald Drew Egbert's *Social Radicialism and the Arts* focused primarily on artists with clearly indicated political interests, he suggested that anarchism and socialism as well as mysticism and occultism influenced the development of twentieth-century abstract art.[1] His study illuminates connections between various occultists, anarchists, socialists, and artists in the late nineteenth century and the early years of the twentieth. For example, before Annie Besant's conversion to Theosophy, she had been an active Fabian socialist and birth-control advocate. Just prior to her meeting in 1889 with Helena P. Blavatsky, the founder of the modern Theosophical Society, Besant, along with the English socialist designer William Morris and the Russian anarchist-communist or communalist Piotr Kropotkin, had spoken at a demonstration in London in support of the American anarchists accused of bomb throwing in Haymarket Square, Chicago.[2] Drawing from the work of Eugenia Herbert and others, Egbert stressed the role Kropotkin played in persuading socially concerned artists and critics in the late nineteenth century to support a style that was not based on the realism of past art.[3]

According to Egbert, Kropotkin had called upon artists, poets, and intellectuals to create works that would deal with the struggle of the masses, urging artists to ignore previously discovered sources in antiquity, Renaissance art, and nature in order to search for a style that could infuse their work with revolutionary fervor. Egbert discussed the impact of Kropotkin on Neoimpressionists such as Signac and on Symbolists such as Fénéon and Mallarmé, and he noted the concern of Gauguin and the Nabis with Theosophy. Although Egbert did not discuss the now-acknowledged interest of Symbolists in occultism,[4] he emphasized that the Theosophical belief in a universal brotherhood of man and its attack on the evils of commercialism were part of its appeal to socially concerned artists. Egbert also referred to František Kupka's interest in spiritualism and anarchism as a prelude to his development of abstraction.[5] Virginia Spate, in *Orphism*, examined Kupka's interest in mysticism and, somewhat more briefly, in anarchism, mentioning Kupka's illustrations for the anarchist-geographer Elisée Reclus's study *L'Homme et la terre*.[6]

There has been far more written in the past twenty years on the importance of Theosophy and Symbolism for Wassily Kandinsky's development of an abstract style of painting before World War I.[7] Yet, the influence of anarchistic attitudes[8] in conjunction with occultism on Kandinsky's ideas and their possible reflection in the structure of his work have not received serious consideration. In fact, Kandinsky used the term "anarchistic" in the *Blaue Reiter* almanac to describe the direction of his own work and that of other contemporary artists whom he admired.[9] Many artists, poets, and intellectuals with whom Kandinsky associated before 1914 in Germany and Russia found inspiration in both occult thought and various anarchistic attitudes for their search for an underlying, unifying force that would emerge after the artificial structures of society were removed. Overlapping circles of intellectuals who were willing to explore new processes of thought in religion, science, art, and politics created a climate in which experiment in the arts could be envisioned as a challenge to the established authoritarian societies in both countries.[10] Before turning to an examination of Kandinsky and his relation to others searching for a better society, it may be helpful to suggest why the interconnections of mysticism-occultism, anarchism, and artistic change have often been ignored.

For most art historians, turn-of-the-century mysticism, occultism, and anarchism have been considered too irrational and chaotic to be viewed as serious influences on modernist artists. Reports of spiritism and seances led to much distrust of occultists, and the terrorists acts of some anarchists brought disapproval to anarchism as well. In addition, the frequency with which various occultists and anarchists moved from one group to another, or formed factions within a larger group, lent itself to much confusion over their activities and programs. Before World War I, although certain occult groups, such as the Theosophists and the Rosicrucians, agreed that knowledge of esoteric wisdom could help mankind to advance to a higher state, they frequently disagreed over the significance of various Christian and Eastern sources. Arguments of this nature led, for example, to the formation of the Anthroposophical Society in 1913 when Rudolf Steiner, the head of the German Theosophical Society, broke with the International Theosophical Society after disagreeing with Annie Besant, its director.

Although anarchists, envisioning themselves as inspiring the masses to remove authoritarian and repressive structures, were more specifically concerned with direct social and political change than were occultists, they shared with the occultists a similar tendency towards internationalism and anticommercialism as well as towards factionalism.[11] Frequently disagreeing with the Socialists, with whom they were at first allied, a number of anarchists rejected Marx's analysis of historical change. In addition, they disagreed with one another as to the direction and nature of their new society. Some argued for a moral revolution arising from strict libertarian individualism, while others argued for violent change arising from militant workers' units. Still other anarchists emphasized the nonviolent restructuring of society into decentralized rural communes or small autonomous Christian groups. Kropotkin, whose ideas were drawn from French utopian socialism and from the Russian populist tradition, exerted considerable influence on artists and writers in Germany and Russia[12] as well as in France and England at the end of the century. Tolstoy's ideas also had considerable prominence in the years before World War I. Nonetheless, the resistance of most anarchists to clearly structured organizations made their existence not only perilous but also subject to derision.

In the 1920s and 1930s, German political groups of the left and right used the terms "anarchism" and "mysticism" to ridicule modern art, particularly abstraction. Critics on the left, abandoning the notion that vanguard art should be nonrealist, began to attack the perceived elitist direction of Expressionism and abstraction.[13] From the right, modernist artists and schools, such as the Bauhaus, were denounced as "full of mysticism" and were charged with artistic Bolshevism, responsible for anarchy and disorder.[14] By the late thirties, while the National Socialists were characterizing modernism as "entartete" (degenerate) as well as anarchistic,[15] the left was attacking modernism, particularly Expressionism and abstraction, for its decadence, anarchism, mysticism, and bohemianism.[16]

The Marxist critic George Lukács, reflecting the Stalinist rejection of modernism in favor of socialist realism and a determination to extend a "popular front" to all the arts, suggested in 1934 that the bourgeois bohemianism, anarchism, and mysticism of the avant-garde had contributed to the rise of fascism by creating such chaotic conditions.[17]

After World War II, critical thinking was marked by a clear retreat from the politicalization of the arts that had characterized the thirties. In Germany, for example, the utopian political interests of many artists who had actively committed themselves to reformist and radical politics after World War I were ignored as was their interest in mysticism.[18] In addition, historians such as George Mosse, who wrote in the sixties about the supporters of National Socialism who had been involved with mystical utopian groups before their involvement with fascism, contributed inadvertently to the already present tendency of artists and their admirers to ignore past explorations of mysticism.[19] It should not be surprising then that accounts of Expressionism and studies of Kandinsky written in the fifties and after did not mention his interest in occultism and anarchism.[20] Even the Symbolist sources were overlooked, perhaps because both occultism and anarchism were so much a part of Symbolist thought.

Despite the negative associations of mysticism, anarchism, and abstraction in the 1920s and 1930s and the later denials of this influence by scholars, much evidence indicates that an artist such as Kandinsky was familiar not only with occultism, particularly Theosophy, but also with contemporary thought on socialism and anarchism in both Germany and Russia.[21] From the time he arrived in Munich in 1896 until he left Germany in 1914, and during his return visits to his native land, Kandinsky associated with artists, poets, writers, and critics who explored occultism, medieval mysticism, anarchism, pacifism, and socialism to find ways to change the direction of society. In a 1914 letter to Franz Marc, his collaborator on the Blaue Reiter almanac, Kandinsky recalled their days together in the artists' quarter—Schwabing—in Munich, when the "genuine Schwabingers living in their farmhouses" had no idea what "was growing" in the earth near them.[22]

During this period, occultists and mystics, anarchists, socialists, and pacifists did not exist in completely separated camps. Theosophists such as Rudolf Steiner, whom Kandinsky praised in *On the Spiritual in Art,* had worked with German socialists and anarchists. Steiner had lectured several times a week from 1899 to 1904 at the school for workers' education, founded by Wilhelm Liebknecht, one of the organizers of the German Social Democratic Party.[23] He was friendly with John Henry Mackay, who had written the book *Die Anarchisten* and had studied the individualist-anarchist theories of the mid-nineteenth-century German Max Stirner. Steiner had also lectured on the monist theories of the Darwinian biologist Ernst Haeckel at the Liebknecht school and had led a literary group, Die Kommende, where young artists such as Else Lasker-Schüler and Herwarth Walden read their works.[24]

Intellectuals who espoused various communalist aspects of anarchism, such as the political theorist Gustav Landauer, who was to become in 1919 one of the leading members of the Bavarian Socialist Räterepublik, and the Russian Symbolist poets and critics Georgii Chulkov and Viacheslav Ivanov, were also interested in mystical thought. Landauer, for example, who translated Kropotkin into German for publication in 1904, had a year earlier edited the writings of the German mystic Meister Eckhart.[25] Chulkov and Ivanov, who sought to combine individual freedom with collective responsibility, were known to be interested in the occult[26] and shortly after the brief Russian revolution of 1905 referred to themselves as mystical anarchists.[27]

Although they were all concerned with the radical transformation of a society they considered too materialistic and authoritarian, these intellectuals differed in the areas they felt would most affect change. Steiner advocated study of Eastern religions as well as the major Christian mystics, believed in meditation, and emphasized that artistic activity growing out of these studies would assist with the regeneration of society. Chulkov and Ivanov, whose friend the poet Mikhail Kusmin contributed to the Blaue Reiter almanac,[28] were determined to have a direct effect on Russian life after the revolution of 1905. They urged that the artificial restraints of governments, religious dogma, and traditional morality be removed in order for a new society based on the natural law of voluntary service and sexual love to evolve. Viewing political activity as petty, they believed the theater could increase communion between the artist and the "crowd" by evoking the mystical unity that existed among all people. They encouraged experimental plays in which music, color of sets, and costumes would reflect the universal and timeless elements of the national myths on which they believed much of the theater should be based.[29]

Landauer, who moved among writers and poets whom Kandinsky knew,[30] was more directly involved with radical politics than was Chulkov or Ivanov. Although Landauer called Marx "the curse of the Socialist movement,"[31] he wanted the terms "socialist" as well as "anarchist" connected to his ideas and formed in 1908 an activist group he called the Socialist Bund. Martin Buber, who was part of the circle of Karl Wolfskehl,[32] a neighbor of Kandinsky's since 1909, was one of the leaders of Landauer's Bund in Berlin. The Munich leader was the anarchist writer Erich Müsham, who in 1909 organized a group of impoverished café outcasts into meetings called Die Tat, which Wolfskehl is reported to have attended.[33] For Landauer, the basic question was how to revive the communal spirit in the modern world, and he advocated restructuring society into small, autonomous rural communes. Like Kropotkin, he viewed writers, poets, artists as having the vision to lead the people, and equated realism with the decline of spirituality. In *Die Revolution,* published in 1908, Landauer praised the Middle Ages, and set the medieval guild as a model of communitarian organization. He also discussed in that work how medieval spirituality declined as realism in the arts became predominant.[34]

In 1908, Kandinsky returned to Germany after a yearlong stay in Paris, during which he had agonized over his goals and direction. After a period of rest, Kandinsky began to work increasingly in oil, with larger-scaled canvases, brighter colors, and looser, more blurred images. It was during 1908 that he is reported to have heard Steiner lecture in Berlin.[35] In Munich, he renewed his friendship with Wolfskehl, and began developing a series of compositions for the stage with the Russian composer Thomas von Hartmann, who was also interested in occult phenomena.[36]

During the summers of 1909 and 1910, Kandinsky and his companion Gabriele Münter shared their house in rural Murnau with Alexei Jawlensky and Marianne von Werefkin, two other Russians living in Munich. Both Jawlensky and Von Werefkin were interested in Steiner as well as in the writings of many Russian Symbolists such as Chulkov, about whom Von Werefkin made notes in a journal.[37] During the summer of 1909, Münter became interested in Bavarian folk art, particularly the religious *Hinterglasmalerei* and began to collect them and to experiment herself with painting on glass. Kandinsky, too, soon collected these examples of folk art as well as Russian *lubki*. Both provided him with simplified and primitivizing interpretations of apocalyptic motifs, which he was beginning to use in a veiled, non-naturalistic manner in his major paintings and in his theatrical compositions to suggest the themes of struggle and regeneration so central to his world view.

During this period, Kandinsky maintained close ties with the Russian avant-garde.[38] In June 1910, he began to correspond with Nikolai Kulbin, the music and art theorist, exhibition organizer, and painter.[39] In the fall of that year, he made a lengthy trip to Moscow, and visited Saint Petersburg as well. He referred in *On the Spiritual in Art* to the innovative production of a Maeterlinck play in Saint Petersburg that forced the imagination of the spectator to complete the scenery.[40] This production may have been at Ivanov's "tower" apartment, where experimental plays and productions were occasionally performed, an activity in keeping with Ivanov's belief in the religious and communal power of the theater.[41] In Saint Petersburg, Steiner's Russian emissaries, many of whom had lived in Germany, could be found at Ivanov's apartment, where the intelligentsia of that city gathered.[42] By 1910, Steiner's name and writings had become more widely known in Russia, and his focus on the Apocalypse as the significant document for modern times coincided with the assumption of many Russian intellectuals, intensified by the 1905 revolution, that the Apocalypse was nearing.[43]

Nearly a year after his trip to Russia, Kandinsky prepared two messianic documents: *On the Spiritual in Art,* completed in 1911, and the Blaue Reiter almanac, published in 1912. Both were conceived for the purpose of awakening the spiritual in all mankind[44] through the suggestion of alternatives to the decadence and darkness of contemporary life. Kandinsky blamed materialists, positivists, scientists unwilling to seek information outside established

sources and "recognizing only what can be weighed and measured"[45] for the anxiety and insecurity of the people around him, and for the confusion of his age. Although he believed that art had the potential to lead the way to the future, he described most artists as savagely competing with one another for success with a small group of "patrons and connoisseurs"[46] who were searching for profits.

To avoid such self-centered degradation, and to move away from blind uncertainty, Kandinsky suggested that the public turn to the Theosophical Society, which he described as "one of the greatest spiritual movements" of his day.[47] Although he explained that some were wary of its "tendency to theorize," he emphasized that it offered "a note of salvation" that touched many who were "enveloped in darkness and night."[48] According to Kandinsky, a few artists could understand these "new truths," and he compared his and his friends' absorption of the lessons of folk, medieval, and primitive art to the Theosophists' search for sustenance in the cultures of other civilizations such as India.[49] For the almanac, Kandinsky and his coeditor, Franz Marc, drew on an international array of artists, writers, dramatists, and musicians who represented all that was new and unconventional— "the anarchistic" tendencies in the various arts, as Kandinsky explained in an essay in the almanac. In this text, **"On the Question of Form,"** Kandinsky wrote that "contemporary art, which . . . may rightly be called anarchistic, reflects not only the spiritual standpoint that has already been attained, but also embodies as a materializing force that spiritual element now ready to reveal itself."[50]

Kandinsky's use of the term "anarchism" is related to his messianic determination to change society not only by exploring religions, such as Theosophy, that the establishment considered heretical but also by examining other attitudes, such as anarchism, that were also considered taboo. Both of these intentions supported his quest to turn to artistic sources such as folk, medieval, and primitive art, examples of which filled the pages of the almanac, by their concentration on areas outside conventional doctrines. Anarchistic thought especially supported Kandinsky's abhorrence of artificial rules and his commitment to free choice as a way to enlightenment and as a means of overcoming the limitations of the present age.

Kandinsky was remarkably well read, and his writings indicate his familiarity with late-nineteenth-and early-twentieth-century political theory. He believed that political institutions, like nature, science, and art, had their own timeless law, and he stated that each of these separate realms would at some point in the future work together to "constitute that mighty kingdom" which at present could only be imagined.[51] But Kandinsky viewed politicians and political parties with skepticism. When discussing the socialists, he commented on their "various shades" and their tendency to use multiple quotations to support every concept.[52] He gave socialists a low position in his well-known spiritual triangle in *On the Spiritual in Art.* He explained that they wished "to deal the fatal blow to the capitalist hydra and cut off the head of evil," but that they could not themselves solve problems since they would accept nothing less than "infallible remedies."[53] He revealed his respect for anarchism when he attacked politicians for directing their hatred against it: he claimed they knew "nothing save the terrifying name."[54] Kandinsky insisted that the popular definition of "anarchy" as "aimlessness" or "lack of order" was incorrect. In **"On the Question of Form,"** he wrote: "Anarchy consists rather of certain systematicity and order that are created not by virtue of an external and ultimately unreliable force, but rather by one's feeling for what is good."[55] His interpretation reflects a central anarchist tenet that an underlying law of nature or truth lies hidden beneath the artificial structures imposed on mankind by established, authoritarian systems.

Kandinsky did not normally refer to political events in either Russia or Germany, but he did mention in his 1913 **"Reminiscences"** the significance the student protests had for him when he was at the university in Moscow in the 1880s. His memoirs indicate that he was radicalized by this event: he explained that the government ban on the university's international student organization made him much more sensitive and more receptive to new ways of looking at his country.[56] Indeed, these memoirs suggest that even in 1913 Kandinsky viewed disruption and discord as powerful tools for change. In the discussion of his student days, Kandinsky praised activism whether it was individual or collective, stating that it would "undermine the stability of our form of existence."[57] Committed to making ordinary people receptive to change, he stressed his support for actions that contributed to stirring up "a critical attitude toward accustomed phenomena."[58] Without critical stimuli, Kandinsky believed that change would be difficult. But for Kandinsky, it was the artist, not the politician or the political theorist, who could most powerfully evoke these discordant stimuli. At the end of **On the Spiritual,** Kandinsky reminded the artist that he had "great power," but that he also had "great responsibilities."[59]

Although he viewed the artist as a prophet, like a Moses leading his people to the promised land, Kandinsky drew moral sustenance and visual strength from indigenous peasant cultures, particularly from the Russian peasant, whose love of color and ornament he called "magical" and whose flexible attitude to legal matters he much admired.[60] As a student, Kandinsky had studied economics and ethnology and had traveled to the remote Vologda region. He later recalled the religious feeling he had experienced in the homes of these peasants, particularly from their icon corners, and he compared this somewhat mystical experience to the feelings he had in the great Moscow churches and more recently in Bavarian and Tyrolean chapels.[61] That Kandinsky preferred the intuitive Russian peasant law to codified law reflects not only his abhorrence of centralized authority and rule but also his knowledge of anarchist theories such as Kropotkin's and Landauer's that praised the natural law of the peasant in contrast to the artificial law of the state.

Kandinsky's discussion of the natural or internal law of the peasant is related to his belief in an underlying law or principle for all art forms that counters the superficial rules "discovered in earlier art, together with those discovered later."[62] He called this basic principle the "internal necessity," explaining that it grew from "three mystical necessities" that allowed art to move beyond time and space, beyond the personal and the national, to the eternal and the universal.[63] Although he made his own commitment to abstraction as the most transcendental and universal of art forms very clear in all his essays written before World War I, Kandinsky insisted that contemporary painting could also move in the direction of the "Great Realism." He also suggested that the artist could work towards both ends.[64]

Kandinsky refused to demand a fixed style for other artists. He was committed to the individual artist's freedom of choice, explaining that the artist should know "best by which means he can most clearly put into material form the content of his art."[65] But, he did suggest that the artists look for a guide to evocative form in their own age, which he described as one of "clashing discords," "stress and longing," "opposites and contradictions." He urged artists to reflect these discordant qualities of their time by using contrasting stimuli or the "principles of contrasts."[66] Drawing from French Fauve, German Brücke, and Russian Neo-Primitivist experiments with color, Kandinsky used brilliant, clashing colors placed over images to create spatial dislocations and feelings of chaos in his paintings. During this period, Kandinsky also used repetition of increasingly dematerialized images, many derived from folk art, both to heighten the sense of mystery and to intensify the evocation of the themes of conflict and hope so central to his beliefs. His embrace of a theory of contrasts is revealed not only in his choice of opposing colors but also in the arrangement of his compositions. A number of large oils, for example, **Improvisation 28** and **Black Spot** of 1912, have remnants of motifs derived from folk-art depictions of the Last Judgment and of Paradise, arranged beneath veils of startling color, on opposite sides of the canvas.[67]

Kandinsky believed that the constraints artificially imposed on artists were loosening in all the arts, and he wrote in the almanac that this "ever-increasing freedom . . . opens the way for further revelations."[68] The essays and the illustrations in the Blaue Reiter almanac make it clear that composers, dramatists, and choreographers, as well as painters, could free themselves from the academic requirements of basing their work on a narrative or an anecdote and from conventional notions of beauty and harmony. He found musicians most responsive to the stimuli of contrast of his age, and as a result, he included several articles on contemporary music, including one by Von Hartmann, one by Kulbin,[69] and one by the Austrian Arnold Schoenberg, whom Kandinsky praised in several essays.[70]

All three musicians argued for the right of the artist to use certain combinations of notes and chords that might at first seem discordant or unpleasant but that would, they hoped, eventually lead the audience to a new understanding of their work. The titles of Hartmann's and Kulbin's essays—"On Anarchy in Music" and "Free Music," respectively—are particularly revealing of their authors' point of view. Schoenberg, in his essay on relating texts to music, argued against strict parallels between text and music by comparing such a rule to one that limited the painter to copying from nature.[71] Kulbin, who believed that "discord" was the principle that excited and aroused mankind, focused in his essay on the musical intervals that could create this effect.[72] Hartmann urged the reader to "welcome" the principle of anarchy in art: he explained that the composer must "shock" the audience by using "opposite sound combinations" to make the observer react strongly.[73] Hartmann emphasized the numerous possibilities that could result from a variety of methods, and, like Kandinsky, he referred to the judgment of the mystical "inner necessity." Moreover, he did not argue for one "absolute" direction in art, but urged the use of both conscious and unconscious elements and suggested that discovery of unconventional approaches to music would lead to a "new Renaissance."[74] Each of these artists believed that the abandonment of past conventions would lead to the enriching freedom necessary for the creation of a work of art that could have a regenerative effect on all mankind.

Kandinsky found the concept of dissonance in music as liberating as the student disturbances at the university. Like Kandinsky, Schoenberg, Kulbin, and Hartmann advocated the use of contrasting stimuli. For Kandinsky, the parallelism of Wagner was too rooted in the past,[75] and he advised painters not to find exact correspondences of color and motifs but to use opposing colors and motifs in addition to "'forbidden' combinations, the clash of different colors"[76] to produce effects equivalent to dissonance in music.

In *On the Spiritual,* Kandinsky noted that the first effect of his painting might be one of chaos, of "forms apparently scattered at random upon the canvas, which—again apparently—have no relationship one to another." But he emphasized that "the external absence of any such relationship" constituted "its internal presence."[77] Hoping the viewer would be startled by the conflicting colors, the disorienting space, the remnants of barely decipherable apocalyptic and paradisiacal images, Kandinsky wanted the viewer to be shocked into mediating on the mysterious themes of struggle and regeneration in the paintings. In so doing, Kandinsky believed he could involve the viewer in the process of replacing confusion with understanding. If both content and form were too readable and the painting did not reflect the chaotic conditions of the time, Kandinsky believed, the work could not have the impact on the public that he envisioned.

Kandinsky was an internationalist and a universalist. Believing that nationalism brought "decline,"[78] he was sympathetic to the interests of friends in forming a transnational union of art and politics. Correspondence from 1914 with the Serbian writer and lecturer Dimitri Mitrinovic, who referred to Kropotkin's works and planned to visit the English socialists Wells and Shaw,[79] and with the Berlin writer Erich Gutkind,[80] who would meet with Buber, Landauer, and other pacifists in June of 1914,[81] suggests his involvement. But Kandinsky indicated that he could be of the greatest assistance through his artistic efforts. He hoped to create a new edition of the almanac, one not only for the arts but for "all spiritual fields," and he wrote to Marc about using Mitrinovic to assist with the new edition.[82]

Above all, Kandinsky believed his approach to art would lead to a better future. The anarchist vision of a revolution that not only would avoid capitalism but also would transform values and regenerate humanity was not in conflict with the Theosophical vision of a coming utopia—a paradise—where all mankind would live in harmony and love. Both viewed the materialism and acquisitiveness of modern civilization as pitting man against man in artificial strife where collective humanitarianism was lost. Both were part of a confluence of messianic thought that contributed to convincing Kandinsky that the discovery of basic truths or natural laws that lay hidden beneath the artificial structures of established governments, religions, and art would change the direction of human life. Theorists of both groups gave support to Kandinsky's interest in folk art, in an art emanating from the indigenous, unspoiled people of all countries, as a powerful transforming source for his work. The emphasis of anarchist and occult groups, in all their varied guises, on opposing traditional conventions to create an appropriate climate for change also gave support to Kandinsky's search for a new way to "shock" his audience out of lethargy into involvement, to prepare them for the struggle for the great utopia.

NOTES

[1] Donald Drew Egbert, *Social Radicalism and the Arts. Western Europe: A Cultural History from the French Revolution to 1968,* New York, 1970, p. 435.

[2] Ibid.

[3] Ibid., p. 226. See also: Eugenia W. Herbert, *The Artist and Social Reform: France and Belgium, 1885-1898,* New Haven, 1961, esp. pp. 5-6, 13-28; and John Rewald, *Post-Impressionism: From Van Gogh to Gauguin,* New York, 1962 (2nd ed.), pp. 154-58.

[4] See: Alain Mercier, *Les Sources ésotériques et occultes de la poésie symboliste (1870-1940),* 2 vols., Paris, 1969, 1974; and Filiz Eda Burhan, "Vision and Visionaries: Nineteenth-Century Psychological Theory, the Occult Sciences, and the Formation of the Symbolist Aesthetic in France (Ph.D. diss., Princeton University, 1979).

[5] Egbert (cited n. 1), pp. 281-83.

[6] Virginia Spate, *Orphism,* Oxford, 1979, pp. 85-159.

[7] For a survey of some of the literature on the influence of Theosophy and Symbolism on Kandinsky's thought and work, see: Rose-Carol Washton Long, *Kandinsky: The Development of an Abstract Style*, Oxford, 1980, pp. viii, 5, 14-46. See also: Sixten Ringbom, "Die Steiner-Annotationen Kandinskys," *Kandinsky und München: Begegnungen und Wandlungen, 1896-1914*, exh. cat., Munich, Städtische Galerie im Lenbachhaus, 1982, pp. 102-5.

[8] Peter Jelavich, in "Theater in Munich, 1890-1914: A Study in the Social Origins of Modernist Culture" (Ph.D. diss. Princeton University, 1982), discusses Kandinsky's theatrical experiments in the contexts of the political and social upheavals in Germany, see: pp. 366-88. In his 1985 book, *Munich and Theatrical Modernism: Politics, Playwriting, and Performance, 1890-1914*, Cambridge, Mass., 1985, pp. 217-34, he refers more specifically to anarchism and Kandinsky.

[9] Wassily Kandinsky, "Über die Formfrage," *Der Blaue Reiter*, Munich, 1912; English translation in *Kandinsky: Complete Writings on Art*, ed. Kenneth C. Lindsay and Peter Vergo, Boston, 1982, vol. 1, p. 242.

[10] For a summary of some of these overlapping groups in Berlin, see: Janos Frecot, "Literature zwischen Betrieb und Einsamkeit," *Berlin um 1900*, exh. cat., Berlin, Akademie der Künste, 1984, pp. 319-47, 351-53.

[11] Literature on European anarchism of the late-nineteenth- and early-twentieth centuries emphasizes the multiple directions of anarchists, ranging from the ego or individualist anarchism of Max Stirner and John Henry Mackay, the anarcho-communism or communalism of Kropotkin, the Christian anarchism of Tolstoy, and anarcho-syndicalism. For a general introduction, see: Andrew Carlson, *Anarchism in Germany*, vol. 1, *The Early Movement*, Metuchen, N.J., 1972, pp. 1-11. Ulrich Linse, in "Individualanarchisten, Syndikalisten, Bohémiens," *Berlin* (cited n. 10), mentions that all these various anarchist groups in Germany offered a leftist "ideological and organizational alternative" to the Social Democratic Party, p. 440.

[12] For a discussion of Kropotkin's influence in Russia and for a survey of the varied anarchist groups that developed there in the early years of the century, see: Paul Avrich, *The Russian Anarchists*, Princeton, 1967, pp. 3-119.

[13] See: Rose-Carol Washton Long, "Expressionism, Abstraction, and the Search for Utopia in Germany," *The Spiritual in Art: Abstract Painting 1890-1985*, exh. cat., Los Angeles, Los Angeles County Museum of Art, 1986, pp. 201-17. See also: Ida Katherine Reigby, *An alle Künstler! War-Revolution-Weimar*, exh. cat., San Diego, San Diego State University, 1983, pp. 35-7, 65-66.

[14] "Die staatliche Bauhaus in Weimar," *Beilage zur Thüringer Tageszeitung*, January 3, 1920, Bauhaus Archiv, Berlin. See also: Istvan Deak, *Weimar Germany's Left-Wing Intellectuals: A Political History of the Weltbühne and Its Circle*. Berkeley, 1968, pp. 1-5.

[15] See the guide to the 1937 exhibition, *"Entartete" Kunst*, reprinted in Franz Roh, *"Entartete" Kunst: Kunstbarbarei in Dritten Reich*, Hannover [1962].

[16] The "Expressionist debate" in the German emigré periodical *Das Wort* of 1937-38 reflects some of these attitudes. Most of the essays are reprinted in *Die Expressionismusdebatte. Materialien zu einer marxistischen Realismuskonzeption*, ed. Hans Jurgen Schmitt, Frankfurt am Main, 1973. For the clearest discussion of the "debate," see: Franz Schonauer, "Expressionismus und Fascismus: Eine Diskussion aus dem Jahre 1938," 2 parts, *Literatur und Kritik* 7 & 8 (Oct. and Nov. 1966), pp. 44-54, 45-55.

[17] Georg Lukács, "'Grösse und Verfall' des Expressionismus," *Internationale Literatur*, 1 (1934); English translation in *Georg Lukács. Essays on Realism*, ed. Rodney Livingstone, Cambridge, Mass., 1980, pp. 77-113.

[18] For example, Lothar Günther Buchheim in *The Graphic Art of German Expressionism*, New York, 1960, focused his discussion of Max Pechstein on his work done before World War I and reproduced none of his politically inspired prints such as the cover of the November-gruppe publication *An alle Künstler!*

[19] G. L. Mosse, "The Mystical Origins of National Socialism," *Journal of the History of Ideas*, Vol. 22, No. 1 (1961), pp. 81-96.

[20] For a brief overview of the reservations of scholars about the influence of Theosophy on Kandinsky, see: Long (cited n. 7), p. 159 n. 17, and p. 160 and n. 27.

[21] Anarchism and mysticism have recently been connected with Kandinsky's abstract painting in *Arnold Schönberg—Wassily Kandinsky: Briefe, Bilder und Dokumente einer aussergewöhnlichen Begegnung*, ed. Jelena Hahl-Koch, Munich, 1983. However, in the introductory essay, "Kandinsky und Schönberg: Zu den Dokumenten einer Künstlerfreundschaft," Hahl-Koch characterizes their work as "instantly subjective and anarchical" and as reflecting "mystical negativity," pp. 184, 185. This essay has been translated into English, London, 1984; see: pp. 142, 143. Hartmut Zelinsky's essay, "Der 'Weg' der 'Blauen Reiter': Zu Schönbeg Widmung an Kandinsky in die 'Harmonielehre,'" pp. 223-70, which was not reprinted in the English edition, refers more specifically to the influence to Theosophy and anarchism upon Schoenberg and Kandinsky. But he overemphasizes the significance of the German ego-anarchism of Stirner and Mackay to the exclusion of anarchist communalism and other communitarian and internationalist interests. In addition, he does not discuss Russian anarchist thought.

[22] Kandinsky to Marc, March 10, 1914, in *Wassily Kandinsky/Franz Marc—Briefwechsel*, ed. Klaus Lankheit, Munich, 1983, p. 254.

[23] Johannes Hemleben, *Rudolf Steiner,* Reinbek bei Hamburg, 1963, p. 71; and also Walter Kugler, "Rudolf Steiner in Berlin," *Berlin* (cited n. 10), pp. 394-404.

[24] Frecot (cited n. 10), pp. 337-38. Walden, whose Sturm Gallery would feature Kandinsky's works before World War I, also knew the poet Paul Scheerbart and the anarchists Gustav Landauer and Erich Mühsam from these early years. See also: Erika Klüsener, *Else Lasker-Schüler,* Reinbek bei Hamburg, 1980, pp. 44-68.

[25] Landauer attacked private ownership of property and bureaucratic authority in favor of a local, grass-roots, and communitarian socialism. Eugene Lunn's *Prophet of Community: The Romantic Socialism of Gustav Landauer,* London, 1973, offers a clear summary of Landauer's sources; see: pp. 3-16, and passim.

[26] Aleksei Remizov, *Kukkha: Rozanovy pis'ma,* Berlin, 1923, p. 23; and James West, *Russian Symbolism: A Study of Vyacheslav Ivanov and the Russian Symbolist Aesthetic,* London, 1970, pp. 76-81.

[27] Bernice Glatzer Rosenthal, in "The Transmutation of the Symbolist Ethos: Mystical Anarchism and the Revolution of 1905," *Slavic Review,* Vol. 36, No. 4 (Dec. 1977), pointed out that Chulkov attacked individualism and referred to Max Stirner's theories as decadent, p. 613, and passim.

[28] Andrei Belyi in *Nachalo veka,* Moscow, 1933, stated that Kusmin lived at Ivanov's apartment, p. 322. Kandinsky translated a 1908 poem by Kusmin for the Blaue Reiter almanac. For a discussion of others such as Aleksei Remizov in Ivanov's circle whom Kandinsky knew, see: Long (cited n. 7), pp. 36-39.

[29] See: Rosenthal (cited n. 27), pp. 608-27; and idem, "Theater as Church: The Vision of the Mystical Anarchists," *Russian History* 4, pt. 2 (1977), pp. 122-41.

[30] Landauer, for example, introduced Kandinsky's friend Dimitri Mitrinovi to the writings of Kropotkin; see: Mitrinovi to Kandinsky, June 19 (?), 1914, Gabriele Münter–Johannes Eichner Stiftung, Städtische Galerie im Lenbachhaus, Munich. Landauer knew Walden from the Berlin Neue Gemeinschaft circle, and he also knew Martin Buber and Erich Mühsam from the early years of the century; see: Frecot (cited n. 10), pp. 337-38; and Lunn (cited n. 25), pp. 142-47. Iain Boyd White believes Landauer influenced the communalist ideas of Bruno Taut; see: *Bruno Taut and the Architecture of Activism,* London, 1982, pp. 9-12. 53-57. For additional discussion of the influence of mysticism and anarchism on Taut and his connection with Kandinsky, see: Marcel Franciscono, *Walter Gropius and the Creation of the Bauhaus,* Urbana, 1971, pp. 101-26; and Rosemarie Haag Bletter, "The Interpretation of the Glass Dream—Expressionist Architecture and the History of the Crystal Metaphor," *Journal of the Society of Architectural Historians,* Vol. 40, No. 1 (March 1981), pp. 20-43.

[31] Gustav Landauer, *Aufruf zum Sozialismus,* Berlin, 1911, as quoted in Lunn (cited n. 25) p. 201. Since the mid 1890s, especially after the Social Democrats excluded anarchists from the International Socialist Congress, and the Stirner followers such as Mackay insisted that anarchism and socialism were not connected, Landauer wanted to justify the anarchosocialist label. He wrote numerous articles in defense of this concept; see: Lunn, pp. 104-5, 190-94, and passim.

[32] Buber, a lifelong friend of Landauer's, was admired by the Wolfskehls, who were interested in Jewish mystical writings; see: *Karl Wolfskehl, 1869-1969: Leben und Werk in Dokumenten,* exh. cat., Darmstadt, Hesse Landesbibliothek, 1969, p. 164-65, 231. For a discussion of Wolfskehl's relation to Kandinsky and other members of the Blaue Reiter, see: Long (cited n. 7), pp. 17-25. See also: Peg Weiss, *Kandinsky in Munich,* Princeton, 1979, p. 81-91.

[33] Ulrich Linse, *Organisierter Anarchismus im Deutschen Kaiserreich von 1871,* Berlin, n.d., p. 92. Will Grohmann reports that Mühsam's name appears in Kandinsky's notebooks; see: *Wassily Kandinsky, Life and Work,* New York, 1958, p. 36.

[34] Lunn (cited n. 25), pp. 178-86.

[35] Alexander Strakosch, *Lebensweg mit Rudolf Steiner,* Strasbourg, 1947, pp. 22-24. Emy Dresler, who had been a schoolmate of Strakosch's wife, and who exhibited with Kandinsky's Neue Künstlervereinigung, became interested in Steiner in 1908 and painted stage scenery for several of his plays.

[36] Hartmann is most well known for the music he composed for Kandinsky's *Yellow Sound.* In two interviews (June 18, 1965, and Sept. 8, 1965) with Olga von Hartmann in New York, she recalled her husband's and Kandinsky's interest in extrasensory phenomena, their reading of Steiner and Blavatsky, and their experiments with writing and receiving answers although the letters were not mailed. Kandinsky felt very close to the Hartmanns and in a letter of 1911 he compared the warm feelings he had towards Franz Marc and his wife to the feelings he experienced when he was with the Hartmanns. See: Kandinsky to Gabriele Münter, Aug. 10, 1911, Gabriele Münter–Johannes Eichner Stiftung, Städtische Galerie im Lenbachhaus, Munich.

[37] Notes dated c. 1909-1913 and reprinted in Jelena Hahl-Koch, *Marianne Werefkin und der russische Symbolismus,* Munich, 1967, pp. 96-101. For a discussion of Steiner's impact on Jawlensky and Werefkin, see: Clemens Weiler, *Alexei Jawlensky,* Cologne, 1969, pp. 68, 70-73.

[38] For a summary of the many links, see: John E. Bowlt, "Vasilii Kandinsky: The Russian Connection," *The Life of Vasilii Kandinsky in Russian Art: A Study of "On the Spiritual in Art,"* ed. Bowlt and Rose-Carol Washton Long, Newtonville, Mass, 1980, pp. 1-41.

[39] Kandinsky's letters to Kulbin beginning June 24, 1910, have been edited by E. F. Kovtun in *Monuments of Culture, New Discoveries,* Academy of Sciences of the USSR, Leningrad, 1981, pp. 399-410.

[40] Kandinsky, *Über das Geistige in der Kunst,* Munich, 1912; English translation in Lindsay and Vergo (cited n. 9), I, p. 146.

[41] Mark Slonim, *Russian Theater from the Empire to the Soviets,* Cleveland, 1961, pp. 184, 191, 196, 204.

[42] Margarita Woloschin, *Die grüne Schlange,* Stuttgart, 1956, pp. 173ff, 180ff, 207; and Nikolai Berdiaev, *Sampoznanie: Opyt filosofskoi avtobiografi,* Paris, 1949, p. 207.

[43] Nikolai Berdiaev, "Tipy religioznoi mysl v Rossii. Teosofiia i antroposofiia. Dukhovnoe Khristianstvo. Sektanstvo," *Russkaia mysl,* Vol. 37, No. 11 (Nov. 1916), p. 1. See also: letter from Andrei Belyi to Aleksandr Blok, 1/14 May 1912, *Aleksandr Blok— Andrei Belyi, Perepiska,* Munich, 1969, p. 295.

[44] Kandinsky explained his goals for both books in "Rückblicke," Berlin, 1913; English translation in Lindsay and Vergo (cited n. 9), I, p. 381. He believed his essay, "On the Question of Form," in the almanac to be an updated and freer continuation of ideas begun in *On the Spiritual in Art;* see: foreword to the second edition (cited n. 40), p. 125.

[45] Kandinsky, *On the Spiritual in Art* (cited n. 40), p. 140.

[46] Ibid., p. 137.

[47] Ibid., p. 143.

[48] Ibid., p. 145.

[49] Ibid., p. 143.

[50] Kandinsky, "On the Question of Form" (cited n. 9), p. 242.

[51] Kandinsky, "Reminiscences" (cited n. 44), p. 376.

[52] Kandinsky, *On the Spiritual in Art* (cited n. 40), p. 140.

[53] Ibid., p. 139.

[54] Ibid. Although Kandinsky did not like Tolstoy's emphasis on naturalism in art (p. 130), he was in Moscow at the time of Tolstoy's death. He commented on the peacefulness and order of the civil funeral service, explaining that even the police couldn't arouse disorder. Kandinsky letter to Münter, 10/23 Nov. 1910, Gabriele Münter– Johannes Eichner Stiftung, Munich.

[55] Kandinsky, "On the Question of Form" (cited n. 9), p. 242.

[56] Kandinsky, "Reminiscences" (cited n. 44), p. 361. For a brief discussion of student protests in Russia in the late 1880s, see: Avrich (cited n. 12), p. 13. Peter Jelavich points out that Kandinsky came from a family with a heritage of political protest. His father had lived in eastern Siberia where his ancestors had been forced to move. Jelavich believes that Kandinsky first studied law and economics rather than art from a commitment to become closer to the Russian people; see: "Theater" (cited n. 8), pp. 367-68.

[57] Kandinsky, "Reminiscences" (cited n. 44), p. 361. Jelavich parallels Kandinsky's directions in *The Yellow Sound* and in his painting with Mühsam's call for "chaos," see: "Theater" (cited n. 8), pp. 432-34. It is interesting to note that Kandinsky's "Reminiscences" were written during the year in which Mühsam published the short-lived journal *Revolution,* where he listed some metaphors for revolution: "God, life, lust, ecstasy, chaos," Vol. I, No. 1 (1913), p. 2.

[58] Kandinsky, "Reminiscences" (cited n. 44), p. 362.

[59] Kandinsky, *On the Spiritual in Art* (cited n. 40), p. 214.

[60] Kandinsky, "Reminiscences" (cited n. 44), pp. 362, 368.

[61] Ibid., p. 369.

[62] Kandinsky, "On the Question of Form" (cited n. 9), p. 248.

[63] Kandinsky, *On the Spiritual in Art* (cited n. 40), p. 173.

[64] Kandinsky, "On the Question of Form" (cited n. 9), p. 242. Kandinsky also mentions both possibilities very briefly in *On the Spiritual in Art* (cited n. 40), p. 207.

[65] Kandinsky, "On the Question of Form" (cited n. 9), p. 248.

[66] Kandinsky, *On the Spiritual in Art* (cited n. 40), pp. 193-94. Harriet Watts suggests that the principle of contrast in Kandinsky's work reflects the approach of the German mystic Jakob Böhme. She believes that Steiner's emphasis on the Christian mystic contributed to the interest among many intellectuals of this period in both Böhme and Meister Eckhart; see: "Arp, Kandinsky, and the Legacy of Jakob Böhme," *The Spiritual in Art* (cited n. 13), pp. 239-55.

[67] For a discussion of Kandinsky's concept of hidden imagery, his utilization of folk art, and for specific analysis of *Improvisation 28* and *Black Spot,* see: Long (cited n. 7), pp. 66-67, 77-87, 131-33.

[68] Kandinsky, "On the Question of Form" (cited n. 9), p. 242.

[69] A fourth essay, on Scriabin's *Prometheus,* was written by Leonid Sabaneev, a music critic who frequented Russian Symbolist circles.

[70] Kandinsky first wrote to Schoenberg on January 18, 1911; see *Schönberg–Kandinsky* (cited n. 21), p. 21. He may have been aware of Schoenberg's writings before

this; see: "On Parallel Octaves and Fifths," *Salon 2*, Odessa 1910-11, in Lindsay and Vergo (cited n. 9), I, pp. 91-95. Schoenberg, like Hartmann and Kulbin was also interested in social issues and in the occult; see, for example: Schoenberg's letter to Richard Dehmel of Dec. 13, 1912, where he wrote of moving from "materialism, socialism, anarchy" to "becoming religious," in *Arnold Schoenberg Letters,* ed. Erwin Stein, New York, 1965, pp. 35-36.

[71] Arnold Schönberg, "Das Verhältnis zum Text," *Der Blaue Reiter,* Munich, 1912; English translation in *The Blaue Reiter Almanac,* ed. Klaus Lankheit, London, 1974, pp. 90-102. Hahl-Koch (cited n. 21), pp. 135-70, believes that Schoenberg's concept of dissonance had the greatest impact of all the contemporary composers on Kandinsky. But the influence of Kulbin needs also to be evaluated, since he was a major source for the Russian avant-grade, especially the Cubo-Futurist Alexei Kruchenykh; see: Charlotte Douglas, "Evolution and the Biological Metaphor in Modern Russian Art," *Art Journal,* Vol. 44, No. 2 (Summer 1984), pp. 154, 160; see also: Long (cited n. 7), pp. 63-64.

[72] Nikolai Kulbin, "Die freie Musik," *Der Blaue Reiter* (cited n. 71), pp. 141-46. Kulbin's essay is an abridged version of one that appeared in 1910 in *Studiia impressionistov;* an English excerpt appears in *Russian Art of the Avant-Garde: Theory and Criticism, 1902-1934,* ed. John E. Bowlt, New York, 1976, pp. 11-17.

[73] Thomas von Hartmann, "Über Anarchie in der Musik," *Der Blaue Reiter* (cited n. 71), pp. 114-16.

[74] Ibid., p. 118.

[75] In his essay, "Über Bühnenkomposition," in the almanac (cited n. 71), p. 195, Kandinsky criticized Wagner for using "parallel repetition," although in *On the Spiritual in Art,* which was written earlier, he had briefly but clearly praised Wagner.

[76] Kandinsky, *On the Spiritual in Art* (cited n. 40), p. 194.

[77] Ibid., p. 209.

[78] Letter with no salutation in Münter's handwriting, July 30, 1914. Gabriele Münter–Johannes Eichner Stiftung, Munich. Münter wrote drafts for almost all of Kandinsky's correspondence.

[79] Mitrinovi to Kandinsky, June 25, 1914, June 30, 1914, and undated. Gabriele Münter–Johannes Eichner Stiftung, Munich. Mitrinovi also referred to D. S. Merezhkovsky, whose concept of a "third revelation" had become increasingly important to Kandinsky.

[80] For a discussion of Kandinsky's relationships with Gutkind, who, under the pseudonym of Volker, wrote *Siderische Geburt,* urging humanity to end its isolation and acquisitiveness through a transcendent sexuality, see: Long, "Kandinsky's Vision of Utopia as a Garden of Love," *Art Journal,* Vol. 43, No. 1 (Spring 1983), pp. 50-60.

[81] For a discussion of this conference, see: Lunn (cited n. 25), p. 245.

[82] Kandinsky to Marc, March 10, 1914, *Briefwechsel* (cited n. 22), p. 253.

Roger Lipsey (essay date 1988)

SOURCE: "Wassily Kandinsky in the Years of 'On the Spiritual in Art'," in *An Art of Our Own: The Spiritual in Twentieth-Century Art,* Shambhala, 1988, pp. 40-50.

[*In the following essay, Lipsey provides an overview of the major themes of Kandinsky's seminal essay, contending that "its essential achievement was to identify the new art as a legitimate language of the spirit and to lay groundwork for a way of thinking, particularly about abstract art, that made sense."*]

More deliberately than any artist of our time, Kandinsky explored the spiritual in art through his work as a painter and through writings—articulate, generous, impassioned—which circulated the idea of the spiritual more widely than his paintings ever did. It was his central idea, and he regarded it as the central idea of the art emerging all around him in 1912 when his small masterpiece, *On the Spiritual in Art,* was first published. In his eyes the spiritual was also the emerging task of the twentieth century, which he thought destined to correct the materialism of nineteenth-century culture. His prewar work as a painter and printmaker may not fully demonstrate for all viewers the vision captured in his writings, but he was prompt to recognize that art had only begun to find its way along a new path. His early writings need to be sifted for ideas that have stood the test of time and even gained in substance. But Kandinsky does not disappoint at the conclusion of this process. Some of his art is very beautiful, and much of his thinking.[1]

Born in Moscow in 1866 in comfortable circumstances, schooled in Odessa and at the University of Moscow, Kandinsky abandoned a promising career in law at age thirty to study painting in Munich, to which he moved in 1896. In a graceful autobiographical essay, **"Reminiscences,"** he evoked a childhood and adolescence filled with precursor experiences that marked him as a born artist.

> When I was thirteen or fourteen I bought a paintbox with oil paints from money slowly saved up. The feeling I had at the time—or better: the experience of the color coming out of the tube—is with me to this day. A pressure of the fingers and jubilant, joyous, thoughtful, dreamy, self-absorbed, with deep seriousness, with bubbling roguishness, with the sigh of liberation, with the profound resonance of sorrow, with defiant power and resistance, with yielding softness and devotion, with stubborn self-control, with sensitive unstableness of balance came one after another these unique beings we call colors. . . . [2]

It is a splendid passage—and notification to us here in the cynical residue of the century that we are attending to a Romantic from its flower-fresh debut.

"Reminiscences" chronicles Kandinsky's groping evolution from a richly decorative pictorial world, in which knights and their ladies were at home, to a fully abstract visual language such as the world had never seen. Arguably the father of abstraction, which was to become a dominant visual language of our time, he was an observer and born teacher; hence the extraordinary record he kept and the ease with which he assumed leadership in the world of art. In his journey from depicting known objects to the discovery of pure abstraction, perhaps most important for him was the realization that painting need not attempt to imitate the grandeur of Nature. It can conjure up a world of its own, prompted only by the artist's sense of "inner necessity." In a striking passage in **"Reminiscences,"** he related this discovery to his conviction that humanity had reached the threshold of a new age.

> For many . . . years . . . , I was like a monkey in a net: the organic laws of construction tangled me in my desires, and only with great pain, effort, and struggle did I break through these "walls around art." Thus did I finally enter the realm of art, which like that of nature, science, political forms, etc., is a realm unto itself, is governed by its own laws proper to it alone, and which together with the other realms ultimately forms the great realm which we can only dimly divine.

> Today is the great day of one of the revelations of this world. The interrelationships of these individual realms were illumined as by a flash of lightning; they burst unexpected, frightening, and joyous out of the darkness. Never were they so strongly tied together and never so sharply divided. This lightning is the child of the darkening of the spiritual heaven which hung over us, black, suffocating, and dead. Here begins the epoch of the spiritual, the revelation of the spirit. Father—Son—Holy Spirit.[3]

How did Kandinsky understand the spiritual in art, in these years before World War I when he made his greatest contributions as a thinker? The answer to this question lies for the most part in the pages of *On the Spiritual in Art.* He shows there that he had no doubt about the crucial role of the guide ("a man like the rest of us in every way, but who conceals within himself the secret, inborn power of 'vision'").[4] He had personally responded to the guiding influence of Theosophy and Steiner and became in turn a guiding influence in the world of art. He shucked off the paralyzing notion that he himself might be a "great initiate" by reasoning that some artists stand in a special relation to inspiring guides, better able to hear them, more quick to respond. The voice of Moses, he wrote, inaudible to the crowd dancing around the Golden Calf, "is heard first by the artist. At first unconsciously, without knowing it, he follows the call."[5]

Apart from the inspiration of a Moses, a teacher, Kandinsky found value in contemplative watchfulness, guided from within by what he insistently called "inner necessity." This watchfulness, not a physical listening but similarly receptive, led in his experience to awareness of the "inner sound" of each thing, be it a color on the palette, a composition on canvas, or an object in the world. "Inner necessity" within the human being and the "inner sound" of all things are the complementary realities that showed him the way to abstract art.

> . . . It must become possible to hear the whole world as it is without representational interpretation. . . . Abstract forms (lines, planes, dots, etc.) are not important in themselves, but only their inner sound, their life. . . .

> *The world sounds. It is a cosmos of spiritually active beings. Even dead matter is living spirit.*[6]

The concluding sentence, more than any passage in his writings, is his credo—Romantic, to be sure, but clean in its affirmation and never betrayed in his art.

The ideas of inner necessity and the inner sound, expressed by Kandinsky in what may seem old-fashioned terms, deserve a restorer's attention. They are in fact powerful ideas, more ancient by far than the early twentieth century and important to creative people in any era. The idea of inner necessity was cast into Western tradition by Socrates, who spoke of the guiding *daimon* within that arrested him at the edge of a misstep and plunged him into thought while others moved on. "I am subject to a divine or supernatural experience . . . a sort of voice which comes to me."[7] He could only obey. This was internal necessity at work. "Internal necessity," wrote Kandinsky, "which might be called honesty"[8]—of the most demanding kind, obliging the artist to search, to wait, to pay close attention.

> [The artist's] eyes should be always directed to his own inner life, and his ears turned to the voice of internal necessity. Then he will seize upon all permitted means and just as easily upon all forbidden means. This is the only way of giving expression to mystical necessity.[9]

He speaks here of a discipline, and speaks with the freshness of rediscovery. Kandinsky rediscovered art as a way austere in method yet potentially ecstatic and liberating in its results. In his experience, attention to the inner life promises to free the artist from superficial self-centeredness:

> . . . The artist works not to earn praise and admiration, or to avoid blame and hatred, but rather obeys that categorically imperative voice, which is the voice of the Lord, before whom he must humble himself and whose servant he is.[10]

The concept of the inner sound of all things is found among the earliest recorded instructions to artists in Chinese tradition. The first of the Six Canons of Hsieh Ho reads "Spirit Resonance, which means vitality," in the

Bush-Shih translation of *ch'i-yün-sheng-tung*.[11] Gnomic words translated in various ways over the years, they clearly call on artists to attend to *ch'i-yün,* "spirit resonance," and it isn't stretching matters to recognize in this phrase Kandinsky's "inner sound." The eye defines, searching and poking among things, while the ear tends toward greater breadth and more constant openness. Hearing is less "material," telling us not how things appear but what vibration they emit. The ear reports on the invisible. This difference between eye and ear confers metaphorical power on hearing. To perceive the "inner sound" is to make use of eyes as if they were ears. Kandinsky's rather mystical expression in fact summons artists to a practical discipline of perception which does not ignore details but cannot rest until it apprehends the fine intrinsic signature of each phenomenon.

On the Spiritual in Art remains the largest fragment of the still incomplete whole of twentieth-century thought on the theme. Establishing Kandinsky as a central figure in the world of the avant-garde, it attempted to gather up many aspects of his own experience and that of artists around him. Liberal in praise of others, it speaks sincerely to the general condition without boosting its author's merit before a general public that still hardly knew or valued his art. Its essential achievement was to identify the new art as a legitimate language of the spirit and to lay groundwork for a way of thinking, particularly about abstract art, that made sense.

The key element in Kandinsky's reading of the historical moment was his conviction that a spiritual awakening had begun and would make its way in spite of dramatic clashes within individuals and the culture at large. Shared with other artists of his generation, Piet Mondrian and Franz Marc among them, his intuition of a general change in the quality of life and persons would be betrayed by later events many times over, but its force of sincerity at the time cannot be overestimated. The damnable nineteenth century was giving way. "Only just now awakening after years of materialism," wrote Kandinsky,

> our soul is infected with the despair born of unbelief, of lack of purpose and aim. The nightmare of materialism, which turned life into an evil, senseless game, is not yet passed; it still darkens the awakening soul. Only a feeble light glimmers, a tiny point in the immense circle of darkness. This light is but a presentiment; and the mind, seeing it, trembles in doubt over whether the light is a dream and the surrounding darkness indeed reality.... Our soul rings cracked when we sound it, like a precious vase, dug out of the earth, which has a flaw.... The soul is emerging, refined by struggle and suffering. Cruder emotions like fear, joy, and grief, which belonged to this time of trial, will no longer attract the artist. He will attempt to arouse more refined emotions, as yet unnamed. Just as he will live a complicated and subtle life, so his work will give to those observers capable of feeling them emotions subtle beyond words.[12]

No doubt, many readers will be put off by the excesses of this passage—its tendency to confuse autobiography with history, hope with necessity. On the other hand, passion of this kind is essential in human affairs; it is the passion of a good man dreaming. Creative people often call out the names of things loudly, like Adam, to confirm their existence. Kandinsky is doing magic in this passage, not scholarship, incantation rather than cogitation, and he keeps his dignity as he does so. His concluding reference to "refined emotions, as yet unnamed . . . subtle beyond words" within lives subtle and complicated, is quintessential Kandinsky; he could be a prophet of the inner life because he had an inner life, pressing on him.

He had a scholar's temperament as well. In *On the Spiritual in Art* and other publications, he regularly took note of other artists' work, provided pocket analyses, and allied the best in them to his presentiment of emerging spiritual vision. Of Cézanne, for example, whom he described as "a great seeker after a new sense of form," Kandinsky wrote that "he was endowed with the gift of divining the internal life in everything." Wary of Matisse's charm, Kandinsky nonetheless perceived enormous value in his work:

> He paints "pictures," and in these "pictures" endeavors to render the divine. To attain this end he requires nothing but the subject to be painted . . . and means that belong to painting alone. . . . [13]

In this brief appraisal, Kandinsky implies the aversion to organized religion and conventional sacred imagery true of most twentieth-century artists who cared for the spiritual at all. Some would try "to attain this end"; few would rely on tradition. Artists were asking the materials of art itself, approached with few certainties apart from "inner necessity" and the answering "inner sound," to reveal what religion no longer revealed.

It is worth remembering that many of the opinions Kandinsky offered in his book were extraordinarily prescient. The year was 1912, much of the book was written in 1910, and yet he already knew much:

> Matisse—color. Picasso—form. Two great signposts pointing toward a great end.[14]

He labored patiently in *On the Spiritual in Art*—sometimes wisely, sometimes with what now seems a wobbly, subjective method—to develop a new art theory that would allow reasoning about abstract and near-abstract form. His ideas about composition were prescient: in one swoop he recognized how to think about forms in art that modify or depart altogether from forms in Nature.

> The flexibility of each form, its internal, organic variation, its direction (motion) in the picture, the relative weight of concrete or of abstract forms and their combination; further, the discord or concord of the various elements of a pictorial structure, the handling of groups, the combination

of the hidden and the stripped bare, the use of rhythmical or unrhythmical, of geometrical or non-geometrical forms, their contiguity or separation—all these things are the elements of structure in drawing.[15]

Thinking of this kind moved on to the Bauhaus and later schools and evolved into a reasonably standard approach to compositional analysis not only in the fine arts but also in commercial design.

Color, about which Kandinsky cared so much, was more resistant to hard-headed analysis. Not that he didn't try. He was conversant with classical nineteenth-century color theory as well as fringe experiments ranging from medical chromotherapy to the Theosophists' clairvoyant studies. The challenge was to account for his own extreme sensitivity to color and to find a way of reasoning about color as an element of the spiritual in art. As always, he drew from the notion of the evolution of consciousness, relayed to him from Hindu and Buddhist sources largely by Theosophy. He did not expect much of the "average man"—and did expect much of the developed man.

> Only with higher development does the circle of experience of different beings and objects grow wider. Only in the highest development do they acquire an internal meaning and an inner resonance. It is the same with color. . . . [16]

Building on established color theory but rapidly departing from it, Kandinsky found himself expressing the impact of color in poetic and metaphorical terms. For example, "The unbounded warmth of *red* has not the irresponsible appeal of yellow, but rings inwardly with a determined and powerful intensity."[17] Such observations do not add up to a science, but they bear witness to brave effort, providing a rudimentary grammar of color in itself apart from forms in Nature. At the conclusion of the exercise he himself was not fully persuaded, but his general sense of direction hadn't failed him. Toward the end of *On the Spiritual in Art,* he could return to fundamentals with great simplicity:

> Construction on a purely spiritual basis is a slow business, and at first seemingly blind and unmethodical. The artist must train not only his eye but also his soul, so that it can weigh colors in its own scale and thus become a determinant in artistic creation.[18]

The other great literary effort of this period in his life, *The Blaue Reiter Almanac* (Munich, 1912) represented a further attempt to explain and celebrate the new orientation of art, not only in painting and sculpture but also in music and theater. It was the first "textbook" on twentieth-century art. Serving as an author and as coeditor with his friend Franz Marc (1880-1916), Kandinsky anthologized the works and ideas of many of the founders of the new art, together with illustrations from the ancient, tribal, and folk arts from which they drew inspiration. The message of *The Blaue Reiter Almanac*, parts of it delivered most attractively by Franz Marc, was consistent with that

of *On the Spiritual in Art*: humanity was entering upon a new spiritual adventure to which artists had much to contribute. The new art, far from capitulating to the forces of materialism and academic convention, would renew the spiritual in grand, partially unforeseeable ways. Already, wrote Marc about certain artists featured in the anthology,

> their thinking has a different aim: to create out of their work symbols for their own time, symbols that belong on the altars of a future spiritual religion. . . . [19]

He enlarged on this striking thought in his introduction to the second edition of *The Blaue Reiter Almanac*, published in 1914, two years before he lost his life in the war:

> We know that everything could be destroyed if the beginnings of a spiritual discipline are not protected from the greed and dishonesty of the masses. We are struggling for pure ideas, for a world in which pure ideas can be thought and proclaimed without becoming impure. Only then will we or others who are more talented be able to show the other face of the Janus head, which today is still hidden and turns its gaze away from the times.

> We admire the disciples of early Christianity who found the strength for inner stillness amid the roaring noise of their time. For this stillness we pray and strive every hour.[20]

"The other face of the Janus head" remains a powerful image, implying a reserve of love, sensibility, and artistry. Franz Marc himself embodied his feeling for life in visionary paintings of horses and other creatures that stand apart from human violence. He was, one might say, a Nature mystic—in any case a man of great sweetness and intellectual capacity who recognized in animals an innocence something like his own.

Kandinsky's art in the years of *On the Spiritual in Art* has been studied in detail by gifted, persevering art historians.[21] I will not attempt to summarize the research of Ringbom, Washton Long, Peg Weiss, H. K. Roethel, and others. It may seem something of an indecency that an artist of our own time has required such extensive interpretation; common sense whispers that a near-contemporary should be more transparent. On the other hand, in creating his first partially (and soon fully) abstract works, Kandinsky moved into an ambiguous imaginative world. Not quite willing to abandon all reference to real objects and familiar ideas, he often dissolved objects in his paintings so that, as he once put it, they could not be immediately recognized.[22] Scholars have naturally been drawn to provide interpretive keys, and their work has been both necessary and effective.

The fully abstract works of these years, such as the especially beautiful *Black Lines* of 1913, can be approached without fear of misperceiving hidden imagery. Such works swirl. Seemingly suspended in turbulent liquid, broad color patches and a nervous linear network stream freely across the canvas—colliding, blending, moving on. The viewer looks in vain for the classical elements of composition, finds instead a passionate clash of color and abstract form, a dominant mood, and in time a theme that can be more or less clearly stated. ***Black Lines*** resolves into a combat between the positive, joyful energies of color and the scratchy, threatening overlay of lines. The painting surely conveys Kandinsky's experience of positive energies rising and dark energies subverting their expansion in a struggle between joy and constraint.

Is this the height of the spiritual in art? The inspiration, the sense of impending greatness, the untiring insistence on spirit in Kandinsky's Munich writings are not quite matched by the art of those years. Kandinsky's passion to break free and soar seemed unable to tolerate a more deliberate order in the world of his paintings. In these earlier years, he had broken down the old order of pictorial signs but had not yet evolved a new order. Obeying his sense of inner necessity, he brought brilliant color and dynamic interactions to the canvas—in a somewhat melted, unstructured visual language. In time this would change. In the art of his Bauhaus years, the 1920s and early 1930s, we will encounter more fully realized work in which Kandinsky's love of color and movement is contained but not constrained by geometric forms.

Yet in the years before World War I Kandinsky discovered and explored much of the pictorial vocabulary that would reappear in the late 1940s as Abstract Expressionism. The Munich works were intensely original, while the Bauhaus works were derivative of the art of Russian colleagues whom Kandinsky came to know in the early years of the Revolution. The Bauhaus works nonetheless represent his artistic maturity, if maturity means a mobile balance between passion and reason, impulse and restraint. Kandinsky, author and thinker, matured earlier than Kandinsky, painter, although the passionate turmoil in his early paintings exerted a great influence on the future.

"In the final analysis," he wrote in 1912,

> every serious work is tranquil. . . . Every serious work resembles in poise the quiet phrase, "I am here." Like or dislike for the work evaporates; but the sound of that phrase is eternal.[23]

Here again is the voice of his early writings, which in their great passages have lost none of their appeal. In those writings, Kandinsky conveyed many of the ideas that inevitably govern and nourish the spiritual in art—ideas about human consciousness and the inner life, about the obvious and subtle in Nature, about the artist's discipline as seer and technician. To all of this he gave a new voice, sometimes Romantic and of its age, sometimes echoing the timeless affirmation, "I am here."

NOTES

[1] Major Kandinsky bibliography includes listings under his name in the bibliography, as well as Bowlt/Washton Long (1984), Guggenheim Museum (1972), Herbert (1964), LA Catalogue, Poling (1983), Ringbom (1970), Rudenstine (1976), Washton Long (1980), Weiss (1979), and the publications of Hans Konrad Roethel.

[2] Herbert (1964), 34

[3] Herbert (1964), 38-39. Ringbom (1970) explains that the epoch of the great spiritual was associated in Kandinsky's thought with a new revelation of the Third Person of the Trinity, the Holy Spirit.

[4] Kandinsky CW, 131

[5] Kandinsky CW, 137

[6] Kandinsky/Marc (1974), 164-65, 173 (italics in original)

[7] Plato, *Apology* 31D

[8] Kandinsky (1974), 74n; cf. Kandinsky CW, 211n. The 1947 translation of *On the Spiritual,* while surely less accurate in places, is often more polished than the version in Kandinsky CW. It is also the voice of Kandinsky heard in English for many decades, given that the 1947 translation was a revision of the original 1914 version. Where I quote the 1947 translation, as here, the note gives the corresponding pages in Kandinsky CW.

[9] Kandinsky CW, 175-76

[10] Kandinsky CW, 400. Kandinsky's reference to the categorical imperative recalls Kantian ethics, evoked here to shed light on inner necessity, which Kandinsky took to be the heart of the artist's ethic.

[11] Bush/Shin (1985), 40; cf. 10-17, 39

[12] Kandinsky (1947), 39; cf. Kandinsky CW, 152

[13] Kandinsky (1947), 36-39; cf. Kandinsky CW, 151-52

[14] Kandinsky (1947), 39; cf. Kandinsky CW, 152

[15] Kandinsky (1947), 51; cf. Kandinsky CW, 171

[16] Kandinsky (1947), 44; cf. Kandinsky CW, 157

[17] Kandinsky (1947), 61; cf. Kandinsky CW, 186

[18] Kandinsky (1947), 67; cf. Kandinsky CW, 197

[19] Kandinsky/Marc (1974), 64

[20] Kandinsky/Marc (1974), 259

[21] See Washton Long (1980)

[22] Kandinsky CW, 396

[23] Kandinsky (1947), 77n; cf. Kandinsky CW, 218

Michael Faherty (essay date 1992)

SOURCE: "Kandinsky at the Klavier: Stevens and the Musical Theory of Wassily Kandinsky," in *The Wallace Stevens Journal,* Vol. 16, No. 2, Fall, 1992, pp. 151-60.

[In the following essay, Faherty explores Wallace Stevens's interest in Kandinsky's work.]

In June 1952, Stevens wrote to the Irish poet and art historian Thomas McGreevy:

> It made Kandinsky for me. I had not seen much of his work up to then and certainly not enough to make it possible to see it as a minor cosmos, which it is. It is the sort of thing that is wholly esthetic and wholly delightful. And from that point of view it seemed valid. (Brazeau)

While it is clear from this comment to McGreevy that Stevens was by no means unfamiliar with the Russian painter, it is also clear that he had been reserving his judgment on Kandinsky's achievement until he had had a chance to see a considerable collection of his work. Stevens does not name the exhibition he refers to in the letter, but he does tell McGreevy that he saw it during a visit to New York to look at some paintings by Jack Yeats.[1] The only considerable collection of Kandinsky's work on exhibit in New York at this time would have been a show hosted by the Knoedler Galleries from May 10th to June 6th of that year. The exhibition was organized by the Institute of Contemporary Art in Boston, which had the paintings on exhibit earlier that spring before sending them on to New York. It was not until after this exhibition, which included forty-five canvases spanning the artist's entire career, that Stevens began to add Kandinsky's name to his rather short list of modern artists whom he found "easy to like."[2]

As was true with the handful of other modern painters whom Stevens embraced—such as Braque, Picasso, Matisse, Brancusi, and Klee—his interest in Kandinsky was inextricably bound with his interest in the aesthetics that justified the artist's modernist experiments. In a subsequent letter to McGreevy in October of the same year, Stevens sings Kandinsky's praises once again, expressing an interest in his theories of abstraction while maintaining reservations for much of the rest of abstract expressionism:

> Much of it is arresting. It is easy to like Klee and Kandinsky. What is difficult is to like the many minor figures who do not communicate any theory that validates what they do and, in consequence, impress one as being without validity. And non-objective art without an aesthetic basis seems to be an especially unpleasant kettle of tripe.

Although Stevens was a great frequenter of the galleries and museums in New York his entire life, his attraction to a particular work was almost always dependent upon the theories that the painter had used to create that work. He repeatedly instructed Paule Vidal, who served as his buyer in Paris, to seek out the intentions of the painters whose works she purchased for him. For example, after taking an interest in the paintings of Camille Bombois, Stevens wrote to Vidal asking her to see if she might be able to find something by Bombois that he could afford, suggesting that she visit the painter's studio where she could also "ask him to comment on whatever you buy so that I can have some idea of what he, himself, intended." In fact, in a letter to Barbara Church in which he describes a less than satisfying visit to an exhibition of sculpture by Hans Arp and laments the weakness of Arp's imagination, Stevens even goes so far as to suggest that "what really validates modern art is not so much its results as its intentions and purposes."

Although it is clear from his correspondence with McGreevy that Stevens was familiar with Kandinsky's theories of abstraction and that he found these theories validated by the exhibition at the Knoedler Galleries in the spring of 1952, it is not clear exactly when and where he first learned of Kandinsky and what it was about his aesthetics that he found so "wholly delightful." According to James Johnson Sweeney, an acquaintance of Stevens who served as director of the Guggenheim Museum from 1952 to 1959, the poet had taken an interest in Kandinsky's aesthetics long before the Knoedler show. Stevens was in the habit of stopping by the Guggenheim to chat with Sweeney about painting when he was in New York and it was apparently during one of these informal conversations that Stevens first indicated to him that he had had an early interest in the Russian expressionist. When asked to confirm the fact that Stevens liked to talk about Kandinsky, Sweeney replied: "Yes, he was interested in the musical theory of Kandinsky's painting. It stimulated a good many people in those early days, 1912 and right after. I think that's what appealed to him" (Brazeau). The "early days" that Sweeney refers to would have been about the time that Stevens became acquainted with a small group of writers (including Donald Evans, Allen and Louise Norton and, somewhat later, Carl Van Vechten) who came together partially as the result of a shared enthusiasm for the modernist innovations of the Armory Show in the winter of 1913. The group served as Stevens' primary contact with the New York avant-garde until they themselves were absorbed into the considerably larger and more artistically mixed social circle that began to gather at the apartment of Walter and Louise Arensberg, whose own interest in modern art included a private collection which rivaled that of Gertrude and Leo Stein in Paris.[3] Although it is impossible to determine exactly what was discussed when either of these groups met, their conversations seem to have covered nearly every aspect of modern art and, as Sweeney has noted, this certainly would have included Kandinsky.[4]

With the publication of his first book, **Über das Geistige in der Kunst,** in Munich in the spring of 1912, Kandinsky became a central figure of the avant-garde in both Europe and America. However, it was not until the publication of Michael Sadler's translation in 1914, **The Art of Spiritual**

Harmony, that artists in New York took a real interest in Kandinsky, including his so-called "musical theory."[5] In *Über das Geistige in der Kunst,* Kandinsky argues that as all the arts at the beginning of this century began to move together toward greater and greater abstraction, artists naturally turned to music for instruction since it is this art form, above all others, that is free of the mimetic dictates of natural phenomena:

> Ein Künstler, welcher in der wenn auch künstlerischen Nachahmung der Naturerscheinungen kein Ziel für sich sieht und ein Schöpfer ist, welcher seine *innere Welt* zum Ausdruck bringen will und muß, sieht mit Neid, wie solche Ziele in der heute un-materiellsten Kunst—der Musik—natürlich und leicht zu erreichen sind. Es ist verständlich, daß er sich ihr zuwendet und versucht, dieselben Mittel in seiner Kunst zu finden.

> [An artist who is creative and sees no point in the copying of natural phenomena, no matter how artistic that copying may be, and who desires to and must express his *inner world* sees with envy how natural and easy it is to achieve such an aim in the most non-material art there is today—music. It is obvious why he turns to music and tries to find the same means in his art.]

Kandinsky argues that although painting and music will naturally move closer together during a period of abstraction in the arts, each will still retain some specific qualities inherent to its art form that the other art will never be able to imitate. Kandinsky cites, for example, music's ability to make use of the duration of time and painting's ability to present itself whole at one glance.[6]

Kandinsky was not only convinced that painting can imitate music but that painting and music can also produce similar effects on the "soul," which he considered to be the center of aesthetic experience. For Kandinsky, there is essentially no difference between a form or color in an abstract painting and a note in music; moreover, this is true whether the note is a sound produced by a musical instrument or the musical notation of that sound on a sheet of paper. In either case, the note itself is merely the "material" expression of a particular emotion, not unlike a form or color in painting, registered by either the sense of sight or hearing. In fact, in *Punkt und Linie zu Fläche,* which includes his most extended discussion of his "musical theory," Kandinsky argues that it is possible to read the forms and colors of an abstract painting much in the same way that one reads the notes of a musical score, with each form or color signifying its own particular *Klang.*[7] Just as it is possible for a trained musician to read a musical score and hear a "sound" internally, it is likewise possible for a sensitive eye to read the "sounds" in an abstract painting. The history of naturalist art, according to Kandinsky, has been a smothering of these "sounds" and an attempt to force the abstract elements of painting to serve a utilitarian end—the representation of natural phenomena—rather than allowing them to stand alone:

> Ihre Entstehung verdanken sie der Unfähigkeit, das Innere der Dinge im Äußeren zu erkennen—die wie eine leere Nußschale hartgewordene Seele hat ihre Tauchfähigkeit verloren und kann nicht mehr in die Tiefe der Dinge durchdringen, wo der Pulsschlag unter der äußeren Hülse hörbar wird. (*PLF*)

> [This sort of painting owes its emergence to the inability to perceive the internal life of an object in its external appearance—the soul has become as hard as an empty nutshell and has lost its ability to dive into and penetrate the depths of the object where, below its external shell, its pulsebeat can be heard.]

However, Kandinsky suggests that for those who have not been completely desensitized by naturalist art, it may still be possible to "hear" the forms and colors of abstract painting. Just as the written note in music is no more than a symbol of a tone of definite pitch—indicating the pitch by its position on the staff and the duration by its shape—Kandinsky argues that an individual form or color is, in a very similar sense, a "symbol" of its own unique "sound" capable of communicating a particular emotion as specifically as a written quarter note can signify an F-flat.[8]

In order to explain how a form or color can have an effect on the soul similar to that of a musical note, Kandinsky often cited his metaphor of the piano. It is this metaphor that is at the heart of Kandinsky's "musical theory" and which was excerpted in the November 1914 issue of *The Little Review* (53), a journal in which Stevens later published and where he might have come across it for the first time.[9] In this metaphor, Kandinsky suggests that the aesthetic experience in abstract art functions in much the same fashion as a piano, in which the colors are the keys and the eye the hammer which causes vibrations in the strings of the soul:

> Im allgemeinen ist also die Farbe ein Mittel, einen direkten Einfluß auf die Seele auszuüben. Die Farbe ist die Taste. Das Auge ist der Hammer. Die Seele ist das Klavier mit vielen Saiten.

> Der Künstler ist die Hand, die durch diese oder jene Taste *zweckmässig* die menschliche Seele in Vibration bringt. (*ÜG*)

> [In general, color is a medium that has a direct influence on the soul. The color is the key. The eye is the hammer. The soul is the piano with many strings.

> The artist is the hand that brings the human soul into vibration by playing the *appropriate* keys.]

It is crucial here to note that the senses in this metaphor serve merely as the "hammers" which cause the vibrations of the "soul." For Kandinsky, this is true whether or not the "keys" themselves are forms, colors, sounds, individual words, or any other signifier. Although there is no doubt that the initial impression of both painting and music is a function of the senses and, therefore, largely a "physical" sensation, this is of value only if it leads to a corresponding internal or "spiritual" vibration:

> Hier kommt die psychische Kraft der Farbe zutage, welche eine seelische Vibration hervorruft. Und die erste, elementare physiche Kraft wird nun zur Bahn, auf welcher die Farbe die Seele erreicht. (*ÜG*)

> [Here the psychic force of color becomes evident, which gives rise to a spiritual vibration. And this initial, elemental psychic force now becomes the transport by which the color reaches the soul.]

Kandinsky argues that too much contemporary art, particularly "decorative" art, appeals only to the senses and not to the soul:

> Die Nervenvibration wird freilich vorhanden sein . . . sie bleibt aber hauptsächlich im Bereiche der Nerven stecken, weil sie zu schwache Gemüts-vibrationen, Erschütterungen der Seele hervorrufen wird. (*ÜG*)

> [There will, of course, be vibrations of the nerves . . . but for the most part they will not get beyond the domain of the nerves because the vibrations of the soul that they call forth will be too weak.]

It is these "vibrations of the soul," and the emotions awakened there, that are the aesthetic experience of any abstract art form, according to Kandinsky, and not the sensual stimulation of vibrations in the air or pigments on a canvas.

Whether Stevens first learned of Kandinsky's "musical theory" at a gathering of the New York avant-garde or from the short excerpt in *The Little Review,* he borrowed the metaphor of the piano to explain his aesthetic views in one of his earliest and most important poems, "Peter Quince at the Clavier." Although the poem was not published in *Others* until August 1915, Van Vechten reports that Stevens showed him a copy of the poem during a luncheon at the Brevoort on November 21st, 1914—the same month the excerpt appeared in *The Little Review* (42). The date stuck in Van Vechten's memory not only because it was the first time he met Stevens or because he had resigned as editor of *Trend* earlier that day (two events memorable enough in themselves), but also because the luncheon eventually stretched into somewhat of a "pseudo-debauch," ending with Arensberg inviting Stevens up to his apartment for the first time for a few more drinks and both Stevens and Van Vechten attempting to "make music" on the piano (44). The poem was an immediate success among the avant-garde and included in *Others* anthologies in both 1915 and 1916, as well as Harriet Monroe's anthology of new poetry in 1917. Kandinsky's metaphor of the piano provides the central metaphor of the poem and is the subject of its very first stanza:

> Just as my fingers on these keys
> Make music, so the selfsame sounds
> On my spirit make a music, too.
> (*CP* 89)

Even though all the elements of Kandinsky's own metaphor are there in the opening lines of the poem, it is not clear that Stevens definitely has this particular metaphor in mind until the reader comes to the conclusion contained in the first line of the following stanza:

> Music is feeling, then, not sound . . .
> (*CP* 90)

It is this basic understanding—that music, and by implication the other arts as well, is essentially emotion rather than its "material" components—which becomes the basis of argument for the rest of the poem.

Stevens quickly turns Kandinsky's metaphor around by suggesting that since music itself is essentially feeling rather than vibrations in the air, the "internal vibrations" caused by any object in nature have an aesthetic effect not unlike that produced by music. Addressing an unidentified *you,* the speaker of the poem argues that if music is emotion, emotion is, likewise, music:

> And thus it is that what I feel,
> Here in this room, desiring you,

> Thinking of your blue-shadowed silk,
> Is music.
> (*CP* 90)

In order to explain this side of the argument, Stevens extends the metaphor by drawing upon the apocryphal story of Susanna who, quite innocently, was spied upon by the elders of her village while bathing. Just as a particular color in Kandinsky's example can cause a corresponding "vibration of the soul," Susanna is the unwitting "key" that "touched the bawdy strings / Of those white elders" (*CP* 92):

> Of a green evening, clear and warm,
> She bathed in her still garden, while
> The red-eyed elders watching, felt

> The basses of their beings throb
> In witching chords, and their thin blood
> Pulse pizzicati of Hosanna.
> (*CP* 90)

For Susanna, too, the emotion of the evening is pure music until it is "muted" by a "breath upon her hand" at which she turns to discover the elders: "A cymbal crashed, / And roaring horns" (*CP* 91). Although Stevens argues in this rather discursive poem that, as he suggests in its final stanzas, our notion of beauty comes from the external world, he also acknowledges that there is essentially no difference between an emotion that is stimulated by an object in nature and an emotion that is the effect of a work of art. In much the same way that Stevens, in the role of Peter Quince, is capable of producing music that can penetrate to the "soul" of those who hear it, nature itself can play upon the keyboard of his "soul," whether through Susanna, the unidentified *you* of the poem, or any other natural object.

Kandinsky makes the same point in his second reference to the metaphor of the piano in *Über das Geistige in der Kunst.* He argues that the metaphor applies equally well to the general experience of life if the object in nature takes the place of color:

> Jeder Gegenstand (ohne Unterschied, ob er direkt von der "Natur" geschaffen wurde oder durch menschliche Hand entstanden ist) ist ein Wesen mit eigenem Leben und daraus unvermeidlich fließender Wirkung. Der Mensch unterliegt fortwährend dieser psychischen Wirkung. . . . Die "Natur," d.h. die stets wechselnde äußere Umgebung des Menschen, versetzt durch die Tasten (Gegenstände) fortwährend die Saiten des Klaviers (Seele) in Vibrationen. (*ÜG*)

> [Every object (regardless of whether it is a direct creation of nature or made by a human hand) is an entity with its own life and its inevitably resultant effects. Man is continually subject to these psychic effects. . . . "Nature," that is to say the constantly changing external surroundings of man, continually sets the strings of the piano (the soul) into vibration by means of the keys (the objects).]

In fact, Kandinsky argues that the perception of an object in nature is nothing more than the perception of its individual forms and colors, but with the additional perception of their combined effect, which is the object itself. Just as the painter has all of nature at his disposal from which to pick and choose the forms and colors of his composition—like Peter Quince selecting which keys to strike and in what combination—nature plays the instrument of his soul, bombarding it with an incessant array of natural objects whose own forms and colors suggest a music not unlike that created by the artist himself.

It was precisely this aesthetic that Stevens found validated by the Knoedler exhibition in the spring of 1952. Surely, he must have been pleased to find that a painter who had claimed years ago in his "musical theory" that it was possible for an artist to set up a music in the soul through the arrangement of forms and colors alone was able to do so. However, this was not something that Kandinsky accomplished quickly. Even though his early paintings are still considered his breakthrough into the realm of pure abstraction, scholars have decoded their images and, in comparison to his later work, many of them no longer look abstract.[10] Even an untrained eye can detect traces of clashing armies, crumbling towers, and other apocalyptic and religious folk images. However, these early, less abstract works are not the paintings Stevens saw at the Knoedler Galleries in New York. Of the forty-five works by Kandinsky displayed at the Knoedler exhibition, all but eight were from his later Bauhaus and Parisian periods. As many art historians have pointed out, it is these later paintings rather than his earlier, better-known works that validated the theories first enunciated in 1912. And it was these later works with their bright, fauvist colors and childlike imagination that Stevens found so "wholly aesthetic and wholly delightful," confirming his best expectations. He must have been

pleased that he could actually "hear" the forms and colors of these paintings, to let Kandinsky—like Peter Quince—put his fingers here and there along the keyboard and set the strings of his "soul" into vibration.

NOTES

[1] The quotation is from an unpublished letter that Brazeau cites in the notes to his book. The letter is held by the Manuscripts Department at Trinity College in Dublin. I am grateful to Stuart O'Seanóir of Trinity College Library for confirming my suspicion that Stevens does not specifically identify the exhibition and providing this additional information.

[2] A list of the paintings included in the exhibition can be found in an appendix at the end of this essay.

[3] Although the Arensberg collection eventually included three paintings by Kandinsky (*Improvisation 29, Kleines Bild mit Gelb,* and *Kreise im Kreis*), it is unlikely that the Arensbergs acquired any of these canvases before leaving New York, particularly *Kreise im Kreis,* which was not completed until 1923. The individual histories of all three works can be found in the catalogue raisonné of Kandinsky's oil paintings by Roethel and Benjamin cited in the appendix (431, 481, 656).

[4] For the best discussion of these "early days" and Stevens' relationship to both circles, see the first two chapters of Glen MacLeod's *Wallace Stevens and Company: The* Harmonium *Years, 1913-1923* (Ann Arbor: UMI Research Press, 1983).

[5] The notable exception was the small circle of artists surrounding Alfred Stieglitz who took an almost immediate interest in Kandinsky's theories, with Stieglitz printing a translated excerpt in his journal *Camera Work* as early as July 1912 (see Works Cited).

[6] However, Kandinsky also notes that these differences are only relative and that painting, in particular, can make use of time in a manner quite similar to music. This becomes the basis of much of his argument in his next book, *Punkt und Linie zu Fläche.*

[7] Kandinsky explains that he uses the word *Klänge* (sounds) to describe the *innere Eigenschaften* (internal qualities) of the individual elements of any art form (*PLF* 89).

[8] In *Über das Geistige in der Kunst,* Kandinsky often compares colors or variations in the shading of colors to musical instruments, suggesting, for example, that a light blue color resembles the sound of a flute, a darker blue that of a cello, an even darker blue that of a contrabass, while the darkest shade of blue can be compared to the sound of an organ (93). The Russian composer Aleksandr Scriabin took this even a step further, arguing that there is a direct correlation between colors and tones of music. For example, he suggests that the note C is comparable to the color red in painting, while a D-flat suggests purple

and G a shade of orange-pink. His chart comparing musical tones to colors first appeared in an issue of the Soviet journal *Music* published in Moscow in January 1911, which Kandinsky had seen.

[9] This issue of *The Little Review* also contains a satirical essay written by Alexander Kaun under the pseudonym of Ibn Gabirol comparing Kandinsky's aesthetics to those of Gertrude Stein in *Tender Buttons* (see Works Cited). The essay almost certainly caught the attention of Donald Evans and other members of Stevens' early circle since, as MacLeod has noted, they shared an enthusiasm for Stein on par with their love for the Armory Show (7-10).

[10] For a comprehensive discussion of Kandinsky's use of hidden images in his early paintings, see Rose-Carol Long's *Wassily Kandinsky: The Development of an Abstract Style* (Oxford: Clarendon, 1980).

WORKS CITED

Brazeau, Peter. *Parts of a World: Wallace Stevens Remembered.* New York: Random House, 1983.

Gabirol, Ibn (Alexander Kaun). "My Friend, the Incurable." *The Little Review* 1 (November 1914): 42-44.

Kandinsky, Wassily. "Extracts from *The Spiritual in Art.*" *Camera Work* 39 (1912): 34.

———. *Punkt und Linie zu Fläche: Beitrag zur Analyse der malerischen Elemente.* 1926. Bern: Benteli, 1973.

———. *Über das Geistige in der Kunst.* 1912. Bern: Benteli, 1965.

MacLeod, Glen. *Wallace Stevens and Company: The Harmonium Years, 1913-23.* Ann Arbor: UMI Research Press, 1983.

Stevens, Wallace. *The Collected Poems.* New York: Vintage, 1982.

———. *Letters of Wallace Stevens.* Ed. Holly Stevens. New York: Knopf, 1966.

Van Vechten, Carl. "Rogue Elephant in Porcelain." *The Yale University Library Gazette* 38.2 (1963): 41-50.

Michael Faherty (essay date 1992)

SOURCE: "The Third Dimension: Ezra Pound and Wassily Kandinsky," in *Paideuma*, Vol. 21, No. 3, Winter, 1992, pp. 63-77.

[*In the following essay, Faherty determines the influence of Kandinsky's theoretical writings on the work of the poet Ezra Pound.*]

The very first English critic to review Wassily Kandinsky's *Über das Geistige in der Kunst* was also the first to recognize its potential impact on the future of modern poetry. Writing in the arts journal *Rhythm* in the spring of 1912, shortly after Kandinsky's book first appeared on the shelves of Munich bookshops, Michael Sadler predicted that Kandinsky's theories of abstraction would not only alter the course of modern painting but modern verse as well. A writer himself, Sadler argued that poets need no longer concern themselves with description and mimesis but should feel free to experiment with the abstract possibilities of verse. However, Sadler was not the only one to recognize the value of Kandinsky's aesthetics for modern English poetry. In his crucial "Vorticism" essay, first published in the *Fortnightly Review* in September 1914, Ezra Pound also called for an end to the naturalistic tendencies of modern poetry, offering Kandinsky's theories of abstraction as a viable alternative to the earlier impressionist analogies put forward by Ford Madox Ford and T. E. Hulme. For Pound, neither the "neo-impressionism" of the cubists nor the "accelerated impressionism" of the futurists provided a satisfactory alternative to the growing restrictions of imagism since they not only maintained the relation between painting and external phenomena but cherished it.

It is now clear to many art historians that the emergence of abstractionism in the visual arts in this century was directly related to an attempt by artists to express what they regarded as finer and subtler emotions than naturalistic art was capable of. It was the inability of mimesis to communicate such emotions that led to experiments with form and color alone. In his chapter on the language of form and color—the chapter Pound cites in his "Vorticism" essay—Kandinsky argues that words have always been able to communicate such basic emotions as fear, joy and grief, but are completely inadequate when it comes to more subtle and complex feelings. It is precisely this will to express these finer emotions that has brought on a search for abstract forms capable of such expression. While certain shades of color and tones of music may approach such expression, argues Kandinsky, words cannot:

> Die Töne der Farben, ebenso wie die der Musik, sind viel feinerer Natur, erwecken viel feinere Vibrationen der Seele, die mit Worten nicht zu bezeichnen sind. Jeder Ton kann sehr wahrscheinlich mit der Zeit einen Ausdruck auch im materiellen Wort finden, es wird aber immer noch ein übriges bleiben, was vom Worte nicht vollständig ausgeschöpft werden kann, was aber nicht eine luxuriöse Beigabe des Tones ist, sondern gerade das Wesentliche in demselben. *Deswegen sind und bleiben Worte nur Winke, ziemlich äusserliche Kennzeichen der Farben.* (*ÜG*)

> [Tones of color, like musical tones, are of a much finer nature and awaken much finer vibrations in the soul than words are capable of. With a bit of effort, every tone can probably be expressed in words. However, there will always be something left over that words cannot entirely express and

this something will not be insignificant but rather the essence of the tone itself. *That is why words are and will remain mere hints and superficial indications of colors.*]

Although this may suggest that Kandinsky does not think his theories of abstraction applicable to the verbal arts, it is clear from other arguments in **Über das Geistige in der Kunst** as well as his own poetry that Kandinsky is speaking here of words only as they were being used in literature at that time. Kandinsky is not suggesting that verse is incapable of expressing such fine emotions but that its own literary and mimetic nature give it even greater obstacles to overcome than painting confronted.

The emotion at the metro station at La Concorde that Pound describes in his "Vorticism" essay is a good example of what both Pound and Kandinsky considered to be a complex modern emotion. Pound notes that it was his struggle to write his "In a Station of the Metro" poem which first alerted him to the inadequacy of the impressionist model for poetry. The complex and subtle nature of the emotion prevented Pound from expressing this feeling in verse form and nothing he had learned about the workings of poetry was able to break this impasse:

> . . . I could not find any words that seemed to me worthy, or as lovely as that sudden emotion. And that evening, as I went home along the Rue Raynouard, I was still trying and I found, suddenly, the expression. I do not mean that I found words, but there came an equation . . . not in speech, but in little splotches of colour.

Pound notes that these "little splotches of colour" did not present themselves to him in an impressionistic manner or in any form suggesting mimeticism, but in pure abstraction. Pound goes on to explain that he immediately understood the significance of his experience:

> That evening, in the Rue Raynouard, I realized quite vividly that if I were a painter, or if I had, often, *that kind* of emotion, or even if I had the energy to get paints and brushes and keep at it, I might found a new school of painting, of "non-representative" painting, a painting that would speak only by arrangements in colour.

It is at this point in the essay that Pound claims that when he first came to read Kandinsky, "I found little that was new to me. I only felt that some one else understood what I understood, and had written it out very clearly."[1]

Even prior to the publication of this essay, Pound claimed that he understood that color alone could effectively communicate such complex emotions. However, it took Pound some time to be able to fully express himself on this. Even after the publication of the first issue of *Blast* with its extensive excerpts from **Über das Geistige in der Kunst** in June 1914, by which time Pound had surely read at least the chapter cited in his "Vorticism" essay, he was still having some difficulty putting his aesthetic experi-ence into words. In his essay on Edward Wadsworth written for *The Egoist* in August 1914, Pound describes a Wadsworth painting before him in his flat at Holland Place Chambers that he considered to be an "arrangement in pure form":

> This picture does not "look like" anything, save perhaps a Chinese or Japanese painting with the representative patches removed. The feeling I get from this picture is very much the feeling I get from certain Eastern paintings, and I think the feeling that went into it is probably very much the same as that which moved certain Chinese painters. (Zinnes)

Although Pound was not ready to state his belief in the expressive capabilities of pure form more strongly than this in August 1914 and still felt the need to compare the abstraction to a parallel in Eastern art, he quite quickly came round to a much bolder conviction in the ability of individual forms to carry meaning. By the summer of 1916, Pound was confidently stating that "A circle or a triangle has just as much form as the Albert Memorial" and, in an explanation of what he had meant by "formless form" in an earlier essay, he contends that "it is manifestly ridiculous to say that you cannot take pleasure in a form *merely because* it is not the form of a man, an animal or a bunch of asparagus" (Zinnes). But even a quick perusal of Pound's art criticism written shortly before and after the "Vorticism" essay makes it clear that although Pound may have found "little that was new" to him in Kandinsky's writings, he was still far from comfortable with these new theories of abstraction when he wrote the essay.

In the "Formen- und Farbensprache" chapter which Pound cites in his essay, Kandinsky argues that each color conveys a particular emotion. Although he admits that the emotional equivalents he assigns to certain colors are based on no more than a "spiritual" analysis, he does include a number of rather scientific-looking charts which graphically describe the various properties of those colors, including their contrasting tendencies toward warmth or coldness, excentricity or concentricity, motion or stasis. Kandinsky argues, for example, that yellow has an essentially aggressive and unsettling nature, tending to move excentrically toward the viewer, while blue emits a feeling of spiritual peace and moves concentrically away from the viewer; a combination of the two colors, creating green, causes all movement either toward or away from the viewer to cease and is, therefore, the most restful of the colors (*ÜG*). Although Kandinsky limits his discussion of these characteristics to the primary colors, he suggests that given the almost unlimited number of shades of these colors as well as the limitless possibilities of combining colors, the ability of the artist to express the most complex and subtle of emotions through the use of color alone seems to know no bounds. Kandinsky points out some of the finer subtleties involved in juxtaposing various colors on a canvas as well as the emotional equivalents of certain geometrical and non-geometrical forms.[2] Like the colors themselves, each form suggests a particular emotion, and the expression conveyed by that form changes substantially with even the smallest alteration:

> Jede Form ist so empfindlich wie ein Rauchwölkchen: das unmerklichste geringste Verrücken jeder ihrer Teile verändert sie *wesentlich.* (*ÜG*)

> [Every form is as delicate as a puff of smoke: the slightest, most imperceptible alteration of any of its parts changes its *entire character.*]

Kandinsky suggests that such expression in abstract form and color is limited only by the artist's ability to sense these characteristics in the forms and colors themselves as well as the ability of the modern audience to appreciate such subtleties of expression.

In *Über das Geistige in der Kunst,* Kandinsky argues that colors are perceived in two stages. In the first stage, the viewer perceives the color as a physical thing: blue is registered on the retina as blue, for example. Although this physical impression may at first have a soothing effect on the eye (as blue usually does), this effect is only temporary:

> Ebenso wie man bei Berührung von Eis nur das Gefühl einer physischen Kälte erleben kann und dieses Gefühl nach dem Wiedererwärmen des Fingers vergiât, so wird auch die physische Wirkung der Farbe vergessen, wenn das Auge abgewendet wird. Und ebenso, wie das physische Gefühl der Kälte des Eises, wenn es tiefer eindringt, andere tiefere Gefühle erweckt und eine ganze Kette psychischer Erlebnisse bilden kann, so kann auch der oberflächliche Eindruck der Farbe sich zu einem Erlebnis entwickeln.

> [In the same way that the mere physical sensation of coldness can be experienced by touching ice and this same sensation quickly forgotten when the fingers warm up again, the physical impression of color is forgotten when the eye turns away. And in the same way that the physical sensation of the coldness of ice—if it penetrates deeper—awakens other, deeper feelings and can begin a whole chain of psychic experiences, the initially superficial impression of a color can generate a similar experience.]

According to Kandinsky, only this deeper psychic experience is of any importance and those painters who work exclusively on the physical level—such as those who are often labeled "colorists" in contemporary art circles—create nothing more than decoration. It is the artist capable of using colors psychically or "spiritually" who can work in a language of form and color to express emotions and spiritual states directly.

While even those who were most critical of Kandinsky admired his attempt to free form and color to work abstractly in painting, nearly all of those who discussed his theories in the pre-war years expressed a concern with the apparently "associative" nature of his color equivalents.[3]

Many of those who reviewed Kandinsky's book in the avant-garde journals in both England and America praised his attempt to use individual forms and colors as *things* capable of their own expression rather than as means toward representation, but they also warned that his charts and diagrams were a dangerous attempt to assign specific emotions to the colors and thereby limit their power of expression rather than expand it. However, Kandinsky also asked himself whether his color equivalents were merely the result of associative memory or whether they had a deeper basis. For some colors, Kandinsky admits, the emotion communicated by that color seems related to an associative reference:

> Z.B. die rote Farbe kann eine der Flamme ähnliche seelische Vibration verursachen, da das Rot die Farbe der Flamme ist. Das warme Rot wirkt aufregend, dieses Rot kann bis zu einer schmerzlichen Peinlichkeit steigen, vielleicht auch durch Ähnlichkeit mit flieâendem Blut. Hier erweckt also diese Farbe eine Erinnerung an ein anderes physisches Agens, welches unbedingt eine peinliche Wirkung auf die Seele ausübt. (*ÜG*)

> [For example, the color red can produce a psychic vibration similar to that produced by a flame because red is the color of flames. Warm red has an agitating effect that can even become extremely painful, perhaps due to its similarity to flowing blood. In both these instances, the color recalls another physical agent which clearly has a painful effect on the soul.]

Kandinsky argues that these associations may not be limited to the sense of sight alone, citing the example of yellow, which may seem "sour" since it is associated with the taste of lemon, or "shrill" when thought of in connection with the sound of the canary.

However, Kandinsky suggests that if the psychic effect of colors was limited to association alone, it would be fairly easy to assign emotional equivalents to each of the colors and this exercise would become little more than a memory game. Kandinsky argues that associative explanations are only valid for a limited number of colors and cannot withstand scientific and artistic analysis. Red, for example, may remind one both of a flame and running blood but, in a painting, red can communicate either warmth or coldness, depending on slight alterations of a single shade. Whereas Kandinsky argues that one light shade of red can communicate a feeling of coldness and parallels the sound of the violin, the slightest alteration of that same shade of light red will suggest warmth and the sound of trumpets. Mixed with brown, red can be described as the thundering of a drum while, when combined with azure, it becomes more like the sound of a cello. Kandinsky contends that these emotional values cannot be the result of associative memory alone, but are a matter of direct communication.

Like Pound, Kandinsky thought that this sort of abstraction was not limited to forms and colors alone. Kandinsky argues that a word can be separated from its meaning much the way the color red can be disassociated from a cherry. Although our idea of the color red comes from the natural objects themselves, red may be abstracted from them and, set free in this manner, used in painting in a purely expressive fashion. Kandinsky suggests that words may come to function in a similar manner:

> Schlieâlich bei öfterer Wiederholung des Wortes (beliebtes Spiel der Jugend, welches später vergessen wird) verliert es den äuâeren Sinn der Benennung. Ebenso wird sogar der abstrakt gewordene Sinn des bezeichneten Gegenstandes vergessen und nur der reine *Klang* des Wortes entblöât. (*ÜG*)

> [Eventually, through the frequent repetition of a word (a popular children's game that is later forgotten), the external meaning of the word is lost. Moreover, the meaning of the object the word denotes will be forgotten, having become more and more abstract, and the pure *sound* of the word exposed.]

Once a word has been freed from its everyday association, argues Kandinsky, even the most common word, such as "hair," can be used to express the most intense and complex emotions. As with colors, Kandinsky believed that individual words as well as the individual sounds of words are capable of communicating an emotion that is neither associative nor completely arbitrary.[4]

In his "Vorticism" essay, Pound suggests that if one accepts that the image is for the poet what form and color are for the painter, "you can go ahead and apply Kandinsky, you can transpose his chapter on the language of form and colour and apply it to the writing of verse." However, like the English and American critics before him, Pound was anxious to avoid any system of language—whether of form and color or of words—which would assign fixed meanings to its abstract elements. Pound agreed with those who cautioned Kandinsky that any sort of system of equivalents will only limit expression rather than expand it. But he did agree with Kandinsky that words, like colors, could convey a complex emotion without relying solely on the association of past sensuous experiences. Unlike Kandinsky, however, Pound was not interested in the expressive capabilities of individual words or sounds, but in the image. In his essay, Pound explains that the emotion communicated by the image, upon successive readings, has little to do with the words which contain it: "The image is itself the speech. The image is the word beyond formulated language." Pound made a similar comment concerning the abstract colors that appeared to him on the Rue Raynouard in Paris, calling this arrangement of colors "a word, the beginning for me, of a language in color." Pound suggests here that the image works in much the same way as forms and colors do for Kandinsky. As in a painting, each element of an image conveys a particular emotion and has its emotional equivalent. However, it is the combination of these elements that constitutes the final image.

It is also important to Pound that the emotion conveyed by the image, as well as its individual elements, not be reduced to the level of a symbol. Pound argues that any attempt to fix values in language will result in a very restrictive sort of symbolism:

> The symbolists dealt in "association," that is, in a sort of allusion, almost of allegory. They degraded the symbol to the status of a word. They made it a form of metonymy. One can be grossly "symbolic," for example, by using the term "cross" to mean "trial." The symbolist's *symbols* have a fixed value, like numbers in arithmetic, like 1, 2, and 7. (*GB*)

It is precisely this metonymic relationship that Pound wishes to avoid in imagist verse. Although it is certainly more difficult to abstract words from their everyday meanings than it is to abstract the color red, for example, from a cherry, Pound did believe it possible for an image to convey a meaning divorced from the fixed values of the words which contain that image. The image, Pound argues, has a "variable significance, like the signs a, b, and x in algebra." Unlike a symbol, an image cannot be said to have a fixed meaning and cannot be decoded as readily as the metonymic relationship of "cross" and "trial." Instead, it conveys what might be called a boundary of meaning within which its complex emotions operate.

Although Pound may have understood this concept before he read Kandinsky, it is clear that Kandinsky not only helped Pound refine his thinking on this subject but had a significant influence on Pound's ideas concerning the conceptual nature of modernism and the importance of the role emotion plays in creating a work of art. For Kandinsky, a true work of art is never the objective expression of a subjective emotion. Instead, Kandinsky argues just the opposite in his discussion of the principle of *innere Notwendigkeit:* the emotion itself is the *objective* element in a painting and the arrangement of the forms and colors on the canvas is nothing more than the *subjective* expression of this emotion (*ÜG*). Kandinsky suggests that this becomes clear if one looks at the development of art through the ages and in various cultures; while each culture and each age seems to have its own peculiar style and means of expression, the emotions and feelings expressed in them are relatively constant and, in a sense, eternal. The objective emotion borrows, as it were, the style of its time and culture in order to find expression.

Pound also makes this distinction in his "Vorticism" essay. In the essay, Pound states that it is the emotion that seeks expression in verse and not an object in nature or some external reality. This is particularly clear in his "autobiographical" account of writing the "Metro" poem:

> Three years ago in Paris I got out of a "metro" train at La Concorde, and saw suddenly a beautiful face, and then another and another, and then a beautiful child's face, and then another beautiful woman, and I tried all that day to find words for what this had meant to me, and I could not find any words that seemed to me worthy, or as lovely as that sudden emotion. (*GB*)

It is clear from this description of his experience at La Concorde as well as his subsequent musings along the Rue Raynouard that Pound does not wish to capture the "beautiful faces" themselves in his poem, but "that sudden emotion." It is the complex emotion brought on by the people that he sees that is the creative impetus for the poem and not the external scene itself. The year-long process that Pound went through in order to achieve his "Metro" poem—first as a thirty-line poem, then a fifteen-line poem and finally the two lines that have survived—was not a struggle to capture faithfully such "beautiful faces" in verse, but to create a poem capable of expressing this feeling in an abstract manner:

> The apparition of these faces in the crowd:
> Petals, on a wet, black bough.
>
> (GB)

Whether or not the "faces" themselves appear in the poem is almost of no consequence other than biographical interest. In fact, Pound notes that the emotion "should have gone into paint" in a non-representative design since that is how he first "perceived" it. The emotion is the objective element seeking expression in a subjective form, and whether or not Pound chose to include the "faces" themselves in the poem is entirely dependent on whether or not they serve this end. Only the emotion expressed abstractly in an arrangement of colors was Pound's original impulse, and his decision to retain the allusion in the poem to the natural objects that inspired the emotion depended on the *emotion itself* and not the external scene.

The difference between this approach to poetry and that of the early imagists becomes clear when compared to Hulme's early ideas concerning the use of the image in modern verse. In his early lectures and essays, Hulme argues that the essence of imagist poetry is the metaphor based on an impressionistic attitude toward nature. The poet's task is to discover a metaphor capable of communicating an impression of an external scene in order to "arrest you and to make you continuously see a physical thing" (*Spec*). It is important for Hulme that the reader have the feeling that "the poet is constantly in presence of a vividly felt physical and visual scene." The poet uses the metaphor to make the reader see and feel what the poet himself had previously seen and felt, to express the emotion created by the sight of a particular concrete vision. As Hulme argues in his personal notebook: "All emotions depend on real solid vision or sound. It is physical" (*FS*). For Hulme, a poet cannot write without something before his eyes: "It is this image which precedes the writing and makes it firm." The creative process begins on the street where the poet looks about for his material:

> The effort of the literary man to find subtle analogies for the ordinary street feelings he experiences leads to the differentiation and importance of those feelings. What would be unnoticed by others, and is nothing when not labelled, becomes an important emotion. A transitory artificial impression is deliberately cultivated into an emotion and written about.

As Hulme rather significantly notes, the impression is "deliberately cultivated into an emotion" and does not necessarily have anything to do with whatever original emotion was attached to the impression itself.[5] This is quite different from Pound's own "street feeling," which was not only retained in the final poem but conditioned the elements that would contain it.

The difference between the impressionistic bias of early imagism and the ideas expressed by Pound in his "Vorticism" essay also becomes clear when one looks at some of the poetry produced by these two attitudes toward art. While much of early imagist verse is still perceptual in its approach and insists upon its connection to "real solid vision or sound," many of the later poems have moved away from this early impressionistic attitude and toward a conceptual style of composition. As one of Hulme's own early poems demonstrates, the primary function of the poem is not to convey any particularly complex emotion but to capture an external scene:

> Above the quiet dock in mid night,
> Tangled in the tall mast's corded height,
> Hangs the moon. What seemed so far away
> Is but a child's balloon, forgotten after play.
>
> (*Personae*)

Hulme uses the metaphor of the "child's balloon" here merely to make the scene more vivid and alive, suggesting that it resembles the moon not only in proximity but in its helpless entanglement in the ship's rigging. For Hulme, metaphor is essential to the poem's ability to capture the scene and its attendant emotion.

Although Pound had not yet dismissed metaphor from his poetry, it is evident that he is moving toward a style of poetry which neither compares dissimilars nor seeks to discuss one object in terms of another. Even as late as his editing of Fenollosa's manuscript on the Chinese written character and his own adoption of the more abstract structure of the ideogram as a basis for composition, Pound still believed in the importance of metaphor in poetry (Fenollosa). His discussion of a Japanese *hokku* in his "Vorticism" essay likewise relies on the convention of metaphor:

> The footsteps of the cat upon the snow:
> (are like) plum-blossoms.
>
> (GB)

However, Pound notes that he inserts the comparative "are like" between the two "ideas" of the poem simply for "clarity" and his explanation of the image that follows—in which Pound argues that a one-image poem is "a form of super-position, that is to say, one idea set on top of another"—makes it clear that Pound is discussing a type of poetry whose essential function is not metaphoric. Without the autobiographical account of how the poem came into being and an unfortunate colon, it would be very difficult to identify the tenor and vehicle in Pound's "Metro" poem. Significantly, the colon was edited to a semi-colon in the first edition of *Lustra* and the relation between the two "ideas" in the poem becomes much less metaphoric and considerably more abstract.

It is not out of any particular generosity that Pound cites the work of other poets in his discussion of vorticist aesthetics. Although Pound eventually mastered this style of composition and used it to great effect in many of the cantos, he had yet to produce many poems which he himself considered good examples of this approach to verse. Even in his "Vortex" in the first issue of *Blast*, Pound cites H.D.'s "Oread" rather than one of his own poems as an example of this sort of poetry, comparing it to both Kandinsky and Picasso in painting. It is clear to Pound that the function of this poem is not metaphoric:

> Whirl up sea—
> Whirl your pointed pines,
> Splash your great pines
> On our rocks,
> Hurl your green over us,
> Cover us with your pools of fir.
>
> (Zinnes)

Unlike the poem by Hulme in which a "vividly felt physical and visual scene" is described in terms of metaphor, this poem is not attempting to paint the scene itself but to express a complex emotion, which contains elements of both surrender and assertion. In his "Vorticism" essay, Pound calls this sort of poem an *equation:* "not an equation of mathematics, not something about *a, b,* and *c,* having something to do with form, but about *sea, cliffs, night,* having something to do with mood" (*GB*). The various elements of the poem do not create an impressionistic scene despite the presence of a strong physical image, but function as emotional equivalents for the feeling expressed.

Like Kandinsky's forms and colors, these images work in two stages: the first physical and the second psychic or "spiritual." Just as one must see Kandinsky's colors for what they are before proceeding to their spiritual significance, Pound's images must be allowed to assert their physical impression before their fuller meaning is revealed. Unless one fully visualizes the faces and petals of the "Metro" poem, the emotion contained in that image will not be communicated. The emotion is grounded in the "ideas" themselves and their subsequent contemplation. Pound was discovering this sort of emotion in Chinese poetry even prior to his interest in Fenollosa; and, in a poem entitled "Ts'ai Chi'h," first published in *The Glebe* in February 1914, he presents an image which does not depend on metaphor or ideogrammic juxtaposition for its effect:

> The petals fall in the fountain,
> the orange-coloured rose-leaves,
> Their ochre clings to the stone.
>
> (*Personae*)

Although this is almost certainly a translation from an unidentified Chinese poet, Pound clearly considered this to be an imagist poem like those of the other Eastern poets that he was also rather loosely translating at the time. For its effect, it depends upon the reader first visualizing the objects themselves: the petals' floating motion as they drop into the fountain, their bright color and its traces on the stone. Once this process is complete, the abstract significance of the poem begins to assert itself and the emotion contained in the image becomes the focus of attention rather than the concrete visualization of the fountain. This is quite different from Hulme's conception of the image in which the metaphor draws the reader closer to the physical objects rather than beyond them.

Like Kandinsky, Pound was convinced that there was a language of form and color which could communicate emotions directly without lapsing into either the one-to-one correspondences of symbolism or, on the other hand, mere caprice. Pound also learned from Kandinsky that poetry must begin with the emotion and not with the portrayal of an external reality, and that the essence of abstraction was not a function of perception but conception. While both poetry and the visual arts could make use of natural objects if they satisfied what Kandinsky called an *innere Notwendigkeit,* the final interest was not in the objects themselves but in their emotional and "spiritual" content. This emotional content is what Pound later referred to as poetry's "third dimension." In an article in *The Criterion,* written more than twenty years after the publication of his "Vorticism" essay, in which he reflects on the vorticist years in London and laments the stagnation of modern verse since 1914, Pound reiterates his belief in a poetry of form and color. Citing the same *hokku* that he also drew upon in his earlier essay, Pound explains that this sort of poetry is more than a metaphor or a "bilateral" image:

> The foot-steps of the cat upon
> The snow:
> Plum blossoms.
>
> (*SP*)

Pound notes that while it may seem to a careless reader that this poem consists of no more than two visual images, "they are so placed as to contain wide space and a stretch of colour between them. The third element is there, its dimension from the fruit to the shadow in the foot-prints. No moral but a mood caught in its pincers." This "third dimension" is the emotion beyond the words, the essence of a poetry of form and color.

NOTES

[1] Pound's professed familiarity with Kandinsky apparently did not extend to his paintings. Kandinsky's paintings and woodcuts were included regularly in exhibitions of the Allied Artists' Association, including shows in 1908, 1909, 1913 and 1914. These exhibitions also included works by Jacob Epstein, Wyndham Lewis and Henri Gaudier-Brzeska; and it was at the 1913 exhibition, which included a number of works by Kandinsky, that Pound first met Gaudier-Brzeska. Yet even in January 1915 Pound

felt unable to make an educated appraisal of Kandinsky's painting. Writing in *The New Age,* Pound suggests that Lewis is a "more significant artist than Kandinsky" but admits that "I have not yet seen enough of Kandinsky's work to use a verb stronger than 'think'" (Zinnes 9).

[2] I use the term "non-geometrical" here cautiously, since Jakobson has shown that there is no such thing as non-geometrical painting. Just as a poem is either grammatical or anti-grammatical but never agrammatical, Jakobson argues that a painting either makes use of geometrical forms and geometrical principles of composition or it rebels against them, but it cannot do away with them (94).

[3] Although Sadler was the first, he was not the only critic to draw attention to Kandinsky's book in the small journals in England and America. Alfred Stieglitz printed a translated excerpt in his journal, *Camera Work,* as early as July 1912. However, most critics, like Pound himself, did not take an interest in Kandinsky's theories of abstraction until after the publication of Sadler's translation in 1914, *The Art of Spiritual Harmony.* Huntly Carter reviewed the book in *The Egoist* only a week before the first issue of *Blast* was published with its extensive excerpts and commentary by Edward Wadsworth. The Sadler translation also attracted attention in America, with short excerpts and a comparison of Kandinsky's aesthetics with those of Gertrude Stein appearing in the November 1914 issue of *The Little Review* (see Works Cited).

[4] Jakobson discovered a similar phenomenon with certain sounds in poetry. In his essay on "Linguistics and Poetics," Jakobson reports that when people are asked whether they find the phoneme /i/ or /u/ to be the *darker,* "some of the subjects may respond that this question makes nosense to them, but hardly one will state that /i/ is the darker of the two" (44).

[5] Hulme confirms here what Gage refers to as "the fallacy of accident." Gage argues that "either one feels an emotion and *seeks* for a proper way to communicate it, or one comes across an *unsought* resemblance which has no connection with one's *original* intuition" (82-83).

WORKS CITED

Carter, Huntly. "New Books on Art." *The Egoist* 1 (1914): 235-36.

Fenollosa, Ernest. *The Chinese Written Character as a Medium for Poetry.* Ed. Ezra Pound. 1936. San Francisco: City Lights, 1983.

Gabirol, Ibn (Alexander Kaun). "My Friend, the Incurable." *The Little Review* 1 (November 1914): 42-44.

Gage, John T. *In the Arresting Eye: The Rhetoric of Imagism.* Baton Rouge: Louisiana State UP, 1981.

Hulme, T. E. *Further Speculations.* Ed. Sam Hynes. Lincoln: Nebraska UP, 1962.

————. *Speculations: Essays on Humanism and the Philosophy of Art.* Ed. Herbert Read. New York: Harcourt, 1924.

Jakobson, Roman. *Selected Writings III: Poetry of Grammar and Grammar of Poetry.* Ed. Stephan Rudy. The Hague: Mouton, 1981.

Kandinsky, Wassily. "Extracts from *The Spiritual in Art.*" *Camera Work* 39 (1912): 34.

————. *Über das Geistige in der Kunst.* 1912. Bern: Benteli, 1965.

Pound, Ezra. *Ezra Pound and the Visual Arts.* Ed. Harriet Zinnes. New York: New Directions, 1980.

————. *Gaudier-Brzeska: A Memoir.* 1916. New York: New Directions, 1970.

————. *Personae: The Collected Shorter Poems of Ezra Pound.* New York: New Directions, 1926.

————. *Selected Prose, 1909-1965.* Ed. William Cookson. London: Faber, 1973.

Sadler, Michael. "After Gauguin." *Rhythm* 1 (1912): 23-29.

Wadsworth, Edward. "Inner Necessity." *Blast* 1 (1914): 119-25.

Carol McKay (essay date 1994)

SOURCE: "Kandinsky's Ethnography: Scientific Field Work and Aesthetic Reflection," in *Art History,* Vol. 17, No. 2, June, 1994, pp. 182-208.

[*In the following essay, McKay discusses Kandinsky's ethnographic essay "From Materials on the Ethnography of the Sysol and Vechegda Zyrians: The National Deities" and relates it to his autobiographical essay "Reminiscences."*]

This article explores how, in two essays written at separate moments of his adult career, Wassily Kandinsky represented the same ethnographic fieldwork experience in quite differing terms. The first of these essays is a scientific one: Kandinsky's **'From Materials on the Ethnography of the Sysol and Vechegda Zyrians: the National Deities (According to Contemporary Beliefs)'** appeared in 1889 in the *Ethnographic Review,* a newly established forum for Russian ethnographic studies.[1] This was based on fieldwork research which he undertook in the late spring of 1889, whilst a student at Moscow University.[2] This ethnographic treatise is the main object of my initial investigation, and I consider it as an historical document, one produced outside the 'history of art', but with reverberations within it. The first and main section of my article attempts to locate Kandinsky's ethnographic training and his 1889 publication within the prevailing discourses of the discipline at the time.[3] The later part of my article has a different focus, its aim being to compare and contrast this scientific essay with an 'artistic' one: with Kandinsky's autobiographical **'Reminiscences'** published in 1913 by Herwarth Walden's *Der Sturm* press, where he presented a distant recollection of his youthful ethnographic researches.[4] The initial analysis of his ethnographic essay in the first part of my article, in other words, will constitute the framework, the perspective, for my narrowly focused reading of those passages in **'Reminiscences'** which give a strongly poeticized and personalized account of his 1889 field work,[5] where 'science', passing through the filter of memory, is transformed into 'art'. The purpose of this comparison, however, is not only to highlight the discrepancies between Kandinsky's two ethnographic representations; more interestingly, it also allows me to suggest some surprising points of contact between the apparently discrete discourses of art and science.

KANDINSKY AS ETHNOGRAPHER

The main goal of Kandinsky's ethnographic research was to document any remaining traces of old Zyrian religious conceptions. The first section of my analysis focuses on this aspiration, combining close reading of Kandinsky's treatise with wider inspection of the disciplinary context in which it was researched and published. Firstly, however, I would like to step back a little, to consider why Kandinsky's relatively obscure scientific essay merits attention at all by art historians. My turning to his article was, of course, mediated by something else: in this instance, by my understanding of recent critical work which explores the 'textuality' (the 'poetics') of twentieth-century ethnographic writing. James Clifford's introduction to the series of essays collected in the volume *Writing Culture: the Poetics and Politics of Ethnography* summarizes the principles behind much of this work. These authors, he writes:

> See culture as composed of seriously contested codes and representations; they assume that the poetic and the political are inseparable, that science is in, not above, historical and linguistic processes. They assume that academic and literary genres interpenetrate and that the writing of cultural descriptions is properly experimental and ethical . . . (they draw) attention to the historical predicament of ethnography, the fact that it is always caught up in the invention, not the representation, of cultures.[6]

From such a perspective, the boundaries of science and art are unstable, and ethnographic writing as much as literary writing is open to textual and historical analysis. The work of Clifford and others, whilst primarily concerned with twentieth-century ethnographies, has prompted me to consider Kandinsky's Zyrian essay as embedded in the academic politics of the time and place in which it was produced, and as shaped by specific institutional constraints. Moreover, it also suggested that Kandinsky's scientific article could be approached in the same way as his artistic writings, employing the same critical apparatus.

Kandinsky's essay appeared in *Ethnographic Review*, a newly established forum for ethnographic studies published under the auspices of the Imperial Society for the friends of the Natural Sciences, Anthropology and Ethnography.[7] The ethnographic section of the society was centred at Moscow University and, as witnessed by its publications, it brought together students of diverse disciplines: legal historians as well as linguists, anthropologists alongside archaeologists.[8] In the Russian version of **'Reminiscences'**, Kandinsky recalled the help and support he had received as a student from A. N. Fillipov. More than an academic mentor, Fillipov was also a colleague in the Imperial Society for the friends of the Natural Sciences, Anthropology and Ethnography, and his influence on Kandinsky's ethnographic research was certainly pervasive.[9] The year prior to Kandinsky's publication, the ethnographic section of the Imperial Society had published an extensive appendix in Volume VIII of its journal;[10] this addendum claimed to be a major contribution to the institutional development of ethnography as a scientific discipline. It consisted of two elaborate programmes of questions and guidelines, designed to aid empirical researchers engaged in ethnographic field work. Both programmes were dated 1887, though the second was prefaced by an introduction dated 1886. This second programme was the more specialized of the two, being a set of guidelines specifically for assembling legal customs. The introduction, written by N. M. Charusin, the secretary of the ethnographic section, acknowledged a number of members who had contributed in devising the projects, giving special thanks to A. N. Fillipov.[11]

The first version in the appendix appeared under the general title 'Programme for Collecting Ethnographic Information'; it was based on Western models such as the so-called *Circular of Enquiry*, published in 1884 by the American Bureau of Ethnography, or the equivalent British programme of *Notes and Queries on Anthropology*, the first edition of which appeared in 1874 but which was subsequently much up-dated and frequently re-issued.[12] The 1874 British compilation was edited by the eminent Victorian, General Pitt-Rivers, and contained contributions from such evolutionary cultural theorists as E. B. Tylor. The preface to this British volume set out the ambitions of the programme, unconvincingly submerging imperialist and racial sentiments in a call for increased scientific exactitude and objectivity:

> Travellers have usually recorded only those customs of modern savages which they have chanced to observe; and, as a rule, they have observed chiefly those which their experience of civilised institutions has led them to look for . . . owing to these and other causes the imperfections of the anthropological record surpass those of other sciences, and false theories are often built upon imperfect bases of induction. . . .
>
> It is hoped that the questions contained in the following sections . . . may be a means of enabling the traveller to collect information without prejudice arising from individual bias. To this end it is

particularly requested that he will endeavour to answer the questions as fully as possible. . . . [13]

Like its models, the Russian questionnaire was divided up into a series of sections, in accordance with natural scientific principles of taxonomic classification. It encompassed sections dealing with geography and history, for example, as well as sections on physical anthropology, architecture and technology, dress, food and drink, occupations, etc. Yet the most comprehensive classification, with internal subsections, focused on religion and beliefs. And the latter, of course, was precisely the category of Kandinsky's ethnographic investigation. His field work took him to the fringes of Western Siberia, where the immediate object was to study:

> the national deities of the Sysol- and Vechegda-Zyrians. When I chose this subject out of the field of general research into religious conceptions, it was with the intention of reconstructing as far as possible traces of the pagan past, insofar as these traces can be established in the chaos of present-day religious ideas, which are so strongly influenced by Christianity. [14]

Kandinsky's fieldwork research was part of a systematic Russian programme of ethnographic inquiry, a programme which coincided with a period of accelerated change in the theory and practice of the anthropological sciences. [15] The last decades of the century bore witness to growing dissatisfaction with the conventional nineteenth-century division of work, between academic theorists, on the one hand, and practical collectors of cultural and anthropological data on the other. In the British context, for example, stereotypical nineteenth-century 'armchair' academics (described by one historian, referring to the likes of Herbert Spencer, as 'evolutionary titans' [16]), rarely if ever undertook empirical research in the field or even among archival data. On the other hand, amateur research in the second half of the nineteenth century comprised a wide range of individual contributions from people with quite different interests and experience. Before the 1880s the scholars' 'evidence' might consist of notes and memoirs of explorers, travellers or tourists, the data compiled by government officials and colonial administrators, or supplied by private traders, merchants and missionaries. Such second-hand material did, in fact, remain important for ethnographic studies beyond the nineteenth century, and provided important precedents for later institutionally trained or guided field workers. However, the British, American and, later, the Russian programmes all evince a growing impetus to achieve more satisfactory integration of the empirical and theoretical components of anthropological inquiry. In Russia, the programmes produced by Fillipov and his colleagues took on board the example of Western projects which attempted to implement more rigorous measures to control the collection of cultural data. The ideal was to establish objective scientific research practices in order to ensure socio-academic respectability for the anthropological sciences. This was stated, for instance, by a leading Russian anthropologist, Professor D.

N. Anutschin, in his opening contribution to the first number of *Ethnographic Review,* also in 1889. [17]

One persuasive image, then, might be of Kandinsky as an eager young academic, setting off on a voyage of cultural exploration, armed with his diary and notebooks and also equipped with a copy of the brand new Russian research programme. He was taking part in a co-ordinated project aiming to document, describe and classify the variousness of ethnic groups comprising the Russian Empire. However, this image needs to be handled with caution, as it can lead to associations with Western-style imperialism, and with a view of the researcher as colonial explorer and perhaps also governor or administrator. [18] In the Russian context, this aspect of the nineteenth-century ethnographic disciplines was out of step with that other function of the 'intelligentsia', as critic of Russian imperial autocracy. [18] The next section of my article will argue this latter point in more detail, considering the ideological complexities of Kandinsky's publication, whilst suggesting how, in particular respects, it reflects the transitional state of ethnographic scholarship in the late nineteenth century. In other words, I will endeavour to show how Kandinsky's research brought together what at the time were contradictory perspectives: namely, that of evolutionary anthropology and that of political history.

Kandinsky's treatise unites, on the one hand, a marked concern for the systematic morphological derivation of the names of Zyrian deities, with, on the other, a highly coloured rendition of the substance of Zyrian legends. The latter, as I demonstrate shortly, was partly shaped by earlier historical accounts of the Zyrians and also by the underlying political message of Kandinsky's essay. The former, his interest in the etymologies of words, is apparent throughout the Zyrian article, and might be considered in the light of Foucault's analysis of the human sciences in the nineteenth century. Focault identifies a 'vast shift' away from biological models, with their hypotheses of instinctual force, leading to 'the reign of the philological . . . when it is a matter of interpretation and the discovery of hidden meanings . . .'. [19] We might suppose this refers, for instance, to the importance of linguistic analysis in Franz Boas's work on North West Coast American Indians. [20] Of more immediate relevance for Kandinsky is the example of the linguist V. F. Müller, a leading member of the ethnographic section of the Imperial Society, whose work in the Caucasus was widely reported, for instance, in the *Internationales Archiv für Ethnographie,* the same international journal which also referred to Kandinsky's work in its bibliographical round-up of 1891. [21] As the evidence of his essay indicates, Kandinsky was aware of the importance of linguistics in ethnographic investigation, viewing words, proverbs and sayings as puzzles in need of decoding. He was particularly fascinated by the way in which linguistic signs could remain constant, changing only slightly in form over history, while their conceptual meanings varied independently. At the end of the article, for example, he considered two old Zyrian terms for gods: Forest-Man [*lesak-mort*] and *Poloznicha.* [22] The latter, the name of a protector of the rye, was of Russian origin, stemming from *poludnica* [midday], and hence the further meaning of 'midday-goddess'.[23] From the same root, he noted, was derived the term for cornflowers: *Poloznicha*-blue, or 'eye of the midday-goddess'. More fantastically, he also explained that, at one time, the power of *Poloznicha* was so revered that no one dared to cut the rye until after St Elijah's day, for fear of retribution. This superstition had almost vanished, except among children and some local elders, who, for his benefit, reminisced about the golden old days of *Poloznicha* when the corn was much better, whilst blaming Zyrian unbelievers for driving the goddess away in anger.[24]

Lesak-mort was more mysterious still. While some Zyrians still believed that *lesak-mort* had once been a fierce god, no one could offer an explanation for this definition. Kandinsky claimed that the term was now often used to designate particularly heroic and fearless men, though until comparatively recently it had been a term of abuse. Typically, he also looked for an historical and sociological explanation of this conceptual turn-around:

> Perhaps the influence of Christianity was responsible for changing the name of the old Deity into an insulting term; this commonly occurs with religious upheaval. . . . [25]

With this latter remark, Kandinsky linked his closing observations back to the beginning of his article, where he investigated a local saying: 'churki never die.' The proverbial village elder of ethnography offered guidance, explaining that the word *churka* derived from *Churila*, an old Chud name for their principal god (the Chuds being original occupants of the lands currently inhabited by Zyrians). The sage's information was fittingly ancient. According to Kandinsky, the grand old man had heard the story as a child from his own elders.[26] At the same time, however, Kandinsky observed how *churka* had completely changed meaning; in bastardized form, it now signified 'illegitimate child'.

These observations in turn acquired considerable imaginative force thanks to Kandinsky's initial consideration of Chud history, which he represented romantically as a history of indigenous struggle for cultural independence. According to Zyrian legend, he noted, the Chuds had been wiped out in the thirteenth century, after valiant but futile resistance to a combination of St Stephen of Perm's missionary fervour and Russian territorial expansionism.[27] Kandinsky seems to have derived much of his information about the rapid conquest and conversion of the region from a long account of the Zyrian peoples published earlier in the century by the Finnish phililogist and historian J. A. Sjögren.[28] Influenced by Herderian ideals, Sjögren specialized in the diverse Finno-Ugric languages and cultures of northern Russia, including Zyrian, and in his numerous publications he paid particular attention to the pre-Russian history of the north.[29] Kandinsky repeated from Sjögren the legendary story about the Chuds' final solution in defence of their own religion and

culture, as they thwarted St Stephen by burying themselves alive with their possessions. These burial spots, he noted, became known to the Zyrians as 'Chud-trenches'. Although many of the older people claimed to know the sites of these graves, they were fearful of excavating them because they were 'impure'. The Zyrians, according to Kandinsky, were sure of one thing about their own history; they knew their ancestors had not followed the Chud example. The Zyrians had survived, as they saw the light and were converted.[30]

Kandinsky, however, also obtained an alternative 'on-the-spot' ethnographic insight from an elderly informant, who claimed that the Chuds and the Zyrians were originally one and the same people, the *Komi*. According to this venerable sage, the conquering Russians, because they could not understand the language of the indigenous people, enforced the name *Chud*, derived from the Russian word for 'incomprehensible'.[31] In Kandinsky's work, then, etymological investigation coupled with investigative field work illuminated a suppressed history of cultural resistance. Moreover, as I demonstrate below, he believed that the complex Zyrian/Chud history of subordination to an invading power and enforced religious conversion explained why present-day Zyrians had repressed virtually all memories of their earlier religious conceptions.

I have been suggesting that Kandinsky's Zyrian essay reveals heterogeneous loyalties. This is also indicated in the way he shaped his article according to recognizable criteria of scientific objectivity. The meticulous academic followed his programmatic guidelines thoroughly; his essay endeavoured to fulfil the requirements not only of the Russian questionnaire directions but even those of its English research paradigm. In his contributions to the 'Cultural' sub-section of *Notes and Queries*, E. B. Tylor offered instruction on how to gather information relevant to the history of ethnic groups. Whilst reminding future researchers to take heed of oral legends and myths as well as written records, Tylor offered specific questions:

> What account do they give of themselves, and their connexion with other nations, wars, alliances, etc? . . .
>
> What names does the tribe, nation, or race go by? and which are native names used by themselves and which terms given by other people? . . . Do they consider other tribes related to them by language, as having branched off from them, or vice-versa, or all from some other national source? . . .
>
> What do they have to say as to the introduction and change of their religion, invention of new ceremonies, etc? . . .
>
> Have they traditions to account for monuments, such as old graves, mounds, sites of villages, etc? . . . [32]

My earlier discussion suggests Kandinsky pondered such precise questions at length—even if some of his answers came courtesy of earlier investigators like A. J.

Sjögren. Moreover, as investigating 'man-on-the-spot', he not only sought to align his investigation with a pre-existing programme, but he also recognized a given set of methodological assumptions. These assumptions as to historical reconstruction are indicated by Kandinsky's remarks on what he believed to be the scientific function of his ethnographic task; he wished to peel back the layers of historical accretion to reconstruct, as far as possible, the original pre-Christian belief system of the Zyrians.[33] If, as a number of historians have noticed, nineteenth-century students of ethnography were obsessed with the development of religious ideas,[34] then Kandinsky was no exception. He adhered to the familiar conceit of ethnography as a form of historical detective work, with the ethnographer teasing out and tracing back surviving clues to the past, such clues being the remains of the past in the present. As the published essay demonstrates, he believed such useful cultural clues were to be found in unusual customs and practices, in the testimonies of village elders, as well as in proverbs and sayings.

The precedents for this way of conceiving cultural practices were legion. Tylor, for one, had urged ethnographers to attend to 'peculiar forms of language' as well as to any remarkable ceremonial customs or ritual prohibitions, all of which could be 'in various ways instructive' in throwing light on the past.[35] Moreover, according to this Victorian theorist, gathering information on religious beliefs demanded particularly acute detective skills on the part of the ethnographer:

> It is often a matter of difficulty to obtain precise information on the religion of uncivilised people, who conceal their doctrines for fear of ridicule, and will purposely put the inquirer off the track. After long and friendly intercourse, however, a clue might generally be obtained; and when something is known, it serves as a means of raising farther questions. . . . Information should be obtained from as many sources as possible. . . .[36]

This was a model procedure and Kandinsky even employed it when setting out parts of his essay. In one section, he considered the possibility of an original sun cult, which was, of course, something to which he would have been alerted by his guidelines. Until Elijah's day in July, he noted, the Zyrians superstitiously refrained from transporting ice uncovered. As for the reason, he offered an unattributed Zyrian statement: 'To ensure that the sun cannot see it; otherwise the sun will send hail.'[37] The present Zyrians, especially those in outlying areas, he argued, still attributed anthropomorphic qualities to the sun, believing that he could see and grow angry or jealous. Ever the good researcher, Kandinsky reported that he had attempted to pursue the origin of the idea further, though, as a result of the resolute nature of peasant faith, this proved unavailing. When he pressed the Zyrians with the implausibility of the concept,

> Many simply answered that they had heard it from their fathers and grandfathers; therefore it had to be true that the sun can see.[38]

According to Tylor's classificatory principles, this was superstitious belief of an absurd kind. Kandinsky followed the trail through by noting evidence for other Zyrian animistic beliefs. The wind was thought to be male, he recorded, citing how old women would exhort the wind to blow; when such entreaties came to naught, they might say: 'He is angry.' Always mindful of his research guidelines, Kandinsky attended to other 'tell-tale' ritual habits, such as those which seemed to indicate early fire-worship: for instance, it was taboo to spit into the hearth.[39] As with his interest in the conceptual vagaries of words, he was also attentive to the way in which cultural practices varied. One custom, again linked to fire-worship, regulated the extinguishing of fires. In its most common form, the practice demanded the fire be put out with water, and never by an 'impure' person trampling on the flames. Yet in a few places the prohibition was turned on its head and the opposite was the case. According to Kandinsky, this indicated that the custom was now merely a matter of form, a mere cipher; the original ritual context that gave the practice meaning had vanished.[40]

Kandinsky's indebtedness to existing patterns of cultural analysis is also indicated in the section of his essay covering Zyrian respect for the souls of their ancestors, which he linked to their adoration of hearth and home.[41] For some Zyrians, he claimed, the whole of the house adjacent to the hearth was sacrosanct. He discovered a remarkable indicator of such reverence, in that numerous new houses in the town of Ust-Sysol'sk remained unoccupied, testimony to Zyrian fears that a move might raise the wrath of the house spirit, that ancient protector of hearth and family.[42]

Characteristically for nineteenth-century ethnographers, Kandinsky declared that all the signs amassed were fragmentary traces of a rapidly disappearing non-Christian culture. Less characteristically, however, he judiciously avoided the loaded terms 'primitive' or 'savage'. For his Western evolutionist exemplars, such terms embodied the assumption of 'civilized' Christian superiority—and that hardly fits with the ideological complexities of Kandinsky's essay. Only once, in fact, did he use 'primitive'; remarkably, he did so at the one point, falling in the second half of his essay, where he referred directly to a paradigm of Western theoretical synthesis, namely the philosophical sociology of Herbert Spencer.[43] This was the point where, in turning his attention fully to Zyrian concepts of 'the soul', he addressed one of the biggest issues for nineteenth-century students of pre-industrialized peoples.[44] The central theme of E. B. Tylor's widely admired *Primitive Culture* (1871), for instance, was the evolution of 'Animism', which Tylor identified as the revering of souls, ghosts and the like.[45] He traced the root of such concepts to belief in the human soul, which in turn derived from the subjective experience of dreams or visions. Tylor's rational exegesis of 'primitive' soul concepts was an exemplary one for contemporary scholars, similar in a number of respects to Herbert Spencer's handling of the theme in the *Principles of Sociology*.[46] Tylor, at least indirectly, provided the empirical guidelines for

Kandinsky's own study of Zyrian soul concepts, whilst Spencer's *Principles* was the more immediate theoretical scheme: the debt to Spencer is most marked, perhaps, in Kandinsky's ambitions to understand religious phenomena 'holistically', in their relationships to specific historical—social and political—factors.[47]

Kandinsky focused on the Zyrian concept of *Ort*, which he theorized as a non-Christian soul concept. He argued that the concept was peculiarly and originally Zyrian. This claim, though, was scarcely justified by the evidence he offered, as more recent studies have demonstrated,[48] and at best it can be taken as a creative misrepresentation on his part. The claim, nonetheless, enabled him to point an accusing finger at the twin forces of enforced Russification and religious conversion, which, he argued, had disrupted the authentic 'native' belief system. This is a case of inventive interpretation, yet one tempered by the nature of the empirical investigation. Tylor's propositions lie behind Kandinsky's approach to *Ort,* as can be seen from a sample of Tylor's instructions for uncovering concepts of the soul:

> Is something of the nature of a human soul believed in? . . . What is its name? is it associated with the breath, shadow, etc? . . . does it depart when the body dies? . . . What is the soul considered to be? what is its form, substance, voice, power, etc? . . . [49]

Kandinsky's investigation of *Ort* amounted to a sustained discussion along these lines, as he considered and juggled the possibilities. For instance, he disavowed conventional equations between the concepts of *Ort* and of Christian 'spirit', the opposite of matter. While allowing that, in modern Zyrian usage, *Ort* usually meant spirit (*dukh*) or soul (*loi*), nevertheless he argued that one should not conclude that the 'substance' of *Ort* was of the nature of spirit:

> Even today the Zyrians are possessed of a completely unclear conception of spirit, and undoubtedly they can thank the processes of Russification and Christianisation for this. All their Forest and Water Deities, etc., have a substantial form. All these beings can be seen and they can incur physical injury. Even their concepts of the human soul are extraordinarily unclear, or are entirely absent . . . [50]

If this was cultural relativism on Kandinsky's part, it was of a highly ambiguous kind, as he assumes in this passage that a clearer—and presumably superior—'conception of spirit' was to hand. The ambiguity is hardly surprising, though, given the diverse models on which his socio-cultural investigation depended.

Kandinsky also marshalled evidence of contemporary Zyrian practices in order to support his contention that '*Ort* is a material thing';[51] this, he implied, distinguished the Zyrian conception from Christian dualism. Dealing with Zyrian notions of the deceased, he noted a peculiar twist in the Zyrian belief in ghosts; they believed that the

dead could wander in this world in their same corporeal form. This was particularly the case, according to the Zyrians, when the dead person was a magic-man or shaman. Kandinsky described a peculiar burial custom, whereby if the deceased was a shaman, the body would be shackled. The desired effect was to prevent the dead shaman from returning to disturb his relatives; no one, he noted in some surprise, doubted that the 'soul' could be bound in this way.[52]

At the same time, Kandinsky endeavoured to make his empirical investigation of Zyrian soul concepts conform to a Spencerian theoretical model—though without great success. Focusing on Spencer's idea that evolution in religious ideas entailed progressive differentiation of the notions of Mind and Matter, he cited from Spencer's chapter 'Ideas of Death and Resurrection' in *Principles of Sociology,* vol. 1.[53] This chapter was part of Spencer's large sub-section 'Primitive Ideas', forming one category in his so-called synthetic philosophy. Religious concepts, according to Spencer's classificatory principles, were, like all ideological forms, subject to hierarchical laws of developmental progress. This schema was supposedly not arbitrary but natural; ideas were subject to 'natural' evolutionary processes in the same way as all biological and sociological forms. On the basis of empirical evidence amassed and supplied by numerous travellers and men on the spot, Spencer had classified 'Primitive Man' under separate headings: 'Physical', 'Emotional' and 'Intellectual', on the basis of which he developed his sociological study, outlining laws of mental development according to his 'psychological principles'. In all three categories of the system articulated in his *Principles of Sociology,* the 'primitive' was considered inferior to the civilized Westerner; only members of civilized Western nations could ideally exemplify his principles of psychology.

Spencer's ideal psychological condition was twofold: it required both a highly developed moral faculty and a rational, reflective consciousness, an abstract Mind. In the circuitous arguments of his philosophy, psychological 'progress' was in turn dependent on the stage of social evolution attained; it required social stability and systematic state regulation. Only such an order of things ensured those immensely desirable Victorian sentiments of duty, responsibility, industry and, above all, justice.[54] In his sociological and psychological principles, Spencer spoke a pre-eminently Victorian language of power and control, and the *Principles of Sociology* which Kandinsky read were imbued with an evolutionary ideology justifying imperial superiority:

> Throughout long past periods . . . there has been going on a continuous differentation of races, a continuous overrunning of the less powerful or less adapted by the more powerful or more adapted, a driving of inferior varieties into undesirable habitats, and, occasionally, an extermination of inferior varieties.[55]

Kandinsky learned from Spencer that many 'primitive' peoples had a more advanced conception of the duality of matter and spirit—and therefore clearer concepts of the soul—than the Zyrians.[56] Yet he clearly had some trouble reconciling this with his sense that, in other respects, the Zyrians had travelled far along the evolutionary ladder: he could only postulate that enforced Russification and conversion to Christianity explained Zyrian backwardness in their soul concepts.[57] With this suggestion he attempted—unconvincingly—to marry Spencer's principles of scientific classification with his own historical critique of the 'survival of the fittest': the cultural suppression of one people by a more powerful neighbour.

Thus, despite Kandinsky's having recourse to a Spencerian model and to precise programmatic guidelines, his published ethnographic essay does not conform straightforwardly to a 'scientifically' evolutionist pattern of sociocultural investigation. I am suggesting, in other words, that Kandinsky's 1889 essay was shaped by specific disciplinary precedents, yet also 'escaped' them. The next section attempts to add substance to this argument, by considering the way in which his Zyrian essay qualified one set of conventions by means of another. Kandinsky's powerful authorial presence, a traveller on a mission of discovery, filtered into his ethnographic essay, undermining the 'norm of a scientific discourse whose authority resides in the absolute effacement of the speaking and experiencing subject'.[58] M. L. Pratt has demonstrated how pre-scientific ethnographic writings, including travelbooks, personal memoirs and explorers' tales, continued to inform the language of nineteenth- and twentieth-century ethnography, effectively undermining the paradigms of objective fact-finding and impersonal reportage. Characteristic of all such 'pre-scientific' writings, she argues, is the combination of narrative and descriptive modes, and at the same time she demonstrates how personal narrative was never fully excluded from formal 'scientific' ethnographies of the late nineteenth and early twentieth centuries. Personal narrative, as a convention of ethnographic writing, 'plays the part of anchoring the "scientific" description in the intense and authority-giving personal experience of fieldwork'.[59] Pratt's analysis is particularly apt as a characterization of Kandinsky's ethnographic publication, and this is hardly surprising, as we know that he also read and used exemplary 'travel-accounts' in preparation for his field trip, such as the one by A. J. Sjögren.[60]

From the outset, Kandinsky's 'personal voice' erupted in his article, as he declared his reasons for undertaking the research and also endeavoured to establish the originality and reliability of his 'on-the-spot' work in comparison with existing studies:

> Anyone who happens to be familiar with the existing literature on the Zyrians is bound to be astonished by the numerous inaccuracies and frequent contradictions. These shortcomings are due to the fact that many investigators do not specify their area of investigation, but speak of the Zyrians in general terms. Such generalizations are inadmissable because the various clans of the Zyrian people are quite distinct one from the other. . . .

> Therefore, I firmly stress that, when I refer to the Zyrians in this article, I mean specifically the Sysola and Vychegda Zyrians. . . . [61]

Throughout the first part of his article Kandinsky repeatedly asserted his personal experience, as if to establish the validity of his field work and of his eclectic observations ('I know, because I was there'). He related anecdotally, for instance, how he had made the mistake, as an alien, of carrying ice uncovered before Elijah's day, suggesting that this subjective experience, and particularly the warning it earned him, was yet another telltale sign of the Zyrians' original sun cult.[62] Moreover, he appealed to personal dialogue as a means of adding weight to his more contentious observations, such as the one about invading Russians enforcing the 'alien' term *Chud* on the native *Komi*, this being a story he heard directly from a wise old informant.[63] Kandinsky's article, then, indicates important tensions between empirical field work on the one hand and theoretical synthesis on the other, and he might have been indicating as much when, in concluding his article, he noted that the materials he had amassed were still 'unsystematic.'[64]

ARTISTIC ETHNOGRAPHY

My analysis so far has attempted to identify some of the complexities (historical and disciplinary) of Kandinsky's ethnographic writing. From this, I have shown that Kandinsky's ethnographic work cannot be fitted into a single theoretical paradigm. The scientific framework for his ethnographic research comprised questionnaire-type guidelines for interrogating an unfamiliar research object and thus collecting relevant cultural data. I now want to develop my suggestion that this framework suppressed many aspects of his fieldwork experience; these 'suppressions', I will argue, were given expression in his semi-fictional **'Reminiscences'**, published in 1913. Here, instead of following a written questionnaire in order to hunt out remnants of indigenous religious concepts, he focused on things that he saw, specifically material culture, art and architecture. As recent scholars have recognized, the study of art and aesthetics continues to be marginalized within cultural anthropology, and this was even more the case at the turn of the century.[65] I will attempt to understand Kandinsky's move from an ethnographic study of religious conceptions to an aesthetic appreciation of traditional artistic cultures within this disciplinary context. Hence the following section concentrates on the visualist quality of his ethnographic remembrances, whereby Kandinsky foregrounded the aesthetic/sensory aspects of his field work and, in particular, focused on his experience of colour. At the same time, I consider how, in the process of rewriting his ethnographic experiences within **'Reminiscences'**, Kandinsky abandoned his earlier aspirations for scientific objectivity. He represented his ethnographic work instead as a first-person narrative of subjective enlightenment, one embedded within a series of revelatory artistic experiences: **'Reminiscences'**, in other words, emphasizes the reflexive, experiential dimension of his ethnographic work.

The ethnographic references in **'Reminiscences'** are woven into the fabric of an essay which, like most of Kandinsky's contemporary writings, aimed to elucidate his sense of the autonomous power of art. I will consider Kandinsky's ethnographic memories, therefore, in so far as they epitomize his notion of a universal 'language of colour'.[66] The culminating passage in his account of his trip to the province of Vologda, 'where . . . I was sent by the Imperial Society for Science, Anthropology and Ethnography', is characteristically ecstatic:

> I shall never forget the great wooden houses. . . . In these magical houses I experienced something I have never encountered again since. They taught me to move within the picture, to live in the picture. I still remember how I entered the living room for the first time and stood rooted to the spot before this unexpected scene. The table, the benches, the great stove (indispensable in Russian farmhouses), the cupboards, and every other object were covered with brightly coloured, elaborate ornaments. Folk pictures on the walls; a symbolic representation of a hero, a battle, a painted folk song. The 'red' corner (red is the same as beautiful in old Russian) thickly, completely covered with painted and printed pictures of the saints, burning in front of it the red flame of a small pendant lamp . . . existing in and for itself. When I finally entered the room, I felt surrounded on all sides by painting, into which I had thus penetrated.[67]

I want to consider this account of his experience of 'folk' art, and specifically his reference to the 'red' icon-corner, in comparison with the work of the Russian Byzantist and historian N. P. Kondakov. This passage from **'Reminiscences'** can be matched almost point for point with Kondakov's discussion of the same icon-corner in traditional Russian houses, in his widely admired study of the Russian icon.[68] Both Kandinsky and Kondakov stressed how the icon-corner was completely covered with painted and printed pictures of the saints, and both drew out the semantic dimensions of the Russian term for this icon oratory ('fair corner'), noting that the etymological root *kras* signified both 'beauty' and the colour red.[69] We know from references in *On the Spiritual in Art* (1911) that Kandinsky read Kondakov's publications with considerable enthusiasm.[70] This enthusiasm is significant precisely because Kondakov approached art 'scientifically', as a form of cultural anthropology. In other words, Kondakov's work was exceptional for its time. My reconstruction of Kandinsky's interest in Kondakov's work begins, therefore, with this 1911 reference, and my overarching aim is to demonstrate the extent to which Kandinsky's art-theoretical formulations were intimately bound up with the concerns of his earlier ethnographic studies.

As an archaeologist and an historian, Kondakov was concerned to elucidate cultural objects—Byzantine miniatures and Russian icons—in terms of their socio-historical and religious functions: at the beginning of his *Histoire de l'art byzantine considérée principalement dans les miniatures* he pointedly rejected formal and stylistic versions of art 'history'.[71] In his chapter on 'The Languages of Colours and Forms' in *On the Spiritual in Art* Kandinsky quoted a passage from the French edition of this work by Kondakov, which discussed colour symbolism in Byzantine miniatures of the tenth century.[72] Kondakov explained the conventional meanings of the colours used, noting that the Emperor was signified by his gold halo in contrast to the blue haloes of 'les personnages symboliques, comme pour indiquer leur origine céleste'. Kandinsky was quoting from the second volume of Kondakov's work, where the author dealt with the so-called second 'Golden Age' of Byzantine art, designating this as some three centuries, from the end of iconoclasm until the late twelfth century. Kandinsky's enthusiasm for Kondakov is hardly surprising, given Kondakov's argument that Byzantine art in this period was remarkably unified, extending across the whole of the Byzantine world, and that this unity could be understood in terms of the 'tendance à l'abstraction' in the art of the time.[73] The 'Golden Age' of Byzantine art was veritably universal, indeed was capable of uniting diverse cultures and peoples. It was based, he suggested, on a common system of formal and colouristic significance, and on firmly established levels of technical attainment.[74]

Of particular interest to Kandinsky was Kondakov's discussion of the 'popular' characteristics of both miniatures and icons. In his discussion of the earlier period of Byzantine miniature painting, for instance, Kondakov stressed a continual intertwining of art, popular culture and religion. He believed that a history of Byzantine art should be based on an understanding of the theological underpinning of culture: complex moral and spiritual ideas inevitably lay behind the production of both texts and images.[75] Miniature painting tended to be cultivated in monasteries, by monks who, he suggested, created the intellectual and philosophical energy of society. This vigorous art he contrasted with that of the imperial courts, which tended to be 'elegant and brilliant', but short on ideas.[76] That produced by the miniaturists, on the other hand, fulfilled the 'true religious needs of the people'.[77] In other words, Kondakov suggested to Kandinsky an extraordinary instance of a spiritual culture produced by an 'intelligentsia' for 'the people'. He even suggested that the monastical centres were major sites of opposition during the period of iconoclasm, an era which witnessed a sustained and effective attack on images, supported by a succession of emperors. The strength of the resistance was marked, for Kondakov, by the subsequent popularity of illustrated psalm books in the post-iconoclast period. The triumph of the orthodox faith was assured and a free religious-artistic culture 'served to instruct the ignorant masses, to explain the faith, to act on the heart, to develop the love of God and of man'.[78]

In other publications, Kondakov also analysed the 'popularity' of the Russian icon, again in terms which Kandinsky could appreciate.[79] As in his study of Byzantine art, he emphasized Pagan-Christian continuities of religious and ritual practice, in which images played a central role. In particular, he stressed the non-Christian origins of icon worship, using terms quite familiar to Kandinsky:

> The Church accepted the use of the icon as a pious popular custom, which helped faith and gave it general support among the people, and she allowed the icon to establish itself and spread, like some other customs. . . . All this arose and developed on soil saturated with survivals of the ancient and oriental worlds.[80]

The study of Russian icons was a logical progression for Kondakov, as he stressed their Graeco-Byzantine origins. He even traced the pious popularity of icon worship back to ancient Egyptian burial and mummification practices, and he explicated this non-Christian ideology of soul-life. The similarity with *Ort* would not have been lost on Kandinsky:

> According to the sepulchral inscriptions, a man at death is divided into body, soul, and the bright essence of the double ('*Ka*'), which was the link between the corruptible body and the soul. The '*Ka*' is a coloured shadow, a bodiless shape.[81]

The substance of *Ka,* as coloured shadow, supposedly partook simultaneously of the nature of matter and spirit, and Kondakov also contended that, in the immediately pre-Christian era, *Ka* became identified with the painted images or icons of funerary furnishings. These, he argued, 'retained the powers of a mystic and vivifying image which maintained the link between the departed soul and the deserted body preserved in the form of a mummy.'[82] This mystic popularity of the image continued into the Christian period:

> When the pictured portrait of a saint became an icon the position it took was that of a devotional icon . . . that voiceless friend in the faith to whom people turned with their prayer. . . . As they prayed they made the sign of the cross upon the breast and kissed the icon and this became the regular practice. . . . [83]

Kondakov argued that the icon retained its quasi-magical and popular function as sanctified matter, partaking directly of the spiritual essence of that which was represented. Indeed, as more recent Byzantine historians have noted,[84] in Eastern Orthodox religion the iconic image was in some sense a sacrament or emanation of the thing represented; in Orthodox liturgy the icon became the primary access door through which man could behold the holy and the holy could descend on man. In his demonstration of Pagan-Christian continuities, moreover, Kondakov presented icon worship as a manifestation of cultural flexibility as well as of religious faith. At the same time, he emphasized that icons were integral forms of popular folk culture; the devotional icon, for example, was also a household protector and defender against evil spirits. As already indicated, Kondakov's discussion of the 'icon-corner' in traditional Russian houses[85] is uncannily similar to the passage in Kandinsky's *'Reminis-*

cences' in which he described his first encounter with folk art in traditional Russian houses.

Having identified some links between Kondakov and Kandinsky, I will now address points of contrast; despite his quoting and paraphrasing of Kondakov, Kandinsky's notion of a universal 'language' of colours was quite at odds with the cultural relativism central to Kondakov's historical methodology. In his pre-war writings, Kandinsky argued that art forms created in socially distinct cultures shared a trans-historical form of aesthetic meaning, having a direct inner effect on the sensitive soul. In *On the Spiritual in Art,* for instance, he maintained that the purely artistic effects of an art object gained in strength the more it was removed from its historical and social origins. Egyptian sculpture, for example, had a more powerful aesthetic effect for 'us' than for its contemporaries, because 'we' are immune to the particular socio-cultural symbolic meanings of Egyptian sculpture;[86] the further removed in time and space, supposedly the greater was the possibility of immediate rather than mediate pure art experience. In the third chapter of *On the Spiritual in Art,* he also offered musings on the possibility of immediate—non-conventional—aural sensations, this time with 'pure sound' transcending the arbitrary limitations of the spoken word, to return to a realm of universal inner affectiveness:

> Words are inner sounds. . . . Skilful use of a word (according to poetic feeling) . . . manifold repetition of a word (a favourite childhood game, later forgotten) makes it lose its external sense as a name . . . and only the pure sound of the word remains . . . this pure sound comes to the fore and exercises a direct influence upon the soul. The soul experiences a non-objective vibration that is more complex . . . than the effect on the soul produced by a bell, a vibrating string, a falling board, etc. Here, great possibilities open up for the literature of the future.[87]

This was an aesthete's aesthetic if ever there were one, grounded in Symbolist principles. It defined artistic excellence as that which transcended cultural relativism to partake in a realm of natural, and therefore universal, human sensitivity.

In the process of expounding his theory of the 'inner' power of art, Kandinsky borrowed ideas from Kondakov. In doing so, however, he effectively undermined Kondakov's insistence on socio-cultural relativism. His was never more than a partial reading of Kondakov; he interpreted the latter's explication of the ritual and symbolic meaning of icons and miniatures in his own terms, according to his own modernist ideals of universal aesthetic experience. This is especially clear in one of the essays Kandinsky wrote for the St Petersburg journal *Apollon.* In his 'Letter from Munich',[88] of October-November 1910, he reviewed an exhibition of Eastern art in the city, conflating miniatures with icons in his discussion of it. He explicitly compared Persian miniatures to 'the old icons',[89] rhetorically evoking his 'inner experience' of miniatures and structuring his account of aesthetic experience as a form of direct spiritual revelation. His sensation was of being inwardly uplifted, like a believer before an icon:

> And suddenly, I seemed to see before my eyes the embodiment of that dream, that reverie I had long carried around with me, unknowing. . . . Standing before it, I felt it had come into being of its own accord, as if it had come down from heaven, like a revelation. This was one of those occasions when the spirit partakes of spiritual refreshment for which it has been waiting, searching, without knowing where to find it. It was as if a curtain had parted before one, revealing new depths of happiness. . . . [90]

In discussing the linear and colouristic qualities of these images, Kandinsky evoked Kondakov's stress on the ornamental abstraction of Byzantine art in the second 'Golden Age':

> Its simplicity is almost barbaric, its complexity bewildering. . . . It has a seriousness, a strength, and occasionally a crudity of draughtsmanship such as one finds in the old icons. And a gentle, pliant, at times cunning beauty of line. The primitive use of colour appears an added adornment. And so keen is the understanding of, so delicate the feeling for, the combination of different tones, so inevitable their unification and division that this primitive ornament suddenly turns into the highest form of painting. [91]

According colour primary significance, he imagined an animate force engendering quasi-ecstatic resonances in the sensitive beholder: 'The colours sing, the costumes, flowers, turbans, rocks, shrubs, palaces, deers, butterflies, horses resound with colour.' [92]

This 'revelation' of the power of Persian miniatures, we might say, prompted his subsequent literary memory of the way in which he had experienced ethnographic art during his 1889 field trip. In both cases, Kandinsky's account of his responses to strange cultural artefacts echoes Kondakov's more objective explication of the mysteries of miniature painting and devotional icons. However, Kandinsky transformed Kondakov's discourse into something more subjective, more artistic. This 'subjectifying' of science is the key theme finally in my more focused reading of **'Reminiscences'**. In this next section, I suggest that Kandinsky's belief in a universal language of art should be seen as a response to his earlier ethnographic dilemma: how to transcend social and historical barriers in order to participate sympathetically in other, unfamiliar cultural experiences?

ETHNOGRAPHY IN 'REMINISCENCES'

Within anthropological discourse, Johannes Fabian has identified, 'a persistent and systematic tendency to place the referent(s) of anthropology in a Time other than the present of the producer of anthropological discourse'. [93]

In evolutionary systematics, for instance, the investigative ethnographer was not only travelling in geographical space (away from—and then back to—the metropolitan centre); he was also travelling backwards in time, via a putative evolutionary ladder. Being based on the episteme of natural history, evolutionary anthropology is, according to Fabian, founded on distancing and separation:

> [It] . . . promoted a schema in terms of which not only past cultures, but all living societies were irrevocably placed on a temporal slope, a stream of Time—some upstream, others downstream. Civilization, evolution, development, acculturation, modernization (and their cousins, industrialization, urbanization) are all terms whose conceptual content derives, in ways that can be specified, from evolutionary Time. [94]

In my reading of Kandinsky's 1889 essay, I suggested that his 'on-the-spot' fieldwork experience undercut such hierarchical separation. I will now argue that in his **'Reminiscences'**, written more than two decades after his initial ethnographic encounter, Kandinsky again imagined the bridging of temporal and spatial distances—this time by means of his heightened artistic sensitivity.

'Reminiscences' is structured as a series of remembered tableaux which are thematically interwoven but not chronological. In a number of places these tableaux move repeatedly from ethnography to art and back again, in such a way that the boundaries of each—science and art—are undermined. Likewise, **'Reminiscences'** calls into question the categories of objectivity (science) and subjectivity (art). As a literary synthesis of personal experiences, **'Reminiscences'** purports to uncover the natural 'archaeological' layering of Kandinsky's modernist artistic persona; it juxtaposes and correlates comforting childhood memories and remembrances of student days in Moscow with experiences from the more recent past in Munich, presenting all of these as but stages in the inexorable development of an artistic initiate. But **'Reminiscences'** is much more than artistic biography; it is also a modernist eulogy to the unifying power of aesthetic experience. Kandinsky structured the whole of the essay as a series of 'revelations' of synthesis. The first narrative section immediately cuts through barriers of time and geography, establishing a continuity between a vanished idyllic past in 'old Russia' and modern urban Munich. The magical connecting powers are colouristic sensations, of course, and also remembrances of horses. Suitably, in fact, for this self-conscious *Blaue Reiter*, this modernist St George, horses are a deliberate thematic leitmotif throughout Kandinsky's **'Reminiscences'**. A child's toy, a wooden hobbyhorse carved out of a stick by 'our coachman', is remembered as a secular transubstantiation; while natural material, in the form of a stick with its bark stripped away to give a spiral pattern of layers, turns animistically into a primal synaesthetic experience:

> My horses usually consisted of three colours: the brownish yellow of the outer bark . . . the juicy green of the second layer of bark (which I loved

most particularly and which, even in a withered state, still had something magical about it) and finally the ivory-white wood of the branch (which smelt damp, tempting one to lick it, but soon withered miserably and dried . . .).[95]

This image of the horse-stick conflates biography, ethnography and aesthetics. It echoes, for instance, an essay published in 1892 by Kandinsky's fellow Russian ethnographer V. M. Mikhailovskii. In this study of Siberian Shamanism, Mikhailovskii graphically described how, in shamanistic practice, the shaman's instruments, including his horse-stick, were replete with ritual significance.[96] Like the child Kandinsky's horse, the shaman's stick was usually carved from the sacred birch tree and, according to Mikhailovskii, supposedly turned into a living horse, which then carried the shaman off on his creative flights beyond this world.[97]

'Reminiscences' has yet another colourful toy horse, this time a piebald stallion from a childhood racing set with yellow ochre on the body and a bright yellow mane, which turns into a 'real' horse in modern Munich. Kandinsky combines memory, imagination and reality, recalling one of his 'first impressions' in Munich, when he encountered such a piebald horse in the streets of the city. In self-imposed exile, he was yet able to identify with his new home through the familiar power of aesthetic remembrances: 'A half-conscious but ebullient promise stirred in my heart. It brought to life the little lead horse within me, linking Munich to my childhood.'[98] His childhood in Old Russia is one of the focal points for Kandinsky's synthesizing project in 'Reminiscences'. He suggests that, even as a child, he possessed remarkable credentials for a future ambassador of modernist abstract art, especially as he was accustomed from a young age to a trans-cultural and bi-lingual role in speaking German with his maternal grandmother and aunt. Around these childhood remembrances Kandinsky elaborated a magical amalgam of fiction and reality. The German fairytales he loved as a child came to life, so he claimed, when he moved to Munich, with powerful colour experiences once more facilitating the conflation:

> The blue trams threaded their way through the streets like an incarnation of the air of a fairy-story, which one inhales with delightful ease. The yellow mailboxes sang their shrill, canary-yellow song from the street corners. I . . . felt I was in the city of art, which for me was the same as being in fairyland.[99]

This literary amalgamation of past and present, dream and reality encapsulates the whole syncretic message of 'Reminiscences'.

As a piece of literature, 'Reminiscences' narrates one thing in order to tell something else. Thus, the remembered 'story' of his 1889 field trip is here also a fable about self-transcendent aesthetic (specifically colouristic) experiences, as Kandinsky presents the transforming power of art through two narratives of artistic-ethnographic trips.

Within the structure of 'Reminiscences', the more recent of these 'transports' is presented first, in a recollection of a visit to the old town of Rothenburg ob der Tauber during his early years in Munich. Kandinsky the intrepid modernist venturer vacated the metropolis for a voyage across time and space. Leaving behind the modern fast train, he experienced progressively more archaic conveyances, firstly a slow train, then a stopping train:

> with its overgrown tracks, the thin whistle of the long-necked engine, the rattling and squeaking of the sleepy wheels, and the old peasant with big silver buttons, who insisted on talking to me about Paris, and whom I had great difficulty in understanding. It was an unreal journey. I felt as if a magic power had, contrary to all the laws of nature, transplanted me from century to century, ever deeper into the past.[100]

This was, indeed, a peculiar experience. Far from the madding city, fixed barriers of reality and illusion were occluded. He remembered 'gateways, ditches, narrow houses, bending their heads across the narrow streets and gazing deep into each other's eyes . . . ';[101] from a suitably distant vantage-point at his bedroom window, this animistic townscape was further transformed into living colour, into a 'sea of bright red rooftops'.[102] It rained all the time he was there, he recalled, this adding an aesthetic twist to his attempts at *plein-air* landscape painting:

> Big, round raindrops fell on my palette, shook hands waggishly from afar, shook and shivered, suddenly and unexpectedly uniting to form thin, cunning threads, which scampered quickly and boisterously between my colours and now and again ran up my sleeves.[103]

He finally managed to paint a sunny *Old Town* from memory, making the 'roofs just as bright a red as I then knew how',[104] but only after returning to the metropolis. This particular literary-artistic anecdote of travel (temporal and spatial) ends with a transcontinental flourish. Kandinsky's colouristic memories transported him back to an idyllic Moscow. Even while struggling with the Rothenburg studies, his unconscious artistic goal was to capture Moscow's sunset hour, which he recalled in a startling passage:

> The sun is already getting low and has attained its full intensity. . . . This image does not last long: a few minutes, and then the sunlight grows red with effort, redder and redder, cold at first and then increasing in warmth. The sun dissolves the whole of Moscow into a single spot, which, like a wild tuba, sets all one's soul vibrating. No, this red fusion is not the most beautiful hour! It is only the final chord of the symphony, which brings every colour vividly to life, which allows and forces the whole of Moscow to resound like the fff . . . of a giant orchestra. Pink, lilac, yellow, white, blue, pistachio green, flame red houses, churches, each an independent song—the garish green of the grass, the deeper tremolo of the bare branches, the red, stiff, silent ring of the Kremlin

walls, and above, towering over everything . . . the long, white, graceful, serious line of the Bell Tower of Ivan the Great. And upon its tall, tense neck, stretched up toward heaven in eternal yearning, the golden head of the cupola, which among the golden and coloured stars of the other cupolas, is Moscow's sun . . . These impressions were repeated on each sunny day. They were a delight that shook me to the depths of my soul. . . . [105]

These magical colours, he claimed, were so powerful that they even 'raised me to ecstasy'.[106] Throughout **'Reminiscences'**, Kandinsky related a series of similar aesthetic experiences, where colours enabled his transportation beyond empirical reality.

The second journey of **'Reminiscences'** was even more extreme than the first, taking the artist-ethnographer on a voyage out of present time and space and also beyond the conventional categories of art and science. He reminisced specifically about his trip to the province of Vologda. Modes of time travel took him even further into the past, almost out of the world, through a primeval, surreal landscape, with colours again contributing to the transport:

> I travelled initially by train, with the feeling that I was journeying to another planet, then for several days by boat along the tranquil and introverted Sukhona river, then by primitive coach through endless forests, between brightly coloured hills, over swamps and deserts.[107]

This time, with no distracting strangers to disrupt the experience, he was able to effect a two-fold absorption 'in my surroundings and in my own self'.[108] Repeating a device used elsewhere in the essay, he wrote of his field trip as if it were a mystery initiation. The journey itself was an ordeal:

> It was often scorching hot during the day, but the nights, despite the almost complete absence of darkness, were so cold that even the sheepskin coat, felt boots and Zyrian hat, which I had procured on the way . . . sometimes proved not entirely sufficient. . . . [109]

The tribulation was well worthwhile, at least from his subsequent perspective as a modern colourist, for he journeyed to places remote enough for colours to have their own reality and force. The populace, in this memory, dissolved into animated colours:

> I would arrive in villages where suddenly the entire population was clad in grey from head to toe; with yellowish-green faces and hair, or suddenly displayed variegated costumes that ran about like brightly coloured, living pictures on two legs.[110]

But, above all, it was the magical colouristic spaces inside old Russian peasant houses which prophesied his future ideals of transcendent aesthetics. As he remembered it, the living spaces of these strange people provoked extraordinary aesthetic experience. He stepped into these unfamiliar folk environs and found their colour and decoration so overwhelming that henceforth he wished to make his own modern spectator '"stroll" within the picture, *forcing him to become absorbed in the picture, forgetful of himself*' (my emphasis).[111] The 'lesson' of this ethnographic encounter, then, is one of self-transcendence through aesthetic contemplation. Kandinsky was conveying an image of himself as artistic-ethnographer, his heightened artistic perception enabling him to cross cultural and historical barriers, to participate in an aesthetic realm of universal oneness.

CONCLUSION

This artistic memory seems remote from my starting point in the disciplinary complexities of Russian ethnography. In the first part of my article, I argued that Kandinsky's 'on-the-spot' investigation was thoroughly textual, at a time when the basic procedures and methodologies of professional ethnographic field work were not fully established. He left Moscow equipped with questionnaire-type guidelines for interrogating an unfamiliar research object and thus collecting relevant cultural data; on his return, he wrote up his findings, editing his field-work notes according to existing exemplars of scientific presentation, though tempered by the modes of earlier historical narratives. My aim was to demonstrate the critical complexities embedded in his 1889 treatise, especially the contradictions between empirical fieldwork experience on the one hand and theoretical synthesis on the other. The boldest result of this section would be to question the 'radical orthodoxy' which views nineteenth-century anthropology as typically evolutionist/colonialist/racist (*pace* Clifford et al.).[112]

The second section on 'artistic ethnography' raises other issues. On the one hand, Kandinsky's aestheticizing of traditional material culture in his own modernist terms is precisely what recent anthropologists have been keen to avoid in their attempts to 're-centre' art as a legitimate topic of anthropological study.[113] Within an art-historical framework, however, I will restate my argument that we should consider Kandinsky's artistic theories partly as a response to his earlier ethnographic dilemma of how to participate sympathetically in other, unfamiliar cultural forms. I am suggesting, in other words, that the current critical perception of all 'universalizing' artistic aspirations as forms of cultural colonialism needs to be tested (and contested) more rigorously.

NOTES

[1] 'Iz materialov po etnografii sysol'skikh i vychegodskikh zyryan—natsional'nye bozhestva (po sovremennym verovaniyam)', *Etnograficheskoe obozrenie*, no. 3, 1889, pp. 102-110. ['From Materials on the Ethnography of the Sysol-and-Vechegda Zyrians: The National Deities (According to Contemporary Beliefs)', *Ethnographic Review*, no. 3 (Moscow, 1889), pp. 102-110] (henceforth 'Zyrian Ethnography').

This essay is most easily available in German translation. See J. Hahl-Koch and H. K. Roethel (eds.), *Kandinsky: Die Gesammelten Schriften*, Band 1 (Bern, 1980), pp. 68-75 (henceforth *Schriften*).

[2] Some of Kandinsky's fieldwork notes, in the form of a diary, are preserved in the archives of the Museum of Modern Art in the Pompidou Centre, Paris. It forms part of Nina Kandinsky's bequest, acquired by the museum in 1981. As yet the notebook is unpublished.

[3] Recent publications by Peg Weiss have already established the importance of Kandinsky's ethnographic work as a shaping influence on his later painting.

See P. Weiss, 'Kandinsky and Old Russia: An Ethnographic Exploration', *Syracuse Scholar*, Spring 1986, pp. 43-62. Also, idem., under the same title, in G. P. Weisberg and L. S. Dixon (eds.), *The Documented Image: Visions in Art History* (Syracuse, 1987).

[4] 'Rückblicke', in *Kandinsky 1901-1913* (*Der Sturm*, Berlin, 1913). I am using the translation in K. C. Lindsay and P. Vergo (eds.), *Kandinsky: Complete Writings on Art* (2 vols., London, 1982), vol. 1, pp. 357-82 [henceforth, *CW*].

[5] For these recollections, see 'Reminiscences' in *CW*, op. cit., pp. 361-3; 365; 368-9; 379.

As a student, he was 'strongly attracted' to ethnography amongst other disciplines:

> Apart from my chosen specialization (economics . . .), I was strongly attracted . . . by various other disciplines. Roman law . . . criminal law . . . the history of Russian law and peasant law . . . ethnography . . . which, I promised myself initially, would reveal to me the soul of the people . . . (ibid., p. 362).

[6] J. Clifford, 'Introduction: Partial Truths', in J. Clifford and G. E. Marcus (eds.), *Writing Culture. The Poetics and Politics of Ethnography* (Berkeley and Los Angeles, 1986), p. 2.

[7] The Ethnographic Section of the Imperial Society for the Friends of the Natural Sciences, Anthropology and Ethnography was based at Moscow University. *Ethnographic Review*, which published Kandinsky's Zyrian essay, appeared under the auspices of the Imperial Society. Kandinsky published a second article in 1889, in yet another *Imperial Society* journal, namely, 'O nakazaniyakh' po resheniyam' volostnykh sudov Moskovskoi Gub[ernoi]', *Trudy etnograficheskago otdela Imperatorskago, obshchestva lyubitelei estestvoznaniya, antropologii, i etnografii*, vol. 9, 1889, pp. 13-19. ('On the punishments meted out in accordance with the decisions of the district courts of the province of Moscow', *Works of the Ethnographic Section of the Imperial Society for the Friends of the Natural Sciences, Anthropology and Ethnography*, vol. 9 (Moscow, 1889), pp. 13-19. This article is also translated into German in *Schriften*, op. cit., pp. 76-88.

I consider Kandinsky's legal studies in detail in 'Kandinsky: The Sciences of Man and the Science of Art' (Ph.D. thesis, Cambridge University, 1992).

[8] Something of the flavour of Russian ethnography can be gleaned from the Russian literature reviews in the *Internationales Archiv für Ethnographie* through the 1890s. In particular see vol. 3 (1891), pp. 45-7; 135-6; 163-4 and 247-9.

[9] In the Russian version of 'Reminiscences', published in 1918, Kandinsky recalled that he had received support and encouragement in his study of customary law from Fillipov who, at the time, was a *privat-dozent* in Moscow University Law Faculty. For the relevant addition to the published Russian version of 'Reminiscences' (1918), see *CW*, op. cit., vol. 2, p. 888, n. 20.

[10] *Trudy etnograficheskago otdela Imperatorskago, obshchestva lyubitelei estestvoznaniya, antropologii, i etnografii (Works of the Ethnographic Section of the Imperial Society for the Friends of the Natural Sciences, Anthropology and Ethnography)*, vol. 8 (Moscow, 1888), Appendix.

[11] ibid., p. ii.

[12] See J. Urry, '*Notes and Queries on Anthropology* and the Development of Field Methods in British Anthropology, 1870-1920', *Proceedings of the Royal Anthropological Institute*, 1972, pp. 45-57.

[13] Quoted in the 1912 edition of *Notes and Queries on Anthropology* (London, 1912), B. Freire-Marreco and J. Linton Myres (eds.), pp. iv-v.

[14] 'Zyrian Ethnography', in *Schriften*, op. cit., p. 68. All English translations are my own.

[15] I use 'anthropology' and 'anthropological sciences' as generic terms referring to the putative 'sciences of man'. See G. Stocking, *Race, Culture and Evolution: Essays in the History of Anthropology* (New York, 1968).

[16] The term is Stocking's. See 'The Ethnographer's Magic: Fieldwork in British Anthropology from Tylor to Malinowski', in *Observers Observed. Essays on Ethnographic Fieldwork*, vol. 1 in the series *History of Anthropology* (Madison, 1983), pp. 70-120.

[17] See the report of Anutschin's article, 'The Work of Russian Ethnography' in the *Internationales Archiv für Ethnographie*, vol. 3, 1891, pp. 45-6.

Anutschin argued that:

> 'die Unbekanntschaft mit ethnographischen Fakten, die Unkunde des inneren Lebens, der Zustände und Bedürfnisse des Volkes in Russland häufig zur Ursache vielfacher administrativer und legislativer Fehler, wie in Bezug auf die fremden Völkerschaften,

so auf das eigentliche russische Volk selbst ward. Dank ähnlichen Fehlern wurden die Buriäten aus Schamanisten zu Buddhisten, die Kirgisen aber zu Mohammedanern gemacht und ihnen solcherweise, vielleicht auch immer, der Weg zur Verschmelzung mit dem russischen Volke abgeschnitten . . . ', ibid., p. 46.

[18] I pursue this line of argument in more depth in my thesis, op. cit.

[19] M. Foucault, *The Order of Things: An Archaeology of the Human Sciences* (London, 1970), pp. 359-60.

[20] See R. Jakobson, 'Franz Boas' approach to language', *International Journal of American Linguistics,* 10, 1944, pp. 188-95.

Also, G. W. Stocking, 'The Boas Plan for the Study of American Indian Languages', in D. Hymen (ed.), *Studies in the History of Linguistics: Traditions and Paradigms* (London, 1974), pp. 454-84.

[21] See note 8 above. Müller's studies of Iranian myths in the Caucasus, published in 1889 and 1890, are reviewed in the *Internationales Archiv für Ethnographie,* vol. 3 (1891), pp. 135 and 247. Kandinsky's research is mentioned, ibid., pp. 247-8.

[22] 'Zyrian Ethnography' in *Schriften,* op. cit., p. 74.

[23] ibid., p. 74.

[24] ibid.

[25] ibid.

[26] ibid., p. 70.

[27] ibid., pp. 68-9.

[28] Among the bibliographic notes in Kandinsky's travel notebook (see note 2 above), I found his reference to an 1861 edition of Sjögren's work edited and introduced by the Estonian linguist F. J. Wiedemann. *Joh. Andreas Sjögrens Gesammelte Schriften* (new facsimile edition, 2 vols, in 3, Leipzig, 1969. Originally, St Petersburg, 1861).

Sjögren's long essay was entitled 'Die Syrjänen, ein historisch-statistisch-philologischer Versuch', ibid., vol. 1, pp. 230-461.

For further details, see my article, 'Modernist Primitivism?: The Case of Kandinsky', *Oxford Art Journal,* vol. 16, no. 2, 1993, pp. 21-36.

[29] On Sjögren, see in particular M. Branch, 'A. J. Sjögren's Studies of the North', *Mémoires de la Société Finno-Ougrienne* (Helsinki, 1973).

[30] 'Zyrian Ethnography' in *Schriften,* op. cit., pp. 68-9.

[31] ibid., p. 69.

[32] In A. H. Lane-Fox (General Pitt-Rivers) (ed.), *Notes and Queries on Anthropology* (London, 1874), p. 27.

[33] 'Zyrian Ethnography', in *Schriften,* op. cit., p. 68.

[34] M. Harris, *The Rise of Anthropological Theory: A History of Theories of Culture* (London, 1968).

I. Langham, *The Building of British Social Anthropology. W.H.R. Rivers and his Cambridge Disciples in the Development of Kinship Studies, 1893-1931* (London, 1981).

[35] In *Notes and Queries* (1874), op. cit., pp. 66-7.

[36] ibid., p. 50.

[37] 'Zyrian Ethnography', in *Schriften,* op. cit., p. 70.

[38] ibid.

[39] ibid., pp. 70-1.

[40] ibid., p. 71.

[41] ibid., p. 73.

[42] ibid., p. 73.

[43] ibid., p. 72. The editors of *Schriften* are misleading in their transcription of Kandinsky's footnote. Kandinsky refers to Herbert Spencer's *Principles of Sociology,* originally published in London in 1876-96 (3 vols.), and *not* to Spencer's *Descriptive Sociology* (London, 1873).

[44] ibid., p. 72.

[45] E. B. Tylor, *Primitive Culture* (London, 1871, n.ed., New York, 1958).

[46] Spencer, op. cit., vol. 1, 1876.

[47] In his wide-ranging and suggestive study, *Culture and Anomie: Ethnographic Imagination in the Nineteenth Century* (Chicago and London, 1981), C. Herbert discusses Spencer as an early champion of the functionalistic interpretation of culture.

See also G. W. Stocking, *Race, Culture and Evolution: Essays in the History of Anthropology* (New York, 1968), and idem., *Victorian Anthropology* (New York and London, 1987).

Kandinsky published another ethnographic essay in 1889, this being a study of customary law (see note 7 above). This essay clearly demonstrates his understanding of the integral nature of 'culture' and of the need to understand customary practices not as isolated data, but 'holistically'. He specifically warned against seeing the widespread practice of corporal punishment as evidence of distorted or regressive moral values and instead argued that the practice was normal and sociologically positive, being linked to the whole configuration of the society in question, and in particular to the economic determinants of peasant life (*Schriften*, op. cit., pp. 87-8). In my thesis, op. cit., I argue that Kandinsky examined legal institutions and customs in the light of rapid change in rural organization, and in the light of widespread economic distress; his essay demonstrates the historical and sociological approach to the study of legal institutions encouraged by the *Moscow Juridical Society*, of which he was a member.

[48] See, for example, U. Holmberg, *Finno-Ugric Siberian*, vol. 4 of *The Mythology of All Races* (Boston, 1927), and also P. Hajdu (ed.), *Finno-Ugrian Languages and People*, trans. G. F. Cushing (London, 1975).

[49] *Notes and Queries*, 1874, op. cit. p. 50-1.

[50] 'Zyrian Ethnography', in *Schriften*, op. cit., pp. 71-2.

[51] ibid. p. 72.

[52] *Ort*, it seems, was like a tutelary spirit, but of a material nature. Kandinsky recorded some differing ideas about forms *Ort* took. Some Zyrians believed that *Ort* accompanied each person from birth; others held that a person obtained his *Ort* shortly before his death. In all cases, though, *Ort* became important at times of impending death. According to one version, the *Ort* of a sick individual appeared to the person's relatives by night, as a deathly portent. In another version, *Ort* appeared to the ill-fated person, leaving behind a very physical calling-card: the *Ort* would pinch and bruise the doomed individual, and the portentous signs could appear up to three years before the event. Ibid., pp. 71-2.

[53] ibid., p. 72. See note 44, above.

[54] See also Spencer's *The Study of Sociology* (new ed., Ann Arbor, 1961).

[55] *Principles of Sociology*, op. cit., vol. 1, part 1, chap. 1.

[56] 'Zyrian Ethnography' in *Schriften*, op. cit., p. 72.

[57] ibid., p. 71.

[58] M. L. Pratt, 'Fieldwork in common places', in J. Clifford and G. E. Marcus (eds.), op. cit., p. 32.

[59] ibid., p. 32.

[60] Sjögren, op. cit., vol. 1, pp. 230-461.

[61] 'Zyrian Ethnography' in *Schriften*, op. cit., p. 68.

[62] ibid., p. 70.

[63] ibid., p. 69.

[64] ibid., p. 74.

[65] See, for example, the volume edited by J. Coote and A. Shelton: *Anthropology, Art and Aesthetics* (Oxford, 1992).

[66] See chap. 6, 'The Language of Forms and Colours', in *On the Spiritual in Art* (1911/12), in *CW*, op. cit., pp. 161-95.

[67] 'Reminiscences' in *CW*, op. cit., pp. 368-9.

[68] N. P. Kondakov, *The Russian Icon* (Oxford, 1927). All quotes are from this English edition.

The original Russian studies were published between 1905 and 1915. For further details, see the posthumous collected publication in four volumes, N. P. Kondakov, *Russkaya ikona* (Prague, 1928-33).

[69] Kondakov, op. cit., also includes a chapter on 'The Use and Place of Icons in Russia'. See especially p. 34.

[70] *CW*, op. cit., p. 182.

[71] N. P. Kondakoff, *Histoire de l'art byzantin considérée principalement dans les miniatures* (Paris, 2 vols., 1886-91), vol. 1, chap. 1, especially pp. 30-1.

[72] *CW*, p. 182.

[73] Kondakoff, op. cit. (vol. 2, 1891), p. 3.

[74] ibid., chap. 6, for example, pp. 3-4.

[75] Kondakoff, op. cit. (vol. 1, 1886), pp. 30-4.

[76] ibid., p. 33.

[77] ibid., pp. 42-3.

[78] 'l'art . . . servirait a instruire les masses ignorantes, a éclairer la foi, a agir sur les coeurs, a développer l'amour de Dieu et des hommes'; ibid., p. 195.

[79] Kondakov, op. cit.

[80] ibid., p. 18.

[81] ibid., p. 12.

[82] ibid.

[83] ibid., p. 18.

[84] See, for example, J. Elsner, 'Image and iconoclasm in Byzantium', *Art History*, vol. 11, no. 4, Dec. 1988, pp. 471-91.

[85] Kondakov, *The Russian Icon*, op. cit., p. 34.

[86] *CW*, op. cit., pp. 173-4.

[87] ibid., p. 147.

[88] 'Letter from Munich', *CW*, op. cit., pp. 73-80.

[89] ibid., p. 74.

[90] ibid.

[91] ibid.

[92] ibid., p. 75.

[93] J. Fabian, *Time and the Other: How Anthropology Makes its Object* (New York, 1983), p. 31.

[94] ibid., p. 26.

[95] *CW*, op. cit., pp. 357-8.

[96] V. M. Mikhailovskii's 'Schamanstvo' was published in the proceedings of the Imperial Society for the Friends of Natural History, Anthropology and Ethnography in 1892. It was partially translated into English by Oliver Wardrop as 'Shamanism in Siberia and European Russia', *Journal of the Anthropological Institute of Great Britain and Ireland*, 24, 1895, pp. 62-100; 126-58.

Weiss, in her study of the ethnographic aspects of Kandinsky's art (op. cit., 1986, p. 51), first suggested the importance of Mikhailovskii, who was vice-president of the ethnographic section of the Imperial Society.

[97] Wardrop, op. cit., p. 89.

[98] *CW*, op. cit., p. 359.

[99] ibid.

[100] ibid.

[101] ibid.

[102] ibid.

[103] ibid.

[104] ibid., p. 360.

[105] ibid.

[106] ibid.

[107] ibid., p. 368. I discuss these 'ethnographic' passages from 'Reminiscences' in similar terms in my article 'Modernist Primitivism?: The Case of Kandinsky', op. cit.

[108] *CW*, op. cit., p. 368.

[109] ibid., vol. 2, p. 891, n. 45.

[110] ibid., p. 368.

[111] ibid., pp. 368-9.

[112] This 'radical orthodoxy' is represented by the volume edited by J. Clifford and G. E. Marcus, op. cit., and by J. Fabian, op. cit. See also J. Clifford, *The Predicament of Culture: Twentieth-Century Ethnography, Literature and Art* (Cambridge, Mass., 1988).

[113] Apart from the volume *Anthropology, Art and Aesthetics*, edited by Coote and Shelton, op. cit., the journal *Res: Anthropology and Aesthetics* also deals with these issues.

William R. Everdell (essay date 1997)

SOURCE: "Vassily Kandinsky: Art With No Object, 1911-1912," in *The First Moderns: Profiles in the Origins of Twentieth-Century Thought*, University of Chicago Press, 1997, pp. 303-20.

[*In the following essay, Everdell investigates Kandinsky's prolific output during the year 1911-1912.*]

> The tall, narrow roofs of the Promenadenplatz and Maximiliansplatz, which have now disappeared, the old part of Schwabing, and especially the Au, which I discovered by chance on one occasion, turned these fairy-tales into reality. The blue trams threaded their way through the streets like an incarnation of the air of a fairy-story, which one inhales with delightful ease. The yellow mailboxes sang their shrill, canary-yellow song from the street corners. I welcomed the label "art-mill," and felt I was in the city of art, which for me was the same as being in fairyland.
>
> —Vassily Kandinsky, *"Reminiscences"*

The city was Munich, the capital of the southern German state of Bavaria. The artist was Vassily Kandinsky, who in 1911 was living and working in Munich's bohemian suburb of Schwabing. His studio at number 36 Ainmiller Street was a whirlpool of activity, and 1911 was to be his *annus mirabilis*. During the twelve months of his forty-fifth year, Kandinsky was to paint a dozen major paintings, together with innumerable studies and sketches, and show his work in four cities in three countries. In addition, he would publish two articles and a germinal book on the theory of modern art, edit a second book bringing most of the important central European voices in the arts together for the first time, and lead in the planning and execution of an international exhibition that is still considered one of the two most important group shows in the early history of modern art. A final divorce decree would end his first marriage halfway through 1911. Finally, somewhere along the way, Kandinsky would paint one of the first pictures ever to deserve the designation "abstract," "nonobjective," or "nonrepresentational" art.

Kandinsky's marvelous year began when he went to a New Year's party at the home of another pair of Munich artists, and went on with them to a concert of works by a new composer, Arnold Schoenberg. One of the out-of-town guests was a painter named Franz Marc, who there began his lifelong friendship with Kandinsky. Within a month Marc was writing that the "hours spent with [Kandinsky] belong to my most memorable experiences."

> My initial response is to feel the great joy of his powerful, pure, fiery colors, and then my brain starts working; you can't get away from these pictures and you feel your head will burst if you want to savor them to the full. . . . [1]

The maker of these mind-blowing pictures had a mustache, a sharply pointed black beard, and mephistophelean almond eyes behind thick glasses. Kandinsky's housemate, Gabriele Münter, an excellent painter herself, had already made several small portraits of him in which the professorial rumple was set off by an unfathomable reserve and an oddly authoritative, almost prophetic gravity. He was quite sure of what he was doing. He was so assured, in fact, that whenever his fellow artists got together they elected Kandinsky to run the show for them. The fact that he had a bit of an independent income helped. In 1909 the Schwabing avant garde had responded to his call to found an exhibiting society, the New Artists Organization of Munich (NKVM), and promptly elected him president. In that capacity he had mounted a show in the fall of 1910 that for the first time brought work by the French cubists and the new Russian painters to Germany. Kandinsky was Russian himself, a Muscovite, and half the NKVM was Russian too. They had come to Munich to study art, and having studied it, had stayed.

Munich was yeasty with cultural pioneers. The journals *Simplicissimus* and *Jugend* (Youth), together with their art-nouveau style called *Jugendstil,* had begun there. The Eleven Executioners cabaret, one of the first outside of Paris, had been in Munich since 1900, and the playwright Frank Wedekind was part of it. Thomas Mann wrote stories there, and Stefan George wrote poems. But it was the artists, and especially the painters, who were the yeastiest of all. Munich was home to several hundred thousand people, and at times it seemed half of them were artists. Many had come from rather faraway places, like Pittsburgh, Glasgow, and Odessa. At least one Munich art show in 1869 had attracted 100,000 visitors, more than 60 percent of its 1869 population.[2] Munich's Glyptothek was the oldest public museum in Central Europe, and its Neue Pinakothek had been the only German public collection of contemporary art until the 1890s. There was a third museum for art that was neither Antique nor contemporary, a fourth small gallery for the Sezession, a fifth hall dedicated to industrial exhibits but often used for art, and a sixth, the Glass Palace, the largest in Germany, which was used on occasion for great exhibitions. The Munich artists' Sezession had been, in 1892, the first in Central Europe to declare its independence. Though it was a spent force in 1911, and its members had become respectable, a group of new artists were already pushing the envelope. In 1911, people were beginning to call them "expressionists."

The term *Expressionismus* was first used by Germans in 1911 to describe the new trend in French painting[3] that had taken up where Matisse and his co-conspirators had left off—the fauves whose work Kandinsky, who had spent a year in Paris in 1906-7, could describe firsthand. Forms were simplified, colors saturated, and surfaces laden with paint. First in painting and later in theater and poetry, *Expressionismus* would be used after 1911 to describe the German avant garde much as *Futurismo* described the Italian. It would be used retroactively to describe Strindberg's drama. For painters, it represented the replacement of Seurat by Van Gogh as a model; and the assertion of a new goal: to paint not the observed moment in the life of nature, but nature's inner life, and the inner life of the artist as well. The style had come to Germany at the turn of the century, well before the word was coined. Among small artists' associations like Die Brücke (The bridge) in Dresden, the Worpswede Group near Bremen, the Neu-Dachau, Phalanx, and Scholle (Clod) groups around Munich that had succeeded the Sezession, expressionism was already under way. Kandinsky had seen some of this French, German, and Russian work that was about to be dubbed expressionist, and he had liked it. He had, in fact, founded the Munich Phalanx and helped mount all ten of their shows. His new friend Franz Marc painted blue horses and yellow cows in a village not far from Munich, and Münter, Marianne Werefkin, Alexei Jawlensky, and other neighbors who had helped him found the NKVM were making equally proto-expressionist art in Schwabing. Nevertheless, Kandinsky's own work was rather different. Though he had done some excellent woodcuts, often achieving the simplified forms beloved by Die Brücke, he had nearly given it up recently, turning instead to painting on glass the way folk artists of the Munich countryside had done for generations, and simplifying not his forms but his subject matter. Instead of using color as a fauve might, to make a white sailboat orange, Kandinsky splashed primary colors onto scenes from the past, from fairytale and myth. Where he had once painted trains rushing through a recognizable countryside, lately he had been painting mounted archers posting through fantasy landscapes under the outlines of mountains.

Even his picture titles were changing. "The direct impression of 'external nature,' expressed in linear-painterly form" he now called an "Impression," though it rendered something very far from a momentary effect of light. He made the first of his Impressions in 1911. Two years before, in 1909, he had painted the first painting to which he attached the label "Improvisation." The source for an Improvisation, he wrote in 1911, was "chiefly unconscious, for the most part suddenly arising expressions of events of an inner character, hence impressions of 'internal nature.'" Another sort of picture was what he called a "Composition." He had painted his first three of these in 1910. A Composition expressed the same internal events, but took more time because "after the first preliminary sketches," Kandinsky "slowly and almost pedantically worked out" how to express them.[4]

Kandinsky, in other words, was not trying to paint what he saw, but what he felt, or rather what he knew inside himself. Though the things he knew inside had no shape at all, Kandinsky was quite certain they were substantial, and well worth painting. He was convinced they were undergone in turn by a faculty that could be found within himself, and that could be reached in others—something he called the "soul," using an unabashedly religious term. He had been born in 1866, ten years after Freud, who called the soul "psyche" and thought its mysteries were material; but Kandinsky did not think, as Freud did, that the materialist millennium was coming in. He thought it was coming to an end. He saw no conflict between religious belief and the radical remaking of art, and indeed thought the two would reinforce each other. Except for some aging Russian symbolists, not many other artists still felt that way. Perhaps one key to Kandinsky's views was synesthesia, the condition Baudelaire had written of in his sonnet "Correspondences" where the sensations produced by any one of the five senses can evoke corresponding sensations in the others. Kandinsky was a cellist and a poet, and every one of his five senses was resonant. He was acutely sensitive, especially to color.

> As a thirteen or fourteen-year-old boy, I gradually saved up enough money to buy myself a paintbox containing oil paints. I can still feel today the sensation I experienced then—or, to put it better, the experience I underwent then—of the paints emerging from the tube. One squeeze of the fingers, and out came these strange beings, one after the other, which one calls colors—exultant, solemn, brooding, dreamy, self-absorbed, deeply serious, with roguish experience, with a sigh of release, with a deep sound of mourning, with defiant power and resistance, with submissive suppleness and devotion, with obstinate self-control, with sensitive, precarious balance.[5]

Indeed, it was a synesthetic moment of vision that had come to him long ago in his native Russia that had turned Kandinsky into an artist. Sometime between 1891 and 1895, Kandinsky, a newly married, newly hired law school teaching adjunct with research interests in economics and ethnography, had gone to an exhibition of French impressionists in Moscow, and "suddenly, for the first time" seen a picture. It was a Monet painting called *Haystacks,* part of a time-series, fixing the effects of light. But Kandinsky had not seen the haystack. What he had seen, instead, was the picture.

> That it was a haystack, the catalogue informed me. I didn't recognize it. I found this nonrecognition painful, and thought that the painter had no right to paint so indistinctly. I had a dull feeling that the object was lacking in this picture. And I noticed with surprise and confusion that the picture not only gripped me, but impressed itself ineradicably upon my memory, always hovering quite unexpectedly before my eyes, down to the last detail. It was all unclear to me, and I was not able to draw the simple conclusions from this experience. What was, however, quite clear to me

was the unsuspected power of the palette, previously concealed from me, which exceeded all my dreams. Painting took on a fairy-tale power and splendor. And albeit unconsciously, objects were discredited as an essential element within the picture.[6]

It had been the first in a cascade of insights that sent Kandinsky from Moscow to Munich. At about the same time, he recalled, he had been amazed to experience the music of Wagner's *Lohengrin* as colors and lines, and he had learned of "the further division of the atom," probably the discovery of the electron between 1894 and 1897. "The collapse of the atom was equated, in my soul, with the collapse of the whole world. Suddenly, the stoutest walls crumbled. Everything became uncertain, precarious and insubstantial."[7]

In 1911, some twenty years later, Kandinsky, his marriage at an end and his career in law no more than a memory, was still working out the consequences of these sudden revelations. It was the year he painted the first five of his numbered *Impressions,* variously subtitled *Moscow* (no. 2) or *Park* (no. 5). The motifs in them could be found by a viewer, but only by one intent enough to pick them out amid Kandinsky's insistent shapes and colors. *Improvisations* 19 through 22 were still more subjective. **Composition IV** and **Composition V** would take painting to the edge of complete subjectivity. He painted all of them in 1911.

Although few painters waste much time writing, Kandinsky wrote well enough and often enough to make his intentions clear even to some who could not make head or tail of his new work. He had already written a monumental attack on positivism and materialism, the book that was to explain his unique approach to painting. It was called **Über das Geistige in der Kunst** (On the spiritual in art). He had read it to an audience in October 1910, and would persuade the adventurous Munich art publisher, Piper, to print it in 1911. Painting, he wrote, used three distinct instruments—color, form, and subject—to cause what he called "sounds" in the soul. Each instrument worked its own magic; color and form, for example, did not exist merely to serve the subject. Instead each one operated independently, creating consonances and dissonances with the others in the inner responses of a viewer. Arnold Schoenberg had much the same idea of how music worked, and Kandinsky, who had heard Schoenberg's breakthrough *String Quartet* #2 with his Munich friends on New Year's Day 1911, saw the point immediately. He began to write Schoenberg letters about the correspondence between their arts. His book **On the Spiritual in Art** likened painting to music in that both could directly to the soul; but argued that the various means by which painting could do this had never been as well understood as those of music.

All through 1910, Kandinsky painted so as to increase his understanding of the separate roles of color, form, and subject, and as 1911 began he was approaching what he thought of as the next step: how to separate the way he used form or color to delineate a subject from other ways he used it that were more "abstract." The outline of a face, he thought, conveyed two things at once. One was the shape of a known subject—a face; the other was a variation on the ellipse—an absolute, *abstraktes* form that had quite different connotations of its own. The color of a face was yet another sort of abstraction, implying infinite extension in a way form did not. In the half-dozen paintings of 1911 whose subject was a horse and rider, Kandinsky left the subject recognizable, but dwelt more and more on the abstract forms it suggested to him, other shapes whose inner "sounds" set up consonances and dissonances with the "sounds" of a horse and a rider, and were thus much more than the mere outlines of straining man and beast.

Kandinsky began to paint **Composition IV** in February 1911. As he recalled it, his "inner necessity" required that he put eight "basic elements" into play in it, including "acute movements to the left and upward," "contrast between blurred and contoured forms," and "predominance of color over form." In fact, though a viewer is still hard put to see it, **Composition IV** was a painting of a battle, centered on a castle-crowned mountain, with struggling knights and horses to the left, lancers in the middle, and two wanderers and a reclining couple to the right. The only clue to their placement in space is in the overlap of one subject by another. Skeptics, knowing that Kandinsky found his thick eyeglasses indispensable, still try to blame the artist's myopia for their own problems discerning the subjects of his paintings, but this is no solution.[8] Independently of vague representations of people and natural objects in **Composition IV**, overwhelming colors struck "sounds" of their own, much as Kandinsky intended them to: a rainbow-like parabola of red, yellow, green, and dark blue; the intense cold blue of the mountaintop; the bright yellow of the hill on the right behind the reclining couple. Kandinsky saw this yellow in fact as an entirely independent second meaning for the painting. As he recalled it two years later, "The juxtaposition of this bright-sweet-cold tone [yellow] with angular movement (battle) is the principal contrast in the picture."[9]

Kandinsky's colors had been intense for years, but now, as the result of another moment of vision, the true depth of their effects began to become clear to him. It was summer.

> The summer of 1911, which was unusually hot for Germany, lasted desperately long. Every morning on waking, I saw from the window the incandescent blue sky. The thunderstorms came, let fall a few drops of rain, and passed on. I had the feeling as if someone seriously ill had to be made to sweat, but that no remedies were of any use. . . . One's skin cracked. One's breath failed. Suddenly, all nature seemed to me white; white (great silence—full of possibilities) displayed itself everywhere and expanded visibly. . . . Since that time I know what undreamed-of possibilities this primordial color conceals within itself.[10]

White, Kandinsky had discovered, was a color, a color as evocative as the primaries themselves, needing only to be set somewhere in its range, a range no less infinite than all color ranges. The experience also seems to have nudged him over the edge into complete abstraction.

> This revelation turned the whole of painting upside-down and opened up before it a realm in which one had previously been unable to believe. I. e., the inner, thousandfold, unlimited values of one and the same quality, the possibility of obtaining and applying infinite series simply in combination with one single quality, tore open before me the gates of the realm of absolute art.[11]

In August, Kandinsky began to paint **Composition V**.[12] This painting too had a subject—the resurrection of the dead at the Christian Apocalypse; but by the time Kandinsky had arranged his forms and colors to evoke this climactic vision, even less of the actual subject was left to be perceived on the canvas than had appeared in *Composition IV*. The subject had clearly been in the painter's mind for a year or more; and along the way, Kandinsky made one picture of Gabriel himself blowing his horn and several others of the saints in concert that could easily have called up a chorus of "The Saints Go Marching In" from a brass band in New Orleans.[13] Among the many riders Kandinsky painted in 1911 is a *Rider of the Apocalypse* in tempera on glass. There are also two glass paintings and an oil of Saint George that seem related, and another small glass painting of a bird of paradise and a hellhound.[14] All the many aspects of the subject were evoked on a deep level in the final painting, not by representing the subject but by the use of forms and colors. "I deprived my colors of their clarity of tone," wrote Kandinsky, "dampening them on the surface and allowing their purity and true nature to glow forth," as if through frosted glass."[15] By now Kandinsky had finally seen the new Picassos; photographs of some of his cubist paintings had been sent to Kandinsky by the Paris picture-dealer Kahnweiler. Kandinsky, fascinated, wrote to Marc in October that Picasso

> splits the subject up and scatters bits of it all over the picture; the picture consists of the confusion of the parts. . . . This decomposition is very interesting. But frankly "false" as I see it. I'm really pleased with it as a sign of the enormous struggle toward the immaterial thought.[16]

About this time Kandinsky found the immaterial thought for himself, a picture that was neither an Impression, nor an Improvisation, nor yet a Composition. He called it, simply, *Bild mit Kreis* (Picture with a circle). It was pretty big, roughly three and a half by four and a half feet. Until quite recently, it lay in storage in the State Museum of Art in Tbilisi, Georgia, while a little watercolor focused the attention of scholars, an apparently purely abstract watercolor dated to 1910 by its owner, Kandinsky's second wife. This watercolor, however, looked so much like Kandinsky's first fully abstract Composition of 1913 that when **Picture with a Circle** was finally brought out in

1989, after sixty years, the "First Abstract Watercolor" was relabeled "Study for *Composition VII*," and the debate became moot.[17] According to Kandinsky himself, **Picture with a Circle** was "my very first abstract picture of 1911," the first picture he ever painted that had no subject at all.[18]

He seems to have painted it sometime after **Composition IV** and perhaps after **Composition V,** which probably means the winter of 1911. As Kandinsky remembered it, **Picture with a Circle** was "a very làrge picture, almost square, with very vivid shape, and a large, circular shape top right."[19] A memory without color, in other words; but that was when he had not seen it for years. The "circular shape top right" is yellow with an almond-shaped navy blue spot in the middle, like an animal's pupil, impossible to overlook. Equally compelling are the lower edge of the picture with its pink on one side and its deep rose on the other, the great yellow proto-sphere on the left split by a red zigzag, or the dark blue bubble with its black armature intruding from the right. Kandinsky was "dissatisfied" and did not feel that the colors and the forms quite achieved his aim of setting off the deepest resonances in the soul, so he neither signed the picture nor entered it into his home catalog. He did remember it later, however, as "a 'historic picture' . . . the first abstract picture in the world, because no other painter was painting abstract art at that time."[20]

But that was not quite the case. In that same year, 1911, in a little house in the village of Puteaux, a mile or two up the Seine from Seurat's Grande Jatte, Frantisek Kupka was also moving down the long road toward abstraction. Indeed, he had embarked on it before Kandinsky. He had been working on a single large painting in stages for nearly three years now. In his modest studio at 7, rue Lemaître, studies for it had piled up, some in pencil, others in crayon or pastel. The latest studies in early 1911 were oil paintings of discs with colored sectors, abstractions in themselves, and there was an enormous oil study that had become, in 1909, a painting on its own, a great purplish canvas with paler discs overlaid on it in a majestic spiral. One might guess that its subject, if it had one, was the evolution of the solar system, but Kupka's title was simply *The First Step.* Finally, looking a bit forlorn in the back of the studio, there was Kupka's oil portrait of his stepdaughter, Andrée, awkwardly, immaturely nude, poised to play in the back garden with a red and blue striped ball. Kupka had painted that piece of realism in 1908, the year Braque and Picasso had stepped off from the *Demoiselles* into cubism, but *Girl with a Ball* was the picture that had become the trigger for Kupka's whole project,[21] a project that would reach completion in the middle of 1912 under the title *Amorpha*—Greek for shapeless.

Kupka was another of Paris's immigrants, a Czech who had dropped out of both the Prague and the Vienna schools of fine arts to come to Paris because it was the capital of the new. He had starved for a while on Montmartre, had a brief affair with the former cancan star La Goulue, and made large oil paintings of Rubenesque women in symbolic settings, one of which had won a prize at the St. Louis World's Fair. Eventually he had found a way to make his living as an illustrator, picturing everything from popular science to the poems of Mallarmé. For an occasional pittance he made cartoons for the anarchist papers, including three entire series of full-page cartoons for *L'Assiette au beurre* (The butterplate)—which also employed Vlaminck—on the themes of peace, religion, and that old corrupter, money. In an unguarded moment in 1909 he had made a classic "artist's reconstruction" of anthropologist Marcellin Boule's Neanderthal Man of La Chapelle-aux-Saints—a wild, brutish, stooped ape—for the mass-circulation weekly *L'Illustration.* He was a convinced evolutionist himself, and politically on the left; but he was no more a materialist than Kandinsky was, and he had plucked from the various spiritualisms at large in the 1890s a sense of hidden meanings in the universe—meanings that could be painted by the methods of the symbolists.

Not that *Amorpha* was Symbolist. If anything it was cubist or even futurist. What Kupka had decided to do after painting Andrée standing with her ball was to try to paint the motion that would have followed the snapshot: a moving ball, a moving girl, throws and catches, stops, starts, and reversals of field—everything the movies were just beginning to capture in the first decade of the twentieth century. As the cubists had painted all sides of an object on one picture plane, so Kupka conceived of painting all moments of a complex motion on one unmoving canvas. In his first sketches of 1908, he had suggested the outlines of the girl and of the ball in swirling strokes of pencil. Then, in each succeeding sketch, he made the arms and legs less recognizable, as he added positions they might assume in play. Black crayon sketches suggested an interplay of color, the ball's red and blue stripes whose constantly changing positions would also have to be painted somehow. When Giacomo Balla and his fellow Italians—the futurists—began to paint motion in 1911, they used a technique suggested by double-exposed photographs, but this idea does not seem to have occurred to Kupka. Instead he seems to have tried to find a way of sampling all the curves described by all the moving points of Andrée's game and melding them together into just one or two complex curves. The oil studies of red and blue discs he made in 1911 were stills of a spinning color wheel intended to explore how the red and blue stripes of the ball might blend in motion. *Amorpha* was well under way before the futurists published their first technical manifesto in 1910 or mounted their first shows in Milan in 1911 and Paris in 1912, and Kupka's project owed little to them.[22]

If Kupka owed anything to anyone else, it was to the other members of a group of mostly cubist artists that had slowly found each other in Puteaux, including Francis Picabia, Fernand Léger, Albert Gleizes, Jean Metzinger, Emile Le Fauconnier, and the Duchamp-Villon brothers. One of the brothers, Jacques Villon, had befriended Kupka when they were both still living in Montmartre, and another, Marcel Duchamp (who would in 1911 paint

Nude Descending a Staircase), had met Kupka back in 1904 in the year his picture had gone to the World's Fair.[23] There was still another member of this group who was not a painter but an insurance actuary, Maurice Princet. Fascinated by mathematics and proud of his friendships with artists, Princet was the theoretician of the Puteaux Group, taking the same role Charles Henry had played in the Laforgue-Seurat circle. It was Princet who talked most about things like the classical ratio of the golden section, and Princet who read and recommended to his friends the writings of people like Charles H. Hinton, René de Saussure, and Einstein's mentors Henri Poincaré and Karl Pearson on the subject of non-Euclidean and multidimensional projective geometries.[24] Kupka must have understood early on that the problem of painting complex motions was a dimensional problem in which time was a fourth dimension, and that representing four-dimensional events on a two-dimensional canvas could be accomplished only by analysis into elements and some sort of projection routine. If Kupka had been as mathematical as Princet he might have worked out a sort of four-dimensional version of the Renaissance rules of linear perspective, but instead he worked largely intuitively, as Giotto had. *Amorpha,* which would resolve itself in 1912 into two paintings—*Amorpha: Chromatiques chauds* (Hot chromatics) and *Amorpha: Fugue à deux couleurs* (Fugue for two colors)—defies step-by-step analysis as serenely as Picasso's cubist *Ma Jolie,* painted at the same time. Both *Amorpha*s are full of continuous curves, but this is especially true of the second, where a sharply defined central swath of bright purple suggests where the red and blue stripes of Andrée's spinning ball ended up. The paintings would finally be exhibited at the Salon d'Automne in Paris in 1912, where they would seem much more abstract than the Kandinsky Improvisations seen earlier that year at the Salon des Indépendants.

Kupka was a central European who had become part of the French art world and remained on its edges, but Robert Delaunay was French by inheritance. In 1910 and 1911 he was painting things no less French than the rooftops of Paris and the Eiffel Tower. One subject was the little medieval church of Saint Severin in the Latin Quarter, close enough to walk to, a few blocks up the Left Bank of the Seine from his studio on an upper floor of number 3, rue des Grands-Augustins. All his pictures of Saint Severin were of its interior, a dark forest of recognizable Gothic pillars and ogives, but every painting in the series portrayed those verticals as bowed out, the interior fantasized. His pictures of the Eiffel Tower showed the Tower increasingly broken up into red modules and surrounded by patches of white and pastel, patches that may have begun as representations of clouds but ended up representing no more than themselves. Cubism had reached Delaunay early, but unlike Picasso and Braque, he had persisted with color and stuck to an intuitive rather than a precise analysis of space.

Delaunay knew Maurice Princet and Princet's friends in the Puteaux group. When their work went on show in Room 41 of the Salon des Indépendants in March 1911, the first "Cubist Room" in exhibition history, Delaunay's paintings were there. In October he came to know Kandinsky when his wife persuaded one of her art-school friends, who was also a friend of Kandinsky's, to write and bring them together. Sonia Terk Delaunay, Robert Delaunay's wife, was more than a mere helpmeet. Russian-born like Kandinsky, she was a particularly adventurous painter who got into abstract art early in 1911 by way of design. When she presented Robert with their first and only child, Charles, on January 18, she made the baby a quilt of sharp-cornered patches dyed in primary colors that her friends instantly dubbed "Cubist." Soon after, she painted Charles a toy box in the same style.[25] Who influenced whom we cannot say, for the Delaunays always cheerfully supported each other's efforts, but we do know that very late in 1911, after he and Kandinsky had begun writing to each other, Robert Delaunay set to work on a new series of paintings called *Windows* made of interesecting planes of bright color. Playing with the time dimension, he called one of them *Simultaneous Windows.* By 1912 they would bring him into the same new world of pure abstraction that Kandinsky and Kupka had entered just before him.

There was yet a fifth artist in this new world in 1911, and he was an American. A laconic upstate New Yorker, Arthur Dove had thrown up his job as a commercial illustrator in 1907 and gone to Paris, where he had had a momentous encounter with the work of Cézanne. After two years he returned, married, and never painted another representational picture. However, Alfred Stieglitz, the photographer who had established what he called the "Photo-Secession" in a storefront at 291 Broadway, had arranged for Dove to show a painting and managed to convince him to go on. In 1910 and 1911, while Dove was living and working in a house in what is now the New York City suburb of Westport, Connecticut, he made six paintings historians now agree are the first abstract or nonrepresentational paintings ever made by an American. Indeed, if they were made in 1910, they would be the first ever made in the West. The pictures are all owned by a private collector and rarely seen or studied, but enough is known to make it likely that when Kandinsky was painting **Picture with a Circle** in 1911, Dove's *Six Abstractions* were already leaning against the studio wall in Westport.

There were even a few seemingly abstract pictures made before 1910. In fact they were in Kandinsky's own native country, all made by a rather mysterious artist named Čiurlionis who had been born and brought up in what was then the Russian province of Lithuania. 1911, as it happens, was the year he died. Mikalojus-Konstantinas Čiurlionis, nine years younger than Kandinsky, had started out as a musician. After graduating from the conservatory and composing some successful tone poems on nature themes, he had given it up at thirty and turned to painting. The pictures had begun to appear in 1906 in series of from four to thirteen at a time, under a musical title, with each individual picture given a tempo marking, like a musical movement: *Sonata of the Stars, Andante*, or *Sonata of the Sea, Allegro*.[26] Since the medium Čiurlionis used, tempera on paper, was fragile, the pictures never traveled and have rarely been reproduced. Kandinsky is unlikely to have seen them, even after 1909, when Čiurlionis had moved to St. Petersburg and become better known. In St. Petersburg, Čiurlionis had been accepted easily as a late-arriving symbolist, championed in fact by Vyacheslav Ivanov, Russian symbolism's leading critic. These strange paintings seemed quite symbolist to Ivanov, and probably were to Čiurlionis; but although some shapes vaguely recalled objects fraught with symbolism—mountains, water, planets, pyramids, networks of bubbles—few had subjects that were recognizable from either the natural or the man-made world. Čiurlionis's pictures were "about" transcendent universes; but rather than representing transcendent things on canvas the way earlier symbolists like Mikhail Vrubel had tried to do, or reproducing them in the soul as Kandinsky had, Čiurlionis made his paintings point toward the transcendent in the same indirect way as Alexander Blok's poetry or Maeterlinck's plays. Ivanov had begun to believe they reflected the fourth dimension.[27] One so charmed young Igor Stravinsky around 1909 that he bought it. Were they the first abstractions? If the symbolist esthetic can be understood to produce pictures entirely without subjects, it seems that they were.

Then there is Piet Mondrian, who is more or less familiar to everyone as the creator of the primary-color rectangles outlined by straight black stripes. Mondrian was in Paris in 1911. The Dutch painter and spiritualist had gone to the French capital and seen works by Cézanne and the cubists. Then, as the story goes, Mondrian slowly but surely simplified the Dutch trees and waterways in his memory until he had brought them down to the simplest linear elements. Thereafter he kept the elements and dropped the subjects. The story has an irresistible dramatic shape, and a clarity that matches Mondrian's late paintings, but it occupies the wrong historical stage. In 1911 Mondrian's trees were still trees, and the nearest thing to an abstraction that Mondrian worked on that year was the incipiently cubist *Ginger Pot* he showed in 1912 in the Salon d'Automne. Mondrian was in fact the last of all the canonical founders of abstractionism to arrive in the new world; and he would not complete a purely abstract painting until his *Composition no. 7* of 1914.[28]

There is, of course, something puerile in determining priority in art. Unlike new science, new art does not replace the old, and the greatness of an artist, like that of a novelist, is not in the innovation but in the execution. Critics who know both artists have invariably found, for example, that there is more in the abstractions of Kandinsky than in those of Arthur Dove. A drift of opinion continues to find the Delaunays' work to contain more riches than Kupka's, even when they all painted the same nonsubject, the color disks of 1911-13.[29] But it is not the priority that makes the difference so much as the effect of the innovation. Frantisek Kupka had little effect

on his fellow artists, and Dove and Čiurlionis almost none at all. In the end it was Kandinsky whose hallucinatory color harmonies made the first impression and carried the day for "abstract" art.

Abstract art has always been a gift to skeptics. It is perennially necessary to contend against them that the first abstraction was not made by the Chat Noir wit Paul Bilhaud when he painted a canvas black and hung it at the first Salon of Les Arts Incohérents in 1882 under the label *Negroes Wrestling in a Cave at Night*. Nor was the first abstraction made by backing a donkey up to a canvas and putting paint on its tail. It is true that a certain Joachim-Raphael Boronali exhibited this asinine picture at the Paris Salon d'Automne in 1910 under the title *And the Sun Dozed Off over the Adriatic*. The title, however, gave away the game. Boronali's idea was to reserve his joke and keep the painting's secret for a while; but the effect of it was to give the painting a subject—in the visitors' minds certainly, and in Boronali's too, though perhaps not in the ass's. In that case, one can legitimately wonder whether it is possible in any philosophically precise sense to paint a picture without a subject. Did not Kupka's *Amorpha* have as its subject a girl and a ball in motion? Did not Čiurlionis put stars in *Sonata of the Stars?* Did not Delaunay paint *Windows* as he said they were, windows in the light? Did not every expressionist at least paint states of mind? Did not even Kandinsky, who snorted at the idea that he might be painting music, claim to strike notes in the soul and there compose something, however ideal? Kandinsky painted colors, as did every other painter; and are not colors in some sense a subject?

We might call this art "nonobjective," but if the philosophical meaning of "abstract" is a problem, the philosophical meaning of nonobjective is a bigger problem. "Objective," for philosophers, at least since Frege, is a condition of thoughts or things thought about that makes it possible for two or more minds to communicate about them, instead of just one. It is the contrary of "subjective," which is the condition of a thought or a thing that restricts it to one mind only. Kandinsky, however, was convinced that he was painting in a way that would evoke the same "sounds" in every soul that it did in his own—or in every soul that was sufficiently evolved. In its intent, therefore, philosophically speaking, his painting was objective. Robert Delaunay was among the first to use the adjective "nonobjective," or rather "inobjectif," in the nonphilosophical way that gives this [essay] its title.[30] This separate sense of the word describes a painting offering a viewer no object that he or she is expected to be able to name or to recall from nature. A similar struggle with meaning leads to the term "nonrepresentational" art. A nonrepresentational picture would be one that deliberately does not represent anything we can agree is part of a "reality" external to paintings, and possibly anything external to the mind. This would at least leave out Boronali's ass and Allais's putons, but could it not also threaten to exclude Kandinsky?

Better than philosophical wrangling is the careful study of where this impulse to nonrepresentation began, and one source must certainly be the cabaret-born irony that inspired Bilhaud. (Alphonse Allais had followed up Bilhaud's black painting in 1883 with one that was all gray and titled *Drunkards Dancing in a Fog.*) Another influential source of nonrepresentational art must be its arch-representational opposites, photography, illustration, and cartooning, the last two of which were the bread and butter of Arthur Dove and Frank Kupka.[31] There was considerable appeal for many artists in doing the contrary of what they had to do for a living. There may have been still more appeal in being first with the new, especially in an art market as crowded as that of some twentieth-century cities—Munich, for example—and it may well turn out that crowded markets can explain the birth of the "avant garde" more satisfactorily than an innovative spirit.[32]

By and large, however, the inventors of abstraction were a solemn group. Irreverence was rare, and even irreverence was taken seriously. Čiurlionis, for example, read some theosophy and cast himself as one of the prophets of a new spiritual epoch. Others too, including Mondrian, were attracted by theosophy, the new religion founded by Madame Blavatsky at a series of table-rappings in a New York apartment in 1875. Kandinsky took it seriously as well, and in 1905, as historians of art have since noticed, the theosophists published a book in which the abstract experience of thought was represented by Kandinskyesque colors, abstract shapes, and the complex curves formed by metal filings on a vibrating plate.[33] Frank Kupka was also interested, despite his biological and political materialism, in drawing an intricate and eclectic spiritualism of his own from Blavatsky, the French guru Sâr Péladan, and anyone else with a pipeline to the ideal universe. Even Robert Delaunay, who was no fan of spiritualisms, wrote about trying to transcend the medium of painting in order to approach an ideal truth.

Often allied with theosophy, artistic symbolism made an even more powerful contribution to nonrepresentational art, seemingly from beyond the grave. Art, said the symbolist esthetic, was an attempt to point to the ineffable using symbols of the occult, the primitive, or the bygone. Gauguin and his friend Mallarmé had shown the way. The idea was hostile to positivism and not at all uncongenial to theosophy, but it was no longer very popular in 1911. Čiurlionis owed much to Russia's lateness in giving up symbolism, and so did Kandinsky, who exhibited with the Russian symbolist group Blue Rose after 1900, admired Maeterlinck, and seems to have brought the symbolist esthetic with him to Munich. Kupka too adopted symbolism, which he found in painter predecessors, in theosophical speculation, and in the writings of Mallarmé, which he illustrated. As the word "expressionism" came into use in 1911, it became clear that some of the more prominent of the old symbolist ideas of art were being absorbed into the new style, whose idealist premises were similar. Where symbolists found ultimate reality in alternate universes, expressionists found it in their own souls; and both made nonrealist art. Then, as the word "expressionism" began to mean anything new or French, or avant-garde, some of the old symbolism went along with it.

The abandonment of representation was also helped along by the rising status of ornament, which had rarely been more than a stepsister to architecture. In the 1870s William Morris's Arts and Crafts movement had become the first to reconstitute decoration as "decorative art." In the late 1890s, with styles like *Jugendstil* and art nouveau, and the founding of institutes like the Vienna Werkstätte (Workshops) and Kunstgewerbeschule (Handcrafter school), decorative art began to become what we now call "design." *Jugendstil* decorative art in particular, very strong in Munich, moved the work of Hermann Obrist and Hans Schmithals quite close to abstraction around 1900.[34] Short of wallpaper patterns, or art nouveau's mania for plant forms in cabinetry, there wasn't much in decorative art that could be called representational, and at one time or another virtually every nonrepresentational pioneer described how decoration had helped him or her see the nonrepresentational light.

The emancipation of color by the fauves, of course, was another influence. So was the study by both artists and scientists of the foundations of geometry. The paintings of cubists and futurists depended on four-dimensional thinking as much as did the physics of Einstein and the mathematics of Hilbert and Poincaré. Kandinsky himself, following his compatriot Peter Ouspensky, thought of the spiritual world as more than three-dimensional;[35] and Kasimir Malevich, who would paint his first abstraction, *Black Square,* in Russia in 1914, came to believe that he was painting entities of four or more dimensions geometrically projected onto his two-dimensional canvas.[36]

What is ultimately clear about abstraction, however, is not where it came from, but how it was done. The analysis of the subject of a picture into its smallest components, a procedure that had begun with the impressionists and was systematized by Seurat, reached a final point with the abstractionists of 1911. They broke up the subject into parts, and then used the parts more and more selectively. Finally the subject itself disappeared as the parts no longer recalled it.

By the time autumn came to Munich, Kandinsky was working nearly full time on the Blaue Reiter, the exhibiting and publication society he had conjured up in a letter to Franz Marc in June, choosing the name "Blue Rider" because Marc liked horses, he liked riders, and both liked them in blue. Already in January he wrote about getting one or more letters in each of Munich's five daily mail deliveries.[37] By September he was in correspondence with artists in every art capital in Europe, soliciting pictures for the exhibition and essays and cuts for the "almanac" Blaue Reiter would publish summing up the situation in the world of Western art. He asked Delaunay for pictures. He asked two Russian music critics to write essays. His correspondence with Schoenberg having revealed that the composer was also a painter, Kandinsky asked him for everything: pictures to exhibit, an essay on music, and some of the music itself, by himself or his disciples, for publication in the almanac. He gave himself the agreeable but time-consuming task of writing the article on the combination of theater and music, adding an example of his own composition, *Der gelbe Klang* (The yellow sound), a symbolist-expressionist play.

The painter Paul Klee, who was living and working two doors down from Kandinsky at 32 Ainmillerstrasse, wrote in his diary that autumn about the strange man

> who lives in the house next to ours, this Kandinsky, whom Luli [Klee's friend] calls "Schlabinsky." . . . Luli often goes to visit him, sometimes takes along works of mine and brings back nonobjective pictures without subject by this Russian. Very curious paintings.

Eventually these two future founding members of the Bauhaus met in a Munich café and Klee became a cautious believer. "Kandinsky wants to organize a new society of artists," Klee continued in his diary. "Personal acquaintance has given me a somewhat deeper confidence in him. He is somebody and has an exceptionally fine, clear mind. . . . in the course of the winter, I joined his 'Blaue Reiter.'"[38]

By December the Blaue Reiter, both the almanac and the exhibition, was ready to go, but the NKVM artists' society was mounting its show at the same time. Kandinsky, who was still a member, made a final offer of his *Composition V* for the NKVM show; but on December 2 the picture was rejected, ostensibly because it was a little larger than their rules allowed. Kandinsky and his friends resigned immediately and *Composition V* was brought over to Thannhauser's Moderne Galerie in time for the opening of the Blaue Reiter show on December 18, two weeks after Kandinsky's forty-fifth birthday.

The Exhibition was a triumph. On the dark walls at 7 Theatinerstrasse, Munich, hung forty-three avant-garde paintings and drawings from half a dozen countries. There was a fantasy by the *douanier* Rousseau, a *Saint-Severin* and two *Eiffel Towers* from Delaunay in Paris, two of Schoenberg's *Visions* from Vienna, several canvases in the primitivist style by the Russian Burliuk brothers, another from the Swiss Jean Niestlé, several from Gabriele Münter, August Macke, and other German Expressionists, and several major pictures by Franz Marc, including the exuberant *Yellow Cow.*[39] Kandinsky himself showed *Composition V, Improvisation 22,* and *Impression-Moscow,* all on the brink of abstraction. Reviewers were fascinated and artists were galvanized. It felt like a whole new era.

The same month of December, Piper published **On the Spiritual in Art,** and in January the long-awaited *Blue Rider Almanac.* Kandinsky had clearly caught a wave. As 1912 unfolded, show after show in country after country affirmed expressionism and launched abstraction. Early in 1912, the Blaue Reiter itself went to Cologne and then on to Berlin, Bremen, Hagen, and Frankfurt am Main, shocking the academy at every stop and changing the direction of German art. To everyone's surprise and delight, several of the paintings sold, including three of the five Delaunays.

It was as if a signal had been given. In February 1912, Arthur Dove had a one-man show at Stieglitz's "291" in New York that included ten pastels with titles like *Based on Leaf Forms and Spaces* (or *Leaf Forms*) and *Movement No. 1;* the show later went on to Chicago.[40] The "Ten Commandments," as they came to be called, were the next generation of Dove abstractions after the original six of 1910-11, and neither city could make much sense of them. It was Dove's first one-man show—and his last—but it was also the first show of abstract paintings ever mounted, at a time when Kandinsky's new pure abstractions had yet to leave his studio.

One month after Dove's show, a world away in Moscow, painters Mikhail Larionov and Natalia Goncharova named their new artists' society The Ass's Tail, in honor of Boronali's hoax, and put on another scandalous art exhibit in Moscow. They accused the Munich crowd of being already "decadent" and ready to be superseded. At the same time, Blue Rider exhibitor David Burliuk and a small band of Russians soon to be labeled "Cubo-Futurists" published a doubly outrageous *Blue Rider Almanac* of their own called *A Slap in the Face of Public Taste.* (Kandinsky had to write to them protesting that they had used his poems without permission.) From May to September the fourth Sonderbund Special Exhibition of "Expressionisten" brought together Munchs, Kandinskys, and works by Die Brücke, amazing the Rhineland city of Cologne. In December the Russian "Slap in the Face" group became an exhibiting society and mounted an expressionist art show, while the newest Russian art society, "Soyuz Molodezhi" (Union of youth), put on its own first show. It was at the Union of Youth that Larionov showed a work whose subject had been almost completely turned into painted rays of light. Exhibiting another like it at the Society of Free Esthetics show later that same month, Larionov called the approach Luchist or Rayonnist and founded yet another school of abstract painting.[41]

Kandinsky wrote that he had no wish to displace representational painting, and representational painting has indeed survived; but so has the nonrepresentational. Since Kandinsky's **Picture with a Circle** there has been no going back.

NOTES

[1] Franz Marc, *Papers,* 10 February 1911; in Susanna Partsch, *Franz Marc, 1880-1916* (Cologne: Benedikt Taschen, 1991), 30; cf. Hajo Düchting, *Kandinsky* (Cologne: Benedikt Taschen, 1991), 30.

[2] Maria Makela, *The Munich Secession: Art and Artists in Turn-of-the-Century Munich* (Princeton: Princeton University Press, 1990), 6.

[3] A critic in the English *Tait's Magazine* 17, no. 394/2 (1850) had referred to "the expressionist school of modern painters" (entry on "Expressionist" in *Oxford English Dictionary*). The French critic Louis Vauxcelles had used "expressioniste" earlier to describe work by Matisse; and in 1901 the painter Julien-Auguste Hervé had described the style of a group of his nature studies as "expressionisme" (Wolf-Dieter Dube, *Expressionism* [New York: Praeger, 1972], 18). These swallows seem to have failed to make a summer.

[4] Kandinsky, *Über das Geistige in der Kunst* (On the spiritual in art) (1911), trans. in Kandinsky, *Complete Writings on Art*, ed. Kenneth Lindsay and Peter Vergo (New York: Da Capo, 1994), 218.

[5] Kandinsky, *Rückblicke* (Reminiscences) (1913), trans. in *Complete Writings on Art*, 371-72.

[6] Ibid., 363.

[7] Ibid., 364.

[8] Jelena Hahl-Koch, *Kandinsky* (New York: Rizzoli, 1993), 168-69. This is the indispensable biography of Kandinsky.

[9] Kandinsky, "Three Pictures," appended to *Reminiscences* (1913), in *Complete Writings on Art*, 384.

[10] Kandinsky, "Cologne Lecture" (1914), ibid., 397.

[11] Ibid., 398.

[12] Kandinsky, *Composition V* (oil on canvas), private collection, Switzerland.

[13] Kandinsky, *Allerheiligen* (All saints) I (oil on card); *Allerheiligen* I (glass painting); *Allerheiligen* II (oil on canvas); *Engel des jüngsten Gerichtes* (Angel of the Last Judgment) (glass painting), all in Städtische Galerie im Lenbachhaus, Munich.

[14] Kandinsky, *Apokalyptischer Reiter* (Rider of the Apocalypse) (tempera on glass); *St. Georg I, II,* and *III* (glass paintings and an oil); *Höllenhund und Paradiesvogel* (Hound of hell and bird of paradise) (glass painting). All are in the Städtische Galerie im Lenbachhaus, Munich.

[15] Kandinsky, "Cologne Lecture," October 1914, in *Complete Writings on Art*, 399.

[16] Kandinsky to Franz Marc, 2 October 1911, in Hahl-Koch, *Kandinsky*, 196.

[17] Hideho Nishida, "Genèse de la première aquarelle abstraite de Kandinsky," *Art History* 1 (1978), 1-20.

[18] Kandinsky to J. B. Neumann, 4 August 1935, in Hahl-Koch, *Kandinsky*, 181.

[19] Ibid.

[20] Kandinsky to J. B. Neumann, 28 December 1935, ibid., 184.

[21] Kupka, *Girl with a Ball*, Musée national d'Art Moderne, Paris. The long genesis of *Amorpha* has been traced with great intelligence by Ludmila Vachtová in *Frank Kupka: Pioneer of Abstract Art* (New York: McGraw-Hill; London: Thames and Hudson, 1968).

[22] Umberto Boccioni, Carlo Carrà, Luigi Russolo, Giacomo Balla, and Gino Severini, *Technical Manifesto of Futurist Painting,* Milan, 11 April 1910, and in *Comoedia* (Paris), 18 May 1910; trans. in Herschel B. Chipp, ed., *Theories of Modern Art: A Source Book by Artists and Critics* (Berkeley: University of California Press, 1968), 289-93.

[23] Marcel Duchamp's *Nude Descending a Staircase II* (Philadelphia Museum of Art) was first exhibited in January 1912. Kupka's 1904 picture was *Ballad/Joys.*

[24] Picasso, wrote Jean Metzinger, "defines a free, mobile perspective, from which that ingenious mathematician Maurice Princet has deduced a whole geometry." *Pan* (Paris), October-November 1910, 650; in Chipp, ed., *Theories of Modern Art,* 223. Princet's sources probably included: Charles Howard Hinton, *Scientific Romances* 1st and 2d ser. (London: Swan Sonnenschein, 1884-5, 1896); René de Saussure, "Les Phénomènes physiques et chimiques et l'hypothèse de la quatrième dimension," *Archives des sciences physiques et naturelles de Genève* (January-February 1891) and *Revue scientifique* (9 May 1891). . . . Chapter 7 of Karl Pearson's *Grammar of Science* (London: Walter Scott, 1911) discusses motion with an extended example that may well have specificallyinspired Marcel Duchamp's most celebrated painting: "Let us take . . . the case of a man ascending a staircase" (Pearson, *Grammar of Science,* 222 ff.). Lynda Dalrymple Henderson's wonderful book, *The Fourth Dimension and Non-Euclidean Geometries in Modern Art* (Princeton: Princeton University Press, 1986) collects most of the popular references to the fourth dimension with which the turn of the century was crowded. Michio Kaku's *Hyperspace: A Scientific Odyssey Through Parallel Universes, Time Warps, and the 10th Dimension* (New York: Oxford University Press, 1994) finds more. The plurality of dimension was probably better understood and described for a broader public in 1900 than it is now. . . .

[25] Sonia Delaunay, *Nous irons jusqu'au soleil* (Paris: Laffont, 1978), 33. A biographical profile based primarily on these and other memoirs is Stanley Baron, with Jacques Damase, *Sonia Delaunay, the Life of an Artist: A Personal Biography Based on Unpublished Private Journals* (New York: Harry N. Abrams, 1995). The quilt, much faded, is now in the Musée national de l'Art Moderne in Paris.

[26] Camilla Gray, *The Russian Experiment in Art, 1863-1922,* 2d ed. (New York: Thames and Hudson, 1986), 119. Short of a visit to the Čiurlionis Museum in Kaunas, Lithuania, one's best chance to see Čiurlionis's work is probably in a portfolio of reproductions: *M. K. Čiurlionis,*

32 Reprodukcijos (Vilnius: Grozines Literaturos Leidykla, 1961). For accounts of his career in English there is a special issue of the journal *Lituanus* 7, no. 2 (1961), with articles by George M. A. Hanfmann, Aleksis Rannit, Vyacheslav Ivanov, Raymond F. Piper, and Vladas Jakubenas; and notes by Romain Rolland, Bernard Berenson, Jacques Lipchitz, and Igor Stravinsky.

[27] "This geometrical transparency seems to be an attempt to approach the possibilities of visual signalization of such conception that the three dimensions we have on disposal are insufficient." Vyacheslav Ivanov, "Čiurlionis and the Problem of the Synthesis of Arts," *Apollon* 3 (1914); in *Lituanus* 7, no. 2 (1961), 45.

[28] *Composition no.* 7 is in the Gemeentemuseum in The Hague. John Golding dates it to 1914 but puts it in the Guggenheim Museum in New York. John Golding, "Mysteries of Mondrian," *The New York Review of Books* 42, no. 11 (22 June 95), 59-65.

[29] Frank Kupka, *Disks of Newton:* Study for *Amorpha: Fugue à deux couleurs,* 1911-12 (oil on canvas), Musée national d'Art Moderne, Paris; Robert Delaunay, *Disque, première peinture inobjective, ou disque simultané* (Disk, first nonobjective painting, or simultaneous disk), 1912-13 (oil on canvas), private collection. Sonia Delaunay's *Prisme électrique* (1913; oil on canvas, Musée national d'Art Moderne, Paris) is said to have been inspired by the newly installed electric streetlights on the boulevard Saint-Michel.

[30] Delaunay, *Disque, première peinture inobjective, ou disque simultané* (Disk, first nonobjective painting, or simultaneous disk), 1912-13 (oil on canvas), private collection.

[31] The American cartoonist Stuart Blackton, in fact, brought filmed animation to Paris in April 1907, a year before Kupka made his initial study of Andrée and her ball.

[32] This suggestion was in fact made at the time about the crowded art world of Germany. A member of Strindberg's Black Pig Café circle in Berlin, the art critic Julius Meier-Graefe, wrote in 1904, "The art exhibition [is] an institution of a thoroughly bourgeois nature, due to the senseless immensity of the artistic output, and the consequent urgency of showing regularly what has been accomplished in the year." Meier-Graefe, *Modern Art* (1904), trans. Simmonds and Chrystal, in F. Frascina and C. Harrison, eds., *Modern Art and Modernism: A Critical Anthology* (London: Harper, Open University, 1982), 208.

[33] Sixten Ringbom, "Transcending the Visible: The Generation of the Abstract Pioneers," in *The Spiritual in Art: Abstract Painting, 1890-1985* (New York: Abbeville Press in association with Los Angeles County Museum of Art, 1986).

[34] Peg Weiss (*Kandinsky in Munich,* Exhibition Catalogue [New York: Guggenheim Museum, 1982], plates 52-71) reproduces work by Obrist and Schmithals.

[35] Peter Demianovich Ouspensky, *Chetvertoe Izmierenie* (The fourth dimension) (St. Petersburg, 1909). The book drew on earlier books by Hinton.

[36] Malevich, *Black Square* (1913-15); *Black Circle; Black Cross; Black Square and Red Square,* Russian Museum, St. Petersburg).

[37] Kandinsky to Schoenberg, 13 January 1911, in Arnold Schoenberg and Vassily Kandinsky, *Letters, Pictures, and Documents,* ed. Jelena Hahl-Koch, trans. J. C. Crawford (Boston: Faber and Faber, 1984).

[38] Klee, *The Diaries of Paul Klee, 1898-1918,* ed. Felix Klee (Berkeley: University of California Press, 1968), 265.

[39] Marc, *Die gelbe Kuh,* now in the Guggenheim Museum, New York.

[40] Arthur Dove, *Leaf Forms,* private collection; *Movement No. 1,* Columbus Museum of Art, Columbus, Ohio. For more, see William Innes Homer, "Identifying Arthur Dove's 'The Ten Commandments,'" *American Art Journal* 12 (summer 1980), 21-32.

[41] Mikhail Larionov, *Glass,* Guggenheim Museum, New York. See Gray, *The Russian Experiment in Art,* 145.

Robert C. Williams (essay date 1997)

SOURCE: "Concerning the Western Spiritual in Russian Art: Vasily Kandinsky," in *Russia Imagined: Art, Culture, and National Identity,* 1840-1995, Peter Lang, 1997, pp. 45-59.

[*In the following essay, Williams chronicles Kandinsky's interest in religious mysticism and theosophy and discusses its influence on his work.*]

In the early days of the Russian Revolution Bolshevism coexisted with Bohemia. Hundreds of artists and intellectuals rushed to help build a new society in which they might play a role, painting Agitprop trains, erecting monuments, composing symphonies for conductorless orchestras, reading Futurist poetry, filming the storming of the Winter Palace, directing workers' plays, and designing skyscrapers. Much of their art, however, was neither new nor Russian, but a development of pre-1914 *avant-garde* tendencies which many Russians had encountered in Europe. Munich was especially important as a transmitter of such tendencies. A number of young Russians studied art there before the First World War and returned to Russia with both technical training and ideas of a "new age" for an artistic elite. The Munich cartoonist for *Simplicissimus,* Olaf Gulbrandson, inspired the revolutionary poster art of D. Moor; the director of the Munich Art Theater, Georg Fuchs, had a major impact on Meyerhold; and the mystic Rudolf Steiner made a great impression on the painter Vasily Kandinsky. Indeed, it was while living in Munich before 1914 that Kandinsky developed both the abstract art and mystical language which later helped make early Russian revolutionary art appear to be a radical departure from bourgeois precedents.

Vasily Kandinsky must be counted among the leading revolutionaries in this cultural upheaval. As much a product of European as of Russian culture, Kandinsky lived most of his life in exile in Germany, where he was a major figure in the expressionist movement and at the *Bauhaus* of Walter Gropius. Between 1910 and 1914, while living in Munich, he helped create a revolution in art that seemed no less dramatic than the contemporary movements in Cubism and Futurism: he removed the physical object from his paintings, and thereby attempted through pure form and color to affect the viewer's emotions in a new way. He also theorized about his work in a book entitled *Concerning the Spiritual in Art,* which he began to write in 1910 and which was published by the Piper-Verlag in Munich in 1912. Yet in both his painting and his aesthetics, Kandinsky remained very much a product of his time and of his Munich environment. In this case, at least, the Russian revolution in art developed in the West before 1914, to which it later returned nurtured by the revolution in politics inside Russia.

I

The prevailing opinion among many artists and art historians has been that Kandinsky's breakthrough to abstract painting before 1914 was something radically new. His wife Nina called him "perhaps the greatest revolutionary in the field of plastic art"; the surrealist André Breton referred to him as "one of the first and one of the greatest revolutionaries of vision"; the Hungarian artist Moholy-Nagy considered Kandinsky "the great initiator of abstract painting, whose theoretical work represents the beginning of a new art history." Yet both Kandinsky's "Russianness" and his "revolution" are open to question. The painter Ernst Kirchner reflected confusion on his nationality when he named Kandinsky as "the finest in color of all the Germans"; a more recent art historian has questioned his originality in describing Kandinsky's work as "the culmination of an historical process which could not be averted."[1]

The claim to both Russianness and newness was that of Kandinsky himself. It appeared in his autobiographical *Rückblicke,* published in Munich in 1913, as well as in other writings and remarks made throughout his life. Kandinsky often mentioned his Mongol ancestors, the city of Moscow, his ethnographic work among the peasants of Vologda province, and the flat space of religious icons. He also recalled his love for horses, great sensitivity to colors, early exposure to the German language and fairy tales through a Baltic German grandmother, and the Rembrandt collection at the Hermitage. Kandinsky described these experiences as always personal and without mediation: His early training in law and economics helped him to think abstractly; in 1895 he saw an exhibit of Monet's haystack paintings in Russia and had a "dull feeling that the object was missing"; the Moslem art he encountered on a trip to Tunisia in 1904 devalued the visual element too; one of his own paintings lying on its side at dusk in his Munich apartment on the Ainemillerstrasse was also objectless but attractive; the breakdown of Newtonian physics and the idea of matter seemed to Kandinsky like "the destruction of the whole world." These intense personal experiences were undoubtedly important for Kandinsky, and he also made clear his debt to other people's ideas in both art and religion in his work. But there is a key element in his makeup which remained Kandinsky's secret and which reflected his exposure to European thought in Munich, namely mysticism in general and theosophy in particular. It is in this sense that Kandinsky could say that *Concerning the Spiritual in Art* "wrote itself more than I wrote it."[2]

II

The movement toward abstraction was common to all the arts in Russia around 1910. As early as 1907 the Lithuanian painter Curlionis tried eliminating physical objects from his pictures, and the Rayonnist painters Larionov and Goncharova were working in this direction on the eve of the war. The same urge toward non-representation was visible in the "pure word" and "transsense language" (*zaumnyi iazyk*) of the Futurist poets, who sought to emancipate words from any external correspondence or meaning. "Art is not a copy of nature," wrote Mayakovsky, "but the determination to distort nature in accordance with its reflections in the individual consciousness." The same tendency appeared in the theater, in the black squares and abstract shapes of Malevich's sets for Kruchenykh's *Victory over the Sun* (1913) and in Meyerhold's attempts to portray "inner dialogue," mystery, and the "world of the soul" in his sets and wordless pantomimes. The object was becoming neither reality nor symbol, but a thing-in-itself.[3]

The turn to religious mysticism after the 1905 Revolution was another characteristic of Russian intellectual life, revealed in the cult of Vladimir Soloviev, the Dionysian ecstasy of the symbolist poet Viacheslav Ivanov and the composer Scriabin, and the discovery of Rudolf Steiner's anthroposophy. In 1905 the Russians had a preview of the epoch of war and revolution which would sweep over Europe in 1914, and thus felt the insecurity of modern life which they frequently compared with life on a volcano. "The youth of our generation," recalled the writer Marietta Shaginian, "used to refer to the first fifteen years of our century as timeless. Time seemed to have stopped, seemed to have moved outside of history. In the very air, in the mood of the people there was an expectation—the seemingly passionate desire for something to happen so that the rhythm and movement of history might again become perceptible."[4] The Third Kingdom of Soloviev, Scriabin's great mystery play scheduled for the end of the world in India, and talk of the timeless moment of ecstasy all reflected this apocalyptic mentality. Not surprisingly Steiner's prophecy of a coming age of spirituality had a great appeal for some

Russian intellectuals after 1905, and it was in Munich that they encountered Steiner.

For intellectuals Munich meant Schwabing, the Bohemia located around the university and the Alte Pinakothek museum to the north of the city center. Kandinsky himself described Schwabing at the turn of the century as not a part of Munich but a state of mind. "Everyone painted—or wrote poetry, or composed music, or began to dance," he wrote. "In every house one could find at least two studios under the roof where people often discussed, disputed, philosophized, and got thoroughly drunk (depending more on how much money they had than on any moral compunctions) more than they painted."[5] Both Franz von Stuck and the Slovak painter Anton Azbe had their art schools there, and art was as much a part of Munich life under King Ludwig III as *Fasching* and *Oktoberfest.* Between 1900 and 1914 Schwabing was the home of Lenin, Hitler, Heinrich and Thomas Mann, Oswald Spengler, Franz Marc, Paul Klee, Giorgio Chirico, the poet Karl Wolfskehl, Stefan George, and the "uncrowned king" of Schwabing—the American-born playwright Frank Wedekind, whose approach to sex in plays such as *Lulu* was as shocking to good burghers as the art of Kandinsky, or the cartoons and satire of the journals *Jugend* and *Simplicissimus.* The fact that so many radical intellectuals were not Bavarians, nor even Germans, was not lost on the Munich public, which not only spat on some of the paintings of the *Neuekunstlervereinigung* exhibit of 1909 but described them as both "anarchist" and "Russian."[6]

In 1896 a group of young Russians arrived in Munich to study painting with Azbe. They included Aleksei Iavlensky, a 32-year-old former army officer, the painter Igor Grabar, Marianna Verefkina, 36, the daughter of the governor of the Peter and Paul Fortress and a student of Repin, and Dmitrii Kardovsky. It was in Verefkina's rooms on the Giselastrasse that they began to gather after the arrival a year later of Kandinsky, then a 31-year-old lawyer who had just turned down a professorship in law at the University of Dorpat. Between 1901 and 1903 they were joined by three more Russians—Vladimir Bekhteev, another army officer in his mid-twenties, and two brothers from Odessa, David and Vladimir Burliuk, who went on to Paris in 1904. It was this group of Russians who were to fertilize German expressionist painting over the next decade, culminating in the *Blaue Reiter* exhibit of 1912.

Like most Russian intellectuals, Verefkina and Iavlensky were under the spell of the religious philosopher Vladimir Soloviev and of mysticism in general. They contrasted realism in art and materialism in philosophy with a Nietzschean hope for some sort of "transvaluation of values" and a new epoch for mankind. For Verefkina, art was transcendence, a creative fantasy that substituted for reality. "To love, to believe, to create," she wrote, "means to deny the world and its absurd and cruel Gods." Art was simply "that which makes life disappear." "Art, thought, love—out of these I will make a religion, a cult. I am its temple, its priest, its God. And the life under my feet is small and hateful." The artist himself is "a person who has made beauty a God and seeks forms to make this God visible." He should strive to express emotions, not to portray the visible world, to express out of his "inner necessity" artistic laws accessible only to geniuses. It was this theme of art as esoteric religion which dominated the mood of Verefkina's Schwabing salon, frequented by both Russians and Germans, including Kandinsky and Iavlensky.[7]

In Munich at the turn of the century the decorative curved lines and artifacts of *Jugendstil*, or *Art Nouveau,* were giving way among young artists to the sharper colors and deformed shapes of what would later be called "expressionism." Expressionism was a movement in art, literature, and drama characterized by an emphasis on the vision of the individual artist, the childlike simplicity of primitive art, a distaste for urban life and bourgeois standards, and a desire to express emotions rather than to portray external reality. Its aesthetics had deep roots in the nineteenth century, however. Conrad Fiedler (1841-95), Theodor Lipps (1851-1914), C. G. Carus (1789-1869) and Alois Riegl (1838-1905), were all German art theorists who had argued that the artist should not strive to imitate reality but to express his "inner necessity," linking the observer's soul with the spiritual forces of nature through a process of empathy (*Einfühlung*). Colors should be used according to their emotional or even musical associations, as Goethe pointed out in his *Farbenlehre* of 1810. "For every lovely painting," wrote the romantic poet Ludwig Tieck, "there is without doubt a complementary piece of music and the two together have but one soul."[8]

The idea that the emotion mattered far more than the object in a painting fascinated Munich artists after 1900. August Endell, a student of Lipps, as early as 1898 envisaged new art forms which "meant nothing, which would excite our souls so deeply and so strongly in a way which was previously only the domain of music." In 1906 the painter Alfred Kubin tried drawing the patterns of biological organisms he saw through a microscope, and a year later August Macke formed colors on a board without thinking of any particular object. Throughout the nineteenth century there had been sporadic attempts at objectless painting, but only after 1900 was there a conscious movement in this direction, best expressed in the popular book by a young art historian Wilhelm Worringer entitled *Abstraction and Empathy,* published in Munich in 1908. Worringer noted that every new phase in art began with an "urge to abstraction" which reflected a "psychic attitude toward the cosmos" and a "greater inner unrest inspired in man by the phenomena of the outside world"; he agreed with Lipps' statement that "geometrically uniform figures are an object of pleasure because the apprehension of them, as of a whole, is natural to the soul" and criticized a "narrowly European outlook" in art which emphasized the portrayal of physical reality. "Abstract forms, liberated from all finiteness," concluded Worringer, "are the only ones, and the highest, in which man can find rest from the confusion of the world picture."[9]

The removal of the object from the painting was thus intimately bound up with religious seeking. Removing reference to physical reality was in fact a means of reaching spiritual reality, of expressing the artist's soul, or of linking the viewer's soul with the cosmos. "Between nature and ourselves, nay between ourselves and our own consciousness," wrote the philosopher Henri Bergson in 1900, "a veil is interposed, a veil that is dense and opaque for the common herd—thin, almost transparent for the artist and poet." Bergson's view was echoed in England before World War I by the philosopher T. E. Hulme, whose influence on the Imagist movement of Ezra Pound and Wyndham Lewis was considerable. In poetry as in painting the reduction of art to its hard essentials—form and color, words and letters—seemed to promise a new way of communicating the artist's vision "I hardly see an object," wrote Hulme, "but merely notice what class it belongs to—what ticket I ought to apply to it." A follower of Worringer in aesthetics, Hulme saw a new "geometrical art" as the sign of a coming "breakup of the Renaissance humanistic attitude."[10]

In London, as in Munich, a number of intellectuals were seeking a new art form after about 1910 which would be precise and abstract in its style and religious in its desire for an elitist vision of reality beyond that offered by science and the material world. It was this search which led to the immersion of a number of artists and writers in the waters of theosophy.

III

Carl Jung has noted the "unbelievable rise of occultism in every form in all cultured parts of the western world" since the late nineteenth century, and has argued that people have flocked to such movements because such modern gnostic systems meet the need for expressing and formulating wordless occurrences going on within ourselves "*better* than any of the existing forms of Christianity, not excepting Catholicism."[11] In England the appeal of mysterious "eastern" religious truths was revealed in the Theosophical Society of the Russian mystic, Madam Blavatsky, whose book *Isis Unveiled* (1877) and other writings borrowed liberally from mid-nineteenth century English novels while claiming to be the secret wisdom handed down by Tibetan mahatmas to an esoteric elite. Commanded by Annie Besant and the Reverend C. W. Leadbeater before 1914, the Society offered solace in spiritualism, table-tipping, ghosts, séances, and secret doctrine for those disoriented by rapid changes and uncertainties in science, technology, and urban life. Theosophists claimed clairvoyance and a key to the spiritual reality which lay hidden behind the veil of material appearances. Around 1900, they predicted, a new age would arrive, a new cycle of world history that would usher in a new type of human being, esoterically defined only as the sixth sub-race of the fifth root-race. A number of intellectuals were dabblers in this doctrine on the eve of the war, a doctrine which provided pre-war Europe with a new mood of anti-intellectualism and spiritual hope.[12]

Such mystical doctrines were plentiful in Munich. The circle of Stefan George spoke of an elite of poets and seers which would save the German soul from the perils of urbanism and material civilization, an order of knight-templars bound together by Eros. One of his followers, the Munich philosopher Ludwig Klages, told the great gathering of German youth at the Hohen Meissner mountain in 1913 that western civilization was "drowning" the soul of man, and that a reunion with earth and soil was needed. Another follower, Alfred Schuler, gave lectures in Munich on the dangers of the city and materialism, while praising the "idealism" of an elite whose inner life-forces could be manipulated through spiritualism. Others, including most of the young artists, rejected the *Völkisch* cult of the national soul in favor of the individual one, as emphasized in theosophy. The artist Karl Hoppner, known as Fidus, did theosophical "temple art" which made visible the invisible by painting in symbols such as the sphinx or the sun higher worlds transmitted through him by a cosmic life force. What all these intellectuals shared was a common belief in the primacy of the inner spiritual world over the outer material world, and the accessibility of that spiritual world to an elite of initiates.[13]

The central figure in Munich theosophy in these years was the Austrian mystic Rudolf Steiner. A scholar specializing in Goethe and Nietzsche, Steiner claimed to have had spiritual visions since childhood although it was only in 1900 that he began attending theosophical lectures in Berlin at the age of 39. Critical of organized Christianity, Steiner nonetheless accepted the mystery of Golgotha as the pivotal fact in history, and found the English theosophical emphasis on esoteric eastern wisdom somewhat distasteful. His hope was to reconcile science and religion through a "spiritual science." In 1902 Steiner was asked by the London Theosophical Society to form a German branch in Berlin, which he did together with his future wife, the Baltic German Marie von Sievers. In 1907 an international Theosophical Congress was held in Munich, where a rift began to emerge between the Christ-centered mysticism of Steiner and the Buddhist and Indian leanings of Annie Besant. When Besant presented the Indian boy Krishnamurti as Christ reincarnate in 1910, the breach widened and in the winter of 1912-13 Steiner organized his own Anthroposophical Society which subsequently established its headquarters in the village of Dornach near Basle on the eve of the war.[14]

According to Steiner, man had once in the Age of Atlantis lived a spiritual life guided by a group of Initiates who expressed their truth through various mystery centers and oracles. After a great flood, the surviving Initiates moved to Central Asia where they had maintained their methods for training successively higher levels of consciousness in order to perceive true reality in the spiritual, astral or ethero-physical world. For the rest of mankind, these ancient truths had been lost, and were only now beginning to be rediscovered. Through these truths the facade of material reality could be penetrated by the elite to which the Initiates had passed on their wisdom.

In March 1910 Steiner gave a cycle of lectures in Vienna which revealed the implications of his doctrine for art. "There are definite methods," Steiner maintained, "which a man may apply to his life of soul and which enable him to awaken certain inner faculties slumbering in normal daily life, so that he is finally able to experience the moment of Initiation." Like Bergson, he maintained that physical reality was merely a veil "drawn over everything that man would behold were he able spiritually to see through the spectacle presented to him in space." The "vibrations" which produce colors, for example, represent a world beyond that from which our "Sentient Body" receives sensations; it is our "Sentient Soul" which determines what we "experience and feel inwardly as a result of the impressions made upon us by the red, violet or yellow color." This deeper "soul-and-spiritual reality" is accessible only to the "seer," a man of vision who "directs his gaze into the Imaginative world; there was the impression, let us say, of something blue or violet, or he hears a sound or has a feeling of warmth or cold. He knows through the thinking of the heart that the impression was not a mere vision, a figment of the mind, but that the fleeting blue or violet was the expression of a soul-spiritual reality, just as the red of the rose is the expression of a material reality."[15]

Not surprisingly, theosophy was popular among a number of Russians before the First World War. Iavlensky was a follower of Steiner, read books on yoga, and sought treatment at an anthroposophical clinic in Stuttgart when he fell ill in 1929. Steiner's wife Marie Sievers, an actress who became interested in mysticism through the French Wagnerian Eduard Schuré in Paris, was well versed in the writings of Soloviev, which she translated into German in the 1920s. When the composer Scriabin first read Madam Blavatsky's *Key to Theosophy* in 1905, he found it very close to his own thinking. Scriabin hoped for a coming spiritual revolution directed by the "consciousness of geniuses" which would render the masses "more perceptive of finer vibrations than usual" and would "shake the souls of peoples and force them to perceive the idea hidden behind the outer event."[16] Similar ideas were popular in the "tower," the poet Viacheslav Ivanov's apartment in St. Petersburg, between 1905 and 1910. Like Scriabin, Ivanov spoke of "ecstacy," the moment of "self-forgetting" in which the unconscious unity of a primal world was recovered. The poet was the keeper of the word, *Logos,* the "microcosm" which reflected the universal "macrocosm" of occult truth. Andrei Belyi later succumbed to the teachings of Steiner himself, whom he met in Cologne in 1912 and followed to Munich that summer. "In 1912-1913," recalled Belyi's wife, "our entire life was under the sign of Rudolf Steiner's lectures." Belyi, like the Russian painter Trapesnikov, even followed Steiner to Dornach at the outbreak of the war.[17]

The attraction of Steiner for Russians before 1914 is best illustrated by the case of Margarita Voloshina, the daughter of a Moscow tea merchant and a student of the painter Ilya Repin, who came to Paris in 1902 at the age of twenty to study painting. "Through Soloviev," she recalled, "I had found my way to Christianity, but I did not see in its ascetic ideal any method for transforming our modern culture." Nor did the intuitionism of Bergson satisfy her. "Where are those who know how to extricate mankind from the dead-end in which it finds itself?" she asked. In Paris she met Trapesnikov, another seeker, and Anna Mintslova, a Russian theosophist attending a congress there. Mintslova was a heavy-set woman of about forty-five with blue eyes, red-blond hair, a large nose, and lips, who wore black dresses, practiced palmistry and graphology and claimed to be clairvoyant. In 1905 Voloshina decided to follow her to Berlin to join the circle of Steiner, who had impressed her by his lectures in Switzerland.

For Voloshina Steiner provided long-awaited answers. He defined a meaningful spiritual reality behind the material world, spoke of a coming catastrophic war of all against all, considered the Slavonic peoples as destined to solve the "social question" and predicted a great future for Russian culture in creating a universal brotherhood of man such as that anticipated by Tolstoy. And his teachings seemed relevant to her painting. When she moved to Munich in January 1909 she was already considering the possibility of a "new landscape painting" which would express "cosmic reality." By the spring of 1910, as Kandinsky was beginning to write *Concerning the Spiritual in Art,* a number of her Moscow friends were also turning from Soloview to Steiner and anthroposophy. Not only did Steiner offer a new religion, but he counterposed the "young soul of the Russian people" to the materialism of Western civilization. Having joined the Munich Steinerites, Voloshina helped establish a branch of the Anthroposophical Society in Moscow in September 1912, and then met Belyi and Trapesnikov at Dornach during the war.[18]

The mood of many Russian middle-class intellectuals after the defeats of the Russo-Japanese War and the 1905 Revolution was thus one of pessimism and desperation. Many escaped into art and mysticism and among those for whom the search for esoteric truths ended in theosophy was Vasily Kandinsky.

IV

As early as 1915 Wyndham Lewis drew attention to the theosophical sources of Kandinsky's art, characterizing him as a "medium-like" artist with a "Blavatskyish soul" who was "the only purely abstract painter in Europe." An English visitor to Kandinsky's home in Murnau in August 1912 also recalled that Kandinsky "was inclined (though not at all obtrusively) to talk about religious things, and is much interested in mystical books and the lives of saints. He has had strange experiences of healing by faith." A more recent art historian has noted that as early as 1899 Besant and Leadbeater had tried to have an artist paint their thoughts, an experiment described in their book *Thought Forms* (1905), and concluded with regard to Kandinsky that "non-objective art began with Annie Besant and Leadbeater in the early 1900s. It is a by-product of astral manifestations as revealed by theosophy, spiritualism, and occultism." What is the evidence for such a claim?[19]

Until 1910 Kandinsky was essentially a landscape painter, whose early works revealed the attraction of old Russian life, a Fauve-like use of bright colors and free lines, and the churches, hills and railroad trains of Bavaria, visible in such paintings as *Troika* (1906) or *Landscape with Church*(1909). Then in 1910 he slowly began painting a series of "improvizations" in which there was no recognizable object, a wild, swirling mass of colors without apparent shape, form, or object. Later he continued on occasion to paint using visual objects and Russian themes, as in *Painting with Troika* (1911) or the Chagallesque *Moscow Lady* (1912). Only in revolutionary Russia and at the *Bauhaus* under the influence of Russian Constructivism did he move to the pure geometric shapes of *White Line* (1920) and *Chessboard* (1921) and the cold lines of *Circles within Circles* (1923) or *Arrow Forms* (1923).

It is clear from Kandinsky's writings between 1910 and 1912 that his apparently non-representational painting had religious and theosophical overtones. At the very beginning of *Concerning the Spiritual in Art* Kandinsky criticizes pre-war Europe as a "nightmare of materialism" and calls for a new art which will give to "those observers capable of feeling them . . . emotions subtle beyond words" by establishing "vibrations" in the soul of the observer. An aesthetic elite with a "secretly implanted power of 'vision'" must drag along a "heavy weight of resisting humanity" with "cold hearts and souls asleep" to a new vision capable of striking down the enemy—atheists in religion, socialists in economics, leftists in politics, positivists in science, and realists in art. While criticizing their "excessive anticipation of definite answers," Kandinsky admires theosophy as "one of the most important spiritual movements" which seeks to "approach the problem of the spirit by way of inner knowledge."[20]

But theosophy is only part of a much broader "spiritual revolution" going on in literature, art, and music, in the plays of Maeterlinck, the painting of Picasso and Cézanne, and the compositions of Scriabin and Schönberg. Maeterlinck uses words such as "inner sound," received by the listener not in any relation to some material object but as an "abstract impression" which sets up a vibration in the heart, and even the simple repetition of words may bring out "unsuspected spiritual properties of the word itself." Like the *leitmotif* of a Wagnerian opera or a Debussy tone poem, the "pure sound" of words without external of symbolic reference may produce a "direct impression on the soul." Matisse in color and Picasso in form have fragmented and juxtaposed visual reality; Scriabin and Schönberg have abandoned conventional tonality. All the arts have "never been closer to each other than in this recent hour of spiritual crisis," concludes Kandinsky. All of them are moving toward a "non-representational, abstract and internal structure" which breaks down the barriers between sound, sight, temperature, and touch for those "sensitive souls" endowed with synaesthesia, the ability to hear colors or see sounds.[21] The function of the artist is to develop a new language, a "grammar of painting" capable of expressing out of the artist's "inner necessity" an art which is eternal and independent of the artist's nationality, age or surroundings.[22]

For Kandinsky the artist would be the high priest of a new religion which, by the use of abstraction, would develop a "power which must be directed to the development and refinement of the human soul," transforming society by transforming individuals. "We have before us," he predicted, "a new age of conscious creation, and this new spirit in painting is going hand in hand with thought towards an *epoch of great spirituality*." Like Bergson he felt that "the veiling of 'the spirit in the material is often so dense that there are generally few people who can see through to the spirit." It would be the function of this elite of artists to create a revolution, the "breaking-up of the soulless-material life of the 19th century" and the "building-up of the psychic-spiritual life of the 20th century."[23]

Kandinsky's friends were well aware of his predilection for theosophy. We know that from 1900 on he engaged in Yoga contemplation, and that in 1908 he began to attend some of Steiner's lectures. There is also evidence that he was familiar with Steiner's book *Goethe as the Father of the New Aesthetics* (1909), which argued that the artist sees beyond the philosopher or scientist to the "secret laws" of the cosmos and called for an "aesthetics of the future" in which the artist would raise the world to a new spiritual level. Steiner also developed the Besant-Leadbeater theory of thought forms, noting that every human body is surrounded by an aura of vibrations produced by thoughts and emotions of the inner life and revealed in the aura's free-floating lines and colors. Finally, the library of Kandinsky and his mistress, Gabrielle Münter, made public in 1957, reveals not only some of Steiner's writings annotated by Kandinsky, but a number of other works on the occult, spiritualism, yoga, vegetarianism, and hypnosis.[24]

Like a number of other Russian artists in Munich, Kandinsky was thus deeply involved with mysticism and anthroposophy. Steiner's movement, in fact, appears to have stimulated his search for both a spiritual faith and an abstract art to express that faith. Unlike the contemporary Dutch abstract painter Piet Mondrian, Kandinsky did not actually join a theosophical group, but like him he may well have thought of himself not as a "non-representational" painter but as an artist painting spiritual, rather than material, reality. Theosophy, of course, did not necessarily imply abstraction, as evidenced by the symbolic canvases of Fidus. Given the independent tendency toward object-less or cosmic painting on the part of his Russian and German friends in Munich, however, it seems unlikely that Kandinsky would have turned to symbols in his works.[25]

v

Like Worringer in aesthetics, Kandinsky's greatness lies not in his personal genius, independence, or Russian background, but in his sensitivity to the intellectual and artistic currents which swirled around him in pre-war Munich and his ability to synthesize them into a coherent painting style and aesthetic theory. He owed a good deal to the "abstraction" and "empathy" of Worringer, the veiled reality of Bergson, the African and Oceanic primitivism of Gauguin, Picasso, and the Trocadero Museum in Paris, the "soul" of German romanticism, the color-organ of Scriabin, the "inner necessity" of Verefkina, the "cosmic painting" of Voloshina, and the emotional "vibrations" of Steiner and anthroposophy. Some of these influences are cited by Kandinsky himself in his written portrait of the intellectual revolution of his age; others reveal themselves through his language and metaphors; still others may only be surmised by the historian from what we know of prewar Munich.

To the German art critics of 1912 the work of Kandinsky and the *Blaue Reiter* group appeared to be "a repetition of the anarchist movement in art," madness, ultra-painting, the destruction of painting by the intellect.[26] Yet the importance of theosophy in Kandinsky's work indicates that his art involved the creation of a new world as much as the destruction of an old, and that this urge toward art as a new religion was common to Europeans and Russians alike. It was this mood which he brought back to Russia. Kandinsky himself remained tied to his native land in many ways, visiting Moscow and Odessa frequently before the war, attending Orthodox church services in exile, and returning to Russia to live and paint between 1914 and 1922. Yet in later years Kandinsky realized that he was as much a product of German as of Russian culture. "We are not leaving Germany for good," he wrote optimistically upon his departure for Paris in 1933; "I couldn't do that; my roots are too deep in German soil."[27]

For several years after 1917 Kandinsky was active in the artistic development of the Russian Revolution, joining the Department of Fine Arts of A. V. Lunacharsky's Commissariat for Public Enlightenment, founding a Museum for Pictorial Culture, and joining the art faculty of the University of Moscow. For a time the Bolsheviks seemed to share both his distaste for academic art which had developed in Munich and his mystical anticipation of a new era of spiritualism. Kandinsky had come to Munich simply to study painting with Azbe; he returned to Russia with a mystical view of the artist as a member of an esoteric elite which would guide mankind toward a new age. Only in 1921 would he finally realize that Lenin was not the architect of that age, and return as an exile to the Germany which had helped nurture both his art and his mysticism. For Kandinsky imagined a spiritual revolution that was beyond national boundaries.

NOTES

[1] W. Kandinsky, *Concerning the Spiritual in Art* (New York, 1947), 10; P. Overy, *Kandinsky: The Language of the Eye* (New York, Washington, D.C., 1969), Vol. 2; D. E. Gordon, *Ernst Ludwig Kirchner* (Cambridge, Mass., 1968), 132; F. Whitford, "Some Notes on Kandinsky's Development toward Non-Figurative Art," *Studio*, Vol. 173 (January 1967), 16; see also L. D. Ettinger, *Kandinsky's 'At Rest,'* (London, 1961), which relates Kandinsky's work to the ideas of Gestalt psychology, showing similarity but not direct influence. More recent works on Kandinsky include: Rose-Carol Washton-Long, *Kandinsky. The Development of an Abstract Style* (Oxford: Clarendon Press, 1980), and Peg Weiss, *Kandinsky and Old Russia. The Artist as Ethnographer and Shaman* (New Haven: Yale University Press, 1995).

[2] W. Kandinsky, *Rückblicke* (Munich, 1913), 15-17, 21, 25, 34; Overy, *Kandinsky,* 35-36.

[3] V. Erlich, "Russian Poets in Search of a Poetics," *Comparative Literature*, Vol. 4 (1952), 69; Iu. Annenkov, *Dnevnik moikh vstrech*, Vol. 2, (New York, 1966), 213-14; V. Markov, *Russian Futurism: A History* (Berkeley, Los Angeles, 1968); E. Braun, ed., *Meyerhold on Theater* (New York, 1969); H. Rischbieter, ed., *Art and the Stage in the Twentieth Century* (Greenwich, Conn., 1968), 137.

[4] V. Serov, *Rachmanninoff* (New York, 1950), 131.

[5] W. Kandinsky, "Der Blaue Reiter," *Das Kunstblatt*, Vol. 14 (1930), 57.

[6] L. Hollbeck, ed., *Unser München* (Munich, 1967); R. Piper, *Mein Leben als Verleger* (Munich, 1964), 297-9.

[7] J. Hahll-Koch, *Marianne Werefkin und der russischer Symbolismus* (Munich, 1967), 53-54, 62, 70. On the Azbe school see M. Dobuzhinsky, "Iz vospominanii," *Novyi zhurnal*, Vol. 52 (1958), 109-39.

[8] O. Walzel, *German Romanticism* (New York, 1932), 121, 125, 128; P. Selz, *German Expressionist Painting* (Berkeley, Los Angeles, 1957), 5, 7, 8.

[9] Whitford, "Notes," 15; O. Stelzer, *Des Vorgechichte der Abstrakten Kunst* (Munich, 1964), 115; W. Worringer, *Abstraction and Empathy* (London, 1963), 15, 65, 134.

[10] H. Bergson, *Laughter* (Paris, 1900), cited in T. Hanna, ed., *The Bergsonian Heritage* (New York, London, 1962), 88; T. E. Hulme, *Speculations* (London, 1924), 75-109; A. R. Jones, *The Life and Opinions of T. E. Hulme* (Boston, 1960), 43, 45, 60.

[11] C. G. Jung, *The Collected Works*, Vol. 4, *Freud and Psychoanalysis* (1932), (Princeton, 1961), 326; Vol. 7, *Two Essays on Analytic Psychology* (Princeton, 1953), 77; Vol. 10, *Civilization in Transition*, (Princeton, 1964), 90.

[12] W. Martin, *The New Age under Orage* (New York, 1967), 162; on Orage, see also P. Mairet, *A. R. Orage* (New Hyde Park, New York, 1966), and P. Selver, *Orage and the New Age Circle*, (London, 1959).

[13] G. Mosse, *The Crisis of German Ideology* (New York, 1964), 84-86, 210-12; "The Mystical Origins of National Socialism," *Journal of the History of Ideas,* Vol. 22 (January-March 1961), 83-85.

[14] On Steiner, see A. P. Shepherd, *A Scientist of the Invisible* (London, 1954).

[15] R. Steiner, *Macrocosm and Microcosm* (London, 1968), Vol. 2, 36, 57, 163. A translation of eleven lectures given by Steiner in Vienna, March 21-31, 1910.

[16] C. Weiler, *Alexei Jawlensky* (Cologne, 1959), 125; H. Weisberger, *Aus dem Leben von Marie Steiner-von Sivers* (Dornach, 1956); F. Bowers, *Scriabin* (Tokyo and Palo Alto, 1969), Vol. 2, 52, 63, 266.

[17] A. Turgeneva, "Andrei Belyi I Rudol'f Shteiner," *Mosty,* 1968, 245; Belyi himself does not mention Steiner in connection with his 1906 Munich visit, *Mezhdu dvukh revoliutsii* (Leningrad 1934), 103-40. On Trapesnikov, see A. Steffen, *Auf Geisteswegen* (Dornach, 1942), 65.

[18] M. Woloschin, *Die Grüne Schlange* (Stuttgart, 1954), 143-8, 158, 212.

[19] *Blast,* 2 (July 1915), 40; M. Sadler, *M. E. Sadler* (London, 1949), 238; A. Nethercot, *The Last Four Lives of Annie Besant* (Chicago, 1963), 52-53, 89-90; T. H. Robsjohn-Gibbings, *Mona Lisa's Mustache* (New York, 1947), 85-87, 130, 151-2, 161.

[20] W. Kandinsky, *Concerning the Spiritual in Art* (New York, 1947), 24-26, 29-31.

[21] Kandinsky himself was synaesthetic, and the subject of "color-hearing" was also of great interest to various nineteenth-century writers and artists. Overy, *Kandinsky,* 45; Kandinsky, *Rückblicke,* 15; Walzel, *German Romanticism,* 125; Stelzer, *Vorgeschichte,* 130-6; A. W. Rimington, *Colour-Music,* New York, 1911?).

[22] Kandinsky, *Concerning,* 33-35, 39-40, 50.

[23] *Ibid.,* 77; W. Kandinsky, "Über die Formfrage," *Der Blaue Reiter,* 1912, as cited and translated in H. B. Chipp, ed., *Theories of Modern Art* (Berkeley, Los Angeles, 1968), 155, 164, 170.

[24] S. Ringbohm, "Art in 'The Epoch of the Great Spiritual': Occult Elements in the Early Theory of Abstract Painting," *Journal of the Warburg and Courtauld Institute,* Vol. 29 (1966), 388, 392, 394, 398-9, 406.

[25] On Mondrian see F. Elgar, *Mondrian* (New York, 1968).

[26] O. Bie, "Die Verwirrungen der Malerei," *Neue Rundschau,* Vol. 23 (1912), 878-83; *Münchener Allgemeine Zeitung,* Vol. 30 (1912), 549; *Der Kunstwart,* Vol. 5 (1912), 308-12.

[27] W. Grohmann, *Vasily Kandinsky* (New York, 1958), 221. Letter to Will Grohmann, Paris, 4 December 1933.

FURTHER READING

Biography

Grohmann, Will. *Wassily Kandinsky: Life and Work.* New York: Harry N. Abrams, Inc., 1965, 428 p.
  Critical biography that includes a catalog of works, color reproductions, and photographs of the artist.

Lassaigne, Jacques. *Kandinsky.* Translated by H. S. B. Harrison. Geneva: Editions d'Art Albert Skira, 1964, 131 p.
  Richly illustrated biographical and critical study of the artist.

Weiss, Peg. *Kandinsky in Munich: The Formative Jugendstil Years.* New Jersey: Princeton University Press, 1979, 268 p.
  Chronicles Kandinsky's Munich years and studies how that time affected his work.

Criticism

Art Journal 43, No. 1 (Spring 1983): 9-66.
  Special issue on Kandinsky includes essays on various aspects of his work by Peg Weiss, Kenneth C. Lindsay, Wolfgang Venzmer, Monica Strauss, Edward J. Kimball, Susan Alyson Stein, and Rose-Carol Washton Long.

Kobialka, Michal. "Theatre of Celebration/Disruption: Time and Space/Timespace in Kandinsky's Theatre Experiments." *The Theatre Annual* XLIV (1989-1990): 71-96.
  Analyzes Kandinsky's experimental treatment of time in *The Yellow Sound.*

Long, Rose-Carol Washton. *Kandinsky: The Development of an Abstract Style.* Oxford:Clarendon Press, 1980, 200 p.
  Chronicles Kandinsky's espousal of abstraction and ensuing struggle to reach a wide audience through his art.

Overy, Paul. *Kandinsky: The Language of the Eye.* New York: Praeger Publishers, 1969, 192 p.
  Examines color, form, and symbolism in Kandinsky's later abstract paintings.

Roskill, Mark. *Klee, Kandinsky, and the Thought of Their Time: A Critical Perspective.* Urbana: University of Illinois Press, 1992, 279 p.
  Considers the careers of Klee and Kandinsky, their interaction, and how it affected modern art.

Weiss, Peg. "Kandinsky and the Symbolist Heritage." *Art Journal* 45, No. 2 (Summer 1985): 137-45.
  Suggests an association between the "Blue Rider"— the symbol Kandinsky chose to represent the artistic

coterie and periodical he founded in Munich—and St. George, a prominent character in Russian folklore.

————. *Kandinsky and Old Russia: The Artist as Ethnographer and Shaman*. New Haven, Conn.: Yale University Press, 1995, 291 p.

Considers "Kandinsky's ethnographic experience as a fundamental key to his life's work."

The following sources published by Gale contain additional coverage of Kandinsky's life and career: *Contemporary Authors,* Vols. **118, 155.**

Joseph Stalin

1879–1953

(Born Iosif Vissarionovich Dzhugashvili) Soviet dictator.

INTRODUCTION

Stalin led the Union of Soviet Socialist Republics as absolute dictator for twenty-four years. While he is credited with transforming the USSR into a world superpower, Stalin's use of mass execution—called "purgings"—and terror made him one of the most reviled political figures in history. As a writer and editor at the Communist Party newspaper *Pravda,* as well as the author of books and articles, Stalin contributed to the body of works delineating Soviet ideology. However, critics are divided over the importance of his writings; some maintain that Stalin simply regurgitated Marxist doctrine as it had already been interpreted by Vladimir Lenin, leader of the Bolshevik movement. Nonetheless, Stalin created for himself as leader a supreme status that gave rise to a cult-like following despite his renowned tyranny.

Biographical Information

Stalin was born in the small town of Gori, in czarist Georgia, in 1879. His father, a poor shoemaker, was an abusive alcoholic who was killed in a brawl when Stalin was eleven years old. His mother was an illiterate peasant who, after his father's death, prepared Stalin to enter the Orthodox priesthood. Stalin entered the Tiflis Theological Seminary when he was fourteen, but he was expelled in 1899 because of his involvement in a revolutionary anti-czarist group. In 1901 he officially joined the Russian Social Democratic Workers Party. A year later he was arrested and sent to a prison in Siberia, from which he escaped in 1904, returning to the underground Marxist movement in Tiflis. When Russian Marxism split into two factions—the radical Bolsheviks and the more moderate Menshiviks—Stalin sided with the Bolsheviks, thus aligning himself with Lenin and other major party leaders. Beginning in 1905 he attended several international conferences of the Russian Social Democrats, where he was first introduced to Lenin. In the following years Stalin was arrested and imprisoned on several instances; each time he escaped. In 1912 he went to Vienna to study Marxism; at that time he wrote *Marxism and the National Question.* The following year he began writing for the party newspaper *Pravda,* under the pseudonym Joseph Stalin, which means "man of steel." During the Russian Revolution of 1917 Stalin concentrated his efforts at the paper's editorial offices, rather than taking part directly in the events. In fact, most historians agree that Stalin played a rather insignificant role in the first years following the revolution; he was appointed People's Com-

missar for Nationalities and was a military commissar during the civil war of 1918-1921. Although Lenin valued Stalin for his organizational abilities and appointed him to the post of general secretary, a powerful position, Stalin's emphasis on Russian nationalism made Lenin uncomfortable. Leon Trotsky also quarreled with Stalin on policy and theoretical issues at this time; Lenin usually sided with Trotsky, but as general secretary Stalin's position of power was secure. Lenin, before his death, allegedly warned other party members about Stalin's potential for abusing power but was too ill to take action. Lenin died in 1924, and within five years Stalin had total control of the party. His first act was to extinguish Lenin's New Economic Policy (NEP)—intended to introduce a limited amount of free trade to the Soviet system in order to revive the economy after the civil war—and replace it with his own policy of collectivization, which nationalized the agricultural industry. Collectivization was an unmitigated disaster: peasants who refused to turn over their livestock and farms to the state were executed or sent to Stalin's prison work camps, called gulags. With agricultural production cut in half, mass famine ensued, and at least three to ten million peasants died of starvation. Stalin denied blame for the failure of collectivization, accusing others of misunderstanding his directives. His other major goal was to introduce widespread industrialization to the USSR, in order to move the country from an agriculture-based to an industry-based economy. In this he succeeded—initiating the machinery that would eventually make the Soviet Union a superpower nation—in large part because of the slave labor provided by the millions of Soviet citizens imprisoned in the gulags. Around 1934 Stalin launched the period that would be known as the Great Terror. Throughout the 1930s about one million old Bolshevik party members (those who had taken part in the pre-Stalin revolutionary era) and countless millions of citizens were accused of sabotage, treason, and espionage and were arrested, tortured, and either executed or sent to the gulags. This massive effort to ensure Stalin's absolute power was called "purging." Dramatic purge trials of party officials and senior members of the Red Army were set up. Defendants were accused of treason and other trumped-up charges and were always found guilty. The purging of the army had particularly devastating effects when the Soviet Union became involved in World War II. Stalin signed a Non-Aggression Pact with German dictator Adolf Hitler in the summer of 1939. The Pact included secret plans for the two leaders to control the European territories each considered essential to his country's expansion. But when Germany invaded Poland in September of that year, Stalin sought to increase the Soviet Union's presence in western Europe by invading Finland in November; Finland surrendered, and in June of 1941 Hitler broke his Pact with Stalin and invaded the Soviet Union, which, because of the military purgings, suffered devastating losses for nearly two years. Historians are divided over the degree of Stalin's success as a military commander during the German invasion. Many blame the huge Soviet losses on his increasing paranoia and megalomania. Nonetheless, the Red Army did hold off the Germans until they surrendered in 1945. After the war Stalin moved quickly to seize control of Eastern European countries to create the Soviet bloc. In 1949 the Soviet Union detonated its first atomic bomb, ushering in the arms race and Cold War with the United States that would last into the late 1980s. In 1953 Stalin was planning another series of purges, this time because of an alleged traitorous plot among the mostly Jewish Kremlin physicians. He died of a cerebral hemorrhage before the new purge trials could take place.

Major Works

Stalin produced a number of works on Soviet ideology—including *Marxism and the National Question, Marxism and Linguistics, Dialectical and Historical Materialism,* and his collected lectures on *Foundations of Leninism*—but whether or not he added anything new or innovative to theoretical communism is debatable. Many critics consider his writing unoriginal and repetitive. He did, however, transform Soviet communism, in his writings and his practices, from a revolutionary system to a strategy of conservative, isolationist authoritarianism. His talent for

propaganda allowed him to establish an astonishingly effective cult of personality despite his reputation for brute violence. By neutralizing anyone he considered or suspected of being an enemy, Stalin opened an avenue to total control of both his party and his people, whether they were followers or not. Pictures and statues of him were placed in all public places, as well as in private Soviet homes. His writings were studied, and poems and songs were written to glorify him. He encouraged his image as "Father of the Soviet People" and the "Great Teacher," and, after the Germans were driven out of the USSR in World War II, he exploited the role of savior of his country. After his death Stalin was still revered by Soviet citizens, many of whom wept openly when they heard he had died. Although he continued to receive credit for advancing Soviet society into the technological age to successfully compete with other world powers, in 1956 his successor Nikita Khrushchev and other Soviet leaders officially denounced Stalin and his actions. His policies were directly responsible for the deaths of as many as thirty million Soviets.

PRINCIPAL WORKS

Marxism and the National Question (nonfiction) 1913
Trotskyism or Leninism? (nonfiction) 1924
Leninism. 2 vols. (nonfiction) 1928-1933
The October Revolution: A Collection of Articles and Speeches (essays and speeches) 1934
Dialectical and Historical Materialism (nonfiction) 1938
Foundations of Leninism (lectures) 1939
The Great Patriotic War of the Soviet Union (nonfiction) 1945
Marxism and Linguistics (nonfiction) 1950
Selected Works of Joseph V. Stalin (nonfiction) 1971
The Essential Stalin: Major Theoretical Writings, 1905-1952 (nonfiction) 1972
Stalin's Letters to Molotov, 1925-1936 (letters) 1995

CRITICISM

Michael Karpovich (essay date 1934)

SOURCE: A review of 'Leninism,' in *Political Science Quarterly,* Vol. 46, No. 4, 1934, pp. 634-36.

[*In the following review, Karpovich finds* Leninism *valuable because of its contemporaneity with Stalin's early years in power but otherwise finds the theories espoused "monotonous" and unoriginal.*]

Those interested in political theory will not find anything new in this collection of Stalin's articles and speeches

Leninism. He himself does not claim authorship of new and original ideas. His position is that of a faithful interpreter of the revelation, a guardian of orthodoxy. The fundamentals of the dogma cannot be questioned, and discussion is permissible only within its limits. In every case final authority is the word of the master. "Lenin says", with an appropriate quotation, is used again and again to prove the correctness of the "general line" of the party and to confound the dissenters. Neither was Lenin an originator of new theory. He merely developed the basic ideas of Marx in accordance with the conditions of his times. Consequently, Leninism is defined as "Marxism of the epoch of imperialism and of the proletarian revolution". It is an international doctrine, and it should not be looked upon as a "product of Russian primitiveness". The core of Leninism is the dictatorship of the proletariat, and not the solution of the peasant problem, which is of a derivative and subsidiary nature. The historical fate of the Russian peasantry is to serve as a "reserve force for the proletariat". A similar part is assigned to the oppressed nationalities of the colonial and dependent countries. All this is familiar from Lenin's writings.

Opinion has been expressed that Stalin's original contribution consists in the theory of "socialism in one country". Stalin himself has no such claim to make. Here too he merely tries to follow Lenin. The genesis of the idea is characteristic. As late as April 1924 Stalin still shared the belief that the final victory of socialism could not be gained in one country alone, and "without the joint efforts of the proletarians in several of the most advanced countries" (vol. I, p. 52). But only six months after that he found himself forced to "rectify" his position by giving a new and ingenious interpretation to the conception of "final victory of socialism" in Russia. By such a victory one should understand a complete guarantee against the restoration of capitalism by means of foreign intervention, and for this a proletarian revolution in other countries was necessary. But as to the upbuilding of a socialist system in Soviet Russia, this was "possible and necessary by the unaided forces of that country". Apparently, during these six months Stalin's attention was called to Lenin's pamphlet on "Coöperation" in which the master had proclaimed "the indisputable truth that we have all the requisites for the establishment of a fully socialized society" (vol. I, p. 54). "Lenin said"—and the new interpretation became the "general line" of the party, while Stalin's own original position assumed the character of a dangerous heresy. Neither was a "new doctrine" a departure from internationalism, as it was described by some writers. Stalin is emphatic on this point. "For what else is our country, the country that is building up socialism, but the base of the world revolution?" (vol. I, p. 63). The change, in other words, was in tactics, not in aim or in spirit. And we get a revealing light on the psychological motive behind it. With the hope for an immediate world revolution gone, a substitute was needed. "We cannot upbuild socialism without a belief in the possibility of what we are trying to do" (vol. I, p. 56). Indeed, how can one?

The book derives its importance from the fact that the author is the dominating figure in Soviet Russia. Stalin himself is very modest as to his personal position. Apparently his ambition does not go beyond being the principal spokesman for the Political Bureau of the party. "The only way of leading the party is by a collectivity of some sort. Now that Lenin is dead, it is absurd to think, or talk, or dream of anything else" (vol. I, p. 457). Behind this appearance of "collectivity", however, there is hiding a formidable personal power, surely no less absolute than that of Hitler in Germany or Mussolini in Italy. It is curious to watch throughout the pages of these two volumes, covering the period of 1924-1931, the growth of Stalin's prestige and authority. In the beginning he is still one of the several forces contending for the control within the party, and occasionally we find him on the defensive, trying to explain his position and to rectify his errors. At the end he is the indisputable leader of Soviet Russia, laying down the law, and making final pronouncements *ex cathedra*.

The impression which most of these pronouncements make upon the reader is somewhat monotonous. With few exceptions they are variations upon one and the same theme. It is significant that during all this period the Soviet government was moving within a vicious circle, facing essentially the same problems and experiencing the same difficulties. The fundamental paradox can be described, in Trotsky's words, as "contradictions inherent in the position of a workers' government functioning in a backward country where the large majority of the population is composed of peasants." In its attempts to get around this difficulty the communist dictatorship tried different methods, all of which are recorded in Stalin's speeches and articles. We can follow the gradual change from the conciliatory attitude of 1924-1925, when even the kulaks were not to be provoked, to the new socialist offensive in the rural districts, with its "mass collectivization" of peasantry and its policy of "liquidating the kulaks as a class." One of the last chapters in the second volume, Stalin's political report to the sixteenth conference of the Communist Party, is a paean of victory, full of assurances of final success. Perhaps, to some readers it might appear convicing. To the present reviewer, who is frankly skeptical, it is primarily an exhibition of official optimism, and as such belongs to the least valuable parts of the book.

Walter Sandelius (essay date 1936)

SOURCE: A review of 'Marxism and the National and Colonial Question,' in *The American Political Science Review*, Vol. XXX, No. 5, October, 1936, pp. 1026-27.

[*In the following review, Sandelius finds Stalin in* Marxism and the National and Colonial Question *"persuasive" and "orderly."*]

Among the publications prepared by the Marx-Engels-Lenin Institute appears now, in English, **Marxism and the**

National and Colonial Question by Joseph Stalin, being a collection of articles, reports, and speeches, ranging in date from 1913 to 1935, on the subject—one may say—of Stalin's most distinctive interest and experience. A rather central thread appears throughout, though in the Marxian vein, yet in a certain judicious adjustment of the objectives of proletarian dictatorship with those "rights of nationalities" which, on the whole, have found in Stalin a consistent champion. The working class interest must come first. But the Great-Russian Communists, again and again, are charged with failure, in their party work, to reckon with the peculiarities of historical background of the lesser nationalities. War must be waged against Great-Russian chauvinism. On the other hand, the Native Communists, haunted still by the horrors of the period of national oppression, tend to exaggerate the importance of national peculiarities, and so to deviate toward bourgeois-democratic nationalism. This tendency, in the eastern regions, assumes at times the form of Pan-Islamism and Pan-Turkism. So, historical context, whether within or without the Soviet Union, may require a varying assertion or denial of the national idea. Essentially, the Union today may be thought of as consistently socialist in content, while varying and national in form. Outside, particularly in the Far East, which represents the "heavy reserves of our revolution," it is necessary continually—though always on guard against premature emphasis—to encourage the nationalism in states dependent upon imperialist powers. But there is no one formula for all things. This caution, persistent and in the spirit of true science, is not, to be sure, without paradoxical consequence. Stalin accepts paradox. Stalin, however, is less the philosopher than the effective controversialist steeped in history. There is convincing evidence of a tenacious, informed, forceful use of the historical argument; testimony, too, particularly in the living presence of extemporaneous speech and its proximity to events, to a personality greater than may have appeared to distant observers. The more popular of the speeches offer, now and again, a pedantic and tiresome classification of categories. But whether in the polemical or the more expository vein, always, without Caesar-pose, it is the persuasive and the orderly mind at work. Also, it is an orderly and attractive arrangement of the principal materials, appendices, and explanatory notes that has been made available.

Edmund Wilson (essay date 1937)

SOURCE: "Stalin, Trotsky, and Willi Schlamm," in *From the Uncollected Edmund Wilson,* Ohio University Press, 1995, pp. 217-27.

[*In the following essay, which was originally published in the* Nation *in 1937, Wilson provides a critical examination of the report of the Trotsky Commission.*]

The report of the Trotsky Commission is a remarkably interesting document, which makes one realize the inadequacy, if not frivolity, of the newspaper accounts of the Mexican hearings.

In regard to the question of Trotsky's guilt on the charges brought against him at the Moscow trials, these hearings made public a great deal of material which helps to establish his innocence. As is already well known, the Oslo airdrome reported that no foreign planes had arrived at the time of Pyatakov's supposed visit to Trotsky; and the Hotel Bristol in Copenhagen, where Torosky's son was alleged to have met Holtzman, no longer existed at that time. The Stalinists later discovered a Bristol Cafe; but Holtzman had testified that he had *stopped* at a Hotel Bristol, and subsequent investigation on the part of the Defense Committee showed that what actually existed was a Konditori Bristol, which had a Grand Hotel with its cafe several doors away.

It is asserted that in a photograph of these buildings published in *Soviet Russia Today* the door of the cafe was blackened out in order to make it appear that the pastry-shop directly adjoined the cafe, and that the words, "Konditori" and "Grand" had apparently been suppressed on the signs. Trotsky gives a detailed chronology of his movements and activities during the time when he was supposed to have been conspiring to overthrow the Soviet Union, and a record of his relations or lack of relations with the persons with whom he was supposed to have conspired.

It is always open to the Stalinists to maintain that the conspirators have covered up their traces, that all the persons who have furnished statements and all the members of the commission are Trotskyists and all the documents which emanate from them forgeries. But what seems to me of overwhelming impressiveness is the review of Trotsky's whole career which is presented in the course of the proceedings. The real argument for Trotsky's innocence is indicated by him in answer to a question as to whether it is not conceivable that his desire "to achieve" his "motives" might not have led him to involve himself with Hitler:

> I write articles and letters [replies Trotsky] absolutely hostile to Hitler, to fascism, and to the Japanese militarists. But in secret I enter into relations with Hess. My work, however, according to that opinion, signifies that ninety-nine or, more, nine hundred and ninety-nine thousandths of my time is devoted to camouflage. My whole life is a camouflage, but my real work and action take only one or two hours. . . . I am alleged to have found Hess and discussed with him the manner of the dismemberment of the Soviet Union. After the discussion, I write a new article, in effect contrary to my supposed real work.

No doubt it is true at the present time that the only people outside Russia who swallow the Moscow trials are naïve persons who cannot believe that Soviet officials could do such things as would be implied by the frame-up of the old Bolsheviks, persons so ignorant of Russian politics and history that they are disqualified from holding an opinion, and fanatical or job-holding partisans who, if they do not belong to either of the other categories, take the position that all methods are permissible for the maintenance of the Stalinist power. But if there is anyone who is still puzzled by the trials, he should compare the official accounts with these hearings. He should also look into "The Stalin School of Falsification," an old book now first translated into English and important for students of the revolution, which includes documents on the last days of Lenin, suppressed by the Stalinist authorities, and the suppressed minutes of a Bolshevik committee meeting of 1917, and shows the continual plastic surgery on past events which has been going on since Lenin's death.

What is perhaps most shocking in this whole affair is the abysmal degree of credulity assumed by the official caste on the part of the worker population. The widening gap in the Soviet Union between the insiders at the top, who have access to information never allowed to reach the masses, and the public which reads the boiler-plate propaganda unloaded on them by *Pravda* and *Izvestia* is a fact which gives the key to many happenings likely to seem incomprehensible to an American.

Aside, however, from the light that it throws on the charges of conspiracy, the report of the Trotsky Commission is one of the greatest political interviews ever printed. The commissioners managed to cover in the course of their questions an enormous amount of ground—Trotsky's personal career, the politics of the revolution, the history of the Comintern, the present condition and prospects of the world, and the general philosophy behind Trotsky's opinions. Many of the questions that one would like to ask Trotsky if one were able to subject him to an unlimited interview were asked him in the course of these hearings; and I am not sure that from the point of view of the ordinary non-Marxist reader Trotsky's world-view is not here presented more impressively and more effectively than in his pamphlets and other writings, where the technical language of Marxism sometimes gets between us and the events.

The Soviet Union in its present disturbed phase has become, as Trotsky says, more completely cut off from the outside world than perhaps any great Western nation has ever been. The document called "Letter of an Old Bolshevik," which reaches New York by way of Paris, where it was published by the *Socialist Messenger*, the organ of the Russian Social Democratic Labor Party, purports to give the political developments inside the Communist Party which have resulted in the propaganda trials. If the document is authentic—and it sounds as if it were—it is of great interest to everyone interested in Russia.

At the end of 1932, says the author of the "Letter of an Old Bolshevik," the situation in Russia was critical. The effects of the famine were so terrible that the workers, with almost nothing to eat, seemed no longer to be capable of producing. Inside the Central Committee and the Politburo there was a strong and predominant feeling that Stalin ought to go out with his program, which

had hopelessly antagonized the rural population, and a counterprogram was even prepared demanding the abolition of the collectives and granting the peasants economic self-determination. Stalin got hold of a copy of the program and set the G. P. U. on the author and those who had circulated it. There was at this time a growth of terrorist sentiment among the young people of the Komsomol, who had been taught to regard the political assassins as heroes in the struggle against the Czar and who had decided that they were now confronted with an officialdom of the same obdurate kind. Stalin, on his side, with Oriental suspicion connecting these tendencies with the movement inside the party, insisted that the opposition program was practically a provocation to take his life; but Kirov, the president of the Leningrad Soviet, dissuaded the Politburo from condemning the author to death.

Then the harvest the next year turned out abundant, and Stalin, acutely conscious that his political future hung in the balance, saw to it that the peasants brought in the crop. The party—the Russians are always overawed by displays of executive energy—decided that he had justified himself, and there was no longer any question of removing him; but a struggle now began among cliques as to who was to have his ear and control him. In the meantime, at the end of 1933, a genuine Nazi conspiracy was uncovered. The Russians were forced to abandon their expectation of a revolutionary Germany next door and to look for support to the democratic countries; the Soviets entered the League of Nations and created the Popular Front in France. A movement in the direction of democracy was thus in order in the Soviet Union, and this movement was led by Kirov, a loyal follower of the Stalinist line but a relatively independent individual. He advocated conciliation with former political oppositionists, tried to make Leningrad an intellectual center. He was made a secretary of the Central Committee, with complete control of the party "ideology," a post which would have brought him to Moscow. His popularity began to rival Stalin's.

Then suddenly Kirov was shot. The motives of his assassin remained a mystery; the man, who was neurotic and exalted, seemed to have acted entirely on his own. But he had been babbling indiscreetly about the necessity of someone's "sacrificing himself"; and yet nobody had restrained him from his crime. He had been able to go straight to Kirov, with no hindrance from the Smolny guards. It was certain that the group around Stalin, the group which Kaganovich headed, had no reason to welcome Kirov to Moscow. They cared nothing about ideologies; they only wanted to hang on to their jobs; and they were afraid of the new movement toward liberalism, which would certainly have cost them their places. Kaganovich, says the author of the "Letter," though able, is a man of no principle; indeed, with the hypocrisy imposed by the lack of democracy inside the party, principle has pretty much gone by the board. And Yezhov, another leader of this group, is the perfect type of the self-seeking informer who fattens on suspicious despots.

The whole development went into reverse. Yezhov, playing on the worst instincts of Stalin, proceeded to clean up on the old Bolsheviks, who had persisted, though with entire futility, in grumbling about the repressions of the government and whom he had his own reasons for disliking. The officials of the Commissariat of Home Affairs who had been responsible for Nikolaiev's reaching Kirov were let off with easy sentences, but a persecution was started by Yezhov against the former political oppositionists, who were accused of having inspired the crime. The dissidents now fell in with the sycophants in a great carnival of flattery for Stalin in the hope that his fury would subside. But the "best disciple of Lenin" now gave rein to all his vindictive instincts; the moral code of the Georgian mountains evidently resembles that which prevails among the feudists of Kentucky. Stalin now even refused to see Gorki, who had sometimes been able to restrain him; and Gorki not long afterward died. The butchering of the old revolutionaries began.

The Kamenev-Zinoviev affair had been prepared without the knowledge of Yagoda, the head of the G.P.U., and when he objected, he was arrested himself. Yezhov briskly stepped into his place and stands today at Stalin's right hand.

But now we come to something new and quite distinct from the type of old Bolshevik, whether Kamenev or Trotsky or Stalin. We come to Herr Willi Schlamm, the author of "The Dictatorship of the Lie." Herr Schlamm is an Austrian Socialist, the former editor of the *Weltbuhne*. Herr Schlamm is trying to find a new political base—he is, I am told, in his middle thirties—and he feels strongly the necessity of cutting himself loose not merely from Stalinism but from the whole tradition of Russian Marxism. His book is not a political program, nor is it properly even a manifesto. It is rather in the nature of a sermon. But it may be that what socialism needs at the moment is a few sermons like this of Schlamm. Certainly "The Dictatorship of the Lie" is one of the most bracing and air-clearing documents which have yet come out of the crisis of the left.

It is impossible to do it justice in a summary, because its power depends on its eloquence and on its tone of moral candor. Herr Schlamm believes that the Moscow trials have played a catalytic role, like that of the Dreyfus case, in precipitating a division of opinion. The time has come for genuine Socialists to throw off all pious hopes and pretensions and face the fact that the government of Stalin has no longer anything to do with socialism. Stalin himself and his associates no longer represent anything much different from what Hitler represents; his example is an encouragement to Hitler, and he may very soon be Hitler's ally. What is the point, then, of raging against the repressions of Hitler after the horrors of the Moscow executions? (I am not sure, however, that Herr Schlamm is right in believing that the trials were anti-Semitic.) Why should the Marxist assume that historical forces will eventually break down the lies of Hitler and at the same time expect that the lies of Stalin can direct the eventual

development of Russia? Not so can the Marxist guide history. "History does not read the newspapers—certainly not those of the Comintern."

At the time of the degradation of the old Bolsheviks, the Soviet government imported to Russia expert perfumers from Paris—the author of the "Letter" discussed above asserts that there was a deliberate attempt to associate the political terror with the idea of a more luxurious standard of living—but all the expert perfumers in the world will be powerless to sweeten the moral atmosphere. What kind of a new socialist humanity is to be expected from the tutelage of a regime, which, after making abortion impossible for the poor in a country overrun with parentless waifs, subjects children from twelve up to the death penalty, and trains the inmates of its asylums for the homeless to subscribe to bloody manifestos demanding the deaths of the original Socialist leaders? And why should the workers of any country be expected to be delighted at the prospect of having "Herr Vyshinsky's Grand Guignol" perform in their midst?

But what is really behind all this, says Schlamm, is the elimination of moral principles from socialism. What are the claims to moral authority of an advance guard of social regeneration which has shown itself to be devoid of the primary human virtues of kindliness, fair-dealing and veracity? There is no morality in the "Dialectic": from a more or less useful philosophical instrument it has been turned first into an incantation and then into the vulgar patter by which the salesman of the "correct line" succeeds in unloading his goods on the stupid. The left intellectual who exploits it is a tick in the sore flesh of the working-class movement. An intellectual, he provokes pogroms against intellectuals. He courts the workers because he hopes to manipulate them, and he despises them because he sees they can be deceived.

And they, on their side, have no "historic role" which will stimulate them inevitably to struggle. Nor does our social science of Marxism take us far. In that field our scientific knowledge is in reality still very meager, and the little we have succeeded in acquiring can never do duty for human initiative and human character. We must recognize that society has to be saved, not by the processes of a mystic dialectic, but by the influence of human beings who are self-respecting and morally sound.

"The Dictatorship of the Lie" has already had its repercussions in certain quarters. Trotsky himself has just published a pamphlet—"Stalinism and Bolshevism"—which is partly devoted to answering Schlamm (as well as some Anarchists, who have seized the occasion to raise their ideological heads). From Trotsky's point of view, Willi Schlamm is dealing in "moth-eaten metaphysical absolutes." The disasters in Russia are not due to Marxism but to the backwardness of the country. Herr Schlamm is trying to return to pre-Marxist socialism in its "German" and "most sentimental" form. Trotsky seizes on the fact that Schlamm's tract has been welcomed by the organ of Kerensky and more or less tries to drown him by tying him and Kerensky together—thereby, himself the victim of many "amalgams," being guilty of a bit of an amalgam himself.

For Herr Schlamm, who pays his respects to Trotsky, the latter represents the Leninist tradition, but he regards both Lenin and Trotsky as obsolete. Herr Schlamm is well aware, he says, that his opinions will cause him to be branded as a "Trotskyist": "Poor wretches! That is all they can do. For them, the whole great world of thought and spirit comes down finally to a Politburo, in which a couple of factions squabble." But he is really on another track.

It is not clear to me that Schlamm, as Trotsky says, has completely repudiated the class struggle. On the contrary, he speaks in one passage as if he assumed it as an elementary fact. It is true that he asserts later on that the great ideas which move and mold humanity are "incorporated in true and strong individuals" who may be "workers, peasants, intellectuals, women, or bourgeois." But does this reject the class view of society? Certainly, Schlamm has not as yet got very far in formulating his social philosophy. But I believe that the reaction he represents is more important than Trotsky supposes.

W. J. Oudendyk (essay date 1938)

SOURCE: A review of 'The History of the Civil War in the U. S. S. R.,' in *International Affairs,* Vol. XVII, 1938, pp. 581-82.

[*In the following review, Oudendyk finds* The History of the Civil War in the U.S.S.R. *interesting but unfortunately too biased to leave the reader with anything but a distorted picture.*]

A New generation has grown up in Soviet Russia of men and women who have never lived under any other régime. The old generation has practically disappeared. The days of revolution and civil war are now considered sufficiently remote for the successful partisan of those days to write a history of them as seen exclusively from his point of view. Much if not most of the material from which this book has been compiled is already known (partly thanks to the publications of the Soviet Government), but here it is presented not in an objective manner (as, for instance, in Serge Oldenbourg's *Le Coup d'État Bolchéviste*), but is full of class hatred and vituperation against the Bolshevik's political opponents. Of course the very names of the authors preclude their treating this subject with the broadness of vision of a scientific historian. For them there exists only the narrowest party point of view. Nevertheless the book provides much interesting reading matter, as it is the product of the diligent and painstaking collection of material from many sources, not the least interesting of which are the minutes of the meetings and congresses of the Bolshevik party. These give the reader an insight into the ceaseless labours of the Bolsheviks to undermine the existing Russian State edifice which had already been so severely shaken by the February revolution of 1917. One cannot help asking, however, while reading all this self-glorification, what would have become of these much-vaunted successes if the despised capitalistic Allies had not defeated the Central Powers in spite of the disappearance—under Bolshevik influence—of the Russian front, and after the Bolsheviks had already been obliged in Brest-Litovsk to accept a treaty under which Russia would, virtually, have become a semi-colonial country.

The only heroes in this history [*The History of The Civil War in The U.S.S.R.*] are the Bolsheviks; the rest of the world consists of villains, bent on betraying, cheating and robbing the "toilers." There are the Mensheviks, the socialist-revolutionaries, the petty-bourgeois, the bourgeois, the cadets, the imperialists and what not else; one and all are traitors, counter-revolutionaries, enemies of the proletariat, actuated only by the vilest and basest motives. But worse than all these are the "Kornilovites," and no words are bad enough to depict General Kornilov; it is even insinuated that he was a traitor who maliciously surrendered Riga to the Germans (p. 339 and p. 343).

The general picture that the authors draw is a distorted one, however true their dates and quotations may be. What they evidently want to impress on the minds of present-day Russia and of their sympathisers abroad is that it was the Bolsheviks who put an end to Tsarism (p. 92); that a Provisional Government arose—as a usurper—side by side with the Soviets (p. 114); that it took power only with the purpose of combating the revolution (p. 173); that the bourgeois leaders were hostile to the revolution and attacked it (p. 200); that they established their dictatorship (p. 219); and that it was by their counter-revolution that the economic disintegration of the country took the proportions it did (p. 321).

The sabotage of the capitalists (p. 368) and their offensive against the working class by striving to bring about a famine (p. 358), together with the utter vileness of the Socialist-Revolutionaries' and Mensheviks' treachery (p. 296), moved the country irresistibly towards disaster (p. 399). Only the self-sacrificing fight of the (Bolshevik) party (p. 401) could bring about an improvement. Any interference with their activities constituted a violation of elementary civil rights (p. 449). One of those elementary rights was to "raspropagandirowat" (dissolve by propaganda) the regiments at the front, and one cannot help wondering what would happen to any one who claimed that right to-day in the U.S.S.R.

The above picture—grotesque as it is to anybody who, like the reviewer, lived through those days in Russia—is cleverly, even in a masterly way, worked out, and the book is to be recommended to everyone who wishes to obtain an insight into, and understand, the Bolshevik mind. The same material, however, could be used to draw a picture in exactly the opposite colours.

The book calls itself "the first comprehensive and authoritative history of the period." Authoritative it naturally is;

but comprehensive it certainly is not. Too much has been left out which a real historian would have put in.

The English translation is perfect.

C. D. Burns (essay date 1941)

SOURCE: A review of 'Leninism,' in *Ethics: An International Journal of Social, Political, and Legal Philosophy*, Vol. LII, 1941-42, pp. 118-20.

[In the following review, Burns finds the English translation of Stalin's Leninism *a valuable source for Westerners studying the socio-political climate of the Soviet Union.]*

This volume [*Leninism*] is an authorized translation of the eleventh Russian edition of *Problems of Leninism.* It contains speeches and articles which were not in the two-volume edition of 1933 or in the volume, also called *Leninism,* published in 1938. But the more important speeches of Stalin, included in the earlier English editions, are republished here. The speeches and articles included represent the views of Stalin from 1934 to 1939 (March 10). The development of Stalin's views will no doubt continue, but it appears to be an established tradition that whatever changes of policy are adopted by him, or by the Communist party under him, must be justified by quotations taken from the sacred texts of Marx and Lenin. Western Europe went through a similar stage of dependence for political ideas upon the sacred scriptures during the controversies about tyranny and liberty in the late Renaissance. Probably, therefore, Russian political theory is only about three hundred years behind that of western Europe. But it is interesting that this book should contain the views, not of an external observer, but of a very subtle politician. The most obvious parallel in the history of political thought is between Stalin's *Leninism* and the treatise on *The True Law of Free Monarchies* by King James I of England, first published in 1598. This is not the place for an analysis or discussion of the theory of government expounded by Stalin in his speeches and articles. But one or two notes may be made upon the peculiar form of Marxian orthodoxy before the outbreak of war between the two great dictatorships on June 22, 1941. Stalin, in his article on the problems of Leninism, quotes (p. 129) Lenin as saying that the alliance between the proletariat and the peasants aims at retaining for the proletariat "its leading role and its political power"; and also two completely contradictory statements by Lenin about dictatorships, in one of which he says, "Dictatorship is unrestricted power, absolutely unimpeded by laws and regulations . . . based on force and not on law"; and in the other that "the Dictatorship of the Proletariat is not only the use of force and not even mainly the use of force" because the proletariat represents the higher type of social organization. The reason thus given, in the second quotation, is obviously a reference to a moral principle. But the eye of faith has always been able to see contradictions in terms as mysterious truths. Thus, Stalin, in two of the articles in this

book, appears to be worried by the old Marxian doctrine that the state will "fade away." In his treatment of the results of the first five-year plan, he says, "the State will die out . . . as a result of its utmost consolidation." Apparently the stronger the state becomes, the weaker it becomes. But this is due to "capitalist encirclement." We are told also that Trotsky and other such leaders were conspiring in the service of foreign spies—even in October, 1918, although nobody noticed it! Another interesting point refers to the so-called Stakhonov movement in 1935, which was an effort to speed up Russian workers. We are told (p. 548) that socialism involves payment "not according to needs, but according to work done," whereas communism involves payment "according to needs." Who is to decide what a man needs is a question that is not discussed. It is unfortunate that a politician of the great ability of Stalin should find it necessary to publish in this book a study in metaphysics written in September, 1938, on "dialectical materialism," which would hardly deserve a third class if written by a student in philosophy in any Western university. In this strange article Stalin informs us that matter is the source of sensation and that "thought is the product of matter." He is evidently not familiar with work that has been done in philosophy since Marx and Engels wrote a century ago. But one would not expect either Mr. Roosevelt or Mr. Churchill to publish an article on metaphysics; and that Stalin should do so is a sign of the very peculiar climate of opinion in which the Russian communists live. Indeed, the speeches and articles contained in this book are valuable documents for the study of a climate of opinion which is entirely strange to the more highly developed civilization of the West.

Edmund Wilson (essay date 1946)

SOURCE: "Trotsky's Stalin," in *From the Uncollected Edmund Wilson*, Ohio University Press, 1995, pp. 231-40.

[In the following essay, which first appeared in the New Yorker *in 1946, Wilson reviews the English translation of Leon Trotsky's biography* Stalin, *finding it a volume of great historical and political importance.]*

Leon Trotsky, during the later years of his exile, set out to write a life of Lenin. The first volume of this biography, which ends with Lenin's graduation from law school, was brought out, in a French translation, in 1936, but Trotsky did not get very much further with it. Needing money, he was persuaded by a New York publisher, on the strength of a considerable advance, to break off and do a life of Stalin. It was thought that such a book could not fail to be a timely and lucrative exploit, but, like so many bright ideas of publishers, this turned out to be very much less sound than the author's own ideas for his work. A life of Lenin was needed; a life of Stalin was not. There was no full-length study of Lenin which was not either a mere journalistic job or a reflection of Soviet propaganda, and the first section of Trotsky's life seemed to indicate that the book, had it been finished, would have been one of his most remarkable works, as this installment of it constitutes what is probably the most brilliant piece of biography that pure Marxism has ever produced. In the case of Stalin, however, documentation is so meagre on his career before 1917 that Trotsky is largely obliged to confine himself to going over the same historical ground that he has covered already in his books on the 1905 and the 1917 revolutions, and pointing out that, through the years of preparation for the Bolshevik seizure of power, Stalin was scarcely known and that no credible evidence exists of his ever having done anything of importance. For the story of the years in which Stalin served as a member of the Central Committee, the years in which, behind the scenes, he was manipulating the political machine that was to make him supreme master of the government, Trotsky, whose own career in this period had all been acted on the public stage of history and thought out in terms of theoretical Marxism, cannot go behind the scenes with Stalin but can only present the latter's role as he has already done with somewhat more vividness in his story of his own life and in his polemics on Soviet politics.

This book, too, has been left unfinished, with great gaps and loose ends not tied up, for the author was assassinated, while writing it, in the summer of 1940, by a young man whom investigation seems to have shown to have been a G.P.U. agent. Then America found herself in the war as an ally of the Soviet Union, and the publishers who had commissioned the book thought it better to withhold its publication. It has thus only now appeared—*Stalin,* by Leon Trotsky (Harper)—in a translation, smooth and lucid, by Charles Malamuth, who has done also a careful job of editing in supplying supplementary information and, in the case of the later chapters, expanding Trotsky's notes and piecing together his fragments.

The book makes very good reading, like almost everything that Trotsky wrote, and I believe it will take its place with that body of Trotsky's work which is likely to have permanent interest. The problem of writing a biography of a Soviet political figure presents difficulties of a peculiar kind. The historian is confronted with official panegyrics that make no attempt at scholarly accuracy and that are sometimes invented out of the whole cloth, the authors of which feel no obligation even to square themselves with authoritative data provided by earlier accounts (since, for Soviet readers, the Soviet government is in a position to suppress these accounts), and he has nothing to check them but chance memories and notes by participants in or observers of the Revolution, who are sometimes themselves biassed by political animosities or loyalties, together with such incomplete records as are to be found in the Soviet press. Trotsky had, of course, his personal archives on the official transactions of the Revolution and his personal impressions of men and events, but it is difficult for him to put together any chronicle that is at all reliable on the early life of Stalin. His method here, as in the case of Lenin, is to scrutinize one by one every supposed fact that has anywhere been recorded and to try to come to some conclusion as to its probable or possible truth. With Stalin, of whom fantastic romances

have been written by the professional eulogists, this process becomes mainly negative—that is, Trotsky is occupied in showing that what is asserted cannot conceivably have happened: Stalin was not a great organizer in the Caucasus, he did not always maintain a Bolshevik position, he did not serve on committees among the members of which his name has since been inserted, etc., etc. On such questions, Trotsky's demonstrations are usually acute and convincing. His analysis of evidence is reasoned with the effectiveness of a brilliant lawyer's brief. (It should be mentioned that Trotsky's dealings with what he calls the official hagiography are just as ruthless in the case of Lenin, whom he followed and admires, as with Stalin, whom he opposed and dislikes.) The only point of view from which, in general, it is possible to object to his procedure is one's feeling that he may be sometimes misled by his desire to see the workings of human life as consecutive and logical processes, the continuous exemplification of a single set of well-grasped principles. If anything sounds at all queer, Trotsky is likely to conclude that it cannot be true. His is a world which can allow no anomalies.

In the same way, the principles of Marxism—the laws of class and group behavior—have to be made to explain all the phenomena in Trotsky's intellectual world. He admits that a great leader like Lenin may affect, in a vital fashion, the outcome of a "historical situation"; but the discipline of Marxism has developed in him so strongly an abstract and international way of approaching mankind's confusion that he tends to leave out of account, in his story of the metamorphosis of the democratic councils of Lenin into the Oriental despotism of Stalin, factors that seem to a foreigner as plain as the nose upon Stalin's face—that is, the national characteristics of the Russians that have disqualified them for political democracy. If it is true, as Trotsky says, that Stalin was ambitious for power and inexhaustibly patient and persistent in accomplishing his ends, that he became a master politician of the familiar Tammany type, who makes deals, distributes patronage, and plays rivals off against one another, that he managed to do all this very quietly, without ever sticking out his neck and always waiting to see which way the cat would jump, and that he is hardboiled and unscrupulous to the last degree, contemptuous of human ties and caring nothing about human life, it is also true that these latter qualities are not calculated to endear him to the people, and that he is also, according to Trotsky, uneducated and unimaginative, with none of the instincts that make civilization, as well as so envious, vindictive, and cruel that he cannot tolerate the presence of anyone who is superior to him in these respects, and will never, so long as he reigns, allow, in the Soviet Union, either free political contests or real general education. He has had not merely the spur to rebellion of the "underprivileged" man of spirit but also the habit of silent hatred implanted by a drunken father, who continually beat him as a child.

Why, then, did the Russians allow him—a Georgian, besides, and an alien—to become their supreme master? That is what Trotsky does not tell us. There is a Russian satirical poem by the first Alexei Tolstoy, the nineteenth-century writer, which throws a kind of light on Stalin that we cannot get from Trotsky's account. Tolstoy takes for his text the saying of an ancient chronicler that "Russia is a great and rich country, but in it there is no order," and he makes this the refrain for a long comic poem that summarizes the history of Russia. It is seen that there were only two eras when order was established in Russia—the reign of Ivan the Terrible and the reign of Peter the Great. When the people were coerced and herded, frightened, tormented and slaughtered, subjected to the caprices of a terrible czar, then, and only then, for a time there was order in Russia. Reading the poem today, we find, when we have got to the end, that a third establisher of order inevitably pops up in our minds: he is what is needed to round out the story. "It is no accident," to use a favorite phrase of Trotsky's, that the publicity agents of the Soviet Union first exploited the cult of Peter the Great and then revived and glorified Ivan. It is the Russians who have created Stalin as much as Stalin has molded the Russians. They have created him through their inveterate dislike of accepting responsibility and through their almost religious need for the authority of a great earthly father. An American travelling in the Soviet Union is amazed to find in Soviet officialdom the same characteristics of timidity, evasiveness, and inaction that he has read about in pre-revolutionary memoirs. In comparison, he comes to realize, the pettiest position in America involves a sphere, however narrow, in which the individual must make his decisions for himself. The bank teller must decide himself whether or not he will cash your check, but in Russia he cannot decide; he has to appeal to the officials above him, and these appeal to higher officials. Everybody passes the buck, and it finally lands with Comrade Stalin, who presently becomes Marshal Stalin. Now, what democracy really depends on, the only thing that can make the word real, is distribution of responsibility, and the soviets (councils) of a Socialist state in a country where this is unknown can no more be democratic than the dumas of the czardom could.

Trotsky had never been concerned about democracy, which for him had never meant anything else than the fraudulent side of bourgeois institutions, and it is curious to see him in this book at last looking around and trying to figure out what it is that went wrong and how. There is a section toward the end—only a sketch, no doubt—in which he tries to retrace the development of Stalin's murderous practice out of Lenin's good intentions. People complain, he says, about the brutal measures of the Bolsheviks in putting down the Kronstadt revolt, but surely that had been all right, the mere suppression of a handful of troublemakers, and what the authorities had done had been done "reluctantly." Then they had "erred on the side of tolerance and forbearance in the treatment of all the non-Bolshevik political parties," till these had become absolutely impossible and the Social Revolutionaries had taken a shot at Lenin. "It was in those tragic days that something snapped in the heart of the revolution. It began to lose its 'kindness' and forbearance." (These sentences do not sound much like Trotsky; and

the phrasing is perhaps that of the editor.) Lenin himself had been extremely indignant when the death penalty for soldiers had been repealed: "How can you expect to conduct a revolution without executions?" he demanded. "The line of development," Trotsky reflects (or Mr. Malamuth so formulates what he finds in Trotsky's notes), "from Soviet democracy and democratic centralism within the Bolshevik party itself to totalitarianism in both spheres is not always clearly traceable." But—as Trotsky will not admit, rather, as he cannot see—what happened was that Marxist authoritarianism combined with the Russian habit of despotism to give Russia a new, streamlined tyrant.

What life got to be like in Russia after Trotsky and the other old Bolsheviks had been exiled or suppressed you may find out from *I Chose Freedom,* by Victor Kravchenko (Scribner). I am sorry that I have left myself so little space to write about this hair-raising book. Kravchenko is the son of a revolutionary father and grew up on the revolution. He became an able engineer, was put in charge of important work, and finally rose to the top layer of officialdom. When, in the summer of 1943, he was sent to the United States to supervise the selection of metal goods under the lend-lease plan, he had already made up his mind to leave the service of the Soviet Union, and he did so nine months later. The reasons for this conclusion form the subject of a long and detailed narrative. *I Chose Freedom,* as a piece of writing, is not so remarkable as *One Who Survived,* Alexander Barmine's rather similar book, but at this moment it is a document of first-rate interest. It covers the familiar and gruesome ground of the collectivization and famine, of the chaos of Soviet industry, of the purges of the later thirties (which Kravchenko managed to survive, through months of third degree and torture, by steadfastly refusing to sign a bogus confession of sabotage.) But it gives also the first inside uncensored story of what has been happening in Moscow since the war, and a revelation of the workings of the Soviet Embassy, a small Moscow lodged in Washington, that is likely to cause a sensation. The picture of slave labor in the Soviet Union, where there were twenty million prisoners in 1938, is absolutely appalling and shows that in this respect Russia was no different from Nazi Germany, except that, as Kravchenko notes, the Germans enslaved foreign workers, whereas the Russians enslaved their own people.

Kravchenko insists that it is no thanks to Stalin that the Russians did such a good job on the Germans. Though the Russians had for years been led to believe that they would eventually have to fight the Nazis, they were left quite unprepared for the invasion. The Red Army and the Soviet factories had been demoralized and crippled by the purges, and Stalin himself put so fatuous a trust in the Soviet-Nazi pact that he would not even believe our State Department when it told him that the Germans were about to attack. Only the bravery and resourcefulness of the people and the equipment supplied by lend-lease saved a desperate situation.

Kravchenko was very much surprised at the extent to which Soviet Russia was idealized in the United States. "The prevailing American notions about the wonders of Sovietism in practice were truly extraordinary. Great chunks of the Communist reality . . . seemed to have completely escaped American attention. These were things of which everyone inside Russia was deeply conscious. Some of us might explain them as necessary or unavoidable or even noble, but it would not occur to us to *deny* them. Yet when I ventured to mention such things (at times when candid conversation was possible), Americans looked at me incredulously and some even hastened to enter cocksure denials. . . . In America today, I was to learn slowly and incredulously, those who venture to tell some truth about the Stalin tyranny, who speak up *for* the Russian people and against their oppressors, are discounted and dismissed and sometimes pilloried as 'anti-Russian.' I became aware that my resolve to escape into the free world and to use the freedom to defend my people would not be as simple as it had seemed at a distance. I realized that I must expect to be denounced and ridiculed by precisely those warmhearted and high-minded foreigners on whose understanding and support I had counted."

Åke Sandler (essay date 1953)

SOURCE: "Stalin and Hitler: A Lesson in Comparison," in *The Pacific Spectator,* Vol. VII, No. 2, Spring, 1953, pp. 152-66.

[*In the following essay, Sandler argues that Stalin's Soviet Union more closely resembled Hitler's Germany than the socialist society proposed by Karl Marx.*]

One day en route to Tiflis a guest of the Soviet government, André Gide, stopped at Gori, a small village where Josef Stalin was born. To the great French writer, who for years had followed the "experiment" in Russia with enthusiasm, the arrival in Gori was an occasion charged with emotional impact. Impulsively he decided to send the Russian leader a telegram expressing his gratitude for the lavish hospitality with which he had been treated.

At the post office Gide wrote out a message which began: "Passing through Gori on our wonderful trip I feel the impulse to send you—" The translator interrupted him with the information that the use of the address "you" was neither proper nor sufficient. He suggested as a better form of address, "You Lord of the people." Gide thought the suggestion absurd, for surely Stalin was not a vain man and did not need flattery, but to no avail. The translator was adamant.

This incident, which in other ways and situations has been experienced by other visitors to the Soviet Union, is suggestive of a prevailing concept of government that is fascist rather than communist in nature. It reveals an attitude of mind that is more akin to the *Führerprinzip* than to the idea of the dictatorship of the proletariat.

This is not a new discovery, but neither has it been given sufficient attention and emphasis. Rather, students of Russia are habitually but falsely regarding and treating present-day Russia as the product of a communist revolution, and its form of government as Marxist in origin and nature. Although discrepancies between communist theory and communist practice have been pointed out and although the anachronistic element in the Marxian dialectic has been recognized in explaining the Russian Revolution as the inevitable result of the historical process, many historians and political scientists and economists, by force of habit, indifference, or ignorance persist in treating the U.S.S.R. basically as a communist state.

We are not talking here about the technical and theoretical distinction between a "socialist" and a "communist" society but the much more fundamental difference between a state that calls itself, and is so labeled by many of us, a communist (or socialist) state and one that has no resemblance to or connection with communism, socialism, or any other form of Marxism. For the forms of government developed by Lenin and Stalin—particularly those of the latter—are no more the historical application of or continuation of Marxian concepts, the dialectic, the *Communist Manifesto,* or any other Marxian, socialist, or communist principle or program than was Hitler's or Mussolini's form of government. From its first motivating impulse, Leninism strayed from the Marxist road and employed non-Marxian means to obtain non-Marxian ends. The New Economic Policy is only one example of this departure from the main highway. Lenin was the first "deviationist," and under Stalin this "deviation" has turned into a complete abandonment and rejection of Marxism.

In reality, of course, the Russian revolutionaries never adhered, even from the outset, to the philosophy of Karl Marx. By their actions they became instead the forerunners of fascism, of Mussolini and Hitler. The Italian Duce and the German Führer, true followers of Lenin and Stalin, added ideas and methods of their own. These innovations and adjustments altered superficially the *form* and *system* of government, but the fundamental realities remained in substance the same, namely a political and economic organization based on the *Führerprinzip*, on the concept of one all-powerful, infallible personality. The modern version and perversion of Plato's philosopher-king, this Great Man (Russian, Italian, or German) moves unguided and unrestrained by law; possesses the two chief virtues of the statesman, Knowledge and Truth; and knows what is best for all concerned. Invariably he does what is right because Truth is on his side.

It was in 1903, at the Social Democratic Congress in Brussels, that Lenin took the step which ultimately led to a rejection of all egalitarian principles and the development of authoritarian ones with the leadership principle as the dominant one. For in that year the international Social Democratic movement was split into those who followed Lenin (Bolsheviks) and those who rejected his leadership (Mensheviks). Immediately thereafter, Lenin organized a revolutionary conspiracy of a small group of dedicated, fanatical, ruthless, and well-disciplined men and women, all of them personally loyal to their leader.

This group became the nucleus of the revolutionary "movement" and was largely responsible for plotting, rehearsing, and executing the October Revolution, which was no more than an enlarged Munich *Putsch*. The "proletarian" element of the Revolution was accidental and coincidental rather than the result of spontaneous social generation. A war-weary, bread-hungry, land-thirsty people assisted the conspirators unaware of their real designs. Lenin was after the only thing in history that has motivated would-be dictators: Power—power and control over what the British geopolitician Sir Halford Mackinder in 1904 (note the date) called the pivotal area or "the heartland," which constituted the core of the "world-island" (Europe, Asia, and Africa, which cover two-thirds of the world's land mass). From Mackinder, Lenin, who was a prodigious reader, had learned the aphorism: "Who rules East Europe commands the Heartland. Who rules the Heartland commands the World-Island. Who rules the World-Island commands the World."

Lenin and even more so his successor, Stalin, were engrossed in realizing ambitions of power and rule, not in carrying out a program of social justice and economic equality. Lenin had no detectable intention of transferring power to the proletariat in form of "a dictatorship of the proletariat" as envisioned and planned by Marx and Engels and, possibly, Trotsky, had the latter had an opportunity to do so; and Stalin not only followed in Lenin's footsteps but carried Lenin's ambitions to their logical conclusion: Absolute Power.

Ultimately this power, as it was accumulated and concentrated in the hands of one man, Josef Stalin, became indivisible and undelegatable; it could not and was not shared by anyone, whether it be the state, the party, or the proletariat; it had to be exclusive. This was the end result envisioned by fascism—but it was already an accomplished fact in Russia before it was realized in Germany under Hitler. It Italy, Mussolini never completely achieved this ultimate goal of dictators because he had to share his power with the Monarchy and the Church—a fact partially responsible for his "premature" undoing.

It is precisely because of the power motives stated above that communism and fascism—that Stalin and Hitler—are fruits off the same tree; these fruits may differ in form but not in substance; so-called "ideological differences" have amounted to nothing more than different shadings of color. Now that both men are dead, one might properly and without reverence for the dead contemplate their misdeeds and compare the master with his pupil to see what lesson can be derived from a comparison.

We shall refer to a man called Malenkov only in passing, as he might be nothing more than a passing phenomenon concealing the real and intense struggle for power that, I am sure, must be taking place behind the scenes; for if such a power struggle is not already going on, Soviet Russia has changed character suddenly (and I do not believe in that Darwinism-in-reverse called "Lysenkoism").

It was the power factor that united Stalin and Hitler in 1939 against what the German Foreign Minister von Ribbentrop called "the unforgiving enemies of both National Socialist Germany and of the U.S.S.R.," thereby precipitating World War II. It is clear from the following declaration by Von Ribbentrop, made on August 14, 1939, and included in a Department of State publication called *Nazi-Soviet Relations 1939-1941*, that a union of interests between Germany and Russia was not only possible but desirable.

> The ideological contradictions between National Socialist Germany and the Soviet Union were in past years the sole reason why Germany and the U.S.S.R stood opposed to each other in two separate and hostile camps. The developments of the recent period seem to show that differing world outlooks do not prohibit a reasonable relationship between the two states, and the restoration of cooperation of a new and friendly type. The period of opposition in foreign policy can be brought to an end once and for all and the way lies open for a new sort of future for both countries.

To this invitation to co-operate, Soviet Foreign Minister Molotov responded that "the Soviet Government warmly welcomed German intentions of improving relations with the Soviet Union. . . ." Nine days later when the friendship pact with Russia was signed in Moscow in the presence of Von Ribbentrop, Molotov, and Stalin, the German Foreign Minister said that "all strata of the German people, and especially the simple people ["proletarians"], most warmly welcomed the understanding with the Soviet Union. The people, he said, felt instinctively that between Germany and the Soviet Union no natural conflicts of interests existed, and that the development of good relations had hitherto been disturbed only by foreign intrigue, in particular on the part of England.

Stalin replied that he "readily believed this," and "spontaneously proposed a toast to the Führer: 'I know how much the German nation loves its Führer; I should therefore like to drink to his health.'" He added: "The Soviet Government takes the new Pact very seriously." He said he "could guarantee on his word of honor that the Soviet Union would not betray its partner."

In November 1940 when Molotov conferred with Hitler in Germany, the latter confirmed his belief that friendly cooperation between his country and the Soviet Union was possible inasmuch as they "had at their helm men who possessed sufficient authority to commit their countries to a development in a definite direction." He stressed that they "need not by nature have any conflict of interests, if each nation understood that the other required certain vital necessities without the guarantee of which its existence was impossible." He believed that Russia and Germany could "achieve a settlement between them, which would lead to peaceful collaboration between the two countries beyond the life span of the present leaders."

Less than a year later Russia and Germany were at war with one another. Stalin provoked. Hitler attacked. That Hitler was a "fascist" and Stalin a "communist" was immaterial and irrelevant. Their falling out was the result of their failure to agree on how to divide the spoils of power. Just as they could not share their power with anyone at home, so they could not share their power with anyone abroad. Hitler and Stalin fought each other for that reason alone and not because of political, economic, or ideological differences.

Stalin's concept of international relations, as has been revealed on many occasions, was purely Machiavellian; it was not based on the solidarity of the working class in all countries, nor on Marx's and Trotsky's idea of world revolution, nor on the idea of "socialism in one country first," but on principles of power politics. His conduct of foreign affairs was totally unrelated to the purposes, aims, plans, and motives of international communism, with which it might accidentally coincide. His actions abroad were calculated on the basis of (1) what served his interests best and (2) what served the interests of his country, which he regarded as his own property. The power politics of the Soviet Union in no substantial way differs from that of Nazi Germany. While Hitler's foreign policy has been described as "panther imperialism" because of the Führer's catlike way of springing on his foes without warning, Stalin's has been called "jackal imperialism" because of the Soviet leader's natural habit of waiting till the victim was dying or had died before he devoured it. Sometimes he might actually attack a victim—Finland, for example—which was too small and too weak to defend itself effectively. But in most cases he proceeded as he did in Poland—let someone else do the job and then reaped the harvest of victory. Or as he did in Korea. His "liberation" of the Baltic States and the Balkans was only a further example of Machiavellian "Marxism."

Stalin's admiration for Hitler, which he expressed upon several occasions, was one tyrant's admiration for another. *Asinus asinam fricat.* In his own judgment, he differed from Hitler only in his superior ability and keener comprehension of the business of power politics. He told Anthony Eden that Hitler did not know when to stop. Stalin, by inference, knew when to stop, when to begin, when to stop again, and when to begin again. The "cold war" may well be an application of this idea. Witness, for example, the new "peace offensive" which began in March. No one knows when or how it will end—or when it will begin again. Similarly, frequent changes in outlook, when forced upon an individual, would tend to make him neurotic. It may be that states, too, become neurotic under such "psycho-ceramic" (crackpot) treatment. This tactic has had the effect of largely blotting out the differences between "peace" and "war," thereby confusing our concepts and leading to the bizarre circumstances wherein we have been, in one very real sense,

actually at war—shooting war (Korea)—with the Soviet Union and in another sense, equally real to us, at peace with Russia in Europe. To Stalin war was diplomacy by other means; but "peace" was also diplomacy by other means (than war), to reverse Clausewitz' maxim. The so-called "peace appeals" which he issued from time to time derived from the latter concept. Like a true Machiavellian he made no distinction between "peace" and "war," except as being different attributes of diplomacy or power politics.

To assume as do our naïve native Communists and their advisers that there were any idealistic undertones in Stalin's "diplomacy," to equate reality with ideals, hopes, and visions long ago vanished—all this is the height of quixotic irony. No man posing in the cloak of a statesman was ever more void of idealism than Stalin. With Churchill, he has been described as a "realist." But compared to Stalin's "realism," Churchill's is blue-eyed idealism. This was brought out at the Yalta Conference, where Stalin discussed the problems of a bleeding mankind with unhuman unsentimentality; Churchill revealed his human "weakness" when, while speaking of the future of the small states, he said: "The eagle should let the small birds sing and care not wherefor they sang," while at an after-dinner snack in his private apartment in the Kremlin, Stalin, without noticeable emotion, told Churchill how he had "liquidated" millions of Kulaks. It was only a matter of statistics. No wonder Churchill called Stalin "a man completely free of illusions"—meaning, I suppose, a man without ideals or human sentiment.

Yet the Russians more than other people pride themselves on their "understanding" of small peoples. It is paradoxical that while Russia in 1939 was "negotiating" with her small neighbor Finland over land concessions to Russia, concessions the Finnish people refused to grant, with Soviet aggression resulting, A. I. Mikoyan, a member of the Politburo, now the Presidium, told one of the Finnish negotiators, Vaino Tanner: "Stalin is a Georgian, I am an Armenian, and many others among us belong to small peoples. We understand the position of small people well." He implied that without this "understanding," much larger concessions would have been exacted from Finland.

What Stalin's real position in Russia was has not been examined properly, nor has his permanent "monarchical" role in Soviet life been fully appreciated. Indeed, many so-called "serious" students of the Soviet government—I do not exclude myself—have behaved like the people in Hans Christian Andersen's "The Emperor's New Clothes": They thought the emperor was dressed in a dazzling uniform when in reality he was naked. It took the eyes of a child to disclose this fact. So, let us look at this recently "expired" Russian "emperor" through the eyes of a child.

Dr. Ley, head of the Nazi Labor Front, said of Hitler that he was Germany and that Germany was Hitler. Malenkov has not to my knowledge said that Stalin was Russia and that Russia was Stalin, although as the temporary or permanent successor (more likely the former), he has paid the tribute of a primitive votary to the god whose place he would like to take and will take if his career is not cut short by *force majeure*—the usual malady of tyrants. The reason is not that Stalin was not so regarded by those around him and by the Russian people. But such allusions were discouraged and possibly forbidden because it was felt they would sound too much like Hitlerism. The Russians have had other ways of expressing practically the same concept. Constant reiteration of his great virtues, ideals, and accomplishments at the slightest pretext and in every conceivable situation and the lavish, slavish display of his picture blown up to enormous proportions and paraded on a thousand and one occasions instilled in the Russian people essentially the same feeling for their Führer that Dr. Ley sought to convey to the German people by his sublimely ridiculous reference.

The most convincing illustration of Stalin's incarnation in the flesh of "Mother Russia" was the divine appearance of the ruler of all Russians at the May Day parade in the Red Square, when he took his place on top of Lenin's Tomb and his chieftains grouped around him in accordance with their importance at the moment. He remained a fixed star, but his chieftains—like satellites—never kept their old positions for long, and would sometimes even disappear from sight, all depending on their fortunes.

An examination of a picture of those assembled on Lenin's Tomb gave one an idea of the hierarchal nature of a despotic regime falsely labeled "government." This picture showed better than anything the clear and present manifestation of the *Führerprinzip* in all its rawness and in stark contrast to the teachings of Marx and Engels on whose teachings, by the way (and we want to make this clear!) we are not here passing judgment. The author, it must be understood, is in no way advocating or defending Marxism, whatever its totalitarian form. He merely insists that any resemblance between Marxism and the Soviet system is to a large degree coincidental.

By way of comparison, Lenin for all his prestige was never so far removed in terms of power from his colleagues in the party as was Stalin from his. Nietzsche spoke of "the pathos of the distance"—meaning the distance in power and prestige. That "distance" was far greater between Stalin and his associates than it ever was in Lenin's days. Although a Trotsky, a Stalin, and a Zinoviev looked upon Lenin as their rightful and acknowledged leader, they were for all practical purposes his equals. At least there was more equality than inequality in the top echelons of those days. Trotsky and Stalin exercised real authority, possessed genuine responsibility, exerted tangible power within their own jurisdictions—Trotsky over military affairs, Stalin over party matters.

Stalin's "men" have had no real power of their own—and still do not. This is true even of Malenkov, who has already proceeded to divide the little power he has. All the power they possessed was delegated power—delegated by Stalin as a reward for loyal service. This power was not something Stalin gave up; it could always be retrieved; and on numerous occasions he reclaimed the power he delegated, sometimes with the death of those who held this temporary power. Like Hitler he could at will promote, demote, remove, and dispose of party and state officials of seemingly the highest prominence and the finest reputations. Witness, for example, his treatment of Marshal Tukhashevsky, chief of staff, who, following a rigged trial, was put to death. His "crime" was identical with that committed by Stalin himself a few years later: Nazi collaborationism. This "crime," of course, was a mere pretext for removing a man who, unfortunately for him, had become too popular, too influential. The *Führerprinzip* tolerates no competitor.

Absolute as Stalin's power was, he varied his use of it according to the place, the circumstance, the individual, and his own personal need—with the result that his inflictions ranged from mild criticism to violent death. In the case of Maxim Litvinov, to take an example from the opposite end of the power scale, Stalin was content with demoting the man and promoting another, Molotov, for two reasons primarily: (1) Litvinov was a Jew (he needed a non-Jew to make the deal with the Nazis); (2) Molotov was less "Western-minded."

Actually it is doubtful if anyone in Russia ever asked for real authority. So much fear was instilled by this one man that few dared to challenge his authority. Not a single member of the Politburo, the most powerful policy organ in Russia, ever suggested that he might be or ought to be Stalin's successor. Nearly every Soviet Communist from time to time was mentioned as a potential heir, but such speculation showed that Stalin's power was personal and that it was the only concrete reality in the Soviet Union. Being indivisible, it could not be shared, nor delegated, nor inherited, nor given away.

Hitler solved the problem of succession by publicly designating his successors: first Göring, then Hess, and then Goebbels—one, two, three, in that order. Why did not Stalin do the same? Because as a despot he was much more clever than Hitler was. As a true Machiavellian, he trusted no one but himself; and he had seen the case histories of tyrants who had violated this rule of Machiavelli and disappeared. He saw what happened to Hitler, betrayed by his number-one successor, Hermann Göring, who, during the final stages of the war, quite uselessly usurped Hitler's power. Outwardly Stalin might care what happened to Russia after he died. He might speak and act as though the future—the future that would exist without him—would be of great importance. But in all likelihood he believed with Louis XV: *"Après moi le déluge."*

Ultimately (as was true of Hitler), the Russian dictator's power rested on brute force or, more precisely, on the Soviet secret police. Prestige, respect, veneration, loyalty, and personal allegiance carried him a long way. Remove his secret police, and the prestige he enjoyed would no longer have been enough. It would not have protected him from ambitious men who sought his crown, for they had been taught to live by the laws of the jungle, where the weak are the prey of the strong.

Men who rule by brute force are often destroyed by the same force that keeps them in power. Force is always an erratic and unreliable element in power politics, as many dictators have found out, from Caesar to Mussolini. "Bayonets are good for many things," Talleyrand said, "except to sit on." If eternal vigilance is the price a free people has to pay for its freedom, constant command and control of the sources and resources of force is the price despots have to pay to keep their peoples enslaved. Mussolini told Emil Ludwig he knew how to avoid the pitfalls of dictators. He would never, he boasted, die at the hand of an assassin. And Hitler thought he led a charmed life, that he was immune to that fatal malady that frequently, suddenly, and happily takes tyrants from us at an unexpected turn of history—a visitation we must bear with equanimity.

Mussolini and Hitler both met violent deaths. Why was Stalin an exception? Or was he? The medical reports sounded convincing, but so did Lenin's. Few students of Russia now doubt that Stalin "helped" his chief across the "line." It is not inconceivable that there may have been those who were willing to give Stalin similar "assistance"—perhaps just as another purge was about to "get" them.

If this indisputably Great Tyrant escaped assassination, it was due in part, I think, to the efficiency of the MVD—an organization far more effective than the Gestapo; in part to the fact that assassins are few in the U.S.S.R.—fewer even than they were in Hitler's Third Reich; and in part to the fact that Stalin, for all his tyranny, was accepted, taken for granted, and even liked by millions. I am thoroughly convinced that he was more loved than hated by his people; that, in fact, most Russians looked upon him as their father and protector, accepted his leadership and followed him wherever he took them, in peace and in war.

This philosophy of politics is possible only in a country where the price of freedom is astronomical; where there exists no libertarian tradition; where the people have no standards against which to measure their freedoms and rights; and where rights and freedoms are entirely expendable. For such people collective obedience comes naturally, and Lenin and Stalin, when they took over, were faced with no problem in this respect, as the Russians for generations under the czars had grown accustomed to obeying.

In one of his essays on liberty Bertrand Russell quotes a Russian to the effect that the people of Russia need none of the "external" freedoms that seem so indispensable to the English and the Americans because the Russians have "free souls" whereas the souls of these Western peoples are in a strait jacket and consequently have need of "external" freedoms. Dostoevski would probably have agreed with this observation; in fact he might have first made it. And because of a preoccupation with their souls the Russians, like the Germans, have overlooked their minds. Or, more to the point, they have scorned the free mind. In two countries otherwise dissimilar—Russia and Germany—the concept, the ideal, and the practice of freedom have been strangely similar for more than four hundred years. Their contempt for unhindered freedom as we understand it in the West has been vehement. I refer, of course, to individual freedom, the only kind of freedom the West truly cherishes. Fear of power in the West has been as strong as indifference to individual freedom in Germany and Russia. Only in the West could the maxim have been born that power corrupts and absolute power corrupts absolutely. And only in the West could effective measures have been taken to thwart the ambitions of would-be dictators.

Russians must have found it difficult to comprehend a President of the United States compelled by a court of the country to surrender powers he thought he possessed. Even more incredible must have been the President's acceptance of the court's verdict with little or no "loss of face"! If reported at all in the Soviet press, all this must have been attributed to "democratic insanity." In Russia it could not happen.

The concept of unconsolidated power, if understood at all, would be repugnant to the Russians. The very possibility of having power split three ways into various departments or compartments would seem preposterous to them. Government and dictatorship are synonymous to them, and the possibility of a great many people sharing power of decision in important matters of state would be laughable—just as it has been laughable to the Germans. In a way the Germans killed their democracy—what there was of it in the Weimar Republic—by ridicule and scorn. When Hitler told them how he sat in the Vienna Reichstag and watched the ludicrous proceedings on the floor, how they "talked and talked," millions of Germans laughed with him. Democracy became a hilarious joke, and *Der Stürmer* and other Nazi publications poked fun in their caricatures at that asinine phenomenon called democracy.

The Russians could not laugh democracy out of existence as the Germans did because they have never experienced it. But as it was described to them by their leaders, by the party, and by the press, democracy appeared as a proposition deserving contempt.

The concept of delegated authority was particularly inconceivable to them. When visiting Moscow on his several wartime missions, Harry Hopkins found that no one in the government, whether an important civilian or military functionary—not even a marshal of the Soviet Union—could speak or dared to speak with finality on any subject. Each referred again and again to Stalin as the only man who could speak with authority.

The usefulness of Stalin's associates depended not on the authority they possessed, nor on their capability, but on their loyalty to Stalin personally. He had built his party and state on the basis of personal loyalty. This was not the way Lenin wanted it. Before his death Lenin warned his associates against Stalin. But the Georgian, thanks to Trotsky's attitude in taking personal succession for granted, succeeded in putting his own men in key positions. By the time the enfeebled Lenin was proposing "to find a way of removing" Stalin, the Georgian was already entrenched, and Trotsky's "magnetic personality," "electrifying oratory," and "spellbinding influence" were of no use.

Leon Trotsky never was given an opportunity to prove whether his brand of communism would have become less tyrannical than Stalin's, but what he predicted before the Revolution, what he did during the Revolution, and what he criticized after the Revolution convinces at least this writer that his critique of Stalin was dictated not so much by his concern for "pure" communism as by his bitter disillusionment over his personal failure to take the place in Russian history and in world history to which, as Lenin's "natural" heir, he thought himself entitled. It was not until his break with his chief rival for Lenin's mantle that he spoke of the "betrayal" of the Revolution. All available evidence strongly suggests that he might have "betrayed" it himself had he, not Stalin, succeeded Lenin. At any rate, an objective student of communist Russia is not justified in concluding that Trotsky and his policies would have been less dangerous to democracy and Western civilization than Stalin has been. On the contrary, because of his greater shrewdness and fanatical dogmatism he might have become an even greater peril than Stalin, especially had he been able to drape his intentions in a camouflage of "pure" communism.

With his only serious rival for Lenin's mantle out of the way, Stalin dedicated himself to the only task worthy of his complete attention—namely, to make his position of power so impregnable that neither man nor event could unseat him. By 1937 he had his first real test of strength. His second came in 1941. Not only did he survive the Nazi invasion and defeat Hitler, but he emerged from this calamity far more powerful—and as a result, far more ruthless, far more tyrannical—than he had been before. And, *mirabile dictu*, we saluted him, greeted him as our friend, and treated him as a man of honor.

This was the man whom Franklin Roosevelt and Winston Churchill referred to as "Uncle Joe," and whom Harry Truman even after the cold war had begun described as "a prisoner of the Politburo." It was said that we could "reason" with Stalin; he seemed receptive to our point of view. He might not always agree with us, but he seemed like an "agreeable" sort of person—an impression that Harold Stassen brought back from his interview with Stalin in 1947. In this interview Stalin spoke of the "will to co-operate," and Stassen—our new Mutual Security Administrator—recorded and reported it as though he earnestly and sincerely believed he was dealing with a sensible man not very different from himself.

The recent purges of Jews in Russia and in the satellites were only one more demonstration of the close spiritual kinship between the Communists and Nazis.

Hitler was our enemy at a time when Stalin was our friend, and yet there was no moral difference between the two; one was as evil as the other, and their systems were equally repugnant. There was no moral difference between Buchenwald and Katyn Forest; between the killing of Jews and the slaughter of Kulaks; between the Nazi purges of 1934 and the Communist purges of 1936; between the systematic terror of the Third Reich and the terroristic system of the Union of the Soviet Socialist Republics; between the psychopathology of one dictator and the pathological psychology of the other; between the "mass" philosophy contained in Hitler's statement, "The German has not the slightest notion how a people must be misled if the adherence of the masses is sought," and that displayed in Stalin's "one must not lag behind a movement, because to do so is to become isolated from the masses"; between NKVD and Gestapo; between the rape of Czechoslovakia and the rape of Finland; between the Berlin-Rome axis and the Moscow-Peiping axis; between *Foundations of Leninism* and *Mein Kampf*. They are all fruits off the same tree; and by their fruits ye shall know them.

Ronald L. Meek (essay date 1953)

SOURCE: "Stalin as an Economist," in *The Review of Economic Studies*, Vol. XXI, No. 56, 1953-54, pp. 232-39.

[In the following essay, Meek examines Stalin's economic theory.]

Whenever great changes in basic economic and social institutions are brought about, the theoreticians of the new order begin seeking to express its experience in generalised form. And sometimes—but only very rarely—it happens that the political leaders who usher in the changes are themselves men with a taste for theoretical generalisation, in which case both the new order and the theory of the new order may come to be constructed under the guidance of one and the same hand. This was the position with Joseph Stalin.

Stalin's work in building the theoretical foundations proceeded more or less concurrently with his direction of the work of "building socialism". In part, it took the negative form of criticism of various economic theories which in Stalin's opinion were inappropriate to the new conditions.[1] And in part, it took the positive form of the systematic expression of new concepts and theoretical propositions designed to illuminate the essential character of the new society which finally took shape in the U.S.S.R. in the 'thirties. An article in *Bolshevik* on **"Economic Problems of Socialism in the U.S.S.R.",**[2] published a few months before his death, represents the culmination of Stalin's work in this field.[3]

The immediate occasion for the publication of Stalin's article was a conference of Soviet economists held at the end of 1951 to discuss the first draft of a new textbook on political economy. In form, the article consists of a set of "Remarks" on various questions which came up at this conference, together with a number of replies to individual economists who had criticised Stalin's views. But the significance of the article is obviously much wider than its form and the immediate occasion for its appearance might at first sight suggest. The question with which Stalin is primarily concerned—the nature and content of the economic laws which operate under socialism in the U.S.S.R.—appears on the surface to be fairly remote from policy issues. But in no society, and least of all in the U.S.S.R., can the discussion of such a question really be divorced from considerations of practical policy. Stalin's statements about the economic laws of socialism in the U.S.S.R. are also, inevitably, statements about contemporary economic policies and opinions in the U.S.S.R. and about the policies to be adopted in the future. For this reason, even if for no other, Stalin's article deserves the closest scrutiny by economists in the West. The aim of what follows is to discuss selected passages from Stalin's article which may be of interest to Western economists.

I. THE CHARACTER OF ECONOMIC LAWS UNDER SOCIALISM

Echoes of several well-known Soviet economic debates of the inter-war years are to be found in Stalin's article.[4] But in essence the article represents the culmination of one particular controversy of the decade just past which hitherto had been carried on largely behind the scenes. Controversy had centred around a viewpoint first consistently expounded in an article of 1943 on **"The Teaching of Political Economy in the Soviet Union"** which caused a considerable amount of speculation in the West at the time.[5] The basic thesis was that the economic laws of socialism "in their character, content, (and) method of action are fundamentally different from the economic laws of capitalism".[6] In particular, it was argued that it was "quite un-Marxist" to think that "only those laws can be considered economic laws which manifest themselves independently of man's will and consciousness."[7] In view of the unique role played by the state in the U.S.S.R., activities such as "industrialisation," "collectivisation" and "planning," it was said, must be regarded as "laws of the socialist development of our society."[8] The article as a whole gave the impression that the author was trying to extend the concept of economic law under socialism so as to embrace the conscious actions of the state and planning bodies. Certainly this was the meaning read into it by many Soviet economists. N. Voznesensky, then the head of the Soviet planning organisation, affirmed (in a book which gained a Stalin Prize in 1947) that "the state plan has the force of a law of economic development. . . . Socialist planning, based on the rational utilization and application of the economic laws of production and distribution, is in itself a social law of development and as such a subject of political economy."[9]

In Stalin's last article, this whole thesis is decisively rejected. The economic laws of socialism, Stalin affirms, possess exactly the same objective character and operate in exactly the same way as the economic laws of capitalism. The *content* of the laws specific to socialism and to capitalism certainly differs,[10] but not the *character* of these laws as such. "The laws of political economy," says Stalin, "whether in the period of capitalism or in the period of socialism . . . are objective laws, reflecting processes of economic development which take place independently of the will of man."[11] It is quite wrong to argue that "in view of the specific role assigned to the Soviet state by history, the Soviet state and its leaders can abolish existing laws of political economy and can 'form,' 'create,' new laws."[12] To argue thus is simply to confuse the "laws" of science with the "laws" issued by governments. Thus "socialist planning" is not in fact "a social law of development," as Voznesensky and others had maintained. There does exist, it is true, a certain objective economic law of socialism—the "law of balanced, proportionate development of the national economy"—of which the yearly and five-yearly economic plans are (or ought to be)[13] a reflection. But the plans themselves must on no account be confused with the law.[14]

It is tempting to consider this rejection by Stalin of the 1943 thesis solely in terms of a victory of common sense over confusion—which, in large part, it undoubtedly is. The problem of the character and method of operation of economic laws under socialism is by no means an easy one to solve. In essence, the 1943 thesis was the expression in the field of economic theory of an over-abundant confidence in the power of the Soviet system to overcome all obstacles standing in its way. It reflected a feeling, natural enough at the end of the war, that the Soviet government could do anything it set its mind to in the economic sphere—that it could, in fact, virtually make its own economic laws.[15] Stalin's attack on this idea—in terms which are sometimes reminiscent of his much earlier **"Dizzy with Success"** article[16]—does indeed represent a victory of common sense over confusion, or, more specifically, a victory of realism over "adventurism". But this does not fully explain why the trend of ideas inspired by the 1943 article was considered sufficiently important in 1952 to call for one of Stalin's carefully rationed interventions. It seems reasonable to suggest that the 1943 thesis must have become closely associated with the advocacy of some particular economic policy which eventually came to be regarded as unrealistic and "adventurist."

One must beware here of proceeding too far into the realms of pure speculation, but it seems at least possible that this policy difference, if it did in fact exist, related mainly to the question of agricultural organisation. Stalin is concerned to emphasise that the continued existence of the collective-farm sector (in which the product is produced and disposed of by the individual collective farms rather than by the state) side by side with the state sector, implies, among other things, that obstacles are set up to "the full extension of government planning to the whole of the national economy, especially agriculture."[17]

Eventually, therefore, collective-farm property must be "raised to the level of public property." How, then, is this task to be carried out? Stalin's solution (to be further discussed below) visualises a series of *gradual* transitions operating over a fairly long period of time. And it seems possible that this solution may in recent years have won a victory over certain alternative solutions, more radical in character, which perhaps visualised a much more *sudden* transition, similar in character to that "revolution from above" by means of which mass collectivisation was originally effected. Certainly Stalin goes out of his way on several occasions to criticise, expressly and by implication, the proposals made by "some comrades" "to nationalise collective-farm property, to proclaim it public property, in the way that was done in the past in the case of capitalist property."[18]

It is with more radical policy proposals of this type, then, that the 1943 thesis may have become associated. Certainly the thesis would at least have *encouraged* the advocacy of such proposals. If the Soviet government can "do anything," if it can make its own economic laws, why should it not raise collective-farm property to the level of public property at one stroke? If "collectivisation" is a "law of socialist development," why should not "nationalisation of collective farms" also be a "law"—to be carried out in a similar manner? Stalin's intervention may have been called for, then, not only because the 1943 thesis was confused and unrealistic, but also because it was encouraging the advocacy of an over-hasty and adventurist policy towards the peasantry.[19]

II. COMMODITY PRODUCTION, THE LAW OF VALUE AND THE TRANSITION TO COMMUNISM

Stalin's discussion of the economic laws of socialism is based on the assumption that the form of economic relationship at present existing between the town and the country in the U.S.S.R. will continue to exist substantially unaltered for some time. The transformation of collective-farm property into public property is visualised as a gradual process stretching over a fairly long period. The first thing which Stalin has to do, therefore, is to provide a set of theoretical concepts capable of dealing with a form of socialist society, not specifically envisaged by Marx and Engels, in which a state sector and a collective-farm sector continue for some time to exist side by side.

The key passage here is the following:

> To-day there are two basic forms of socialist production in our country: state, or publicly-owned production, and collective-farm production, which cannot be said to be publicly owned. In the state enterprises, the means of production and the product of production are national property. In the collective farm, although the means of production (land, machines) do belong to the state, the product of production is the property of the different collective farms, since the labour, as well as the seed, is their own, while the land, which has been turned over to the collective farms in perpetual

tenure, is used by them virtually as their own property, in spite of the fact that they cannot sell, buy, lease or mortgage it.

> The effect of this is that the state disposes only of the product of the state enterprises, while the product of the collective farms, being their property, is disposed of only by them. But the collective farms are unwilling to alienate their products except in the form of commodities, in exchange for which they desire to receive the commodities they need. At present the collective farms will not recognise any other economic relation with the town except the commodity relation— exchange through purchase and sale. Because of this, commodity production and trade are as much a necessity with us to-day as they were thirty years ago, say, when Lenin spoke of the necessity of developing trade to the utmost.[20]

The most interesting feature of this passage is Stalin's use of the Marxian concepts of "commodity" and "commodity relation" to describe the existing state of affairs in the U.S.S.R. "Commodities," in the Marxian sense, are those products of labour which are produced not for the personal use of the producers but for exchange through sale and purchase. Commodity production requires two main conditions: first, separate ownership of such of the means of production, or such separate rights of productive use over them, as are necessary to provide a basis upon which productive activity can be carried on by more or less independent units; and, second, separate ownership of the products of this activity. "Only such products can become commodities with regard to each other," Marx wrote, "as result from different kinds of labour, each kind being carried on independently and for the account of private individuals."[21] A "commodity relation" is the basic socio-economic relation which exists between the producers of "commodities" (as so defined) and which is reflected in the relations manifested between the commodities themselves in the markets where they are exchanged. What Stalin is doing is to apply this concept of a "commodity relation" to the existing economic relationships between the collective-farm sector and the state sector in the U.S.S.R. to-day (and also, by implication, to the relationships between the separate productive units within the collective-farm sector). The collective farms, although they do not actually own the land on which they work, have been granted separate rights of productive use over it, and on this basis they carry on productive activity more or less independently, each unit having a substantial degree of freedom to decide what it is going to produce and on which of the available markets it is going to sell its surplus. Thus the surplus products of the collective farms (and private plots), and the manufactured goods for which they are directly or indirectly exchanged, are alike *commodities*, and the relation between their producers is essentially a *commodity relation*.[22]

This analysis is primarily intended as a prelude to Stalin's consideration of the operation of the "law of value" in the U.S.S.R. For according to Marxian political economy, "wherever commodities and commodity production exist, there the law of value must also exist."[23] The "law of value" sums up those economic forces which (according to Marx) regulate the prices of "commodities" and the allocation of resources to their production. Broadly speaking, the leading idea behind Marx's theory is that the basic socio-economic relationships existing between the producers of commodities generate certain "objective necessities" which assert themselves decisively in the process whereby the exchange-ratios of these commodities on the market are determined.[24] Typically (but not universally) these "necessities" manifest themselves by bringing it about that exchange-ratios are broadly determined, directly or indirectly, by embodied-labour ratios.

Now it was formerly believed by many Marxists that the "law of value" could apply only in pre-socialist forms of society. It was often said that in a socialist society, where productive activity was consciously controlled by the state, exchange-ratios would be regulated not by the law of value but simply by the decisions of the planning authority. Behind such statements there usually lay the assumption, express or implied, that the victory of socialism would mean the abolition of commodity production within a relatively short space of time. Socialism in the U.S.S.R., however, differs in certain important respects from the typical Marxian model, and, if Stalin is correct, a form of commodity production still exists there. Does the law of value, then, continue to exist and operate? It does indeed, says Stalin. The fact that certain goods are still produced as commodities in the U.S.S.R. means that (within certain definite limits) the exchange-ratios of these goods are determined by economic forces which are to some extent outside the control of the planning authority. The degree to which the law of value operates as a regulator of exchange-ratios will of course vary from market to market, and it is evident that in general it will have very much less influence in the U.S.S.R. than in Western countries. But Stalin is obviously more concerned with the danger of under-estimating its influence in the U.S.S.R. than with that of over-estimating it. "Our business executives and planners," he writes, "with few exceptions, are poorly acquainted with the operations of the law of value, do not study them, and are unable to take account of them in their computations"; and he goes on to give a horrific example of what he calls "the confusion that still reigns in the sphere of price-fixing policy."[25] What he appears to be saying here, in essence, is that in so far as the prices of commodities are fixed by the state, they must be fixed with careful reference to what we in the West might call the "economic realities." The prices of commodities cannot be fixed arbitrarily: incentives which depend upon them must be preserved (particularly in agriculture), and the general balance of the economy maintained.

But the law of value, according to Stalin, is not a universal law: like the state, it is eventually destined to wither away. "Value," says Stalin, "like the law of value, is a historical category connected with the existence of commodity production. With the disappearance of commodity production, value and its forms and the law of value also disappear."[26] And commodity production will finally disappear only when "instead of the two basic production sectors, the state sector and the collective-farm sector, there will be only one all-embracing production sector, with the right to dispose of all the consumer goods produced in the country."[27] How is this end to be achieved? Stalin, as we have seen, sets his face strongly against any form of action which might be construed by the collective farmers as "expropriation." Instead, he advocates a long-term policy of "gradual transitions carried out to the advantage of the collective farms."[28] The first step, he argues, should be an extension of the system of "products-exchange" or "merchandising." The rudiments of products-exchange which at present exist in the U.S.S.R. do not appear to amount to much more than forward contracts for the sale of the whole crop, the payment consisting not only of money but also of a certain quantity of consumer goods. Stalin's idea seems to be that "as the products of the town multiply" these rudiments should be extended and developed into "a broad system, under which the collective farms would receive for their products not only money, but also and chiefly the manufactures they need."[29] Apparently the differential advantages of products-exchange contracts with the state are considerable, and Stalin evidently assumes that as the state offers more and more of them all the surplus produce of agriculture will gradually come into its hands. At the same time "a single *national* economic body (comprising representatives of state industry and of the collective farms)" is to be set up, "with the right at first to keep account of all consumer product in the country, and eventually also to distribute it, by way, say, of products-exchange."[30] What happens after that is left a little vague (no doubt deliberately), but Stalin apparently envisages that as a result of the strengthening of the ties between the collective farms and the state, the increase of productivity in both town and country, and the extension of communist education, the collective farms will be more and more prepared to accept state direction of their productive activities, so that eventually the "single national economic body" will become merged in that "one all-embracing production sector" which appears at the moment as the ultimate aim. When this stage has been reached, commodity production, and therefore the reign of the law of value, will finally cease.[31]

At this point it should perhaps be noted in passing that the "measures for the further development of agriculture in the U.S.S.R." promulgated in September, 1953, on the basis of a report by Kruschev, although they make no mention of Stalin's **Economic Problems,** clearly come within the framework of general attitudes outlined in that work. Stalin was concerned above all to emphasise (*a*) that the collective-farm system was "already beginning to hamper the powerful development of our productive forces"[32]; (*b*) that remedial measures in the countryside must not depart from the principle of material incentives; and (*c*) that each collective-farm household has *as its personal property* a subsidiary husbandry, a dwelling-house, livestock, etc.[33] The main emphases in Kruschev's report are very much the same: agriculture is lagging behind heavy industry; the principle of material incentive has been ignored in certain branches of agriculture; and there has been excessive pressure on the private plot. It is true that there is no mention in Kruschev's report of the broad system of products-exchange (which, as Stalin said, should be introduced "without any particular hurry, and only as the products of the town multiply"[34]);but there is little doubt that Stalin's article was intended to lay the theoretical basis for economic changes of the general type of those indicated in the report. The same can be said of the recent change of emphasis from heavy industry to light industry and the food industry. Stalin said in the **Economic Problems** that primacy should continue to be given to heavy industry,[35] but at the same time he went out of his way, in his discussion of the "basic economic law of socialism" and (more specifically) in his reply to Yaroshenko, to point out very emphatically that production is not an end in itself, but merely a means to the end of increasing the output of consumer goods.[36] In addition, his statement that the requirements of "the law of balanced (proportionate) development of the national economy" are not "fully reflected by our yearly and five-yearly plans"[37] takes on a new significance in the light of recent changes. Finally, mention should also be made in this connection of Stalin's argument that the struggle of the capitalist countries for markets, and their desire to crush their competitors, may at present prove to be stronger in practice than the "contradictions" between the capitalist and socialist camps"[38]—a statement which must have helped appreciably to create the new atmosphere in which the present economic changes are taking place.

Stalin's analysis of the conditions of agricultural development in the U.S.S.R. is directly linked with his interesting account of the preconditions of the transition from socialism to communism.[39] Communism will not be possible, he argues, until "collective-farm property (is raised) to the level of public property."[40] In his discussion of the transition, Stalin is primarily concerned to combat the idea that communism is just around the corner—that "it is only necessary to organise the productive forces rationally, and the transition to communism will take place without particular difficulty."[41] It is not such a simple matter as some comrades imagine, says Stalin—and in particular it is not just a *technical* matter. It is true that a continuous expansion of all social production will be required, in order to produce an abundance of products. But "neither an abundance of products, capable of covering all the requirements of society, nor the transition to the formula, 'to each according to his needs,' can be brought about if such economic factors as collective-farm, group, property, commodity circulation, etc., remain in force."[42] And, as a third precondition, it is also necessary to bring about a great cultural advance, which will require a shortening of the working day to five hours, a radical improvement in housing conditions, and at least a doubling of real wages. This is clearly a much more sober and realistic blueprint than many which have been drawn up by writers in the U.S.S.R. (and elsewhere) in recent years.

NOTES

[1] One of the most interesting early examples of this was Stalin's speech on *Questions of Agrarian Policy in the Soviet Union* (27th December, 1929), published in *Leninism*, Vol. II (Modern Books), pp. 253-74.

[2] *Bolshevik*, October, 1952. The references below are to the English translation published by the Foreign Languages Publishing House, Moscow.

[3] On the question of Stalin's personal authorship of this work, see my review of it in the *Economic Journal*, September, 1953, pp. 717-8.

[4] For accounts of some of these debates, see A. Kaufman, "The Origin of 'The Political Economy of Socialism'", in *Soviet Studies*, January, 1953, p. 243.

[5] An English translation of this article will be found in the *American Economic Review* of September, 1944, pp. 501 ff. Articles commenting upon it appeared in the June, September and December, 1944, and March, 1945, issues of the same journal. See also the discussion by A. Zauberman in *The Review of Economic Studies*, Vol. XVI (1), No. 39, pp. 2 ff.

[6] *American Economic Review*, September, 1944, p. 518.

[7] Ibid., p. 513.

[8] Ibid., pp. 515-9.

[9] N. Voznesensky, *War Economy of the U.S.S.R. in the Period of the Patriotic War* (English translation by Foreign Languages Publishing House, Moscow), pp. 115 and 120.

[10] Cf. Stalin's treatment of the "basic economic laws" of modern capitalism and socialism (*Economic Problems*, pp. 42-6).

[11] *Economic Problems*, pp. 7-8. It does not follow from the objective character of economic laws that society is helpless in the face of them. "Man may discover these laws," Stalin insists, "get to know them and, relying upon them, utilise them in the interests of society" (*Economic Problems*, p. 8).

[12] Ibid., pp. 5-6. It is true, of course, that man can change the particular economic system which gives rise to the existing laws, in which case the existing laws will give place to new laws. Here, however, according to Stalin, the existing laws "are not abolished, but lose their validity owing to the new economic conditions and depart from the scene in order to give place to new laws, laws which are not created by the will of man, but which arise from the new economic conditions" (ibid., p. 8).

[13] Stalin complains (ibid., p. 11) that "it cannot be said that the requirements of this economic law are fully reflected by our yearly and five-yearly plans."

[14] Ibid., p. 11.

[15] Stalin says (ibid., p. 13) that thousands of enthusiastic young people, who are "dazzled by the extraordinary successes of the Soviet system," begin to imagine that "Soviet government can 'do anything,' that 'nothing is beyond it,' that it can abolish scientific laws and form new ones."

[16] *"Dizzy with Success"* was an article published in *Pravda* in March, 1930, designed to halt the excesses which were taking place in the carrying out of the collectivisation policy. The emphasis of the article was upon the *consolidation* of the successes which had been achieved.

[17] *Economic Problems*, p. 76.

[18] Ibid., p. 96. Cf. p. 20, where Stalin suggests that "the swallowing up of the collective-farm sector by the state sector . . . would be looked upon as the expropriation of the collective farms"; and p. 75, where a "wrong policy" put forward by Yaroshenko is mentioned (but not specified). Cf. also Stalin's emphasis on the *acceptability* of certain policies to the peasants (p. 17) and on their *unwillingness* to accept others (p. 19).

[19] The extent to which the 1943 thesis was influencing opinion in this sphere may not have been fully revealed until the campaign for the amalgamation of collective farms, which began in the second half of 1949, had got under way.

[20] Ibid., pp. 19-20. A summary of Lenin's practical proposals is given by Stalin on pp. 16-17.

[21] Marx, *Capital*, Vol. I (Allen & Unwin), p. 9.

[22] Stalin emphasises that "*our* commodity production is not of the ordinary type, but is a special kind of commodity production, commodity production without capitalists." Its sphere of action is relatively narrow, and it "cannot possibly develop into capitalist production." (*Economic Problems*, pp. 20-1.)

[23] Ibid., p. 23.

[24] Cf. my fuller discussion of this question in the *Economic Journal*, September, 1953, pp. 721-3.

[25] *Economic Problems*, pp. 24-5.

[26] Ibid., p. 26.

[27] Ibid., p. 20.

[28] Ibid., p. 75.

[29] Ibid., pp. 103-4.

[30] Ibid., p. 20.

[31] Strictly speaking, one ought to say that commodity production will disappear when an internal "all-embracing production sector" has been achieved, *and* when, in addition, *world* production is controlled by a single international economic organisation. For goods which enter into international trade as it is at present constituted can be said to be "commodities" according to Stalin's interpretation of the concept, and "commodity production" will therefore not disappear so long as the countries exchanging goods with one another constitute independent producing units. Stalin explicitly mentions the case of countries like Britain, which are dependent to a large extent upon international trade, in this connection (pp. 14-5).

[32] Ibid., p. 76.

[33] Ibid., pp. 47-8.

[34] Ibid., p. 104.

[35] Ibid., p. 28.

[36] Ibid., pp. 42-6 and 83-7.

[37] Ibid., pp. 11 and 46.

[38] Ibid., pp. 37-41.

[39] According to Marxist theory, society passes through two phases after the termination of capitalism. In the first phase, usually described as "socialism" or "the first phase of communism," there is still a relative scarcity of goods, there are many survivals of capitalist attitudes regarding labour, etc., and the national product is distributed according to the value to society of each individual's *work*. In the second phase, usually described as "communism" *simpliciter* or "the second phase of communism," there is an abundance of goods, labour is regarded as a matter of honour, and the national product is distributed according to each individual's *needs*.

[40] *Economic Problems*, p. 75.

[41] Ibid., p. 73.

[42] Ibid., p. 74.

The World Today (essay date 1956)

SOURCE: "Anatomy of Tyranny: Khrushchev's Attack on Stalin," in *The World Today*, Vol. 12, No. 6, June, 1956, pp. 265-71.

[*In the following essay, the anonymous writer discusses Khrushchev's criticism of Stalin's policies.*]

Rarely has a document aroused more interest and speculation than the paper issued by the State Department purporting to be the text of the speech delivered on 25 February 1956 by Mr Khrushchev, first secretary of the

Communist Party of the Soviet Union, to its twentieth Congress. The United States Government does not vouch for its authenticity; nevertheless it has been received everywhere as plausible; it is in keeping with the tenor of statements made by responsible officials of non-Soviet Communist parties, and Communist newspapers in the West have made no attempt to denounce it as a forgery. On the contrary, they have treated it as genuine.

To read this paper is to recall a dozen highlights of Soviet history between the assassination of Kirov in 1934 and Stalin's death in 1953. Of these two events the first is presented in a highly equivocal light, suggesting a plot by the secret police in collusion with Stalin, the second as a release from unparalleled tyranny. Overshadowing all the rest is the sombre horror of the great purge of the later 1930s.

The ostensible purpose of the speech was to destroy Stalin's reputation, or, in its own terms, to destroy the 'cult of the individual'. Mr Khrushchev's picture of the Soviet Union between 1934 and 1953, as given here, bears a startling resemblance to the more lurid efforts of the extreme anti-Communist school. They, too, spoke of Stalin's dictatorship by terror, of mass injustice, of the execution of thousands of innocents, of cringing judges and confessions, extorted by torture, to crimes that were never committed, of the distortion of history, of the paralysing rule of fear—all of it smothered under choking clouds of servile adulation.

In contrast to Lenin, Mr Khrushchev is alleged to have said, Stalin 'abandoned the method of ideological struggle for that of administrative violence, mass repressions, and terror.' Whoever opposed him was 'doomed to moral and physical annihilation'. But not only those who opposed him. Stalin used terror against 'many honest Communists, against those party cadres who had borne the heavy load of the civil war and the first and most difficult years of industrialization and collectivization'. It was enough to be 'suspected of hostile intent'. Mass arrests and executions without trial 'created conditions of insecurity, fear, and even desperation'; in his 'intolerance and brutality' Stalin condemned to summary death many thousands who had committed no crimes at all, but who were forced to confess to the most 'unlikely crimes' by the use of 'cruel and inhuman tortures'. The military collegium of the Soviet Supreme Court is now reviewing these cases. Since 1954 it has 'rehabilitated 7,679 persons, many of whom were rehabilitated posthumously'.

Stalin is also declared to have been responsible for 'the mass deportation from their native places of whole nations'. These actions were 'not dictated by any military considerations'; others, by implication, were, and it is therefore not surprising that Mr Khrushchev did not include in his list of the uprooted the Volga Germans, the Poles, and the Balts. For these, apparently, the Stalin regime is not yet at an end.

To attribute to Stalin alone the responsibility for these and innumerable other acts is to carry the cult of the individual far indeed. It imposes too great a strain on credulity to believe that for twenty years one man could terrorize 200 million, while his colleagues in the Party, the Government, and the Army remained utterly helpless. Mr Khrushchev deplored the tendency to 'elevate one person, transform him into a superman possessing supernatural characteristics akin to those of a god'; in his own fashion this is precisely what he himself has done.

Mr Khrushchev's was a curious contention for a Marxist. No revolutionary of Tsarist days would have accepted as a reason for inactivity the plea that the tyrant 'treated all others in such a way that they could only listen and praise him', or that 'a situation was created where one could not express one's own will'. It is tantamount to an admission that the revolutionary terror had succeeded—where Tsarist persecution had failed—in destroying the spirit and traditions of the party which elevates revolution against oppressors to the highest level of social obligation.

The alternative plea of ignorance, of Stalin's failure to convene the Central Committee, or to inform his colleagues of action about to be taken, cannot even have been intended seriously; it might have some validity for a few months, but not for twenty years. The present rulers of the U.S.S.R. saw their colleagues, their superiors, and their subordinates fall by the thousand. It is difficult to believe that they had to wait for Stalin's death to learn that the victims were innocent. In any case, the plea of ignorance cannot be advanced to excuse inactivity when, on Mr Khrushchev's own showing, Stalin's policies threatened the country, in the opinion of the Army chiefs, with immense losses and dangers during the war. (Neither ignorance nor obedience to orders was accepted as a valid plea at Nuremberg; in his final speech there the Chief Soviet Prosecutor, General Rudenko, said that the Nazi leaders 'were necessary to Hitler just as much as he was necessary to them. Göring, Frick, Rosenberg . . . are inconceivable without Hitler, just as Hitler is inconceivable without them'.[1])

In fact neither plea was meant to be taken at face value. Mr Khrushchev was not talking to a gathering of schoolchildren but to his country's outstanding political figures. What he was in effect saying was that they were *all* equally responsible. As witnesses and accomplices, none had the right to claim a preeminence on moral or historical grounds. If there was collective leadership, there was also collective guilt.

There were two interesting exceptions. Mr Khrushchev appeared to go out of his way to suggest that Mr Malenkov's guilt was greater than average by recalling two occasions during the war when he acted as Stalin's spokesman, and to display in a favourable light Marshal Zhukov, whom Stalin denigrated. (Mr Malenkov, it may be remembered, was highly critical of Khrushchev's agricultural policies at the nineteenth Congress in 1952.)

Why was the risk taken of bringing the details of this nightmare of tyranny out into the open? Why not have continued the policy of silence which was pursued up to the twentieth Congress, while eradicating the worst abuses of the earlier years? For three years the Party leaders had been cautiously refashioning many facets of Soviet society, executing or getting rid of leading officials of the secret police, encouraging local initiative, loosening the stranglehold that had virtually killed the arts, and generally reducing the extreme tensions and fears of the Stalin era. It might have been thought that this was a settled policy, and would be followed until the present itself denied the past and the dead tyrant's name sank unremarked into oblivion without explicit disavowal.

There is no convincing answer to be found in the 'objective situation', for reasons that were valid in the spring of 1956 were equally valid three years earlier. The answer can lie only in the situation within the Communist Party itself, and here there are only slender indications to support speculation.

In the published records of the 20th Congress there is only one speech which departed from the practice of silent repudiation. That is the speech of Mikoyan which contained the first explicit attack on Stalin. It seems reasonable to assume either that this section of Mikoyan's speech came as a surprise to his colleagues, or that it had been inserted by agreement 'to test audience reaction'—the first being the more likely. It was presumably a step in the manœuvring for position within the leadership. The popularity of the measures taken after Stalin's death to mitigate the harshness of the regime suggested that support could be won by the open denunciation of its chief architect, and if prestige was to be enhanced by these means, Mr Khrushchev was unlikely to allow it to be won by a colleague. The response to Mikoyan's attack probably convinced the Party presidium that the risks were smaller than they had supposed. (There is in fact a strong suggestion, implicit in the parentheses indicating the mood of the audience which occur in the report of the speech, that the Party cadres welcomed this opportunity to purge themselves of feelings of guilt, to find a more telling and significant scapegoat than Beria.)

There was no suggestion, in Mr Khrushchev's opening speech at the Congress, of any crisis of authority. The forces making for change, embodied in the technical and administrative personnel of the country, received full recognition. But it must be assumed, *post facto,* that the air of confidence was in part fictitious, that the Communist leaders still felt the need to create fresh bonds between themselves and the members generally, to build relations of confidence and understanding between the rulers and the mass of the ruled. No better way could have been found—given the political narrowness of the regime—than to denounce the man who had destroyed all earlier bonds and made a virtue of mistrust.

In any case, once the conspiracy of silence was broken, it would have been difficult to stop at the point to which

Mr Mikoyan ventured. Whether a landslide has been set in motion by this drastic action it is too early to say. But the subterranean forces were already there, imprisoned within the petrified Stalinist mould. They would in any case have sought an outlet, and it is more likely that they can be kept under control and guided if the initiative in their release comes from above.

What cannot be in doubt is that the dual process—of establishing a hierarchy within the leadership, and reaching a new social equilibrium—will take time to work itself out. The Soviet rulers must hope that the revelations—or rather admissions—will prove no more than a nine days' wonder, that their own part in the twenty years of tyranny and misrule will be overlooked in thankfulness that it has ended, and that they will be able to go ahead untrammelled by the discarded garments of their past.

It is difficult, unless one has lived in a totalitarian country, to understand the pressures to which its inhabitants are subjected. But what of the Communist leaders in the decadent democracies, over whom no secret police kept watch? They found no difficulty in approving the purge, and apparently as little in approving there habilitation of its victims. They were prepared to subscribe to the belief in Stalin's infallibility and now appear equally prepared to tread his reputation into the mud. Was none of them capable of distinguishing between theory and dogma, between dissent and treason? What of their historians, for whom the records were available, their scientists, technicians, writers, and artists, who were in a position to compare the Soviet output with that in other countries? It is not Stalin's writings, or genetics, or the quality of Madame Pankratova's history, or the technical standing of Western industry that have changed, but the Party line, and in following it Communist leaders outside the Soviet bloc show themselves as subservient, with backbones as flexible and pens as docile, as in the past.

This is not to suggest that the leaders of Communist Parties in the West will have as little freedom in the future as they have had hitherto. On the contrary, it seems probable that they will have a far wider scope for initiative thrust on them. The Soviet leaders have emancipated themselves from the cramping obsession that there is only one pattern of revolution; it will now be up to the leaders of other parties to seek, under licence, their own road.

Mr Khrushchev dates Stalin's degeneration from the seventeenth Congress of the C.P.S.U., that is from 1934. The choice of the date is significant, not because more than half the delegates who attended the Congress, and 70 per cent of the members of the Central Committee it elected, fell victims to the purge, but because it implies endorsement of the policy with which Stalin's name will always be associated, the policy of 'revolution from above', of forced collectivization and industrialization—whose victims were probably no fewer than those of the great purge. To have denounced him wholly, as Beria is denounced, would have destroyed too much. To deny him altogether would be to deny the present leaders' own legitimacy and the very essence of the system they are operating. For if it would be foolish not to admit that Stalin's insanely suspicious and envious character, his megalomania, ignorance, and vanity account for some of the worst abuses of his rule, it is equally incontestable that a policy which imposed such burdens, pains, and punishments could not have been applied except in a society where there are no alternative parties, alternative policies, and alternative rulers. How indeed, except in a totalitarian system, could Stalin have concentrated such power in his own hands?

This is the cardinal feature of the Soviet system which Mr Khrushchev could not attack. And it is to preserve this that Stalin's crimes were said to have been committed from a mistaken view of the interests of the Party and the masses. 'In this lies the whole tragedy.'

The more striking excrescences of the dictatorship, the paralyzing rigidity and conformity of Stalin's last years, can be condemned and abandoned now that the painful and costly stage of 'primitive accumulation' is past. There is no risk that relaxation will start the whole system sliding backwards. (In the same way the forced labour camps have largely fulfilled their economic function and can be in part dissolved: the roads and railways and houses have been built, the mines have been mechanized. Inducements can now be combined with pressure in varying degrees to get labour to the uninviting wastes of the Arctic region.) Industry now has a broad enough basis and sufficient momentum to expand without subjecting the population to conditions which only brutal terrorism could persuade them to endure in silence. The endorsement of Stalin's earlier policies implies that criticism of the Communist Party, of its position in the country, and of its monopoly of power, will still not be tolerated.

The resignation of Molotov and Kaganovich from their ministerial posts (while remaining deputy premiers) continues the programme of disavowing the past, leaving, of Stalin's old guard, only Mr Mikoyan and the figurehead President, Marshal Voroshilov. The balance of power within the presidium has shifted, and Mr Malenkov now seems to hold a fairly isolated position. While the newly-released forces find channels of expression, and eventually settle down into a pattern that reflects the Soviet Union's changed position, internally and externally, the machinery of political power remains unchanged and the new élite appear to have full control of its operations. They are aware of the need for experiment and adaptation, and are prepared to initiate it themselves. Stalin is said not to have visited the rural areas after 1928, whereas Mr Khrushchev spends a good deal of his time travelling round his own as well as other countries.

The men who now rule were the beneficiaries of the policy they have discarded. They are operating a new policy. For the inhabitants of the Soviet Union and its East European bloc, the change is most welcome. The extent to which 'controlled relaxation' may be permitted can perhaps be gauged from the way in which this policy

has operated in Yugoslavia; there nothing has been allowed to encroach on the unique position of the Communist Party, and the reduction in the size of maximum landholdings testifies to the belief that an independent peasantry is potentially an enemy of the Communist regime.

Externally, the change in policy antedates the twentieth Congress. The rapprochment with Yugoslavia—the quarrel was singled out by Khrushchev as a glaring example of 'Stalin's shameful role' for which the Soviet Union 'paid dearly'—and the rapid development of friendly relations with the countries of Asia were all set in motion before the Congress. Broadly, Soviet foreign policy continues to aim at the neutralization of Europe, the isolation of America, and advance through the under-developed countries. But these aims are pursued with far greater flexibility and in more conventional terms than before; 'during Stalin's leadership our peaceful relations with other nations were often threatened'. There is basically no difference between competitive coexistence and cold war, but the current term emphasizes that the struggle will be waged by other than military means. For its part, the U.S.S.R. cannot begin to compete successfully until it approximates to the level of productivity achieved in the United States, and to do this it requires, not the sullen acquiescence of an intimidated working class, but voluntary co-operation, and the belief that initiative and independence will not have fatal consequences. The largest obstacle of all—the stagnation of agriculture—remains, and there is no sign that in this respect the essentials of Stalin's policy have been abandoned. Twenty-five years of collectivized agriculture have failed to attract the peasants, who, after all, represent nearly half the working population.

NOTES

1 *Trial of the Major War Criminals,* vol. xxii, p. 358 (Nuremberg, 1948).

Robert D. Warth (essay date 1960)

SOURCE: "Stalin and the Cold War: A Second Look," in *The South Atlantic Quarterly,* Vol. LIX, No. 1, Winter, 1960, pp. 1-12.

[*In the following essay, Warth contends that Stalin's notorious personal defects—including vanity, deceit, and brutality—did not necessarily have a negative impact on his political skills or his leadership ability.*]

The image of Joseph Stalin in the Western world was never a pleasant one—except, obviously, during the war years when the heroic achievements of the Red Army in the common cause lent a glow of enchantment to the Soviet Union and its paternal "Uncle Joe." Through the prism of the cold war his image was refracted to become one of calculated deceit, monstrous vanity, and senseless brutality, a view which Nikita Khrushchev's celebrated "secret" speech of February, 1956, did much to confirm.

These unsavory traits Stalin undoubtedly possessed, though to what extent they warped his political judgment is far from clear. Without seeking to rehabilitate a deceased tyrant—even to the extent that Khrushchev and his colleagues have felt is expedient—this essay will suggest that popular and even well-informed opinion about Stalin, at least in relation to the onset of the cold war, is not necessarily correct.

I

However one assesses his personal defects, Stalin was a skilled politician—at times a master at his trade. His blunders cost his country dearly; but if greatness is judged in the purely utilitarian terms of success, then Stalin was one of the great dictators of history. Devoid of the demagogic *mystique* with which his bankrupt contemporaries, Hitler and Mussolini, seemed so lavishly endowed, the Soviet autocrat outlived his era; and at the time of his death he was a kind of fossil remain from the Russian past—a symbolic relic of the backward society which had brought him to power and which he himself had undermined so energetically with the Five Year Plans.

It is a kind of conventional homily that Stalin dissipated with heedless abandon the vast reservoir of good will which the Soviet war effort had stored up in the West; that by his headlong drive to master eastern Europe he plunged the world into a new crisis which has become a durable and apparently permanent feature of mid-century civilization. This is by no means a fallacious judgment; but it is also an oversimplification of what actually occurred, for history is a subtle mosaic whose basic patterns can seldom be traced in monistic terms.

Stalin was never a reckless man who gambled, as did his fascist counterparts, with the safety of the state. In diplomacy his ultimate aim was to avoid war even at the cost of appeasement—as with Japan in the early thirties and with Germany in the spring of 1941. This is not to say that he declined to take risks: he alarmed conservative Westerners by intervening in the Spanish Civil War, though with a timidity which was scarcely acknowledged at the time; he decreed the Berlin blockade but eventually backed down when his bluff was called by the airlift; and he ordered—or at any rate did not veto—the North Korean attack which very nearly ignited World War III. Yet in every case he was unwilling to commit Soviet armed forces to the struggle.

If it is conceded that Soviet policy has never displayed those characteristics of aggressive militarism by which Germany, Italy, and Japan bullied their way to transitory success two decades ago, there is the obvious answer that it was not necessary, that Communism as an international secular faith has provided the perfect disguise to conceal the Kremlin's designs for world domination. Although the Communist International was formally abolished in 1943, there is indeed no reason to suppose that Stalin intended to renounce the long-range goals of world revolution. Nor is there at the present time when even

that pale ghost of the Comintern, the Communist Information Bureau, has been allowed to collapse without a successor. It is evident, however, that the revolutionary romanticism of the original Comintern died out long ago with the abortive revolt in Germany in 1923 and the near-extermination of Chinese Communism in 1927. The consolidation of Stalin's dictatorship forcefully accelerated the means by which the Comintern became an instrument of Soviet foreign policy: the tired shibboleths of Trotsky's "permanent revolution" gave way to the incipient nationalism of "socialism in one country." "One Soviet tractor is worth more than ten good foreign Communists" was the kind of remark heard in Stalin's entourage during the first Five Year Plan.

In the thirties world depression and the rise of fascism concealed from party members abroad (and a much larger circle of fellow travelers) the extent to which the original aims of the Comintern had been perverted. The cynicism with which Stalin abandoned Popular Front ideology and a policy of collective security by striking a bargain with Hitler was a shattering blow to international Communism—at least to its Western acolytes. Even the Grand Alliance of the Second World War never quite restored the glossy finish of dedicated idealism to a movement which had become so blatantly a manipulated subsidiary of the Kremlin.

Yet the cumbersome machinery of the Stalinist bureaucracy failed to crush the revolutionary potential of Communism. In China, a set of historical circumstances wholly different from those familiar in the West—and which none of the Soviet leaders ever properly understood—allowed Mao Tse-tung and his colleagues virtually a free hand in consolidating their revolution against the crumbling regime of Chiang Kai-shek; in Yugoslavia, Marshal Tito became the only Communist chieftain in Europe to achieve power without Moscow's help; and in France, Italy, and Greece, Communist-led resistance movements sprang up which were an embarrassment to Stalin as the war neared its end.

II

If the battle of Stalingrad was the turning point of Hitler's Russian campaign, it was also the great watershed of the wartime alliance. Querulous to the point of rudeness in chastising his allies for the absence of a second front in 1942, Stalin's protests became more dignified in 1943 as it began to dawn on him that the Red Army was capable of holding its own against the Wehrmacht. In the same year, Moscow began to show its hand in the Polish question. A subservient "Union of Polish Patriots" was organized and relations were severed with the Polish government in London. At the Teheran Conference in November, Roosevelt and Churchill virtually committed themselves to the Curzon Line as an equitable Soviet-Polish frontier. Stalin's hint to Polish Premier Wladyslaw Skorski in December, 1941, that a settlement might be arranged on the basis of the prewar boundary with some "slight alterations" was a theme to which Stalin never reverted.

By the spring of 1944, the European balance of power had shifted so markedly in Moscow's favor that Churchill's latent mistrust of Communism—which he equated with Soviet power—had begun to revive. Always more concerned with the nuances of *Realpolitik* than Roosevelt, the British premier hoped to arrive at a mutually agreeable solution to the approaching East European power vacuum. Without a specific understanding among any of the Big Three, such a development had already been implied by the course of the war. Stalin was in no mood for revolutionary adventurousness. Postwar security was his watchword. When the Red Army crossed the prewar frontiers of the Soviet Union, it did so as Tsar Alexander I's troops had once invaded Napoleonic Europe, not as revolutionary zealots bent upon propagating a new faith. The only eager Communist missionaries were outside the Soviet orbit: Mao, Tito, and the anonymous antifascist guerrillas of occupied Europe. Stalin expended a great deal of effort—sometimes in vain—in attempting to curb these overly enthusiastic votaries of the Communist cause. It was not simply the act of a clever dissembler when he asserted that Poland would remain a capitalist state because "Communism does not fit the Poles"; that "Communism on a German is like a saddle on a cow"; and that Mao and his associates were "margarine Communists."

In the expectation that Soviet primacy would be conceded in eastern Europe, Stalin went out of his way to reassure London and Washington about the "menace" of Communism. In the spring of 1944, the Italian Communist leader Palmiro Togliatti, who had spent many years of exile in Moscow, was dispatched to Naples by plane and soon curbed the party militants who were attacking the monarchy and the "fascist" regime of Marshal Pietro Badoglio. After the liberation of France and the Low Countries there was a similar concern about the party's errant "radicalism," though there was no need for crash methods *à la* Togliatti.

The only other country in which Communism represented a serious threat to the status quo was Greece, long a bastion of British security in the Mediterranean and the Near East. In May, 1944, the British Foreign Office broached the subject of a *quid pro quo* in the Balkans: Greece to fall within the British sphere, Romania—already partly occupied by the Red Army—within the Russian. Moscow assented provided Washington's approval was forthcoming. Roosevelt's original response was cool. To the State Department, "spheres of influence" was an obscene phrase, and Churchill's adroitness in disguising the proposal as a temporary wartime expedient failed to obliterate the taint of power politics. Without the knowledge of Secretary of State Cordell Hull, Roosevelt was persuaded to withdraw his objections for a trial period of three months upon the understanding that no permanent spheres were to be carved out of the Balkans and that American interests in the area would be preserved.

As Hitler's satellite empire collapsed in ruins about him, Churchill hastened to the task of implementing his Balkan entente with Stalin. The two had tentatively agreed during the summer that Bulgaria lay within the Soviet domain and Yugoslavia within the British. Meanwhile Soviet influence had continued to grow as the Red Army pushed onward, while Anglo-American forces were still meeting strenuous opposition. At their conference in Moscow on October 9, 1944, Churchill proposed and Stalin immediately accepted the notorious "percentage plan" for the Balkans: the Soviet Union to have 90 per cent predominance in Romania and 75 per cent in Bulgaria; Britain (theoretically in accord with the United States) to have 90 per cent predominance in Greece; and Yugoslavia and Hungary to be split on a fifty-fifty basis. Such a precise delineation of their respective spheres was a rather academic exercise since it was not intended as a guide to proportionate representation in future governments. But the political implications were clear enough in outline, and both Stalin and Churchill were quite satisfied not to probe too deeply into the other's interpretation of the agreement—"to let well enough alone," as the latter put it in his memoirs.

Roosevelt held aloof from any explicit rejection or affirmation of the plan. By the tactics of procrastination he defaulted on a unique opportunity for a political settlement in the Balkans before Soviet power, based on the *de facto* position of the Red Army, could consolidate itself. But Churchill's initiative did pay a handsome dividend just two months later: Greece was preserved as a Western outpost when the Communist-led army of the National Liberation Front was forced out of Athens by British troops. While incapable of documentary proof, the presumption is strong that Moscow's fiat restrained the Communists from attempting to seize power. Churchill later acknowledged with gratitude the Kremlin's forebearance: "Stalin . . . adhered strictly and faithfully to our agreement of October, and during the long weeks of fighting the Communists in the streets of Athens not one word of reproach came from *Pravda* or *Isvestia*."

In the case of Marshal Tito, Stalin uncovered a streak of stubbornness in his subordinate which undoubtedly confirmed his later prejudice that "Muscovites"—Moscow-trained Communists—were infinitely preferable to antifascist resistance leaders whose loyalty and doctrinal purity was more likely to have become polluted by long years away from the socialist fatherland. Stalin's aides were aghast at Tito's independent attitude toward "the boss" when the two met for the first time in Moscow in September, 1944. Their initial encounter was in fact so chilly that Tito ascribed it to his acrid telegrams in 1942-43 when Moscow had timidly refused to assist the Partisans because the Western powers were then supporting the Chetniks of General Mihailovich. Tito was shocked and offended by Stalin's insistence that the exiled King Peter be reinstated but reluctantly signed an accord several months later with the king's premier, Dr. Ivan Shubashich, promising a coalition government. That the agreement meant very little was clear by mid-1945, yet it would seem that Stalin was anxious to uphold his end of the bargain with Churchill by curbing Tito's burgeoning power.

III

The controversy about the Yalta Conference (February, 1945) has been so thoroughly aired that it would be superfluous to review the proceedings once again. But it would not be amiss to emphasize that it was not human frailty but the disruption of the Grand Alliance which was to make an obscure Crimean city a term of abuse in the lexicon of American politics. Whereas the simple and personal becomes enshrined in the folklore—a crafty Stalin hood-winking an ill and naïve Roosevelt—the complex and impersonal is duly registered in forbidding tomes of neglected scholarship. Stalin too made concessions and displayed a flexibility which was not to be duplicated by Soviet diplomacy during the aging dictator's remaining years. However painstakingly the Yalta literature is scrutinized for clues as to the motives, aspirations, and personalities of the leading protagonists, the conclusion is inescapable that the Yalta failure lay elsewhere: in the rapid erosion of military necessity—always the best cement for unstable alliances; in the hidden rivalry to fill the political vacuum left by a collapsing Germany; and in the "normal" resurgence of ideological hostility between two disparate systems.

That in 1945 Stalin contemplated a Communist eastern Europe may be doubted—not because his frequent protestations to the contrary should be taken at face value but because of his actions. His insistence that the "Polish goose"—Churchill's phrase—be stuffed with German territory and that the ethnically "correct" Curzon Line become Poland's eastern frontier; his demand for heavy reparations from Germany and her tributary states; his willingness to partition the Balkans; and his tight rein upon the European Communist parties all bespoke the language of nationalism, not of revolution. The hobbling of capitalist Germany to insure against future aggression was the key to his strategy in Europe—a far cry from Lenin's day when Germany had been the lodestar of world Communism. In return for his disavowal of revolutionary aims, Stalin continued to expect Anglo-American recognition of Russia's developing "security zone" in the East and to be deeply chagrined by the refusal of his allies to accept what he considered just recompense for the unparalleled sacrifices which the Russian people had made.

At the Potsdam Conference (July-August, 1945) Allied unity was already beginning to crack, for the war against Japan, which the Soviet Union was soon to enter, was insufficient to halt the process of disintegration. Stalin presented a host of complaints and demands which remained unsatisfied, and the bitter Anglo-American criticism of Soviet policy in eastern Europe was likewise passed over without action. Stalin's attitude was that it was "unjust" to complain about the situation in Romania and Bulgaria because "he was not meddling in Greek affairs."

In the end nothing was done to alter the political complexion of the vassal empire which the Russians were already erecting. Indeed, the possibilities for effective countermeasures were severely limited. Stalin was not a man to be swayed by moral exhortation, and a show of force was neither politically nor militarily feasible. The only realistic alternative lay in exploring the opportunities which the Stalin-Churchill pact presented. Precisely the opposite course was pursued. It became clear at Potsdam, if it had not been before, that the United States would never countenance spheres of influence in Europe. To Stalin it must have seemed that Britain was drawing closer to the American position; certainly Churchill was beginning to have his doubts about the scheme, for Stalin's inability to discipline Tito was a serious flaw which Churchill took as a sign of bad faith. Since the agreement had been an informal and personal transaction, the election victory of the Labour party before the conference ended could only arouse concern as to the continuity of British policy. While neither country specifically disavowed the sphere arrangement, Potsdam was an important way station in a general retreat from the supposed evils of "power politics" and "secret diplomacy" to a "democratic" concern for moral rectitude and hollow propaganda triumphs.

Stalin returned to Moscow to fulfil his Yalta promise by declaring war on Japan. The protracted negotiations with China for a treaty of friendship and alliance were brought to a speedy conclusion on August 14, by which time the first two articles were already obsolete. Because the Soviet government promised material and moral support to the Nationalist regime "as the central government of China," the pact came as a stunning rebuff to the Chinese Communists, though they obediently acquiesced in what must have seemed a betrayal of the revolutionary heritage of the Soviet state. The dazzling vista of a Communist China, so natural to the Bolshevik elite in the mid-twenties, was a utopian fantasy to the hard-bitten oligarchs of the mid-forties. Stalin was too much the "realist" to perceive the revolutionary currents which more than two decades of disappointment had taught him were mere figments of overwrought Marxist imaginations. It was left to Western commentators to enshrine the undeserving Stalin as a super-Machiavellian who could simultaneously aggrandize the Russian state on a scale never conceived by the most ardent imperialist of Tsarist times and nurture a revolution of the dimensions of the Chinese upheaval.

American intervention in the Chinese civil war for the ostensible purpose of disarming the defeated Japanese troops prompted misgivings in the Kremlin. The Red Army delayed its occupation of Manchuria and continued to strip the area of its industrial assets on the principle that this was enemy "war booty." Moscow was already indignant at its virtual exclusion from Japanese affairs and had recalled its Tokyo representative because, as Stalin complained, he was "treated like a piece of furniture." (The remark recalls Churchill's similar protest to Stalin at Potsdam that the British mission in Bucharest had been "penned up with a closeness approaching internment.") Nevertheless the Russians were usually circumspect in their relations with the Nationalist government and repeatedly advised Mao to abandon the futile struggle with Chiang. Kuomintang charges that their opponents were receiving Soviet aid were never confirmed by an independent source, and the probability is strong that they were intended for American as well as domestic consumption.

The Communist victory in China, which already looms as one of the transcendent events of Asian if not of world history, reflects no credit upon Stalin's revolutionary acumen. It reveals him instead as a conservative imperialist much more anxious to consolidate Soviet gains in Manchuria than to gamble upon what was to become one of the "blue chips" among Communist investments. In the end the Soviet dictator was able to avoid a repetition of his Yugoslav blunder of 1948—but only by the narrowest margin and with the grating knowledge that his Chinese comrades considered themselves junior partners in a joint enterprise, not wage slaves in a monopoly run for the benefit of the Soviet Union.

IV

At the first postwar conference of the powers, a meeting of the Council of Foreign Ministers in London (September-October, 1945), nothing had yet occurred to dramatize to any of the future cold-war protagonists the increasingly perilous but still outwardly friendly relationship among them. The attempt to agree on the minor European peace treaties proved abortive. The underlying point of friction, though it was never stated in so many words, was the refusal of the Atlantic powers to acknowledge Soviet preponderance in eastern Europe. Secretary of State James F. Byrnes, with the adherence of Foreign Secretary Ernest Bevin, insisted on the letter of the Yalta declaration on liberated Europe and clung to the ritualistic formula of "governments both friendly to the Soviet Union and representative of all the democratic elements of the country." Byrnes knew, or should have known, that his statement was a contradiction in terms. No democratic government in the Western sense, except perhaps in Bulgaria (and in Finland as it turned out), could have satisfied the Soviet or any other reasonable definition of "friendly." Nor did the prospects for democracy in an underdeveloped area whose people had never become familiar with civil liberties, an effective parliament, or a fluid social order seem to trouble the Anglo-American representatives. The Russians were hardly prepared to admit their own unpopularity either as Communists or as imperialists, although Stalin had posed the issue bluntly enough at Potsdam when he declared that "a freely elected government in any of these countries would be anti-Soviet, and that we cannot allow." But they could—and did—suspect with good reason that it was not so much the state of democracy in eastern Europe which was the matrix of the dispute as the expansion of Russian power into a region where the tsars had been unable to penetrate save for brief and transitory interludes.

The Kremlin's foreign policy became increasingly rigid as the afterimage of the Grand Alliance gradually faded from view. In domestic affairs a return to Marxist first principles—Soviet style—smoothed the way for the later excesses of the *Zhdanovschchina*, a far more drastic cultural straitjacket (instituted in the name of Stalin's chief henchman, Andrei Zhdanov) than the United States was to endure in the Age of McCarthy. A strata of reason lay beneath the aberrant tendencies of Soviet xenophobia. The prewar experiences of the Soviets, with memories stretching back to Allied intervention in 1918-20, were not such as to inspire confidence in the Western democracies; and during the war itself the bitterness engendered by the prolonged delay in opening the second front was not wholly a product of the inequality of bloodshed. It also stemmed from the belief that while the material wealth of the homeland—created at such a heavy cost to the living standards of the Russian people—was being wantonly pillaged, the United States and to a lesser extent Britain were privileged sanctuaries where capitalists of the Wall Street image waxed fat and sleek on the blood of the Soviet worker and soldier. That such enrichment was an accident of geography rather than a calculated conspiracy was perhaps emotionally indigestible, but the Marxist axiom that war is the health of the capitalist order was a valid commentary as far the United States was concerned. The Great Depression had been transformed into general prosperity by the clash of arms, not by the natural workings of a free economy. The irony of the situation was that the postwar crisis in the capitalist West, which Moscow had every reason to expect from its theoretical extrapolations, was postponed into the indefinite future, first by the pent-up demand for consumer goods and then by a rearmament program designed to counter the threat of Soviet aggression.

It may be that there was nothing which the West could have done to reverse the trend of Soviet policy. But given the traditional European state-system of competing sovereignties, each a law unto itself, there does seem to have been an opportunity for realistic negotiations of the kind which Churchill pursued with such vigor and then abandoned, presumably in the face of American objections. Admittedly it would have been "immoral" to permit limited Soviet expansion into eastern Europe by negotiated agreement. But would that not have been preferable, considering the impossibility of establishing any countervailing power, to introducing a policy of "containment" which only fed the Kremlin's anxiety neurosis and induced Stalin to weld over the last remaining chinks in the Iron Curtain? At the very least, Greece could have been spared the horrors of civil war in 1946-48 and Czechoslovakia—provided Stalin's eastern preserve was legitimized—salvaged as a democratic oasis in central Europe.

There is no more delusive sagacity, however, than the wisdom of hindsight; and it is less my purpose to find fault with Western policymakers than to revise in a minor way the "good *vs.* evil" stereotype which has tended to pervade American thinking about the rest of the world— a kind of provincialism which evades a sober appraisal of what a foreign policy can and cannot do in a world which is, unhappily, still a jungle arena of competing nation-states.

William Henry Chamberlin (essay date 1962)

SOURCE: "Khrushchev's War with Stalin's Ghost," in *The Russian Review*, Vol. 21, No. 1, January, 1962, pp. 3-10.

[*In the following essay, Chamberlin examines the possible motives behind Nikita Khrushchev's decision in the early 1960s to openly denounce Stalin and his tyranny by having Stalin's body exhumed and removed from its exalted spot next to Vladimir Lenin's.*]

There was high historical drama and some political risk in Nikita Khrushchev's decision to carry his war with the ghost of Josef Stalin to the point of removing the embalmed corpse of the deceased dictator from what was, until recently, the Lenin-Stalin Mausoleum, the great secular shrine of the Soviet Union. Even more challenging was the decision to erect a memorial to the innocent victims of Stalin's tyranny.

Eloquent proof of the powerful spell Stalin cast upon the country he ruled with a rod of iron for twenty-four years is the fact that only now, more than eight years after his death, are the Russian people being told the truth about his grim record of brutal criminality. It is true that about three years after Stalin's death, at the Twentieth Congress of the Soviet Communist Party, in February, 1956, Khrushchev took the first step toward destroying the image of Stalin as the all-benevolent, all-wise, all-powerful "father of peoples" and "sun of the universe," to recall two phrases of Byzantine flattery which were frequently used about Stalin in his lifetime.

At that time Khrushchev's indictment of Stalin's crimes was selective. He said nothing about those acts of mass cruelty which might be regarded as enhancing the power and interests of the Soviet state, the "liquidation of the kulaks as a class," the man-made famine of 1932-33, the deportations from Poland and the Baltic States, the massacre of some 15,000 Polish officer war prisoners in the Katyn Forest and elsewhere in 1940. What he emphasized was Stalin's habit of torturing and killing devoted Communists, his miscalculations in the planning and conduct of the war.

However, this speech was not officially published in Russia. It remained in the category of Lenin's famous Political Testament, something known to sophisticated Communist Party members, but a matter of rumor and hearsay to the majority of the Soviet people. Khrushchev even tried to soften the impact of his own indictment, delivered behind closed doors, by publicly referring to Stalin as "a great fighter against imperialism," leaving the impression that he had rendered great services to the Soviet Union, even if he had been led astray by what was euphemistically referred to as "the cult of personality."

But now the declaration of war on Stalin's ghost is uncompromising and implacable. What was authorized by the Twenty-Second Congress is comparable with the practice of the impotent Roman Senate, in the time of the absolute power of the Emperors, in decreeing the throwing down of the statues of those Emperors who had behaved as tyrants—once they were safely dead. The most remote collective farm, the loneliest mountain village in the Caucasus will hear that the body of Stalin, once adored as a mortal god, has been excluded with infamy from its place next to Lenin in the Soviet pantheon.

The motivation for this spectacular denigration is not altogether clear, although three factors seem to have played a part.

First, the Twenty-Second Party Congress, hailed as a demonstration of unity of the triumphant "builders of Communism" in the Soviet Union with the fraternal Communist parties of some eighty countries, may be remembered as an occasion which emphasized the rift between Moscow and Peiping, for which the ostensible issue of tiny backward Albania is scarcely the most important explanation. Peiping and its sympathizers in the world Communist movement have always refused to accept the downgrading of Stalin. For Khrushchev to emphasize this downgrading is a natural reaction to strained relations with Peiping.

Second, it has apparently seemed expedient to stigmatize as "Stalinists" the "anti-Party" group of Khrushchev's open and secret opponents in the Communist Party. To associate Malenkov, Molotov, Voroshilov and other individuals who have opposed Khrushchev as closely as possible with Stalin's acts of arbitrary cruelty is a normal maneuver in inner-Party in-fighting.

Third, Khrushchev, in trying to exorcise the ghost of Stalin, may be hoping to win popular support by creating the impression that he is completely dissociating himself from Stalin's policies. As against the risk of administering a traumatic shock to those Soviet citizens who are still indoctrinated with the cult of Stalin's unique virtue and wisdom, there is the possibility of rallying the allegiance of those who remember with bitterness the undeserved suffering Stalin brought to the uncounted thousands whom he slaughtered, to the millions whom he banished to slave labor concentration camps.

To be sure, Khrushchev cannot assume the role of Stalin's accuser with clean hands. Like every prominent political figure in the Soviet Union, he survived the purges of the Stalin era only by obsequious sycophancy and by zealously carrying out any purging assignments which the dictator entrusted to him. Here is the voice of Khrushchev, greeting Stalin on his seventieth birthday in December, 1949:

> Comrade Stalin, the genius leader of our party, rallied the peoples of our country and led them to the triumph of socialism. . . . Stalin stood at the cradle of each Soviet Republic, protected it and paternally helped it to grow and flourish. . . . This is why all the peoples of our country, with extraordinary warmth and filial love, call the great Stalin their dear father and genius teacher.

To-day the peoples of the great Soviet Union and all advanced progressive mankind wholeheartedly greet our dear Comrade Stalin, inspirer of the indissoluble friendship of peoples.

Glory to our dear father . . . the genius leading the Party, the Soviet people and the working people of the whole world, Comrade Stalin. .

The following passage in the most authoritative biography of Khrushchev[1] brings out the present Soviet dictator's full identification with Stalin's method of rule by unlimited terror, directed against the ruling Communist Party, as well as against the Soviet peoples as a whole:

In 1937 Khrushchev became a member of a "purge troika," sent to liquidate "the enemies of the people" in the Ukraine. The other members were Molotov and the dreaded NKVD chief, Ezhov. The purge-team worked effectively. Most members of the Ukrainian Cabinet, of the Ukrainian Supreme Soviet and of the Ukrainian Central Committee were summarily executed. According to conservative estimates, sixty percent of the Ukrainian CP apparatus was liquidated, not to speak of the thousands of ordinary Party members, and their accomplices, the "class-hostile" elements among non-Party people.

According to the official Soviet "History of the Ukraine":

"With the arrival in the Ukraine of the close comrade-in-arms of Stalin, N. S. Khrushchev, the eradication of the remnants of the enemy and the liquidation of the wrecking activities proceeded particularly successfully."

Stalin was a most vivid living illustration of the eternal truth of Lord Acton's dictum: "Power corrupts and absolute power corrupts absolutely." He was a figure of blood and horror in Russian history unmatched since the paranoid Tsar Ivan the Terrible, whom in many ways he resembled. In the violent twentieth century the only man who might rival him in the number of human lives he blighted and destroyed was Adolf Hitler. Stalin also represented the most emphatic refutation of Lenin's utopian dream that, after a period of absolute dictatorship, the very need for the existence of the state would disappear and men would live in perfect freedom. This theory presupposes a measure of selfless dedication on the part of the wielders of the dictatorship which is contrary to all historical experience of human nature. When entrusted with unlimited power, Stalin's proved record of criminal super-gangsterism, now at last revealed to the Russian people, warrants every word of George F. Kennan's eloquent indictment:[2]

This was a man of incredible criminality, of a criminality effectively without limits; a man apparently foreign to the very experience of love, without pity or mercy; a man in whose entourage no one was ever safe; a man whose hand was set against all that could not be useful to him at the moment; a man who was most dangerous of all to those who were his closest collaborators in crime. . . .

By way of response, apparently, to what seems to have been some opposition to his purposes on the part of the Seventeenth Party Congress in 1934, Stalin killed, in the ensuing purges of 1936 to 1938, 1108 out of a total of 1966 of the members of the Congress. Of the Central Committee elected at that Congress and still officially in office, he killed 98 out of 139—a clear majority, that is, of the body from which ostensibly he drew his authority. These deaths were only a fraction, numerically, of those which resulted from the purges of those years. . . .

All this is apart from the stupendous brutalities which Stalin perpetrated against the common people: notably in the process of collectivization, and also in some of his wartime measures. The number of victims here—the number, that is, of those who actually lost their lives—runs into the millions. But this is not to mention the broken homes, the twisted childhoods and the millions of people who were half killed, who survived these ordeals only to linger on in misery, with broken health and broken hearts.

It might also be noted that Stalin killed all his six colleagues in the Politburo at the time of Lenin's death (Trotsky, Zinoviev, Kamenev, Rykov, Bukharin and Tomsky), thereby giving rise to the grim joke that, having killed all his friends, he was beginning on his acquaintances. After the end of the war, enraged by the cordial reception which Moscow Jews gave to the Ambassador of Israel, Mrs. Golda Meir, he let loose a wave of anti-Semitic terror and persecution, in which some of the best known Russian Jewish writers and intellectuals perished.

It is perhaps understandable that a cunning tyrant, possessed of the two mighty weapons of the totalitarian state, unlimited terror and unlimited propaganda, could have fooled a considerable number of his own people. But one of the most depressing aspects of the Stalin story is the way in which he fooled considerable numbers of people in the West. The United States Ambassador to the Soviet Union, Mr. Joseph E. Davies, described Stalin as a man so kindly that a child would sit on his lap and a dog would sidle up to him. Although the list of Stalin's broken treaties and promises is endless, this same Ambassador Davies, in a speech in Chicago in February 1942, offered the following endorsement:

By the testimony of performance and in my opinion, the word of honor of the Soviet Government is as safe as the Bible.

There is nothing in the memoirs or in the available historical material to show that either Roosevelt or Churchill realized that, in Stalin, they were dealing with a monster, with one of the greatest mass murderers of all time. Had this been realized, even when military expediency dictated co-operation against Hitler, Western policy in the concluding phase of the war and in the immediate postwar period might have been shaped along more realistic lines.

Stalin's career is another historical illustration of the point that revolutions are usually made against weak, rather than strong governments, that the most terrible tyrants are likely to die peacefully in their beds. (Whether Stalin's own death was due to natural causes is a mystery that may never be cleared up with certainty. His personal secretary Poskrebyshev mysteriously disappeared at the time of his death and was never heard of again. As Stalin's paranoid mind was apparently tending in the direction of another big purge, with the arrest of a number of prominent Russian physicians on poisoning charges as a macabre curtain-raiser, his death was distinctly convenient to his lieutenants, none of whom could be sure of not being one of the victims of the new purge.)

It is by no means certain that Khrushchev has finally banished Stalin's ghost, even though he felt politically strong enough to evict the deceased dictator from the shrine which his body had occupied since his death. Stalin has become such a gigantic myth in Soviet history that its elimination seems bound to leave a big spiritual and psychological vacuum. His belated condemnation poses distinctly awkward questions.

What, for instance, was Khrushchev doing in the Stalin era to thwart Stalin's crimes? What about the Communist Party, which is supposed to be the highest source of authority and the supreme repository of political wisdom? What went wrong with its functioning when a bloody tyrant could place himself above all restraint and put to death large numbers of veteran Party members who were innocent of any crime? If so many of Stalin's judgments were nothing but a despot's whims, what about the trials of an earlier period which sent to their deaths Lenin's old comrades, Zinoviev and Kamenev, Bukharin and Rykov? What about Trotsky? Once Stalin's method of extorting false confessions by torture is officially established, who can be sure of the genuineness of any political trial that took place under his rule?

It is sometimes reported from Germany that parents avoid talking about the Nazi period, because of fear that their children will reproach them for not having done something to prevent the monstrous crimes that took place in the concentration camps. This moral and psychological problem is compounded in the Soviet Union, because there has been no break in continuity, because Khrushchev and his associates are the direct political heirs of Stalin.

"The truth shall make ye free" is a famous Biblical phrase. It would probably be too much to hope that the final moment of truth about Stalin and his crimes will immediately free the Soviet people from the effects of forty-four years of totalitarian indoctrination and regimentation. But this moment of truth will probably make it more difficult for a new Stalin to arise. It will almost certainly sow seeds of doubt among the more intelligent young Soviet citizens about the infallibility of their system. And the exposure of Stalin for what he was, not a "father of the peoples," not a "genius leader of progressive humanity," but an amoral monstrous tyrant, seems calculated to shake the cocky self-confidence of the most indoctrinated Young Communist.

Nor will the dual role of Stalin's faithful henchman and Stalin's belated accuser be altogether easy to play, even for a politician of Khrushchev's audacity, bounce, and ingenuity.

NOTES

[1] George Paloczi-Horvath, *Khrushchev*, p. 92.

[2] *Russia and the West Under Lenin and Stalin*, pp. 256-258.

Antón Donoso (essay date 1965)

SOURCE: "Stalin's Contribution to Soviet Philosophy," *International Philosophical Quarterly*, Vol. V, No. 2, May, 1965, pp. 267-303.

[*In the following essay, Donoso traces Stalin's place in the development of Soviet philosophy, arguing that his most significant contribution was "his ability to bring theory in line with practice."*]

It has been said that "throughout the whole of the Stalinist period Stalin himself was the only person in the Soviet Union who ever dared to say anything new."[1] This was especially true in the field of philosophy. The history of Dialectical Materialism in the Soviet Union from the death of Lenin on January 21, 1924 until the ascendency of Khruschev in the later 1950's is largely the history of Stalin's philosophical activities. It will be the purpose of this paper to present an account of these activities, to examine any significant contribution made by Stalin to Soviet Dialectical Materialism, and, finally, to attempt to determine how the so-called "de-Stalinization" has affected this contribution in respect to the contents of selected, current Soviet textbooks in philosophy.

In order to place his contribution to Soviet Marxism in its proper historical context I shall preface my remarks with a short prologue dealing with the origins of Russian Marxism and the philosophical situation in the Soviet Union at the time of Stalin's rise to power.

PHILOSOPHICAL SITUATION BEFORE STALIN

The spread of Marxism in Russia as an economic theory began in the 1870's but it did not emerge *as a social movement* until the 1880's. As a consequence of the revolutionary activities of certain Russian exiles and their polemic with a Russian form of socialism known as *Narodnichestvo*, there arose that socio-political phenomenon later to be known as Soviet Marxism.

The acknowledged leader in the emergence of Russian Marxism was Georgy Valentinovich Plekhanov (1856-1918). Son of a prosperous landowner, he left Russia both to escape the government and to learn the sources of influence that European socialism was having upon other exiled Russians. He went (1881) as a Narodnik but in ten years he had entered wholly into the Marxist camp. His works attack the Narodnik position on the "subjective" method in history and sociology (denying that the social sciences involve "ideals"), on the role of the individual in history (denying that history is made by heroes and not the masses), and on the idea that Russia possessed some sort of peculiar historical destiny (denying that, unlike the rest of Europe, Russia would by-pass capitalism on its way to socialism because of the peculiar Russian *obschina* system of peasant communes).

This polemic gained for Plekhanov the respect of Lenin, a respect that remained unabated when Plekhanov became a Menshevik. In 1914 Lenin remarked: "The best exposition of the philosophy of Marxism and of historical materialism is given by G. V. Plekhanov."[2] In 1921, in a discussion of the role of trade unions in Soviet society, Lenin wrote:

> It is appropriate, I think, to observe for young members of the Party that one *cannot* become a class-conscious *real* Communist without studying— and I mean *studying*—everything written by Plekhanov on philosophy, for it is the best of all the international literature on Marxism.

And, in a footnote, he added:

> Incidentally, I cannot but express the wish, first, that the edition of Plekhanov's works now appearing should separate out all the articles on philosophy into a special volume or special volumes, with a more detailed index, etc. For this must form part of a series of obligatory text-books of Communism. Secondly, a workers' state in my opinion ought to require of professors of philosophy that they should know Plekhanov's exposition of Marxism and be able to pass on this knowledge to students.[3]

It must be pointed out that Plekhanov's legacy, for the Soviets, excludes the works of his later *menshevik* period (after 1903). Unlike Lenin's application of Marxism to the imperialistic state of capitalism, so the Soviets say,

> Plekhanov proved unequal to the tasks of the new era. [He] was too much under the sway of the traditions of the Second International, and in his later works he not only resisted the further development of Marxism, but deviated from the Marxist philosophy and distorted it in several respects.[4]

In 1903 ideological differences divided the infant group into two main factions. Lenin came to control the majority group, known as the *Bolsheviki*. In the decade before the First World War Lenin had reason for grave concern within the very ranks of the Bolsheviks. It took all his talents to offset the attempts of certain intellectuals to salvage the practical aspects of Marxism by putting them on a new theoretical basis, one called "empirio-criticism."

This was the name given to a group of positions based on sense experience and tending toward epistemological idealism. The group included men such as Mach, Avenarius, Poincaré, Bogdanov, and certain Neo-Kantians. Out of this controversy grew Lenin's famous *Materialism and Empirio-Criticism* (1909), a book in which he attempted to destroy any efforts at Marxist philosophical revisionism and to show that a theory of knowledge and a theory of matter can be developed from the principles of Marxism.

Recent Soviet historians of philosophy tell us that, although the book generally was praised as dealing a deathblow to Machism (empirio-criticism),

> Stalin did not understand the scientific character and the importance . . . of the battle that Lenin decreed against this revision of Marxism. In contradiction to the facts, Stalin characterized the fight by Lenin against Machism and *Ostzovism* as a "tempest in a glass of water."[5]

Certain letters of Stalin tell us that he considered Lenin's *Materialism and Empirio-criticism* as a "unique summary of its kind of the theses of the philosophy (epistemology) of Marxism," but at the same time to contain "certain errors." He even expressed a sympathy for Bogdanov's attack against Lenin (in *Science and Faith,* 1910). We are told by these same Soviet sources that the position of Stalin during this controversy was that of an eclectic, in that he was for the assimilation by Dialectical Materialism of the "positive aspects" of Machism, an assimilation Lenin had declared revisionistic.

In the years immediately following the Bolshevik victory of October, 1917 it was not considered obligatory for the members of the Party to follow Lenin's philosophy. In fact, such freedom in the field of philosophy existed that not only materialist philosophy but a variety of idealist systems were put forward and allowed to be taught. When the positive work of reconstruction began, these views came into open conflict and the non-Leninist professors of philosophy were dismissed from their positions.

When Stalin came to power in 1924 there were two trends in materialism in philosophical circles in the Soviet Union. The most prevalent variety was the "mechanistic" view that all higher-order phenomena, including psychic and social phenomena, could be reduced ultimately to mechanical processes. The other trend was rather positivistic in temper and denied philosophy had any right to existence now that science had developed.[6]

STALIN'S PHILOSOPHICAL CONTRIBUTION

It was in such an atmosphere that Stalin took the reins of power, although it would be six years before he could consolidate that power. Previous to 1924 he had written little in general and almost nothing on philosophy. His literary career began in 1901 and consisted for the most part of articles published in various newspapers. R. H. McNeal, speaking of Stalin's early career, reports:

As a political writer he attracted little attention. His compositions appeared only in exceedingly obscure newspapers in the Caucasus and many of them (including the largest single essay he ever wrote, *Anarchism or Socialism*) were written in the Georgian language, which neither Lenin nor other leading Bolsheviks could read.[7]

Contemporary Soviet historians of philosophy, speaking of the contribution of Georgia, have the following to say concerning this early work by Stalin:

> The articles of J. V. Stalin, *Anarchism or Socialism?*, published during 1906 and 1907 in the Georgian Bolshevik newspapers *Ajaili Tsjovreba* (New Life), *Ajali Droeba* (New Times) and *Dro* (The Times), contributed to the battle against the anarchists and towards the diffusion of the fundamentals of dialectical materialism and of historical materialism in Georgia. These articles were considered later by Stalin himself as the work of a novice Marxist. In this work are popularized certain theses of dialectical materialism. Nevertheless, there is also grave error found therein. The author of this work affirmed, for example, that nature exists in two distinct forms: the material and the ideal, and that "we are not able to imagine one without the other." Consequently, in this he departed from the materialistic solution of the fundamental problem of philosophy, that is to say, of the recognition of the primary character of matter, and of the derived character of consciousness [mind]; and, as such, conceded to idealism. Also erroneous was his manner of viewing Darwinism, even accusing it of rejecting development in a dialectical sense; that is, Darwinism was interpreted as a vulgarly evolutionistic doctrine. Such a coarse error was in contradiction with the appreciation of Marx, Engels, and Lenin in regard to Darwinism. This error of Stalin had its origin in his identification of evolutionary changes with quantitative and revolutionary changes with qualitative changes. He also was mistaken in presenting neo-Lamarckism as a progressive dialectical doctrine, considering it as part of a tendency as idealistic and reactionary as psycholamarckism; the other current (mechano-lamarckism) was frankly mechanistic, that is, antidialectic.[8]

Actually, Stalin's debut as a theoretical (i.e., ideological or philosophical) writer came in 1913 with his contribution to a journal of an article entitled **"The National Question and Social Democracy"** (later known as **"Marxism and the National Question"**). He had been replaced earlier as editor of *Pravda* and given a short leave to try his ability as a theoretician.

> Although this did not establish him as a peer of the prolific and theoretically minded leaders of Russian socialism, it was successful enough to be reprinted as a booklet a year after its publication in a journal, and it gave Stalin some standing as a Bolshevik expert on the problem of nationalities, to which his long service in the Caucasus also entitled him.[9]

Of Stalin's pre-1924 works the only one even remotely significant for philosophy is the series of articles of 1906-07 entitled *Anarchism or Socialism?* However, reference for philosophical purposes is seldom made to it and I will omit it in my more detailed consideration. I shall concentrate instead on the following four major philosophic works by Stalin: *Foundations of Leninism* (1924), *Dialectical and Historical Materialism* (1938), *Marxism and Linguistics* (1950), and *Economic Problems of Socialism in the U.S.S.R.* (1952).[10]

Beginning in April, 1924, three months after Lenin's death, Stalin delivered a series of lectures at the Sverdlov University in Moscow. The lectures, dedicated to the new members of the Communist Party of the Soviet Union recruited in the Lenin memorial enrollment, were published as *Foundations of Leninism.* As Stalin rightly observed, "the foundations of Leninism is a big subject." Omitting an exposition of those Marxist aspects of Lenin's philosophy, Stalin discusses only those points Lenin contributed *as new* to the "general treasury of Marxism." In answering the question "What is Leninism?" Stalin tells us that it is more than just an application of Marxism to the peculiar conditions of Russia, for Leninism is an international phenomenon. Also, Leninism is more than just a revival of the revolutionary elements of the early writings of Marx, for Lenin developed Marxism under the new conditions of imperialistic capitalism. What, then, in the last analysis, is Leninism? Here are the words of Stalin:

> Leninism is Marxism of the era of imperialism and of proletarian revolution. To be more exact, Leninism is the theory and tactics of the dictatorship of the proletariat in particular. Marx and Engels pursued their activities in the pre-revolutionary period (we have the proletarian revolution in mind), when developed imperialism did not yet exist, in the period of the proletarians' preparation for a revolution, in the period when the proletarian revolution was not yet a direct, practical inevitability. Lenin, however, the disciple of Marx and Engels, pursued his activities in the period of the unfolding proletarian revolution, when the proletarian revolution had already triumphed in one country, had smashed bourgeois democracy and had ushered in the era of proletarian democracy, the era of the Soviets.[11]

These lectures on Leninism were the extent of Stalin's participation in the philosophic activity of the times. It was to be four years before he stepped, in 1929, into the disputes concerning interpretation of Dialectical Materialism.[12] At that time he complained, in a speech, that the theoreticians had not kept pace with the practical developments of Marxism in the Soviet Union and accused philosophers in general of dragging their feet in the battle on the two fronts against Rightist and Leftist deviationism. By 1931 he was instrumental in having the Central Committee of the Party condemn both mechanism and its positivistic ally, as well as the "menshevizing idealism" of a third faction.

This double condemnation by the Central Committee marks a decisive turning point in the history of Soviet philosophy.

Whereas previously there had at least been a continuing opposition between rival tendencies within Soviet philosophy, and a resultant conflict of schools and opinions, with discussion and controversy, all such contention is from this time forward abolished; the course of philosophy flows in the narrow channel of officially prescribed opinion; all controversy is now directed outwards merely, against the "bourgeois" ideology which is striven against as a class enemy. To be sure, "discussions" are still conducted to promote the emergence of truth from an interchange of conflicting opinions, being devoted merely to discovery and "rooting-out" deviations on the part of individual authors from the course laid down by the "classics of Marxism," Marx, Engels, Lenin and Stalin.[13]

Nothing much happened philosophy-wise for a long time, but when it did it was associated with the name of Stalin. Indeed, to read the journals of the times, we are lead to believe that there was really only one productive philosopher in all of the Soviet Union. As Mitin wrote:

> The further advancement of Marxist-Leninist theory in every department, including that of the philosophy of Marxism, is associated with the name of Comrade Stalin. In all Comrade Stalin's practical achievements, and in all his writings, there is set forth the whole experience of the world-wide struggle of the proletariat, the whole rich storehouse of Marxist-Leninist theory.[14]

A criticism of philosophy was included in the general political and social house-cleaning that marked the new Soviet Constitution of 1936. Soviet philosophy was told that it was "out of date," too abstract and too scholastic in presenting the subject, too polluted with quotations from such deviationists as Trotsky. Like all conscientious Bolsheviks, the leading philosophers acknowledged these faults, thanked the government for setting them straight "just in time," and set out to repair the damage. Soviet philosophers at last came to acknowledge the dictatorship of the proletariat in their sphere.

In the years that followed there was a striking decline of philosophical literature and discussion. It is probably inaccurate to attribute this entirely to fear of Party criticism, although this factor had its effect. That any member of the Party should have feared criticism was extremely bourgeois and unbolshevik. It was the required norm in the Soviet Union that all phases of socialist activities should progress only and solely by the dictum of "criticism and self-criticism." This meant that in every field the members of the Party were to cooperate for the advancement of socialism and the realization of communism by working together, by acknowledging their own faults and shortcomings for the benefit of all, and by criticizing each other. As a matter of historical fact, what actually occurred is that criticism came from *above,* from the superiors, and self-criticism came from *below,* from the subordinates who acknowledged this criticism. This occurred throughout the last fifteen to twenty years of Stalin's rule. And periodically the philosophical

journals would be full of such criticism and self-criticism—a philosophical chapter of faults!

Exactly what was lagging on the part of philosophy in socialist construction may be seen in the following:

> It should also be borne in mind that ideology was underrated in many Party organizations, and propaganda and agitation work neglected. For a long time a part of the Party cadres did nothing to improve their knowledge of Marxism-Leninism. The result was that, as a whole, ideological work lagged behind the scale of the Communist construction going on. Taking into consideration the general requirements of Communist construction and the specific circumstances of the post-war [Second World War] period, the Party launched an *offensive* on the ideological front.[15]

The most important philosophical work to appear after 1936 and before the end of the Great Patriotic War was *The History of the Communist Party of the Soviet Union (Bolsheviki).* It was published in 1938 and at first was listed as edited by a Commission of the Central Committee headed by Stalin. However, and especially since 1948, the entire work was attributed to his personal authorship. This is probably so only in an indirect way; but there has never seemed to be any doubt that Stalin himself did write Section 2 of Chapter 4, **"On Dialectical and Historical Materialism,"** for it would have been the most dangerous portion of the history to have been entrusted to a subordinate.[16]

Soviet philosophical circles greeted its appearance as epoch-making, as having raised Dialectical Materialism "to a new and higher level" and as being "one of the pinnacles of Marxist-Leninist philosophical thought."[17] At any rate, the essay is extremely easy reading and its clarity and conciseness makes it excellent for pedagogical purposes, its main use in the Soviet Union until a few years after Stalin's death. For the purpose of a brief exposition, the work can be divided into three parts: Marxist Dialectical Method, Marxist Philosophical Materialism, and Marxist Historical Materialism. In speaking of the dialectical method, Stalin discusses its four principal features: (1) nature is an integrated whole; (2) nature is in a state of continuous change; (3) quantitative changes lead to qualitative changes; and (4) natural phenomena contain internal contradictions. These four principles then are applied to the study of the history of society to show us that: (1) each society must be studied contextually; (2) societies are not eternal; (3) a change in the way we make our living leads to a change (called "revolution") in our thinking; and (4) the contradictions in society are the economic classes of exploiter and exploited.

In presenting Marxist philosophical materialism Stalin lists its three principal features: (1) the world is material, not spiritual; (2) matter or nature exists outside and independent of our consciousness of it; and (3) the world and its laws are fully knowable, i.e., there is no "thing-in-itself" forever barred to the human mind. He then applies the materialism to the study of society and history to show that, just as it is possible to have a science of living things, or biology, and to predict and control by means of its laws, so it is possible to have a science of society and history and to predict and control by means of *its* laws. This new science is socialism; and it tells us that there are two aspects to society, the spiritual and the material. The spiritual aspect includes a society's political, moral, religious, philosophical, and cultural ideas or ideals. This aspect is secondary in origin to the material aspect, which includes all the factors that enter into the way a society makes its living.

This is not to say that the spiritual aspects are of no significance to a society. Far from it! Historical materialism, Stalin tells us, stresses the importance of these factors. The old social ideals are significant because they hamper the development and progress of society; the new social ideals are important because, once they have emerged from the material conditions, they hasten the further development of these same material conditions. For example, modern technologically advanced capitalism has engendered a cooperative and social mode of making a living by bringing together a great number of individuals to work in huge corporations. Thus, the material conditions of society are social, at least in this respect. Such a condition has given rise to new socialistic spiritual ideals, which once they have emerged must be re-applied in an orderly manner by the Party of the Proletariat to bring into balance the superstructure with the basis or foundations of the society.

With the above as his background Stalin launches into an examination of the "conditions of material life of society," to determine, in the final analysis, what precisely determines the ideas and views of a given society. He lists three determining factors of the material life of a society: (1) geography, (2) population, and (3) mode of production. Of these, the mode of production, or the method of procuring the means of life necessary for human existence, is the chief factor that ultimately determines the way a society thinks, its ideological superstructure. A change in the mode of production will generate, eventually and necessarily, a corresponding change in ideology in an effort to yield a synthesis of the contradictions existing between antithetical superstructure and basis. There have been, in the course of history, five main relations of production or ideological superstructures: the primitive communal, the slave, the feudal, the capitalist, and the socialist systems. In each case, the change in system occurred because of a change in the mode of production, which change began with a modification of the old productive forces.

During the period from 1938 to 1950 the many incursions of the Party into the philosophical sphere were made by subordinate personalities or party institutions.[18] It was twelve years before Stalin personally found it necessary to take pen in hand and lay down the law on matters of Marxist ideology. The occasion was the current "free discussion" in the seemingly innocent subject of linguistics.[19] On May 9, 1950 such a discussion was opened in *Pravda* on linguistic problems, an area hitherto dominated by Marr's theory of languages, a theory formulated after the Bolshevik Revolution and before his death in 1934.

In brief, the theory considered language to be part of the super-structure of society, along with religion, art, ethics, etc. Accordingly, language is the result of class structure. Before the rise of classes there had prevailed a system of hand-signals or gesture-language. This passed into articulate speech, reflecting formal thinking, which, in turn, reflected the split-up of society into classes. This formal logic and its speech will be superseded, once the classless society is reached, by dialectical materialist thinking. In this classless society "thought gains the upper hand over language, and will continue to gain it, until in the new classless society not only will the system of spoken language be done away with, but a unitary language will be created, as far, and even further, removed from articulate language as the latter is from gesture."[20] Thought will no longer be dependent on its phonetic and material expression in language; thought itself will replace language to give a universal means of communication to the members of the new classless and universal society.

Stalin's entrance into the discussion followed more than a month of "free discussion" by others.[21] The first point that he stressed is that, contrary to Marr, language is not to be assigned to the super-structure of society since it is not the outcome of the mode of production but of society as a whole. Moreover, language is not part of the basis of society.

Language, as has been said, is created by society in general, for the benefit of the whole of society, not in the interests of any one class and at the expense of other classes. In fact, class-conditioned words constitute barely one percent of the total vocabulary. *Language grows according to the developmental laws of society as a whole* and not by the laws of either the superstructure or the basis.

This means that unlike ideology, which develops by sudden eruptions or explosions, language grows by way of a gradual accumulation of new elements and the equally gradual dying away of old ones. And, as far as the unitary and universal thought-language predicted by Marr, according to Stalin this is no "language" at all, but rather a soundless and immediate communication of thoughts implying idealism and leading to the destruction of Marxist materialism. To separate material language from thought would make thought immaterial— to Stalin, plainly a contradiction.

These letters of Stalin on linguistics had a most important effect on Soviet philosophy and were to dominate the field until his death.

The last important work by Stalin bearing on philosophy appeared in October 1952. It was his ***Economic Problems*** *of Socialism in the U.S.S.R.,* originally published in the periodical *Bol'shevik.* In its external trappings the work purported to be Stalin's concluding comments on a discussion begun in 1951 on a new textbook on political economy.[22] However, as it came immediately prior to the XIXth Party Congress that met in the same month,[23] the comments are much more pertinent and were an opportunity for Stalin of rebuking the impatience of certain youthful party-members who supposed that the Soviet regime "can do anything" in the area of economics. On the contrary, says Stalin, the Soviet regime is bound by objective economic laws, existing independently of the will of man, and can create no new laws of its own. Even under socialism these economic laws retain their objective, necessary character, just as do the laws of physical nature. Man can do no more in economics than he can do in any other science—he can do nothing but recognize economic laws, utilize them by guiding their operation into particular channels willed by him, and "impart a different direction to the destructive action of some of the laws."

The work contained many other questions, but all are of lesser philosophic interest.

EVALUATION OF STALIN'S CONTRIBUTION

I now turn to an evaluation of Stalin's contribution to Marxism. Concerning any evaluation of Stalin's definition of Leninism, as given in his 1924 lectures on the *Foundations of Leninism,* it must be pointed out that, due to Stalin's political position, his definition managed to become the official one among the many advanced by various individuals. Stalin took great pains to dispel the misinterpretation of Leninism as practical Marxism *only.* He quotes from Lenin to show that for his predecessor "without a revolutionary theory there can be no revolutionary movement."[24]

Anyone who wishes to be scientific in his attack on contemporary imperialistic capitalism must be a Leninist, says Stalin. And anyone who wishes to be a Leninist must adopt the "special Leninist style" in his revolutionary activities. This "style" has two specific features: (1) the Russian revolutionary sweep and (2) American efficiency.

> The Russian revolutionary style is an antidote to inertness, routine, conservatism, mental stagnation and slavish submission to ancestral traditions . . . without it no progress is possible.

This characteristic runs the danger of degenerating into empty revolutionizing, i.e., to empty slogan-making and a lack of plain everyday work. American efficiency is the antidote to this.

> American efficiency is that indomitable force which neither knows nor recognizes obstacles; which with its business-like perseverance brushes aside all obstacles; which continues at a task once started until it is finished, even if it is a minor task; and without which serious constructive work

is inconceivable. But American efficiency has every chance of degenerating into narrow and unprincipled commercialism if not combined with the Russian revolutionary sweep.[25]

The combination of the two is the "essence" of Leninism in Party and State work.

Of the works I have considered, the first to be praised by the Soviet philosophers themselves in the most glowing terms was the short essay of 1938, *On Dialectical and Historical Materialism.* Stalin was praised not so much for *what* he said concerning dialectical method but more for the fact *that* he said something. After all, Engels was unable to bring to completion his projected *Dialectic of Nature:* and Lenin was not able to correlate into book-form his collected material on the dialectical method. "To Stalin alone it has been reserved to give the first comprehensive, systematic account of the doctrine of the materialist dialectic."[26]

In previous treatments of Marxism, philosophical materialism had always been examined *before* dialectical method. That Stalin reversed the order was deemed highly significant as an indication of the importance of the dialectic. It is generally recognized, however, that in the portion of his essay dealing with historical materialism Stalin is much more in his element. When the work first appeared, Soviet philosophers discovered in its very appearance something significant for historical materialism, namely, that Stalin was the first to disclose the laws of development of socialism after its victory in the U. S. S. R. and to establish the road to communism—socialist industrialization and collectivization of agriculture.

> He was also held to have improved upon Leninism in regard to a number of problems, such as those of the State, social classes, labour, the driving-forces of social development, and the position of nationalities under socialism and communism.[27]

Discounting the characteristic Soviet exaggeration of the times, Stalin does indeed show some originality in these areas and makes considerable departure from the original Marxist views. This is true especially in three areas: (1) the great emphasis he places on the "retroactive" influence of the superstructure; (2) an elaboration of the developmental laws in a socialistic classless society; and (3) the great stress he placed on the "national" factor. I shall now examine these in more detail.

Once the new ideological superstructure has arisen from a change in the basis of society, it acts in a "retroactive" manner to organize and carry the changing mode of production to its completion. That is, once ideas have arisen they can react, in turn, upon the material basis to contribute powerfully to its further development. This is seen, in principle, in Lenin; but the great emphasis placed by Stalin upon the "subjective factor" in completing the process of socialization has led some to conclude that he held this factor to be the *decisive* force in history. If true, nothing could be further from Marx. There seems to have been little change in official Soviet doctrine on this point as a result of the "de-Stalinization" policy.[28]

In a classless or socialist society any further development of the basis does not take place by "leaps" or revolutions; otherwise the dictatorship of the proletariat would be overthrown. Rather, the development now occurs according to a different type of "leap," *a gradual change,* since socialism is the end of the explosive type of dialectic. Certain further changes in the mode of production, such as complete collectivization of agriculture, take place now, not by "revolution from below" as in non-socialist societies, but by the process termed "revolution from above." This means, as Stalin was to point out in *Marxism and Linguistics,* that the socialist government takes the initiative in such actions.

Nowhere is Stalin's teaching seemingly more different from the original intention of Marxist historical materialism than it is on the national question. This emphasis on the "national" is coupled with his drive to reinstate the individual in his old rights. He still held, in general, that the driving force of social development is the proletariat as a class and not specific individuals, but he put a new interpretation on the individual.

From 1934 onward there was an ever-increasing degree of national patriotism spreading in the Soviet Union. Certain figures of the country's history were resurrected to places of honor, as seen in the literature of the times. This provided an opportunity for the deification of the founders of Marxism-Leninism and later for the glorification of Stalin himself.

By the early forties this Soviet emphasis on the national became clearly visible. In the political and military sphere the Second World War was declared a contest between socialism and imperialism and turned into the "Great Patriotic War." It is probably no exaggeration to say that Stalin's marriage of communism and nationalism (especially the Russian variety) prevented the defeat of the Soviet Union. In the historical and cultural sphere the Soviet Union was depicted increasingly as the "heart and backbone of human history." Everything of historical importance that ever had taken place within its territories, as far back as the ancient Chaldeans and Assyrians, was declared as evidence for the superiority of socialism. Everything occurring outside its boundaries was reckoned as more or less marginal. The exaggerated, often ludicrous, reports that the Russians had first discovered or invented "such-and-such" stem from this era.

Stalin had been concerned especially with the national question for a long time, and had come to be acknowledged as an expert in that area (the field of nationality affairs or the relations of peoples in the multinational Soviet Union), even while Lenin lived. At the XVIth Party Congress of 1930 he coined the celebrated formula that national cultures should be "national in form but socialist in content." He was to maintain that the period of building socialism in the U. S. S. R. is the opposite of the

period of the collapse and abolition of national cultures—it is a period of the "flowering" of national cultures so as to fulfill their potentialities and create the appropriate conditions for merging them into one common culture with one common language in the period of worldwide socialism. Is this contradictory? Certainly, says Stalin, but "anyone who fails to understand this peculiar feature and 'contradiction' of our transition period, anyone who fails to understand these dialectics of the historical process, is dead as far as Marxism is concerned."[29] Stalin, despite his apparent intellectual crudity, seemed to have sensed that nationalism goes a long way in cementing any society, socialist or otherwise. His marriage of communism and nationalism was to be of the greatest practical advantage to the Communist regime in the U. S. S. R., and one of his shrewdest strokes of practical genius in politics.

When Stalin's booklet on *Marxism and Linguistics* appeared, it was greeted as a "new, world-historical contribution to the treasury of Marxism." It is quite possible that this time the praise was accurate, for Stalin appeared to have introduced an entirely new theory in his amplification of historical materialism. What was so history-making in these letters of 1950 was the implication that a phenomenon, language in this case, could belong to neither the superstructure nor the basis of society, nor to an "intermediate" area but to *society as a whole.* This third area had never before been referred to in Marxist theory.[30]

All in all, it is not difficult to agree that "what he [Stalin] said was sensible, temperate, and on the whole far better linguistics doctrine than much that had preceded it" in the Soviet Union.[31] In this consideration of language Stalin was led to an examination of the development of socialism. In reality this was a further elucidation of his 1938 contribution of the active role of the superstructure and the manner in which the dialectic occurs in a socialist society, namely, by gradual and not by explosive leaps.

The main contribution of Stalin to the development of Soviet Marxism in this essay, as well as in all his others, is, in my considered opinion, his practical genius *to justify in theory what he had been doing already in fact.* The new course in the field of Bolshevik politics that Stalin had been pursuing for at least sixteen years was to find a theoretical anchorage in Marxist-Leninist theory as a result of this essay. According to Marxism-Leninism, theory and practice must proceed *simultaneously.* That this was not always the case in actual fact can be seen from the periodic rebukes by the Party to Soviet philosophers. It is to Stalin's credit that he saw the importance of grounding his practices in theory, of making his decisions according to Marxist theory. And he was not adverse to amplifying the main body of Marxism to accomplish this, for he recognized that it gave his decisions a sort of "scientific" necessity. More than anyone in the history of Marxism, Stalin has proven himself nimble in replacing out-dated formulas with new ones. In Stalin we see the *relativism* and *pragmatism* of Soviet Marxism.[32]

Is this the hated heresy of "revisionism?" Your answer will depend on who you are. Trotsky called Stalin a "revisionist"; but, on the other hand, Stalin called Trotsky a "falsifier" of Marxism. Stalin himself would have answered the charge of "revisionism" by reminding us that Marxism, above all else, *is not dogmatic!* Stalin is emphatic (dogmatic?) in his denial of dogmatism in his *Marxism and Linguistics.* Marxism is not a collection of unchanging dogmas. He who thinks so sees only the letter of Marxism but not its essence or content.

> Marxism is the science of the laws of development of nature and society, the science of the revolution of the oppressed and exploited masses, the science of the victory of socialism in all countries, the science of the building of the communist society. Marxism is a science and cannot stand still; it develops and perfects itself. In the course of its development Marxism cannot but be enriched by new experience, by new knowledge; consequently, its separate formulas and deductions cannot but change in the course of time, cannot but be replaced by new formulas and deductions corresponding to the new historical tasks. Marxism does not recognize any immutable deductions and formulas, applicable to all epochs and periods. Marxism is the enemy of dogmatism.[33]

Again: in an effort to embarrass Stalin, Trotsky and Kamenev attempted to show that Marx, Engels, and Lenin did not believe in the possibility of socialism in one country.

> Stalin, who normally depended heavily on scriptural authority, neatly shifted his ground and argued that "Marxism is not a dogma but a guide to action," that if Engels were alive he would say, "To the devil with all old formulas! Long live the victorious revolution in the U.S.S.R.!" And if Lenin had plainly said that the victory in one country is impossible, said Stalin, he must have meant merely that the 'complete' victory is impossible.[34]

The entire series dealing with *Economic Problems of Socialism in the U.S.S.R.* (1952) is most interesting, but the most important part of it, philosophically speaking, is the first section wherein the Soviet economists, especially the younger and often over-enthusiastic ones, are told that the laws of economics are as objective for a socialist society as are the laws of physical nature. To think otherwise is to be a "subjective idealist."[35]

Some historians see in this emphasis by Stalin on complying with reality, or the objective character of laws, a sign of pessimism and conservatism. True, Stalin by this time had learned by practice that the inevitable communist society was not just around the corner, and that unrealistic views in a centralized economy could cause national crises. However, in my opinion, this issue is part of the greater, overall problem of how the laws of the dialectic affect socialism as a society. The dilemma remains that *either* the laws of the dialectic apply to all societies, including socialism (and it, too, will pass away), *or* socialism is not a true society.[36]

The booklet on *Economic Problems of Socialism in the U.S.S.R.* is virtually Stalin's last testament. His death is recorded as follows in the 1960 edition of the *History of the Communist Party of the Soviet Union:*

> On March 5, 1953 soon after the [19th Party] Congress Joseph Vissarionovich Stalin died. The enemies of socialism counted on confusion breaking out in the ranks of the Party and in its leadership, and on vacillation appearing in the conduct of home and foreign policy. But their hopes were dashed. The Communist Party rallied still closer round its Central Committee, and raised the all-conquering banner of Marxism-Leninism higher than ever. The Leninist Central Committee successfully led the Party and the entire people forward, along the road to Communism.[37]

STALIN AND SOVIET TEXTBOOKS

The downgrading of Stalin began openly at the XXth Party Congress in 1956.

> The months leading to this event in February, 1956 were full of subtle bargaining and maneuver [between those seeking the leading position of power in the Party], in which the major issue was Stalin. Ever since the old man's death his status had been ambiguous. His bemedalled corpse had been placed beside Lenin's in the public mausoleum, under the direction of mortician Khrushchev ("Chairman of the Commission for the Funeral of Joseph Vissarionovich Stalin"), and remained enshrined in statue, picture, book, and toponymy. But his sanctity had been called into question in a number of implicit but fairly clear respects.[38]

An immediate and important reversal of Stalinism was the retreat from rule by terror. The revelation of the sorrowful state of the agricultural situation cast doubts on Stalin's ability as planner in this field. Stalin's charge of heresy was discredited with the renewal of friendly relations with Yugoslavia. More important for the purposes of philosophy was the so-called thaw in intellectual life.

From the opening session of the XXth Party Congress on February 14th until February 25th the only speaker to raise any specific criticism of Stalin was Mikoyan. On the last day Khrushchev delivered his famous attack on Stalin at a meeting closed even to foreign Communist observers.[39] He attacked Stalin for his vanity, arbitrariness, brutality, and blundering. The *H.C.P.S.U.* speaks of the event as follows:

> The question of overcoming the personality cult, alien to Marxism-Leninism, and of eliminating its consequences, occupied an important place in the proceedings of the Twentieth Congress. . . . It criticized, from the standpoint of principle, the mistakes brought about by the cult of Stalin, and planned measures to eradicate its consequences completely.
>
> In criticizing the personality cult, the Party was guided by the well-known propositions of Marxism-

Leninism on the role played in history by the masses, parties and individuals, and on the impermissibility of the cult of the personality of a political leader, no matter how great his services.

The Party was aware that open criticism of the errors stemming from the cult of the personality would be used by the enemies for anti-Soviet purposes. Nevertheless, it decided on that step, which is regarded as a matter of principle and prompted by the interests of Communist construction. It proceeded from the fact that, even if its criticism gave rise to some temporary difficulties, it would indisputably yield positive results from the point of view of interests of the people and of the ultimate goal of the working class. The personality cult had to be denounced above all in order to provide sure guarantees that *phenomena of this kind would never again arise in the Party and the country,* that Party leadership would be based on the collective principle and on a correct, Marxist-Leninist policy with the active, creative participation of millions of people. The criticism of this cult was of tremendous importance for the consolidation of the Party and the creative development of Marxism-Leninism, the extension of Socialist democracy, and also for the whole of the international Communist movement.[40]

During all this criticism Khrushchev was emphatic on the point that:

> He had many defects but Stalin was a devoted Marxist-Leninist, a devoted and steadfast revolutionary. Stalin committed many mistakes in the later period of his activity but he also did much that was useful for our country, for our party, for all international workers' movements. Our party, the Soviet people, will remember Stalin and give him his due.[41]

The de-Stalinization never meant to deny that Stalin rendered great services to the cause of Communism and was "an outstanding theoretician."[42] Stalin was attacked more for his political methods than for his theoretical contributions to Soviet Marxism. Nevertheless, there have been significant changes since the so-called de-Stalinization in the presentation of Dialectical Materialism, as seen from the various current Soviet textbooks we shall presently examine.

The definition of Leninism presented by Stalin in the *Foundations of Leninism* (1924), with his apologia for the coming of the proletarian revolution to relatively backward Russia, continues to dominate ideology.[43] The greatest change in Stalin's philosophical contribution has been in connection with his famous essay of 1938 on *Dialectical and Historical Materialism.* Within a year of his death reviewers of textbooks on Marxism, which books followed the method of exposition inaugurated by Stalin in his booklet, "now declared that it would have been more to the purpose if the exposition had begun, not by dealing with problems of method, but with a description of Marxist philosophical materialism."[44] The reason given by one critic is that "it is not possible to throw light

on the manner and method of investigating the material world without having previously explained what this material world itself consists in."[45] Soviet philosophers had come to recognize the pedagogical advantages of presenting the dialectic, as the rhythm of development in reality, *after* it has been explained what reality is.

One critic, B. M. Kedrov, of the Moscow Academy of Social Sciences, went further in his criticism and declared that textbooks on Marxism would be better to dissociate themselves entirely from the exposition by Stalin. The four points listed by Stalin as the principal characteristics of the dialectical method are said to omit a whole series of important problems. (This will be the same reason for objecting to Stalin's exposition of philosophical materialism.) Foremost among the omitted problems of dialectics is the "law of the negation of negations," the characteristic Lenin especially emphasized in his great admiration of Hegel's methodology. Briefly, it explained the re-emergence of the old negated aspect in a form higher than the original. Although not examined, this category of the dialectic is recognized as a fundamental law in a recent Soviet text on the *Categories of Dialectical Materialism.*[46] The book appeared after the XXth Party Congress and exhibits the ideological theses proposed by that meeting. It is significant that the lengthy bibliography contains no reference to Stalin's works. While Lenin is cited throughout the text, there is only one brief reference to Stalin, in connection with the cult of the personality.[47]

A text that does illustrate the return to the Leninist mode of presentation, of philosophical materialism first[48] and then dialectical method, is F. V. Konstantinov, editor, *The Fundamentals of Marxist Philosophy.* Its "Prologue" tells us that the authors are against idealism and metaphysics (which means the same in Soviet Marxist thought) as well as revisionism, "which actually constitutes the principal danger in the bosom of the worker and communist movement and against dogmatism." They emphasize their agreement with the declaration made by the representatives of the Communist and Workers' Parties of the Socialist countries at their conference in Moscow, November 14-16, 1957, namely, that the basic theory of Marxism-Leninism is Dialectical Materialism and that its application is the task of the workers' parties. The book is divided into an introduction and two parts. The first part, dealing with Dialectical Materialism, introduces the subject by first speaking of matter, its forms of existence, and consciousness before presenting the fundamental laws of the dialectic. An entire chapter (IX) is devoted to the "law of the negation of negation." The only work by Stalin included in the bibliography is *Questions of Leninism,* to which reference is made in connection with an attempt to show the indissoluble unity of Marxism-Leninism.[49]

However, that Stalin has not lost all his recognition as a "classicist" in Soviet philosophy can be seen from the following.

> After Lenin, the philosophy of Marxism was developed and carried forward by his disciples,

among them including the eminent Marxist J. V. Stalin. Except for a series of statements and errors, in relation to the cult of the personality, into which Stalin slipped during the last period of his life, *his works constitute a valuable contribution to Marxist thought.*[50]

F. V. Konstantinov, presently Director of the Institute of Philosophy, Academy of Sciences of the U.S.S.R., is also general editor of a textbook on *Historical Materialism.* There is no mention of Stalin in connection with the reference to the cult of the personality as idealistic, as seen in section four (dealing with the role of the leaders of the worker class) of the chapter.[51] This can be explained by the fact that the Prologue of the text is dated March 1954. However, there also is no reference to Stalin in the chapter (VIII) dealing with "The Role of the Popular Masses and of the Individual in History." This may be taken as an indication of the ambiguous position Stalin had in the years preceding the XXth Party Congress and his official re-evaluation.

The only recent textbook on Marxism-Leninism to appear in English translation has been *Fundamentals of Leninism-Marxism.* It, too, is authored by "a group of scholars, Party officials and publicists." The "Authors' Note" reminds us that criticism is still very much a part of the philosophical science in the U.S.S.R. Note the following:

> The authors are fully aware of the complexity of their task, which was to provide a scientifically competent and, at the same time, popular exposition of Marxism-Leninism, a science which is being constantly developed and enriched owing to changing historical conditions. It is only natural, therefore, that this attempt, the first in many years, to summarize in a single book the basic propositions of Marxism-Leninism cannot be free from shortcomings and defects. All readers' criticisms and advice for improving the book will be gratefully taken into account in preparing the second edition.[52]

Of the numerous footnotes only three refer to Stalin. One, from *Problems of Leninism,* deals with the fact that the rising bourgeoisie did not realize that their innovations in production means would lead eventually to a re-grouping of social forces.[53] The second deals with Stalin's definition of "nation;"[54] and the third is a reference to Stalin's realization (in 1931) that a high rate of industrial growth for the Soviet Union was a matter of life or death for the first socialist state in the world.

The text exhibits the non-Stalinist form of presentation of Marxism, philosophical materialism first (Chap. 1) and materialist dialectics secondly (Chap. 2). In the chapter dealing with the role of the masses and the individual in history there is a consideration of the contradiction between the cult of the individual and Marxism-Leninism and a mention, in the usual words, of Stalin as an example of the harm of such a cult.

A significant departure in form can be detected in the latest edition of the *History of the Communist Party of the Soviet Union.* Historically speaking, the book has been rewritten to place Stalin in proper perspective in history and to avoid the exaggerations and lies connected with the cult of the personality. Philosophically speaking, there is absent a section that summarizes the theory of Soviet Marxism. Stalin's exposition in the 1938 edition has been removed but not replaced. The only references to ideology are of a historical nature, namely, sections of Lenin's development of Marxist philosophy and theory of the party, as well as his theory of socialist revolution.[55]

There has also been a notable lessening of the cultural isolationism between the Soviet Union and the West. Thus, the 1960 edition of the *H.C.P.S.U.* acknowledges (p. 630) that, while patriotism has led to a rise in the ideological level of the people,

> . . . at the same time certain mistakes were made in propagating Soviet patriotism. The press frequently portrayed all life in the capitalist world as being a mass of corruption. The activity of the progressive forces was underrated and achievements in science and technology abroad were ignored. This hindered the speedy utilization of major discoveries made in science and technology abroad, limited creative contacts between Soviet and foreign scientists and engineers, and impeded the establishment of close ties with the democratic, progressive section of the people in the capitalist countries.

This lessening of isolationism in regard to philosophy has taken, among other means, the path of participation, in an ever-increasing degree, in the last three world congresses of philosophy. In an effort to extend its participation to the greatest possible number of attending delegates, the Soviet Union, unlike any other country, had translated into English and distributed gratis copies of the papers delivered by her delegation at the latest congress, the XIIIth, held in Mexico City, September 7-14, 1963.[56]

This does not mean that peaceful co-existence has entered the area of philosophy. According to the late Premier Khrushchev, in the course of his castigation of those comrades who signed a "petition" calling for such co-existence, those who wish to propagate ideological co-existence are the enemies of the Soviet people, for they wish to replace the "cement" of communist ideology, which unites the Party into a monolithic whole, with the "salt" of a bourgeois ideology that would destroy all that the Soviets have built and hold dear.[57]

Despite the lessening of cultural isolationism, the Communist regime has continued Stalin's emphasis on nationalism, without acknowledging him as its source.[58] Lenin's name increasingly is attached to this policy. For example, N. S. Khrushchev, in his report to the Extraordinary Twenty-First Congress of the Party (1959), tells us: "The Leninist national policy, which provides ample opportunities for the all-round economic and cultural progress of all peoples, finds vivid expression in our plans."[59] This continued emphasis on Soviet patriotism does not, however, interfere with what the 1960 edition of the *H.C.P.S.U.* calls "proletarian internationalism." This name refers to the fraternal co-operation, mutual aid and sincere mutual support in the struggle for Communism to be found between the U.S.S.R. and the Peoples' Democracies of Europe and Asia.

Stalin's booklet on *Marxism and Linguistics,* greeted as a "new, world-historical contribution to the treasury of Marxism," was not considered much of a reference work by the time D. P. Gorski, among others, wrote *Thought and Language.* This series of essays is based on the thesis that thought and language constitute an indissoluble organic unity; that it is impossible to understand either the naturalness of thought as a generalized reflection and mediation of reality or the naturalness of language as a means of communication, of an exchange of thoughts between persons, if thought and language are considered isolated and separated from each other.[60] Of the six essays only two mention Stalin. D. P. Gorski, in his "Language and Knowledge," quotes Stalin when discussing language as a means of exchanging thought. V. Z. Panfilov, in his "On the Correlation Existing between Language and Thought," refers to and discusses Stalin's position that: (1) phonetic language constitutes the only material basis for abstract and generalized thought; and (2) given the fact that deaf mutes are deprived of a phonetic language, their abstract and generalized thoughts are founded on images of perception and representation. Panfilov disagrees with Stalin's contention that sign language is not, properly speaking, a language.[61]

In the recent Soviet *Manual of Political Economy,* Stalin's *Economic Problems of Socialism in the U. S. S. R.* (1952) is referred to approximately twice, the second time in order to point out not only the important problems it raises but also its errors. We are told that:

> . . . in his last work, *Economic Problems of Socialism in the U. S. S. R.,* Stalin expounded some important problems of Marxist-Leninist theory: of the objective character of the economic laws of socialism, of the law of planned and proportional development, and others. It must be pointed out, nevertheless, that in this work and in certain others by Stalin are contained erroneous theses, such as, for example, that the mercantile traffic already represents, in actuality, a curb for the development of productive forces and that the time already has come for the necessity of a gradual passage to direct change of products between industry and agriculture; an insufficient appreciation of the force of the law of value in the sphere of production, in particular that touching on the means of production, etc.[62]

The singularly most valuable essay in English on some of the developments in Soviet philosophy since the XXth Party Congress is an article of that same title translated from the Russian original. It informs us that:

> During the years that have elapsed since the 20th Party Congress, changes of great importance have occurred . . . in ideological developments. . . . All this has produced a creative environment in our country and has stimulated activity in the field of philosophy. It may be stated without exaggeration that the 20th Congress of the Party, by creatively solving pressing problems of the present epoch, marked the beginning of a new stage in the development of social sciences generally in our country.[63]

It is said that ". . . research in the field of philosophy has increased in variety and deepened in content, that its ties with life and with those great tasks which the Party is fulfilling in organizing extensive communist construction [Khrushchev had called the post XXth Party Congress period a time of "taking apart and cleaning up"] have been strengthened."[64] The greatest evil of the Stalinist cult was that "works of commentary were elevated to first place." This meant that "only one person had the right to create anything new or original." That "one" person was, of course, Stalin.

Philosophic writings degenerated into "gray" works "in which elementary declarations and philosophical definitions are repeated *ad nauseam* in place of profound study and analysis of . . . [current] reality."[65] This "citationism," as Okulov refers to it, resulted in *separation of theory from practice,* for "many workers in philosophy ceased to deal with pressing problems of the day in terms of historical philosophical subject matter," and *dogmatism,* for which the "dictation of theory" and "a subjective evaluation of certain writings among the classics of Marxism-Leninism" prevented an accurate understanding of these same classics.[66]

Okulov maintains that the Soviet philosophers, unshackled by the cult of the personality of Stalin, are remedying this situation. He reminds us that the finest philosophical works of the past speak of their own epoch; and this "contemporaneity," the very "soul of progressive philosophy and a major source of its development," is what Soviet philosophy must exhibit and is exhibiting once more. In his words: "Today, more than at any previous time, the problem is that of rendering philosophy a moral weapon in the struggle of the Soviet people for the construction of communism."[67]

In summary, it might be pointed out that the so-called de-Stalinization has affected Soviet philosophy mainly by freeing it from the dictatorship of any one individual and subordinating it to the dictatorship of the proletariat.[68] The *renewed* emphasis on cooperative writing of philosophical texts (most textbooks had been so written even during the Stalin epoch) aims to eliminate, through criticism and self-criticism, a recurrence of the cult of the individual. Stalin still is recognized as having contributed to the development of Marxism-Leninism but is rarely quoted,[69] and is not considered the "classic" he once was thought to be. Gone is any reference to Marxism-Leninism-Stalinism. His main theoretical work, *On Dialectical and Historical Materialism,* has been omitted from the latest edition of the singularly most important book in the Soviet Union, namely, the *History of the Communist Party of the Soviet Union;* and his method of the presentation of theory has been abandoned in favor of a return to Lenin.[70] In spite of all this, Stalin still remains the most "realistic" of all the contributors to the "treasury" of Marxism, and this by his ability to bring theory (by "developing" it) in line with practice (his own political activities).[71]

NOTES

[1] Gustav A. Wetter, *Dialectical Materialism* (London: Routledge & Kegan Paul, 1958), p. 209. The "Stalinist period" coincides with the years during which Stalin held totalitarian powers, from approximately 1930 onward, rather than from the death of Lenin in 1924. The 'twenties' were years in which Stalin had to combat the ambitions of the other powerful Bolsheviks. He did not succeed in consolidating his power until at least December, 1929. Wetter's book is not without its limitations and shortcomings. For a critical review of the work, see John Somerville, "Approaches to the Critique of Soviet Philosophy," *Philosophy and Phenomenological Research,* 23 (1962), 269-73. For an example of Soviet criticism of Wetter, see F. T. Tarjiptsev, *La Materia como Categoría Filosófica* (Mexico, D. F.: Grijalbo, 1962), pp. 18, 138, 151-53, 168-69, 178, 190, 204, 227-28, 235. Also, see A. F. Okulov, "Some Developments in Soviet Philosophy since the 20th Party Congress" *Soviet Studies in Philosophy,* 1 (1962), 5, where both Wetter and Bochenski (see n. 12, below), are referred to as "well-known falsifiers of Marxism."

[2] *The Teaching of Karl Marx,* as quoted in the "Introduction" by Andrew Rothstein of his English translation of Plekhanov's *On the Development of the Monist View of History* (London, 1947), p. 25. The other two important works of Plekhanov on historical materialism are *The Materialist Conception of History* and *The Role of the Individual in History.*

[3] *Ibid.,* p. 21. There is a five-volume *Selected Philosophical Works* of Plekhanov in Russian (Moscow, 1956) that is being translated into English. Each volume contains an introductory essay. At present only the first volume has been completed; it contains an informative essay by V. Fomina. Also in Russian is the study by V. Fomina, *The Philosophic Ideas of G. Plekhanov* (Moscow, 1955). Besides the English translations of Plekhanov mentioned above, see his *Unaddressed Letters* and *Art and Social Life* (Moscow, 1957) and *The Bourgeois Revolution,* a pamphlet issued by the American Socialist Labor Party (New York, 1955). His *Fundamental Questions of Marxism* exists in French translation (Paris, 1947). Studies on Plekhanov have been made by S. H. Baron. See his "Plekhanov and the Origins of Russian Marxism," *The Russian Review,* 14 (1955) 315-30; "Plekhanov's Russia: The Impact of the West Upon an 'Oriental Society,'" *Journal of the History of Ideas,* 19 (1958), 388-404. A truly major contribution is his *Plekhanov, The Father of Russian Marxism*

(Stanford: Stanford Univ. Press, 1963), especially pp. 286-95 for the treatment of his philosophy.

[4] Unsigned "Editor's Preface" in G. Plekhanov, *Essays in Historical Materialism:* "The Materialist Conception of History" and "The Role of the Individual in History" (New York: International Publishers, 1940), p. 9.

[5] M. A. Dynnik y Otros, eds. *Historia de la filosofía,* Tomo V, "Desde finales del siglo XIX hasta la revolución socialista de octubre de 1917" (Mexico, D. F.: Grijablo, 1963), pp. 155-56. The Russian edition was published in 1957.

[6] For a recent critique of contemporary positivism by a Soviet philosopher, see B. M. Kedrov, "Philosophy as a General Science," *The Soviet Review,* 4 (1963), 49-70. The article, of which this is an English translation, is an attack prompted by A. J. Ayer's article on "Philosophy and Science" that appeared in *Voprosy filosofii,* 1962, No. 1. Kedrov's own reply originally appeared in *Voprosy filosofii,* 1962, Nos. 5 and 6.

[7] R. H. McNeal, *The Bolshevik Tradition* (Englewood Cliffs, N. J.: Prentice-Hall, 1963), p. 78.

[8] Dynnik, *op. cit.,* V, pp. 319-20.

[9] McNeal, *op. cit.,* p. 79. See also n. 54.

[10] Fourteen volumes of Stalin's official *Works* were planned. Only thirteen have appeared. It required eleven volumes to contain his works prior to 1934. After January 1934, when Stalin's political supremacy was assured, his public speeches and published writings dwindled greatly. According to McNeal, *op. cit.,* p. 107, "the rarity of his addresses or writings made it easier to build up gigantic campaigns of acclaim for these 'classics.'" More will be said about Stalin's "genius" on matters of theory in the concluding portion of this paper.

[11] Josef Stalin, *Foundations of Leninism* (New York: International Publishers, 1939), pp. 10-11.

[12] One other contribution during these years (1926) by Stalin to Marxism should be mentioned. This is the weighty essay entitled "On Questions of Leninism," published as a discourse on theory after his victory against various oppositions in the ruling circles of Leningrad. Later the essay was printed as part of a larger anthology of didactic works, *Problems of Leninism.* "The book, from that time until Stalin's death, served as the basic reference work on Stalinism." McNeal, *op. cit.,* 95. The Stalinism mentioned is a reference to matters more political than philosophic. This is probably the reason why J. M. Bochenski considers it a "misinterpretation" to cite *Problems of Leninism* as a philosophical work. According to him, the book does not deal with philosophy except in a few marginal comments. See *Soviet Russian Dialectical Materialism* (Dordrecht, Holland: D. Reidel, 1963), p. 34. The philosophic nature of the work is due to the inclusion of *Foundations of Leninism,*

which is said to form the nucleus of the celebrated collection. See Wetter, *op. cit.,* p. 210.

[13] Wetter, *op. cit.,* p. 175.

[14] M. B. Mitin, *Dialektichesky materialiszm* (Dialectical Materialism) (Moscow, 1933), p. 347. English translation in Wetter, *op. cit.,* p. 177. Earlier Stalin had been praised as a loyal disciple of Marxism-Leninism, especially after December 1929 when he successfully crushed the last serious attempt against Bolshevik unity and his power. On December 21 Stalin was honored with the following birthday message by *Pravda:* "To the true continuator of the cause of Marx and Lenin, to the staunch fighter for the purity of Marxism-Leninism, for the steel-like unity of ranks of the All-Union Communist Party (of Bolsheviks) and the Communist International, for international proletarian revolution; to the organizer and leader of socialist industrialization and collectivization of the Soviet land; to the old *Pravada*-ist; to Comrade Joseph Vissarionovich Stalin from *Pravda*—militant Bolshevik greetings." Cited by McNeal, *op. cit.,* p. 102.

[15] B. N. Ponomaryov et Al., *History of the Communist Party of the Soviet Union* (Moscow: Foreign Languages Publishing House, 1960), p. 629 (hereafter referred to as *H.C.P.S.U.,* 1960).

[16] The Russian title of this work has been translated also as *History of the All-Union Communist Party.* In the first ten years of its appearance at least thirty-six million copies were printed. The essay on "Dialectical and Historical Materialism" was reprinted in periodicals, as a brochure, and later as part of Stalin's anthology, *Problems of Leninism,* to increase its printing to many more millions. It was mainly upon this essay that Stalin's claim to theoretical omniscience was based.

[17] J. Stalin, *A Short Biography* (London, 1943), p. 56.

[18] From a low of 1.9 million in 1938, due to expulsion and terrorism, Party membership increased by 1946 to approximately 6 million, of whom half had joined during the war. *H.C.P.S.U.* (1960), pp. 629-30, 632, tells us that since "a sizeable section of the Party membership had not had time to receive the necessary theoretical training," it was decided not to press for further growth but to organize education on a large scale. "Between 1946 and 1952 the bulk of Party and government workers went through refresher training" in an effort to destroy "the survivals of bourgeois views and ideas." "On the initiative of the Central Committee, discussions were held on philosophy (1947), biology (1948), physiology (1950), linguistics (1950), and political economy (1951). Serious shortcomings in the elaboration of Marxist-Leninist philosophy were revealed and criticized during the discussion of philosophical problems. These shortcomings were disregard of Party principles, attempts to gloss over the contradictions between Marxism-Leninism and philosophical trends alien to it, isolation from urgent problems of the day, and manifestations of scholasticism.

The discussion mapped out ways of reorganizing the front of philosophical science."

[19] A "free discussion" is an open debate on those matters or points upon which the Party has not pronounced definitively.

[20] N. Y. Marr, *Izbrannye raboty* (Selected Works), III, p. 118; English translation in Wetter, *op. cit.,* p. 196.

[21] On June 20, 1950 he sent a letter to *Pravda,* followed by four others published on July 4 and August 2. That same month the letters appeared for the first time in booklet form, under the title of *Marxism and Linguistics.*

[22] Of the discussions initiated by the Central Committee, that on political economy began in 1951. According to *H.C.P.S.U.* (1960), pp. 632-33: "The economic discussion dealt with the features distinguishing the economic development of modern capitalism, the basic laws governing the socialist reorganization of society, and the ways of effecting the gradual transition from Socialism to Communism. Subjective and voluntarist views were condemned. The advocates of these views denied the objective character of economic laws; they could be made, transformed or abolished at will. This point of view led to an arbitrary approach to economic management and to adventurism in politics. The discussion revealed the serious consequences of the prolonged isolation of the economic sciences from the actual development of socialist society."

[23] The XIXth Party Congress was held in October 1952. It was the first such meeting in thirteen years. By then the membership of the Party was 6,013,259, with 868,886 candidate members. For a résumé of what occurred see *H.C.P.S.U.* (1960), pp. 633-36. It will be seen that it was at this congress that the name "Bolshevik" was dropped from the Communist Party of the Soviet Union.

[24] Stalin, *Foundations of Leninism,* p. 29. While Lenin lived Stalin played a most limited role in the high-level discussions of theory within the Party. "But after the demise of the chief dogmatist, Stalin began to promote himself as the prime interpreter of Leninist theory. His effectiveness was all the greater among the masses of new and less sophisticated party members because he presented himself as a simple apostle of Lenin, too modest to be an original theoretician in his own right, as were Trotsky, Zinoviev and Bukharin, among others. In this spirit Stalin delivered a series of lectures at the Sverdlov University in Moscow. . . . In this didactic work he presented what came to be the official Bolshevik apologia for the coming of a 'proletarian' revolution in a country which had not achieved the high level of capitalism that Marx had predicted as the basis for the dialectical upheaval. Stressing Lenin's theory that the most advanced stage of capitalism was the worldwide development of imperialism, Stalin argued that Russia, although not very advanced economically, was the country in which all of the 'contradictions' of world capitalism were most highly concentrated. This justified the Bolshevik revolution and

moved toward the dogma of 'socialism in one country,' set forth in December, 1924. . . . It might be quite a while, he argued, before revolution would come in the West, owing to Lenin's 'law of uneven development of capitalism,' which Stalin interpreted to mean that revolution comes in successive waves rather than all at once." McNeal, *op. cit.*, pp. 91-92.

[25] Stalin, *The Foundations of Leninism,* p. 126. With this definition Stalin places Bolshevik revolutionary practice firmly upon a theoretical foundation. Marxism-Leninism cannot deemphasize theory in favor of practice only. Contemporary Soviet Marxists continue to stress the union of theory and practice. Note the following, from a paper given at the recent XIIIth World Congress of Philosophy: ". . . Although at times people may achieve practical successes before they are aware of the inner workings of the phenomena and things they are using, in the long run knowledge and ability to act tend to merge. The boundless possibilities of action and cognition merge in the infinite progress of mankind." Y. K. Melvil, "Man in the Space Age" (Moscow, 1963), p. 14.

[26] Wetter, *op. cit.*, p. 212 and n. 2. It is with this essay that Stalin laid aside his role of mere continuator and loyal disciple of Marx and Lenin and took up the task of elaborating the science of Marxism-Leninism. His contribution entitled him to be listed among the "classics" of Dialectical Materialism. Henceforth began the practice of referring to Marxism-Leninism-Stalinism. "The veneration of Stalin especially emphasized the versatility of the leader's genius. Stalin's program for Soviet Russia was comprehensive in scope, omitting no department of life and culture, and it is natural that an all-embracing program should be directed by an all-round genius." McNeal, *op. cit.*, p. 107.

[27] Wetter, *op. cit.*, p. 215.

[28] Note the following: "In the conditions of transition from Socialism to Communism, when the importance of the subjective factor, the conscious guidance of society, increases, the Party, equipped with the theory of Marxism-Leninism, is called upon to direct the creation of new economic and political relations on the basis of the principles of Communism." *H.C.P.S.U.* (1960), p. 684.

[29] Reviewing the results of the Party's activity at the head of the Soviet People for forty years, the 1960 edition of the *H.C.P.S.U.* reminds us, with no reference to Stalin, that: "the Party ensured the all-round development of culture that is national in form and Socialist in content. The culture of each people influences that of other peoples, and shares in the common process of creating a Soviet socialist culture (p. 691)."

[30] This innovation seems to have eluded most students of Soviet Marxism. In my opinion it provides an opportunity to examine critically the possibility that many more social phenomena, hitherto considered a reflection of class struggle, may be the result of the development of society

as a whole. The revolution within Marxism that such a re-evaluation could bring about cannot be overstated.

[31] These are the words of Professor Margaret Schlauch, one-time professor of New York University and then (1951) of the University of Warsaw. Her article on Stalin's contribution to linguistics is reprinted as Appendix III of Joseph Stalin, *Marxism and Linguistics* (New York: International Publishers, 1951), pp. 57-58. She reminds us that the implication ". . . that Stalin's statement came as a fiat unexpectedly imposed on linguistics from without; that they [the linguists] had no voice in the matter at all, and no choice but to accept an unwelcome decree issued from above by a non-specialist; in fact, by an unqualified interloper"—this implication is all quite the opposite of the truth. According to her: "Stalin is actually a student and specialist in those fields of sociology which border immediately on linguistics (nationalities, minorities, and so on). . . . Moreover, he did not suddenly descend upon the body of Soviet linguists with an unsolicited decree concerning their special subjects. A lively debate on the matter had been going on for some weeks, chiefly in the columns of *Pravda.* Stalin entered it upon invitation, in response to questions posed to him directly by several young students."

Concerning Stalin's qualifications, these are his own words, in the opening paragraph (p. 9) of the booklet under discussion: "A group of comrades of the younger generation have asked me to give my opinion in the press on questions relating to the science of language, particularly in reference to Marxism in linguistics. I am not a linguist and cannot of course satisfy these comrades fully. But as to Marxism in linguistics, as well as in other social sciences, this is a subject with which I have a direct connection."

[32] For a critique of American pragmatism and relativism, see the following: Harry K. Wells, *Pragmatism, Philosophy of Imperialism* (New York: International Publishers, 1954); and Maurice Cornforth, *Science versus Idealism* (London: Lawrence & Wishart, Ltd., 1955), Chap. 18.

[33] Stalin, *Marxism and Linguistics,* p. 47.

[34] McNeal, *op. cit.,* p. 97.

[35] Joseph Stalin, *Economic Problems of Socialism in the U.S.S.R.* (New York: International Publishers, 1952), p. 63. Soviet philosophers took the hint from this warning to the economists and resolved to pay greater attention themselves to the objective laws of social development, and especially to avoid *subjective* conceptions of these laws—all of which set off another series of criticisms and self-criticism in philosophic circles.

[36] Various solutions have been proposed, examples of which range from the affirmation that the contradictions existing in a socialist society are not of the type ("antagonistic" economic exploitation) that find their resolution in revolution to the assertion that socialism *as a society*

does not exist and hence is not a violation of the law of dialectics. This latter view stems from an interpretation of history *as the development of socialism.* Once socialism is reached, history *as revolutionary transitions* has ended. Still others would have it that the socialist society is the beginning of history and that all "pre-societies" leading to it are part of "pre-history." The presence of economic contradictions is characteristic of prehistory only.

See: V. Pirozhkova, "Problems of Historical Materialism," *Bulletin, Institute for the Study of the U. S. S. R.* (1958), pp. 31-37; I. V. Malyshev, "The Motivating Forces of the Development of Socialist Society," *Voprosy filosofii,* (1953) No. 5; V. I. Gazenko and M. N. Rutkevich, "A Profound Study of the Problems of Dialectical Materialism," *Ibid.* (1954), No. 2; T. A. Stepanyan, "Contradictions in the Development of a Socialist Society and Ways of Overcoming Them," *Ibid.* (1955), No. 2; D. F. Krivoruchko, "On the Basic and Chief Contradictions of a Communist Structure," *Ibid.* (1957), No. 4; and O. G. Yurovitsky, "The Basic Economic Law and the Basic Economic Contradiction of Socialism," *Ibid.* (1957), No. 6.

[37] *H.C.P.S.U.* (1960), p. 636.

[38] McNeal, *op. cit.,* p. 150.

[39] This was the same man who had exclaimed in 1939: "Hail the greatest genius of mankind, teacher and leader, who leads us victoriously to Communism, our own Stalin!" N. Krushchev, *18th Congress of the All-Union Communist Party* (Russian edition, Moscow, 1939), p. 174. Translation in *Soviet World Outlook* (Washington, D.C.: U. S. Government Printing Office, 1959), p. 43.

[40] *H.C.P.S.U.* (1960), pp. 669-70. Herein the reasons for the rise of Stalin's personality cult are given in such a manner that it is made to appear to have been historically inevitable.

[41] N. Khrushchev, "For a Close Tie of Literature and Art with the Life of the People," *Kommunist* (1958), No. 12, p. 17. Translation in *Soviet World Outlook,* p. 44. Also, see N. Khrushchev, "Speech at Reception in Chinese Peoples' Republic Embassy," *Pravda,* January 19, 1957; English translation in *Soviet World Outlook,* p. 47. Finally, see *H.C.P.S.U.* (1960), p. 671, for a quote from Khrushchev that appeared in *Pravda,* August 28, 1957. What stands out in all this is Krushchev's "prayer" that "God grant that every Communist will be able to fight as Stalin fought."

[42] *H.C.P.S.U.* (1960), p. 670.

[43] In *The Fundamentals of Marxist Philosophy* the only reference made to Stalin's works is to his *Questions of Leninism,* in connection with an attempt to show the indissoluble unity of Marxism-Leninism. "As J. V. Stalin has shown, Leninism is the direct continuation of Marxism in the new historical conditions, in the epoch of imperialism and the proletarian revolution." F. V. Konstantinov, ed., *Los Fundamentos de la Filosofía Marxista* (Mexico: D. F.: Grijalbo, 1960), p. 107.

[44] Wetter, *op. cit.,* p. 237. See Bochenski, *op. cit.,* pp. 60-61.

[45] *Voprosy filosofii* (1954), No. 5, p. 199; English translation in Wetter *op. cit.,* p. 237.

[46] See "Prologo," M. M. Rosental y G. M. Straks, ed., *Categorias del Materialismo Dialectico* (Mexico, D. F.: Grijalbo, 1960). This work is the Spanish translation of a 1957 Russian edition. The text was written by members of the Chair of Philosophy of the State Pedagogical Institute, "K. D. Ushinski" of Yaroslavsk, U. S. S. R., in collaboration with other investigators from other scientific institutions. The basis of the text was an elaboration of an article entitled "Categories of Dialectical Materialism" published in 1954 in *Scientific Sketches* by the aforementioned Institute. We are told that the book does not pretend to be a complete exposition of all the categories of the Marxist dialectic. In particular, there is not included a study of the categories that express the fundamental laws of the dialectic (quality, quantity, contradiction, negation, etc.), for these had been the object of a more lengthy examination. Chapter headings are: the categories of dialectical materialism; phenomenon and essence; cause and effect; necessity and causality; laws; content and form; possibility and reality; the singular, the particular and the universal; the abstract and the concrete; and the historical and the logical.

A more recent book, M. M. Rosental, *Principios de Lógica Dialéctica* (Montevideo: Pueblos Unidos, 1962), devotes the last section of Chap. III (p. 171) to the law of the negation of negation. In his "Prólogo" the author tells us that this book is, "in a certain sense," the continuation of an earlier work by himself, namely, *Los Problemas de la Dialéctica en "El Capital" de Marx* (Montevideo: Pueblos Unidos, 1961). An entire chapter (7) is devoted to this law in A. D. Makarov, A. V. Vostrikov, y E. N. Chesnokov, eds., *Manual de Materialismo Dialéctico* (Montevideo: Pueblos Unidos, n. d.). Finally, for a recent treatment of the dialectic of the development (evolution) of inorganic matter, see: S. Meliujin, *Dialéctica del Desarrollo en la Naturaleza Inorganica* (Mexico, D. F.: Grijalbo, 1963). The references are to Engels and Lenin, with no mention of Stalin.

[47] Rosental and Straks, *op. cit.,* pp. 151-52, in which Stalin's cult of the personality and the errors resulting therefrom are said to have been inevitable once Stalin stopped taking into account the role of the popular masses in history ". . . Isolating himself from the masses, believing in his own infallibility, he began to fall into arbitrariness and committed a series of grave faults. . . . "

[48] For a recent treatment of philosophical materialism, see F. T. Arjiptsev, *La Materia como Categoría Filosófica* (Mexico, D. F.: Grijalbo, 1962). Stalin is not listed in the

lengthy bibliography nor is he quoted. Lenin's *Material-ism and Empirio-Criticism* is referred to constantly.

[49] F. V. Konstantinov, ed., *Los Fundamentos de la Filosofía Marxista* (Mexico, D. F.: Grijalbo, 1960), p. 107. This text was published first in Russian in July 1959 and is authored by a board of thirteen. Its "Prologue" tells us that "the manuscript of the book was read by many scientific workers and professors of Marxist philosophy, and discussed in a full session of the Institute of Philosophy of the Academy of Sciences of the U. S. S. R. with participation by the most active philosophic sector, by the professors of the establishments of higher learning. It also was submitted to a discussion in the chairs of philosophy of the higher schools of Moscow and Leningrad." *Ibid.,* p. 11. This shows the care taken to avoid doctrinal error and the Soviet principle of criticism and self-criticism in cooperative endeavors.

See Okulov, *op. cit.,* pp. 5a and 8a. Herein we are told that: "Textbooks on dialectical materialism have been published in a number of the constituent republics. In these texts, the authors have overcome many of the short-comings of previous years when works differed from each other only in the number of examples or quotations cited. In the past, these books were largely monotonous both in theoretical content and in style of presentation. The new textbooks are much more varied, lively, and stocked with factual materials." We are told what care went into the authoring of *Fundamentals of Marxist Philosophy*. Note the following: "A very important step in the stimulation of work in philosophy has been the holding of competitions for the writing of textbooks on philosophy. These contests have received active support from our scholars. It is well known, for example, that about 100 groups of authors entered into the competition to take part in the writing of the popular book entitled *Fundamentals of Marxist Philosophy*. More than 100 applications were submitted for participation in the contest for the preparation of a popular book devoted to the fundamentals of communist morality. It may be assumed that in the years immediately ahead competitions will become one of the most important means of bringing out interesting and creative works in philosophy."

[50] Konstantinov, ed., *op. cit.,* p. 110. The only reference to Stalin is to be found on pages 593-94 in connection with the cult of the personality. The attack is substantially the same as that found in all books in the post-Stalin (post-XXth Party Congress) period.

[51] F. V. Konstantinov, *El Materialismo Histórico* (Mexico, D. F.: Grijalbo, 1960), p. 296. This work is the Spanish translation of the second Russian edition dated in the "Prologue" March 1954 but published in October 1956. The first edition appeared in 1951. For a Soviet critique of bourgeois (idealistic?) philosophy of history, see the extremely interesting I. S. Kon, *El Idealismo Filosófico y la Crisis en el Pensamiento Histórico* (Buenos Aires: Platina, 1962).

[52] O. V. Kuusinen, ed., *Fundamentals of Marxism-Leninism* (Moscow: Foreign Language Publishing House, 1961), p. 14. This manual is indeed a summarization of the entire position of Marxism-Leninism. It is divided into five parts: I. The Philosophical Foundations of the Marxist-Leninist World Outlook; II. The Materialist Conception of History; III. Political Economy of Capitalism; IV. Theory and Tactics of the International Communist Movement; and V. Socialism and Communism. The Spanish edition appeared the previous year as *Manual de Marxismo-Leninismo* (Mexico: D. F.: Grijalbo, 1960).

[53] This is reminiscent of the portion of Stalin's *Dialectical and Historical Materialism* dealing with the third feature of production and the fact that the new productive forces and relations arising from old ones do not do so as a result of the deliberate and conscious activity of man, but spontaneously, unconsciously, independently of the will of man. That is, "when improving one instrument of production or another, one element of the productive forces or another, men do not realize, do not understand or stop to reflect what *social* results these improvements will lead to, but only think of their everyday interests, of lightening their labour and of securing some direct and tangible advantage for themselves." Stalin, *Dialectical and Historical Materialism,* p. 41.

[54] Stalin's definition of "nation," given as early as 1913 in "Marxism and the National Question," is still considered a classic. It is interesting to note that when referring to this work, contemporary Soviet historians of philosophy emphasize the fact that it was written "with the advice of Lenin." This, by implication, accounts for its orthodoxy and accuracy. See: Dynnik, *op. cit.,* V, 185-86.

[55] B. N. Ponomaryov, et Al., *History of the Communist Party of the Soviet Union* (Moscow: Foreign Language Publishing House, 1960). For Lenin's development of Marxist philosophy and his theory of the Party, see Chap. 4, sect. 3, p. 147. For his theory of socialist revolution, see Chap. 6, sect. 3, p. 199.

[56] For an observation of Soviet participation at this Congress, see Carl Cohen, "The Poverty of a Dialogue," *Problems of Communism* 13 (1964), 11-20. Also, see George L. Kline, "Soviet Philosophers at the Thirteenth International Philosophy Congress," *Journal of Philosophy,* 40 (1963), 738-43. Professor John Somerville took exception to some of Professor Kline's observations and sought to make these known through the same *Journal of Philosophy*. His "Comment" was declined publication. Consequently, he sent it in mimeographed form to various of his fellow philosophers. For a published account of this Congress, with its meeting between American philosophers and the Soviet "delegation," see Professor Somerville's "The American-Soviet Philosophic Conference in Mexico," *Philosophy and Phenomenological Research* 25 (1964), 122-30. For the Soviet account of this much publicized American-Soviet meeting, see M. B. Mitin and M. E. Omel'ianovskii, "Soviet-American Philosophic Discussions," *Soviet*

Studies in Philosophy 3 (1964), 1-4 in its reprint form. However, the article, translated from the original Russian that appeared in *Voprosifilosofii* (1964), No. 5, deals mainly with Soviet participation in the meetings of the Society for the *Philosophical Study* of Dialectical Materialism. This is an American society, founded largely through the efforts of Professor Somerville at the Detroit meeting of the American Philosophical Association (Mid-Western Division) in the Spring of 1962. At the symposia organized by the Society, held in connection with the meetings of the American Philosophical Association, philosopher-guests are invited from the U.S.S.R. for a most interesting and frank exchange of ideas with their American colleagues.

[57] See N. Khrushchev, *El Marxismo-Leninismo Es Nuestra Bandera, Nuestra Arma Combativa* (Marxism-Leninism Is Our Banner, Our Fighting Arm) (Mexico, D. F.: Embassy of the U. S. S. R., n.d.), especially pp. 11-12, 14-15. This is a speech delivered on January 21, 1963 by the then Premier before the Plenary Session of the Central Committee of the C.P.S.U.

[58] *H.C.P.S.U.* (1960), p. 630.

[59] N. Khrushchev, *Control Figures for the Development of the U.S.S.R. for 1959-1965.* English edition, pp. 49-50, cited in *H.C.P.S.U.* (1960), p. 724. Note the following: "Distortions of the *Leninist* policy on nationalities, committed during the Great Patriotic War [certainly referring to Stalin's policies], were eradicated. The national autonomy of the Balkars, Kalmyks, Chechens, Ingushes and Karachais was re-established and they were thus enabled to develop unhampered in the fraternal family of peoples of the U. S. S. R. The friendship of the Soviet peoples benefited thereby." *H.C.P.S.U.* (1960), p. 657; italics added. No mention is made of Stalin in connection with what is the State in the recent Soviet text on the topic, namely, N. C. Alexandrov y Otros, *Tería del Estado y del Derecho* (Mexico, D. F.: Grijalbo, 1962).

[60] D. P. Gorski y Otros, *Pensamiento y Lenguaje* (Mexico, D. F.: Grijalbo, 1962), p. 7. This is the second edition in Spanish, the first having appeared in 1958, Ediciones Pueblos Unidos, Montevideo (Uruguay). The work consists of six essays: A. G. Spirking, "The Origin of Language and Its Role in the Formation of Thought"; D. P. Gorski, "Language and Knowledge"; V. Z. Panfilov, "On the Correlation Existing between Language and Thought"; A. S. Ajmanov, "Logical Forms and Their Expression in Language;" V. M. Boguslavski, "The Word and the Concept"; P. V. Kopnin, "The Naturalness of the Judgment and Its Forms of Expression in Language"; and E. M. Galkina-Fedoruk, "Form and Content in Language." Not only do the authors invite criticism from their readers but they include the address at the Institute of Philosophy to which it may be sent.

[61] For the reference by Gorski, see *ibid.*, p. 70; and for that by Panfilov, see *ibid.*, pp. 138-39.

[62] K. V. Ostrovitianer y Otros, *Manual de Economía Política* (Mexico, D. F.: Grijalbo, 1960), p. 706. Translated from the corrected and enlarged third Russian edition, according to the "Prologo," it incorporates the decisions of the XXth and XXIst Congresses of the Communist Party of the Soviet Union, as well as of the Central Committee meetings. There are approximately eight references to Stalin in this gigantic manual. The only one of significance is an earlier reference made to the contributions and erroneous theses of Stalin, as part of the chapter on "The Economic Doctrines of the Epoch of Capitalism." Herein, pp. 328-29, Stalin is credited with "clarifying" certain issues, as well as with expounding certain errors.

[63] Okulov, *op. cit.*, p. 3b. This work appeared originally in *Voprosy filosofii* (1962), No. 1.

[64] *Ibid.*, p. 4a. For an interesting article on how philosophy is taught in the Soviet Union, see S. Kaltakhchyan and Y. Petrov, "The Teaching of the Philosophical Sciences," *University of Toronto Quarterly* 28 (1958), 37-46. For a syllabus of the courses on Dialectical and Historical Materialism that are taught in the Soviet Union, see *Administration of Teaching in Social Sciences in the U. S. S. R.,* "Syllabi for Three Required Courses: Dialectical and Historical Materialism, Political Economy, and History of the C. P. S. U," (Ann Arbor: Univ. of Michigan Press, 1960). It will be of interest to non-Soviets that up to 140 hours in the study of philosophy is required in Institutions of Higher Learning. See pp. 7-35.

[65] Even in 1962 there were said to be not a few of these "stereo-type" books "which contain nothing but description and in which the essence of phenomena and their causes and fundamental principles and tendencies of development are not revealed." Okulov, *op. cit.*, p. 13a.

[66] *Ibid.*, p. 14a.

[67] *Ibid.*, p. 13a.

[68] Both the XXth and XXIst Party Congresses have emphasized that the role of ideology is to further the cause of socialism and that the task of the Party is to guard the *purity* of Marxist-Leninist theory by combating the survival of bourgeois ideology. Ideological work still is criticized, as in the days of Stalin, primarily for its lack of connection with the practical tasks of Communism, as well as for dogmatism (not changing according to new historical situations) and for "quotation-mongering" (lacking creativity or being too scholastic). For reference to the XXth Congress and ideology, see *H.C.P.S.U.* (1960), pp. 672-75, 700, 706-07; for such references in connection with the XXIst Congress, consult pp. 719, 731-32, 741-44.

[69] See Bochenski, *op. cit.*, p. 53.

[70] See C. Olgin, "Lenin's Philosophical Legacy: The Reconstruction of Dialectical Materialism," *Bulletin, Institute for the Study of the U. S. S. R.* (1959), pp. 3-15; also, Okulov, *op. cit.*, p. 10a.

[71] As a final word, I wish to refer to the existence of Volume VI of the *History of Philosophy,* edited by M. A. Dynnik and others, which treats of philosophy after the October Revolution of 1917. Thus, it treats of the four main works by Stalin that I considered in my essay. Unfortunately, I was unable to locate a copy before this essay had to go to press, either in Spanish translation from Editorial Grijalbo of Mexico City (who implied that they had not even begun their translation) or in the original Russian from Moscow (my booksellers having been unable to locate it and my inquiries directed to the Institute of Philosophy, Academy of Sciences of the U.S.S.R., having brought no reply). Frankly, I have no way of knowing if it has been published. Professor Okulov, *op. cit.,* p. 10b, tells us that "the sixth volume, which went to the printers early in 1962, is devoted chiefly to the history of the development of Marxist-Leninist thought in the present epoch." Even if it returned from the printers, it may have been in a "trial" form to be circulated for criticism until the corrected final copy was approved. If this was the case, the "trial" copy may still be circulating. (This would not be surprising because the volume is the most pertinent in the series, dealing as it does with issues still not quite settled.) If it has appeared (or when it will appear), it is the singularly most valuable volume in determining current Soviet appraisal of the philosophic contribution of Stalin to Marxism. Compared with this volume, the current Soviet textbooks I have examined can only be regarded as "secondary" means to determine this appraisal. Likewise, I have no way of knowing if the planned multi-volume history of philosophy in the Soviet Union has been written. (The six-volume work deals with the history of philosophy throughout the whole world.) Professor Okulov also tells us (p. 10a) that: "In the years immediately ahead, a multi-volume history of the philosophy of our own country will be written." When this work appears (or, if it has appeared), it will be even more valuable than the Dynnik-edited series.

Thomas B. Larson (essay date 1968)

SOURCE: "Dismantling the Cults of Stalin and Khrushchev," in *The Western Political Quarterly,* Vol. XXI, No. 3, September, 1968, pp. 383-90.

[In the following essay, Larson examines the differences in retrospective opinion of the leadership of Stalin and his successor, Nikita Khrushchev.]

Whatever else Communist power brought to Russia, it did not guarantee rule by "good" leaders. The toppling from their pedestals of Stalin and then Khrushchev forced the introduction of a very sobering note into the treatment of the past history of the Soviet regime. The present top leaders can point to no honorable predecessors in the chief party and government posts for the entire period between Lenin's death in 1924 and the ouster of Khrushchev forty years later. The list of fallen chiefs included every single chairman of the Council of Ministers (formerly Peoples Commissars) of the period.

These government chiefs were not much celebrated during their tenure of office, however, so the only serious problems of iconoclasm related to Stalin and Khrushchev, the principal party secretaries during the four decades. It is now admitted even by party ideologists that Stalin amassed and retained almost absolute power despite a long catalogue of costly mistakes and serious abuses. Despite this experience, the system allowed his successor Khrushchev to impose his impulsive ideas and "hare-brained" schemes on Soviet society without even having to resort to the terror that stilled opposition to Stalin.

In their effort to lighten the great shadow cast on the "heroic" past of the Soviet regime, the spokesmen have focused attention on the peerless father of the Soviet order, Lenin, while doggedly insisting that Soviet institutions remained basically sound even in the period when errant successors ruled. Nevertheless, it has not been easy to combine a repudiation of past leaders with glorification of the Soviet past, and the tension between these seemingly irreconcilable tendencies has continued to trouble Soviet ideological policy.

These past leaders left; of course, rather different legacies. Stalin could take years to nourish his "cult of personality." Although it took major form by 1929, in the succeeding decades it went to lengths far beyond anything achieved (or perhaps contemplated) under Khrushchev, who attained a lofty eminence at a much later age and could not have expected to occupy the top post for a period comparable to Stalin's. Stalin died in honor and only later lost his good standing, in a gradual shift punctuated by outbursts of accusations at the 1956 and 1961 Party Congresses. Khrushchev was removed from office in silent disgrace as he was consigned to virtual oblivion. Stalin was always credited with some virtues and some good deeds, but recognition of these from 1961 became infrequent. In October 1964, there was an abrupt and complete halt to acknowledgement of Khrushchev's virtues and an almost complete ban on mention of his name, whether in a negative or positive context.

These differences in handling the two ex-leaders were due not only to the fact that one was safely buried and the other still living. Stalin's faults were on a grand scale, as were the virtues formerly attributed to him. Tragedy did not become farce with Khrushchev, but certainly the faults laid on Khrushchev were pedestrian compared to those of Stalin. To successor-leaders concerned about morale the major difference between the Stalin problem and the Khrushchev problem lay in the impact of Stalin as the source of practices and policies deeply imbedded in Soviet life, of formulas woven into the orthodox ideology, and of habits of veneration going far beyond anything fostered under Khrushchev. Dislodging Stalin from the gallery of great heroes, pinning errors and crimes on him, and reducing his good deeds to humdrum proportions proved difficult. Furthermore, the toppling of Stalin had traumatic effects on Soviet Communists and citizens, not to speak of foreign comrades, which had no parallels after Khrushchev's downfall, despite its suddenness and lack of precedent.

Differences in these leaders' cults of personality must be noted, because they dictated differences in the tactics of deflation. Stalin and Khrushchev were alike in being presented as overarching leaders who left all their colleagues in the background. Though attention was occasionally directed (more under Khrushchev than under Stalin) to the principle of collectivity of leadership at the top echelon, i.e., the principle that the Soviet party and government were headed by groups and not by individuals, the role of the individual top leader came to dominate the symbolism of the regime. Each of these spotlighted leaders was not only accorded a matchless current role but was also endowed, through a rewriting of history, with a past full of good deeds and free of errors. Khrushchev's past was, of course, on a modest scale compared to that attributed to Stalin.

One striking difference between the Stalin and Khrushchev "cults" was that Stalin—particularly in his later years—was identified with the "permanent" institutions of the Soviet Union, Khrushchev only with current policies of the Soviet regime. The latter-day Stalin image was that of a remote and somewhat mystical being, present everywhere as an immanent but ordinarily invisible force. Khrushchev's image was that of an active, earthily human leader who traveled widely inside the country and to other countries, who voiced ideas and policies on a wide range of questions, who served as the spokesman of the regime.

To take an example, a comparison of *Pravda*'s treatment of Stalin in a fairly typical month of his last year (September 1952) with the same paper's treatment of Khrushchev twelve years later (September 1964) illustrates some of the differences of cult practice. Only one photograph of Stalin appeared in *Pravda* during the month, but more than two-thirds of the issues in September 1964 contained at least one photograph of Khrushchev. In September 1952, *Pravda* published very little material specifically tied to Stalin: two messages to leaders of ruling Communist parties (Mao Tse-tung and Chervenkov), a brief account of a visit to Stalin in the Kremlin on the part of Mongolian leader Tsedenbal, and an account of the signing in the presence of Stalin of a Soviet-Chinese agreement. The only other item directly connected with Stalin was an article on the twenty-fifth anniversary of a 1927 Stalin interview with an "American workers' delegation." All of these materials concerned Soviet relations with foreign Communists.

In contrast, Khrushchev material abounded in *Pravda* of September 1964. There were numerous lengthy messages to such foreign political leaders as President de Gaulle and the Communist chiefs of North Vietnam, North Korea, and Bulgaria. Khrushchev's signature was on messages of some length to four international meetings. Full texts were printed of seven Khrushchev addresses to various audiences in the U.S.S.R. and of one interview with a Japanese delegation. The range of interests, audiences, and countries represented was thus far wider than in the comparable month involving Stalin.

While this comparison illustrates Khrushchev's far greater involvement in current affairs, it would be misleading if taken alone. Even in *Pravda* the name Stalin appeared repeatedly, usually in adjectival form, to associate the leader with the country, the U.S.S.R. Constitution, the ideology, and, above all, the Communist party. This linkage was almost obligatory in Soviet communications of the period, and was designed to place Stalin among the permanent features of the political and physical landscape. It was obviously a conscious decision of propaganda strategy not to associate Stalin closely with domestic and foreign policy moves of transient significance.

In the postwar years Stalin tended to expound in public basic principles rather than current policy, or to focus on long-range rather than day-by-day affairs. Examples of major Stalin statements include his well-known speech of February 9, 1946, as a candidate for election to the U.S.S.R. Supreme Soviet, his contributions to the linguistics discussion of 1950, and the papers on economic problems made public shortly before the XIX Party Congress in the fall of 1952. At the Congress itself Stalin spoke only briefly and couched his statements on a very broad plane. In contrast to this style, Khrushchev as party chief was much more oriented to programs or campaigns, and published no works devoted to general theoretical problems.

The difference of style is also illustrated in the handling of foreign policy questions. Sometimes Stalin did express himself on issues in this field, usually in interviews, but he was somewhat detached from the specific policy pronouncements which occupied such a large place in Khrushchev's output. The difference can be seen in the Soviet handling of the Berlin crises of the Stalin and Khrushchev periods. Stalin personally never identified himself publicly with the effort to force, through a land blockade on communications between Berlin and West Germany, a change in Western policy toward Germany. In the second Berlin crisis Khrushchev tied his prestige to the Soviet effort to bring about a change in the status of West Berlin. When the U.S.S.R. acceded to pressure in 1946 to remove its troops from Iran, nothing in the affair touched any public stance taken by Stalin. When the U.S.S.R. was forced to remove its IRBM's from Cuba in 1962, the affair clearly redounded to the discredit of Khrushchev, who publicly involved himself in the negotiations. Stalin took no prominent role either in the successful effort to dissuade the Bulgarian leader Dmitrov and other Eastern Europeans from plans for an Eastern European federation, or in the unsuccessful effort to overthrow Tito by expelling the Yugoslavs from the Communist camp. In contrast, Khrushchev engaged himself deeply at one time against the Yugoslavs and later against the Albanians and Chinese.

Both Stalin and Khrushchev saw to it that their pronouncements were widely disseminated in propaganda media, but only Stalin's writings dominated the formal indoctrination system. There was much writing about Stalin, including a highly flattering biography, while writings *about* Khrushchev were relatively unimportant, as compared especially to utterances *of* Khrushchev. If it seems surprising that Khrushchev looked out from the pages of the newspaper so often, it must be remembered that Stalin did not need to have his photograph in the newspapers every day, because representations of him were everywhere in the Soviet Union. Stalin loomed up outdoors and indoors, in statues, paintings and photographs, in ceramics, in flower-beds, in carpets. Beginning with Stalingrad in 1925, hundreds of places from villages to cities bore Stalin's name as did the highest mountain of the U.S.S.R., an important canal, and literally thousands of institutions. There was little comparable to this in regard to Khrushchev. He dominated the Soviet scene by seizing opportunities to make news and to appear as the spokesman of the Communist party and—from 1958—the Soviet government.

A comparison of the treatment given to each leader's seventieth birthday is illustrative. The celebration of Stalin's in December 1949 began a month earlier, rose to a tremendous peak on December 21, the anniversary, and only slowly tapered off. To take *Pravda* again for illustration, the "birthday party" lasted a full month in significant volume, and well over a year later the press was still publishing lists of those sending birthday greetings. Although Khrushchev's seventieth birthday celebration in April 1964 was elaborate enough to indicate how far the Soviet Union had gone toward establishing a new cult around a new leader, it was a much briefer affair than Stalin's. *Pravda* gave it coverage for only four or five days before cutting it off completely, and never gave it exclusive attention.

These differences in cult-styles were due in part to the rather different personalities of the two leaders, one preferring night-work, the other a day shift; one disposed to shield himself from the public, the other to find or create crowds and action; one leader perhaps suspecting his colleagues too much, the other certainly suspecting them too little. The cult-style reflected differences in degree of power and methods of rule of leaders whose general policy orientations had different emphases.

Because of the differences in the extent and kind of personality cults developed under Stalin and Khrushchev the problems for successor regimes in their dismantling were not at all the same. However awkward the operation, Khrushchev's associates decided simultaneously to oust him from power and consign him to oblivion. None of the major published attacks from October 1964 to the present has mentioned Khrushchev's name. As with Stalin, a major element of de-Khrushchevization was the reversal of policies instituted under Khrushchev's influence. These changes, in economic policy, especially regarding agriculture, in the reorganization of party and government institutions, and in other domestic and foreign areas, were usually accompanied by references to "subjectivism" or

another phrase designating Khrushchev; the target was made crystal clear by favorable allusion to the October 1954 plenum of the CPSU Central Committee, whose only known subject was the change of leadership.[1] On a more personal level the ouster brought to an end the glorification of Khrushchev's past in accounts of his prewar party activities in Moscow and the Ukraine, in his wartime service on various military councils, and in his postwar assignments in the Ukraine and on the national level. His pre-1953 activities have now been shrunk to modest proportions, where mentioned at all. They have not so far been criticized often, though Khrushchev's wartime role has been denigrated in some writings, for example, the war diaries of the prominent Soviet novelist Konstantin Simonov.[2]

The very occasional positive or negative references to a named Khrushchev are among the few exceptions to the rule that Khrushchev's name is not to be mentioned. He is still listed occasionally and inconspicuously among other party figures playing a role in the war, and documentary collections permit references to the fact that he gave the Central Committee reports at the XX and XXII Party Congresses.[3] On the negative side, critical references to Khrushchev by name occurred at the December 1964 session of the U.S.S.R. Supreme Soviet (though excised from the published records) and at the March 1965 plenum of the Central Committee, as recorded in the stenographic report.[4] No stenographic reports have been published—or are likely to be published—for the plenums occurring in October and November, 1964, and in September 1965. Certainly the first two of these must have heard a good deal about Khrushchev's faults. There are some borderline cases in which specific acts of Khrushchev, such as speeches to creative artists, appearances at meetings, and visits to agricultural or other enterprises were subjected to criticism which stopped just short of mentioning his name.

In view of the role of Khrushchev as the spokesman for the party and regime in the years before October 1964, the virtual ban on use of his name and writings makes the task of propagandists and historians difficult. They have to resort often to party documents, such as the Program of the CPSU adopted in October 1961, or to statements of an unnamed chairman of the U.S.S.R. Council of Ministers, in order to cite an untainted source from the period of the ex-leader's hegemony.[5] They still confront the task of writing the history of the Khrushchev decade in such a way as to endorse many of the reforms introduced into Soviet society while simultaneously criticizing the leader who sparked the changes.[6]

While specific references to Stalin have also become infrequent, there has never been as complete a blackout on mention of him, either in a positive or negative context, as that imposed regarding Khrushchev. Deficiencies of specific writings or speeches of Stalin have been discussed, and some credit allowed to individual works or positions taken by Stalin. In the post-Khrushchev period there has been a shift toward favorable mention of Stalin.

Even today the over-all treatment, however, continues to be negative, whether in references explicitly naming him or in those condemning the "cult of personality" with only indirect reference to Stalin.

The demolition of the Stalin "cult," a process which began in 1953 and underwent a basic change in 1956 with open attacks on Stalin, gave rise to one problem which recurred in the disposal of the Khrushchev "cult" after 1964. The leaders who managed to oust Khrushchev did not want to suggest a general abandonment of the policies characteristic of the Khrushchev era. Though the Soviet citizenry in general reacted with equanimity to the fall of the former chief, there was some apprehension abroad, both inside and outside Communist circles, that the shift in Soviet leadership meant a resurgence of "Stalinism." The post-Khrushchev leaders took care to stress the continuity of the policy lines adopted at the three Party Congresses from 1956, and reaffirmed the general thrust of criticism of the Stalin leadership. On the topic of de-Stalinization, the authoritative journal *Party Life* in its issue No. 2 of 1965 asserted that the general line worked out at the XX and XXII Party Congresses and the criticism of Stalin's personality cult were irreversible, whatever "fables" might be circulated by "some people" abroad. These post-Khrushchev reaffirmations of continuity followed the pattern set earlier in regard to Stalin of distinguishing between praiseworthy developments under the former regime, for which the ex-leader would no longer receive much credit, and the errors of the past, which were blamed explicitly (in the case of Stalin) or implicitly (as with Khrushchev) on the leader then in power.

In the past, when individual leaders within the top echelon have lost their standing and come under criticism, the dominant party leaders have invested great effort in securing endorsement of the criticism by the victims. Nothing appeared to illustrate better the monolithism of the party than the endorsement by victors and vanquished alike of the wisdom of the former and the deficiencies of the latter. Such self-criticism marked the settling of accounts after leadership disputes not only in the 1920's and 1930's, but also in the postwar period with Premiers Malenkov and Bulganin. Although an admission of fault was secured from Molotov in 1955 regarding his underestimation of the advancement achieved by the U.S.S.R. in establishing socialism, Molotov stubbornly refused in 1957 to add his vote and his voice to the condemnation of the "anti-Party group." Subsequently, taking advantage of the improved conditions for "factionalism" which existed in the post-Stalin period, Molotov made at least two moves to circulate his dissenting views on post-1957 developments.[7] The example of Molotov's recalcitrance was apparently good enough for Khrushchev, who has not been quoted as endorsing the low evaluation of his leadership expressed by his successors. Probably the anti-Khrushchev forces employed heavy persuasion to secure an admission of fault. In fact, it seems likely that the awkward solution adopted (retiring Khrushchev on honorable grounds of health and age while avoiding mention of his name in the strong criticism of his leadership) resulted from Khrushchev's resistance to a solution in which he would have been shunted from the top job to the accompaniment of criticism made unanimous by Khrushchev's participation.

In the criticism first of Stalin and then of Khrushchev the successors have had to confront the embarrassing question: Where were you? In each case the successors had been the intimate collaborators of the erring leader. The question was brought more into the open in regard to Stalin than in regard to Khrushchev. The answer on Stalin was compounded of references to his standing in the party and country and of discreet allusions to his use of strong-arm methods. Khrushchev's collaborators could not even point to the terror as an explanation of their acquiescence in his erroneous policies. To the limited extent that they faced up to this question of their responsibility for errors committed before October 1964, the answer stressed the seductiveness of some of the innovations which Khrushchev promoted.[8] In any event, the de-personalization of the criticism subsequently leveled against the former leadership was probably calculated to blunt the effect of questions embarrassing to those who had been supporters of Khrushchev, his associates if not his protégés.

Brezhnev has paid modest public tribute to Joseph Stalin on occasion since assuming the leadership. In May 1965, before a Moscow audience he recalled Stalin's role in the war, and in November 1966, speaking in Georgia, he mentioned Stalin among early Bolshevik revolutionaries. Neither Brezhnev nor any of the other leaders has alluded since 1964 to Stalin's errors and crimes. Clearly, however, Stalin is not to be restored to the gallery of Communist saints, but is to be accorded a minor role in Soviet history. In this and other areas involving past and present leaders of the country, de-personalization is the order of the day. This de-personalization lies behind the almost faceless image presented by the current group of leaders; it dictates the strategy of criticism directed to the Khrushchev era; and it guides the present efforts to eliminate Stalin—the "good" Stalin and the "bad" Stalin—as an issue in Soviet political life.

NOTES

[1] The communiqué announcing Khrushchev's relief was published in *Pravda* and other newspapers on October 16, 1964. A Central Committee plenum on October 14 was said to have elected L. I. Brezhnev to Khrushchev's job as Party First Secretary, and a meeting of the Presidium of the U.S.S.R. Supreme Soviet on October 15 to have substituted A. N. Kozygin for Khrushchev as chairman of the Council of Ministers. The announcement was followed by editorials in *Pravda* (October 17) and *Party Life* (No. 21, 1964) which spelled out the criticism of Khrushchev without mentioning his name. While these editorials were clearly anti-Khrushchev, the phraseology was routine. Thus, the principal Soviet public law journal included the following statement: "A business-

like Leninist style of work and of vital initiatives does not have anything in common with groundless, hare-brained schemes, with window-dressing and empty talk." Although this sounds like an attack on Khrushchev, in fact it appeared in April 1963. The author, P. T. Vasilenko, writing in *Sovetskoe Gosudarstvo i Pravo* (No. 4, 1963, pp. 29-39), followed the sentence cited with another quoting Khrushchev in support of the author's position.

[2] *New Times*, No. 8, February 24, 1965.

[3] In the one-volume history of the "Great Patriotic War," which appeared in July 1965, Khrushchev was pictured once and mentioned several times. This history was compressed from the five-volume edition, which celebrated Khrushchev's war record in such a fulsome manner that the first volume had to be toned down and re-issued after Khrushchev's ouster. The five-volume history gave about equal prominence to Khrushchev and Stalin.

[4] Plenum of the Central Committee of the CPSU, March 24-26, 1965, *Stenograficheskii Otchet* (Moscow 1965), speeches by Novosibirsk Obkom First Secretary F. S. Goriachev, p. 83, by Georgian Party First Secretary V. P. Mzhavanadze, p. 89, and by Kazakh Party First Secretary D. A. Kunaev, p. 104.

[5] Although the 1961 Program is still cited with approval, it is obvious that the current leaders are dubious about some of the doctrinal innovations, particularly references to "the Party of the whole people." This formula appears to have been dropped, though the leaders continue to refer to "the state of the whole people."

[6] One attempt to do this is represented in *Ocherki Istorii KPSS* (Moscow, 1966), pp. 372-428. This textbook of party history discreetly acknowledges the leading role played by Stalin and Khrushchev, but is more severely critical of the former than of the latter. Endorsing the steps to eliminate the personality cult of Stalin, it criticizes the way this was done as too much of a "campaign," in a one-sided way. The criticism of Stalin's "mistakes" was presented in a fashion, the book argues, to minimize Soviet successes in building socialism and in winning World War II.

[7] According to L. F. Ilichev at the XXII Party Congress in 1961, Molotov on April 18, 1960, submitted an article on Lenin to *Kommunist* (apparently for publication in the April issue commemorating Lenin's birthday). P. A. Satiukov, then-editor of *Pravda*, told the Congress that Molotov in October 1961 circulated a letter to the Central Committee, just before the Congress assembled on October 17, criticizing as "anti-revolutionary" the new Program which the Congress was to adopt. See XXII Congress CPSU, *Stenograficheskii Otchet* (Moscow 1962), II, 186, 353.

[8] This note was sounded in a *Party Life* editorial (No. 23, 1964, pp. 3-8), explaining why the party had adopted in 1962 the proposal to divide party (and government) organizations into industrial and agricultural components.

Edith Rogovin Frankel (essay date 1976)

SOURCE: "Literary Policy in Stalin's Last Year," in *Soviet Studies*, Vol. XXVIII, No. 3, July, 1976, pp. 391-405.

[*In the following essay, Frankel discusses the period of "liberalization" regarding literary activity during Stalin's last year in power.*]

In recent years Western scholars have been deeply interested in determining the nature and degree of change which has taken place in the Soviet Union since Stalin's death. Numerous works have analysed and assessed the transformation of post-Stalin Russia: changes in economic policy, in the effectiveness of group pressures on policy-making, in the use and role of terror, and in the area of public discourse, debate, and cultural creativity. But relatively little effort has been made to establish a reliable gauge with which to measure change. Studies of what was happening in specific areas of interest during the late Stalin years—studies in detail—have been few and far between, so that comparisons have often been based on well-documented research covering recent years but on generalizations about the Stalin era. One exception has been Marshall Shulman's study of Stalin's foreign policy,[1] which emphasized its complexity and broad range of options. It is the purpose of this brief study to investigate another specific field—literature—within a highly limited time span (the last year of Stalin's life) in order to examine the degree of uniformity prevailing at that time. Was the totalitarian regime as monochromatic as is often assumed? Or was the literary field, too, of a complex nature?

The general view of internal Soviet politics in the early 1950s is that the increasing repression and pre-purge tension were irreconcilable with a loosening of literary bonds. And yet an examination of the period shows that both trends—a policy of mounting intimidation by the state and an officially sanctioned 'liberalization' in the literary sphere—co-existed in 1952.

Soviet internal policy at this time was characterized by the renewed attack on bourgeois nationalism, the instigation of the Doctors' Plot and the proliferation of the vigilance campaign. On the other hand, foreign policy provided a contrast—the broad alliance policy and the development of the peace movement after 1949 represented a 'rightist' approach.[2] A similar absence of consistent correlation between all phases of Soviet policy had been seen at other times: in the mid-1930s, for example, the beginning of the Great Purge was coupled with an official veneration of law and order, with propaganda for the new Constitution and, in foreign affairs, with the pursuit of the Popular Front.

In 1952 the contrast was not limited to an emphasis 'on "peaceful co-existence" in foreign policy and strict ideological conformity at home'.[3] A moderated policy was also to be seen in the field of literature. For approximately ten months an atmosphere of relaxation, albeit strictly limited, was felt in the literary world.

This modification in the firm attitude of the party to literature was first felt as early as February 1952.[4] Although prose was the object of some of the reforming criticism, the main brunt of the campaign was felt by drama. There ensued a series of articles condemning the so-called no-conflict theory which had dominated postwar Soviet drama. The single most famous—and most outspoken—statement on the subject was made by the playwright Nikolai Virta in March of that year.[5] In it he tried to explain his own role in the development of the 'theory'.

> . . . It arose as a consequence of 'cold observations of the mind' on the manner in which those of our plays which contain sharp life conflicts passed through the barbed-wire obstacles of the agencies in charge of the repertoire . . . everything living, true to life, sharp, fresh and unstereotyped was combed out and smoothed over to the point where it was no longer recognizable. Every bold, unstereotyped word in a play had to be defended at the cost of the playwright's nerves and the play's quality . . . each of us [has] accumulated a great deal of bitter experience in ten years about which, for some reason, it has been the custom to keep quiet. . . .

Virta placed much of the blame on those people who killed plays and who were guided 'not by the interests of Soviet art but by a wild rabbit fear of the hypothetical possibility of a mistake, mortal fear of taking any risk or responsibility for risk'. His own initial adherence to the no-conflict theory had been the result of his search for 'a creative way out'. Perhaps, he had thought, the period of sharp conflicts in drama really had passed. But,

> no, this stupid and spurious theory did not arise because 'everything was fine'! It is not because 'everything is fine' that Pogodin writes a play about the beginning of the century, while Virta, who spent two years in a Russian village, wrote a play about peasants of the people's democracies!

Although, of course, the atmosphere of suppression which Virta here described does not surprise us, what is notable is that he expressed his views publicly—and in the way that he did. His candid remarks during what was assuredly an extraordinarily repressive period, his attack on problems of censorship and publication policy, and the fact that his statement was not a unique utterance but part of a concerted campaign in the press to revise established literary doctrine, all make this a most noteworthy article. What is interesting is not that a writer in the Soviet Union in the early 1950s should have felt bitterness and helplessness at his plight, nor necessarily that he should have committed these thoughts to paper, but that a publication such as *Sovetskoe iskusstvo,* of conservative leanings and quite orthodox editorial policy, should have taken it upon itself to publish them. One can only assume that the editors—and there had

been no recent significant changes of the board—deemed the article appropriate to the current literary mood.

Although Virta's article, and others, were subsequently attacked in the Soviet press,[6] the crusade against the no-conflict theory continued throughout the summer and into the autumn, with the concomitant demands for the portrayal of more well-delineated negative characters and for more and better comedies. It proceeded with varying degrees of fervour beyond the XIX Party Congress and extended to include not only drama but other prose forms as well. Malenkov's speech at the XIX Party Congress in October did little to clarify the literary situation.[7] Nothing really new was said in the few paragraphs devoted to the subject. One thing that his speech did not do, however, was to put any further brake on the dim process of innovation which had been emergent since the spring. Literary events were apparently to proceed along their course without a strong directive from the top at this point.

In January 1953—on the same day that the Doctors' Plot was announced in the press—I. Pitlyar published an article demanding that more attention be paid to the material details of life: 'What enormous artistic and editorial possibilities open up before the writer who is not afraid to be truthful in portraying the material conditions of people's existence. . . . Those writers who wave aside the so-called "details of life" are sinning against the truth of life.'[8] This sentiment, uttered here at the beginning of a repressive swing in Soviet literature, would later be a central theme in the literary criticism of the early 'thaw'.

A situation in which articles calling for conflict, for innovation, for a description of negative characteristics of Soviet life appeared simultaneously with attacks on nationalism in literature, with Great-Russian chauvinism, with virulent anti-semitism and a campaign to induce mass paranoia, was clearly anomalous. There was a build-up of fear and distrust, but there existed the other side of the coin which cannot be ignored. Explaining it is by no means simple.

There are a number of possible explanations and there is probably some truth in each. First was the state of drama itself. It is certainly plausible that the attack on the no-conflict technique was nothing more than an attempt to cure the ills which had beset the theatre for some time. Evidence of the low level of dramatic endeavour (half-empty theatres and the popularity of the classics in contrast to contemporary plays) is overwhelming and it is not unlikely that a main goal was to raise the theatre to the point where it could at least be a meaningful instrument of education or propaganda. Demands for more constructive criticism, for a re-organization of responsible committees, and attacks on dull insipid plays all point in this direction.

If, however, one considers the period preceding Stalin's death as a whole, and not just in terms of literary development, one perceives other possibilities. Seeing the build-up of insecurity and tension throughout the year

1952, reaching a frenzy early in 1953, one is struck by a certain similarity between the vigilance campaign and the attack on the 'no-conflict' theory. The vigilance campaign, in essence, warned that no one was to be trusted, that all sorts of subversive elements lurked in the background of Soviet society, that one should be on guard against every conceivable danger, whether from doctors, embezzlers, bourgeois nationalists or petty criminals. Implied in the campaign against the doctrine of no-conflict was the assertion that it was wrong to assume that Soviet society had reached that point of development where there was no socio-political danger left. Drama could not yet be written so that the only opposition present in a play was that between good and better. Evil remained in society and ought to be presented in the theatre, with the aim of rooting it out. In other words, in order to expose enemies the Soviet citizen had to know how to recognize them.

There is, finally, the possibility which we cannot entirely discount, that this 'liberal' swing was simply to be used as a bait to draw out what Anatolii Surov had referred to as the 'keepers of silence'[9] from their lairs, with the ultimate intention of repression. It is widely held that a major purge was in the offing on the eve of Stalin's death; perhaps this campaign was simply to be used as a mouse trap.

Whatever the ulterior motives may have been, the fact is that in 1952 writers and editors did find that they had somewhat more scope, more 'elbow room', limited though it still was. This became evident not only in the remarkable candour of some writers, but also in the demands made on the writers as a whole. The attack on the no-conflict theory permitted a less stereotyped publication policy. In order to demonstrate this point, let us look at the output of the literary journal *Novyi mir*, the most experimental journal in the fifties and the one quickest to reflect a change of policy.

Two major works appeared in its pages in the summer and early autumn of 1952—as well as some lesser items—which distinguished that literary season and differentiated it from the Stalinist model. Almost predictably, *Novyi mir* was to be the object of a severe concerted attack launched against it by the party press and the Writers' Union several months later.

In the July 1952 issue of *Novyi mir* the first instalment of Vasilii Grossman's *Za pravoe delo* (For the Just Cause) appeared.[10] This was a lengthy novel which centred on the Battle of Stalingrad and followed the thread of a number of individuals and families whose lives were caught up in the war and whose fates were interrelated. Long sections of the book were devoted to discussions of a philosophical nature among the participants—soldiers, professors, students—on the causes of the war.

It is indicative of the indecisive official attitude—and the amount of permissiveness—that the novel received some excellent, or at worst mixed, reviews at the end of 1952. Indeed, *Za pravoe delo* was virtually ignored in the beginning. Ilya Ehrenburg noted this fact in his memoirs, recalling that he considered this a positive development. 'I have been looking through the files of *Literaturnaya gazeta* [for 1952],' he wrote. 'Everything appeared most satisfactory. The paper noted that Grossman's novel *Za pravoe delo . . .* had appeared in *Novyi mir*, but the reviewers ignored it.'[11]

In fact—as Ehrenburg clearly understood—the novel did contain sections which could well have been alarming to the Soviet reviewer. The following two excerpts are from a passage in which an academic, Chepyzhin—one of the central characters—propounded his views in a conversation with Professor Shtrum.[12]

> Look, imagine that in some little town there are people known for their learning, honour, humanity, goodness. And they were well known to every old person and child there. They enriched the town life, enlarged it—they taught in the schools, in the universities, wrote books and wrote in the workers' newspapers and in scientific journals; they worked and struggled for the freedom of labour. . . . But when night fell, out onto the streets came other people whom few in the town knew, whose life and affairs were dirty and secret. They feared the light, walked stealthily in the darkness, in the shadow of buildings. But there came a time when the coarse dark power of Hitler burst into life, with the intention of changing its most fundamental law. They started to throw cultured people, who had illuminated life into camps, into prisons. Others fell in the struggle, others went into hiding. They were no longer to be seen during the day on the streets, at factories, at schools, at workers' meetings. The books they had written blazed. But those who had been hidden by the night came out noisily into the light and filled the world with themselves and their terrible deeds. And it seemed that wisdom, science, humanity, honour had died, disappeared, had been destroyed. It seemed that the people had been transformed, had become a people of evil and dishonour. But look here, it isn't so! Understand that it isn't so! The energy contained in a people's wisdom, in a people's moral sense, in a people's goodness is eternal, whatever fascism might do to destroy it. [It continues to live, temporarily dispersed. It accumulates in nodes. It gathers around itself indestructible microscopic diamond crystals which can cut both steel and glass. And those popular champions who were killed transmitted their spiritual strength, their energy to others, teaching them how to live and how to die. And their strength was not destroyed together with the corpses of the dead, but continues to live in the living. I am convinced that the Nazi evil is powerless to kill the energy of the people. It only disappeared from view, but its quantity in the people has not diminished. Do you understand me? Do you follow my line of thought?]

Chepyzhin then went on to discuss the psychology of social change:

> You see, all sorts of things are mixed in man, many of which are unconscious, hidden, secret, false.

Often, a man, living under normal social conditions, doesn't himself know of the vaults and cellars of his soul. But a social catastrophe occurred, and out of the cellar came every evil spirit, they rustled and ran out through the clean, light rooms. [The flour fell and the chaff rose outside. It wasn't the relationship of things that changed, but the position of the parts of the moral, spiritual structure of man which was altered.]

It is not at all surprising that, when the attack finally came, the critics singled out these passages. Chepyzhin, wrote one, taught an 'idealist philosophy', which the author himself obviously espoused.[13]

It does not require great imagination to see Grossman-Chepyzhin's description of the coming of Hitlerism as a commentary on Stalinist Russia. Especially in the light of his later work *Vse techet* (Everything Flows),[14] it is clear that Grossman was highly sensitive to, and understandably obsessed with, the evils which had been committed in Soviet Russia during his lifetime. His concentration in this section on the intelligentsia and their difficult fate was at least as applicable to the Soviet as to the German situation. This is a striking example of the not infrequent practice of political criticism by analogy in which the dissenting writer attacks a feature of his own contemporary society through reference to tsarist times or to foreign and hostile countries. Of course, the official critics could not directly expose this type of invidious comparison, for to do so would be to admit that they themselves had recognized the forbidden parallel.

The critics in general—and the February article in *Literaturnaya gazeta* was in this typical—had therefore to confine their criticism within safe ideological bounds. Specifically, in the case of Grossman, they concentrated most of their fire on his universalistic moralism, his apparent indifference to Marxist dialectics and his preference for a class-free, science-based philosophy. 'It adds up,' said *Literaturnaya gazeta*,

> to the idea that there is an eternal struggle of good and evil, and good is the personification of perpetual energy—whether the cosmic energy of the stars or the spiritual energy of the people. It is completely clear that these ideological, unhistoric fumblings of reasoning can in no way explain the existence of social phenomena.[15]

Chepyzhin, the article went on, talks abstractly, and unhistorically, about fascism and the idea of war. He measures everything according to his 'unhistoric categories' of the struggle of light and darkness, of good and evil. Shtrum, it continued, nods his agreement, and not one of the main characters replies to this argument with a Marxist-Leninist explanation of the war and the nature of things. So one may assume that Grossman did not want Chepyzhin's reactionary philosophy refuted. Grossman, through Chepyzhin, seemed to follow the idea of the Pythagoreans that there is an eternal rotation of events, that '. . . there is an eternal circulation of the very same beginnings, conditions, events'.[16]

It should be noted here that when the novel was published in book form, as it was after Stalin's death and again in the 1960s, the two passages quoted above had been considerably altered. Moreover, the entire dialogue between Chepyzhin and Shtrum had been transformed. Although Chepyzhin's views had not been essentially changed—only toned down and attenuated—Shtrum now emerged as an advocate of Soviet Marxist orthodoxy. For example, he now objected vigorously to the idea that Nazism was to be explained as the work of 'a handful of evil men with Hitler at their head', arguing instead that it was the result 'of the specific peculiarities of German imperialism. . . .'[17] Again, Shtrum now pointed out that Chepyzhin's theory of science and history if applied 'not to fascism . . . but to progressive phenomena, to liberating revolutions, . . . [implies that] the revolutionary struggle of the working class also cannot change society, also cannot raise man to a higher level. . . .'[18]

Besides the criticism of the excerpts quoted here, many general features of Grossman's novel were attacked. Grossman had not 'succeeded in creating a single, major, vivid, typical portrait of a hero of the battle of Stalingrad, a hero in a grey greatcoat, weapons in hand'.[19] He 'had not shown the Communist Party as the true organizer of victory. . . .'[20] A feeling of doom pervaded the work.[21]

The campaign continued unabated until a month after Stalin's death.[22] In fact, pressure became so great that several members of *Novyi mir*'s editorial board—Tvardovsky, Tarasenkov, Kataev, Fedin and Smirnov—publicly apologized for their 'error' in publishing Grossman's novel.[23] It was a vain attempt to stem the tide of criticism directed at the journal. The climax of the letter was the admission by the editors that the fault lay with the editorial board—that is, with themselves—for not having gone into the work more thoroughly, for having failed to ferret out its ideological-artistic faults. They asked the Secretariat of the Writers' Union as soon as possible to 'take measures towards strengthening the composition of the editorial board of *Novyi mir*'. As for Grossman, he never made any kind of apology.[24]

The last major attack on Grossman's novel—and on the journal which had published it—was made by Fadeev at the end of March.[25] The focus of his criticism did not differ sharply from that which had preceded it, except for a rather pointedly anti-semitic undertone, but what is especially significant in terms of history is his account of the publication process through which the novel had passed.

According to Fadeev,[26] the novel had been discussed for a number of years before its appearance in print, and there had been numerous objections to it. But the discussion did not reach the broad public. 'It was conducted in the narrow circle of the editorial board and the Secretariat [of the Writers' Union], and only after the novel was printed did it creep into the Presidium of the Union of Soviet Writers—the body which should have decided these matters of principle.'

Evidently, when the novel first came to the editorial offices of *Novyi mir* it had been strongly criticized by B. Agapov, then a member of the board.[27] As we know that Agapov left the editorial board of *Novyi mir* in February 1950, it is clear that the novel must have been under discussion for a minimum of two-and-a-half years, and probably for much longer. It was when the new editorial board was appointed that discussion of the novel flared up again. The new editorial board, which brought out its first issue in March 1950, had been significantly changed. Tvardovsky took the place of Simonov as editor-in-chief. Agapov and Aleksandr Krivitsky were replaced by three new members: M. S. Bubennov (an abject conformist under Stalin—and afterwards), S. S. Smirnov, and A. K. Tarasenkov.[28]

When the manuscript of *Za pravoe delo* was submitted for examination to the new board, Bubennov brought the issue to the Secretariat of the Union of Writers. Fadeev reported: 'The novel was changed many times. Discussion once more developed in the Secretariat and the above-mentioned comrades[29] held to their point of view.' Fadeev then asked why the novel had been published despite all the adverse criticism.

> Because a situation has risen in the Union of Soviet Writers and in editorial boards in which the solution of many ideological questions—the evaluation of works, the formulation of one or another serious problem—very often depends on the opinion of a few leaders. We rarely apply the normal collegium principle in our work.

It must be assumed that, in the face of a good deal of opposition, someone on the *Novyi mir* board was keen on seeing *Za pravoe delo* published. The likelihood is—in view of his reputation and courage—that that man was Tvardovsky. Had he, as editor-in-chief, been unfavourably inclined towards the novel there would never have been a struggle to have it printed.

One cannot ignore the basic facts of the Grossman affair. First, the author was not an unknown. On the contrary, he had a reputation and, by the official standards, a dubious one. Born in Berdichev in 1904, Grossman had been a war correspondent during World War II for both *Krasnaya zvezda* and for *Einekeit*, the Yiddish-language journal of the Jewish Anti-Fascist Committee. His story 'Narod bessmerten' (The People are Immortal), which appeared in *Krasnaya zvezda* in 1942, was one of the earlier, more powerful works on the war. However, his play *Esli verit' pifagoreitsam* (If We Believe the Pythagoreans)—written before the war, but not published until 1946—had been severely criticized by the press. After the war he had collected materials on heroic and tragic facts concerning Jewish victims of the Nazis. They were to have been published in what was to be called the Black Book, as a tribute to the Jews who had suffered during the war. The book, although set in type, was never published in the Soviet Union, and the plates were destroyed in 1949, when the Soviet Jewish cultural community was closed down.[30] Grossman was hamstrung by

Soviet criticism during the postwar Stalin years. Disliked by Stalin[31] and dogged by hack critics, Grossman never won the acclaim he deserved.

Second is the undeniable fact that, as the novel had been under consideration for so long, the *Novyi mir* editorial board, members of the Writers' Union and of the literary—and censoring—community must have been well aware of the objections to it. It was thus a deliberate and not a random, decision to publish that particular novel by that particular author during the summer of 1952. It is quite clear that Tvardovsky took the step of publishing the novel then because he felt—correctly—that this was an opportune time, that the literary atmosphere warranted it.

Indeed, another remarkable aspect of this case is that *Za pravoe delo,* published during a period of mounting fear, under the unyielding influence of the Zhdanov tradition, was never republished in its original form in Russia. As has been noted above, passages published under Stalin were considered unfit to print in later years.[32] Nor did Part II of the book ever appear at all, even in the 'best' of literary periods to follow. Grossman died in 1964, some six months after the manuscript of the second part had been confiscated by the secret police.[33]

All this indicates that the literary situation during 1952 was in a state of flux. The Virta statement provided one example of the subtle change which was evident and *Novyi mir*'s publication of *Za pravoe delo* another. Whatever the motivation behind the anti-'no-conflict' campaign, the end result had been a different publishing policy.

One of the outstanding literary events of the whole decade was the publication in 1952 of Valentin Ovechkin's 'Raionnye budni', the first of a series of sketches on contemporary kolkhoz life.[34] It was concerned primarily with party work in a rural area and specifically attacked the complacent attitude of the district secretary, Borzov, whose sole aim was to see that the plan was fulfilled. Ovechkin contrasted him with the second-in-command, who was interested in the long-term goal of achieving communism and in treating fairly those kolkhozniki who did manage to fulfil their quota. He supported the principle of incentive, if this would encourage the kolkhozniki to work harder and more effectively.[35] Ovechkin emphasized the fact that these characters were not products of his imagination, but real people. The implication was that the Borzov approach was not uncommon and that the political direction of rural work was a real problem which the party must solve.

It is significant that the sketch, far from being passively accepted, was warmly received in spite of the fact that it incisively censured the work of party officials in the rural areas.[36]

Tvardovsky would later note the innovative nature of Ovechkin's sketch. In his article on the occasion of the fortieth anniversary of *Novyi mir* he called the appearance of 'Raionnye budni' a literary turning point.[37] Noting that it had been published before the September Plenum of the Central Committee in 1953 (which had dealt with problems of agriculture), Tvardovsky said that its truthfulness and ideological orientation were only fully appreciated afterwards. He pointed out that until then criticism had tenaciously attacked the slightest deviations of prose writers from 'conventional and legitimized norms, as it were, of interpreting rural life in literature. It seemed that maintaining these norms of well-being in the reflected picture was more important than reality'.[38] The fact is that 'Raionnye budni' was to serve as a model for works on the rural scene throughout the mid-fifties and became symbolic of the 'new approach' of thaw writing. Tvardovsky's other mention of 'Raionnye budni' was in a letter to Fedin about *Cancer Ward*.[39] The letter, written in January 1968, came after the refusal to publish Solzhenitsyn's novel. Tvardovsky wrote: 'Solzhenitsyn, incidentally, outstanding as he is, is not unique or unprecedented in our literature. We should not forget the courage of Ovechkin's ['Raionnye budni'], which appeared in *Novyi mir* as early as 1952 and marked a turning point.'[40]

All indications—Tvardovsky's remarks, Malenkov's discussion of agriculture at the XIX Party Congress, the very fact of the publication of Ovechkin's sketch, and an assertion that Stalin himself had called for it[41]—point to the fact that the ruling group had recognized the serious weaknesses of the agricultural situation and was seeking remedies. The coincidence of Ovechkin's first sketch and Malenkov's speech in the autumn of 1952 indicate a coordinated introduction of forthcoming changes in agricultural policy. (In fact, however, agricultural problems and a corrective programme were to be dealt with only six months after Stalin's death, in September 1953.)

There were other items published in *Novyi mir* during the last year of Stalin's life which contributed to the general atmosphere of moderation in publishing policy.[42] Thus, the combination of the Virta statement, along with the concerted attack on the no-conflict theory, the publication of Vasilii Grossman's novel and of Ovechkin's first sketch in the series, as well as the appearance of some lesser articles in *Novyi mir,* establishes a view of the Soviet literary scene clearly redolent of variety, limited experimentation, and of chance-taking on the part of the editors. Whatever was in the offing—and, by January 1953 attacks on *Novyi mir* had already begun—the fact remains that an atmosphere of some give-and-take had existed in 1952.[43] In literature (as well as in the field of foreign affairs) official policy did not on the surface proceed in consonance with the obviously repressive environment.

We are thus confronted by some curious but, I submit, not random, facts. The events described do present a cumulative image of literary life in 1952 which is far more variegated than is usually recognized. The year selected for examination was one that is generally assessed as oppressive to a degree at least typical of Stalin's postwar years. And there is no reason to doubt this overall judgement. On the contrary, indications do point to a vicious situation in the internal life of the Soviet Union, one

headed towards a new phase of mass terror. But our recognition of this fact should not lead us to the conclusion that there was complete uniformity in all aspects of Soviet life. Comparative studies which cover both the Stalinist and post-Stalinist years—Ploss's work on agriculture, for instance, or Conquest's on politics[44]—have shown in specific cases the intricacies and contrasts present within the monolithic Stalinist system, thus providing a realistic basis on which to assess the actual changes which subsequently took place. Certainly, the literary life in the one year examined here suggests that there, too, complexity was the norm.

There is often an assumption in Western writing, encouraged by the image of the totalitarian model, that the Stalin period must have been monochromatic. Thus, whenever one meets a clash of opinion, or an indication of variety or innovation in the post-Stalin period, the natural tendency is to assume that it is 'new'. But the presence of terror did not necessarily mean an absence of variety. People willing to take a chance—and the risks were far greater then—could still manage, as Tvardovsky did with Grossman's novel, to find the means of publishing a particular work. And men like Grossman could still refuse to bow to official criticism, though his bravery could well have been suicidal had Stalin not died when he did. The examples provided were from the last year of Stalin's life, but detailed studies of other years would probably yield similar 'anachronisms'.

It is generally accepted that the 'thaw' began in the late autumn of 1953—after the September Plenum and after the Fourteenth Plenary Session of the Board of the Writers' Union in October—and that the period was marked by a sharp break with previous literary life. In fact, signs of the post-Stalin relaxation were already evident earlier. Ovechkin's third sketch in the series was published in *Pravda* in July 1953;[45] Tvardovsky's attack on literary restrictions in his poem 'Za dal'yu dal' ' (Horizon beyond Horizon) came out in *Novyi mir* the month before.[46] In September Mikhail Lifshits published an outspoken book review in *Novyi mir*.[47] The truth is that, while the atmosphere of the 'thaw' period was markedly different from the Stalinist era, many of its roots can be traced—despite the hiatus produced by the attacks on *Novyi mir* during the first months of 1953—directly to the preceding era.

Let there be no misunderstanding. The absence of arbitrary terror in the post-Stalin years made an enormous difference in the lives of people in all spheres—the difference between night and day, between madness and a measure of normality. But the absence of terror no more signals the existence of a 'pluralistic' society than the fact of a 'totalitarian' regime implies complete uniformity. Certain people in certain fields were able on occasion to publish or say what was important to them even at the worst of times. The abandonment of the mass purge as a method of attaining compliance has not put an end to the coercive pressure enforcing conformity on the writer (or scientist, or lawyer). He is not at an opposite pole from his colleague of Stalinist times; he must still toe the line if he wishes to be published and paid. The writer who 'sticks his neck out' is still taking a grave chance, even if this is not usually a chance of life or death. In the literary sphere, as in many other areas of Soviet life, the dichotomy between the Stalinist and post-Stalinist periods should not be taken for granted, but analysed and measured.

NOTES

1 Marshall Shulman, *Stalin's Foreign Policy Reappraised* (Cambridge, Mass., 1963).

2 This is a theme to which Shulman devoted his book. He points out that, in order to find means of dividing its foreign adversaries and maximizing its own influence, 'the Soviet Union reintroduced tactical and ideological formulations that had been associated with earlier periods identified as "Right" in Soviet terminology' (*ibid.*, p. 7).

3 *Ibid.*, p. 6.

4 A literary review criticized an author who 'writes in only two colours—black and white. Her positive characters are good unto holiness, while from the bad character's very first appearance in the story he is completely unmotivated and a scoundrel' (G. Kalinin, 'Zhurnal i sovremennost' ', *Pravda*, 4 February 1952, p. 2).

5 *Sovetskoe iskusstvo*, 29 March 1952, p. 2, translated in *The Current Digest of the Soviet Press (CDSP)*, vol. IV, no. II, pp. 6-7.

6 The first significant attack came in a *Pravda* editorial. It discussed the crisis in drama, but cautioned against overcorrecting the situation, and then went on to criticize *Sovetskoe iskusstvo* for not taking a solid stand on the issue; see 'Preodolet' otstavanie dramaturgii', *Pravda*, 7 April 1952, pp. 2-3.

7 *Ibid.*, 6 October 1952.

8 I. Pitlyar, 'About the "Details" of Life as Handled in Literature—Let Us Discuss Questions of Craftsmanship', *Literaturnaya gazeta*, 13 January 1953, p. 3, translated in *CDSP*, vol. V, no. 14, pp. 13-14.

9 *Sovetskoe iskusstvo*, 12 March, 1952, p. 12.

10 Part I of the novel was published in four instalments from July to October 1952.

11 Ilya Ehrenburg, *Post-War Years: 1945-54* (Cleveland and New York, 1967), p. 293.

12 *Novyi mir*, 1952, no. 7, p. 102. The lines within square brackets were omitted in later editions.

13 'Na lozhnom puti—O romane V. Grossmana, "Za pravoe delo" ', *Literaturnaya gazeta*, 21 February 1953, pp. 3-4. See also A. Lektorsky, 'Roman, iskazhayushchii obrazy

sovetskikh lyudei', *Kommunist*, 1953, no. 3, pp. 106-15. Lektorsky wrote: 'He sees the whole history of culture, all social phenomena, the history of peoples, through the anti-scientific understanding of the idealistic-mechanistic philosophy of "energetics" and the Freudian theory of the dark, subconscious instincts. . . . '

14 Vasilii Grossman, *Everything Flows* (New York, 1972).

15 *Literaturnaya gazeta*, 21 February 1953, p. 3.

16 *Ibid.*

17 V. Grossman, *Za pravoe delo* (M., 1955), p. 137.

18 *Ibid.*, pp. 139-40.

19 Mikhail Bubennov, 'O romane V. Grossmana "Za pravoe delo" ', *Pravda*, 13 February 1953, pp. 3-4.

20 *Ibid.* This criticism echoed the notorious attack on Fadeev's novel *The Young Guard*. The fact is that during the early fifties Fadeev was rewriting the entire novel in order to give credit to the party leadership which, according to official doctrine, had been responsible for the war effort in the Krasnodon area. Grossman does not appear to have heeded the warning issued to his colleague.

21 A. Fadeev, 'Nekotorye voprosy raboty Soyuza pisatelei', *Literaturnaya gazeta*, 28 March 1953, pp. 2-4.

22 See also Marietta Shaginyan, 'Korni oshibok', *Izvestiya*, 26 March 1953, pp. 2-3.

23 'O romane V. Grossmana "Za pravoe delo" ', *Literaturnaya gazeta*, 3 March 1953, p. 3. In this letter the editors were also apologizing for other articles the journal had published which had been severely criticized.

24 Grossman was criticized at least twice for having failed to own up to his errors. See, for example, *Literaturnaya gazeta*, 21 February 1953, p. 3, which reported that at a meeting held at the *Novyi mir* offices on 2 February 1953 Grossman had responded 'scornfully' to the 'completely justified' criticism made by various literary representatives. See also 'V Soyuze sovetskikh pisatelei', *Literaturnaya gazeta*, 28 March 1953, p. 3, in which A. Perventsev expressed 'general indignation' that Grossman had not replied to criticism.

25 The end of the campaign against *Novyi mir*—and against *Za pravoe delo*—was not simultaneous with the death of Stalin. Indeed, it is interesting to note that the literary campaign extended longer than other facets of the repressive onslaught characteristic of the last months of Stalin's life. Even after the official halt of the Doctors' Plot, articles criticizing *Novyi mir* works continued to appear. Ehrenburg discussed Fadeev's role in the publication of, and later in the attack on, Grossman's novel:

> In March 1953, soon after Stalin's death, I came across an article in *Literaturnaya gazeta* in which

Fadeev sharply attacked Grossman's *Za pravoe delo*. This puzzled me because I had several times heard him speak well of this novel *which he had managed to get published*. It had aroused Stalin's displeasure and there had been some scathing reviews of it. But Fadeev had continued to defend it. . . . And now suddenly Fadeev had come out with his article.

Only by mid-April had the attacks on *Novyi mir* finally stopped. Ehrenburg mentioned the continuation of the literary campaign in his memoirs:

> The announcement about the rehabilitation of the doctors appeared: changes were obviously in the air. Fadeev came to me without ringing the bell, sat down on my bed and said: 'Don't be too hard on me . . . I was frightened.' 'But why after his death?' I asked. 'I thought the worst was still to come', he replied (Ehrenburg, *op. cit.,* p. 166, emphasis added).

[26] *Literaturnaya gazeta,* 28 March 1953, pp. 2-4.

[27] Agapov was a Simonov associate who followed him on and off a number of editorial boards—including a return to *Novyi mir* in the mid-fifties.

[28] The only members remaining from the old board were the well-known writers Valentin Kataev, Konstantin Fedin, and Mikhail Sholokhov. But these three members were figure-heads (or, as Soviet critics chose to call them, 'wedding generals'), and did not perform active roles on the journal.

[29] Bubennov and Kataev objected to the novel, and Kozhevnikov joined them.

[30] See Yehoshua A. Gilboa, *The Black Years of Soviet Jewry 1939-1953* (Boston, 1971).

[31] See Ehrenburg, *op. cit.,* p. 165.

[32] See footnote 12 above.

[33] See, for example, Svetlana Alliluyeva, *Only One Year* (London, 1969), p. 44: 'In the U.S.S.R. one could expect anything: the search of one's home by warrant, the confiscation of books from one's shelves, of manuscripts from one's desk. In this way the government had confiscated the second part of Vasily Grossman's novel. . . . ' Other sources report that the KGB confiscated the manuscripts after the author's death. One copy at least was preserved by friends. Although Part II has never been published in Russia, excerpts of the novel have begun to appear in the West. See, for example, *Posev,* no. 7, 1975, pp. 53-55, *Grani,* no. 97, 1975, pp. 3-31, and *Kontinent,* nos. 4, 5.

[34] *Novyi mir,* 1952, no. 9, pp. 204-21. (Amongst possible translations are 'District Routine' and 'The Daily Round in a Rural District'.) Ovechkin's series continued, in *Novyi mir* and *Pravda,* until 1956.

[35] Ovechkin's sketches have been described frequently in Western studies. See, for example, Harold Swayze, *Political Control of Literature in the U.S.S.R.* (Cambridge, Mass.), pp. 95-97. Ovechkin's sketch was partially translated in *Soviet Studies,* vol. IV, no. 4 (April 1953), pp. 448-66. The subsequent instalments in the series were also translated or summarized in *Soviet Studies.*

[36] See, for example, Marietta Shaginyan, 'Kritika i bibliografiya—"Raionnye budni" ', *Izvestiya,* 26 October 1952, p. 2; 'Shirit' front boevoi publitsistiki!—V sektsii publitsistiki i nauchno-khudozhestvennoi literatury Soyuza sovetskikh pisatelei', *Literaturnaya gazeta,* 17 January 1953, p. 2; 'Chitatel'skaya konferentsiya ob ocherkakh V. Ovechkina', *ibid,,* 19 February 1953, p. 3.

[37] A. Tvardovsky, 'Po sluchayu yubileya', *Novyi mir,* 1965, no. 1, pp. 3-18.

[38] *Ibid.,* p. 6.

[39] *Survey,* vol. LXIX (October 1968), pp. 112-21.

[40] *Ibid.,* p. 113. For further discussion of the innovativeness of Ovechkin's 'District Routine' see B. Platonov, 'Novoe v nashei zhizni i literature', *Zvezda,* 1954, no. 5, pp. 160-74 and Gennadii Fish, 'Na perednem krae', *Novyi mir,* 1957, no. 4, pp. 203-4. Fish wrote: 'Already in 1952, in the days preceding the XIX Congress, when the adverse situation in agriculture, the disastrous condition of many kolkhozy and kolkhozniki was hidden under the froth of official reports of "unprecedented" successes—the writer bravely, with precise, spare lines, showed the true picture of life of one artistically generalized agricultural region of Central Russia' (p. 203).

[41] See Arkadii Belinkov's statement in 'The Soviet Censorship', *Studies on the Soviet Union* (Munich), vol. XI (new series), no. 2, 1971, p. 17.

[42] See, for example, V. Komissarzhevsky, 'Chelovek na stsene', *Novyi mir,* 1952, no. 10, pp. 210-24, in which the author was relatively outspoken in extending the general lines of the attack on the no-conflict theory; N. K. Gudzy and V. A. Zhdanov, 'Voprosy tekstologii', *Novyi mir,* 1953, no. 3, pp. 232-42, which discussed the censor's arbitrary destruction of texts in nineteenth-century Russia—a veiled comparison between that censor and his Soviet counterpart; V. Ognev, 'Yasnosti!', *ibid.,* 1953, no. 1, pp. 263-7; E. Kazakevich, 'Serdtse druga', *ibid.,* 1953, no. 1, pp. 3-125. Much of the criticism launched against Grossman was applied to Kazakevich as well, although the works were distinctly different and the Kazakevich story was far less ideologically interesting.

[43] See, for example, reports of a conference on Mayakovsky in 'Osnovnye voprosy izucheniya tvorchestva V. V. Mayakovskogo (Soveshchanie v Soyuze sovetskikh pisatelei SSSR)', *Literaturnaya gazeta,* 22, 24, 27, 29 January 1953 (p. 3 in all cases). What is striking about the record of the meeting is the atmosphere of pro-and-con

discussion which seems to have prevailed there. Ognev, for example, who was criticized there a number of times for his *Novyi mir* article and for oral statements he had made, was quoted in *Literaturnaya gazeta*—both his own statements and his attacks on others present.

[44] Sidney Ploss, *Conflict and Decision-Making in Soviet Russia* (Princeton, N.J., 1965); Robert Conquest, *Power and Policy in the U.S.S.R.* (London, 1962).

[45] Valentin Ovechkin, 'Na perednem krae', *Pravda*, 20, 23 July 1953, pp. 2-3.

[46] Aleksandr Tvardovsky, 'Za dal'yu dal' ', *Novyi mir*, 1953, no. 6, pp. 59-83.

[47] M. Lifshits, 'Krepostnye mastera', *ibid.*, 1953, no. 9, pp. 220-6.

Albert Parry (essay date 1976)

SOURCE: "Stalin's Archipelago," in *Terrorism: From Robespierre to Arafat*, by Albert Parry, The Vanguard Press, Inc., 1976, pp. 187-202.

[*In the following essay, Parry discusses changes in the policy of terror instituted by Stalin, most notably the policy of arresting and executing loyal followers of Stalinism in addition to those openly against it.*]

From Lenin and Trotsky the path of terror led to Stalin and Stalin's heirs. Over these decades the character and organization of Soviet terror underwent certain changes. The transformation can be traced through the vast literature by survivors and scholars, available not in Russian alone but also in other languages, especially by such writers as Alexander Solzhenitsyn, Roy Medvedev, and Robert Conquest.[1]

In the reminiscence of one little-known survivor of the Lenin-Stalin camps, Nikolai Otradin, now residing in the United States, we find a concise analysis of the Red terror from Lenin on up to the end of Stalin's rule as consisting of essentially three periods.[2]

During the first period, that of the civil war of 1918-21, the arrests, executions, and other repressions were the combined result of both the spontaneous anger of the lower classes against the middle and upper ones and the calculated action of the revolutionary government. Many shootings were done by men of the masses, on the spur of the moment, with neither trials nor formal sentences. Yet there is no doubt that Lenin and Trotsky deliberately fanned such mob outbursts so as to create and intensify the revolutionary atmosphere.

As in Robespierre's terror, so in this first Lenin-Trotsky period, all classes were represented in prisons and on execution rolls. Otradin recalls: "We were rounded up both selectively and nonselectively." And so numerous were the arrested that during the civil war there were not enough old Tsarist jails to hold these new Soviet captives. So, in addition, barges moored on the rivers, monasteries lost in the forests or on northern islands, and other makeshift detention sites were used.

Amid the cruelty of it all there was still a chance and thus a hope. If a victim escaped the firing squad by drawing a 10- or 20-year sentence, and if somehow he did not succumb to starvation or epidemic in those cells, barge-holds, or barracks, he could perhaps gain freedom in just a few months—thanks mainly to the energetic pleas, influence, or bribes by their kin or friends still at large. In many cases, Cheka commissars accepted (or even demanded and received) bed-services of the female relatives of the political convicts as payment for the latter's release.

The terror's second period lasted from the end of the civil war in 1921 to the First Five Year Plan of 1928. Early in this period, with the Red victory won over the Whites and foreign foes, voices were raised by the more humane Communist leaders that perhaps the Cheka should be abolished and the Red terror at last terminated.

These would-be humanists were overruled. Yet through the 1920s and their New Economic Policy until 1928-29, there were in the Soviet Union but two large concentration camps: in the sequestered monasteries of Solovki, the island in the White Sea north of Arkhangelsk with branch barracks on the nearby mainland; and on the Vishera River shores on the continent, in the Perm region of the European slope of the Urals. From these two camps thousands of men were sent to various railroad- and canal-building or other work areas throughout the north. The total of all such convicts up to 1919 was no more than some 20,000, although outside the camps, all over Russia, the numbers of those shot by the Cheka were by that time in the hundreds of thousands.

Compare this with the estimated millions of victims in Stalin's time, most of whom were killed during the third or main period of the Soviet terror, lasting from 1928-29 to the dictator's death in March 1953. Otradin states that the mass terror of this third phase was no sudden development. It had been carefully prepared during those comparatively mild 1920s when the New Economic Policy gave the Communist leadership an opportunity to pretest and organize the terror of the succeeding decades quietly. Thus the gigantic Archipelago of Solzhenitsyn's description—of thousands of concentration camps, of millions destined to die of slave work and malnutrition if not by firing squad—would become the awful reality of the third period.

To these three periods we should add the fourth, from 1953 well into these mid-1970s, the time of Nikita Khrushchev and Leonid Brezhnev, which Otradin does not discuss and which stands quite distinctly separate from the first three phases. At a later point of this narrative it will be discussed.

II

Born on December 21, 1879, as Iosif Dzhugashvili, the son of a hard-drinking Georgian shoemaker in the small Caucasian town of Gori, Stalin[3] in his boyhood was sent by his pious mother to a theological seminary in Tiflis (now Tbilisi). He later claimed he was expelled for his early revolutionary activity, but his mother denied this, saying she removed him from the seminary because of his weak health.

Becoming a clerk in the Tiflis observatory, he devoted most of his effort to underground work for the Russian Social Democratic Party, which he joined in 1898, when he was not yet 19. The Tsarist police soon knew him as an agitator and strike organizer; his first arrest came in 1902. It was in Siberia, to which he was exiled in 1903, that he learned of the split between the Bolsheviks and the Mensheviks, and chose the former as the more militant. Escaping from Siberia in early 1904, he returned to the Caucasus to resume his revolutionary activity. He adopted the name Stalin, meaning Man of Steel.

He first met Lenin in 1905 at the Party conference in Finland. Two years later, with Lenin's secret approval, Stalin organized the first major Bolshevik terrorist act: on June 25, 1907, in Tiflis, his men attacked and robbed a State Bank carriage, causing bloodshed and getting away with 340,000 rubles ($170,000). Arrested in April 1908 in Baku, he was exiled again. Altogether, the years 1902-17 meant for Stalin six arrests, repeated imprisonments and exiles, and several escapes. The revolution and fall of Tsarism in March 1917 freed him from his last Siberian exile. He came to Petrograd to take charge of the Bolshevik newspaper *Pravda* and to join Lenin on his return from Switzerland in April.

In years to come, from his position of power, as he rewrote history, Stalin asserted that from the spring of 1917 he was Lenin's closest aide. In fact it was Trotsky, not Stalin, who shared Lenin's fame as his second-in-command and often as his equal. Stalin was obscure throughout the civil war, as Commissar of Nationalities; he also collected food supplies for the Red Army and played a role in the defense of Tsaritsyn on the Volga against the White offensive. (On becoming the Soviet dictator, Stalin renamed Tsaritsyn Stalingrad. After his death in 1953 and denigration by Khrushchev in 1956, Stalingrad became Volgograd.)

Stalin's gradual rise to power began in 1922, when Lenin made him secretary general of the Communist Party, with the task of bringing it out of its post–civil war disarray. Stalin shrewdly used the job to pull his aides—mostly nonintellectuals—up the bureaucratic ladder, thus creating his own political machine. This alarmed Lenin but, already on his deathbed, he could do little except to urge, in his last will, Stalin's removal. Lenin wrote: "He is too rude . . . insufferable." Stalin, now in command, suppressed the document.

Lenin died on January 21, 1924. From then on, for nearly 30 years, until his own death at the age of 73 on March 5, 1953, Stalin wielded his untrammeled and terrible tyranny over the vast empire. Sending multitudes to slavery and death, he was quoted as saying: "One death may be a tragedy, but millions of deaths are only statistics." He was frank about his sadism, on one occasion remarking that he derived the greatest pleasure from planning in detail precisely how he would do away with an intended victim and then going off to bed for his sweet and sound sleep, knowing that in the morning he would put the death sentence into effect.

At a whim, Stalin reclassified comrades as enemies to be executed. He turned upon his aides and staunchest supporters, either on what Khrushchev was later to call "distrustful" and "sickly" suspicion or on the cold-blooded premise that intimidation works best when terror is highly indiscriminate. Not a single one of Stalin's favorites was ever sure of his continued favor, nor of his own liberty or even life. These favorites were in mortal fright, trembling each time they were called into Stalin's presence. When thus summoned, they said their grim farewells to their families, not knowing whether they would return. Some, in fact, did not. Aware of their fear, Stalin played on it with relish, asking a henchman: "Why do you turn around so much today and avoid looking at me directly in the eye?"

Increasingly in his three decades of dictatorship, as he ordered a mass chorus of praise from the people high and low, he at the same time formalized on a grand scale the insanely cruel terror initiated in Russia by Lenin and Trotsky. Through the swirling madness of mass murder, he displayed for all the world to see the irrational purposes of this terror that, in a much more flagrant way than any other Soviet leader before or after him, Stalin used as the main basis of his power.

Not that the two leaders before him, Lenin and Trotsky, should be absolved to any degree. Nor should we concede that in their terror Lenin and Trotsky were more rational than Stalin. All three should be judged as one phenomenon. And far from being a late or sudden development, their rule of mass-scale murders from 1918 to 1953 had been largely predetermined by the trio's psyches (at the root of their politics), inherent and unfolding long before their coming to power.

And yet, in modern literature, very little has been done to show the necessary connections between the mentalities of Lenin, Trotsky, and Stalin. Thus, in *The Anatomy of Human Destructiveness* by Erich Fromm, we find that Stalin is classed with Hitler and Himmler in the chapters on "Malignant Aggression." Stalin and the two Nazis are described as sadists; in addition, Stalin is defined as possibly suffering "from paranoid tendencies in the last years of his life." With all that, Fromm's analysis of Stalin's aberration is quite inadequate—surely not so full or original as are his depictions of Hitler's necrophilia and Himmler's sadomasochism. Lenin is not even included in this company. Astonishingly, all that Fromm has to say about Lenin is that, like Marx, Engels, and Mao Tse-tung, Lenin had "a sense of responsibility." As for Trotsky, there is not a single mention of him in all the 526 pages of Fromm's book.

While we wait for a truly expert study of the dementia of the founders of the Soviet state and terror, we see that at least on the surface the aims of the Soviet secret police over their nearly six decades have been soberly practical. They have been threefold: First, to remove actual and potential enemies of the Communist dictatorship. Second, through this to intimidate the rest of the population. Third, to secure manpower for the work projects run by the secret police.

The "show trials" of the 1930s, where terrorized and often innocent defendants vied with one another to heap slander and malice upon themselves while confessing the most fantastic "crimes" invented by the secret police, did intimidate most of the populace. But they also convinced some gullible citizens that wholesale arrests and harsh punishment were truly deserved—until that time, of course, when these naive men and women were in their turn themselves arrested, starved, beaten, tortured, and sent to slave camps or shot dead.

An explanation of that terror was once given by a perceptive victim. A Russian engineer sentenced to a long term in a Stalinist concentration camp (we do not know whether he survived it) said to a fellow inmate (who did survive and brought his reminiscences to the West): "We are accused of wrecking. Wrecking there is, in fact, but it is the regime's own wrecking, not ours. Those power-hungry amateurs, those incompetents, have made such a mess of the nation's political body and above all of the nation's economy that they need scapegoats. We are the scapegoats for the years and years of their mistakes. Hence this terror."

At the same time we must remember that this terror, this slavery, was more than a purely political tool. It was and still is an important economic resource of the Soviet regime, or at least an attempt to make it such a resource.

The Red regime's need for labor was at certain times a predominant reason for terror. From a secret 750-page book of Soviet economics, published in Moscow in 1941, that fell into Nazi hands during the initial Soviet retreat in the Second World War and was eventually found in Germany by the American victors, we glean the following:

On the eve of that war, slave labor cut and finished 12.5 per cent of all Soviet timber, built 22.5 per cent of the country's railroads, and mined 75 per cent of its gold, 40.5 per cent of its chrome, and 2.8 per cent of its coal. The secret police were also in charge of all capital construction.

From other reliable sources we know that it was common for the headquarters of the secret police in Moscow to apportion in periodic instructions to its provincial offices the arrest of so many engineers of a certain specialty, so many lumberjacks or tailors or railroad men, so many skilled hands for whatever the secret police enterprises needed in the coming months of their own Five Year Plans.

Special slave laboratories, established for captive scientists and engineers, were meant to contribute toward the Soviet Union's technological progress. Thus, in the 1930s, one of the most valued Soviet sites of radioactive ore mining and processing was made into a property of the secret police, with large numbers of professors, engineers, and other experts arrested for the express purpose of this particular production. The extraction and processing of radium by highly qualified slaves was done in the extreme Arctic north of European Russia, in the Pechora region near the White Sea. The concentration camp contained radium mines, eight chemical plants, and three laboratories—chemical, radiometrical, and physiological—among other units.

The slaves manning this huge compound included Professors F. A. Toropov and G. A. Razuvayev, both celebrated chemists; engineers A. N. Kazakov, G. S. Davydov, S. A. Savelyev, and M. D. Tilicheyev; and many others, almost all eventually perishing in their cages. Kazakov was a renowned flyer and specialist in aeronautics; Davydov was a metallurgist, sentenced to ten years of hard labor on his return from a mission to the United States; Savelyev had pioneered in radio; Tilicheyev was well known in oil mining. Together with nonexperts, the number of prisoners here reached 1,000. Yet their total production was ridiculously low: by the testimony of a surviving slave of this camp who later reached the West, the annual output of radium totaled 4.7 grams in 1936 and 6 grams in 1937.

In 1938 the world-renowned Soviet aircraft builder, Andrei Tupolev, was arrested. On trumped-up charges he was sentenced to five years in jail—first in Moscow, then at Omsk in western Siberia where a *sharashka,* or a special design and test laboratory-prison, was established by the secret police for him and more than 100 other scientists and engineers to help Tupolev create his efficient airplanes for both war and civilian purposes. Mikhail Gurevich, one of the two inventors of the celebrated MiG plane, was among these slaves. So was Sergei Korolyov, the famous pioneer of Soviet rocketry.[4]

Solzhenitsyn's great novel *The First Circle* is about one of these prison-laboratories for Soviet slave-scientists and engineers of Stalin's era. It is based on the novelist's own experience as a mathematician-physicist incarcerated in a slave pen and forced to do research.

III

Today, side by side with such regular Soviet law agencies as the court system, the network of state attorneys known as procurators, the Ministry of Justice, and the Ministry of the Interior, but in actuality overshadowing all of them, there reigns the Soviet institution called KGB, which is the current embodiment of the secret police and which, as an organization, though under other names, realized its greatest power under Stalin.[5]

The initials stand for *Komitet Gosudarstvennoi Bezopasnosti,* or Committee for State Security; it is nominally attached to the federal Council of Ministers, but in reality subject to the Politbureau, which is the supreme organ of the Communist Party, and to its Secretary General Leonid Brezhnev. The head of the KGB is Yury Andropov, a personal friend of Brezhnev and a neighbor of his: Andropov's apartment is one floor below that of Brezhnev in one of Moscow's best sectors, on Kutuzov Prospect (Number 24). The two and a few of their intimates often get together in one or the other of the pair's apartments for supper parties, at which Brezhnev likes to cook.

Let us look back at the list of the predecessors of the KGB and Andropov. The first such security force with arbitrary powers of life and death was established by Lenin on December 20, 1917, six weeks after his seizure of power. It was usually referred to as the Cheka, or Ch. K., after the Russian initials of the first two words of its long name, the Extraordinary Commission for Combating Counterrevolution and Sabotage. Dzerzhinsky, its first chief, was soon widely dreaded as a cold-blooded, ruthless exterminator. No regular trials were held by the Cheka; death sentences were decreed either by a three-man tribunal (*troika*) or by a provincial or regional head of the agency, each such powerful individual acting on his own. One report estimated the total of those executed in the four years of the Cheka's existence at more than 1,760,000. Sentences were usually carried out by shooting, in prison basements. (Executioners on the White side during the civil war sometimes used firing squads but, quite often, gallows as well.)

The adjective "Extraordinary" in the Cheka's official name was a near-ironic Red promise that terror was a temporary tool, to be discarded when the civil war ended and the new Soviet republic was certain of its survival. Indeed, on February 6, 1922, the Cheka was disbanded, but, as it turned out, only nominally. Now it was the GPU, later called OGPU, for the name *Ob'yedinennoye Gosudarstvennoye Politicheskoye Upravleniye,* or the United State Political Administration. In fact, it was the same Cheka merely rechristened in the direction of greater permanency, with the same deadly staff and under the same Feliks Dzerzhinsky.

After Dzerzhinsky's death in 1926, the OGPU was headed by another Russian-Polish Communist, Vyacheslav Menzhinsky. This man, a devotee of mathematics and Persian art, was once called by Lenin "the decadent neurotic." Between executions he read pornographic novels and wrote erotic poetry. His own death, in 1934, was reportedly arranged by his assistant and successor, Genrikh Yagoda.

On July 10, 1934, the OGPU was made part of the People's Commissariat of the Interior, at once feared as the sinister

NKVD, the initials of the Commissariat's Russian name (*Narodny Komissariat Vnutrennikh Del*). Under Dzerzhinsky and Menzhinsky the old Cheka and the OGPU had already added to the terror at home an elaborate system of espionage in foreign lands. Now, under Yagoda, the new NKVD expanded its activities abroad at the same time extended enormously the use of slave labor in concentration camps in the country's northern and eastern provinces. [In addition, in 1934 a Main Administration of State Security was formed (within the NKVD) that, in time—February 1941—was made into the NKVD's twin—the NKGB, which after March 1946 became MGB, now KGB. At the same time the name Gulag emerged, for *Glavnoye Upravleniye Lagerei,* or the Main Administration of Camps; hence the title of Solzhenitsyn's book, *The Gulag Archipelago.*]

The son of an artisan, Yagoda first joined the Bolsheviks in 1907 at 16, was arrested by the Tsarist police at 20, and was drafted into the army during the First World War. In the civil war he held a noncombatant post in the Red forces and shifted to the secret police in 1920. Rising to the very summit, he became known and feared for his ingenious cruelty. It was he who prepared the first two major trials of such fellow Communists incurring Stalin's displeasure as Zinovyev, Kamenev, and others. Under Stalin's own guidance, Yagoda succeeded in exacting from these high-rank defendants astonishingly abject confessions of crimes they had not committed against Stalin and the Party—so starkly depicted in Arthur Koestler's novel, *Darkness at Noon.* Yagoda picked his staff shrewdly; one of his assistants was known to boast that with his methods of interrogation he could force Karl Marx himself to admit his guilt as Bismarck's agent.

Yagoda was removed by Stalin in September 1936, in Stalin's usual pattern of demonstrating his power by demoting and killing his most loyal aides. In March 1938, Yagoda was tried, along with some of the top-level Communist leaders he himself had earlier arrested and harassed. Among other charges of Stalin against Yagoda was that he had poisoned the writer Maxim Gorky. Soon afterward Yagoda was shot, along with those other fallen Old Bolsheviks.

His post at the NKVD pinnacle was assumed by Nikolai Yezhov, whom Stalin had discovered at a provincial post and brought to Moscow. A native of St. Petersburg, of humble origins, Yezhov joined the Bolsheviks in March 1917 at 23, later served as a Red Army political commissar, and moved into the secret police in the mid-1930s. Because of his phenomenal sadism and his short stature (only five feet), Yezhov was called—in frightened whispers—"the bloodthirsty dwarf." Among his practices was that of personally killing his victims in his office.

Always the secret police had the right, introduced by Lenin and continued by Stalin, to kill people at will. But in the great campaign of terror launched by Yezhov on Stalin's orders in 1936-38, death or jail sentences were formalized in a show of legality, which, however, was limited in its pretense. Even before the Yezhov period, Stalin gave the NKVD's Special Board the authority to mete out "administrative" terms of up to five years in exile or forced-labor camps, in the defendants' absence and with no counsel present to plead the victims' cases. In the purge period of '36-'38, the Board increased such sentences to 25 years. Death sentences were numerous. The entire mind-boggling span of these years became known colloquially as *yezhovshchina:* "the horrible time of Yezhov."

Then came Yezhov's own doom. In 1938 he was transferred by Stalin from his NKVD post to head the Soviet Union's water transport, and in 1939 he disappeared. Soon he was executed by his successors, although Stalin had the rumor spread that Yezhov had died in an insane asylum. This was clearly Stalin's clumsy attempt to disassociate himself from the terror he was in fact responsible for and to explain Yezhov's mass tortures and murders by Yezhov's sheer madness.

In 1938 the secret police chieftancy devolved upon Stalin's fellow Georgian, Lavrenty Beria.[6] He remained at this job until a few months after Stalin's death in March 1953.

A peasant's son, Beria had some minor technical education and became a Bolshevik in 1917 at 18. In secret police work since 1921, within ten years he was Stalin's merciless satrap for all of Transcaucasia. Like Yezhov, he particularly enjoyed having important victims—Communists and others—shot in his presence in his own office. In 1935 he ingratiated himself with Stalin by writing a fraudulent history of the Caucasian revolutionary movement with outrageous flattery for Stalin's role. This proved to be the main factor in his transfer to Moscow and his replacement of Yezhov.

Thin-faced, wearing a pince-nez, Beria seemed an austere figure, but even before the promotion he had been notorious for hard drinking and lechery. Now, in Moscow, he gave full vent to his proclivities. Among other pastimes he would on afternoons cruise the streets of the Red capital, spot a pretty girl of a good family in her early teens hurrying from school or to her music lesson, and order his guards to seize and bring her to his bedroom. He would violate the captive, at times—in case of desperate resistance—first drugging her or making her drunk. After several days of his pleasure he would sometimes release the girl, upon warning her and her family to be quiet about it, but sometimes he would kill her and the family so as not to leave any possible complainants.

Prominent in Beria's activity was his organization of Trotsky's murder in Mexico in 1940. In time he received in his Moscow office and personally thanked on their return from Mexico his two chief aides in the assassination, one of them the Spanish Communist Caridad Mercader, the murderer's mother. He then presented her to Stalin, who bestowed a decoration upon her.

When, in March 1946, all the Soviet commissariats were renamed ministries (after the old Imperial and general Western custom), the NKVD became the MVD, or the Ministry of the Interior. By the MVD's side, the MGB, or the Ministry of State Security, grew into a mighty organ, the distribution of the police functions between the two never entirely clear, but both under Beria until just before his death in 1953.

On Stalin's death there was a distinct possibility that Beria, with the help of his plentiful special secret police troops, would seize all power in the land. But somehow he lacked the nerve to do this.[7]

In June 1953, Beria was grabbed by Khrushchev and his associates, charged with treason (including an accusation that he had spied for the British!), and condemned to death, his execution taking place in December 1953, according to an official communiqué, or several months earlier—in the summer of that year, immediately upon his arrest—according to other, informal accounts.

Heartbreaking reminiscences by survivors and by relatives of victims exist now for every phase of the Lenin-Trotsky-Stalin terror. But the greatest sufferings appear to have been experienced when, under Stalin's guidance, Yezhov was in charge. In his *The Great Terror,* Robert Conquest states that at the peak of the Stalin-Yezhov purges in 1937-38 some 8,500,000 people, or 5 per cent of the nation's population, were arrested, and that most of these were sent to slave camps where the annual death rate was 20 per cent. Nor was Yezhov's successor Beria much milder. At the height of the Beria period, the concentration camps held as many as 20 million people—according to the statement made on April 4, 1955, by John H. Noble, an American released from a Soviet slave camp after more than four years of imprisonment. This is more than three times the figure given later, for the same time, by Solzhenitsyn. As his source, Noble cited a statement he had heard from a Russian prisoner with access to such statistics because of his employment as a bookkeeper at the central Gulag headquarters.

Other Stalin-era reports estimate that about 10 per cent of this human mass of misery were women (most of them sentenced for being wives, daughters, and other kin of the imprisoned or executed men); and that 90 per cent of the captives were men of working age, representing 15 to 30 per cent of the country's total male working population. From his experience as a long-time American diplomat in the Soviet Union, George F. Kennan declares that in the purges of the 1930s there were destroyed "a full 75 per cent of the governing class of the country, a similar proportion of the leading intelligentsia, and over half of the higher officers' corps of the Red Army."[8]

A distinguishing characteristic of the Stalin reign was its mass slaughter of Communists by Communists, which had not been so common in the years of Lenin and Trotsky. So all-embracing, in the mid-1930s, were the arrests and executions of Communists in the Soviet Union that a French magazine printed a cartoon showing a demented man in a desert chasing himself with an ax, the caption below reading: "The Last Communist."

Torture of prisoners by the Soviet secret police, interrogators, and guards had already been known in the Lenin-Trotsky period, but under Stalin it was refined and expanded into regular, incessant practice. The methods of torture were many:

Placing a prisoner on the so-called "conveyor"—keeping him or her sleepless for days and nights at a stretch while being questioned by a series of interrogators taking their turns, until the victim signed a false confession.

Tearing off the prisoner's nails. Crushing his fingers between doors. Holding him and other prisoners in a tightly packed cell, with standing room only, for several days and nights, with neither food nor water, until the few survivors were taken out to sign whatever was demanded of them. Or putting the prisoner against a wall with arms raised, the guards beating him each time he dared to move, until the man's legs swelled and after several fainting spells he collapsed completely.

Urinating into the prisoner's mouth during his interrogation.

Administering brutal beatings to the children of prisoners in the parents' presence until "confessions" were signed.

Raping the prisoners' wives and daughters in the prisoners' full view, with similar results.

In the camps, allowing and even encouraging nonpolitical criminals to beat, rob, and rape political prisoners. One method of abusing a woman prisoner was *poslat' yeyo pod tramvai,* or "send her under a trolley car"—subject her to mass rape by 20 or 30 nonpolitical criminals and sometimes by guards.

IV

Following Stalin's death in 1953, arrests decreased greatly, a limited amnesty was announced, and, after Beria's downfall, measures were taken to treat prisoners more humanely. Gradually there came reviews of sentences and numerous "rehabilitations" of victims, in many cases—alas—posthumous. The reasons for the new Khrushchevian policy of mitigation and even apology were several:

Concessions to the people were essential, for hardly a family in the land had by 1953 remained unaffected by the state-decreed and -maintained terror. The many years of Soviet repression had had its calculated effect of intimidating the populace—but it had also rendered them so terrorized as to make them listless. People did their work poorly and ineffectively. Particularly in the slave camps productivity was low. Stalin's heirs in the Kremlin now knew that, economically, slavery did not really pay. Besides, the hardest job of pioneering in the north and east had already been accomplished—by the millions of slaves, so many of whom were by then dead. Free labor could now be induced by wages and bonuses, not by armed guards and vicious dogs, to migrate to those remote, poor-climate areas, to live in relative comfort in barracks built by slaves and to work in mines dug and improved by those who had perished.

The slaves' strikes and rebellions in Vorkuta in the northeast and in Karaganda in Central Asia in 1953, although bloodily quelled, were one more reason for Stalin's heirs to relax the repressions. For in those slaves' insurrections they saw a specter of nationwide uprisings.[9]

And there was the world's opinion, too. Stalin had not worried about it; so powerful he had deemed himself to be, and had indeed been. But the new leaders were not so sure. And by then, unlike Stalin's time (and the earlier Lenin-Trotsky years), the world knew and at last believed the stories brought West by the escaped survivors of the unprecedented terror.

Nor were only the people living in fear. The leaders were also afraid. Stalin's high-placed aides too, as it now became known, had not felt safe in the face of the terror machine they themselves were managing. Respite and assurance were needed by everybody in the nation, of all classes and stations. Beria's downfall was brought about by his Kremlin colleagues' apprehension that, unless eliminated, he would become another Stalin. And Khrushchev and his group also needed a scapegoat to offer to the now restless Soviet masses and classes for Stalin's crimes—and their own. What handier scapegoat than this hated chief of the dreaded secret police?

Thus in 1953 a new, milder policy was introduced, reaching its height in February 1956, when Khrushchev delivered his famous "secret" anti-Stalin speech to the Twentieth Congress of the Communist Party.

The danger of new arrests was diminished, first of all, for Communist Party members who, from the initial post-Stalin time on, could no longer be seized by the secret police without the knowledge and clearance on the part of their Communist superiors. The ill-famed *troika,* the three-man MVD tribunal with arbitrary powers to sentence Soviet citizens in secrecy and in the victims' absence, was abolished. As numerous surviving prisoners were released and fewer new slaves were brought in, certain forced-labor camps were closed. In some of the remaining ones, army guards took over from the MVD slave drivers, and the prisoners' treatment became noticeably more bearable.

From the mid-1950s, the KGB, or the Committee for State Security, as the successor of the MVD and MGB (and of the earlier Cheka, OGPU, and NKVD), has been the top organ of the Soviet secret police, in implacable charge of the continuing arrests and their victims as well as the never-ceasing espionage and sabotage in foreign countries the world over.

A watershed in the renewal of terror was the Hungarian revolt and its suppression by Soviet tanks in late 1956. Soon after the Budapest events, arrests of suspect or restless Russians and non-Russians were resumed in the Soviet empire. By 1958 such arrests, although not publicized, were occurring *en masse*. The new wave included not only "first offenders," but also rearrests of many of those freed only a short time before. Western researchers of the phenomenon estimated that in 1961 there were some three to four million prisoners in Soviet concentration camps. This figure was in time judged to remain constant for the next 14 years, except that by 1976 it also included the growing numbers of those political dissenters who were kept in the KGB's special insane asylums, even when such prisoners were entirely sane. Nor should we forget the additional contingents of prisoners in the jails and camps of Czechoslovakia (particularly numerous after the suppression of that country in August 1968 by Soviet tanks), Poland, East Germany, and other so-called "people's democracies," where the native secret police usually act with the guidance or at least cooperation of the Moscow KGB.

It is true that, although the prisoners' beatings, tortures, and killings in the prisons and concentration camps of the Soviet empire have not stopped completely, these now occur less frequently and in most cases are not perhaps as brutally sadistic as they commonly were in Stalin's era. On the other hand, the number of fresh arrests is higher, and the treatment of prisoners is harsher than in Khrushchev's time. Instances of inmates' suicide are on the increase.

The dominant role of the KGB over the nation's regular courts is once more quite definite. It is the KGB that decides which of the political trials in these mid-1970s are to be conducted behind closed doors, even if held in regular courts. Sentences by such courts in the defendants' absence are on the increase, sternly reminding the population of Stalinist times. A regular court sometimes swiftly turns over a prisoner to the KGB's keeping. Often there is not even a formal charge and any legal condemnation—only the court's finding that the prisoner must be demented since he does not like the Soviet regime. Such was, for instance, the case of the poetess Nataliya Gorbanveskaya when, in July 1970, the Moscow city court committed her to the infamous Serbsky Insane Asylum, which is within the KGB network, staffed by "psychiatrists" officially employed by the KGB, and even wearing their KGB uniforms and insignia as colonels and majors of the secret police beneath their unbuttoned white coats. Since 1970 such commitments of political dissidents to mental hospitals have been common. Treatment of these perfectly normal prisoners include forcible injections of drugs, in the KGB's hope that this will soon make the unfortunates truly insane.

The maximum term in present-day concentration camps appears to be 15 years, but cases are known where prisoners are being held well beyond this limit. The death penalty is still on the Soviet law books, for treason to the state (such as caused Colonel Oleg V. Penkovsky's execution in May 1963), and for major economic crimes (the law of May 5, 1961), as well as for murder and banditry. While a high court of the Ministry of Justice may be the agency that passes a sentence of capital punishment, the penalty is carried out by a firing squad of the secret police, as in the Stalinist era.

By the middle 1970s the protesting voices of Amnesty International and other Western organizations on behalf of Soviet dissidents became a strong chorus. The Soviet dictatorship has responded to it reluctantly and sparingly. Often it has disregarded the protests of Western intellectuals completely, though at times it has yielded by allowing a few dissidents to leave the Soviet Union for good. Sometimes it has deported them against their will. Thus, in February 1974, the KGB arrested Alexander Solzhenitsyn and at first threatened him with execution. Then, realizing the furor this would arouse abroad, the KGB expelled him to Western Germany.

Some Soviet and Western intellectuals attempted to use the détente, then being negotiated by the United States President Richard M. Nixon and the Soviet leader Leonid Brezhnev, toward the lessening of the Soviet terror in its latest phase. In late June and early July 1974, as Nixon and Brezhnev met in Moscow and Yalta, the Soviet nuclear physicist Andrei D. Sakharov appealed to them:

> Do what you can, at least for some of the prisoners—the women, the old people, those who are ill, those who have been tried more than once (the courts punish them with special perversity). Bring about the immediate release of all who have been incarcerated for more than 15 years, the maximum term fixed by law. Encourage international supervision of places of confinement in all countries—in these places human rights and humanitarian principles are violated most often.[10]

To strengthen his plea, Professor Sakharov went on a hunger strike that he kept up for almost a week. The only response from Brezhnev was his order to the Soviet television technicians to cut off at its very beginning the interview with Sakharov that American broadcasters tried to relay from Moscow to the world at large.

As for President Nixon, there is no evidence that he interceded with Brezhnev in any way on behalf of Soviet prisoners and other dissidents. On the contrary, in a public speech prior to his flight to meet with Brezhnev, the President warned that there should be no interference with the domestic affairs of any nation, no matter how much we may sympathize with the victims of such a nation's terror.

From August 1974 on, the new President Gerald R. Ford, having inherited Secretary of State Henry Kissinger, has on the whole continued this Nixon-Kissinger policy of noninterference with the severe repressive course of the Soviet government within that country.

But a welcome contrast came in October 1975, when a special committee of the Norwegian parliament awarded Sakharov the year's Nobel Peace Prize, citing the Russian scientist for his fearless advocacy of human rights, particularly the right to dissent and the right to freedom from oppression and terror: "His basic principle is that universal peace cannot have a lasting value if not based on respect for every individual in society."

V

There remains for humanitarians and demographers as well as for historians the grave problem of the exact or even approximate total toll of Soviet terror from Lenin's seizure of power in November 1917 to Stalin's death in March 1953.

On the eve of the revolution of 1917, political prisoners in Tsarist jails totaled fewer than 800. In the first volume of his *Gulag Archipelago,* Solzhenitsyn estimates that as many as six million political convicts were held in Soviet prisons and concentration camps at any one time (while another six million were nonpolitical inmates and slaves). This high figure, according to Solzhenitsyn, was reached just before Stalin's death. In his second volume, Solzhenitsyn writes that from late 1917 to early 1953 between 40 and 50 million humans passed through Soviet jails and slave camps, including men, women, and children who never came out alive. Those dead totaled between 15 and 25 million.

Hitler's victims of gassing, gallows, firing squads, and other means of extermination (not counting those lost in battles and bombings) totaled between 10 and 12 million, of whom six million were Jews. But then, the Nazis had only 12 years to establish their grisly record, whereas the Lenin-through-Stalin period lasted more than 35 years.

In early 1974, Western intelligence sources put the Soviet prison population under the Brezhnev-Kosygin regime as anywhere between one million and 2,500,000, of whom only 10,000 were considered political convicts. But defectors and émigrés from the Soviet Union in 1974-76 ridiculed this figure as entirely too low.

The number of those politicals who are unjustly confined to Soviet insane asylums is unknown.

Thus the grand promise of Russia's terrorists, from the Narodniki through the Terror Brigade of the Socialist Revolutionaries to Lenin's launching of mass murders, which sought to justify their bloodshed by their aim of making mankind happy, was never even close to realization. In the Soviet Union and other Socialist-Communist countries there may have been economic gains, but even these could have been achieved by peaceful means. The human rights of the original dream and promise—equality, justice, personal liberty—have not been enhanced. Far from it; whatever such rights did exist in pre-terror times have by now been trampled into the bloody mire by the hobnailed boots of torturers and firing squads.

NOTES

[1] On the Stalinist period in Soviet terror, in addition to the pertinent parts of the already cited Solzhenitsyn's *The Gulag Archipelago,* see:

Roy A. Medvedev, *Let History Judge: The Origins and Consequences of Stalinism,* transl. by Colleen Taylor and edited by David Joravsky and Georges Haupt (New York: Alfred A. Knopf, 1971). Unfortunately, while blaming Stalin for terror, the author tends to exonerate Lenin.

Robert Conquest, *The Great Terror: Stalin's Purge of the Thirties,* revised edition (New York: The Macmillan Company, 1973). One of the best accounts and analyses of the Stalinist terror.

An earlier, thorough, and well-documented study is David J. Dallin and Boris I. Nicolaevsky, *Forced Labor in Soviet Russia* (New Haven: Yale University Press, 1947). More embracive geographically is Alexander Dallin and George W. Breslauer, *Political Terror in Communist Systems* (Stanford University Press, 1970).

Among the innumerable individual memoirs by survivors of the Stalinist terror, three of the latest and most impressive are:

Alexander Vardy, *Das Eisloch* [The Icehole], transl. from the Russian by Josef Hahn (Stuttgart: Henry Goverts Verlag, 1966).

Joseph Berger, *Nothing But the Truth* (New York: The John Day Company, 1971).

Alexander Dolgun with Patrick Watson, *Alexander Dolgun's Story: An American in the Gulag* (New York: Knopf, 1975).

Much of my knowledge and understanding of the Stalinist terror came from my acquaintance and long talks, over the years, with numerous survivors of the Soviet concentration camps. Among others, I am indebted to Alexander Vardy for the recollections he so readily and fully shared with me during our many get-togethers in his Munich home.

[2] N. Otradin, "Po ostrovam 'Arkhipelaga'" [On the islands of the 'Archipelago'], *Novoye Russkove Slovo,* March 3, 1974.

[3] For biographies of Stalin, besides the already cited Trotsky, *Stalin,* and the relevant parts of Wolfe, *Three Who Made a Revolution,* see:

Boris Souvarine, *Stalin: A Critical Survey of Bolshevism,* translated by C. L. R. James (New York: Alliance Book Corporation, Longmans, Green & Co., 1939).

Adam B. Ulam, *Stalin: The Man and His Era* (New York: The Viking Press, 1973).

Robert C. Tucker, *Stalin As Revolutionary, 1879-1929: A Study in History and Personality* (paperback, New York: Norton 1974).

[4] A. Sharagin (pseudonym of Georgi A. Ozerov, one of the victims), *Tupolevskaya sharaga* [Tupolev's secret camp-laboratory], (Frankfurt, West Germany: Published by the Posey House, [1971]), *passim.*

[5] John Barron, *KGB* (paperback, New York: Bantam Books, 1974).

[6] Despite the historical importance of Beria's life and activity, there is not a single comprehensive biography of him in any language. The book by Thaddeus Wittlin, *Commissar: The Life and Death of Lavrenty Pavlovich Beria* (New York: Macmillan, 1972), notwithstanding its size—566 pages—is a complete failure.

[7] How close in those March days of 1953 Beria came to seize all power in the Soviet Union, may be seen from Harrison E. Salisbury, *American in Russia* (New York: Harper & Brothers, 1955), Chapter X, "The Seventy-five Hours," particularly pp. 170-72.

[8] George F. Kennan, *Memoirs: 1925-1950* (Boston: Little, Brown, 1967), pp. 503-04.

[9] The fullest story of the slaves' uprising at Vorkuta is Joseph Scholmer, *Vorkuta,* translated from the German by Robert Kee (London: Weidenfeld and Nicolson, 1954).

[10] *The New York Times,* July 5, 1974, the Op-Ed Page, accompanied by Arthur Miller's short essay, "Sakharov, Détente and Liberty." For the role of Soviet courts as instruments of terror in the current Brezhnev period, see Telford Taylor, *Courts of Terror: Soviet Criminal Justice and Jewish Emigration* (New York: Knopf, 1976).

Robert C. Tucker (essay date 1979)

SOURCE: "The Rise of Stalin's Personality Cult," in *The American Historical Review,* Vol. 84, No. 2, April, 1979, pp. 347-66.

[*In the following essay, Tucker discusses the reasons behind Stalin's rise to the status of cult figure despite the objections of earlier Soviet leaders, particularly Lenin, to public adulation.*]

The cult of Lenin, which Lenin himself opposed and managed to keep in check until incapacitated by a stroke in March 1923, subsequently became a pervasive part of Soviet public life. No single cause explains its rise. Undoubtedly, the Bolsheviks genuinely venerated their *vozhd'* as the man whose personal leadership had been critically important for the movement from its origin to its assumption of power and for the creation and consolidation of the Soviet regime in the ensuing years. But it is also true that after Lenin's death that regime had a pragmatic need for a prestigious unifying symbol. The Lenin cult, whose obvious religious overtones were at variance with the Communist Party's professed secularism, is likewise an example of how Soviet culture came to incorporate certain elements of the Russian past, in this case the ruler cult. For centuries the Russian people, overwhelmingly composed of peasants, had been monarchist in outlook. The Revolution had opened the door for many peasant sons to have careers in the new society. Industrialization and collectivization resulted in the recruitment of millions of people of peasant stock into the working class. They brought with them, along with their Soviet schooling and experience, residues of the traditional peasant mentality, including respect for personal authority, whether it emanated from the immediate boss or from the head of the party and state. The social condition of Russia at the time of the "great turn" (1929-33) was, therefore, receptive to the cult of a deceased leader—or a living one.

Lenin refused to tolerate public adulation—save, with extreme reluctance, on his fiftieth birthday in 1920—and even then he showed dry disapproval of the eulogizing to which his comrades subjected him. Thus, as the public adulation of a living leader, the Stalin cult deviated from previous Bolshevik practice. How and why, then, did the Stalin cult arise?

Realpolitik fused with psychological needs. Politically, a Stalin cult alongside of and integrated into the Lenin cult promised to make Stalin's position more impregnable than it was at the start of the 1930s. Although he had won considerable support and even popularity inside party circles during the early post-Lenin years, Stalin never enjoyed a prestige even remotely comparable to Lenin's. His popularity, moreover, plummeted in the early 1930s as a result of forced collectivization and the concomitant famine of 1932-33. No evidence suggests that he was then in danger of being overthrown; still, his power was not yet absolute, the argumentative-critical tradition lived on (at least in higher party circles), and he had no guarantee against the rise of new opposition in response to new tribulation. So Stalin was undoubtedly concerned to forestall future trouble by making his political supremacy more unassailable. He was shrewd enough to realize that his elevation to a Lenin-like eminence in the regime's publicity would be useful for this purpose. But, important as it was, the political motive does not provide a sufficient explanation. Not only did the cult continue to grow after Stalin's power became increasingly absolute later in the 1930s, but both direct and indirect evidence indicates that it was a prop for his psyche as well as for his power. Boundlessly ambitious, yet inwardly insecure, he had an imperative need for the hero worship that Lenin found repugnant.

That the name "Stalin" symbolized a lofty idealized self to its seemingly earthy bearer was not widely known in Russia. In part, this reflected Stalin's studied effort to emulate in public Lenin's example of modestly unassuming deportment. In private, moreover, Stalin repeatedly affected disdain for adulation. For example, he concluded a letter to an Old Bolshevik, Ia. M. Shatunovskii, in August 1930 by saying, "You speak of your 'devotion' to me. Perhaps that phrase slipped out accidentally. Perhaps. But if it isn't an accidental phrase, I'd advise you to thrust aside the 'principle' of devotion to persons. It isn't the Bolshevik way. Have devotion to the working class, its party, its state. That's needed and good. But don't mix it with devotion to persons, that empty and needless bauble of intellectuals."[1]

But the man behind the mask of modesty was hungry for the devotion he professed to scorn. He showed it by his own actions and by those of functionaries representing him—and by his acceptance of the officially inspired adulation as it rose in intensity during the 1930s. Indeed, in the very month in which he wrote the letter to Shatunovskii, Stalin, also in private, gave lie to that same advice. In June-July 1930 the Sixteenth Party Congress witnessed an outpouring of public tributes to him. Louis Fischer, who covered that event for *The Nation,* concluded his post-Congress dispatch by saying,

> A good friend might also advise Stalin to put a stop to the orgy of personal glorification of Stalin which has been permitted to sweep the country. . . . Daily, hundreds of telegrams pour in on him brimming over with Oriental super-compliments: "Thou art the greatest leader . . . , the most devoted disciple of Lenin," and the like. Three cities, innumerable villages, collectives, schools, factories, and institutions have been named after him, and now somebody has started a movement to christen the Turksib the "Stalin Railway." I have gone back over the newspapers from 1919 to 1922: Lenin never permitted such antics and he was more popular than Stalin can ever hope to be. It exposes a weak side of Stalin's character which his enemies, who are numerous, are sure to exploit, for it is as un-Bolshevik as it is politically unwise. If Stalin is not responsible for this performance he at least tolerates it. He could stop it by pressing a button.[2]

A press section officer of the Foreign Commissariat, whose duties included the briefing of Stalin on foreign press coverage of Soviet affairs, later confided to Fischer that, when he translated the passage just quoted, Stalin responded with an expletive: "the bastard!" (*svoloch'!*).[3] Evidently, he was stung by the truth of Fischer's observation that he himself bore responsibility for the emerging Stalin cult.

Precisely when this cult took on a life and momentum of its own is not easy to pinpoint. If the official celebration of Stalin's fiftieth birthday in 1929 is taken as the opening episode, there is no immediate sequel. The marking of Lenin's fiftieth birthday had been a one-time affair, and many in high positions may have assumed that Stalin's fiftieth would be similarly observed. Six months later came the acclaim at the Sixteenth Congress. But again the wave subsided. Although his name appeared often in the Soviet press, no steady stream of Stalin idolatry appeared in Soviet publicity in 1930 and most of 1931. Shortly afterwards, however, the cult began to grow. And Stalin himself took certain steps to make it happen.

One such step was in philosophy, one of the numerous fields in which different schools of thought contended for primacy in the relatively pluralistic atmosphere of the period of the New Economic Policy (NEP). In the mid-1920s the so-called mechanistic materialists lost their previously influential position, and a school of devotees of Hegelian dialectics, led by A. M. Deborin, won dominance. Theirs was a positive response to Lenin's invitation to Soviet philosophers in 1922 to constitute themselves a society of "materialist friends of Hegelian dialectics."

Although Lenin had some philosophical writings to his credit, it was not uncommon in the 1920s to place him below Georgii Plekhanov as a Marxist philosopher. Deborin's disciples, moreover, tended to rate Deborin as the Engels of his own time in the field of philosophy.[4] Stalin, by contrast, was widely regarded in Communist Party circles as a *praktik,* save for his theoretical work on the nationalities problem and his codification of Leninist doctrine in *The Foundations of Leninism;* thus, his standing in Marxist philosophy was virtually nil. Interesting evidence on this point exists in the form of a list, published in 1929, of writings with which students entering graduate work in the Communist Academy's Institute of Philosophy were supposed to be familiar in advance. Thirty-three works were listed under dialectical and historical materialism—that is, philosophy. Six works by Marx and Engels came first, followed by six works by Lenin, then four by Plekhanov, and then seven by Deborin. Then came entry number 23, Stalin's *Problems of Leninism,* which even at that low ranking was very probably included for diplomatic reasons. The list ended (Western philosophers will be interested to note) with Descartes, Hobbes, Hume, and Berkeley.[5]

For both political and personal reasons, Stalin could not be content with this situation. As the party's *vozhd'* in succession to Lenin, he was duty-bound, in terms of Bolshevik culture, to be a creative Marxist theoretical mind of the first rank—in the political if not in the technical philosophical sense. But beyond those political expectations imposed by the *vozdh'*-role, Stalin had a personal craving for renown as a Marxist theoretician. Nikolai Bukharin, who knew him well, saw this and stressed it in his clandestine conversation with Lev Kamenev in 1928. For many years Stalin had harbored pretensions in Marxist philosophy. He had set forth what he saw as the fundamentals of dialectical materialism in his treatise of 1906-07, *Anarchism or Socialism?* In correspondence in 1908 that vexed Lenin, Stalin had characterized Lenin's philosophical polemics with the Bogdanov group over Machism as a "tempest in a teacup" and commended A. A. Bogdanov for pointing out some "*individual* faults of Ilyich."[6]

Stalin quietly continued, in the midst of intense political activities of later years, to try to enhance his command of

Marxism as philosophy. He called upon Jan Sten, a leading philosopher of the Deborin school, to guide him in the study of Hegelian dialectics. Sten's teaching method, the one then used in the Institute of Red Professors, involved the parallel study of Marx's *Capital* and Hegel's *The Phenomenology of the Mind*. Stalin continued to have twice-weekly sessions with Sten from 1925 until some time in 1928, after which Stalin called a halt. Sten reportedly was depressed by the difficulty Stalin had in mastering Hegelian dialectics.[7]

Stalin sounded the characteristic note of the future Stalin school when he told a conference of agrarian Marxists on December 27, 1929 that Marxist theory always needed to keep in step with current practice. Not long afterwards, two young, clever, opportunist-minded philosophers from the Institute of Red Professors, Pavel F. Iudin and Mark B. Mitin, took up the same theme. Along with a third professor, V. Ral'tsevich, they published in *Pravda* on June 7, 1930 a long article that championed the notion that philosophy should apply itself in a new way to the theoretical problems of practice in building socialism. They lauded Stalin for showing an example of "deepened understanding of Marxist-Leninist dialectics" in his theoretical formulation of the idea of a struggle on two fronts—that is, against deviations of both Left and Right—and called for a corresponding philosophical struggle on two fronts. Although the authors did not openly attack Deborin, the article pointed to his school as the enemy on the philosophical second front. The authors came forward, in effect, as the nucleus of a new, Stalin school in Soviet philosophy. Stalin's approbation—if not inspiration as well—was reflected in the unusual note, published along with the article, that claimed that "the editors associate[d] themselves with the main propositions of the present article."

Soon Stalin personally intervened on the philosophical front. On December 9, 1930 he spoke out on philosophical matters in an interview with a group of philosophers from the Institute of Red Professors. Mitin later quoted him as saying that it was necessary to "rake and dig up all of the manure that has accumulated in questions of philosophy and natural science." In particular, it was necessary to "rake up everything written by the Deborinite group—all that is erroneous on the philosophical sector." Deborin's school was a philosophical form of revisionism that according to Stalin, who had a special talent for coining caustic neologisms, could be called "Menshevizing idealism." It was necessary, he continued, to expose a number of erroneous philosophical positions of Plekhanov, who had always looked down upon Lenin. Stalin kept emphasizing in the interview that Lenin had raised dialectical materialism to a new plane. Before Lenin, he said, materialism had been atomistic. On the basis of new scientific advances, Lenin produced a Marxist analysis of the electronic theory of matter. But, although he created much that was new in all spheres of Marxism, Lenin was very modest and did not like to talk about his contributions. It was incumbent upon his disciples, however, to clarify all aspects of his innovative role.[8]

Stalin was assuming the role of the premier living Marxist philosopher. Albeit coarsely, he spoke as one philosopher, and the authoritative one, to other philosophers. He was clearing the way for self-elevation by mobilizing the subservient, young, would-be disciples to dethrone Deborin and Plekhanov from their positions of eminence in the minds of Soviet Marxist philosophers. "Deborinism" along with "Menshevizing idealism" now became polemical by-words for philosophical heresy in the philosophical journal, *Under the Banner of Marxism*, and other publications. Future lists of mandatory advance reading for graduate students in philosophy no longer put Stalin in twenty-third place, and Deborin's learned treatises did not figure in them at all.

In the interview Stalin did not directly refer to his own philosophical credentials, although he implied them by his pronouncements. But he employed an indirect strategy of cult-building by the way in which he dealt with Lenin. Since he did not actually harbor much enthusiasm for Lenin's philosophical merits, why did he studiously praise Lenin as a philosopher and warn the audience not to be put off by Lenin's modest forbearance to speak about his contributions in this field? For one thing, there was the subtle Aesopian message, which could not have escaped the minds of the alert Iudin and Mitin, that *they* should not be put off by Stalin's own modesty on the same count. But, more importantly, Stalin was promoting Lenin's primacy in philosophy as a vehicle for his own claim to similar primacy. The party's erstwhile politico-ideological chief was presented as its philosophical chief as well—in place of Plekhanov, the acknowledged father of Russian Marxism, who had later become a Menshevik. By thus putting supreme philosophical authority into Lenin's *vozhd'*-role, Stalin helped the philosophers to grasp this broadened conception of that role as applicable to Lenin's successor.

They were quick to do so. In 1931 the organ of the Central Committee, *Bolshevik,* carried a bitter criticism of "Menshevizing idealism" as found in the *Great Soviet Encyclopedia*. Deborin's *Encyclopedia* article on Hegel was the first object of attack. In castigating Deborin and others of his school as carriers of Menshevizing idealism, the *Bolshevik* author stated, "Materialist dialectics really must be elaborated. But this elaboration must be carried out on the basis of the works of Marx, Engels, Lenin, and Stalin. . . ."[9] Here appeared the holy quartet—Marx, Engels, Lenin, Stalin—who together became the symbolic centerpiece of Stalinist thought and culture, replete with the four huge, equal-sized portraits on the facade of Moscow's Bolshoi Theater for May Day, November 7, and other special occasions.

The cult of Stalin as Communism's first philosopher in succession to Marx, Engels, and Lenin had now been founded. But this was not all. Embryonic in this development was the monolithism that became a hallmark of Stalinist intellectual culture in all fields and that distinguished it from pre-Stalinist Bolshevism. To treat, for example, Lenin's philosophical writings, much less Stalin's, as sacrosanct dogma had never before been mandatory.[10] Stalin himself became not only the first philosopher but also the authority figure in some other fields, and in still others a Stalin-surrogate—Andrei Vyshinskii, for example, in jurisprudence—was, so to speak, subenthroned as the authority figure. Part of the role of such Stalin-surrogates was to glorify Stalin's thought in the process of hunting for heresy and establishing Stalinist truth for their own disciplines. Consequently, those chosen as Stalin-surrogates were scholars who combined intellectual acumen, in most cases, with absolutely reliable servility. Anyone with any independence of mind, no matter how zealous a servitor of Communism, was unacceptable.

If Marxist philosophy was the first area Stalin selected for building the stately edifice of the Stalin cult, party history was the second. Here he moved into a field of great political sensitivity, for the annals of the Bolshevik past were the movement's inner sanctum. But he also trod on ground of intense personal concern, namely his own revolutionary biography. Nothing was of more importance to a man who felt driven to view himself as Bolshevism's second Lenin, in the past as well as the present. He made his move in the familiar manner that so many have chosen in their effort to set the record straight: he wrote a letter to the editors.

At the outset of the 1930s, research on the history of the Marxist movement was still pursued with a certain freedom, contentious issues were seriously debated, and work of genuine scholarly character was still produced in Soviet Russia. One set of questions, those concerning the German Social Democratic Party (SPD) and the pre-1914 Second International, was deemed of sufficient interest that in 1929 the Communist Academy's Institute of History established a special group to study them; the group's academic secretary was A. G. Slutskii. Various articles by members of the group were published, one of which appeared in the journal *Proletarian Revolution* in 1930. Slutskii's main topic was Lenin's position in connection with the internal divisions in the pre-1914 SPD. The revisionist wing of that party, led by Eduard Bernstein, was opposed by a dominant centrist group, whose leaders were Karl Kautsky and August Bebel and whose viewpoint was taken by many—Lenin included—to be genuine revolutionary Marxism. On the extreme Left was a group of radicals led by Rosa Luxemburg. Slutskii claimed that as early as 1911 she had grasped and openly discussed the basically "opportunist" nature of Kautskyan centrism, whereas Lenin, though he had shown a certain critical caution toward the Kautsky-Bebel leadership ever since 1907, had continued to base his hopes on it. Lenin himself admitted in a letter of October 1914 that "Rosa Luxemburg was right"; he had not seen through Kautsky's pseudo-revolutionism as early as had the German left radicals. Slutskii concluded that Lenin had displayed "a certain underestimation of the centrist danger in the German party before the war."[11]

The publication of this article demonstrates that, although a Soviet Lenin cult existed in the early 1930s, it was still possible to publish an article that did not treat Lenin as an icon—infallible, preternaturally foresightful, beyond human limitations. True, the editors of *Proletarian Revolution*—the Old Bolsheviks M. Saveliev, V. V. Adoratskii, M. S. Ol'minskii, D. Baevskii, and P. Gorin—seemed to sense the potential danger, for they inserted an introductory footnote disclaiming any agreement with Slutskii's interpretation of Lenin and announcing the printing of his essay "for purposes of discussion" only. But they clearly were unprepared for the thunderbolt that its appearance provoked from on high. Stalin was infuriated. He wrote a letter of article length, entitled "On Some Questions of the History of Bolshevism," which was simultaneously printed in *Proletarian Revolution* and *Bolshevik* at the end of October 1931.

First, Stalin mauled Slutskii's position beyond recognition, contending that to accuse Lenin of underestimating the danger of "veiled opportunism" was to accuse him of not having been a "real Bolshevik" before 1914: a real Bolshevik could never underestimate the danger of veiled opportunism. It was simply axiomatic that Bolshevism arose and grew strong in its ruthless struggle against all shades of centrism. Thus, the editors should never have accepted Slutskii's "balderdash" and "crooked pettifogging" even as a piece for discussion; the genuineness of Lenin's Bolshevism was not discussable. Second, Stalin protested Slutskii's favorable treatment of Rosa Luxemburg and the left radicals in the pre-1914 SPD. He was profoundly irked by the very idea that Lenin might have had something to learn from these people.

The strong Russian-nationalist tinge of Stalin's Bolshevism was also evident in his letter. He presented a Russocentric view of the history of the European Marxist movement: "Russian Bolsheviks" had a right to treat their own positions as the test of the Marxist revolutionary validity of those of left Social Democrats abroad. Lenin's forecast of 1902 in *What Is To Be Done?*—that the Russian proletariat might yet become "the vanguard of the international revolutionary proletariat"—had been brilliantly confirmed by subsequent events. "But does it not follow from this that the Russian Revolution was (and remains) the key point of the world revolution, that the fundamental questions of the Russian Revolution were at the same time (as they are now) the fundamental questions of the world revolution? Is it not clear that only on these basic questions could one really test the revolutionism of the left Social Democrats in the West?" Neither before nor after the war were Western Marxists to give lessons to their Russian brethren, but vice versa.

To say or imply otherwise, as Slutskii did, was "Trotskyist contraband." To give weight to this ugly charge, Stalin asserted that Slutskii's thesis about Lenin's pre-1914 underestimation of centrism was a cunning way of suggesting to the "unsophisticated reader" that Lenin had only become a real revolutionary after the war started and after he had "re-armed" himself with the help of Trotsky's theory that bourgeois-democratic revolutions grow into socialist ones (the theory of permanent revolution); Lenin himself, Stalin recalled had written in 1905 that "we stand for uninterrupted revolution" and "we will not stop half way." But "contrabandists" like Slutskii were not interested in such facts, which were verifiable from Lenin's writings. Slutskii, Stalin noted elsewhere in the letter, had spoken in his article of the unavailability of some Lenin documents pertaining to the period in question. "But who except hopeless bureaucrats can rely on paper documents alone? Who but archive rats fail to realize that parties and leaders must be tested by their *deeds* primarily and not simply by their declarations?"

Toward the end of the letter, Stalin's language shifted from the rude to the sinister. In giving Slutskii a forum for his contraband, the editors were guilty of that "rotten liberalism" toward Trotskyist tendencies that was current among a segment of Bolsheviks who failed to understand that Trotskyism had long since ceased to be a faction of Communism but had turned into a forward detachment of the counterrevolutionary bourgeoisie, making war on Communism, the Soviet regime, and the building of socialism in the USSR. Such, for example, was the purpose of the Trotskyist theses on the impossibility of building socialism in Russia and the inevitability of Bolshevism's degeneration.

Here Stalin repeated in public the argument of a memorandum he had written in 1929.[12] Its purport had been to transfer Trotskyist affiliation or sympathies from the category of political error to that of crime against the Soviet state and, hence, to justify repressive action against persons accused of being Trotskyist. As Stalin now spelled out the conclusion to his argument, "Liberalism toward Trotskyism, even though defeated and masked, is thus a form of bungling that borders on crime, treason to the working class." Hence, the editors' task, Stalin continued (mixing his metaphors), was "to put the study of party history onto scientific Bolshevik rails and to sharpen vigilance against Trotskyist and all other falsifiers of the history of our party, systematically ripping off their masks." This task was all the more necessary in that certain genuinely Bolshevik party historians were themselves guilty of errors that poured water on the mills of the Slutskiis. Unfortunately, said Stalin at the end, one such person was Comrade Emelian Iaroslavskii (the dean of Bolshevik party historians as well as the secretary of the Central Party Control Commission), whose books on party history, in spite of their merits, contained a number of errors in principle and of historical character.[13]

Considering what Stalin had said earlier about centrism, it is easy to see why he was outraged by Slutskii's argument that Lenin had underestimated the centrist danger in the German Social Democratic Party. To fight against deviations of the Left and Right was not to be a centrist, Stalin had contended in 1928, any more than it had been centrist of Lenin to combat both Menshevism on the Right and the sectarianism condemned in *Left-Wing Communism* on the Left. Centrism meant "adaptation" and on

that account was "alien and repulsive to Leninism."[14] How then—no matter what documents the archive rats might turn up—could a real revolutionary (that is, a Bolshevik), ever, even briefly, underestimate the centrist danger? To a mind that so reasoned, people like Slutskii fully deserved the merciless bawling out that the letter gave them and severe punishment as well. Slutskii was arrested in the later Stalin terror and spent many years in a concentration camp.[15]

But Stalin's letter, in addition to expressing his rage, pursued a tripartite purpose in cult-building. Though it did not mention his own name (how could it?), the letter solicited a Stalin cult in party history just because Stalin wrote it and by the tone and content. First, in writing it (or, conceivably, having it written to his specifications and issued in his name), he arrogated to himself the position of premier party historian and arbiter of contentious issues in that sensitive area. For this the letter did not have to mention Stalin's name, but only to be the thoroughly dogmatic document that it was and to bear his signature. Merely by publishing the letter Stalin asserted his place as the supreme authority on the very subject that formed the core of the personality cult as it mushroomed in the 1930s: Bolshevism's past and the parts that he and others had played in it.[16]

Second, in the letter just as in the earlier interview with the Mitin-Iudin group of philosophers, Stalin followed the strategy of cult-building via the assertion of Lenin's infallibility. By making the party's previous *vozhd'* an iconographic figure, beyond limitation and beyond criticism, Stalin's letter implicitly nominated the successor-*vozhd'* for similar treatment. Since Stalin was the man whom the party had saluted in 1929 as its acknowledged chief in succession to Lenin, it behooved party historians to be as careful not to find lapses or blemishes in his political past as the letter in effect ordered scholars to be where Lenin's past was concerned. People as experienced in reading delphic utterances as were Bolshevik party intellectuals were bound to draw this inference as they pondered or discussed with one another the implications of the letter. Stalin even gave them a broad hint with a phrase used twice in the letter: "Lenin (the Bolsheviks)." Lenin, by Stalin's fiat, stood for true Bolshevik revolutionism as distinct from any and all false varieties—left, right, or center. The words in parentheses pluralized his revolutionary rectitude; they made it more inclusive without giving names. But anyone with intelligence enough to be a party historian could guess whose name ought to come next on the list of "Bolsheviks" in Stalin's normative sense of the term.

Third, the letter demanded quite explicitly that the party pasts of real revolutionaries be evaluated not on the basis of documents that archive rats might turn up or fail to uncover but on the basis of their "deeds." Naturally, such deeds would have to be documented insofar as possible. Stalin was to become the arch-archive rat of the Soviet Union or, more precisely, the leader of a whole pack, although he often hungered as much for the destruction or concealment of documents as for their discovery or publication. To those capable of discerning his letter's implications, they were that a party historian should not be guided, as had Slutskii, by what he could document, but by what he knew *a priori* must be true—that Lenin, being a "real Bolshevik," could never have underestimated centrism or that Stalin, also a "real Bolshevik," could never have taken an un-Bolshevik position at any juncture. The function of documentary materials, or of their concealment, was to help establish such higher truths. To use them otherwise was to slander and to falsify. Consequently, the message of Stalin's tirade against falsifiers was that scholars had to be ready to falsify (in the normal meaning of the word) whenever *a priori* party-historical truth—as revealed by word from Stalin or his spokesmen—should so dictate.

The cult-building purport of Stalin's letter may be shown further by reference to one work—namely that of Iaroslavskii—that it criticized. Stalin did not clearly specify the nature of the errors to which he was alluding, and Iaroslavskii himself seems to have been somewhat baffled. He wrote Stalin several letters requesting clarification but received no answer.[17] In various party discussions prior to the appearance of Stalin's letter, Iaroslavskii had defended every Leninist's right to voice his view on "any controversial question" without fear of being branded a "revisionist."[18] From Stalin's standpoint, such a position was certainly "rotten liberalism" and, hence, an error in principle. As for historical errors, a quick glance through volume four of the party history, covering the period 1917 to 1921 and published under Iaroslavskii's editorship, could have indicated to Iaroslavskii at least one area of difficulty: while poisonously anti-Trotsky in its account, for instance, of Trotsky's position in the Soviet trade-union controversy of 1920, the book treated Trotskyism as the (wrongheaded) faction of Communism that Stalin now said it had "long since" ceased to be; the book did not show Trotskyism to be, even incipiently, the forward detachment of the counterrevolutionary bourgeoisie that Stalin declared it had become. Even the reprinted photographs seemed ill chosen in some cases. Here, for example, was Lenin's original fifteen-man Council of People's Commissars; Trotsky appeared to the left of Lenin (and Alexei Rykov, appropriately, flanked Lenin on the right), while Stalin appeared in the bottom row, next to the Kremlin wall. And here, too, on another page, was an old photograph of the Soviet delegation to the Brest talks, with Trotsky, its leader, looking handsome and impressive in the top row.[19] What Iaroslavskii may have been a little slow in grasping was that affirmation of Stalin necessitated the retrospective denigration of many others who had played more prominent roles in the Revolution than had Stalin.

Further, this volume of the party history made brief reference to the well-known fact, acknowledged by Stalin himself in a speech in 1924, that in March 1917, prior to Lenin's return to Russia and the issuance of his "April Theses," Stalin had shared with Kamenev and M. K. Muranov "an erroneous position" on policy toward the Provisional Government (they had advocated that the party merely put pressure on the government to leave the war). This easily documentable truth of party history as written before 1929 was one of the Iaroslavskii "mistakes" to which Stalin's letter alluded. It became an "unfact" in party history as rewritten in the 1930s by Iaroslavskii and others. The system of falsification extended to retrospective censorship by or for Stalin of his own earlier writings—the deletion, for example, from later printings of **Problems of Leninism** of Stalin's reference in 1924 to the position he took in March 1917. Subservient writers falsified actual party history in conformity with an idealized image of the "real Bolshevik" for whom straying from the path of revolutionary rectitude was clearly impossible—an image representing Stalin's self-concept. The logical groundwork of this system of falsification was laid in Stalin's letter to *Proletarian Revolution.*[20]

Hell broke loose on the party history and theory fronts as soon as Stalin's letter appeared. The Communist Academy's institutes hastily called meetings to discuss the document's implications for their work. Many editors and scholars were dismissed from their jobs and expelled from the party. *Proletarian Revolution,* after putting out the issue containing the letter, suspended publication in 1932. On reappearing in early 1933, it had a wholly new editorial board, one of whose members was Ivan Tovstukha, Stalin's one-time personal secretary.

Soviet archival sources reveal that all of the Soviet historical journals received instructions to print the text of Stalin's letter and to carry appropriate editorials on its meaning for their respective areas. In a confidential letter of November 26, 1931 to the editorial board of one such journal, *The Class Struggle,* Stalin's erstwhile personal assistant—by then secretary of *Pravda's* editorial board—L. Z. Mekhlis said that materials in preparation should be written through the prism of Stalin's propositions. The Communist Academy's presidium met on November 31 to review its affiliates' responses to the Stalin letter. K. G. Lur'e, academic secretary of the Society of Marxist Historians, reported that all of the society's sections had been instructed to review the whole literature on the party's history critically in the light of Stalin's "article."[21] Trotskyist contraband had already been brought to light in numerous works. Many writers, for example, had failed to show the earlier leading role of the Russian Bolsheviks on the international Marxist arena. And Lur'e combined the unmasking of contrabandists with criticism of three well-known party figures—Iaroslavskii, Karl Radek, and I. I. Mints.

Proceedings and reports from other academic groups show that not only historians and their histories but all members and sectors of the theoretical front were being brought into line with higher-level, authoritative interpretation of Stalin's letter. A representative of literary criticism denounced the "Menshevik-Trotskyist view" of Maxim Gorky's writings, without indicating what that view was, and said that Stalin's letter necessitated criticism of the literary policy—also not identified—of the Second International. A writer named Butaev reported that the Institute of Economics had set up a special brigade to re-examine economic theory in light of Stalin's letter and to "bring to light Trotskyist contraband in the literature on economics." Examples of such contraband were the still-prevalent petty-bourgeois and Trotskyist ideas that equated socialism with equal remuneration and the view, voiced in a book published in 1931, that Henry Ford's factories and assembly lines were a model for Soviet rationalization of labor processes. The legal theorist E. B. Pashukanis, speaking for the Institute of Soviet Construction and Law, criticized a textbook by two authors (one of them Butaev) that contained no account of what Stalin had said in 1927 about the proletarian state. K. V. Ostrovitianov, an economist, objected to the hitherto-accepted notion that the writings of Lenin and Stalin belonged to "politics" as distinct from "economics," whereas in fact they presented the basic laws of socialism's construction and Soviet economic life. Not surprisingly, Ostrovitianov in later years became the Stalin-surrogate for economics.[22]

A speaker from the Institute of Technology assailed the "narrow technicism" that he said was characteristic of Trotskyism, condemned the "technological policy of social-fascism," and asserted that a review of "literally the entire technological literature" was now needed. A representative of the Institute of Philosophy, in addition to discussing its new tasks, remarked that the Institute of Technology should produce in short order "a work systematizing all of the basic theses of Marx, Engels, Lenin, and Stalin on technology." The representative of the Association of Natural Science wondered why the basic methodological postulates about physics provided by Lenin in *Materialism and Empirio-Criticism* were not being taken as a guide in an attempt "to create a conception of physics, to produce our Marxist-Leninist conception of the structure of matter."[23] Nadezhda Mandelstam, then working in the editorial offices of the journal *For a Communist Education,* recalled later how "all of the manuscripts were rechecked in great panic and we went through huge piles of them, cutting mercilessly. This was called 'reorganization in the light of Comrade Stalin's remarks.'"[24]

The pell-mell rush to ferret out "Trotskyist contraband" and "rotten liberalism" was deeply troubling to many in responsible posts, in part, no doubt—but only in part—because of the pressure and embarrassment they themselves were in some cases experiencing. Stalin was not yet an absolute dictator; some in high places failed to realize that he was on the way to becoming one or to understand what was driving him to it. Several prominent Old Bolsheviks—including Ol'minskii, Iaroslavskii, V. Knorin, and N. Lukin—sought to restrain those "glorifiers" (as Iaroslavskii called them in a handwritten note found decades later in the party archives) who were taking Stalin's letter as a new gospel. Knorin suggested to a meeting of the party group of the Society of Marxist Historians on November 11, 1931 that the letter should simply be seen as a restatement of some basic Leninist

tenets. Lur'e, on the other hand, said that party history had lacked all methodology before Stalin's letter appeared and that historians did not grasp the relation between theory and practice. I. I. Mints, who was present at the meeting, wrote a letter to Iaroslavskii, who was out of town, saying that Lur'e, in her "nasty and unsound" speech, had put things less charitably: "Before Stalin's letter there was nothing, and only now does she understand the relation between theory and practice." Yet three weeks later Lur'e reported to the Communist Academy's presidium on the situation in the Society of Marxist Historians. At about the same time, Iaroslavskii warned against certain unprincipled people who wanted "to make capital on this question" of the Stalin letter. But this statement, along with his handwritten note recalling "how the glorifiers 'worked me over' in 1931," did not see publication until 1966.[25]

One month after Stalin's letter appeared, his headquarters began to take action against those who pleaded for restraint. Lazar Kaganovich gave a long speech at the Institute of Red Professors on December 1, 1931—the occasion of its tenth anniversary. When the text appeared in *Pravda* some days later, it became clear that the address was meant to reach the whole Soviet intelligentsia. But "address" is a misnomer. The document is best described as a several-thousand-word, peremptory command by drill sergeant Kaganovich ordering the army of the intelligentsia to snap to attention in the light of General Stalin's letter.

Kaganovich introduced his discussion of the letter by stressing the great importance of Marxist-Leninist indoctrination at a time when individuals who had only been members of the party for three to five years comprised one and a half to two million out of a total of two and a half million party members and when the Komsomol numbered five and a half million Young Communists. No one in the party would have disputed the statistics and their general implications, but Kaganovich quickly made it clear that what was at issue was the specific content of party indoctrination. The millions of new members must learn that, if the country once thought the most backward in the world was now the land of socialism, "We owe this to the selfless struggle waged for decades by the best people, headed by Lenin, against the *narodniki,* legal Marxists, economists, Mensheviks, Trotskyists, rightists, and conciliatory elements in the party." Clearly, Stalin was the best of "the best people." Kaganovich then spoke of the "criminality" of slanderer-falsifiers like Slutskii. Radek, Kaganovich continued, had acknowledged his own errors to the party group of the Society of Marxist Historians: he had recognized, furthermore, that Rosa Luxemburg did not always take "a correct Bolshevik position" but had argued that Rosa was a "bridge" to Bolshevism for the best Social Democratic workers. In fact, Kaganovich charged, Radek himself had been a bridge between Rosa Luxemburg and Trotsky.

The importance of Stalin's letter, Kaganovich said, did not lie in its attack on the insignificant ex-Menshevik

Slutskii, whom Stalin had pulverized in passing, but in exposing the rotten liberalism shown by the editors of *Proletarian Revolution* toward deviations from Bolshevism and distortions of party history. And this journal was not the only weak spot. A still weaker one was Comrade Iaroslavskii's four-volume history, criticism of the errors of which would "undoubtedly develop further." Among his illustrations of the history's grave errors, Kaganovich mentioned its "erroneous and harmful assessment of the role of the Bolsheviks in the first period of 1917, [its] foul slander of the Bolsheviks." Kaganovich delivered this veiled rebuke to Iaroslavskii for his reference to Stalin's "erroneous position" in March 1917. Then came a methodological pointer: the key to a comprehensive party history was the "flexibility of Lenin's tactics," not passages in which Lenin said, in so many words, "Kautsky is a bastard." What, in short, a "real Bolshevik" said or failed to say at a particular time was not the touchstone of party-historical truth; the documents must be interpreted according to the canons of the real-Bolshevik-revolutionary-can-do-no-wrong school.

Kaganovich ended with an implicit call for an intensification of the ongoing hunt for heresy. Difficulties were rife, the fight was not over, the class struggle was continuing. "Opportunism is now trying to creep into our ranks, covering itself up, embellishing itself, crawling on its belly, trying to penetrate into crannies, and trying, in particular, to crawl through the gates of the history of our party." In his recent speech Radek was wrong to describe the Comintern as a channel through which many different currents and brooklets flowed into the Bolshevik party. The party was no meeting place of turbid brooklets but a "monolithic stream" capable of smashing all obstacles in its path. The meaning was as clear as the metaphor was mixed: fall in line or be destroyed.[26]

The pleaders for restraint—and others—fell into line. Within the twelve days following Kaganovich's speech of December 1, *Pravda* carried letters of recantation from Radek, Iaroslavskii, and the party historian Konstantin Popov. Radek pleaded guilty to all of Kaganovich's charges and joined the attack on "Luxemburgianism." Iaroslavskii acknowledged a whole series of "the grossest mistakes" in the four-volume history, including "an objective, essentially Trotskyist treatment of the Bolsheviks' position in the February-March period of the Revolution of 1917" (Trotskyist, presumably, because Trotsky was one of those who had called attention to the generally known facts about Stalin's position at that time). He also disavowed the view, reportedly expressed by Mints in a recent speech, that the authors of the four-volume history had erred in their objectivity and that what was now being asked of party historians was "not so much objectivity as political expediency." No, lied Iaroslavskii, the party had not and could not demand that historians surrender their objectivity; the problem was that the authors of the four-volume work had sinned against objectivity.[27] Resigning himself to the situation, Iaroslavskii started work on the glorifying biography of Stalin that was published in 1939.

Plainly, to confess to heresy was not enough; the heretic had to join the inquisition. Only by entering the ranks of the accusers could he expect to have his recantation taken seriously. To denounce Trotskyist contraband on the part of others demonstrated the genuineness of one's own "real" Bolshevism—that is, Stalinism. Recantation followed by denunciation was becoming a ritual of Soviet political culture. Iaroslavskii's public disavowal of his friend Mints was but one of many examples.

Still, Stalin did not yet wield absolute power. Those higher in the hierarchy of power than Iaroslavskii could suggest the need for restraint. Among them was P. P. Postyshev, then a full member of the party Central Committee, a member of its Orgburo, and one of four Central Committee secretaries serving under General Secretary Stalin. As a secretary, Postyshev was in charge of the Central Committee's Organizational Department and its Department of Agitation and Propaganda, whose functions included oversight of the press. In a speech at a district party conference in Moscow, he stressed the great significance of Stalin's letter and then took various party cells to task for their failure to distinguish between an individual's particular mistakes and a "system of views." Of course, there were concealed Trotskyists in the party's ranks, who must be exposed and expelled. But there were also comrades who had simply erred. Instead of denouncing them as deviationists and kicking them out of the party—as did some who had been asleep but now wanted to "show themselves" (and then go back to sleep)—errant comrades should be criticized in a comradely way. Postyshev's fate after trying to curb the excesses of the heresy hunt was instructive: arrested in 1938, he was killed in 1940 in one of Stalin's concentration camps.[28]

The master-builder of the Stalin cult was the cult-object himself. But many others, ranging from men in Stalin's entourage like Kaganovich and Mekhlis to obscure ideological workers like Lur'e, assisted. Who, we may now ask, were the glorifiers? Some, without doubt, were persons devoted to Stalin or to the man they idealistically perceived him to be; others were simply careerists who may have lacked strong qualification in intellectual work but who were shrewd or, perhaps, cynical enough to grasp the opportunities for self-advancement inherent in the Stalin-glorifying enterprise. One climber who made his way to the top by this route was the head of the Georgian secret police, Lavrentii Beria, who with Stalin's backing became party chief of the Transcaucasus in 1932. The one indispensable quality shared by all of the glorifiers, high and low, was pliability. In very many ways the aggrandizement of Stalin required the twisting of truth and the falsification of historical fact. As Iaroslavskii himself expressed it, the glorifiers had to be "unprincipled," pliable enough to ignore their scruples and still their consciences insofar as the cult-building enterprise required.

The letter to *Proletarian Revolution* was a turning point in the cult's evolution. From the time of its appearance forward, idolatry of Stalin became one of Russia's major growth industries. No field of Soviet culture was exempted from finding inspiration for its activities in Stalin's letter. The journal *For Proletarian Music,* for example, devoted its editorial in January 1932 to "Our Tasks on the Musical Front" in light of the letter, and the corresponding editorial in the February 1932 issue of *For a Socialist Accounting* bore the title, "For Bolshevik Vigilance on the Book-Keeping Theory Front." But revolutionary history and Stalin's place in it remained the central concern. A small example, typical of many, was an article published in *Pravda* shortly after Stalin's letter appeared. It denounced a book on Comintern history on the grounds that Stalin's name was only mentioned twice and said, "Without showing Comrade Stalin's leading role in the history of the Comintern, there can be no Bolshevik textbook on the history of the Comintern."[29]

Having asserted himself as premier party historian, Stalin delivered another lecture in reply to two party members, Olekhnovich and Aristov, who had written separately to him in response to the letter; and his answers, dated January 15 and 25, 1932, were published in *Bolshevik* (and then in other publications) the following August. Olekhnovich, apparently, had tried to show himself more Stalinist than Stalin and suggested that "Trotskyism *never was* a faction of Communism" but "was *all the time* a faction of Menshevism," although for a certain period of time the Communist Party had wrongly *regarded* Trotsky and the Trotskyists as real Bolsheviks. In knocking this construction down, Stalin showed the hair-splitting quality of his mind. Undeniably, he said, Trotskyism was once a faction of Communism but oscillated continually between Bolshevism and Menshevism; even when the Trotskyists did belong to the Bolshevik party, they "were not *real* Bolsheviks." Thus, "in actual fact, Trotskyism was a faction of Menshevism before the Trotskyists joined our party, temporarily became a faction of Communism after the Trotskyists entered our party, and again became a faction of Menshevism after the Trotskyists were banished from our party. 'The dog went back to its puke.'"[30]

These further pronouncements only confirmed to professionals that they should look to Stalin's writings and sayings as scripture. As if to meet their need, party publications in 1932 started printing early Staliniana, such as Stalin's virtually unknown letter of 1910 to Lenin from Sol'vychegodsk exile and his little-known **"Letters from the Caucasus"** of that same year. Meanwhile, the glorifiers set about rewriting history in accordance with Stalin's canons and in a manner calculated to accentuate his role and merits in the party's revolutionary past, while discrediting those of his enemies. The skewed Stalinist version of Bolshevism's biography began to emerge. Grosser falsification still lay ahead.

The rise of the Stalin cult did not bring the eclipse of the Lenin cult, only its far-reaching modification. Instead of two cults in juxtaposition, there emerged a hyphenate cult of an infallible Lenin-Stalin. In some respects, Lenin now "grew" in stature: he became the original "real Bolshevik" who could not have erred. But by being tied like a Siamese twin to his successor, he was inescapably diminished in certain ways. Only those facets of his life and work that could be connected with Stalin's were available for full-scale idealization, and whatever did not in some way include Stalin had to be kept in the background. In effect, some parts of Lenin's life had to be de-emphasized and others rearranged, modified, or touched up to put Stalin in the idealized picture.

Thus, Stalin was now portrayed as sharing in Lenin's exploits, was declared to be from an early time Lenin's right-hand man, on whom the leader leaned for counsel and support at key points in the development of the Revolution and after. The marking on May 5, 1932 of the twentieth anniversary of *Pravda*'s founding may be taken as an illustration. At the beginning, said *Pravda*'s anniversary editorial, Lenin "wrote articles for the paper nearly every day—with the closest participation and guidance of Comrade *Stalin,* particularly when Lenin was hiding underground." So in the dual cult the younger figure emerged as Lenin's alter ego, who naturally took over when Lenin himself was away from the immediate scene of action. Symptomatically, the article was accompanied by a large portrait not of Lenin but of Stalin and contained a lengthy quotation from Stalin's recollection of 1922 on the paper's early days.

By now Iaroslavskii had not simply fallen in line but had joined the vanguard of the glorifiers. Invited to contribute an article in commemoration of the twentieth anniversary of the Prague Conference of January 1912, he found a shrewd way of enthroning Stalin in retrospect practically as a founder of the Bolshevik party. As Lenin had testified, Bolshevism had existed as a political current from 1903, when the Bolshevik-Menshevik schism occurred at the Russian Marxist party's Second Congress. But the Bolshevik Party's formal existence dated only from the all-Bolshevik Prague Conference of 1912, at which Lenin converted what had been a faction into a separate party no longer organizationally tied to the Mensheviks. In the aftermath of the Prague Conference Stalin was elevated (by co-optation, not election) for the first time to membership in the party's Central Committee. Iaroslavskii obscured the embarrassing fact of Stalin's co-optation by saying, "At the conference a Bolshevik Central Committee was elected in the persons of Lenin, Stalin, Zinoviev, Ordzhonikidze, Belostotskii, Shvartsman, Goloshchekin, Spandarian, and Ia. M. Sverdlov (some of these comrades were co-opted into the Central Committee subsequently)." And by writing with heavy emphasis—"The Prague Conference was a *turning point in the history of the Bolshevik Party*"—he contrived to portray Stalin by indirection as having been present at the party's creation.[31]

Even clever party theorists were in some cases slow in comprehending the transformed personality cult and in applying its special canons. One person who illustrates the early confusion was S. E. Sef, a zealous glorifier, who was managing secretary of the journal *Marxist Historian.* He gave the provisional title "Marx, Engels, Stalin" to the lead article of a planned special issue commemorating the upcoming fiftieth anniversary, in March 1933, of the death of Marx. His omission of Lenin was corrected before the issue appeared.[32] Sef had failed to grasp that Lenin *qua* co-leader remained a cult-object. In the dual cult, however, the figure of the successor in some ways now began to tower over that of the predecessor. For example, a foreign correspondent's count of "political icons" (portraits and busts of leaders) in display windows along several blocks of Moscow's Gorky Street on November 7, 1933 showed Stalin leading Lenin by 103 to 58.[33]

Stalin was now being sung, especially by poets from the Orient, where versified flattery of rulers is a centuries-old art. "To the *Vozhd'*, to Comrade Stalin" was the title of a long poem by A. A. Lakhuti, translated from Persian into Russian. A typical stanza reads,

> Wise master, Marxist gardener!
> Thou art tending the vine of communism.
> Thou art cultivating it to perfection.
> After Lenin, *vozhd'* of Leninists.[34]

Meanwhile, scholars in Oriental studies were enjoined to apply the works of Stalin as well as those of Lenin to problems of the national-colonial revolution in the East. A pamphlet on the history of the Georgian Communist Party was attacked for treating the period from 1917 to 1927 in a spirit of "national deviationism" (that is, Georgian nationalism) contrary to Stalin's orientation; and among those who were later reported from Tbilisi to have condemned the offensive pamphlet was Lavrentii Beria.[35] Stalin's early revolutionary years in Transcaucasia now began to attract reverent attention. A pamphlet published in Georgia portrayed the young Stalin as a heroic leader directing underground revolutionary activities in Batum in 1901-02.[36]

The cult kept growing in official publicity during 1933. *Pravda* marked the fiftieth anniversary of Marx's death on March 14 by lauding Stalin's theoretical contributions to materialist dialectics and concluded, "Stalin's name ranks with the great names of the theoreticians and leaders of the world proletariat—Marx, Engels, and Lenin." The phrase "classical works of Marx, Engels, Lenin, and Stalin" was now commonplace. Partizdat, the party publishing house, was savagely criticized for its failure to eliminate a series of minor misprints in the latest printing of the fastest selling of the classics, Stalin's *Problems of Leninism.* "As if 'minor' misprints are allowable in a book by Comrade Stalin!" the critic parenthetically exclaimed.[37] Overall figures released in early 1934 show that the classics had been published in 1932-33 in the following numbers: seven million copies of the works of Marx and Engels, fourteen million of those of Lenin, and sixteen and a half million of those of Stalin, including two million copies of *Problems of Leninism.*[38] That collection of Stalin's articles and speeches was by then well on the way to becoming probably the world's best seller of the second quarter of the twentieth century.[39]

From that time forward, to the end of Stalin's life, his aggrandizement through the personality cult continued incessantly.

NOTES

[1] I. V. Stalin, *Sochineniia,* 13 vols. (Moscow, 1946-52), 13: 19. The letter was first published in Stalin's collected works after the Second World War.

[2] *The Nation,* August 13, 1930, p. 176.

[3] Louis Fischer gave me this information in a personal conversation in 1965.

[4] David Joravsky, *Soviet Marxism and Natural Science, 1917-1932* (New York, 1961), 170.

[5] *Vestnik kommunisticheskoi akademii,* 1929, Kn. 35-36, p. 390. For note of this list, see Joravsky, *Soviet Marxism and Natural Science,* 227.

[6] I. Dubinskii-Mukhadze, *Ordzhonikidze* (Moscow, 1963), 93. For Bukharin's comment, see the Bukharin-Kamenev Conversations of July 11-12, 1928, Harvard University, Cambridge, Mass., Trotsky Archives, T 1897.

[7] Roy A. Medvedev, *K sudu istorii: Genezis i posledstviia Stalinizma* (New York, 1974), 433. The information on the Stalin-Sten sessions came to Roy Medvedev from Sten's friend, E. P. Frolov.

[8] Mark B. Mitin, *Boevye voprosy materialisticheskoi dialektiki* (Moscow, 1936), 43-44, and "Nekotorye itogi i zadachi raboty na filosofskom fronte," *Pod znamenem Marksizma,* 1 (1936): 25-26. For the date of the interview, see the chronology in Stalin, *Sochineniia,* 13: 401. The full text of his remarks to the philosophers remains unpublished.

[9] P. Cheremnykh, "Men'shevistvuiushchii idealizm v rabotakh BSE," *Bol'shevik,* no. 17, September 15, 1931, p. 85.

[10] For a discussion by a former Soviet economist of this aspect of Stalinism and the use of "monolithism" to describe it, see Aron Katsenelinboigen, "Conflicting Trends in Soviet Economics in the Post-Stalin Era," *Russian Review,* October 1976, pp. 374-76.

[11] A. Slutskii, "Bol'sheviki o germanskoi s.-d. v period ee predvoennogo krizisa," *Proletarskaia revoliutsiia,* 6 (1930): 37-72.

[12] Stalin, "Dokatilis'," in *Sochineniia,* 11: 313-17. This document has the appearance of an internal Politburo memorandum.

[13] Stalin, *Sochineniia,* 13: 84-102.

[14] Stalin, *Sochineniia,* 11: 281-82, 284.

[15] I am indebted to Roy A. Medvedev and Stephen F. Cohen for the information on Slutskii's subsequent arrest and imprisonment.

[16] On the effect of the letter's rude style and tone, see, for example, V. A. Dunaevskii, "Bol'sheviki i germanskie levye na mezhdunarodnoi arene," in *Evropa v novoe i noveishee vremia: Sbornik statei pamiati Akademika N. M. Lukina* (Moscow, 1966). A modern Soviet historian, Dunaevskii has claimed that "the form of Stalin's pronouncement—sharp expressions against the authors he mentioned and politically characterizing them as 'rotten liberals,' 'Trotskyist contrabandists,' and the like—led to the impossibility of creative discussions on matters of principle and subsequently to repressions against individuals whom he had subjected to criticism"; *ibid.*, 508.

[17] *Vsesoiuznoe soveshchanie o merakh uluchsheniia podgotovki nauchno-pedagogicheskikh kadrov po istoricheskim naukam. 18-21 dekabria 1962 g.* (Moscow, 1964), 363.

[18] Paul H. Aron, "M. N. Pokrovskii and the Impact of the First Five-Year Plan," in John Shelton Curtiss, ed., *Essays in Russian and Soviet History in Honor of Geroid Tanguary Robinson* (New York, 1962), 301.

[19] E. M. Iaroslavskii, gen. ed., *Istoriia VKP(b)*, 4 (Moscow-Leningrad, 1929): pt. 1, 230, pt. 2, 291. Iaroslavskii explained in his editorial foreword that the volume had been in preparation for the tenth anniversary of the Revolution (1927) "but for a whole series of reasons was delayed for a year." He did not explain what those reasons were.

[20] For a different interpretation of the key purpose of Stalin's letter, see John Barber, "Stalin's Letter to the Editors of *Proletarskaya Revolyutsiya*," *Soviet Studies*, 28 (1976): 21-41. Ignoring the cult question, Barber has suggested that the letter was chiefly occasioned by the "falling quality of party recruits" and an insecure regime's "concern over the tendency of its Marxist intellectuals to engage in too much controversy and speculation," and he has questioned whether the letter was intended to have the effect it did or was conceived as the vital turning point it proved to be. To me Barber's position is unpersuasive.

[21] *Vsesoiuznoe soveshchanie*, 19, 362, 457, 75. Also see Dunaevskii, "Bol'sheviki i germanskie levye na mezhdunarodnoi arene," 508-09.

[22] According to Katsenelinboigen, "In the forties, K. V. Ostrovitianov was appointed as the curator of economics. All he did was provide commentaries for Stalin's work; he had no opinions of his own, and made no practical recommendations." "Conflicting Trends in Soviet Economics in the Post-Stalin Era," 375.

[23] *Vestnik kommunisticheskoi akademii*, nos. 1-2 (1932): 40-66.

[24] Nadezhda Mandelstam, *Hope against Hope: A Memoir*, trans. Max Hayward (New York, 1970), 259. Although she spoke of it as a letter of 1930 in *Bolshevik*, it is clear from the context that Mandelstam was referring to the 1931 letter to *Proletarian Revolution*, also printed in *Bolshevik*.

[25] Dunaevskii, "Bol'sheviki i germanskie levye na mezhdunarodnoi arene," 509-12. The Russian word here translated as "glorifiers" is *alliluishchiki*.

[26] *Pravda*, December 12, 1931. Dunaevskii has observed that "Kaganovich's speech, filled with shouted threats, was designed to pin the label of Trotskyist on all from now on who would dare to deviate from Stalin's propositions"; "Bol'sheviki i germanskie levye na mezhdunarodnoi arene," 511.

[27] Iaroslavskii's letter appeared in *Pravda* on December 10, 1932; Radek's on December 12; Popov's on December 8.

[28] T. Mariagin, *Postyshev* (Moscow, 1965), 299-300. The speech in question was reported in *Pravda* on January 11, 1932.

[29] *Pravda*, December 29, 1931.

[30] Stalin, *Sochineniia*, 13: 126-30.

[31] *Pravda*, January 22, 1932.

[32] Dunaevskii, "Bol'sheviki i germanskie levye na mezhdunarodnoi arene," 511-12.

[33] Eugene Lyons, *Moscow Carrousel* (New York, 1935), 140-41.

[34] *Pravda*, November 29, 1932. Iranian by origin, Lakhuti had emigrated to the USSR and become a Soviet citizen.

[35] *Pravda*, March 21 and 25, 1932.

[36] *Stalin i Khashim (1901-1902 gody): Nekotorye epizody iz batumskogo podpol'ia* (Sukhum, 1934).

[37] *Pravda*, February 22, 1933.

[38] *XVII s"ezd vsesoiuznoi kommunisticheskoi partii (b) 26 ianvaria-10 fevralia 1934 g. Stenograficheskii otchet* (Moscow, 1934), 620.

[39] By 1949 almost seventeen million copies in fifty-two languages were in print. See *Bol'shevik*, no. 23, December 1949, p. 48.

Susan Layton (essay date 1979)

SOURCE: "The Mind of the Tyrant: Tolstoj's Nicholas and Solzenicyn's Stalin," in *Slavic and East European Journal*, Vol. 23, No. 4, Winter, 1979, pp. 479-90.

[*In the following essay, Layton finds parallels between Leo Tolstoy's portrayal of Czar Nicholas I in* Xadzi-Murat

(1912) and Aleksandr Solzenicyn's depiction of Stalin in The First Circle *(1968).]*

Repeatedly Solzenicyn has paid tribute to Tolstoj as the grand master of Realism in the nineteenth century and as a philosopher concerned with the moral service of art. The concept of the artist as teacher and conscience of the nation has acquired major importance for Solzenicyn and has given particular coloring to his assessment of Tolstoj.[1] As a writer determined to bear witness to the history of injustice in the Soviet Union, Solzenicyn perceives a heritage in the role Tolstoj assumed in tsarist Russia in the latter part of his career.

The First Circle (1968) pursues the moral task of the writer in a manner strongly reminiscent of Tolstoj's *Xadzi-Murat* (1896-1904; pub. 1912). In the novella Tolstoj presents imperial Russia of the 1850s as a ruthless power bent on assimilating or exterminating the relatively primitive culture of the Chechens, and he gives a central place to the condemnatory portrait of Nicholas I in order to show the essence of the state. As represented in *The First Circle,* Stalin displays a psychology akin to Nicholas' mentality (Feuer, 134), but the similarity between the works of Solzenicyn and Tolstoj does not end here. In conveying the nature of Stalin, Solzenicyn relies on stylistic techniques used by Tolstoj as well, and in the structure of *The First Circle* the portrait of the dictator serves a function equivalent to the function of the portrait of Nicholas in *Xadzi-Murat.* In thought and language each tyrant appears as the guiding spirit of a rationalistic political system and stands in opposition to shapes of mind which resist the characteristic mode of the state. By placing the mind of the tyrant at the center of attention, Tolstoj and Solzenicyn both explore an ultimate, shared concern with the relationship between politics and language.

Xadzi-Murat focuses on the conflict between the savage and the Russian state. The story stands as recollection within a frame which establishes identification between Xadzi-Murat and the crushed but tenacious thistle plant. Within the main body of the text, however, Tolstoj operates against this somewhat sentimental metaphor of a mutilated creature of nature and gives remarkable insight into a process which Max Weber analyzed as the shift from traditional to bureaucratic forms of authority.[2] Rather than express a pastoral vision,[3] Tolstoj recreates the complex psychic being of Xadzi-Murat as a charismatic figure, shaped by a pre-scientific, proto-state society. As the diametrical opposite, Nicholas appears as the rationalistic, bureaucratic leader who bears ultimate responsibility for the death of the savage. On the basis of extensive research into Chechen culture and the reign of Nicholas I,[4] Tolstoj makes the Tsar and Xad i-Murat stand forth as the representatives of two cultures or cultural "languages." In an expanded sense of the term, the language of the Russian state is comprised of distinctive codes, procedures, modes of thought and communication. Tolstoj shows this language as the embodiment of cruelty, mendacity, and artificiality. The

contrasting language of Xadzi-Murat is personal, authentically engaged with human realities and expressive of an aesthetic sensibility.

In the opening chapters Xadzi-Murat (in flight from Šamil') emerges as a charismatic figure within the context of his distinctive culture. The power of Xadzi-Murat is conveyed largely through the quality of relationships that obtain between him and those loyal followers who risk danger by helping him in the house of a village and on the journey to the Russians' fort. Tolstoj also penetrates the mind of Xadzi-Murat to reveal a confidence in the mysterious working of benevolent fate: the savage feels great faith in his fortune and dreams of triumph over Šamil'. By showing Xadzi-Murat in interaction with the other Chechens and by touching the deepest level of his mind, Tolstoj immediately conveys a powerful impression of authority as a God-given attribute.

In subsequent episodes, when Xadzi-Murat places himself in the hands of the Russians in hope of receiving assistance against his enemy Šamil', the charismatic fugitive leaves the context of primitive society and enters a bureaucratic system in which power derives from office. In contrast to rejected variants, which gave a detailed chronological treatment of Xadzi-Murat's entire life, the final text allots most space to the critical period spent among the Russians; and through a so-called "peep-show method" Tolstoj projects a multi-faceted picture of the savage in an alien realm.[5] Xadzi-Murat's inability to speak Russian helps to define his distance from the characteristic mode of the state. The illiterate savage cannot understand most of the words spoken in officialdom (French as well as Russian); instead of communicating verbally, he often conveys the truth with his eyes and gestures. Xadzi-Murat's longest utterance is the autobiography which the Russian interpreter transcribes for the Tsar (chapters XI and XIII). In telling his story in his own words, Xadzi-Murat employs diction which is concrete and forthright (occasionally even vulgar), he does not follow complex syntactical patterns typical of standard literary Russian, and he makes effective use of colorful aphoristic phrases characteristic of a folk idiom ("in body he was strong as a bull and brave as a lion, but in spirit he was weak as water"). Tolstoj strove to fashion an effective, distinctive idiom for Xadzi-Murat (Sergeenko, 604-5) and pointedly contrasts the autobiography with the actual official document written (originally in French) in the chancellary style by Voroncov (chapter XIV).

As an alien within Russian culture, Xadzi-Murat cannot comprehend the split between "public" as opposed to "private" dimensions of being, and accordingly he is snubbed by officials on social occasions when he tries to discuss his strategy for rescuing his family from Šamil'. Ultimately the charismatic savage is thwarted by the efforts of the Russians to channel his complex, fully human project into the prescribed legalistic procedures and forms. As defined by Tolstoj, Xadzi-Murat's cultural language conveys a noble, humane spirit at odds with corrupt civilized men: Xadzi-Murat's speech itself, his manner of dress, his love for his family, his religious faith, the barbaric grandeur of his traditions of war, his appreciation of the beauty of nature, and his response to the Chechen songs all combine to project an integrity and authenticity which clash absolutely with the rationale of the Russian state.

As Tolstoj explores the character of the various Russians, he constructs a hierarchy of moral corruption. In this hierarchy the old parents of the soldier Avdeev stand closest to Xadzi-Murat and farthest from the pinnacle of bureaucratic power. In chapter VIII Tolstoj represents the existence of the peasant not only by giving attention to details of dress and by describing at length the collective work of threshing grain, but also by capturing the distinctive idiom of the village. In *Xadzi-Murat* the peasants' speech and their illiteracy isolate them from the characteristic modes of discourse of aristocrats (who speak French as well as standard Russian) and bureaucrats (the official notification of the beloved son's death is couched in the hackneyed rhetoric of the state and must be relayed orally by a clerk who can read). Within the Russian army, Tolstoj focuses upon Butler, a congenial, morally weak cadet who finds romance in the "poetry of warfare" (*voinnstvennaja poèzija*) in the Caucasus. In contrast to the traditions of the Chechens, which Tolstoj represents in chapter XXIII, this false "poetry" consists of drunkenness, gambling, vulgar sexual escapades, and impersonation of the natives (chapter XXIV). Butler operates fully in accord with this code of the typical Russian soldier and eventually finds himself gazing with morbid fascination at Xadzi-Murat's severed head, which a fellow officer has brought back to the fort as proof that the savage is dead. Although Butler had developed a friendship with Xadzi-Murat during his stay among the Russians, he now shows blind acceptance of the notion that "war is war" and acquiesces in the state's policy of subjugating or exterminating the native tribes of the Caucasus.

At the top of the hierarchy stands Nicholas as the embodiment of cruel, self-aggrandizing bureaucratic power. In chapter XV Tolstoj first shows the Tsar's quarters at the palace, where everything has been arranged to create an impression of imperial grandeur. As an actor on this stage, Nicholas appears as a repulsive, dissipated figure whose "senile sensuality" emerges as the truth behind a mask of religious rectitude and the dignity of a statesman. Since Nicholas himself can no longer see behind the public facade, he is enveloped completely by an aura of inauthenticity. He exists by performing appropriate roles (brilliant general, devout sovereign, family man) and by surrounding himself with subordinates who will play to his deluded self-image. (Between the two extremes of Nicholas and Xadzi-Murat, Tolstoj in chapter XIX represents Šamil' as a traditional leader of a proto-state society who is losing authenticity and learning to operate by the duplicitous practices of modern statecraft.) Nicholas' courtiers are skilled in reading the exterior signs which indicate the mood of the tyrant, and they are quick to tell him what he wants to hear. In particular, they play to his vanity about being a military leader of genius. All in all,

Nicholas regards himself (in the mirror and in his mind's eye) as the savior of Russia: "Yes, what would Russia be without me?" he asks himself; and with an air of martyrdom he recognizes the need to terrorize people who dare to think that they "could govern themselves better than he, Nicholas, governed them!"

The true inner dimension of Nicholas emerges tellingly as a matter of language: in writing a cruel, hypocritical order which will result in a man's execution, the Tsar makes orthographic mistakes which signify total corruption of thought and moral fiber. *Xadzi-Murat* displays keen insight into the relationship between corrupt language and corrupt politics, but Tolstoj's conception cannot be extracted from the representation of Nicholas alone. *Xadzi-Murat* is a perfectly realized structure in which the architectonics and the stylistic nuances draw a complex pattern of linkages. The chapter on Nicholas stands almost exactly in the middle of the text—as a center of the rationalistic power of the state. The Tsar's mental dynamics radiate outward and are made evident everywhere. His spiteful orders to continue attacks against the Chechen villages are translated into murder and destruction in the next chapter; the old General Voroncov appears as a little Nicholas who also will not call things by their real names; the official communiques about the death of the soldier Avdeev hide human suffering; the impersonal document written by Voroncov cannot convey the unique, full truth of Xadzi-Murat's project to save his family. Through juxtapositions and particulars of style, Tolstoj explores a central antithesis between the rationalistic, bureaucratic mode of the state and the personal, concrete mode of consciousness embodied most fully in Xadzi-Murat. The language of the Russian state (bureaucratic idiom, legalistic procedures, policy of military aggression) stands forth as a complex structure which is used to dominate or exterminate an alien shape of mind (the savage, the peasant).

In form and function the three chapters on Stalin in *The First Circle* closely approximate the model of *Xadzi-Murat*. The data come from the Soviet period and corroborate information contained in Xruščev's secret speech and memoirs, Djilas' *Conversations with Stalin,* and Medvedev's *Let History Judge,*[6] but Solzenicyn selects and assembles details in much the way that Tolstoj does in treating Nicholas. At the beginning of the first chapter ("The Birthday-Hero") he makes Stalin's quarters speak of his personality and his reign of terror. Initially the tyrant appears in the inner sanctum, which embodies his paranoia. Later he moves into the large daytime office that has been stage-designed as a setting for public contacts. After describing the small, sparsely decorated night office, Solzenicyn focuses upon the physical appearance of Stalin himself. Whereas Nicholas is dissipated, Stalin is decrepit, and this important difference in psychology[7] lends distinctive coloring to each of the portraits of the tyrants. In Tolstoj's representation, the Tsar tries to fill the void of his existence with sexual escapades, while Solzenicyn's Stalin has senile longings for immortality. Despite this difference in conception, the means of characterization are identical: description of the exterior moves toward revealing an inner dimension which is at variance with an official image. As in the case of Nicholas, Stalin can no longer distinguish the truth behind his public image, and in particular he cherishes the notion of himself as a military leader of genius. Subordinates display the behavior of the courtiers of Nicholas: Abakumov reads exterior signs to ascertain Stalin's mood, and his thoughts and words take shape through a mechanism that tries to register the desires of the dictator. Stalin duplicates the Tsar's habit of contemplating his greatness in the mirror, and he also conducts a similar kind of dialogue about himself within his head. In the same spirit of martyrdom that Tolstoj attributes to Nicholas, Stalin believes that he simply must "suffer another twenty years for the sake of humanity" and is outraged by independent thinking ("Better socialism? In *some other way* than Stalin's?").

In Solzenicyn's portrait the idiom of the tyrant announces the total inner corruption. Nicholas' lie about capital punishment calls attention to itself through sub-standard orthography, while Stalin's Georgian accent is approximated through incorrect, phonetic spelling. On a superficial level of the text this device signifies the more fundamental distortions in the thought, language, and moral character of the tyrant. In a distinctive manner Solzenicyn examines the process whereby politics mutilates language in the chapter entitled "Language is a Tool of Production."[8] Here he parodies the turgid style of Stalin's writing (cataloguing, repetition which adds no new semantic content) and shows how his muddled mind does violence to words. The very concept of language has little real importance in the mind of Stalin. He merely wants to aggrandize himself by making "his indelible contribution to a science other than philosophy or history." In deciding to end the Cikobava-Marr debate about the relationship between language and superstructure, Stalin proceeds in a purely mechanical way. He views "philology" as "grammar," which in turn is perceived as a quasi-mathematical set of relations that can be manipulated and used to generate formulas. Within such a conceptual framework he brings various clichés into alignment as a structure which is internally coherent and makes no appeal beyond itself in order to substantiate its "message." In parodying the efforts of Stalin as a writer, Solzenicyn thus seeks to reveal a quite terrifying mode of abstraction which operates in isolation from human concerns and transforms language into an instrument of political control.

In a way that is analogous to Tolstoj's representation of Nicholas, Solzenicyn defines Stalin as the embodiment of the totalitarian state and poses relationships to other types of consciousness which are more or less distant from the dictator's. Within Stalin's realm of thought stand all the members of the establishment who serve him. These creatures include the *apparatciki* as well as the slick literary critic Lanskij, who uses the computer-technician's language ("increment of victims") to speak of the inequities in the Soviet system of justice. With the exception of Galaxov, the members of the establishment are short-sighted and seek no philosophical grounding

for their existence. They appear almost as emanations, as puppets who take their cues and make Stalin's words their own in a relatively mechanical way.

In contrast to these types of characters, the high-minded Communist Rubin more complexly displays Stalin's cast of mind. Rubin's background, scholarly pursuits, and moral dilemma differentiate him from his Mavrino comrades and from Stalin himself, but he has made the tyrant's language his own. Both Rubin and Stalin are grounded in the thorough rationalism which allows abstract structures to keep moral questions and existential despair at a distance. In an argument about the laws of dialectics, Rubin becomes befuddled and leaves the impression that he is committed to a self-referential structure that has virtually no meaning for human experience. As a dogmatic Communist who defends his jailer, he shows Stalin's tendency to downgrade other human beings into objects governed by the laws of history. The individual personality (Volodin, or a cousin against who Rubin informed) is lost in a process of objectification whereby concepts such as the "proletariat," "enemy of the people," and "progressive forces" are elevated into substantially existing realities.

Through such a process of abstraction and obfuscation Rubin arrives at his project for "civic temples." Without recognizing his self-deception, he seeks to find some home in a realm of spirit—in churches called by another name. Solzenicyn attributes the same yearnings to Stalin, who longs for spiritual comfort and notes in himself an undying predisposition toward Orthodoxy. But whereas the plan for "civic temples" appears as a prisoner's futile exercise, the tyrant transforms the traditions and the idiom of religion into instruments of political control. By calling attention to the state's appropriation of an entire system of religious signs, Solzenicyn clearly seeks to present Communism as a false, secular faith. In contrast to the false faith of Stalinism, a genuine spirituality emanates from the secondary character Aginja. Through association with her in his youth, the police agent Jakonov felt the power of religion at a service in a beautiful church. But in opposition to his religious girl friend, Jakonov ultimately sided with the Bolsheviks' "realm of reason," and his complete abnegation of the soul was signaled by willingness to sign an article full of clichés about Communism's struggle with the decadent West. In *The First Circle* Solzenicyn does not give an elaborate projection of traditional religious faith, but a consideration of the power and the abuse of the language of the church (religious idiom, architecture, ritual, mythology) helps define affinity or hostility to the characteristic mode of Stalin.

Art, the realm of Solzenicyn's own endeavors, also comes under direct discussion as a mode of expression alien to the characteristic language of the state. As in the treatment of religion, *The First Circle* affirms the value of genuine art by contrast to a sham product. The inauthentic writers of Russia are represented by Galaxov, an acclaimed winner of Stalin Prizes who has learned to rationalize his servility and moral cowardice. In opposition stands the painter Kondrašev-Ivanov, who serves the same function that an authentic novelist could as a character in Solenicyn's book. In discussion with other prisoners, Kondrašev-Ivanov voices the idea that art provides a way of knowing the most significant human realities. Ner in concurs, and praises *Anna Karenina* as an unsurpassed work of literature. By contrast, he notes, the technological innovations of the 1870s now seem primitive. The remarks of Nerzin, which are directed against Rubin, convey Solznicyn's own view of the power of art and underline the limitations of the "objective," scientific mode of cognition promoted by the ideology of the Soviet state. Throughout *The First Circle* Solzenicyn upholds art as an eternal way of knowing moral truths and voices his condemnation of Socialist Realism as an artistic code which cannot embody the actuality of life in Stalinist Russia as he sees it. The mode, not merely the message, is at issue. As for Solzenicyn himself, for the inauthentic writer Galaxov the art of Tolstoj stands as a compelling, challenging model which the winners of Stalin Prizes seem only to parody, as they continue to fashion a literature which lends support to an unjust political system.

In contrast to the loyal Communist Rubin, Nerzin and Solzenicyn's other major characters exhibit a personal, existential type of consciousness which stands diametrically opposed to Stalin's mode of thought and language.[9] Nerzin, Volodin, Sologdin, and Spiridon have an individualized psychology, but their minds diverge in the same direction away from the laws of abstraction and obfuscation which govern the mentality of the tyrant. In an argument with Rubin, Nerzin explicitly protests against the obtuse, pretentious style of Stalin which seeks to disguise monstrous stupidity. Nerzin's mistrust of rationalistic structures as a source of values is elaborated in counterpoint with the experience of Volodin, who recognizes the inadequacy and irrelevance of the philosophical system of Epicurus only as he confronts the existential horror of being a prisoner. At the end of the novel, Volodin has suffered a drastic reorientation and entered the school of the Gulag. As the actuality of imprisonment supplants book-learning, he begins to recapitulate the experience of Nerzin, who claims that fellow *zeks* and intense introspection have revealed to him the knowledge he considers most meaningful.

In charting the development of Volodin, Solzenicyn makes significant reference to conflicting modes of discourse. The attempt to find some grounding for his existence leads Volodin not only to the thought of the ancient Greeks but also to the predominant sensibility of the era of Russian Symbolism. His mother's diary and her journals from the *fin de siècle* period arrest his attention through language itself:

> The very words in which his mother and her women friends had expressed themselves were old-fashioned. They wrote in all seriousness with capital letters: Truth, Good, Beauty; Good and Evil, the

ethical imperative. In the language Innokentij and his friends used, words were more concrete, and therefore more comprehensible: ideological substance (*idejnost'*), humaneness, loyalty, purposefulness.[10]

In this episode Solzenicyn shows Volodin's confused attraction to a new language. The very concern with ethical imperatives appears alien in Stalinist Russia and helps prompt Volodin to search for a code of justice. But the Symbolist mode of discourse, which promoted its own form of "poetic" abstraction and obfuscation, cannot give him firm guidelines. As they stand in abstract shape, the capitalized words seem available as categories, as containers to be filled with meanings that match Volodin's ill-defined personal longings. By contrast to the Symbolist mode, the words in the second series in the quotation only seem more "concrete" to Volodin because in Stalinist Russia they have been transformed into unambiguous signs.[11] Through a process of appropriation by the state, words have been locked onto their referents; as signs, they are weighed down with specific meanings so that they can no longer signify in different ways. As in the treatment of Communism as a false religion and Socialist Realism as false art, in dealing with Volodin Solzenicyn suggests that the state can pervert words such as "humane," "just," "loyal," and effectively impair a citizen's capacity to define true meaning.

In connection with the chapters on Stalin, the contemplation of language by Nerzin and Volodin acquires special force and furthers Solzenicyn's major concern with the salvaging of words as instruments of genuine communication—particularly as means of giving shape to the inner life of the individual. In contrast, Sologdin's "Language of Maximum Clarity" actually confuses the main issue of the relationship between corrupt politics and corrupt language. The refusal to use words of foreign origin leads Sologdin to expunge from his vocabulary "poet" as well as references to science, technology, and Soviet Communist ideology. In speech he (or Solzenicyn) sometimes completely forgets his linguistic program, and his most successful "Russianizations" consist largely of Church Slavonic forms.[12] Despite the resulting incoherence, Sologdin's protest against political jargon helps to further Solzenicyn's concern with the debasement of language in Stalinist Russia.

As a projection of the consciousness which diametrically opposes the state's language of abstraction and obfuscation, the peasant Spiridon stands as one of Solzenicyn's most effective creations. The mentality of the peasant is conveyed in his own words and from the perspective of Nerzin, who is reexamining the whole tradition of Russian intellectuals' looking to the people for moral edification. Again the recoiling from abstract structures characterizes Nerzin. In their own way, the Populists elevated a concept of the People into the substantially existing reality. By dealing with various representatives of the peasantry during his imprisonment and by seeking out Spiridon in particular, Nerzin looks for those who get lost in the intellectual process of formulating categories. In distinction from Nerzin as well as Sologdin and Volodin, Spiridon himself recognizes no need to speculate on matters of philosophy. But in elaborate detail Solzenicyn represents his existence as a series of life-threatening confrontations in which the peasant made decisions on the basis of his family ties and some obscure sense of relation to a scheme of natural law. This personal, existential mode of thought finds expression in the idiom of Spiridon, who speaks of the concrete, misuses "learned words," and finds meaning in the pithy language of proverbs. Rubin, the dialectical materialist, rages against this whole shape of mind which resists rationalistic abstraction. In debate with Sologdin, who self-consciously opposes the language of the state, Rubin shouts that discussion with him is as boring "as trying to pound the fact that the sun doesn't circle the earth into the head of some dottering old fool (*starik-pesocnik*). He'll never learn no matter how long he lives." (227.) As in *One Day in the Life of Ivan Denisovic* and "Matrena's Home,"[13] in *The First Circle* the particulars of the peasant's language best show Solzenicyn's ability to explore Russian as a living, whole system which endures as the most significant, cherished element of continuity in the history of his country.

Both Solzenicyn in *The First Circle* and Tolstoj in *Xadzi-Murat* project the mind of the tyrant as the very source of the corruption, impersonality, and cruelty writ large in society. With the tyrant defined as the central point of reference, other characters in *The First Circle* and *Xadzi-Murat* take shape within artistic structures which establish linkages (between Stalin and Rubin, between Nerzin and Spiridon; between Nicholas and General Voroncov, between Xadzi-Murat and the peasants) and oppositions (between Stalin and Agnija, Stalin and Kondrašev-Ivanov, Stalin and Spiridon; between Nicholas and Xadzi-Murat).

While Solzenicyn's treatment of Stalin does display notable stylistic and structural parallels with Tolstoj's treatment of Nicholas, *The First Circle* and *Xadzi-Murat* provide different perspectives on the issue of politics and language. Solzenicyn attacks the issue with an intensity born of his experience in Soviet Russia. While all significant Russian writers have prized the unique resources of their native tongue, Solzenicyn felt compelled to formulate a set of guidelines[14] which authors could follow in order to salvage a linguistic edifice undermined by Stalinist Russia. His concern about the debasement of language finds various forms of expression in *The First Circle*. Within the scope of this loosely structured novel, Solzenicyn shows that tyranny involves the appropriation of words as state commodities and the transformation of language into a set of sign-systems (official historiography, controlled journalism, Socialist Realism). Full of righteous indignation against such power, he urges his readers to learn to decode the language of the state. Volodin, the man who attempts to communicate a sympathetic message by telephone in chapter one, will be defined as an "enemy of the progressive forces of history"; the parody of Stalin's language seeks to unmask the utter

mediocrity of the mind and spirit of the dictator; "civic temples" speak of a false religion; the story "Buddha's Smile" figures as a literary amusement which illustrates the novel's central concern with decoding; the final chapter ("Meat") underlines the effectiveness with which the state uses mendacious language. In *The First Circle* Solzenicyn aspires to bear witness to history, and frequently his own impassioned voice rings out in commentaries (on the value of *valenki*, on Dostoevskij's *Notes from the House of the Dead*) which are reminiscent of passages in *The Gulag Archipelago*.

By contrast, Tolstoj does not take such a tendentious approach to the question of the relationship between corrupt politics and corrupt language. In *Xadzi-Murat* the life of the state and the making of history under Nicholas I provide Tolstoj with the occasion for giving his final artistic depiction of death. In this tightly structured novella which moves through a series of scenes full of significant visual detail, he draws the reader toward that final moment of death, when Xadzi-Murat's integrity and harmony of being blaze forth against the background of the whole morally corrupt culture that has destroyed him. Unlike Solzenicyn, Tolstoj does not raise his own voice to condemn history in the main body of *Xadzi-Murat*. He strived for the objectivity achieved in the final text and rejected variants which did include authorial commentary (on the nature of imperialism).

With the facts of history before him and with an understandable sense of urgency, Solzenicyn shows the corruption of language in an advanced stage not attained in Tsarist Russia. In *Xadzi-Murat* the subordinates of Nicholas worry about being dismissed or demoted, whereas *The First Circle* documents Stalin's casual murders, full-scale purges, and the total collapse of a legal system in Russia. At the dinner party in *Xadzi-Murat* the guest's insistence on describing a military campaign as the disaster that it really was produces annoyance and embarrassment in General Voroncov, while in Stalin's time calling things by their right names might result in exile or death. When Stalin proceeded to build Socialism in Russia, the "increment of victims" escalated drastically, and the state's control over language also reached an unprecedented degree: as massive social transformation was effected, the state fashioned language into an instrument for defining truth and justifying policy.

In Tsarist Russia, Tolstoj did not confront the totalitarian state and the brand of Newspeak which became its distinctive idiom. Given his place in history, his artistic insight into the relation between socio-political change and the debasement of language appears all the more remarkable: Xadzi-Murat uses words as a means of authentic communication, Šamil' as leader of a proto-state society has begun to play roles and use language to manipulate his subjects, while Nicholas as the head of a vast bureaucratic empire quite cynically employs language to rationalize acts of murder. Without witnessing the terror of Stalinism or the perfecting of the Stalinist mode of discourse, Tolstoj in *Xadzi-Murat* brilliantly represented the earlier phases of that process whereby language becomes another institutionalized structure wielded by the state to control the defining of truth and to exercise absolute authority over the individual.

NOTES

[1] See for example Kathryn B. Feuer, "Solzhenitsyn and the Legacy of Tolstoy," and Richard Haugh, "The Philosophical Foundations of Solzhenitsyn's Vision of Art," in *Aleksandr Solzhenitsyn: Critical Essays and Documentary Materials,* ed. John Dunlop, Richard Haugh and Alexis Klimoff (Belmont, MA: Norland Publishing, 1973), 129-46; 168-84. See also A. Obolensky, "Solzhenitsyn in the Mainstream of Russian Literatures," *Canadian Slavonic Papers,* 13 (1971), 131-38; and Deming Brown, "*Cancer Ward* and *The First Circle,*" *Slavic Review,* 28 (1969), 304-13.

[2] See especially *Max Weber on Charisma and Institution Building. Selected Papers,* ed. S. N. Eisenstadt (Chicago: Univ. of Chicago Press, 1968).

[3] For an analysis of the distinction between the pastoral and the primitive in Tolstoj's writings, see my essay, "Concepts of the Primitive in Russian Literature: from Tolstoy to Pasternak," in *Concepts of the Primitive in Western Civilization,* ed. Stanley Diamond (New York: Pergamon Press, forthcoming).

[4] A. P. Sergeenko, "Kommentarii," in L. N. Tolstoj, *Polnoe sobranie socinenii* (90 vols.; M.: GIXL, 1935-58), XXXV, 583-633; see also L. Semenov, ed., "Material k istorii sozdanija povesti 'Xadzi-Murata,'" *Literaturnoe nasledstvo,* 37-38 (1939), 633-50. For an assessment of the historical accuracy of the work, see V. A. D'jakov, "Istoriceskie realii 'Xadzi-Murata,'" *Voprosy istorii* (1973), no. 5, 135-48.

[5] For the variants, see Tolstoj, XXXV, 284-556. On the peep-show method, see the entry of 21 March 1898 in Tolstoj's diary, LIII, 188.

[6] Gary Kern, "Solzhenitsyn's Portrait of Stalin," *Slavic Review,* 33 (1974), 1-22.

[7] See Feuer, 134, who draws no distinctions between the psychology of Stalin and the psychology of Nicholas.

[8] See Edward J. Brown, "Solzenicyn's Cast of Characters," *SEEJ,* 15 (1971), 162-63.

[9] By using this term, I mean to characterize a mode of thought and language which recoils from abstract structures. For discussion of the characters' philosophies of life, see John Dunlop, "The Odyssey of a Skeptic: Gleb Nerzhin," in *Aleksandr Solzhenitsyn,* 241-59; Natalia Rea, "Nerzhin: A Sartrean Existential Man," *Canadian Slavonic Papers,* 13 (1971), 209-16; and Helen Muchnic, "Solzhenitsyn's *The First Circle,*" *Russian Review,* 29 (1970), 154-66.

[10] Solzenicyn, *V kruge pervom* (New York: Harper and Row, 1968), 306.

[11] On the distinction between "signs" and "signifiers," see Roland Barthes, *Mythologies,* tr. Annette Lavers (London: Cape, 1972), 113. Compare Nadezda Mandel'štam's remark on her husband's famous portrait of Stalin: the authorities said that the poem was a "usurpation of the right words and thoughts that the ruling powers reserved exclusively for themselves." *Hope against Hope: A Memoir,* tr. Max Hayward (New York: Atheneum, 1976), 83.

[12] Boris O. Unbegaun, "The 'Language of Ultimate Clarity,'" in *Aleksandr Solzhenitsyn,* 196-98.

[13] L. R evskij, "Obraz rasskazcika v povesti Solzenicyna 'Odin den' Ivana Denisovica,'" *Studies in Slavic Linguistics and Poetics in Honor of B. O. Unbegaun* (New York: New York Univ. Press, 1968) 165-78; "Tvorceskoe slovo u Solzenicyna," *Novyj zurnal,* 96 (1969), 76-90; T. G. Vinokur, "O jazyke i stile povesti A. I. Solzenicyna 'Odin den 'Ivana Denisovica,'" *Voprosy kul'tury reci,* 1965, no. 6, 16-32; Roman B. Gul', "A. Solzenicyn, socrealizm i škola Remizova," *Novyj zurnal,* 71 (1963), 68-74; and Ludmila Koehler, "Solzhenitsyn and Russian Literary Tradition," *Russian Review,* 26 (1967), 176-84.

[14] Solzenicyn, "Ne obycaj degtem šci belit', na to smetana," *Literaturnaja gazeta,* 4 November 1965.

George Urban with W. Averell Harriman (interview date 1981)

SOURCE: "Was Stalin (the Terrible) Really a 'Great Man'?: A Conversation with W. Averell Harriman," in *Encounter,* Vol. LVII, No. 5, November, 1981, pp. 20-38.

[*In the following interview, Urban discusses with Harriman, who was Franklin Roosevelt's special ambassador to Churchill and Stalin from 1941 to 1946, Stalin's behavior and activities during World War II, particularly his wartime leadership abilities.*]

W. Averell Harriman was born in November 1891 and, after the usual "Eastern Establishment stations" (Groton, Yale), made a career first in the railroad business which his father, the pioneer of the Illinois Central and the Union Pacific, had established, and then as a prominent Wall Street banker. He was, during the liberal New Deal days, a close adviser to Franklin D. Roosevelt, later becoming the President's Wartime Ambassador-at-large. He served after the War in various high governmental posts (including a period as Ambassador to Britain), taking time out only to be elected Governor of New York State (1955-58). Ten years later he was the US representative at the Viet Nam Peace Talks in Paris. He is the author of a number of books and has recently published his memoirs.

I. CHURCHILL AND ROOSEVELT

[*George Urban:*] *What were President Roosevelt's reasons for believing that he knew how to handle Stalin whereas Churchill, as he thought, did not? On 18 March 1942 Roosevelt wrote to Churchill:*

> *I know you will not mind my being brutally frank with you when I tell you that I think I can personally handle Stalin better than either your Foreign Office or my State Department. Stalin hates the guts of all your top people. He thinks he likes me better and I hope he will continue to do so. . . .*

There is evidence of Stalin's dislike of the "top" British in your own memoirs (Special Envoy, with Elie Abel). Stalin took an unenthusiastic view of Britain's first wartime ambassador, Sir Stafford Cripps (a socialist, a teetotaller, and a bit of an ascetic), and refused to accept Lt-General M. B. Burrows on the tripartite military committee on the grounds that Burrows had no respect for the Soviet military and regarded them as "savages."

Roosevelt's letter to Churchill has given rise to much speculation. Historians have asked: What was it in Roosevelt's policies and personal attitude that might have appealed to Stalin? Was it Roosevelt's generosity, goodwill, and perhaps naivety? his dislike of Churchill's unabashed view of Empire? his apparent disinclination to get too deeply involved in the post-war European settlement? the scale of American economic power?

Did personal observation during your many Wartime meetings with Roosevelt, Churchill and Stalin give you reason to think that Roosevelt did indeed have better access to Stalin's mind than Churchill?

[*W. Averell Harriman:*] Oh yes! One could, for example, see at the Teheran Conference that when Roosevelt talked, Stalin listened very carefully and with what one might call a certain deference. His rapport with Churchill was different. In 1942, when Churchill and I visited Moscow to tell Stalin that the "Second Front" could not be launched in 1942, Stalin was furious and gave Churchill a rough time. He accused the British of being too much afraid of fighting the Germans. On one occasion, speaking to me out of Churchill's hearing, Stalin complained that the Arctic convoys had been stopped because the British Navy had lost the initiative and that the British Army was not fighting either (mentioning the British defeat at Singapore). He made a similar accusation direct to Churchill's face, questioning whether the British Navy had any sense of glory—to which Churchill responded in no uncertain terms but with great dignity.

These were, of course, unjustified accusations. The postponement of the "Second Front" was a joint Anglo-American decision, as were in fact all the other things Stalin took exception to; and my presence in Moscow on behalf of Roosevelt was the President's way of saying that there was complete solidarity between the Western Allies. But as Churchill was the one to break the news, Stalin's anger was concentrated on him.

For all that, Stalin did admire Churchill's qualities as a Wartime leader. He once toasted Churchill as a comrade-in-arms and a man of indefatigable fighting spirit; and the two men cooperated closely in the pursuit of the War. But that exhausted Churchill's usefulness for Stalin. He did not think that Churchill would be of any value after the War. He suspected his motives.

There was (to come back to Roosevelt) nothing personal about Stalin's deference to Roosevelt—although, for some reason, Roosevelt appeared to think that there was. Stalin simply realised that the USA possessed the greatest productive machinery the world had yet seen in a single country. He needed the help of this machinery to keep the Red Army fighting and therefore had great respect for it. This was the *real* reason why Roosevelt was given more consideration than Churchill when the three leaders met. American supplies were vital to the survival of the Soviet Union.

How do you react to the view that Roosevelt as President of a country which had itself been a colony had a certain tacit emotional affinity with Moscow's long-term anti-colonial objectives? Or, to put it another way, that he and Stalin were both uncomfortable with Churchill's (unreconstructed, as they thought) concept of Empire? If so, might this have accounted for Roosevelt's feeling that he could handle Stalin better than Churchill, to say nothing of the fact that in 1919 Churchill had tried to thwart the Bolshevik Revolution, whereas Roosevelt suffered from no such handicap in dealing with Stalin?

Stalin was no sentimentalist. He would not be led by considerations of this kind even if Roosevelt would. It was the practical things in life that affected Stalin—American trucks, tanks, aircraft, and other supplies.

Roosevelt did feel, to my mind rather optimistically, that he could influence Stalin; but the fact was that he could only influence Stalin when Stalin had something at risk that Roosevelt was in a position to deny him. Every now and then Stalin felt that if he did not do what Roosevelt wanted, his relationship with the President would be adversely affected and his American war-supplies might dry up. In such cases he would give way; but this is the only sense in which we can speak of Roosevelt's special influence over Stalin.

Did Stalin's esteem for Roosevelt rub off on yourself as the President's personal representative?

Stalin was always courteous to me. In October 1946 I called on him while he was on vacation at Gagra in the Crimea to discuss with him serious differences which had arisen between our governments on the question of calling a peace conference with Hitler's former satellites and settling Allied control in Japan. Although our talks had been controversial and inconclusive, Stalin remained extremely cordial. As I was getting up to leave after our last discussion, Stalin said: "I have received you not only as an Ambassador of the United States but as a friend. It will always be so."

This was the expression of something more than cordiality extended to Roosevelt's representative as US Ambassador. It went back to the circumstance that in the 1920s I had, together with other American businessmen, taken manganese concessions in the Caucasus.

When I returned to the Soviet Union as Roosevelt's representative, some of my friends feared that Stalin would resent my earlier role as "a capitalist" who had come to "exploit" the new Soviet state at a time when it was undergoing grave difficulties. But this was not at all Stalin's attitude. On the contrary, he observed to me on one occasion: "You came to our country at a time of need and ready to help us. . . . " What I am saying is that Stalin had a fine appreciation of people who were prepared to work with him, as distinct from those who were strictly antagonistic. He was astute. He had a good understanding of the other man's point of view.

You say: "He had a good understanding of the other man's point of view." Were you conscious, in negotiating with Stalin, that you were talking to the greatest tyrant of modern times with a fearful record of savagery to his name?

I was not concerned about what sort of a man Stalin was or how he had dealt with his rivals. My concern was to achieve my objective which was to be able to show Stalin that we could give him enough help to keep the Red Army in the War. I was interested in him as the leader of a country which was vital to the security of my own. I did not go to Russia as a sightseer or as an historian. It was not my job to assess Stalin's character or to ascertain where he stood historically. I looked upon him as the head of the Soviet Union and therefore had to deal with him as I found him.

Nowadays everybody thinks I went to the Soviet Union concerned to see who this great man was. That sort of consideration never entered my head. Roosevelt's hope was—and I fully agreed with it—that the Red Army would destroy enough of Hitler's forces so that our men would not have the ghastly job of doing it themselves. Roosevelt knew that the US would get into the War sooner or later. He was mindful of the terrible losses we had suffered at the hands of Germany in World War I and was anxious that our troops should never again be exposed to that sort of blood-letting. So my job was to supply Stalin with whatever he needed and keep the Red Army fighting Hitler's troops. . . .

—in which you succeeded only too well—

Yes—but the point I want to stress is that I didn't give a damn about Stalin's character or the 1936-38 "Show Trials" or the collectivisation campaign. I was concerned

to get him to do the things we wanted him to do. For me he was simply the leader of a country we had some very important business with.

Obviously I knew about Stalin's past deeds, the brutalities of the 1930s and so on, but I had a mission to perform, and it wasn't that of a tourist or a student of Communist history.

But could the job of understanding, supporting and influencing the Soviet War-effort be completely divorced from an historical assessment of Stalin's character and his record as a dictator? Two points immediately come to mind.

First, historians of the Second World War tell us that the Red Army would have performed a great deal better in 1941-42 if in 1937 Stalin had not exterminated many of its most senior generals and the cream of its officer corps. Stalin's war on Finland foundered for precisely that reason.

Second, Stalin's post-War expansionism—which you foresaw even before the European War ended and reported to the President in a number of warnings—was the expansionism of the same man who had incorporated the Baltic states, some of the Eastern territories of Poland and Rumania, and made an unsuccessful bid to grab Finland. Didn't these aspects of Stalin's record have some bearing on your estimate of his post-War policies? Weren't they an early warning of what could be expected of him if and when his forces reached deep into Europe?

In 1941-43 we were not interested in what Stalin's peace policies might turn out to be. We were at war with Hitler. We were interested in Stalin's *war* policies, and that was enough to keep us busy. Later on, I was much concerned about Stalin's plans for a post-War European settlement and was able to give some advice to President Roosevelt which proved to be correct—

—absolutely prophetic. I read your despatches with great admiration. For example, commenting on Stalin's policy vis-à-vis *the 1944 Warsaw Uprising you told Roosevelt that there was every indication that the Soviet Union would "become a world bully" wherever their interests were involved.*

I appreciate your comments. It was not that I was particularly eagle-eyed or brilliant. I only happened to have an opportunity which few people had: a chance to see Stalin in action at close quarters. He would talk bluntly to me, and I was able to talk bluntly to him. I could get to the heart of the matter and report my thoughts frankly to the President.

But, as you report in your memoirs, even after a personal talk with Roosevelt later in the year in Washington, you did not think you convinced the President "to be firm and vigilant" in dealing with the Soviets in Eastern

*Europe . . . although you do say that the State Depart-
ment was fully alive to the necessity and did not want to
see Eastern Europe surrendered to Soviet domination.*

The President did not have as sure a grasp of the realities
in Central and Eastern Europe as he did in the Far East.
For example, he still thought that he could personally
arbitrate the Soviet-Polish and the Soviet-Finnish boundary, which was to my mind quite out of the question.
When I told the President that Stalin was hoping to split
the Japanese armies in China by driving a wedge direct to
Peking, he responded with the question: "If the Russians
go in, will they ever go out?" He did not, however, bother
to ask a parallel question about the Soviet penetration of
Central and Eastern Europe because, I think, he felt that
he was powerless to affect the issue.

I was always hopeful that when I got to see the President
I could persuade him that my reading of Soviet intentions
was right. I was unhappy that he did not see them as
I saw them; but I knew Roosevelt well and realised that
he made up his mind sometimes without full information—but then, he was always ready to discuss his
decisions. Roosevelt was unduly optimistic. He failed
to understand that Stalin, with the terrible damage that
had been done to the Soviet Union, would not be as
anxious to have our help in the post-War period as he
had been during the War. He did not realise how
tough-minded the Russians would be and with what
determination they would stick to the long-term goals
of world revolution.

*One adjective often used by historians to describe
Roosevelt, and especially his attitude to Stalin, is "na-
ive." you knew Roosevelt from your common childhood.
Was he naive?*

This is a complex question. Roosevelt was hopeful that
his personal relationship with Stalin could carry on after
the War, but Stalin had no regard whatever for personal
relationships. He was thinking in a framework of ideology
and power which was alien to the President. Roosevelt
was confident in his ability to get other people to do
things for him, and he was not entirely wrong in that—
his ability to persuade people to change their minds was
very considerable. But he was over-confident.

Naive? I do not like using the word to describe the character of a great man, but he was certainly over-optimistic
about what he could achieve personally, as distinct from
what he could as head of a powerful government.

*Was Roosevelt's "over-confidence" vis-à-vis Stalin due
to his lack of any profound knowledge of Bolshevik
history and the world Communist movement generally?*

I don't know—I have never bothered to find out.

*You talk in your book of Roosevelt's inclination to "ro-
mance"—to engage in flights of the imagination which
you personally tended to ignore.*

He would "romance" when you went to see him and he
did not want to tell you what was on his mind because
his mind was not made up. He would talk all round the
subject but would not give you an answer. He never said
"I refuse to give you an answer", but you could sense
very quickly that he had no intention of telling you. He
had a strong belief that the President had the right, and
in many cases the obligation, of not making up his mind
until the last minute, because if he made a decision too
soon, information might come in that would invalidate it.

This was in a sense highly frustrating for one who had
to work with him, because it meant the lack of precise
instructions. In another sense, however, it was very
stimulating, because Roosevelt would give you the general line of his thinking, leaving it to you to use your own
judgment in turning it into practical policy. This was an
exciting thing to do. The responsibility was yours. If you
made a mistake, you were out on a limb; but as I did not
need a job to support myself, I did not mind running the
risk of being fired!

*When I mentioned Roosevelt's inclination to day-dream
I had one example especially in mind—his thoughts
about the future of Lvov. He observed to you in 1944
that the Soviet-American-British controversy over the
future of Lvov could be resolved by the simple expedient
of appointing Lvov as a "Polish capitalist island"
within the Soviet Union. He thought Stalin might agree
to have the city governed by an international committee,
leaving it to a future plebiscite to decide whether Lvov
should finally belong to Poland or the Soviet Union.*

*This strikes me as a good example of Roosevelt's naivety.
Anyone who could believe this after the Warsaw Uprising would have no difficulty with another and even less
likely idea—that Stalin would permit parliamentary
democracy to flourish in Eastern Europe after the War.*

As you know, I tried to tell Roosevelt that Stalin would
never permit a Polish capitalistic enclave within a Soviet-
Ukrainian environment. But Roosevelt thought this would
present no problem: the Ukrainian peasants would come to
Lvov and sell their produce to the Poles for roubles. . . .

Without question, Roosevelt did not fully understand
Soviet thinking, and I do not know if any of us did when
it came to talking to the Soviet side directly. Roosevelt,
to be fair to him, knew how to handle Stalin, as one could
see at both Teheran and Yalta. Nevertheless, he was, as
I say, more optimistic about being able to deal with Stalin
than the facts justified. In the Spring of 1945 it was a
great shock for him to find that Stalin was turning his
back on the "Declaration on Liberated Europe" signed at
Yalta, first, by installing a minority government of his
own choosing in Rumania, and then trying to do the same
in Poland—a case we regarded as being much more serious, and one which brought the Alliance close to breaking point. Roosevelt's telegrams to Stalin and Churchill,
and his instructions to myself as his representative on the
Anglo-American-Soviet commission dealing with the

problem of the Polish government, show the depth of his concern. But even then, he did not allow his disappointment to run away with him. He was very firm with Stalin, but not angry to the point of wanting to slash back.

Roosevelt is on record as having said: "There is no doubt in my mind that after the War American and Soviet societies are going to converge." Was this not a gross misjudgment?

Of course it was—it was nonsense. Roosevelt said this, and I think he believed it. He never understood the ideological vigour (as it then was) of the Communist faith. He never grasped the fact that Communism in Russia was not merely a political and economic system but an ideological faith.

Did you point this out to him at the time?

No, it was not for me to correct the President. From time to time I did remark to Roosevelt that I did not share his judgment of the Soviet system and Soviet intentions; but one had to accept Roosevelt as he was.

I knew Roosevelt pretty well. His brother was in my class at school, and I used to have meals with the Roosevelts in the first decade of the century. So I knew Roosevelt before he acquired the great qualities he did in fighting off the effects of polio; for there is no doubt that his victory over polio strengthened his character. I knew him before he had become as vigorous a man as he was when he was President. I was, therefore, not surprised by these lapses of his judgment. People expected the great man to be perfect in every way. But, of course, he was not—nobody is perfect.

II. PORTRAIT OF STALIN

So much has been written about Stalin's "cult of the personality" that I'd be curious to know a little more about Stalin's character as he appeared to you at the time.

Some historians, Isaac Deutscher for example, have stressed Stalin's coolness and "impersonality." He is described as a pragmatist—a doer rather than a thinker.

Stalin was very impersonal when you first met him. He did not go around shaking hands. But when he got interested he warmed up and shed his impersonality. But I agree that to the casual observer, and those who only saw him in public, he was cool.

But, then, there was also a warmer side to Stalin which I saw displayed in his attitude to Harry Hopkins. Hopkins, as you know, was a sick man. Nevertheless he made the long and hazardous trip to the Teheran Conference. When Stalin saw him enter the conference room, he got up, walked across the room, and shook hands with him. I never saw him do that to anybody, not even Roosevelt. He was the only man that I ever saw Stalin show personal emotion for. Hopkins had

won Stalin's admiration earlier in the War. He was one of the first Western envoys to go to Moscow shortly after the Russians had been attacked by Hitler. He made the difficult trip all the way around the North Sea to Archangel and down to Moscow. He had lost his pills and was not very well. Stalin saw all this and showed personal respect for Hopkins's courage.

But was it not also that Hopkins brought Stalin, extremely hard-pressed as he was at the time, the vital news that Roosevelt "regarded Hitler as the enemy of mankind and that he therefore wished to aid the Soviet Union in its fight against Germany"? Whereupon Stalin asked for 20,000 anti-aircraft guns, thousands of fighter planes and bombers and a long list of other war materials?

No—he respected Hopkins's courage as a human being, not as a representative of the American President. I am only telling this story to show that Stalin did have a softer side to him which, I agree, did not come out very often, for we know well enough that he could be callous and brutal.

Joseph E. Davies, US Ambassador to Moscow in 1936-38, saw a different Stalin from the one Isaac Deutscher describes.

> *His brown eye is exceedingly kind and gentle. A child would like to sit in his lap and a dog would sidle up to him . . .*

he wrote in Mission to Moscow. *Stalin was "clean-living, modest and retiring." Even Lord Beaverbrook commented after your joint meetings with Stalin in 1941 that Stalin was "a kindly man" who "practically never shows any impatience at all." And H. G. Wells: "I have never met a man more candid, fair and honest, and to these qualities it is, and to nothing occult or sinister, that he owes his tremendous undisputed ascendancy in Russia. . . . No one is afraid of him and everybody trusts him."*

The reverse side of this coin is best represented by Djilas. Stalin, for him, was

> *the greatest criminal of all time, for in him was joined the criminal senselessness of Caligula with the refinement of a Borgia and the brutality of Czar Ivan the Terrible.*

Davies's view is utter nonsense, as indeed is his whole book. He never understood what was going on.

Beaverbrook was an enthusiast and a backer of the Soviet Union at almost any price—so much so that his "Russia-First" attitude worried Churchill. He wanted our joint mission to Moscow to sound like a great success and used it to build up his reputation with his Cabinet colleagues in London. In one of his cables from Moscow he boasted to the British War Cabinet that "the campaign laid down by Harriman and me" had been carried out without "any hitch." None of this was quite true. I took a much more sober view of what had been transacted and said so in a personal note to Roosevelt. Beaverbrook's exuberance sometimes carried him way beyond the facts. Hence his somewhat overdrawn characterisation of Stalin.

What about Djilas's lapidary words?

For me, Djilas's witness carries much more importance. He was a dedicated leading Communist, but his disappointment with Stalin and the Stalinist system caused him to reject Communism and his own past with particular bitterness. So I would discount his judgment, too, or at least I would express my disenchantment with Stalin (if I were in Djilas's shoes) in a different way. Stalin was, to be sure, cold and highly suspicious, and when he acted on his suspicions he could be cruel and brutal; but I would have thought that comparing him with the sanguinary madman Caligula was not quite justified. I am more inclined to think that Khrushchev's account of Stalin's way of dealing with his associates was accurate and struck the right note.

You may not agree with Djilas's reference to Caligula, but I should imagine you would not quarrel with his reference to Ivan the Terrible, seeing that in Peace with Russia? *(1960) you quote with apparent approval an observation which Alexey Tolstoy once made to you:*

> *If you want to understand the Kremlin of today . . . you must first understand the Kremlin of Ivan the Terrible.*

This is, incidentally, also a view strongly held by Professor Robert C. Tucker, one of Stalin's best-known American biographers.

Yet little in your memoirs reminds the reader that the man with whom you had so many crucial discussions in the Kremlin and elsewhere was a latter-day Ivan the Terrible who, in fact, cast himself in that role quite consciously. You portray a shrewd, well-informed, determined and somewhat home-spun politician with his eye on the main chance; but there is nothing terrifying or repulsive about him.[1] Your book, if I may say so, did not leave me with the impression that its author was a privileged eyewitness at the court of a fearsome dictator and loathsome individual, no admirable though I found your memoirs in all other respects.

You must understand that my business in Moscow was not to look at Stalin with the curiosity of an historian or the questioning eye of a political philosopher. I was sent there by the President to keep Russia in the War and save American lives. And as ideology had nothing to do with Roosevelt's decision to help Russia, I was not concerned with Soviet Party history, Stalin's record as Party leader, and the like.

People studying Stalin now are looking for evidence of blood and murder. *I* was looking for vigorous action in Stalin's war with Nazi Germany, and I did find in him a

man of action and a man of leadership. I expected him to be tough, and he was tough, although (as I have said) he was also very polite. But his blunt words did not bother me nearly as much as they did Beaverbrook, for example. I went to see him as an equal. I had met so many important men in my time that I was not going to be awed by Stalin.

Now, Alexey Tolstoy did not say that Stalin was *like* Ivan the Terrible. He merely observed that "If you want to understand the Kremlin of today . . . you must first understand the Kremlin of Ivan the Terrible." This simply means that one could not understand Stalin's Russia without understanding Russian history and appreciating some of the, for us, appalling things which the Russian people were brought up with and were prepared to put up with. It wasn't that the Kremlin I saw somehow bore traces of the court of Ivan the Terrible, for (if I am not mistaken) Ivan was the monarch who murdered his son in a fit of anger. Stalin was not like that.

On the other hand, Stalin knew well enough that the Russian people's tremendous War effort had little to do with their support of the Communist system. Stalin—this is a point I want to stress—was a realist. He said to me in September 1941:

> We are under no illusion that they [the Russian people] are fighting for us. They are fighting for Mother Russia.

Stalin was aware that the Party was unpopular and he himself hated in his capacity as Party leader. That is why he thought he had to protect himself against the germ of counter-revolution. He had himself been a revolutionary, so he knew how underground movements began and developed. He was not going to let one come into being directed against himself. In this respect, then, there was something in Stalin's political behaviour that runs parallel with Ivan the Terrible's campaign against the boyars.

Stalin the War Leader, however, was popular, and there can be no doubt that he was the one who held the Soviet Union together after it had been smashed by Hitler's invasion. I do not think anyone else could have done it, and nothing that has happened since Stalin's death induces me to change that opinion.

It is quite true that Stalin made a desperate blunder in not preparing for Hitler's invasion. He evidently could not believe that Hitler would attack without talking to him again, because he was ready to make further concessions. The British had sent him several warnings, all of which he disregarded. He thought these were a provocation, the British trying to get him to mobilise and thus to bring on Hitler's attack (he was conscious of 1914, when the Czar's mobilisation caused the Kaiser to mobilise and made war inevitable). All this showed a serious lack of judgment. Both the British and we knew through our intelligence networks that Hitler was preparing to attack Russia; and we repeatedly communicated this information to Stalin in precise detail, including the actual date of the attack. But then, Stalin refused to believe his own agents too, some of whose warnings (Richard Sorge's above all others) had been just as categorical.

But once Stalin had overcome the shock of invasion (I was not there, but I accept the story that he had fallen into a mental collapse and cut himself off from his closest associates), he moved fast and vigorously to assert his leadership. It was amazing that after the great losses he had taken he was able to redevelop his armed forces, move his industrial production to the East, restore morale and eventually defeat the Germans.

I must also give credit to Stalin as military leader. He attacked only when he had accumulated the necessary reserves to break through the German lines, but then he was prepared to take enormous losses in order to achieve a decisive victory. My military friends tell me that although these losses were quite shocking, they were smaller than they would have been if Stalin had repeatedly attacked with smaller forces and less resolution. So I'd like to emphasise my great admiration for Stalin the national leader in an emergency—one of the historic occasions where one man made so much difference. This in no sense minimises my revulsion against his cruelties; but I have to give you the constructive side as well as the other.

Let's be fair to Stalin and add in parenthesis that when the War was over he acknowledged his early blunders. On 24 May 1945, at a victory celebration in the Kremlin, Stalin said:

> Our government made not a few errors, we experienced at moments a desperate situation in 1941-1942, when our army was retreating, because there was no other way out. A different people could have said to the government: "You have failed to justify our expectations. Go away. We shall install another government which will conclude peace with Germany. . . . " The Russian people, however did not take this path. . . .

These were not the words of a man whose head had been turned by victory.

One should perhaps add for the record that Stalin's unpreparedness for the German attack may well have had its roots in his ambivalent psychological attitude to Germany and the Nazi system.

> *If there is one nation to which we are attracted— to the whole people or at least to a majority—they are the Germans.*

Stalin said this to Emil Ludwig. And, responding to Ribbentrop's congratulatory wire on his 60th birthday in December 1939, Stalin said: "The friendship of the peoples of Germany and the Soviet Union, cemented in blood, has every reason to be lasting and firm"—words that will be quoted against him as long as history is written.

This may have been no more than a rhetorical flourish to cover a holding operation and gain time, as Soviet historians would like us to believe; but, equally, it may have expressed Stalin's genuine conviction that he could (to put it no higher) stay out of the War. Indeed, we have it on the authority of Stalin's daughter, Svetlana, that "even after the War he was in the habit of repeating, 'Ech, together with the Germans we would have been invincible.' . . ."[2]

I was not there—your comment is as good as mine.

Our most famous character portrait of Stalin comes from Trotsky. This is the image of Stalin as a bureaucrat: not a man who fought his way to power through revolutionary activity of his own, as Mussolini and Hitler did, but one who manipulated his way to power using the post-revolutionary bureaucratisation of Soviet life as his escalator—a creature of the machine and symbol of Thermidor.

Did this "bureaucratic" side of Stalin come across in your talks with him (and, of course, "bureaucratic" for Trotsky meant the betrayal of the revolution)?

It is a travesty of the facts to call Stalin a mere bureaucrat. He had an enormous ability to absorb detail and act on detail. He was very much alert to the needs of his whole war machine. He had his finger on the pulse of the country. He was not just sitting in the Kremlin glorying in his power.

In our negotiations with him we usually found him extremely well informed. He had a masterly knowledge of the sort of equipment that was important for him. He knew the calibre of the guns he wanted, the weight of the tanks his roads and bridges would take, and the details of the type of metal he needed to build aircraft. These were not characteristics of a bureaucrat, but rather those of an extremely able and vigorous war leader. Trotsky's prejudice against Stalin was as strong as Stalin's against Trotsky.

Wasn't your confidence in Stalin's competence as a War Leader a little shattered when you heard Stalin remark to you: "In the Soviet Army it takes more courage to retreat than to advance"? Was this not a clear pointer that the Russian people's willingness to fight was not self-evident and that terrible things must have been going on behind the Soviet lines?

Or did Stalin's toughness and realism perhaps give you additional reasons for trusting his leadership?

This remark of Stalin's shows that he was fully conscious of the realities prevailing in the Red Army. We knew that Stalin had his security agents behind the lines ready to shoot down their own troops if they turned and retreated. We were appalled by this, but we realised that it did make the Red Army fight. That was the thing that mattered.

But wasn't Stalin's remark a very damaging confession about the morale of his forces?

It was not a question of morale—he wanted them to do the impossible; he was determined to give his attack that extra punch which could be done with no other means. Our military people, who consulted the Germans after the War, told me: the devastating thing about a Russian offensive was its mass character. The Russians came in wave after wave. They would all be mown down by the Germans until, by the force of sheer attrition, one wave would eventually break through and achieve the Russian objectives. Now, there is a theory in military tactics which says that you should take your big losses right away, this being, in the last analysis, a better way of economising on your manpower than any other method. I am not qualified to judge it; but this is the theory on which the Russians worked. It was not for us to question it or the manner in which Stalin enforced it.

Did you find Stalin a man of keen intelligence?

Oh, very. He was a man of simple purposes ready to use devious means to attain them, but these he would use doggedly and intelligently.

Boris Bazhanov, Stalin's secretary in the mid-1920s, described Stalin as a man of poor education, incapable of producing "an orderly train of thought in speech or writing" and with a very short attention-span. Would you agree with his judgment?

No—Stalin was certainly not like that in the 1940s. I would, however, not put him down as deeply intellectual. I do not think he spent much time in trying to figure out things philosophically. He was not the creative genius that Lenin was. He was an operator. He accepted Communist ideology as he had received it from Lenin and built on that. He inherited a situation and took control of it. He was a practical man who knew how to use the levers of power, but he was no innovator or ideologue.

Did you find Stalin a "silent" man? Bazhanov stresses Stalin's inclination to listen, wait for the consensus of his colleagues to emerge, and then come up with their conclusions as though they were his own. Emil Ludwig says:

> *He is the most silent man I ever saw, silent until he suddenly rises to attack you. This silence, this slowness, show him an Asiatic.*

Stalin was no chatterbox. He was "Asiatic" perhaps in the sense that he was inscrutable, even enigmatic. He would not often look you in the eye. The contradiction between his personal courtesy and his wholesale liquidations always puzzled me.

Practically everyone who had to deal with Stalin agrees that he was extremely suspicious, even paranoid. Khrushchev quotes Stalin as saying: "I trust no one, not even myself."

I have no reason to doubt that Stalin did say that to Khrushchev. He never made a similar statement in my presence, but there is nothing that I know about Stalin which would have made it impossible for him to say it. He would say almost anything to make a point, even indulge in a bit of self-mockery. He was not at all pompous. He was in no sense holding himself up as someone hard to approach. He was very blunt, and he did not resent bluntness in return—which he certainly got from me when the situation so required.

Professor Robert C. Tucker, in his penetrating analysis of Stalin's character, sums up Khrushchev's indictment of Stalin as abuse of power, and Stalin's mental state as one of paranoia. You were at the receiving end of Stalin's mistrust of his friends and allies, as for example his refusal to grant landing rights to US planes to supply the Poles in the Warsaw Uprising; his reluctance to allow the American military to locate US prisoners in the liberated areas; and countless other displays of Stalin's suspicious nature. Would you agree that he suffered from some form of persecution mania?

He was certainly very suspicious. One of Roosevelt's instructions to me was to "talk him out of his shell", away from his aloofness and secretiveness, which takes us back to September 1941 when Beaverbrook and I, representing Churchill and Roosevelt, went to Moscow to ascertain Stalin's needs and offer whatever help we could. On the second day of our talks, on 29 September 1941, we ran into rough weather. Stalin was most dissatisfied with what we had to offer and questioned our good faith, which upset Beaverbrook more than it upset me. Stalin expressed the view that we wanted to see his regime destroyed—otherwise we would have offered more assistance. "The paucity of your offers clearly shows", he said, "that you want to see the Soviet Union defeated." Whether this was just a tactical move to smoke us out and make us increase our offer, I do not know; but the fact that he said what he did reflected his deep distrust.

There was an even graver display of Stalin's misgivings later in the war when General Karl Wolff, a senior SS-commander in Italy, attempted to make contact with the Anglo-American Command to negotiate the surrender of German forces in Italy.

Yes, known as the "Berne Incident", this really showed Stalin's mistrust of his allies in an ugly light. To cut a long story short: Stalin was gripped by the bitter suspicion that the US and Britain were negotiating to accept without Soviet participation the surrender, not only of German forces facing them on the Italian front, but of Germany as a whole. Despite Roosevelt's repeated and painstaking assurances to the contrary, Stalin in fact accused the Western Allies of betraying the Alliance. In his note of 3 April 1945, he told Roosevelt that he, Stalin, had reliable information that Marshal Kesselring had agreed to open the Western front and permit the Anglo-American troops to advance to the heart of Germany and then to the East.[3]

There was, of course, absolutely no truth in this. In any case, nothing ever came of General Wolff's suggested negotiations; but the incident did show up Stalin's morbidly suspicious nature.

Roosevelt was furious. Having trusted Stalin, he expected Stalin's trust in return. He now saw himself accused as a traitor to the Alliance, a liar and a dupe. He gave Stalin as good as he got, telling him of his "bitter resentment" for the "vile misrepresentations" of his [Roosevelt's] actions.[4]

Didn't Roosevelt's hope to have his "trust returned" betray a less than adequate knowledge of what constitutes "morality" for a Marxist-Leninist?

The incident was a rather devastating display of Stalin's suspicious nature and had little to do with the actual facts of the suggested negotiations, but it went a lot deeper than that. Stalin, like other Soviet leaders, believed in the ultimate inevitability of a confrontation between the Soviet system and "capitalist imperialism." He did not trust us, and he could not believe that we would deal with him fairly.

Stalin's cable to Roosevelt was the most insulting I had seen. The President was deeply offended. It made him suddenly realise what the post-War world was going to be like. Yet, as always in dealing with Stalin, he left the door open.

Was Stalin's mistrust reciprocated? Did you feel at any time that Stalin might come to terms with Hitler, or accept a German surrender from other German leaders behind the backs of Britain and the US?

No, I never had any basis for suspicion that Stalin would not fight it out to the end. I do not think that was possible. Too much bitterness had accumulated between the Russians and Nazi Germany—too many terrible things had happened. Some Pentagon generals, however, feared that if America got too tough with the Russians, Stalin might break up the Alliance and make a separate peace with Hitler. But, as I say, I was convinced that a second Stalin-Hitler pact was not on the cards.

Hitler himself, in his final months in the Berlin bunker, certainly thought that he could come to terms with Stalin more easily than with the Western Allies. His argument was—and this was not unreasonable—that Stalin could turn the tide by the stroke of a pen, whereas Roosevelt and Churchill were prisoners of democratic public opinion and could therefore not change course as swiftly.

If Hitler thought that Stalin could be turned, he was certainly wrong.

He was; but doesn't his reasoning tell us something about the kinship of dictators—even when they find themselves in mortal combat with each other? We have quite a bit of evidence that Roosevelt, and Churchill too,

felt, at least in 1942, that the affinity between the two totalitarian systems, and Stalin's terrible losses in 1941-42, might persuade Stalin to seek a separate understanding with Hitler, as he had done in 1939.

This is a matter for speculation.

Our most telling evidence of Stalin's morbid mistrust of his Allies comes from Charles Bohlen, Roosevelt's wartime interpreter (and later US Ambassador to Moscow). He recalls "a rather acrimonious accusation by Stalin, at one of the dinners, that Churchill had secret sympathies with the Germans. . . ."

Bohlen ascribes Stalin's outburst to his irritation at the postponement of the Second Front and Churchill's refusal to set a definite date for the invasion. If so, doesn't this show Stalin at his most arrogant (or purposely provocative)? For it was Britain that fought Germany single-handed after the fall of France, while Stalin was enjoying the benefits of his Pact with Hitler. Indeed, as you show in your memoirs, when, in the late summer of 1941, Churchill received Stalin's first demand for a Second Front, he was moved to tell the Soviet Ambassador in London:

> *Remember that only four months ago we in this Island did not know whether you were not coming in against us on the German side. Indeed we thought it quite likely that you would. You of all people have no right to make reproaches to us.*

I was in Moscow with Churchill when the words Bohlen cites must have been spoken. I have no recollection of them, but it is quite possible that Stalin made the remark on some occasion when I was not present. Stalin would use shock-tactics as well as flattery if he felt that either could further his purpose.

Professor Tucker, to return to him for a moment, quotes in corroboration of his view of Stalin's paranoia the testimony of such friendly witnesses as Stalin's daughter, Svetlana, who uses the words "persecution mania" to describe her father's condition. Did you see any sign of this in Stalin's behaviour?

No, I don't think Stalin was paranoid—nothing, at least, that I could observe during our negotiations and personal talks led me to believe that he was.

The remarks he made to Churchill were probably intended to annoy the British leader, to draw him out and get him to come up with a better offer. Stalin made a habit of being somewhat rude to Churchill in front of Roosevelt too, as for example at the Yalta conference. He never took liberties with Roosevelt. Of course, Churchill was a master of the pen and the word, and knew how to fend for himself. Stalin's accusations of British disloyalty on the second night of our 1942 Moscow talks induced Churchill (as I have already said) to make one of the most extraordinary speeches I have ever heard. With great composure, very quietly, and without losing his temper, Churchill told Stalin what Britain had done during the War and completely refuted Stalin's accusations. I was really surprised that Churchill preserved his calm so well, seeing the criticism Stalin had hurled at him. It was a masterly performance by a great statesman and orator.

Much has been written about Stalin's behaviour at dinner and after dinner, both on formal occasions with foreign statesmen such as yourself, Roosevelt and Churchill, and among his Communist cronies. Were these enjoyable occasions?

"Enjoyable" is not quite the word that would come to my mind. I would say they were fascinating experiences. Stalin took tremendous interest in these formal banquets. He was very conscious of protocol. He showed concern for everybody. He went round the room at different times, toasting everyone involved in any kind of official activity. No one was ignored. He made these dinners very lively—he brought everybody in.

Stalin's parties were known for their inordinate length, the amount of alcohol consumed, and their rather earthy baiting and bantering. Did you ever see Stalin not fully in control of himself? Khrushchev in his The Last Testament *speaks of one such occasion: ". . . soon he [Stalin] was so drunk that he didn't even know who this Petru Groza was any more." Svetlana, too, records: "One day . . . my father did have too much to drink and sang folksongs with Smirnov, the Minister of Health."*

No, I never saw Stalin out of control; but, then, the accounts you are hinting at refer to Stalin's rather more intimate sessions with his comrades and foreign Communists. It was there that Khrushchev was made to dance a Ukrainian dance, and Beria disgraced himself on a variety of occasions. Molotov, too, was rather fond of taking a little more than was good for him. I never saw Stalin less than fully in control of himself. When I sat next to him at dinner I noticed that he would drink one glass of pepper vodka; but the rest of the toasts were drunk in white wine in very small glasses so that during the course of a long evening he consumed very little. Stalin was very careful in his relations with other people. He kept a watchful eye on them. I can well imagine that if he was suspicious of someone he would try to get him drunk to see how he behaved. But, as I say, he would never put himself in a position where he was not master of the situation.

Milovan Djilas feels that the desperate indulgence of the cabal around Stalin in drink and bravado was an expression of the conspiratorial nature of the Soviet Leadership. They drank and talked to excess because they were unsure of their legitimacy. Would you agree with that?

I was not there, hence it is not my business to say whether he is right or wrong. I always found Stalin controlled and self-confident.

You spoke of Stalin's great sense of realism. I wonder how this accords with Djilas's account of an after-dinner

film-show he attended in Stalin's company. "Throughout the performance", Djilas reports, "Stalin made comments—reactions to what was going on, in the manner of uneducated men who mistake artistic reality for actuality." Did Stalin behave in a like manner during the film-shows you attended?

No, I never saw him behave like that. Stalin had a great liking for the Viennese type of operettas and waltzes and certain American musicals written in that style. I saw him enjoying those. But I never saw him egg on a film's hero or berate the villain. I take Djilas's account with a grain of salt. I find it hard to reconcile with Stalin's realism.

Would you say that Stalin was a formative influence in your political career? Would your life-experience be poorer and thinner if you had not met Stalin and not worked with him?

I never thought of Stalin in that framework. I have had so many fascinating experiences in my life that I would only say that my dealings with Stalin were among many *other* fascinating ones.

Not the outstanding experience in the sense of adding some new dimension to your knowledge of human affairs?

No, I would not say so. My relationship with Roosevelt was much more important and more interesting.

"History does not know a despot as brutal and as cynical as Stalin was", Djilas writes in Conversations with Stalin. *"He was all-embracing, and total as a criminal. He was one of those rare and terrible dogmatists capable of destroying nine-tenths of the human race to 'make happy' the remaining tenth."*

I would have thought that working with a man like that would be a memorable and rather mind-expanding occasion even though the "monster" in Stalin (to use Djilas's word) was carefully hidden from the eyes of foreign visitors.

It was, of course, memorable to work with Stalin, but it was not an experience I would hold up as unique and put way above the others. I had to deal with Stalin as head of the Russian government. He was important to us and we were important to him. I was not interested in the psychology of his character, the secret of his rule, or any of the other philosophical matters that exercise your curiosity. I would summarise my relationship with Stalin in a single phrase: a contest of wills. That was all.

Have you ever puzzled over Stalin's doodlings? Beaverbrook reports that Stalin was in the habit of drawing pictures of wolves and filling in the background in red pencil. Emil Ludwig also saw him draw images in red pencil but never using the blue end.[5] Would you have an explanation for his doodlings?

Stalin was a doodler—that's all. He did it all the time. I did not pay as much attention to this as Beaverbrook did.

He was more curious about that sort of thing than I was. I don't know why people doodle. Psychologists claim to have explanations. I don't. Have you?

I would hazard that Stalin's wolves were the "enemy" about to be consumed by the red fire of Soviet power and revolution.

It is too much of a guess. I would not want to speculate.

III. THE SECOND FRONT & EASTERN EUROPE

Hindsight, as you rightly say, is a treacherous perspective, yet I find it difficult to resist asking you: If Churchill and Roosevelt had known in 1942 or 1943 what they were to know in 1945, would they not have done well to pick up Stalin's urgent appeals for a Second Front and launch the invasion of Europe in 1943 rather than 1944? This would have changed the entire post-War map of Europe, admittedly at some cost to the Western allies, but also to their immense advantage in terms of the post-War world balance of power. One can say with as much certainty as anything is certain in history that an invasion in 1943 would have seen the whole of Germany, Austria, Czechoslovakia, Hungary and Yugoslavia liberated by the Anglo-American forces.

My question, then, is: Was the postponement of the Second Front, first from 1942 to 1943 and then to 1944, really inevitable, and did Roosevelt and Churchill have a realistic appreciation of the price they would have to pay for the delays?

The story of this harassed chapter of Anglo-American-Soviet relations is well known; so I will restrict myself to saying that in 1942 we were militarily unprepared to go in. The Russians had some legitimate grounds for complaint because a statement approved by President Roosevelt at the time of Molotov's visit to Washington in June 1942 did speak of the "urgent tasks of creating a Second Front in Europe in 1942", even though Churchill was more cautious and refused on his part to promise that a Second Front would, in fact, be launched that year.

Plans were being made for major action in Europe in 1943, but this would have meant building up large US forces in Britain over a long period of time and keeping them inactive until all was ready for the actual invasion. Moreover, Churchill and the British generals were unenthusiastic. Their troops and equipment were inadequate, and Churchill had a predilection for not striking at the heart of Europe at that particular time, but rather going round it via North Africa, Italy and the Balkans. Roosevelt's great worry was that if large American forces remained idle in the United Kingdom he would find it impossible to fend off demands inside the US for a Pacific-First strategy. That was the reason why Churchill's plan for a North African operation as a substitute had a great appeal for Roosevelt and was eventually accepted, even though our Chiefs of Staff were unenthusiastic about it.

For all these reasons, and in the tenth of Stalin's bitter charges that the Western Allies were not pulling their weight and were too cowardly to tangle with the Germans, the Second Front could not be launched until June 1944. Even then, Churchill and his generals were worried and diffident. I saw Churchill a month before the invasion and found him, even at that late hour, torn by doubt. He was deeply worried about the disaster that might flow from the operation if the landings should fail. He told me that if the Anglo-American forces were pushed back into the sea, the Americans would have lost a battle but the British would have incurred the loss of their whole military capability.

I don't like to indulge in the might-have-beens of history. Roosevelt was convinced that it was in our national interests to defeat Hitler first and not to enter into premature speculation as to whether the Soviets might outflank us in a post-War settlement, or we them. People who now tell us that we ought to have had more foresight and pre-empted this or that Soviet move are wise after the event. They don't realise the political pressures of the time.

Nevertheless, looking back from the comfortable position we are now in and permitting ourselves the luxury of some speculation, would you not agree that if Roosevelt had been strong enough to fend off the Pacific-Firsters, the invasion might have been successfully launched in 1943 despite British military weakness and British hesitation? In which case the Russians would never have reached Berlin or perhaps even got as far West as Warsaw?

General Marshall put all the heat he possibly could on the British, but he did not realise just how weak the British were. They had some 28 divisions, none of them fully equipped, some of them only 25% up to strength. They were paper divisions. It would have been a disaster to go ashore with them. We had difficulty enough achieving what we did in 1944—remember the Germans' Ardennes offensive. In 1943 it was militarily just not possible to launch the Second Front with any prospect of success.

Macmillan made a speech the other day in which he, too, said that we should have gone into Germany from the South much earlier in the War, taken Vienna and advanced from there to the heart of Germany. All sorts of people are now telling us how we should have fought the War. I'm not going to indulge in any second-guessing. My obligation to history is to record what happened and why, and not to speculate what might have been a better course of action seen with the wisdom of hindsight.

Isn't it rather ironic, though, that Stalin was pressing so hard and with such bitterness for the Second Front from 1941 all the way to 1944! If Britain and the US had been able and willing to do what he was asking, an early Second Front would have boomeranged back on his own expansionist ambitions. I do, of course, realise, that Stalin was under extreme military pressure and had no choice but to ask for military assistance from any quarter he could get it.

Precisely. After Hitler's attack had taken him by complete surprise, Stalin lost a large part of his armies, many of his best generals and officers. He was facing disaster, hence he was most anxious to have some of the pressure taken off his forces. That is why he was so doggedly pleading for a Second Front. The prospect of victory was very distant, and any post-War jockeying for advantage in Europe was more distant still. The first priority was to avoid defeat. That explains Stalin's insistence.

When General Eisenhower reached some 120 miles into what was to become the Soviet Zone of Occupation, Churchill urged President Truman that the Western Allies should make the withdrawal of Eisenhower's forces conditional on correct Soviet behaviour in Central and Eastern Europe. He wanted the Americans to stand pat on the Elbe and thus force Stalin to live up to his Yalta obligations. On the advice of the US State and War Departments, however, Churchill's suggestion was turned down by President Truman. Do you feel that this was the right decision?

I had nothing to do with that decision. I was always for maximum pressure on the Soviets. I thought, however, that Churchill's suggestion was not very practical because agreements made under duress generally do not hold. It is hard enough to get an agreement with the Soviets that is freely entered into and make it stick! Also, acceptance of Churchill's idea would have landed us with clear responsibility for the Cold War without ultimately changing things much in Eastern Europe; for in the last analysis there was nothing we could have done to prevent unilateral Soviet action in Eastern Europe short of going to war with the Russians. Some American officers and some of the French were talking of doing just that, but I do not think that American public opinion would have stood for it. The mood in America was one of solidarity with the Soviet Union, and there was a war to be won with Japan.

But would it not have been in line with your own thinking for the Anglo-American forces to penetrate as far to the East as they could and force Stalin's hand from a position of strength—force him, that is, to respect the Yalta agreement? We learn from your memoirs that in April 1945, in your talks with the Pentagon and State Department, you expounded the view that

> *Stalin's insistence upon a belt of weak, easily dominated neighbouring states was not limited to Eastern Europe. Once the Soviet Union had control of the bordering areas . . . it would probably attempt to penetrate the next layer of adjacent countries. [I] saw no virtue in waiting; the issue was best fought out as far to the East as possible.*

I felt at the time that we ought to have taken Berlin, which was well within our grasp. Hanging on to 120 miles of German territory, however, did not seem to me anything as exciting. Berlin would have been something tangible and well worth holding, and I do regret that we did not take it. But remember that we were bound by the agreement we had made with the Russians about the division of Germany into national zones of occupation, and the rationale of that agreement was not so much to parcel out German territory as to avoid any fighting between the Soviet and Western Allied forces. For all these reasons, and also because he overestimated the strength of German resistance further south, Eisenhower held back and then withdrew to the zonal boundary. There was, furthermore, another important factor. If we had refused to evacuate the Soviet zone of occupation, the Soviets would most probably have retaliated in Austria by refusing to withdraw from *our* zone of occupation there, in which case Austria today would be a Soviet satellite.

More generally: you must remember that we were not looking for a fight with the Russians. We were looking for the defeat of Hitler with the minimum cost in American lives. That was what Roosevelt was trying to do, and I think history will say that he did it very well. I am, of course, interested in how we could have done better; I am interested in listening to it, but not in joining the discussion.

But wouldn't you agree that Churchill's sombre forecast, soon to be borne out by events, could have been turned to good account if American government thinking had been informed by a more sophisticated sense of history? On 12 May 1945 Churchill wrote to Truman:

> *An iron curtain is drawn upon their [the Russians'] front. There seems little doubt that the whole of the regions east of the line Lübeck-Trieste-Corfu will soon be completely in their hands. To this must be added the further enormous area conquered by the American armies between Eisenach and the Elbe, which will, I suppose,, in a few weeks be occupied, when the Americans retreat, by the Russian power. . . .*

Both the State Department and the Pentagon were against using the presence of American troops in the Soviet zone as a bargaining counter. Harry Hopkins advised the President that an American failure to withdraw would be violating an agreement made in good faith only a short time earlier. There was also the consideration that the Russians would not permit the Allied Control Council to function in Berlin until we evacuated the Soviet zone. On 11 June 1945, therefore, Truman told Churchill that he was "unable to delay the withdrawal of US troops from the Soviet zone in order to use pressure in the settlement of other problems."

Even in retrospect, I don't think we could have forced the Russians to allow freely elected governments to function in Eastern Europe if we had done what Churchill suggested. Churchill's gloomy vision was borne out by events, but the factors I have listed militated against accepting his counsel.

Just how strongly did you feel about the suggestion you had made to the Pentagon and the State Department that the Western Allies' quarrel with the Russians should be "fought out as far to the East as possible"?

Another distinguished observer of the Soviet scene, Mr George Kennan, felt (as he tells us in his Memoirs) that the US did not have the power to affect Soviet behaviour in Eastern Europe and that it would be a mistake for America to make a big fight over it. The US, he suggested, should not share any of the moral opprobrium for what the Russians were doing in Eastern Europe.

My own feeling was that unless we fought it out in Eastern Europe, the Russians would be moving to the next area further West. Having given up our first line of defence, we would then have to make a stand anyway, but under conditions far less favourable.

I remember meeting Stalin at Potsdam in 1945 and congratulating him on arriving in Berlin after all the trials his country had gone through. He looked at me meaningly and said: "Czar Alexander I got to Paris!"

What I suppose he intended to convey was not, as many people now think, that he wanted his armed forces to conquer the rest of Europe, but that he felt that the Communist Parties of France and Italy were strong enough to take control of the governments there, which would then open the way for Stalin to move in.

It was precisely to counter that threat and to work out a programme for European recovery that President Truman appointed a Committee under my chairmanship. We were very active trying to prevent the expansion of Soviet power to Western Europe and, as you know, our work was not unsuccessful. A second volume of my memoirs, which is now in preparation, will give the details of this story.

Was it not surprising in the light of the "Berne Incident", and the Nazis' justified (and one might say well-deserved) fear of the Russians that they did not open the Western front to the Anglo-American forces and permit a much larger part of Germany to be occupied than the Western Allies actually succeeded in doing?

I was, from the very beginning, not very happy about the division of Germany into zones of occupation, because I thought the Germans would fight the Russians every inch of the way but would let us in and enable us to occupy a much larger part of Germany or indeed the whole of it. They did, in fact, put up a tremendous fight against the Russians; but they fought us too.

Why did they mount the Ardennes offensive? Was it a last desperate attempt to raise morale in Germany, or was Hitler entertaining hopes on the lines I have suggested, i.e. that he might pull off a sudden cease fire with Stalin, in which case he would want to hold off the Americans as far to the West as he could?

I don't suppose anyone in Hitler's forces had the courage to let the enemy in, no matter which enemy. The Ardennes offensive? I cannot explain it, but as I keep telling my friends, I was never hired to be a prophet. It is an interesting question, and if you have a good answer, I'd be glad if you'd let me know. In any case, in the last few weeks of the War the Germans no longer put up a great fight against us, whereas they did fight the Russians.

Hitler hoped and to some extent believed to the very end of the War that the Allies would fall out with each other, in which case either Stalin or the Western Allies would want to enlist the Germans on their side; and, as we know, he was anxiously examining every scrap of information that appeared to support his hopes, as well as reading and re-reading the story of Frederick the Great, who in the Seven Years War snatched victory out of the jaws of defeat by the sudden disintegration of the unity of his enemies. This is the only theory I can come up with, and it is, of course, widely held by historians. Hitler, on this showing, ordered the Ardennes offensive to gain time and raise morale in the hinterland. There was always some straw in the wind a desperate man could clutch at. If he took a large enough view, he could, for example, take some general comfort from Senator (as he then was) Truman's words: "If we see that Germany is winning we ought to help Russia, and if Russia is winning we ought to help Germany and that way let them kill as many as possible. . . . "

Ah, but Truman also said that he would not want to see Hitler victorious under any circumstance! "Neither of them thinks anything of their pledged word. . . . "

On 14 December 1944 (as you tell us in your memoirs) you saw Stalin and discussed with him Eisenhower's difficulties in reaching the Rhine before the winter set in. You asked him to acquaint you with his plans for winter operations so that Eisenhower might make his own arrangements accordingly. Stalin explained the causes of delay on the Polish front (bad weather etc.) and made the "astonishing suggestion" (already, in fact, made to Churchill in October) that five to six Allied divisions, later to be increased to eight to ten, should be landed in Northern Yugoslavia, advance on Zagreb, and eventually join up with Soviet troops on Austrian soil. You replied that this was something Churchill had been advocating for a long time, warning that an amphibious operation of this kind would take very careful preparation.

Stalin's proposal was indeed astonishing, for at the 1943 Teheran conference he had fought off Churchill's plan for just that kind of an operation as an alternative to a Second Front in France. We can only speculate about its meaning. Does it suggest to you in retrospect that as late as December 1944 Stalin was not sure whether Yugoslavia, Hungary, Austria and Czechoslovakia would come within his sphere of influence, and that he was prepared to settle for far less than he got in 1945? Stalin must have known that if eight to ten Western divisions drove a wedge from Zagreb to Vienna, the future of the Communist régime in Yugoslavia, and of

Hungary, Austria and Czechoslovakia as possible satellites, would be jeopardised.

You must remember that in October-December 1944 extremely bitter fighting was still going on on all fronts. My guess would be that Stalin was anxious to get German divisions diverted from the Eastern front. If we could be persuaded to land in Dalmatia at short notice, he would get large German forces off his neck. This might admittedly have limited his penetration in the South, but it would have made it easier for him to advance rapidly in the North and take a great deal more of German territory than he eventually did manage to occupy. I am as certain as anybody can be that Stalin at that stage did not have a master plan to turn Yugoslavia, Hungary, Austria and Czechoslovakia into Communist buffer states and satellites. He did so, or attempted to do so, once his forces were there. But in December 1944 he would have been just as glad to see his way made a little less arduous in the North. Germany was, after all, a greater prize than any other part of Europe.

There is also an alternative and rather Yugo-centric explanation which I put to Milovan Djilas in embryonic form in 1979. By the autumn of 1944 there were tensions and misunderstandings between Tito and Stalin. Stalin would not allow that a "Communist" revolution was taking place in Yugoslavia; he was gravely suspicious that Tito might puncture his monopoly. Moreover, Stalin went on recognising and maintaining diplomatic relations with the Yugoslav monarchy, which was anathema to Tito. Stalin's initiative for an Anglo-American landing in Yugoslavia was, according to this theory, a veiled threat to Tito: If you don't toe the Moscow line you will come under Anglo-American occupation and that will be the end of your régime. (Tito, we must remember, was extremely hostile to the Western Allies and especially apprehensive about a British landing in Dalmatia.)

Would this make sense to you?

What was Djilas's reaction?

"Possibly so", he said rather laconically, but said no more.

I would not even go as far as that. It is, to my mind, unlikely that Stalin would have suggested so big an operation with such unforeseeable consequences just to threaten Tito. I am, of course, in no position to analyse fully the Yugoslav point of view, but my guess would be that Stalin was led by purely military considerations. He was anxious to reach the northern parts of Germany via Poland as rapidly as he could, and for that he needed some pressure to be taken off his central front. In any case, the landings were never made. Incidentally, I don't know Djilas. I always wanted to meet him because I'd like to see into the mind of a man who, having been an avid Communist, then decided that Communism was not for him. I once asked Tito (after Djilas's second imprisonment, if I remember correctly) whether I could meet Djilas, but he said "Better not. . . . "

IV. CZAR & COMMISSAR

You have pointed out repeatedly in this conversation that your job in Moscow was to keep the Russians fighting and save American lives. This may have been an entirely justified policy in terms of American national interest, but it did make the Soviet Union bear the brunt of the War both in material devastation and human sacrifice. Soviet losses in dead alone were about twenty times those of the US and the British Empire combined.

My impression is that some of the US indulgence shown towards Soviet expansionism in the final phases of the War and for a short time after the War was due to a tacit American recognition that the Russians had done most of the bleeding and taken most of the punishment. In other words: the American public was, perhaps only subconsciously, burdened with a feeling of a "debt unpaid" which it was anxious to pay off in some form.

The Soviets, of course, have never stopped claiming in their propaganda that they won the War either single-handed or with minimal assistance from the Allies. Indeed, during the War, it was already (in the words of Deutscher) Stalin's "stock argument that the place any nation was to be allowed to keep in peace should be proportionate to the strength it had shown and the sacrifices it had borne during the War. . . . " Accordingly, Stalin never permitted the Soviet public to be informed of Lend-Lease; and he kept it in the dark about the Anglo-American bombing of Germany and the magnitude of the American and British War effort.

I should imagine it was not difficult for you and your colleagues in Moscow to infer that every time Stalin launched one of his bitter recriminations against the Anglo-American side for being too slow and too much afraid to take on the Germans, he was building up credit for himself as head of a country which was bearing most of the sacrifices and thereby earning the right to present the bill at the appropriate time?

I was not conscious that American public opinion did show such indulgence towards the Russians. Apart from occasional visits to the States, I was in Europe throughout the War, so I cannot speak from experience; but I was not conscious of it at all.

Now, Stalin never reprimanded us for not pulling our weight in the War. I would have answered him if he had; I would have given him a very strong reply. The Soviets would not have survived if we had not helped them, and on at least one occasion Stalin himself acknowledged his debt. Speaking in Churchill's presence in the British Embassy in October 1944, Stalin said that there was a time when Great Britain and Russia between them could handle the affairs of Europe. Together they had fought the Germans in World War I; but in World War II, Britain and Russia could not have prevailed over Germany. He doubted, Stalin said, whether Germany could have been defeated without the full weight of the United States on the side of the Allies.

Stalin said Germany could not have been defeated without American help. Is this quite the same as saying that Russia could not have survived without American assistance?

If we had not sent them the massive supplies we did, the Russians could not have survived. When I say "survive", they would perhaps not have been thoroughly conquered, but they *would* have been pushed back to the Urals and probably beyond. We supplied them with an enormous amount of war materials—worth about twelve billion dollars at Wartime prices.

We have already spoken of your inability, in 1944, to convince Roosevelt of "the importance of a vigilant, firm policy in dealing with the political aspects in various Eastern European countries." Would it be too wild a conjecture that Roosevelt's attitude was at least coloured by the indulgence which (in my assumption) American public opinion and much of the American political class showed towards the Soviet Union at that particular time?

I think it would. America was suffering from no guilt complex *vis-à-vis* the Russians. President Roosevelt just did not have a very good understanding of the problems of Eastern Europe; and he realised, as the Russians were moving deeper and deeper into Eastern Europe, that he would be powerless to exert any real influence there.

What was the President's reaction to the division of Eastern Europe into spheres of influence on a by now extremely famous piece of paper on which Churchill wrote down the percentages? The story as told by Churchill is well known:

> *The moment was apt for business, so I said: "Let us settle about our affairs in the Balkans. Your armies are in Bulgaria and Rumania. We have interests, missions and agents there. Don't let us get at cross purposes in small ways. So far as Britain and Russia are concerned, how would it do for you to have ninety percent predominance in Rumania, for us to have ninety percent of the say in Greece, and go fifty-fifty about Yugoslavia?*

While his words were being put into Russian, Churchill wrote down these percentages on a piece of paper, adding a 50-50 division for Hungary and giving the Kremlin a 75-25 predominance in Bulgaria.

> *I pushed this across to Stalin. . . . There was a slight pause. Then he took his blue pencil and made a large tick upon it, and passed it back to us. It was all settled in no more time than it takes to set down. . . .*
>
> *After this there was a long silence. The pencilled paper lay in the centre of the table. At length I said, 'Might it not be thought rather cynical if it seemed we had disposed of these issues, so fateful to*

millions of people, in such an offhand manner? Let us burn the paper.' 'No, you keep it,' said Stalin.

I never took this thing seriously, and I don't think it was important as it did not affect the future. Stalin, as we know, ignored it even though Churchill always claimed that Stalin respected the Greek side of the bargain in the sense that the Greek Communists received their aid from Yugoslavia, not Russia. This so-called agreement was one of those rather spectacular non-events that historians tend to pick up and make much of. The United States was not party to the bargain. Indeed Roosevelt dissociated himself in *advance* from any understanding Churchill might reach with Stalin during their Moscow talks in October 1944.

You see, Churchill was anxious to have a *tête-à-tête* with Stalin on two principal topics: Russian participation in the war against Japan and the future of Eastern Europe. He wanted to have full American participation, which Roosevelt, however, refused. Indeed he sent a message to Stalin through myself, making it absolutely clear that Churchill was not authorised to speak for the United States.

"I am firmly convinced", Roosevelt wrote, "that the three of us, and only the three of us, can find the solution of the questions still unresolved. In this sense, while appreciating Mr Churchill's desire for the meeting, I prefer to regard your forthcoming talks with the Prime Minister as preliminary to a meeting of the three of us. . . . Mr Harriman naturally will not be in a position to commit this Government in respect to the important matters which very naturally will be discussed by you and Mr Churchill." Churchill was, of course, disappointed that Roosevelt declined to authorise American participation, and Stalin, too, expressed his embarrassment. He expected that Churchill was coming to Moscow on the strength of agreements reached at the Quebec conference and thus fully authorised to speak for the US too. But this was not so. When Churchill put his spheres-of-influence ideas on the table I was not even present. I was informed about it by Churchill several days after the event, even though (quite mistakenly) Churchill in his book lists me as one of the participants.

But once the spheres-of-influence agreement (if that is what it was) had been reached, Roosevelt did not disown it.

He knew nothing about it and had nothing to do with it. He had (as I say) disowned everything Churchill said or agreed to *before* Churchill undertook his trip to Moscow. He made it very plain to Churchill and very plain to me that he didn't want Churchill to go and see Stalin in the first place, and then that he would not be bound in any way by anything Churchill told Stalin or agreed with Stalin. It never crossed Roosevelt's mind that Churchill would come up with a spheres-of-influence proposal.

In any case, I did not take this so-called agreement seriously, and if I did not take it seriously at the time it could not have been very serious, because I was there on the spot, quite able to judge what was important and what was not.

Did the spheres-of-influence agreement have any impact on your work in 1945 in Rumania as member of the Harriman-Clark Kerr-Vishinsky Commission?

None whatever. The Russians, of course, imposed their government on King Michael in any case, despite our repeated protests, but Churchill's agreement with Stalin never came up as a point of reference. We insisted on completely free elections as agreed at Yalta, under the Atlantic Charter and in the Rumanian Armistice Agreement, but the spheres-of-influence agreement just did not come into the picture. Even the Russians made no reference to it although they might have quoted it in their favour as Churchill had given them a 90% interest in Rumania. In a message to Churchill of 11 March 1945 Roosevelt said that he was determined not to let the Yalta decisions slip through his fingers in Rumania; and he commented with some bitterness that the Russians had installed a minority government of their own choosing. He refrained, however, from so much as mentioning the Churchill-Stalin understanding. So much for the importance of that famous piece of paper.

Historians are divided on the question whether Russian national interest or Communist ideology was the motor behind Stalin's expansionism and indeed whether one or the other is the motor behind the expansionism of Stalin's successors. Without necessarily assuming that the choice has to be "either/or", let me ask you whether you thought Stalin was exploiting the patriotism of the Russian people in order to advance world revolution, or whether, on the contrary, he was using Communist ideology to advance Russian national, not to say imperial, interests?

Stalin and the Soviet government had and have both objectives. The expansion of Russia as a national state promotes, in their eyes, the triumph of Communism, and the advance of Communism serves old-fashioned, Czarist, imperial ends. Whether the first or the second took precedence in the mind of Stalin I was not able to judge. He was certainly convinced that the Soviet type of system was the one which the whole of mankind was sooner or later destined to adopt and that it was his responsibility to put maximum pressure on whomever or whatever stood in the way. I doubt whether he or his colleagues ever stopped to ask themselves which of the two was their principal motivation, and I doubt whether anyone in the present Soviet leadership does.

Yet Stalin was a cautious revolutionary and a cautious imperialist. He believed in the inevitability of world revolution, but he was not prepared to endanger the Soviet state by pushing the revolution too far to the West. Poland, however, was a different matter for him. This was the traditional invasion route for both Napoleon and Hitler. He was determined to keep control of it.

Would you agree that Stalin and his successors have been able to use the message of Communism as an excellent tool for Russian expansionism—a much more effective weapon than Orthodoxy and Panslavism with their necessarily limited appeal?

I would not disagree with that. My own view, however, is that Bolshevism has no appeal, or should have none, because it is a reactionary development. The dictatorship of the proletariat is an historically regressive idea for it makes the individual a servant of the state, robs him of his power of decision, and is thus at odds with the aspirations of mankind. This was my view after I had first visited Russia in 1926, and I have had no reason to change it.

How did Roosevelt see the relative importance of Russian national ambition and Communism in the mind of Stalin?

Roosevelt was a religious man. He did not think that the atheist Communist system could permanently suppress the Russian people's religious instincts and traditions. He thought that in time the Soviet system was bound to become more liberal.

He looked upon Stalin's international policies as a combination of traditional Russian imperialism and an ideological drive to advance world Communism. He felt that, after the War, Soviet revolutionary evangelism would slowly recede and self-interest would increasingly become the guide to Soviet policy.

But in your personal judgment this hope has clearly not been borne out by facts, because in your book Peace with Russia? *(and the question-mark in that title already tells us something about your views) you observed in 1960 that the Soviet leaders' "plans for developing Russia for the Russians are subordinate to the main goal of world revolution. Though their methods have changed since Stalin's time, their aims remain the same. . . . "*

Yes, Roosevelt would have been disappointed. He would have been disappointed on another score too. He believed that our intimate cooperation with the Russians during the War could and should serve as a basis for post-War collaboration. He was determined to establish a close personal relationship with Stalin so that after the War the Soviet leaders would have confidence in the West. He was aware that the devastation of vast areas of Russia would call for a great effort at reconstruction, and he was prepared to offer generous American help. He was anxious to help Russia establish itself as a leading and respected member of the family of nations.

I did not disagree with Roosevelt's approach, but I was convinced that it would be far more difficult to establish a basis of confidence with Stalin than Roosevelt thought. Churchill was even more cautious. He too wanted a post-War understanding with the Kremlin, but he despised Communism and all its works and had his eye on specific political problems. He foresaw much greater political difficulties with the Soviet leaders after the War than Roosevelt did.

What were your thoughts when you first discovered that several thousand American war-prisoners, whom the Soviet forces had found in Poland, weren't treated at all well by their Soviet liberators—that the Russians could not be moved to expedite their return to the US, that American food and medical supplies were not allowed to reach them, and that in many cases their belongings had been stolen by Russian troops and their lives threatened?

Well, of course the callousness of the Soviet attitude did not augur well for the prospects of post-War collaboration with the Russians. But I did not spend my time worrying about what would happen after the War. My job was to get our supplies to these men and to see them brought home, and I did just that. I was not really surprised that the Russians treated our men so badly. They knew no better. They treated their own people just as callously. There was a great deal of suffering on all sides.

Did you ask yourself: If this is the way they treat their allies who have supplied them with arms, raw materials and food in their hour of need, how are they going to treat their enemies and indeed their own war-prisoners in German hands?

I had no responsibility for the prisoners they took from enemy countries. My responsibility was for and to our own people, and I could not go beyond that. I should think you realise that I was extremely busy dealing with the War. I was not going to assume responsibility for people who were no concern of mine.

After a great deal of frustration, the Russians were eventually persuaded to sign an agreement with the US and British military representatives on the repatriation of Allied prisoners. General John R. Deane and his Soviet counterpart signed the relevant agreement shortly before Yalta. Your purpose was to get the 75,000 US servicemen located in territories overrun by the Russians back to America in the shortest possible time. But the agreement also provided for the repatriation of Soviet war-prisoners and other Soviet citizens found in territories occupied by the Western Allies. Were you aware of the implications of this agreement for millions of Russian soldiers and civilians found on German territory in May 1945?

The negotiations leading up to the agreement were exclusively the responsibility of General Deane and his British counterpart, General Burrows. They had been started some eight months before Yalta and were no part of the Yalta agreement.[6] Roosevelt never saw the document, and I got to know about it much after the event. When I did get to know about it, however, I was concerned; but I knew that General Deane's primary business was to get food and medical supplies to our men and get them out. It would have been a little too much to expect us to worry about Russian prisoners-of-war on German territory.

I don't think it ever occurred to anyone on our side that these Russians would refuse to return home because they had good reason to suspect that they would be sent to their deaths or to prison camps. In any case, if we claimed (as we did) the right to our prisoners in Russian hands, we could not very well deny the Russians their right to the repatriation of their own men in Germany. We could not have demanded something for us that we were not willing to grant them.

Did the United States Government have no information as to how Stalin was dealing with Soviet soldiers who had fallen into German captivity? With all due respect— Stalin's denunciation and the NKVD's treatment of these as "traitors" was public knowledge in Russia from the beginning of the German-Soviet war. So was the fact that when Stalin's son, Jacob, fell into German captivity and the Germans offered to exchange him, Stalin disowned his son as a traitor, and Jacob eventually died in a German war-prison.[7]

All that knowledge came later. At the time we could not be expected to prejudge the issue by assuming that the Russians would regard their prisoners-of-war as traitors and treat them as such. We could not guess that. The criticism is unjustified.

Nothing in the Soviet-Allied agreement required the US and British commanders to repatriate Soviet soldiers against their will. Unfortunately, the Russians insisted on this cruel interpretation of the agreement, and the Western Allies went along with it until about the spring of 1946, sending back hundreds of thousands of Russian men, women, and children. The US and British commanders were fearful that if these people were not forcibly repatriated, the Russians might refuse to repatriate our own men from Eastern Europe. It was a sorry business and easy to condemn in retrospect. But at the time our first concern was the fate of our own men.

Whatever one may think of the deeds and misdeeds of Joseph Stalin, the historian's job is to acknowledge that he left his "footprints in the sands of time." Was he liked? Was he feared? Was he worshipped? Was he hated?

My personal impression is that the ordinary Russian's attitude to Stalin in his life-time is well summed up by Ilya Ehrenburg (and I quote him with some reluctance because his integrity is not unimpeachable, but then, that may be the very thing that makes him so representative):

> *It would be too much to say that I liked Stalin, but for a long time I believed in him and I feared him. When I talked about him, I, like everybody else called him "The Boss." In the same way Jews in the past never pronounced the name of God. . . .*

How would you as a distinguished American who probably saw more of Stalin than any other Western statesman, sum up your mental image of Stalin?

Soon after the death of Stalin, Khrushchev and I discussed the self-same topic. Khrushchev said: "Like Peter the Great, Stalin fought barbarism with barbarism, but he was a great man."

That, I believe, is the truth about Stalin.

NOTES

[1] Svetlana Alliluyeva tells a different story of Stalin:

> . . . the cruel tragedies of those years didn't spare our family. In 1937 the brother of my father's first wife, an old-time Georgian Bolshevik, A. S. Svanidze, and his wife Maria were arrested. His sister Mariko was arrested, too. After that the husband of my mother's sister was arrested—the Polish Communist Stanislav Redens. The three Svanidzes and Redens perished in prison. Mama's sister was forbidden to visit us children. Her brother Paul died of a heart attack, shaken by the arrests of his relations and numerous friends, for whom he had vainly pleaded with my father. . . .

> My mother's sister, Anna, had gone mad in prison and had come home a sick woman. Yevgenia Alliluyeva, the widow of Mother's brother, bore it all, but she said she had signed all the accusations set before her: spying, poisoning her husband, contacts with foreigners. "You sign anything there", she would say, "just to be left alone and not tortured! At night no one could sleep for the shrieks of agony in the cells. Victims screamed in an unearthly way, begging to be killed, better be killed. . . ."

Only One Year (1969), pp. 148, 162

[2] On 23 August 1940, as the Battle of Britain was beginning in earnest, *Pravda* reminded its readers that the day coincided with the first anniversary of the Soviet-German Pact:

> The signing of the Pact put an end to the enmity between Germany and the USSR, an enmity which had been artificially worked up by the warmongers. . . . After the disintegration of the Polish state, Germany proposed to Britain and France the termination of the war—a proposal which was supported by the Soviet Government. But they would not listen, and the war continued, bringing hardships and suffering to all the nations whom the organisers of the war had dragged into the bloodbath. . . . We are neutral, and this Pact has made things easier for us; it has also been of great advantage to Germany, since she can be completely confident of peace on her Eastern borders.

[3] You insist that there have been no negotiations yet. It may be assumed that you have not been fully informed.

As regards my military colleagues, they, on the basis of data which they have on hand, do not have any doubts that the negotiations have taken place and that they have ended in an agreement with the Germans, on the basis of which the German commander on the Western front, Marshal Kesselring, has agreed to open the front and permit the Anglo-American troops to advance to the East and the Anglo-Americans have promised in return to ease for the Germans the peace terms. . . .

I understand that there are certain advantages for the Anglo-American troops as a result of these separate negotiations in Berne or in some other place, since the Anglo-American troops get the possibility to advance into the heart of Germany, almost without any resistance on the part of the Germans, but why was it necessary to conceal this from the Russians . . . ?

Stalin to Roosevelt, *Foreign Relations of the United States Diplomatic Papers* (1945, vol. III, p. 742

[4] . . . It would be one of the great tragedies of history if at the very moment of the victory, now within our grasp, such distrust, such lack of faith, should prejudice the entire undertaking after the colossal losses of life, material and treasure involved.

Frankly, I cannot avoid a feeling of bitter resentment towards your informers, whoever they are, for such vile misrepresentations of my actions or those of my trusted subordinates.

Foreign Relations, vol. III, p. 746

[5] He seemed to use the red end of his pencil to give free rein to his imagination as a man of power, and *did* in fact use the blue end, for settling administrative detail—for example, in approving Churchill's 1944 "spheres of influence" paper.

[6] The Yalta Agreement did in fact provide for the repatriation of all Soviet citizens, saying nothing, however, about the future of those who did not want to return. Ed. Note.

[7] Svetlana Alliluyeva records: "To my father the fact that Jacob had become a prisoner of war was nothing but a 'disgrace' before the whole world. In the USSR the news was kept under cover both during the War and after, although the press in the rest of the world was writing about it. And when a foreign correspondent officially asked for information on the subject, my father said that '. . . in Hitler's camps there are no Russian prisoners-of-war, only Russian traitors, and we shall do away with them when the War is over.' About Jacob he said, 'I have no son called Jacob.'" *Only One Year,* p. 370

Gregory Freidin (essay date 1982)

SOURCE: "Mandel'shtam's 'Ode to Stalin': History and Myth," in *The Russian Review,* Vol. 41, No. 4, October, 1982, pp. 400-26.

[In the following essay, Freidin examines the mysterious circumstances surrounding the writing and publication of Osip Mandel'shtam's "Ode to Stalin."]

If manuscripts do not burn, as Mikhail Bulgakov once suggested, they at least get hot sitting in the fire, which is more or less what happened to the "Ode to Stalin" by Osip Mandel'shtam.[1] The first indication that Mandel'shtam might have written something like the "Ode" came from Anna Akhmatova's recollections of Mandel'shtam and had the effect of a minor literary bombshell.[2] Two years later, in 1967, the issue was taken up in print by Clarence Brown who had been working on Mandel'shtam for nearly a decade.[3] In order to determine whether Mandel'shtam had actually written the "Ode," Brown analyzed some twenty-four poems composed during the Voronezh exile (1935-37), relating them to what he had been able to find out about the poet's life at that time. The conclusion of this first thorough and by no means outdated study of the later Mandel'shtam was largely negative. Hard as he tried, Mandel'shtam—it would seem—was unable to twist the arm of his muse even though he knew very well that a panegyric to Stalin might prolong his precarious existence. Yet, some pieces of the puzzle, such as Akhmatova's authoritative statement and the poem "Esli b menia nashi vragi vziali,"[4] did not fit the otherwise satisfying picture of a poet incapable of violating the integrity of his talent, and Brown decided to defer his final judgement, hoping that more conclusive evidence might eventually turn up.

The uncertainty was resolved by Nadezhda Mandel'shtam. In the first book of her memoirs, published in 1970, the poet's widow acknowledged the fact of the composition of the "Ode," adding that she had preserved the complete text of it for fear it would otherwise have survived in the "wild versions circulating in 1937."[5] However, it was not until 1975 that the poem itself, albeit seven lines short of complete, made its first appearance in print, published in the *Slavic Review* by an anonymous contributor.[6] A few months later a fuller version was included in a brief essay by Bengt Jangfeldt. In one important respect, Jangfeldt's account complemented, if not contradicted, the account of the poet's widow. Contrary to her assertion, an unnamed friend of the Mandel'shtams whom Jangfeldt cites, maintained that the poet "was not at all ashamed of the 'Stalin verses' . . . and read them on several occasions after his return from the Voronezh exile."[7]

The complete version of the "Ode," coming, one assumes, from Nadezhda Mandel'shtam herself, had to await the publication of the fourth volume of Mandel'shtam's *Collected Works* issued in Paris in 1980. But the controversy that had accompanied the "Ode" at least since Akhmatova's off-hand remark continued. A reviewer writing for *Russkaia mysl'* found it objectionable that the editors included the "Ode" in the main part of the volume instead of placing it with the annotations and setting it in "small type as it is ordinarily done."[8]

To use Pushkin's locution from the "Table Talk," the story of the "Ode's" publication is not savory but it does provide a credible picture of the ideological habits shared by many readers of Osip Mandel'shtam. Indeed the "Ode" clashes with the readers' image of Mandel'shtam all too powerfully, and if this image is to remain intact, if it is to continue to serve as a prism through which Mandel'shtam's poetry is perceived, a poem like the "Ode" (and there are others) will have to be stowed away in some dark corner (or is it a furnace?) reserved for the least pleasant among Russian literary curiosities. Whatever the practical merits of such an approach to poetry, it is inadequate if one wishes to account, at least in principle, for all the known facts and to accommodate Mandel'shtam's legacy in its entirety. The aim of the present study is to contribute to such an enterprise by finding a place for the "Ode to Stalin" in the ideological and mythological framework of Mandel'shtam's writings.

What we know about the events surrounding the composition of the "Ode to Stalin" comes from the poet's correspondence and the memoirs of Nadezhda Mandel'shtam, who, alone among her husband's companions in Voronezh, has chosen to make her recollections public.[9] The poem was composed some time in January 1937, which places it in the middle of the *Second Voronezh Notebook*,[10] the period when the term of Mandel'shtam's exile was coming to an end. Increasingly apprehensive—indeed desperate—about his future, Mandel'shtam decided to buy his way out by paying Stalin in poetic kind, that is, by composing a paean in his honor. This was a realistic response to a situation that was growing grimmer by the day. Mandel'shtam's fellow-exiles whom he befriended in Voronezh were being re-arrested one by one.[11] The Voronezh Theatre that had previously offered Mandel'shtam an opportunity to earn a meager income no longer wanted to have anything to do with him. Graver still, the Voronezh Section of the Writer's Union, supposed to supervise the poet's ideological re-education, was beginning to accuse him in print of such literally mortal sins as Trotskyism.[12] But perhaps worst of all for Mandel'shtam, the fear of dealing with a poet in disgrace was now threatening to sever the last links connecting him with the literary community on the "mainland."[13] Reading Mandel'shtam's correspondence of those months, it is especially painful to realize that many of his pleas, and not just for financial assistance or intercession but merely for an acknowledgement of his existence, remained unanswered. This social isolation, intense to begin with, was made doubly unbearable by the state of Mandel'shtam's health, which was deteriorating rapidly under the stress of continuous harrassment. Even following his arrest in 1934, Mandel'shtam was still enjoying the stature of a major literary figure—recall Stalin's conversation with Pasternak[14]—but by 1937 the transformation of a poet of the first magnitude into a nonperson was, for all intents and purposes, complete.

Any one of these factors might serve as a good excuse for bowing to the authorities and in combination they no doubt justify an outward display of contrition and awe before an almighty tyrant. Yet, the circumstances under which the "Ode" was composed appear to be more complex, and Nadezhda Mandel'shtam went further to suggest that her husband for awhile (but how long?) assumed the mentality of the contemporary crowd.[15] In her own words, Mandel'shtam "tuned himself like a musical instrument." The "Ode's" tone of profound sincerity and the consummate skill that apparently went into its composition demonstrate that the poet's absolute pitch worked, even in this instance, without fail.

But perhaps the word "even" is inappropriate here, for there is hardly anything unusual in a poet's, or for that matter anybody's, fascination with an omnipotent leader enjoying a litany of praise for almost a decade. Poetry of the Napoleonic era abounds in such examples. Nor is it unusual for a victim to identify with his tormentor, especially if the tormentor happens to be exalted and the victim either physically or psychologically isolated. Bruno Bettelheim's analysis of the "Heil Hitler" salute and the effect of its adoption on anti-Nazi Germans is instructive in this regard,[16] and so are the pleas of Ovid, the archetypal exile for poets and especially for Mandel'shtam. It may also be worth recalling that Dostoevskii's political conversion occurred under similar circumstances. The composition of the "Ode," then, as that of any significant work of art, appears overdetermined: the fear and the fascination must have combined with considerations of a more practical sort as Mandel'shtam was "tuning himself" for the composition of this, in my opinion, magnificent paean. But there was even more to it than that.

For the "Ode" to come into being, the emotional state that the poet was experiencing had to be objectified, had to locate itself in that ideological space where contemporary consciousness overlapped with the frame of reference which the poet superimposed onto the world—that is, his poetics, his myths, and broadly, his ideology. Without such an objectification, Mandel'shtam's expressive resources would have remained untapped, and the "Ode," had it come into existence at all, would not have risen above the Stalin doggerels of the kind that Akhmatova produced after the Second World War when the noose around her neck once again was beginning to tighten.[17] Was there anything in Mandel'shtam's frame of reference capable of accommodating such an enterprise?

A review of his writings shows that his attitude toward the October Revolution, indeed the entire Soviet project including Stalin's role in it, was far more complex than has often been assumed and cannot be reduced to a romantic notion of a poet as David continuously fighting his Goliath. After all, Mandel'shtam is known to have relegated the Wrangel Army to the Antechamber of the Inferno where the souls of the undistinguished fall like leaves from the Tree of Life;[18] to have praised Lenin as "the people's leader assuming in tears the fateful burden" of state power;[19] and finally to have ridiculed his own pre-revolutionary affinities in *The Egyptian Stamp* (1928).[20] In 1929, wrongfully accused of plagiarism by a powerful faction of the literary establishment, he counterattacked

in *Izvestiia* and *Na literaturnom postu* with a verbal barrage painfully reminiscent of the cannibalistic rhetoric of the First Five-Year Plan.[21] In the wake of the Shakhty trial, to describe the literary hacks as "wreckers" (or "pests," *vrediteli*) and to demand criminal prosecution for those whose only sin was a slap-dash translation job[22] amounted to more than an unimaginative use of invective. Even in his famous Jeremiad, *The Fourth Prose* (1930-31?), we see Mandel'shtam appealing to the pure revolutionary values that, in his view, were now being betrayed by the increasingly bourgeoisified and bureaucratized establishment.[23] Similar sentiments, couched in the rhetoric of War Communism, were being exploited at the same time by the Stalin side in the industrialization debates, as we know now, all too effectively.[24]

Read against this background, many of Mandel'shtam's poems of 1931-32 display an ambiguous attitude to what historians have now come to define as the Stalin Revolution. While finding some of its aspects distasteful, not to say repulsive, Mandel'shtam was yet unwilling to declare himself squarely against it. In poem after poem, he projected the image of a man fatefully torn between a profound commitment to the cause of the "fourth estate"—which he identified with the continuing revolution—and the growing horror at the violent and distorted form this cause was now taking.[25] The ideological frame of reference that he had previously developed left him with a limited choice: either to accept the "march of history" or to join those whom in a 1922 poem he himself presented as the "parasites trembling at the threshold of the new days."[26] Mandel'shtam's inability to reject this Procrustean dilemma altogether helps to explain why he found it necessary in 1931 to reaffirm his pledge, indeed a spell (*chur*), of allegiance to the fourth estate,[27] to insist on his alienation from the Imperial world that had reared him,[28] and even to doubt—a rarity in Mandel'shtam—his own rectitude.[29] The famous "wolf" poem[30] exemplifies, perhaps better than any other poem of the period, the state of mind Mandel'shtam wished to project at the beginning of the 1930s. In this regard, it merits closer consideration.

The bill of particulars that the poem presents to the epoch reads approximately as follows: the revolution that has sacrificed the present for bombastic future glory has deprived him of "the cup at the feast of the fathers, of merriment and honor," has wrongfully assaulted him ("The age-hound leaps on my shoulders"), and finally, has created such a violent, filthy and cowardly world that the sight of it has become unbearable for the poet. His only wish now is to be led away by some unnamed guide as far away as possible from this scene, even to Siberia. The poem concludes on a spell-like repetition, or incantation, in which the poet once again denies that he is "a wolf by blood," by implication an inappropriate target for the "age-hound," and insists that he can be killed only by one who is his equal. In the literature on Mandel'shtam, at least in the tradition established by his widow, this poem has been perceived as an indictment of the times.[31] Yet, a closer scrutiny reveals a far more complex picture in which the poet's aversion to the brutality of the epoch is combined with an historical and moral justification of the very cause of his distress.

As many poems by Mandel'shtam, this one is constructed around an allusion to Dante, specifically Virgil's prophecy in Canto I of the *Inferno,* which helps to identify the prototypes of the protagonists in Mandel'shtam's poem. Thus, behind the "age-hound" of Mandel'shtam one discerns Dante's *Veltro* (the Hound) who, according to Virgil, will rid Italy of the covetous and corrupt *lupa* (the she-wolf). It was this she-wolf who terrified Dante's Pilgrim as he was trying to find his way out of the "dark wood." Virgil's prophecy also helps explain Mandel'shtam's metaphor "I am not a wolf by blood," since Virgil predicted that before the Hound's appearance many creatures would have mated with the she-wolf. Finally, the Hound himself embodied the ideals of social justice which in Mandel'shtam's time were associated with the revolutionary "messianic" class: "he shall not feed on land or pelf but on wisdom, and love, and valor." Against this background, the repulsive sights of Mandel'shtam's poem might constitute a good enough reason for the poet not to participate in the social life of his time and to prefer instead a Dante-like pilgrimage. But these "excesses," as the "cowardice, slushy filth and the bloodied bones in the wheel" might have been qualified at the time, do not justify for him a wholesale rejection of the Revolution, or so, at least, the allusion to Dante suggests.[32]

Only later did alternative viewpoints begin to appear in Mandel'shtam's poetry. The epigraph that he chose for his *Conversation about Dante* (1933) offers a concise definition of the poet's contemporary stand: "Cosí gradai con la faccia levata." The words are taken from a telling passage in Canto XVI of the *Inferno* (the dialogue with Farinata) where the Pilgrim delivers one of his invectives against his native city: "'The new people and the sudden gains have begot in thee, Florence, arrogance and excess so that already thou weepest for it.' *This I cried with lifted face.*" Any one familiar with Mandel'shtam's iconography will recognize the poet in this pose, and Mandel'shtam himself, actually, recorded it in one of his rare verbal self-portraits.[33] The poet, it seems, was prepared now to pit himself against the whole world, very much in the manner of his Florentine mentor. Indeed, the voice one hears in a series of poems composed in 1933 is neither muted nor twisted by doubt. One poem composed contemporaneously with the *Conversation* speaks with a supreme clarity not often encountered in Mandel'shtam about the devastation of the countryside in the terror of forced collectivization. Another poem about a newly acquired Moscow apartment bursts with anger at the brave new world as Mandel'shtam refuses, among other things, "to teach executioners how to twitter."[34] Finally, in November 1933, Mandel'shtam decides to point an accusing finger at Stalin himself, producing a searing epigram[35]—to my knowledge the only contemporary document of its kind—that a few months later would result in his arrest, with its profound psychological trauma, and subsequent exile.

It would be gratifying to think that Mandel'shtam, once he perceived the inexcusable brutality of the new state, would never give up his insight. The record speaks otherwise. The poems of 1933 that have just been mentioned from an exception rather than the rule and, at least judging by the poetry composed in Voronezh, Mandel'shtam once again was reaching for the rationalizations familiar from his writings of the 1920s and the early 1930s. What is more, the figure of Stalin, like the specter of Hamlet's father, now comes to haunt the poet, confronting him again and again with the transgression for which he had been so severely punished.

Mandel'shtam wrote a number of poems beginning in 1935 that deal with Stalin either directly or indirectly, expressing the poet's remorse and a desire to atone for his offense. In a 1935 poem, Mandel'shtam already calls himself a "non-party Bolshevik, like all [my] friends [and] like this foe."[36] "I must live, breathing and bolshevizing myself [*bol'sheveia*]," are the words from another 1935 poem where he refers to the causes of his present predicament—his bourgeois social origins and the epigram—as "the damned seam, the clumsy prank" that had rendered him a pariah among people.[37] He even accepts the "corrective" nature of his exile: "Measure me, land, *repattern* me—oh the miraculous heat of the attached earth!"[38] The person of Stalin, or rather, his iconic features, begin to appear early in 1937, either simultaneously with or shortly after the "Ode" was finished. In "Sleep defends my Don drowsiness," one finds Stalin's metonyms pulled out of a propaganda poster: "The brow and the head of the militant armor are lovingly combined with the eyes."[39] Another poem alludes directly to the plea for mercy represented by the "Ode" and to its addressee: "It is to him—into his very core—I came, entering the Kremlin without a pass, tearing the canvas of distance, bowing my head heavy with guilt."[40] In another Voronezh poem, Mandel'shtam refers to Stalin by name: "Lenin will rustle like a ripe thunder storm, and on this earth that shall avoid decay, Stalin shall keep awakening life and reason."[41] Stalin even enters a love poem, addressed to a singer, Elekonida Popova: "My black-browed glory, tie me up with your thick brow, you, who are ready for life and death, who utter lovingly the thunderous name of Stalin with the tenderness of a vow, with love." This and a companion poem, both addressed to the "black-browed" admirer of Stalin, are tucked away in the Addenda of volume four of Mandel'shtam's *Collected Works.*[42]

It is not my intention to represent the entire spectrum of the Voronezh poems in this brief survey, not even those that deal with the theme of exile. Many are politically neutral. Some have nothing to do with exile. Among those that do, several are free from official rationalization as are the "little demon" poems where the Pushkinian-Gogolian trickster is blamed for Mandel'shtam's misfortune (perhaps not without an echo from Dostoevskii's *The Possessed*).[43] Nevertheless, the *other* poems do represent a coherent entity, demonstrating that Mandel'shtam was more of a contemporary of his times than either he[44] or

many of those who have written about him have been
willing to admit. Even Nadezhda Mandel'shtam to whom
we owe the canonical image of the poet has insisted: "All
of us led a double existence, and no one could avoid that
fate." The "Ode to Stalin" shows how intimately inter-
twined these two sides of existence actually were.

No other Stalin-related poem possesses the scope of the
"Ode." Its size makes it the third longest poem ever composed by Mandel'shtam (after "Verses on the Unknown
Soldier" and "He Who Found the Horseshoe"), and its
thematic breadth offers a unique entry into the conceptual and mythic world of his later poetry. Mandel'shtam's
idea of himself and his art, his view of his "crime" and
approaching death, his vision of Stalin and the posthumous life of his poetry—are all contained in the "Ode"
and are presented with the kind of skill that would have
been appreciated in the Greece of the tyrants or Au-
gustan Rome. Indeed, to judge by formal features alone,
the poem belongs to one of the most difficult genres of
panegyric poetry, the Pindaric ode. The exuberance of
imagery framed in the rhetoric of praise, triadic divisions
within stanzas which follow the pattern of strophe,
antistrophe and epode,. and finally the lines of unequal
length combining hexameter, pentameter and tetrameter
conform to the basic scheme of the ancient genre of
glorifying a supreme leader.[45] Such a strict adherence
to the Pindaric rules is unknown to the mainstream of
the Russian odic tradition, which may in part explain
why the editors published the poem under a provisional title, "Verses on Stalin." It is safe to assume that
Mandel'shtam, who must have been aware of his priority
in the genre, wished to produce something unique—a
fitting tribute from a great master of verbal art to a great
master of political power.

The "Ode" begins with a traditional poetic conceit for
expressing the ineffable: if only the poet possessed the
limitless power of representation, he would sketch with a
charcoal across the firmament of heaven the portrait of
the one "who had shifted the world's axis." The purpose
of this conceit, needless to say, is to convert the poet's
confessed inadequacy into an affirmation of his creative
gift at a higher rate of exchange. In an unspoken competition, Mandel'shtam invites Aeschylus to watch him
"weep as he is drawing"—now with the flaming coal of
Prometheus. Transcending pain, the poet will offer a pictorial tribute to Stalin, as it were, in atonement for
Prometheus's transgression that had once angered the
Stalin of Mount Olympus. The second stanza, as it continues the theme of representation, introduces another
conceit central to the "Ode," namely, a rapturous search
for Stalin's likeness.

His aim shall be achieved, Mandel'shtam says enigmati-
cally, after he produces a twin (*bliznets*) whose identity
he pointedly refuses to disclose. Yet, in his features, one
would be able to recognize the "father's" face:

> . . . I v druzhbe mudrykh glaz naidu dlia bliznetsa,
> Kakogo ne skazhu, to vyrazhen'e, blizias'

K kotoromu, k nemu,—vdrug uznaesh' ottsa
I zadykhaesh'sia, pochuiav mira blizost'. . . .

The third stanza exhorts artists not to misrepresent the
leader, now named as the "warrior" (*boets*) and once
again as the "father" (*otets*).

The main part of the poem begins with the fourth, yet
another painterly stanza: Stalin is addressing the "hillocks of heads" from a mountain-like podium. Remarkably,
this portrait seems to derive from a newsreel of Lenin
addressing a crowd in Sverdlov Square on 5 May 1920—
a prototype for many a Lenin poster. This is doubly significant: first because Stalin was not known for his oratorical
skill and second because Lenin, who was a skillful speaker,
is missing from the "Ode" (except as a modifier of the
word "October" in the last stanza). In 1937 such an omission was rare and therefore meaningful even in the unabashedly worshipful Soviet folklore of those days.[46]

In the fifth stanza, Mandel'shtam returns to the subject
of his craft and speaks about the technique he employs
in drawing the portrait of Stalin. It is only in this section
that Mandel'shtam discloses the nature of his relation to
his subject whose portrait is once again composed out of
bits and pieces of propaganda placards.

In the sixth stanza, Mandel'shtam goes on to describe the
transformation of the earth under the power of Stalin's
vision: a mountain comes apart to make way for a cultivated plain with furrows stretching into the sunset. The
six-fold oath, referring to Stalin's funeral oration after
Lenin's death, has been fulfilled.[47] In order to emphasize the magical, or miraculous, nature of the transformation, Mandel'shtam suddenly shifts to trochee—
Chudo narodnoe! ("People's miracle!")—creating a metrical equivalent of the Greek spondee which served as a
mark of epiphany in sacred Greek poetry.[48] Appropriately,
this line also contains an element of the formula with
which God brought forth the universe: *Da budet zhizn'
krupna* ("Let life be large").

The seventh stanza, the poem's coda, has three distinct
parts. In the first, the poet recalls Stalin's life six times,
partly in reference to the six-fold oath and partly in allusion to the six days of Creation. He then expresses the
hope that his own art will survive him and will benefit
future generations, and, finally, he thanks fate for having
allowed him to be a contemporary of the man who embodies honor and love, valor and steel-like firmness.

Obviously, Mandel'shtam constructed the "Ode," at least
in part, out of contemporary official rhetoric in all of its
maniacal verbosity.[49] It is less obvious, although equally
significant, that the poem forms a nexus—a lexicon and a
grammar of sorts—for a cycle of poems composed in the
Voronezh period.[50] A cycle, or a group of poems in which
the poet works through a set of key rhythms, images, and
ideas, constitutes a basic unit of Mandel'shtam's poetry,
especially in the middle and later periods of his career.[51]
Within such a cycle, the poems do not merely follow one

another like beads on a string but interact as entities belonging to a single structure, contradicting, developing, and complementing one another like elements in a complex musical composition or, to use Mandel'shtam's simile, "like stones in a groined arch."

The "Ode to Stalin" functions as a keystone in such a cycle which consists of some twenty-four poems written between December and February 1936-37. Some of them, such as numbers 330 and 331 dealing with a statue of a Buddha-like deity residing inside a mountain, are barely comprehensible without the "Ode," while others acquire a new, fuller meaning which otherwise would have been lost. For example, one is tempted to see features of Stalin in the "cat" from the "Kashchei" poem.[52] A particularly striking insight is produced when the "Ode" is juxtaposed with the "wasps" poem. Clarence Brown suspected a link between this poem and the "Ode,"[53] and Nadezhda Mandel'shtam, who unlike him had access to both texts, pointed out that the two have a central image in common: the "axis," or *os'*.[54] In the "Ode," Stalin is called the one who "had shifted the world's axis" (stanza 1), and the word appears once again in stanza 5 where Mandel'shtam develops the theme of his relation to Stalin. Attempting to "catch the likeness of his subject," the poet isolates the essence of Stalin's appearance, the core, to which he refers as the "axis of likeness" (*skhodstva os'*). The nature of this latter axis is broached in the second stanza (cited above) where Mandel'shtam introduces a mysterious "twin" of his subject in whose features one is bound to recognize the father.

The choice of the word "twin" for the poet's representation of Stalin is far from random,[55] for, above all, it personifies the portrait or, to use the more appropriate Russian term, *odushevliaet*, animates it, that is, endows it with spirit or soul. That Mandel'shtam pointedly refuses to name the "twin" ("I won't say who he is," stanza 2, line 6) only emphasizes the animate nature of the created representation, and the fact that the "twin" here rhymes with "father" establishes a relationship of equivalence between the two key words (lines 5 and 7). The three main entities in the poem—the poet, the look-alike, and Stalin—emerges as a curious kind of triad, and as the "Ode" proceeds, we begin to get the sense of what Mandel'shtam had in mind.

In the third stanza, the father and the twin are presented in their martial aspect, emphasized by the rhyming scheme: *otets-bliznets-boets*. In the fourth stanza, where the first real portrait of Stalin appears—a poster-like image of Stalin addressing the crowd—Mandel'shtam refers to his subject as a "debtor more powerful than any debt" (*dolzhnik sil'nee iska*) and, once again, as father. This insistence on the paternity of Stalin generates, needless to say, some echoes of the Old Testament with its paternalistic symbolism, and one indeed encounters a similar "debtor" formula in the *Psalms:* "The Lord hath sworn and will not repent"[56] or "My covenant will I not break . . . Once I have sworn by my holiness that I will not lie unto David."

But how does the poet define himself in relation to Stalin the father? The answer is contained in stanza V which becomes transparent when juxtaposed with the "wasps" poem:

>   Szhimaia ugolek, v kotorom vse soshlos',
> 50 Rukoiu zhadnoiu odno lish' skhodstvo klicha,
>   Rukoiu khishchnoiu—lovit' lish' shkodstva os'—
>   Ia ugol' iskroshu, ishcha ego oblich'ia.
>   Ia u nego uchus', ne dlia sebia uchas',
>   Ia u nego uchus' k sebe ne znat' poshchady,
>   Neschast'ia skroiut li bol'shogo plana chast',
>   Ia razyshchu ego v sluchainostiakh ikh chada . . .
>   Pust' nedostoin ia eshche imet' druzei,
>   Pust' ne nasyshchen ia i zhelch'iu i slezami,
>   On vse mne chuditsia v shineli, v kartuze,
> 60 Na chudnoi ploshchadi s schastlivymi glazami. . . .

Compare this with the way Mandel'shtam presented himself, or rather his persona, in the "wasps":

> Vooruzhennyi zren'em uzkikh os,
> Sosushchikh os' zemnuiu, os' zemnuiu,
> Ia chuiu vse, s chem svidet'sia prishlos',
> I vspominaniu naizust' i vsue. . . . [57]

Even though the choice of "wasps" may have been determined by Mandel'shtam's reading of Bergson, according to whom these insects were the paragons of intuitive perception,[58] the poem's "poetics" are defined by Mandel'shtam's favored device, paronomasia,[59] in this case a play on the phonetic similarity between the genetive plural of *osa, os*, the accusative singular of the word. axis, *os'*, the ending of the verb signifying an unpremeditated encounter, *prishlos'*, and of course, the vocative form of his own first name Osip, *Os'*, a contraction of Joseph, the name he happened to share with Stalin.[60] "Solominka," a famous poetic declaration of the earlier Mandel'shtam, is constructed on such a play on first names,[61] and in the "Ode" the poet exploited the potential of the remarkable coincidence, transforming it into a likeness. A careful reading of the fifth stanza demonstrates that Mandel'shtam made the coincidence work for him with supreme mastery.

The similitude, then, that Mandel'shtam was seeking with such fervor, as he was sketching in the air the portrait of Stalin, as he was creating the "twin," involved not only the morphological essence of Stalin's face (a portrait arranged around the axis of facial symmetry) but also, and indeed primarily, the identity between his famous tormentor and himself. This kind of an identification of the poet's *persona* with the subject of his poetic portrait is common in poetic iconography[62] and is not unrelated to confessional literature, both mediaeval and modern.[63] The identity Mandel'shtam establishes between himself and his subject in the "Ode" is that of the son and the father. To be more specific, it is the identity between the two and the father's personified, "inspired" likeness generated in the course of the representation—the twin whom the poet refuses to name. Needless to say, patriarchal terminology applied to Stalin permeated the panegyric literature of the 1930s,[64] and it could have been dismissed in this instance as a *locus communus* had it not been woven by Mandel'shtam into a rather remarkable triad.

Stanza 5 contains a significant elaboration on the nature of these three. A subtle but unmistakable reference to the Crucifixion—"Granted, I have not been sated with either gall or tears" (line 10)—defines the artist with a burning coal in his hand (recall Prometheus, Pushkin's "The Prophet," and the calling of Isaiah) in terms of the One who accepted the bitter cup predestined for Him by His Father.[65] To leave no doubt about the parallelism—a kenotic *imitatio Christi*—Mandel'shtam offers a prophecy concerning his own resurrection in the final stanza: ". . . in the tender books and in the children's games, I shall be resurrected to say that the sun is shining." More important, this *imitatio* does not end with Christ but is extended to include the other two members ofthe Trinity: the Father and the One "in whom one recognizes the father, choking and short of breath"—*zadykhaias'*—namely, *Sviatoi dukh*, the Holy Ghost. But what can the Trinity have to do with the pagan myth of Prometheus with which the poem commences?

The apparent incongruity dissolves if one turns for help to Mandel'shtam's earlier writings where he interpreted the Greek world-view (as it is expressed in myths, among them the myth of Prometheus) as a far more important and congenial component of Christianity than the Old Testament faith. Influenced in his thoughts on this subject by Tadeusz Zielinski,[66] Mandel'shtam attempted to elaborate this concept of an Helleno-Christian conjecture in an essay, "Pushkin i Skriabin," that he drafted late in 1915.[67] In subsequent years, even though he occasionally took a more favorable view of the Judaic heritage, his affinity with the ideas spelled out in this essay remained undiminished. Responding to Skriabin's death and in part reacting to Viacheslav Ivanov's thoughts concerning tragedy, Mandel'shtam produced the following telling formulation of the alignment of cultural "essences" at the origins of Christianity:

> . . . Hellas has to be saved from Rome. [If Rome prevails in defining the meaning of the Crucifixion,] it will not even be Rome but Judaism. Judaism has always stood behind Rome's back, waiting for its appointed hour. [And if this hour strikes,] the terrifying, unnatural trend will triumph: history will turn backward the flow of time—the black sun of Phaedra.[68]

While the Judaic filiation of Christianity represented an incestuous act on a world-historical scale, the unblemished Hellenic lineage of Christianity constituted for Mandel'shtam a promise, indeed a fulfilled promise, of a blissful and carefree "communion of the Father with His children."[69] Unlike the Hebrews, constrained in their "legalistic morality and countless rules,"[70] the Greeks had enjoyed this blessed state, if only on those occasions when their gods were taking a rest from supplying material to the writers of tragedies. But Christianity, Mandel'shtam believed, had rendered this undesirable aspect of Greek life obsolete. By accepting the bitter cup, Christ focussed upon himself and redeemed the fatal flaw of mankind, thereby relieving once and for all the tension between the divine and the human that had hitherto made universal participation in tragedy an inevitable fact.[71]

It is this view of Christianity that defines the use of myth in the "Ode to Stalin." The story of Prometheus, recalled at the outset, passes almost imperceptibly into another mythic register where the guilty poet, his once misused creative gift, and the Zeus of the Soviet Olympus can be presented, respectively, as Christ, the Holy Ghost and God the Father. After all, Prometheus, like Christ, was a transgressor with respect to established authority. But while his offense, even though beneficial for mankind, served to set the tragic cycle in motion, Christ's much later violation of the Law and His subsequent Crucifixion put the tragic cycle to rest. Taking account of this *transformation* of one frame of reference into another, it becomes possible to see that Mandel'shtam was projecting his personal misfortune along the metaphoric and metonymic axes: horizontally, or by analogy, onto the stories of Prometheus and Christ; and vertically, or by contiguity, onto an historical continuum through which the Greek worldview culminated in Christianity, for him the essence of humanity's millenarian quest. To reverse the famous formula, in the case of the "Ode," ontogeny recapitulated filogeny in more ways than one.

Emphasizing the dynamic aspect in the development of the "Ode's" central myth, that is, by having the Christian view supersede its Greek counterpart, Mandel'shtam was pleading for a different interpretation of his predicament, integrating it into the framework of the universal Christian redemption, forgiveness. "Where is the bound and nailed-down groan, Where is Prometheus—the rock's support and likeness? . . . That is not to be—tragedies cannot be brought back . . . ," wrote Mandel'shtam shortly after completing the "Ode" as if to exorcise the tragic pattern from his own life.[72] The "Ode to Stalin," too, seems to have been meant as an exorcism, and it does indeed appear to be modelled on a magic spell.[73] The "magic" coincidence in the first name of the poet and his addressee and the talismanic "charcoal" point in the direction of such a pattern. Prior to Mandel'shtam, the burning coal of the archetypal rebel had touched the lips of the prophet Isaiah, replaced the heart of Pushkin's Prophet, and in more recent times, mined in fabulous quantities, earned a singular fame for Stakhanov (one can expect an acmeist Mandel'shtam to outline his paradigms with this kind of precision). Such a history is bound to confer transcendent powers on the mineral, transforming it, by contagion,[74] not only into a magical tool with which to fashion a fitting image of Stalin, but also into a talisman that would grant the poet his wishes. Mandel'shtam, no doubt, remembered Pushkin's incantation: "Guard me, my talisman, Guard me in the days of persecution, In the days of remorse and agitation: You were given me on the day of sorrow."[75] Finally, the structure of the poem provides an even stronger indication of a magical subtext, for the "Ode" follows the two-fold formula of a homoeopathic spell,[76] that is, one based on analogy or comparison.[77] The first part of such a spell recounts a phenomenon that has already taken place—here the development of tragedy into the Christ event—while the second contains a wish for a similar outcome with respect to an unrelated but in some ways comparable situation— Mandel'shtam's desire to have his predicament interpreted within the Christian, rather than Promethean framework. Thus the initial analogy with Prometheus yields to the desired *imitatio Christi*, the "stolen fire" to the divine gift, the Holy Ghost, and the angry Zeus-Stalin to God the Father.

Behind this wish projected in the "Ode," there stands an eclectic but a peculiarly Mandel'shtamian understanding of the imitation of Christ in relation to life and artistic creation. Some of the ideas that he committed to paper in "Pushkin i Skriabin" may have lost their validity by 1937, and this is not surprising, but some seem to have remained significant for Mandel'shtam, and they help to interpret the phenomenon of the "Ode." Arguing against Skriabin's view of art as an act of self-sacrifice that would result in universal rebirth (Skriabin did actually intend such a pandemonium[78]), Mandel'shtam wrote:

> . . . Consequently, not sacrifice, not redemption through art, but a free and joyous imitation of Christ—this is what constitutes the cornerstone of Christian aesthetics. Art cannot be a sacrifice because the sacrifice has already taken place, cannot be redemption because the world together with the artist have already been redeemed—what is left then? A joyous communion with God, a game of hide-and-seek, as it were, of the Father with his children, the hide-and-seek of the spirit. The divine illusion of redemption implied in Christian art can be explained precisely by this play of God with us, the Deity who allows us to wander along the paths of mystery so that we, as if on our own, suddenly find redemption, having experienced a catharsis—redemption in art. Christian artists are in a sense the freedmen of the idea of redemption, but not its slaves or preachers. The entire two millenia of our culture, thanks to the miraculous mercy of Christianity, is an act of *releasing the world into freedom* for the sake of play, for the sake of spiritual merriment, for the sake of the free "imitation of Christ."[79]

It is hard to imagine that as late as 1936, Mandel'shtam could believe that imitation of Christ was, in his case, a joyous affair or that he could consider the hide-and-seek with Stalin to be just a game. On the contrary, the scenario he outlined for himself in the "Ode" in such gruesome detail (stanza 5) did include, as in the case of Christ, humiliation, suffering, and death. And yet, whatever other reasons for the composition of the poem, he clearly sought in it a "catharsis, redemption," as he put it, not through but "in art": a justification of his fate in Christ's likeness and image. Indeed, while the "Ode," as an article of exchange, did not fetch a high premium on the political

market, as a magic spell, it proved to be quite, if not excessively, effective. Of course, one hardly required any magical powers to have Stalin preside over one's final kenosis, but they may have helped to reaffirm the mythic framework of the "Ode" as a major pattern for interpreting Mandel'shtam's life and art during the remarkable literary resurrection that has returned the poet to his readers. One may recall in this connection another of Pushkin's incantations: "Dear friend! from crime, From new heart wounds, From treason, from oblivion Thou shall be guarded by my talisman."[80]

This Helleno-Christian myth, tragic and heroic as well as kenotic and redemptive in the specific way it was generated in the "Ode," became the foundation (a concealed one as myths require[81]) of a book which more than any other work contributed to Mandel'shtam's posthumous fame: the two volumes of Nadezhda Mandel'shtam's memoirs. There, of course, Stalin was revealed as a false god, but the "Ode's" trinity could persist without him and the "prodigal son" could practice his divine gift and even return to his Father.[82] The very first paragraph of the memoirs defines the reader's frame of reference, tuning him to the right myth, once again imperceptibly as myths require, establishing a theme that will inform the entire narrative like a Wagnerian leit-motif:

> . . . Having slapped Aleksei Tolstoi [the author of the famous *Road to Calvary*], O. M. without delay returned to Moscow and there telephoned Anna Andreevna [Akhmatova] every day, pleading with her to come to Moscow. She tarried; he was getting angry. With her ticket purchased and ready to go, she paused by the window and became pensive. "Praying that this cup may pass you?" asked Punin, an intelligent, bilious, and brilliant man. It was he who suddenly said to Akhmatova, as they were strolling through the Tretiakov Gallery: "And now let us look how you are going to be conveyed to the execution" [reference to Surikov's "Boiarynia Morozova"]. This prompted the poem "A posle na drogakh . . ." But she was not fated to make this journey: "They are saving you for the very end," Nikolai Nikolaevich Punin would say and his face would become distorted by a tic. But at the very end, they forgot about her and did not arrest her . . .

The scandalous slap cannot but be read in the Dostoevskian tradition of unmasking an antichrist in a sudden breakdown of social conventions (viz. scandals in *The Possessed*). Here, the slap exposes the "other" Tolstoi as a false prophet and, by implication, his famous trilogy *Khozhdenie po mukam* as a diabolical perversion of the *Road to Calvary* or the apocryphal story of the Virgin's Descent into Hell (the Russian title alludes to both) which will be set aright in Nadezhda Mandel'shtam's own narrative. As befits an imitator of the One who prayed at Gethsemane, Mandel'shtam pleads with his friend Akhmatova to come and keep vigil with him; and as befits one assigned the role of the poet's apostle, she delays. The third sentence contains an allusion to the prayer at Gethsemane, and Punin's biliousness once again reminds the reader of the "bitter cup" (*zhelch* is bile and/or gall). Punin's reference to Surikov's painting of the Archpriest Avvakum's disciple functions as another metonym of Christ's Passion and alludes directly to Russia's most famous autobiography of an imitator of Christ. Along the way and without any apparent motivation, the narrator finally focuses on Punin's nervous tic. In part a mimetic ploy, this singled out detail begins to generate its own associations in a densely allusive context. Punin, formerly a militant member of LEF, is represented by a feature that he shares with Mikhail Bulgakov's Pontius Pilate, as he is interrogating Ieshua, and with Dostoevskii's Tikhon, as he is listening to the most inspired portions of Stavrogin's confession.[83] Punin, as most other "intelligent and brilliant" people that one encounters in the memoirs, is marked by a sign of possession, or so the context seems to suggest. The symbolism of Gethsemane would once again reappear in the chapter devoted to the "Ode" where the poem itself would be referred to as the "prayer of the cup."[84]

There is no way to determine to what extent the poet and his wife, whose writings are permeated with Mandel'shtam's conceptualizations, were conscious of their appeal to the Helleno-Christian myth as their ultimate referent, the cornerstone on which the narrative meaning of their art and life rests. But perhaps the question of awareness is beside the point here. What is more important is that the appeal to the myth informed the two works, each addressed to distinct and incompatible audiences: one to Stalin and his henchmen, the other to the public eager for an exposé of the brutalities of the Stalinist regime. This suggestion of compatibility between the mentalities of these two groups, of the common ideological ground (not in the political sense) that they shared should make us pause.

After all, Mandel'shtam was not the only poet of the Soviet period to use the Gospel narrative extensively as the ultimate referent. Beginning with Blok (*The Twelve*), other poets, including Maiakovskii and Pasternak, made similar appeals to the Scripture, though they did not necessarily imply the vision of Stalin as God the Father. Finally, Stalin himself demonstrated that he, too, was adept at using similar rhetoric, as he was making his famous "six vows" at Lenin's funeral—an oration reminiscent of the Lord's Covenant and one to which Mandel'shtam alluded in the "Ode" twice. The rhetoric of these vows and of the subsequent Stalin cult with all of its eschatology and patriarchal transcendence must have struck a responsive chord, not only in the hearts of the "simple people,"[85] but also in the hearts of some of the best minds among the members of the intellectual elite. In this respect, the "Ode" helps to isolate a number of important elements in the nation's ideological vocabulary that originated in the years before 1917 and were shared by the society at large in the 1930s, during perhaps the most cataclysmic decade in Russia's history.

Of course, the "Ode" is offensive to our sense of Mandel'shtam—a victim of Stalinist terror and one of the great poets of this century. The careful mastery that went into its composition, its range, and its brilliance clash harshly with what one considers to be Stalin's due. But neither our sensibility nor the brutal pressures of Mandel'shtam's life in Voronezh, nor the blinders of our historical hindsight should prevent us from seeing the common root of the "sacred" and "profane" uses of religious belief in the mentality of contemporary Soviet society and state. While the workings of this belief may often be concealed, when detected in rhetoric, narrative structure or allusion, they begin to speak eloquently about a culture's unacknowledged needs that can rarely tolerate the light of reason. As the "Ode to Stalin" demonstrates, they are bound to turn up in the most unlikely, and therefore most likely, places.

APPENDIX

1

Were I to take a charcoal for the sake of
    supreme praise—
For the sake of the eternal joy of drawing—
I would divide the air into clever angles
Both carefully and with alarm.
To make the present echo in his features
(My art bordering on audacity),
I would speak about him who has shifted the
    world's axis
Honoring the customs of one hundred and
    forty peoples.
I would lift a small corner of his brow
10 And lift it again, and redraw it differently:
Oh, it must be Prometheus blowing on his
    coal—
Look, Aeschylus, how I weep as I am drawing.

2

I would take a few thunderous lines,
His youthful millenium entire,
And would bind his courage with his smile,
And let it loose again, illuminated softly.
And in the friendship of his wise eyes, I shall
    find for the twin
(I won't say who he is) that expression,
    drawing close to
Which, to him—you suddenly recognize the
    father
20 And gasp, sensing the proximity of peace
    [world?].
And I want to thank the hills
That have shaped this bone and this hand:
He was born in the mountains and knew the
    bitterness of jail.
I want to call him, not Stalin,—Dzhugashvili!

3

Artist, cherish and guard the warrior:
Surround him entire with a damp blue forest
Of moist concern. Do not upset the father
With an unwholesome image or an inferior
    thought.
Artist, help him who is with you completely,

30 Who is thinking, feeling and building.
Not I, no, not another—his dear people—
The Homer-people will offer him a triple praise.
Artist, cherish and guard the warrior:
The forest of mankind growing ever denser is
singing behind him,
The future itself is this wise man's retenue
And it needs him more often, with greater
courage.

4

He is bending over a podium as if over a
mountain
Into the hillocks of heads. A debtor—more
powerful than any debt.
His mighty eyes are decisively kind,
40 His thick eyebrow is glaring at somebody,
And I would like to point out with an arrow
The firmness of his mouth—the father of
stubborn speeches
Whose sculpted, complicated and abrupt eyelid
Is projecting itself, it must be, out of a
million frames.
He is all sincerity, he is all brass of fame.
And his far-sighted hearing is intolerant to
muffling.
His gloomy little wrinkles are playfully
stretching
To reach out to all those who are ready to
live and die.

5

Grasping the charcoal, the focus of everything,
50 Summoning with a greedy hand the likeness
alone,
With a rapacious hand—to catch only the axis
of likeness—
I shall make the coal crumble, searching for
his features.
I am learning from him, but learning not for
my own sake,
I am learning from him to be merciless to
myself.
Shall misfortunes conceal even a part of his
great plan,
I shall seek it out in the confusion of their
fumes . . .
Granted, I am still unworthy of having friends,
Granted, I have not yet been sated with gall
or tears,
Still, I sense his presence: in his military coat
and cap
60 He is standing in the miraculous square, his
eyes happy.

6

Stalin's eyes made the mountain come apart,
And the plain is squinting into the distance.
Like the sea without wrinkles, like tomorrow
out of yesterday—
The furrows of a colossal plough reach to
the sun.
He is smiling with the smile of a harvester
Of handshakes during the conversation

Which has begun and continues without end
On the expanse of his six oaths.
And each threshing-floor, and each sheaf
70 Is strong, fit and clever—live wealth—
People's miracle! Let life be large.
The core of happiness keeps forever turning.

7

And six times over I guard in my mind's eye—
The slow witness of labors, struggles,
harvests—
The enormous distance he traversed across
the taiga
And Lenin's October—to the fulfillment of
his oaths.
The hills of people's heads are running into
the distance,
In them I am growing smaller; soon I won't
be noticed,
But in tender books and in children's games,
80 I shall be resurrected to say that the sun is
shining.
There is no truer truth than the sincerity of a
warrior:
For honor and love, for valor and steel.
There is a glorious name for the taut lips of a
rhapsode—
We've heard it, and him [it] we have
encountered.

NOTES

[1] An earlier version of this essay was delivered at the Annual Meeting of the Modern Languages Association in December 1981. While preparing this draft for publication I greatly benefited from discussion of its subject with Victoria E. Bonnell, Joseph Brodsky, Clarence Brown, Edward J. Brown, Boris Gasparov, Olga R. Hughes, Robert P. Hughes, Herbert Lindenberger, Robert A. Maguire, William Mills Todd III, and Reginald Zelnik. I am also indebted to the members of the Mellon Seminar on Interpretation, Stanford University, for many stimulating discussions concerning ideology and myth.

All references to Mandel'shtam, unless noted otherwise, are made to Osip Mandel'shtam, *Sobranie sochinenii*, ed. G. P. Struve et al., 4 vols. (1967-71, 1981) hereafter cited as SS. References to Mandel'shtam's prose are made to volume and page (e.g., SS, 2:315); poems, to volume and a poem's number (e.g., SS, 1:250). Translations from the Russian are mine.

[2] Anna Akhmatova, *Sochineniia*, 2 vols. (1967-68), 2:181. Originally, these reminiscences appeared in *Vozdushnye puti*, 4 (1965).

[3] Clarence Brown, "Into the Heart of Darkness," *Slavic Review* 26, no. 4 (1967): 584-604.

[4] SS, 1:372.

[5] Nadezhda Mandel'shtam, *Vospominaniia* (New York, 1971), pp. 216-20, or the chapter entitled "Oda."

[6] Anonymous, "Mandelstam's 'Ode to Stalin,'" *Slavic Review* 34, no. 4 (1975): 683-91.

[7] Bengt Jangfedt, "Osip Mandel'štam's 'Ode to Stalin,'" *Scando-Slavica* 22 (1976): 35-41.

[8] Efim Etkind, "Razmyshleniia o poslednem tome O. Mandel'shtama i pervom tome M. Tsvetaevoi," *Russkaia mysl'*, no. 3359 (7 May 1981).

[9] N. Mandel'shtam, pp. 216-220. See also *Osip Mandelstam: The Later Poetry* (Cambridge, 1976), pp. 174-98, by Jennifer Baines whose account, although more detailed, follows closely that of Nadezhda Mandel'shtam.

[10] For the list of poems constituting *The Second Voronezh Notebook* see Baines, pp. 242-43. The same list with only minor variations may be found in Osip Mandel'shtam, *Voronezhskie tetradi,* ed. annot. Viktoria Shveitser (Ann Arbor, MI, 1980), pp. 35-80.

[11] N. Mandel'shtam, p. 212ff and elsewhere.

[12] SS, 4: 143-45.

[13] Most of Mandel'shtam's letters of this period end with an urgent plea for an answer by telegraph—a good indication of the sense of isolation Mandel'shtam was experiencing. See his letter to K. I. Chukovskii (SS, 3: 279-80) or a letter to Iurii Tynianov (SS, 3:280-81) which begins: "I want to see you. What can I do? A legitimate wish. Please do not consider me a shadow. I still cast a shadow. . . . "

[14] N. Mandel'shtam, pp. 152-57.

[15] Ibid., p. 220.

[16] Bruno Bettelheim, "Remarks on the Psychological Appeal of Totalitarianism," *Surviving and Other Essays* (New York, 1979), p. 319ff.

[17] Akhmatova, 2:147-54.

[18] "Gde noch' brosaet iakoria" (SS, 2:458).

[19] "Proslavim, brat'ia, sumerki svobody" (SS, 1:103). For an analysis of this poem see Steven Broyde, *Osip Mandel'stam and His Age* (Cambridge, MA, 1975), p. 47ff., and Aleksandr Morozov, "Mandel'shtam v zapiskakh dnevnika S. P. Kablukova," *Vestnik russkogo khristianskogo dvizheniia* 129, no. 3 (1979): 135-55, specifically p. 134.

[20] Mandel'shtam's novella, in this respect, bears comparison with a whole series of prose works mocking the cultivated intellectual of Mandel'shtam's generation which were published almost simultaneously with *The Egyptian Stamp.* Among them are Olesha's *Zavist',* Vaginov's *Kozlinnaia pesn',* and Zoshchenko's *Mishel' Siniagin,* not to speak of the somewhat more popular novels by Il'f and Petrov. This subject is discussed in a yet unpublished essay by Irina Reyfman, "Mikhail Bulgakov and Osip Mandel'shtam."

[21] SS, 2:425-41. "Potoki khaltury" was published in *Izvesiia* (7 April 1929); "O perevodakh," a much calmer and reasoned article, in *Na literaturnom postu* 13 (July 1929).

[22] "Potoki khaltury" contained the following passage:

Poisoning of wells, wreckage and pollution of sewers and water mains, poor maintenance of cauldrons in communal kitchens are all crimes liable to prosecution by the courts. But the ugly, unbelievable to the point of indignation, state of the shops in which world literature is produced for our reader, the wreckage of the transmission belts which connect the mind of the mass Soviet reader with the aesthetic production of the West and the East, of Europe and America, indeed of the whole of mankind in its past and its present—all this unheard-of wreckage has so far gone unpunished, has been treated as something innocent, as a matter of course. (SS, 2:428)

[23] Take, for example, this passage: "We mooch cigarettes from one another and continue our Chinese games, encoding into the formulae of animal cowardice the great, powerful, forbidden concept of class" (SS, 2:179). The "Chinese games" (*kitaishchina*) most likely represents an allusion to Dostoevskii's famous comparison of Russian bureaucracy with the Chinese Imperial state: "I would say that we are just like China only without her orderliness. We are only beginning what the Chinese have already accomplished. Doubtless, we will achieve the same accomplishment, but when? In order to accept a thousand volumes of ceremonies, in order to win the right never to think about anything once and for all, we will have to live for at least another thousand years of pensiveness, . . ." F. M. Dostoevskii, *Polnoe sobranie sochinenii,* 30 vols. (Leningrad, 1972-), 21:7. Given this subtext, to use the terminology of Kiril Taranovsky, Mandel'shtam's invective can hardly represent a wish for the return of the good old days before 1917. Rather, it has much in common with the mentality of War Communism when one did not have to "encode" into the formulae of "Chinese" servility the "great and powerful concept of class." Compare this with a 1922 essay, "'The Furcoat'": "This was a severe and beautiful winter of 1920-21, the last harvest-time winter of Soviet Russia; and I miss it, remember it with tenderness. . . . I feel oppressed by my heavy furcoat, just as the whole of Russia feels oppressed by the fortuitous satiety, fortuitous warmth, the ill-gotten second-hand wealth. . . . " SS, 4:95. This is about the first glimmers of economic recovery under NEP. On the "context-subtext" approach see Kiril Taranovsky, *Essays on Mandel'štam* (Cambridge, MA, 1976), pp. 1-20.

[24] Stephen F. Cohen, *Bukharin and the Bolshevik Revolution: A Political Biography, 1888-1938* (New York, 1973), pp. 313-15 and elsewhere.

[25] "I ianvaria 1924" (SS, 1:140) is perhaps the most elaborate of the early representations of this dilemma. On this

poem and, specifically, on the use of the "fourth estate" in Mandel'shtam see Omry Ronen, "An Introduction to Mandel'štam's *Slate Ode* and *1 January 1924:* Similarity and Complementarity," *Slavica Hierosolymitana* 4 (1979):146-58, and "Cetvertoe Soslovie: Vierte Stand or Fourth Estate? (A Rejoinder)," *Slavica Hierosolymitana* 5-6 (1981):319-24. Ronen's insistence on interpreting the term *chetvertoe soslovie* as the proletariat is supported, if indeed it needs any additional support, by the following instance of contemporary usage: ". . . Kuskova writes: 'the growing "fourth estate" cannot give up its hope for a distant paradise for labor, for the great promised land where there will be neither the rifles that shoot nor any inequality. . . . '" A. S. Izgoev, "Na perevale. Zhizn' i publitsistika," *Russkaia mysl'* 33, no. 27 (1912):142 (2nd pagination).

26 "Vek" (SS, 1:135).

27 "Polnoch' v Moskve" (SS, 1:260).

28 "S mirom derzhavnym ia byl lish' rebiacheski sviazan" (SS, 1:222).

29 "Ia s dymiashchei luchinoi vkhozhu" (SS, 1:231).

30 "Za gremuchuiu doblest' griadushchikh vekov" (SS, 1:227). A number of drafts of this poem may be found in the Mandel'shtam archive at Princeton University. They indicate that during the initial stages of composition, Mandel'shtam was working on a text that would later yield three separate poems: the one mentioned above, "Ia s dymiashchei luchinoi vkhozhu" (SS, 1:227), and "Net, ne spriatat'sia mne ot velikoi mury" (SS, 1:232). Other lines and whole stanzas belonging to these drafts, though not all, have been published in SS, 1:242-46. The "wolf" poem is dated by Nikolai Khardzhiev "17-28 March 1932." Osip Mandel'shtam, *Stikhotvoreniia* (Leningrad, 1973), p. 153. The dates for the other two in SS 1 are 4 April 1932 and April 1932, respectively. Khardzhiev also cites four different versions of the concluding stanza of the "wolf" poem (p. 288). For a discussion of the composition of the poem see N. Mandel'shtam (pp. 158, 197, 201-202, 204) and Baines (pp. 20-24).

31 "As to the wolf cycle, it did not bode any special hardship—a labor camp at worst." N. Mandel'shtam, p. 16. See also N. Mandel'shtam, *Vtoraia kniga* (Paris, 1972), p. 603ff., which refers the composition of the "wolf cycle" to the period when the Mandel'shtams "thought that the screws had been tightened to the limit and it was time to expect an improvement." This ambivalence is, of course, detectable in much of Mandel'shtam's poetry written after his return from Armenia in the fall of 1930.

32 The last stanza of the third version cited by N. Khardzhiev (see note 30) contains another allusion to Dante in the second line (*Inferno* 32:46-8). Mandel'shtam: Take me away into the night where the Enisei flows And a tear on the eyelashes is like ice, Because I am not a wolf by blood And a human being will not die in me." Cf.

Dante: ". . . their eyes, which before were moist only within, gushed over at the lids, and the frost bound the tears between and locked them up again." *The Divine Comedi of Dante Alighieri,* tr. and comment. John D. Sinclair; *Inferno* (New York, 1961), p. 397. Dante's description refers to the traitors frozen in the ice of the Caina. Following the logic of the poem, it appears that Mandel'shtam was prepared to accept a possible damnation as a "traitor" of the Revolution (?) from the authorities but not their definition of himself as a man guilty of such treason. If this misfortune were to befall him, the lines suggest, he would interpret it in the same way as Dante—another poet accused of treason—interpreted his exile by transforming it into the pilgrimage of *The Divine Comedy.*

33 "Avtoportret" (SS, 1:164).

34 These poems are "Kholodnaia vesna. Golodnyi Staryi Krym" (SS, 1:271) and "Kvartira tikha, kak bumaga" (SS, 1:272) which was prompted by Pasternak's incautious congratulations when he visited the Mandel'shtams at their newly acquired apartment. See N. Mandel'shtam, *Vospominaniia,* p. 157, and Anonymous, "Zametki o peresechenii biografii Osipa Mandel'shtama i Borisa Pasternaka," *Pamiat'.* Istoricheskii sbornik 4 (Moscow, 1979, Paris, 1981): 314ff., which gives a fairer interpretation of the incident.

35 "My zhivem, pod soboiu ne chuia strany" (SS, 1:286).

36 "Ty dolzhen mnoi povelevat'" (SS, 4:515).

37 "Stansy" (SS, 1:312).

38 "Ot syroi prostyni govoriashchaia" (SS, 1:311).

39 "Oboroniaet son moiu donskuiu son'" (SS, 1:371).

40 "Sred' narodnogo shuma i spekha" (SS, 1:361).

41 "Esli b menia nashi vragi vziali" (SS, 1:372). The correct version of the poem's coda, cited here, appears in a draft copied by Nadezhda Mandel'shtam's hand (deposited at the Mandel'shtam archive at Princeton University). Baines (p. 202), however, follows the poet's widow in insisting that the poem ends instead in "Budet *gubit'* razum i zhizn' Stalin" (Stalin will keep *destroying* reason and life). But as previously noted by Brown (pp. 601-3) and Jangfeldt (pp. 39-41), this reading, or version, contradicts the logic of the rest of the poem. The edition of Mandel'shtam's *Voronezhskie tetradi* prepared by Shveitser follows Brown and Jangfeldt, attributing the other version to "the memory of Nadezhda Mandel'shtam" (p. 85).

42 SS, 4:147-48.

43 See Baines, pp. 174-78. The poems are SS, 1:346-48.

44 "Net, nikogda nichei ia ne byl sovremennik" (SS, 1:141).

[45] The subtitle of another of Mandel'shtam's longer poems, "Pindaricheskii otryvok" (Pindaric fragment, "Nashedshii podkovu, SS, 1:140) identifies this most "irregular" of his poems as belonging to the Pindaric tradition, not via, but bypassing Russian classical poetry. On this poem see Broyde (note 19), pp. 169-99.

[46] Frank J. Miller, "The Image of Stalin in Soviet Russian Folklore," *The Russian Review* 39, no. 1 (1980): 60ff.

[47] Iosif Stalin, *Sochineniia*, 13 vols. (Moscow, 1949-52), 4:46-61. The speech containing these famous six vows was made the day before Lenin's entombment, on 26 January 1924. The formula Stalin used runs as follows: "We vow to thee, Comrade Lenin, that we shall with honor fulfill this thy testament" (*My klianemsia, tovarishch Lenin, chto my s chest'iu vypolnim etot tvoi zavet*) And so six times. The words *klianemsia* and *zavet*, needless to say, belong to the Scriptural vocabulary, the first to The Old Testament, the second to both The New and The Old Testament (*Novyi i Vetkhii Zavet*). They emphasize the sacred nature of the leadership transition, sanctify its legitimacy and correspond to Stalin's self-image that he would later so assiduously cultivate. As the "Ode" demonstrates, Mandel'shtam knew well how to "read" Stalin's speeches. Compare Stalin's vows to Genesis 26:3: ". . . for unto thee and thy seed I will give all these countries, and I will perform the oath (*kliatvu*) which I swear (*klialsia*) unto Abraham thy father."

[48] Viacheslav Ivanov, "Pindar, Pif. 1," *Zhurnal Ministerstva narodnogo prosveshcheniia*, no 7-8 (1899), Otdel klassicheskoi filologii, pp. 50-51.

[49] To what extent Mandel'shtam followed the contemporary official rhetoric in composing the "Ode" may be judged from a greeting to Stalin "telephoned" to Moscow by the Congress of Iakutian Soviets which had just finished debating the project of the Stalin Constitution: ". . . and our first thought, our first word are addressed to you, our dear leader and teacher, father and friend Iosif Vissarionovich! We have no words to express our gratitude and love for you, the creator of the new Constitution—this charter [Magna Carta?] of the socialist peoples. . . . You have made a vow over Lenin's sepulcher to fulfill Lenin's commandment. . . . Have the Iakutian people ever dreamed that they would have in abundance, not only bread, meat, and butter, but vegetables whose growth on a massive scale has until recently been considered a miracle. . . . We vow a holy vow: to cherish, to preserve, . . . to broaden further the Stakhanovite movement that you have brought forth. . . . " *Izvestiia*, 2 October 1936. Mandel'shtam's incorporation into the "Ode" of the myth of Prometheus was also *au courant*. Compare "Prometheus Unbound" by Iakub Kolos which was published in the same issue of *Izvestiia*: ". . . Stretching his shoulders-wings, Prometheus is free. The days have become an epic poem, A fairy tale come true. Who and where from are these heroes—Demchenko, Stakhanov—That are marching in a triumphant formation At the pace of giants?" Stakhanov, it may be recalled was

a miner, whence his association with the Titans imprisoned in the bowels of the earth (Kolos's *velikany*). Prometheus was the son of one of the Titans (*Apollodorus* 1, 2:2). There may be another, metonymic or contiguous, association of Stalin with the myth of Prometheus, which is focused on the Caucasus, the place of Stalin's birth and Prometheus's punishment.

[50] Baines, pp. 174-98.

[51] N. Mandel'shtam, *Vospominaniia*, pp. 198-212.

[52] Cf. Omry Ronen, Mandel'stam's Kascej," *Studies Presented to Professor Roman Jakobson by His Students* (Cambridge, MA, 1968), pp. 252-64, and Baines, pp. 170-73. The poem is "Ottogo vse neudachi" (SS, 1:337).

[53] Brown, 598-600. "Vooruzhennyi zren'em uzkikh os" (SS, 1:367).

[54] N. Mandel'shtam, *Vospominaniia*, pp. 216-20, and Baines, pp. 174-98. Nadezhda Mandel'shtam, for example, insists that the words of the "wasps" poem "I neither draw, nor sing . . ." are in direct opposition to the persona assumed by the poet in the "Ode" where he indeed draws. This observation, although backed by the authority of, perhaps, the sharpest reader of Mandel'shtam's poetry, has the flaws of any literal interpretation. In the "wasps," Mandel'shtam neither "draws nor sings," but in the poem written on the same day, 8 February 1937, he "sings while the soul is moist and the throat dry . . ." (SS, 1:365). The same may be said about another poem (one among many) where a similar reversal takes place: "Do not compare, a living man cannot be compared" (SS, 1:352). But on 4 February, that is, seventeen days later, the poet breaks his own vow: Like the martyr of chiaroscuro Rembrandt, I have gone deep into the mute time, But the sharpness of my burning rib Is guarded neither by those guards Nor by this warrior who are asleep under the thunder storm . . . (SS, 1:364). Here the poet compares himself, not only with his brother artist, but also with the subject of the artist's painting: either the Crucifixion or Christ's resurrection from the tomb (viz., the "burning rib", the "sleeping warrior," the "guards"). Cf. Brown, p. 385. On this subject see also Kiril Taranovsky, p. 113ff.

[55] Pasternak's "Stalin" poem provides a tantalizing example of contemporary poetic usage of the "twin" image and may help to account in part for Mandel'shtam's enigmatic trope "bliznets" (even though Pasternak resorted to a more colloquial synonym, "dvoinia"). This poem, "Ia ponial: vse zhivo," published in *Izvestiia* on 1 January 1936 together with Dem'ian Bednyi's variation on Stalin's "life has become better, life has become merrier" could not have been overlooked by Mandel'shtam, who all throughout his exile maintained contact with Pasternak. Like Mandel'shtam's, Pasternak's "twin" is a mysterious creature whose identity is nowhere explicitly established. Thanks to his "nightingale" attribute, he may be identified as a poet, perhaps an archetypal poet, Homer or, more appropriately, Virgil, the author of the

prophetic *Fourth Eclogue* ("Ne on li, prorocha, nas s vami predrek?"). Further, his association with the "precursors" (*predtechi*) and "leaders" (*vozhdi*) as well as his birth in the vicinity of *anno domini* suggest a composite Christological image. The poem's potential for such an interpretation did not go unnoticed. In the version that appeared later in the year in *Znamia,* the "twin" stanzas were altogether missing while the transparent "two thousand years" (stanza 4) were increased to a vaguely folkloric "three thousand." It is tempting to think that the poetic idea generated by the author of *Bliznets v tuchakh* (*A Twin in the Clouds*) struck a responsive chord in Mandel'shtam who, in a true Acmeist fashion, responded to it with a learned and appropriately enigmatic elaboration (cf. Pasternak's "zagadannyi vprok"). In a letter to Pasternak written on 2 January 1937, when the "Ode" had been almost or entirely completed, Mandel'shtam may have even alluded to this borrowing: ". . . spasibo za *vse* i za to, chto eto 'vse'—eshche 'nevse'" (SS, 4:140). If this is so, then the "Ode" represents another instance in an intense dialogue between the two poets in the 1930s. After all, the "wolf cycle" was prompted by among other things Pasternak's "Krasavitsa moia, vsia stat'," while certain lines in Pasternak's "Vse naklonen'ia i zalogi" read like an admonition to Mandel'shtam put together from bits and pieces of Mandel'shtam's own poetry (The "Ariosto" cycle; SS, 1:267-70). The admonition may have actually had an effect on Mandel'shtam, since its echoes are audible in "Esli b menia nashi vragi vziali" (SS, 1:372). For the text of Pasternak's "Stalin" poem and its versions see his *Stikhi 1936-1956. Stikhi dlia detei. Stikhi 1912-1957, ne sobrannye v knigi avtora. Stat'i i vystupleniia* (Ann Arbor, MI, 1961), pp. 138-39 and 256. For a careful review of Mandel'shtam's relationship with Pasternak see Anonymous (note 34).

[56] "Klialsia Gospod' i ne raskaetsia . . ." (*Psalms* 109:4); "Ne narushu zaveta Moego . . . Odnazhdy Ia poklialsia sviatostiiu Moeiu: solgu li Davidu?" (*Psalms* 88:35-36).

[57] An English rendering of this stanza: "Armed with the eyesight of the slender wasps, Sucking the earth's axis, the earth's axis, I sense all that I have happened to encounter And recall by heart and for no reason. . . . "

[58] Henri Bergson, *Creative Evolution,* trans. Arthur Mitchell (New York, 1944), pp. 153, 188-94.

[59] On the function of paronomasia in Mandel'shtam see Omry Ronen "Leksicheskii povtor, podtekst i smysl v poetike Osipa Mandel'shtama," *Slavic Poetics: Essays in Honor of Kiril Taranovsky* (The Hague, 1973), pp. 367-87.

[60] N. Mandel'shtam, *Vospominaniia,* p. 218, Baines, p. 175. Curiously, neither author mentions this coincidence of Mandel'shtam's and Stalin's first names.

[61] SS, 1:86-87. For an analysis of this poem see Clarence Brown, *Mandelstam* (Cambridge, 1973), pp. 237-45, and

Gregory Freidin, "Time, Identity and Myth in Osip Mandelstam," Doctoral dissertation, University of California, Berkeley, 1979, pp. 164-68.

[62] Cf Derzhavin's ode "Bog."

[63] St. Augustin's *Confessions* and those by J. J. Rousseau.

[64] Katerina Clark, "Utopian Anthropology as a Context for Stalinist Literature," *Stalinism: Essays in Historical Interpretation,* ed. Robert C. Tucker (New York, 1977).

[65] Apart from the "prayer of the cup" at Gethsemane, compare line 10 of stanza V with *Matthew* 27:34: "Dali Emu pit' uksusa, smeshannogo s *zhelch'iu* i, otvedav, ne khotel pit'.''

[66] Tadeusz Zielinski (F. F. Zelinskii) was a classical scholar of great stature and one of the most successful popularizers of classical antiquity at the turn of the century. One of Mandel'shtam's professors at St. Petersburg University and a frequent visitor at Viacheslav Ivanov's "tower" where Mandel'shtam may have met him for the first time in 1909, Zielinski had a profound influence on the poet's "Hellenistic" philosophy. Disagreeing with Ivanov's strong emphasis on the Dionysian, orgiastic aspect of Hellenism, Mandel'shtam must have found Zielinski's more decorous and Catholic version of it far more appealing. There are a number of significant ideological and even textual coincidences between Mandel'shtam's "Pushkin i Skriabin" and Zielinski's treatise *Drevne-grecheskaia religiia* (Petrograd, 1918). Despite the apparent anachronism, Mandel'shtam's reliance on his professor's views should not be dismissed even in this instance. Zielinski was a prolific writer and often published the same text under different titles, feeling free to borrow from himself. Mandel'shtam's passage from the essay in SS, 4:100, follows, at times almost verbatim, Zielinski's words (p. 156): ". . . During the second and, especially, the first century before Christ, the *ring* of Hellenism around the country governed by Zion *was growing tighter and tighter. . . . Its* teaching was a protest against the Judaic legalism in the spirit of Hellenic freedom, Hellenic humaneness, Hellenic filial attitude towards a beloved god . . . whence the fateful Judaization of Christianity which has imparted to it that quality from which it has not been able to liberate itself— intolerance. . . . " On the subject of Zielinski's influence on Mandel'shtam see G. A. Levinton, "'Na kamennykh otrogakh Pierii' Mandel'shtama: materialy k analizu," *Russian Literature* 5, no. 2 (April 1977): 123-70 and no. 3 (July 1977): 201-38. See also Gregory Freidin, "Osip Mandelstam: The Poetry of Time (1908-1916)," *California Slavic Studies* 11 (1980): 168n.

[67] SS, 2:313-19, 4:100.

[68] SS, 4:100. Viacheslav Ivanov whom Mandel'shtam visited in Moscow early in 1916 (Morozov, note 19) had just finished his tragedy *Prometei* and given a lecture on Skriabin at the "concert-meetings of the Skriabin Society

in Petrograd in December 1915 and in Moscow in January 1916." Viacheslav Ivanov, *Sobranie sochinenii*, vol. 3 (Brussels, 1979), p. 736. This lecture, "Vzgliad Skriabina na iskusstvo" (ibid., pp. 172-189), provides a necessary, if negative, context for Mandel'shtam's essay. Ivanov's essay "K ideologii evreiskogo voprosa" (1915, ibid., pp. 308-10) in which he criticizes high-brow antisemitism may give another interesting clue to Mandel'shtam's engimatic formulations.

[69] SS, 2:315.

[70] Zielinski, p. 154.

[71] "While there is death in the world, Hellenism will continue to exist, because Christianity Hellenizes death . . . Hellenism fertilized by death—this is what constitutes Christianity. . . . " SS, 2:318.

[72] "Gde sviazannyi i prigvozhdennyi ston" (SS, 1:356).

[73] It appears that Mandel'shtam's contemporaries were attuned to the poet's reliance on the attributes of verbal magic in his poetry even though it is not clear whether their descriptions of his poetry as "shamanistic," "exorcist," "prayer-like," or "spell-binding" (in the etymological sense) referred to his recitation style of his poetics. "Mandelstam presided as a shaman for two and a half hours . . . They [his poems] were such exorcisms that many people took fright. . . . " This is from a letter by Nikolai Khardzhiev to Boris Eikhenbaum written in November 1932 (Brown, *Mandelstam*, p. 129). "He sang like a shaman possessed by visions." This is about Mandel'shtam's reading at "Prival komediantov" in 1917. Elena Tager, "O Mandel'shtame," *Novyi zhurnal* 85 (1965):184. ". . . Mandelshtam's nostalgic spells: 'Remain foam, Aphrodite, . . . '" Benedikt Livshits, *Polutoroglazyi strelets* (New York, 1978). Similar statements may be found in Vladimir Piast, *Vstrechi* (Moscow, 1929), p. 157, and Georgii Ivanov, *Peterburgskie zimy* (New York, 1952), p. 120. Blok's well-known impression of Mandel'shtam's performance in 1918 belongs to the same genre and resembles closely a description of a shamanistic performance. Cf. E. R. Dodds, *The Greeks and the Irrational* (Berkeley, 1951), p. 140ff. For a scholarly discussion of this aspect of Mandel'shtam's poetry see Omry Ronen, "An Introduction . . ." (note 25) and "K siuzhetu 'Stikhov o neizvestnom soldate' Mandel'shtama," *Slavica Hierosolymitana* 4 (1979):214-21. It may be appropriate to add here that there was nothing idiosyncratic in this aspect of Mandel'shtam's poetry. Among his contemporaries, Sologub, Bal'mont, Belyi, Blok, not to speak of Gumilev and Khlebnikov took a special interest in the "magic of words." Scholarly interest in the problem, too, was quite intense. For a review of contemporary scholarship on the folk uses of verbal magic see V. P. Petrov, "Zagovory," *Iz istorii russkoi sovetskoi fol'kloristiki,* ed. A. A. Gorelov (Leningrad, 1981), pp. 77-142.

[74] Sir James Frazer, *The New Golden Bough* (an abridged edition), ed. Theodore H. Gaster (New York, 1959), p. 35 ("The Roots of Magic").

[75] "Khrani menia, moi talisman."

[76] Frazer, p. 35.

[77] To cite A. A. Potebnia with whose theories Mandel'shtam was more than familiar (viz. "O prirode slova," SS, 2:255ff.), the "fundamental formula of a spell (*zagovor*) . . . constitutes a verbal representation in which a given or contrived phenomenon is compared to one that is desired, with the purpose of fulfilling the latter." *Malorusskaia narodnaia pesnia* (Voronezh, 1877), p. 21.

[78] Igor' Glebov (B. V. Asaf'ev), *Skriabin. Opyt kharakteristiki* (Petersburg-Berlin, 1923), p. 15 and elsewhere. See also "Zapisi A. N. Skriabina," *Russkie propilei* 6, ed. M. O. Gershenzon (Moscow, 1919):202-47, which contains Skriabin's own text of the *Preliminary Act* that was to prepare humanity for the ultimate *Mystery*.

[79] SS, 2:315.

[80] "Talisman" ("Tam, gde more vechno pleshchet").

[81] I am relying here on Roland Barthes, *Mythologies,* trans. Annette Lavers (New York, 1972), especially pp. 117-21. Significantly for the history of myth in contemporary culture, Mandel'shtam praises myth in "Pushkin i Skriabin" in virtually the same words as Barthes uses to damn it:" It is this constant game of hide-and-seek between the meaning and the form which defines myth" (p. 118). Compare this with Mandel'shtam's idea of a poet "playing hide-and-seek with God." On the problem of this sort of concealment fundamental to texts in general see Jacques Derrida, "La pharmacie de Platon," *La dissémination* (Paris, 1972), where one finds the following definition of a text: ". . . un texte n'est un texte que s'il cache au premier regard, au premier venu, la loi de sa composition et la règle de son jeu . . ." (p. 71).

[82] "Prodigal Son" is the title of a chapter in Nadezhda Mandel'shtam, *Vtoraia kniga.*

[83] "The Procurator's cheek twitched and he said: 'Bring me the accused. . . . '" Mikhail Bulgakov, *Belaia gvardiia. Teatral'nyi roman. Master i Margarita* (Moscow, 1973), p. 438. Dostoevskii, *Polnoe sobranie sochinenii* 11:28.

[84] N. Mandel'shtam, *Vospominaniia,* p. 220.

[85] Isaac Deutscher, *Stalin: A Political Biography* (New York, 1967), p. 270. See also Robert C. Tucker, *Stalin as Revolutionary, 1879-1929* (New York, 1973).

Richard Nickson (essay date 1984)

SOURCE: "The Lure of Stalinism: Bernard Shaw and Company," in *The Midwest Quarterly,* Vol. XXV, No. 4, Summer, 1984, pp. 416-33.

[*In the following essay, Nickson uses an examination of the adherence of George Bernard Shaw to Soviet-style communism under Stalin as an example of such adherence among many artists and intellectuals of the time.*]

"I am not a fascist; I am, and have been all throughout my political life, a Communist." That was George Bernard Shaw in 1935. But ten years later he was still having to answer the question "Are you a Fascist, Mr. Shaw?" Patiently replying to a newspaper reporter, Shaw said: "No: I am a Communist. That is, I advocate national control and ownership of land, capital, and industry for the benefit of all of us. Fascists advocate it equally for the benefit of the landlords, capitalists, and industrialists." Finally, in the summer of 1950, the question got reshaped for one of his last press interviews: "Are you a Communist, Mr. Shaw?" The nonagenarian replied: "Yes, of course I am. A war on Communism is ignorant, blazing nonsense. . . . The future is to the country that carries Communism farthest and fastest."

Do we have here Tweedledum and Tweedledee? This popular viewpoint has been carried one curious step further by Susan Sontag, who recently declared, "Communism *is* fascism—successful fascism." In a much-publicized speech Sontag argued, "not only is fascism (and overt military rule) the probable destiny of all Communist societies . . . but Communism is in itself a variant, the most successful variant, of fascism." According to Shaw, such political labels as these are "understood by only a few specialists"—labels that get "continually misplaced by politicians and journalists who do not know what they are talking about." Because it pleases Soviet Russia to wear the label "Communism"—even as Germany opted for "National Socialism"—some politicians and journalists today are happy to fall in with Sontag's call to abandon what she terms old and corrupt rhetoric; the tug of disillusionment results in seeing the distinctions explained by Shaw as passé, meaningless. Ardor and cynicism in political attitudes may both be all too easily attained. As Issac Deutscher remarked about the ex-communist three decades ago, "As a communist he saw no difference between fascists and social democrats. As an anti-communist he sees no difference between nazism and communism." The German Thomas Mann, on the other hand, chose to agree with the Irish playwright that these labels are quite significantly distinguishable. Rejecting though he did any absolutist partisanship, Mann yet affirmed,

> communism remains an idea—albeit a utopic one—with roots far longer than those of Marxism and Stalinism; its untarnished realization will never quite cease to present itself to humanity as a task and a demand. Fascism, however, is no idea at all; it is mere badness, and one can only hope that no nation will ever again succumb to it.

As a lifelong, passionate advocate of socialism, Shaw was decidedly a more partisan figure than Mann, just as he was a good deal less partisan than his Irish playwright friend Sean O'Casey. Furthermore his partisanship was flaunted at a time when the notion (or romance, as he

would have it) was widely held that the direct cause of the extinction of freedom in many lands was the allegiance of some Western intellectuals to communism. To what degree was Bernard Shaw partisan? To what degree guilty?

Assessing his property for the National Trust the month after the playwright's death, Harold Nicolson found one picture of Mahatma Gandhi and two of Joseph Stalin hanging in a collection otherwise given over to one of Mrs. Shaw and many of her husband. Shaw had a brief visit with Gandhi in London; in Moscow he once spent several hours with Stalin. Since he extended so much praise for Stalin and the Soviet Union in the last two decades of his life, a summary of that praise alongside views of the same leader and government expressed by others—especially views contemporary with Shaw's—seems in order and perhaps helpful in throwing some light, three decades after his death, on his fixed bias. As an important, extraordinary man and writer, he merits close attention. The focus here, however, is on Shaw as a representative figure, as one of so many artists and intellectuals caught up in enthusiasm for the Soviet state as manipulated by Stalin.

With only a modicum of historical perspective, one can make out Shaw's polemical stance in offering favorable remarks, in varying degrees, about Mussolini and Hitler. Were the fascist leaders to be condemned? Not—Shaw was determined—by the self-righteous plutocrats who had made their rise possible, nor by the European statesmen who had inflated their reputations. In any event, he never made a pilgrimage to either Mussolini, Franco, or Hitler: a British gesture that became remarkably common. Shaw's equivocal commendations of certain qualities of the fascist leaders and governments were made for the sake of invidious comparison with the government he knew best, the British parliamentarian.

Writing in 1930 the Preface for the 1931 reprint of *Essays in Fabian Socialism,* Shaw expressed doubt about the "resolute constitutionalism" of the Fabians and, as usual, about parliamentarian government. His doubts had been amplified by the First World War and the tendency of many European countries to resort to either revolution or dictatorship, depending on whether they were led by what he called "the revolutionary Left" or "the Fascist Right." "But dictatorships, like proclamations of martial law, are emergency measures," he argued; "and they are subject to the standard objection to martial law that it is no law at all." On the other hand, citing the Russian Revolution, he declared it "a most beneficent event in spite of the incidental horrors which attend all too long delayed revolutions." Seven years later he was doggedly reminding us: 1. "There is no remedy in fascism, but there is in Communism, and Communism is precisely what fascism teaches to abhor." 2. "Russia is an example to all the world of the enormous superiority of Socialism to capitalism, economically, socially and politically." With these distinctions resolutely in mind, Shaw in his many references to twentieth-century dictators never included Stalin.

The Shavian pledge of allegiance was sounded early. In the very year of the Bolshevik Revolution, in the face of volleys of denunciation of the Bolshevists, especially from British socialists and labor leaders, Shaw rose at a public meeting of the Fabian Society to declare simply, "We are socialists. The Russian side is our side." All the same, Shavian allegiance being distinctly non-doctrinaire, Shaw throughout the decade following 1917 as often as not scoffed at the failure of socialism in the Soviet Union. Laudatory appraisals then followed, as did his nine-days visit to the Union of Federated Sensible Societies. Thus that land is referred to in *Too True to Be Good,* the play he completed in the summer of 1931 shortly before his departure on the trip he was persuaded to take by the Marquis of Lothian (Phillip Kerr) in the company of a few other friends, including Viscount and Lady Astor and their son.

In the Hall of Columns in Moscow (the scene, but a half dozen years later, of the infamous treason trials), a spectacular reception for Shaw was held on July 26 to celebrate his seventy-fifth birthday. The white-haired but ruddy Fabian responded by saying:

> It is a real comfort to me, an old man, to be able to step into my grave with the knowledge that the civilization of the world will be saved. . . . It is here in Russia that I have actually been convinced that the new Communist system is capable of leading mankind out of the present crisis, and saving it from complete anarchy and ruin.

A letter to Shaw from Maxim Gorky was read aloud at the reception at Shaw's request, and three days later Shaw and Lady Astor paid a visit to Gorky.

Then at eight o'clock the night following that visit, they and Lord Astor (who had made all the arrangements), Lord Lothian, Maxim Litvinov (the Soviet Commissar for Foreign Affairs), and a British Foreign Office interpreter visited for over two hours with Stalin, who paid a gracious tribute to Shaw as they parted. No mere visitors had been granted an interview with Stalin before. The next day Bernard Shaw and Nancy Astor, at their request, visited Lenin's widow. Finally, that evening Shaw wrote in the visitors' book in the Metropole Hotel, "Tomorrow I leave this land of hope and return to our Western countries of despair."

Before turning to Shaw's impressions of Stalin, readers may care to pause at these references to "crisis" and "despair"—at least long enough to recall that soon after Shaw returned home, Ramsay MacDonald, the Fabian Socialist, resigned as prime minister only to be immediately recommissioned by the king to deal with the great depression and the government crisis as prime minister of a "National Government" composed of Tories and a sprinkling of Laborites. The 1933 "Political Comedy" *On the Rocks* provides further reflections by the disillusioned Fabian on crisis and despair at home; and it is in part that disillusionment which impelled Shaw throughout his remaining years to pin his hopes on a socialist future elsewhere, on a country he knew precious little about, the U.S.S.R.

"I expected to see a Russian working man," Shaw said of his visit with the General Secretary of the Communist Party of the Soviet Union, "and I found a Georgian gentleman. He was not only at ease himself, but he had the art of setting us at our ease. He was charmingly good humored. There was no malice in him; but also no credulity." He also said: "There is an odd mixture of the Pope and the field-marshal in him; you might guess him to be the illegitimate soldier son of a cardinal. I should call his manners perfect if only he had been able to conceal the fact that we amused him enormously." Shaw, who had listened to such fellow Irishmen as Wilde and Yeats, went so far as to say, "I never met a man who could talk so well." And he was pleased to observe of that man, "virtually the Lord Protector of Russia," that he lived with his family in three rooms.

Ten years later, in an interview, Shaw stated: "When I met Stalin in 1931 I knew I was face to face with the greatest statesman in Europe. And the personal impression he made on me did not change my opinion." Still later, in *Everybody's Political What's What?* he wrote of "Russia under the exceptionally clever, politically well read, and heroically public spirited Bolshevik statesmen, led by Lenin and Stalin, now recognized as beyond question the ablest rulers our age has produced." After commenting in that book on such "Great Men" as Cromwell, Peter the Great, Napoleon, Kemal, Mussolini, Hitler, and Stalin, he wrote: "Of these only Cromwell with his Bible and Covenants of Grace, and Stalin with his Marxist philosophy, held themselves within constitutional limits (as we say, had any principles); and they alone stand out as successful rulers." Two years after his enthusiastic address to the Fabian Summer School upon his return from Moscow, Shaw wrote the Preface to *Too True to Be Good.* It is there we come upon this astonishing passage:

> Mr. Stalin is not in the least like an Emperor, nor an Archbishop, nor a Prime Minister, nor a Chancellor; but he would be strikingly like a Pope, claiming for form's sake an apostolic succession from Marx, were it not for his frank method of Trial and Error, his entirely human footing, and his liability to removal at a moment's notice if his eminence should upset his mental balance.

It is likely that Shaw's enthusiasm contributed in part to the decision of his longtime friends and Fabian associates Beatrice and Sidney Webb to conduct their researches in Sovietland. But their interest in the U.S.S.R. was of long standing; Lenin himself had translated their *History of Trade Unionism;* and for them as well as Shaw Fabian gradualism had been getting to seem all too gradual. They engaged a Russian-speaking secretary and were given the services of a Foreign Office interpreter during their stay in Moscow in July and August 1932. Then in September and October 1934 Sidney Webb was there again to check up on their findings. At about that time Stalin announced: "Life has grown better, life has grown merrier."

The Webb findings did not ring with such brevity. Their two-volume *Soviet Communism,* published in

1935, consists of 1,257 pages. It was pronounced by Shaw to be "the first really scientific analysis of the Soviet State." The Webbs succeeded in finding all the *documents* commendable; their research was restricted to reading. Beatrice Webb, in particular, became a Stalin enthusiast. In 1942, the year before her death, she wrote: "Stalin is not a dictator." That same year, in the course of writing about the Webbs, Shaw stated, "The history of Communist Russia for the past twenty years in the British and American press is a record in recklessly prejudiced mendacity."

Three summers after the Shaw visit, H. G. Wells, one-time Fabian, interviewed Stalin for nearly three hours in Moscow. The text of this interview as approved by Wells testifies to masterly political acumen and seemingly frank modesty on Stalin's part. Without agreeing with the General Secretary, Wells yet declared, "I never met a man more candid, fair, and honest, and to these qualities it is, and to nothing occult and sinister, that he owes his tremendous undisputed ascendancy. . . . No one is afraid of him and everybody trusts him." As Boris Pasternak's wife used to say (according to Nadezhda Mandelstam in *Hope Against Hope*), "My children love Stalin most of all, and me only second."

In the recently published notebooks and diaries of Edmund Wilson one can read about a 1935 sports parade in Moscow in which 115,000 people stood up and shouted greetings to Stalin—a parade that struck Wilson at the time as more inspiring than any parade he had seen at home. Early in that decade in France, André Gide began affirming *his* sympathy for communism and admiration for Soviet Russia. A trip through that country in 1936 led, however, to his deploring in his *Retour de l'U.R.S.S. and Retouches à mon Retour de l'U.R.S.S* the poverty he found there, the intellectual regimentation, and the lack of personal liberty. Gide's vehement criticism of the "adoration" of Stalin prompted Lion Feuchtwanger to venture an explanation, or justification. "It is obvious," he wrote, "that this excessive veneration is bestowed upon Stalin not as an individual but simply as the representative of Socialism. . . . When the people say, 'We love Stalin,' that is the most natural and naive human expression of their approval of Socialism and of the government." Feuchtwanger's 1937 book *Moscow* also proved to be the best explanation of the treason trials—in the eyes, anyway, of Bertolt Brecht: the Brecht whose anti-Stalin poems are only now coming to light. These poems, written in 1956 shortly before his death (and three years after Stalin's), were discovered among Brecht's papers. Feuchtwanger's opinion was shared, in 1937, by another notable writer, André Malraux. "Just as the Inquisition did not detract from the fundamental dignity of Christianity," Malraux declared, "so the Moscow trials do not detract from the fundamental dignity [of communism]."

A resumé of Shavian and a few other foreigners' views of Stalin may be rounded out by noticing those of American statesmen who knew Premier Stalin. Thus even Stalin the music lover emerges, a Stalin attuned to the impromptus of Chopin. "The night Stalin was host I had some very nice conversations with him," in the words of Harry Truman in his oral biography. "I liked him. I didn't like what he did, of course, but I liked him. . . . He was just like me about Chopin. He liked Chopin. Churchill didn't." And Averill Harriman, who probably saw more of Stalin than any other American or Briton, has recently written:

> It is hard for me to reconcile the courtesy and consideration that he showed me personally with the ghastly cruelty of his wholesale liquidations. Others, who did not know him personally, see only the tyrant in Stalin. I saw the other side as well—his high intelligence, that fantastic grasp of detail, his shrewdness and the surprising human sensitivity that he was capable of showing, at least in the war years. I found him better informed than Roosevelt, more realistic than Churchill, in some ways the most effective of the war leaders. At the same time he was, of course, a murderous tyrant.

As for Soviet appraisals of Stalin—prior, that is, to the Khrushchev revelations—the bulk of the denunciatory ones is but gradually emerging, for obvious reasons. The year after Shaw's Moscow visit, an anti-Stalinist political comedy by Nikolai Erdman titled *The Suicide* was banned by Moscow censors, despite Gorky's praise of it and Meyerhold's wanting to produce it; it remains unproduced in the Soviet Union to this day. A 1980 New York production of the play unearthed the sobering line, "Only the dead can say what the living think." Then there is Shostakovich's *Lady Macbeth of Mtensk District* (revised as *Katerina Ismailova* in the 1940s), which was first produced early in 1934 with an enormous popular success through its first two years. But in January 1936 Stalin attended a performance and was displeased. An attack on the opera appeared in *Pravda* later that month, and the production was straightway withdrawn.

In recent years much has been heard from the stalwart Alexander Solzhenitsyn. His writings and his program (advocating a withdrawal from the totalitarian state, a return to the authoritarian one) scarcely require replication. Remarking other, less famous artists and victims may seem to be a duty more in order today, though it is a daunting one. Merely listing their names would require so many millions of entries as to leave the mind boggled. Assuredly Stalin had more communists put to death than did Hitler. Did he in fact "liquidate" more people? The answer appears to be a grim "yes."

An often published photograph of Shaw in Moscow shows him seated alongside about a dozen Soviet writers, one of whom was Karl Radek, the Polish Jew who had become the foremost Soviet press propagandist, one of the editors of *Izvestia* and a leading writer of *Pravda*, soon to appear on Stalin's "little list" and hence to disappear. He was one of those placed on trial for one week at the beginning of 1937; he was sentenced (provisionally) to ten years imprisonment. Mass imprisonments and liquidations continued up to the year of Stalin's death in 1953. During the night of August 12, 1952, for example, twenty-four Jewish writers and political figures were executed in the basement of Moscow's Lubianka Prison.

In 1933 a poet chanced to write a brief poem about Stalin—the poet Osip Mandelstam, considered by many Russian readers to be their finest poet of the century. The poem, quoted in his widow's *Hope Against Hope,* describes the leer of the great man's "cockroach whiskers" and the "fawning half-men" around him: distinctly not a publishable poem in Soviet circles then or now. Yet circulate it did. And shortly it fell into the hands of the exterminating profession (even the first draft of the poem that referred to Stalin as "the murderer and peasant-slayer"). In the late Nadezhda Mandelstam's two volumes of memoirs we learn of the torment meted out to her husband, who evidently perished in a transit camp near Vladivostok at the close of 1938.

Interestingly, Shaw in the 1935 Preface to *The Millionairess* alluded to "the miserable plight of the great men neglected, insulted, and occasionally put to death, sometimes horribly, by the little ones." But then he was looking back, at history. Regarding the present, he had a reassuring lecture: "the power to exterminate is too grave to be left in any hands but those of a thoroughly Communist Government responsible to the whole community." The lecture may be found in the Preface to *On the Rocks* which, though principally a plea for tolerance, candidly confronted the fact that "every government, out of necessity, has exterminated people and is exterminating people." Analyzing killing as a political function, Shaw singled out the Soviet Union as "the only country which has yet awakened to this extension of social responsibility" because it had set up the Cheka for the purpose—as he described it—of asking these questions (and of liquidating persons who did not answer them satisfactorily): "Are you pulling your weight in the social boat? are you giving more trouble than you are worth? have you earned the privilege of living in a civilized community?" All reasonable questions. The trick is being able to answer them "satisfactorily" to reasonable judges. Neither the dead poet Osip Mandelstam nor the living poet Joseph Brodsky would be relieved to learn from Bernard Shaw that the security against the abuse of the power of life and death in the Soviet Union lay in this: "the Cheka had no interest in liquidating anybody who could be made publicly useful. . . . "

In 1980 the Nobel prize for literature went to another poet, one born in what is now the Lithuanian Soviet Republic, the Polish author Czeslaw Milosz, who has lived in this country for the past two decades after quitting the Communist diplomatic service of Poland. Much as he dreaded exile, he dreaded more the imposition of so-called socialist realism, requiring artists to serve "the Revolution" in their work, thus rendering inoperable what Milosz believes to be the writer's unique responsibility—"to look at the world from his own independent viewpoint." According to Milosz: "socialist realism is nothing more than a different name for a lie."

Lenin had early on demanded "party-mindedness" of writers in conformity with the Revolution. According to Roy A. Medvedev, "By 1929 there was not a single non-Party publication left, nor any privately owned publishing houses that might have served as vehicles for oppositionist views." Then in the mid-thirties the Writers' Union was created to impose orthodoxy. At the First Congress of Soviet Writers in 1934, Andrei Zhdanov, Stalin's commissar of cultural affairs, made a speech in which the doctrine of socialist realism was initially propounded as the official Party line in literature: "the representation of reality not as it is but as it ought to be." Gorky, who died two years later, found it possible to embroider this doctrine with romantic fustian. The practical results of such doctrines swiftly followed: conformity, the Great Purge, the trials, and the terror of 1937-38.

Yet the 1936 Constitution of the U.S.S.R. most certainly makes for inspirational reading—and not only for such researchers as Beatrice and Sidney Webb. There was, however, a "Catch 22," which Mandelstam, Babel, Pasternak, Akhmatova, Bulgakov, and millions of other Soviet citizens learned could be applied to *everything:* Article 58 of the Criminal Code, which covered "anti-Soviet propaganda" and "counter-revolutionary activity." Can it be that such tyranny of the state was a-borning in the theories of Father Marx, the ones which held that political authority could not be a problem once private ownership of the means of production had been abolished, a theory which seemed to ensure the transient nature of political authority after a communist revolution?

In the Soviet Union, which claims to be a socialist country on the way toward communism, some freedom for the working class and some degree of equality had been effectively destroyed by Lenin as early as 1921; and a theoretical foundation for the role of "leader" was provided at the very outset of Stalin's rule. In short, Lenin cemented the cornerstone of Soviet communism with the suppression of dissent and the persecution of political opponents; Trotsky lent his fanatic support with forcible labor conscription; Stalin and Stalinism followed, with the imposition of forced collectivization on the peasants together with the rise of the General Secretary's personal dictatorship and the formation of a bureaucratic, arbitrary regime.

The lineaments of a Victorian gentleman unprepared to credit the terrible tidings of the twentieth century can sometimes be glimpsed in the later political assessments of Shaw, especially those questioning the possibility of mass brutalities. This is the gentleman who wrote a letter to the Secretary of the British Committee for the Defense of Leon Trotsky in the summer of 1937. Esteeming Trotsky as a writer, Shaw proceeded to argue that Trotsky was spoiling his defense by making the same sort of attacks on Stalin that the Stalinists were making against Trotsky. "Now I have spent nearly three hours in Stalin's presence and observed him with keen curiosity," Shaw wrote, "and I find it just as hard to believe that he is a vulgar gangster as that Trotsky is an assassin."

Yet Angus Wilson, in his recent biography of Kipling, has suggested that Shaw was guilty of accepting "the brutalities carried out in the Stalinist name of collectivist efficiency." Wilson finds nothing in Shaw's work that demonstrates a "proper realization of the meaning of individual suffering." Shaw, who wrote comedies, has himself testified: "Life cannot bear thinking of for those who know what it truly is." And in his "Chronicle" play *Saint Joan* he gave sensitive expression to individual suffering. All the same, for Wilson, and others, Shaw may be seen as one of the "professional humanists" described by Nadezhda Mandelstam as not interested in the fate of individuals.

Shaw once wrote an incisive preface to Dickens's *Hard Times,* in which Josiah Bounderby, a caricature of a capitalist exploiter, regards his dissatisfied employees as expecting to be fed on both turtle soup and venison with a silver spoon. Oddly, in his Preface to *On the Rocks,* after remarking the constant clamor of Soviet workers for more varied food and more of it, Shaw added: "As Stalin said quaintly 'They will be demanding silver watches next.'" Thus spake Josiah Stalin.

Bertrand Russell went so far as to describe the aging Shaw as acquiescing in systematic Marxism. Yet to an interviewer's question—"Are you not a friend of the Russian people?"—put to him in Moscow, Shaw replied with a thunderous "No!" He explained: "I am not the friend of any people as a whole. I reserve the right to criticize every people—including the Russians." Still, it must be owned that Shaw's criticism of the Russians was never so severe as that of Russell, who once recommended dropping the atom bomb on the Soviet Union. Although Shaw chose to affirm that he was a communist in theory and a playwright by profession, the theorist remained an undogmatic one who doubted (as had Marx) that Marx himself was a Marxist. He unswervingly disdained creeds as holding that—like the Athanasian Creed as described by himself—"certain things are so, and that anybody who doubts that they are so cannot be saved."

Shaw's non-doctrinaire espousal of the Soviet cause was chiefly another tactic in his essentially artistic campaign: the exposure of capitalism in the society he knew best, the British. He maintained till his death in 1950 at the age of ninety-four his invidious comparison of British parliamentarianism with what he took to be the relative equalitarianism of a *bona fide* socialist country. That illusion is comparable to the one recently ascribed by Isaiah Berlin to Shaw's friend Albert Einstein: "His [Einstein's] hatred of the cruelty and barbarity of reactionaries and fascists at times led him to believe that there were no enemies on the left—an illusion of many decent and generous people, some of whom have paid for it with their lives."

What did such elderly Western intellectuals as Shaw and the Webbs, for example, actually know about Soviet society? Next to nothing. Jean-Paul Sartre refused to condemn the concentration camps of the Soviet Union; Shaw considered them to be a creation of the venal Western press. The poet Robert Bly recently noted how Pablo Neruda "loved matter, and the poor, was suspicious of gods and ended up praising Stalin. What can one say about that?" Apparently the motes dimming human eyes sometimes have to await hindsight to be exposed for all to see. After all, till the end of the conflict, unbelievable as it now seems, astonishingly few people—other than the murderers and the murdered—were aware of the implementation by the Germans of a policy of total extermination of European Jews during World War II. Moreover, only after a score of years have we attained some detailed knowledge of the atomic bombings of Hiroshima and Nagasaki.

At the time of that war Shaw wrote: "there is no hope for civilization in government by idolized single individuals." He believed that absolute authority (that is, the "last word") should be vested in councils of qualified persons, not in an individual—and that the councils should stand accountable to public criticism. Therefore he had honest reasons for scolding his biographer Hesketh Pearson for repeating "the silly complaint that I have collapsed into dictator-worship in my old age." His political thinking always had a solid base in socialist theory; and the Shavian program was a constructive one, aimed at securing "substantial democracy" for the benefit of everybody. Nevertheless, he is most notable, and most readable, for his destructive criticism. As an artist first and a theorist last, he could always write better about what he knew and deplored than about what he sought and advocated. Whether as advocate or denunciator, Shaw and his matter should not in any case be viewed apart from his customary manner, prominently featuring levity, hyperbole, and paradox.

The complex artist that is Shaw has been misunderstood by shoals of critics, including some dotty ones calling themselves Marxists. Yet two distinguished British Marxians have declared that Shaw "exposed capitalist society with a passionate intensity that has never been equalled by any writer of English" (R. Palme Dutt) and that he has produced "the most remarkable running critique of imperialist civilization from within that has so far appeared" (E. J. Hobsbawn).

Obviously, a running critique of Soviet civilization was *not* supplied by Shaw. In the light of what is now known about it, his guesses, glosses, and good wishes make painful reading, even though one may agree with that other Fabian, the acute Leonard Woolf, who has said, "Communism has its roots in some of the finest of human political motives and social aspirations." He added that the corruption of such motives and aspirations is repulsive, for the *greatest evil is the good corrupted* (a Latin saying quoted by Woolf in his autobiography). It is possible that the greatest of the manifold evils of Stalin and Stalinism is located precisely here, in this shattering corruption.

The good that could be in communist aspiration remains in the future. Regarding the past and present, one can no more judge communism by the Soviet Union than one can judge Islam by the present Islam Republic of Iran or judge Christianity by . . . The Country of Your Choice.

Likewise, Shaw should not be judged exclusively by such a passage as this, from the Preface to *Far-fetched Fables*, written in his nineties:

> The Soviet system . . . includes all the conventional democratic checks and safeguards against despotism now so illusory, and gives them as much effectiveness as their airy nature is capable of. Incidentally it gives Stalin the best right of any living statesman to the vacant Nobel peace prize, and our diplomatists the worst. This will shock our ignoramuses as a stupendous heresy and a mad paradox. Let us see.

The ignoramus in these matters was, alas, Bernard Shaw—tragically duped as have been so many other staunch world betterers. The shock is a great one indeed.

Daniel Rancour-Laferriere (essay date 1985)

SOURCE: "The Deranged Birthday Boy: Solzhenitsyn's Portrait of Stalin in 'The First Circle'," in *Mosaic: A Journal for the Interdisciplinary Study of Literature*, Vol. XVIII, No. 3, Summer, 1985, pp. 61-72.

[*In the following essay, Rancour-Laferriere attempts a psychoanalytical reading of the character Stalin in Solzenicyn's* The First Circle.]

Since Alexander Solzhenitsyn personally experienced the concentration camps of Stalinist Russia, it is not surprising that his extended portrait of Stalin in *The First Circle* should be "bitter" and "sarcastic."[1] What is surprising is that this portrait nonetheless succeeds on an esthetic level and is convincing psychologically. Solzhenitsyn's Stalin is just as real and just as likely to move the reader as his Ivan Denisovich, his Matryona and his Oleg Kostoglotov.

What I propose to do is to psychoanalyze the character of Stalin created by Solzhenitsyn. Any correspondences between this character and the historical Joseph Stalin are merely coincidental for my purposes (though they could hardly have been coincidental from Solzhenitsyn's personal viewpoint).

The portrait begins with Stalin lying on a couch, free-associating (in literary parlance, having an "interior monologue") about his past, and ends with him continuing to free-associate as he falls asleep. Solzhenitsyn thus seems to have *invited* a psychoanalytic discussion of this tyrant. Furthermore, Solzhenitsyn's Stalin is a sick man, mentally,[2] and psychoanalysis is (among other things) a method of understanding mental illness. There may not be much sex and violence in Solzhenitsyn's books, but there is much sickness and much perversity—indeed, how could there not be in a writer whose major concern has been the Soviet *univers concentrationnaire?*

The text for the present analysis will be the new, uncensored 96-chapter version of the novel which was published only in 1978.[3]

I will focus on the long passage devoted to Stalin as he appears shortly after the celebration of his seventieth birthday. This passage comprises chapters 19-23, of which chapter 20, "Sketch of a Great Life," was entirely absent from the earlier, 1969 edition.[4]

I will be concerned specifically with the pathological aspects of Solzhenitsyn's Stalin. This is not to say that every single thing about this Stalin is abnormal. Indeed there is much about him that is ordinary and even rather mediocre for someone who is supposed to be the Leader of All Progressive Mankind.[5] But Stalin is more than mediocre. He is truly twisted and this is what is upsetting. The reader has an opportunity—like it or not—to witness a florid and completely unchecked display of pathological symptoms, symptoms which in any ordinary Soviet citizen would have immediately led to confinement in a mental hospital or a prison.

Basically, these symptoms fall into seven clinical clusters: paranoia, hyperdeveloped narcissism, megalomania, agoraphobia, obsessive power hunger, sadism (with associated masochism), and defective conscience (underdeveloped superego). Other scholars have noticed some of these symptoms, but have not given them systematic study.[6] I want to emphasize that the symptoms, though they are allowed to develop to extreme proportions in Solzhenitsyn's Stalin, just as they do in various mental patients, nonetheless are familiar and understandable to all of us because we have all experienced them within ourselves in rudimentary form. No one is innocent in the Freudian world. Nor for that matter is anyone even innocent in the often insistently self-righteous world of Alexander Solzhenitsyn, for he himself has confessed:

> In the intoxication of youthful successes I had felt myself to be infallible, and I was therefore cruel. In the surfeit of power I was a murderer, and an oppressor. In my most evil moments I was convinced that I was doing good, and I was well supplied with systematic arguments. And it was only when I lay there on rotting prison straw that I sensed within myself the first stirrings of good. Gradually it was disclosed to me that the line separating good and evil passes not through states, nor between classes, nor between political parties either—but right through every human heart—and through all human hearts. This line shifts. Inside us, it oscillates with the years. And even within hearts overwhelmed by evil, one small bridgehead of good is retained. And even in the best of all hearts, there remains . . . an unprooted small corner of evil.

> Since then I have come to understand the truth of all the religions of the world: they struggle with the *evil inside a human being* (inside every human being). It is impossible to expel evil from the world in its entirety, but it is possible to constrict it within each person.[7]

Evil is thus a universal of the human heart. The human task, says Solzhenitsyn, is to "constrict" evil. Freud would have said "repress," and he would have dispensed with the religion, too. But we can hardly expect a man who has done time in the prisons of an atheist state to dispense with religion.

Extending Solzhenitsyn's metaphor, Edward Ericson says of Solzhenitsyn's portrayal of Stalin: "a soul in which the line dividing good and evil has been pushed so far over to one side that evil overwhelmingly predominates must be painted in very dark colors if the depiction is to be accurate."[8] Again, Freud would have said that an individual whose repressive mechanism was as defective as Stalin's was must be depicted as a psychopath if the depiction is to be believable. I would add that the frequent characterization of Solzhenitsyn's Stalin as a *Satanic* figure,[9] a personification of the evils of Soviet society, is also fully in line with a Freudian perspective: "the devil is certainly nothing else than the personification of the repressed unconscious instinctual life."[10]

Let us examine, then, Stalin's psychopathologies one by one. The symptoms in each category are presented according to the order of their appearance in the narration.

Indicative, first, of Stalin's paranoia is his dislike of curtains, recesses and other places where someone might hide (p. 122). He marvels at how many hindrances and enemies fate has sent him (p. 124). After his religious training is over, he feels that God has *deceived* him (p. 125), and then, after getting bored with revolutionary activities, he feels the revolution has *deceived* him (p. 126). When the (1905) revolution actually takes place, he feels the Czarist police, for whom he has been working, have *deceived* him (p. 128). In the 1937 trials he accuses fellow party members of having been Czarist informants (paranoid projective reversal, p. 132), and believes his revolutionary colleagues are laughing at him for his ineptness in theoretical discussions (p. 133). He formulates a strict principle never to believe what anyone says (pp. 137-38). He exerts unrelenting efforts to purge the party and the country of *enemies* (p. 142), and even finds it necessary to sacrifice close friends such as Sergo, and devoted assistants such as Yagoda and Yezhov (p. 143).

To the same effect, Stalin sees himself as long ago having turned the Soviet Union into a communist country *if it were not for* . . . —there follows a half page list of problems and enemies that Stalin has been fighting, including such unlikely items as "greedy housewives," "spoiled children" and "streetcar chatterboxes" (p. 146). Most of this passage is done in a thick Georgian accent (misplaced stresses, etc.), and by the end of the passage Stalin has gone from thinking silently to talking aloud, and nearly has a shaking fit.

Secret passages and one-way mirrors have been installed in his residence just as his bedroom is without windows, and the walls are armor-plated (p. 148). Elsewhere in his residence, where there are windows, they are bulletproof

(p. 174). Disliking people who reach into their inner pockets in his presence (p. 150), he loves to hear Abakumov's regular revelations about hostile political groups (p. 154). No matter to whom he is talking, he always wonders whether the person is to be believed, and whether it is yet time to kill this individual (p. 155).

Solzhenitsyn's Stalin has never trusted anyone—not his mother, not God, not the revolutionaries, not the peasants, not the workers, not the engineers, not the soldiers and generals, not his intimates, not his wives and lovers, not his children (p. 155). Only Hitler was trusted, mistakenly, as we will see.

At the sight of the portraits of Zhelyabov and Perovskaya (terrorists who are made to shout "Kill the tyrant!"), Stalin has a coughing fit and orders the portraits removed (p. 158). The more lives Stalin takes, the more he fears for his own, the more he fears assassination plots, the more complicated becomes the guard system around him, the more security measures he orders for himself and his subordinates (p. 159).

The conversation with Abakumov, in which Stalin again speaks at length in a heavy Georgian accent, is primarily about counter-revolutionaries, terrorists, political sabotage (especially among youth), and the need to re-introduce capital punishment. At one point he declares that "The whole world is against us," that a "big war" will be necessary, and that such a war would have to be preceded by a "big purge" (p. 164). Again he thinks that everyone is trying to deceive him (p. 171), and in this case he is at least partially correct, since Abakumov has just managed to speak with the aging and forgetful leader for an hour and still avoid bringing up the crucial topic of secret telephones.

Indicative, in turn, of Stalin's pathological narcissism are the following. He reads and rereads incessantly his own biography, and he expects everyone to carry the conveniently sized biography around with them all through life; he warmly agrees with everything in the sycophantic biography—he is a genius of war strategy, he was Lenin's deputy from 1918 on, he is terribly modest, etc.; moreover, he helps his biographers write the biography (p. 117). The photographs of himself in the biography (p. 125) fuel his self love and recall those years when, as one of Lenin's henchmen, he traveled about in his smart officer's uniform and calf boots, with a clean-shaven face and moustache, and with the women adoring him (p. 135); in love with his voice, he likes to sit and listen to his old recorded speeches at night (p. 153). Extreme security measures he therefore feels are necessary because his person is priceless for human history (p. 159); in his view, he has to survive until he is ninety, because he is irreplaceable (p. 165).

Symptoms of Stalin's megalomania similarly abound. He wants his biography to be published for a third time, in an edition of ten or twenty million (p. 117), with his motive stemming from his belief that the revolution left the people without a god (p. 118). Feeling that he constantly has to correct the misguided Lenin (p. 119), in 1918 he believes that he is superior to Lenin, Trotsky and all those other "bookish dreamers" (pp. 133-34). Comparing himself to Napoleon, he imagines himself being called "Emperor of the Planet" and "Emperor of the Earth" (p. 166). He fantasizes living forever, but decides to settle for monuments, the heads of which will soar above the clouds on the Kazbek and the Elbrus (p. 166). Everyone is below him, only God is above him. He and God are alone (p. 167). He imagines that he has abilities in the area of linguistics, and takes it upon himself to write a tract supporting Chikobava against Marr (pp. 172ff). He has fantasies about conquering West Europe just as soon as he has built atom bombs and purged the rear. He will take over the whole world without bothering with revolutions (p. 177).

If Stalin is megalomanic, however, he is also agoraphobic. He feels he can easily avoid the *space* of the outside world, though he cannot avoid the passage of time (p. 116). Russia is to him a huge, unpeopled space (p. 174). When he steps out of his cozy quarters to go to a banquet in a large hall, when he has to cross the "frightening space" between the automobile and the door, and when he has to cross the "too broad" foyer—he feels ill (p. 175). Having gained power over one-sixth of terrestial space, he has become afraid of it.

Another set of Stalin's pathological symptoms takes the form of obsessive power hunger. The first time he leads a revolutionary political demonstration he becomes ecstatic, telling the followers what to do and where to go. He decides that giving orders is much better than being rich (p. 126). After working as a Czarist secret agent for a while, he is made a member of the Central Committee, and decides to rejoin the revolutionaries on the ground that a TsK member has more power than a petty secret agent (p. 130). Already at an early stage of the revolution he notices how much *respect* he gets from people when he signs this or that order for an execution (p. 135). He believes that he alone (not Lenin nor Trotsky) can direct the revolution (p. 134). He tricks Churchill and Roosevelt into giving him control of Poland, Saxony, Thüringen, Sakhalin, Port Arthur, etc. (p. 144). Only the death of one's enemy assures one of real power, he thinks (p. 163).

Nor is Stalin without sado-masochistic traits. He displays a (to the reader) false sense of pity for the Russian people, thinking that the revolution has made them orphans (p. 118), and that they therefore are in need of his guidance and help. Solzhenitsyn's heavy-handed irony here is almost a caricature of the psychoanalytic principle according to which "pity is . . . a character trait connected with an original sadism," as Otto Fenichel puts it.[11] Stalin celebrates his birthday by arranging for Traicho Kostov to be beaten to death (p. 119). He feels obliged to live and suffer for another twenty years for the sake of the people. This way of accepting the pains and infirmities of old age may be thought of as a masochistic delusion on Stalin's part, but it also appears to be a kind of *identification* with

the abused object typical of sadism, since the suffering is expressed specifically as a twenty-year *prison term* (p. 121). He takes great pleasure in not informing the people he investigates whether they will be executed or not (p. 137; cf. p. 150). He takes sadistic pleasure in developing facial expressions and gestures which terrorize people around him (p. 154). He takes sadistic pleasure in Hitler's destruction of Europe (p. 156). While conversing with Abakumov, he jokingly suggests that when capital punishment is reinstated, it first be applied to Abakumov (p. 163).

A final set of pathological traits concerns Stalin's defective conscience (underdeveloped superego). He is often referred to as having an "iron will" (e.g. p. 117, p. 148). His Russian alias "Stalin" (from *stal,* steel) is also aimed at conveying the impression of a determined, unstoppable leader. But the rigid determination and lack of hesitation in executing and imprisoning his (real or imagined) enemies in fact indicates a complete lack of guilt feelings about perpetrating such horrors, or at best a thorough repression of what faint voice of conscience he might have heard. Although some rudimentary functions of conscience may be detected in the passage where Stalin secretly locks himself up in his room and prays on his knees, this behavior is not a request for forgiveness for having let Hitler invade. Nor does Stalin want to be forgiven for all the other crimes he has committed. He wants only to be saved from Hitler's invasion, and makes a vow to let the Russian Orthodox Church function and not to persecute believers if God will grant his wish. God does, of course—or that is how Stalin sees it—and, in one of the few mildly positive acts that Solzhenitsyn has Stalin do, Stalin keeps his vow.

Many of the acts of aggression, cruelty, deception, etc. which are listed in the previous categories could not have been carried out by Stalin if he had had the normal ability to feel guilty. I say "many" rather than all these acts because in a wartime or revolutionary situation even the normal person does things which the superego would not under normal circumstances permit. Also, at some point in his ascent to power it may have become absolutely impossible for Stalin to stop committing horrors, because power itself would have been an antidote to whatever guilt he may have felt; as Fenichel observes, "the more power a person has, the less he needs to justify his acts. . . . the struggle against guilt feelings through power may start a vicious circle necessitating the acquisition of more and more power and even the commitment of more and more crimes out of guilt feelings in order to assert power. . . . These crimes may then be committed in an attempt to prove to oneself that one may commit them without being punished, that is, in an attempt to repress guilt feelings . . ." (p. 500).

Some of the pathologies I have described may, to the reader, look more like the narrator's ironical jabs at Stalin. The repeated use of the verb "deceive" to characterize how Stalin perceives the world, for example, may seem to be a satirical pseudo-identification on the narrator's part rather than a personal problem of Stalin's.[12] But there is no *a priori* reason why it cannot be both. The numerous grandiose epithets for Stalin (e.g., "Father," "Master," "Leader," "the Highest," "the All-Powerful," "the Greatest of the Great," "the God-Chosen Leader," "the Wisest of the Wise," etc.) can be interpreted as simultaneously revealing Stalin's megalomania and the narrator's satiric hostility—the latter especially because these epithets tend to appear in contexts where the opposite of their literal meaning is clearly intended. Similarly, Stalin's pretense at doing linguistics is not only a symptom of his megalomania, but is a manifestation of what Edward Brown calls the narrator's "fierce satiric intent" (p. 363). The fond reading of the biography is both a symptom of Stalin's hyperdeveloped narcissism and another sign of the narrator's negative attitude (Kern describes the passage as "lightly laced with acid," i.e., the acid of satire, p. 11). The narrator's remark about Stalin's fear of all the space he has conquered is a particularly successful combination of clinical diagnosis (without using the technical term "agoraphobia") and ironic aggression. Note that when Stalin seems *most* deranged, namely, when he fantasizes starting a Third World War and becoming "Emperor of the Planet" is precisely when the narrator seems—to some readers at least—to have gone *too* far with his satiric thrust.

Not all of the horrors depicted in the Stalin chapters are necessarily the personal psychological problems of Joseph Stalin. Many of them are pathological features of the people around him, or collective aberrations of the entire Soviet society (as depicted by Solzhenitsyn), aberrations which harmonized nicely with the personal psychopathology of Stalin. Hence what Kern describes as the wonderfully Tolstoyan and hyperbolic description (p. 8) of how widely Stalin is pictured is not a part of Stalin's megalomania *per se*, but is a way of telling us how the Soviet masses *fed* that megalomania: "On the ottoman was reclining a man whose likeness had so often been sculpted in stone; painted in oil, water colors, gouache, sepia; drawn with charcoal, chalk, crushed brick; formed from road-side pebbles, sea shells, glazed tiles, wheat grains and soy beans; carved on bone; grown from grass; woven in rugs; formed by flying airplanes; photographed on motion picture film—more than any other likeness for the three billion years of the existence of the earth's crust" (p. 115). Similarly, the thousands upon thousands of gifts and greetings Stalin receives for his seventieth birthday *encourage* his narcissistic need to be loved (a particularly strong need, since the acting out of his paranoia has eliminated any possibility of having real friends). The simple fear of Stalin in most of his colleagues *gratifies* his obsession with gaining power over them. The very real hostility which some of these colleagues (e.g., Trotsky) have toward Stalin seems to *justify* his paranoia.

Stalin's illness, in other words, comes into existence and flourishes only because a specific social context permits it to. It is, of course, obvious that Stalin cannot personally carry out every arrest, every execution, every beating, every sentencing to hard labor that is perpetrated in Solzhenitsyn's depiction of Soviet reality. However, there are plenty of police personnel, as sick or sicker than Stalin, who are ready and willing to do these things.

There are some more forms of neurotic behavior in Solzhenitsyn's Stalin that do not fall into the general categories described above. For example, Stalin is very prone to denial. When a doctor warns him about his deteriorating health, the doctor is shot (p. 118). When an oblast committee secretary informs him about the tendency for young people to flee the kolkhozes, this secretary is shot (p. 121). These are not particularly sadistic acts, but manifestations of a refusal to deal with reality.

A rather mild neurotic symptom is Stalin's temper tantrums. He will step on a comrade's foot, or spit at him, or blow hot ashes into his face (p. 150). There are also behaviors which are not even particularly neurotic, though we may find them quite repellent. For example, Stalin's participation in extorting large sums of money from capitalists (the so-called expropriations) seems to be just plain greed. His panicky flight from Moscow at the height of Hitler's invasion is pure cowardice, a natural enough human trait, and not a psychopathology.

There is also, of course, much overlap in the categories of pathology I have charted. For example, many of the items listed under paranoia have the *effect* of furthering Stalin's megalomania and gratifying his lust for power. Thus, to imagine that many of his close collaborators are "enemies" leads Stalin to kill them off, but their absence then leaves less competition and thereby encourages his megalomania and leaves him with more power. His passionate striving for power can itself be understood as a route to narcissistic gratification (Fenichel says power hunger reveals a need for narcissistic reassurance, p. 479). Also, there is considerable overlap between the items listed under pathological narcissism and those under megalomania. It is difficult to decide, for example, whether Stalin's repeated view of himself as irreplaceable is the expression of a deeply wounded narcissism or a megalomanic delusion.

Freud did observe that megalomania may constitute a regression to a primitive, infantile form of narcissism (XII, 72; XIV, 86). Indeed, our impression that many of Stalin's pathologies overlap with one another makes sense in light of what psychoanalysts believe is an intrinsic relatedness of many forms of pathology. To take another example, Freud says that "the majority of cases of paranoia exhibit traces of megalomania," and that "megalomania can by itself constitute a paranoia" (XII, 72). But what is interesting from the psychoanalytic viewpoint is *how* various psychopathologies can be related to one another. In his famous essay on the Schreber case (XII, 62-65), Freud comes up with the idea that one particular constellation of pathologies might be thought of as variations on one, essentially homosexual proposition,

I (a man) love him.

The relations of pathologies to one another are relations of propositions.[13] Stalin's paranoid delusions of persecution, for example, might be arrived at by the progression

I *do not love* him (negation).

I *hate* him (reversal).

He hates (persecutes) *me* (subject-object inversion).

His grandiose narcissism, on the other hand, might be derived as follows:

I do not love *any one* (categorical negation).

I love only *myself.*

For Stalin to trust no one and to believe everyone is an "enemy" (he hates me) is just two propositional steps (contradicted verb, reversed subject) away from his megalomanic/narcissistic belief that he is a precious and irreplaceable personality (I love myself).

One gets the impression from Solzhenitsyn's portrait (especially from the new, uncensored and much more complete portrait) that Stalin's narcissism had been wounded at a very early stage, and that he carried this wound with him for the rest of his life. Perhaps it was the birthday boy's illegitimate and low origin which first did the damage: "Hopelessly did this life come into being. An illegitimate son, supposedly fathered by an impoverished, drunken shoemaker. An uneducated mother. The grubby child Soso did not exactly come out of the pools beside the hillock of Queen Tamara. Not that he wanted to become lord of the earth, but how in the world was this child supposed to escape from a most vile, most degrading situation?" (p. 124). Right from the start, then, everything was wrong. Later, after Stalin had become "leader of the world proletariat," his mother on her deathbed would confront him .with the words: "It's a shame you didn't become a priest" (p. 166). This Stalin interprets as the worst possible criticism. He is a failure.

Solzhenitsyn's Stalin thus could not have had a very positive image of himself. He was a Narcissus looking into very muddy, very disturbed waters, and he would have to spend the rest of his life trying to improve the faulty image, inflating it and often replacing it with the *projected* images of enemies deliberately stirring up the waters. Stalin nicely illustrates Freud's belief that "paranoics have brought along with them a *fixation at the stage of narcissism . . .*" (XII, 72). In Heinz Kohut's terms, Stalin appears to be suffering from a generalized "narcissistic personality disorder."[14]

Psychoanalysts know that the narcissistic mirror which gives rise to paranoia also gives rise to a duality of the psyche. The paranoid personality is a personality observed by itself. It is a double personality, a split personality. The imagined persecutor is one's double, as Dostoevsky understood quite well sixty-five years before Freud's analysis of Senatspräsident Schreber.

Dostoevsky was probably not consciously aware, however, that persecutory delusions can camouflage a latent homosexuality. The paranoic individual fears that the persecutor seeks sexual union with him. It took Freud, Rank and later experimental psychologists to bring *this* ego-distonic material to the surface.[15]

Applying the idea to Solzhenitsyn's Stalin, we would have to say that the mentally ill old tyrant has spent most of his life liquidating potential sex objects. Better to kill them than to admit possibly erotic feelings about them. For, if they cannot be killed, they will prance about, mocking the self by duplicating the self.

Take Tito, for example. Joseph Tito is Joseph Stalin's double and his nemesis. Trotsky, Kirov, Kamenev, Zinoviev, Churchill, Roosevelt and others were all problems that were solved in one way or another. Kolchak and Nicholas II could come back from the grave, for all Stalin cared. But Tito was something else. Tito did not budge: "Joseph had tripped on Joseph." Joseph the Yugoslav was proposing a "better socialism" than Joseph the Georgian had to offer: "A better socialism?! Different than Stalin's?! The snotnose! Socialism *without* Stalin is just Fascism pure and simple!" (p. 145). A page later Stalin is reading that "pleasant book" by Renaud de Jouvenal, *Tito, the Traitors' Marshall,* which completely corroborates his feelings about his rival. Tito is described as a "vain, touchy, cruel, cowardly, revolting, hypocritical, base tyrant" (p. 147). If this sounds familiar, I am not sure Solzhenitsyn meant it to be. The crude caricature of Tito by de Jouvenal is embedded within Solzhenitsyn's own hatchet job on Stalin, and seems to be that hatchet job all over again, in miniature. Just as Stalin did, Tito shows cowardice in the face of the German onslaught, engages in intrigue, destroys his enemies, covers himself with medals, etc. Stalin would only like to add: "Didn't Tito have some sexual deficiencies too?" What could those deficiencies be, and why is Stalin interested in them? Solzhenitsyn does clearly intend a parallel between the Stalin biography (described earlier in the chapter) and the Tito biography—both of which Stalin has difficulty putting down.

Another double of Stalin's is Adolph Hitler. Stalin had a special place in his heart for Hitler. Whether this was true of the real, historical Stalin is irrelevant here, though there have been some interesting differences of opinion on the subject.[16]

What matters for the reader of Solzhenitsyn's novel is this paradox: Stalin fears persecution from everyone but the one person whom he *should* fear, the one person who does in fact attack. Stalin's "idiotic faith in Hitler"[17] is based on an *affirmation* of his similarity to Hitler, while his hatred of Tito is based on a *denial* of his similarity to Tito. Paranoia cannot survive without denial of the identification-based doubling effect, and the open identification with Hitler temporarily cancels Stalin's usual paranoia. Hitler is a "man of action," just as Stalin is. Hitler smashes Poland, France and Belgium, and invades the skies over England, just as Stalin would like to be doing. Stalin is so carried away by his sadistic identification with Hitler that he pays no heed to the warnings of his subordinates about a possible German invasion. And sure enough, Hitler catches him with his pants down. Or, as I have put it elsewhere, there seems to be a "hole" in Stalin's paranoia, a spot where the usual mistrust is perversely inverted into trust, a spot where Stalin seems to invite anal penetration by the aggressor.[18]

The most fundamental of Stalin's doubles is of course Stalin himself. For example, was he a Czarist agent or a Bolshevik? The narrator says: "Not only was his will not made of *steel* in those days, but it became completely double, he lost himself and could see no way out" (p. 128). Is this former seminarian a believer in God, or is he the self-proclaimed leader of the avowedly atheistic international Communist movement? Is Stalin a Georgian or is he a Russian? Is he Djugashvili or is he Stalin? We know he sincerely admires the Russians (who have always been "faithful" to their "Father"). We know he would *like* to be a Russian: "Stalin had, with the passage of years, wanted to be taken as a Russian as well" (p. 168). But the narrator's savage parody of his heavy Georgian accent tells us that Stalin could never really make it as a Russian. He can identify with the Russians in his sentimentally sadistic way, but he can never *be* a Russian. He is thus rather like two other famous tyrants who figure in the Stalin chapters, namely, the non-German Adolph Hitler and the non-Frenchman Napoleon Bonaparte.

Solzhenitsyn's Stalin is a fragmented, perverse and pathological personality. The author does gain some distance from this personality by being satirical and ironic. As Vladislav Krasnov says, ". . . Solzhenitsyn shows great sympathy for many characters, including Communists, but not for the 'leader'."[19] We too, as readers, are relieved of too painful an involvement with the sick birthday boy by the author's ironic distance.

Yet the very need to be relieved bespeaks a profound involvement on our part. There is something much too engrossing about Solzhenitsyn's Stalin. Alexander Schmemann speaks of "the life *we* live during those several unforgettable hours in Stalin's cell. . . ."[20] We are all too easily sucked into the vortex of Stalin's free associations, into what is really the innermost circle of hell in Solzhenitsyn's deliberately Dantean novel. As Sergei Dovlatov contends in his *Zone*, another novel of the prison genre: "hell is us ourselves. . . ."[21]

NOTES

[1] These terms are from Gary Kern, "Solzhenitsyn's Portrait of Stalin," *Slavic Review*, 33 (1974), 2.

[2] Kern speaks of Stalin as "diseased" (p. 7) and says the reader has "an impression of a mental structure falling to pieces" (p. 15). Deming Brown says Stalin is, among other things, "sick"; see his *Soviet Russian Literature Since Stalin* (Cambridge, 1978), p. 316.

[3] Aleksandr Solzhenitsyn, *Sobranie sochinenii: V kruge pervom*, vols. 1 and 2 (Vermont/Paris, 1978). Translations are mine; quotations are from volume I.

[4] Solzhenitsyn, *V kruge pervom* (New York, 1969).

[5] Edward Brown refers to Solzhenitsyn's Stalin as a "mediocre man" and a "banal nonentity"; see his "Solzhenitsyn's Cast of Characters," in *Major Soviet Writers: Essays in Criticism*, ed. E. Brown (London, 1973), p. 365.

[6] See, for example, Brown, pp. 360-65. Brown says that "Solzhenitsyn's purpose is . . . to examine the psychic makeup of one of history's great criminals" (p. 361). What a psychoanalyst would call pathological narcissism Brown calls the "chronically festering *amour-propre*" in Stalin. Other literary studies which mention Stalin's pathological behaviors (usually his paranoia), and which I have found helpful, are: Susan Layton, "The Mind of the Tyrant: Tolstoy's Nicholas and Solzenitsyn's Stalin," *Slavic and East European Journal*, 23 (1979), 479-90; Helen Muchnic, "Solzhenitsyn's 'The First Circle'," *Russian Review*, 29 (1970), 154-66; Sviatoslav Ruslanov, "*Epigon Velikogo Inkvizitora,*" *Grani*, 92-93 (1974), 279-94; Deming Brown, p. 316; Kern, "Solzhenitsyn's Portrait."

[7] Solzhenitsyn, *The Gulag Archipelago, 1918-1956*, trans. T. Whitney (New York, 1975), IV, 615. The original is: *Arkhipelag GULag, 1918-1956* (Paris, 1974), IV, pp. 602-03.

[8] Edward Ericson, Jr., *Solzhenitsyn: The Moral Vision* (Grand Rapids, 1980), p. 73.

[9] See, for example: Ruslanov, pp. 284ff; David M. Halperin, "The Role of the Lie in *The First Circle*," in *Aleksandr Solzhenitsyn: Critical Essays and Documentary Materials*, ed. J. Dunlop, R. Haugh, A. Klimoff (Belmont, Mass., 1973) p. 262.

[10] Sigmund Freud, *Standard Edition of the Complete Psychological Works of Sigmund Freud*, trans. and ed. J. Strachey (London, 1953-65), IX, 174. For a more detailed study of the demonic from a psychoanalytic perspective, see my *Out From Under Gogol's Overcoat* (Ann Arbor, 1982), pp. 62ff.

[11] Otto Fenichel, *The Psychoanalytic Theory of Neurosis* (New York, 1945), p. 476.

[12] There are at least two historically real, *non*-paranoid uses of this verb in the Stalin chapters: "Hitler *deceived* him . . ." (p. 143), and "to *deceive* the experienced investigators . . ." (p. 148)—the last a reference to Traicho Kostov's public retraction of an earlier, forced confession.

[13] For a discussion of psychoanalyses based on propositional relationships, see my "'*Ja vas ljubil*' Revisited," in *Russian Poetics*, ed. Dean Worth, Thomas Eekman (Columbus, 1983), pp. 305-24.

[14] Heinz Kohut, *The Analysis of the Self: A Systematic Approach to the Psychoanalytic Treatment of Narcissistic Personality Disorders* (New York, 1971).

[15] See Freud, XII, 12-82; Otto Rank, *The Double: A Psychoanalytic Study* (1914), trans. H. Tucker (Chapel Hill, 1971); Seymour Fisher and Roger Greenberg, *The Scientific Credibility of Freud's Theories and Therapy* (New York, 1977), pp. 255-70.

[16] For example, Adam Ulam strongly doubts that Stalin had "faith" in Hitler before Hitler's invasion of Russia, while Christopher Moody is inclined to believe that Solzhenitsyn's Stalin is true to life. See Ulam, *Stalin: The Man and his Era* (New York, 1973), p. 529; Moody, *Solzhenitsyn*, rev. ed. (New York, 1975), pp. 108-09.

[17] Moody, *Solzhenitsyn*, p. 108.

[18] Daniel Rancour-Laferriere, "The Boys of Ibansk," *Psychoanalytic Review*, 72 (1985), 528.

[19] Vladislav Krasnov, *Solzhenitsyn and Dostoevsky: A Study in the Polyphonic Novel* (Athens, 1980), p. 33.

[20] Alexander Schmemann, "On Solzhenitsyn," in *Critical Essays and Documentary Materials*, p. 38.

[21] Sergei Dovlatov, *Zona: zapiski nadziratelia* (Ann Arbor, 1982), p. 7.

Rosalind Marsh (essay date 1989)

SOURCE: "The Image of Stalin in Soviet Literature During Stalin's Lifetime," in *Images of Dictatorship: Portraits of Stalin in Literature*, Routledge, 1989, pp. 17-53.

[*In the following essay, Marsh reviews portrayals of Stalin in Soviet literature written and published during his leadership.*]

With the exception of Lenin,[1] no historical figure in modern times has been the subject of as many literary and dramatic portrayals as Joseph Stalin. Many writers in the USSR, including both hack writers and the best writers in the country, have chosen—or been forced—to treat this subject. In Stalin's time Soviet writers were obliged to contribute to the ever-growing cult of Stalin's personality; and after his death Stalin became a subject of intense speculation by Soviet writers, as a result of the party's reassessment of Stalin's achievements and the need of individual writers to come to terms with their own and their country's past. Hence a sharp dichotomy exists between literary portraits composed in Stalin's lifetime and after his death. Another useful distinction can be drawn between works published in the USSR, where portrayals of Stalin are subject to a rigorous scrutiny for ideological purity, and works published elsewhere, where there are no such restrictions. The latter group includes a wide spectrum of western writers and dissident and émigré Russian authors with different approaches to Stalin, but they are all united by their freedom to depict Stalin in any way they wish.

Solzhenitsyn's portrait of Stalin in the new version of *The First Circle* manifests some similarities to, but also considerable differences from, other fictional depictions of Stalin both in the USSR and in the west. An examination of other literary portraits of Stalin will help to highlight the originality of Solzhenitsyn's conception, as well as to provide a measure by which the literary qualities and historical accuracy of his portrait can be judged.

EARLY HOSTILE PORTRAITS

Not surprisingly, few Soviet writers are known to have expressed opposition to Stalin during his lifetime, since derogatory references to Stalin could mean persecution, imprisonment, or even death. Paradoxically, this reflects the high regard in which literature has been held in the USSR: as Osip Mandelstam said in the 1930s, 'Poetry is respected only in this country—people are killed for it. There's no place where more people are killed for it'.[2] Nevertheless, in the 1920s, before Stalin's rise to uncontested leadership of the party, three prominent Soviet authors, Kornei Chukovsky, Evgeny Zamyatin and Boris Pilnyak, inspired by the long-standing Russian tradition of using literature for the scrutiny of socio-political issues, were drawn to treat the subject of Stalin.

One of the first Soviet writers to make an oblique allusion to Stalin was Chukovsky, in his narrative poem for children, *The Big Bad Cockroach* (1923).[3] Chukovsky paints an allegorical picture of an idyllic animal kingdom terrorised by 'a dreadful giant . . . A big bad cockroach' which rages and twitches its moustache, snarling 'I'll devour you, I'll devour you, I won't show any mercy'. As Lev Loseff has shown, the tyrant-cockroach is an image common in Russian folklore: the etymology of the Russian word 'cockroach' (*tarakan*) is linked with the Turkic word 'dignitary' (*tarkan*); and the figure of Torokanchik, the representative of an alien and hostile power, appears in a number of folk epics.[4] The Russian cockroach has whiskers, so 'Tarakan' is often used as a nickname for any man possessing a thick, bristly moustache. Moreover, the word 'moustache' (*usy*) was in use up to the nineteenth century as a slang term for 'thieves' in a cycle of folk ballads depicting thieves who pillage and torment the simple people, the *muzhiki*. Thus the images of 'moustache' and 'cockroach' combine to form a single, powerful image evoking coercion and unlawfully acquired power. Chukovsky composed his poem before Stalin became dominant, at a time when several of the contenders for power in the party had moustaches (Zinoviev and Trotsky, for example, as well as Stalin), so his satire was aimed not at any specific ruler, but at any dictatorship imposed by a small political faction against the will of the majority of the population. It was only with hindsight that Chukovsky's vision could be seen as prophetic, and was clearly regarded as such in the USSR. Stalin's nickname 'The Cockroach', which was in use from the beginning of the 1930s, was taken from Chukovsky's poem; and in the 1950s, in a performance based on *The Big Bad Cockroach* at the Leningrad Young People's Theatre, the title character was played as an undisguised caricature of Stalin. Chukovsky's work, moreover, established a whole genre of successful anti-Stalinist Aesopian satire in the guise of children's literature.

One of the first Soviet prose writers to portray a character bearing some resemblance to Stalin was Zamyatin, in his comic story *X* (1926), a satire on the superficial adaptation of some people to the new Soviet environment.[5] Zamyatin depicts Comrade Papalagi, a terrifying member of the Cheka (secret police), whose foreign-sounding name and huge, black, pointed moustache are reminiscent of Stalin (whose real name was Djugashvili). Zamyatin emphasises Comrade Papalagi's ruthlessness: his moustache is like 'a pair of horns ready to gore' his hapless victims, and he shouts 'Confess!' to Deacon Indikoplev, who admits to making the sign of the cross in public.[6] Stalin was not formally connected with the Cheka in the 1920s, but since 1919 he had been Commissar of the Workers' and Peasants' Inspectorate which supervised the machinery of government, and, as General Secretary of the Central Committee from 1922, he had co-ordinated the work of the Central Control Commission, the body responsible for purges in the party. Although there is no definite proof that Zamyatin had Stalin in mind, by 1926 he would have had some reason to express hostility to Stalin, because his anti-utopian novel *We* (written in 1920-1), with its idea of 'infinite revolutions' (an echo of the concept of 'permanent revolution' advocated by Stalin's rival Trotsky), had been banned in the USSR in 1924.[7] Moreover, the prophetic talent displayed by Zamyatin in *We,* which proved to be a fairly accurate prediction of some aspects of Stalinist Russia, renders it legitimate to interpret the character of Papalagi, who shines a light into his victims' eyes and forces them to confess to absurd crimes, as a precursor of Stalin and his NKVD interrogators during the purges of the 1930s.

Zamyatin's *We,* which has often been interpreted as a powerful satire on Stalin's Russia, cannot be cited as the first Soviet novel to contain a portrait of Stalin, since it was written too early for the figure of the all-powerful Benefactor to bear any direct relation to Stalin. Zamyatin's Benefactor can rather be seen as a generalised picture of a dictator of the future, and his 'Socratically bald' head gives him, if anything, a greater resemblance to Lenin. However, Zamyatin's frequent use of metallic imagery in his portrait of the dictator, and, particularly, the repeated image of 'steel' to describe the Benefactor's supporters and the One State that he rules: 'Everything was new, of steel: a steel sun, steel trees, steel people', make it not entirely fanciful to suspect a veiled reference to Stalin, who chose the revolutionary name 'Man of Steel'. More significantly, Zamyatin's portrait of the Benefactor demonstrates that already, in the early 1920s, he was keenly aware of the dangers of a 'cult of personality'. By 1926, when *X* was written, the cult of Lenin was growing, and excessive reverence for the party leaders was becoming a more serious problem in the USSR. Zamyatin's contempt for the burgeoning 'cult of personality' is evident in *X,* when he comments ironically: 'Before Papalagi stood a plate with the most ordinary millet gruel, and it was a marvel to see him eating it in the most ordinary manner, like everybody else'.[8]

A character more obviously recognisable as Stalin was depicted by Boris Pilnyak, in his *Tale of the Unextinguished Moon* (1926).[9] This story was closely based on the death of M. V. Frunze, People's Commissar for Military and Naval Affairs, who died in October 1925 during an operation for a stomach ulcer undertaken at the behest of the party. It was rumoured that Stalin had ordered Frunze to be murdered because he resisted the domination of the army by the GPU, and because his power and popularity represented a threat to Stalin's ambition. Although in real life Stalin's complicity has not been proven, Pilnyak suggests in his story that Commander Gavrilov was killed on the orders of his superior, the shadowy 'Number One' (*Pervyi*).[10] Pilnyak uses the epithets 'Number One' and 'the Unbending Man' (*negorbyashchiisya chelovek*) interchangeably to evoke the powerful bureaucrat in whom many Soviet readers recognised a resemblance to Stalin. Vera Reck contends that Pilnyak depicted this Stalin-like character because of 'his artist's instinct rather than any deliberate attempt at portraiture'[11]; he did, however, take pains to inform himself about the details of Stalin's life and conduct during Frunze's illness, acquiring information both from the newspapers and from two friends, the critic A. K. Voronsky and the Communist leader Karl Radek. Pilnyak's Unbending Man shares several characteristics with the real Stalin: his posture is stiff, his movements quick and angular; he lives like a recluse in Moscow in a silent, curtained room whose only luxuries are a carpet and a fireplace;[12] and he justifies the liquidation of people in the name of the Revolution: 'It is not for us to talk about the grindstone of the Revolution, Gavrilov. The wheel of history, unfortunately, I suppose, is turned mainly by blood and death—particularly the wheel of revolution'.[13] The epithet 'Unbending Man' is reminiscent of the Soviet phrase 'inflexible Bolshevik' (*nesgibaemyi bolshevik*); and Number One is the senior figure in the ruling *troika* at a time when Stalin too was a member of a *troika,* but rapidly gaining ascendancy over his colleagues Zinoviev and Kamenev. Although Pilnyak 'covers' himself by crediting Number One with several traits which differentiate him from Stalin—he does not smoke, and is an educated man with a knowledge of foreign languages—these differences only serve to accentuate the parallel. In particular, Pilnyak's evocation of the dictator's ruthless lust for power, indifference to human life and willingness to annihilate his rivals, who were old revolutionaries, former comrades in the 'glorious band of 1918',[14] testifies to the author's prophetic talent.

Vera Reck considers that Pilnyak was only able to write such a work as a result of 'political naïveté';[15] and indeed, Pilnyak's preface, which warns the reader: 'It is not at all the point of my story to report on the death of a Commissar of Military Affairs. I feel I must inform the reader of all this, lest he seek real persons or events in my story.',[16] seems to be an example of extreme naïveté, since it had just the opposite effect from that explicitly intended: many readers associated Gavrilov with Frunze and his murderer with Stalin. Pilnyak's camouflage is so thin that it is legitimate to speculate that the preface may have been an attempt to alert readers to the reasons for Frunze's death, or to point to other, wider philosophical ideas in the text. As Elena Semeka has demonstrated, it is an oversimplification to view the Unbending Man as merely a portrait of Stalin; with his angular movements, his monotonous speech in which 'every phrase was a formula',[17] his absence of emotions, immobility, loneliness and silence, he is associated both with machinery and with death. The Unbending Man is more than Stalin: 'a generalised portrait of the dictator of the future who has ceased being human and has become a machine'.[18] Everything in his study is red, the colour of blood and violence; and when he travels in his car, the embodiment of soulless mechanisation, which is like a spaceship or a 'whip', he gazes with 'a cold glance' on the city which suffers under his scourge.[19] The moon in Pilnyak's story is an ambiguous symbol with multiple possible meanings, which has variously been interpreted as signifying death, or the unfathomable spirit of nature and eternity which cannot be extinguished.[20] When Number One rushes out of the city in his car, he is able to change the direction of the moon, which, like him, remains solitary and immobile until it is eventually chased beyond the clouds. The Unbending Man can be seen as the master of the universe who glimpses higher eternal values, but is unable to sustain the vision; he is able to stop life and set death in motion, although he is ultimately powerless to exert full dominion over nature and death.

The wider philosophical significance of Pilnyak's story was ignored when the author's personal fate was being decided. Although many details of Pilnyak's case remain obscure, it would seem that Stalin recognised himself in the story; Pilnyak's tale was not republished in the USSR for over half a century; and Pilnyak himself, despite his contacts with senior party and secret police officials, including Ezhov, disappeared in mysterious circumstances in the purges (he was probably shot in 1937). It has been assumed that Pilnyak's fate was sealed because Stalin never forgave him for the unflattering portrait; but since he was arrested on other charges, and so many other literary figures were purged at the same time, the precise contribution made by *The Tale of the Unextinguished Moon* towards Pilnyak's ultimate fate still remains unclear.

Another writer who dared to express a hostile attitude to Stalin was Osip Mandelstam. According to Nadezhda Mandelstam, her husband composed his famous epigram on Stalin in November 1933,[21] at a time when the cult of Stalin was beginning to blossom, because he had been deeply affected by collectivisation and 'the terrible sight of the hungry, wraith-like peasants he had recently seen on the way through the Ukraine and the Kuban'. The opening lines of the poem:

> We live, deaf to the land beneath us,
> Ten steps away no one hears our speeches,

express Mandelstam's feeling that he could no longer remain silent about the evils of Stalinism, as exemplified by the mass deportation of the peasantry and the herding of writers into a single Union of Soviet Writers, subservient to Stalin. Mandelstam's wife relates that, although he suspected that his fate was already sealed, 'he did not want to die before stating in unambiguous terms what he thought about the things going on around us'. The poem, which was written in a comprehensible, accessible style 'with a view to a wider circle of readers than usual', was a deliberate act of suicide on Mandelstam's part; it led directly to his first arrest in 1934, although after Stalin's personal intervention he was only sentenced to exile. Mandelstam describes Stalin with imagery taken from the most primitive forms of life. His reference to Stalin's fat greasy fingers like grubs has a basis in reality: the poet Demyan Bedny fell into disgrace because he was unwise enough to note in his diary that he did not like lending books to Stalin because of the dirty marks left on the white pages by his greasy fingers.[22] Mandelstam's line 'his great cockroach moustache laughs' is a highly condensed and powerful use of the image first employed by Chukovsky; and Stalin's cronies are depicted as subhuman creatures who fawn around their master mewing and whining like animals. In the first version of the poem which came into the hands of the secret police Mandelstam had emphasised Stalin's responsibility for the tragedy of collectivisation, calling him a 'murderer and peasant-slayer'[23] (the word *muzhikoborets* again evokes the 'moustaches', or thieves in folk tales who robbed the peasantry). Stalin's unlimited power and ruthlessness are evoked by imagery of heavy metal; his words resemble 'lead weights' and, like some infernal blacksmith, he forges iron laws like horseshoes which are flung at vulnerable parts of the human body. He takes a malign pleasure in terror: 'Every killing is a treat'. The epithet 'Kremlin mountaineer' applied to Stalin has been explained by Nadezhda Mandelstam: 'In Russian there is a clear phonetic trail of association leading from "Kremlin" to "mountain" via the words *kremen'* ("flint") and *kamen'* ("stone")'.[24] In this poem, as in one of Mandelstam's later poems of 1936 describing an idol living in the middle of a mountain which tries to remember the days when it still had human shape,[25] the image of the mountain evokes Stalin's remoteness, immobility and isolation.

The personal interest which Stalin took in Mandelstam's case, as in Pilnyak's, once again demonstrates the seriousness with which Stalin regarded literary references to himself. Mandelstam recognised this when he said, 'That poem of mine really must have made an impression, if he makes such a song and dance about commuting my sentence'.[26] It has been claimed that the question Stalin asked Pasternak on the telephone after Mandelstam's arrest, 'He is a genius, he is a genius, isn't he?', and Stalin's initial decision to spare Mandelstam's life, were a result of his desire to be immortalised in verse by a real genius, rather than by innumerable hacks.[27] The epigram of 1933, however, represented Mandelstam's true feelings about Stalin; as we will see, when in 1937 he forced himself to write an ode glorifying Stalin it turned out to be an artistic failure and did not save his life.[28]

The highly personal manner in which Stalin read fiction is also demonstrated by the experience of the satirist Mikhail Zoshchenko. In the original version of his story *Lenin and the Sentry* (1940) Zoshchenko had presented Lenin as a kind, gentle, wise man; for contrast, he had described a crude party official with a moustache and beard. His editor suggested that in subsequent editions the beard should be omitted, in case people thought the crude official was based on Mikhail Kalinin, the President of the USSR. Unfortunately, however, Zoshchenko made the horrific mistake of removing the beard, but leaving the moustache. Allegedly Stalin read the work and took offence, imagining that it was about him; subsequently a series of troubles began for Zoshchenko, culminating in the famous attack on him by Andrei Zhdanov, Stalin's aide on cultural matters, in 1946.[29] Whether or not this story is true, it aptly illustrates Stalin's sensitivity to any slight, real or imagined, and the extreme caution with which all Soviet writers had to operate in Stalin's time.

THE CULT OF PERSONALITY

The cult of Stalin's personality in the 1930s grew out of and became integrated into the cult of Lenin, which Lenin himself opposed and managed to keep in check until incapacitated by a stroke in March 1923. The Lenin cult, while undoubtedly based on the Bolsheviks' genuine veneration for their leader, whose personal influence had been vital from the formation of the movement to the seizure and consolidation of power, was also a result of the party's need for a unifying symbol after Lenin's death. Moreover, as Robert Tucker and Nina Tumarkin have convincingly shown, the Lenin cult, with its religious overtones which clashed with the professed secularism of the Soviet state, also grew out of certain elements of the Russian past, notably traditional peasant respect for personal authority, and, particularly, veneration for the Tsar as a divinely appointed ruler.[30] Stalin had been fully conscious of the power of such feelings from the moment of Lenin's death, ensuring that he posed at Lenin's funeral as Lenin's faithful disciple and natural successor. Although he possessed considerable support and even popularity within party circles in the years after Lenin's death, Stalin knew that his prestige was not remotely comparable with Lenin's; hence it was in his interests to associate himself as closely as possible with Lenin. The Stalin cult was already in evidence by 21 December 1929, Stalin's fiftieth birthday, when the press was full of adulation of Stalin, the 'glorious leader' and 'staunch fighter'. During the ceremonials of 21 January 1930 to mark the anniversary of Lenin's death an idealised view of Stalin's close relationship with Lenin was frequently expressed.

Since Stalin's popularity subsided somewhat in the early 1930s as a result of forced collectivisation and the concomitant famine of 1932-3, he resolved to prevent the growth of opposition to him by making his political position more unassailable. Conscious that his elevation to a status similar to that of Lenin would be useful for this purpose, he actively assisted the creation of his own cult. Stalin's letter to the journal *Proletarian Revolution*, 'On Some Questions of the History of Bolshevism', published in October 1931, was a turning point in the building of the cult.[31] The underlying aims of this letter, which attacked an article by A. S. Slutsky suggesting that Lenin had underestimated the Centrist danger in the German Social Democratic Party before the First World War, were to solicit a Stalin cult in party history; to assert the infallibility of Lenin, and hence of Lenin's successor; and to falsify the position of other revolutionaries by proposing that they be judged by their deeds, rather than by documents discovered by 'archive rats'. The influence of this letter was so far-reaching that idolatry of Stalin became universal in all fields of culture in the 1930s, rising to heights of extravagance on such occasions as the Seventeenth Congress of 1934, the promulgation of the Stalin Constitution of 1936 and the purge trials of 1937 and 1938. Political expediency alone, however, does not explain why Stalin found it necessary to allow the cult to grow after his power became increasingly absolute later in the 1930s. It must be assumed that Stalin had a psychological need for adulation; as Tucker suggests, 'Boundlessly ambitious, yet inwardly insecure, he had an imperative need for the hero worship that Lenin found repugnant'.[32] The image of Stalin projected in the cult must have borne some relation to Stalin's own self-image, since, while outwardly assuming a demeanour of modesty, he was angry when Louis Fischer suggested in 1930 that he should put a stop to the personal glorification.[33] Evidently Stalin, the ordinary man, needed the idealised picture of 'Stalin' evoked by his sycophants. Once the cult had been established, its continuation can be ascribed to several factors: Stalin's personal encouragement, the servility of his followers and the psychology of mass conformism engendered by a totalitarian state. Above all, the cult persisted because it was highly effective; just as tyrants of the past had solicited flattery and worship in order to retain their power, the personality cult enabled Stalin to survive until his death in 1953.

It would be an impossible and thankless task to attempt to encompass the ceaseless flood of hack literature eulogising Stalin which flowed from the pens of Soviet writers from the early 1930s to the end of the dictator's life. Nevertheless, it is worth considering certain literary genres which were specifically engendered by the cult of Stalin's personality. Alexander Tvardovsky, the poet and editor of the journal *Novy Mir* in the post-Stalin era, had these in mind when he said scornfully: 'By 1936 every issue [of *Novy Mir*] opened with a portrait of Stalin, a *skaz* [folk tale] on Stalin, "folk songs" on Stalin'.[34]

The 'poem' or 'song about Stalin', which attributed exceptional human virtues or even superhuman powers to him, was a unique new genre which emerged in the 1930s.[35] Such tributes were produced in great quantities in all the languages of the USSR, particularly by poets from the east, where the tradition of flattering rulers in verse dates back to ancient times. An early example was *To the Leader, to Comrade Stalin,* a long poem by A. A. Lakhuti, an Iranian who emigrated to the USSR and became a Soviet citizen, which was translated from Persian into Russian in 1932:

> Wise master, Marxist gardener!
> Thou art tending the vine of communism.
> Thou art cultivating it to perfection.
> After Lenin, leader of Leninists.[36] .

Other exponents of the genre who received decorations and prizes were the Kazakh bard Dzhambul Dzhabaev, to whom were ascribed the oriental dithyrambs *My Stalin, I Sing this Song to You* and *The Immortal Name—Stalin;*[37] and Suleiman Stalsky from Dagestan, who received a special ovation when he was presented to the First Congress of Soviet Writers in 1934. Deutscher describes their conquest of Moscow: 'Both were the last of the oriental tribal bards, illiterate nonagenarians, long-bearded, picturesque composers of folk-songs, belated native Homers. From their highland and steppe they came to Moscow to sing, to the accompaniment of their harps, Stalin's praise at the Lenin Mausoleum'.[38]

The case of Dzhabaev is particularly curious and instructive. As Shostakovich relates in his memoirs, Dzhabaev was entirely a creation of the 'personality cult'; he embodied the strange phenomenon of 'a great poet, known by the entire country, who doesn't exist'. The promotion of Dzhambul began in the 1930s when a Russian poet and journalist working on a Kazakh newspaper brought to his editor a few poems which he claimed to have written down from the words of some folk singer and translated. The party leader of Kazakhstan happened to read the poems of the 'unknown poet', whereupon he ordered him to be found and immediately made to write a song in Stalin's honour. At this point the journalist admitted that he had lied and that the poems he had submitted were his own, but he managed to extricate himself from the dilemma by discovering Dzhambul, a picturesque old man who sang and played the *domba,* a Kazakh folk instrument. Shostakovich relates: 'They found Dzhambul and a hurried song in his name praising Stalin was sent to Moscow. Stalin liked the ode, that was the main thing, and so Dzhambul Dzhabaev's new and incredible life began'. Dzhambul was illiterate, but he was handsomely paid for his poems, which existed only in Russian translation, not in the Kazakh original. Shostakovich comments sarcastically, 'An entire brigade of Russian poetasters laboured for Dzhambul, including some famous names like Konstantin Simonov. And they knew the political situation well and wrote to please the leader and teacher, which meant writing mostly about Stalin himself'. After Dzhabaev's death some young Kazakh poets wanted to expose the myth, but they were ordered to keep quiet, and the non-existent poet's anniversary was celebrated with pomp.[39]

Apart from labouring for Dzhabaev, many well-known Russian poets produced in their own names popular lyrics about Stalin intended to be sung. These included Mikhail Isakovsky, Aleksei Surkov, who likened Stalin to 'the flight of our youth' (a phrase later used ironically by the dissident Alexander Zinoviev as the title of his 'literary and sociological study of Stalinism'),[40] and Vasily Lebedev-Kumach, whose famous *Song of the Motherland,* written in 1935 and published in editions of 20 million copies, quotes Stalin's 1936 Constitution:

> A person always has the right
> To study, rest and labour.

(this verse was omitted from the 1977 text of the song).[41] The Soviet national anthem, which was composed in 1943 by the poet Sergei Mikhalkov and the journalist Gabriel El-Registan after taking Stalin's corrections into account, and set to music by A. Aleksandrov, after a national competition, contained a third verse eulogising Stalin:

> Stalin raised us—faithfulness to the people,
> Work and heroic deeds he inspired in us.[42]

When the 'cult of personality' was exposed in the post-Stalin period the anthem became known as the 'song without words', until in 1977 a new text was approved in which Stalin's name was replaced by Lenin's.

Songs about Stalin are highly stylised in language and imagery, using elements divorced from popular speech. The emotional range is very restricted: no satire or humour could be included, and the poet could only express positive emotions such as joy, happiness, gratitude, veneration, pride and fidelity, or defiance towards the enemies of the USSR. Some epithets and images are those associated with God or gods in religious literature: Stalin is constantly addressed as 'father', and is seen as a 'sun', a 'star', a source of light; and the words 'immortal' and 'eternal' are sometimes used in connection with his youth or his fame.[43] Other images evoke the earthly power and majesty of the ruler and shaper of human destinies: he is an architect, a helmsman, a military leader ('our fighting glory'),[44] or an incalculable treasure:

> You are more dear than all diamonds
> You are more valuable than all pearls.[45]

Other images are more closely connected with Stalin's own life and achievements. He is frequently depicted against a specific geographical background: either the mountains, sun and snows of his native Georgia[46], or the fields and steppes of Russia.[47] Bird imagery is also commonly used to evoke Stalin's Georgian background and soaring genius. Stalin had once characterised Lenin as a mountain eagle, and in the 1930s this image was taken up by the Old Bolshevik N. Antonov-Ovseenko to eulogise Stalin.[48] Subsequently, innumerable poets employed the image of the eagle, sometimes coupled with a reference to aeroplanes, to evoke Stalin's paternal encouragement of the long-distance pilots such as the Arctic flier Valery Chkalov, popular heroes whose feats enhanced Soviet national prestige in the 1930s, and who were known as 'Stalin's falcons' or 'Stalin's fledgeling children'.[49] While most imagery is taken from archaic rural folklore rather than from modern urban life, Stalin is sometimes depicted in Moscow, where he is seen as the embodiment of Russia's capital city and of the Kremlin, the symbol of imperial Russian power;[50] the light in the Kremlin window at night symbolises his fatherly concern for his people.[51] In the 1940s, in homage to Stalin's interest in Lysenko's agricultural schemes and his sponsorship of the 'Great Stalin Plan to Transform Nature' (1948), another set of images depicted Stalin as a 'gardener' before whom the abundant kolkhoz fields extend in sunny profusion;[52] the promise of new life which he offers is conveyed by images of dawn and spring. While most poets treat Stalin with awe, some present a more approachable Stalin, describing him as a 'friend', a genial figure who blows smoke rings;[53] and his role as the mentor of youth is frequently evoked:

> He loves youth
> He himself is young.[54]

Another unique genre engendered by the cult of personality in the 1930s was the folk tale in prose or verse about Stalin and other Soviet leaders. A renewed interest in folklore was stimulated by Gorky, who in his speech to the First Writers' Congress of 1934 called on literature to model its heroes on those of 'folklore, i.e. the unwritten compositions of the toiling man'.[55] Considerable resources were invested in the collection and dissemination of oral folklore; and an attempt was made to create a genuine contemporary folk literature. The main aim of these latter-day *byliny* (traditional heroic poems) or folk tales was to extol and legitimise the Stalin leadership. In 1937 the publishing house 'Two Five Year Plans' invited some singers of *byliny* to travel from their remote villages to Moscow to create new tales in praise of the present age. Professional writers were usually assigned to the bards to help them compose their epics or tales. The best known example is *Tale of Lenin* (1937) by Marfa Kryukova, the granddaughter of the *bylina* singer used as a source by the great nineteenth-century collector of folklore, Rybnikov.[56] Kryukova's epic poem depicts three meetings between 'the red sun Vlademir' (Lenin) and 'Stalin-svet' (light), after which Lenin sends Stalin out into the world to accomplish his work. The poem, which closely follows the Stalinist version of Bolshevik history, is intended to legitimise Stalin's succession.[57]

Other folk tales are either designed to provide a general eulogy of Stalin as a wise leader, or to glorify specific aspects of his life and achievements. In *The Dearest Thing* (1937) by F. A. Konashkov, a story-teller from a Karelian kolkhoz, the three best workers from a collective farm are sent to resolve an argument about the identity of 'the dearest thing'. They follow an enchanted ball of thread until it leads to Moscow, to Stalin; and the moral

of the story is: 'The best and dearest thing we have on earth is the word of Comrade Stalin'.[58] The Chuvash tale *About Happiness* (1935) is designed to praise Stalin's collectivisation policy. An old Chuvash sends his son away to find happiness; he meets an eagle (Stalin) who tells him to kill, successively, a bear, a wolf and a fox; each time the life of the peasants improves until, after the third heroic deed, the kolkhoz is established. The conclusion leaves the reader in no doubt as to how the story should be interpreted: 'Thus the poor Chuvash Endri, having killed the bear-Tsar, wolf-landowner and fox-kulak, at last found his happiness'.[59]

Other tales, such as V. Bespalikov's *Three Sons* (1937) and *The Sun* by the Chuvash V. Khramov, celebrate Stalin's role as father and mentor of heroic young people.[60] In Khramov's tale an old kolkhoznik says he will give his blessing to whichever of his three sons reaches the sun; one becomes a pilot, the other a sailor and the third a soldier, seeking the sun by air, sea and land. Finally all three are rewarded by Stalin, and the old man gives his blessing to them all, as 'The brightest of all suns in the world is our Stalin'.[61] Other tales, such as I. Kovalyov's *Icy Hill* and a tale by the old story-teller Ayau from Dagestan, *How the Heroes Subdued Ilmukhanum*, celebrate the exploits of the Arctic pilots, depicting the conquest of icy northern regions by young heroes inspired by Stalin.[62] One aspect of Stalin's early life emphasised in adulatory biographies was his daring escapes from exile. This was dramatised in a Nenets tale from a Siberian kolkhoz, *Stalin and Truth* (1936), in which Stalin is sent to the tundra by the wicked Tsar because he is friendly with Truth; Stalin fraternises with the peoples of the tundra, and because he is 'not a simple man, but a hero' (*bogatyr*) and 'the gods have invested him with the strength of a bear and the wisdom of a polar falcon' he manages to send a letter to Truth discussing 'how the poor people can live better on earth'. Stalin tells the people to fight for Soviet power, and when it is achieved, their life becomes happier.[63]

The revival of folk genres did not prove to be a particularly successful method of inculcating praise of the leader or of portraying a model of the new man, because, in Katerina Clark's words, 'the crudity of the engrafted folksiness and the transparency of the devices reduced its effectiveness as a repository of myth'.[64] In 1947 critics came out against the folk bards, quoting a phrase in Zhdanov's speech of 1946, 'Russia is not the same', to argue that the policy of encouraging folk epics was misconceived.[65]

One work which presents a striking contrast to the artificially sponsored adulatory songs and tales about Stalin is an ironic song, *Comrade Stalin, You're a Real Big Scholar* (first published abroad in 1964), which circulated in the prison camps and became a genuine folk song of the late Stalin era. The composer subsequently turned out to be Yuz Aleshkovsky, a former convict, who had been published in the USSR only as a children's writer, and who emigrated in 1979.[66] The song parodies various aspects of the 'cult of personality' by juxtaposing them with the hard life of the prisoners in Stalin's camps:

> Comrade Stalin, you're a real big scholar
> You know what's going on in linguistics
> But I'm a simple Soviet convict
> And my comrade is the grey Bryansk wolf.[67]

The singer, incarcerated in the Turukhansk region where Stalin himself had been imprisoned under Nicholas II, calls himself a fool for not being able to escape even once, when Stalin managed to escape from exile six times (this is an ironic reference to the far harsher conditions for prisoners and exiles in the Stalin era than in Tsarist times).

Aleshkovsky's irony is aimed against those party members who remained loyal to the party and Stalin in the camps and even accepted Stalin's ideological justification for the purges:

> What I'm in for, I swear I don't know,
> But the procurators are right, it would seem . . .
> Naturally, I understand all this
> As an intensification of the class struggle.

The song ridicules those 'loyalists', to use Solzhenitsyn's term,[68] who remained convinced that when the all-wise Stalin found out what crimes were being committed in his name by the security organs, he would investigate the cases of party members and set them free. The song tells of a dying Marxist:

> And before he passed away forever,
> He willed you his tobacco pouch and all his words,
> He asked you to get to the bottom of all this here,
> And screamed out quietly: 'Stalin's so clever!'
>
> Live a hundred years, comrade Stalin,
> And though it may be my fate to kick the bucket
> 　　here,
> I only hope the production of steel can rise
> Per head of population in the country.

A genre which proved particularly effective in inculcating Stalinist values, especially pride in Holy Mother Russia, was the historical epic, or film. Aleksei Tolstoy's *Peter the Great*, published in serial form from 1929 to 1945, a portrait of the ruthless Tsar who transformed Russia from a backward country into a European power, was a skilful attempt to create a parallel with Stalin and an apologia for his tyranny.[69] Similarly, numerous historical films of the 1930s, such as Petrov's *Peter the First*, Pudovkin's *Minin and Pozharsky*, Dovzhenko's *Shchors* (made in response to Stalin's request for a Ukrainian version of *Chapaev*) and Eisenstein's *Alexander Nevsky*, featured a powerful and charismatic leader.[70] Film was Stalin's own favourite art form, and he was fond of quoting Lenin's dictum: 'Cinema for us is the most important of the arts'.[71] Stalin's awareness of the value of films on historical subjects was demonstrated in 1947 when he summoned Eisenstein and instructed him to make a film showing Ivan IV as a 'great and wise ruler'; of all the leaders in Russian history, he claimed, Ivan and Lenin were the only two who had introduced a state monopoly of foreign trade. According to Ehrenburg, Stalin contrasted Ivan favourably with Peter the Great, who did not cut off enough heads.[72] In Part I of *Ivan the Terrible* Eisentein followed Stalin's instructions, glorifying autocracy and putting into Ivan's mouth what Stalin could not say to anyone: 'O God, am I right in what I do?', to which God seems to answer that he *is* right.

However, if historical works could be used to extol Stalin, they could also be subverted to express criticism of him. Vera Alexandrova, writing in 1943, recognised a similarity between the Russia depicted in the first part of V. Kostylev's trilogy *Ivan the Terrible* (1943-55) and contemporary Soviet reality.[73] Part II of Eisenstein's *Ivan the Terrible* was banned by the Soviet authorities, as it represented a clear attempt to attack Stalin and tyrannical rule. Eisenstein himself in his autobiographical notes compared the 'black forms of the *oprichniki* of Ivan the Terrible' with the 'soulless automatons of the *apparatchiki* of Stalin the terrible'.[74] The film director Mikhail Romm, a witness to the first showing of Part II, saw Ivan's henchman Malyut Skuratov as Beria; and the victim in the film, Vladimir Staritsky, can be interpreted as an image of Eisenstein, the victim in real life.[75]

It was not only hack writers who contributed to the personality cult; some of the best Soviet poets also felt obliged to write poems about Stalin. The better poets, such as Nikolai Zabolotsky, treated this theme obliquely, with greater subtlety than the majority of Soviet writers. Zabolotsky's poem *Gori Symphony* (1936) provides a good description of Stalin's birthplace, the small town of Gori in Georgia, with its trees and encircling mountains.[76] The poet's attention is attracted to a poor dark hut, and he tries to understand how in such a remote place unutterable thoughts first formed in Stalin's head, and how:

> The original structure of his soul
> Was formed by the action of nature.

Most of the poem is a hymn in praise of Georgia, and only the final stanza bows to the prevailing literary climate with a conventional eulogy of the revolution, the birth of the new world and the Five Year Plan. Unfortunately, Zabolotsky's willingness to write a poem in praise of Stalin did not save him from persecution: he spent the years 1938 to 1946 in camps and exile.

Another unconventional work which includes a reference to Stalin is Alexander Tvardovsky's long narrative poem *Muravia Land* (1936), which skilfully combines elements of the *bylina* with the flavour of peasant speech.[77] Rumour spreads through the countryside that Stalin is coming, and he appears like a fairytale *bogatyr'* 'on a raven-black horse', 'in a greatcoat, with his pipe'. He looks around, speaks to the people and takes note of conditions. (This is, of course, an idealised picture of Stalin, who rarely travelled into the countryside). The hero Nikita Morgunok tells Stalin everything in his heart:

he admits that conditions are improving and agrees to join the kolkhoz one day, but regrets the loss of his own land. Stalin listens in silence as Nikita asks if he can make allowances for him and 'for the time being' leave him his farm. The rest of the poem concerns Nikita's search for the peasants' Utopia where he will be allowed to keep his small holding; but experience and the advice of a mysterious old man teach him that there is no Muravia Land, and he must join a collective farm. This poem, which demonstrates Tvardovsky's understanding of the psychology of the peasant, perhaps represents the poet's attempt to smooth over his own doubts about collectivisation (his father was deported as a kulak). Tvardovsky was subjected to some criticism for alleged 'peasant anarchism';[78] and indeed, *Muravia Land* is by no means an orthodox embodiment of Stalinist ideology, as at times the author appears sympathetic to Nikita's dream. Nevertheless, the poem was eventually awarded a Stalin Prize.

In order to understand Tvardovsky's real feelings about Stalin and collectivisation it is salutary to contrast *Muravia Land* with his posthumously published poem *For the Right of Memory,*[79] which evokes both the guilt that Tvardovsky was made to feel in the 1930s as 'the son of a kulak', and the guilt he subsequently felt in relation to his father's persecution when he had reassessed the experience of collectivisation.

One of the most tragic aspects of the effect of the personality cult on literature was that the best and most independent poets in the country were obliged to join in the chorus of praise. A brief discussion of some of the darkest pages in the biographies of Pasternak, Mandelstam and Akhmatova (without any intention of passing judgement on their actions) will help to illuminate the impact of politics on literature in Stalin's time.

Pasternak's poetic inspiration declined in the 1930s; he did not himself write 'poems about Stalin', but his decision to translate Georgian poetry as a refuge from the need to create original works meant that it was difficult to avoid references to Stalin in his translations. Some of his translations of the 1920s, for example P. Yashvili's *On the Death of Lenin* (1924) and V. Gaprindashvili's *October Lines* (1929), contained passing references to Stalin;[80] but a new departure occurred in 1934, when Pasternak's translations of two poems dedicated to Stalin by N. Mitsishvili and P. Yashvili became widely known through their publication in the journals *Novy Mir* and *Krasnaya Nov'.*[81] The poems were written at the beginning of 1934 and rapidly translated by Pasternak so that they could be published before the Seventeenth Party Congress (the 'Congress of Victors'). Mitsishvili's *Stalin,* with its grandiose tone and ornate symbolism, is particularly alien to Pasternak's own style. Lazar Fleishman argues that Pasternak's decision to translate these odes cannot be ascribed to bureaucratic compulsion; rather, in 1934 his views did not significantly diverge from those of the Georgian poets. He saw Stalin as a unifying force in the country after the troubled period of the 'Great Turning-Point', and hoped that the development of fascism in Europe would inspire the socialist state to move in the direction of greater civilisation and humanity. Pasternak's decision may also have been inspired by a desire to help his fellow poets in the Georgian 'Blue Horn' group whose work had suffered neglect; and possibly also represented a reaction against Mandelstam's epigram about Stalin, which horrified Pasternak as a 'suicidal' act. Moreover, in 1934 the cult of Stalin was only in its infancy; Pasternak could not have foreseen the extravagant proportions it would reach in later years.[82] These odes are an exception in Pasternak's *oeuvre;* most of his translations, while published in collections containing eulogies of Stalin, are remarkably free from references to Stalin. In general Pasternak deliberately avoided political themes, concentrating on personal or nature lyrics.[83] Nevertheless, these odes to Stalin may have played their part in ensuring Pasternak's survival and cementing his enigmatic personal relationship with Stalin (as witnessed by the famous phone call from Stalin to Pasternak after Mandelstam's first arrest in 1934).

Although Pasternak, like many other people in the USSR, was 'morbidly curious about the recluse in the Kremlin',[84] in his later work he preferred to pass over the subject of Stalin in silence. *Doctor Zhivago,* however, contains a reference to 'pockmarked Caligulas', which may well express Pasternak's considered judgement of Stalin as the latest in a long line of tyrants.[85] It is true, as Neil Cornwell points out, that Pasternak was being particularly cautious if he placed a reference to Stalin in the mouth of Zhivago's uncle Vedenyapin, who was speaking in 1903;[86] but this argument does not invalidate the allusion, since Pasternak frequently displayed caution in his literary activities, and may have been resorting to deliberate camouflage in the hope that *Doctor Zhivago* would be published in the USSR. Isaiah Berlin mentions a theory current among the Soviet intelligentsia that Evgraf, Yuri Zhivago's mysterious half-brother, was intended to represent Stalin—a theory apparently dismissed by Anna Akhmatova.[87] The parallel is valid only in the limited sense that Evgraf is a high official who acts as a *deus ex machina* in Yuri's life, as Stalin did in the lives of such writers as Pasternak, Mandelstam and Bulgakov. Although there have been many other more plausible and complex interpretations of the figure of Evgraf,[88] the theory nevertheless possesses some interest as an example of the highly political interpretations accorded to literary works by the Soviet reading public.

The case of Mandelstam is more tragic. Nadezhda Mandelstam describes how in the winter of 1936-7, foreseeing the impending catastrophe, her husband made an attempt to save himself by writing an *Ode to Stalin.*[89] The artificiality of the whole project was evident from the fact that Mandelstam forced himself to sit down at their table with paper and pencil and waited for words to come, 'like Fedin, or someone of that kind'. Since he had never in his life composed in that manner, the plan was bound to fail; 'his attempt to do violence to himself met stubborn resistance', but the artificially conceived poem about Stalin led to the creation of other poems, antagonistic to the Ode, which formed part of the *Second Voronezh Cycle.* Mandelstam asked his friend Natasha Shtempel to destroy the Ode when they left Voronezh, but some indications of its content can be extrapolated from Nadezhda Mandelstam's memoirs. The word *os'* ('axle') which featured in the ode, perhaps connected with Stalin's first name 'Iosif', led to a scattering of words containing the syllable 'os' throughout the cycle. In the Ode an artist, with tears in his eyes, draws a portrait of the leader; but another poem of 8 February contained the line: 'I do not draw and I do not sing'. A reference to Aeschylus and Prometheus in the Ode led in the other poems to a treatment of the theme of tragedy and martyrdom; and the Caucasus, mentioned as Stalin's birthplace in the Ode, occurs again in the reference to Tbilisi as the place which remembers not the Great Leader but the poor poet with his worn shoes. Nadezhda Mandelstam concludes: 'To write an ode to Stalin it was necessary to get in tune, like a musical instrument, by deliberately giving way to the general hypnosis and putting oneself under the spell of the liturgy which in those days blotted out all human voices. Without this, a real poet could never compose such a thing: he would never have had that kind of ready facility. M. thus spent the beginning of 1937 conducting a grotesque experiment on himself. Working himself up into the state needed to write the 'Ode', he was in effect deliberately upsetting the balance of his own mind. "I now realise that it was an illness", he said later to Akhmatova.'

Although Nadezhda Mandelstam was advised not to speak of the Ode, as if it had never existed, she insists on telling the truth about the double life that she and her husband were forced to live in Stalin's time. She comments bitterly that, unlike other poets who 'wrote their odes in their apartments and country villas and were rewarded for them, M. wrote his with a rope around his neck'. The Ode did not achieve its aim of saving Mandelstam's life, but it may have been instrumental in saving his wife's life and enabling her to preserve his poems.

Another poet who wrote poems to Stalin in similar tragic circumstances was Anna Akhmatova. She had suffered persecution since 1946, when she had been singled out for attack in a speech by Stalin's henchman Zhdanov. She was subsequently expelled from the Union of Writers, and in 1949 her husband Nikolai Punin and her son Lev Gumilyov were arrested. It was in order to save her son's life that she wrote for Stalin's seventieth birthday in December 1949 *In Praise of Peace,* a cycle of poems extolling Stalin, which was sent directly to Aleksei Surkov, Secretary of the Writers' Union, for prompt publication.[90] Akhmatova regarded the cycle as a sacrifice, and expressly requested that it be omitted from her *Collected Works.*[91] Earlier, in a poem of her *Requiem* cycle written in 1939, she had recognised the inner necessity of surrendering to the authorities and begging for forgiveness, despite the futility of the sacrifice:

> For seventeen months I have cried
> I call you home.
> I have thrown myself at the feet of the
> executioner,
> You are my son and my terror . . .[92]

Akhmatova was aware that she could not write the panegyric to Stalin in any remotely literary style; it is striking in its banality. The poems are a contribution to the peace movement launched by the Soviet Union in 1949-50, which was intended to suggest to world public opinion that America's possession of atomic weapons rather than Soviet policies constituted the major threat to peace. Akhmatova demands 'peace' on Soviet terms, praising the Stockholm peace charter of 1950, a document calling for a ban on the atom bomb which was allegedly signed by 500 million people, and attacking the imperialists for their participation in the Korean War. She praises Stalin in many of the current clichés; he is an eagle, the transformer of nature,

> The true master of life,
> The sovereign of mountains and rivers,

who utters the 'radiant word—peace'.[93] There is a bitter irony in her words:

> Legend speaks of a wise man
> Who has saved each of us from a terrible death.[94]

Akhmatova's real feelings had been expressed in a poem of the 1930s, *An Imitation of the Armenian,* in which an oriental tyrant is asked:

> And was my son to the taste
> Of yourself and your children?[95]

In Praise of Peace is one of the most tragic documents of the age, but Akhmatova's sacrifice may have saved her son's life (he was released in 1956). The very artistic poverty of the cycle makes it an ironic work: in Amanda Haight's words, it was 'a joke on the very times themselves when a handful of bad poems by someone who had written the poems of *Requiem* could actually result in saving someone's life'.[96] As Nadezhda Mandelstam says of her friend Akhmatova and her husband: 'Who can blame either her or M.?'.[97]

Prose fiction was the most important genre for the inculcation of Stalinist values; and during the period of the 'personality cult' writers were unanimous in their extravagant eulogies of Stalin. As Katerina Clark has shown, in the mythology of the 1930s sightings of Stalin or meetings between Stalin and young pilots or Stakhanovite workers, which were extensively reported in the press, played the role of 'ritual exchanges between "mentor" and "disciple", between "father" and "son", which conferred greater consciousness' on the young heroes.[98] Such climactic moments were also important for characters in fiction. In P. Pavlenko's *In the East* (1936), for example, the heroine Olga feels great joy when she sees Stalin's 'calm figure' and 'severe' countenance, and listens to 'the voice of our motherland, the simple, clear, infinitely honest, boundlessly kind, unhurried and fatherly voice of Stalin'.[99]

In the 1930s writers of fiction, like historians, fulfilled the function of rewriting history to legitimise the Stalinist succession. One of the most effective promoters of the Stalin cult was Aleksei Tolstoy, who enjoyed a good personal relationship with Stalin and, according to Ilya Ehrenburg, would go to any lengths to achieve 'peace and quiet'.[100] His novel *Bread* (1937), an adulatory account of Stalin's allegedly single-handed defence of Tsaritsyn in the Civil War, contains some of the clichés with which we are already familiar from poetry and folk epics, and some which became the stock-in-trade of the prose writer for the next decade. The most prominent is Tolstoy's evocation of Stalin's 'calm' voice and manner; as Katerina Clark demonstrates, the epithet *spokoinyi* ('calm, confident') is frequently used in Soviet novels as a sign of complete self-control and firmness in the revolutionary faith.[101] Tolstoy's Stalin first appears as Lenin's close comrade-in-arms, and gives Lenin advice in the 'even, quiet, calm voice in which he conducted all conversations'; when he arrives in Tsaritsyn his face is 'serious and calm', and he greets everyone without distinction 'not too warmly and not too drily'.[102] Stalin's good nature and courage are stressed: his eyes are 'cheerful', and when under fire he merely laughs and says: 'It happens'.[103] It is Stalin who alerts Lenin to the importance of Tsaritsyn; his role as Lenin's equal is emphasised by the orders which are issued in the names of 'Lenin and Stalin'. He tackles his job as organiser of the food supply in south Russia in a business-like manner; he is firm, decisive and knowledgeable, with a 'penetrating gaze'.[104] He stresses the importance of the political preparation of his soldiers and of hardwork to produce armaments. Although he does not immediately use his emergency powers, he is ruthless in dealing with enemies: he comes into conflict with the Supreme Military Council headed by Trotsky, and has several officers and specialists shot for counter-revolutionary activities. Tolstoy rewrites history in order to contribute to the mythology surrounding Stalin in the 1930s: Trotsky's role as creator of the Red Army is ignored, and Tolstoy emphasises Stalin's part in revitalising the Red Army by purging its command of saboteurs. Tolstoy also anachronistically projects on to Stalin an interest in aviation: he predicts that one day Soviet people will fly like birds.

During the first, disastrous period of the war, July-December 1941, Stalin's name was notable for its absence from newspapers and war stories. Ehrenburg relates: 'Stalin's name was hardly mentioned; for the first time for many years there were neither portraits nor enthusiastic epithets; the smoke of nearby explosions banished the smoke of incense'.[105] Even Stalin appeared to understand that he needed to take a back seat, since his unpreparedness for war had led to the initial heavy defeats. For a long time Soviet writers kept silent about the first months of the war and began their account with the counter-offensive of December 1941.

After the shock of the invasion had subsided, however, Stalin returned to prominence. Alexander Korneichuk's play *The Front,* published in *Pravda* in August 1942, was commissioned by Stalin himself to improve his image—a striking example of the political use of literature.[106] Korneichuk attempts to exonerate Stalin, laying the blame for the defeats of 1941-2 at the door of generals with old-fashioned ideas and practices. Although stalin himself does not appear as a character in the play, he is shown to be supremely well-informed and actively concerned with introducing new technology and replacing inefficient commanders with younger, more talented men. Another work of the same year, Leonid Leonov's play *The Invasion* (1942), emphasises the patriotic and near-religious aspects of Stalin's leadership. Before Stalin's speech of November 1941 an old man tells his grandson about a previous meeting at which Stalin was present; 'It was an enormous great hall and there were more than a thousand of us, but it felt empty and cold somehow. Then one man entered, and it felt as though there weren't an empty seat. His presence set us on fire.'[107] Another aspect of Stalin's leadership which was emphasised in wartime fiction was his ability to organise industrial production. A. Karavaeva's *Fires* (1943) also evokes Stalin's speech of November 1941, emphasising his claim that Germany's resources will be more quickly exhausted and that Soviet tanks, although less numerous, are of better quality; Stalin's 'calm' voice with its 'deep trust' in the Soviet people makes a great impression on the listening workers, who vow to produce tanks more rapidly.[108] Works published later in the war, such as Simonov's *Days and Nights* (1944), also concentrated on the inspiration inculcated by Stalin's speeches, perhaps because it was easier to portray Stalin as a national and spiritual leader than as a military strategist.[109] By 1945 adulation of Stalin had become more intense. The climax of V. Kataev's novel *A Son of the Regiment* (1945) is a boy's dream of ascending a marble staircase, at the top of which stands Stalin with his brilliant marshal's star and his 'severe paternal smile'.[110]

After the victory, during the oppressive 'Zhdanov period' in literature until Stalin's death in 1953, the cult flourished with renewed vigour; and writers once again extolled Stalin's military genius. In Vsevolod Ivanov's *At the Capture of Berlin* (1946), Marshal Zhukov asks an artist to give him a sketch of Stalin's face so that he can look at it during the capture of Berlin: 'I always look at Stalin! We conquer through his genius. Always!'.[111] In the conclusion of Ivanov's novel the panegyric rises to hagiographic proportions. Stalin mounts the Mausoleum steps with 'a thoughtful gait, the gait of a thinker and wise soldier, sure of every step' and 'all rapturously applaud Stalin, the father of the people, the happiness of humanity, the greatest military leader in the world. . . . And everybody can clearly see love written on his face, an inextinguishable love for his people, for their lives, for their happiness, and those in the square, realising his feelings, applaud again and again'.[112]

Nikolai Virta's play *Great Days,* written in 1947 and allegedly edited by Stalin himself, depicts Stalin making all the

major decisions about the battle of Stalingrad. Virta includes a theory widely disseminated in the post-war years
to explain the events of 1941: the myth that the retreat of
the Soviet troops was a deliberate strategy conceived by
Stalin to draw the Germans deep into the country prior to
the launching of a counter-offensive, a plan allegedly
based on the example of the ancient Parthians. Moreover,
Virta suggests that already in August 1942 Stalin had
devised the precise tactics through which the Red
Army's offensive in November would trap the Germans in
Stalingrad (Marshal Zhukov, who at the time of the victory at Stalingrad was recognised as the chief planner, is
not mentioned). One innovation introduced into Virta's
play is the shadowy character of 'Stalin's Friend', whose
function is to humanise him. The Friend comments sympathetically on 'Joseph's' grey hair and tiredness, advises him to rest more and not to smoke (although Stalin
admits he cannot give it up) and recalls his escapes from
exile and the battle near Tsaritsyn (about which Stalin
comments modestly: 'I always have to undertake something'). Stalin is cordial and polite with his Friend, inviting him to his dacha to talk about old times; when his
comically solicitous secretary Poskryobyshev reminds
him of the urgent business that awaits him, Stalin protests
wearily: 'Don't I get any free time, even at night?'.[113]
Virta's play, although set in the war, reflects the atmosphere of the post-war years: the emphasis laid on
Churchill's refusal to open a second front in Europe is
redolent of the confrontation of the Cold War period; and
Virta implausibly depicts Stalin reflecting in the middle of
the war both on post-war car production and the need to
make contact with Lysenko about a new type of grain in
order to double agricultural production by 1950. Other
incongruous elements in Virta's play are Stalin's solici-
tude and respect for Molotov (notwithstanding the arrest
of Molotov's wife in 1948), and an anachronistically
friendly reference to the Americans, who are presented as
good, if naive people who call Stalin 'Uncle Joe' (a name
which never became popular in the USSR). It is not surprising that Virta's play was singled out for satirical treatment by Solzhenitsyn in *The First Circle*.[114]

Another work satirised by Solzhenitsyn is V. Vishnevsky's
play *Unforgettable 1919* (1949), which also depicts past
events in order to provide lessons for the present.
Vishnevsky's portrayal of Stalin's stern treatment of
spies in Petrograd in 1919 and his arrest of members of
the Military Council, a body headed by Trotsky, is an
attempt to justify the renewed campaigns in the late forties against anti-cosmopolitanism and bourgeois nationalism. Stalin's final threat that 'if anyone is to be bloodied' he will make sure that it is 'the bourgeois camp and
not the Soviet state' is clearly aimed against the USA.[115]
According to Shostakovich, Stalin was particularly fond
of the film *Unforgettable 1919,* based on Vishnevsky's
play. As he watched his young self riding by on the
footboard of an armoured train with a sabre in his hand,
he was heard to exclaim, 'How young and handsome
Stalin was!'. Shostakovich comments ironically, 'He
talked about himself in the third person and gave an
opinion on his looks. A positive one'.[116]

In the late 1940s and early 1950s the cult of Stalin reached
new heights. In Alexander Kron's *Party Candidate*
(1950), the hero, in the middle of a love scene, when asked
by the heroine if he has one 'sacred dream' . . . a fantastic
dream, an almost impossible one', responds: 'I would like
to have a talk with Comrade Stalin'.[117] In A. Gribachev's
Spring in 'Pobeda' (1948) Stalin's sainthood is established when he personally escorts the party organiser
Zernov across the threshold of death, with the words:

> 'You have struggled not in vain.
> You have laboured not in vain.
> Your last day is your first step into the commune.
> Here comes its dawn.'
> Thus, at dawn
>   in "Pobeda"
> Zernov, the party organiser,
>   died.[118]

Since apparently orthodox works such as A. Fadeyev's
The Young Guard and V. Kataev's *For the Power of the
Soviets* came under attack in the late 1940s for under-
estimating the role of the party in the war, it was inevitable that history would be rewritten to present Stalin
as a supreme military genius. Two extreme examples of
'varnishing reality' are the first part of G. Berezko's
Peaceful Town (1951) and the second part of M.
Bubyonnov's *White Birch Tree* (1952), which contain
frequent, extravagant depictions of Stalin.[119] Both writers dramatise the myth of Stalin's counter-offensive
strategy, suggesting that Stalin's aim in 1941 was to
conserve reserves, not to weaken them in defensive
fights, and to defeat the enemy outside Moscow.
Berezko describes Stalin in a 'large bright room' in the
Kremlin, poring over maps with a 'concentrated face'
and an 'enormous energy of thought . . . analysing,
comparing, predicting, creating'. Stalin's speech on 7
November 1941 is seen as 'a father's blessing'; Stalin,
as always, is 'attentive, very serious, very calm', and
his omniscience is emphasised: 'He had thought of
everything, predicted everything'.[120] Bubyonnov depicts Stalin on the night of 16 November 1941: he is
concerned about the forthcoming battle, but confident
that Moscow will stand; and he plans an improvement
in the war industries in the Urals.[121] Both writers suggest, with hindsight, that Stalin's defensive strategy in
1941 marked the beginning of the Soviet victory.

The hagiography in which Soviet writers indulged during
the 'period of the personality cult' now appears absurd,
but the main reason for the cult's survival is that it was
highly effective. Just as tyrants of the past had solicited
flattery and worship in order to retain their power, the
personality cult of Stalin, which perhaps corresponded to
Russia's deep-rooted autocratic traditions, enabled Stalin
to survive unchallenged until his death in 1953.

AESOPIAN LANGUAGE

Apart from the anonymous composers of folk songs and
anecdotes, only very few writers explicitly expressed
hostility to Stalin in his lifetime—and, of these, Pilnyak

and Mandelstam perished. After the war the only writer to compose and recite verses against Stalin while Stalin was still alive was the young poet Naum Mandel (Korzhavin). One of his poems was:

> There in Moscow in a whirlpool of darkness
> Wrapped in his greatcoat,
> Not understanding Pasternak
> A hard and cruel man stared at the snow.

Korzhavin was exiled, but Evtushenko claims that the very fact that he did recite his verses openly saved his life, because the authorities thought him insane.[122] More frequently, although still very occasionally, writers made derogatory references to Stalin obliquely, through Aesopian devices, although works containing such allusions only rarely achieved publication in the USSR.

Mikhail Bulgakov's play *Batumi,* which concerns Stalin's early life and, particularly, his activities during the strikes and demonstrations in Batumi in 1902, followed by his imprisonment, exile to Siberia and escape, at first sight appears to be yet another tragic example of a great writer's sacrifice of his artistic integrity. The play was conceived in March 1936 under the title *The Pastor,* but was put aside until September 1938 when well-meaning friends from the Moscow Arts Theatre, the literary consultant P. Markov and the theatrical scholar V. Vilenkin, suggested that Bulgakov complete the play to coincide with the celebrations for Stalin's sixtieth birthday in 1939. Bulgakov finally agreed, and the play was finished on 24 July 1939. Vilenkin states in his memoirs that the aim of giving the subject to Bulgakov was that there would be 'no varnishing, no speculations, no incense; the emotional content of the drama could arise from the truth of the authentic material, if only a dramatist of Bulgakov's stature took it up'.[123] Bulgakov's decision to write the play, which gave the author no pleasure, and is not particularly successful, can be ascribed to several factors. Firstly, *The Pastor* was originally conceived at a time when Bulgakov's play *Molière,* which implies a parallel between Molière's relationship with Louis XIV and Bulgakov's relationship with Stalin, had been subjected to criticism in the press and eventually taken off. It is possible, as Ellendea Proffer suggests, that the first version of the play about Stalin was 'far from icon-painting'.[124] Secondly, Bulgakov's life and works testify to his interest in tyrants. He had a strange personal relationship with Stalin, which began on 18 April 1930 when a letter he had sent to the Soviet government was followed by a telephone call from Stalin offering Bulgakov a choice between emigration and the possibility of working in a consultative capacity in the Soviet theatre. Subsequently Stalin took an interest in Bulgakov's literary career, and in particular, became fascinated by Bulgakov's play *The Days of the Turbins,* (first produced in 1926 and restaged in 1932 at Stalin's personal request), which he went to see fifteen times. Moreover, as an artist Bulgakov was interested in Stalin in the same sense that he was interested in other absolute rulers such as Louis XIV or Nicholas I. Another factor was the strong pressure exerted on

Bulgakov by his friends in the Moscow Arts Theatre to write something for the Stalin jubilee. Bulgakov's wife Elena Sergeevna also supported the idea, hoping that it would assist the publication and production of Bulgakov's other works. Personal reasons were, however, perhaps the decisive factor: Bulgakov was ill and knew he was dying, so although he himself had no further need for protection, he hoped the play might secure the future for his widow and her son.

Vilenkin describes the character of Stalin in Bulgakov's play as 'a young, fearless, intelligent revolutionary who had already won authority among the workers, a recent pupil of a theological seminary. Without a halo. With the right to ordinary human feelings, a living, authentic daily life and humour'.[125] This is an apt characterisation: Bulgakov's Stalin is an unimpeachable hero, but he is also a realistic character, unlike the idealised stereotypes who were later to appear in plays by Virta and Vishnevsky.[126] Bulgakov's play was fated to have an unsuccessful outcome: on the very day when Bulgakov and other members of the theatre were going to Batumi to collect more material for the production, he received a telegram in the train informing him that the play had been banned. According to one commentator, Stalin decided that all young people were alike and saw no need for a play about his youth;[127] but the real reason may have been that the contrast between Stalin's youthful democratic ideals portrayed in the play and the USSR of the 1930s was too great for comfort.

Although *Batumi* appears on the surface to follow the pattern of Soviet hagiography, Bulgakov was unable to write a truly servile play. As Lev Loseff demonstrates, the ease with which Bulgakov's Stalin implements his schemes is absurd, and all his enemies, from the police informant to the governor and Tsar Nicholas himself, are ludicrously inept.[128] The primitivism of Bulgakov's style in this work contrasts markedly with the psychological subtlety of his other plays. Moreover, the text itself contains hints that the work can be read on another level of Aesopian parody. As Loseff points out, the rector of the theological seminary from which Stalin is expelled uses phrases which could be construed as critical of Stalin, such as 'wrongdoers', 'crazed people clanging the cymbal of their barren ideas', and 'human society proclaims an anathema on the noxious tempter'.[129] The scene at the end of Act II where Stalin is beaten on stage by his jailers also diverges from conventional depictions of Stalin. Furthermore, as Loseff demonstrates, Bulgakov makes a subtle equation between Stalin and the imbecilic Nicholas II through their use of the word 'miraculous': Nicholas refers to miracle cures and his 'miraculous trained canary'; and Stalin says that his rescue from the icy river during his escape from Siberia, after which he has not coughed once, was 'miraculous'.[130]

Loseff's Aesopian reading of the play can be taken even further. A Moslem worker relates a dream in which he watched the Tsar swimming, and makes a comment which recalls Hans Christian Andersen's tale *The Emperor's*

New Clothes, 'But how would he [the Tsar] walk naked if someone stole his uniform?'. Then the Tsar drowns and everyone shouts: '"The Tsar has drowned! The Tsar has drowned!" And all the people were joyful'.[131] This dream is reminiscent of Stalin's 'miraculous' escape from drowning at the end of the play (although Stalin himself also appears in the worker's dream, perhaps in an attempt to deceive the censor). Furthermore, the prison scenes in the play evoke the imprisonment of many people under Stalin. At one point a prisoner sings:

> The Tsar lives in great halls,
> He walks and sings;
> Here in grey overalls,
> The people croak in prison cells.[132]

The Tsarist police report read out in the play which states that Stalin's appearance 'makes no impression' may indicate Bulgakov's own feelings about Stalin's mediocrity; and Stalin's story about the 'black dragon' which 'stole the sun from the whole of humanity' could refer to Stalin's terror of the 1930s. Moreover, the Tsar's trained canary which sings the first line of 'God save the Tsar' could be interpreted as an allegory of the Soviet writer in the 'period of the personality cult'.[133]

In his novel *The Master and Margarita,* written during the period 1928-40, but first published in the USSR post-humously in a censored version in the years 1966-7,[134] Bulgakov chose to approach the figure of Stalin obliquely, through allegory and fantasy. Donald Piper has argued that much in Bulgakov's portrait of the Devil, Woland, suggests Stalin, who was also 'aloof, mysterious, rarely seen in the thirties, having difficulty with the Russian language, destructive when affronted, demanding subservience, impressive in his self-control'.[135] Other scholars dispute Piper's interpretation;[136] and, indeed, it is difficult to sustain, as Woland is not a sufficiently independent force of evil to be an adequate personification of Stalin. He is, rather, a fallen angel who frequently acts as the agent of the 'other department' of light, tempting people, but not compelling them to do evil, and using black magic for beneficent ends.[137] Bulgakov does, however, draw an ironic comparison between the servility of Woland's retinue and the cult of Stalin's personality. The cat Behemoth speaks of the grandeur of Satan's ball, but, after being contradicted by Woland, immediately hastens to agree with his master: 'Of course, messire . . . If you think it wasn't very grand, I immediately find myself agreeing with you'.[138] The Soviet censorship was evidently conscious of this allusion, since the passage was deleted in the version of the novel published in the journal *Moskva* in 1966-7. The censor also heavily cut passages in Chapter 26 containing Pilate's ambiguous conversation with his secret policeman Aphranius during which he explicitly warned against, but implicitly proposed, the murder of Judas. These passages must have been removed because they would have suggested to Soviet readers Stalin's dealings with his security services, notably in the case of Kirov's assassination in 1934, widely believed to

have been committed by the Soviet security police on Stalin's secret instructions.[139]

There is more evidence to suggest that Bulgakov intended a parallel between the Rome of Tiberius and the Moscow of the 1930s. Both societies are permeated by philistine values, spies, denunciations and the power of the secret police; and the eulogies of Tiberius, for example Pilate's insincere toast: 'For us, for thee, Caesar, father of the Romans, most beloved and best of all men!', are reminiscent of the praise of Stalin in the period of the 'personality cult' (although they were also characteristic of contemporary references to Tiberius).[140] Significantly, the phrase 'most beloved and best of all men' was omitted in the journal edition, in order to remove the implied parallel with Stalin. Furthermore, the comment on the nature of political power which Bulgakov puts into the mouth of Yeshua (Jesus), 'Every form of authority means coercion over men and . . . a time will come when there shall be neither Caesars, nor any other rulers'[141] is a general statement which is clearly applicable to Stalin's Russia. Although the interpretations of Piper and others who see *The Master and Margarita* as a 'cryptotext' for Stalin's Russia are highly debatable,[142] it is indisputable both that the Soviet censorship in the 1960s read the novel in an Aesopian fashion, and that some Soviet intellectuals perceived a parallel between Woland and Stalin (although some readers appear to have been disappointed by Part II of the novel which did not seem to bear out this interpretation as clearly as the first part). One prominent Soviet intellectual to support this reading was Andrei Sinyavsky, who compared Woland's relationship with the Master to Stalin's strange relationship with Bulgakov.[143] Although Bulgakov's love of ambiguity and mystification makes it impossible to prove conclusively any definite parallels between either Woland or Tiberius and Stalin, it should be remembered that Bulgakov was fully aware of the subversive nature of his manuscript, suspecting that he would have been shot if the novel had been discovered, and feeling it necessary to burn a draft of the manuscript at the time that he wrote his letter to Stalin and the government in March 1930. Moreover, Bulgakov was a close friend of Zamyatin, and the multiple possible implications of such Aesopian, but not entirely precise parallels with contemporary society as Zamyatin's *We* would have been familiar to him.

As we have seen, one of the most successful forms of anti-Stalinist satire was that conceived on the basis of children's literature. In 1941 Daniil Kharms used the children's magazine *The Siskin* (*Chizh*) to parody stereotyped May-day verses to Stalin. Kharms's *May Song* displays all the hallmarks of the military-patriotic song, with its simple metrical patterns and frequent repetitions:

> We'll get to the reviewing stand
> We'll get there
> We'll get to the reviewing stand
> First thing in the morning
> So that we'll shout the loudest
> Shout the loudest

So that we'll shout the loudest
'Hooray for Stalin!'[144]

As Loseff has shown, the exaggerated urgency of the repetitions and the illogicality of the content are disproportionate even by the usual standards of the 'song about Stalin': the lyric hero longs not to accomplish heroic deeds but merely to shout 'Hooray!', and his faith in the invincibility of the USSR is based only on the belief that Voroshilov will lead the Soviet army into battle 'on a horse'.[145]

The most skilled exponent of the genre of 'fairy tales for adults' was Evgeny Shvarts, whose play *The Dragon* can read on several levels: as a fairy story, a morality play and an Aesopian satire.[146] *The Dragon* was written for the Leningrad Comedy Theatre at the request of the theatre's director, chief set designer and artist Nikolai Akimov; it was begun during the period of the Nazi-Soviet Pact and the first version was completed by November 1943. On the surface the play is an obvious satire against Nazism: the Dragon is related to Attila the Hun; he persecutes gypsies (a reference to Hitler's persecution of gypsies, and, by implication, his much more extensive repression of Jews); his proclivity for sudden invasions, aerial tactics in battle and use of 'poisonous smoke' are reminiscent of the methods of the German armed forces; moreover, the names of the townspeople, such as Müller and Friedrichsen, as well as the Gothic lettering on the town hall, help to create a Germanic atmosphere. However, Shvarts's use of typically Soviet words, phrases and plot situations suggests that the allegory was also intended to point to Stalin and Stalinism.

Shvarts was clearly not unaware of the possibility of equating the Dragon with Stalin, since his earlier plays *The Naked King* (1935) and *The Shadow* (1940) had established a pattern of introducing elements which could apply equally well to the west or to the USSR. (In particular, *The Naked King,* based on Andersen's story *The Emperor's New Clothes,* could be interpreted as a satire on the 'personality cult'). In *The Dragon* the stage direction in Act I which precedes the Dragon's entrance states: 'At this point a middle-aged, but robust, man, looking younger than his years, enters the room. He is towheaded and has a military bearing. He wears his hair in a crew-cut. On his face is a broad smile. Despite its coarseness, his manner is in general not without a certain appeal'.[147] The portrait of the leading villain is so drawn that it combines traits which could apply equally to the typical Nazi or the typical Soviet leader of the 1930s: the crew-cut hair, military bearing and genial appearance of a father-commander. However, the Soviet slang of the Dragon's opening lines: 'Hello, lads!' ('*Zdorovo, rebyata!*') points the reader in the direction of Soviet, rather than German, reality. Another double-edged reference is made by Charlemagne: 'The only way of getting free of dragons is to have one of your own'.[148]

Shvarts parodies many specifically Soviet situations: for example, the Burgomaster's address to an empty chair, as he appeals to the Dragon to act as the meeting's 'honoured head', is reminiscent of the Soviet ritual of electing an 'honoured presidium' at ceremonial gatherings to demonstrate loyalty to the Politburo; and Heinrich's direction of the townspeople in a rehearsal of 'greetings to the leaders' recalls a time-honoured Soviet custom. The battle scene contains a satire on Soviet wartime information and propaganda: the Burgomaster and Heinrich issue communiqués which try to prove, against the evidence of the citizens' own eyes, that the Dragon is winning the battle, and that all his efforts to evade the invisible Lancelot, including the loss of his three heads, are well-planned military manoeuvres. This is particularly reminiscent of the theory of Stalin's tactical withdrawal of Soviet troops in 1941. In Act III Shvarts even includes a veiled reference to the Stalin terror: the conversation between the Burgomaster and the jailer contains a pun on the Soviet term *sazhanie,* which means both the 'planting' of seeds and the 'planting' of men in prison.

Shvarts's play met a fate as unsuccessful as that of Bulgakov's *Batumi.* There was one preliminary showing of the play in Moscow in August 1944, in the course of which Akimov was summoned by an official who told him the production was to be discontinued. Akimov later commented: 'There were no motives, and indeed they could not be expressed: a long time later it became clear that some excessively vigilant official of that time had seen in the play what was not in it at all'.[149] This is the only suggestion that the play was banned for any more specific reason than a lack of *ideinost':* the unsuitably trivial treatment of a subject as serious as fascism. *The Dragon* remained banned until after Shvarts's death in 1958; it was performed in Leningrad during the theatrical season of 1962-3, but, despite its great popularity with the audience, was soon taken off (perhaps because the character of the Burgomaster who rules the town after the Dragon's death could now be identified with Khrushchev). Shvarts's play can certainly be interpreted as an anti-Stalin satire, but, as Amanda Metcalf reminds us, it is more than that: 'a play about a tyrant—especially one which uses allegory—can always support as many different meanings as there are tyrants in the world'.[150]

The last phase of Stalinism was an unpromising period for anti-Stalinist satire, but one rare example of a children's story of the 1940s which uses 'Aesopian language' to criticise Stalin was Lev Kassil's *Tale of the Three Master Craftsmen* (1949).[151] Kassil's portrayal of King Vainglorious, whose kingdom is ruled by winds, implicates Stalin and the time-serving sycophants of the 'personality cult'. The tale of the three master craftsmen seized by the King's 'weathercocks' suggests the persecution of talented people and the success of pragmatists and intriguers in Stalin's time.

In the year before Stalin's death *Novy Mir* published Vasily Grossman's *For the Just Cause* (1952), ostensibly a conventional war novel which emphasised Stalin's brilliant strategy in the battle of Stalingrad and juxtaposed a favourable depiction of Stalin and Molotov with a satirical picture of Hitler and his generals. There were, however, certain passages in the novel, notably the views expressed by an academic, Chepyzhin, which hinted at a parallel between Nazi and Stalinist obscurantism.[152] Grossman's novel aroused Stalin's personal displeasure and was criticised in the press; some of the offending passages were removed from subsequent editions. That a parallel between Nazism and Stalinism was indeed in Grossman's mind has only become evident since the appearance of the sequel, originally entitled *Stalingrad,* but published abroad in 1980 under the title *Life and Fate.*[153] In this novel Chepyzhin's dismissal is presented as a harmful result of Stalin's repressive cultural policy.

NOTES

[1] M. Friedberg, 'Solzhenitsyn's and other literary Lenins', *Canadian Slavonic Papers,* 1977, no. 2, pp. 123-37.

[2] N. Mandelstam, *Hope Against Hope,* transl. M. Hayward (Harmondsworth, 1975), p. 190.

[3] K. Chukovsky, *Tarakanishche,* in *Sob. soch. v 6 tomakh,* vol. 1 (Moscow, 1965), pp. 173-80.

[4] L. Loseff, *On the Beneficence of Censorship. Aesopian language in Modern Russian Literature* (Munich, 1984), pp. 201-2.

[5] E. Zamyatin, *Iks, Novaya Rossiya,* no. 2 (February 1926), pp. 49-62. The 'spoof on Stalin' has been noted in A. Shane, *The Life and Works of Evgenij Zamyatin* (Berkeley and Los Angeles, 1968), p. 177.

[6] E. Zamyatin, *The Dragon and Other Stories,* transl. M. Ginzburg (Harmondsworth, 1975), pp. 227, 234.

[7] E. Zamyatin, *We,* transl. B. Guerney (Harmondsworth, 1983), p. 169. See also E. Zamyatin, 'O literature, revolyutsii i entropii', first published 1924, reprinted in *Litsa* (Munich, 1967), pp. 249-56.

[8] Zamyatin, *The Dragon and Other Stories,* p. 226.

[9] B. Pil'nyak, *Povest' nepogashennoi luny, Novy Mir,* 1926, no. 5, pp. 5-33.

[10] Most commentators have emphasised Number One's responsibility for the murder; for an alternative view, see G. Browning, *Boris Pil'niak: Scythian at a Typewriter* (Ann Arbor, 1985), pp. 153, 201 (n. 19), which stresses the ambiguity of details in the story.

[11] V. Reck, 'Introduction', in B. Pilnyak, *Mother Earth and Other Stories,* transl. and ed. V. Reck and M. Green (London, 1968), p. xii.

[12] S. Allilueva, *Dvadtsat' pisem k drugu* (New York and Evanston, 1968), pp. 150, 19; A. Barmine, *One who Survived* (New York, 1945), p. 198. These and other similarities to the real Stalin are discussed at length in V. Reck, *Boris Pil'niak. A Soviet Writer in Conflict with the State* (Montreal and London, 1975), pp. 29-38.

[13] Pil'nyak, *Povest', Novy Mir,* 1926, no. 5, p. 13.

[14] Ibid., p. 10.

[15] Reck, 'Introduction', p. xii.

[16] Pil'nyak, 'Predislovie', *Novy Mir,* 1926, no. 5, p. 5.

[17] Ibid., p. 18.

[18] E. Semeka, 'The Structure of Boris Pil'njak's "Povest' nepogasennoj luny": From the Structure to a Determination of the Genre', in A. Kodjak, M. Connolly and K. Pomorska (eds), *The Structural Analysis of Narrative Texts* (Columbus, Ohio, 1980), p. 161.

[19] Pil'nyak, *Povest', Novy Mir,* 1926, no. 5, pp. 31, 32.

[20] Semeka, p. 168; cf. Browning (see note 10), pp. 152-8.

[21] O. Mandel'stam, 'My zhivyom, pod soboyu ne chuya strany', no. 286 (November 1933), in Mandel'stam, *Sob. soch. v tryokh tomakh,* ed. G. Struve and B. Filippov, vol. 1 (Washington, 1967), p. 202.

[22] N. Mandelstam, *Hope against Hope,* pp. 191-2, 29.

[23] Ibid., p. 189.

[24] Ibid., p. 239.

[25] O. Mandel'stam, *Sob. soch.,* vol. 1, p. 227.

[26] N. Mandelstam, *Hope against Hope,* p. 177.

[27] A. Ulam, *Stalin. The Man and his Era* (New York, 1974), p. 436.

[28] See below, p. 86.

[29] L. Chukovskaya, *Pamyati Anny Akhmatovoi. Stikhi, pis'ma, vospominaniya* (Paris, 1974), p. 160; D. Shostakovich, *Testimony. The Memoirs of Dmitri Shostakovich* as related to and edited by Solomon Volkov, transl. A. Bouis (London, 1979), p. 210. See also M. Zoshchenko, *Lenin and the Sentry,* transl. with an afterword by R. Sobel, *Irish Slavonic Studies,* no. 4, 1983, pp. 106-8.

[30] N. Tumarkin, *Lenin Lives!* (Cambridge, Mass., 1983), pp. 1-23; R. Tucker, 'The Rise of Stalin's Personality Cult', *American Historical Review,* 84 (April 1979), pp. 347-8.

[31] I. V. Stalin, *Sochineniya,* vol. 13, pp. 84-102; discussed in Tucker, pp. 353-63.

[32] Tucker, p. 348.

[33] Ibid., pp. 348-9. For Louis Fischer's article, see *The Nation,* 13 August 1930, p. 176.

[34] A. Werth, *Russia, Hopes and Fears* (New York, 1969), pp. 305-6.

[35] *Pesni o Staline* (Moscow, 1950).

[36] A.A. Lakhuti, 'Vozhdyu, tovarishchu Stalinu', *Pravda,* 29 November 1932.

[37] D. Dzhabaev, 'Moi Stalin, tebe etu pesnyu poyu', in *Pesni o Staline,* pp. 48-9; D. Dzhabaev, 'Imya bessmertnoe—Stalin', in *Samoe dorogoe, Stalin v narodnom epose,* ed. Yu. Sokolov (Moscow, 1939), pp. 10-13.

[38] I. Deutscher, *Stalin: a Political Biography,* 2nd edn (Harmondsworth, 1970), p. 366.

[39] Shostakovich, pp. 161-2, 171.

[40] A. Surkov, 'Na prostorakh rodiny chudesnoi', in *Pesni,* pp. 16-17; A. Zinov'ev, *Nashei yunosti polyot* (Lausanne, 1983).

[41] V. Lebedev—Kumach, 'Pesnya o rodine', in *Pesni,* pp. 9-11; on the author, see G. Smith, *Songs to Seven Strings: Russian Guitar Poetry and Soviet 'Mass Song'* (Bloomington, Indiana, 1984), pp. 14-15.

[42] *Pesni,* p. 3; discussed in Smith, p. 60; Shostakovich, pp. 201-5. V. Aleksandrov, 'Kak sozdavalsya gimn Sovetskogo Soyuza', *Moskva,* 1988, no. 3, pp. 190-3.

[43] For references to Stalin as 'father', see, for example, S. Alymov, 'Rossiya'; L. Olshanin, 'Rozhdyonnyi v gorakh', in *Pesni,* pp. 12-13, 30-1; for other godlike attributes, see A. Churkin, 'Est' na svete strana'; M. Isakovsky, 'Shumyat plodorodnye stepi'; A. Kovalenkov, 'Pesnya o yunosti vozhdya', in *Pesni,* pp. 18-19, 22-3, 32-3.

[44] A. Surkov, 'Na prostorakh rodiny chudesnoi'; Ya. Shvedov, 'Noch'yu zvezdnoi', in *Pesni,* pp. 16-17, 147-8.

[45] From the Georgian folk song 'Slavnyi kormchii', in *Pesni,* p. 49.

[46] M. Inyushin, 'Ot kraya do kraya'; L. Olshanin, 'Rozhdyonnyi v gorakh'; M. Lisyansky, 'Pesnya o Staline'; A. Kovalenkov, 'Pesnya o yunost vozhdya', in *Pesni,* pp. 20-1, 30-1, 36-7, 32-3.

[47] M. Isakovsky, 'Shumyat plodorodnye stepi'; M. Matusovsky, 'Spasibo Stalinu!', in *Pesni,* pp. 22-3, 165-6.

[48] Tucker, *Stalin as Revolutionary,* p. 470; A. Antonov-Ovseenko, *Portret tirana* (New York, 1980), p. 281. On bird imagery in Stalinist culture, see M. Ziolkowski, 'The Reversal of Stalinist Literary Motifs: The Image of the Wounded Bird in Recent Russian Literature', *Modern Language Review,* vol. 83, part 1 (January 1988), pp. 106-20.

[49] M. Inyushin, 'Ot kraya do kraya'; A. Kovalenkov, 'Pesnya o yunosti vozhdya', in *Pesni,* pp. 20-1, 32-3. On Stalin's relationship with the young pilots, see Katerina Clark, *The Soviet Novel: History as Ritual* (Chicago and London, 1981), pp. 124-9, 137-9.

[50] V. Lebedev-Kumach, 'Pesnya o stolitse'; 'Moskva, Moskva!'; A. Zharov, 'Golos Kremlya', in *Pesni,* pp. 59-60, 154-6, 149-51.

[51] Ya. Shvedov, 'Noch'yu zvezdnoi', p. 147.

[52] V. Lebedev-Kumach, 'Sadovnik'; D. Suleimanov, 'Velikii sadovod'; A. Surkov, 'Na prostorakh rodiny chudesnoi'; M. Isakovsky, 'Shumyat plodorodnye stepi', in *Pesni,* pp. 59-60, 61-2, 16-17, 22-3.

[53] N. Nezlobin, 'Kolechko', in *Pesni,* pp. 159-60.

[54] V. Lebedev-Kumach, 'Spoyom, tovarishchi, spoyom', in *Pesni,* p. 28.

[55] *Doklad A.M. Gor'kogo o sovetskoi literature, Pervyi s'ezd pisatelei: stenograficheskii otchot* (Moscow, 1934), p. 6.

[56] Clark (see note 49), pp. 148-50.

[57] M.S. Kryukova, *Skazanie o Lenine, Krasnaya nov',* 1937, no. 11, pp. 97-118.

[58] F. A. Konashkov, *Samoe dorogoe,* in *Samoe dorogoe. Stalin v narodnom epose,* ed. Yu. M. Sokolov (Moscow, 1939), p. 31.

[59] *O schastye,* in ibid., p. 36 (first published *Pravda,* 4 July 1935).

[60] V. Bespalikov, *Tri syna,* in ibid., pp. 48-52; V. E. Khramov, *Solntse,* ibid., pp. 53-6.

[61] Ibid., p. 56.

[62] I. Kovalyov, *Ledyanoi kholm,* ibid., pp. 65-72; Ayau, *Kak bogatyri pokorili Il'mukhanum,* ibid., pp. 73-8.

[63] *Stalin i pravda,* ibid., pp. 79-91.

[64] Clark, p. 150.

[65] See, e.g., N. Leontiev, 'Zatylok k budushchemu', *Novy Mir,* 1948, no. 9, pp. 248-66. For Zhdanov's speech, see *Oktyabr',* 1946, no. 9, pp. 5-20.

[66] 'Tovarishch Stalin, vy bol'shoi uchonyi', in anon., *Narodnye sovetskie pesni, Student,* 2/3 (1964), pp. 81-4; see also M. Mihailov, *Leto moskovskoe 1964* (Frankfurt, 1967), pp. 58-9; the song is attributed to Vysotsky in *Pesni russkikh bardov* (Paris, 1977), vol. 3, p. 31. The first authorised publication is Yu. Aleshkovsky, *Pesni, Kontinent.* no. 21 (1979), pp. 146-7. The reference to

linguistics is an ironic allusion to Stalin's famous article of 1950, 'On Marxism in Linguistics'.

[67] As translated in G. Smith, *Songs to Seven Strings*, p. 76.

[68] A. Solzhenitsyn, *The Gulag Archipelago*, vol. 2 (Fontana, London, 1976), pp. 308-38.

[69] A. N. Tolstoy, *Pyotr pervyi*, in A. Tolstoy, *Pol'noe sobranie sochinenii*, 15 vols (Moscow, 1946-53), vol. IX.

[70] R. Taylor, *Film Propaganda: Soviet Russia and Nazi Germany* (London, 1979). p. 119. See also M. Ferro, 'The fiction film and historical analysis', in P. Smith (ed.), *The Historian and Film* (Cambridge, 1976), pp. 80-94.

[71] H. Marshall, *Masters of Soviet Cinema: Crippled Creative Biographies* (London, 1983), p. 174.

[72] I. Ehrenburg, *People, Years, Life*, vol. 3 (New York, 1963), p. 226. See also Marshall, pp. 228-32.

[73] V. Kostylev, *Ivan groznyi*, 3 vols (Moscow, 1955); discussed in V. Alexandrova, *Literatura i zhizn'. Ocherki sovetskogo obshchestvennogo razvitiya* (New York, 1969), pp. 430-1.

[74] Cited in M. Seton, *Sergei M. Eisenstein* (New York, 1960), pp. 436-7.

[75] M. Romm, *Besedi o kino* (Moscow, 1964), p. 91.

[76] N. Zabolotsky, *Goriiskaya simfoniya, in Sob. soch.*, vol. 1 (Moscow, 1983), pp. 184-6.

[77] A. Tvardovsky, *Strana Muraviya, in Stikhotvoreniya i poemy* (Moscow, 1954), pp. 283-6.

[78] M. Friedberg, *Reading for the Masses: popular Soviet fiction, 1976-80* (Washington, DC, 1981), p. 29.

[79] On Tvardovsky's *For the Right of Memory;* see above pp. 74-5.

[80] P. Yashvili, *Na smert' Lenina, Tridtsat' dnei*, 1934, no. 1, p. 13; V. Gaprindashvili, *Oktyabrskie stroki*, transl. B. Pasternak, in *Poety sovetskoi Gruzii* (Tbilisi, 1946), p. 49.

[81] N. Mitsishvili, *Stalin, Novy Mir*, 1934, no. 3; P. Yashvili, *Stalin, Krasnaya nov'*, 1934, no. 6.

[82] L. Fleishman, *Pasternak v tridtsatye gody* (Jerusalem, 1984), pp. 151-2.

[83] See, for example, *Poety sovetskoi Gruzii*, pp. 50, 81, 116, 132, 152, 154.

[84] N. Mandelstam, *Hope against Hope*, p. 173.

[85] B. Pasternak, *Doctor Zhivago*, transl. M. Hayward and M. Harari (Fontana, London, 1961), p. 19.

[86] N. Cornwell, *Pasternak's Novel: Perspectives on 'Doctor Zhivago'* (Keele, 1986), p. 112.

[87] I. Berlin, *Personal Impressions* (London, 1980), p. 204.

[88] Cornwell, pp. 65-7, 137, n. 50.

[89] N. Mandelstam, *Hope against Hope*, pp. 237-44.

[90] A. Akhmatova, *Slava miru*, first published *Ogonyok*, 1950, nos. 14, 36, 42.

[91] A. Haight, *Anna Akhmatova: A Poetic Pilgrimage* (Oxford, 1976), p. 159. Her wishes were ignored: see A. Akhmatova, *Sochineniya*, vol. 2 (Munich, 1968), pp. 147-54.

[92] A. Akhmatova, *Sochineniya*, vol. 1 (Munich, 1967), p. 364.

[93] Akhmatova, vol. 2, p. 147.

[94] Ibid., p. 150.

[95] Akhmatova, 'Podrazhanie armyanskomu', cited in *Sochineniya*, 2, p. 139.

[96] Haight, p. 159.

[97] N. Mandelstam, *Hope against Hope*, p. 244.

[98] Clark, *The Soviet Novel*, p. 127.

[99] P. Pavlenko, *Na vostoke* (Moscow, 1937), pp. 438-9.

[100] I. Ehrenburg, *Lyudi, gody, zhizn', Novy Mir*, 1962, no. 4, p. 61.

[101] Clark, pp. 61-3, 79.

[102] A. Tolstoy, *Khleb* (Moscow, 1937), pp. 35, 191, 192.

[103] Ibid., pp. 194, 257.

[104] Ibid., pp. 35, 192.

[105] I. Ehrenburg, *Lyudi, gody, zhizn', Novy Mir*, 1963, no. 1, pp. 70-1.

[106] A. Korneichuk, *Front, Pravda*, 24-7 August 1942. On Stalin's role, see A. Werth, *Russia at War 1941-45* (London, 1964), pp. 423-6.

[107] L. Leonov, *Nashestvie, Novy Mir*, 1942, no. 8, p. 84.

[108] A. Karavaeva, *Ogni, Novy Mir*, 1943, no. 12, pp. 38-40.

[109] K. Simonov, *Dni i nochi* (M., 1946), pp. 167-8.

[110] V. Kataev, *Syn polka, Oktyabr'*, 1945, nos. 1-2, pp. 67-8. See also V. Kozhevnikov, *Blizost', Oktyabr'*, 1945, no. 3, p. 62, which depicts Stalin's great interest in testing a

gun, and stresses how important it is for soldiers to gain strength by thinking of Stalin's face.

[111] V Ivanov, *Pri vzyatii Berlina, Novy Mir,* 1946, no. 3, p. 22.

[112] Ibid., *Novy Mir,* no. 6, p. 32.

[113] N. Virta, *Velikie dni,* in *P'esy,* (Moscow, 1950), pp. 113-15.

[114] A. Solzhenitsyn, *V kruge pervom,* in *Sob.soch.,* vol. 1 (Vermont and Paris, 1978), p. 119.

[115] V. Vishnevsky, *Nezabyvaemyi 1919-yi,* in *Dramaturgiya i izbrannoe* (Moscow, 1953), pp. 399-400; mentioned in Solzhenitsyn, *Sob.soch.,* vol. 1 (1978), p. 119.

[116] Shostakovich, pp. 197-8. See also Tucker, p. 436, on Stalin's liking for other films such as *Lenin in October* and *Man with a Rifle,* in which he himself figured as a character.

[117] A. Kron, *Kandidat partii, Novy Mir,* 1950, no. 10, p. 19.

[118] A. Gribachev, *Vesna v Pobede, Znamya,* 1948, no. 12, p. 48.

[119] G. Berezko, *Mirnyi gorod,* Book I, *Znamya,* 1951, nos. 2-4; Books 1 and 2, Moscow, 1955; M. Bubyonnov, *Belaya beryoza, Oktyabr',* 1952, nos. 3-5.

[120] G. Berezko, *Mirnyi gorod, Znamya,* 1951, no. 3, p. 49; no. 5, pp. 77-8.

[121] M. Bubyonnov, *Belaya beryoza, Oktyabr',* 1952, no. 4, pp. 71-4.

[122] E. Evtushenko, *A Precocious Autobiography,* transl. A. MacAndrew (London, 1963), pp. 77-8.

[123] M. Bulgakov, *Batum,* in *Neizdannyi Bulgakov. Teksty i materialy,* ed. E. Proffer (Ann Arbor, 1977), pp. 137-210 (for a discussion of the circumstances surrounding its conception, see the Preface by E. Proffer, pp. 7-8); V. Vilenkin, *Nezabyvaemye vstrechi,* in ibid., p. 58.

[124] Ibid., p. 8.

[125] Ibid., p. 58.

[126] See above, pp. 42-3.

[127] V. Petelin, 'M.A. Bulgakov i "Dni Turbinykh" ', *Ogonyok,* 1969, no. 11, pp. 26-8. It is true that works about Stalin's youth were not encouraged. An exception to this general rule was a children's play by two Georgians, G. Nakhutsreshvili and B. Gamrekeli, *Lado Ketskhoveli* (Moscow, Leningrad, 1940), first performed in Tbilisi, subsequently translated into Russian and produced in Moscow in 1939, which presents the twenty-year-old Soso Djugashvili as a leading figure in the Trans-Caucasus who was responsible for setting up a clandestine printing press. See E. J. Simmons, *Through the Glass of Soviet Literature* (New York, 1953; 1972 reprint), pp. 184-5.

[128] L. Loseff, *On the Beneficence of Censorship,* pp. 223-6.

[129] *Neizdannyi Bulgakov,* p. 141.

[130] Ibid., pp. 201-2, 204, 209.

[131] Ibid., p. 182.

[132] Ibid., p. 195.

[133] Ibid., pp. 163, 156, 203-4.

[134] M. Bulgakov, *Master i Margarita, Moskva,* 1966, no. 11; 1967, no. 1.

[135] D. Piper, 'An Approach to Bulgakov's *The Master and Margarita',* *Forum for Modern Language Studies,* 7, no. 2 (1971), pp. 146-7.

[136] For criticism of Piper's interpretation, see E. Proffer, *Bulgakov. Life and Work* (Ann Arbor, 1984), p. 647, n. 45; A. C. Wright, *Michael Bulgakov. Life and Interpretations* (Toronto, 1978), p. 266.

[137] M. Bulgakov, *Master i Margarita* (Frankfurt, 1969), p. 359. See also the epigraph, taken from Goethe's *Faust:*

> That power I serve
> Which wills forever evil
> Yet does forever good.

A. Barratt, *Between Two Worlds. A Critical Introduction to The Master and Margarita* (Oxford, 1987), pp. 171-2, makes quite a convincing case for interpreting Woland as a 'gnostic messenger'.

[138] Barratt, p. 70.

[139] Bulgakov, *Master i Margarita,* p. 351.

[140] Ibid., p. 383. G. El'baum, *Analiz yudeiskikh glav 'Mastera i Margarity' M. Bulgakova* (Ann Arbor, 1981), p. 114, points out that this toast bears a close similarity to a passage in Suetonius referring to Tiberius.

[141] Ibid., p. 41.

[142] See, in particular, Piper; E. Mahlow, *Bulgakov's 'The Master and Margarita': The Text as Cypher* (New York, 1975).

[143] A. Sinyavsky, 'Literaturnyi protsess v Rossii', *Kontinent,* no. 1 (1974), pp. 158-61.

[144] D. Kharms, *Maiskaya pesnya, Chizh,* 1941, no. 5.

[145] Loseff, pp. 205-7.

[146] E. Shvarts, *Drakon*, ed. with an introduction by A. J. Metcalf (Canberra, 1984). The first version was completed by November 1943. For a discussion of the play, see Loseff, pp. 125-42; A. Metcalf, *Evgenii Shvarts and his Fairy-tales for Adults* (Birmingham, 1979), pp. 47-68.

[147] Shvarts, *Drakon*, p. 9.

[148] Ibid., p. 8.

[149] M. Slonimsky *et al., My znali Evgeniya Shvartsa* (Leningrad, 1966), p. 183.

[150] A. Metcalf, 'Introduction' to *Drakon*, p. vii.

[151] L. Kassil', *Povest' o tryokh masterakh,* in *Dorogie moi mal'chiki* (Moscow, 1949).

[152] V. Grossman, *Za pravoe delo, Novy Mir,* 1952, no. 7, p. 102. For a translation of this passage and a discussion of the attacks it engendered, see E. R. Frankel, *Novy Mir. A case study in the politics of literature* 1952-1958 (Cambridge, 1981), pp. 9-14.

[153] V. Grossman, *Zhizn' i sud'ba* (Lausanne, 1980). See above, pp. 116-18.

Margaret Ziolkowski (essay date 1991)

SOURCE: "A Modern Demonology: Some Literary Stalins," in *Slavic Review,* Vol. 50, No. 1, Spring, 1991, pp. 59-69.

[*In the following essay, Ziolkowski examines the depiction of Stalin in literature published both in and out of the Soviet Union, arguing that such literary representations are particularly important in the absence of accurate historical and biographical documents on Stalin.*]

The publication of Anatolii Rybakov's *Deti Arbata* (1987) was heralded with much fanfare both in the Soviet Union and abroad. In the novel Rybakov seeks to capture the essence of Stalinism as it affected the day-to-day existence of Soviet citizens, a theme that commands intense interest in the Soviet Union today. Yet it seems unlikely that *Deti Arbata* would have attracted the attention it has were it not for its lengthy passages devoted to the actions and thoughts of Stalin. The novel's protagonist Sasha Pankratov remains curiously flat, too reminiscent of socialist realist paragons; it is instead Rybakov's Stalin who holds the reader's attention.

Few reliable Soviet histories of the Stalinist period or biographies of Stalin exist. Dmitrii Volkogonov and others are trying to rectify this situation, but literature has attempted to fill the gap and to respond to the national desire for some insight into the mysteries of Stalinism and its creator.[1] Writers of fiction like Rybakov and Mikhail Shatrov try to fulfill the roles of historian and novelist or

playwright simultaneously, as they overwhelm the reader with a mass of painstakingly researched details. For the moment, Rybakov's Stalin is the most thoroughly revisionist portrait of the dictator officially available to the Soviet reading public.[2] This fact invests the novel with a prestige sometimes difficult for the western reader to grasp.

Outside the Soviet Union, Rybakov's Stalin draws the attention of readers as an extensive portrayal of one of the most significant personages of the twentieth century. Much of the curiosity surrounding *Deti Arbata,* especially in the west, undoubtedly stems from the fact that the novel was published in the Soviet Union. At the same time, on western ground Rybakov's Stalin has competitors who are only beginning to be acknowledged within the Soviet Union. For a historical appraisal of Stalin, western readers may turn to one of dozens of studies produced by émigré and other historians, like Adam Ulam, Robert Tucker, Roy Medvedev, Boris Souvarine, and Anton Antonov-Ovseenko.[3] In literature, Aleksandr Solzhenitsyn's Stalin chapters in *V kruge pervom* (1968) create a portrayal that has been famous in the west for twenty years.

Deti Arbata and *V kruge pervom* are not isolated productions. Rather, they are part of a large corpus of literary Staliniana, most of which has only been published abroad. The shared features that typify this body of writings are the subject of this article. A long series of works has sought to deglamorize Stalin and, in order to achieve this end, has used surprisingly similar physical, verbal, and psychological characterizations. The result is often a series of commonplaces. Read in isolation, *Deti Arbata* may appear to offer an incisive psychological portrait; examined in context, it emerges as a typical product of a tradition of literary stereotyping.[4]

V kruge pervom was published in 1968. In 1969 a pseudonymous work, P. N. Anonimov's *povest'*-length *Utro v mae 1947 goda,* appeared, purporting to describe a typical day in the life of Stalin and his associates. In 1971 Aleksandr Bek's *Novoe naznachenie,* a novel about the bureaucratic upper echelons of heavy industry under Stalin, was published; it finally appeared in the Soviet Union in 1986.[5] In 1973 the émigré author Vladimir Maksimov produced a parablelike tale entitled "Preobrazhenie tikhogo seminarista," which is included in his novel *Karantin.* Maksimov later published another novel containing several passages devoted to Stalin, *Kovcheg dlia nezvanykh* (1979), which concerns Soviet attempts at postwar settlement of the Kurile Islands. Anatolii Gladilin's "Repetitsiia v piatnitsu," a fantastic story of Stalin's resurrection from freezer storage in the 1970s, appeared in 1977, and in 1979 "V krugu druzei" appeared—it is a satirical spoof about Stalin and his associates on the eve of World War II by another member of the third wave emigration, Vladimir Voinovich. Another tamizdat publication of 1979 was "Piry Valtasara," one of the stories in Fazil' Iskander's *Sandro iz Chegema* cycle; this segment describes a gathering of dignitaries in the Caucasus in the mid-1930s and

Sandro's boyhood memories of inadvertently encountering Stalin in the prerevolutionary years. Significantly, "Piry Valtasara" recently appeared in *Znamia*.[6] Another story by Iskander in which Stalin figures, "Diadia Sandro i ego liubimets," was also published abroad in 1979. In 1980 Vasilii Grossman's *Zhizn' i sud'ba*, a massive treatment of the Battle of Stalingrad and Soviet society of the war years that contains a brief sketch of Stalin, was published. Like *Novoe naznachenie*, Grossman's novel recently appeared in the Soviet Union.[7] In 1981 two collections appeared that, like several of the works described above, had long circulated in samizdat, Il'ia Suslov's anecdotal portrait, *Rasskazy o tovarishche Staline i drugikh tovarishchakh,* and Aleksandr Galich's "Poema o Staline."

The works just mentioned were first published abroad between the 1960s and the early 1980s. In the Soviet Union during these years, critical portraits of Stalin—literary portraits of any sort—were rare. A notable exception is Iurii Bondarev's novel *Goriachii sneg* (1969), a war novel that includes a brief encounter between one of the novel's major characters and Stalin. A few poems dating from the early 1960s also deserve mention: Andrei Voznesenskii's lengthy "Oza" (1964), which in one passage attempts to capture the essence of Stalin's attitude towards his citizens, Boris Slutskii's "Bog" (1964?), and Bulat Okudzhava's "Chernyi kot" (1960). Okudzhava's poem is often thought to be an allegorical representation of Stalin, while Slutskii's, as the title suggests, focuses on the apotheosis of the dictator.

More recently, Stalin has figured as a character within the Soviet Union in the plays of Shatrov. In *Brestskii mir* (1987), for example, the dictator is an unscrupulous participant in the controversy over the Bolshevik acceptance of the terms of the Treaty of Brest-Litovsk. In *Dal'she, dal'she, dal'she . . .* (1988) he is one of numerous disputants of the significance of Soviet history. With the advent of glasnost, other portraits may be expected. Indeed, the sequel to *Deti Arbata, Tridtsat' piatyi i drugie gody,* has already appeared.[8]

This brief catalog of works containing critical portraits of Stalin, while not exhaustive, does show that a large body of such writings exists.[9] The image of Stalin presented in these stories, poems, and novels is complex and requires an awareness of two major, generally antithetical, bodies of cultural material. One is official Stalinist-era literary and other propaganda that surrounds the person and personality of Stalin. The other is composed of the historical and memoiristic works devoted to Stalin and Stalinism and largely published abroad; these works contain a significant component of political gossip that has long circulated orally within the Soviet Union and in émigré circles. The interaction between these very different bodies of material has decidedly affected the literary portrayal of Stalin in the past three decades.

The genesis of Stalin's official persona can be traced in large part to Stalin himself. As early as the 1920s Stalin singled out for praise certain of Vladimir Lenin's qualities that he later sought deliberately to have ascribed to himself. In a speech given shortly after Lenin's death in 1924, for example, Stalin discussed how he came to understand that Lenin's "simplicity and modesty . . . , [his] striving to remain inconspicuous . . . was one of Lenin's strongest features as a new leader of the new masses" (pp. 54-55).[10] Describing Lenin's rhetorical manner, Stalin speaks of his "simplicity and clarity of argumentation, short phrases comprehensible to everyone, the absence of posing, the absence of dizzying gestures and phrases produced for effect. . . . —all this advantageously distinguished Lenin's speeches from the speeches of ordinary 'parliamentary' orators" (p. 55). He was most captivated, however, by "the irresistible force" (p. 55) of Lenin's logic.

These enthusiastic observations echo eerily in a work published three decades later, the *Kratkaia biografiia* of Stalin, which Nikita Khrushchev asserted was composed to a great extent by the dictator himself:[11]

> Everyone knows the indefinable, shattering force of Stalin's logic, the crystal clarity of his intellect, his steel will, devotion to the party, ardent faith in the people and love for the people. His modesty, simplicity, sensitivity to people and mercilessness to enemies are well-known to everyone. His intolerance for sensation, for phrase-mongers and chatterboxes, for grumblers and alarmists is well known. Stalin is wise, unhurried in the solution of complex political questions.[12]

Many of the characteristics here are the same as those granted Lenin—modesty, simplicity, clarity, logic. Other desirable traits are only hinted at in Stalin's comments about Lenin but are made explicit in the description of Stalin himself. Thus Lenin's purported oratorical restraint suggests an implicit criticism of rhetorical brilliance and its authors, while Stalin is overtly intolerant of both. Lenin's comprehensibility and position as "a new leader of the new masses" point to a harmonious relationship with the people, while Stalin is ostentatiously devoted to them. Where the description of Stalin differs from that of Lenin is in its insistence on the former's "steel will" and other manifestations of toughness of character, such as an appropriate intolerance and mercilessness. Stalin's official persona tends towards stylized reproduction of a stylized Lenin, but the former implicitly exceeds the latter in his refusal to compromise.

Stalin's desire to be admired for the same qualities attributed to the near-deity Lenin was readily apparent to the Soviet intelligentsia of the 1930s and 1940s. In 1950 the literary scholar G. S. Cheremin asserted in *Obraz I. V. Stalina v sovetskoi khudozhestvennoi literature* that Soviet writers had striven to reproduce Stalin's characteristic traits, which, Cheremin happily reported, are precisely those that Stalin himself singled out as typical of Lenin: "simplicity and modesty, 'an irresistible power of logic,' unshakeable confidence in victory, an ability to 'weigh soberly the strengths of the opponent,' a supreme adherence to principles, a faith in the masses, 'a brilliant perspicacity, an ability quickly to grasp and divine the internal sense of approaching events'" (p. 4).[13] In its obsession with simplicity, modesty, pretensions to unique intellectual acuity, and a special relationship with the people, this statement is fully compatible with the remarks by and about Stalin cited above. Cheremin later noted additional characteristic traits: Stalin's "love for the truth, his negative attitude towards any kind of farfetched thinking . . . his calm" (p. 25). A similarity with Lenin is not cited here, but the image of calm practicality is consistent with the absence of oratorical fireworks elsewhere attributed to Stalin's predecessor.

Many Soviet writers participated in the creation of a literary Stalin compounded of the traits described above. In Iakov Il'in's novel *Bol' shoi konveier* (1934), for example, Stalin delivers a speech slowly and quietly, with restrained gestures and a seemingly enviable talent for simplifying the complex: "Posing questions, he would answer them, and the very repetition of this device, the clear, precise development of thought contributed to everyone's ability to repeat after him his complex generalizations, the result of gigantic intellectual labor."[14] Another gift is apparent in *Schast'e* (1947), Petr Pavlenko's optimistic saga of the 1940s, in which Stalin's rapport with the people achieves truly mystical proportions: "Stalin's face could not help changing and becoming somewhat different, because the people looked into it as in a mirror, and saw in it themselves, and the people had changed, in the direction of even greater majesty."[15] Yet Pavlenko's Stalin does not succumb to pomposity. A soldier's boast about the achievements of the Soviet army inspires a characteristic rejoinder: "It is wrong to think that we did more than we could. Let us say more modestly: we did everything that was in our power" (p. 97).

Many recent literary portrayals of the leader seem to have been composed in direct opposition to this image of the wise, calm, unassuming leader of the people, for they single out for satire precisely the positive qualities he was supposed to possess. To achieve this subversion of what was once Stalin's near divine status, writers often make use of the other corpus of material mentioned above, the great and rapidly growing number of historical and memoiristic works that have been published since the death of Stalin and that have sought to demolish his received image. Works like Antonov-Ovseenko's *Portret tirana* (1980), Nadezhda Mandel'shtam's *Vospominaniia* (1970), Khrushchev's secret speech to the Twentieth Party Congress in 1956, Roy Medvedev's *K sudu istorii* (1971), and even chapters of Robert Conquest's *The Great Terror* (1968) have reached a large audience both abroad and in the Soviet Union.[16] Nor should one overlook the writers' familiarity with critical commentary on Stalin from the 1920s and 1930s, like the famous observations about his rudeness and capriciousness in Lenin's "Testament."[17] How much each work uses gossip and rumors varies, but much of this informal information surfaces in literary depictions of Stalin. Solzhenitsyn's reference to "moist, greasy fingers which left traces on papers and books" suggests a familiarity with Dem'ian Bednyi's

observation along these lines.[18] In Maksimov's *Kovcheg dlia nezvanvkh* Stalin humiliates an aging friend of his youth by making him dance the *lezginka*. In his memoirs, Khrushchev tells of being made to dance the *gopak*. This incident is directly incorporated by Voinovich in his story. Such anecdotal fidelity is in general characteristic of critical portrayals of Stalin.

The Stalin who emerges from these literary works is often a synthesis of traits antithetical to those in orthodox writings of the Stalinist era and of details, largely unflattering, culled from historical and memoiristic literature and, presumably, word of mouth. Such syntheses are generally remarkably consistent in physical, verbal, and psychological terms. Taken together, they point towards shared and stereotyped assumptions about Stalin's malevolent personality.

The similarities in the various depictions of Stalin begin with the delineation of his physical characteristics, appurtenances, and mannerisms. Suslov captures much of the essence of this portrait in one of his anecdotes: "Comrade Stalin never presided over the Politburo. He would walk softly around the table in his soft, box-calf boots and smoke his little pipe."[19] The boots, the pipe, and the catlike walk are recurrent motifs in the portrayal of Stalin. Other common motifs include his short stature, mustache, low forehead, pockmarked skin, and disturbing eyes. A characteristic description appears early in *Utro v mae 1947 goda*: "The door opens. Out comes a rather short old man in a light tussore jacket . . . and wide trousers . . . tucked into soft calf-skin boots. Gray, wiry hair over a low, yellow forehead and dark, intent eyes . . . , a heavy pockmarked nose, a gray mustache."[20] Another common motif is Stalin's handicapped arm, which Sandro notices with great interest in "Piry Valtasara." Sandro feels that "this little disablement somehow lowered the image of the leader."[21] In "Diadia Sandro i ego liubimets," the phrase, *usykhaiushchaia ruka*, occurs so many times that it becomes nearly formulaic.[22]

References to Stalin's boots perform a different function, serving as a physical reminder of the easily ignited violence in his personality. In *V kruge pervom*, for example, on Stalin's first appearance, he is lying down "with his feet raised a little in soft Caucasian boots which were like thick stockings" (p. 115). Later Stalin thinks of the Yugoslav Communist Traicho Kostov: "Rage flooded his head, and he struck out hard with his boot—into Traicho's snout, into his bloody snout" (p. 147). References to the oppressive quality of Stalin's gaze also serve to underscore how dangerous he was to those around him. In the 1968 text of *V kruge pervom*, his eyes betray his viciousness: "Stalin was terrifying because he did not listen to excuses, he didn't even make accusations; his yellow tiger eyes only brightened balefully and his lower lids narrowed a bit—and there, inside, sentence had been passed."[23] A similar menace characterizes Stalin's glance in Gladilin's "Repetitsiia v piatnitsu." When confronted by the resurrected, previously innocuous-seeming old man, a guard initially cannot understand why the familiar face seems so different. Then he realizes: "The eyes! The eyes had lit up—and at once the harmless little old man had disappeared, and HE, the real Master, had risen."[24]

These motifs may not all appear simultaneously but often several occur in the initial description of Stalin in a given work. When Onisimov, the protagonist of *Novoe naznachenie*, remembers meeting Stalin in 1938, he recalls his first glimpse of the leader "walking up and down in his soft boots."[25] More details emerge from Onisimov's memory: Stalin "still retained the undemanding clothing of a front-line soldier— . . . his pants of military cut, tucked into his boots, . . . —but he had already acquired a seemingly deliberately unhurried habit, a slowness of step" (p. 34). The deliberate quality of Stalin's gait enhances its ominousness. When Stalin finally turns toward Onisimov, the oppressive sensation increases: "A rather heavy stare . . . measured Onisimov. . . . At that moment nothing changed in his motionless . . . face, well-known from many canvases and photographs, in which of course, however, no one had dared to reproduce the prominent pockmarks noticeable on his cheeks and beneath his . . . mustache" (pp. 34-35). The allusion to artistic and photographic renditions of Stalin points to the gap between the myth and the reality perceived by Onisimov in spite of his devotion to the leader. Other literary characters strive actively to ignore this reality. In *Kovcheg dlia nezvanykh*, the ambitious young bureaucrat Zolotarev, watching a slow-moving Stalin, attempts a conscious selection of observation and tries to force himself to ignore physical defects he has heard mentioned, like the leader's pockmarks, and instead "to remember other traits and details more essential for himself and his future."[26]

In *V kruge pervom*, physical characteristics that undercut Stalin's grandeur are also emphasized. For example, the narrator speaks of Stalin's "brownish-gray, smallpox-pitted face, with its large plow of a nose" (p. 175). He also describes him as "a little yellow-eyed old man with reddish, . . . thinning hair (represented [in portraits] as thick); with traces of smallpox here and there on his gray face [and] a desiccated double chin (they were not pictured at all)" (p. 116). As do *Kovcheg dlia nezvanykh* and numerous other works, *V kruge pervom* adduces such details to demonstrate the falsehood of Stalin's official portraits, both artistic and literary. . . .

The remarkable coincidence of physical details employed in literary depictions of Stalin achieves an unusually high level of predictability in *Deti Arbata*. When the plant director Mark Riazanov first visits Stalin, he sees a familiar sight:

> Stalin was walking up and down the study and stopped when the door opened. He was wearing a service jacket of khaki, almost brown, material and pants of the same material tucked into his boots. He seemed shorter than average height, thickset, somewhat pockmarked, with slightly Mongolian eyes. In the thick hair over a low forehead grey hairs were showing.[27]

Almost immediately, mention of another, disliked plant director evokes a characteristic reaction: "His eyes suddenly became yellowish, heavy, tiger-like, malice flashed in them" (4: 13). Describing how Stalin listens to Riazanov, the narrator writes: "Stalin listened carefully, clasping his left arm to his chest with his pipe gripped in his fist; it seemed that his arm straightened out badly" (4: 13). Physical imperfections and flashes of malevolence again undermine the received image of the leader.

Cumulatively, these descriptions show a remarkably formulaic quality in the use of physical detail in literary portrayals of Stalin. The repetition evokes medieval iconographical handbooks. While some recent Russian authors appear to engage in this practice without self-consciousness, others assume a deliberately ironic stance. Voinovich, for example, mocks the necessity for including the famed mustache and pipe when he writes that Stalin "smoked a pipe only in company, and he wore a false mustache."[28]

A similar, if less mechanical, consistency informs recent critical literary treatments of Stalin's verbal manner and intellectual ability. A favorite source of ridicule is Stalin's purported verbal and intellectual facility. This attitude is in direct opposition to the mainstream authors' descriptions of Stalin's remarkable mental powers and simple yet powerful oratorical manner. Widespread assertions about Stalin's astounding intellect and rhetorical flair appear at times to have had an almost hypnotic effect on his contemporaries. Milovan Djilas effectively captures the essence of this phenomenon:

> we waxed enthusiastic not only over Stalin's views but also over the "perfection" of their formulation. I myself referred many times in discussions to the crystal clarity of his style, the penetration of his logic, . . . But it would not have been difficult for me, even then, to detect in any other author of the same qualities that his style was colorless, meager, and an unblended jumble of vulgar journalism and the Bible.[29]

Some, like Konstantin Simonov, remained positive in their appraisal of Stalin's style.[30] Others are more reserved. Volkogonov writes: "[Stalin] was a mediocre publicist from the point of view of literary style. But there was no denying that he had consistency, precision, and an immutable categoricality in his conclusions."[31]

Volkogonov may be evenhanded in his assessment of Stalin's style and implicit appraisal of his intellect, but others are scathing in their criticism. Antonov-Ovseenko refuses to grant Stalin the least trace of rhetorical sophistication, although he grudgingly acknowledges the dictator's ability to win over some listeners. He dismisses Stalin's use of the question and answer method as a seminary device: "a ready-made answer followed a ready-made question."[32] He later reiterates this popular notion of the seminary roots of Stalin's style, speaking of his "childishly bombastic style and grammar on the level of a half-educated seminarian" (p. 170) and of how "the seminary's imprint lies on all of Stalin's actions . . . his question-and-answer style of exposition, and his use of expressions like 'the mere wafting of a hand,' 'would fain do,' and 'brothers and sisters.'"[33]

The kinds of accusations leveled against Stalin's style by Antonov-Ovseenko and like-minded others form the basis for negative literary appraisals of Stalin's linguistic and intellectual talents. Typically, the two are related, for, as Susan Layton points out in regard to *V kruge pervom,* "the parody of Stalin's language seeks to unmask the utter mediocrity of the mind and spirit of the dictator."[34] Touching on Stalin's forays into linguistic theory, Solzhenitsyn singles out certain of the leader's stylistic foibles—his weakness for enumeration and repetition, for example—as well as his poor grasp of the existence or absence of causal relationships. "Language was created in order to . . . ," Stalin writes in *V kruge pervom,* for example (p. 175).

In *Kovcheg dlia nezvanykh,* Maksimov also casts aspersions on Stalin's intellect, and notes that "he did not like details, which prevented him from seeing things as a whole without the ballast of circumstances and circumlocutions" (p. 69). Maksimov's Stalin is ignorant but vain; learning inadvertently that he has omitted a comma in an inscription on one of Maksim Gor'kii's manuscripts, he later has the manuscript retrieved from a museum so that he can correct his mistake. Such vanity may degenerate into smug self-satisfaction. "The Kuriles," he says, "are our far eastern underbelly." "The word obviously pleased him," (p. 35) observes the narrator, pointing simultaneously to Stalin's fondness for crude, even vulgar, language (often mentioned in memoir accounts) and to his exaggerated enjoyment of his own speech. The implication is that such vanity regarding his verbal talents hampers meaningful attention to issues.

In "Repetitsiia v piatnitsu," Gladilin's resurrected old man delivers a speech larded with the trite expressions typical of the worst Soviet officialese. Ironically, much of his rank and file party audience responds enthusiastically. Anonimov also portrays the leader as an orator dependent on unsophisticated listeners in *Utro v mae 1947 goda.* When he speaks to his immediate entourage, the narrator observes: "Every word solidly, weightily sinks into the guarded, but now also admiring attention. He knows, they like it when he thinks aloud" (p. 100). Here, too, there is a keen sense of smug self-satisfaction. Elsewhere in Anonimov's work, Stalin revels in a belief in his own intelligence. Constant expressions of gushing approval by his subordinates foster the development of an unbridled vanity.

The truly pernicious aspect of Stalin's verbal manner is perhaps best illustrated by Bek, who in *Novoe naznachenie* exceeds even Maksimov in depicting a Stalin infatuated with his own intellect. Unwilling to acknowledge the advice of metallurgical experts, Stalin reacts with irritation when pet projects do not appear feasible. Later, when he finds a suitable aphorism to use in combating the experts,

he is complacent and self-assured: "'Experience is a good thing. . . . But new conditions demand a new technology as well, new experience, isn't that so?' Satisfied by his speech, its clarity, logic, he pronounced the last words without any irritation" (pp. 54-55). He reacts in similar fashion on another occasion. "'Why substitute trifles for the main thing? Can something significant really be born without tribulations?' Satisfied by his formula, he was silent for a while" (p. 100). One of the characters thinks to himself, "Every means *is* trifles, subtleties, details" (p. 100). Yet Bek's Stalin is so filled with a consciousness of his own rhetorical self-importance that this trait is apparent, even to someone unversed in Georgian, when the dictator is overheard speaking only in his native language.

As with physical details, the portrayal of Stalin's verbal manner in *Deti Arbata* adheres to time-honored critical tradition. The assessment of Budiagin, one of his old acquaintances from exile, is characteristic: "A heavy Georgian accent and ponderous turns of speech did not make him a good orator" (4:98), thinks Budiagin, but he concedes Stalin a certain effectiveness: "In his straightforwardness, his seminary penchant for commentary, his unshakeable confidence that his learning was the limit of wisdom, there was a persuasiveness that impressed Budiagin at the time [in exile] more than the erudite eloquence of others" (4:98). Sergei Kirov later concurs in this assessment: "[Stalin's] simplified seminary logic, his seminary dogmatism, are comprehensible and impress people" (6:123).

The ability of Rybakov's Stalin to make an impression on some listeners is only a screen for ineptitude, however. Budiagin finds certain of Stalin's verbal and intellectual tendencies downright dangerous: "all complicated problems are simple: on the one hand—England, France, Japan, on the other—the USSR, USA, Germany. To reduce the complex to the simple Stalin considered his great talent. [Budiagin] considered Stalin's conception . . . obsolete, and Stalin's ability to simplify everything—a catastrophe" (4:105). While Budiagin fears terrible consequences because of Stalin's simplistic misunderstanding of Hitler's Germany, Stalin himself remains confident of his talent for generalization: "He always attached importance to trifles, . . . he was proud of his ability to generalize [on the basis of] trifles, to draw conclusions from them" (4:109). These "trifles" are implicitly very different from the significant details willfully ignored by Bek's and Maksimov's Stalins. Indeed, on one level, Rybakov's entire novel is an illustration of the frightening results of Stalin's misplaced obsession with trivialities. Rybakov's Stalin does generalize, but his generalizations are severely flawed.

When Stalin actually speaks in *Deti Arbata,* he reveals a fondness for the hackneyed devices that elicit admiration from orthodox writers and scorn from his detractors. These devices purportedly stem from his seminary days, the use of the question and answer method, for example (5:123):

Pacing up and down the office, Stalin said:

"To what does your report attest? Your report attests to the fact that comrade Zaporozhets is not coping with his responsibilities. . . . "

Slowly and inaudibly Stalin paced up and down the carpet.

"What is the peculiarity of this situation? . . . The peculiarity of the situation in Leningrad consists not only of the fact that many Zinov'evites have been retained in the Leningrad party organization."

In this same passage, Rybakov's Stalin also reveals a predilection for tired metaphors. "Kirov is harboring a Trotskyite snake in his bosom against Stalin," he tells Iagoda, "but might it not bite comrade Kirov himself?" (5:124). That this observation is less a question than a directive is confirmed by Stalin's final statement to Iagoda: "The party needs deeds, not scraps of paper" (5:124). The use of a trite aphorism to express a desire for Kirov's destruction is typical of the verbal mediocrity of many literary Stalins.

In addition to common presumptions about Stalin's unattractive appearance, ominous physical habits, hackneyed manner of speech, and smug intellectual mediocrity, critical portraits of the dictator also often share additional assumptions about his psychology—about, for example, his suspiciousness, even paranoia, his capriciousness, sadism, anti-Semitism, and hostility toward Lenin. Often most attention is given to his suspiciousness. Far from being depicted as the courageous mountain eagle of Soviet mythology, Stalin emerges as the thrall of an intense paranoia, particularly in his later years. This perception reflects an assumption prevalent in both western historical literature and memoir accounts.

In some fictional portraits Stalin's purportedly extreme suspiciousness acquires truly epic proportions. Commenting on Stalin's unique attitude toward Hitler, Voinovich observes: "The most suspicious person on earth, in his relations with Dolph [Hitler] he was credulous as a child" (169-170). In V kruge pervom, Solzhenitsyn makes a similar observation: "He had trusted only one person—the only one in his entire unerringly mistrustful life. . . . That man was Adolf Hitler" (p. 155). In both cases, Stalin's attitude toward Hitler is the exception to the rule of complete lack of trust. "Distrust of people was the determining trait of Iosif Djugashvili's character. Distrust of people was his world view" (p. 96), asserts Solzhenitsyn's narrator in the 1968 text. In Deti Arbata Rybakov describes Stalin's suspiciousness as a pathological state: "Puny and weak since childhood, he was morbidly sensitive to everything that put his physical strength and bravery into doubt,—a spiritual condition from which later grew his suspiciousness" (4:106).

Several writers link the leader's notorious insomnia to his paranoia and describe this combination in hyperbolic terms. "On odin, a emu nemozhetsia, / . . . Sto postelei emu posteleno,/ Ne usnut' emu ni v odnoi" (p. 273), writes Galich in "Poema o Staline." In Maksimov's "Preobrazhenie tikhogo seminarista" the ecclesiastical narrator describes how "fear ensnares his soul with oppressive alarm, fear tightens his chest with suffocating cold, fear deprives him of sleep and peace."[35] Anonimov speaks of "evil, disquieting thought. . . . The sudden nauseating cold of nocturnal fear" (p. 24).

Wracked by fear, the Stalin described in such works keeps not only supposed enemies, but also doctors, family, admirers, and subordinates at bay. In Kovcheg dlia nezvanykh, he locks up a diary in a wall safe and has a recurrent fear of being robbed while lying helpless and paralyzed. In V kruge pervom, he feels ill when he must attend a large banquet, and his favorite office is small and virtually windowless. In Deti Arbata, Stalin feels completely isolated even in apparent moments of success and thinks to himself: "They stand and applaud, but they don't like him, they are afraid of him, that is why they stand and applaud" (5:77). The cumulative portrait that emerges from these representations is of a man baleful in his distrustfulness and utterly isolated from real human contact.

An ironic consequence of Stalin's alienation as described in Kovcheg dlia nezvanykh and V kruge pervom, for example, is his regret and fantasies about the true friend he has never had. In the former, he imagines meeting a friendly stranger on the Kuriles and revealing his identity "with his characteristic modest dignity" (p. 60). He finds his secret watching of an encounter between the Cossack commanders Petr Krasnov and Andrei Shkuro intolerable largely because he bitterly envies the pair's ability to speak openly and frankly to each other. In V kruge pervom he longs for a friend like the one given him in the screenplay of The Battle of Stalingrad, a friend he cannot have "because of the constant insincerity and perfidy of people" (p. 119). In these literary portraits, paranoia and isolation are inextricably linked.

The works mentioned here can be categorized in various ways. One obvious way is to consider the times they cover. "Preobrazhenie tikhogo seminarista" provides an overview of Stalin's entire life, but most of these works are more temporally limited. Rybakov has thus far focused on the mid-1930s. Iskander also concentrates on this period, with flashbacks to the prerevolutionary period. Voinovich describes the eve of World War II, while Bek deals primarily with the 1930s with some reference to the postwar period. Grossman and Bondarev portray the war years, while Solzhenitsyn, Anonimov, and Maksimov in Kovcheg dlia nezvanykh all treat the late 1940s. Galich describes an unspecified time but also one that is clearly the postwar period, while Suslov's anecdotes refer to various eras. Gladilin portrays a resurrected Stalin, but one who embodies the leader as he was in old age.

Several of these works focus on the last few years of the dictator's life. Why is this period highlighted, rather than the Great Terror, which tends to be the focal point of much critical memoiristic and historical literature? Doubtless each writer has an individual reason for choosing this period, but a general rationale may be at work as well. The satirical mode may be best suited to the later period for reasons that lie within popular psychology. Writers like Solzhenitsyn, Maksimov, Galich, Bek, and others seem to share the implicit assumption, a psychological truism, that personality traits become more rigid and exaggerated with age. The dictator of the postwar years, their accounts suggest, did evolve from the young Stalin, but his essential personality crystallized, as it were, in the 1940s. From this point of view, the old man is indeed the quintessential Stalin. Moreover, the perceived hyperbolic quality of his negative features in old age renders them even more ready targets of mockery and sarcasm.

The most important generalization about these literary portrayals of Stalin, however, is in the remarkable coincidences in their physical, verbal, and psychological depictions of the leader. Solzhenitsyn's Stalin and Dante's Satan have been compared before,[37] and other authors' portrayals permit further generalization. The accumulation of recurrent negative imagery in recent works points toward a coherent demonology that is directly opposite to the hagiographical perspective long typical of a wide variety of portraits of Stalin. Commenting on Stalin as a personification of socialism, the historian Iurii Borisov observes that after 1956 Stalin "remained as before a symbol, however no longer of the victories of socialism, but of deviations from it. This is a kind of Dorian Gray phenomenon."[38] A character in Galich's poem expresses a similar idea in much cruder terms, when he says: "Okazalsia nash Otets / Ne otsam, a sukoiu" (p. 276). Both observations point toward the frequent pattern of complete reversal that dominates revisionist thinking about Stalin. Literature repeatedly exhibits literary Stalins who are the mirror images of their 1930s and 1940s predecessors and carbon copies of their contemporaries. It becomes difficult to speak of realism, although some portrayals, for example, Bek's, have been praised for their greater realism.[39] The tendency toward stylization that often dominates hagiography in general is also characteristic of demonological portraits of Stalin. In delineating the contours of evil these portraits often resort to evocative topoi that may appear to be realistic detail but are stock motifs. Readers who are unaware of the literary tradition connected with the portrayal of Stalin and its recurrent patterns of imagery may be convinced by the patina of realism that distinguishes a novel like *Deti Arbata*. Such failure to identify the stereotype can occur as easily in the Soviet Union as in the west. Yet analysis of fictional writings devoted to the dictator leads to the conclusion that, at least for the present, in literature Stalin remains a predominantly abstract, symbolic figure.

NOTES

[1] See Dmitrii Volkogonov, *Triumf i tragediia [Politicheskii portret I. V. Stalina],* 2 vols. (Moscow: Izdatel'stvo Agentstva pechati Novosti, 1989).

[2] *Moskovskii rabochii* is planning to publish Anton Antonov-Ovseenko's harshly critical portrait of Stalin, *Portret tirana* (New York: Khronika, 1980), in the Soviet Union.

[3] Adam Ulam, *Stalin: The Man and His Era* (New York: Viking, 1973); Robert Tucker, *Stalin as Revolutionary 1879-1929: A Study in History and Personality* (New York: Norton, 1973); Roy A. Medvedev, *Let History Judge: The Origins and Consequences of Stalinism,* ed. David Joravsky and Georges Haupt, trans. Colleen Taylor (New York: Knopf, 1971), and Roy A. Medvedev, *On Stalin and Stalinism,* trans. Ellen de Kadt (Oxford: Oxford University Press, 1979); Boris Souvarine, *Stalin: A Critical Survey of Bolshevism* (London: Alliance, Longmans, Green, 1939); Anton Antonov-Ovseenko, *The Time of Stalin,* trans. George Saunders (New York: Harper and Row, 1981).

[4] Irving Howe describes Rybakov's Stalin as being "pretty much the same monster we have come to know from [various] biographers and historians" (*The New York Times Book Review,* 22 May 1988, 7).

[5] *Znamia,* 1986, nos. 10-11.

[6] *Znamia,* 1988, no. 9.

[7] *Oktiabr',* 1988, nos. 1-4.

[8] *Druzhba narodov,* 1988, nos. 9-10. Other works that appeared too recently to be incorporated here are Ales' Adamovich's "Dubler: Snys otkrytymi glazami," *Druzhba narodov,* 1988, no. 11, and Vladimir Uspenskii's *Tainyi sovetnik vozhdia, Prostor,* 1988, nos. 7-9. An important critical study that also appeared too recently to be incorporated into my discussion is Rosalind Marsh's *Images of Dictatorship: Stalin in Literature* (London: Routledge, 1989).

[9] See, for example, Iuz Aleshkovskii's "Pesnia o Staline," quoted in Iurii Mal'tsev, *Vol'naia russkaia literatura 1955-1975* (Frankfurt a. M.: Possev, 1976), 320, and Vladimir Gornyi's [pseud.] "Palach i ego master," *Novyi zhurnal,* no. 114, 1974. Also noteworthy is Andrei Siniavskii's *Sud idet* (1960), which contains brief sections in which the "Master," easily recognizable as a stylized Stalin, appears. See *Fantasticheskii mir Abrama Tertsa* (New York: Inter-Language Literary Associates, 1967), 199-276.

[10] "O Lenine," in I. V. Stalin, *Sochineniia,* 13 vols. (Moscow: OGIZ / Gosudarstvennoe izdatel'stvo politicheskoi literatury, 1946-1951) 6:52-64. Page of exact quotation is indicated in parentheses in the text.

[11] Bertram D. Wolfe, *Khrushchev and Stalin's Ghost: Text, Background and Meaning of Khrushchev's Secret Report to the Twentieth Congress on the Night of February 24-25, 1956* (New York: Praeger, 1957), 214.

[12] *Iosif Vissarionovich Stalin (kratkaia biografiia)* (Moscow: OGIZ / Gosudarstvennoe izdatel'stvo politicheskoi literatury, 1945), 74.

[13] G. S. Cheremin, *Obroz I. V. Stalina v sovetskoi khudozhestvennoi literature* (Moscow: Vsesoiuznoe obshchestvo po rasprostraneniiu politicheskikh i nauchnykh znanii, 1950). Cheremin quotes here from Stalin's "O Lenine."

[14] Iakov Il'in, *Bol'shoi konveier* (Moscow: Molodaia gvardiia, 1934), 161.

[15] Petr Pavlenko, *Schast'e* (Moscow: Gosudarstvennoe izdatel'stvo detskoi literatury, 1950), 165.

[16] On the underground dissemination of some of these writings, see, for example, Peter Reddaway, ed., *Uncensored Russia: Protest and Dissent in the Soviet Union* (New York: American Heritage, 1972), 377, 417, and Robert M. Slusser, "History and the Democratic Opposition," in *Dissent in the USSR: Politics, Ideology, and People*, ed. Rudolf L. Tökés (Baltimore: Johns Hopkins University Press, 1975), 334, 343, 345, 346. Most of this material has either recently become or will soon be officially available to the Soviet reading public.

[17] Lenin's "Testament," a letter addressed to the Twelfth Party Congress, is found in V.I. Lenin, *Polnoe sobranie sochinenii*, 5th ed., 55 vols. (Moscow: Izdatel'stvo politicheskoi literatury, 1958-1965) 45:344-346.

[18] Aleksandr Solzhenitsyn, *Sobranie sochinenii* (Paris: YMCA Press, 1978-), vol. 1, *V kruge pervom*, 1:116. Bednyi's observation is in Nadezhda Mandel'shtam, *Vospominaniia* (New York: Chekhov, 1970), 29-30.

[19] Il'ia Suslov, *Rasskazy o tovarishche Staline i drugikh tovarishchakh* (Ann Arbor, Mich.: Hermitage, 1981), 9.

[20] P. N. Anonimov, *Une matinée de Joseph Staline (Utro v mae 1947 goda)*, bilingual edition (n.p.: L'Herne, 1969), 18.

[21] Fazil' Iskander, "Piry Valtasara," in *Sandro iz Chegema* (Ann Arbor, Mich.: Ardis, 1979), 187-229, quotation on 206.

[22] Fazil' Iskander, "Diadia Sandro i ego liubimets," in ibid., 285-319.

[23] Aleksandr Solzhenitsyn, *V kruge pervom* (New York: Harper and Row, 1968), 93. In the 1978 text, reference to Stalin's eyes has been replaced by mention of his mustache, ibid., 150.

[24] Anatolii Gladilin, "Repetitsiia v piatnitsu," *Kontinent* 12 (1977):47-84, and 13 (1977):91-131; quotation on 12:55.

[25] Aleksandr Bek, *Novoe naznachenie* (Frankfurt a. M.: Possev, 1971), 30.

[26] Vladimir Maksimov, *Kovcheg dlia nezvanykh* (Frankfurt a. M.: Possev, 1979), 36.

[27] Anatolii Rybakov, *Deti Arbata, Druzhba narodov*, 1987, no. 4: 3-133; no. 5: 67-161; no. 6: 23-151; quotation on 4: 13.

[28] Vladimir Voinovich, "V krugu druzei," in his *Putem vzaimnoi perepiski* (Paris: YMCA Press, 1979), 166.

[29] Milovan Djilas, *Conversations with Stalin*, trans. Michael B. Petrovich (New York: Harcourt, Brace and World, 1962), 12.

[30] See Konstantin Simonov, *Glazami cheloveka moego pokoleniia, Znamia*, 1988, no. 3, 33.

[31] Dmitrii Volkogonov, "Fenomen Stalina," *Literaturnaia gazeta*, 9 December 1987, 13.

[32] Antonov-Ovseenko, *Portret tirana*, 73.

[33] Antonov-Ovseenko, *The Time of Stalin*, 234. The chapter from which this quotation is taken is not included in the Russian edition. In much the same vein as Antonov-Ovseenko, Edward J. Brown observes that "Stalin the orthodox seminarian, as Trockij long ago pointed out, developed a style which is a weird miscegenation of content and form: communist ideas couched in quasi-religious, catechetical style. The drearily repetitive questions and answers come readily to mind" ("Solzenicyn's Cast of Characters," *Slavic and East European Journal* 15 [1971]: 162).

[34] Susan Layton, "The Mind of the Tyrant: Tolstoj's Nicholas and Solzenicyn's Stalin," *Slavic and East European Journal* 23 (1979): 488.

[35] Vladimir Maksimov, *Karantin* (Frankfurt a. M.: Possev, 1973), 83-90, quotation on 88.

[36] See, for example, Gary Kern, "Solzhenitsyn's Portrait of Stalin," *Slavic Review* 33 (March 1974): 16-17; and Vladimir Grebenschikov, "Les cercles infernaux chez Soljénitsyne et Dante," *Canadian Slavonic Papers* 13 (1971): 154-58.

[37] Iurii Borisov, "Chelovek i simvol," *Nauka i zhizn'*, 1987, no. 9, 63.

[38] Mal'tsev, *Vol'naia russkaia literatura*, 213; and Rosalind J. Marsh, *Soviet Fiction since Stalin: Science, Politics and Literature* (London: Croom Helm, 1986), 33. Josephine Woll argues that Rybakov is "relentlessly realistic" (*The Atlantic*, June 1988, 103).

Lionel Abel (essay date 1991)

SOURCE: "On the Crimes of Lenin, Stalin, and Hitler," in *Partisan Review*, Vol. LVIII, No. 1, Winter, 1991, pp. 78-87.

[*In the following essay, Abel rejects Marxism and national socialism as the moral doctrines they were purported to be by their adherents and focuses the blame for crimes and brutality committed for these causes on those who, Abel believes, mistakenly held them up as rooted in morality.*]

In the late summer of 1945, I took issue with James Burnham (in Dwight Macdonald's *Politics*) for having maintained earlier that year (in the January issue of *Partisan Review*) that Stalin was the logical and appropriate successor to Lenin in the Communist hierarchy. A Marxist—and much more long-winded—argument to the same effect was given during the seventies by Jean-Paul Sartre (in the second volume of his *Critique de la raison dialectique*). Here Sartre tried to show that Stalin was chosen to be Lenin's successor, not just by the will of the Communist Party, arbitrary and manipulable as that no doubt was, but by the October Revolution itself, whose needs *required* the Party to reject Trotsky's bid for power and to endorse Stalin's.

I am convinced today that I was wrong in my condemnation of Burnham's article, and that he was substantially correct in his evaluation of Stalin as Lenin's appropriate successor, as was Sartre in his more recent discussion of the matter. Burnham was of course aware of Stalin's crimes, as was Sartre too, but each had his own prudential reasons for not saying in so many words that the dictator was a criminal, something any hack journalist, even of the left, may now do regularly. Which brings me to a question *not* regularly asked: if Stalin for all his criminality was the rightful heir of Lenin, then can Lenin have been innocent of crime?

More than a decade ago, when Lenin, and Stalin, too, had armies of journalistic defenders, Solzhenitsyn told us that in his judgment Lenin was a criminal. In fact, Burnham and Sartre have said the same, at least by implication. For to authenticate Stalin politically as Lenin's heir is to deauthenticate Lenin morally. Certainly Lenin was responsible, along with Trotsky, for the crime of *Kronstadt,* the pilot massacre in the long series of executions, one of whose latest episodes, "Tiananmen Square," we were able to watch on June 3rd of 1989, appropriately enough on television.

Lenin was—or thought himself to be—an orthodox Marxist. But is Marxism *in any sense* a moral doctrine? To those who regard it as such, Lenin, as things stand now, can hardly be an exemplary figure; he can remain a hero, however, to those who have always regarded Marxist indignation against capitalism and imperialism as so much political propaganda, possibly poetry of a sort. So before trying to judge Lenin morally, one must answer this question: in what sense is Marxism moral?

Professor Kai Nielson, the author of a philosophical work, *Why Be Moral?*, tried to answer this question in the Fall 1989 issue of *Social Research*. His article is entitled, "Arguing for Justice," and this is just what Marxists, according to Professor Nielson, are arguing for. Let me say at once that his discussion of the issue is a thoroughly academic one. I feel entitled to say this in criticism, because Professor Nielson has shown that he is fully aware of the insufficiency of academic argument on a political matter of this kind. To do him justice, when he condemned American foreign policy during our war with

North Vietnam, he did not restrict himself to academic argument but actually renounced his American citizenship and betook himself to Canada, in one of whose colder provinces, Calgary, he is now teaching philosophy. Now to show in nonacademic fashion that Marxism argues for justice, Nielson would not have had to go anywhere: certainly he would not have had to leave Calgary for an even colder province. But he would have had to face up to a very warm political fact, namely that leading Marxists—and I include among them the compassionate and ethically-minded Rosa Luxemburg—have argued *against* the idea of justice. It was Rosa who called justice "that old Rosinante, on which our Don Quixotes ride forth to save the world, only to come back with their eyes blackened," which is hardly something to say about justice if what you are doing is to be called "arguing" for it.

According to Nielson, Marxism argues for justice in this sense; it condemns the capitalist's profit, which it claims has been subtracted from the worker's wage, and should properly be called "theft." Should not "theft" be condemned in the name of justice? Quite so. But what Nielson has failed to note is that Marx's objection to the capitalist profit was linked conceptually by him with the prediction that the system entailing it was going to founder, and that its end was already in sight. Were it not—such is my reading of Marx—capitalist wages might be objected to, but the only point of such objection would be to relieve one's feelings. When Marx called capitalist wages "theft," he was trying to change the system determining them. And in fact, unionized labor has indeed changed the wage system, at least under democratic governments.

But was it ever right to call the capitalist's profit "theft," whatever Marx's motive may have been in calling it that? I think not. On this point Kai Nielson does give a fair restatement of Jon Elster's argument against Marx's view, an argument I think irrefutable. Here it is: the worker's wage does not exist until he is paid it by the boss; Marx's assumption is that he is robbed before being paid, which is just not possible. Let us assume the worker is not paid enough, at least from his point of view. This is by no means the same thing as being robbed. I must add that Nielson, having stated this argument, makes no effort to meet it. Moreover, he has ignored Marx's intellectual purpose, even as he has ignored Marx's political motive in characterizing the capitalist wage system as "theft." In addition to making a moral point against capitalism, Marx wanted to explain how the system worked. He was trying to give an *explanation* of capitalist profit, which would also serve as propaganda against it, and the notion he hit on was that profit was taken from the worker's wages. But according to this view, the more workers employed in a given enterprise, of whatever type, the greater would be the profit. That such cannot be shown to be the case led certain Marxists (during the thirties) to suggest that all the profits of capital investment—subtracted from all the workers' wages—were piled in one kitty, divvied up by all the capitalists like the bills and bonds taken from a bank by robbers. Thus the profits of an enterprise with a few workers would be percentage-wise equal to those of an enterprise with many employees. But this was a hopeless argument, for there is simply no such kitty of capital. The Marxists who claimed this were simply extending metaphorically Marx's unjust characterization of capitalist profit. And if Marx's characterization of profit is unjust, can it be said that in making it he was "arguing for justice"?

In fact, however immoral or amoral Marxists have been in revolutionary action, this at least can be said for them: they were striving for power, not just arguing for justice. If we were to agree with Professor Nielson, to the other moral claims made against Marxists, we would have to add the charge of hypocrisy.

This brings me back to the question of Lenin's character, raised by the contention that for all his criminality, Stalin was Lenin's proper successor. Here I will not take up again Burnham's arguments, which I dealt with in 1945. For if Burnham's arguments were poor he was still correct in his conclusion. But I do want to look for a moment at Sartre's argument for Stalin's leadership, which amounts to a choice, long after the choice was important, of Stalin's actual as against Trotsky's possible policies. Sartre claims that Stalin represented the *particularity* of the October Revolution, Trotsky the *universality* which the Bolsheviks hoped would crown their efforts, their aim being nothing less than an international revolt against capitalism. But even had the revolution spread over the continent of Europe, while incontestably "international" it would not have been "universal" in scope. *Many* countries is not the same thing as *all* countries, many places is not everywhere, and the general is something other than the universal. *An international revolution in 1917 would have been a particular revolution to no less a degree than the one the Bolsheviks led.* Sartre's error here lies in thinking the difference between a national and an international revolution can instance the dialectical division of the particular and the universal. This seems to me a variant of the error Benedetto Croce long ago detected in Hegel's philosophy, when he noted that Hegel had constructed a dialectic of distinctly *different* terms which could hold only for terms that are *logically* opposed. And I must add that this error of Hegel is not unlike that in the economic dialectic of Marxism which sets up a *logical* opposition between wages and profits, a view which Marxists have been unable to defend.

For Sartre, Stalin represented the nationalist—Sartre calls it *particularist*—bias of a revolution which was intended to be international, but was stranded in a backward country, and Trotsky the internationalist aims of the Bolsheviks, which Sartre has called universalist. The two positions were summed up in different theories, Stalin's being the theory that socialism can be achieved in a single country, Trotsky's that the revolution would have to spread to succeed, and which has become known as the Theory of Permanent Revolution. Oddly enough, Sartre asserts both that the October Revolution itself opted for Stalin's theory of socialism in one country, and also that the theory was a monstrosity. He also holds that the

theory was false when it was formulated, and only after that became true. He holds, too, that Trotsky's contrary theory was true when formulated and has since lost none of its truth. Then how could the theory of socialism in one country have become the kind of truth he, Sartre, may have disliked, but felt he had to abide?

Now in point of fact the theory of socialism in one country is not only monstrous but false. And the Theory of Permanent Revolution is also a monstrosity and also false, at least in part, as has been amply shown by events. And note this: the character and meaning of the October Revolution, and also the moral character of the Bolshevik leaders, Lenin and Stalin—Trotsky's role was more complex than theirs in view of his long struggle against Stalin—cannot but be affected by what we think of these theories, both of which Sartre claimed were true, both of which I hold in important respects are false.

Let me look at the Theory of Permanent Revolution. It consists of two propositions: 1) it is easier to make a revolution against capitalism in a country where such a revolution could not succeed than in a country where it might succeed, being on the order of the day, and 2) if made in a country in which it could not succeed, such a revolution would spread to a country or countries where it could not be initiated but might have every chance of success. Now proposition number one was vindicated if not proved by the October Revolution, which, aimed at capitalism, took place not in an advanced but in a backward country. The second proposition was of course not vindicated by the revolution, which did not spread from Russia to any other country of Europe. And all the problems of the Soviets: the deliberately imposed famine, the Trotsky-Stalin controversy, the purges, the crimes of Stalin, followed from the nontruth of this second proposition of the Theory of Permanent Revolution. What also follows is a possible charge of crime against Lenin himself. He acted finally on the supposition that the Theory of Permanent Revolution was substantially correct; if that theory is false, then the bloody actions he undertook on the basis of its assumed truth can hardly be justified.

One more point about this theory. Why could not a revolution against capitalism take place in a country where it had some chance of success, why was it *necessary* to start such an action in a country where it was almost certainly bound to fail? This question the Bolsheviks never replied to when it was raised by Martov. Moreover, they never considered what was to be done if the revolution did *not* spread. In not considering these matters the Bolshevik leaders, Lenin included, are open to the charge of criminal behavior which Maxim Gorky leveled against them immediately after their seizure of power in October of 1917.

I have found the two theories on the basis of which Lenin and Stalin justified their political deeds to be invalid, if not completely false. But this judgment is hardly enough to prove their immortality. If guilty of crimes, they are to be judged criminals. What follows from the validity or invalidity of the theories discussed is not whether or not Lenin and Stalin were guilty of criminal deeds; that they were. What follows from our judgment of their theories is an answer to a related question: are their crimes forgivable? Let us suppose for a moment that the theory of socialism in one country had proved true, the evidence for this being that the Soviet Union, instead of verging on economic catastrophe today could offer a higher quality of life to its citizens than obtains in the democracies of the West. It still would be the case that judged strictly, Lenin and Stalin would have to be found guilty of crimes. But who, under the circumstance I have supposed, would be interested in judging them strictly? I think they would be forgiven their deeds. Hegel (interpreted by Kojève) puts the matter thus: an action, however criminal, may be forgiven, if thanks to it some great purpose can be achieved.

It may be instructive to relate this notion of Hegel's to Macbeth's reasoning in Shakespeare's tragedy. For is not Hegel's thought Macbeth's thought, too? He assumes, because of the witches' prophecies, that if Fleance lives he, not Macbeth, will become king; thus his own venture in kingship must end in failure. He will not have established a line of kings, and thus will not be forgiven the murder of Duncan. Or, for that matter, of Banquo. Shakespeare, with his customary depth, shows us Macbeth most wracked by guilt right after he has been told that Fleance has escaped his killers. He might have felt less guilt for murdering the father had his men also succeeded in murdering the son. One guilt more might mean less guilt finally, and possibly forgiveness. That is how tyrants, also modern dictators like Lenin and Stalin, often thought.

Suppose we apply Hegel's reasoning about the morality of great action to the deeds of the Bolsheviks, and most particularly to those of their extraordinary leader, Lenin, whom Solzhenitsyn has called a criminal. Now is it proper to call him that? No doubt Lenin was responsible for the killing of thousands of innocent persons whose deaths brought no advantage to him personally or to the regime he headed. Was then Lenin guilty of crime? But the question has still not been properly put in the terms Hegel has suggested. For what we must ask now is this: Did Lenin succeed? Was the purpose for which the October Revolution was undertaken ever realized, even in part? We are now alerted to the fact that the present-day leaders of the Soviet Union are beginning to think their revolution anything but a success. (I was told some years ago by Andrea Caffi, an Italian socialist, who had visited Moscow in 1923, and there read Lenin's famous article "On Cooperation" just as it came off the press, that anyone who read the piece in Moscow at just that moment, and had some capacity to read between the lines, would have understood that for Lenin the revolution had already failed.)

We must note that the crimes committed by the Bolsheviks before Stalin came to power, and seldom regarded by radicals as crimes, provided the model for those acts of Stalin which the present-day Soviet leaders today call criminal. What Lenin ordered, which was not characterized as crime, justified for Stalin the actions Khruschev and the present Soviet leaders admit were criminal. The praise accorded the ruthless acts of Lenin no doubt provided inspiration for Stalin.

And yet, in a way, Stalin was trying (he had other objectives, to be sure) to prove Lenin's and his own deeds forgivable, when he claimed that socialism in one country could be achieved. If it were, then the failure of world revolution would not invalidate morally the decision of Lenin to overthrow the Kerensky government, from which followed all the crimes of the Soviet leaders.

Solzhenitsyn has detailed many of these crimes in his book, *The Gulag Archipelago*. But there are two stories about Lenin, told to me by Andrea Caffi in Paris in 1949, and attested to by Ignazio Silone in Rome in 1962, which for me at least best convey the attitude which made the Bolshevik's crimes possible, and accepted. The first tells of Lenin at a Party affair in Finland, before the revolution. A young recruit announced to Lenin that he was quite ready to die for the Party, and Lenin was unimpressed. "Many are," he replied, "so my question to you is this: 'are you ready to pimp for the Party?'" The other tale has to do with executions after the revolution. A comrade, well known to Lenin, came to see him with a complaint against the secret police. They had arrested his son and were about to execute him. And the man swore his son was innocent. "I do believe you," replied Lenin, "but I know that nine out of every ten persons shot by the G. P. U. are innocent. Why should I intervene just for your son? And since I need the G. P. U., I have to put up with their mistakes and injustices." In these tales we may grasp the criminal thinking of the Bolshevik leader from which followed the particular illegalities and cruelties catalogued by Solzhenitsyn. What we have here is the denial of moral experience as such.

Once again, despite their enormity are these crimes forgivable? By Hegel's standard, yes, if something great was achieved which could not have been brought into being otherwise, for instance: an international revolt against capitalism or socialism in Soviet Russia. The first was no longer possible in the early thirties, when Hitler came to power, the second Trotsky and his followers claimed was contrary to Marxist theory. But in that case there was no possible exculpation of the Bolsheviks, and to say as much was also a crime. From this thought we may get some sense of Stalin's hatred for Trotsky and his supporters, of Stalin's reasons for staging the show trials and for ordering Trotsky's assassination.

That the Bolsheviks did not achieve their declared goal is incontestible, but there were positive developments throughout the world as a result of their actions, which should moderate our judgment if not excuse their crimes. So I must insist here on the clear difference between communism under Lenin, even under Stalin, and the Nazism of Hitler, the fascism of Mussolini. This difference has been blurred of late. There was Susan Sontag's remark in a speech just a few years back in which she dubbed Soviet communism—which the Russians tell us has been a failure—"successful fascism." And there was the equally absurd counter-judgment of Soviet communism by Michael Walser, a respected professor of political science. He dubbed the Soviet state an instance of "failed totalitarianism," as if the goal of the Bolsheviks had been totalitarianism, rather than the international revolution, or alternatively, socialism in one country.

And on October 31st of 1988, Marjorie Brady, Director of the Russian Research Foundation in London, told us in a column in *The Wall Street Journal,* that there may be a fascist element in *perestroika,* so that what we take to be a democratic development in the Soviet Union may be in fact a turn towards the corporate state Mussolini brought into being. And the London sociologist, Zygmunt Bauman, in his recently published (and much overpraised) book, *Modernity and the Holocaust,* has stressed what he finds similar in the criminal procedures of Hitler and Stalin. Their victims, Bauman claims, were executed ". . . because they did not fit, for one reason or another, the scheme of a perfect society. They were eliminated, so that an objectively better human world—more efficient, more moral, more beautiful (sic!)—could be established. A Communist world. Or a racially pure, Aryan world."

Were the Communists and the Nazis similar in their grandiose aims as in their criminal deeds? If Bauman is right in the judgment I cited, it would be impossible to distinguish morally between the Bolsheviks and the Nazis. To do so one would have to show—and I think this can be shown—that the Bolsheviks regretted the terrible methods employed by the G. P. U., and *one cannot say this of the Nazis,* who for the most part thought the world more beautiful and more human *because of the methods employed by the Gestapo.* And there are these indirect results of the October Revolution: independent nations in Asia and Africa. One cannot imagine the slightest increment of freedom or independent sovereignty for any nation in any part of the world had Hitler been the victor in the late war. So Bauman's equalization of the Nazis and Bolsheviks simply does not hold. And I must add one other point, which I take from a great story of Borges. A Nazi officer, who has overseen the gassing of a Jewish dramatist, applauds the execution, noting that by such deeds he and his colleagues have introduced into the world a moral coldness which no one will be able to expunge. What Borges the poet has seen and Bauman the sociologist has missed, is that the Nazis did not differentiate their methods from their goals, which in fact the Bolsheviks did. The Nazis thought themselves great because they were 'capable of deeds the rest of humanity regarded as unforgivable. The Bolsheviks believed they were creating a world such that their efforts in constructing it could be forgiven or forgotten.

In judging the deeds of the Bolsheviks, I have used a literary model, bringing up Macbeth's effort to justify his murder of Duncan by eliminating Banquo and his son. Now to judge Hitler, I will need a different model, and I have chosen Raskolnikov, the murderer described by a modern novelist, and I shall contrast him with Macbeth in just one respect. Raskolnikov had no great purpose in mind when he killed the pawnbroker. His aim was murder and nothing more, murder as the reward for murdering. Lady Macbeth reproaches her husband with: "What you would highly you would holily," as if this were a character defect in him. But this is in fact an accurate description of Macbeth's attitude prior to his first crime. At a similar moment in his career, Raskolnikov cannot be so described. What he wants is precisely to act unholily. He murders to prove himself capable of murder. If Macbeth in his subsequent murders sought forgiveness for his initial crime, Raskolnikov's first murder was an attempt to prove himself capable of other, equally unforgivable deeds.

Here we may glimpse a moral difference between the Nazi and Communist dictators. I grant that Stalin ordered the torture or death of many more persons than did his opposite number in the Reich. Yet I do not think we have to place the two dictators on the same moral plane. Stalin at least wanted to justify the October Revolution, and all of the Bolshevik crimes that followed from its failure. Hitler, in destroying Europe's Jews, could not have wanted to do anything more than prove himself inexorable, for no military advantage was achieved or even aimed at in the Holocaust. And let us speculate: What if Hitler had been victorious in the Second World War? Would his name have been sacred fifty years after victory, as Caesar's was in the Roman Empire set up by Octavius? To be sure, we cannot know what might have followed from what never occurred. But it is at least possible to think that after the success of German armies, with the passage of time, there would be some investigation of Nazi deeds and a critical appraisal of Hitler. Did anyone expect Khruschev to denounce Stalin only three years after the dictator's death? Some fifty years after a Hitler victory there might indeed be motivation for a closer scrutiny of the dictator's deeds. We have just had the admission by Soviet leaders that the execution of the Polish officers in the Katyn forest was ordered by Stalin himself. What about Hitler's war on the Jews? It is at least thinkable that some German scholars would sort out the true facts about the Holocaust and advance the thought that this adventure in crime had played no part in Germany's military successes, and that the Auschwitz and Treblinka exterminations were without military meaning, being motivated solely by the German dictator's desire to commit inexpiable deeds, and to position himself, proud of being unforgivable, in the pages of history.

But I do not want to terminate these reflections without expressing regret for the judgment I have been forced to make of Lenin, whom before this, like others of my generation, I greatly admired. And regret occasions recollection. More than forty years back, Harold Rosenberg, who had not yet ventured into the art criticism which later made him widely known, confided to me that he had begun to write a play. He had always wanted to write plays, he said, but the particular play he had in mind to write then was to be about Lenin's burial. His script called for Stalin and the other Communist Party leaders to follow the hearse bearing the body of Lenin to the tomb where it is still exhibited. Lenin's widow, Krupskaya, would halt the procession with the demand that Lenin's corpse be given a modest grave like any Soviet citizen's. An argument would then develop between Krupskaya and Stalin, the former stressing Lenin's identity with the masses he led, the latter pointing to the propaganda value of investing Lenin's corpse with pharaonic splendor. In Rosenberg's script, Stalin would of course fail to convince Krupskaya, and then would have her dragged away by his police. I remember that I thought the idea a marvelous one, and for some time kept asking Harold about his script. I urged him to complete it and offer it to a producer, and in the new period of off-Broadway theater right after the war, an intellectual play of that sort could have made the stage. But Harold was afraid, I think, of being charged with anticommunism, dropped his script and turned to his other projects. He did say to me, though, after Khruschev's attack on Stalin, and the removal of Stalin's body from the tomb where it had been placed beside Lenin's: "You see, I was right to connect the positioning of Lenin's corpse with bureaucratic policy. . . . When there is freedom in Soviet Russia, Lenin's corpse will be given private burial. . . . "

Should this indeed occur, what feelings will be expressed? Rosenberg still assumed that the Soviet experiment would succeed and that when the weight of the regime was lifted, its citizens would be able to enjoy much better lives than in what was then called "the capitalist world." But such optimism about the Soviet future is no longer possible. I believe that Lenin's corpse will be removed from his present tomb and be given private burial. But this will not take place in an atmosphere of respect for the Bolshevik leader, rather in one of unrelenting polemic against his ideas and his deeds. He will not be forgiven for all of those deeds, and he may even be condemned for an act not his, and for which he was in no way responsible: the exhibition of his corpse, enshrined like Pharaoh's, for the masses to worship.

Russell J. Reising (essay date 1993)

SOURCE: "Lionel Trilling, 'The Liberal Imagination,' and the Emergence of the Cultural Discourse of Anti-Stalinism," in *Boundary* 2, Vol. 20, No. 1, Spring, 1993, pp. 94-124.

[*In the following essay, Reising investigates the later impact on American cultural studies of the "discourse of anti-Stalinism" that emerged in the 1950s alongside the study of Soviet communism in the American academy, exemplified by Lionel Trilling's* The Liberal Imagination.]

In the concluding remarks to her excellent study of McCarthyism and the universities, Ellen W. Schrecker reiterates one of her central points—that university professors were not only not "isolated from the political repression that touched their institutions" but that, "in fact, many of the nation's leading intellectuals were directly involved with one or another aspect of McCarthyism."[1]

Lionel Trilling is one of the few of these intellectuals to whom Schrecker calls our attention for his having "chaired a Columbia committee that developed guidelines for congressional witnesses" (339), guidelines that informed Columbia professors of ways in which they were expected to cooperate with the goals of the committee grilling them on any given day.[2] Just how the activities of Trilling and others like him affected university work is, as Schrecker notes, "certainly worth considering" (340). In his introductory remarks to *Postmodernism and Politics,* Jonathan Arac issues a similar call. After a summary of the more interesting and potentially damaging contradictions that marked some of Trilling's most strenuously held aesthetic/political beliefs, Arac suggests, "We lack the history of American intellectuals from the thirties through the sixties that will allow us fully to make sense out of these crossings back and forth, yet they continue to haunt our current situation."[3] And in his introductory essay to a special issue of *boundary* 2 dedicated to New Americanist revisions of American literary studies, Donald E. Pease performs an exemplary dissection of the ideological dimension of Trilling's terms of discussion in *The Liberal Imagination* and proposes that Trilling's "redefinition of the basis of the field [American Studies] elevates the liberal imagination (and the liberal anticommunist consensus) into the field's equivalent of a reality principle."[4]

These are but examples of some recent work on the ideological histories, dilemmas, and futures of American literary, theoretical, and historical culture. Lionel Trilling has, not surprisingly, figured prominently as a subject for such studies, playing a decisive role in the transformation both of American literary thought and historiography during the politically volatile decades of the forties, fifties, and sixties. This essay is an attempt to *begin* a particular line of inquiry into Trilling's place in the ideological history of American cultural criticism, namely, his relationship to the history and practices of Soviet communism that Trilling and others understand as "Stalinism" and to the emerging discourse of anti-Stalinism during those decades, as well as to the subsequent impact of that discourse on American cultural production.[5] While my focus is on Trilling, I do not mean to suggest that he was alone in his integration of anti-Stalinism and literary criticism, nor that he alone was responsible for subsequent trends along those lines. Indeed, as Richard Pells has demonstrated, the roster of cultural spokespeople with similar track records is disturbingly long, including such influential figures as Leslie Fiedler, Mary McCarthy, Irving Kristol, and James Burnham, to name only a few noteworthy anti-Stalinists of the era.[6] I would, instead, argue that Trilling is important precisely because his work was *representative*. While I recognize the importance and interest of an inquiry into the origins of Trilling's anti-Stalinism, of the complex aesthetic imperatives and sociopolitical pressures surrounding it, and of its relations to his other interests, obsessions, and agendas, my focus will be on the particular constellation Trilling's political thinking takes in *The Liberal Imagination.*

1

Jacques Barzun remembers Lionel Trilling responding to the ideological certainty of Stalinized American liberals by advancing the view that "it's complicated. . . . It's much more complicated. . . . It's very complicated."[7] A definitive, if redundant, statement of Trilling's valorization of complexity as a key word in literary and cultural analysis. Trilling's politics are, in many ways, complex. Stalinism is, however, generally regarded as the enemy for Trilling in some of his most influential literary and cultural thought. In fact, Trilling may have elevated complexity as *the* literary value *because* of Stalinism, in a way parallel to the American New Critics, whose valuation of ambiguity, irony, and complexity has been seen as a direct response to political and economic change.[8] Whereas Mark Krupnick believes that "Trilling's self-assigned task *in the forties* was to redefine 'reality' so as to wrest it from the Stalinists" (*FCC*, 64; my emphasis), William Chace argues that Trilling's "*whole career* was spent in evaluating Stalinism" and that, throughout that career, "Trilling patiently developed a mind that could oppose the Stalinist mind."[9] Daniel T. O'Hara has recently suggested that Trilling wrestled with a nightmarish figure of totalizing and repressive authority (eventually to be figured as Stalinism) throughout his career, even in his earliest short stories, and that Trilling was, "since at least the late thirties, staunchly, even blindly anti-Communist and antirevolutionary."[10] Following O'Hara's example, we might argue that Stalinism was merely the most politically compelling and (perhaps, therefore) culturally influential avatar of the experience of the sublime for Trilling. The continuing influence of Trilling's perspectives and the leakage of the anti-Stalinism impulse throughout American culture suggest, however, that O'Hara's autobiographical reading of the psychodynamics of Trilling's career does not account for the broader cultural acceptance of Trilling's idiosyncratic psychoideological animus. While Cornel West associates Trilling's Arnoldian view of culture with his need "to articulate and elaborate this conception of culture for the educated middle class in order to combat the encroachment of Stalinist politics and philistine culture," he has also demonstrated that, late in Trilling's life, "the major culprits [against which he directed his animus] were no longer Stalinism and philistinism but rather *their latest forms and manifestations*—the New Left and black revolt, rock 'n' roll, drugs, and free love."[11] Whatever their views on the duration of Trilling's anti-Stalinism, Krupnick, Chace, O'Hara, West, and others agree that the essays collected in *The Liberal Imagination* are written directly and powerfully against Stalinism and Stalinized American writers and critics. As Trilling himself declares, "All my essays of the Forties were written from my sense of this [Stalinist,] dull, repressive tendency of opinion which was coming to dominate the old ethos of liberal enlightenment."[12] While one might argue that Trilling represses the extent to which *The Liberal Imagination* also attacks anti-Semitism, bad writing, and, perhaps most importantly, the middlebrowism against which he directed his energy for much of his career, we should remember that Trilling had already situated bad writing and pervasive middlebrowism as exemplary of the putative Stalinist dominance of American culture in the thirties and forties. The vagueness of Trilling's image of Stalinism—an umbrella term for everything Trilling disdains—paradoxically empowers such a flaccid definition of the cultural terrain in the United States.

I would like to consider the impingement of Trilling's anti-Stalinism on several major tenets in Trilling's literary/ political program. These principles are all related to Trilling's elevation of complexity and include his notion of the *literary idea* and the literary crime he termed *ideological thinking*. I would also like to consider three major critical perspectives on Trilling's aesthetics: Robert Boyers's suggestion that, for Trilling, society and social issues need, "like persons in the given society, to be read, to be interpreted, to be studied with an imagination capable at once of candor and affection";[13] Krupnick's accounting for Trilling's complex, seemingly contradictory views by arguing that Trilling was a "reactive critic who characteristically defined himself against what he took to be the dominant cultural tendencies of his time" (*FCC*, 173); and O'Hara's position that Trilling's "generally magnanimous style of mind" enabled him to deal generously and compassionately with "his experiences, his own abilities and limitations, *and those of his intellectual opponents,*" and that for Trilling the "function of criticism . . . [was] this ability to imagine amidst the least fortuitous circumstances as noble a motive for the Other as one can imagine for oneself" (*WL*, 27, 12, and passim; my emphasis). I agree with each of these overviews—they provide valuable angles from which to approach the Trilling corpus. (This is not to suggest that they are all compatible.) In fact, the strengths of these studies are even more significant and provocative when we realize that Trilling's assaults on Dreiser, Parrington, and Stalin violate their theses so thoroughly and with such vituperation as to suggest that the issues around which these writers cluster constitute, for Trilling, an enormous and terrifying Other, an Other that has permeated American cultural thought at least since Trilling's influential dicta, and an Other that Trilling is incapable of regarding with compassion, complexity, or magnanimity. Trilling's notion of Stalinism (and the related crimes he attributes to Dreiser and Parrington) becomes *the* point at which Trilling violates his own most consistently maintained literary principles. It is strange that Trilling, a critic dedicated to complexity and, as Krupnick wittily notes, "allerg[ic] to closure" (*FCC*, 188), sees little, if any, complexity in Theodore Dreiser, V. L. Parrington, and Joseph Stalin, and is all too ready to close his cases on them in strikingly uncharacteristic ways. Everything and everyone, it seems, is "too complicated," except these three figures, a strange grouping, to be sure, though a virtual triumvirate of Trilling's primary targets and the focal points of the most significant moments of ideological blindness in all Trilling's work.

2

Trilling's polemic against Dreiser has exerted substantial pressure on American literary study. Krupnick is representative when he refers unquestioningly to "Trilling's famous demolition of Theodore Dreiser" (*FCC,* 65). Yet, we learn very little about Dreiser from "Reality in America" other than that he is a bad writer; that he is "crude," "vulgar," and "offensive"; that he dealt with difficulties in a simplistic, often stupid, way; and that he joined the Communist party. Dreiser and his elevation by the liberal establishment are indicative both of the American "political fear of the intellect" and of the chronic American belief that "reality is always material reality, hard, resistant, unformed, impenetrable, and unpleasant."[14] Hardly the stuff of a literary "demolition"; nevertheless, Trilling's attack has been regarded as influential in de-centering Dreiser and clearing the cultural space for a revival of interest in Henry James (and later Faulkner) in postwar American literary studies.

Primary in Trilling's attack, however, is his imputation that Dreiser was guilty of "ideological thinking"; that is, he never had any ideas that were genuinely *literary.* It is on this charge that Trilling indicts Dreiser, and it is this element in Trilling's critique that cascades throughout *The Liberal Imagination* as an issue of central literary and political importance. In fact, Trilling's contempt for what he terms "ideological thinking" is not fully articulated until "The Meaning of a Literary Idea," the volume's concluding essay. An idea is "what comes into being when two contradictory emotions are made to confront each other and are required to have a relationship with each other" (*LI,* 298). "Ideological thinking," the antithesis to the "literary idea," is the primary symptom of the malaise plaguing American culture:

> But to call ourselves the people of the idea is to flatter ourselves. We are rather the people of ideology, which is a very different thing. Ideology is not the product of thought; it is the habit or the ritual of showing respect for certain formulas to which, for various reasons having to do with emotional safety, we have very strong ties of whose meaning and consequences in actuality we have no clear understanding. (*LI,* 286)

Elsewhere in "The Meaning of a Literary Idea," Trilling specifies the hall-marks of *ideological thinking* as intellectual passivity, the inability to "remain in uncertainties, mysteries, and doubts," and the insistence on "formulated solution[s]" (*LI,* 299). As Trilling remarks in "Reality in America," a culture's true artists "do not submit to serve the ends of any one ideological group or tendency" but rather contain the contradictions of their culture within themselves (*LI,* 9). It is this belief that informs Trilling's later defense of his remarks during the McCarthy era:

> It is clear to us [Trilling's Columbia committee] that membership in Communist organizations almost certainly implies a submission to an intellectual control which is entirely at variance with the principles of academic competence as we understand them.[15]

Thus, Dreiser's joining the Communist party, his literary and intellectual passivity before the complex facts of

modern existence, and his simplistic pitting of crude experience as an adequate refutation of the "mind of gentility" (*LI,* 15 and passim) are all, according to Trilling, evidence of Dreiser's mind having been violated by an idea. If Krupnick is correct that, for Trilling, "as the forties began, the Stalinists were generally thought to be the legitimate heirs of the realist revolt of the twenties and thirties against formalism and gentility" (*FCC,* 64), it is at this point that Trilling's focus on Dreiser blurs and assumes the burden of Trilling's immense hostility to the so-called Stalinization of the American intelligentsia.

While Trilling's most significant articulations of his theory of ideological thinking are offered in the essays that frame *The Liberal Imagination,* that theory and its corollaries inform the entire volume. Most thoroughly, Trilling's reading of Hyacinth Robinson in James's *The Princess Casamassima* examines Hyacinth's moral heroism in terms reminiscent of the categories of negative capability versus ideological thinking. Whereas the Princess imposes revolutionary ideas onto the future, Hyacinth resists such easy and ideological solutions:

> By the time Hyacinth's story draws to its end, his mind is in a perfect equilibrium, not of irresolution but of awareness. . . . And just as he is in an equilibrium of awareness, he is also in an equilibrium of guilt. He has learned something of what may lie behind abstract ideals, the envy, the impulse to revenge and to dominance. (*LI,* 85)

It is not surprising that both Boyers and Krupnick perform elaborate readings of Trilling's analysis of this James text, capable as it is of embodying their respective visions of Trilling himself as a hero of civilization who resisted ideological thinking amid the pulls of a partisan social moment.

If Dreiser has seemed to vanish as a particular literary force, we need to realize that Trilling's critical practice is primarily concerned with the general drift of American culture (rather than with specific manifestations), though he does trace that drift from Dreiser into the Cold War. It may actually be the sketchy nature of "Reality in America," however, that has enabled that essay to remain so influential. Dreiser, in all his particularities (literary and political), might not finally be important for Trilling. Dreiser *is* important as a representative of the deterioration of American literary values in the wake of Parringtonian progressivism and of the ideological thinking that Trilling associates with Stalinism. As Krupnick notes, "Trilling was not just responding to texts but to Dreiser's involvement in Communist propaganda campaigns in the thirties and the use that was made of him in the forties by Stalinist literary criticism" (*FCC,* 67). Trilling proposes writers like Hawthorne, Melville, and James as alternatives to Dreiser because these writers refused to cave in to ideological pressures. Dreiser is thus perceived ideologically in the service both of Trilling's literary *and* of his political interests (though to separate the two areas of Trilling's practice is to miss their mutually reinforcing role).

Trilling's attack on Dreiser needs to be examined in terms of Trilling's own priorities. In one troubling way, Trilling simply ignores the complexity of Dreiser's thinking and life. For example, while partisan thinkers may have "Stalinized" the reception of Dreiser, Dreiser the individual had a sustained ambivalence, at least toward the USSR and communism. Dreiser's 1927-1928 visit to the Soviet Union violated his expectations so violently that the not only growled, "What a lousy country anyway," but remarked to his guide, "If I ever get out of this country alive, I'll run as fast as I can across the border, and . . . yell 'You're nothing but a damned Bolshevik.'"[16] On Dreiser's thinking about the USSR, W. A. Swanberg notes that Dreiser's "efforts . . . were less misguided than those of the party-serving fellow travelers, for he usually retained an independence of thought, however blurred, that kept him from skidding outright into the communist fold" (*D*, 391).[17] Furthermore, Dreiser himself showed outright contempt for the notion of ideological thinking. In a letter to Evelyn Scott, Dreiser scoffed, "Only the other day some young writer was telling me that a man could write a better book if he had read and understood the Marxian dialectic! Imagine!" (*D*, 449). If Dreiser held the reductive views for which Trilling accuses him, it is strange that such views are so thoroughly contradicted in some of Dreiser's explicit remarks about Soviet communism.

We need to ask whether Trilling had grappled very much at all with Dreiser. By denying Dreiser's work anything like the care and attention he affords, say, to James's *The Princess Casamassima*, Trilling quite literally silences Dreiser, preventing him from emerging with anything like the complexity his work offers. Following Philip Fisher, and a host of other recent critics on Dreiser, we could argue that Dreiser's work engages (with what some might call prophetic lucidity) the transformation of American consciousness within a new economic and cultural frame.[18] One might, then, not accuse Dreiser of opposing "crude experience to mind" (*LI*, 15) and siding with crude experience, and one might not oppose James and Dreiser but rather account for them as two complementary and interdependent responses to cultural transformation. By polarizing Dreiser and James, Trilling exposes his own incapacity to grasp the two writers dialectically.

In another respect, Trilling's attack on Dreiser is not the work of Krupnick's "reactive critic." Far from resisting the dominant cultural tendencies of his time, Trilling may simply be resituating an already fairly common indifference to Dreiser. By the time Trilling launches his attack, Dreiser's influence, not to mention his public standing, had waned. He had, in Swanberg's words, "been out of the mainstream for twenty years" (*D*, 523). For example, while Trilling complains about "the doctrinaire indulgence which liberal intellectuals have always displayed toward Theodore Dreiser" and about the "liberal severity toward Henry James" (*LI*, 10), the sheer number of articles and books on James compared to those on Dreiser calls Trilling's assumptions into serious question. In the years from 1930 to 1950 (the decades of Trilling's focus), a rough count of items in the *MLA Bibliography* comes up

with almost one hundred articles on James and only seventeen on Dreiser, with book publications also corresponding roughly to this 5:1 ratio. Granted, mere numerical advantage does not tell the entire story, but such a difference points to James's favored status, even in the heyday of the so-called liberal criticism Trilling attacks. In 1941, the literary world totally ignored Dreiser's seventieth birthday, and, in 1946, "fewer than a hundred persons, some of them strangers" attended Dreiser's funeral (*D*, 525). It was only a few years later that Ginger Rogers's mother, Lola, turned down a role for Ginger in the film version of *Sister Carrie,* because "Dreiser's novel was open propaganda for Communism."[19] We could draw meaningful distinctions between Trilling's denunciation of Dreiser and the remarks of Ginger Rogers's mother. Trilling's attack and its timing (coming a few years after Dreiser's death), however, may have more in common with such crude reductions than we are wont to admit. We might even suggest that Lola Rogers wouldn't have such ready access to a prepackaged anticommunist vocabulary without Trilling paving the rhetorical path for such reductions.

3

Trilling's very closely related polemic against Parrington is another example of lapses in an imagination that elsewhere embodies candor, affection, and magnanimity. According to Trilling, Parrington held an arrogant and positivistic conception of reality and believed that an artist's relation to reality is a simple, mimetic one. "Whenever he was confronted with a work of art that was complex, personal and not literal, that was not, as it were, a public document," Trilling argues, "Parrington was at a loss" (*LI*, 4). Trilling issues a still influential dictum when he argues:

> Separate Parrington from his informing idea of the economic and social determination of thought and what is left is a simple intelligence, notable for its generosity and enthusiasm but certainly not for its accuracy or originality. (*LI*, 3-4)

In his concluding remarks on Dreiser, Trilling returns to Parrington. Attacking the "logic of the liberal criticism that accepted [Dreiser] so undiscriminatingly," Trilling cites such a lapse as a logical extension of the "liberal criticism, in the direct line of Parrington, which establishes the social responsibility of the writer and then goes on to say that, apart from his duty of resembling reality as much as possible, he is not really responsible for anything, not even for his ideas" (*LI*, 21).

This line of Trilling's argument (in some cases an extension of his assault on ideological thinking and in others a clarification of its implications) surfaces periodically throughout *The Liberal Imagination,* always as a point of contempt and dismissal. In his most extended and influential extension of this critique, Trilling examines *The Princess Casamassima,* which, as we have seen, allows him to articulate and to substantiate some central assumptions.

Whereas Trilling's admiration for Hyacinth Robinson pivots on that character's fully embracing a life of negative capability, the bulk of Trilling's criticism of the Princess rests on her Parringtonian conception of reality. The Princess, according to Trilling, is a "perfect drunkard of reality":

> She is ever drawn to look for stronger and stronger drams. . . . She cannot but mistake the nature of reality, for she believes it is a thing, a position, a finality, a bedrock. She is, in short, the very embodiment of the modern will which masks itself in virtue, . . . that despises the variety and modulations of the human story and longs for an absolute humanity, which is but another way of saying a nothingness. (*LI*, 91-92)

Trilling returns to the James novel in "Manners, Morals, and the Novel," again to expose the shallowness of the Princess's understanding of reality:

> She seeks out poverty, suffering, sacrifice, and death because she believes that these things alone are real; she comes to believe that art is contemptible; she withdraws her awareness and love from the one person [Hyacinth Robinson] of her acquaintance who most deserves them, and she increasingly scorns whatever suggests variety and modulation, and is more and more dissatisfied with the humanity of the present in her longing for the more perfect humanity of the future. It is one of the great points that the novel makes that with each passionate step that she takes toward what she calls the real, the solid, she in fact moves further away from the life-giving reality. (*LI*, 218)

Aside from what objections one may make to Trilling's rendering of James's ambiguous character as one simple pole in a political morality play, the terms of his argument are clear in their relationship to his leadoff reading of Parrington. Those who believe in reality as a solid and stable point of reference violate the variety of life and actually (and paradoxically) move away from the "life-giving reality" of the conditioned, Trilling's counter-construction to the ideological diminution of reality by those like the Princess. The Princess's reformist zeal (like that which Trilling ascribes to Parrington and Dreiser) replaces the contingency of lived experience with the abstract and life-denying "ideology" of revolutionary politics.

We might well agree with Trilling that Parrington's literary history is informed by political ideals and that those ideals at times impinge on what some critics would like to isolate as the purely literary significance of literature. We might similarly remark that many transformations in the sphere of literary criticism and theory are marked by rhetorical hyperbole. We might also note that Trilling was only one of many thinkers whose attacks on Parrington ushered in a new approach to theorizing about American literature and culture. In these respects, as in many others, Trilling is representative rather than "reactive" in the general drift of his argument. The consistency and the intensity of Trilling's attack on the Left, the near Left, and ideas forcibly attributed to the Left, however, is notable.

Trilling's judgment of Parrington is, quite simply, flawed. Trilling ignores, for example, Parrington's historical milieu, a strange lapse for a self-declared historical and *dialectical* critic such as Trilling. Parrington's so-called denigration of (perhaps oblivion to) belles lettres did not at all disturb most critics of his era (Progressive or otherwise), and even Howard Mumford Jones, who did fault Parrington's literary tastes, could comment on the originality and force of Parrington's work. "Who could forget," Jones muses, "the tingling sense of discovery with which we first read those lucid pages!"[20] Of course, it might be this critical (or uncritical) response against which Trilling reacts, but Parrington's originality (or lack of it) is not merely a subjective matter. As Kermit Vanderbilt notes, in tracing American romanticism, "Parrington ranged outside the common literary-historical treatment of New England by describing and documenting the less familiar aspect of movements in the Middle and Southern states, pages in *Main Currents* whose freshness has never been fully appraised."[21] Trilling's attack on Parrington has been largely responsible for this neglect. If Parrington lacked originality, it was only in Trilling's sense of the word.

Trilling also ignores several similarly important directions in Parrington's aesthetic thought. Again, Vanderbilt puts Parrington's contribution in terms that point out just how original the latter was:

> Parrington has moments of aesthetic demonstration that hint at a further range that he might have achieved as a literary historian were it not for the demands of his intellectual history. We need only recall the vapid impressionism—or no aesthetic commentary at all—by our earlier literary historians to appreciate what Parrington does accomplish in literary explication.[22]

Trilling fails to note Parrington's achievement largely by ignoring a different kind of historical context than that in which he is interested. One can hardly imagine Trilling's Parrington writing:

> If literature be the product of estheticism and not of protest and propaganda; if it has had its birth out of that persistent love of beauty which is the mainspring of creative art, it is a thing spiritual or esthetic rather than economic.[23]

Even a few remarks from *Main Currents* reveal a Parrington who was by no means blind to the complex, personal and aesthetic side of American literature, as Trilling would have us believe. Parrington criticizes Harriet Beecher Stowe because "she never trained herself in craftsmanship . . . her work has suffered the fate that pursues those who forget that beauty alone survives after emotion subsides." In other cases, Parrington anticipates Trilling's position on writers who subordinate their craft to their ideas. He faults the "art submerged by propaganda" in Upton Sinclair and criticizes those Dreiser novels in which "the artist suffers at the hands of the disputant."[24] This catalog could be expanded. If Parrington was ever the crude ideologue represented by Trilling, we would still need to account for these and other similar remarks throughout *Main Currents.*[25] Once separated from his governing idea of the "social and economic determination of thought," a Parrington sensitive to literary and intellectual nuance *does* exist, but Trilling never recognized *that* Parrington.

In fact, Trilling seems capable of missing the entire drift of Parrington's study. He criticizes Parrington for imagining his study as one of "main currents" in American thought. As he charges,

> Parrington's characteristic weakness as a historian is suggested by his title, for the culture of a nation is not truly figured in the image of a current. A culture is not a flow, nor even a confluence; the form of its existence is struggle, or at least debate— it is nothing if not a dialectic. (*LI,* 9)

One can only respond that Parrington's study foregrounds nothing more than it does struggle and debate. In fact, in his emerging dialectic between progressive and conservative elements in American culture, Parrington locates struggle at the heart of American literature—an innovation that constitutes one of his major advances over such literary historians as Moses Coit Tyler, who represented American literature emerging in one seamless, evolutionary whole. Trilling's attack responds to Parrington's title page only, not in any meaningful way to Parrington's work.

4

The figure looming behind Trilling's readings of Dreiser and Parrington and generating their bizarre misprisions is Stalin. In Trilling's work, Dreiser and Parrington are guilty of aesthetic crimes for which Stalin and Stalinism are the political foundations. Who was Stalin and what, for Trilling, was Stalinism? While the name *Stalin* is conspicuously absent from *The Liberal Imagination*, Trilling alludes several times in politically pregnant terms to ominous political forces. Stalin figures as a powerful, almost determining presence, largely by virtue of the absence of *Stalin* as signifier in Trilling's text. We should recall that Trilling himself admitted that "all [his] essays of the Forties" were written with Stalin as their implicit antagonist. Perhaps Trilling's remark in a letter to Eric Bentley, that Stalinism requires "the death of the human spirit" if it is to succeed politically (*FCC,* 61), best captures the nature of his animus. O'Hara proposes the cultural extension of this drift in Trilling. "A final monolithic order or totalitarian scene of ultimate persuasion with either I or IT as the presiding deity" permeates Trilling's American culture, O'Hara argues, because

> whether the artist is thought capable of subsuming reality within his will, or the individual will thought to be subsumed by some deterministic historical process or structure of culture, the underlying desire or hidden motive in both cases is the apocalyptic urge to put an end both to the incessant conflict of wills that is society and to the repeated

> need to overcome personal passivity in the face of this adverse reality. (*WL,* 286)

Thus, Trilling's political allusions can be understood as oblique broadsides against the oppression and danger alive in the Stalinist ethos.

While acknowledging the omnipresence and irrationality of Trilling's anti-Stalinism, O'Hara would nonetheless argue that Stalin is merely a latter-day manifestation of a life-long preoccupation of Trilling's. In his shrewd reading of Trilling's 1929 short story, "Notes on a Departure," O'Hara concludes,

> in [the narrator's concluding] apocalyptic vision of America, the Uncanny is the great original of all Trilling's subsequent nightmare images of a tempting, totalizing dream, to be rediscovered in Stalinism, the adversary culture of modernism, and the "madness" of postmodern orthodoxy, all of which would obviate the need for further personal development or struggle, and so put an end to the basis of and purpose for "liberal" culture. (*WL,* 35)

O'Hara (like West in the remarks quoted earlier) is correct in positing a resilient vision at the heart of Trilling's career. The very capaciousness of their readings, while revealing crucial continuities in Trilling's diverse corpus, may, however, also gloss over the important differences between those moments when Trilling's vision of a totalizing Other is *primarily* a personal and psychological matter and those years when it resonates with (perhaps aids in constructing) a vision more strategically and more aggressively polemical and ideological.[26] It is with such socio-ideological and cultural issues that I am presently concerned, though I would not separate the personal from the political in any absolute way in my reading of Trilling. In some ways, my own perspective exists in dialectical solution with those of O'Hara, Krupnick, and Boyers, and I hope to illuminate the darker areas of Trilling's long and complex literary career.

In his preface to *The Liberal Imagination*, Trilling calls attention to the political subtext of his literary-critical text. "These are not political essays," he cautions, "they are essays in literary criticism. But they assume the inevitable intimate, if not always obvious, connection between literature and politics" (*LI,* xi-xii). In "Reality in America," while Trilling vaguely alludes to "the disasters that threaten us" (*LI,* 12), his essays place us "at the dark and bloody crossroads where literature and politics meet" (*LI,* 11). And elsewhere he develops the political context of his essays in equally ominous and suggestive terms. For instance, the aura of politics looming barely beyond the critical page persists in "The Function of the Little Magazine," where Trilling alerts us to his belief that "unless we insist that politics is imagination and mind, we will learn that imagination and mind are politics, and of a kind that we will not like" (*LI,* 100). And, in the final sentences of "Manners, Morals, and the Novel," Trilling warns that the waning of the novel as a literary form capable of representing the moral imagination has dire consequences:

There never was a time when its [the novel's] particular activity was so much needed, was of so much practical, political, and social use—so much so that if its impulse does not respond to the need, we shall have reason to be sad not only over a waning form of art but also over our waning freedom. (*LI*, 222)

Trilling reserves his most explicit cautionary analysis for "The Meaning of a Literary Idea." In that essay, he completes the political subtext of his study with an assault on "ideological thinking." The "language of non-thought" (that attitude which he also calls "ideological thinking") "is the language which is developing from the peculiar status which we in our culture have given to abstract thought. There can be no doubt whatever that it constitutes a threat to the emotions and thus to life itself" (*LI*, 285).

While the drama of such remarks may be a function more of hyperbole than of Trilling's genuine political thought, these declarations are more than mere rhetorical asides—they focus and punctuate some of Trilling's most reflective and influential passages. Such passages *are* rhetorically marked, however, by their directness and political passion in a study otherwise noted for its carefully modulated and cautiously balanced sentences, essays, and thoughts, and for its valorization of such modulation and equipoise as both literary and political virtues. In each of these (and numerous other such passages), Trilling represents the political reality to which the essays of *The Liberal Imagination* respond, and that reality is bloody and threatening. Throughout *The Liberal Imagination*, Stalin is roughly synonymous with monolithic, reductive, ideological thinking and with the simplistic politics that, as Chace and Krupnick argue, Trilling spent his career attacking. It is the Stalin whose reductions of reality dramatize the dangers of "ideological thinking" who generates such passages and against whom Trilling may ultimately have formulated his influential doctrine of "the literary idea." Dreiser and Parrington, then, may be mere pretexts for Trilling's political subtext.

Trilling's sacrifice of referential specificity for ideological vigor has recently been subjected to serious scrutiny and criticism. Arac touches on some significant lapses in Trilling's cultural-political thinking. Trilling's construction of Stalinism, Arac argues, prevented him from recognizing that Tess Slesinger's *The Unpossessed* (1966), a novel Trilling greatly admired, was more "a Communist satire on halfhearted intellectual leftists" than the supposed attack on communism for which Trilling took and admired it (*PP*, xxxiii). Noting the ideological nature of Trilling's critical blindness to Slesinger's work, Arac remarks:

> Trilling here may have failed in his own appreciation for the complex variety of views. So too his opposition to "Stalinist" principles of art led him to exclude from serious consideration certain modes of writing, to downgrade realism, and in the effect of his own authority become to a younger generation "the mirror image of Zhdanov" [quoting Aronowitz], independent only in relation to his chosen opponent. (*PP*, xxxiii)

Remarking similarly on the narrowness and surprising failures of dialectical thinking in Trilling's own program (along with that of the New Critics), Stanley Aronowitz concludes:

> It was but a short step to the recruitment of the critics to the side of the cold war where every realist was equated with Stalinism, and every attack on expressionism, subjectivism, and high art immediately condemned as mass authoritarian culture.[27]

Even Krupnick's very generous study notes that Trilling's reading of *The Princess Casamassima*, while "certainly a brilliant performance," flattens James's work as it "tells more about Trilling's [political] preoccupations in the forties than it does about the novel that Henry James wrote" (*FCC*, 69).

Trilling's version of Stalinism (as with his readings of Dreiser and Parrington) needs serious and sustained reexamination. We might go so far as to say that as long as Trilling's notion of Stalinism (which, in many ways, postwar American culture shares) remains an undeconstructed and unchallenged representation, we won't have access to the various effects it has had on either Trilling's cultural-critical work or its influence on subsequent critics of American literature and culture. Trilling's Stalin is, in many ways, our Stalin, just as Trilling's Dreiser and Parrington have, until fairly recently, been *our* Dreiser and Parrington. Krupnick seems representative when he speaks several times of "the murder of millions in Stalinist purges" and of "Stalin's . . . barbarities" as "major *facts* of which [Trilling's] essays try to take account" (*FCC*, 62, 97; my emphasis).

These "facts," however, are not by any means accepted as such by an increasingly large number of Sovietologists (both political scientists and historians) in the United States and Europe. Some recent work has challenged the Cold War totalitarian thesis of Stalinism along lines that suggest a cautious revision may now be in order. While recent trends in Sovietology question most of our central assumptions concerning Stalin and Stalinism, there is general agreement that serious political mistakes, paranoia, and factional infighting *did* have catastrophic results. It is important to note that even on these crucial figures Western historians differ drastically in their estimates of how many people may have perished (from 20,000 to 60,000,000), just as they offer explanations for the deaths that range from diffused political paranoia and mistakes to iron-handed and carefully orchestrated murder. With the former USSR now as interested as the West in condemning Stalin and in distancing itself from all vestiges of "Stalinism" as it paves the way for reentering the world capitalist economy, and given the political biases that historians, political scientists, and literary thinkers of both East and West bring to bear on their reconstructions, it may well be impossible ever to represent the Stalin era carefully and accurately. It is particularly interesting and problematic that Moscow's own aggressively anti-Stalinist reconstructions of the Stalinist past contradict those of bourgeois scholars from Western Europe and the

United States, just recently exposing many of the received and arguably mythic versions of Cold War historiography.

This summary of revisionist work in American Sovietology is not an attempt to "rehabilitate," to "defend," or to "exonerate" Stalin.[28] My interest is in challenging and complicating the Trilling thesis on Dreiser, Parrington, and Stalin by foregrounding moments in their lives and works contrary to, and often excluded from, Trilling's readings of them. The nature and influence of his observations, not merely their accuracy, is at issue. Trilling's blindness to complications in their works is more than a simple lapse in his otherwise careful reading of American culture; these exclusions mirror those of American Cold War culture in general. This discussion, like my discussions of Dreiser and Parrington, is meant only to subject some of Trilling's most consistently maintained and influential critical programs to renewed scrutiny and to remind those who would take Trilling (or Robert Conquest) at his word that "it's much more complicated."

One of the most highly charged controversies in the field of Soviet Studies in the West centers on the issues of Stalin and Stalinism. Both the *Slavic Review* and the *Russian Review* have recently published the proceedings of symposia on "new perspectives on Stalinism," and scores of articles and books reexamining the Stalin era in the Soviet Union from a variety of perspectives have been published over the past two decades.[29] While no consensus seems to be emerging among Sovietologists on the crucial questions of what Stalinism was, how and why it emerged when and how it did, and what its impact on subsequent Soviet politics has been, even Robert Tucker, who was among the scholars who brought the term into wide use in the 1950s and 1960s, has announced that "years of work on the Stalin era have taught me to use the term sparingly, because its referent is unclear."[30] In fact, the recent revisions of our understanding of Stalin have provoked Henry Reichman to advocate a moratorium on using the term *Stalinism* because the "indiscriminate labeling of 'isms' has too long allowed ideologues—Soviet and Western—to avoid concrete historical analysis" and because the wide and ideologically charged misuse of the term has distorted our sense of Soviet history.[31] It would be foolish, Reichman grants, to make too much of a word; however, as an explanatory concept, *Stalinism* lacks historical and conceptual power, covering more than it uncovers about the multidimensional reality of Soviet history—and, ironically, about Stalin's own role in that history.[32] And, as Alfred G. Meyer notes, in using the totalitarian model that most American Sovietologists have used to conceptualize Stalinism, they "were also celebrating Americanism and at the same time succumbing to cold war hysteria."[33] Both Reichman and Meyer stress that the study, the very imagining, of Stalin and Stalinism has been obscured (some contend to the point of serious error) by the emerging and consolidating discourse of Cold War anticommunism. Many now believe that these "facts" disseminated by the Cold War ideologists (and often accepted by literary historians) have been provided by scholars who have accepted

payments from British intelligence agencies for "consciously falsifying information about the Soviet Union"[34] and who have intentionally substituted fraudulent photographic evidence and testimony for actual research.[35]

Responding to the anti-Stalinist animus driving much work on the Soviet Union, Roberta Manning has issued a statement of purpose for her work and that work being done by an increasing number of Western Sovietologists. By extending the critique of the embattled "totalitarian thesis" on Stalinism to the prewar era, Manning declares, revisionist historians

> eschew the political goals espoused by many American Soviet specialists, who are unable to conceive of scholarship other than as an enterprise undertaken to "indict" and/or "rehabilitate" particular individuals or movements. The body of work that we are beginning to produce presents a correspondingly detailed, complex, and nuanced view of Stalinism.[36]

While the particulars of the debates now raging among Sovietologists are many and sometimes seem focused more on methodological than on informational issues, I will briefly summarize a few points that press significantly on the anti-Stalinist position common to Trilling and many subsequent American literary historians. First, Western views of the "great purges" associate them with mass slaughter. All available documentation suggests, however, that the purges were largely ordinary membership operations designed to *expel*, not to murder, hangers-on, careerists, drunks, and those who abused their official positions, usually by demanding sexual favors (Getty, 99). The usual view of the purges as organized mass murder akin to Hitler's slaughter of the Jews are flawed, John Arch Getty suggests, by misinterpretation of Soviet documents and by the uncritical acceptance of defector and émigré horror stories, by relying, in short, on obviously one-sided (ideological, in Trilling's sense) reports. The theory of the so-called terror famine, which Stalin is charged with orchestrating, has also been exposed, in most of its central assumptions, as a hoax, the promotion and distribution of which has been sponsored and funded by organizations with suspicious ties to the Nazis and with great political clout in "Soviet studies, where rigor and objectivity count for less than the party line, where fierce anti-Communists still control the prestigious institutes and first-rank departments."[37] The Sovietologists whom Jeff Coplon cites (including some self-declared anti-Stalinists) refer to Robert Conquest's *The Harvest of Sorrow* (the most celebrated document on the famine), as "crap," "rubbish," "totally out of keeping with what we know," and they accuse Conquest of "misus[ing] sources, [and] twist[ing] everything."[38] As Coplon clarifies,

> there was indeed a famine in the Ukraine in the early 1930s. It appears likely that hundreds of thousands, possibly one or two million, Ukrainians died—the minority from starvation, the majority from related diseases. By any scale, this is an

enormous toll of human suffering. By general consensus, Stalin was partially responsible [for making mistakes, not for consciously producing or directing a famine]. By any stretch of an honest imagination, the tragedy still falls short of genocide.

It is possible, in other words, that there were no purges and no famine as we have understood them and as they have underwritten a vision of Stalin as equal to or worse than Hitler.[39]

In addition, the view of Stalinism as an all-controlling, all-deciding formation of organized and systematic terror is also seriously challenged by scholarly scrutiny. As Reichman suggests, "the picture of the Stalinist state beginning to emerge from some recent research is . . . a far cry from the powerful monolith of Soviet propaganda and Cold War scholarship."[40] Robert W. Thurston, for example, has argued that there is simply no evidence to support the "Great Terror" totalitarian thesis of the late thirties. At the conclusion of one discussion based on the examination of volumes of recently available documentation, Thurston notes:

> In the coming years [World War II] a "broken" people would not have fought effectively, let alone put up the tremendous resistance that the Soviet population by and large displayed during World War II. Nor can this idea explain why people evinced genuine affection for Stalin during and after the war, lasting down to the present in some quarters or strata. Soviet society demonstrated truly remarkable strength in the late 1930s, despite the grave injustice and hysteria that gripped it for a time; the sources of that strength should be the subject of many more studies.[41]

Roberta Manning, to cite one more example of the recent work to which Reichman refers, argues that in the collective farms "we find at the grassroots a government far more human, more fragile, more prey to events outside of its control and more vulnerable to the vagaries of public opinion than any of us have hitherto dared to imagine."[42] Rather than an iron-fisted party machine in full control, the Soviet Communist party under Stalin "was in reality a disorganized collection of often conflicting interest groups with little influence outside the cities" (Getty, 79). Furthermore, Getty argues, Stalin could not have exercised the kind of control most often attributed to him, even had he so desired:

> The situation was characterized less by efficiency, discipline, or obedience [to Stalin] than by sloth, chaos, inertia and disunity. In this polycentric environment various social and political groups and institutions supported various policies (including Stalin's) at various times, and there were conflicting and mutual hostile trends even among the pro-Stalinists. (Getty, 46)

While no one is denying that errors, losses, miscalculations, and tragedies were rampant in the Soviet Union during Stalin's putative rule, most of these historians are arguing that attributing such travesties and mistakes to the unified, coherent, and intentional construct of *Stalinism* actually impedes and distorts the complexity and virtual chaos of the historical record and experience. The totalitarian thesis shuts down, rather than makes possible, historical inquiry.

The question still remains as to the character of Stalin himself. Gabor T. Rittersporn has suggested that, given the factional dissension and power struggles rife within the Soviet Union during Stalin's leadership, Stalin himself may have served more as a powerless icon than as a totalitarian dictator. Rittersporn goes so far as to liken Stalin to Mao Tse-tung on the eve of the Chinese Cultural Revolution, more a figure for convenient mythical appropriation (by the Left or the Right) than an influential player in the action.[43] Getty, too, posits a figure very different from the totalitarian megalomaniac of the institutionalized American mythology. The idea that Stalin presided over a virtual dictatorship is untenable, Getty suggests; in fact, Stalin played a role almost the antithesis of that usually attributed to him. For example, he repeatedly curbed or condemned radicals and enthusiasts who had been carried away over ideological matters. Stalin's position among warring factions,

> as always, was that of a balancer or political makeweight. The various opinions, factions, interests . . . were each important and necessary. When he intervened, it was usually to restore a balance—in several of his speeches he spoke forcefully in favor of *both* contending points of view. (Getty, 531)

As Getty elsewhere puts it, "although the inner politics of the Kremlin still eludes us, it is clear that in the thirties Stalin's lieutenants represented policy alternatives and options."[44] I would like to recall Trilling's definition of a literary idea as "what comes into being when two contradictory emotions are made to confront each other and are made to have a relationship with each other." To border on the perverse, one could deduce from recent work in Sovietology that Stalin fully *lived out* Trilling's ideal of negative capability, of the sensitive mind capable of existing amid the stress and pull of contradictions without caving in to one side or the other. As Krupnick notes, Trilling's mind worked dialectically "to keep the culture on a steady course and maintain an always threatened equilibrium" (*FCC*, 58). According to at least one recent perspective, so did Stalin's.

5

My purpose has been to observe, in Trilling's thinking about three of his declared antagonists and in some of the major scholarly assessments of Trilling's career, tendencies that call into serious question the consistency and coherence of both Trilling's position and his scholarly reputation. That Trilling was complex, valued complexity, and explicated complexity is a given of Trilling scholarship. Yet, in the cases of Dreiser, Parrington, and the Ur-villain, Stalin, Trilling seems strangely blind to the complexities surrounding their work's historical status and ignores implications of their work along lines that corroborate Trilling's critical program. In a related manner, the fact that Trilling valued the ability to reside tenuously, almost vertiginously, amid contrary pulls without deciding "ideologically" on an issue similarly unites critics of Trilling, whether they value or attack Trilling for his stance. In his responses to Dreiser, Parrington, and Stalin, however, Trilling demonstrates none of the negative capability he finds so valuable in Keats, James, and others and, instead, flattens their work or reputations in ways that suggest his mind had been violated by an idea. Boyers argues that Trilling was "scrupulously fair and responsive to [all] rival points of view."[45] In the cases of Dreiser, Parrington, and Stalin, Boyers's view is simply wrong; the fact that Boyers can seriously advance the position is evidence of just how thoroughly Trilling's views have infused American literary and cultural thought. His readings have become institutionalized.

Finally, that Trilling was a reactive critic struggling against popular cultural trends and against the simplification of complex issues is another tenet that unites Trilling scholars, again whether they attack Trilling's elitism or praise his Arnoldian high-mindedness. Trilling's reactions to Dreiser, Parrington, and Stalin, however, are all of a very different nature. At the conclusion of his essay "Lionel Trilling and the Conservative Imagination," Joseph Frank challenges Trilling's "reactive" or "adversarial" role by arguing that in "defending the conditioned on the level of middle-class values, and in endowing the torpid acceptance of these values with the dignity of aesthetic transcendence, Mr. Trilling is merely augmenting the already frightening momentum making for conformism and the debilitation of moral tension."[46] Here Frank joins Delmore Schwartz and others in suggesting that Trilling's valorization of certain values corroborates a tendency toward conformity and homogeneity (Robert Lowell's "tranquilized fifties"). My point is similar, but I am more concerned with Trilling's impact on American cultural studies. Rather than articulating a literary critical vocabulary capable of distinguishing (when possible or desirable) literary and cultural criticism from immediate political pressures, Trilling ushers into American literary criticism an entire array of values and priorities that mirror those of a culture nearly paralyzed by McCarthyite paranoia. Polls taken in the early fifties, for example, reveal that Americans tended to suspect that friends and neighbors who had maps of Russia in their homes, who brought "foreign looking" people into their homes, or "who were always talking about world peace" were Communists.[47] Rather than countering and resisting such trends in American popular culture, Trilling's work in *The Liberal Imagination* can be read as restating, reshaping, and intellectualizing some of the basic, though usually more crudely stated, assumptions of the Cold War and postwar American anticommunism. Whereas advocacy of radical causes represents "dangerous" thinking for some, for Trilling it represents "vulgar" thinking, or, worse yet, no thinking at all.

What makes such a development significant is that Trilling's major tenets were all formulated as ways of saving literary discourse from caving in to immediate political pressures. Trilling's formulations of a vocabulary to swerve around overt politicization are troubled from the beginning by his own political biases. In this respect, one would need to qualify Irving Howe's correction of Frank's charges. Howe argues "that Frank did not perhaps see [that] Trilling's views did have an 'immediate practical and political relevance.'" Rather than being the conservative that Frank criticizes, Howe counters, "Trilling's critique of 'the liberal imagination' eased a turning away from all politics, whether liberal, radical, or conservative."[48] Yet, if Trilling did ease the turn toward apolitical quietism (itself an oxymoron), it may have been by helping construct an image of Stalinist terror to rival that of Nazi terror in order to discredit any extreme political positions and to usher in "the end of ideology." Whatever Trilling's motives may have been, the quietism Howe credits him with merged quickly with the very political "deradicalization of twentieth-century American intellectuals."[49]

This is not merely to argue that Trilling's position is inherently political. R. W. B. Lewis and others pointed that out long before it became a commonplace of recent politicized literary theory. In Trilling's case, the politics are more than implicit; they constitute a political perspective so powerful and coherent as to blind Trilling to the violations of his own literary program. Trilling nowhere registers the drama of a mind violated by an idea more than when he succumbs to the very crimes for which he indicts Dreiser, Parrington, and Stalin.[50]

The difficulties inherent in Trilling's thinking about Dreiser, Parrington, and Stalin point out the need to assess Trilling's relationship to a developing Cold War rhetoric and the impingement of the Cold War on the academic study of American literature and culture. As Michael Paul Rogin has claimed, "McCarthyism has not so much suppressed opinions as changed them; it has significantly altered the tone of intellectual discussion about politics in general and American politics in particular."[51] David Caute and Ellen Schrecker have noted disturbing examples of American universities submitting to direct political pressures in the forties and fifties. In essence, what I have tried to suggest in this essay is one way in which Trilling's intellectual work in the forties and fifties changed (to use Rogin's term) opinions and provided intellectual respectability for a wide range of opinions and beliefs rampant in mass culture, ideas which, when pushed to their McCarthyite limits, generated investigations and harassments, and shattered many careers, marriages, and lives.[52] It is also possible, however, that the origins, mutations, and contradictions of Trilling's animus point to a more complex *participation* in Cold War ideology than has yet been acknowledged. Both Schrecker and Alan Wald, for example, have called attention to Trilling's cooperation with HUAC and with the American Committee on Cultural Freedom.[53] Wald stresses that Trilling's participation in drawing up a Columbia University statement on academic freedom made a gentle case against "the real practice of McCarthyism" but "offered a powerful statement that implicitly bolstered the rationale for the McCarthyite campaign."[54]

One might also speculate on less obvious ramifications of the politico-cultural survival of Trilling's literary work in American politics and pop culture (if the two can now be distinguished with any precision). How big a step is it from Trilling's simplifications of his enemies to Ronald Reagan's "Evil Empire" speech? How big a step is it from Trilling's powerful reduction of his enemies to those of the Pentagon systematically falsifying reports of Soviet, Vietnamese, Nicaraguan, and Iraqi military power in order to divert billions of dollars away from medical research, housing, and hunger relief to defense spending? How big a step is it from Trilling's casting his enemies as monolithically crude, vulgar, and "dreary" (a key word in Trilling's anti-Stalinist vocabulary) to the cartoon character Murky Dismal (an animated, Saturday morning Stalinist complete with bushy moustache and eyebrows) threatening the color and variety of Rainbow Brite's kingdom with his gray vision of a world without color? These suggestions are, of course, extreme—I advance them as areas of possible inquiry, not as substantiated assertions. If Trilling's vision was ever "reactive" or "adversarial," however, we need to think more about how it became so thoroughly *part* of the prevailing views of postwar American popular culture.

This absorption might be ascribed to the power of what Donald Pease calls a "Cold War scenario," which "manages to control, in advance, all the positions objectors can occupy. And all the objectors—whether the Batista regime against Cuban rebels, the Israelis against the Palestinians, or Ishmael against Ahab—can be read in terms of 'our' freedom versus their totalitarianism."[55] This is to say that Trilling's cultural thought may well have formulated a position for American writers and critics not *merely* compatible with the more blatantly reductive directions of postwar American cultural and political thought but a position many of whose particulars were absorbed and appropriated (after the fashion of the blob from the 1950s anticommunist sci-fi film) by the flexible parameters of Cold War discursive practices. The consonance, however, between some of Trilling's major tenets and trends in postwar culture may also point to an essential coherence between Trilling's thought and the general reductive drift in popular American politics. This is not to accuse Trilling of causing the problems, but rather to suggest that the relationship between Trilling's work, its impact on recent thinking about American literature, and the market for that work in postwar, Cold War American culture is far more complex than we have yet realized. We would profit enormously from a thorough study of the reception of Trilling's work by a postwar audience very much in the market for ideas such as those advanced by Trilling and many others.

6

I would like to conclude by briefly considering the contemporary vitality of a post-Trilling anti-Stalinist vocabulary in contemporary literary thought. It is especially troublesome

to consider that the same set of terms and significations that have been under increasing scrutiny, debate, and attack by the historical community have become increasingly reified in their usage by literary theoreticians and historians. Henry Reichman has complained that "for just about everyone [in the Sovietological community] 'Stalinism' and 'Stalinist' serve as ready and convenient epithets."[56] And, as Stephen F. Cohen comments, revisionist historians have rejected the idea of Stalinism popularized by political scientists in the 1950s, largely because it assumed a malignant "inner logic" and "unbroken continuity" within the narrative of Soviet experience, "thereby largely excluding the stuff of real history—conflicting traditions, alternatives, turning points, and multiple casualties."[57] If literary studies were currently wedded to a naïve model of seamless historical evolution, Cohen's charge might have little relevance for us. However, from Trilling's valorization of complexity, ambiguity, and irony as the "key words" in historical (like literary) analysis, to Hayden White's exemplary work on metahistory reminding us of the figurative nature of historical discourses, to Foucaultian historiography with its stress on discontinuity and the multiplicity of points of dispersion in history, literary histories have been increasingly informed by the ideas of rupture, revolution, and conflict. Yet, amid the various notions of history current among literary theorists and for all the stress on discontinuity, on conflict, and on the figurative and representational nature of historical discourse, *Stalin* and *Stalinism* continue to exist as unexamined reference points of horror.

Stalin and *Stalinism* are figured as a complex *historical* origin, almost literally a *given* and irrefragable truth, by a community of literary thinkers that otherwise questions all such designations of a historical origin as functions of representational practice, not referential accuracy or truth. How has it come to pass that Stalin and Stalinism have escaped the same deconstructive interrogation that current literary theory applies to any and all references to history? If among historians Stalinism no longer carries any weight as a historical signifier, and if the totalitarian thesis has been widely rejected as inadequate to represent Soviet historical experience, where does that leave Trilling's work in the forties, especially his influential "demolitions" of Dreiser and Parrington, which are predicated on their resemblances to an untenable notion of Stalinism. How does that require us to reexamine some of the truisms of poststructuralist Marxism? If Stalin and Stalinism are no longer valid, or even plausible, signifiers for the historical moments used to underwrite the anti-Stalinist polemics of Trilling and recent theory, precisely what is it that has been repudiated under the names of Stalin and Stalinism? Does Trilling's elevation of complexity—as well as the arguments against master discourses, realism, and other negative touchstones of post-structuralist politics—depend on the construction of a mythic antagonist whose oppositional endurance has been secured by its supposed rootedness in the actual fabric of history?

The construction and maintenance of Stalin as the undeconstructed locus of horror needs to be reexamined *as* a representation, saturated with the residues and pressures of numerous historiographical, political, and cultural struggles. Such an investigation into the history and ideology of the Cold War representations of "Stalinisms" in literary and historical discourse may well have to precede any articulation of a principled rapprochement between poststructuralism and Marxism. Stalin and Stalinism seem to be reemerging, however, as a monolithic and heavily interested ideological target even within the former Soviet Union. Both East and West, in other words, may be constructing ideological identities against a myth of Stalinism that has little historical, little political, and little referential accuracy, and we will need to interrogate the struggles and concealments being enacted by both sides. Unless we question the adequacy of any representation of Stalinism and of its impact on subsequent literary and political culture, our access to anything like a counter-hegemonic version of the Soviet 1930s and our ability to perform any archaeology on the historical and political struggles inscribed within the concept of Stalin may be impaired even more, Trilling may yet have the last word— it *is* very complicated. We, in fact, may be just beginning to realize how complicated it is.

NOTES

[1] Ellen W. Schrecker, *No Ivory Tower: McCarthyism and the Universities* (New York: Oxford University Press, 1986), 339.

[2] Daniel O'Hara glosses this episode somewhat more generously, granting that Trilling's influence may have prevented more Columbia professors from losing their jobs. See, however, Alexander Bloom's detailed discussion of the events and of Trilling's letter to the *New York Times* clarifying his committee's position on Communists in the universities. Bloom stresses that Trilling's need to publish the letter at all not only reaffirmed "several central notions of liberal anticommunism" but revealed Trilling's gratuitous stress on *"anticommunism itself rather than on academic freedom"* (my emphasis). According to Bloom, Trilling wanted to remove any sense that his committee was "'soft' on communism." See Daniel T. O'Hara, *Lionel Trilling: The Work of Liberation* (Madison: University of Wisconsin Press, 1988), 25. See also Alexander Bloom, *Prodigal Sons: The New York Intellectuals and Their World* (New York: Oxford University Press, 1986), 249, 250.

[3] Jonathan Arac, ed., *Postmodernism and Politics* (Minneapolis: University of Minnesota Press, 1986), xxxiii. Subsequent references to this work are cited parenthetically in my text as *PP*.

[4] Donald E. Pease, "New Americanists: Revisionist Interventions into the Canon," *boundary 2* 17 (1990): 7.

[5] Virtually every major recent study of Trilling's work (including those by Robert Boyers, Mark Krupnick, Cornel West, and Daniel O'Hara, all of whom are cited in other footnotes) posits anti-Stalinism as a crucial determinant

for Trilling's work, though only West and O'Hara work through the contradictions I am interested in.

[6] Richard H. Pells, *The Liberal Mind in a Conservative Age: American Intellectuals in the 1940s and 1950s* (New York: Harper & Row, 1985). See especially "Are You Now, Have You Ever Been, and Will You Give Us the Names of Those Who Were?" chap. 5, 262-346.

[7] Barzun is quoted in Mark Krupnick, *Lionel Trilling and the Fate of Cultural Criticism* (Evanston: Northwestern University Press, 1986), 58. Subsequent references to this work are cited parenthetically in my text as *FCC*.

[8] For an original and enlightening discussion of the emergence of an ideological-aesthetic consensus between the New York Intellectuals and the New Critics, see Lawrence H. Schwartz, *Creating Faulkner's Reputation: The Politics of Modern Literary Criticism* (Knoxville: University of Tennessee Press, 1988).

[9] William M. Chace, *Lionel Trilling: Criticism and Politics* (Stanford: Stanford University Press, 1980), 48, 47 (my emphasis).

[10] Daniel T. O'Hara, *Lionel Trilling: The Work of Liberation* (Madison: University of Wisconsin Press, 1988), 25, 35, 195-96. O'Hara's entire study is sensitive to nuances in Trilling's career. For O'Hara's reading of Trilling's early stories, see especially 32-38. Subsequent references to this work are cited parenthetically in my text as *WL*.

[11] Cornel West, *The American Evasion of Philosophy: A Genealogy of Pragmatism* (Madison: University of Wisconsin Press, 1989), 165, 177, my emphasis.

[12] Lionel Trilling, *The Last Decade: Essays and Reviews, 1965-75* (New York: Harcourt Brace Jovanovich, 1979), 141.

[13] Robert Boyers, *Lionel Trilling: Negative Capability and the Wisdom of Avoidance* (Columbia: University of Missouri Press, 1977), 26. Daniel O'Hara's stress on Trilling's magnanimous response to any and all opposing ideas is a more sustained and plausible version of the generosity and affection Boyers posits as central to Trilling's career.

[14] Lionel Trilling, *The Liberal Imagination: Essays on Literature and Society* (New York: Viking, 1950), 12, 13. Subsequent references to this work are cited parenthetically in my text as *LI*.

[15] Lionel Trilling, letter to the *New York Times,* 26 Nov. 1953, 30.

[16] W.A. Swanberg, *Dreiser* (New York: Scribner's, 1965), 334. Subsequent references to this work are cited parenthetically in my text as *D*.

[17] Swanberg's own formulation participates in the liberal anticommunism that I am addressing. His equation of "inde-

pendence of thought" with resistance to "skidding . . . into the communist fold," while meant to rehabilitate Dreiser, also reinforces the Trillingesque condemnation of communism as inimical to freedom of thought and expression.

[18] Dreiser also played an instrumental role in inspiring women to new forms of literary expression. Consider, for example, Blanche Gelfant's remark that "for [Emma] Goldman, as for other radical women autobiographers, the authorizing male writer of their times was Theodore Dreiser" ("Speaking Her Own Piece: Emma Goldman and the Discursive Skeins of Autobiography," in *American Autobiography: Retrospect and Prospect,* ed. Paul John Eakin [Madison: University of Wisconsin Press, 1991], 252). Henry James played virtually the opposite role, commonly savaging in his early book reviews the works of mid-nineteenth-century women novelists, silencing their literary energies while borrowing significantly from their themes; see Alfred Habegger's *Henry James and the "Woman Business"* (New York: Cambridge University Press, 1989). The stark contrast between Dreiser's support and James's contempt for women writers may even suggest a subtext of hostility toward women in Trilling's work.

[19] David Caute, *The Great Fear: The Anti-Communist Purges under Truman and Eisenhower* (New York: Scribner's, 1978), 493.

[20] Howard Mumford Jones, *The Theory of American Literature* (Ithaca: Cornell University Press, 1948), 141-42.

[21] Kermit Vanderbilt, *American Literature and the Academy: The Roots, Growth, and Maturity of a Profession* (Philadelphia: University of Pennsylvania Press, 1986), 311.

[22] Vanderbilt, *American Literature and the Academy,* 323.

[23] Vernon Parrington, Jr., "Vernon Parrington's Views: Economics and Criticism," *Pacific Northwest Quarterly* 44 (1953): 99.

[24] V. L. Parrington, *Main Currents in American Thought,* 3 vols. (Norman: University of Oklahoma Press, 1987), 2: 378, 3:353, and 3:354.

[25] Krupnick, O'Hara, and others repeatedly return to this passage to reconfirm and substantiate Trilling's initial assessment. See my "Reconstructing Parrington," *American Quarterly* 41 (1989): 155-64, for a more thorough discussion of the reception and repression of Parrington's work.

[26] Lawrence Schwartz (*Creating Faulkner's Reputation*) provides important materials from which to explore more thoroughly the economic and political subtexts of the fossilization of Stalin in Trilling's imagination. See especially chap. 5, "Forging a Postwar Aesthetic: The Rockefeller Foundation and the New Literary Consensus," 113-41.

[27] Stanley Aronowitz, *The Crisis in Historical Materialism: Class, Politics, and Culture in Marxist Theory* (New York: Praeger, 1981), 249.

[28] It is important to stress this point. One recent biographer of Lionel Trilling referred to an earlier version of this essay as an attempt to "rehabilitate" Stalin, despite the presence in the version he read of the sentence to which this note is appended. Another reader suggested I delete any and all references to Stalin in the paper. Another wrinkle of this hostility came when the editor of an ostensibly progressive periodical rejected an earlier version of this essay on the grounds that s/he regarded Trilling as a "minor figure," and s/he couldn't believe anyone had ever read him anyway. The very need to defend an attempt such as this to clarify and to question some important historical issues and to synthesize recent Western scholarship on Stalin in order to demonstrate the extent of Trilling's adherence to a palpably ideological version of history points to the depth to which the Cold War version of Stalin has sunk in the American psyche. Many revisionist historians have come under similar criticism by traditional Soviet historians and political scientists. To cite just one example, Peter Kenez goes so far as to imply that the "quantitative stress on terror in a scholarly work is a barometer of the author's moral sensibility" (quoted in J. Arch Getty, *Origins of the Great Purges: The Soviet Communist Party Reconsidered, 1933-1938* [Cambridge: Cambridge University Press, 1985], 395). The specific remark to which Getty responds reads as follows: "It is true, there are no morally correct or incorrect topics. However, once we choose the social and political history of the Soviet Union in the 1930s as a topic, whatever aspect we emphasize inevitably has a moral dimension. If the stress on terror betrays a certain moral sensibility, so does the denial of its significance" (399).

[29] In addition to those works listed in these notes, see Robert C. Tucker, ed., *Stalinism: Essays in Historical Interpretation* (New York: Oxford University Press, 1977) and Stephen F. Cohen, *Rethinking the Soviet Experience: Politics and History since 1917* (New York: Oxford University Press, 1985). See also Werner G. Hahn, *Postwar Soviet Politics: The Fall of Zhdanov and the Defeat of Moderation, 1946-1953* (Ithaca: Cornell University Press, 1982), for a new and challenging perspective on Zhdanov, whom postwar literary culture has regarded as the cultural version of Stalin. Hahn argues for a revision of Zhdanov similar to that currently being done on Stalin. As Hahn notes, "In reexamining the Soviet press of this period and studying the extensive source material that has appeared more recently, I find much evidence that divergent viewpoints, rather than monolithic orthodoxy, characterized Soviet officialdom after the war, and the dominant political forces in 1946—Zhdanov and his followers—were dramatically overturned by 1949, as part of a historic defeat of moderate elements in the Soviet political establishment" (9). According to Hahn, not only did Zhdanov not impose narrow ideological restraints on Soviet cultural production, he actually encouraged more creativity in fields such as philosophy and science.

[30] Robert C. Tucker, "The Stalin Period as an Historical Problem," *Russian Review* 46 (1987): 425.

[31] Henry Reichman, "Reconsidering 'Stalinism,'" *Theory and Society* 17 (1988): 74.

[32] Reichman, "Reconsidering 'Stalinism,'" 59.

[33] Alfred G. Meyer, "Coming to Terms with the Past . . . And with One's Older Colleagues," *Russian Review* 45 (1986): 402.

[34] J. Arch Getty, "The 'Great Purges' Reconsidered: The Soviet Communist Party, 1933-1939" (Ph.D. diss., Boston College, 1979), 47. I quote frequently from the dissertation version of Getty's work. In a phone conversation of 25 Aug. 1988, Getty affirmed that he still adheres to the specific wording in the passages I quote from the dissertation. See the conclusion to his *Origins of the Great Purges*, 196-206, for more specific discussions of the trends and characteristics noted in the passages I quote. I would like to thank Professor Getty for his time and his bibliographic references that greatly assisted me in researching this essay. Subsequent references to Getty's work are cited parenthetically in my text as Getty. I would also like to thank Ellen W. Schrecker and Gregory Meyerson for their valuable advice and suggestions. Their input made this a much more informed essay.

[35] See Jeff Coplon, "In Search of a Soviet Holocaust: A 55-Year-Old Famine Feeds the Right," *Village Voice*, 12 Jan. 1988: 29-33.

[36] Roberta T. Manning, "State and Society in Stalinist Russia," *Russian Review* 46 (1986): 408.

[37] Coplon, "In Search of a Soviet Holocaust," 31.

[38] Coplon, "In Search of a Soviet Holocaust," 31.

[39] On this point, see also Coplon, "Rewriting History: How Ukrainian Nationalists Imposed Their Doctored History on Our High-School Students," *CAPITAL Region* (March 1988): 44-46, 66.

[40] Reichman, "Reconsidering 'Stalinism,'" 62.

[41] Robert W. Thurston, "Fear and Belief in the USSR's 'Great Terror': Response to Arrest, 1935-1939," *Slavic Review* 45 (1986): 233-34.

[42] Roberta T. Manning, "Government in the Soviet Countryside in the Stalinist Thirties: The Case of Belyi Raion in 1937," *The Carl Beck Papers in Russian and East European Studies*, no. 301 (Pittsburgh: Russian and East European Studies Program, 1983), 43-44.

[43] Gabor Tamas Rittersporn, "Rethinking Stalinism," *Russian History* 11 (1984): 343-61.

[44] Getty, *Origins of the Great Purges*, 199.

[45] Boyers, *Negative Capability*, 1.

[46] Joseph Frank, *The Widening Gyre: Crisis and Mastery in Modern Literature* (New Brunswick: Rutgers University Press, 1963), 271.

[47] See Caute, *The Great Fear*.

[48] Irving Howe, *A Margin of Hope: An Intellectual Autobiography* (New York: Harcourt Brace, 1982), 231.

[49] Alan M. Wald, *The New York Intellectuals: The Rise and Decline of the Anti-Stalinist Left from the 1930s to the 1980s* (Chapel Hill: University of North Carolina Press, 1987), 4.

[50] One possible exception to this general assertion might be found in Trilling's own *The Middle of the Journey* (1947), a novel which, even by Trilling's own standards, would have to be termed ideological. Aronowitz refers to the work as "a dreary anti-drama of disillusionment and betrayal which might have been the manifesto of the cold war intellectual elites, but instead remained a symptom of their malaise" (*The Crisis in Historical Materialism*, 273).

[51] Michael Paul Rogin, *The Intellectuals and McCarthy* (Cambridge: MIT Press, 1967), 2.

[52] See Caute, *The Great Fear*.

[53] See Christopher Lasch, "The Cultural Cold War: A Short History of the Congress for Cultural Freedom," reprinted in *Towards a New Past: Dissenting Essays in American History*, ed. Bartram Bernstein (New York: Pantheon, 1968), 322-59, for a detailed discussion of "the cultural Cold War" and its impact on academic studies.

[54] Wald, *The New York Intellectuals*, 274.

[55] Donald E. Pease, *Visionary Compacts: American Renaissance Writings in Cultural Context* (Madison: University of Wisconsin Press, 1987), 245.

[56] Reichman, "Reconsidering 'Stalinism,'" 57.

[57] Cohen, *Rethinking the Soviet Experience*, 7.

Piers Gray (essay date 1993)

SOURCE: "Totalitarian logic: Stalin on linguistics," in *Critical Quarterly*, Vol. 35, No. 1, Spring, 1993, pp. 16-36.

[*In the following essay, Gray examines Stalin's position on linguistics in* Marxism and Problems of Linguistics.]

> No, no: arrests vary very widely in form. In 1926 Irma Mendel, a Hungarian, obtained through the Comintern two front-row tickets to the Bolshoi Theatre. Interrogator Klegel was courting her at the time and she invited him to go with her. They

sat through the show very affectionately, and when it was over he took her—straight to the Lubyanka.

(Alexander Solzhenitsyn, *The Gulag Archipelago, 1918-1956*, chapter 1, 'Arrest')

Go to, let us go down, and there confound their language, that they may not understand one another's speech.

(Genesis 11:7)

1

Confronting evil men, areas of human experience are often deemed sacrosanct in order to preserve them from the minds we are casting out. Thus it is a commonly held belief that Adolf Hitler was a 'house-painter'. This assertion is made in order to preserve the transcendental dignity of the concept 'artist'. The irony of the canard's refutation is that Hitler was not only a 'painter' but also an aspiring architect: a water colourist who, at one point in his early Viennese years, attempted to survive by selling paintings on postcards in the streets by day, returning to the doss-house at night.[1] In the history of black propaganda this is an interesting example of a major value-distortion: the idea of 'house-painter' as an honest occupation can snobbishly be discredited in order to preserve the lofty ideal of artist. Vegetarian dog-loving Hitler could not have become a 'house-painter' since he never did an honest day's work in his life. Except in the trenches.

The same principle applies to the following from a review in the *Times Literary Supplement* of books about Khrushchev. 'He did not express his beliefs in the way of his predecessors. Not for him the theorizing of Lenin's *State and Revolution* or the incantatory rantings of Stalin's **Marxism and Linguistics**.[2] In this we have the 'house-painter' principle preserving a valued area of human activity from contamination by evil genius: for it may be that the only incantatory rantings to be found here will be in the incantatory rantings of 'incantatory rantings': the phenomenon of high seriousness's folly is, in fact, not Stalinesque whimsy but rather a studied response to particular political questions with the Man of Steel being a lot less than loony and rather more than merely rational. Which is always where the real trouble begins.

2

With Stalin's **Marxism and Problems of Linguistics**, Isaac Deutscher confesses to being perplexed: suddenly this peculiar subject is taken up at the very moment of the Korean War:

For about five years he made not a single public utterance (apart from a few trite interviews accorded to foreign journalists; but the journalists were hardly ever admitted to his presence; they received in writing his answers to their questions). When in the anxious early days of the Korean war he chose to make a pronouncement, it was on—linguistics. In a series of letters, filling many pages

in an enlarged edition of *Pravda,* he attacked the academic school of N. Y. Marr, which had for nearly three decades been the authorized Marxist interpreter of language. Stalin, uninhibited by the scantiness of his own knowledge—he had only the rudiments of one foreign language—expatiated on the philosophy of linguistics, the relationship between language, slang, and dialect, the thought processes of the deaf and dumb, and the single world language that would come into being in a remote future, when mankind would be united in communism. Sprinkling his Epistle with a little rose water of liberalism, he berated the monopoly the Marr school had established in Soviet linguistics and protested against the suppression of the views of its opponents.[3]

Linguistics after five years' silence? What was the unpredictable Georgian up to apart from being, of course, predictably unpredictable? The incident certainly haunted Solzhenitsyn: that Stalin is found in chapter 19 of *The First Circle*—'Language Is a Tool of Production'—to be engaged with the problems of linguistics seems grotesquely appropriate in its very incongruity. The tone is Olympian condescension, observing the little monster attempting to struggle with a crushing problem: is language of the superstructure or the base?

. . . if language is a superstructure, why doesn't it change with every epoch? If it is not a superstructure, what is it? A basis? A mode of production?

Properly speaking, it's like this: modes of production consist of productive forces and productive relationships. To call language a *relationship* is impossible. So does that mean language is a productive force? But productive forces include the instruments of production, the means of production, and people. But even though people speak language, language is not people. The devil himself doesn't know—he was at a dead end.

To be really honest, one would have to recognize that language is an instrument of production like—well, like lathes, railroads, the mail. It, too, is communications, after all.

But if you put the thesis that way, declaring that language is an instrument of production, everyone will start snickering. Not in our country, of course.

And there was no one to ask advice from; he alone on earth was a true philosopher. If only someone like Kant were still alive, or Spinoza, even though he was bourgeois . . . Should he phone Beria? But Beria didn't understand anything at all.

Well, he could put it more cautiously: 'In this respect language, which differs in principle from superstructure, is not distinguishable, however, from instruments of production, from machines, let us say, which are as indifferent to class as language is.'

'Indifferent to class'—that, too, could never have been said before.

He placed a period after the sentence. He put his hands behind his head, yawned and stretched. He had not got very far, but he was already tired.[4]

Perhaps this passage is powerful because the novelist has to control his revulsion before an odious truth: nothing lies beyond the tyrant's Godly interference; not even the language of Solzhenitsyn's own contradictory act—this novel—can unironically transcend the totalitarian Communist state's Satanic Comedy. The monster at its heart (in all the paranoid megalomania of his historical certainty) will sort out the only means of rebellion against his own tyranny—the *Russian* language itself. Thus the dignity of Solzhenitsyn's indignation animates his writing, giving his voice that historical authority setting him apart from ordinary attempts to wish away the significance of Stalin's linguistic excursion, as in the following:

Was Stalin aware of the grotesque nature of this business? Did he really believe that the platitudes he enunciated constituted a fundamental contribution to knowledge? Or did he simply enjoy having all those professors and academicians jump through the hoop? Did he take in good faith the chorus of sycophantic praise that rang through the Communist World, celebrating his immortal work? By now, even in his own mind, Stalin would have been incapable of answering these questions. The linguistics affair, despite its apparent triviality, is one of the most telling episodes of Stalin's entire career. The urge to struggle, to seek out and destroy enemies, which had prompted young Soso Djugashvili to enter the revolutionary path, continued unabated in the aging tyrant. The middle-aged Stalin, like all successful politicians, advanced his career by seeking and gaining allies, by impressing people with reasonableness and tolerance. But in the end as in the beginning there was the terrible passion to destroy the 'impure' ones, be it a loyal servant . . . or a professor he had never known. . . .[5]

And yet to see all this linguistics simply as one more incident—however important—in an individual psychodrama, underestimates the phenomenon's whole wretchedness: in fact, something significant—affecting nations and their histories—is being played for by the Great Genius: so to start again . . .

. . . four letters to a total of five scholars in linguistics were far removed from any pressing practical matter. It was evidently a reflection of Stalin's amateur interest in the field, which appeared in his editing of Georgian-to-Russian poetic translation, his enquiries of Enver Hoxha concerning the Albanian language, and his questions to the Indian ambassador Menon about the languages of India. The main point of Stalin's disquisition on linguistics was to overturn the prevailing theory in Soviet scholarship since the early 1930s, the eccentric notions of the Georgian N. Ya. Marr, who had died in 1934.[6]

Returning to the sceptical Deutscher, his account suggests that the young Stalin was hardly father to the enfeebled buffoon of Solzhenitsyn's portrait: at the age of sixteen, 'only a year after leaving the Gori school, he was already publishing verses in a leading Georgian periodical';[7] a year after his arrival at the Seminary at Tiflis—the leading institute of higher education in Georgia—Deutscher reports that his literary ambitions flourished:

While he was still in the first form, Djugashvili must have made frequent half-stealthy excursions into town and got in touch with the members of the opposition. This can be seen from the fact that a poem by him was published in the Georgian periodical *Iberya,* edited by the liberal patriot Ilya Chavchavadze, on 29 October 1895, almost exactly a year after Djugashvili's arrival at Tiflis. He dedicated the verses, patriotic in character but coloured with social radicalism, to a well-known Georgian poet, R. Eristavi. They appeared under the signature 'Soselo' ('little Joe'), for the author must have been anxious to conceal his identity from the seminary authorities. His other offence was to borrow books from a circulating library in town. Apart from Georgian poetry, the masterpieces of Russian and European literature were his favourite reading. Most of all he enjoyed the three great Russian satirical writers, Saltykov-Shchedrin, Gogol, and Chekhov, whom he afterwards frequently quoted in speeches and articles. Victor Hugo's novels and Thackeray's *Vanity Fair,* in Russian translations, figure among the foreign books he read. Of greater importance to his development were popular books on Darwinian biology, on economics and sociology.[8]

One more fact about the young tyrant: the linguistic patriot was equally a realist; at school in Gori, he assiduously mastered the language of power: 'His success in learning Russian is attested by his survival in a school that operated in this language, and one fellow-pupil . . . recalls how hard Iosif worked on this, "how absolutely flawlessly he wrote in Russian, what clear handwriting he cultivated on his own".[9] On the other hand, he spoke Russian with 'a Georgian accent . . . swallow[ing] his case-endings, hoping . . . that this would cover his uncertainties concerning the mysteries of Russian grammar'[10]—suggesting a subject already aware of the linguistic act's deep resonances.

Solzhenitsyn's art argues that the man must ultimately have been orphaned by such a child as this: nevertheless his interest in literature, particularly foreign literature ('by 1896 he was caught reading in Russian translation a variety of forbidden western books, novels by Hugo and Thackeray, general works on culture and the social sciences'[11]), was a genuine factor in leading him away from the monks' control as he descended the underworld of dissidence, coming finally to rest within a socialist circle in Tbilisi, the 'Third Group'.

Having made some progress in such studies, in August 1898 Iosif joined an organization that was attempting to move beyond mere 'circle' activity to political action among the workers of Tbilisi, the so-called 'Third Group'. In undertaking this activity, which exposed him to the risk of arrest,

Dzhugashvili had need of a pseudonym and chose 'Koba'. This was somewhat pretentious, for that was the name of the hero of a well-known romantic nationalist Georgian novel . . . *The Patricide*. It is possible that Soso had been called Koba as a lad in Gori, having been impressed then by this heroic figure, but it is unlikely that he was called that in his seminary days. A revolutionary could not conceal his identity from the police by using his well-established nickname. 'Koba' was the first of many cover-names which he utilized in the following years, but the only one, apart from 'Stalin', that stuck. At least a few of his old friends still called him 'Koba' in the years of his eminence.[12]

'Koba' reinforces a sense of the young Stalin's alertness to the talismanic power of the word. Koba was not, of course, 'Stalin' but still Iosif Djugashvili, i.e. that son of his own father: of the name Stalin, there is one more story yet to consider.

Iosif Djugashvili first used the pseudonym which he made famous on 1 December 1912, when he signed an article in the Bolsheviks' St Petersburg newspaper *Pravda* as 'K. Stalin'. His biographers generally point out that the name 'Stalin' is based on the Russian word for steel and hence was meant to signify that Djugashvili-Stalin was a 'man of steel'.[13] In fact, 'Stalin' was the final version of three earlier attempts to establish a nominal identity following 'Stefin', 'Salin', and 'Solin'.[14] The orthodoxy regarding the word's shape is that Stalin was attempting to create a name which would give him an irrefutable linguistic identity with Lenin. Robert Himmer, however, offers a different explanation:

> . . . what then was the relationship between 'Stalin' and 'Lenin'? . . . [T]he answer [lies] in the record of Djugashvili's attitude toward Lenin in the years prior to the adoption of the name 'Stalin' in December 1912 . . . [F]ollowing Lenin's retreat from advocacy of insurrection after the revolutionary failures of 1905, Djugashvili became increasingly disenchanted with Lenin—a disenchantment that sprang from Djugashvili's uncompromising hatred of class enemies, his mistrust of émigrés and intellectuals, and his self-image as a man of destiny. While the émigré intellectual Lenin turned to parliamentary politics, Djugashvili continued to favor armed revolt and strove to enhance the role within the party of ordinary workers, whom he represented in his writings as the real heroic leaders of revolutionary socialism. When, a few days before his thirty-third birthday, he took the name 'Stalin,' he was proclaiming himself the truest of these true revolutionaries, the new champion of the 'hard' revolutionary creed that Lenin had once represented. 'Stalin' was an expression of Djugashvili's belief in a revolution of class war, of his self-image as its rightful hero, and of his consequent dissatisfaction with the leadership of the temporizing Lenin.[15]

On his way to becoming the Man of Steel, Iosif had realigned certain characteristics: Georgians—like Jews, intellectuals and émigrés—were deemed to be 'deficient in the revolutionary consciousness . . . essential for a real

Bolshevik'.[16] Did it then follow that the fully created hard man abandoned all the linguistic sensitivities so conspicuous in childhood and adolescence? On the contrary: the first article to appear above that notorious name

> was flawed by grammatical errors, gross stylistic awkwardness, and poor choice of words—as if written by an ordinary proletarian trying to make sense of the confusion within the party. Djugashvili's pose as an ordinary working man when he first used the name 'Stalin' expressed a belief that he, not Lenin, was the rightful leader of the revolutionary proletariat.[17]

Such dissimulation reinforces the thesis that Stalin knowingly manipulated language's immense power; it was a phenomenon over which he had complete control: creating or recreating the self and its world was simple. Nevertheless, in and of itself, language remained a matter of great significance: indeed even more ironically perhaps than Solzhenitsyn realised in chapter 19 of *The First Circle:* 'Language is a tool of production'. It was exactly that: an instrument of political power. And if suddenly he was made aware that Marxist linguistics had got into a muddle over how that should be so, then it was entirely natural that *he* should correct error and see the people right, which is precisely what he does in **Marxism and Problems of Linguistics.**

3

In the world of Stalin, if there was a problem then *somebody* must be to blame: that's only fair, after all. The whole of *The First Circle*'s Mavarino Institute—i.e. prison—in which various intellectuals toil over the elusive vocoder (the telephone scrambler) which will make sure that the Great Genius's conversations are secure from treacherous eavesdroppers is dedicated to that principle. The history of an isolated peripheral figure like Mamurin, the Man in the Iron Mask, makes the point:

> It happened that the Leader of All Progressive Humanity once talked with Yenan Province and was dissatisfied with the squeals and static on the telephone. He called in Beria and said in Georgian: 'Lavrenty! What kind of an idiot have you got as head of communications? Get rid of him.'
>
> So they got rid of Mamurin; that is, they imprisoned him in the Lubyanka.[18]

In the case of language, the idiot in charge was one Nikolai Yakovlevich Marr. He fits the insane world of Stalin's Soviet Union exactly—indeed Marr is character enough to torment one of Solzhenitsyn's hells. His dates—1865-1934—saved him from experiencing correction at the hand of the Leader of All Progressive Humanity but his posthumous reputation ultimately reserved him a place in the collective demonology. The son of an eighty-seven year old Scot and a Georgian mother,

> Marr grew up in Gerogian surroundings. He attended the Classical Gymnasium at Kutaisi, and

while at school he endeavoured to mend the 'broken' speech which he had acquired in early childhood, when immersed in that atmosphere of faulty Russian combined with Georgian which had served his parents as a medium of communication. (It appears, however, that Marr—like Stalin, who was also of Georgian origin—never quite achieved perfection in Russian stress and intonation patterns.) After successfully completing his schooling, Marr finally decided to read Oriental languages, despite attempts (recorded in an autobiographical sketch of 1927, published in the periodical *Ogonëk,* No. 27/223) on the part of both teachers and fellow pupils to dissuade him. He qualified for entry to the Faculty of Oriental Studies of the University of St. Petersburg in 1884, and embarked on the comparative study of Persian, Georgian, Hebrew, Syriac, Arabic and Turkish. Two years later, having acquired a knowledge of Semitic language structures, he was struck by an apparent similarity between Georgian and Arabic, and in 1888 he published an article on the nature and characteristics of Georgian which appeared in [a] Tbilisi paper . . . In this article, written in Georgian, Marr attempts to correlate Georgian, both lexically and structurally, with Semitic: 'The Georgian language, both flesh and spirit, i.e. in its lexical roots and grammatical conformation, is related to the Semitic languages, but the relationship is not so close as that among the Semitic languages themselves.' (A much fuller formulation was to come ten years later, in his preface to the *Paradigms of Old Georgian grammar,* under the heading 'Preliminary remarks on the relationship of Georgian to the Semitic languages' . . . which was published in 1908.)

After completion of his initial course at the Faculty of Oriental Studies (1888), Marr turned his attention to an ever increasing extent to aspects of Armenian folklore, history, literature and philology. He made repeated visits to Armenia, and in 1892-1893 participated in excavations at Ani, ancient town of Armenia near Lake Van (now in Turkey). He appears to have aroused the hostility of the Georgian nationalist Prince Chavchavadze, who took exception to Marr's discovery that the Georgian Bible had been translated from the Armenian, and that the fable underlying Shota Rust'aveli's twelfth century heroic poem 'The knight in the tiger's skin' ('Vityaz' v tigrovoi shkure') was actually of Persian origin. In 1901, in the face of some considerable opposition, he was appointed to the chair of Armenian at the University of St. Petersburg; and he was awarded his doctorate two years later, in 1903. In 1909 he was recommended for membership of the Imperial Academy of Sciences, and his election followed in 1912.

Marr's work in the Caucasus, and his numerous field studies, lie at the base of his early linguistic theories. 'All my creative linguistic ideas', he writes in *Ogonëk* (op. cit.), 'are not the outcome of work in the study. They were conceived and moulded in the course of my contacts with man and nature, in streets and market-places, in deserts and on the seas, in the mountains and in the steppes, by rivers and springs, on horseback and in trains—

anywhere but in the study.' He was particularly concerned with detecting, in the South Caucasian languages and in living Armenian, where Indo-European had overlaid the original Urartian (an idiom probably related to Hurrian, and written in cuneiform), traces of those archaic elements which could establish a link with Semitic.[19]

Fair enough—although the obsessive quality of Marr's life, his refusal to be dissuaded by teachers and students from following his destiny, is in ironic contrast to the casually arbitrary reasoning by which Solzhenitsyn imagines the World's Greatest Marxist being drawn into linguistic controversy: the whole business is actually no more than a squabble among Georgians.

> He had, in fact, chanced upon just such a felicitous concept in a completely different field, in linguistics, in connection with the recent case of Professor Chikobava of Tiflis. Chikobava had written some apparently anti-Marxist heresy to the effect that language is not a superstructure at all but simply language, that it is neither bourgeois nor proletarian, but simply national speech—and he had dared to cast aspersions openly on the name of Marr himself.
>
> Since both Marr and Chikobava were Georgians, there was an immediate response in the Georgian University journal, a gray, unbound copy of which, printed in the characteristic Georgian alphabet, lay at this moment in front of Stalin. Several linguistic disciples of Marr had attacked the insolent scholar. In the wake of their accusations he could only sit and wait for the midnight knock of the MGB. It had already been hinted that Chikobava was an agent of American imperialism.
>
> Nothing could have saved Chikobava if Stalin had not picked up the phone and let him live. He would let him live—and would himself give the man's simple, provincial thoughts an immortal exposition and a brilliant development.
>
> True, it would have been more impressive to refute the counterrevolutionary theory of relativity, for example, or the theory of wave mechanics, but because of affairs of state he simply did not have the time. Philology, however, was the next thing to grammar, and, in respect to difficulty, Stalin had always put grammar on a level with mathematics.[20]

To Solzhenitsyn, Stalin's grotesque interest in linguistics is an exact synecdoche for the multiple betrayals of language which cancerously tissue Soviet life: the phonologist Rubin ultimately identifies Innokenty Volodin from the tapes of his bugged telephone conversation as the voice warning a medical researcher about to visit Paris not to let French scientists in upon his secret discovery of a possible cure for some particularly wretched disease. Marr's ridiculous part in the novel's moral scheme is scornfully alluded to:

> 'The transitory nature and unreality of the concept are implicit in the word itself. The word "happiness"

is derived from the word that means this hour, this moment.'

'No, dear Professor, pardon me. Read Vladimir Dahl. "Happiness" comes from a word that means one's fate, one's lot, what one has managed to hold on to in life. The wisdom of etymology gives us a very mean version of happiness.'

'Just a minute! My explanation comes from Dahl, too.'

'Amazing. So does mine.'

'The word ought to be researched in all languages. I'll make a note of it!'

'Maniac!'

'Never mind! Let me tell you something about comparative philology—'

'You mean the way everything is derived from the word "hand"—as Marr would say?'

'Go to hell. Listen—have you read the second part of *Faust?*'[21]

The narrative's sustained objection, at one level, is to rationality's perversion: the phonologist Rubin's specialist knowledge means no more than the ruination of another human life. And, at another, there is a hostility to Marr's reductionism: fining language down to a single source is a shabby way of decoding life's plurality. The ultimate example of this evil is centred upon Stalin himself: everything in Russia comes down to one sadistically arbitrary jester. And so Marr deserved his place in the lunatic hells of *The First Circle*. N. S. Trubetskoi, reviewing an article by Marr, asserted that the piece should properly be examined 'by a psychiatrist. Marr's theories were worthy only of Martynov . . . a Russian mental patient at the end of the nineteenth century who published a pamphlet . . . [proving] that the words of all human languages can be traced back to the one root word meaning "to eat" '.[22] The spectre of that reductionism haunts Solzhenitsyn: Marr's work is simply another example of its evil.

Once lunacy gets through the door it proves an ample presence: Marina Yaguello devotes a whole chapter to Marr in *Lunatic Lovers of Language*—a title fairly predicting the book's contents:

> The only thing left to him by his father . . . to see him on his way was the following remark: 'You'll always be a good for nothing'. He found a father-substitute twenty years later in the person of the Arabic scholar Rosen, the only one of his teachers at the university to be well-disposed towards him, although he, just like the others, predicted that Marr would be a failure in a scholarly career. In his autobiography Marr tells how, when he succeeded after twenty years in getting his thesis on the relationship between the Caucasian and Semitic languages published, he went to seek Rosen's approval as he lay dying.

Right from childhood Marr seems to have provoked widespread hostility. He was a permanent rebel, and put everyone's back up. He clearly had a very high opinion of himself. Poor and humiliated, a fatherless child and a foreigner (although his native language was Georgian, he was registered as 'English' at school), always left out, aggressive, full of himself and revengeful, he seemed right from the start to display, at least in embryonic form, all the elements of the classic picture of paranoia: repressed homosexuality, persecution mania, and megalomania, the salient social causes of which are instances of humiliation and social rejection, especially where men are concerned.[23]

Whatever; the repressed, megalomaniac, paranoid Georgian ultimately—despite (or because of) these odds—made a hugely successful career out of two particular theories: the Japhetic explanation of language and a Marxist linguistics. The former took its name from Japhet—Noah's third son: if Shem and Ham had lent their names correspondingly to the Semitic (e.g. Arabic, Hebrew, Aramaic, Syriac etc.) and Hamitic languages (e.g. Coptic, Ancient Egyptian etc.) then what other name could be given to the speech of 'those ancient peoples who lived to the West and North of the Hebrews—principally those dwelling in the regions adjacent to the Aegean, Black and Caspian Seas'?[24] There must have been a language closely related to Semitic and Hamitic (Genesis 11:1—'And the earth was of one language, and one speech') in this geographical area which functioned as a pre-Indo-European Ursprache. As his work developed, Marr came to believe that a Caucasian based proto-language could be traced from pre-hellenic Etruscan to living Basque.

> Originally . . . —according to Marr—there was one primeval substratum or common means of human communication in the Mediterranean world, Japhetic; and the *coup de grâce* to Japhetic unity was administered by the emergence of Indo-European, which induced the process of hybridization, in itself a form of re-creation. In this way, he concludes, Japhetism had contributed, if only vicariously, to the constructive remodelling of European world-culture.[25]

Parallel to this genetic explanation of linguistic families was Marr's theory about the development of speech:

> Adopting a monogenetic approach, he conceived one common origin for all languages. This he envisaged as comprising two stages: (i) a manual or gestural (pre-phonic), which he described as linear kinetic; and (ii) a vocal or phonic, which he linked to phylogenesis, or the early formation of tribes, where an articulate form of intercommunication became essential. In connexion with the second phase, he even claimed to have identified the four monosyllabic elements which lay at the base of all future language development: [sal], [ber], [y (j) on] and [roš]; and these were allegedly uttered—in the first instance—as an aid to magic, in totemic-tribal rituals. Innumerable variations were possible (i.e. sal, zal, tsal, dal, gal, tkal, dgal, tskal, dzgal, etc.); and the eventual emergence of more differentiated combinations was attributed

to the crossing of tribes as ethnic groups began to crystallize.

Marr's views on the origin of language were essentially phylocentric (or tribal-oriented) in the first instance, and closely connected with his early field studies.[26]

But with Marr there is always another step down the explanatory ladder:

> . . . when we turn our gaze back towards the dark ages with the aim of elucidating the fundamental principles of human language . . . we are faced with a crucial and highly tricky question: which are the most primitive representations? Which is primary, the sky or the hand? Japhetic linguistics takes us back, following the laws laid down by the paleontology of speech, from the 'heavens' to the 'hand', which therefore really is the primitive word, the hand of toiling man, of *homo faber,* of this creator of the whole of our material culture, including language. The hand is the unique and natural primitive vehicle of communication, just as it is the unique tool of all production, up until the moment when this force of production belonging to *homo faber* creates substitutes for him in the form of tools of production, artifacts, and objects of material culture; and it is then, and then alone, that the role of language tool is quite naturally shifted to the tongue, which, as the paleontology of speech shows us, bears the same name as the hand.[27]

Solzhenitsyn's scornful dismissal in *The First Circle*— 'Go to hell'—of the materialist thesis that speech descended from the word 'hand' laconically brings us to the point about Marr and his theories: any assertion about correctness is manifest nonsense—the theories themselves are obviously meaningless; indeed, one might just as well go back to Genesis for a plausible account of language's origin. Marr may have been a repressed homosexual paranoid whose work ought to be examined by a psychoanalyst but that diagnosis is as irrelevant as his own theories which brilliantly demonstrate that in this peculiar area anything goes: genetic explanations can never escape the follies of reductionism. Equally, it must be said, there is nothing with which to replace them. For the other absurd fact of life is that language is random and its evolvers, sole makers and users, are unable to explain its origins other than—apparently—mythically.

Nevertheless, out of this, Marr had an ideal academic career: from humble origins and early derision, he gradually became the Stalin of linguistics wreaking revenge on his earlier critics: 'Thus from 1924 onwards, in addition to his chair at the University, he was in charge of the Leningrad Library and *six* research institutes. After 1930 when the cult of his personality began, the "Japhetic" institutions directed by Marr were quite simply named after him'.[28] He was even luckier in death. Stalin's critique appeared in 1950: sixteen years after his death; sixteen years beyond the hell of the Lubyanka. So why did Stalin bother? The answers to which question can be found in his pamphlet *Marxism and Problems of Linguistics.*

4

QUESTION. *Is it true that language is a superstructure on the base?*

ANSWER. No, it is not true.

The base is the economic structure of society as the given stage of its development. The superstructure is the political, legal, religious, artistic, philosophical view of society and the political, legal and other institutions corresponding to them.

Every base has its own corresponding superstructure . . . If the base changes or is eliminated, then, following this, its superstructure changes or is eliminated; if a new base arises, then, following this, a superstructure arises corresponding to it.

In this respect language radically differs from the superstructure.[29]

Thus Stalin *in medias res:* twenty-seven pages later we discover the source of this grotesque misconception about language as a superstructure:

> N. Y. Marr introduced into linguistics the incorrect, non-Marxist formula that language is a superstructure, and got himself into a muddle and put linguistics into a muddle. Soviet linguistics cannot be advanced on the basis of an incorrect formula.
>
> N. Y. Marr introduced into linguistics another and also incorrect and non-Marxist formula, regarding the 'class character' of language, and got himself into a muddle and put linguistics into a muddle. Soviet linguistics cannot be advanced on the basis of an incorrect formula which is contrary to the whole course of the history of peoples and languages.
>
> N. Y. Marr introduced into linguistics an immodest, boastful, arrogant tone alien to Marxism and tending towards a bald and off-hand negation of everything done in linguistics prior to N. Y. Marr.
>
> N. Y. Marr shrilly abused the comparative-historical method as 'idealistic.' Yet it must be said that, despite its serious shortcomings, the comparative-historical method is nevertheless better than N. Y. Marr's really idealistic four-element analysis, because the former gives a stimulus to work, to a study of languages, while the latter only gives a stimulus to loll in one's arm-chair and tell fortunes in the tea-cup of the celebrated four elements.
>
> . . . . .
>
> To listen to N. Y. Marr, and especially to his 'disciplines,' one might think that prior to N. Y. Marr there was no such thing as the science of language, that the science of language appeared with the 'new doctrine' of N. Y. Marr. Marx and Engels were much more modest: they held that their dialectical materialism was a product of the development of the sciences, including philosophy, in earlier periods.[30]

These denunciations follow on from a logical sequence of theoretical positions starting from an obvious question: if language is not of the super-structure where, within a Marxist analysis, must it function?

> In this respect language radically differs from the superstructure. Language is not a product of one or another base, old or new, within the given society, but of the whole course of the history of the society and of the history of the bases for many centuries. It was created not by some one class, but by the entire society, by all the classes of the society, by the efforts of hundreds of generations. It was created for the satisfaction of the needs not of one particular class, but of the entire society, of all the classes of the society. Precisely for this reason it was created as a single language for the society, common to all members of that society, as the common language of the whole people. Hence the functional role of language, as a means of intercourse between people, consists not in serving one class to the detriment of other classes, but in equally serving the entire society, all the classes of society. This in fact explains why a language may equally serve both the old, moribund system and the new, rising system; both the old base and the new base; both the exploiters and the exploited.

> It is no secret to anyone that the Russian language served Russian capitalism and Russian bourgeois culture before the October Revolution just as well as it now serves the socialist system and socialist culture of Russian society.

> The same must be said of the Ukrainian, Byelorussian, Uzbek, Kazakh, Georgian, Armenian, Estonian, Latvian, Lithuanian, Moldavian, Tatar, Azerbaijanian, Bashkirian, Turkmenian and other languages of the Soviet nations; they served the old, bourgeois system of these nations just as well as they serve the new, socialist system.[31]

But how significant is the ultimate consequence of the view that language is extra-revolutionary: if not part of the dialectic, where does it exist? The answer is—in a word—everywhere; Stalin, it seems, is, if anything, a vulgar Wordsworthian:

> Language, on the contrary, is connected with man's productive activity directly, and not only with man's productive activity, but with all his other activity in all his spheres of work, from production to the base, and from the base to the superstructure. For this reason language reflects changes in production immediately and directly, without waiting for changes in the base. For this reason the sphere of action of language, which embraces all fields of man's activity, is far broader and more comprehensive than the sphere of action of the superstructure.[32]

If Marr's first error was to associate language with superstructure, his second was to link it to social class:

> *Is it true that language always was and is class language, that there is no such thing as language which is the single and common language of a society, a non-class language common to the whole people?*

> ANSWER. No, it is not true.[33]

The reason it is not true is as follows: 'History shows that national languages are not class, but common languages, common to all the members of each nation and constituting the single language of that nation.'[34] This is a refutation of another Marr error: 'languages used by members of the same class of society in countries with identical social structures showed greater topological kinship with one another than with "different-ranking" dialects or sociolects from their native environments'.[35] Taken to extremes, on this argument there could only be—according to Stalin's interpretation—class languages. Marr's excessive zeal in serving the Party has only led to error, for the truth is that 'the upper strata of the propertied classes . . . [who] detest the people'[36] while having their own fashionable cant must draw 'all the fundamentals, that is, the overwhelming majority of the words and grammatical system . . . from the common, national language'.[37] Moreover 'Marx . . . recognize[d] the necessity of a *single* national language, as a higher form, to which dialects, as lower forms are subordinate'.[38] Misinterpreting Engels's remarks in *The Condition of the Working Class in England* concerning the chasms between the proletariat and the bourgeoisie (that the former 'speak other dialects, have other thoughts and ideals, other customs and moral principles, a different religion and other politics'[39] from the latter) Marr's confusion of superstructure with language excludes class dialects from the *whole* of a national language. Language and culture are not the same: 'language, as a means of intercourse, is always a language common to the whole people and can serve both bourgeois and socialist culture'.[40] Stalin's insistence upon a national language is the significant point and it is important to register what he is willing to forgo in order to reject the 'class-character' language formula. On the one hand:

> The mistake our comrades commit here is that they do not see the difference between culture and language, and do not understand that culture changes in content with every new period in the development of society, whereas language remains basically the same through a number of periods, equally serving both the new culture and the old.

Hence:

> *a)* Language, as a means of intercourse, always was and remains the single language of a society, common to all its members;

> *b)* The existence of dialects and jargons does not negate but confirms the existence of a language common to the whole of the given people, of which they are offshoots and to which they are subordinate;

> *c)* The 'class character' of language formula is erroneous and non-Marxist.[41]

Which means, on the other hand, that language falls outside of the dialectical process:

> The further development of production, the appearance of classes, the introduction of writing, the rise of the state, which needed a more or less well-regulated correspondence for its administration, the development of trade, which needed a well-regulated correspondence still more, the appearance of the printing press, the development of literature— all this caused big changes in the development of language. During this time, tribes and nationalities broke up and scattered, intermingled and intercrossed; later there arose national languages and states, revolutions took place, and old social systems were replaced by new ones. All this caused even greater changes in language and its development.

> However, it would be a profound mistake to think that language developed in the way the superstructure developed—by the destruction of that which existed and the building of something new. In point of fact, languages did not develop by the destruction of existing languages and the creation of new ones, but by extending and perfecting the basic elements of existing languages.[42]

The matter of linguistic change had yet again been misinterpreted by Marr and so, in a second *Pravda* article, Stalin denounced him for arguing that thought must ultimately dissociate itself from speech, evolving an abstract language, a future realm of pure concepts, the first examples of which would be demonstrated by 'the latest inventions which are unreservedly conquering space'.[43] This is a corruption of Marx's formulation that language is the immediate reality of thought, a *material phenomenon*, the natural matter of thought. Marr is thus an idealist. Language's existence outside the base-superstructure dialectic actually lies in its identification with national materiality. Stalin is willing to forgo the dialectic, base and superstructure, so long as the natural matter of thought is preserved. Thus if Marr had erred in the higher reaches of Marxist thought he had, according to Stalin, nevertheless 'conscientiously and, one must say, skillfully investigate[d] individual languages'.[44] Which, in the end, was not simply a redeeming feature mentioned in casual passage: the dangers Stalin was alert to in Marr's Marxism were not merely theoretical—indeed, as the Chinese Communists saw in their own way, the national language is absolutely a matter of practical power and political control: exactly the sort of thing to be got right.

5

The edition from which I have quoted Stalin's linguistic theories was published in Peking, in 1972. It is a reprinting of the English language text published in Moscow in 1954: 'Changes have been made according to other English translations'.[45] The obvious question here is this: why should the Chinese Government be so keen to keep in circulation a foreign language edition of Stalin's corrections of Marr's misinterpretations of Marxist linguistics? The answer to that question can be found within the constraints of Chinese 'speech reform' and the political control of individual nationalities: the true matter at hand.

In 1913, the new republic organised a conference on the unification of pronunciation at which it was decided to adopt Mandarin—educated Peking speech—as the national tongue. 'This standard form of speech, which it was hoped would replace regional forms of speech as the medium of instruction and eventually in ordinary usage as well, was given the name *Guóy*. This term is generally translated as "National Language", a literal rendering of the two syllables, but it can also be rendered as "State Language" since *guó* can be translated as "state" as well as "nation".'[46] Thus, in 1927, one wing of the Guomindang saw *Guóy* as the standard language of the entire state—that being the group deemed ethnically Chinese or related by blood to a single *mínzú*, variously translated as 'ethnic group', 'nationality', 'nation'. This would include Mongols and Tibetans. On the other hand, the left argued that China was 'made up of various nationality groups . . . which should be permitted education in [their] own language'.[47] The term *Mínzúy* — 'national language'—should therefore be replaced by *Putonghuà*—'Common Speech' or 'Common Language'— as '*an addition to,* rather than *a replacement of,* other forms of speech' (italics added).[48] Needless to say, upon actually getting power, the Communists had a severe change of heart: language policy among the ethnic minorities could continue but 'toward the regionalects, however, [it] became almost identical with that of the ousted Guomindang regime'.[49]

It was highly fortuitous that Stalin published his thoughts in 1950 on linguistics, with their radical emphasis upon the essential 'national' characteristics of a language. The Chinese translation appeared a month after the publication of the Russian original. The new rulers of the PRC, struggling to survive in the face of international hostility, had no time to mess with pluralistic niceties of regionalects or—according to Wang Li—reactionary American linguists, like Bloomfield, who held that 'the term "Chinese language" actually refer[red] to a . . . family made up of a great many varieties of mutually unintelligible languages'.[50] To deny that the Chinese have a common language was tantamount to denying the fact that they constituted a common nation.

The irony of all this is that while Wang Li saw Stalin brilliantly reworking Marxist orthodoxy to serve his own Chinese ends—namely the articulation of principles upon which uniform speech could be imposed—it appears that Stalin had the opposite end in view: namely, the legitimation of as many regionalects as possible in order to preserve the dominance of one central language—Russian. In 'Stalin on Linguistics', Ian Bedford argues that the Great Leader's real problem was the large minority, within the Soviet Union, of Turkic speakers and the spectre of a pan-Turkic movement held together, on the one hand, by their hostility to Russian and, on the other, by the strength of their own mutually intelligible languages:

The aim of . . . the pan-Turkic movement was to establish a standard literary language. The task did not seem [impossible]. One characteristic of Turkic languages has been widely remarked on, and is fundamental to any discussion of Soviet linguistic policy. The languages are 'remarkably uniform' . . . and slow to change. Only Chuvash (which so fascinated Marr) and Yakut, spoken in Siberia, are 'aberrant'. Various classifications have been proposed and . . . real differences exist, but it is possible to speak of similarity and even of mutual intelligibility among languages spoken 'in Adrianople, in the Turkish-speaking parts of Cyprus, in Chinese Turkestan [and in] Samarkand' (Lewis 1977).

If these differences were minimised (as they were in the programme of pan-Turkism) then it would appear credible to speak of Turkish (or some such name) as the second language of the Soviet Union. In a sense, so it is. But the danger was avoided. In Soviet usage and to all administrative intents and purposes, there is today no Turkish, but Uzbek, Turkmeni, Kirghiz, Kazakh and so on, the national and regional languages of the respective republics, autonomous republics, autonomous provinces (*oblasti*) and autonomous regions (*okrugi*). Each of the major languages is furnished with its separately devised alphabet, in cyrillic script since 1939-41 but unregularised with respect to all the others so that minor differences flourish to such a degree that 'the languages look far more different from each other than in fact they are'. . . . In persevering through thick and thin with the concept of a national language, Stalin forged a redoubtable instrument of policy. If it were not for Stalin, Pushkin might still be read almost exclusively in his native tongue. He would never have become the most famous poet in the Uzbek language.[51]

So much for Stalin's rantings. Hence his rejection of whatever might actually have seemed essential to any Marxist account of linguistics: now the pragmatic relation between language and land is supreme, for only by reaffirming the plurality of languages, cultures and hence nations, could Stalin ensure that Russian—his borrowed tongue, the language of administration and control—made possible the continuous central domination of Moscow over its linguistic others and their fragmented ethnic groups.

6

The seminary student certainly knew the significance of Genesis: he was particularly aware that God was the first linguist: incomprehensibility is necessary to ensure worship—the survival of the One through confusing the many. The reductionist—the one God—understands the need for linguistic pluralism if He is to survive. Solzhenitsyn had direct experience of the megalomaniac cult of personality: guilty of blasphemy, he 'was arrested and sentenced to eight years of forced labor for derogatory remarks about "the man with the moustache" made in a letter to a friend.'[52] God knows all, sees all; the Great Linguist

realised that language was a crucial area of political experience to be set in disorder. At the end of his treatise on linguistics Stalin wearily looks ahead to the ultimate merging of languages into one common language:

> . . . *after the victory of socialism* on a world scale, when world imperialism no longer exists; when the exploiting classes are overthrown and national and colonial oppression is eradicated; when national isolation and mutual distrust among nations is replaced by mutual confidence and rapprochement between nations; when national equality has been put into practice; when the policy of suppressing and assimilating languages is abolished; when the co-operation of nations has been established, and it is possible for national languages freely to enrich one another through their co-operation. It is clear that in these conditions there can be no question of the suppression and defeat of some languages, and the victory of others. Here we shall have not two languages, one of which is to suffer defeat, while the other is to emerge from the struggle victorious, but hundreds of national languages, out of which, as a result of a prolonged economic, political and cultural co-operation of nations, there will first appear most enriched unified zonal languages, and subsequently the zonal languages will merge into a single international language, which, of course, will be neither German, nor Russian, nor English, but a new language that has absorbed the best elements of the national and zonal languages.[53]

As knowing a lie as you could ask for: linguistic heaven. But of course, until then—Babel. God has spoken. He is the first linguist; the first linguist is God. Quite properly did Solzhenitsyn's instincts lead him to portray the man with the moustache hunched over his manuscript as a lunatic, even if he radically underestimated what was going on while the Great Linguist's mind devised a wonderland logic that, under the illusion of liberation, would continue to imprison his very own subjects. And so, while Saussure's point about the significance of language and the linguist—

> In the lives of individuals and of societies, language is a factor of greater importance than any other. For the study of language to remain solely the business of a handful of specialists would be a quite unacceptable state of affairs. In practice, the study of language is in some degree or other the concern of everyone. But a paradoxical consequence of this general interest is that no other subject has fostered more absurd notions, more prejudices, more illusions, or more fantasies. From a psychological point of view, these errors are of interest in themselves. But it is the primary task of the linguist to denounce them, and to eradicate them as completely as possible[54]

—is relevant, it is even more important to realise that this warning carries in turn an ironically unrecognised judgment against itself. We mislead with assumptions of correctness lodged neatly within the smooth glove of intellectual custom: the history of courageous reactions against monotone normative discourses flatters self-deceptions. The idea that linguistic plurality must *necessarily* be a good thing is, as the case of Stalin shows, profoundly deceptive: there is no linguistic reassurance against the uncertainties of life. Unfortunately, being nice to others may be feelgood in an intellectually secular world but it can equally cover dobad in the real version: God or the Devil's ways are infinite and cunning in their varieties.

The 'house-painter's fallacy' should warn us against the danger of becoming successful victims to our own propaganda. Orwell's observation that totalitarianism promises 'an age of schizophrenia'[55] is overwhelmingly confirmed by Stalin's essays. One thing is said in order to contradict itself—that is the logic of totalitarian schizophrenia: attempting to hoodwink entire peoples about the nature of their own languages might appear to be a truly grand act of folly; nonetheless it was, at the time, nothing if not grotesquely logical.

NOTES

I am extremely grateful to Christopher Hutton, of the Department of English, and to Grant Evans, of the Department of Sociology, at the University of Hong Kong, for their extreme generosity with advice and information concerning matters linguistic and anthropological.

[1] Norman Stone, *Hitler* (Boston and Toronto, 1980), p. xi.

[2] Robert Service, *Times Literary Supplement,* 15 November 1991, p. 14.

[3] Isaac Deutscher, *Stalin, A Political Biography* (Penguin Books, 1979), p. 600.

[4] Aleksandr I. Solzhenitsyn, *The First Circle,* translated by Thomas P. Whitney (New York and Evanston, 1968), pp. 97-8. Gisela Bruche-Schulz—in personal communication—informs me that Bulthaup, the editor of the translation of Stalin's articles on linguistics into German, doubted his authorship and that V. Kiparsky, in 'Comparative and Historical Slavistics', *Current Trends in Linguistics,* edited by T. S. Sebeok (Mouton, The Hague, 1963), p. 96, suggests that 'Chikobava . . . initiated the "famous linguistic discussion" '. Kindly translated by G. Bruche-Schulz from her own book, *Russische Sprachwissenschaft. Wissenschaft im historisch-politischen Prozess des vorsowjetischen und sowjetischen Russland* (Tuebingen: Niemeyer, 1984), p. 133.

[5] A. B. Ulam, *Stalin: The Man and His Era* (London, 1973), pp. 718-19.

[6] R. H. McNeal, *Stalin: Man and Ruler* (London, 1989), p. 276.

[7] Isaac Deutscher, *Stalin,* p. 27.

[8] Ibid., p. 36.

[9] R. H. McNeal, *Stalin: Man and Ruler,* pp. 6-7.

[10] Ibid., p. 7.

[11] Ibid., p. 8.

[12] Ibid., p. 10.

[13] Robert Himmer, 'On the Origin and Significance of the Name Stalin', *The Russian Review,* vol. 45, 1986, p. 269.

[14] Ibid., p. 270.

[15] Ibid., pp. 270-1.

[16] Ibid., p. 278.

[17] Ibid., p. 284.

[18] Aleksandr I. Solzhenitsyn, *The First Circle,* p. 46.

[19] K. H. Phillips, *Language Theories of the Early Soviet Period,* vol. 10, Exeter Linguistic Studies (University of Exeter, 1986), pp. 69-71.

[20] Aleksandr I. Solzhenitsyn, *The First Circle,* pp. 96-7.

[21] Ibid., p. 31.

[22] K. H. Phillips, *Language Theories of the Early Soviet Period,* p. 86.

[23] Marina Yaguello, *Lunatic Lovers of Language; imaginary languages and their inventors,* translated by Catherine Slater (London, 1991), p. 69.

[24] K. H. Phillips, *Language Theories of the Early Soviet Period,* pp. 71-2.

[25] Ibid., p. 76.

[26] Ibid., pp. 78-9.

[27] N. Y. Marr, *On the Origins of Language* (1926), quoted in Maria Yaguello, *Lunatic Lovers of Language,* pp. 174-5.

[28] Maria Yaguello, *Lunatic Lovers of Language,* p. 77.

[29] J. V. Stalin, *Marxism and Problems of Linguistics* (Peking, 1972), pp. 3-4.

[30] Ibid., pp. 31-2.

[31] Ibid., pp. 5-6.

[32] Ibid., p. 9.

[33] Ibid., pp. 9-10.

[34] Ibid., p. 11.

[35] K. H. Phillips, *Language Theories of the Early Soviet Period,* p. 84.

[36] J. V. Stalin, *Marxism and Problems of Linguistics*, p. 11.

[37] Ibid., p. 12.

[38] Ibid., p. 13.

[39] Ibid., pp. 13-14.

[40] Ibid., p. 18.

[41] Ibid., p. 20.

[42] Ibid., p. 25.

[43] Ibid., p. 36.

[44] Ibid., p. 39.

[45] Ibid., Publisher's Note.

[46] John de Francis, *The Chinese Language: Fact and Fantasy* (University of Hawaii Press, 1986), p. 224.

[47] Ibid., p. 225.

[48] Ibid.

[49] Ibid., p. 226.

[50] Ibid., p. 227.

[51] Ian Bedford, 'Stalin On Linguistics', *Canberra Anthropology*, 8 (1 and 2) *Special Volume: Minorities and the State*, 1985, pp. 78-80.

[52] Aleksandr I. Solzhenitsyn, *The First Circle*, 'About the Author'.

[53] J. V. Stalin, *Marxism and Problems of Linguistics*, pp. 51-2.

[54] F. de Saussure, *Course in General Linguistics*, translated and annotated by Roy Harris (London, 1983), p. 7.

[55] George Orwell, 'The Prevention of Literature', in *Collected Essays* (London, 1961), p. 334.

Eugene D. Genovese (essay date 1995)

SOURCE: "Stalin's Letters to Molotov, 1925-1936," in *The New Republic,* Vol. 213, No. 10, September 4, 1995, p. 34.

[*In the following review, Genovese finds* Stalin's Letters to Molotov *an important source to understanding the Soviet ruler's motivations and methods.*]

In 1969, Viacheslav Molotov released eighty-six letters written to him by Josef Stalin between 1925 and 1936. Seventy-one of those letters, which now appear in English in **Stalin's Letters to Molotov,** were written between 1925 and 1930, years of bitter intraparty struggles and the onset of the bloody collectivization of agriculture and forced-march industrialization. The Bolsheviks were building 'socialism in one country,' as hopes waned for Communist revolutions in Western Europe and China. As might be expected, **Stalin's Letters** contain only hints of the atrocities that were mounting during the 1920s and rose to a horrifying magnitude in the 1930s. No doubt Molotov winnowed his collection carefully, and he included none of his own letters to Stalin; and to add to the frustration, there are no letters for 1928 and 1934, both years of particular interest. The year 1934 saw a concerted attempt in the party to rein Stalin in, as well as the Kirov assassination. It offered a foretaste of the sweeping purges to come.

Most of the letters were handwritten. Some were written in obvious haste, others were carefully crafted. To the extent that Stalin trusted anyone, Molotov was the man, and so Stalin wrote about state and party issues frankly. Still, these few letters are only a tease. They reveal just enough to fire our fancy and then leave us to stew. And the actual texts of the letters take up less than half the pages in the book, though their value is considerably enhanced by Lars Lih's long and illuminating introduction and annotations, which contain valuable additions from other correspondence and documents.

Lih's introduction offers a penetrating interpretation of Stalin, the political leader and the man, and Robert C. Tucker adds a thoughtful foreword. Stalin emerges as a man whose acute intelligence, political and administrative talent and boundless energy matched his ruthlessness. He won the allegiance of many able party leaders at least partly because he offered the most cogent analyses of the political and economic problems of the day. These letters testify to his effort, generally although not always successful, to face the hard facts others resisted. Stalin's painstaking attention to the smallest details is particularly impressive.

The letters show, as Lih insists, that Stalin by no means turned his back on the world revolution. In particular, he continued to work for a revolutionary policy in China. A heavy dose of cynicism may well have gone into Stalin's strategic calculations, but it remains difficult to separate Stalin's cynicism from his commitment. For, much as Stalin came to identify the cause of Soviet socialism with his own person, so, by extension, did he personify the cause of world revolution. As Lih writes, 'All in all, Stalin comes out of the letters with his revolutionary credentials in good order.'

The letters support Lih's argument that Stalin worked with an 'antibureaucrat scenario' that was predicated on the Soviet Union's coming into possession of everything that was necessary to effect a socialist industrialization. Hence, Stalin regarded every setback and failure as evidence of bureaucratic opposition to, or lack of faith in, the party's program. Before long, he was attributing every failure to 'wrecking,' that is, willful sabotage by class enemies who had insinuated themselves into the state apparatus, especially economic management, and into the party itself. His endless bloody purges were not merely struggles for personal power, they were extensions of the class war.

Contrary to his reputation, he displayed a fiery temper that sometimes transformed towering hatreds and vendettas into political mistakes. The arrest and trial of 'bourgeois' specialists in 1928, for example, sent the country reeling; but it was only the beginning of a prolonged process of mutilation. In 1930, forty-eight specialists in the meat industry were made scapegoats for an industrial failure, tried in secret and executed. Trials and executions of engineers and others followed. Then and afterwards, Stalin seems to have convinced himself that the accused were guilty, even when he ordered the tortures that provoked their confessions.

Stalin saw every failure as a betrayal, no matter how loyally or even heroically the comrades on the ground may have performed. If a factory or collective farm did not meet a quota assigned by party leaders, its managers were saboteurs or men who had grown lazy and corrupt. From the beginning, factories, farms and procurement agencies could not meet quotas, follow directives and stay within the law all at the same time. They improvised as best they could and, in effect, placed the interests of their own sector above that of what the party regarded as the general interest. In 1926, Stalin exploded: 'The virtual impunity of these obvious criminals is grist for the mill of the Nepmen and other enemies of the working class. . . . This can't be tolerated any further if we don't want to be captured by these bastards who claim to 'accept' our directives but really mock us.' The party had to make an example of them. Throughout his career, Stalin exhibited an utter disregard for human life and an obsession with the 'Cause.' Like countless radicals before and after, he never doubted that the party's program served mankind, but he had little time for the lives of individual men and women.

To the day he died, Stalin remained a revolutionary leveler who despised the bureaucracy that he could not do without. Did any leader in modern history do remotely as much as Stalin to rein in the privileged, bring down the haughty and create such marvelous opportunities for the upward mobility of mediocrity? At first blush it may appear absurd to view Stalin as an egalitarian of any kind. He comes through in these letters, however, as a sincere champion of radical egalitarianism. True, he mocked the Marxist-Leninist vision of a classless society by imposing a dictatorship based upon a wide array of privileges and de facto social stratification; but Stalin hated elitist pretensions no less than Mao Tse-tung, and no less than Mao he constantly provided new and (to some) surprising evidence of a readiness to shoot those who settled into a life of comfort and privilege. He especially praised the 'moral aspect' of Lenin's exhortations to create a genuinely revolutionary leadership. Lenin, according to Stalin, 'wanted to get to the point where the country

contained not a single bigwig, no matter how highly placed, about which the man in the street could say, 'that one is above control.''

The tragedy of the Soviet experience lay right there. Stalin distrusted all elites and, most particularly, the former tsarist bureaucrats and 'bourgeois specialists' who crossed over and joined the party or at least served the Soviet state. He sorely needed them to build a socialist economy, but his distrust and his resentment easily passed into a self-defeating wrath. He could not wait to get rid of them, and get rid of many of them he did. This is not surprising. Every time something went wrong, as it usually did, the reason had to be found not in real difficulties or in the socialist system itself, the soundness of which could not be questioned, but in the subversion that one had to expect from class enemies who yearned for a counterrevolution. The sooner the party overcame its misplaced tolerance of error—that is, its concessions to a rotten bourgeois sentimentality—and the sooner it ruthlessly purged these contemptible wreckers, the sooner it could get on with the business of building socialism.

Thus Stalin railed at '"Communists" who have burrowed into our organization like thieves and have maliciously helped to wreck the cause of the workers' state.' Thus he congratulated the Politburo for 'smashing the nest . . . of bourgeois politicians ensconced in Gosplan, the Central Statistical Administration, and so on. Hound them out of Moscow and put in their place young fellows, our people, Communists.' And the devil of it was that no one could ever be sure whether responsibility for a failure did not, in fact, rest with saboteurs, corrupt officials and time-serving imbeciles.

The party planners had at their disposal the brilliant insights of high theory, but they were lacking the vital mundane information that only a market structure could provide. The managers had to fulfill the plan in the teeth of endless shortages and miscalculations, to patch things together as best they could. If the job got done—however it got done—they were on their way to (momentary) fame and fortune. If the job did not get done, they were on their way to the Gulag or a firing squad.

Armed with a first-rate mind, Stalin knew much more about the world than all except his best biographers usually give him credit for. But his intelligence and his knowledge availed little when the system revealed itself as essentially unworkable. The party's vision of a New World was sustained by dialectical reason, and its materialist philosophy could not be criticized. Its political economy and social theory were scientifically grounded. Historical law guaranteed the triumph of socialism. 'The Party makes mistakes, but the Party is never wrong': so said the slogan of communist parties everywhere. No one seemed to notice, as Stalin, a former divinity student, doubtless did notice, that the party was appropriating, transforming and corrupting St. Cyprian's dictum that 'outside the Church there is no salvation.'

Increasingly, the party of the working class became the party of the central committee, and then of the Politburo, and then of its all-wise leader: 'The Leader of All Progressive Mankind,' as he came to be called. The 'Cause' became identified with a single leader. To fail the party meant to fail Stalin, who evinced nothing so clearly as an inclination to play the God of Wrath. Under such conditions, failure was sin, as Stalin noted in outbursts such as this one, in 1930: 'There can be no doubt that Kalinin has sinned.' And more often than not, his opponents did not commit just any sin. They committed a sin against the Holy Ghost, the one sin Jesus pronounced beyond repentance and redemption.

No political leader in modern history, perhaps no political leader in world history, displayed so little human feeling. Hitler at least retained a small measure of sentimentality toward old party comrades; when he purged the Nazi storm-troopers, he wailed that the execution (or forced suicide) of Ernst Rohm made that day the most painful day of his life. If Stalin ever had such a moment (which we may doubt), he kept it well hidden. Stalin provided all the evidence that sane men need about where the belief that 'the personal is the political' sooner or later must end.

Few tyrants so thoroughly relished revenge as a dish best eaten cold. In 1930, Stalin zeroed in on L. M. Kinchuk and G. K. (Sergo) Ordzhonikidze for fouling up their assignments: 'Do people pity Kinchuk? But the cause should be pitied even more. Do they not want to offend Sergo? But what about the cause—can such an important and serious matter be offended?' When serious financial difficulties developed, he proposed his favorite solution: 'Definitely shoot two or three dozen wreckers from these apparaty, including several dozen common cashiers.'

Stalin knew that shooting people, while enjoyable, does not solve problems however much it may create favorable conditions for solutions. The solution, he said explicitly, lay in training 'honest Communists' to take over the administration of the economy and, indeed, of all social life. The building of socialism required ruthless and incorruptible Communists who tolerated no excuses and had the will (and the infallible ideology) to overcome all obstacles. Stalin, the seminarian turned revolutionary, did not doubt that man had the power to storm heaven and make himself the only god that matters. The tension in Marxism-Leninism's combination of an allegedly scientific doctrine of the inevitability of a communist victory with an extreme voluntarism was never resolved. How could it be resolved? It could not be made a subject for discussion. In all this Stalin proved himself a good Marxist and Leninist, who could plead that he was merely finding the indispensable means to effect the ends that his predecessors had espoused.

He did find honest Communists, real Bolsheviks, dedicated revolutionaries, and he did open the road to power to them, sort of. Heroic efforts impelled a forced collectivization and an astonishingly rapid industrialization that transformed a wretched country into a world power strong enough to defeat the Nazi onslaught. The costs included an unprecedented human carnage, which the Soviets and their foreign admirers justified as the price necessary to end oppression and establish the foundations for a just and equitable social order. But it was not to be. One after another, the Communist New Men and New Women, worn down by impossible demands and unattainable goals, looked very much like the old time-servers. No amount of revolutionary elan and selfless dedication could overcome the weaknesses inherent in an economy that stifled initiative and productivity and sacrificed economic efficiency to unattainable social goals.

The denouement came after Stalin's death, when a more relaxed regime had to make good on its endless promises to 'overtake and surpass' the capitalist countries. And that denouement unearthed the terrible truth that socialism did not work. The social-democratic and labor parties that promised an economically efficient and democratic socialism fared no better. They may be credited with many things, but a viable socialist society is the one thing they were never able to deliver.

For all his crimes, Stalin died in bed. He always boasted that no one could fool him, and up to a point he had reason to crow. Yet the one thing that he seemed to covet was lasting fame as the great architect of the social system of the future. He died before it all crumbled, but he was always beset by fears. Since he trusted no one in life, how could he trust anyone in death? The men around him may well have been largely his own creatures (that depends upon how you read them), but he had little faith in them. He was too serious a Marxist to cry, Apres moi le deluge, but late in life he lashed out at the 'fools' who would inherit his mantle. How on earth would the Soviet Union survive their weaknesses and their blunders?

The illusions of Stalinism long predated Stalin, and they have never completely abated. When the ramparts of heaven do not yield to human assault, and the latest version of the Cause lies in ashes, the refrain returns: we failed for this reason or that, and we were betrayed from within. Next time we will be thorough and leave nothing to chance. Whatever went wrong, the Cause will ever remain a shining beacon to future generations. That much cannot, must not, be questioned.

A master psychologist, Stalin knew, as few others have ever known, how to attach a man's strength and how to manipulate his weakness. He regarded most people as fools, and he knew how to prey upon them with supreme cunning and heartlessness. No one would ever fool Stalin, and perhaps no one, with the possible exception of Hitler on the eve of the Nazi invasion, ever did fool him. But Stalin fooled himself. He was utterly deluded about the inevitable outcome of the great struggle on which his movement had embarked. Let us pray that we shall not see his likes again.

Probably, we shall not; and his 'ism,' too, is probably over. But its mentality lives on, however much its ravages are restricted by circumstances. It has been with us since ancient times, espousing ostensibly noble ideals of human greatness, all the while driven by fierce hatreds spawned by the impossibility of every attempt at self-deification. It has taken wantonly cruel political form whenever the gnostic vision of a man-centered universe has called upon masses of men to storm heaven and become like the gods.

Nikolai Bukharin, leader of the party's right wing, criticized the Stalinist majority in the Central Committee and said: 'Doubt everything.' Stalin, the true believer, was incensed. That slogan, Stalin wrote in 1929, 'was deployed by Marx to destroy capitalism and overthrow the bourgeois government,' whereas Bukharin, by invoking it against the party's leadership, 'completely violates the Marxist method of dialectics.' Here, as always, Stalin preached 'class truth,' which was a precursor, mutatis mutandis, of what postmodernists have come to call 'situational truth.'

In dealing with his underlings, Stalin showed that he really was no fool. The Father of Political Correctness rallied to his Cause everyone from the most vile opportunist to the most selfless idealist. He knew that the opportunists, having whored for him, would whore for his enemies, and he knew that the revolutionaries, in words he once used for the Western communists, would 'swallow anything.' He knew, in short, that he could never trust the men who carried out his orders. It was common sense that dictated a policy of shooting them after they had served their purposes and replacing them with a new wave. He eyed them all warily, for idealists, being prone to delude themselves, were as likely as opportunists to ruin everything.

Credit where credit is due: a true leveler, Stalin did more than any man in world history to make sure that society constantly opened room at the top for every aspirant with a raised consciousness. He turned every political position into a lifetime job (when he did not end the job with a bullet to the head). A true idealist, he gave the world an unforgettable taste of life in a society dedicated to the elimination of all oppressive elites, all slavish respect for tradition, all concessions to what Marx called 'the old crap.'

However much Stalin's political talent and iron will attached people to his person, the best of those who rallied to him did so in loyalty to the cause that his person embodied. No matter how great his crimes, he was leading the Soviet peoples and all progressive mankind toward the promised land. He skillfully assimilated to himself the myth of the good tsar who had to contend with bad officials. Thus the people referred to the worst of the purges as the Yezhovschina—the terrible days of Yezhov, the head of the secret police—and never as the Stalinschina. When Boris Pasternak met Ilya Ehrenburg on the street and expressed his horror at the arrest of innocent people, he put it this way: 'Ilya, someone must tell Stalin!'

As for Nikolai Yezhov, who seems, from a clinical standpoint, to have been criminally insane, Stalin dispatched him as he had dispatched his predecessor when the time came to halt the latest purge. When Westerners asked Stalin about Yezhov, he replied that Yezhov was a bad man who actually persecuted innocent people. Molotov himself admitted that Stalin, just before he died, was preparing another purge: 'I think that if he had lived another year or so, I might not have survived, but in spite of that, I have believed and believe that he carried out tasks so colossal and difficult that no one of us then in the party could have fulfilled them.'

The identification of the man with the cause was greatly strengthened by the nationalistic identification with Mother Russia during World War II. Consider Marshall K. K. Rokossovsky, who emerged from the war in the highest echelons of the Polish and then Soviet defense ministries. In the late 1930s, in the purge of the military elite, Stalin had him arrested and sent to the Gulag. In 1941, with Moscow in danger of falling to a Nazi blitzkrieg, Stalin needed Rokossovsky's superior military talent, and Rokossovsky suddenly found himself in Moscow at a meeting with Stalin and the general staff. Stalin greeted him warmly, and Rokossovsky did not skip a beat. He took up his post and turned in the performance expected of him.

In his final sermon to the last party Congress that he would ever address, Stalin expounded his grand vision, exhorting his comrades to fulfill their holy obligation to the Cause. Preaching from the Revelation of St. Vladimir, Stalin brought the Congress to its feet with a prophecy that he doubtless expected would put the final touches to his bid for immortality. It has fallen to us, he exulted, to create 'a radiant future for the peoples.'

Roberta Reeder (essay date 1997)

SOURCE: "Anna Akhmatova: The Stalin Years," in *New England Review*, Vol. 18, No. 1, Winter, 1997, pp. 105-25.

[*In the following essay, Reeder examines the poetry, little known outside of Russia, written by Anna Akhmatova during Stalin's years in power.*]

For a long time now Anna Akhmatova has been known in her own country as one of the most gifted Russian poets of the twentieth century. Yet in the West she is still relatively unknown.

For many the only poems by Akhmatova that have been read and recited have been the love poems which she wrote as a young Russian aristocrat at the turn of the century. These poems have always attracted large numbers of enthusiasts, for Akhmatova was able to capture and convey the vast range of evolving emotions experienced in a love affair—from the first thrill of meeting, to a deepening love contending with hatred, and eventually to violent destructive passion or total indifference. But others before her had turned to these themes. What made Akhmatova so revolutionary in 1912, when her first collection, *Evening,* was published, was the particular manner in which she conveyed these emotions. She was writing against the background of the Symbolist movement, and her poetry marks a radical break with the erudite, ornate style and the mystical representation of love so typical of poets like Alexander Blok and Andrey Bely. Her lyrics are composed of short fragments of simple speech that do not form a logical coherent pattern. Instead, they reflect the way we actually think—the links between the images are emotional, and simple everyday objects are charged with psychological associations. Like Alexander Pushkin, who was her model in many ways, Akhmatova was intent on conveying worlds of meaning through precise details.

What is less well understood, however, is that Akhmatova was not only a poet but a prophet. While throughout her life her style remained essentially the same (except in certain works like *Poems Without a Hero* or her verse dramas), over the years themes of political and historical consequence as well as philosophical themes begin to play an increasingly important role in her writings.

Akhmatova often complained about being immured, "walled in," by critics, into a conception of her enterprise which was limited to the very early period of her career. There was good reason for this: except for a trusted few, no one knew of her poems against the Stalinist Terror. These works certainly were not allowed to be published in the Soviet Union, and only certain examples—a noted one being her famous cycle entitled *Requiem*—were published in the West during her lifetime. Yet many consider these poems to be her greatest. They convey the profound horror as well as the numbness of the average Soviet citizen in response to the vast number of arrests, trials, exiles and deaths of so many innocent sufferers.

Akhmatova could have left Russia after the revolution, as so many of her friends did, but she chose to stay, and in the process took on the burden of speech on behalf of her people. As the poet says in her poem "To the Many," written in 1922:

> I—am your voice, the warmth of your breath,
> I—am the reflection of your face,
> The future trembling of futile wings,
> I am with you to the end, in any case.

In fact, Akhmatova's poetic response to the pressure of historical events began before the revolution. Although until that time her poetry was largely apolitical, when World War I broke out in 1914 she had been moved to write a few extremely powerful poems confronting that development. While her husband, the poet Nicholas Gumilyov, insisted on combining patriotism with a conscious Nietzschean stance of the male seeking situations of utmost danger to prove his Superman status, Akhmatova reacted with a sense of dread and foreboding to the outbreak of the war. In her memoirs, she

observes that the real twentieth century began in 1914 when war broke out, for the war brought not only devastation, but revolution and ultimate ruin to the Russian land. The name of the city Petersburg, with its Germanic associations, was altered to Petrograd, a Slavic term, and the name itself became a metonymic symbol for the transformation in the consciousness of the Russian people of its conception of itself and its relation to its sometimes friendly but often hostile neighbor. Of this first year of the war, Akhmatova writes:

> At the beginning of May the Petersburg season began to fade, and everyone left. This time they left Petersburg forever. We returned not to Petersburg but to Petrograd. We fell from the 19th into the 20th century. Everything became different, beginning with the appearance of the city.

Akhmatova interpreted the war as a spiritual event. She viewed it as a portent of things to come, as God's way of showing His displeasure with the Russian people. As she grew older, she became increasingly convinced of this, and later expressed the belief that war and revolution came to Russia as retribution for the indifference shown by the intelligentsia and upper classes toward the suffering of the common people.

The war began on July 19th, Russian Old Calendar (thirteen days behind our calendar). Written the next day, one of Akhmatova's most striking poems about the war is the first in the cycle entitled "July 1914." Unlike the religious imagery in the poems in her earlier collection *Rosary,* where sacred symbolism was often employed to convey a sense of intense passion, here as in the ancient Russian chronicles, religious imagery serves to elevate the historical immediacies of the war to a more philosophical level. In earlier periods the Russian chroniclers would not only relate facts but interpret historical events (such as the incursion of the Mongols) allegorically, as a punishment of the Russian people for their sins. In this poem the themes of retribution and forgiveness through divine intercession are central. Akhmatova remains secure in her belief that Russia would be compelled to live through a terrible period, but that in the end the Madonna would protect them all, spreading her mantle over them as she had in earlier times, playing the ancient role of Woman as Intercessor between the human and the divine, and bringing forgiveness. This image refers here specifically to an Eastern Orthodox holiday, Pokrov or "Intercession," based on the belief that in the tenth century the Madonna appeared in a vision to St. Andrew the Holy Fool at a church in Constantinople and extended her veil over the people as a symbol of her protection. In the poem it is not the poet who acts as prophet, but a one-legged stranger:

> It smells of burning. For four weeks
> The dry peat bog has been burning.
> The birds have not even sung today,
> And the aspen has stopped quaking.
>
> The sun has become God's displeasure,
> Rain has not sprinkled the fields since Easter.

A one-legged stranger came along
And all alone in the courtyard said:

"Fearful times are drawing near. Soon
Fresh graves will be everywhere.
There will be famine, earthquakes, widespread death,
And the eclipse of the sun and the moon.

But the enemy will not divide
Our land at will, for himself:
The Mother of God will spread her white mantle
Over this enormous grief."

By 1916 patriotic fervor had been replaced by despair in the minds of most Russians, including Akhmatova. Her poem "In Memoriam, July 19, 1914," written in 1916, depicts the poet as a vessel of God Himself, and now she has evolved from a singer of love songs to a prophet of doom:

We aged a hundred years, and this
Happened in a single hour:
The short summer had already died,
The body of the ploughed plains soaked.

Suddenly the quiet road burst into color,
A lament flew up, ringing, silver . . .
Covering my face, I implored God
Before the first battle to strike me dead.

Like a burden henceforth unnecessary,
The shadows of passion and songs vanished from
   my memory.
The Most High ordered it—emptied-
To become a grim book of calamity.

In a poem written in 1915, the poet again takes on the mantel of the prophet:

No, tsarevitch, I am not the one
You want me to be.
And no longer do my lips
Kiss—they prophesy.

During the course of the war the evolution of Akhmatova from a poet of personal themes to a prophet of historical events was noted by the critic Sergey Rafalovich: "Akhmatova has developed into a great poet. . . . She has not changed the former thread or broken it, she has remained herself, but she has matured. Before, they said hers was a narrow circle but great. . . . She has broadened her range to include more universal themes, but has not perceived them on a lofty scale, but the same scale of themes from ordinary, everyday life."

In February, 1917, the year of revolutions, the country as a whole rose up against the Tsar—workers, merchants, aristocrats. A Provisional Government was declared, but the war continued. Another authority arose parallel to the government—the soviets, or councils of workers and soldiers, which wielded enormous power over the masses. When the Revolution began on February 25, Akhmatova was spending the morning at the dressmaker's, oblivious to what was occurring. When she attempted to go home to the other side of the Neva River, the driver nervously

replied that it was too dangerous to go over, so Akhmatova roamed the city alone. She saw the revolutionary manifestoes, the troops, and the fires set by the tsarist secret police in an attempt to keep the masses off the streets. What she captured in recollection, in "Apparition," written in 1919, was the Tsar's inability to comprehend what was happening and why:

The round, hanging lanterns,
Lit early, are squeaking,
Ever more festively, ever brighter,
The flying snowflakes glitter.

And quickening their steady gait,
As if sensing some pursuit,
Through the softly falling snow
Under a dark blue net, the horses race.

And the gilded footman
Stands motionless behind the sleigh,
and the tsar looks around strangely
With light, empty eyes.

Akhmatova spent the summer of 1917 away from the city, on her husband's estate in the province of Tver. But the overall atmosphere of horror and doom hanging over the land continues to assert itself in an evocative poem:

And all day, terrified by its own moans,
The crowd churns in agonized grief,
And across the river, on funeral banners,
Sinister skulls laugh.
And this is why I sang and dreamed,
They have ripped my heart in half,
As after a burst of shots, it became still,
And in the courtyards, death patrols.

Akhmatova was back in Petrograd when the Bolsheviks began the October Revolution. The only record we have of her immediate reaction is a recollection by her intimate friend Boris Anrep, who was saying farewell to her in January, 1918 on his way to London: "For some time we spoke about the meaning of the revolution," he writes. "She was excited and said we must expect more changes in our lives. The same thing's going to happen that occurred in France during the Revolution, but maybe even worse." Her prophecies were beginning to prove true. In verses written in 1917, the poet grieves that her latest poem, which would have been free in the past to take flight, now begs for a hearing:

Now no one will listen to songs.
The prophesied days have begun.
Latest poem of mine, the world has lost its
   wonder,
Don't break my heart, don't ring out.

A while ago, free as a swallow,
You accomplished your morning flight,
But now you've become a hungry beggar,
Knocking in vain at strangers' gates.

Despite the devastation and chaos around her, Akhmatova remained in Russia, at the same time as many of her friends fled. Her reaction to their flight from the homeland figures in her memorable poem titled "When in suicidal anguish," written in 1918. Though the speaker is tempted by the voice calling her to leave her suffering country, she remains, not realizing that the horrors she now faces are small in comparison to those that she and her companions will have to endure in the future. The first few lines may refer to the treaty in which the Bolsheviks capitulated to the Germans, ending their role in the war. (These lines of the poem were not published in Russia until recently.)

> When in suicidal anguish
> The nation awaited its German guests,
> And the stern spirit of Byzantium
> Had fled from the Russian Church,
> When the capital by the Neva,
> Forgetting her greatness,
> Like a drunken prostitute
> Did not know who would take her next,
> A voice came to me. It called out comfortingly.
> It said, "Come here,
> Leave your deaf and sinful land,
> Leave Russia forever,
> I will wash the blood from your hands,
> Root out the black shame from your heart,
> With a new name I will conceal
> The pain of defeats and injuries."
> But calmly and indifferently,
> I covered my ears with my hands,
> So that my sorrowing spirit
> Would not be stained by those shameful words.

The brutal Civil War began in 1918 and lasted three years. No one thought the Bolsheviks would remain in power for long, but by 1919 Akhmatova was beginning to feel the sense of overwhelming dread that permeated the capital.

> *Petrograd, 1919*
>
> And confined to this savage capital,
> We have forgotten forever
> The lakes, the steppes, the towns,
> And the dawns of our great native land.
> Day and night in the bloody circle
> A brutal languor overcomes us . . .
> No one wants to help us
> Because we stayed home,
> Because, loving our city
> And not winged freedom,
> We preserved for ourselves
> Its palaces, its fire and water.
>
> A different time is drawing near,
> The wind of death already chills the heart,
> But the holy city of Peter
> Will be our unintended monument.

When her husband Gumilyov returned from the war, Akhmatova asked for a divorce. Their marriage had disintegrated long before, but they had remained friends. After the revolution, Gumilyov had become an important figure in the world of art, helping writers get food and clothing, organizing poetry readings for the masses, and establishing literary circles and workshops for the

intelligentsia where he trained new poets and new appreciators of the written word. In August, 1921, however, Gumilyov was arrested on the ostensible charge of involvement in a counterrevolutionary plot. No one thought events would move so quickly—some tried to help, but their efforts were in vain. A possible reason for the arrest of Gumilyov and others was that the Bolsheviks were reacting to the Kronstadt Rebellion that had taken place during the previous March, and that they needed to demonstrate vividly what could happen to those who might have any ideas about resisting the regime. On August 25th, at the age of thirty-five, Nikolay Gumilyov was executed.

Gumilyov's death was shattering to Akhmatova: she felt somehow responsible for it, and she grieved for many years. Her horror was conveyed in a moving poem, "Terror, fingering things in the dark," dated August 27, 1921. In it she personifies the abstract feeling of terror, which leads "the moonbeam to an ax." It would be better, she says, to be executed by rifle or to be hanged on the scaffold than to have to endure the prolonged fear of imminent death, or the pain of someone you love dying. This is a theme that will be developed in Akhmatova's poems about the Stalinist terror—the sense that it is not the actual physical event of exile or execution that is most unendurable, but the anxiety of waiting, waiting for the knock on the door to take you to prison, to the camps, to your death:

> Terror, fingering things in the dark,
> Leads the moonbeam to an ax.
> Behind the wall there's an ominous knock—
> What's there, a ghost, a thief, rats?
>
> In the sweltering kitchen, water drips,
> Counting the rickety floorboards.
> Someone with a glossy black beard
> Flashes by the attic window—
>
> And becomes still. How cunning he is and evil,
> He hid the matches and blew out the candle.
> How much better would be the gleam of the barrels
> Of rifles leveled at my breast.
>
> Better, in the grassy square,
> To be flattened on the raw wood scaffold
> And, amid cries of joy and moans,
> Pour out my life's blood there.
>
> I press the smooth cross to my heart:
> Go, restore peace to my soul.
> The odor of decay, sickeningly sweet,
> Rises from the clammy sheets.

Never does Akhmatova mention the revolution directly; her attention remains centered on its effects on the life around her. One poem, "Everything has been plundered . . . ," bears a distinct resemblance to Alexander Blok's famous poem "The Twelve," in which despite the pervasiveness of looting, rape, and rout there is an intuitive feeling that this stage of great suffering will lead inevitably to a glorious dawn—symbolized in Blok's work by Christ and in Akhmatova's by "the miraculous," which is drawing near.

> Everything has been plundered, betrayed, sold out,
> The wing of black death has flashed,
> Everything has been devoured by starving anguish,
> Why, then, is it so bright?
>
> The fantastic woods near the town
> Waft the scent of cherry blossoms by day,
> At night new constellations shine
> In the transparent depth of the skies of July—
>
> And how near the miraculous draws
> To the dirty, tumbledown huts . . .
> No one, no one knows what it is,
> But for centuries we have longed for it.

A new society was indeed created in this new Soviet Union, but it was constructed on the basis of a totalitarian state in which the happiness of the many was to be determined and controlled by the few. In this new order, the role of artists and intellectuals was to be a painful one, as became increasingly clear when, in 1922, over a hundred intellectuals, including the philosopher Nicholas Berdyaev, were arrested and exiled. The poet Osip Mandelstam quickly grasped what the new role of the poet was to be in this society: "He [the modern poet] sings of ideas, systems of knowledge and state theories, just as his predecessors sang of nightingales and roses." But Akhmatova did not wish to express in rhyme the accepted theories of the state; as a result, by 1925 she was no longer published and was considered irrelevant. In 1922 the poet Vladimir Mayakovsky, the mighty Futurist and poet laureate of the Soviet State, who before the revolution had often declaimed Akhmatova's love poems, rang the death knell for her verse:

> The chamber intimacy of Anna Akhmatova, the mystical verses of Vyacheslav Ivanov and his Hellenic motifs—what meaning do they have for our harsh, iron age? Of course, as literary milestones, as the last born child of a collapsing structure, they find their place on the pages of literary history; but for us, for our epoch—these are insignificant, pathetic, and laughable anachronisms.

Poets now had to make a choice—to accommodate themselves to the new regime, or to remain consciously on the periphery. Akhmatova chose the latter. She signals this in an unpublished poem of 1921, in which she recalls the ancient name of Russia—the land of Rus:

> A light beer had been brewed,
> On the table a steaming goose . . .
> The tsar and the nobles are recalled
> By festive Rus—
>
> Strong language, facetious remarks,
> Tipsy conversation,
> From one—a risqué joke,
> From the other—drunken tears.
>
> And fueled by revelry and wine,
> The noisy speeches fly . . .

> The smart ones have decided:
> Our job—stay out of the way.

Although on the periphery, in her unpublished works Akhmatova was unambiguous in her negative attitude toward the aftermath of the revolution:

> Here the most beautiful girls fight
> For the honor of marrying executioners.
> Here they torture the righteous at night
> And wear down the untamable with hunger.

In the same year in which those lines were written, 1924, Akhmatova produced one of her most famous poems, "Lot's Wife." Turning to biblical imagery, she takes on the persona of a woman looking back—on the realistic level, to the familiar locales of her native city. But these specific places become metonymic symbols for "the past" that must be let go if one is to make peace with the future, no matter how terrifying it may be. Although Akhmatova's generation at first thought a return to the former way of life might be possible, by 1924 both the emigrés and those remaining in Russia felt compelled to admit that the Bolsheviks were probably going to remain in power indefinitely—perhaps forever—and each individual had to find a way of coming to terms with this recognition.

Lot's Wife

> *Lot's wife looked back from behind him and*
> *became a pillar of salt.*
>   —Book of Genesis

> And the righteous man followed the envoy of God,
> Huge and bright, over the black mountain.
>
> But anguish spoke loudly to his wife:
> It is not too late, you can still gaze
>
> At the red towers of your native Sodom,
> At the square where you sang, at the courtyard
>   where you spun,
> At the empty windows of the tall house
> Where you bore children to your beloved husband.
>
> She glanced, and, paralyzed by deadly pain,
> Her eyes no longer saw anything;
> And her body became transparent salt
> And her quick feet were rooted to the spot.
>
> Who will weep for this woman?
> Isn't her death the least significant?
> But my heart will never forget the one
> Who gave her life for a single glance.

The suicide of the poet Sergey Yesenin on December 27, 1925 was a shock to Akhmatova, though she had never really liked him as a person or a poet. Of peasant origin, Yesenin hoped one day Russia would become a land of agricultural communes, all committed to sharing the fruits of the earth. But the Social Revolutionaries, who wanted to make this dream come true, lost to the Bolsheviks, who saw the future of the Soviet Union in terms of accelerating industrial progress. Yesenin died a broken, drunken man. In spite of all her criticism of him, however, Akhmatova was upset when she learned the circumstances of his death: "He lived horribly and died horribly," she observed. "How fragile the peasants are when they are unsuccessful in their contact with civilization—each year another poet dies. . . . It is horrible when a poet dies." Although it cannot be proven conclusively, it is possible that her poem, "It would be so easy to abandon this life," written about the death of a poet in 1925, refers specifically to Yesenin:

> It would be so easy to abandon this life,
> To burn down painlessly and unaware,
> But it is not given to the Russian poet
> To die a death so pure.
>
> A bullet more reliably throws open
> Heaven's boundaries to the soul in flight,
> Or hoarse terror with a shaggy paw can,
> As if from a sponge, squeeze out the heart's life.

After her brief time together with Vladimir Shileiko, an Assyriologist whom she married in 1918 and from whom she separated in 1921, Akhmatova eventually went to live with her lover Nicholas Punin, a famous avant-garde art critic and professor, along with his wife and daughter in a wing of the Sheremetyev Palace. During this time, she began writing less poetry and turned instead to a study of the works of the poet whose example remained central to her own ambitions, Alexander Pushkin. In his work and life she saw parallels to her own situation and to that of other contemporary poets persecuted by the State.

By 1930, in any case, it was becoming increasingly difficult for anyone to publish at all. Stalin was now firmly in power and his control of society extended to the arts. In August 1929 there was a concerted attack against the writers Boris Pilnyak and Yevgeny Zamyatin. The condemnation of their work marked a clear turning point in the relationship between the intelligentsia and the state. Henceforth the Stalinist line would become harder, and any trace of criticism of the state would be forbidden. The increasing storm of abuse against Mayakovsky led to his suicide on April 14, 1930. During this period of collectivization, many Party members lost their jobs for showing leniency toward the peasants. The year 1933 saw another vast purge. Stalin's Terror had begun, but the majority of the population were still unaware of the extent to which it would touch their everyday lives. Nadezhda Mandelstam attempts to explain the feeling at this moment:

> There had been a time when, terrified of chaos, we had all prayed for a strong system, for a powerful hand that would stem the angry human river overflowing its banks. This fear of chaos was perhaps the most permanent of feelings. . . . What we wanted was for the course of history to be made smooth. . . . This longing prepared us, psychologically, for the appearance of the Wise Leaders who would tell us where we were going. And once they were there, we no longer ventured to act without their guidance. . . . In our blindness we ourselves struggled to impose unanimity—because in every difference of opinion, we saw the beginnings of new anarchy and chaos. . . . So we went on, nursing a sense of our own inadequacy, until the moment came for each of us to discover from bitter experience how precarious was his own state of grace.

In this situation in the early thirties, Akhmatova began translating *Macbeth,* but in the end she only succeeded in working on Act I, Scene iii, the famous witches' scene. She must have seen parallels between the murders committed by *Macbeth* and his wife to gain power and what was occurring in the Soviet Union; Lady Macbeth, the "Scottish queen," appears in Akhmatova's famous poem written in 1933 evoking the blood spilled by the Bolsheviks:

> Wild honey smells like freedom,
> Dust—like a ray of sun.
> Like violets—a young maid's mouth,
> And gold—like nothing.
> The flowers of the mignonette smell like water,
> And like an apple—love.
> But we learned once and for all
> That blood only smells like blood . . .
>
> And in vain the vice-regent of Rome
> Washed his hands before all the people,
> Urged on by the ominous shouts of the rabble;
> And the Scottish queen
> In vain washed the spattered red drops
> From her slender palms
> In the stifling gloom of the king's home. . . .

One of the first victims of the Stalinist Terror was Osip Mandelstam, who had been her dear and intimate friend from before the Revolution. Akhmatova later called the early 1930s "the vegetarian years," meaning that this would come to be seen as a relatively harmless period in comparison to the "meat-eating" years that followed, but when visiting the Mandelstams in Moscow, she felt that "in spite of the fact that the time was comparatively vegetarian, the shadow of doom lay on this house." She recalls a walk she took with Mandelstam along Prechistenka Street in February, 1934. "We turned onto Gogol Boulevard and Osip said, 'I'm ready for death.'" But when he was finally arrested for the poem in which he portrays Stalin with "cockroach whiskers" and "fingers as fat as worms," the effect on this gentle, sensitive poet was a progressive descent into madness. The secret police came for him when Akhmatova was visiting the Mandelstams in May, 1934. He and his wife were sent away to Voronezh, where in February, 1936 Akhmatova went to visit them.

When her poem reflecting this visit was first published in 1940, the last four lines were omitted. At first glance, the poem seems to be a poetic guided tour of Voronezh, mentioning not only the landscape and townscape, but alluding to the monuments and historical occurrences associated with the place—the statue of Peter the Great, who built his fleet here, and the Battle of Kulikovo, a landmark event in Russian history, which was fought nearby in 1380 (in that encounter, the Grand Prince Dmitry Donskoy defeated the Tatars after many years of domination). As the poem progresses, the mood shifts. At first the images evoke winter stillness, lack of life—crows, ice, a faded dome; but then a sound breaks the stillness—there is a roaring in the poplars, compared in a simile to the sounds of a happy event, to cups clashing together at a wedding feast toasting the joy of the poet and her companions. After the expectation created by this simile—the sense that more happy events are to follow—suddenly in the last four lines anxiety is palpably personified, as in Akhmatova's poem on the death of Gumilyov, "Terror, fingering things in the dark." In the room of the poet in "Voronezh," Fear and the Muse keep watch together:

> And the whole town is encased in ice,
> Trees, walls, snow, as if under glass.
> Timidly, I walk on crystals,
> Gaily painted sleds skid.
> And over the Peter of Voronezh—crows,
> Poplar trees, and the dome, light green,
> Faded, dulled, in sunny haze,
> And the Battle of Kulikovo blows from the slopes
> Of the mighty, victorious land.
> And the poplars, like cups clashed together,
> As if our joy were toasted by
> A thousand guests at a wedding feast.
> But in the room of the poet in disgrace,
> Fear and the Muse keep watch by turns.
> And the night comes on
> That knows no dawn.

Before Mandelstam's death, Nadezhda had experienced what thousands of other women in the Soviet Union endured during those years—hours of standing in endless lines in front of prison windows, waiting for a glimpse of those they loved. Now it was Akhmatova's turn to stand in line. Her son Lev had been arrested in the past and released, but this time, after arresting him on March 10, 1938, he had been tortured. He was sent first to the Leningrad Kresty Prison and condemned to be shot, but then the feared head of the NKVD, Yezhov, was removed, and the beating of prisoners ceased for a time. Lev's sentence was commuted to five years, and he was sent to Siberia. During the period of waiting, Lydia Zhukova, a member of the intelligentsia, had stood in one of those long lines in front of the prison. She remembers seeing Akhmatova. "Wearing something long, dark, and heavy," she recalled, "she appeared to me like a phantom from the past, and it never entered my mind that this old-fashioned lady in an ancient coat and hat would still write so many more brilliant new poems."

Indeed, Akhmatova had begun to throw herself into her work with new energy. Her "mute" period was over, as the impressions of many years of quiet suffering finally rose to the surface. When her creative powers returned, Akhmatova wrote the cycle of poems about the Great Terror that was to capture the attention of the world, *Requiem* (1935-1940). That this work is characterized by a portrayal of intense suffering did not signify, however, that Akhmatova had lost her faith and arrived at unrelieved despair. Inherent in the works of great Russian writers like Dostoyevsky is the Russian Orthodox belief that suffering is at all times an essential aspect of life, a means by which one's faith is continually tested. Never in any of Akhmatova's writings or conversations with trusted friends did she admit to doubt or lack of faith in the mysterious and often incomprehensible ways of a divine Creator.

A short prose piece, entitled "Instead of a Preface," introduces this memorable cycle:

> In the terrible years of the Yezhov terror, I spent seventeen months in the prison lines of Leningrad. Once, someone "recognized" me. Then a woman with bluish lips standing behind me, who, of course, had never heard me called by name before, woke up from the stupor to which everyone had succumbed and whispered in my ear: "Can you describe this?" And I answered: "Yes, I can." Then something that looked like a smile passed over what had once been her face.

In this great work Akhmatova fulfills her destiny as the voice of her people, taking on the persona of the Mourner in the Russian village, and of the Madonna. This poetic cycle is both universal and specifically Russian in its symbolic implications. On the universal level it depicts the suffering of women in general who, like the Madonna, must stand on the side and witness helplessly the suffering of those who are compelled to meet an incomprehensible destiny. In such circumstances, the woman can only provide comfort and prayer so that the pain and agony may be alleviated somehow. But there are specific Russian references here as well. In the first verse of the cycle the poet compares herself to a peasant woman performing the ancient Russian ritual of *vynos*—the carrying out of the dead from the house to the vehicle that will take the body to the cemetery. Instead of a dead body, however, this time it is a live prisoner, someone beloved. Another specifically Russian cultural allusion is to the icons, the sacred images painted on wood to which the Orthodox pray, and the icon shelf, placed in a special corner of the house where meals and rituals take place. At the end of this work, the poem's speaker compares herself to the wives of the *Streltsy* or Archers, the military corps employed by Peter the Great's sister Sophia, whom they supported in her unsuccessful fight for the throne and who were subsequently executed. Their wives grieved for them under the Kremlin towers, and the event was immortalized in the nineteenth century in a well-known painting by Vasily Súrikov. Through this comparison with women caught up in a famous historical event, the poet elevates the actual situation in which she finds herself, transforming the immediate event into one of universal significance:

> They led you away at dawn.
> I followed you, like a mourner.
> In the dark front room the children were crying,
> By the icon shelf the candle was dying,
> On your lips was the icon's chill.

The deathly sweat on your brow . . .
   Unforgettable!—
I will be like the wives of the Streltsy,
Howling under the Kremlin towers.

In another poem not included in *Requiem,* a poem written in 1939, Akhmatova compares her speaker to another Súrikov painting, one depicting the Boyarina Morozova, a seventeenth-century noblewoman in a sleigh, in chains, being taken into exile for her rebellion against the reforms being introduced into the Orthodox church. The poem also alludes to Viy, the chief of gnomes, whose eyelids reach to the ground (the Gogol story "Viy" contains such a creature):

I know I can't move from this place.
Because of the weight of the eyelids of Viy.
Oh, if only I could suddenly throw myself back
Into some sort of seventeenth century.

On Trinity Eve to stand in church
With a fragrant branch of birch,
To drink of sweet mead
With the Princess Morozova.

And then at twilight in the sleigh,
To sink in the dingy snow.
What mad Súrikov
Will paint my last journey?

In some of the poems in *Requiem,* there are allusions to Tsarskoye Selo, the lovely area near Petersburg where Akhmatova grew up. The town is represented by the poet as symbolic of the womb-like existence of the upper classes before the revolution, a time when they attempted to shut themselves off from the sufferings of the people; reflecting on this milieu, the speaker comes to regard her earlier self as a "gay little sinner":

You should have been shown, you mocker,
Minion of all your friends,
Gay little sinner of Tsarskoye Selo,
What would happen in your life—
How three-hundredth in line, with a parcel,
You would stand by the Kresty prison,
Your fiery tears
Burning through the New Year's ice.
Over there the prison poplar bends,
And there's no sound—and over there how many
Innocent lives are ending now. . . .

Other less-known poems written at this time express Akhmatova's pervasive sense of terror and grief. In the simple but powerful quatrain, "And I am not at all a prophet," for example, the simple image of prison keys brings into focus a network of ominous associations linked with the Stalinist terror—associations centered on arrest, exile, and death. Here the poet disowns her claim to be a prophet:

And I am not at all a prophet,
My life is pure as a stream.
I simply don't feel like singing
To the sound of prison keys.

In another unpublished work, "Imitation from the Armenian," Akhmatova pretends merely to be presenting a variation on a theme, reworking a poem by someone else. But the theme of the original (a poem by the Armenian poet H. Tumanjan) has been chosen with great care, and its theme coincides with that of other poems by Akhmatova written during the Terror. Here once again, the vulnerable female, in this case an innocent ewe, witnesses the slaughter of a loved one:

I will appear in your dreams as a black ewe.
On withered, unsteady legs
I will approach you, begin to bleat, to howl:
"Padishah, have you supped daintily?
You hold the universe, like a bead,
You are cherished by Allah's radiant will . . .
And was he tasty, my little son?
Did he please you, please your children?"

One of Akhmatova's most powerful responses to the Terror is her poem "Stanzas" (written in 1940 but not published in the Soviet Union until 1989), in which she indirectly addresses Stalin himself. She enumerates infamous figures in Russian history who have lived in the Kremlin and implies that the leader now in residence there is living up to and even surpassing his predecessors in the enormity of his cruelty. The poem addresses a "Streltsy" or "Archer" moon—which might refer to late winter (associated the astrological sign Sagittarius, the Archer), or to the Streltsy corps rebellion against Peter the Great mentioned earlier, or to both. There are allusions here to tsars like Boris Godunov, the various Ivans, and Dmitry, the Pretender to the Russian throne at the beginning of the seventeenth century who, in attempting to capture Russia with the aid of the Catholic Poles, had alienated the Russian people:

Archer Moon. Beyond the Moscow River. Night.
Like a religious procession the hours of Holy
   Week go by.
I had a terrible dream. Is it possible
That no one, no one, no one can help me?

You had better not live in the Kremlin, the
   Preobrazhensky Guard was right;
The germs of the ancient frenzy are still
   swarming here:
Boris Godunov's wild fear, and all the Ivans'
   evil spite,
And the Pretender's arrogance—instead of the
   people's rights.

In another unpublished poem, "Why did you poison the water?" (1935), the poet complains that instead of being rewarded for staying in her motherland, she is being punished by having her freedom taken away:

Why did you poison the water
And mix dirt with my bread?
Why did you turn the last freedom
Into a den of thieves?
Because I didn't jeer
At the bitter death of friends?
Because I remained true

To my sorrowing motherland?
So be it. Without hangman and scaffold
A poet cannot exist in the world.
Our lot is to wear the hair shirt,
To walk with a candle and to wail.

The implications of the hair shirt and walking with a candle as penance become clearer in Akhmatova's poem on Dante. While Pushkin turned to the Roman poet Ovid as the archetype of the poet in exile, Akhmatova turned to Dante, whom she and Mandelstam were both reading in the thirties. Like the Pushkin poem on Ovid, Akhmatova's work is a thinly disguised reflection on the dignity a poet must retain no matter what external conditions are tormenting him—whether it be the political regime of fourteenth-century Florence or that of twentieth-century Leningrad. After being forced to leave Florence in 1302, Dante was offered the possibility of returning under condition of a humiliating public repentance, which he rejected. He refused to walk "with a lighted candle" in a ritual of repentance:

Dante

Il mio bel San Giovanni

—Dante

Even after his death he did not return
To his ancient Florence.
To the one who, leaving, did not look back,
To him I sing this song.
A torch, the night, the last embrace,
Beyond the threshold, the wild wail of fate.
From hell he sent her curses
And in paradise he could not forget her—
But barefoot, in a hairshirt,
With a lighted candle he did not walk
Through his Florence—his beloved,
Perfidious, base, longed for....

One of those who had gone into voluntary exile abroad after the revolution was Marina Tsvetayeva. She and Akhmatova had never met, but in the 1910s Tsvetayeva had written a series of adoring poems to Akhmatova, calling her the "Muse of Lament." She had spent many years in Prague and Paris, but in 1937 her husband, Sergey Efron, was implicated in the murder of a Western official by the Soviet secret police and fled to the Soviet Union. Two years later Tsevtayeva and her son followed, joining Efron and her daughter, who had returned earlier. The regime turned on the family, arresting her husband and daughter. Tsvetayeva herself continued to live on a meager sum from a job as a translator which Pasternak had obtained for her. She asked a friend of Akhmatova's to arrange for a meeting between them. The meeting took place in 1940; in March of that year, Akhmatova had written a poem to Tsvetayeva, but she did not read it to her. There is an allusion in the poem to the Marinka Tower—the Kremlin tower in the town of Kolomna near Moscow, a town where Akhmatova sometimes spent the summer during the nineteen-thirties. According to legend, this tower was the site of the incarceration of Marina Mnishek, who had the same first name as Tsvetayeva.

She was the aristocratic Polish wife of Dmitry, the seventeenth-century Pretender to the Russian throne:

Belated Reply

My white-handed one, dark princess
                    —M. Ts.

Invisible, double, jester,
You who are hiding in the depths of the bushes,
The one crouching in a starling house,
The one flitting on the crosses of the dead,
The one crying from the Marinka Tower:
"I have come home today,
Native fields, cherish me
Because of what happened to me.
The abyss swallowed my loved ones,
The family home has been plundered."
We are together today, Marina,
Walking through the midnight capital,
And behind us there are millions like us,
And never was a procession more hushed,
Accompanied by funeral bells
And the wild Moscow moans
Of a snowstorm erasing all traces of us.

No one knows what the two poets discussed at their meeting—two women so very different in their attitudes toward life and their conceptions of poetry: one a product of the muted elegance of Petersburg, expressing her emotion through verse distinguished by restraint, and the other reflecting the noisy bustle of Moscow, declaring her feelings in writings charged with raw emotion. Not having read Akhmatova's unpublished poems from the nineteen-twenties and thirties, Tsvetayeva assumed that Akhmatova had remained fixed in the style and themes of her early period, and in her diary she was critical of Akhmatova's verse. They met behind the closed door of Akhmatova's room in the apartment of the poet's friend Nina Olshanskaya. Later on, during the war, Tsvetayeva was evacuated and ended up in Yelabuga, a town near Kazan, where she could find no work. On the afternoon of August 31, 1941, she was found hanging from a hook inside the entrance of her hut.

Along with many other artistic figures such as Shostakovich, Akhmatova herself was evacuated during the war to Central Asia, where she lived for several years in Tashkent. On the way there she learned about Tsvetayeva's suicide. In "Over Asia—the mists of spring," written on June 24, 1942, Akhmatova included the following lines alluding to her sense of the predicament they shared:

I've earned this gray crown,
And my cheeks, scorched by the sun,
Frighten people with their swarthiness.
But the end of my pride is near:
Like that other one—Marina the sufferer,
I will have to drink of emptiness.

As arrest after arrest intruded on the lives of those around her, around 1940 Akhmatova wrote that she wished emphatically to cast a vote in favor of something positive—not something extraordinary, merely a return to an ordinary situation in which a door could once again be seen as nothing more than a door:

> And here, in defiance of the fact
> That death is staring me in the eye—
> Because of your words
> I am voting *for:*
> For a door to become a door,
> A lock—a lock once more,
> For this morose beast within my breast
> To become a heart. But the thing is,
> That we are all fated to learn
> What it means not to sleep for three years,
> What it means to find out in the morning
> About those who have died in the night.

At the end of the nineteen-forties, when the situation was unchanged, Akhmatova wrote "The Glass Doorbell," in which the glass doorbell performs a function similar to that of the lock as a focus of terror:

> The glass doorbell
> Rings urgently.
> Is today really the date?
> Stop at the door,
> Wait a little longer,
> Don't touch me,
>   For God's sake!

In keeping with this persisting sense of anxiety, on August 14, 1946 the Central Committee of the Communist Party passed a Resolution condemning the journals *Zvezda* and *Leningrad* for publishing the works of Akhmatova and Zoshchenko. As Churchill was to observe, the iron curtain had been rung down earlier that year by Stalin, and the Resolution was a symbolic act confirming this. A few weeks later, on September 4th, Akhmatova and Zoshchenko were expelled from the Union of Writers. In his speech that evening to the Leningrad branch of the Union, Andrey Zhdanov, Secretary of the Central Committee, said: "What positive contribution can Akhmatova's work make to our young people? It can only sow despondency, spiritual depression, pessimism, and the desire to walk away from the questions of public life." After her expulsion, and for many years thereafter, Akhmatova retained a few loyal friends, including Pasternak, who helped her and supported her both spiritually and financially; but most of the people she had known avoided her. She expresses her profound state of alienation in her poem "Prologue," written sometime in the nineteen-fifties, in which she presents herself as a leper:

> Not with the lyre of someone in love
> Do I try to captivate people—
> A leper's rattle
> Sings in my hand.
> You will have ample time to exclaim
> And curse and howl.
> I will teach all the "courageous ones"
> To shy away from me.
> I didn't look for any return,
> And glory I didn't expect,

> I have lived for thirty years
> Under the wing of death.

Akhmatova's son Lev also suffered from the effects of the Resolution. Released from the camps to fight in the war, he had taken part in the capture of Berlin. He was allowed to return to Leningrad after the war had ended, but was arrested again in November, 1949 and sentenced to ten years in a camp in Siberia. It was around this time that Akhmatova wrote a series of short poems as part of a cycle entitled "Shards"—as if to suggest that the individual poems were like fragments of an ancient vessel. She begins the cycle with an epigraph, a phrase taken (and misquoted slightly) from Joyce's *Ulysses:* "You cannot leave your mother an orphan." In the brief quatrain serving as the second poem of the cycle, Akhmatova contrasts the various verbal definitions that may be applied to a single person—in this case, in the biographical subtext, Lev Gumilyov. For the regime he bears the signifier "rebel," but for Akhmatova he is designated by another, more personal, name:

> How well he's succeeded, this fierce debater,
> All the way to the Yenisey plains . . .
> To you he's a vagabond, rebel, conspirator—
> To me he is—an only son.

The West knew little of Akhmatova's life or her works written during the nineteen-forties and fifties. Many thought she had stopped writing verse altogether. By not allowing her to be published for so long—except for a book in 1940 that was immediately confiscated and some poems which were permitted to appear during the war— Stalin had condemned Akhmatova to silence, at least to Western readers. She expresses her sense of this choking silence in part V of "Shards," in which, without mentioning him directly, she compares Stalin to a butcher who had hung her (like Marina Tsvetayeva) "on a bloody hook":

> You raised me up, like a slain beast
> On a bloody hook,
> So that sniggering, and not believing,
> Foreigners wandered in
> And wrote in their respectable papers
> That my incomparable gift had died out,
> That I had been a poet among poets,
> But my thirteenth hour had struck.

Akhmatova's lament for her imprisoned son is heard at the end of one of her greatest works, *Poem without a Hero.* It is a long narrative poem, in a style more reminiscent of the complex opaqueness and erudite allusions of the Symbolists at the beginning of the century than representative of Akhmatova's characteristically direct assertions seizing on metonymic symbols from everyday life. In this work the poet looks back to the period before World War I, to the year 1913, when she and her friends had hidden in the cellars of cabarets, devoting themselves to a life of pleasure while the common people suffered. The Epilogue takes place on a white night of June 24, 1942, with Leningrad left in ruins. The text is chanted in the voice of the author—seven thousand kilometers away from the scene, in evacuation in Tashkent. In this Epilogue, Akhmatova's son is depicted as her double, and death takes the form of a Noseless Slut:

> And from behind barbed wire,
> In the very heart of the taiga—
> I don't know which year—
> Having become a heap of "camp dust,"
> Having become a terrifying fairy tale,
> My double goes to the interrogation.
> And then he returns from the interrogation,
> With the two emissaries from the Noseless Slut
> Assigned to stand guard over him.
> And even from here I can hear—
> Isn't it miraculous!—
> The sound of my own voice:
> I paid for you in cash.
> For exactly ten years I lived under the gun,
> Glancing neither to the left nor to the right.
> And after me came rustling ill repute.

There are several stanzas thought to be conceived for possible inclusion in *Poem without a Hero* but not included in the text. In one of these the poet identifies herself and other women suffering during the Stalinist Terror with the ancient heroines of Troy—Hecuba, queen of Troy, who looked on helplessly as her dear son, the hero Hektor, died, and the Trojan princess Cassandra, who was condemned to know the future but whose fate it was to have her prophecies ignored:

> Sealing our bluish lips,
> Mad Hecubas
> And Cassandras from Chukloma,
> We roar in silent chorus
> (We, crowned with disgrace):
> "We are already on the other side of hell".…

But finally, on March 5, 1953 an event occurred that changed the life of Akhmatova and millions of others in the Soviet Union: Joseph Stalin died. Not long afterward, in a closed session of the Twentieth Party Congress that took place in February, 1956, the new First Secretary of the Communist Party, Nikita Khrushchev, denounced Stalin as a cruel, bloodthirsty tyrant. The "Thaw" had begun. While the Thaw certainly did not fulfill all the hopes of the intelligentsia or the people at large, it did at least mean that the harshest aspects of the reign of Terror were ended, and there was a perceptible loosening of the iron rule of the former regime. Lev Gumilyov, Akhmatova's son, was released in May, 1956, and her own works went into circulation again, though it was not until 1958 that a whole collection of her writings would appear.

In 1957, unsure when—or whether—her works would engage a wide audience again, Akhmatova wrote the poem "They will forget?—How astonishing!" It was her equivalent of Horace's "Exegi monumentum"—a poem imitated by Pushkin—in which the poet asserts that while he may be persecuted and unappreciated in his own time, his spiritual legacy, in the form of his works, will be eternal. In this poem Akhmatova turns to an ancient mythical image of death followed by certain rebirth—the image of the phoenix, symbolic of the everlasting nature of verse:

> They will forget?—How astonishing!
> They forgot me a hundred times,
> A hundred times I lay in the grave,
> Where, perhaps, I am today.
> But the Muse, both deaf and blind,
> Rotted in the ground, like grain,
> Only, like the phoenix from the ashes,
> To rise into the blue ether again.

Although Akhmatova spent the last years of her life under the somewhat looser regime of Khrushchev, she never stopped writing about his feared predecessor, and sometime around 1962 she addressed a poem "To the Defenders of Stalin." These defenders are placed in a long historical line of those who supported the despots, who tormented the innocent:

> There are those who shouted: "Release
> Barabbas for us on this feast,"
> Those who ordered Socrates to drink poison
> In the bare, narrow prison.
>
> They are the ones who should pour this drink
> Into their own innocently slandering mouths,
> Those sweet lovers of torture,
> Experts in the manufacture of orphans.

A decade earlier, in 1950, hoping to please Stalin so that he would free her son, Akhmatova had written a cycle of poems, "In Praise of Peace," simple poems with a clear message praising the victory of Russia in the war. Despite this effort on her part, her son remained a prisoner in the camps. These poems in this group were written in the officially-sanctioned style of Socialist Realism, and they include the kinds of trite phrases found in hundreds of poems produced during the Stalinist period. The poem entitled "In the Pioneer Camp," for instance, ends with the lines: ". . . There the children marched by with their banners / And the Motherland herself, admiring them, / Inclined her invisible brow toward them." In a poem called "No, we didn't suffer together in vain," written later (in 1961, five years before her death), Akhmatova seems implicitly to refer to this uncomfortable episode in her life. And yet in her own eyes, throughout this grim period when she felt compelled to make some compromises, she retained her inner freedom even as she outwardly groveled before the "bloody puppet-executioner." She had chosen to stay in her country—and she suffered for it, in many ways; but in the end she affirmed her decision to share this appalling epoch with her own people:

> No, we didn't suffer together in vain,
> Without hopes of even drawing a breath.
> We took an oath, we voted—
> And quietly followed our path.
> Not in vain did I remain pure,
> Like a candle before the Lord,
> Groveling with you at the feet
> Of the bloody puppet-executioner.

No, not under the vault of alien skies
And not under the shelter of alien wings—
I was with my people then,
There, where my people, unfortunately, were.

FURTHER READING

Biography

Deutscher, Isaac. *Stalin: A Political Biography*. Second edition. New York: Oxford University Press, 1967, 661 p.
    Focuses on Stalin's political life.

McNeal, Robert H. *Stalin: Man and Ruler*. Hampshire and London: Macmillan Press, 1988, 389 p.
    Examines Stalin's life and work using sources rarely available outside the former Soviet Union.

Trotsky, Leon. *Stalin: An Appraisal of the Man and His Influence*. Revised edition. Edited and translated by Charles Malamuth. New York: Stein and Day, 1967, 516 p.
    Seminal biography by Stalin's close associate and sometime enemy Trotsky that includes an introduction by Bertram D. Wolfe.

Tucker, Robert C. *Stalin as Revolutionary, 1879-1929: A Study in History and Personality*. New York: W. W. Norton and Company, 1973, 517 p.
    Presents a "psychohistorical" analysis of Stalin's personal and professional life, focusing on the transformation of individual personality during periods of crisis, such as Stalin's rise to power.

Criticism

Conquest, Robert. *The Great Terror: A Reassessment*. New York: Oxford University Press, 1990, 570 p.
    Updates an earlier publication, *The Great Terror*, based on documents and information revealed after the fall of the Soviet Union about Stalin's most violent tyranny in the 1930s.

Daniels, Robert V., ed. *The Stalin Revolution: Foundations of Soviet Totalitarianism*. Second edition. Lexington, Mass.: D. C. Heath and Company, 1972, 233 p.
    Collection of essays on Soviet ideology during Stalin's rule by major thinkers on the subject, including Stalin, Leon Trotsky, and Nikita Khrushchev.

Davies, R. W. "Peaches from Our Tree." *London Review of Books* 17, No. 17 (7 September 1995): 20.
    Reviews *Stalin's Letters to Molotov, 1925-1936*.

Kemp-Welch, A. *Stalin and the Literary Intelligentsia, 1928-39*. Hampshire and London: Macmillan Press, 1991, 338 p.
    Examines Stalin's policies about, effect on, and representation in Soviet literature during the crucial years of his rule.

Kern, Gary. "Solzhenitsyn's Portrait of Stalin." *Slavic Review* 33, No. 1 (March 1974): 1-22.
    Discusses the creative and political problems encountered by Alexander Solzhenitsyn when he presented a direct attack on Stalin in his novel *The First Circle*.

Lewis, Jonathan, and Phillip Whitehead. *Stalin: A Time for Judgement*. London: Thames Methuen, 1990, 254 p.
    Attempts to discover the wide-reaching effects of Stalinism in post-Cold War Russia.

Lipson, Leon. "Stalin's Style." *Yale Review* 70, No. 4 (Summer 1981): 500-05.
    Examines Stalin's writing style, calling it "curiously formal" and "intricately patterned."

Lowenthal, Richard. "Stalin's Testament." *The Twentieth Century* CLIII, No. 913 (March 1953): 180-94.
    Argues that the leaders of the Russian Revolution created the first "permanent revolution," the phenomenon of continued political crisis without periods of stability.

Luck, David. "A Psycholinguistic Approach to Leader Personality: Imagery of Aggression, Sex, and Death in Lenin and Stalin." *Soviet Studies* XXX, No. 4 (October 1978): 491-515.
    Psychoanalyzes several twentieth-century political figures, including Stalin and Lenin, as leaders, concluding that "in important historical cases data were available for psychological comprehension and deathly-aggression prediction well before the attainment of political power."

Marsh, Rosalind. *Images of Dictatorship: Portraits of Stalin in Literature*. London and New York: Routledge, 1989, 267 p.
    Explores Russian and European writers' attempts to come to terms with the aftermath of Stalinism in their fiction.

Medvedev, Roy A. *On Stalin and Stalinism*. Translated by Ellen de Kadt. Oxford and New York: Oxford University Press, 1979, 205 p.
    Posthumous examination of Stalinism by an eminent Soviet historian.

Rancour-Laferriere, Daniel. "From Incompetence to Satire: Voinovich's Image of Stalin as Castrated Leader of the Soviet Union in 1941." *Slavic Review* 50, No. 1 (Spring 1991): 36-47.
    Psychoanalyzes Vladimir Voinovich's satiric portrayal of Stalin in *Zhizn' i neobychainye prikliucheniia soldata Ivana Chonkina: roman-anekdot v piati chastiakh*.

Struve, Gleb. *Russian Literature under Lenin and Stalin, 1917-1953*. Revised edition. Norman, Okla.: University of Oklahoma Press, 1971, 454 p.
    Comprehensive survey of literature written from the Russian Revolution to the death of Stalin.

Tucker, Robert C. *Stalin in Power: The Revolution from Above, 1928-1941.* New York and London: W. W. Norton and Company, 1990, 707 p.

Examines the notion of the "revolution from above"— the continuing Soviet revolution initiated and directed by the state and supported from below by the masses—and the place of Stalin's collectivization.

Volkogonov, Dmitri. *Stalin: Triumph and Tragedy.* Edited and translated by Harold Shukman. New York: Grove Weidenfeld, 1988, 642 p.

Examination of the Stalin years by a Colonel General in the Soviet government.

William Strunk, Jr.

1869–1946

American educator, editor, and author.

INTRODUCTION

Strunk is the author of *The Elements of Style*, known as "the little book" of English grammar. Despite its slight size—only forty-three pages—it has remained a useful tool for students of English composition for decades. E. B. White, a former student of Strunk's, revised and updated the book in 1935 and termed *The Elements of Style* Strunk's *parvum opus*.

Biographical Information

Strunk was born on 1 July 1869, in Cincinnati, Ohio. He attended the University of Cincinnati and received his undergraduate degree in 1890. He became an instructor of mathematics at the Rose Polytechnic Institute in Terre Haute, Indiana but left to pursue graduate studies in English literature. After earning his doctorate at Cornell University in 1896, he studied at the University of Paris in 1898. A year later he returned to Cornell and became an instructor of English literature. During this time he edited several books on English literature and developed an interest in writing a handbook on English grammar derived from his experience with undergraduate students. Privately printed in 1918, *The Elements of Style* garnered critical and popular attention for Strunk. Becoming a full professor in 1909, he remained at Cornell until his retirement in 1937. During his career he was recognized not only as the author of *The Elements of Style*, but also as a respected editor of Shakespearean literature. He died on 26 September 1946.

Major Works

A treatise on the rules of English usage and the principles of composition, *The Elements of Style* is considered the major achievement of Strunk's career. During his years of teaching English literature at Cornell University, he noted that his students often abused certain rules of composition and grammar. In 1918, he self-published a handbook meant to address those abuses, *The Elements of Style*. Referred to as "the little book," it was only forty-three pages long; despite its small size, it soon became an essential handbook for English composition classes throughout the country. Revised and updated by American author E. B. White in 1935, White classified *The Elements of Style* as Strunk's "attempt to cut the vast tangle of English rhetoric down to size and write its rules and principles on the head of a pin."

Critical Reception

The Elements of Style has been praised as an effective tool for writers and an essential handbook for students of English grammar and composition. Critics laud Strunk's wit and engaging style, and they deem his attention to the rules of grammar comforting. For decades the book has remained a popular and critical success. The continuing appeal of the "little book" was explained by White, who wrote, "I still find the Strunkian wisdom a comfort, the Strunkian humor a delight, and the Strunkian attitude toward right-and-wrong a blessing undisguised."

PRINCIPAL WORKS

The Elements of Style (handbook) 1918; revised and updated by E. B. White, 1935
English Metres (handbook) 1922
The Elements and Practice of Composition [with Edward A. Tenney] (handbook) 1935

CRITICISM

E. B. White (essay date 1957)

SOURCE: "William Strunk," in *Essays of E. B. White*, Harper & Row, Publishers, 1977, pp. 256-61.

[*In the following essay, which was originally published in 1957, White offers personal recollections of Strunk and praises* The Elements of Style *for its brevity and significance.*]

AUTHOR'S NOTE. Soon after this piece about Professor Strunk appeared in *The New Yorker*, a publisher asked me to revise and amplify ***The Elements of Style*** in order that it might be reissued. I agreed to do this and did it, but the job, which should have taken about a month's time, took me a year. I discovered that for all my fine talk I was no match for the parts of speech—was, in fact, over my depth and in trouble. Not only that, I felt uneasy at posing as an expert on rhetoric, when the truth is I write by ear, always with difficulty and seldom with any exact notion of what is taking place under the hood.

The Strunk book, which is a "right and wrong" book, arrived on the scene at a time when a wave of reaction was setting in against the permissive school of rhetoric, the Anything Goes school where right and wrong do not exist and there is no foundation all down the line. The little book climbed on this handy wave and rode it in.

It was during the permissive years that the third edition of Webster's *New International Dictionary* was being put together, along new lines of lexicography, and it was Dr. Gove, the head man, who perhaps expressed the whole thing most succinctly when he remarked that a dictionary "should have no traffic with . . . artificial notions of correctness or superiority. It must be descriptive and not prescriptive." This approach struck many people as chaotic and degenerative, and that's the way it struck me. Strunk was a fundamentalist; he believed in right and wrong, and so, in the main, do I. Unless someone is willing to entertain notions of superiority, the English language disintegrates, just as a home disintegrates unless someone in the family sets standards of good taste, good conduct, and simple justice.

Turtle Bay, July 15, 1957

Mosquitoes have arrived with the warm nights, and our bedchamber is their theater under the stars. I have been up and down all night, swinging at them with a face towel dampened at one end to give it authority. This morning I suffer from the light-headedness that comes from no sleep—a sort of drunkenness, very good for writing because all sense of responsibility for what the words say is gone. Yesterday evening my wife showed up with a few yards of netting, and together we knelt and covered the fireplace with an illusion veil. It looks like a bride. (One of our many theories is that mosquitoes come down chimneys.) I bought a couple of adjustable screens at the hardware store on Third Avenue and they are in place in the windows; but the window sashes in this building are so old and irregular that any mosquito except one suffering from elephantiasis has no difficulty walking into the room through the space between sash and screen. (And then there is the even larger opening between upper sash and lower sash when the lower sash is raised to receive the screen—a space that hardly ever occurs to an apartment dweller but must occur to all mosquitoes.) I also bought a very old air-conditioning machine for twenty-five dollars, a great bargain, and I like this machine. It has almost no effect on the atmosphere of the room, merely chipping the edge off the heat, and it makes a loud grinding noise reminiscent of the subway, so that I can snap off the lights, close my eyes, holding the damp towel at the ready, and imagine, with the first stab, that I am riding in the underground and being pricked by pins wielded by angry girls.

Another theory of mine about the Turtle Bay mosquito is that he is swept into one's bedroom through the air conditioner, riding the cool indraft as an eagle rides a warm updraft. It is a feeble theory, but a man has to entertain theories if he is to while away the hours of sleeplessness. I wanted to buy some old-fashioned bug spray, and went to the store for that purpose, but when I asked the clerk for a Flit gun and some Flit, he gave me a queer look, as though wondering where I had been keeping myself all these years. "We got something a lot stronger than that," he said, producing a can of stuff that contained chlordane and several other unmentionable chemicals. I told him I couldn't use it because I was hypersensitive to chlordane. "Gets me right in the liver," I said, throwing a wild glance at him.

The mornings are the pleasantest times in the apartment, exhaustion having set in, the sated mosquitoes at rest on ceiling and walls, sleeping it off, the room a swirl of tortured bedclothes and abandoned garments, the vines in their full leafiness filtering the hard light of day, the air conditioner silent at last, like the mosquitoes. From Third Avenue comes the sound of the mad builders—American cicadas, out in the noonday sun. In the garden the sparrow chants—a desultory second courtship, a subdued passion, in keeping with the great heat, love in summertime, relaxed and languorous. I shall miss this apartment when it is gone; we are quitting it come fall, to turn ourselves out to pasture. Every so often I make an attempt to simplify my life, burning my books behind me, selling the occasional chair, discarding the accumulated miscellany. I have noticed, though, that these purifications of mine—to which my wife submits with cautious grace—have usually led to even greater complexity in the long pull, and I have no doubt this one will, too, for I don't trust myself in a situation of this sort and suspect that my first act as an old horse will be to set to work improving the pasture. I may even join a pasture-improvement society. The last time I tried to purify myself by fire, I managed to acquire a zoo in the process and am still supporting it and carrying heavy pails of water to the animals, a task that is sometimes beyond my strength.

A book I have decided not to get rid of is a small one that arrived in the mail not long ago, a gift from a friend in Ithaca. It is *The Elements of Style,* by the late William Strunk, Jr., and it was known on the Cornell campus in my day as "the little book," with the stress on the word "little." I must have once owned a copy, for I took English 8 under Professor Strunk in 1919 and the book was required reading, but my copy presumably failed to survive an early purge. I'd not laid eyes on it in thirty-eight years. Am now delighted to study it again and rediscover its rich deposits of gold.

The Elements of Style was Will Strunk's *parvum opus,* his attempt to cut the vast tangle of English rhetoric down to size and write its rules and principles on the head of a pin. Will himself hung the title "little" on the book: he referred to it sardonically and with secret pride as "the *little* book," always giving the word "little" a special twist, as though he were putting a spin on a ball. The title page reveals that the book was privately printed (Ithaca, N.Y.) and that it was copyrighted in 1918 by the author. It is a forty-three-page summation of the case for cleanliness, accuracy, and brevity in the use of English. Its vigor is unimpaired, and for sheer pith I think it probably sets a record that is not likely to be broken. The Cornell University Library has one copy. It had two, but my friend pried one loose and mailed it to me.

The book consists of a short introduction, eight rules of usage, ten principles of composition, a few matters of form, a list of words and expressions commonly misused, a list of words commonly misspelled. That's all there is. The rules and principles are in the form of direct commands, Sergeant Strunk snapping orders to his platoon. "Do not join independent clauses with a comma." (Rule 5.) "Do not break sentences in two." (Rule 6.) "Use the active voice." (Rule 11.) "Omit needless words." (Rule 13.) "Avoid a succession of loose sentences." (Rule 14.) "In summaries, keep to one tense." (Rule 17.) Each rule or principle is followed by a short hortatory essay, and the exhoration is followed by, or interlarded with, examples in parallel columns—the true vs. the false, the right vs. the wrong, the timid vs. the bold, the ragged vs. the trim. From every line there peers out at me the puckish face of my professor, his short hair parted neatly in the middle and combed down over his forehead, his eyes blinking incessantly behind steel-rimmed spectacles as though he had just emerged into strong light, his lips nibbling each other like nervous horses, his smile shuttling to and fro in a carefully edged mustache.

"Omit needless words!" cries the author on page 21, and into that imperative Will Strunk really put his heart and soul. In the days when I was sitting in his class, he omitted so many needless words, and omitted them so forcibly and with such eagerness and obvious relish, that he often seemed in the position of having short-changed himself, a man left with nothing more to say yet with time to fill, a radio prophet who had outdistanced the clock. Will Strunk got out of this predicament by a simple trick: he uttered every sentence three times. When he delivered his oration on brevity to the class, he leaned forward over his desk, grasped his coat lapels in his hands, and in a husky, conspiratorial voice said, "Rule Thirteen. Omit needless words! Omit needless words! Omit needless words!"

He was a memorable man, friendly and funny. Under the remembered sting of his kindly lash, I have been trying to omit needless words since 1919, and although there are still many words that cry for omission and the huge task will never be accomplished, it is exciting to me to reread the masterly Strunkian elaboration of this noble theme. It goes:

> Vigorous writing is concise. A sentence should contain no unnecessary words, a paragraph no unnecessary sentences, for the same reason that a drawing should have no unnecessary lines and a machine no unnecessary parts. This requires not that the writer make all his sentences short, or that he avoid all detail and treat his subjects only in outline, but that every word tell.

There you have a short, valuable essay on the nature and beauty of brevity—sixty-three words that could change

the world. Having recovered from his adventure in prolixity (sixty-three words were a lot of words in the tight world of William Strunk, Jr.), the Professor proceeds to give a few quick lessons in pruning. The student learns to cut the deadwood from "This is a subject which . . ." reducing it to "This subject . . . ," a gain of three words. He learns to trim " . . . used for fuel purposes" down to "used for fuel." He learns that he is being a chatterbox when he says "The question as to whether" and that he should just say "Whether"—a gain of four words out of a possible five.

The Professor devotes a special paragraph to the vile expression "the fact that," a phrase that causes him to quiver with revulsion. The expression, he says, should be "revised out of every sentence in which it occurs." But a shadow of gloom seems to hang over the page, and you feel that he knows how hopeless his cause is. I suppose I have written "the fact that" a thousand times in the heat of composition, revised it out maybe five hundred times in the cool aftermath. To be batting only .500 this late in the season, to fail half the time to connect with this fat pitch, saddens me, for it seems a betrayal of the man who showed me how to swing at it and made the swinging seem worth while.

I treasure **The Elements of Style** for its sharp advice, but I treasure it even more for the audacity and self-confidence of its author. Will knew where he stood. He was so sure of where he stood, and made his position so clear and so plausible, that his peculiar stance has continued to invigorate me—and, I am sure, thousands of other ex-students—during the years that have intervened since our first encounter. He had a number of likes and dislikes that were almost as whimsical as the choice of a necktie, yet he made them seem utterly convincing. He disliked the word "forceful" and advised us to use "forcible" instead. He felt that the word "clever" was greatly overused; "it is best restricted to ingenuity displayed in small matters." He despised the expression "student body," which he termed gruesome, and made a special trip downtown to the *Alumni News* office one day to protest the expression and suggest that "studentry" be substituted, a coinage of his own which he felt was similar to "citizenry." I am told that the *News* editor was so charmed by the visit, if not by the word, that he ordered the student body buried, never to rise again. "Studentry" has taken its place. It's not much of an improvement, but it does sound less cadaverous, and it made Will Strunk quite happy.

A few weeks ago I noticed a headline in the *Times* about Bonnie Prince Charlie: "CHARLES' TONSILS OUT." Immediately Rule 1 leapt to mind.

> 1. Form the possessive singular of nouns with 's.
> Follow this rule whatever the final consonant.
> Thus write,
> Charles's friend
> Burns's poems
> the witch's malice.

Clearly Will Strunk had foreseen, as far back as 1918, the dangerous tonsillectomy of a prince, in which the surgeon removes the tonsils and the *Times* copy desk removes the final "s." He started his book with it. I commend Rule 1 to the *Times* and I trust that Charles's throat, not Charles' throat, is mended.

Style rules of this sort are, of course, somewhat a matter of individual preference, and even the established rules of grammar are open to challenge. Professor Strunk, although one of the most inflexible and choosy of men, was quick to acknowledge the fallacy of inflexibility and the danger of doctrine.

"It is an old observation," he wrote, "that the best writers sometimes disregard the rules of rhetoric. When they do so, however, the reader will usually find in the sentence some compensating merit, attained at the cost of the violation. Unless he is certain of doing as well, he will probably do best to follow the rules."

It is encouraging to see how perfectly a book, even a dusty rule book, perpetuates and extends the spirit of a man. Will Strunk loved the clear, the brief, the bold, and his book is clear, brief, bold. Boldness is perhaps its chief distinguishing mark. On page 24, explaining one of his parallels, he says, "The left-hand version gives the impression that the writer is undecided or timid; he seems unable or afraid to choose one form of expression and hold to it." And his Rule 12 is "Make definite assertions." That was Will all over. He scorned the vague, the tame, the colorless, the irresolute. He felt it was worse to be irresolute than to be wrong. I remember a day in class when he leaned far forward in his characteristic pose—the pose of a man about to impart a secret—and croaked, "If you don't know how to pronounce a word, say it loud! If you don't know how to pronounce a word, say it loud!" This comical piece of advice struck me as sound at the time, and I still respect it. Why compound ignorance with inaudibility? Why run and hide?

All through ***The Elements of Style*** one finds evidences of the author's deep sympathy for the reader. Will felt that the reader was in serious trouble most of the time, a man floundering in a swamp, and that it was the duty of anyone attempting to write English to drain this swamp quickly and get his man up on dry ground, or at least throw him a rope.

"The little book" has long since passed into disuse. Will died in 1946, and he had retired from teaching several years before that. Longer, lower textbooks are in use in English classes nowadays, I daresay—books with upswept tail fins and automatic verbs. I hope some of them manage to compress as much wisdom into as small a space, manage to come to the point as quickly and illuminate it as amusingly. I think, though, that if I suddenly found myself in the, to me, unthinkable position of facing a class in English usage and style, I would simply lean far out over the desk, clutch my lapels, blink my eyes, and say, "Get the *little* book! Get the *little* book! Get the *little* book!"

P. F. Baum (essay date 1960)

SOURCE: A review of *The Elements of Style,* in *The South Atlantic Quarterly,* Vol. LIX, No. 1, Winter, 1960, pp. 128-29.

[*In the following essay, Baum provides a favorable assessment of White's revision of* The Elements of Style.

It is a melancholy thought, sometimes, that the language we are born to, which we practice daily—speaking, reading, and occasionally writing—should be so vexatious when we are asked to use it properly. Custom never seems to mitigate its infinite complexity. In the home and in secondary schools something is done about it; but there the Law of Hydrostatics is operant. In the colleges Freshman English is a perpetual trial, when the poor student is faced with all his accumulated handicaps and the poor instructor, in the rôle of Sisyphus, resorts to all the known devices to undo the evils of quotidian habit and overcome the influences of newspaper and radio, of the advertisement writers and, in their own corner, the sports writers. A losing battle, a rearguard action, but never without hope.

The older books of formal rhetoric are out of fashion; they are too heavy for today's youth. Of handbooks (for hand-to-hand fighting) there has never been a dearth. And here we have now two rather special specimens: a rigorous handbook with the cachet of the *New Yorker* and a discursive volume especially intended for "the noble amateur."

Mr. E. B. White, having received a copy of the old textbook [***The Elements of Style***] he used as a Cornell undergraduate, was moved to write about it for the *New Yorker,* in a spirit of nostalgic reverence, two years ago. The original version by Professor Strunk, 1918, had been three times reprinted, with and without revision, and now appears under a new imprint with fresh revisions by Mr. White to give it a modern coloring, with the *New Yorker* piece as Introduction, and with a supplementary chapter nearly half as long as the original work—"the *little* book." Strunk was a forthright teacher. He laid down the rules with authoritative determination. His rules are deliberately elementary, but they have a perennial value: "they are," says Mr. White, "in essence, mere gentle reminders: they state what most of us know and, at times, forget." About some of them the new editor is himself not altogether happy, but he complains of them cheerfully. In the new chapter he writes more freely on the mystery of style, and also authoritatively, as one known to be an accomplished stylist. Surely it is something that this little book has for four months stood in the upper half of the Best Seller list.

If it is a far cry from the Cornell classroom to the *New Yorker* pages, it is a still farther cry to *Say It with Words* by a senior editor of the *Reader's Digest* and the author of a recent biography of Cardinal Wolsey. Here we are to learn "the effective *use*" of words and to "put into daily service the love of language with which we were born." (This love, however, is an ambivalent love, not without a taint of original sin.) We are encouraged to cultivate words as music and as pictures, and to break down "the immensity of language" into "edible fragments for daily fare." In the chapter on Mind Your Verbs we are told that "Knowing the rules of punctuation need put no crimp in our get-along." But the author ends with a pleasing "benediction" on questions of ethics and taste and the courtesy of accuracy—for "The careful writer does precision thinking with tools calibrated down to reasonable tolerances." All this may not be in the tradition of Cicero and Quintilian; it would hardly please Cardinal Newman or satisfy Walter Pater; but it has a message for the noble amateur, even if it is not a safe model for such as aspire to the *New Yorker*.

Robert Kanigel (essay date 1982)

SOURCE: A review of *The Elements of Style*, in *Los Angeles Times Book Review*, August 22, 1982, p. 4.

[*In the following laudatory review, Kanigel deems* The Elements of Style *as a "monument to clear thinking cleanly voiced."*]

The world would be a better place if everybody read ***The Elements of Style;*** if it were read not just by writers and journalists, but by all who write legal briefs, job applications, love letters, or notes to the teacher; read even by those who never write anything. Even a single reading of the Strunk and White classic imparts immunity to bureaucratic gobbledy-gook, technocratic jargon and psychobabble (at least temporarily). If we all wrote and spoke clearly, without resort to weasel words and fuzzy generalities, maybe we'd all feel more at home with one another.

This is not too grand a judgment to make of so slim a book; it is not making too much of it. ***The Elements of Style*** stands as a monument to clear thinking cleanly voiced. Indeed, the big problem any writer takes on in reviewing it is simply living up to its injunctions. As the words click from the typewriter, he's apt to feel Messrs. Strunk and White peering over his shoulder, remarking on each empty phrase and murky thought.

William Strunk Jr. was a Cornell professor who, back in 1918, had his little rule book on prose expression printed privately. A revised edition appeared in 1935. Twenty-two years later, a former student of Strunk, the noted essayist E. B. White, wrote a New Yorker piece about "my friend and teacher" Strunk and his book. In 1959, with that piece to serve as introduction, ***The Elements of Style*** reappeared with revisions, deletions, and a new chapter by White. This is the edition known today more widely as "Strunk and White" than by its formal title.

White's charming introductory tribute to Strunk leads off this guidebook. It is followed by a chapter on rules of usage, another on principles of composition, and a concise rundown of "Words and Expressions Commonly Misused." The final chapter is White's own "Approach to Style," advanced through Strunkian rules such as "Do not affect a breezy manner," and "Write with nouns and verbs."

None of this, of course, hints at the sparkling clarity here; it is a delight to read and offers a sense of revealed wisdom for the first-time reader. "Prefer the specific to the general," is the essential Strunk speaking. For example, he says, the sentence "He showed satisfaction as he took possession of his well-earned reward" just won't do; much better is "He grinned as he pocketed the coin." And we grin in recognition of the Truth.

In the clear, crystalline world of Strunk and White, acts of a hostile character become *hostile acts*. The phrase *in the last analysis* is "bankrupt"; the word *interesting* is "unconvincing . . . Instead of announcing that what you are about to tell is interesting, make it so." As for an occasional colloquialism, "simply use it; do not draw attention to it by enclosing it in quotation marks. To do so is to put on airs, as though you were inciting the reader to join you in a select society of those who know better."

The final chapter on writing style displays all White's own mastery of the essay form. "Writing," he says, "becomes a question of learning to make occasional wing shots, bringing down the bird of thought as it flashes by. A writer is a gunner, sometimes waiting in his blind for something to come in, sometimes roaming the countryside hoping to scare something up." Then come 21 of White's own rules, echoing the voice of his mentor—as when he describes words like *rather, very, little, pretty* as "leeches that infest the pond of prose, sucking the blood of words."

One paragraph appears twice within ***The Elements of Style***. Originally penned by Strunk in advancing his dictum to "Omit needless words," White repeats it verbatim in his introduction. Here it is:

> Vigorous writing is concise. A sentence should contain no unnecessary words, a paragraph no unnecessary sentences, for the same reason that a drawing should have no unnecessary lines and a machine no unnecessary parts. This requires not that the writer make all his sentences short, or that he avoid all detail and treat his subjects only in outline, but that every word tell.

"There you have a short, valuable essay on the nature and beauty of brevity," wrote White. "Sixty-three words that could change the world."

Trish Deitch Rohrer (essay date 1990)

SOURCE: "A Small Masterpiece," in *GQ*, Vol. 60, No. 12, December, 1990, pp. 72, 76.

[*In the following essay, Rohrer praises White's revisions to Strunk's* The Elements of Style.]

It was an instance of fate that, in 1919, young E. B. White found himself in William Strunk Jr.'s English 8 class at Cornell. Strunk was then teaching grammar from a forty-three-page rule book he'd written and privately published and that he called *The Elements of Style.* But it wasn't Strunk's homegrown style manual that made a lasting impression on White (White, in fact, quickly forgot the book), it was the man.

"From every line there peers out at me the puckish face of my professor," White says in the introduction he wrote to Strunk's book in 1971, "his short hair parted neatly in the middle and combed down over his forehead, his eyes blinking incessantly behind steel-rimmed spectacles as though he had just emerged into strong light. . . .

"'Omit needless words!' cries [Strunk from the pages of his book]. . . . In the days when I was sitting in his class, he omitted so many needless words, and omitted them so forcibly and with such eagerness and obvious relish, that he often seemed in the position of having shortchanged himself—a man left with nothing more to say yet with time to fill, a radio prophet who had outdistanced the clock."

In 1957, thirty-eight years after Strunk and White's fateful meeting at Cornell—and long after the good professor had died—White, who was by then an influential and well-respected contributor at *The New Yorker,* was commissioned by the Macmillan Company to revise Strunk's "little book" for the college and general-trade markets.

Surely almost any other man or woman asked to do this job would have polished up Strunk's writing, added a few dry points of his or her own and handed over to the world of aspiring writers another uninspiring (albeit blessedly short) style manual. But White, having been moved and amused by Strunk's odd character and his do-or-die commitment to good writing, brought to the short textbook a kind of loving and vivifying perspective on what he referred to in his introduction as Strunk's "dusty rule book."

It is ironic that what became known as Strunk and White's *Elements of Style*—essentially Strunk's original text sandwiched between White's six-page introduction and his own brief chapter on writing—sold millions of copies over the decades to people searching through the seemingly impenetrable thornbush that is English grammar. It is ironic because Strunk and White's *Elements of Style* is anything but simple; it is, in fact, a riddle, a treasure map whose prize is not an easy understanding of grammar and style but instead the odd and wonderful book itself: the story of what a nimble and irreverent writer such as E. B. White does when faced with the task of whipping into shape and presenting to the world a beloved professor's ornery, pedantic and sometimes wrong-headed little grammar book.

It's true that White does celebrate Strunk's book—he calls it "a tiny thing, a barely tarnished gem"—but if readers listen carefully, they will hear White also whispering in their ear "Take this little book in, if you will, but only with a grain of salt, for the author here is both lovely and suspect. . . . "

White gently pokes fun at Strunk, saying that some of his likes and dislikes were "as whimsical as the choice of a necktie," and describes his old teacher as "Sergeant Strunk snapping orders to his platoon" because of the way Strunk puts all his rules of grammar and style in the form of commands, such as "Do not break sentences in two" and "Use the active voice" and "Omit needless words."

All this good-natured testing is both a kind of eulogy to a man very much admired and a circumspect way of saying that Strunk's word—the word that most people, knowing it or not, turn to *The Elements of Style* to hear—is often exasperating, confusing, priggish, arbitrary and unnecessarily intimidating. (White makes his point with some subtlety when he cautions the reader that "none are so fallible as those who are sure they're right" or that "the trouble with truth is its many varieties.")

That's not to say that a reader won't find, as White puts it, "deposits of gold" running through Strunk's prose. He does offer up the basic rules, which are more often than not lost or broken ("Form the possessive singular of nouns by adding 's," "The number of the subject determines the number of the verb" and so on), and he fights a noble fight in trying to steer us away from using such words as "hopefully" when we mean "I hope," or "aggravate" when we mean "irritate."

But what readers will mainly find is an example of a man—that is, Strunk—trying to write well by using all the right rules of grammar and style but plodding very heavily around his subject. And around this heavy plodder flies White, a light and carefree bird who does not, like Strunk, think of what his readers would like to read but instead sings the song that's on his mind and in his heart.

"The squalor of the streets," says White by way of showing how a colon can introduce a quotation, "reminded him of a line from Oscar Wilde: 'We are all in the gutter, but some of us are looking at the stars.'"

"When we speak of Fitzgerald's style," White says at the beginning of his chapter on writing, "we don't mean his command of the relative pronoun, we mean the sound his words make on paper."

He goes on to say:

> Style takes its final shape more from attitudes of mind than from principles of composition, for, as an elderly practitioner once remarked, "Writing is an act of faith, not a trick of grammar." This moral observation would have no place in a rule book were it not that style *is* the writer, and therefore

what a man is, rather than what he knows, will at last determine his style.

This is the trick, the riddle, that White performed when he gave us Strunk's book: He took such care in describing his old professor in order that we might see that Strunk's book, more thana textbook on grammar, is a very particular picture of and by a very particular man—it is a wonderful example of how you write what you are. White, rather than judging Strunk's book and finding it lacking because it is not beautiful or witty, praises the original *Elements of Style* for being so truly, clearly and honestly an expression of its author.

This, then—that you find your style by finding yourself, and you make something of it by putting yourself on the line—is the main element of any style.

"It is encouraging to see how perfectly a book, even a dusty rule book, perpetuates and extends the spirit of a man," says White of Strunk's *Elements of Style.* This can be said of Strunk and White's *Elements of Style,* as well; Strunk's contribution to the book shows us audacity in action, while White's shows us generosity and ingenuity.

Debra Fried (essay date 1991)

SOURCE: "Bewhiskered Examples in 'The Elements of Style'," in *Western Humanities Review,* Vol. XLV, No. 4, Winter, 1991, pp. 304-11.

[*In the following essay, Fried analyzes Strunk and White's handbook from a feminist perspective.*]

The debate that feminist criticism must hold with Strunk and White's standard composition handbook, *The Elements of Style,* is a version of a polite spat about diction which takes place in the eleventh chapter of *Middlemarch:*

—All choice of words is slang. It marks a class.

—There is correct English. That is not slang.

—I beg your pardon: correct English is the slang of prigs who write history and essays. And the strongest slang of all is the slang of poets.

Feminist criticism has been quick to note that correct English is slang, not only of prigs but of all of us; what I wish to examine is the slang of composition handbooks. To point out that *The Elements of Style* would be more aptly titled *The Elements of the Plain Style* is to say something obvious about the way most traditional style manuals select a single style to teach as normative, correct, the acceptable way to write. The advocated style is characterized in the lingo of these handbooks by clarity, concision, and concreteness. It is the English plain style embodying the empiricist tradition and therefore excluding all but, in Richard Ohmann's words, "the kind of argumentation that is most helpful in preserving the status quo." Where a feminist critique of the teaching of

composition must begin is not with the rules that the rhetoric texts teach, but with the examples they supply to illustrate those rules. Examples may betray the rules they are designed to serve. Ushered in as helpmates, ancillary or secondary to the rules and meaningless outside their context, examples constantly threaten to take over the neat household of rhetorical authority— that is, to confess the power structures necessary to keep the house neat. But then, as Strunk and White admit by way of providing an instance of a compound subject governing a singular verb, "Give and take is essential to a happy household."

Where do examples get their power to subvert the rules they have been invoked solely to support? How can the lowly, subservient example gain mastery over the lordly precept? An example should not mean but be; it should not say, but merely show. And yet an example has to say something as well as illustrate something: there is no colorless, voiceless, value-free language in which to write examples designed to teach writing, no language that doesn't smack of having been written or uttered by someone in some context. It has been argued that prose fiction itself began from this property of illustrative examples to create a world. Richardson's *Pamela* developed from Richardson's writing of a manual of business letters to illustrate how to meet various new occasions for correspondence that arose to task the etiquette and the literacy of a rising middle class. By composing a series of letters to exemplify the correct tone, phrasing, and form for such letters, Richardson could not help but invent characters to write them, individuals to whom such tone and phrasing would be appropriate. The textbook composed of examples becomes a novel. In E. B. White's phrase from *The Elements of Style,* "No writer long remains incognito." The examples a writer chooses will reveal what kind of world he believes that he lives in, and who wields the power in that world, more readily than the precepts that the examples are invented in order to teach. Ideology resides in the illustrations as well as the rules; indeed, is most at home there, where the writer of rules is least on his guard about the content of his sentences because he is to be interested solely in the principles of composition they embody. The examples will tend to reveal that these principles of composition allow only certain things to be said, because those principles structure the world in a certain way.

The Elements of Style hovers on the brink of confessing that rules and examples are often hard to tell apart, that the entire structure of dominating precept and subservient, obedient example is a shaky kingdom. With a readiness to enjoy the fun of an inside joke, Strunk and White at times bring attention to the ways in which their examples mime as well as embody the rules under which they appear. Sometimes the examples are sentences that quietly obey the rule while stating it. According to White, Strunk was master of the rule that is itself an example, as in the economy of his precept "Omit needless words," a phrase that obeys itself, three little words that are a model of how English should sound when it follows the rule it voices. Other times, examples are permitted to disobey their precepts if that disobedience will serve to clarify the precepts. Writing about whether the accepted idiom is "try *and*" or "try *to*," White opts for the standard usage while he playfully admits the current relaxation of this rule: "When you are writing formal prose, try and write *try to*" (62). Under the rubric, "Avoid the use of qualifiers," White illustrates the need for this rule by advocating it in a sentence that repeatedly disobeys it: "We should all try to do a little better, should all be very watchful of this rule for it is a rather important one and we are pretty sure to violate it now and then" (73). To illustrate the rule "Do not construct awkward adverbs," White advises, "Do not write the word *tangledly*. The word itself is a tangle" (75). This is good fun and good teaching, but these examples are by no means the only ones that enact the rule they speak, only the most explicit in that enactment. They invite us to examine, in all the handbook's illustrative sentences or passages, the relationship between what they say and what they are supposed to illustrate. The instances just cited blur the distinction between rule and illustration, precept and example, but in such a way that we can detect the handbook writer's voice and the gentle but firm hold he has on the reins, allowing the instances only so much play as will make them better serve the handbook's rules.

Let me turn to a more guardedly self-referential illustration in order to sketch why this approach to composition texts must be a feminist one. The entry on the use of the colon includes several entries that blur the line dividing rule and example. The rule itself, the sentence explaining how correctly to use the colon, is a sentence that uses the colon correctly to introduce a list of particulars. Here is the rule:

> The colon also has certain functions of form: to follow the salutation of a formal letter, to separate hour from minute in a notation of time, and to separate the title of a work from its subtitle or a Bible chapter from a verse. (8)

The examples that are listed under this rule illustrate in turn each occasion for formal usage of the colon. Thus the last example is assigned to show how to use a colon in order to "separate a Bible chapter from a verse." The example is "*Nehemiah* 11:17." And that should be the end of that; that citation is all we need in order to see where to put the colon: between the 11 and the 7. But that is not the end of that, for here is the seventh verse of the eleventh chapter of the *Book of Nehemiah:* "And these are the sons of Benjamin: Saluh the son of Meshullam, the son of Joed, the son of Pedaiah, the son of Kolaiah, the son of Masseiah, the son of Ithiel, the son of Jesaiah." The verse from Nehemiah itself illustrates the rule for the usage of the colon, rule 7: "Use a colon after an independent clause to illustrate a list of particulars, appositive, an amplification, or an illustrative quotation," although all it was required to exemplify was how to punctuate between chapter and verse in a Biblical reference. In this case, the colon promises a list of the sons of Benjamin, who are themselves listed according to

whose immediate sons they are; joining a patriarch to his male heirs, the colon gathers the tribe. While this Biblical verse does not appear in Strunk and White, if we follow the lead of this final, because most specified, example of formal usage of the colon, we find that the citation to *Nehemiah* 11:7 hides another, more general illustration of the colon that introduces, and thereby joins—in this case, joins sons to their patriarch. For what if we suppose that this hidden illustration has the same self-reflexive force as the example "tangledly" or the advice "try and write *try to*"? We can see how the Biblical sentence is another instance of correct colon usage, but in what sense is it also a sentence *about* correct colon usage? What do the sons of Benjamin have to do with the place-ment of the colon? Could it be that the Nehemiah text implies that genealogy is the originating instance of the colon, the archetypal case of the distinction between a topic and an illustrative list or catalogue? Do we have here a grammarian's just-so story (how the colon came into being; how the need for the colon arose) that teaches us that patriarchy (quite literally here, the lineage of a Biblical patriarch) marked the beginning of the categori-zation that the colon authorizes and makes legible? Things of the same type are those that a single patriarch has begotten; according to this logic, fathering becomes the reigning metaphor for categorizing, and the model for the relation of general to particular, of rule to illustration, is that of a father to his sons.

Categorizing together things of the same type is of course a project central to the enterprise of Strunk and White's manual, as of all guides to standard usage. Without cri-teria by which you can classify like thoughts and struc-tures, you cannot legislate compositional norms such as parallel structure, agreement of noun and modifier, unmixed metaphors, and paragraph unity. Nor, I think, should a feminist composition dispense with such es-sential aids to getting things said. It would be folly to believe that, because order and category are identified as patriarchally begotten, a feminist composition must teach divergences, inconsistencies, and their attendant sloppiness as female, by renaming what the male tradi-tion terms incorrect as a creative insurgence necessary for the invention of a woman's language. My suggestion is rather less ambitious: that in the feminist classroom we can never teach composition by teaching from a hand-book unless we also teach the handbook itself as a text. Since, according to the rule, the colon is the correct notion to introduce "an illustrative quotation," there is always an unwritten colon between text and example throughout *The Elements of Style.* But examples resist such colonization. Strunk and White would like to believe that illustrative sentences are to rules as sons are to their fathers, extensions and legitimations of fatherly counsel. But I want to suggest that examples in the feminist classroom are disobedient daughters, most subversive precisely in their demure appearance of obedience achieved by their shy effacement of them-selves. And it is by scrutinizing the examples that we can enable our students to understand the ideology out of which arise the rules that define standard English.

Strunk and White's ingratiating clubbiness happens to make their handbook a particularly insidious example, and it is probably unfair to take it as typical of the offenses of freshman rhetorics. Yet its own canniness about the potential repercussions of examples beyond the bounds of their precepts makes it an appropriate text for our purposes. This kind of analysis must refuse to pinpoint a rhetoric text's ideology in its explicitly "sexist" examples, and must rather relocate that ideology in the way the text conceives the relationship between rule and example. All the same, it will not be a futile exercise to look at a few of the sample sentences in the handbook in which women are mentioned. In his revisions of earlier editions, White may have deleted, as he claimed, the "bewhiskered entries," but he did not do much about the corseted ones.

What is most pernicious about the following sentences is that they are advanced under the false colors of mere examples:

"Chloe smells good, as a pretty girl should" (51): Not, that is, *like* a pretty girl should. The sentence chosen as an illustration of a rule about grammatical deportment is a sentence about female deportment, dictating how pretty Chloe should smell while dictating how that recommendation should be written. The rhyme lends this example the memorable unassailability of such paideutic jingles as "I before E except after C," with the result that we cannot recall this rule for the use of *as* without also recalling this advice about how pretty girls should smell.

"As a mother of five, with another one on the way, my ironing board is always up" (14): What is wrong with this sentence, according to *The Elements of Style,* is that it is in "ludicrous" (White's word) violation of Rule 11, "A participial phrase at the beginning of a sentence must refer to the grammatical subject." As a dreary picture of female domestic slavery, this example hints at what lies in store for pretty Chloe. It reeks, as an example should, of the assumptions of its culture—here, perhaps, of America's baby boom ethic of the years of the first edition of the Strunk/White collaboration (1959), a period in which women were praised for being prolific. But that fertility here gives birth to a confused sentence. It is as though the very procreative productivity of the post-war wife were incompatible with the spare, crisp style advocated by Strunk and White. Excess is one of the worst stylistic crimes identified by *The Elements of Style,* and here excess is identified with a woman, whose punishment for producing too many children is the Sisyphean labor of never being able to keep ironed and neat the ragged brood whose very number is a kind of raggedness no ironing will smooth. The excess of male desire required to bring forth this brood is not, of course, in evidence; "another one on the way" is a roundabout idiom that ignores where babies come from. And it is a phrase the overworked mother has presumably chosen herself. Unlike "Chloe smells good, as a pretty girl should," which cannot be attributed to Chloe herself, but is the kind of utterance that might be laid at the doorstep of a (male)

advertising copywriter or a lyricist of popular songs, this example is a fictional utterance by a woman. Neither of these examples is in the language of Strunk and White. They are excerpts from a different realm of discourse than that of the writers of style manuals. The fiction that the examples are chosen from the free-floating plenitude of English utterances "out there" in the world of sweet-smelling girls and ever-pregnant housewives is a particularly deceptive one, and I shall have more to say about that deception a bit later.

In some examples, grammatical confusion is figured as female confusion, a woman's inability to choose or distinguish intelligently. "Her father's suspicions were well-founded—it was not Edward she cared for—it was San Francisco" (9): In a confusion of female choice used to illustrate the correct use of the dash, it takes a male authority to figure out what choice the woman really wants to make. To illustrate correct and incorrect pronoun usage, *The Elements of Style* adduces "Polly loves cake more than me" (12). It is somewhat surprising to learn that the correct version of this sentence is "Polly loves cake more than she loves me." "Polly loves cake more than me" is presumably the error a careless speaker would make who meant to say "Polly loves cake more than I do." By insisting that the correct form of "Polly loves cake more than me" must be "Polly loves cake more than she loves me," the handbook reminds us of the silly remarks that careless speakers don't realize they are making. The silliness is not the surreal nonsense yielded by dangling participles, for instance ("Walking along the bank, a fish was jumping"). Rather, it might be argued, this correction makes the example's speaker most plausibly imagined as a man making a judgment about a woman. The corrected version alters the sample sentence in a revealing way that has little to do with pronoun usage. It is no longer a statement distinguishing the speaker's predilections from Polly's, but is now a report of Polly's choice between the speaker and something else. In the light of the book's other oscillating females, the correct sentence conjures up a scenario in which a man is complaining about Polly's failure to respond to him. Even though an incorrect sentence is put in his mouth, his grammatical confusion is overshadowed and figured by Polly's illogical choice, so that the male speaker does not seem taken to task morally for his murky incorrect grammar, as was the mother with her ironing board always up. What does a woman want? The confusion of woman's polymorphously perverse preference—a confusion of classifying together two incompatible choices (cake or me, Edward or San Francisco)—is made the vehicle for illustrating incorrect because unclear stylistic choices.

Examples such as these seem to me sufficiently "bewhiskered" to have been excised from the 1979 edition of *The Elements of Style.* But of course to be bewhiskered is to suffer from a form of old-fashioned bad grooming that only men are privileged to suffer from and correct. The metaphor of good grooming for good writing is a recurrent one in Strunk and White. At the same time there is a clash between this complacently neoclassical figure for style ("True wit is nature to advantage dressed") and the more dominant Romantic myth of style White propounds in his insistence at the end of the manual that style is an unquestionable mark of identity, a writer's "fingerprints" (68), or an unmasking or undressing, "the Self escaping into the open" (67). Style is clothing, but it also unclothes. Two paragraphs after White's promise to delete bewhiskered entries, his sketch of his teacher William Strunk presents a portrait of an impeccably groomed grammarian: "From every line" of the manual, White reminisces, "there peers out at me the puckish face of my professor, his short hair parted neatly in the middle and combed down over his forehead . . . his smile shuttling to and fro under a carefully edged mustache" (xiii). Strunk's view of the universe of rhetoric is as neatly parted down the middle as his short hair, as White suggests in his account of the organization of Strunk's original "little book," which is essentially the structure of the subsequent editions as well:

> Each rule or principle is followed by a short hortatory essay, and usually the exhortation is followed by, or interlarded with, examples in parallel columns—the true vs. the false, the right vs. the wrong, the timid vs. the bold, the ragged vs. the trim. (xiii)

To this list of opposites we may add female vs. male.

This division of the world and the world of language into true and false, ragged and trim, left-hand side of the page vs. right-hand side, with parallel columns of *do's* and *don'ts* curiously begins to affect the way the examples are paired, even when a rule is followed by a series of correct examples. This contrariness forces us to read a horizontal split as a version of the vertical split between right and wrong instances following a rule. Even correct examples are often paired in terms of male and female applications of a rule. To illustrate the rule, "A name or title in direct address is parenthetic," are these two sentences: "If, Sir, you refuse, I cannot predict what will happen" and "Well, Susan, this is a fine mess you are in" (3). The correct placement of the commas seems the least interesting thing about these two sentences. Curiously, I think we tend to posit a male speaker for both, though we could imagine scenarios in which a woman might speak either sentence. For they suggest that men have titles (Sir) and women first names (Susan), that men are adamant in their dealings with other men ("I cannot predict what will happen" is not an admission of confusion about the future but about the certainty of the threatened reprisal). Women, on the other hand, are in a "fine mess," even when their commas are neatly placed; Susan is a close cousin of indecisive Polly and the ironing-board housewife and no doubt of pretty Chloe as well.

The neatness of such paired examples as these shows how even the approved, the trim, falls into categories of the trim vs. the ragged, and reminds us that these sample sentences are not really "samples" of anything except the example-making discourse of the writers of style manuals. They are made objects masquerading as found objects. They are not random samples or overheard snippets plucked from the flow of surrounding talk, or even boners culled from student papers over the years. They are rather bastard sons begotten by a father other than the father they claim, the rules they follow and exemplify. E. M. Forster also divides the world into two parts in a long passage cited in *The Elements of Style* ostensibly to illustrate how to "Avoid a succession of loose sentences." The Forster passage begins, "I believe in aristocracy. . . . Not an aristocracy based on rank and influence, but an aristocracy of the sensitive, the considerate, and the plucky" (26). Even here, I would argue, we have the trim vs. the ragged, male rank vs. female sensitivity. In the world conjured up by the examples in *The Elements of Style,* rank and influence still rule the day. It is in the examples that we find some answers to the question that rhetoric texts usually try to forget to ask: Who decides what is correct English? Whose authority determines standard usage?

NOTES

[1] *English in America* (New York: Oxford University Press, 1974) 159.

[2] Strunk and White, *The Elements of Style,* 3rd ed. 10. The currently available edition is still this 1979 revision. Subsequent references will be given in the text.

[3] Linguistics studies this capacity of language under M.A.K. Halliday's rubric of language's "ideational function," whereby "the speaker or writer embodies in language his experience of the phenomena of the real world," "Linguistic Function and Literary Style," in Seymour Chatman, ed., *Literary Style: A Symposium* (New York: Oxford University Press, 1971) 332. As Roger Fowler explains, "ideational variation distinguishes text from text: each act of language is formed for a specific purpose and in a particular setting, and the text's structure reflects these circumstances" (*Linguistic Criticism* [New York: Oxford University Press, 1986]) 148. Texts may build a world-view through local instances and through the cumulative effect of such instances: "Cumulative ideational structuring depends on regular and consistent linguistic choices which build up a continuous, pervasive representation of the world. This is the major source of point of view in fiction" (Fowler, 150). For a dissenting view, that examples "depict utterances, but not utterances-in-context," see Barbara Herrnstein Smith, *On the Margins of Discourse: The Relation of Literature to Language* (Chicago: The University of Chicago Press, 1978) 50-57.

The following sources published by Gale contain additional coverage of Strunk's life and career: *Contemporary Authors,* Vols. 118, 164.

Louis Wirth

1897–1952

American sociologist, educator, essayist, and nonfiction writer

INTRODUCTION

Although he did not seek to develop a comprehensive social theory, Louis Wirth made a lasting contribution to sociology through his studies of urban communities and their effect on the individuals within them. A committed liberal both in thought and action, Wirth rejected the rigidity of Marxism, but built on Marxist themes of alienation in his urbanism, utilizing a pragmatic empirical framework that had little place for iron-clad predictive theories of human behavior. Other significant influences included Karl Mannheim, whose *Ideology and Utopia* he helped translate, as well as Robert Park, George Simmel, and Albion W. Small. Wirth represented a link between these sociologists of an earlier era and the "urban ecologists" of the mid-twentieth century. He spent much of his professional life at the University of Chicago, where he became a significant member of that institution's burgeoning "Chicago School" of social sciences, and in his most significant work, *The Ghetto,* he examined the lives of individuals and groups within the city's Jewish population. Likewise in his pivotal essay "Urbanism as a Way of Life," Wirth explored the means by which the urban environment exerts its pull even on persons living within tradition-based communities. It was his view—one which would have enormous impact on later work in urban studies—that the city supplants traditional modes with a way of life that at once offers the individual a greater sense of freedom and a heightened awareness of isolation.

Biographical Information

Wirth was born in 1897 into a bourgeois Jewish family in Gemünden, in the Rhineland. In 1911, the Wirths moved to Omaha, Nebraska, and in 1919 Wirth earned his Ph.B. at the University of Chicago. Thus he began a relationship with the university, where he earned his M.A. in 1925 and his Ph.D. in 1926, that would continue for the remainder of his life. He would also remain active in social work and causes, beginning with a period as a social worker from 1919, and continuing in his position as director of the delinquent boys' division of the Jewish Charities of Chicago. In 1925, Wirth made his first significant publication with the contribution of a substantial essay to *The City,* edited by Park, Burgess, and Roderick McKenzie. The following year he became an instructor of sociology at the University of Chicago, but took a position as an associate professor at Tulane in 1928, the same year that *The Ghetto* was published. From 1929 to 1930 he held a Social Science Research Council fellowship in Europe, but returned to the University of Chicago in 1930. Wirth spent most of his remaining life at the university, working successively as assistant professor, associate professor, and from 1940, professor of sociology. He also served as associate dean of social science from 1940 to 1945. Wirth was associate editor of the *American Journal of Sociology* from 1926 to 1928, and he continued in that role from 1931 until his death in 1952. He also took part in numerous Chicago Round Table radio broadcasts from 1938 on, and served as consultant to several boards which made recommendations concerning national policy during World War II, including the Federal Housing Authority and the National Resources Planning Board. In addition, Wirth served as president of the American Sociological Society in 1947.

Major Works

Wirth held that sociology is essential to the proper study of humankind precisely because individuals "everywhere and always" find themselves within groups. His principal works are concerned with the impact of two quite different types of social order: race and ethnicity on the one hand and, on the other, the less organic—but no less influential—structures of human behavior informed by life in the urban community. These dual themes pervade his most significant study, *The Ghetto,* in which he presented the Jewish community of Chicago as a group which both influences and is influenced by its surroundings. "Urbanism as a Way of Life," a pioneering work in sociological understanding of urbanism, dealt with questions of alienation and the means by which the city produces its own modes of behavior. In Wirth's view of the urban environment, not only are individuals challenged as much by a sense of loneliness as by an awareness of freedom, they are equally divided in their response to outside influences. Thus whereas traditional groups—or indeed any groups—fail to hold a determining influence on the lives of persons within an urban setting, those individuals are more vulnerable than their rural counterparts to the appeal of mass movements. In "Consensus and Mass Communication," Wirth explored another theme he considered vital to the study of sociology: "Because the mark of any society is the capacity of its members to understand one another and to act in concert toward common objectives and under common norms," he wrote, "the analysis of consensus rightly constitutes the focus of sociological investigations." Wirth took a pragmatic approach to sociological studies, and thus neither claimed to have developed a comprehensive theory that would predict all the particulars of social life, nor sought to do so; characteristically, he presented much of his most important work in the form of essays rather than books. In 1964, Albert J. Reiss, Jr. collected a number of Wirth's writings in *On Cities and Social Life.*

PRINCIPAL WORKS

The Ghetto (nonfiction) 1928
"Urbanism as a Way of Life" (essay) 1938
"Consensus and Mass Communication" (essay) 1948
On Cities and Social Life: Selected Papers (essays and nonfiction) 1964

CRITICISM

R. D. McKenzie (essay date 1929)

SOURCE: A review of *The Gold Coast and the Slum* and *The Ghetto,* in *The American Journal of Sociology,* Vol. XXXV, No. 3, November, 1929, pp. 486-87.

[*In the following essay, McKenzie reviews* The Ghetto *along with another study of urbanism and ethnicity, Harvey W. Zorbaugh's* The Gold Coast and the Slum.]

These two products from the University of Chicago [*The Gold Coast and the Slum* by Harvey W. Zorbaugh and *The Ghetto* by Wirth] are essentially studies of urban segregation. Zorbaugh approaches the subject from the standpoint of place. He analyzes the changing forms of human segregation within a specific region—the Near North Side of Chicago, an area a mile and a half long and a mile wide, in which live about ninety thousand people. Wirth, on the other hand, focuses his attention on the communal habits of a people, the Jews, and studies the ghetto in its natural development and various manifestations throughout Europe and America.

Zorbaugh's book is a graphic and intimate account of life among the most divergent groups which the processes of city growth have placed side by side in urban structure. Facing the lake is the "Gold Coast," girdled on the west by the "world of furnished rooms," which fades into the "rooming house area" and finally declines into a great "slum" section lying farther west. By direct observation, personal interviews, the use of documents, maps, and some statistical data, the author has succeeded in painting a very vivid picture of life in its contrasts and extremes in this section of Chicago. Dr. Zorbaugh, however, writes from the standpoint of a reporter rather than of a scientist. In his desire for descriptive effect he frequently violates the principles of scientific caution. Too often he yields to the temptation to generalize his illustrations and to explain uncommon behavior by ready-made formula.

For instance, after the quotation "One no longer is born to social position; one achieves social position by playing the social game," it adds nothing but rhythm to generalize, "And this is as true of the society of London or of New York as it is of the society of Chicago." Or again, after having defined the "slum" as "an area of freedom and individualism" (p. 128) it seems anomalous to say later on (p. 141) "It is in the slum, in every city, that one finds Little Italy, Little Poland, Chinatown, and the black belt." And it is certainly a little sweeping to say (p. 234) "Segregated areas of a given type, wherever they may be located in a given city with respect to other such areas, invariably fall, in every city, within one of these larger well defined zones." The zones referred to are those indicated by Burgess in *The City* (p. 55). Zorbaugh states without proof that the concentric circles which Burgess works out for Chicago "represent the typical structure of a modern commercial and industrial city." This may be so, but it has not been proved as yet.

Despite this tendency to unwarranted generalizations the reviewer thinks well of Zorbaugh's book. While it lacks precision in definition and interpretation, it explores actualities with a freshness and literary insight that gives them a vital significance such as could not be portrayed by the ordinary methods of statistical finesse.

Wirth approaches the study of the ghetto from the standpoint of its *natural* history. To him the ghetto is a social institution which evolved out of the peculiar conditions and circumstances in which the Jews have lived throughout history. It arose as a voluntary form of segregation among a migratory people moving from one cultural area to another, just as immigrant colonies arise in our own cities. Later it became sanctioned or decreed by legal enactment. In this regard it assumed the characteristics of a prison and bore the stigma of something to be escaped from. Wirth sees in the ghetto, with its characteristic institutions and patterns of behavior, the basis of the so-called physical, mental, and cultural traits of the Jewish people. It is the core of Jewish solidarity and social organization throughout the world. But the ghetto is always in process of dissolution. Individuals are continually escaping from it and being lost in the larger community. Frequently, however, the escaped individuals segregate in other parts of the city and give rise to new ghettos. It is interesting to note that the great ghettos of history are located in the strategic commercial and trade centers of Europe and America. In playing the rôle of the middleman the Jew has segregated at the focal points of trade and commerce. Not only is the ghetto found in the great commercial centers, but it is usually located in the heart of the city close to the market and trading center. Wirth selects for special consideration the famous ghetto of Europe located in Frankfort-on-the-Main and the Ghetto in Chicago. He shows that now that the compulsory features of ghetto existence have passed, the institution is largely maintained, as all immigrant colonies are, by the importation of new recruits from other cultural areas. Whenever immigration slacks or ceases there is a tendency for the ghetto to disappear.

This is a careful, objective analysis of the conditions associated with a form of human grouping and of the effects of such a mode of life on human nature itself.

William L. Kolb (essay date 1956)

SOURCE: A review of *Community Life and Social Policy*, in *American Sociological Review*, Vol. 21, No. 6, December, 1956, pp. 788-89.

[*In the following essay, a review of* Community Life and Social Policy, *Kolb discusses Wirth's contributions to sociology within the context of a larger tradition.*]

Somewhere in the recent literature it is written that the day of the system-builder in sociology is over. Yet this is true only in the sense that the builder of the "personal" system is no more. The task of testing, broadening, and deepening the theoretical tradition we have inherited goes on, not in isolation from research but in interactive relationship with it. Those who work at this task are frequently criticized, yet they continue to be the source of major research hypotheses and of modes of comprehending the practical social world about us. So it was and is with Louis Wirth.

Wirth was the inheritor of a great tradition in sociology, the Chicago tradition, which shaped immediately several generations of sociologists and at one remove almost all professional sociologists in the United States. The focus of interest of this tradition was the city; the frame of reference, a dual one of biological community and morally ordered society; and the object of moral concern, the uprooted. The essays collected in this volume [*Community Life and Social Policy*] show clearly that Wirth used the tradition in all its aspects and in so doing added to it.

Part III of the volume is made up primarily of articles devoted to the problems of minority groups. The content of these articles may strike the reader who comes to them for the first time as containing little that is new in the specialized area of minority groups and race relations. This can only reflect the dominance of the Chicago tradition in this area, and in particular the contribution made to it by Wirth in his articles and in his classic, ***The Ghetto***.

Wirth's practical and moral concerns constantly deepened and we find in Part IV essays concerned with planning and with the problem of peace. These for the most part are directed toward a lay audience, and are of interest to us as they show the scientist who is not afraid of suggesting policy attempting to break through the walls of ignorance and inertia. **"Chicago: Where Now?"** is a prime example.

But for sociologists Wirth's greatest contributions, whether he wanted them to be or not, are the ways in which he deepened the theoretical aspects of the tradition which he inherited. His great and enduring scientific concern, and perhaps his moral concern also, was with the problem of the city and consensus. To Wirth, as to other students of Park, the city was an object of devotion and yet of fear. The achievements of city civilization were tremendous: the freeing of man from the dead hand of tradition, the growth of rationality, and the recognition of the individual. Yet these all are threatened by the very conditions which make them possible. Population size, density, and heterogeneity and the process of competition are the creators of the city; they may also destroy it. As one rereads **"Urbanism as a Way of Life,"** the classic statement of the consequences of the growth and mixing of population, the fragility of the city way is delineated for all time.

Yet Wirth knew that the city cannot endure without a moral order and a moral consensus. If the older mode of consensus is broken down by the demographic features of urban life, then a new consensus must be established. In what was perhaps the best work of his life, **"Consensus and Mass Communication,"** read as his Presidential Address to the American Sociological Society in 1947, Wirth finally came to full engagement with this problem. How in a society made up of large, impersonal organized groups and of isolated mass individuals is it possible to create the conditions of collective action and solidarity? In a society as empty of consensus as Wirth believes modern society to be, and where the size, density, and heterogeneity of the population militate against the primary group conditions of a new consensus, what are the prospects? The mass media of communication are more likely the tools of a totalitarian consensus than of a shared democratic consensus. And, as Blumer suggests in his foreword, consensus brought about by the typical urban device of propagandizing ideologies "could, be at best only temporary and only segmental." Thus, Blumer continues, "Wirth sought to describe the new form of consensus arising from the indigenous nature of a mass society—a type of consensus which would peculiarly and almost paradoxically allow for complex diversity and incessant change in norms, values, and interests. This new form of consensus, Wirth saw, would necessarily have to be a consensus of means and not of ends."

One must ask several questions of this conclusion. Is a consensus of means possible without a consensus of at least a few ultimate ends? Does not Wirth himself in his devotion to rationality, freedom, and the individual actually set the ultimate ends in terms of which a flexible consensus of means is possible? And are not these ends much more widely and deeply shared than Wirth's picture of the lack of consensus in the city would indicate?

American society has always been a going concern, and although the growth of cities and the influx of immigrants have created problems for consensus through the creation of heterogeneity, there has been a continuing tradition internalized in the minds of substantial segments of the citizenry and objectified in the structure of institutions. It can even be argued that the elements of this consensus have done as much to shape the character of the modern city as have the elements of population size, density, and heterogeneity. If all this be true then we have a larger reserve of consensus than Wirth thought, and a basis on which to build. The problem, however, remains, in that the conditions of urban life threaten the continuation of this reserve. It is, perhaps, even deepened in that elements of the consensus, such as a purely rationalistic individualism, may create the conditions which are destroying consensus.

In any event we can best pay tribute to Louis Wirth by continuing what he carried on as part of his inheritance: the search for the conditions of consensus and a genuinely social life. If the search requires change and modification in the ideas we have inherited from him, this too is part of the tradition by which he lived and did his work.

Amitai Etzioni (essay date 1959)

SOURCE: *"The Ghetto—A Re-Evaluation,"* in *Social Forces,* Vol. 37, No. 3, March, 1959, pp. 255-62.

[*In the following essay, occasioned by the republication of* The Ghetto *more than a quarter-century after its original release, Etzioni critiques the seminal work.*]

The republication of **The Ghetto** by Louis Wirth[1] seems to be an appropriate occasion for a re-evaluation[2] of his thesis. It is of importance to state at the very beginning of this discussion that, although some concepts and conclusions of Wirth will be sharply criticized, in general this is one of the most important studies of the sociology of the Jews, a much neglected field.[3]

Wirth's study presents a theory as well as considerable evidence which disproves it. The theory applied in **The Ghetto** is Park's model of a natural history of race and ethnic relations. The pattern of interaction among different ethnic groups passes through the stages of isolation, competition, conflict, and accommodation. Eventually the last stage is reached, at which minority groups become completely assimilated. This scheme can be criticized from several points of view. First, like many theories of natural history, it is not sufficiently specified to be tested.[4] It is formulated in such a manner that different and even contradictory data can be interpreted to support the theory. The term "eventually," often used by Park,[5] is a good indicator of this fallacy. When an ethnic group is assimilating, it is suggested that the hypothesis is supported; if an ethnic group is not assimilating, it is suggested that it has not yet reached the stage of assimilation. "Eventually," one can still hold, every ethnic group will be assimilated. As no time interval is mentioned and the sociological conditions under which the process of assimilation will take place are not spelled out, the whole scheme becomes unscientific.

It is necessary to distinguish carefully between the description of the stages and the processes which take place at each stage on the one hand, and the analysis of the forces which cause the processes to proceed from stage to stage on the other. This is especially important in understanding Park and Wirth, for their natural history is not presented as a continuous process but assumes that there is a limited number of stages at which intergroup relations can reach an equilibrium. In case no accumulation of changing forces occurs, the system will not move to the next stage. The factor of change which transfers groups from the first to the second stage is the diffusion of civilization which brings hereto isolated societies into contact. Whether one accepts this proposition or not is irrelevant. The point is that one is confronted with a clear hypothesis concerning the nature of the factors of change.

The forces further changing the pattern of interaction are much less clear. According to the theory, contact although it first causes competition and conflict, eventually creates a division of labor and *modus vivendi* among the groups. Open conflict ceases, and a relationship based on cooperation in some spheres and on segregation in others is established. But here the theory runs into difficulties. It is clear that under some conditions this process does not take place, while under others it does. What are these conditions? Park and Wirth seem to have no systematic hypothesis on this point.

This criticism applies even more strongly to the last step, the transition from accommodation to assimilation. The processes of assimilation are clearly analyzed; the major mechanism being intermarriage and conversion. Also peaceful interaction at the accommodation stage leads to the taking over of others' attitudes, intense communication, and mutual understanding. But what are the conditions under which the processes of assimilation are triggered or blocked? Park and his disciples introduce *ad hoc* factors which delay the "natural" process. For Jews, the European tragedy of Hitler is mentioned. An establishment of a Jewish state is considered by Wirth as such a factor. But these factors are not an integral part of the conceptual scheme. Historical accidents can always be found to explain away any data which do not fit the theory. Consequently any alternative to assimilation can be defined as a delay only.

While groups are often forced into contact by the process of technological, economic, and social change, and perhaps this is an unavoidable process, the remaining stages should be seen as *alternative situations* rather than links in an evolutionary process culminating in assimilation. Groups are either in conflict or accommodation or assimilation. It is the task of social science to inquire into the conditions under which this or that alternative is chosen. The a priori assumption that there is no alternative in the long run is not justified by the data and leads to an evaluative approach in which certain processes are defined as natural and others as delaying. Assimilation, it seems, is not more probable than accommodation. Wirth seems to prefer it on nonscientific grounds.

Wirth, who closely follows Park, maintains that the Ghetto, and with it the Jews, are bound to assimilate and to disappear sooner or later as a distinct group.

> The children seem generally to carry the de-Judaization a step farther than their parents.[6] [Note the unilinear assumption.] The Ghetto demonstrates the subtle ways in which this cultural community [the Jews] is transformed by degrees until it blends with the large community about it, *meanwhile* [italics supplied] reappearing in various altered guides of its old and unmistakable atmosphere.[7] . . . Not only does the Ghetto tend to disappear, but the race tends to disappear with it.[8]

Wirth describes and analyzes the process in detail. Assimilation is a double process of external conditions and internal development. First, emancipation breaks down the formal barriers between the Jewish community and the society at large. This in turn causes increased communication between the heretofore isolated group and society. The internal process, which is just the complementary side of the same process, is a development from an orthodox religious attitude (first generation) through Conservative, then Reform Judaism (second and third generation)[9] to, finally, intermarriage, coupled with joining the Unitarian Church, and/or conversion to Christianity.[10] The change is accompanied by general acculturation.

If the Jews still exist as a distinctive group, the theory goes, this is to be explained by two factors: (a) influx of new immigrants, (b) revival of racial prejudice. If the process of immigration should cease, assimilation would "blend" the Jews into the large community in a few generations. If immigration should continue the "menace" of the Ghetto would survive as long as the reservoir of orthodox Jewish immigrants is not exhausted. The revival of anti-Semitism (in Wirth's days) is also only a temporary delaying factor. It is a part of the price of assimilation. Wirth discusses several factors responsible for the new increase in anti-Semitism. But he chooses to emphasize one factor: the assimilating Jews, too anxious to assimilate, are pushing too hard.

> Prejudice from without has revived the ghetto wall, less visible, perhaps, than before, but not less real. . . . As the Jew emerges from the ghetto and takes the character of humanity in the outside world, the ghetto declines. But as this freedom is restricted, *generally* [italics supplied] as a result of *too massed or hasty* an advance, distances between Jews and non-Jews arise and the retreat to the ghetto sets in.[11]

If the Jews leaving the Ghetto would relax, be less sensitive, act more naturally in their relations with non-Jews, one important factor delaying assimilation would be removed. Wirth compares right and wrong behavior. The Jew " . . . sensitive as he generally is even to the slightest gestures of those of whom he is not yet a part has difficulty in acting without restraint and with poise."[12] But this can be overcome, and the right behavior achieved: "His [the Jew's] personality expands and he relaxes somewhat in his studied manners and courtesies, just to be natural and act the part of one who is at home and feels at home."[13] Assimilation may take time, but in the long run there is no way back to the Ghetto, and only one way away from it to assimilation. One should not lose one's courage and escape back to the Ghetto when some difficulties arise on the way out. One should "face the music" of racial hostility; sooner or later it will subside.

So far we have discussed the theoretical scheme; we shall turn now to the facts presented by Wirth. We suggest that much of the evidence does not support and sometimes even contradicts a good part of the theoretical scheme. Wirth analyzes life histories and other "human documents" and dedicates a whole chapter to demonstrate that the Ghetto and the race do not disappear, even in places where immigration has stopped. Third generation Jews return to the Ghetto and to Judaism, some "even" become Zionists. Wirth analyzes with great insight the psychological and sociological factors causing this return. He realizes that not only the Jewish immigration and the Jewish rush to assimilate maintain the "race" but also that the contact with others and others' culture makes the Jew conscious of the positive values of his own tradition. The Ghetto is a source of "warm" intimate social life. When the Jew, who is used to this *Gemeinschaft* life, comes into contact with the external, "cool" impersonal life he misses his Jewish home and realizes its value. But Wirth's theory points to assimilation ("the race disappears"), which he seems to approve, while his evidence shows that the very generation (third) which is supposed to be on the highway to conversion is on the main road back to the Ghetto.

The study of the natural history of the Jews is focused around the concept of the Ghetto, which is problematic in itself. The Ghetto in Wirth's book is both a geographical-physical unit and an ethnic group (a group based on common origin and carrying a separate subculture). It is a place and a state of mind, an area and an institution. This fusion is misleading at a decisive point, namely when the cultural group ceases to be confined to specific geographical boundaries. Wirth sees the geographical criterion as essential. Following Park he assumes that a group which is not concentrated in one area disappears, i.e., assimilates. The third generation Jews seem to be, as Wirth himself demonstrates, a cultural group, based on tradition, organization, and communication, which maintains contact and consciousness of its members without their necessarily being concentrated. The ecological approach reaches its limitations at the same point where the race-relations theory does not suffice. Neither concedes that members of the third (and later) generations of an ethnic minority may maintain a particular subculture,[14] not lose their identity, although they are neither isolated nor concentrated in specific ecological areas.

Wirth analyzes two Ghettos, the European Middle Age Ghetto of Frankfurt and the modern, rapidly changing Ghetto in Chicago. In analyzing the second case, the relationship between area and race are explored in an elaborate manner. The failure, therefore, is only more obvious. Maxwell street is the Ghetto area—the area of the first generation's Orthodox Jews. Lawndale ("Deutschland") is the second area of settlement. Wirth shows that many norms and values have changed in the transition from the first to the second area. Jews in the second area are usually second generation in the United States, secular or Conservative, and much more Americanized. They are already "partially assimilated." The third stage still has a clear geographic designation, although not one clear center like the ones Wirth was able to point out for the first and second stages. The third generation's area is the territory of Reform Jews, a highly Americanized group on the verge of assimilation. But when we reach the "embarrassing" phenomenon of Jews who refuse to give up the "shadows of the Ghetto walls" for the new lights, Wirth fails to find a habitat for this group. These self-conscious Jews do not have a place in the ecology of the city and therefore they seem to Wirth not to have a "place" at all. He tries to find an area for them by suggesting that their return to Judaism (Ghetto as a cultural group) is accompanied by a physical return to the area of settlement (Ghetto as an ecological area).

> Jews . . . whose life begins in the Ghetto and after moving in a circle, finally ends *somewhere* not far from its starting point.[15]

Wirth who as an ecologist is always ready to name streets and quarters is compelled here to remain somewhat vague. The reason may be that he extended his theory a little too far. Obviously Jews return to Judaism without returning to the physical Ghetto, without returning to the immigrant slums. They return to a group without an ecological base, a phenomenon which Wirth's conceptual scheme does not cover.

Using Wirth's data, we would like to suggest that *a group can maintain its cultural and social integration and identity, without having an ecological basis.* The mechanisms which enable the group to maintain its integration are many and complex. Only further research can specify them in a satisfactory way. Still, one can find in Wirth's material some important clues on the nature of these mechanisms. One of the most important seems to be the common tradition reinforced by communication which is not as diffuse as the communication in primary groups, but also not as specific as communication among strangers or persons who have in common only membership in a formal organization.[16] There is common identity, tradition, values, and consciousness.[17] Often there are common sentiments and interests based on past experience, education, and communication. The common bond is reinforced through ethnic newspapers, organizations,[18] clubs,[19] and synagogues, where members meet, even though they do not live next to each other and are not concentrated in one ecological area.

Jews and some other ethnic groups in America seem to pass from ecological, traditional, immigrant "totalistic" groups (which are concentrated in "natural areas" and are based on face-to-face contacts, informal communication, and primary loyalties, limited exclusively to in-group members) to non-ecological, nontotalistic, modern groups. If the following terms are preferred, the process might be described as transition from a membership to a reference group which is maintained by communication and activated in limited social situations and core institutions (e.g., synagogues). A fuller discussion of this process is far beyond the scope of this paper. The main point is that what seems to Wirth a temporary delay in the inevitable process of disintegration of the minority group can be viewed as a process of social change and adjustment, and hence of enduring nature.

By stating that a group is non-ecological, it is not implied that the group is completely randomly distributed in space. Most ethnic groups are relatively concentrated on certain levels of stratification. The stratification structure uses space as one way of segregating groups and symbolizing distance and prestige. Thus Jews are disproportionately members of the middle class[20] which is concentrated in certain residential districts. But this does not mean that these areas are habitats, "substructures" on which social relations are "super structured";[21] or that there is a one to one relationship between habitat and culture or "race," an assumption which Wirth and Park make as a basis of their discussion. Even if the class factor is held constant and a concentration of third generation Jews is still found, this does not show that these areas are "Jewish habitats," in which Jews live a *Gemeinschaft* life, and thereby maintain their self-consciousness, identity, etc.

It seems that third generation Jews—primarily those who "return to the Ghetto," i.e., try to maintain their ties with their ethnic group—are attracted to certain suburbs. Although there seems to be no conclusive evidence, one may suggest that they usually look for a suburb in which there are at least some Jews but not much more than a third of the population.[22] The reasons for the lower limit may be that they prefer not to live in an area in which there is no synagogue, no Jewish Sunday school, no opportunity to have Jewish friends and Jewish mates for their children. Some may not go to a completely non-Jewish suburb because they do not want to have the feeling, or do not want others to have the feeling, that they are hiding their Jewishness. These suburbs may also be less open to Jews. The reasons for the upper limit may be that they would prefer not to live in an area which is clearly identified as Jewish or is about to become predominantly Jewish. Living in such an area would give them a feeling of segregation, of living in a Ghetto.

In the suburbs themselves we would expect Jews not to be concentrated in certain blocks but to be dispersed in them, maintain neighbor relations with non-Jews, participate in local activities such as the country club, PTA, municipal government, etc.—all bases for face-to-face relations between Jews and non-Jews. If these Jews still maintain a group life and self-consciousness, it is of a non-ecological nature.[23] It is a reference group, realized and reinforced in certain social situations, rather than a community or even a subcommunity.

Ecological ethnic groups are often less integrated into society than non-ecological ethnic groups. Ethnic groups concentrated in geographic areas, have often, but by no means always, been a major source of tension and have been considered disloyal to the political regime and endangering the consensus about supreme values. The Germans in Austria and Czechoslovakia were a well-known case. The Arabs in Israel are another.

This might be explained in two ways: (a) The power organization of every society is ecological. The supreme political organization, in most cases the state, aims to maintain a monopoly of power in a certain territory. Every group which concentrates in one part of this territory, and also has a different value system, potentially endangers the monopoly by being able to organize an independent political unit. A group which is ecologically dispersed, on the other hand, has no monopoly over any area and is therefore in no position to create a monopoly of power. (b) An ecological group has higher chances to avoid intimate contacts and informal communication with out-groups than has a non-ecological group and hence can more easily withhold loyalty from the society at large.

Park and Wirth, following the mass society theories, assume that eventually every *Gemeinschaft* will become a *Gesellschaft*. Ecological groups are communal in their nature and therefore will disintegrate. Segregation is therefore evaluated negatively as a source of all that is "sectarian" and "provincial," and assimilation as a progressive force. There is no third alternative between community and "society," between segregation and assimilation. This approach overlooks the pluralist nature of modern society, the importance of partial segregation combined with partial assimilation, not as a transitional stage, but as a basic form of social organization.

Some sociological reasons may be suggested as explaining the long run existence of non-ecological ethnic groups. Ecological groups may be dysfunctional, for reasons discussed above, and therefore under social pressure become acculturated or disintegrate. Groups which refuse may be penalized by limitation on their "success," as Wirth puts it,[24] i.e., by receiving a smaller share of social rewards for the same effort. Non-ecological groups, on the other hand, especially when *partially* acculturated, do not have the above mentioned dysfunctions. The dysfunctional nature of "totalistic" groups is a consequence of their ability to withhold loyalty from society; members of "partial" groups on the other hand are more likely to form primary and reference relations which cross-cut the boundaries of every single group. This is a source of social cohesion and consensus. Thus ethnic groups of this type are less likely to be dysfunctional. Moreover, they may fulfill important social functions.

The American society is not a "society" (in Tönnies' sense, which is close to what is often called a secondary group), and is not a universal melting pot,[25] into which all ethnic groups "blend" sooner or later, by accepting the dominant culture of the one "real" American tradition. It is, as has often been pointed out, a pluralistic society, with many subcultures and subgroups.[26] All integrated groups accept *some* values, the universal values of American society, but at the same time hold their own particularistic tradition and values;[27] they also maintain their segregating norms in many spheres in which the American society is open to alternative values and norms of behavior. Religion is the classic example. Attitudes toward work, leisure, sex, clothing, food, etc., are all highly differentiated, often along ethnic lines.[28] Therefore, a group may pass from more or less complete segregation to partial segregation (a transition which is often accompanied by a change from an ecological to a reference group); it may change from a relatively dysfunctional to a more integrated group without losing its identity and maintaining a subculture.

These groups have important functions in preserving the American society as it is. Their functions are comparable to those of occupational groups, professional associations and voluntary organizations in general. They are sources of the pluralism which is the basis of an open, democratic society. They are sources of consolidation of competing centers of power, which is a vital condition for the maintenance of the democratic process. Moreover, ethnic groups, which cut across other social groups—most important of which are social classes—are an important factor for maintaining the solidarity of American society and avoiding class consciousness and class conflict. If the major ethnic groups will assimilate, American pluralism[29] will be undermined. If at the same time the racial groups will not assimilate—and it seems to be agreed that their rate of assimilation is at least much slower than that of ethnic groups—and their stratificational location will not change drastically, American society will be cut into two by a clear class-race cleavage, a situation which, for instance, prevails in some Latin American countries and is considered detrimental to a balanced society in general and a democratic regime in particular. Park himself, in a different context, points to the South, as a case of a "bi-racial" society.[30] Others have analyzed the not too democratic nature of the southern states.[31]

Although American pluralism is not based on ethnic groups alone, the latter constitute a major component of it,[32] since they cut across class lines and elicit a high degree of involvement. It is therefore questionable if the other factors of pluralism would be strong enough to maintain the structure in case the ethnic groups would be weakened considerably. Others have frequently pointed out that an unlimited melting pot is undesirable from a cultural point of view.

A functional analysis always requires a complementary analysis of the mechanisms which lead to the fulfillment of these functions. The fact that there are functional needs for pluralism in American culture and democracy does not explain what causes these functions to be fulfilled. Wirth himself points to a major mechanism which leads to the fulfillment of these needs. He shows that emancipation can often be merely formal because Jews trying to pass are still rejected. This makes the Jew self-conscious, and

> he tends to return to the flock and become an ardent "Jew" and sometimes even a rapid advocate of orthodoxy and Zionism as the only fitting answer to a world that excludes him and insults him.[33]

Wirth obviously disapproves. He believes that the rejection is temporary. We would suggest that the rejection might be a long-run phenomenon, an offspring of the American tradition of pluralism, which expects everyone to accept certain universal values, but beyond that, to keep his own tradition and identity.

The third generation is often viewed as a kind of test case. Are they one step nearer to assimilation or are they less assimilated than their parents? If it is shown that they view their subculture with more pride and less self-hatred the next question is: this a temporary return or a lasting process?[34] Park and Wirth assume a unilinear process of assimilation, each stage being nearer to this end than the previous one. "Returning" to Judaism is therefore not in line with this basic process. This assumption, we suggest, lacks sound ground. A social process may take many forms and assimilation must not necessarily be the last stage. Lacking sound evidence, one is forced, in this speculative stage, to rely on others' insight and personal experience. On these bases, it seems that some children of converted Jews or mixed marriages return to Judaism. A mixed couple or a convert may be socially rejected as much and even more than a Jew. One way out of this highly marginal position is to return to one's legitimate ethnic group. In the past, at least, there seems to have been little room for "universal Americanism," for Americans who did not have a particular ethnic background. There have been attempts to create social institutions for mixed couples, converts and other assimilationists which legitimatize assimilation or serve as institutional bridges from the minority to the majority group. These institutions seem bound to fail since they rapidly become known as such. When their latent function becomes manifest, it can no longer be fulfilled.

Assimilation not only means rejection of one's own particularism but also acceptance of some other particularism, usually of a group which is considered superior, a group for instance whose values dominate the society. Now it is only natural for such a group to defend its superior status by defending its exclusiveness. This is done by (a) preventing outsiders from achieving the ascribed status by conversion, intermarriage, and joining intimate activities of the group. Hence, for such a group at least, a converted Jew may still be a converted Jew, not a true Episcopalian, etc., and a mixed couple may be classified as such and not according to the higher status of one spouse. As these attempts to assimilate are strongly connected with aspirations and efforts of

upward mobility, their *partial* failure may be related with defense mechanisms of a higher group which opposes too much upward mobility.[35] We emphasize partial failure, because even if mobility succeeds in some areas but fails in the "social" area, the purpose of assimilation has failed. Successful assimilation is based on balanced mobility, including social acceptance by the target group. One cannot lose his old identity, unless one is accepted by a new group, which has the identity sought. When such acceptance is denied we find often a phenomenon which lacking a better term will be referred to as the *"intimate kick."* Starting with secondary and semi-primary relations with members of the target group (calling them by their first names, participating in non-intimate parties of the group, etc.) the assimilationist tries to move closer, to convert these relations into full-fledged primary relations, which are considered the sign of full acceptance and the basis of "blending" into the new group. But here, at least quite often, the superior group's liberalism reaches its limits. Somewhere along the social distance scale there is a limit,[36] and when it is passed, rejection ensues.[37] The more liberal the society and the period, the nearer to the intimate pole the line is drawn,[38] the more intimate the relationship becomes before it breaks down. The more intimate the relationship, the more involved are the parties and the more frustrating the rejection.[39] The return to the ethnic group is therefore only more emotion-laden and more strongly motivated. Those "returnees" may become, as Wirth suggests, fanatically orthodox and Zionists.

This might be a basis for a cyclic process; one generation tries to assimilate, the next returns and so on; the process may take place in one lifetime and create conscious and active members of the ethnic group (the blocking of personal mobility often leads to collective activity). A group may learn. Something may go down into its tradition, a warning to following generations not even to try, to save themselves the frustration of rejection. Heine's biography, for instance, served as such a myth for some German-Jews. To sum up, the third generation may be a temporary delay on the way to assimilation but it may also be the first generation of a long-run process of revival and enhancement of solidarity and ethnic self-consciousness.

At any rate, a theory should not be formulated in a way which does not take into account the problems of pluralism versus complete assimilation; return to Judaism versus conversion; and the problem of the long-run existence of an ethnic group, versus temporary delay in the process of disintegration. The conditions under which one or the other of these phenomena emerges, should be specified, and the functional significance of both explored. An *a priori* preference of one of them cannot be accepted. Considering the empirical evidence collected by Wirth and some of the studies conducted since *The Ghetto* was first published, one may be inclined to accept the pluralist, rather than the assimilationist point of view, as being more adequately supported by the data.

NOTES

[1] Louis Wirth, *The Ghetto* (Chicago: University of Chicago Press, 1928; republished in 1956 in paper back edition).

[2] For earlier evaluations see R. D. McKenzie, *The American Journal of Sociology,* XXXV, p. 487; *The American Historical Review,* 34: 695 (April 1929); Herbert Blumer, foreword to Louis Wirth, *Community Life and Social Policy* (Chicago: University of Chicago Press, 1956).

[3] Seymour M. Lipset, "Changing Social Status and Prejudice," *Commentary* (May 1950), p. 478. See also S. M. Lipset, "Jewish Sociologists and the Sociology of the Jews," *Jewish Social Studies,* XVII, (1955), p. 177.

[4] This fallacy is discussed by Kingsley Davis in "Malthus and the Theory of Population," in *The Language of Social Research,* Paul F. Lazarsfeld and Morris Rosenberg (eds.), (Glencoe, Ill.: The Free Press, 1955).

[5] Park's theory has to be discussed since this is the theory applied by Wirth. See Robert E. Park, *Race and Culture* (Glencoe, Ill.: The Free Press, 1950), esp. p. 104. On the relation of Wirth to Park see Reinhard Bendix, "Social Theory and Social Action in the Sociology of Louis Wirth," *The American Journal of Sociology,* LIX (May 1954), pp. 523-529.

[6] *The Ghetto,* p. 256.

[7] *Ibid.,* p. 5, see also pp. 9, 128, 74.

[8] *Ibid.,* p. 125.

[9] *Ibid.,* pp. 107-108, 256. See also pp. 219, 254, 259.

[10] *Ibid.,* p. 260.

[11] *Ibid.,* p. 279.

[12] *Ibid.,* p. 267.

[13] *Ibid.,* p. 265.

[14] For this concept see Talcott Parsons, *The Social System* (Glencoe, Ill.: The Free Press, 1951), pp. 286-297.

[15] *The Ghetto,* p. 263.

[16] For an analysis of communication processes from this point of view see Amitai Etzioni, "Work Groups in Collective Settlements," *Human Organization,* 16, (Fall 1957), pp. 2-6.

[17] For an insightful report on such a group see M. B. Seider and M. J. Ravitz, "A Jewish Peer Group," *American Journal of Sociology,* Vol. 61, (July 1955), pp. 11-15.

[18] It is of interest to note that Jewish organizations are a recruiting ground for a Jewish professional elite, which has strong vested interests in maintaining and expanding the ethnic consciousness. See Solomon Sutker, "The Jewish Organizational Elite of Atlanta, Georgia," *Social Forces,* 31 (Dec. 1952), pp. 136-43.

[19] See Solomon Sutker, "The Role of Social Clubs in the Atlanta Jewish Community," in M. Sklare (ed.), *The Jews: Social Patterns of an American Group* (Glencoe, Ill.: The Free Press, 1958), pp. 262-270.

[20] See Nathan Glazer, "Social Characteristics of American Jews 1654-1954," *The American Jewish Year Book,* 55 (1955), p. 3.

[21] R. E. Park, *Human Communities* (Glencoe, Ill.: The Free Press, 1952), pp. 155-158, 139-140.

[22] Some impressions may be gained from the following discussions, John R. Seeley, R. Alexander Sim, Elizabeth W. Loosley, *Crestwood Heights* (New York: Basic Books, Inc., 1956); Herbert J. Cans, "Park Forest: Birth of a Jewish Community," *Commentary,* (April 1951). Sklare brings the following material: "According to Rosental, Jews constituted 67% of the total population of North Lawndale in 1931. In third settlement areas the ratios are very different during the same period: 8% for Uptown, 12% for Humboldt Park, and 19% for Hyde Park." M. Sklare, *Conservative Judaism* (Glencoe, Ill.: The Free Press, 1955), p. 265.

[23] Gans' study illustrates this point. See H. J. Gans, "The Origin and Growth of a Jewish Community in the Suburbs: A Study of the Jews of Park Forest," M. Sklare (ed.), *The Jews: Social Patterns of an American Group* (Glencoe, Ill.: The Free Press, 1958), pp. 205-248. See also J. R. Seeley, et al., *op. cit.*

[24] Wirth, *op. cit.,* pp. 240, 215.

[25] See Nathan Glazer, "Ethnic Groups in America: From National Culture to Ideology," in *Freedom and Control in Modern Society,* M. Berger, T. Abel, C. H. Page (eds.), (Toronto: D. Van Nostrand Company, Inc., 1954).

[26] Robin M. Williams, Jr., *American Society* (New York: Alfred A. Knopf, 1952) pp. 14-15.

[27] This is empirically demonstrated by Lubel, who shows that ethnic groups vote on some issues according to their ethnic norms, while on other issues they follow a different line, e.g., their class, their generation, their trade union, etc. See Samuel Lubel *The Future of American Politics* (New York: Harper and Bros., 1952), p. 78, on Jewish voting, pp. 207-208, 229.

[28] For a general discussion see Brewton Berry, *Race Relations* (Boston: Houghton Mifflin Co., 1951), pp. 327-333.

[29] Park and Wirth were, of course, aware of the pluralistic nature of American society. But it seems that they did not relate the process of assimilation to the problems of maintaining pluralism in a way which would show that the two are contradictory.

[30] Park, *op. cit.*, p. 220.

[31] V. O. Key, Jr., *Southern Politics* (New York: Alfred A. Knopf, 1949).

[32] See W. Herberg, *Protestant-Catholic-Jew* (New York: Doubleday and Co., 1956), p. 213.

[33] Wirth, *op. cit.*, pp. 267-268.

[34] This problem is often discussed in *Commentary*. See especially M. L. Hansen, "The Third Generation in America" reprinted in *Commentary* (November 1952); Nathan Glazer, "The Jewish Revival in America" *Commentary* (December 1955 and January 1956); Herbert J. Gans "American Jewry: Present and Future," *Commentary* (May and June 1956).

[35] See E. D. Baltzell "The Development of a Jewish Upper Class in Philadelphia: 1782-1940" in M. Sklare (ed.) *op. cit.*, pp. 271-287.

[36] The best evidence for this may be found in the low rate of intermarriage between Jews and non-Jews, which may, of course, have other important causes as well. See Ruby Reeves Kennedy, "Single or Triple Melting Pot?" *The American Journal of Sociology*, 49 (January 1944), pp. 331-339. The main point for our discussion is: "Jews almost always choose Jewish mates."

[37] W. L. Warner and P. S. Lunt describe these processes in *The Social Life of a Modern Community* (New Haven: Yale University Press, 1941).

[38] The more intimate the relation, the more informal it becomes and the more unclear is the border line. This is another factor in sustaining the unrealistic aspirations of the assimilationist, which lead him to the mistake of trying to force the issue, to bring about full assimilation.

[39] One may suggest that the relationship is asymmetric, the rejected party is more involved than the rejecting one, and the break is therefore more painful for him.

Joan Aldous (essay date 1962)

SOURCE: "Urbanization, the Extended Family, and Kinship Ties in West Africa," in *Social Forces*, Vol. 41, No. 1, October, 1962, pp. 6-12.

[*In the following essay, Aldous, applying methodology pioneered by Wirth, examines the effects of urbanization on family systems in parts of West Africa.*]

The effect of urbanization upon extended family relations has been extensively investigated within the last 10 years. The starting point for many of these studies has been Wirth's analysis of urbanism as a way of life written in 1938. According to Wirth, the city is a social organization that substitutes secondary for primary group relationships.

Though dependent on more people for the satisfactions of his wants, the urbanite, unlike his rural counterpart, is not dependent upon particular persons, and his dependence is limited to a "highly fractionalized" part of other persons' activities. Contacts are segmental and of secondary character; no group can claim the complete allegiance of the individual. The city's effect on the family, consequently, is to strip it to its bare essentials. The nuclear family of father, mother and children replaces the extended family. "The family as a unit of social life is emancipated from the larger kinship group characteristic of the country," so that relationships based on the extended family disintegrate in the city.[1]

Recent urban studies, however, have shown that kinship ties continue to exist. Using a sample representative of the Detroit area, Axelrod found interaction with relatives as manifested in friendship networks and mutual assistance to be important in all age and socioeconomic status groups.[2] Greer's sample of two middle-level census tracts in Los Angeles indicated that 73 percent of the high urban families and 76 percent of the low urban families were a part of family friendship networks.[3] The San Francisco study of Bell and Boat reported a similar finding. In their probability sample of adult males drawn from four census tracts representing different social types, six of ten men had a close friendship tie with at least one relative.[4] Seventy-six percent of the low income and 84 percent of the high income respondents, in addition, expected assistance from relatives even for prolonged illnesses.[5] Of the 195 parent-child relations Sussman studied in his New Haven research, 154 maintained mutual assistance patterns.[6] This was a white, Protestant middle-class sample, but Young and Willmott found much the same thing in London with their working class sample.[7] The same investigators' study of a middle-class London suburb showed that 25 percent of parents in their seventies lived with married children and the percent increased to 41 for those 80 and over.[8] Childless couples also turned to the extended family in old age; 53 percent of those of pensionable age lived with relatives.[9] In contrast to these results, Michel concluded that among the segment of the Parisian working class living in furnished hotels that she studied, kinship ties were disintegrating.[10] Data, therefore, collected from widely varying samples in such disparate cities as Detroit, London, San Francisco, Los Angeles and New Haven have not confirmed the disappearance of kinship ties in the urban milieu. Only in Paris did a study of a small part of the population appear to uphold the hypothesis.

Relevant African studies provide comparative data from different societies on the fate of the extended family in the city. Some variation of the extended family appears in all the basic culture areas of Africa—Mediterranean littoral, Sahara Desert area, western and eastern Sudan, the West Coast, Central-Southern and the East Horn, and the East African cattle area. In fact, the concept of the extended family itself developed from studies of African peoples. Life in the tribal villages follows a traditional pattern. The person is important only as he contributes to the extended family unit. In return he is given the security of not one but several fathers, mothers, brothers, sisters, uncles and grandparents. Such a social organization results in strong group solidarity with an attendant communal spirit. The purpose of this paper is to examine how this "powerful cementing framework" is affected by urbanization.[11]

The analysis will center on the Negro cities of West Africa.[12] Their social organization differs to a considerable extent from that of European and United States cities. Another advantage in using these cities for comparative purposes is that a number of urban studies have been done in this area. To obviate the problem of the varying completeness of the data upon which their conclusions are based, as complete a description as possible is given in this paper of the source of each study's data. The reader can decide for himself how much weight to give to each study's findings.

To test the hypothesis that extended family relations are absent in West African cities, it is necessary to set up some empirical referent for the concept of the extended family. There are several criteria that can be used to establish the existence of this kinship group. Among these is residence where two or more related nuclear family units live together or relatives share the nuclear family's quarters. A second criterion consists of the joint activities engaged in by the extended family members as an organized unit. These activities can be of various types ranging from economic and legal to welfare and leisure. Still another criterion is assistance between individual relatives based on normative expectations whether in the form of gifts or services. Friendship networks joining kinsmen constitute a fourth criterion. The presence of any of these criteria is taken as evidence of the existence of the extended family.

WEST AFRICAN CITIES

The fairest test of the hypothesis that the extended family structure will not be present in the African city would appear to lie in data from a long-settled, stable urban community. Otherwise, it could be argued that the extended family would occur in a city largely because its population is made up of recent migrants from villages who have not had time enough to be influenced by urbanization. Unfortunately for such a test, most of the cities of Africa are experiencing their greatest growth at the present time due to in-migration.[13]

The long-established city of Timbuctoo, however, is an exception. Miner, in his 1940 anthropological study, observed that though the fabled city's Arab, Taureg and Songhoi residents each possessed a distinctive culture, all three maintained extended family ties. Among the Songhoi the extended family's existence was manifested in joint activities, assistance patterns and friendship ties. Gathered in council, the extended family fulfilled a legal function meting out punishment or deciding upon reparations when a kinsman had engaged in robbery or murder

or had himself been murdered.[14] Assistance took a number of forms. Wealthier relatives adopted the poor man's "surplus" children, thereby relieving him of the burden of their support. If this aid proved insufficient, relatives supplied food, clothing or shelter. Helping patterns were also present among the Tauregs, who followed the same adoption practice.[15] Like the Songhoi, they too participated in friendship networks with relatives, as did the Arabs. Arab men, for example, every morning after breakfast would go about the town exchanging greetings with parents, uncles, aunts and siblings. On Fridays they visited more distant relatives.[16] Thus in Timbuctoo the individual, far from being limited to the nuclear family, was involved in various forms of relations with the extended family.

Other examples of long-settled urban people exist among the Yoruba of Nigeria. Though living "long before colonial times" in cities of up to 100,000 residents, the Yoruba have maintained their traditional extended family patterns.[17] Individuals continue to feel strong obligations to give economic assistance to relatives while maintaining social ties, and the customary residential unit remains the lineage. For these reasons the anthropologist Bascom, although noting the weakening of kinship bonds, has declared "the city dweller need not feel lonely or insecure."[18]

In Lagos, a traditional city now subject to industrial influence, the kinship group remains important, though the anthropologist Comhaire described it as "teeming with political and business activities of the most modern kind."[19] This was demonstrated in the study Marris made in 1958-59 of a slum area in central Lagos in which he found the extended family existing according to all four criteria listed above. For his research he interviewed 372 men and women—110 households—intensively. There were still four properties on the four streets Marris surveyed in detail where the children of the founder of the family property followed the traditional custom and occupied it together with their families and descendants. Tenants, however, constituted 60 percent of the population of the area. Though they were less apt than owners to have relatives living with them, 38 percent had at least one brother or sister in the same residence, and among an additional 23 percent a half-brother or sister was present. Moreover, members of extended families when living apart were usually within a 10 to 15 minute walk from each other and showed a high degree of mutual affection. Friendship networks were maintained by daily meetings which served as opportunities to pass on family news and to discuss family problems.[20]

As for assistance patterns, the residents of central Lagos, like their rural counterparts, continued to regard the needs of their kinfolk as their first obligation. They supported aged aunts and cousins as well as parents, so it was customary to present their elderly kinsmen with gifts in cash or kind when visiting them. In addition, they often contributed to the marriage payments of younger brothers, reared nieces and nephews and helped married sisters. Such assistance coupled with open-handed hospitality and gifts to relatives still living in the country often proved a financial burden on the urban dwellers. Over one-half of the persons Marris interviewed, for example, spent at least one-tenth of their income assisting relatives. This aid, however, was not begrudged. The "sense of mutual obligation of the family group is the outstanding loyalty of Lagos social life," Marris concluded.[21] Its residents, therefore, rather than owing their primary loyalty to themselves or to their conjugal families, identified with the extended family.

In addition to the help given because of personal obligations ensuing from kinship ties, the extended family in Lagos as an organized unit engaged in welfare activities. Its members contributed funds which were distributed to relatives in need whether they were the orphaned, the elderly, the unemployed or the young eager for an education. Relatives and the extended family, therefore, substituted for the nonexistent public welfare program. The kinship group as a unit also held frequent celebrations. Funerals, naming ceremonies for the newborn and anniversaries served as such occasions, with each branch of the family paying for a part of the expenses. The extended family was "westernized" to the extent that as a group it often took on the formal character of a voluntary association. When this was the case, all the members met at regular monthly or weekly intervals instead of waiting for special occasions. At these meetings the kinsmen functioned as a legal body discussing family difficulties and settling disputes. At many such meetings the relatives contributed to a subscription fund to be used to repair the family house or to conduct corporate business in the name of the extended family's founder. Two-thirds of the men and women Marris interviewed belonged to families having such regular meetings.[22] Thus the extended family served as the basis for one of the new voluntary associations the residents of Lagos formed to forward their common economic interests.

Africans living in Leopoldville and Stanleyville, Republic of the Congo, have also been studied in some detail. Here too the extended family in various forms continues to remain important to the individual. In Leopoldville, the assistance patterns led to the doubling up of residential units. Comhaire declared, on the basis of his observations while an information officer in the Belgian Congo, that the unemployed or new arrivals to the city turned to relatives for shelter and sustenance.[23] A survey reported by UNESCO indirectly confirmed this observation when it showed that 16 percent of the average couple's food budget went to the support of adult dependents.[24] The extended family also manifested itself in joint religious activities which had an additional recreational function. The week-long funeral proceedings to whose expense even distant relatives contribute were the focus of urban social life, according to Comhaire. These family rites also served to strengthen the solidarity of the extended family as well as serving as an index of it. Even organizations based on professional or territorial interests were usually pseudo-kinship groups. Comhaire concluded on the basis

of this evidence that the extended family institution would probably continue in Leopoldville for some time to come.[25]

In Stanleyville as in Lagos, Nigeria, permanent housing patterns attest to the strength of the extended family. A 1952 survey of a random sample of the population sponsored by the International African Institute showed that 34.9 percent of the tenants who were subletting property were closely related to the owner, while an additional 24.3 percent were more distant relatives. None of the close relatives and only a few of the more distantly related paid rent.[26]

Dakar, Senegal, in another new nation is yet another city whose inhabitants have been studied. The results show the continuing existence of the extended family. One survey described in a UNESCO report pointed to the increasing importance of the nuclear family as the household unit, a finding in line with the hypothesis that the extended family disappears in the urban environment.[27] The extended family continued, however, in assistance patterns, friendship networks and joint activities. Family unity, for example, served to stimulate help to relatives. The same UNESCO survey noted that the obligation to come to the aid of kinsmen was respected in all sections of the population.[28] Many immigrants were only able to subsist because they could take up residence with an already established single relative or family group, and this was also true of the jobless. As Dakar generally has a high unemployment rate—10 percent in 1955—without the assistance its unemployed workers received from kinsmen, many of them would have to leave the city. By this help the extended family substituted for a nonexistent government unemployment compensation program. With only a few exceptions, family friendship ties were maintained through visits with relatives living in various parts of town. Joint celebrations served as occasions for the extended family as a whole to get together. The extended family also engaged in economic activities. The anthropologist Mercier observed that self-employment in such occupations as trading, gardening and fishing made possible the retention of the type of economic organization based on parental relationships almost unchanged from the form found in tribal villages.[29]

Brazzaville, the capital of what was formerly French Equatorial Africa, now Congo, has also been the subject of research. Here too the extended family was present. Mutual aid was prevalent, leading in some cases to persons sharing their residential quarters with relatives. The social anthropologist Balandier, in an intensive study of one African section of the city, found residents expected to take in relatives coming into town for seasonal work or education. They also contributed to the education costs of relatives.[30] If other work were unavailable students or other relatives could turn to trader kinsmen. These middlemen, as much as possible, gave available jobs to kinsmen rather than filling them according to merit, Balandier observed.[31]

So far the discussion has been largely limited to findings concerning specific cities. When one turns to descriptions of African cities in general, some of them are reminiscent of Wirth's analysis. McCall, from his experience in Ghana and Liberia, concluded that status in the city was achieved and not an ascribed status based on family membership. Kinsmen constituted only a small number of those with whom the African urbanite daily interacted. The extended family as a residential unit was breaking down. Other relatives were rarely found in the nuclear family's town dwelling although in the country members of the extended family would live in the same compound.[32] Smythe, who had done field research in West Africa, wrote that emphasis on extended family loyalty, obedience to the tribal elders and devotion to clan and tribe were giving way to the Africans' desire for a big car, a good job having status, a nice home and especially money.[33] Even observers like these, however, who discount the importance of the extended family in the city describe its continued existence and influence. Thus McCall characterized the migrant to the city as preeminently an offshoot of the kinship group. As such he expected to assist through support and shelter other relatives who would follow,[34] a conclusion supported by the studies cited above.

The economist Okigbo, after noting that West African society was formerly based on family linkages, declared that it still retained some of its solidarity. But he added that the kinship structure had felt the weakening impact of growing individualism and new alignments based on similarity of outlook and education. With the rise in living standards, obligations to meet the needs of poor and nonproductive relatives had become an unpleasant duty. Evasions of such responsibilities, in his observations, were more common than formerly.[35] Another economist, Marcus, concluded from her interviews with "over 400" individuals in Tropical Africa that in some African areas the younger generation, "perhaps the third or fourth generation of city dwellers," was rebelling against the extended family system.[36]

CONCLUSIONS

Thus some observers see signs which indicate that individuals are less apt to honor assistance obligations to relatives than formerly. Trade union and other associations also cut across family lines to serve political, occupational and neighborhood interests. Yet, as detailed above, available research on West African cities shows the continued existence of the extended family. As Homans has written, kinship relations are not maintained unless they serve some purpose for those involved.[37] In the African cities of Brazzaville, Dakar, Lagos, Leopoldville and Stanleyville, the extended family is indeed functional. Besides filling recreational, religious, legal or economic needs of urbanites it substitutes for a nonexistent public social welfare program. Kinsmen provide for the elderly and support the sick, the jobless and the destitute. They give the new arrival from the country shelter and food and help him to get work or an education and to adjust to the bustling city. A corollary of this is that the individual urbanite, far from facing the complex urban milieu as a solitary individual, exists in a web of friendship relations in the extended family. It would, of course, be desirable if more information were available concerning urban life in these and other cities in this area. Since it is not, however, one can come to a tentative conclusion on the basis of the evidence at hand. On this basis, the hypothesis that the extended family will disappear would seem not to hold true. Rather, the existing data indicate not only the continued presence of the extended family, but the crucial functions it performs for the African in the urban milieu.

NOTES

[1] Louis Wirth, "Urbanism as a Way of Life," *American Journal of Sociology,* 44 (July 1938), p. 21.

[2] Morris Axelrod, "Urban Structure and Social Participation," *American Sociological Review,* 21 (February 1956), p. 17.

[3] Scott Greer, "Urbanism Reconsidered," *American Sociological Review,* 21 (February 1956), p. 23.

[4] Wendell Bell and Marion D. Boat, "Urban Neighborhoods and Informal Social Relations," *American Journal of Sociology,* 62 (January 1957), pp. 394, 396.

[5] *Ibid.,* p. 396.

[6] Marvin B. Sussman, "The Help Pattern in the Middle Class Family," *American Sociological Review,* 18 (February 1953), p. 23.

[7] Michael Young and Peter Willmott, *Family and Kinship in East London* (Glencoe, Ill.: The Free Press, 1957).

[8] Peter Young and Michael Willmott, *Family and Class in a London Suburb* (London: Routledge and Kegan Paul Ltd., 1960), p. 40.

[9] *Ibid.,* p. 51.

[10] Andrée Michel, *Famille Industrialisation Logement* (Paris: Centre National de la Recherche Scientifique, 1959).

[11] Hugh H. Smythe, "Social Change in Africa," *American Journal of Economics and Sociology,* 19 (January 1960), p. 202.

[12] The Department of State classification system is used which includes the Congo and the Republic of the Congo in West Africa, as well as among others, Nigeria and the Mali Federation, consisting of Senegal and the Sudanese Republic. See G. Etzel Pearcy, *Africa: Names and Concepts* (Washington, D. C.: Department of State Publication 7129, January 1961), p. 9.

[13] Lagos, Nigeria, for example, with a population of 250,000 in 1952, had trebled in 25 years. In 1950 over

one-half of its population was estimated to be immigrants. International African Institute, London, *Social Implications of Industrialization and Urbanization of Africa South of the Sahara* (Paris: UNESCO, 1956), p. 22. Population estimates as of 1959 for this and other cities mentioned in the paper are as follows: Brazzaville, Congo, 93,500; Dakar, Senegal, 185,820; Lagos, Nigeria, 364,000; Leopoldville, The Congo, 402,492; and Stanleyville, The Congo, 126,533. *UN Demographic Yearbook* (New York: United Nations Publications, 1960).

[14] Horace Miner, *The Primitive City of Timbuctoo* (Philadelphia: American Philosophical Society, 1953), p. 140. Miner felt Timbuctoo readily fitted Wirth's definition of a city as a "relatively large, dense and permanent settlement of socially heterogeneous individuals" despite its rather small population of some 6000. *Ibid.*, p. 11, quoting Wirth, *op. cit.*, p. 8.

[15] *Ibid.*, p. 140.

[16] *Ibid.*, p. 147.

[17] Historical descriptions of the cities date from the sixteenth century. See William Bascom, "Urbanization Among the Yoruba," *American Journal of Sociology,* 60 (March 1955), p. 448.

[18] *Ibid.*, p. 451.

[19] Jean L. Comhaire, "Economic Changes and the Extended Family," *Annals,* 305 (May 1956), p. 48.

[20] Peter Marris, "Slum Clearance and Family Life in Lagos," *Human Organization,* 19 (Fall 1960), p. 124.

[21] *Loc. cit.*

[22] *Loc. cit.*

[23] Jean L. Comhaire, "Some Aspects of Urbanization in the Belgian Congo," *American Journal of Sociology,* 62 (July 1956), p. 11.

[24] UNESCO, *op. cit.*, p. 33.

[25] Comhaire, "Some Aspects . . .", *op. cit.*, p. 13.

[26] V. G. Pons, "The Changing Significance of Ethnic Affiliation and of Westernization in the African Settlement Patterns in Stanleyville," in International African Institute, *op. cit.*, p. 644.

[27] UNESCO, *op. cit.*, p. 28.

[28] *Ibid.*, p. 32.

[29] Comhaire, "Economic Changes . . .", *op. cit.*, p. 48, quoting Paul Mercier, "Aspects de la société africaine dans l'agglomération dakaroise," *Études sénégalaises,* No. 5 (1954), pp. 11-40.

[30] Georges Balandier, "Sociological Survey of the African Town at Brazzaville," in International African Institute, *op. cit.*, p. 108.

[31] Comhaire, "Economic Changes . . .", *op. cit.*, p. 48, quoting Georges Balandier, *Sociologie des Brazzavilles noires* (Paris: Armand Colin, 1955).

[32] Daniel McCall, "Dynamics of Urbanization in Africa," *Annals,* 298 (March 1955), p. 154.

[33] Smythe, *op. cit.*, p. 202.

[34] McCall, *op. cit.*, p. 159.

[35] Pius Okigbo, "Social Consequences of Economic Development in West Africa," *Annals,* 305 (May 1956), p. 130.

[36] Mildred R. Marcus, "Some Social Characteristics of Tropical African Peoples," *Sociology and Social Research,* 45 (October 1960), p. 42. If, however, rebellion against the responsibilities of family ties must wait for the third or fourth generation of urbanites, a widespread movement will be long in developing. The overwhelming majority of African urbanites are migrants.

[37] George C. Homans, *The Human Group* (New York: Harcourt, Brace and Company, 1950), p. 265.

Albert J. Reiss, Jr. (essay date 1964)

SOURCE: "Introduction: Sociology as a Discipline," in *On Cities and Social Life,* by Louis Wirth, The University of Chicago Press, 1964, pp. ix-xxx.

[*In the following essay, an editor's introduction to Wirth's selected papers, Reiss provides an overview of Wirth's sociological ideas, and discusses these within the framework of the discipline as a whole.*]

Sociology, for Louis Wirth, is a more or less organized body of knowledge about human behavior—"What is true of human behavior by virtue of the fact that always and everywhere men live a group existence?" Like others from the "Chicago school" of sociology, he held that the discipline of sociology consists of three divisions, loosely defined: demography, ecology, and technology; social organization; and social psychology.

The field of *demography, ecology, and technology* is concerned with the physical, biological, and situational base of human living, and the techniques and tools that man evolved which affect his environment. These circumstances or factors constitute the preconditions of existence at particular times. They are materially ascertainable conditions. At the other pole is *social psychology,* a field concerned with personality and collective behavior. It constitutes the study of the "subjective aspect of culture," the psychic states, attitudes, and sentiments of persons as well as communication, public opinion, consensus, ideas, and collective action. The main field is *social organization,* concerned not only with systems of social life but all their constituent elements, such as groups, associations, communities, institutions, and classes.

Sociology is to be regarded as both a general and a special social science:

> Sociology . . . is a general social science in the sense that the questions it asks about human nature and the social order are of a kind that cut across different specific contexts and accent the group factor in human behavior . . . sociology is a specific discipline in that it focuses on the nature and genesis and forms of the human personality and attitudes (social psychology); in that it is also concerned with the structuring of group life. . . .[1]

As a special discipline, Wirth at times characterized sociology as the "science of left-overs," a collection of special subjects discarded by the other social sciences, e.g., social problems, the family, and rural sociology. These special concerns he felt hindered the development of a genuinely comparative sociology.

Of his own entry into sociology, he said:

> I was enthusiastic and radical in those days in a sense that I believed a science of human behavior not only possible but indispensable. What I read in the course of my studies impressed me as rather disappointing. Through the inspiration and the help of . . . teachers . . . I was impelled to go on and do what little I could to make our knowledge in the field perhaps a little less disappointing to others.[2]

Wirth's papers stand as partial evidence of his success. Though what sociologists *do* may often be disappointing, sociology is an intellectually challenging subject matter.

SOCIOLOGICAL THEORY AND METHODOLOGY

Louis Wirth regarded himself as a sociological theorist, though it is not possible to characterize his own sociological theory. He firmly maintained that sociology had not developed a body of knowledge that merited formulation as a theory. What he offered to others—both to students in classes and in his writings—therefore, was an analysis of sociological writings and of social reality as he saw it, and a strategy for the development of sociological theory. To students, his penetrating negative and critical stance generally emerged as contributing more to their own development than any positive one. This is not surprising perhaps since his own analysis remained essentially unsystematized. The essays in this volume thus do not provide an introduction to the work of a systematist, as that word is generally used. He would have been the first to deny that he was one. Rather, what the reader finds is a number of essays that illuminate several aspects of social life as he defined it, molded by a general perspective of consensus as the basis of social order.

Whether Wirth might have developed a more systematic sociological theory had he lived is perhaps a matter of idle speculation. Yet several things are worth noting in this connection. Though interested in questions regarding formal properties of any theory, what is called metatheory, he was skeptical of the possibilities for a systematic sociological theory. He had the humanist's regard for the central role of values in shaping and reshaping human events, and of history in the unending social drama. Though a political activist, he was disinclined to tackle the problems of politics theoretically. He approached such problems primarily through action research, research that is intimately tied to changing the social order rather than to a theoretical formulation about what that order is like.

The first step to be taken in developing a sound sociological theory Wirth maintained was to develop a coherent set of assumptions and a conceptual framework consistent with the group character of social life.

> By theory, I mean the definition of interests of scholars, the assumptions with which they start, the conceptual framework in terms of which they analyze their materials, and the types of generalizations which they develop as they are related to other generalizations in the field as a whole or knowledge as a whole.[3]

He was rarely sympathetic with attempts to develop deductive sociological theory, speaking of all such endeavors as "mere exercises" in theory construction. As Bendix points out, Wirth contested the validity of most sociological theory on grounds that it was but proof of what had already been assumed.[4] "Most sociological theories," he would say, "ignore the most obvious and obscure thing about human beings, what it is they take for granted." He was especially disenchanted with theories based on a rational means-ends framework, since they failed to treat nonrational behavior as important determinants of behavior.

Theories of social action were generally dismissed on grounds that they focused only on people doing things, i.e., actually behaving, when failure to act was in his judgment an equally significant fact about human social life. Wirth steadfastly refused to limit sociological inquiry to the study of overt behavior or action, contending that values, ideas, attitudes, and motives are equally viable concepts in sociology:

> . . . in the study of human social life generally, while it is desirable to concentrate on overt action— of which language itself is one form—it is not so irrelevant, as some have thought, to take account of what people say. For despite the deflections, distortions, and concealment of their verbal utterances, men do betray, even if they do not always accurately and completely reveal in them, their motives and their values.[5]

Yet he was clearly dissatisfied with most theories of motivation and values. He was particularly critical of psychoanalytic theory, opposing it on grounds that it was incompatible with the group nature of social life and personality in the context of a cultural milieu. Despite his admiration for the Scottish moral philosophers, particularly Adam Smith, he contended that Smith failed to utilize the fundamental insight developed in the *Theory of Moral Sentiments,* that motivation arises through the sharing of common sentiments, for his analysis of the market economy in *The Wealth of Nations.* Notwithstanding his criticism of specific theoretical formulations in *The Polish Peasant,* he was perhaps more sympathetic to Thomas and Znaniecki's basic concerns in developing a theory of motivation resting in values and attitudes than were most of the critics of that work.[6] Though rejecting Thomas and Znaniecki's formulation of the "four wishes," he nevertheless expressed the view that critics had failed to provide viable alternatives for their formulation. For he steadfastly maintained that " . . . if we do not have an understanding of . . . motives and values, we do not know men as social beings."[7]

Values are for Wirth an important concern in sociology for two reasons. They are data of sociology necessary to know men as social beings. But, they are also forces acting upon the sociologist in his study of human behavior. His own position on the sociologist's dilemma regarding facts and valuations in social science is closer to that recorded in Myrdal's *American Dilemma*[8] than that of Weber,[9] as the hitherto unpublished piece, **"On Making Values Explicit,"** in this volume makes clear. Writing to Myrdal in 1939, he said: "Without valuations we have no interest, no sense of relevance or significance, and, consequently, no object."[10] Summarizing his view of values in sociology for Howard Odum, he wrote:

> we are, of course, as scientists, or would-be scientists, interested in understanding what is, rather than what ought to be. But it has been my experience that almost everything we do is tied up with the problem of values. Values determine our intellectual interests, the selection of problems for analysis, our selection and interpretation of the data, and to a large extent also our generalizations and, of course, our application of these generalizations. Therefore, I believe the sociologist, like other social scientists, must make greater efforts than physical and biological scientists to make explicit the value premises from which he proceeds.[11]

Wirth's theoretical position on values is therefore intimately tied to a methodological position. Even the critical examination of another man's contribution to sociology requires a knowledge of the theorist's background and perspective, an examination at the level of the sociology of knowledge. At the Social Science Research Council conference on Herbert Blumer's appraisal of Thomas and Znaniecki's *The Polish Peasant,* Wirth remarked:

> . . . I would say one way to begin the analysis of a given theory is to inquire into the particular perspective which prompted this particular author to arrive at these particular conclusions or hypotheses. Having discovered that, i.e., what he took for granted, I would say, "Now suppose we take

something else for granted, at what conclusions would we arrive?" . . . it might result in two opposing theories. Then I would ask, which one requires the most assumptions and which one is more consistent with what we already know?[12]

Just as it is difficult to characterize Wirth's scholarship in terms of a theoretical position, other than to say that he sought a body of verified knowledge for sociology, so it is not easy to characterize his methodological stance in terms of a recognized position or unified school. Close to the skeptics in his approach to any question, he would have been among the first to question such a procedure, delighting in questioning the assumptions and presuppositions of any and all schools of thought. Given to phenomenological empiricism as was Robert Park, he argued against the pitfalls of "getting too close to the data." Perceiving the relational character of all knowledge, he advocated an assault upon the problem. "Knowledge of the unstated assumptions and premises of our own and other people's premises comprises the foundation of our intellectual house." For him, the sociology of knowledge, or of intellectual life, vied with established schools of epistemology in getting at truth—"a version of reality compatible with reality." He sensed a "real" order to the world, the way things are to human beings, but regarded the nominalist-realist controversy as a straw man.

Apart from the basic methodological position inherent in his sociology of intellectual life, Wirth advocated a union of intimate acquaintance with social life and *sociologically* contrived conceptions of that reality. He continually emphasized the importance of William James's distinction between knowledge of things and acquaintance with them. Acquaintance with things was most likely to stem from actual *experience* and *involvement* with reality. "In my work in theory, especially through my ears of teaching it to graduate students, I have tried to emphasize that theory is an aspect of everything they do, and not a body of knowledge separate from research and practice."[13]

He was unimpressed with most cross-cultural work as a basis for the development of a scientific sociology. Such comparison, in his view, was essentially sterile, since it ignored the most important facts about human life—the changing course of human history and the ways in which societies are changed by civilization. A genuinely comparative sociology must be based in history.

Wirth had a predilection for typological classification, believing it to be the single most important prerequisite to the development of sociological theory. The ideal types of "urban" and "rural" ways of life developed in the essay on **"Urbanism as a Way of Life"**; of pluralistic, assimilationist, secessionist, and militant minorities in **"The Problem of Minority Groups"**; of hegemony, particularistic, marginal, and minority nationalism in **"Types of Nationalism"**; and of social types of Jews in **"Some Jewish Types of Personality"** reflect both his concern for the development of ideal types to facilitate theoretical analysis and his insistence that these types be grounded in experience and observation of social reality.

He rejected the basic methodological distinction of German sociologists between causal and meaningful relationships, suggesting it is a contradiction in terms. Undoubtedly Max Weber's critique of the German school of Verstehen, together with Weber's reformulation of it, and his discussion of ideal type analysis and causal imputation influenced Wirth's thinking. Skeptical of Weber's analysis in *The Protestant Ethic and the Spirit of Capitalism,* he nonetheless sympathized with the method Weber used to approach the problem. Weber's treatment of causal imputation, by construction and verification of a historical individual—the thing to be explained—was of special interest to him. He insisted on viewing social reality in terms of "what would have happened if an event had not taken place," or "what would happen if we altered or changed these conditions." To understand social institutions, he regarded it as important to know what would be altered or disrupted if the institution were taken away. This, for him, was the clue to its function. "We get an institution when we know that its removal will slow up sets of behavior and understandings among people in a society."

Wirth readily questioned what other social scientists take for granted. Students and colleagues alike were aware of his critical skills. Educated men were not necessarily speaking intelligently nor were they intellectuals. He was generally as impatient with the grand theory as with the trivial empirical investigation with precise measurement. Both were usually seen as pretensions that disregarded the nature of social life. If anything could be said to be characteristic of his highly perceptive and usually insightful commentary on social life, it is that it arose from what he liked to term a healthy skepticism, a continuous questioning of what is known or of how things come to be known. "Nothing is ever self-evident; it is not even evident." "The hardest thing to know is what people take for granted." "To say something is a law of nature is to confess ignorance, especially when it is applied to the realm of social life." "Our generalizations can be no more valid than the precision with which our concepts are formulated." "The more precise and unambiguous concepts in social theories become, the less valuable they are." Such statements convey both his impatience with assumptions or generalizations that are accepted without question by sociologists, and the way in which he tried to imbue others with a healthy skepticism.

CONSENSUS

Wirth's theoretical writings center around the problem of consensus as the basis of social order. He defined a society or social group by its capacity to act together, or to take collective action. Collective action rests in "a set of common understandings, a system of reciprocally acknowledged claims and expectations." His presidential address to the members of the American Sociological Society emphasized that collective action rests in consensus.

> I regard the study of consensus as the central task of sociology, which is to understand the behavior of men in so far as that is influenced by group life. Because the mark of any society is the capacity of its members to understand one another and to act in concert toward common objectives and under common norms, the analysis of consensus rightly constitutes the focus of sociological investigation.[14]

The most important thing to know about any aggregate of people belonging together, he contended, is "what they take for granted." The first task for sociology, therefore, he held, is to learn the unstated assumptions of people, the credo by which they live. These are the elements upon which there is consensus, a consensus which does not "rise above the level of consciousness." To know these things about organized entities, he insisted, requires that "we enter into their life." He often paraphrased Kant's dictum: "one should not believe everything that people say, nor should one suppose they say it without reason."

That for Wirth the study of consensus was the central task of sociology is apparent from the way he treated the ends-means (teleological) problem. Although he viewed human beings as essentially goal-directed animals, the crucial fact about them, for him, was their collective pursuit of ends. Only rarely is behavior an individual pursuit. Goal-seeking requires organization and collective action which derives from consensus on ends to be pursued. The paradox this created for Wirth is that while ends cannot be pursued without organization, organizations may monopolize one's loyalties and the very conditions for freedom. He was deeply concerned with the establishment of consensus by democratic means in the mass society. He wanted to know not only what consensus is necessary for individual freedom to be realized but how much freedom is necessary to achieve a genuine consensus resting in voluntary agreement.

Wirth's concern with the analysis of consensus was by no means an interest in some static equilibrium, for consensus is treated as problematic in the social order. Yet he never probed the different meanings of consensus, formally regarding it in only two senses: (1) as a sufficient understanding of the symbols of others to permit communication rather than "talking past one another" and (2) as sharing of the same values. Consensus in the first sense might involve only "an agreement to disagree." A minimum condition for it he thought is tolerance, which in his elfin manner he described as a "suspicion that the other fellow might be right." Following Robert Park, he contrasted consensus in the second sense with symbiosis. "Symbiosis" was defined as a condition in which "men live together by virtue of sheer existential dependence upon one another" while "consensus" is that condition in which men agree with and mutually identify with one another.

His failure to explore the dimensions of consensus is readily apparent in the kind of questions he raised about consensus in the mass society. "The fundamental problem for modern society," he would say, "is how can so many people live together if they have so little in common in the way of moral values or sacred beliefs? How can a mass society exist with so little consensus?" This manner of stating the problem led him to ignore the possibility that there may be more consensus in a modern mass society than in any previous ones, given the myriad consensually legitimate groups within it.

Wirth was particularly critical of simple explanations of the conditions for consensus. He did not regard contact and interaction as necessary and sufficient conditions for consensus. Though he regarded contact as a necessary condition for consensus, since only through confrontation with alternatives could choice be made, he argued that with contact one is as likely to get confusion and conflict as well as friendship and harmony.

Like Robert Park, Wirth saw society as resting on three main types of order. There is first a kind of equilibrium in which people compete with and struggle against one another, what Hobbes termed a *bellum omnia contra omnes*. This is the *symbiotic order*. Society is also a set of symbols or communications resulting in common understandings, a *cultural order*. Finally, society is a group of people accepting a set of common norms, rules of the game, common goals, and agreement upon the achievement of these goals. This was termed the *moral and political order*. For Wirth, these were different orders of *social cohesion*. They exist and grow up, one upon the other. A political order rests upon a cultural order, and there can be no political order without a competitive system. In his lectures, he often remarked, "If we look at a society as being a symbiotic system, a set of common understandings, mutual claims and expectations, and a system of norms, we can say that society exists wherever *consensus* exists among men. A society is as large as the area over which consensus prevails." Reference to the consensual base of society as the moral or political order was by no means a fortuitous choice of words. Wirth, unlike Park, saw the problems of consensus as political problems. The democratic selection of political means and the mobilization of people for a consensual order resting in a democratic creed or ideology was his idea of the "good society."

At times he approached the problem of consensus by first asking what were the bases for concerted action. "On what bases do people coexist?" he would ask. His answer was that they coexist first of all in terms of physical contact and interdependence, an *ecological community*. A second basis for collective action is the division of labor and the struggle for a livelihood, an *economic base*. A consideration of *different or common interests* arising from needs that are incidental to living or working together is a third basis for collective action. The pursuit of interests gives rise to a fourth basis for collective action, the *normative basis*, or the moral area of life as it is regulated by common values. The realm of tradition, a *culture*, provides a fifth basis for collective action since it provides a common framework of language,

ideas, sentiments, and the like. Although he argued that these account for man's coexistence, he concluded they do not deal directly with the problem of how men, although they are different beings, can act concertedly—how consensus is achieved. He emphasized that there is an important difference between the kind of order that arises from the fact that people have similar or parallel aims and that arising from their co-operation to achieve a common end which is seen and shared by everyone. Organizations based upon these two kinds of bonds were fundamentally different for him. In the one case he held that people act alike because they are and think alike while in the other, people work to implement commonly accepted goals even though they are not necessarily alike and may think and act differently as they work to achieve them.

Few issues were as confused in sociology, he thought, as that between "similarity" and "commonness" or between "parallelism" and "shared circumstances of living." He emphasized that people often live similar lives without common goals; they are culturally and socially distant, though spatially and economically interdependent. "A mere aggregate of people does not constitute a social entity," he would say; "Unless people recognize they have the same goals or position in life and act accordingly, unless they develop a consciousness and a capacity for collective action based upon the consensus, they do not have a group life." Perhaps because of this artificial distinction between symbiosis and consensus and his own definition of widespread consensus as the basis for collective action, he was led to underestimate both how much social life is possible without consensus and how much the mass society is organized through consensually legitimated institutions.

For Wirth, the main problems in achieving consensus in modern societies arose from the segmentation of values and interests and their lack of integration with one another, and from the failure of men to participate together in reaching common decisions. He viewed the modern world as atomized into a multiplicity of interests with people failing to communicate meaningfully with one another and to participate in common decision-making, and concluded that the main task of anyone who would forge a democratic consensus is less one of reconciling conflicting interests than of *generating participation in common decisions*. A main difficulty, he felt, in generating participation in the mass society is the fact that people are generally *excluded* from participation in decision-making. He often remarked: "Even if there is a so-called common man by virtue of the fact that as Lincoln said, 'God made so many of them,' there is no discounting the fact that they have little to say in making common decisions; today the common man has no power of original decision, judgment, or initiation." It seems clear that for Wirth democratic consensus lay less in consensually legitimated institutions that make decisions than in mass participation in making them.

Wirth viewed the dissociation of men from full and intimate participation in community life then as an integral aspect of the mass society. The problem of democracy in a mass society for him was how to encourage people to share in decision-making. He argued that today there is only a "superficial" consensus based on similarity and concentration of power whereas a "genuine" consensus is necessary, one based on communication and common participation in making common decisions. Like Dewey, he emphasized that society exists not only *through* communication but *in* communication. Central to an understanding of consensus, therefore, is an understanding of communication and its organization in societies. He was particularly concerned that communication through the mass media is a one-way process, with the media controlled by a small group of men, since he viewed the mass media of communication as a potential means of generating mass participation in common decisions in the mass society. His presidential address, **"Consensus and Mass Communication"** was devoted to this question.

Openly critical of those who nostalgically advocated a return to the "simple life," he maintained that such a situation is possible in modern societies only on the condition of terror. At the same time he was frankly skeptical about the possibility that men can be integrated in a common life in mass societies, emphasizing that the bases for agreement are ever-shifting. To what extent can we enlist the masses of men to participate in some functional activity when we have segmental interest groups, he would ask. In reply, he would say that uncoerced consensus requires some kind of constitution, minimal consensus to arbitrate our differences and a maximum communication of ideas and values. Above all he contended there should be competition in the marketplace of ideas if democracy is to survive. **"Ideas and Ideals as Sources of Power in the Modern World"** is an essay reflecting the importance that Wirth attached to them as a basis for building consensus for a world community.

Wirth never attempted any systematic theory which might be brought to bear on the problem of consensus as the basis of social order. He brought rather a point of view and illuminating discussion of the problem of achieving a democratically based consensus in the mass society. Analytically, he was disposed to view consensus in terms of several main questions: (1) How widely does consensus extend for a given universe of discourse? (2) What is the penetration of consensus? How pervasive or thoroughgoing is it? (3) What is its degree of integration? Is it segmental or comprehensive?

SOCIAL ORGANIZATION

Wirth approached the analysis of social organization from a dual viewpoint: (1) that of *social structure or form* resulting from social interaction and (2) that of *social process* or dynamic qualities underlying any more or less enduring structure. A central task of sociology he contended is to understand how structure and process are interrelated in all social phenomena. He conceptualized social structures as forms of human activity. This led him to reject most current theories of social structure on the

grounds that they dissociated structure and process. He suggested that, for example, if the concept of "association" were looked at as a verb rather than as a noun, one would ask with whom do people associate, and why, rather than what kind of associations do they form. Social organization for Wirth was both structure and equilibrium, and process and interaction.

Wirth emphasized also that an understanding of social organization required that it be compared with other "conditions," those of unorganization, disorganization, and reorganization. Like W. I. Thomas, he viewed such conditions in terms of social process. Much human activity he suggested is unorganized. A main task of sociology, therefore, is to investigate how organization comes into being. He asserted that under unorganized conditions, parts are readily observed but there is no order, regularity, or continuity—no organized relationship among them. He implied that the field of collective behavior in its concern with crowds, mobs, social movements, and related phenomena is generally concerned with this problem of how organization comes into being, although he did not limit the study of unorganized activity to these phenomena.

The concept of social disorganization, like that of social organization, was given a normative basis.

> . . . The degree to which the members of a society lose their common understandings, i.e., the degree to which consensus is undermined, is the measure of a society's state of disorganization. The degree to which there is agreement as to the values and norms of a society expressed in its explicit rules and in the preferences its members manifest with reference to these rules, furnishes us with criteria of the degree to which a society may be said to be disorganized.[15]

Like Durkheim and W. I. Thomas, Wirth did not regard all deviations from norms as prima facie evidence of social disorganization. He asserted that in a society there could be both wide differentiation in norms and deviation from them without disorganization, for in Thomas's terms "Social organization is not coextensive with individual morality, nor does social disorganization correspond to individual demoralization."[16] Societies were viewed as having the capacity to reconstruct and reorganize following disorganization. A focal concern in Wirth's own writing is the reconstruction of modern societies as literate and democratic ones.

Since Wirth viewed social organization and disorganization in terms of norms, he concluded that a main task of social organization was to discern those norms upon which consensus rests. In a Socratic vein he would inquire, "if it were not for norms, values and consensus, would there be mutual understanding, claims and expectations, or communication among men?"

"What we are after when we talk about social organization," he would say, "is something like a set of processes of interaction by means of which social entities retain their structure." To this he added, "There are as many kinds of social organization as there are varieties of human interests that can be expressed in an organized way." Interests for him, were irretrievably bound up with historical situations from which they emerge and are organized. There was for him, therefore, no study of social organization apart from a study of history.

He protested against sociological attempts to develop theoretical schemes in terms of some basic unit. Those who say a social act is the basic unit were reminded that there is no act apart from interaction and that means become ends and ends, means. Those who attempted to define a basic unit of social organization such as the family were brushed aside with the comment that any social group is a basic unit by virtue of its being a group. Nor would he regard persons as the basic unit of social organization: "Insofar as human beings are persons, they are always members of some kind of group; men are persons only by virtue of the fact that they are incorporated in some kind of social structure."

Discontented with much of the empirical work on social structure, he insisted that investigators failed to distinguish structural categories based on people having certain traits in common, such as income or opinion aggregates, from groups as collectivities based on a sense of belonging or solidarity and in sharing common values, claims, and expectations. He firmly maintained a distinction between social aggregates and social groups; groups were not "mere aggregates" but "corporate bodies moving toward common ends."

Wirth suggested that a main task of social organization is to develop a theory which orders and differentiates organized units or groups from one another. Although he never evolved such a theory, he addressed himself to the main criteria which might be used to differentiate types of organized units. In his lectures on social organization, he stressed the following criteria, which he did not see as mutually exclusive: (1) the social bond that holds people together; (2) their stratification or rank as a product of common interests or the roles people play in collective action oriented toward some common end; (3) the amount of difference in human behavior which may be attributed to the role the group plays in the life style of members; (4) the chronological priority the group has upon the formation of, or change in, personality; (5) the permanence of the group and the devices it has to insure or disrupt activity; (6) the transitory or permanent character of its organization; (7) size of the group; (8) the original *raison d'être* for the group, and whether forces other than these must reinforce it; (9) criteria for membership, particularly whether it recruits by appeal or ascription and the exclusiveness or selectivity of membership; (10) whether it is a *Gemeinschaftliche* or *Gesellschaftliche* group.

SOCIOLOGY OF INTELLECTUAL LIFE

A substantive area of considerable interest to Wirth was the sociology of knowledge. He liked to remark that it is

" . . . a field which is misnamed and with the misnaming of which, unfortunately. I have had something to do. . . . It should rather be called the sociology of intellectual life."[17]

Wirth did little writing in this field, although he offered annually a course in "The Sociology of Knowledge" at the University of Chicago. His preface to Karl Mannheim's *Ideology and Utopia* discusses the major problems involved in the relationship of intellectual activity and social existence and concludes with a tentative outline of the major issues of the field.

For Wirth, the sociology of intellectual life " . . . historically and logically falls within the scope of general sociology conceived as the basic social science."[18] When systematically developed, the sociology of intellectual life should deal with a series of subject matters " . . . in an integrated fashion, from a unifying point of view and by means of appropriate techniques."[19]

The leading issues with which the sociology of intellectual life must concern itself, he thought, are these: (1) an elaboration of the theory of knowledge itself, particularly of knowledge as a social product, or of how the context of thought is socially determined by social conditions—the relational character of knowledge; (2) the discovery of the styles and modes of thought characteristic of historical-social situations, particularly the role of belief systems and ideologies, and their comparison across historical situations; (3) the effect of thought upon social life, including examination of whether we can intervene in the world and make a difference, and of how society allocates its resources for the cultivation of types of knowledge; (4) the study of the intellectuals, those whose special function it is to "accumulate, preserve, reformulate, and disseminate the intellectual knowledge of the group"; (5) the social organization of intellectual life, especially an analysis of its institutional organization.

SOCIAL ACTION

Louis Wirth began the quest for sociological knowledge with a fundamental question, "can we do anything about social life, or do we live in a matrix of social forces that elude understanding?" Or, in another vein, "What are the paths open to us in society for intelligent self-direction?" He once concluded his course on social organization with these words:

> We must stay close to the reality of our own life in our own day. We must reshape our technical investigations to consider its problems and to provide the understanding that is needed for the formulation of an enlightened public policy.

Wirth belonged to a cohort of social scientists at the University of Chicago that contended the social sciences are policy sciences: Research without action or policy implications is sterile. Action based on social science knowledge is amenable to intelligent direction.

The central problem of sociology for Wirth, as already noted, is to understand consensus as the basis of social order. The analysis of consensus he argued requires not only an understanding of the conditions generating and stabilizing it but also of the bases for its manipulation. Time and again he emphasized that there is a distinction between knowing how a thing works and knowing how to put such knowledge to work—to know enough to act upon the basis of what is already known. Nowhere did he address himself more eloquently to this problem than when he spoke of the "suicide of civilization in the face of the new physical power":

> There may be some among us who feel that we already have the knowledge to prevent disaster but that we lack the power to put that knowledge into effect. Such a claim, however, is a confession that we lack perhaps the most important knowledge that we need, namely the knowledge to unlock the power requisite to put our existing knowledge usefully to work.[20]

Wirth not only emphasized that some of the most important knowledge sociologists might gain was the knowledge of how to make things work, but also that this kind of understanding could best be gained by involvement in action to change things. Though value and fact might to a substantial degree be separated from one another, he counseled against the separation of social action from either one. Out of the myriad of problems to which sociologists might address themselves, they should, he felt, address themselves to those which are relevant to the social life of man in contemporary societies. There was no room for "knowledge for the sake of knowledge" in his view of the world of social science. Wirth's "competent sociologist" was one who experiences the reality he investigates and assumes the full role of citizen as well as the role of scientist qua scientist. The professional sociologist he recommended should be a scholar in action.

> Perhaps it is a temperamental trait rather than an orthodox turn of science to turn in a period of turmoil away from the problems of the world to the problems of science, and as we customarily say, to take the long view and devote oneself to the building up of a body of knowledge which may or may not be relevant to the problems of life but which satisfied one's intellectual curiosity. It is curious that the reputation of a realist goes to one who never thinks about reality and that the reputation of a social scientist goes to one as far away from the actual problems and aspirations of society as he can get.
>
> Happy are those who can find this refuge. . . . The student of society will be plagued by the difficulties of achieving "objectivity," by the competition with common-sense knowledge, by the limits of his freedom and capacity to experiment, and by other serious and peculiar handicaps which trouble the natural scientist not at all. But the social scientist, whose very subject matter is the social world, can avoid studying the processes and problems of man in society only by pretending to

be something he is not, or by lapsing into such a remote degree of abstraction or triviality as to make the resemblance between what he does and what he professes to be doing, purely coincidental.[21]

The interplay of scholarly interest, citizen role, and sociological expert or investigator are exemplified in Wirth's case both in his writing and in his public and professional life.

The main answer that Wirth gave to the question of what avenues are open to us in democratic societies for intelligent self-direction is that of planning. He regarded the planning process very much in Mannheim's sense as a technique of social organization. His own personal commitment to the central function of planning in mass societies is evident not only in his many writings on cities, regions, intergroup relations and tensions, unemployment, housing, and a broad range of social problems, but it is evinced by his active participation in planning programs and organizations. He founded the Chicago Community Inventory at the University of Chicago to gather information that could be equally useful to action agencies and social scientists. During Franklin D. Roosevelt's administration he served as a member of the Committee on Urbanism of the National Resources Planning Board and wrote a number of their reports. Much of the research and writing in their volume, "Our Cities: Their Role in the National Economy" is his. He served as Director of Planning for the Illinois Post-War Planning Commission, an organization he was active in founding and promoting. At the University of Chicago, he was actively involved in founding an interdisciplinary graduate program in planning and taught several seminars in planning.

His many writings on the urban community reflect his deep involvement in studying and influencing social life. Central to these concerns was an active interest and involvement in planning cities and the urban civilization. The now classic **"Urbanism as a Way of Life"** is a formulation of a sociological framework for the analysis of urban phenomena developed while a consultant to the Committee on Urbanism of the National Resources Planning Board.

Wirth's writings on minorities included in this volume reflect his interest in minority problems and race relations, which he spoke of as his first and main love. He was a founder and director of the American Council on Race Relations and was active in preparing material presented to the U.S. Supreme Court in support of pleas to declare racial restrictive covenants unconstitutional and to desegregate the nation's schools. His **"Problems of Minority Groups in War Time," "The Problem of Minority Groups,"** and **"The Present Position of Minority Groups in the United States"** are among the essays which reflect both a scholarly and a citizenly interest in these matters.

His interest in belief systems, nationalism, and ideology centered around the generic problem of how they undermine consensus as well as build it. Yet he wrote about these topics in terms of the contemporary world, their effect on achieving a "democratic social order and a society of nations." In **"Ideological Aspects of Social Disorganization,"** he tried to show that "through the analysis of ideologies we may be able to discover the clues that indicate the disintegration of our social structure and to spot the areas of life where disorganization threatens to occur."[22] In **"Types of Nationalism,"** he examined the effect of national interest on the possibilities for a unified Europe. Deeply concerned with the problem of establishing a minimum consensus for the basis of world order in the face of mass destruction, he not only wrote upon these topics but became involved with others in their resolution. He was particularly interested in the role which the United States might play in the contemporary world. The essay, **"Freedom, Power and Values in Our Present Crisis"** deals with the effect of the discrepancy between American ideals and reality upon its leadership role in a world polarized by the two great concentrations of power, the United States and the Soviet Union.

He was deeply concerned with maintaining conditions for free exchange in the marketplace of ideas and promoted exchange among intellectuals. For a good many years he participated frequently in the public broadcast discussions of the University of Chicago Round Table. He was influential in the establishment of the International Sociological Association following World War II and served as its first president.

Though he firmly believed in social action he was not altogether optimistic about the prospects for bringing about the kind of consensus and change he sought for democratic societies. To the fraternity of democratic liberals, he observed that "it is almost impossible to live in either a revolutionary society or a reactionary one and be a liberal."

AUTHOR'S NOTE

In preparing this introduction, I have relied heavily upon a variety of sources including Wirth's published papers, course notes, and memories of discussions with Wirth. I am particularly indebted to Bendix's excellent paper, "Social Theory and Social Action in the Sociology of Louis Wirth," *American Journal of Sociology*, LIX (May, 1954), 523-29 and to Wirth's autobiographical statements in Howard Odum, *American Sociology: The Story of Sociology in the United States through 1950* (New York: Longmans, Green & Co., 1951), pp. 227-33. Unless otherwise stated, direct quotation is from transcriptions of his lectures made by students in his classes, 1945-52. All page references to Wirth's essays are to this volume, unless otherwise indicated.

NOTES

[1] Howard W. Odum, *American Sociology* (New York: Longmans, Green & Co., 1951), p. 228.

[2] *Ibid.*, p. 229.

[3] *Ibid.*, p. 230.

[4] Reinhard Bendix, "Social Theory and Social Action in the Sociology of Louis Wirth," *American Journal of Sociology*, LIX (May, 1954), 525.

[5] Louis Wirth, "Ideological Aspects of Social Disorganization," p. 59.

[6] See Part Two, "Transcript of the Conference Proceedings," in Herbert Blumer, *Critiques of Research in the Social Sciences: I, An Appraisal of Thomas and Znaniecki's, The Polish Peasant in Europe and America* (Bulletin 44, New York: Social Science Research Council, 1939).

[7] Louis Wirth, "Ideological Aspects of Social Disorganization," p. 59.

[8] Gunnar Myrdal, *An American Dilemma: The Negro Problem and Modern Democracy* (New York: Harper & Bros., 1944), Appendix 2, pp. 1035-64.

[9] *Max Weber on the Methodology of the Social Sciences.* Translated and edited by Edward A. Shils and Henry A. Finch (Glencoe, Illinois: Free Press, 1949).

[10] Gunnar Myrdal, *op. cit.*, pp. 1063-64.

[11] Howard Odum, *op. cit.*, p. 230.

[12] *Critiques of Research in the Social Sciences: I, op. cit.*, p. 154.

[13] Howard Odum, *op. cit.*, p. 230.

[14] Louis Wirth, "Consensus and Mass Communication," p. 20.

[15] Louis Wirth, "Ideological Aspects of Social Disorganization," p. 46.

[16] W. I. Thomas and F. Znaniecki, *The Polish Peasant in Europe and America* (New York: Alfred A. Knopf, 1927), II, 1129.

[17] Howard Odum, *op. cit.*, p. 231.

[18] Louis Wirth, "Preface to *Ideology and Utopia*," p. 142.

[19] *Ibid.*, pp. 142-43.

[20] Louis Wirth, "Consensus and Mass Communication," p. 18.

[21] *Ibid.*, p. 19.

[22] Louis Wirth, "Ideological Aspects of Social Disorganization," p. 58.

Earl Smith (essay date 1985)

SOURCE: "Louis Wirth and the Chicago School of Urban Sociology: An Assessment and Critique," in *Humanity and Society,* Vol. 9, No. 1, February, 1985, pp. 1-12.

[In the following essay, Smith delineates the particulars of the Chicago School of Sociology and Wirth's model of the city, then discusses these in light of later perspectives in urban studies.]

> The city as a built form can . . . be regarded as a set of objects arranged according to some pattern in space. But there are few who would argue that cities are just that.
>
> —David Harvey
> *Social Justice and the City*

INTRODUCTION

Louis Wirth's essay **"Urbanism As A Way Of Life,"** (Wirth, 1938:1-24) marked the beginning of conventional views in urban sociology on the relationships between the individual and the urban environment. Using the city as an isolated unit of analysis and claiming its study to be the sole province of sociology Wirth and the contemporary proponents of "The Chicago School" advanced a series of related paradigms that attempted to describe and understand the city. Though Wirth's views are no longer appropriate to the analysis of the capitalist city, much urban sociological literature of the last forty years reflects his useful orientation. Through critiquing Louis Wirth one may move beyond the limits of his position to more substantial theories regarding the genesis and persistence of the city as a modern social formation.

WIRTH'S MODEL OF THE CITY

Like other sociologists, Wirth described the city as the embodiment of civilization—the historic center of progress, education, and higher standards of living. Wirth pointed to the city as the locus of slums, poverty, crime, and defined the city as a "relatively large, dense, and permanent settlement of socially heterogeneous individuals" (Wirth, 1938:8) with a universally distinct pattern of behavior.

Urbanism, then, was typified by "secularization, secondary group relations, increased role segmentalization, and poorly defined social norms." (Wirth, 1938:1-24) Furthermore, Wirth saw this way of life as existing only in the city as opposed to the rural community.

Key determinants of this urban behavior pattern were the ecological variables of size, density, and heterogeneity. Wirth posited the following linear relationship: "the larger, the more densely populated and the more heterogeneous a community, the more accentuated the characteristics associated with urbanization will be" (Wirth 1938:9). In other words, the bigger the city the more one should expect to find individual differences, mechanisms of formal control, segmenting of roles, utilitarian social relationships, and what Wirth defined as the "schizoid" character of urban personality—anonymity, superficiality, anomie, lack of participation, and impersonality. Density or physical closeness intensified these segmented social interactions, diversified the social activities, and increased social disorganization.

In Wirth's model, social heterogeneity reinforced the tendency of the individual to pursue their own interest in a competitive setting (over that of the community), thereby weakening community ties, traditions, and commonly acknowledged social norms of behavior. This increased social heterogeneity culminated in the disorganization of the individual and, along with the other variables of size and density, produced higher incidences of social pathologies. Wirth described urbanization as a spatial form solely in terms of the development, intensification, and diffusion of characteristics associated with urbanism. The analysis disregarded the relationship between social processes and spatial form. Furthermore, he made no attempt to relate the city to the larger society. While his paradigm was specific to the inner core during the 1930's, he generalized his analysis into a grand theory purporting to describe a lifestyle indigenous to any city, applicable to all its denizens, regardless of their location in the world.

The characteristics Wirth ascribed to urbanism lacked a clear theoretical framework. They neither demonstrated how cities function nor explained the reason for a city's existence. Wirth's ecological concept of urbanism more successfully described the adaptation of a certain group of urban people to a physical environment than accounted for all social action. Lifestyle reflects the role humans play in a social and political system and therefore, class fractions, not merely residence. Furthermore, the city way of life must be traced to the larger social, economic, and political systems that determine the situations in which it operates. To focus on the internal dynamics of the city without considering the effects on it of dominant political, ideological, and economic systems is far too limiting theoretically.

THE CHICAGO SCHOOL OF SOCIOLOGY

The Chicago School of Sociology, strongly influenced by the European theorists Weber, Durkheim, Simmel, Tonnies and Wirth posited a series of generalizations that idealized rural folk society. Urban life was viewed as somewhat undesirable, while the lifestyle of the "yeoman farmer" was seen not only as the ultimate symbol of American culture, but utopian as well. Rural areas were idealized by these scientists as the embodiment of folkways, desired traditions, social continuity, and cultural conformity. By contrast, the city was characterized by innovation, change, and disorganization. Its more sophisticated, more rational inhabitants had less real warmth and feeling. This estranging sophistication Wirth ascribed to the universal process of urbanism.

The Chicago school developed during an era of extreme and rapid social change. The influx of millions of immigrants at the turn of the century who settled principally in urban areas, along with deteriorating economic conditions culminating in the Great Depression, created a series of social problems (crime, suicide, prostitution, lack of integration, anomie, alcoholism) erroneously assumed to be uniquely urban. The sheer numbers of individuals from highly diverse ethnic backgrounds greatly contributed to the rapid growth and social diversity of not only existing American urban areas, but many new cities plagued by the same social problems.

Widespread concern with urban problems prompted the Chicago School to make these problems the central focus of their research. Their analysis centered solely on Chicago, yet their findings were generalized into a macroscopic urban theory. They developed a series of "natural" laws (zones and processes of invasion, competition, segregation, and succession) and used ecological factors (population, density, technology, size, heterogeneity) to explain the creation, arrangement, way of life, and expansion of cities.

Like other members of the Chicago School, Louis Wirth viewed cities as fostering secondary contacts in place of the primary relationships found in rural areas. He believed that the sources of social control, represented by the family, the neighborhood, and the local community were largely undermined by the demands of an irrational urban existence.

The anthropologist Robert Redfield, a student of Robert Park, a founder of the Chicago School of Urbanization, described a "folk" or "rural" society as having the following characteristics: isolation, a high degree of genetic and cultural homogeneity, slow cultural change, preliteracy, small numbers, minimal division of labor, a simple technology in which every individual is a primary producer, a social organization based on blood and fictive kinship, traditional and uncritical behavior, the viewing of traditional objects and acts as sacred, the importance of magic and religion and the absence of the economic motive (see Mintz, 1953-54:137). Redfield viewed the rural economy as one of status rather than market, with the family group representing the primary production unit. He argued that since this type of society exhibited a strong sense of group solidarity and common understanding, it did not require legislative and formal social control.

Parallel to Redfield's description of a folk society, Wirth's urban society exhibited an extensive division of labor, an emphasis on innovation and individual achievement, lack of primary ties to neighborhoods, reliance on secondary forms of social control such as the police and courts, the breakdown of primary groups, social disorganization, interaction with others as role players rather than as total personalities, the destruction of close family life and transfer of its functions to specialized agencies outside the home, a diversity in values and religious beliefs, social mobility and universal or codified rules applicable to all (Wirth, 1938:1-24). Wirth claimed that while the urban lifestyle was based on rationality, secularism, diversity, innovation, and progress, it was also disorienting to the individual.

Increasing population, size and density especially when accompanied by heterogeneity, decreased the power of informal social controls. These controls, effected largely through the interplay of folkways and mores, gave way to the increased formal control of laws, police, courts, jails, regulations, bureaucracies and orders. Wirth considered the breakdown in informal social controls to be largely responsible for the increase in juvenile delinquency, crime, prostitution, drug addiction, suicide, mental disease, social unrest and political instability. Their sheer urban numbers meant that residents had to rely on representatives rather than themselves in the political process.

Wirth's view of urban life and the urban resident was derived particularly from the slum and ghetto areas of the city. He saw the slums as suffering from acute social disorganization, deteriorating to a state of anomie—the "loss of spontaneous self-expression, the morale, and the sense of participation that comes with living in an integrated society" (Wirth, 1938:12).

Beginning about 1943, sociologists began to study slum areas to test Wirth's hypotheses. The work of Whyte (1943), Gans (1962), and Suttles (1968) focused on the key elements in Wirth's essay and found little to support his hypothesis. Whyte's study, *Street Corner Society*, documents a high degree of social organization and predictability in a Boston Italian slum. Gans' study of social bonds, in *The Urban Villagers: Group And Class In The Life Of Italian Americans*, reveals the presence of strong family life and relationships as strong and as meaningful as bonds found in a village. Gans' salient point was that to find a sense of community one must look beyond the physical appearance of the urban area. And last, Suttles, after studying four major ethnic groups in urban slums (Italian, Black, Mexican and Puerto Ricans), discovered a pattern of social organization in which each group carefully defined its boundaries. These boundaries, not apparent to strangers, were well-known and respected by residents. Members of each ethnic group remained safe and comfortable as long as they stayed in their own territory. These studies undermined Wirth's contention that urbanization bred *disorganization* and the loss of primary group contact. Gans demonstrated that much urban behavior remained traditional rather than irrational, and, in many ways, resembled folk rather than urban characteristics.

Wirth's essay **"Urbanism As A Way Of Life,"** delineated the distinctions between folk and urban societies. In establishing the legitimacy of the rural-urban continuum Wirth posited that "The city and the country may be regarded as two poles in reference to one or the other of which all human settlements tend to arrange themselves. In viewing urban-industrial and rural-folk society as ideal types of communities, we may obtain a perspective for the analysis of the basic models of human association as they appear in contemporary civilization" (Wirth, 1938:3). Like others who tried to define the differences between settlement patterns (Park, Burgess, and McKenzie: 1925), Wirth tended to retain a "rural ethos" in his analysis, preferring the "rural" culture and viewing the city as destroying that culture. He attached a negative value to "urban" life. His distinctions between folk and urban society and urban and rural social order became so widely diffused in the sociological literature, that they were viewed as empirically based.

Wirth, Redfield (1956), Tonnies (1940), Weber (1947) and Durkheim (1938), regarded their typologies as ideal-typical constructs for historical comparative analysis. These constructs were little more than exaggerated, imagined, "pure" societal states with no basis in social reality. In his discussion of typologies, Redfield asserted that "in every isolated little community, there is civilization; in every city, there is folk society" (Mintz, 1953-4:137). As Mintz pointed out, "Redfield does not maintain that either the ideal folk or the ideal urban society can be found anywhere in the world. His conception of an ideal type consists of . . . an enumeration of societies . . . which are then put together to form the type" (Mintz, 1953-54:137).

These theorists cautioned others against using ideal types in an "either-or" perspective, and warned that the generalizations they prompted were subject to the values of the interpreter. Unfortunately, these admonitions have been ignored by many sociologists and students of urban studies. Societies—rural or urban—fall, if at all, somewhere between the two ideal types.

It is in Wirth's leap from an analysis of the social system to conjectures about individual personality (Wirth, 1938:22-24) that his theory is most suspect. The assumption that the urbanite is blasé, indifferent, calculating, utilitarian, rational, anonymous, and anomic, in addition to possessing a heightened and intellectual consciousness compared to the countryside compatriot, has yet to be verified empirically. Wirth also assumed that all people living in cities were affected by this experience in profound and similar ways. For him, the process of urbanization was essentially the process of disorganization. By extending his theory to its logical conclusion, one would have to surmise that the elite, the intellectual and the slum dweller have a similar urban personality—a fallacy requiring no further comments. Social life is not a mass phenomenon. It occurs, for the most part, in small groups—in the family, neighborhoods, formal and informal situations, rural and urban areas. No evidence suggests that secondary relations diminish the strength and importance of primary group relations. Primary groups retain the same importance psychologically for city people as for rural.

No one can doubt that the city differs in important ways from the town. Yet, too rigorous a comparison of urban and small town life has led to a distorted picture of urban social relations. . . . The tendency to view two types of social organization, "gemeinschaft and gesellschaft," as opposites obscures elements in both. Forms of social organization are not static but in a continual state of change. In viewing urban life, one shouldn't focus on whether various features of human relations exist but on *how* they've been or are in the process of being modified. One shouldn't ask whether primary relationships exist in cities as they do in towns, but how they've assumed new forms.

THE MARXIST PERSPECTIVE ON URBANISM

In contrast to the traditional Chicago School, Marxist sociologists see the city as evolving from a particular economic mode. Their view, as it began to emerge in the 1960's and in the research of Manuel Castells and David Harvey, offered a fundamentally different and more systematic method of urban analysis than could be found in Wirth's rural-urban continuum model.

Relying on such Marxian concepts as capital accumulation, over-accumulation, class struggle, surplus value, conflict, circulation of surplus, and modes of economic integration, theorists from this school viewed the city as a social product, defined by an identifiable social, economic, political and ideological structure, and the conjunction of social relations resulting from those structures (Castells, 1977:430). Denying the existence of an autonomous city as the appropriate unit of analysis, to explain urban lifestyles and forms, the paradigm focused on the mode of production dominant in the society and the social relationships which developed from it. Urban economies reflected not only the national social and economic systems, but were mirror images of local and regional systems. One could expect variations in spatial and social form. Unconcerned by the city's effect on behavior, Marxist urbanists, as Goering pointed out, aimed their studies at the control and distribution of scarce resources, associating class antagonism with the management of scarcity (Goering, 1978:78).

In the Marxist view, a city such as Chicago had its roots in the Industrial Revolution and the evolution of the capitalist economic system. In his essay, "Urbanism And The City—An Interpretative Essay," Harvey, for example, reconstructed the evolution of the modern city from Medieval feudal society, attempting to show that a new system of production was responsible for the demise of the established social, economic, and political order of the rural hinterland (Harvey, 1973:195-285).

The Marxist critique of the Chicago School basically revolves around issues concerning the appropriate unit of analysis, the conceptual framework to be used, the restrictions of time and space and the lack of comparative studies. The Chicago School viewed the city as a clearly defined, autonomous spatial form with a specific political boundary and therefore as an appropriate unit of analysis. Urban life, assumed to be formed by the composition, size and density of the urban population, created the forces which shaped the pattern and consequences of urban growth. In contrast, the Marxist position is that cities are no longer, if they ever were, independent, but have become increasingly dependent on regional, national and global political economic forces. For Marxists the laws for the formation of cities and the transformation of urbanism are not embedded in population size and concentration, but are derived from economic and political conditions.

Before the sixteenth century, society in Europe was dominated by a rural-based economy, whose primary mode of production was subsistence agriculture. The rural hinterland established and controlled the social and political structure, social relationships, property and material wealth, and maintained a mode of production which tied people to small, isolated, self-sufficient geographic areas. Organized for religion or defense, medieval cities played a minor role in feudal society.

The development of trade and commerce created a new series of conditions which threatened the existing economic and social order. This crisis was resolved by confirming these activities to the city. The quest of the merchant class for expanded internal and external trade routes, the development of the guilds and the origin of state apparatuses to administer and control trade and commerce posed a challenge to the dominant rural hinterland.

In the Marxist view, subsequent opposition between "town" and "country" and the dominance of the rural order over more concentrated spatial forms was totally transformed by the Industrial Revolution and the changing relationships between capital and labor under the new production mode of capitalism, and the process of market exchange. The factory system separated the worker not only from his work, but removed the production process from the home. Lacking control over the means of production, labor became a commodity exchanged for wages. Control over property, material existence, social relations, the means of production, the political system (including the State), and the wealth derived from production became vested in the hands of a new class, the capitalist entrepreneur.

The development and expansion of profit required that the city became the dominant social form. Capital, needing labor, recruited that commodity not only from the urban population, but increasingly, from the rural areas.

For the Marxist this movement of labor to the city ended the power of the rural feudal order and generated the new urban form, the capitalist or industrial city. This social unit became "a production site, a locale for reproducing the labor force, a market for circulating commodities and realizing profit, and, most important, a control center for these complex relationships" (Hill, 1976:31). The city's purpose then was to organize and legitimize this new mode of production and not only maintain it, but help it to expand by providing those services that foster capital accumulation and labor reproduction; such as transportation routes, communication, utilities,

social control mechanisms, housing and education. As Etzkowitz and Mack put it:

> The Marxist views the transportation, housing, and other city institutions as organized for the benefit of the capitalist class. Such institutions enable capitalists to concentrate workers near factories and enable people and goods to move swiftly from one enterprise to another. . . . The city government to facilitate the coming together of employers and employment . . . in order to create the goods and services necessary for the generation of profits and wages . . . by providing the infrastructure base of municipal services of streets, water, security, sequage, and often transportation and communication. Cities are administered for the benefit of private business activities (Etzkowitz and Mack, 1978:46-47).

As transportation equipment, communication and technology improved, new cities were built nearer to the raw materials and labor needed to produce finished products. They were interconnected to one another, and to the wider society. The expansion of this economic system, put an end to the rural lifestyle as these urban forms and their social relationships absorbed the hinterlands into their sphere of influence. This urbanization of society so transformed the previous social order that the term rural-urban became meaningless.

The conceptual framework of the Chicago School, which David Harvey described as "the fragmentation of knowledge into rigid, academic disciplines" thus ignoring the obvious relationships between the other social sciences: psychology, history, economics, and anthropology. Continued adherence to this fragmented approach resulted in problems of definition and scope. It leads one to the morass of the rural-urban continuum model and to misplaced attention on explaining and defining what is "urban," what is unique about "sociology," and even more so, "urban sociology" (Harvey, 1978:35). The Marxist interdisciplinary framework is a more effective analytic stance for studying the city.

A third Marxist objection is to the limits inherent in sociological concepts of time and space. Studies like Wirth's essay based their generalization on one or at most a few American cities. Microscopic studies like "Ethnicity In Sydney In The 1960's" and "Family Relations In Flint, Michigan, In The Depression Of The 1930s" became, as Harvey put it, "the standard bread-and-butter product and diet of the urban sociologist" (Harvey, 1978:31). These theorists did not pursue comparative studies between different cities within and without a specific culture, region, or society. Had Wirth tried this, for example, his concept of urbanism might have been understood in the context of the effects of the Depression, rather than of urbanization and physical form.

In his critique of traditional urban sociology, Martindale (1958) found added theoretical difficulties with the Chicago School: its orientation toward the "geo-physical aspects" of the city; the unnecessary primitivism of its crucial concepts; and the omission of the sociological concepts of groups, institutions, and social structure (Martindale (Weber), 1958:28-30). Social relationships and action, in his opinion, could not be ascertained by studying transportation routes, buildings, zones, or statistical rates of crime, mental disease, suicide or other social pathology indices.

The characteristics of Wirth's "urbanism," or what Martindale called "the primitivism of concept," is "found as easily in rural life as they were identified in city life. They could apply to social life in the past or the present. The basic conceptualizations were insufficiently precise to differentiate the theory of the city from any other branch of sociological theory" (Martindale (Weber), 1958:29-30). Reducing the city to an itemized list of social problems, traditionalists precluded an analysis of the social groups, institutions and political-economic system which determined the structure, form, and relationships of an urban area.

A key feature of cities is that they offer, "at least potentially, a wider range of alternatives for individuals in most aspects of living than is provided by the non-urban areas of a given nation or society at a given time. Urbanization and urbanism involve the availability of a wide range of services and alternatives in terms of work, food, clothing, educational facilities, modes of travel, medical facilities, voluntary organizations, types of people and ways of life" (Hauser, 1965:499). This value-free recognition of what a city may offer is more appropriate to the study of the city than Wirth's treatment of the "urban mentality." It also moves scholars away from the polarizing and normative judgments of the urban-rural construct, which has, for too long, dominated urban sociological reasoning. Only from within the context of industrial capitalism and the industrial city, says the Marxists, can we define the processes of urbanization and urbanism. Industrial capitalism is seen as rooted in "the production, reproduction, circulation, and overall organization of capital accumulation; while the industrial city is regarded as the particular geographic form and spatial patterning of relationships taken by the process of capital accumulation" (Hill, 1976:31). The concepts of "urbanism" and "urbanization" derived their existence only after the emergence of the industrial city. From the Marxist viewpoint, everything described by Wirth as urbanism was, in fact, the cultural expression of capitalist industrialization, the emergence of the market economy, and the process of rationalization of modern society (Fischer, 1978:12). Or, in other words, that which existed prior to capitalism cannot be considered "urban."

CONCLUSION

Do the Marxist political-economic factors transcend Wirth's ecological variables of size, density, and heterogeneity? Is this paradigm a more systematic method of urban analysis, and does it explain the urban phenomenon? I am, as yet, somewhat unclear on whether the

Marxist approach offers the sound alternative needed for moving beyond Wirth and the overall influence of The Chicago School.

To begin, Marxist concepts and generalizations are abstract and often vague. Marxist theoretical attempts to define and clarify their concepts often fall short. Consider, for example, Harvey's definition of surplus value: "Surplus value is surplus value expressed in capitalist market exchange terms" (Harvey, 1973:238). For those struggling to understand Marxist generalizations, such a definition is unacceptable. Harvey himself observed that "He could testify to some of the extraordinarily complex problems which arise when confronting the Marxian meanings, as it took him almost seven years to acquire a limited fluency in the use of the Marxian concepts . . ." (Harvey, 1978:29). If the Marxist paradigm hopes to gain wider understanding, and just as important use, its proponents must clearly define their concepts and explain how they relate to the generalizations hypothesized.

In addition to vagueness and linguistic complexity, the Marxist perspective has seldom been tested empirically. Few Marxists have engaged in empirical research, and the tools they might use for such research are not at all clear. Castells argued that one can analyze space as an "expression of the social structure by studying the elements of the economic system, the political system, and the ideological system, and by their combinations and the social practices that derive from them" (Castells, 1977:126). He defined the economic system as a composite of the subelements of production, consumption, exchange, and administration, and asserted that "the politico-institutional system could be organized around the two essential relations defining this system (domination-regulation and integration-repression)" (Castells, 1977:127). Castells' following explanation of the ideological system, typifies the abstractness of Marxist language: "The ideological system organized space by marking it with a network of signs, whose signifiers are made up of spatial forms and whose signifieds are ideological contents, the efficacity of which must be construed from their effects on the social structure as a whole" (Castells, 1977:127). How one would apply such propositions to an urban setting or case study within a city remains unclear.

Then too, after a perusal of Marxist readings, especially Harvey and Castells, one is left with a feeling of incompleteness. (The same, obviously, can be said of Wirth and The Chicago School). The question at once arises: where does Marxist urban theory take us? Should one conclude that the social issues of class conflict and inequity exists *only* in capitalist cities? Should one further infer that socialism (socialist mode of production) and socialistic cities have eradicated these conditions and are created and transformed by other factors? If so, what are those factors? Finally, is it not true that from reading the Marxist literature on urban society their policies seem to point in the direction of eradicating the injustices caused by capital accumulation and the capitalist class *within capitalist social formations*? Questions such as these remain unanswered by the Marxist School of the New Urban Sociology.

Joseph Bensman succinctly summarized my concern with the Marxist position: "To support the claim that contemporary urbanism is a product of capitalistic economic development, the Marxists would be required to prove that these developments did not exist in pre-capitalistic societies . . . and that the problematics of advanced capitalism do not exist in contemporary societies labeled as non- or anti-capitalist" (Bensman, 1978:72). One would, therefore, have to show that socialist cities have no competition, no inequities in consumption, services, occupations, housing, and material wealth; and furthermore, performs different functions than the capitalist city. Finally, it must be demonstrated that socialism and its urban system do not display such tendencies ascribed to capitalism as slums, crime, unemployment, mental illness, riots, unemployment, strikes, and suicides.

If comparative urban research cannot demonstrate the differences between the socialist and capitalist city, one may have to conclude with Bensman that the

> problematics of contemporary urban society are not related to Marxian theory, historical materialism, or dialectical materialism . . . (but) are the problematics of urbanization, industrialism, population density, and the struggles for control of the scarce resources by organized elites, classes, regional groups, and rural and urban dwellers in *all* societies, whether capitalistic or socialistic, developed or underdeveloped, colonial or neo-colonial (Bensman, 1978:73).

Summary

This paper was written to examine the major hypothesis of Louis Wirth's essay, **"Urbanism As A Way Of Life,"** (Wirth, 1938) and to discuss what I consider to be some of the weaknesses and criticisms of his approach. His theory reduced the city's complex force of actions to the psychological effects of increase, density, and heterogeneity of population on the individual, their way of life, and the interaction with others (Martindale (Weber), 1948:42). My second objective was to look at the Marxian urban paradigm as a possible alternative model for studying the city. It, too, proves somewhat unsatisfactory. Much to be preferred is the idea of studying the city as one aspect of society. The analysis, therefore, should not be conducted in isolation from the whole of society or the city's historical context. Equally attractive is the Marxist attempt to interrelate the thought and inquiry of economics, history, sociology, psychology and anthropology. However, until some of their generalizations and conclusions are clarified and more empirical research has been conducted to support their hypothesis, and until it can be demonstrated, through comparative studies, that socialism, as a mode of production, does not replicate the conditions found in capitalist cities, the Marxian perspective cannot be acclaimed as a totally workable (alternative) model for the study of the city.

In the final analysis, what Martindale referred to as "the state of city theory" (Martindale (Weber), 1958:28), may pose the same problem for contemporary urbanologists as it did in Lewis Wirth's day:

> In the rich literature on the city, we look in vain for a theory or urbanism presenting in a systematic fashion the available knowledge concerning the city as a social entity. . . . Despite the multiplication of research and textbooks on the city, we do not as yet have a comprehensive body of compendent hypotheses which may be derived from a set of postulates implicitly contained in a sociological knowledge which may be substantiated through empirical research (Wirth, 1938:8).

WIRTH'S URBAN THEORY

Population Size Results In:
1. Increased diversity of cultural characteristics
2. Increased diversity of occupational characteristics
3. Professional structure with advanced division of labor
4. Increase in impersonal human relationships: segmentalized social life based on roles rather than personal characteristics
5. City structure "hardening" into commercial enterprise
6. Moral structure of city "loosening" toward state of anomie intensification of effects noted above

Population Density Results In:
1. Ecological specialization: city as mosaic of differentiated land areas
2. Districts reflecting productive speciality
3. Devices to facilitate visual recognition: status symbols or unusual dress
4. Increased toleration of differences
5. Increased "social distance"
6. Increased antisocial behavior: friction and irritation intensification of effects noted above

Heterogeneity Results In:
1. Acceptance of insecurity and instability
2. Increased physical relocation
3. Increased use of stereotypes and categorical thinking
4. Increased importance of money as basis of social relations

Source: Adapted from Wirth (1938)

REFERENCES

[1] Bensman, Joseph. 1978. "Marxism As A Foundation for Urban Sociology." *Comparative Urban Research* Vol. VI #2,3: 10-19.

[2] Castells, Manuel. 1977. *The Urban Question: A Marxist Approach.* Translated by Ann Sheridan. London, Great Britain. Edward Arnold Publishers, Ltd.

[3] Durkheim, Emile. 1938. *The Rules of Sociological Method.* Edited by George R. G. Cattin. Chicago, Illinois. University of Chicago Press.

[4] Etzkowitz, Henry and Roger Mack. 1978. "Corporations And The City: Oligopolies And Urbanization." *Comparative Urban Research* Vol. VI #2,3: 46-53.

[5] Fischer, Claude S. 1978. "On the Marxian Challenge To Urban Sociology," *Comparative Urban Research* Vol. VI #2, 3: 28-45.

[6] Gans, Herbert. 1962. *The Urban Villagers: Group And Class In The Life Of Italian-Americans.* Glencoe, Illinois. The Free Press.

[7] Goering, John M. 1978. "Marx And The City: Are There Any New Directions For Urban Theory?" *Comparative Urban Research.* Vol. VI #2,3: 76-85.

[8] Hauser, Philip M. and Leo F. Schnore. 1965. *The Study Of Urbanization.* New York City, New York. John Wiley and Sons, Inc.

[9] Harvey, David. 1978. "On Countering The Marxian Myth—Chicago Style." *Comparative Urban Research.* Vol. VI #2,3: 28-45.

[10] Harvey, David. 1973. *Social Justice And The City.* London and Baltimore. John Hopkins.

[11] Helmer, John and Neil A. Eddington. 1973. *Urbanman: The Psychology Of Urban Survival.* New York City, New York. MacMillan Publishing Co., Inc.

[12] Hill, Richard C. Summer. 1976. "Fiscal Crisis And Political Struggle In The Decaying U.S. Central City." *Kapitalistate* #4,5: 31-49.

[13] Mintz, Sidney. 1953-54. "The Folk-Rural Continuum And The Rural Proletarian Community." *American Journal Of Sociology.* Vol. 59: 126-143.

[14] Palen, J. John and Karl H. Fleming. 1972. *Urban America: Conflict And Change.* New York City, New York. Praeger Publishers.

[15] Palen, J. John. 1975. *The Urban World.* New York City, New York, McGraw-Hill Book Co.

[16] Park, Robert E., Ernest W. Burgess and Roderick D. McKenzie. 1925. *The City.* Chicago, Illinois. University of Chicago Press.

[17] Pickvance, C. G. 1978. "Competing Paradigms In Urban Sociology: Some Epistemological Issues." *Comparative Urban Research.* Vol. VI #2, 3: 20-27.

[18] Redfield, Robert. 1956. *The Little Community And Peasant Society And Culture.* Chicago, Illinois. University of Chicago Press.

[19] Simmel, Georg. 1950. *The Sociology Of Georg Simmel.* Edited by Kurt E. Wolff. Glencoe, Illinois. The Free Press.

[20] Suttles, Gerald. 1968. *The Social Order Of The Slums.* Chicago, Illinois. University of Chicago Press.

[21] Tonnies, Ferdinand. 1940. *Fundamental Concepts Of Sociology.* Translated by Charles Loomis. New York, New York. American Book Company.

[22] Weber, Max. 1958. *The City.* Translated and Edited by Don Martindale and Gertrude Neuwirth. New York City, New York. The Free Press.

[23] Weber, Max. 1947. *The Theory Of Social And Economic Organization.* Translated by A. M. Henderson and Talcott Parsons. New York City, New York. Oxford University Press.

[24] Wirth, Louis. July, 1938. "Urbanism As A Way Of Life." *American Journal Of Sociology.* Vol. #44: 1-24.

[25] Whyte, William Foote. 1943. *Street Corner Society.* Chicago, Illinois. University of Chicago Press.

Zane L. Miller (essay date 1992)

SOURCE: "Pluralism, Chicago School Style: Louis Wirth, the Ghetto, the City, and 'Integration'," in *Journal of Urban History,* Vol. 18, No. 3, May, 1992, pp. 251-79.

[*In the following essay, Miller provides an overview of Wirth's career with special attention to the Chicago School and the influence of Karl Mannheim, and divides Wirth's sociology work into two distinct phases.*]

Dick Wade, in 1989, reprimanded me for missing a convention session on the theoretical roots of the "new" urban history, then made his case about the roots of the "old" urban history. He located them in sociology, rather than economics or geography, and specifically in the Chicago school sociology of the 1920s, 1930s, and 1940s. He also suggested that it happened accidentally. The new university had lots of money and large aspirations, but even money could not buy a cadre of established stars in established fields from older and more prestigious institutions. So President Harper persuaded his conservative board of trustees to hire promising people in the unestablished, ill-defined, and arguably subversive field of sociology. In addition, said Wade, Chicago's potential for becoming America's largest and most powerful city attracted the sociologists to the study of the Windy City, which they treated not as a unique city with a unique future but as an exemplar of urbanism generally for the purpose of solving urban problems.

Wade's assertion of the Chicago roots of historical writing about American cities since 1940 sounded reasonable to me. But what especially intrigued me about his case was the nondeterministic nature of his explanation for the creation of the Chicago school and his emphasis on chance and on individuals doing new things in new ways as if unconstrained by larger social or economic "forces" or conventional ways of thinking. This part of Wade's story struck me, as it turns out, because I had already concluded that nondeterminism was a major characteristic of both the old and new urban history and a major trend in American civilization since 1940,[1] although I had not thought much about it in connection with the history of sociology. So I wondered if I might find some suggestions about the origins and significance of this nondeterministic tendency in Chicago school sociology, particularly in the work of Louis Wirth, the member of the Chicago school most concerned with urban theory and urbanism as a way of life.

I think I have found some such suggestions, but I also discovered that Louis Wirth's career may be divided into two periods, a deterministic and a nondeterministic phase. The first began in the 1910s, when he came to the University of Chicago and started the study of sociology.[2] Simultaneously, however, he participated in various social action efforts, activities in his view that provided experience and information useful for the empirical analysis of social processes and problems. In this period he sought to legitimize group pluralism as a way of life by replacing race-based cultural determinism with a social determinism in which social group membership accounted for how people thought and behaved. To accomplish this he developed in the 1920s a theory about the role of cities in social processes that may be found in his historical study of the Jewish ghetto in Europe and America. That theory supported programs for the gradual elimination of prejudice and discrimination against "minority" groups by the adoption of educational activities and social policies that would foster intergroup understanding and tolerance and facilitate natural processes of group interaction leading eventually to "integrated" societies composed of a pluralistic blend of all the cultures that had participated and would participate in a given social system.

The second phase of Wirth's career began in the mid-1930s. Now he edged away from determinism and his social activism intensified and took new directions because of his conviction that the United States and the world faced a crisis of authoritarianism and perhaps a onetime-only opportunity to resolve the crisis in a way that would preserve democratic pluralism as he now understood it. During this second phase of his career he sought a greater role for whimsy in social thought and for individual self-determination in social and cultural life by advocating the democratization of intellectual life. He now concentrated on the promotion of citizen participation in city planning and the management of social organizations and civic agencies, the enactment of laws to secure social group integration, especially racial residential integration, and the establishment of world government as the only means of blending cultures to avoid potentially catastrophic social and ethnic conflict.

Wirth's advocacy of these programs concluded in 1952, in Buffalo, New York, where he died of a heart attack after delivering the closing address to a conference on community living. In that talk he distinguished between the ethics of conscience, which proceeded from an "irrational" and spiritually based sense of responsibility and produced absolutist "true believers," and an ethics of conviction, which proceeded from an empirically and analytically based sense of responsibility and produced pluralistic pragmatists who understood the role and technique of consensus and compromise in a pluralistic world. He then accused those failing to act on their ethics of conviction of hypocrisy, called for the provision of a decent standard of living for all Americans, and declared America vulnerable internationally because of the wide disparity between its creed of equality for all social groups (his reinterpretation of the Declaration of Independence) and its practice of inequality, a stance that made the United States appear hypocritical before the emerging world community that increasingly shared American ideals of equality. Failure of the United States to continue striving for the equality of social groups could only lead to domestic and international skepticism, disillusion, and alienation from the ideal of equality of social groups.[3]

Wirth started on the road that led to these convictions in an agricultural village in western Germany. Born in 1897 into a cattle-raising and trading family, he received a Jewish and a secular primary education. For his secondary schooling his parents in 1911 sent him to live with his uncle, a merchant in Omaha, Nebraska, for whom the boy worked as he attended school and mastered the English language, both as a writer and a skilled debater. After graduating, Wirth neither stayed to work with his uncle nor returned to Germany. Instead, he accepted a scholarship to attend the University of Chicago as a premedical student.

Wirth had a lively time as an undergraduate in Chicago during the later 1910s. He hung out at Hull House. He read W. E. B. Du Bois's *Souls of Black Folk*. He joined the Cosmopolitan Club, which held forums on world affairs, and edited its journal, the *Cosmopolitan Student*. He read German historical sociology and empirical works about cities. He protested the American entrance into World War I and affiliated with various Marxist groups. He dropped medicine for sociology and took courses with Albion Small; with W. I. Thomas, then completing *The Polish Peasant in Europe and America* with Florian Znaniecki; and with Robert Park, Ernest Burgess, and George Mead. He also met Mary Bolton, of Paducah, Kentucky, who had been sent by her middle-class parents to Chicago for a safe Baptist education, and who, with her friend, Wirth, engaged in radical protests on and off campus.

After graduating in 1919, Wirth seemed not sure of what to do next. According to one unverified charge he joined the Communist party, but in any case he had no money and decided to find a job in Chicago. He took a position as director of the division for delinquent boys in the Bureau of Personal Services of the Jewish Charities of Chicago. He held that post until 1922, when he returned to Germany to visit his family and introduce its members to Mary Bolton, whom he married in 1923 and with whom he raised two daughters, encouraging in them, as one of them put it, "agnosticism with quite audible atheistic overtones" and a "'generalized minority' ethnic identification."[4] That meant, she later explained, that Wirth taught them always "to stand up and be counted whenever there were questions that we were Jews."[5]

By 1923 Wirth had also decided on a career in sociology in America, and his salary as a social worker and from part-time teaching at the University of Chicago and the YMCA college made it possible for him to complete his M.A. and Ph.D. degrees at Chicago. As a graduate student he became a naturalized U.S. citizen at the age of twenty-seven, wrote an M.A. thesis (1925) on culture conflict in immigrant families that drew on his work with the Jewish Charities; compiled a large bibliography of the urban community that appeared in R. E. Park, E. W. Burgess, and R. D. McKenzie's *The City* (1925); and published two scholarly articles, one on the sociology of Ferdinand Tonnies and another on some Jewish types of personality. He also completed his doctoral dissertation, which appeared as a book in 1928 titled simply *The Ghetto*, a work that may be seen as a characteristic product of the 1920s.

During that decade Wirth and others defined societies as entities that had been and were becoming socially, culturally, and politically pluralistic and characterized by a "natural" coherence facilitating collective action.[6] Such societies seemed always in the process of organizing, disorganizing, and reorganizing, some at a rapid and others at a glacial pace, as a consequence of the contact and competitive and cooperative interaction of the social groups that composed the entire system. These groups ran the gamut in size from the family to the "nation"-state or empire, although not all societies possessed a formal government or even a common territory. Some of the subgroups that formed these larger wholes came from "outside," such as immigrant groups from various racial stocks and various place-based cultural entities, including rural and urban groups as well as "ethnic" ones. But some groups also stemmed from the processes of differentiation within the larger system. These processes produced regionally based groups, such as Appalachians, within the United States. But they also yielded classes, status groups, castes, occupational groups, and other informally and formally organized groups. These included small ones whose members interrelated on an intimate and face-to-face basis, as in the family or a club, and large ones whose members interrelated on an impersonal basis, as in business corporations or labor unions, in which persons within and outside the group related to one another on the basis of the function of the individual. In such societies, moreover, all individuals participated in and interacted with a variety of groups, some more than others, and acquired habits, customs, ideas, attitudes,

and goals from the groups with which they affiliated most intensely, a process that made social groups both elements of social reality and socially determined states of mind.[7]

One formulation of pluralism also treated all groups as equal, or potentially equal, and suggested that under certain circumstances groups that found themselves in an unequal situation, in a situation defined by their leaders or outside sympathizers as unequal, would become self-conscious as a "minority" and strive to improve their situation in relation to the "dominant" groups. By this definition, dominant groups, although different in some respects, would not constitute a problem because their leaders would not agitate for a change in their situation. Yet resistance by dominant groups to the aspirations of minorities could yield various forms of conflict, including violence. These conflicts could threaten the coherence of the larger pluralistic entity, either in the form of revolution by a class minority or by creating a nationalistic ethnic minority demanding either its own territory and a society it might dominate or the annexation of its current area of dominance to a society controlled by the same ethnic group. Other solutions to social conflict included some form of peaceful accommodation by both dominant and minority groups to the situation of inequality or the granting of socioeconomic or ethnic cultural autonomy to the minority groups.[8]

Yet some students of this form of pluralism thought that the contact and interaction of groups also produced pluralistic "assimilation," what they sometimes called "integration." They conceived of this as stemming from the human capacity to get under the skin of other people, as Wirth liked to put it. By this he meant the human capacity to understand the perspectives, motives, goals, and systems of thought of others even while disagreeing on particular questions. This capacity for empathy meant that the contact and interaction among groups led to a process of interpenetration among some of these various groups, so that they shared traits and outlooks while remaining cognizant of, proud of, and loyal to their heritages. Or, to put it in words that Wirth understood but avoided, assimilative pluralists thought in pluralistic Hegelian terms of theses and antitheses yielding a coherent yet dynamic synthesis in which elements of the theses and antitheses remained. For his audience, at least his public ones in America after 1919, Wirth called this the social "melting pot" and skirted the question of classes and class interaction and assimilation.[9]

Some of the proponents of this form of pluralism also began in the 1920s to look for examples of how it worked in the past and the present as a means of building a science of society. They hoped this science would lead to an understanding of contemporary societies, so that their tendencies might be explicated and projected into the future as guides for leading such societies in directions approved by the social experts and as advice that might be urged upon planners and policymakers. The young Louis Wirth was one of these scientists of society. As he later explained it, "I was enthusiastic and radical in those days in a sense that I believed a science of human behavior was not only desirable but indispensable." What he read in his studies at Chicago, he added, he found "disappointing," but "through the inspiration and help" of his teachers he felt "impelled to go on and do what little I could to make our knowledge in this field [the science of human behavior] perhaps a little less disappointing to others."[10]

The Ghetto was the first product of Wirth's effort to be less disappointing than his predecessors had been to him, and the book contained a theory of social change that made cities the dynamic factor, a theory that rejected or reformulated several notions still current in the 1920s.[11] In this work Wirth considered and rejected the idea of race-based cultural determinism and the notion of the race-based inferiority or superiority of groups. Jews, he argued, should be regarded as a socially determined and therefore mutable rather than a racial "type," a person or thing believed to foreshadow another.[12] Wirth also rejected the notion of the gemeinschaft/gesellschaft rural/urban continuum, the notion that societies evolved in a straight line from simple forms of primary social organization characterized by small groups and intimate relations to complex forms of secondary social organization characterized by large groups and impersonal relations. Instead he treated both as coterminous, located each deep in the past, and suggested that they interacted.[13]

For Wirth, then, cities were "urban" regardless of historical period and contained both forms of social organization, although in them the secondary form especially flourished, the factor that distinguished them from rural places and tribes, nomadic and settled. But he also depicted cities as densely populated and composed of a broad range of subcategories of groups of both the primary and secondary variety. This made cities crucibles for the contact of groups and for group interaction, competition, and cooperation.[14] These processes yielded castes and accommodative, autonomous, and assimilative minorities[15] and made cities dynamic centers of social change and the urbanites and urbanized groups the carriers of that tendency, even when they left the city for nonurban locales. The character of cities also suggested that each would possess its own socially and historically determined "personality," even though all cities in all times ranked as "urban," regardless of their status as predominantly commercial or industrial in economic structure.[16] This approach to cities and social change made "progress" chancy, depending upon the urban mix of cultural and social groups, the availability of material resources, and the disposition of dominant groups toward technological change. "Progress" especially depended on the reaction of dominant groups toward the aspirations of unequal minorities, particularly the willingness of dominant groups to embrace assimilative pluralism, or perhaps their willingness to grant minority groups a measure of cultural or socioeconomic autonomy, something more than a gesture to underwrite the coherence and welfare of the whole.

Indeed, this approach to cities and social change rejected the notions of both unilinear and inevitable progress. In the first place it posited the existence in any given epoch of multiple conceptions of what constituted progress. Various people would define and measure progress from their own perspective, outlooks derived from the social group affiliation with the most influence on the advocates of one version or another of progress. In addition, this relativistic view of progress allowed for reversion, the disintegration of a pluralistic social entity, and its reformulation on the principles of an "earlier" stage as seen by one or another group. It also allowed for stasis, a situation in which competing and cooperating groups "lost" the capacity to envisage a new order of things toward which to strive, the necessary precondition for "synthesis."[17] In this view, then, history might go "forward," "backward," or not at all.

Finally, Wirth treated ghettos, Jewish or otherwise, as cities within cities[18] and began his history of the Jewish ghetto with the ancient diaspora. Uprooted by the Roman destruction of Jerusalem, the Jews became nomadic groups in the pluralistic Christian civilization within which they traveled. As they wandered, however, they carried with them their cultural baggage, including not only their religion, with its tendency toward communal living and its stress on teleology and the importance of learning and the rational explication of texts,[19] but also a considerable experience of living in cities. As nomads, moreover, they interacted closely with a broad range of peoples and shared traits to such an extent that they became known for their cosmopolitanism.

Yet gradually some of the Jews settled in the cities of various countries within Christendom, and there they accommodated their Jewish cultural baggage by forming voluntary ghettos. Here Jews from various places gathered and through the division of labor developed a broad range of interacting social groups and personality types. From these heterogeneous ghettos they continued to interact with their outside neighbors, although increasingly in an impersonal and utilitarian although mutually beneficial way, and became self-conscious as a group and regarded by their hosts as "strangers" with a special and useful talent for rationality in economic matters. But that heightened self-consciousness among Jews, combined with extensive communication among ghettos and with continued impersonal interaction among "outsiders," also created an integrated and pluralistic pan-Jewish community, or civilization that included Jews not resident in a ghetto.[20]

Then came the Crusades, which yielded in some places attempts to expel or eliminate the Jews and in others the creation of compulsory ghettos, complete with walls and badges, to prevent them from converting or contaminating Christians. Compulsory ghettos weakened the pluralistic pan-Jewish community, but even in the age of the involuntary ghetto some Jews continued to interact economically and intellectually with outsiders, a process that funneled traits and ideas from the outside world, including rationalism, capitalism, and nationalism, into the world for which the ghetto served as the center. These same factors eventually produced political emancipation, participation by Jews in civic affairs, and movement toward "enlightenment" among many Jews themselves. In some places, such as Frankfurt, Germany, this led to assimilation, the dispersal of the ghetto, and the emergence of a sophisticated, cosmopolitan, and modern Jewish community, aware of its Jewish identity but characterized by a "duplex culture," one "richer and more iridescent" than its predecessors.[21] But wherever ghettos remained, they continued as sources of resentment among both Jews and their neighbors, obstacles to assimilative pluralism, agencies for the fomenting of mutual distrust, misunderstanding, and conflict, and havens for some assimilative Jews who could not bear the coldness and partiality of their initial reception among outsiders.[22]

In the second part of his book, Wirth presented a history of Jews in America, a story that virtually recapitulated that in Europe, even though Jews in America never confronted the extreme isolation of the walled ghetto. Broadly speaking, Wirth contended that West European and especially German Jews, who had a long and intense urban ghetto experience, tended more readily toward assimilation in America. East Europeans, whom Wirth called a "village people," not only lacked such a long and intense urban ghetto experience but also came later to the United States. Because of their backwardness they re-created ghettos as they arrived and experienced in the United States more extreme isolation than had their German predecessors. Yet their "voluntary" ghetto did not cut off all interaction with outsiders, especially with German Jews, who acted as intermediaries. As such, they assisted East European Jews in moving more rapidly toward assimilation and the acquisition of a duplex culture than contemporary non-Jewish immigrants and black migrants and in the creation of a pluralistic, resourceful, and "competent" pan-Jewish community that established conditions favorable to the even more rapid assimilation of East European Jews.[23]

Wirth's history of the Jews in America concluded with a history of the Jews of Chicago, who seemed to him in the 1920s headed in the same direction as the Jews in Frankfurt,[24] although in Chicago as in other American and European cities, the ghetto persisted, both as a place and as a symbol. It provided a richly human and neighborly way station for some Jews, a symbol of poverty and humiliation for others, and a source of divisiveness that undermined the coherence of the pluralistic pan-Jewish community. It also served outsiders as a symbol of Jewish haughtiness and clannishness[25] and endangered all Jews by arousing the suspicion of outsiders about the civic and national loyalty of the Jews as a uniform race or as a uniform social group or as a uniform international community, ideas Wirth designated as among the "fantastic" conceptions of the Jews in the past and the present.[26]

That parlous situation defined "the Jewish problem," the issue with which Wirth closed the book. Here, as throughout, Wirth posed as the objective social scientist

committed to social determinism and offering expert advice to concerned parties. He repeated his conviction that Jews constituted not a racial but a socially constructed and pluralistic type based on a flexible, resilient, and adaptable self-consciousness encompassing not only residents of the ghetto but also those who had left and those who had never lived in a ghetto. He also presented the Jews as an accommodationist, autonomizing, and assimilative minority as a matter of fact, not theory, in the past and in the present and as an alternative for the future. This analysis of the Jewish problem rendered futile any attempt to make the Jews into "pure" Americans or Germans, for in Wirth's taxonomy all racial and social groups, including Americans and Germans, ranked as hybrids, and any persistent policy of homogenization based on the myth of purity could only lead to frustration and probably to violence. On the other hand, dominant groups could follow accommodationist, autonomizing, or assimilative policies or even all three at once without disrupting the efficient functioning of the larger society, although autonomizing or assimilative policies would lead to the best results from the standpoint of the welfare of the minority group and the whole society. But all three approaches required a measure of mutual understanding and respect among social groups, and accommodationist and autonomizing approaches—to avoid recurring conflicts and the threat of violence—required in addition the provision of separate or separate but equal facilities for those minorities not yet at the assimilative state or for those minority groups with which the dominant groups refused to assimilate.[27]

This analysis, then, provided a benign account of the urban ghetto. In it cultural groups built a sense of self-consciousness, and through their interaction with diverse insiders and outsiders the ghetto groups acquired new traits and the resiliency to devise flexible strategies for survival, including a strategy of pluralistic assimilation, the success of which depended on the willingness of dominant groups to facilitate the trait-sharing process, an outcome that had happened in Frankfurt and that could be expected in Chicago.

This analysis also probably accounts for Wirth's silence on the question of residential integration for blacks in the 1920s and early 1930s and for his acquiescence in city plans accommodating segregation and the migration of minority groups from the inner city through successive bands of less segregated neighborhoods as they moved from an accommodative stance to an assimilative stance. Once established on the periphery of the metropolis, their closer contacts with dominant groups would break down barriers and pave the two-way street of assimilation, a street that would leave both the dominant group and the minority group with a new duplex culture. Such an outcome, after all, seemed only natural, for Wirth's "natural history" of the Jewish ghetto demonstrated that through this gradual process Jews from various European cultures would become Jewish Americans, loyal to both aspects of their heritage and that other minority groups would do the same.[28]

Shortly after completing **The Ghetto**, however, Wirth began to develop doubts about some of its elements, including its deterministic nature, especially with respect to the prospects for the gradual elimination of prejudice and discrimination by natural social processes.[29] He had taught for two years at Chicago but failed to receive a regular appointment, perhaps because of anti-Semitism. He then went to New Orleans to teach at Tulane, where he finished his book but where he also failed to receive a regular appointment, this time because of his advocacy of birth control. He then won a fellowship to study in Germany during 1931 and 1932. There he confronted the virulent anti-Semitism and the myth of race embedded in the Nazi movement. He also met Karl Mannheim, who in 1929 had published *Ideology and Utopia*. On Wirth's return to the United States he received a regular appointment at Chicago, spent the middle 1930s teaching, extricating thirteen members of his family from Germany, engaging more intensively in social activism, and thinking about *Ideology and Utopia* and its implications.

Wirth concluded that Mannheim deserved an Anglo-American audience and helped persuade him to prepare a longer version that Wirth helped translate and for which Wirth wrote a preface. The English edition appeared in 1936, and Wirth in his preface praised the study as a potential solution to the problem of objectivity in a relativistic world of social group pluralism. Mannheim defined the modern crisis as a situation in which some social groups developed ideologies to preserve what Wirth called "the status quo," a situation in which society seemed to be heading in a direction congruent with the expectations of a given ideology. At the same time, however, geographically and socially mobile dissenting groups developed utopias, visions of a new order moving in some other direction, visions that themselves became ideologies with the arrival of a new order, where they once more confronted new utopias. The subjective bias in all groups, however, meant that proponents of both ideologies and utopias left no room in their mental constructs of society for antipathetic positions, an absolutist and authoritarian stance that left them no options but the removal or extirpation of alternative mental constructs and the groups they represented. This situation seemed to doom democracy and pluralism, especially in modern mass societies in which alienation and anomie created a widespread sense of insecurity and a longing for a goal that would give life a purpose, a goal that might be found in an ideology or a utopia.

Yet Mannheim thought he had identified a way to avoid this monstrous stasis and to stimulate artificially the dialectic process of pluralistic social integration. He argued that the mental constructs of social "reality" in both ideologies and utopias failed in fact to encompass the entirety of reality and that no social group could pull off that feat. Yet the pluralistic democratic dialectic process could continue if one could identify a group with a more complete insight into the whole situation than the advocates of particular ideologies or utopias. And he depicted intellectuals as the only persons sufficiently detached from a particular social group to find a middle way between ideologies and utopias that would integrate the benign elements of the current situation into a dynamic synthesis leading to the next phase of the dialectic, which by definition would remain democratic and pluralistic.

Wirth, as it turned out, agreed with Mannheim that assimilative pluralism, or integration, would not work "naturally," as Wirth had proposed in **The Ghetto**. But it also turned out that Wirth now distrusted intellectuals, at least those who isolated themselves within the walls of ivory-towered ghettos and those who dreamed up grand explanatory theories. To Wirth such theories seemed "utopian" in two senses: They tended to become ideologies, and they would prove politically infeasible in the surviving democratic states characterized by a dense variety of utopias and ideologies and by entrenched and inflexible if not yet authoritarian dominant groups.[30] Wirth, as we have seen, also distrusted people animated by an ethics of conscience, for it produced "irrational" true believers, noncompromising absolutists. He preferred those activated by a "rational" and empirically based ethics of conviction, which yielded pragmatic compromisers (pluralists).[31]

Wirth had already moved in this direction in 1938, when he published his famous essay **"Urbanism as a Way of Life."** This widely misunderstood piece helped stamp Wirth as a rabid antiurbanite who depicted cities as seedbeds of uprootedness that engulfed their alienated and anomic residents in loneliness, insecurity, and despair and pushed them into antisocial behavior and toward antidemocratic political movements. Yet reading this essay in the context of his other work after 1935 produces a different picture. From this angle Wirth argued in the urbanism essay not only that modern urban life might move in that dangerous direction but also that it might be made to move in the direction of tolerance, urbanity, integration, cosmopolitanism, and democracy if people decided to act on pressing social and economic problems in ways calculated to realize that vision of the public welfare.[32]

Indeed, this allegedly antiurban essay may be seen as the apotheosis of the city for its historic role as the prime crucible of group mobility, contact, interaction, and communication. This role gave it that density and heterogeneity that made possible both the sharing of traits among groups *and* the recent discovery of the necessity of using law to protect that sort of "integration" as a means of averting intergroup conflict and violence. In this conception the policy from the 1920s of providing merely education in tolerance and intergroup understanding would no longer suffice, a realization by the second Wirth and others that helps explain the sudden emergence in the late 1930s and 1940s of their determination to promote legislation and secure court decisions to foster immediate racial integration, the arrangement of social relations to foster the sharing of traits among groups.

In assessing the urbanism essay it is also useful to remember that Wirth was addressing sociologists and urging them to abandon grand and utopian theories in favor of contributing to the solution of particular problems. He aimed to establish an agenda for the sociological study of urban life and problems and, in so doing, concentrated on the itemization of particular problems, a list that gave the essay a gloomy cast. But this agenda may be viewed as similar to the agenda of the historical study of urban life prepared at about the same time by Arthur Schlesinger,[33] for both started from similar premises about the liberating nature of urban life. Both sought to differentiate urban from rural life. Both presented city dwellers as urbanites by choice and as people liberated by urban life from the mental prison of socially determined identity and thinking. And both suggested that such people invented history or caused it to happen by virtue of their ability to think and act in new ways.

Those skeptical of this reading of the urbanism essay should consult a less famous essay of Wirth's prepared about the same time as a speech to the American Planning and Civic Association. Called **"The Urban Mode of Life,"** it covered much the same ground as the more famous piece. But Wirth concluded it by commenting on the bewildering diversity of urban life as a virtue, a source of democratic pluralistic coherence. The very "complication of urban life, involving similar interests, similar risks and dangers and communal crises," he noted, "tends to mold the urban population into a new community in which common objectives, rational programs and intellectual leadership emerge." He proceeded then to criticize "tender hearted, if not tender-minded romanticists" so staggered by the problems of urban living that they "seek to escape from the city," an impossibility for all but a few and for them only "partially or temporarily" an option, "for the lure of the city and its great cultural advantages is virtually irresistible." Yet Wirth did not stop here. Even "conceding," he added,

> that a few can find refuge in pastoral pursuits or in "rurban" settlements, and admitting that our cities, especially our metropolitan super-cities, could be loosened up considerably in the interest of economy and livability, it is idle utopianism to assume that human satisfactions could be increased by dismantling our great cities. We could not possibly hope to enjoy some of the most cherished advantages that we have come to regard as essential ingredients of modern civilized life without great cities. In the interest of the millions of people who live and work in our cities and of the advancement of our national life a nation-wide program designed to make the cities better and more effective mechanisms in the national economy is urgently needed.[34]

The second Wirth also wrote a great deal about city planning. As early as 1935 he opposed planning for the development of cultural regionalism in the United States on the grounds that it might yield political regionalism, or what he called "nationalist" minorities.[35] This indisposition to plan the culture of other people appeared more stridently in later years. Wirth argued in 1949 that modern civilizations and planners faced three alternatives: "change

the attitude and character of our people . . . , change the situation under which we are working . . . , or . . . alter the rules of the game." Wirth preferred the last two and resisted proposals to tinker with the personalities of people, perhaps a response to contemporary talk about "the authoritarian personality" and ways of engineering democratic personalities. "To paraphrase Vice-President Marshall's famous phrase," wrote the second Wirth, some people think that "what this country needs . . . is a good five-cent psychiatrist; but psychiatrists and psychiatric social workers are not available in the quantity and quality at the prices the masses of men can as yet afford." Instead, he added, we "must work superficially and in large groups, altering the conditions of life and improving the rules of the game. But at no time need we barter security for freedom or freedom for security, for to put one over against the other is to establish a false dichotomy."[36] This same distaste for psychiatric engineering may also account for Wirth's disapproval of Karl Mannheim's book on planning, which not only discussed the democratic personality and how to create it but also proposed a revival of religion as an antidote for anomie.[37]

Beyond this, the second Wirth liked to distinguish between dictatorial and democratic community planning. The former consisted of planning for the community and the second of planning by the community involving "mass participation on the part of the members of the community. . . . The fact is," explained Wirth,

> that unless the planning activities of a community are not from the start the self-energizing activities of the real social forces in the community, and of the people . . . affected thereby, the planning turns out to set for itself obstacles it can rarely hurdle. For if the plan is not the plan that the people really want, and in which they have something to say, it will be an extraneous thing, and it will be out of accord with the wishes and desires of the people.[38]

As for dictatorial planners, including those of the Soviet regime, the second Wirth argued that "there are certain limits beyond which . . . dictators cannot go, and . . . if the conditions of life which they can provide for their people and the hopes they can hold out to them fall below a certain minimum there will be rebellion and counterrevolution."[39]

Yet the second Wirth not only lectured planners. He also participated in planning and even wrote a plan himself, essentially a manual on democratic planning rather than a conventional master plan. In 1945 he and an architect entered a newspaper competition that offered a prize of $25,000 for the best plan for Chicago. Wirth's proposal, which finished second, called for the division of the Chicago area into seventy communities of some fifty thousand people living in smaller neighborhoods. These local communities he said, should be self-governing and offer residential racial, ethnic, and class integration for those who so desired. He also proposed methods for securing maximum feasible participation of local community residents in designing social and physical environments "consistent with the interests of the larger community" of which the local communities formed parts.[40]

So Wirth proposed to resolve the modern crisis by advocating the democratization of intellectual life based on an ethics of conviction, a proposal with an agenda for professional social scientists and for other citizens. He urged social scientists to engage in interdisciplinary work to create an integrative "general" sociology that concerned itself especially with the welfare of whole communities, such as cities, nations, and the emerging world community, and to devote much of their time to teaching that approach to students who would enter community service professions outside academic life. He also exhorted professional social scientists to social activism to engage them in interaction with other groups and the process of getting under the skins of other people to grasp their aspirations, aims, motives, and mentalities. This would assist the social scientists in developing a general sociology centered on the search for democratic integrative policies and make them more effective in suggesting alternative policies to other groups.[41]

At the same time he advocated not only the maximum feasible participation of citizens in community planning and the management of social and civic groups[42] but also the immediate clearing out of legal and economic obstacles to racial and ethnic residential integration and socioeconomic mobility for all groups. Citizens' participation would engage the masses in interaction with other groups and the process of getting under the skins of other people, a process that would be reinforced by the group interaction involved in socioeconomic, racial, and ethnic mobility. But the proper functioning of this mobility required the establishment as a goal of the integration of racial, ethnic, class, occupational groups, and women into the neighborhoods, jobs, and careers of their choice to prevent the recently arrived and the well established from turning on those still "outside" as scapegoats for their own discontents.[43] Wirth especially feared that this fate as perpetual strangers awaited blacks, whom he seemed to have regarded as potential candidates for relegation to a status similar to that of the Jews as virtually everybody's favorite scapegoat and as the special target of antidemocratic social movements.[44]

Community planning with maximum feasible participation in decision making provided a critical component of this scheme, however. For Wirth it ranked as "one of the roads by which we may preserve a democratic society . . . ,"[45] because it obliged citizens to focus on goals for the welfare of the pluralistic whole rather than on the interests of a particular group.[46] Together, Wirth's proposals for the pursuit of social science, integration, and citizens' participation would produce citizen intellectuals. Inspired by an ethics of conviction and interested in perpetuating the pluralistic whole, they would constitute staunch defenders of pluralistic assimilative democracy and an imposing counterforce to proponents of ideologies and utopias.

These propositions for the democratization of intellectual life rested on Wirth's analysis of American history and society. Here, especially in the teemingly heterogeneous cities, the social melting pot had worked tolerably well, despite its defects, in producing an effective sense of local and national community and a sympathetic attitude to the idea of world community. And it worked because the United States constituted a society based on ideals expressed in its Declaration of Independence and Constitution, which he interpreted as the ideals of treating all social groups equally and of tolerating pluralistic dissent under the rule of law. These rules of the game prohibited the suppression of ideals or the extirpation of the social groups that advocated them. They also provided an antidote for the alienating and anomic tendencies in modern life: an empirically derived and secular ideal toward which to strive that gave a "spiritual" meaning to life without promoting or repressing religious or secular ideologies or utopias. The challenge lay in finding a way to keep this social melting pot, which had worked naturally in the past, vital in the present and the future, the pluralistic present and future that had yielded the dilemma of ideologies and utopias, the resolution of which Wirth thought he found in his proposals of the democratization of intellectual life on the basis of an ethics of conviction.[47]

This same analysis led Wirth during and after World War II to advocate the establishment of a world government based on these democratic principles. This did not strike him as American imperialism because the ideal of the equality of social groups and the rule of law had already spread around the world and had been voluntarily embraced, especially among the ascendant minorities beginning to experience intense social and geographic mobility in the backward countries of color.[48] But the chance to crystallize a democratic consensus on the pluralism of equal or potentially equal groups and ideas as the basis for goal setting and the implementation of compromises[49] for the welfare of the whole (while agreeing to disagree on lesser questions) might pass if men and women who shared those convictions did not act to make them a reality. Otherwise, a situation of stasis and murderous authoritarianism and totalitarian planning would rule by default,[50] a situation that might eliminate the rational basis for mid-twentieth-century democratic ideals and lead to the nuclear destruction of modern societies if not humanity itself.

The second Wirth recognized that forging a consensus on which to base world government and other large and pluralistic formal organizations and societies would not be easy. He defined consensus as "a measure of agreement" sufficient to support collective action but insisted that the agreement should be "neither imposed by coercion nor fixed by custom so as no longer to be subject to discussion. It is always partial and developing and has constantly to be won. It results from the interpenetration of views based upon mutual consent and upon feeling as well as thinking together." But it could be done, he asserted, because of his assumption that human beings the world over are sufficiently alike in their basic nature and their life careers that even the most alien groups in contact with one another, no matter how indirectly or remotely, will have some elementary capacity to put themselves in the place of the other, that the common understanding that comes through communication will have a cumulative effect, and that every step toward understanding becomes the basis for a still broader and deeper basis for understanding.[51]

The second Wirth also asserted that a politics of consensus and compromise without repressing "heretical" ideas and their proponents would incorporate and sustain a lively conflict of ideas. As he put it after Harry Truman's dramatic comeback victory in 1948,

> We know that America's liberal forces have already yielded if not surrendered on many . . . issues to a minority of the nation on the ground that higher strategy demands compromise. I, too, favor compromise, when one can foresee the consequences of the battle will be more costly than the actual victory. But to compromise before the battle, and during the battle, and after the battle, too, is to squander one's moral heritage, and in the end to gain nothing but remorse. The measures that are now before the American people for wider coverage of health, education, recreation and other forms of insurance against the vicissitudes of life that the individual cannot control are now the uncompromisable agenda of our society. And on this agenda goes the item of civil rights.[52]

In the final analysis, then, the second Louis Wirth may be seen as seeking to put "whimsy" into social thought, to find a way to detach ideas from groups, from nonintellectual sources. He sought to avoid what Robert Merton called "the functionalization of thought," to avoid regarding ideas as epiphenomena of some deeper reality. The second Wirth wanted to avoid the social determination of thought, the embedding of thought irrevocably in the social needs of a group or the psychological needs of individuals. For Wirth the key rested in human nature, its capacity for empathy and the trait-sharing integration that produced cosmopolitans with the ability to think new things and in new ways. For him community planning with the maximum feasible participation in decision making under the ideal of the equality of groups and the rule of law seemed the safest route to the preservation and exercise of the human capacity for whimsy.[53] Such a process, moreover, possessed the potential to turn assimilative minorities into a majority that shared a variety of cultures but belonged to none,[54] a characteristic providing a well-developed capacity to think in new ways and to integrate the old with the new in a new order of things.

Some of these propositions of the second Louis Wirth still strike some people as good advice, but that is another story, part of the unwritten history of the idea of pluralism since the late 1930s. Yet it might be added that the second Wirth's advocacy of the democratization of intellectual life and of immediate legal steps to encourage

integration marked not only a retreat from expertise-ism, determinism, and gradualism but also a shift in the focus of his concern from groups to individuals as the basic unit of society. This new emphasis also stressed the importance of establishing and maintaining a consensus on a pluralism of ever-expanding visions of "better" and different futures not only as a way out of the deadlock of ideologies and utopias but also as a means of deterring individuals engaged in the self-absorbing task of constructing their own cultures from pursuing merely self-fulfillment without regard to the public welfare.[55]

In this sense the second Wirth may be seen as symptomatic of a major tendency in American civilization and historical writing since 1940. This analysis proposes nondeterministic and integrative democratic pluralism as the vision of the so-called consensus school and questions the suspicion that its adherents longed for homogeneity or sought to homogenize the American past. It also suggests the essentially antideterministic character of most urban historical work since 1940, a characteristic of both the old and the new urban history and, for that matter, of the other old and new specializations as well. Both, that is, sought to analyze the ways in which various persons and groups of people have sought liberation from social or other "forces" to create for themselves a vision of who and what they wanted to become and the social and physical environments in which that becoming might take place.

Finally, analysis of the two Louis Wirths reminds us that the best urban history, like the best of historical writing since the 1920s, has consisted of a commentary on the delights and dilemmas of pluralism, an implicit and sometimes explicit discourse about the cultures of the past intended as a discourse about what the cultures of the present might be and might become. That we may celebrate, but safely only if we remember the persistence since 1952 of ghettos, racial and otherwise, as facts, symbols, and states of minds, here and around the world. That remembering should remind us of our responsibility as historians to understand the persisting ghettos and to lay out the dangers and opportunities their persistence offers for those various communities in which we live. Such studies, in the spirit of Louis Wirth, might benefit from our civic activism as well as research, thinking, and writing as aspects of the pursuit of history as a way of life.

NOTES

[1] I pick 1940 in part because of the publication that year by Arthur M. Schlesinger, of "The City in American History," *Mississippi Valley Historical Review* 27 (June 1940), 43-66, esp. pp. 45-47, which, it seems to me, leaned in this nondeterministic direction. Schlesinger depicted cities as social and physical environments created by ambitious and innovative people in all fields of endeavor that attracted other ambitious and innovative people in all fields of endeavor who strove to promote the common good by improving collective life in the city and in the country. See also Schlesinger's revision of that article,

"The City in American Civilization," in Arthur M. Schlesinger, *Paths to the Present* (New York, 1949), 210-233, which states forcefully the case for the important and beneficent role of cities in the making of both American history and American civilization.

[2] Unless indicated otherwise I am relying for biographical information about Wirth on Roger A. Salerno, *Louis Wirth: A Bio-Bibliography* (New York, 1987), 3-49.

[3] Wirth may have gotten the distinction between the ethics of conscience and the ethics of conviction from Max Weber, who said the former produced "true believers" (noncompromising absolutists) and the latter pragmatic compromisers (pluralists). See Job L. Dittberner, *The End of Ideology and American Social Thought: 1930-1960* (Ann Arbor, 1979), 181, 318. On another occasion Wirth cited Weber as having distinguished between the ethics of conviction and the ethics of responsibility. Wirth this time said the first stood for the enunciation of "noble universal principles" or the establishment of a "Utopian dream." The "ethics of responsibility," on the other hand, required living by one's principles and the establishment of "more modest" goals "for the community or the world," goals that could be realized or partially realized. See Louis Wirth, Ernest R. Hilgard, and I. James Quillen, eds., *Community Planning for Peacetime Living: Report of the 1945 Stanford Workshop on Community Leadership* (Palo Alto, 1946), 88.

[4] The quote is from his daughter, Elizabeth Wirth Marvick, "Louis Wirth: A Biographical Memorandum," in Elizabeth Wirth Marvick and Albert J. Reiss, Jr., eds., *Community Life and Social Policy: Selected Papers by Louis Wirth* (Chicago, 1956), 337.

[5] The quote, from Elizabeth Wirth Marvick, is in Salerno, *Louis Wirth,* 13.

[6] I am indebted to Henry D. Shapiro for alerting me to the catching on of the ideal of pluralism. See, for example, his *Appalachia on Our Mind: The Southern Mountaineers in the American Consciousness, 1870-1920* (Chapel Hill, 1978) and "The Place of Culture and the Problem of Identity," in Allen Batteau, ed., *Appalachia and America: Autonomy and Regional Dependence* (Lexington, 1983), 111-141.

[7] Wirth in 1931 proposed to reform working-class juvenile delinquents by encouraging in them the development of a proletarian class consciousness to wean them from their destructive associations. See James T. Carey, *Sociology and Public Affairs: The Chicago School* (Beverly Hills, 1975), 89.

[8] In 1945 Wirth commended the Soviet Union for handling its "pluralistic" [what I call autonomizing] minorities by offering "recognition" as a matter of national policy. See Wirth, "The Problem of Minority Groups," in Marvick and Reiss, eds., *Community Life and Social Policy,* 248. He thought Europe but not the United States possessed

nationalistic minorities. See Wirth, "Types of Nationalism," in Marvick and Reiss, eds., *Community Life and Social Policy,* 365-367.

[9] In 1946 Wirth wrote that a "man cannot be assimilated unless someone is willing to assimilate him. In assimilating others we take on some of the characteristics of those assimilated." He then drew an analogy to the American diet, noting that one could detect the waves of immigration by studying changes in the American diet. "In other words," he concluded, "by attempting to change someone else we change ourselves. If we recognize that assimilation is this two-way street, we see more clearly the nature of our American culture." Wirth, Hilgard, and Quillen, eds., *Community Planning,* 80-81.

[10] For the quote see Howard W. Odum, *American Sociology: The Story of Sociology in the United States Through 1950* (New York, 1951), 228.

[11] What follows flows not only from my reading of *The Ghetto* and much of Wirth's other work during the 1920s but also from Robert E. Park, Ernest W. Burgess, and Roderick McKenzie, eds., *The City* (Chicago, 1925), and particularly in that volume Louis Wirth's "A Bibliography of the Urban Community" (a misleading title for what amounts to an essay on cities irrespective of time and place); Ernest W. Burgess, ed., *The Urban Community: Selected Papers from the Proceedings of the American Sociological Society* (Chicago, 1925); and Karl Mannheim, *Ideology and Utopia: An Introduction to the Sociology of Knowledge* (New York, 1936), a revised version of Mannheim's earlier work (1929) on the same subject that Wirth helped translate and for which he wrote a preface.

[12] Louis Wirth, *The Ghetto* (Chicago, 1928), esp. 63-71, 287-288, and the index entry for "Jews," 304. This definition of *type* may be found in *Webster's Seventh Collegiate Dictionary* (Springfield, 1971), 960, which lists as the first meaning of the word "a person or thing (as in the Old Testament) believed to foreshadow another (as in the New Testament)." Wirth dealt his most thorough and systematic blow to the "myth" of race in Louis Wirth and Herbert Goldhammer, "The Hybrid and the Problem of Miscegenation," in Otto Klineberg, ed., *Characteristics of the American Negro* (New York, 1969), 249-370.

[13] Years later Wirth wrote a scathing review of Eric Fromm, *Escape from Freedom.* Among other things he questioned the assumption that many Germans willingly consented to the reign of Hitler and suggested that some modern people sought an escape from the responsibility imposed by freedom rather than from freedom itself. For the review see *Psychiatry* 5 (February 1942), 129-131.

[14] This approach to gemeinschaft/gesellschaft, the rural/urban distinction, and urban life is sometimes implicit and sometimes explicit in *The Ghetto* (see especially the index entry for "city life," p. 303). Two years before the publication of this book, Wirth went on record against the

dualism implicit in the community/society distinction, which he attributed to Ferdinand Tonnies. See Wirth, "The Sociology of Ferdinand Tonnies," *American Journal of Sociology* 32 (November 1926), 422, and Carey, *Sociology and Public Affairs*, 95-120, esp. 96-97, for the Chicago school attack on evolutionary unilinearity.

[15] The typology of minorities is implicit in *The Ghetto*, but Wirth made it explicit in 1945. See Louis Wirth, "The Problem of Minority Groups," in Marvick and Reiss, eds., *Community Life and Social Policy*, 237-260. In that essay he defined pluralistic, assimilationist, secessionist, and militant minority groups. I have used the term *autonomizing* for *pluralistic* in an effort to avoid the confusion that hampers the discussion of these two categories. In *The Ghetto* Wirth explicitly points to Horace Kallen as an advocate of "cultural pluralism" and distinguishes it from "assimilative" pluralism, which he there defines by borrowing from someone else the phrase "duplex culture." See *The Ghetto*, 128.

[16] For an example of Wirth treating a particular city as urban from the outset, as unique and characteristic, as a factor in the urbanization of a region, and as a force in the development of national society see his "Chicago: The Land and the People," *Survey Graphic* 23 (October 1934), 468-471, 520-522, 525.

[17] Wirth notes periods in which outsiders, including some Jews, regarded the Jews (as a group) as, in effect, "backwards." See, for example, *The Ghetto*, 97-130. Reversion may be understood as the persistence into the present of ideas from the past. On "reversion" and what I have called "stasis," see Wirth's preface to Mannheim, *Ideology and Utopia*, xxi, xxiii, xxiv. On static modes of thought in Mannheim, see the index listing in *ibid.*, 352. In the situation of stasis, groups lost the capacity to envisage a new order of things because their representatives talked past one another. They lacked, that is, a level of consensus that permitted the ability to understand one another sufficiently to agree on fundamentals while agreeing to disagree on particulars, the situation in which the dialectic process might proceed.

[18] In his foreword to *The Ghetto*, Park called the ghetto a "natural area" of the city and defined "natural areas" as "regions whose locations, character, and functions have been determined by the same forces that have determined the character and functions of the city as a whole" (see *The Ghetto*, x-xi). A natural area should not be confused with a "neighborhood." On this point see Wirth's bibliographical essay in Park, Burgess, and McKenzie, eds., *The City*, 187-195, in which he defines the various spatial elements of the city according to the Chicago school: the natural area, the neighborhood, the local community, and zones (the famous concentric circles).

[19] Wirth observed that the full development of the teleological and rationalistic aspects of the Jewish mind made Jews particularly susceptible to "isms" of various kinds as solutions to their problems. On this tendency Wirth

noted that such Jews had not learned that solutions to problems did not lead to a problemless condition of life for any group, because life was "an ongoing process, in the course of which every day brings new situations which cannot be met by nostrums and magic formulas, but which must be lived, and which reappear again and again and never are finally solved." See *The Ghetto*, 97-110. The quotation is from p. 110.

[20] See *The Ghetto*, 11-18, 75-88.

[21] For the quote see *ibid.*, 127-128.

[22] On the "compulsory" ghetto see *ibid.*, 29-34. ·

[23] In the 1920s the Chicago school sociologists followed W. I. Thomas in defining a "competent" community. Such a community provided for the four fundamental wishes of humans: the wish for security, a home; the wish for new experience, recreations, adventure, sensations; the wish for recognition (status); and the wish for affection. See Robert E. Park, "Community Organization and the Romantic Temper," in Park, Burgess, and McKenzie, *City Life*, 118-119.

[24] Wirth dealt with the Jews of Frankfurt in a separate chapter analyzing a "typical" ghetto. In it he noted that "the Frankfurt Jewish community of today is scattered all over the city. The ghetto seems to have vanished more completely than in most large American cities, where the compulsory ghetto has never been known" (*The Ghetto*, 48). To this he added that "the Jews have left their impress on the life of Frankfurt as they have on no other city of Europe" and in "time of need, it was Frankfurt that came to the rescue of Jews everywhere" (*The Ghetto*, 49). He concluded that "in spite of all the conversions and intermarriages that have taken place in that city, the Jewish community there still remains one of the most influential in the whole of Europe. Its older families are probably more decidedly orthodox than those of any other German city. *They have a noticeable pride of ancestry and strong feeling of group solidarity*" (*The Ghetto*, 50; emphasis added).

These comments on assimilation in Frankfurt help to clarify the last sentence of the next chapter of *The Ghetto*, which deals with the concept of the Jews as a race. That sentence closed with the following phrase: "The so-called Jewish racial type disappears with the disappearance of the ghetto." In other words, the disappearance of the ghetto led to the disappearance of the *concept* of Jews as a racial or social type, not to the disappearance of Jewish culture and community. In 1943 in an article on the survival of the Jews, Wirth wrote that social groups "cannot die even if they try, for, though the entire membership of a group be exterminated, some remnant, at least, of the culture that made them a group will make its influences felt, if on no one else but their would-be exterminators." See Louis Wirth, "Education for Survival: The Jews," *American Journal of Sociology* 48 (March 1943), 682-691.

[25] The later Wirth continued to worry about the myth of the extraordinary solidarity of the Jews and about Jewish

behavior that fed the myth and the anti-Semitism stemming from the myth. In 1941, for example, he reminded the Council of Jewish Federation and Welfare Funds that the "people who constitute the Jewish groups are not only Jews but Americans, business men, laborers, golf players, capitalists, Republicans and a lot of other things. When we take hold of the handle of their Jewishness, we sometimes have hold only of a fragile and tenuous thing" and "can't proceed to organize Jews on the assumption that their Jewishness is equally significant and means the same thing to all of them." He thought organizations professing to represent all Jews might give some Jews "a false sense of security and solidarity which . . . might prove disastrous." Such organizations, as in Nazi Germany, might "collapse like a house of cards when the crisis came," did "not even . . . stop some Jews from supporting the Hitler movement," and might prove just as ineffective in countering "fascist movements" in America. He thought for "some purposes" Jewish leaders should emphasize "Jewish" intragroup cooperation, and for others intergroup cooperation. In dealing with anti-Semitism he proposed to "have Jews participate as individuals in more general movements . . . perhaps led by non-Jews" while working to "change the structure of Jewish life to permit more effective participation of Jews in non-sectarian movements for warding off menaces to society as a whole and for the improvement of life generally." See Louis Wirth, "Appearances of Harmony," *Notes and News* (Council of Jewish Federation and Welfare Funds), January 15, 1941, 8-9.

[26] The second part of *The Ghetto*, 131-281, deals with the ghetto in America and includes three chapters on the Jews in Chicago. For the "fantastic" (as in "fantasy") conceptions of Jews, see *ibid.*, 291.

[27] *Ibid.*, 287-291. Wirth closed his book by arguing that the Jewish problem was not a problem for the Jewish community, which seemed headed for assimilation. It was a problem for non-Jewish dominant groups, who could solve it by agreeing to assimilate with (share traits with) the Jewish community. Intelligent persons—those with an interest in the coherence and welfare of the larger pluralistic community—would follow that course with respect to any assimilative "minority."

The "deterministic" Wirth felt the same way about segregation, including racial segregation, in the United States. He thought that segregation "may have been a useful historical means of establishing a modus vivendi in a static social order." But "under modern conditions of life and communication it seems at best a costly and temporary makeshift in the struggle against an irresistible process through which peoples and cultures are blended." Louis Wirth, "Segregation," in Edwin R. A. Seligman, ed., *Encyclopedia of the Social Science* (New York, 1934) XIII, 643-647, esp. 647, last sentence.

[28] Wirth referred to his book as a "natural history" of the ghetto that intended to throw light on "human nature and on culture." See *The Ghetto*, 5, 10.

[29] As late as 1935 Wirth expressed the view that the integration of social groups could come only gradually. See Louis Wirth, "Types of Nationalism," *American Journal of Sociology* 41 (May 1936), 723-737, esp. 737.

[30] See, for example, the remarks of Wirth in the discussion section of Herbert Blumer, *An Appraisal of Thomas and Znaniecki's* The Polish Peasant in Europe and America: *Critiques of Research in the Social Sciences* (New York, 1939), I, 122-124, 130-131, 147-148, 153-160, 164, 182-183. Wirth in these discussions makes clear the dangers of social theories becoming "cults" and slogans as well as his preference for substituting for grand explanatory theories, generalizations or hypotheses consisting of a collection of propositions, which hypotheses and propositions should be tested by additional research.

In 1938, a year before the appraisal of *The Polish Peasant*, Wirth had himself published such a hypothesis. See Wirth, "Urbanism as a Way of Life," in Marvick and Reiss, eds., *Community Life and Social Policy*, 116-117. In this essay Wirth warned once more of the "danger of confusing urbanism with industrialism and modern capitalism," for "different as the cities of earlier epochs may have been by virtue of their development in a pre-industrial and precapitalistic order from the great cities of today, they were also cities" (pp. 115-116). Wirth said he received more requests for reprints of his urbanism essay than for any other article he published. See Odum, *American Sociology*, 231.

[31] The second Wirth thought that ideologies in contemporary life tended to proliferate and crystallize into dogmatic propaganda that lacked the power to forge consensus under the pluralistic conditions of modern life, especially in great cities. See Wirth, "Ideological Aspects of Social Disorganization" [1940], in Marvick and Reiss, eds., *Community Life and Social Policy*, 192-205. But he insisted on the importance of the sociological analysis of ideologies on the grounds that what people said could be as revealing as what they did.

[32] Wirth, "Urbanism as a Way of Life," in Marvick and Reiss, eds., *Community Life and Social Policy*; Zane L. Miller, "Pluralizing America: Walter Prescott Webb, Chicago School Sociology, and Cultural Regionalism," in Robert B. Fairbanks and Kathleen Underwood, eds., *Essays on Sunbelt Cities and Recent Urban America* (College Station, 1990), 164.

[33] Schlesinger, "The City in American History" and "The City in American Civilization," in *Paths to the Present*.

[34] Wirth, "The Urban Mode of Life," in Harlean James, ed., *American Planning and Civic Annual* (Washington, DC, 1937).

[35] Wirth, "The Prospects of Regional Research in Relation to Social Planning," *Publications of the American Sociological Society* 29 (August 1935), esp. 107-109, 113-114.

[36] Wirth, "Social Goals for Nation and World," *The Survey* 85 (July 1949), 388 and 389 for the necessity of organizing into groups to attain goals.

[37] Reinhard Bendix, "Social Theory and Social Action in the Sociology of Louis Wirth," *American Journal of Sociology* 59 (May 1954), 525; Karl Mannheim, *Freedom, Power, and Democratic Planning* (New York, 1950), 19-21; chaps. 9, 13.

[38] Wirth, "The Planning of Modern Urban Communities," in William C. Reavis, ed., *Forthcoming Developments in American Education* (Chicago, 1945), VIII, 155-156, 161, 169.

[39] Wirth, "Consensus and Mass Communication," *American Sociological Review* 13 (February 1948), 5.

[40] Ernest A. Grunsfeld and Louis Wirth, "A Plan for Metropolitan Chicago," *Town Planning Review* 25 (April 1954), 5-32, esp. 27, 31.

[41] The most succinct statement of the second Wirth's views on sociology may be found in Odum, *American Sociology,* 229-230, and esp. 232. He also said that he best set forth his views on sociology "and its task in the present-day world" in his presidential address before the American Sociological Society, "Consensus and Mass Communication," in *ibid.*, 1-15, in which he posed the problem of achieving consensus in pluralistic formal organizations and societies as the central problem of sociology and of the contemporary world (p. 2). For Wirth on all the social sciences and their social obligations, see "The Social Sciences," in Merle Curti, ed., *American Scholarship in the Twentieth Century* (Cambridge, 1953), esp. 81-82. In these essays and elsewhere Wirth repeatedly urged social scientists and citizens to examine their own assumptions, values, cultural biases, and prejudices as a way to enhance their objectivity (he thought total objectivity an impossibility) and empathy and to bring their grasp of social reality more closely in conformity with true reality, what Mannheim called the total situation.

[42] For Wirth on the obligation to participate in large and formally organized groups see his "Group Tensions and Mass Democracy," *American Scholar* 14 (Spring 1945), 231-235.

[43] Wirth did not write much about women as a social group but he seems to have ranked them as a group that had passed through the various stages of minority group status and that by 1945 constituted an assimilative group whose members possessed the capacity and opportunity to make choices about their roles and identities in life. As such they represented a model for other minority groups. He noted, for example, the problem of "inclination" among wage-earning women in determining how many would continue to work outside their homes after World War II. More tellingly, he talked about Jane Addams, whose work in the slums led some to regard her as "a woman of shady reputation," and noted that people often viewed "the first women doctors, women preachers, [and] women lawyers . . . as eccentric," an attitude that "had to be overcome. If it is easier now for young women to enter professions, it is because these pioneers established the tradition of success. Today's young women can identify themselves with them and say, 'My grandmother did it—my mother did it—so can I.' The same thinking is true for members of minority groups." See Wirth, Hilgard, Quillen, eds., *Community Planning,* 33, 73. Wirth praised the League of Women Voters for its use of "the project method," which he said it got from "progressive educators." See *ibid.*, 83. Wirth may have derived his notions about community participation in planning in part from "the project method," whose advocates stressed learning by doing and urged its use in planning as early as 1926. See Shelby M. Harrison, "Community Participation in City and Regional Planning," in Burgess, ed., *The Urban Community,* 206-218.

[44] Wirth closed his essay on the survivability of the Jews with a section on the survivability of Negroes in America in which he concluded that "for both groups the goal of a happier adjustment to the world in which they must live is seen to be further distant than either had expected. They have the consolation that they can travel at least part of that road in companionship" ("Education for Survival," 691). Wirth also defined education as "part of a process by which societies keep themselves alive and renew themselves in the face of changing membership, changing locality, and changing circumstances" (*ibid.*, 682). The essay amounts to a prospectus for a manual on minority group survival in a pluralistic world of pluralistic societies.

[45] The quotation may be found in Odum, *American Sociology,* 232.

[46] The fullest statement of the second Wirth's views on planning may be found in the eight chapters he contributed to Louis Wirth, Ernest R. Hilgard, I. James Quillen, eds., *Social Policy.* See especially chapter 8, in which he discusses community organization and maximum participation by citizens in civic affairs. Wirth in 1937 referred to the "intellectual" as "typically a marginal man sharing in a plurality of cultures but not fully a member of any one of them." See Wirth, "Discussions," *Social Research* 4 (September 1937), 331.

[47] See, for example, Wirth, "Race and Public Policy," *Scientific Monthly* 54 (April 1944), 311-312; Wirth, "Domestic and International Inter-Group Relations," in *Build the Future: Addresses Marking the Inauguration of Charles Spurgeon Johnson* (Nashville, 1949), 77-83. In "Morale and Minority Groups," *American Journal of Sociology* 47 (November 1941), 415-429, Wirth warned "against the tendency to think of ourselves as a superior race or to identify our nation with the Anglo-Saxon peoples. . . . It would be a sad error to believe that because the Anglo-Saxon peoples and their

institutions were dominant when the nation was young we too are today an Anglo-Saxon people and those of that stock are by virtue of that fact a privileged or superior group. Moreover, in the heterogeneous composition of our national cultural complex, we have potentially the broadest possible base for the development of a civilization which more nearly than any other in the world would embrace all the others" (p. 429). See also Wirth, "The Present Position of Minorities in the United States," in Marvick and Reiss, eds., *Community Life and Social Policy,* esp. 235-236.

[48] The most useful piece by Wirth on world government is his "World Community, World Society, and World Government: An Attempt at a Clarification of Terms," in Quincy Wright, ed., *The World Community* (Chicago, 1948), 9-20, and the discussion that follows. But see also his "Ideas and Ideals as Sources of Power in the Modern World," in Albert J. Reiss, Jr., ed., *Louis Wirth on Cities and Social Life* (Chicago, 1964), 146-156, a reprint of a paper delivered in 1947, esp. pp. 153-156. on the role of mass communications "industries" and intellectuals, and its warning to intellectuals about the danger of their being used by the power groups that dominated the mass communications industries as "paid or unpaid agents" (p. 155). I also found useful his "Integrative Tendencies in International Relations," in Lyman Bryson, Louis Finkelstein, and R. M. Maciver, eds., *Perspectives on a Troubled Decade: Science, Philosophy, and Religion, 1939-1949* (New York, 1950), 267-277, in which he notes that when "we" use the term "integration," we "are not thinking of uniformization and the reduction of the varied cultures of the world to one." He wanted to make the term "world society" more than a mere "figure of speech," while recognizing that "the consensus which is requisite for such a world society [an entity capable of collective action] and the institutions upon which it necessarily must rest are not to be achieved by force or fraud" (pp. 270-271).

[49] Wirth, "Social Goals for Nation and World," 388.

[50] *Ibid.*

[51] Wirth, "Consensus and Mass Communication," 5.

[52] Wirth, "Social Goals for Nation and World," 388.

[53] Henry D. Shapiro started me to think systematically about the role of whimsy in history and human life. But see also Job L. Dittberner, *The End of Ideology,* esp. 293-294, where he proposes "the functionalization of thought" as "the argument of last resort" and an approach to ideas "whose dimensions and implications need further attention" (p. 294).

[54] The second Wirth, had he lived, would doubtless have agreed with E. Franklin Frazier, who in 1957 worried that black businessmen and intellectuals seemed to have chosen to become "anonymous Americans," or what Frazier called *"nobody."* The second Wirth preferred that everybody, but especially minorities concerned about their survivability, should forge duplex cultures. In this connection, it may bear repeating that Wirth advocated racial residential integration, knowing that only more prosperous blacks and whites would experience it immediately, because from these groups of whites and blacks came the leaders, advocates of the two-way street of assimilation, the continuing syntheses of cultures. This would also yield an assimilative black minority, one with the flexibility and adaptability to survive even if the drive for assimilation met rejection and the persistence or revival of antiblack sentiment.

[55] The second Wirth especially tried to emphasize that minority groups were fabricated by the actions of people, not something inevitably given by the social process. They existed, that is, only so long as one group treated another as not only "different" but as deserving an unequal status. The ascription of unequal status made the unequally treated group aware of discrimination and gave it a grievance. The removal of discrimination did not remove the differences among groups, merely the sense of grievance of a persecuted group. The second Wirth also talked about individuals identifying themselves with one or another group as a matter of choice rather than as a matter of an inescapable social heritage. This stance is evident in his essay on "The Present Position of Minority Groups in the United States," cited above, but also in his "Problems and Orientation of Research in Race Relations in the United States," *British Journal of Sociology* 1 (June 1950), 117-125, where it stands out clearly as he tries to explain to foreign readers his thesis that group differences "are not necessarily an insuperable obstacle to a high degree of social integration" and that the outcome depended on what people decided to do and not do rather than on social determinism (p. 117). The second Wirth had lost confidence in the notion that natural social processes would gradually eliminate prejudice. He sought not to eliminate prejudice but to prohibit by law its exercise in action as discrimination, the unequal treatment of a particular group.

Also helpful to an understanding of the Chicago school—although I did not read it until after I wrote this essay—is Vernon J. Williams, Jr., *From a Caste to a Minority: Changing Attitudes of American Sociologists Toward Afro-Americans, 1896-1945* (New York, 1989), especially the quote from Robert Park on p. 162.

FURTHER READING

Bibliography

Salerno, Roger A. "Works about Wirth." In *Louis Wirth: A Bio-Bibliography,* pp. 108-30. Westport, Conn.: Greenwood Press, 1987.

An extensive annotated list of writings about Wirth, including reference books; theses and dissertations; books, journals, periodicals, and papers; criticisms and analyses; and book reviews.

Criticism

Christensen, James A. "Urbanism and Community Sentiment: Extending Wirth's Model." *Social Science Quarterly* 60, No. 3 (December 1979): 387-400.

Applies Wirth's urban model to a study of mostly rural communities in 100 counties of North Carolina.

Fischer, Claude S. "Toward a Subcultural Theory of Urbanism." *American Journal of Sociology* 80, No. 6 (May 1975): 1319-41.

Presents a model of urban life which takes into account both Wirth's views on "the pervasive 'unconventionality' (deviance, invention, etc.) of urban life" and critiques his reliance on "ecological factors."

Guterman, Stanley S. "In Defense of Wirth's 'Urbanism as a Way of Life'." *American Journal of Sociology* 74, No. 5 (March 1969): 492-99.

Examines criticisms regarding Wirth's essay "Urbanism as a Way of Life," and in turn offers a critique of these appraisals.

Review of *The Ghetto*, by Wirth and *The Chosen People: A Short History of the Jews in Europe*, by Jerome and Jean Tharaud. *Times Literary Supplement*, No. 1419 (11 April 1929): 285.

Compares Wirth's "careful and lucid book" with the Tharauds' "more superficial and rather wilful affair."

Twentieth-Century
Literary Criticism

Cumulative Indexes
Volumes 1-92

How to Use This Index

Literary Criticism Series
Cumulative Author Index

See Rolfe, Frederick (William Serafino Austin Lewis Mary)

Barondess, Sue K(aufman) 1926-1977 .... **CLC 8**
See also Kaufman, Sue
See also CA 1-4R; 69-72; CANR 1

Baron de Teive
See Pessoa, Fernando (Antonio Nogueira)

Baroness Von S.
See Zangwill, Israel

Barres, (Auguste-) Maurice 1862-1923**TCLC 47**
See also CA 164; DLB 123

Barreto, Afonso Henrique de Lima
See Lima Barreto, Afonso Henrique de

Barrett, (Roger) Syd 1946- .... **CLC 35**

Barrett, William (Christopher) 1913-1992 **C L C 27**
See also CA 13-16R; 139; CANR 11, 67; INT CANR-11

Barrie, J(ames) M(atthew) 1860-1937 . **TCLC 2; DAB; DAM DRAM**
See also CA 104; 136; CANR 77; CDBLB 1890-1914; CLR 16; DLB 10, 141, 156; MAICYA; MTCW 1; SATA 100; YABC 1

Barrington, Michael
See Moorcock, Michael (John)

Barrol, Grady
See Bograd, Larry

Barry, Mike
See Malzberg, Barry N(athaniel)

Barry, Philip 1896-1949 .... **TCLC 11**
See also CA 109; DLB 7

Bart, Andre Schwarz
See Schwarz-Bart, Andre

Barth, John (Simmons) 1930-**CLC 1, 2, 3, 5, 7, 9, 10, 14, 27, 51, 89; DAM NOV; SSC 10**
See also AITN 1, 2; CA 1-4R; CABS 1; CANR 5, 23, 49, 64; DLB 2; MTCW 1

Barthelme, Donald 1931-1989**CLC 1, 2, 3, 5, 6, 8, 13, 23, 46, 59, 115; DAM NOV; SSC 2**
See also CA 21-24R; 129; CANR 20, 58; DLB 2; DLBY 80, 89; MTCW 1, 2; SATA 7; SATA-Obit 62

Barthelme, Frederick 1943- .... **CLC 36, 117**
See also CA 114; 122; CANR 77; DLBY 85; INT 122

Barthes, Roland (Gerard) 1915-1980**CLC 24, 83**
See also CA 130; 97-100; CANR 66; MTCW 1, 2

Barzun, Jacques (Martin) 1907- .... **CLC 51**
See also CA 61-64; CANR 22

Bashevis, Isaac
See Singer, Isaac Bashevis

Bashkirtseff, Marie 1859-1884 .... **NCLC 27**

Basho
See Matsuo Basho

Bass, Kingsley B., Jr.
See Bullins, Ed

Bass, Rick 1958- .... **CLC 79**
See also CA 126; CANR 53; DLB 212

Bassani, Giorgio 1916- .... **CLC 9**
See also CA 65-68; CANR 33; DLB 128, 177; MTCW 1

Bastos, Augusto (Antonio) Roa
See Roa Bastos, Augusto (Antonio)

Bataille, Georges 1897-1962 .... **CLC 29**
See also CA 101; 89-92

Bates, H(erbert) E(rnest) 1905-1974 .... **CLC 46; DAB; DAM POP; SSC 10**
See also CA 93-96; 45-48; CANR 34; DLB 162, 191; MTCW 1, 2

Bauchart
See Camus, Albert

Baudelaire, Charles 1821-1867 **NCLC 6, 29, 55; DA; DAB; DAC; DAM MST, POET; PC 1; SSC 18; WLC**

Baudrillard, Jean 1929- .... **CLC 60**

Baum, L(yman) Frank 1856-1919 .... **TCLC 7**
See also CA 108; 133; CLR 15; DLB 22; JRDA;

MAICYA; MTCW 1, 2; SATA 18, 100

Baum, Louis F.
See Baum, L(yman) Frank

Baumbach, Jonathan 1933- .... **CLC 6, 23**
See also CA 13-16R; CAAS 5; CANR 12, 66; DLBY 80; INT CANR-12; MTCW 1

Bausch, Richard (Carl) 1945- .... **CLC 51**
See also CA 101; CAAS 14; CANR 43, 61; DLB 130

Baxter, Charles (Morley) 1947-**CLC 45, 78; DAM POP**
See also CA 57-60; CANR 40, 64; DLB 130; MTCW 2

Baxter, George Owen
See Faust, Frederick (Schiller)

Baxter, James K(eir) 1926-1972 .... **CLC 14**
See also CA 77-80

Baxter, John
See Hunt, E(verette) Howard, (Jr.)

Bayer, Sylvia
See Glassco, John

Baynton, Barbara 1857-1929 .... **TCLC 57**

Beagle, Peter S(oyer) 1939- .... **CLC 7, 104**
See also CA 9-12R; CANR 4, 51, 73; DLBY 80; INT CANR-4; MTCW 1; SATA 60

Bean, Normal
See Burroughs, Edgar Rice

Beard, Charles A(ustin) 1874-1948 .... **TCLC 15**
See also CA 115; DLB 17; SATA 18

Beardsley, Aubrey 1872-1898 .... **NCLC 6**

Beattie, Ann 1947- **CLC 8, 13, 18, 40, 63; DAM NOV, POP; SSC 11**
See also BEST 90:2; CA 81-84; CANR 53, 73; DLBY 82; MTCW 1, 2

Beattie, James 1735-1803 .... **NCLC 25**
See also DLB 109

Beauchamp, Kathleen Mansfield 1888-1923
See Mansfield, Katherine
See also CA 104; 134; DA; DAC; DAM MST; MTCW 2

Beaumarchais, Pierre-Augustin Caron de 1732-1799 .... **DC 4**
See also DAM DRAM

Beaumont, Francis 1584(?)-1616 ... **LC 33; DC 6**
See also CDBLB Before 1660; DLB 58, 121

Beauvoir, Simone (Lucie Ernestine Marie Bertrand) de 1908-1986 **CLC 1, 2, 4, 8, 14, 31, 44, 50, 71; DA; DAB; DAC; DAM MST, NOV; SSC 35; WLC**
See also CA 9-12R; 118; CANR 28, 61; DLB 72; DLBY 86; MTCW 1, 2

Becker, Carl (Lotus) 1873-1945 .... **TCLC 63**
See also CA 157; DLB 17

Becker, Jurek 1937-1997 .... **CLC 7, 19**
See also CA 85-88; 157; CANR 60; DLB 75

Becker, Walter 1950- .... **CLC 26**

Beckett, Samuel (Barclay) 1906-1989**CLC 1, 2, 3, 4, 6, 9, 10, 11, 14, 18, 29, 57, 59, 83; DA; DAB; DAC; DAM DRAM, MST, NOV; SSC 16; WLC**
See also CA 5-8R; 130; CANR 33, 61; CDBLB 1945-1960; DLB 13, 15; DLBY 90; MTCW 1, 2

Beckford, William 1760-1844 .... **NCLC 16**
See also DLB 39

Beckman, Gunnel 1910- .... **CLC 26**
See also CA 33-36R; CANR 15; CLR 25; MAICYA; SAAS 9; SATA 6

Becque, Henri 1837-1899 .... **NCLC 3**
See also DLB 192

Beddoes, Thomas Lovell 1803-1849 ...... **NCLC 3**
See also DLB 96

Bede c. 673-735 .... **CMLC 20**
See also DLB 146

Bedford, Donald F.
See Fearing, Kenneth (Flexner)

Beecher, Catharine Esther 1800-1878 **NCLC 30**
See also DLB 1

Beecher, John 1904-1980 .... **CLC 6**
See also AITN 1; CA 5-8R; 105; CANR 8

Beer, Johann 1655-1700 .... **LC 5**
See also DLB 168

Beer, Patricia 1924- .... **CLC 58**
See also CA 61-64; CANR 13, 46; DLB 40

Beerbohm, Max
See Beerbohm, (Henry) Max(imilian)

Beerbohm, (Henry) Max(imilian) 1872-1956 **TCLC 1, 24**
See also CA 104; 154; CANR 79; DLB 34, 100

Beer-Hofmann, Richard 1866-1945 .... **TCLC 60**
See also CA 160; DLB 81

Begiebing, Robert J(ohn) 1946- .... **CLC 70**
See also CA 122; CANR 40

Behan, Brendan 1923-1964**CLC 1, 8, 11, 15, 79; DAM DRAM**
See also CA 73-76; CANR 33; CDBLB 1945-1960; DLB 13; MTCW 1, 2

Behn, Aphra 1640(?)-1689**LC 1, 30, 42; DA; DAB; DAC; DAM DRAM, MST, NOV, POET; DC 4; PC 13; WLC**
See also DLB 39, 80, 131

Behrman, S(amuel) N(athaniel) 1893-1973 **C L C 40**
See also CA 13-16; 45-48; CAP 1; DLB 7, 44

Belasco, David 1853-1931 .... **TCLC 3**
See also CA 104; 168; DLB 7

Belcheva, Elisaveta 1893- .... **CLC 10**
See also Bagryana, Elisaveta

Beldone, Phil "Cheech"
See Ellison, Harlan (Jay)

Beleno
See Azuela, Mariano

Belinski, Vissarion Grigoryevich 1811-1848 **NCLC 5**
See also DLB 198

Belitt, Ben 1911- .... **CLC 22**
See also CA 13-16R; CAAS 4; CANR 7, 77; DLB 5

Bell, Gertrude (Margaret Lowthian) 1868-1926 **TCLC 67**
See also CA 167; DLB 174

Bell, J. Freeman
See Zangwill, Israel

Bell, James Madison 1826-1902**TCLC 43; BLC 1; DAM MULT**
See also BW 1; CA 122; 124; DLB 50

Bell, Madison Smartt 1957- .... **CLC 41, 102**
See also CA 111; CANR 28, 54, 73; MTCW 1

Bell, Marvin (Hartley) 1937- .. **CLC 8, 31; DAM POET**
See also CA 21-24R; CAAS 14; CANR 59; DLB 5; MTCW 1

Bell, W. L. D.
See Mencken, H(enry) L(ouis)

Bellamy, Atwood C.
See Mencken, H(enry) L(ouis)

Bellamy, Edward 1850-1898 .... **NCLC 4**
See also DLB 12

Bellin, Edward J.
See Kuttner, Henry

Belloc, (Joseph) Hilaire (Pierre Sebastien Rene Swanton) 1870-1953 ..... **TCLC 7, 18; DAM POET; PC 24**
See also CA 106; 152; DLB 19, 100, 141, 174; MTCW 1; YABC 1

Belloc, Joseph Peter Rene Hilaire
See Belloc, (Joseph) Hilaire (Pierre Sebastien Rene Swanton)

Belloc, Joseph Pierre Hilaire
See Belloc, (Joseph) Hilaire (Pierre Sebastien Rene Swanton)

Belloc, M. A.
See Lowndes, Marie Adelaide (Belloc)

Bellow, Saul 1915-**CLC 1, 2, 3, 6, 8, 10, 13, 15, 25, 33, 34, 63, 79; DA; DAB; DAC; DAM MST,**

See also CA 1-4R; CANR 5, 20; DLB 88; MTCW 1

Biruni, al 973-1048(?) .... **CMLC 28**

Bishop, Elizabeth 1911-1979 **CLC 1, 4, 9, 13, 15, 32; DA; DAC; DAM MST, POET; PC 3**
See also CA 5-8R; 89-92; CABS 2; CANR 26, 61; CDALB 1968-1988; DLB 5, 169; MTCW 1, 2; SATA-Obit 24

Bishop, John 1935- .... **CLC 10**
See also CA 105

Bissett, Bill 1939- .... **CLC 18; PC 14**
See also CA 69-72; CAAS 19; CANR 15; DLB 53; MTCW 1

Bissoondath, Neil (Devindra) 1955- .. **CLC 120; DAC**
See also CA 136

Bitov, Andrei (Georgievich) 1937- .... **CLC 57**
See also CA 142

Biyidi, Alexandre 1932-
See Beti, Mongo
See also BW 1, 3; CA 114; 124; CANR 81; MTCW 1, 2

Bjarme, Brynjolf
See Ibsen, Henrik (Johan)

Bjoernson, Bjoernstjerne (Martinius) 1832-1910 **TCLC 7, 37**
See also CA 104

Black, Robert
See Holdstock, Robert P.

Blackburn, Paul 1926-1971 .... **CLC 9, 43**
See also CA 81-84; 33-36R; CANR 34; DLB 16; DLBY 81

Black Elk 1863-1950 ..... **TCLC 33; DAM MULT**
See also CA 144; MTCW 1; NNAL

Black Hobart
See Sanders, (James) Ed(ward)

Blacklin, Malcolm
See Chambers, Aidan

Blackmore, R(ichard) D(oddridge) 1825-1900 **TCLC 27**
See also CA 120; DLB 18

Blackmur, R(ichard) P(almer) 1904-1965 **CLC 2, 24**
See also CA 11-12; 25-28R; CANR 71; CAP 1; DLB 63

Black Tarantula
See Acker, Kathy

Blackwood, Algernon (Henry) 1869-1951 **TCLC 5**
See also CA 105; 150; DLB 153, 156, 178

Blackwood, Caroline 1931-1996 .. **CLC 6, 9, 100**
See also CA 85-88; 151; CANR 32, 61, 65; DLB 14, 207; MTCW 1

Blade, Alexander
See Hamilton, Edmond; Silverberg, Robert

Blaga, Lucian 1895-1961 .... **CLC 75**
See also CA 157

Blair, Eric (Arthur) 1903-1950
See Orwell, George
See also CA 104; 132; DA; DAB; DAC; DAM MST, NOV; MTCW 1, 2; SATA 29

Blair, Hugh 1718-1800 .... **NCLC 75**

Blais, Marie-Claire 1939- .. **CLC 2, 4, 6, 13, 22; DAC; DAM MST**
See also CA 21-24R; CAAS 4; CANR 38, 75; DLB 53; MTCW 1, 2

Blaise, Clark 1940- .... **CLC 29**
See also AITN 2; CA 53-56; CAAS 3; CANR 5, 66; DLB 53

Blake, Fairley
See De Voto, Bernard (Augustine)

Blake, Nicholas
See Day Lewis, C(ecil)
See also DLB 77

Blake, William 1757-1827 **NCLC 13, 37, 57; DA; DAB; DAC; DAM MST, POET; PC 12; WLC**
See also CDBLB 1789-1832; CLR 52; DLB 93, 163; MAICYA; SATA 30

Blasco Ibanez, Vicente 1867-1928 **TCLC 12; DAM NOV**
See also CA 110; 131; CANR 81; HW 1, 2; MTCW 1

Blatty, William Peter 1928- . **CLC 2; DAM POP**
See also CA 5-8R; CANR 9

Bleeck, Oliver
See Thomas, Ross (Elmore)

Blessing, Lee 1949- .... **CLC 54**

Blish, James (Benjamin) 1921-1975 ..... **CLC 14**
See also CA 1-4R; 57-60; CANR 3; DLB 8; MTCW 1; SATA 66

Bliss, Reginald
See Wells, H(erbert) G(eorge)

Blixen, Karen (Christentze Dinesen) 1885-1962
See Dinesen, Isak
See also CA 25-28; CANR 22, 50; CAP 2; MTCW 1, 2; SATA 44

Bloch, Robert (Albert) 1917-1994 .... **CLC 33**
See also AAYA 29; CA 5-8R; 146; CAAS 20; CANR 5, 78; DLB 44; INT CANR-5; MTCW 1; SATA 12; SATA-Obit 82

Blok, Alexander (Alexandrovich) 1880-1921 **TCLC 5; PC 21**
See also CA 104

Blom, Jan
See Breytenbach, Breyten

Bloom, Harold 1930- .... **CLC 24, 103**
See also CA 13-16R; CANR 39, 75; DLB 67; MTCW 1

Bloomfield, Aurelius
See Bourne, Randolph S(illiman)

Blount, Roy (Alton), Jr. 1941- .... **CLC 38**
See also CA 53-56; CANR 10, 28, 61; INT CANR-28; MTCW 1, 2

Bloy, Leon 1846-1917 .... **TCLC 22**
See also CA 121; DLB 123

Blume, Judy (Sussman) 1938- **CLC 12, 30; DAM NOV, POP**
See also AAYA 3, 26; CA 29-32R; CANR 13, 37, 66; CLR 2, 15; DLB 52; JRDA; MAICYA; MTCW 1, 2; SATA 2, 31, 79

Blunden, Edmund (Charles) 1896-1974 **CLC 2, 56**
See also CA 17-18; 45-48; CANR 54; CAP 2; DLB 20, 100, 155; MTCW 1

Bly, Robert (Elwood) 1926- **CLC 1, 2, 5, 10, 15, 38; DAM POET**
See also CA 5-8R; CANR 41, 73; DLB 5; MTCW 1, 2

Boas, Franz 1858-1942 .... **TCLC 56**
See also CA 115

Bobette
See Simenon, Georges (Jacques Christian)

Boccaccio, Giovanni 1313-1375 **CMLC 13; SSC 10**

Bochco, Steven 1943- .... **CLC 35**
See also AAYA 11; CA 124; 138

Bodel, Jean 1167(?)-1210 .... **CMLC 28**

Bodenheim, Maxwell 1892-1954 .... **TCLC 44**
See also CA 110; DLB 9, 45

Bodker, Cecil 1927- .... **CLC 21**
See also CA 73-76; CANR 13, 44; CLR 23; MAICYA; SATA 14

Boell, Heinrich (Theodor) 1917-1985 **CLC 2, 3, 6, 9, 11, 15, 27, 32, 72; DA; DAB; DAC; DAM MST, NOV; SSC 23; WLC**
See also CA 21-24R; 116; CANR 24; DLB 69; DLBY 85; MTCW 1, 2

Boerne, Alfred
See Doeblin, Alfred

Boethius 480(?)-524(?) .... **CMLC 15**
See also DLB 115

Bogan, Louise 1897-1970 **CLC 4, 39, 46, 93; DAM POET; PC 12**
See also CA 73-76; 25-28R; CANR 33; DLB 45, 169; MTCW 1, 2

Bogarde, Dirk .... **CLC 19**
See also Van Den Bogarde, Derek Jules Gaspard

Ulric Niven
See also DLB 14

Bogosian, Eric 1953- .... **CLC 45**
See also CA 138

Bograd, Larry 1953- .... **CLC 35**
See also CA 93-96; CANR 57; SAAS 21; SATA 33, 89

Boiardo, Matteo Maria 1441-1494 .... **LC 6**

Boileau-Despreaux, Nicolas 1636-1711 ..... **LC 3**

Bojer, Johan 1872-1959 .... **TCLC 64**

Boland, Eavan (Aisling) 1944- **CLC 40, 67, 113; DAM POET**
See also CA 143; CANR 61; DLB 40; MTCW 2

Boll, Heinrich
See Boell, Heinrich (Theodor)

Bolt, Lee
See Faust, Frederick (Schiller)

Bolt, Robert (Oxton) 1924-1995 .. **CLC 14; DAM DRAM**
See also CA 17-20R; 147; CANR 35, 67; DLB 13; MTCW 1

Bombet, Louis-Alexandre-Cesar
See Stendhal

Bomkauf
See Kaufman, Bob (Garnell)

Bonaventura .... **NCLC 35**
See also DLB 90

Bond, Edward 1934- **CLC 4, 6, 13, 23; DAM DRAM**
See also CA 25-28R; CANR 38, 67; DLB 13; MTCW 1

Bonham, Frank 1914-1989 .... **CLC 12**
See also AAYA 1; CA 9-12R; CANR 4, 36; JRDA; MAICYA; SAAS 3; SATA 1, 49; SATA-Obit 62

Bonnefoy, Yves 1923- **CLC 9, 15, 58; DAM MST, POET**
See also CA 85-88; CANR 33, 75; MTCW 1, 2

Bontemps, Arna(ud Wendell) 1902-1973 **CLC 1, 18; BLC 1; DAM MULT, NOV, POET**
See also BW 1; CA 1-4R; 41-44R; CANR 4, 35; CLR 6; DLB 48, 51; JRDA; MAICYA; MTCW 1, 2; SATA 2, 44; SATA-Obit 24

Booth, Martin 1944- .... **CLC 13**
See also CA 93-96; CAAS 2

Booth, Philip 1925- .... **CLC 23**
See also CA 5-8R; CANR 5; DLBY 82

Booth, Wayne C(layson) 1921- .... **CLC 24**
See also CA 1-4R; CAAS 5; CANR 3, 43; DLB 67

Borchert, Wolfgang 1921-1947 .... **TCLC 5**
See also CA 104; DLB 69, 124

Borel, Petrus 1809-1859 .... **NCLC 41**

Borges, Jorge Luis 1899-1986 **CLC 1, 2, 3, 4, 6, 8, 9, 10, 13, 19, 44, 48, 83; DA; DAB; DAC; DAM MST, MULT; HLC; PC 22; SSC 4; WLC**
See also AAYA 26; CA 21-24R; CANR 19, 33, 75; DLB 113; DLBY 86; HW 1, 2; MTCW 1, 2

Borowski, Tadeusz 1922-1951 .... **TCLC 9**
See also CA 106; 154

Borrow, George (Henry) 1803-1881 ...... **NCLC 9**
See also DLB 21, 55, 166

Bosman, Herman Charles 1905-1951 . **TCLC 49**
See also Malan, Herman
See also CA 160

Bosschere, Jean de 1878(?)-1953 .... **TCLC 19**
See also CA 115

Boswell, James 1740-1795 **LC 4, 50; DA; DAB; DAC; DAM MST; WLC**
See also CDBLB 1660-1789; DLB 104, 142

Bottoms, David 1949- .... **CLC 53**
See also CA 105; CANR 22; DLB 120; DLBY 83

Boucicault, Dion 1820-1890 .... **NCLC 41**

Boucolon, Maryse 1937(?)-
See Conde, Maryse
See also BW 3; CA 110; CANR 30, 53, 76

Bourget, Paul (Charles Joseph) 1852-1935 **TCLC 12**
See also CA 107; DLB 123

1945; DLB 19; MTCW 1, 2

Brooke-Haven, P.
See Wodehouse, P(elham) G(renville)

Brooke-Rose, Christine 1926(?)- .... **CLC 40**
See also CA 13-16R; CANR 58; DLB 14

Brookner, Anita 1928- ... **CLC 32, 34, 51; DAB; DAM POP**
See also CA 114; 120; CANR 37, 56; DLB 194; DLBY 87; MTCW 1, 2

Brooks, Cleanth 1906-1994 ..... **CLC 24, 86, 110**
See also CA 17-20R; 145; CANR 33, 35; DLB 63; DLBY 94; INT CANR-35; MTCW 1, 2

Brooks, George
See Baum, L(yman) Frank

Brooks, Gwendolyn 1917-**CLC 1, 2, 4, 5, 15, 49; BLC 1; DA; DAC; DAM MST, MULT, POET; PC 7; WLC**
See also AAYA 20; AITN 1; BW 2, 3; CA 1-4R; CANR 1, 27, 52, 75; CDALB 1941-1968; CLR 27; DLB 5, 76, 165; MTCW 1, 2; SATA 6

Brooks, Mel .... **CLC 12**
See also Kaminsky, Melvin
See also AAYA 13; DLB 26

Brooks, Peter 1938- .... **CLC 34**
See also CA 45-48; CANR 1

Brooks, Van Wyck 1886-1963 .... **CLC 29**
See also CA 1-4R; CANR 6; DLB 45, 63, 103

Brophy, Brigid (Antonia) 1929-1995 . **CLC 6, 11, 29, 105**
See also CA 5-8R; 149; CAAS 4; CANR 25, 53; DLB 14; MTCW 1, 2

Brosman, Catharine Savage 1934- .... **CLC 9**
See also CA 61-64; CANR 21, 46

Brossard, Nicole 1943- ....**CLC 115**
See also CA 122; CAAS 16; DLB 53

Brother Antoninus
See Everson, William (Oliver)

The Brothers Quay
See Quay, Stephen; Quay, Timothy

Broughton, T(homas) Alan 1936- .... **CLC 19**
See also CA 45-48; CANR 2, 23, 48

Broumas, Olga 1949- .... **CLC 10, 73**
See also CA 85-88; CANR 20, 69

Brown, Alan 1950- .... **CLC 99**
See also CA 156

Brown, Charles Brockden 1771-1810 NCLC **22, 74**
See also CDALB 1640-1865; DLB 37, 59, 73

Brown, Christy 1932-1981 .... **CLC 63**
See also CA 105; 104; CANR 72; DLB 14

Brown, Claude 1937- ..... **CLC 30; BLC 1; DAM MULT**
See also AAYA 7; BW 1, 3; CA 73-76; CANR 81

Brown, Dee (Alexander) 1908-**CLC 18, 47; DAM POP**
See also AAYA 30; CA 13-16R; CAAS 6; CANR 11, 45, 60; DLBY 80; MTCW 1, 2; SATA 5

Brown, George
See Wertmueller, Lina

Brown, George Douglas 1869-1902 .... **TCLC 28**
See also CA 162

Brown, George Mackay 1921-1996**CLC 5, 48, 100**
See also CA 21-24R; 151; CAAS 6; CANR 12, 37, 67; DLB 14, 27, 139; SATA 35

Brown, (William) Larry 1951- .... **CLC 73**
See also CA 130; 134; INT 133

Brown, Moses
See Barrett, William (Christopher)

Brown, Rita Mae 1944- ... **CLC 18, 43, 79; DAM NOV, POP**
See also CA 45-48; CANR 2, 11, 35, 62; INT CANR-11; MTCW 1, 2

Brown, Roderick (Langmere) Haig-
See Haig-Brown, Roderick (Langmere)

Brown, Rosellen 1939- .... **CLC 32**
See also CA 77-80; CAAS 10; CANR 14, 44

Brown, Sterling Allen 1901-1989**CLC 1, 23, 59;**

BLC 1; DAM MULT, POET
See also BW 1, 3; CA 85-88; 127; CANR 26; DLB 48, 51, 63; MTCW 1, 2

Brown, Will
See Ainsworth, William Harrison

Brown, William Wells 1813-1884 **NCLC 2; BLC 1; DAM MULT; DC 1**
See also DLB 3, 50

Browne, (Clyde) Jackson 1948(?)- .... **CLC 21**
See also CA 120

Browning, Elizabeth Barrett 1806-1861**NCLC 1, 16, 61, 66; DA; DAB; DAC; DAM MST, POET; PC 6; WLC**
See also CDBLB 1832-1890; DLB 32, 199

Browning, Robert 1812-1889 **NCLC 19, 79; DA; DAB; DAC; DAM MST, POET; PC 2; WLCS**
See also CDBLB 1832-1890; DLB 32, 163; YABC 1

Browning, Tod 1882-1962 .... **CLC 16**
See also CA 141; 117

Brownson, Orestes Augustus 1803-1876 **NCLC 50**
See also DLB 1, 59, 73

Bruccoli, Matthew J(oseph) 1931- .... **CLC 34**
See also CA 9-12R; CANR 7; DLB 103

Bruce, Lenny .... **CLC 21**
See also Schneider, Leonard Alfred

Bruin, John
See Brutus, Dennis

Brulard, Henri
See Stendhal

Brulls, Christian
See Simenon, Georges (Jacques Christian)

Brunner, John (Kilian Houston) 1934-1995 **C L C 8, 10; DAM POP**
See also CA 1-4R; 149; CAAS 8; CANR 2, 37; MTCW 1, 2

Bruno, Giordano 1548-1600 .... **LC 27**

Brutus, Dennis 1924-.... **CLC 43; BLC 1; DAM MULT, POET; PC 24**
See also BW 2, 3; CA 49-52; CAAS 14; CANR 2, 27, 42, 81; DLB 117

Bryan, C(ourtlandt) D(ixon) B(arnes) 1936-**CLC 29**
See also CA 73-76; CANR 13, 68; DLB 185; INT CANR-13

Bryan, Michael
See Moore, Brian

Bryant, William Cullen 1794-1878 **NCLC 6, 46; DA; DAB; DAC; DAM MST, POET; PC 20**
See also CDALB 1640-1865; DLB 3, 43, 59, 189

Bryusov, Valery Yakovlevich 1873-1924**TCLC 10**
See also CA 107; 155

Buchan, John 1875-1940 **TCLC 41; DAB; DAM POP**
See also CA 108; 145; DLB 34, 70, 156; MTCW 1; YABC 2

Buchanan, George 1506-1582 .... **LC 4**
See also DLB 152

Buchheim, Lothar-Guenther 1918- .... **CLC 6**
See also CA 85-88

Buchner, (Karl) Georg 1813-1837 ...... **NCLC 26**

Buchwald, Art(hur) 1925- .... **CLC 33**
See also AITN 1; CA 5-8R; CANR 21, 67; MTCW 1, 2; SATA 10

Buck, Pearl S(ydenstricker) 1892-1973 **CLC 7, 11, 18; DA; DAB; DAC; DAM MST, NOV**
See also AITN 1; CA 1-4R; 41-44R; CANR 1, 34; CDALBS; DLB 9, 102; MTCW 1, 2; SATA 1, 25

Buckler, Ernest 1908-1984**CLC 13; DAC; DAM MST**
See also CA 11-12; 114; CAP 1; DLB 68; SATA 47

Buckley, Vincent (Thomas) 1925-1988 . **CLC 57**
See also CA 101

Buckley, William F(rank), Jr. 1925- **CLC 7, 18,**

37; DAM POP
See also AITN 1; CA 1-4R; CANR 1, 24, 53; DLB 137; DLBY 80; INT CANR-24; MTCW 1, 2

Buechner, (Carl) Frederick 1926-**CLC 2, 4, 6, 9; DAM NOV**
See also CA 13-16R; CANR 11, 39, 64; DLBY 80; INT CANR-11; MTCW 1, 2

Buell, John (Edward) 1927- .... **CLC 10**
See also CA 1-4R; CANR 71; DLB 53

Buero Vallejo, Antonio 1916- .... **CLC 15, 46**
See also CA 106; CANR 24, 49, 75; HW 1; MTCW 1, 2

Bufalino, Gesualdo 1920(?)- .... **CLC 74**
See also DLB 196

Bugayev, Boris Nikolayevich 1880-1934**TCLC 7; PC 11**
See also Bely, Andrey
See also CA 104; 165; MTCW 1

Bukowski, Charles 1920-1994**CLC 2, 5, 9, 41, 82, 108; DAM NOV, POET; PC 18**
See also CA 17-20R; 144; CANR 40, 62; DLB 5, 130, 169; MTCW 1, 2

Bulgakov, Mikhail (Afanas'evich) 1891-1940 **TCLC 2, 16; DAM DRAM, NOV; SSC 18**
See also CA 105; 152

Bulgya, Alexander Alexandrovich 1901-1956 **TCLC 53**
See also Fadeyev, Alexander
See also CA 117

Bullins, Ed 1935- ..... **CLC 1, 5, 7; BLC 1; DAM DRAM, MULT; DC 6**
See also BW 2, 3; CA 49-52; CAAS 16; CANR 24, 46, 73; DLB 7, 38; MTCW 1, 2

Bulwer-Lytton, Edward (George Earle Lytton) 1803-1873 .... **NCLC 1, 45**
See also DLB 21

Bunin, Ivan Alexeyevich 1870-1953**TCLC 6; SSC 5**
See also CA 104

Bunting, Basil 1900-1985 **CLC 10, 39, 47; DAM POET**
See also CA 53-56; 115; CANR 7; DLB 20

Bunuel, Luis 1900-1983**CLC 16, 80; DAM MULT; HLC**
See also CA 101; 110; CANR 32, 77; HW 1

Bunyan, John 1628-1688 **LC 4; DA; DAB; DAC; DAM MST; WLC**
See also CDBLB 1660-1789; DLB 39

Burckhardt, Jacob (Christoph) 1818-1897**NCLC 49**

Burford, Eleanor
See Hibbert, Eleanor Alice Burford

Burgess, AnthonyCLC 1, 2, 4, 5, 8, 10, 13, 15, 22, 40, 62, 81, 94; DAB
See also Wilson, John (Anthony) Burgess
See also AAYA 25; AITN 1; CDBLB 1960 to Present; DLB 14, 194; DLBY 98; MTCW 1

Burke, Edmund 1729(?)-1797**LC 7, 36; DA; DAB; DAC; DAM MST; WLC**
See also DLB 104

Burke, Kenneth (Duva) 1897-1993 .... **CLC 2, 24**
See also CA 5-8R; 143; CANR 39, 74; DLB 45, 63; MTCW 1, 2

Burke, Leda
See Garnett, David

Burke, Ralph
See Silverberg, Robert

Burke, Thomas 1886-1945 .... **TCLC 63**
See also CA 113; 155; DLB 197

Burney, Fanny 1752-1840 .... **NCLC 12, 54**
See also DLB 39

Burns, Robert 1759-1796**LC 3, 29, 40; DA; DAB; DAC; DAM MST, POET; PC 6; WLC**
See also CDBLB 1789-1832; DLB 109

Burns, Tex
See L'Amour, Louis (Dearborn)

Burnshaw, Stanley 1906- .... **CLC 3, 13, 44**

Clash, The
    See Headon, (Nicky) Topper; Jones, Mick;
    Simonon, Paul; Strummer, Joe
Claudel, Paul (Louis Charles Marie) 1868-1955
    TCLC 2, 10
    See also CA 104; 165; DLB 192
Claudius, Matthias 1740-1815 .... **NCLC 75**
    See also DLB 97
Clavell, James (duMaresq) 1925-1994 **CLC 6, 25,**
    87; DAM NOV, POP
    See also CA 25-28R; 146; CANR 26, 48; MTCW
    1, 2
Cleaver, (Leroy) Eldridge 1935-1998 **CLC 30, 119;**
    BLC 1; DAM MULT
    See also BW 1, 3; CA 21-24R; 167; CANR 16, 75;
    MTCW 2
Cleese, John (Marwood) 1939- .... **CLC 21**
    See also Monty Python
    See also CA 112; 116; CANR 35; MTCW 1
Cleishbotham, Jebediah
    See Scott, Walter
Cleland, John 1710-1789 .... **LC 2, 48**
    See also DLB 39
Clemens, Samuel Langhorne 1835-1910
    See Twain, Mark
    See also CA 104; 135; CDALB 1865-1917; DA;
    DAB; DAC; DAM MST, NOV; DLB 11, 12, 23,
    64, 74, 186, 189; JRDA; MAICYA; SATA 100;
    YABC 2
Cleophil
    See Congreve, William
Clerihew, E.
    See Bentley, E(dmund) C(lerihew)
Clerk, N. W.
    See Lewis, C(live) S(taples)
Cliff, Jimmy .... **CLC 21**
    See also Chambers, James
Cliff, Michelle 1946- .... **CLC 120; BLCS**
    See also BW 2; CA 116; CANR 39, 72; DLB 157
Clifton, (Thelma) Lucille 1936- **CLC 19, 66; BLC**
    1; DAM MULT, POET; PC 17
    See also BW 2, 3; CA 49-52; CANR 2, 24, 42, 76;
    CLR 5; DLB 5, 41; MAICYA; MTCW 1, 2;
    SATA 20, 69
Clinton, Dirk
    See Silverberg, Robert
Clough, Arthur Hugh 1819-1861 .... **NCLC 27**
    See also DLB 32
Clutha, Janet Paterson Frame 1924-
    See Frame, Janet
    See also CA 1-4R; CANR 2, 36, 76; MTCW 1, 2
Clyne, Terence
    See Blatty, William Peter
Cobalt, Martin
    See Mayne, William (James Carter)
Cobb, Irvin S(hrewsbury) 1876-1944 ... **TCLC 77**
    See also CA 175; DLB 11, 25, 86
Cobbett, William 1763-1835 .... **NCLC 49**
    See also DLB 43, 107, 158
Coburn, D(onald) L(ee) 1938- .... **CLC 10**
    See also CA 89-92
Cocteau, Jean (Maurice Eugene Clement) 1889-
    1963 **CLC 1, 8, 15, 16, 43; DA; DAB; DAC;**
    DAM DRAM, MST, NOV; WLC
    See also CA 25-28; CANR 40; CAP 2; DLB 65;
    MTCW 1, 2
Codrescu, Andrei 1946- ..... **CLC 46, 121; DAM**
    POET
    See also CA 33-36R; CAAS 19; CANR 13, 34, 53,
    76; MTCW 2
Coe, Max
    See Bourne, Randolph S(illiman)
Coe, Tucker
    See Westlake, Donald E(dwin)
Coen, Ethan 1958- .... **CLC 108**
    See also CA 126
Coen, Joel 1955- .... **CLC 108**

See also CA 126
The Coen Brothers
    See Coen, Ethan; Coen, Joel
Coetzee, J(ohn) M(ichael) 1940- **CLC 23, 33, 66,**
    117; DAM NOV
    See also CA 77-80; CANR 41, 54, 74; MTCW 1, 2
Coffey, Brian
    See Koontz, Dean R(ay)
Coffin, Robert P(eter) Tristram 1892-1955 **TCLC**
    95
    See also CA 123; 169; DLB 45
Cohan, George M(ichael) 1878-1942 ... **TCLC 60**
    See also CA 157
Cohen, Arthur A(llen) 1928-1986 ..... **CLC 7, 31**
    See also CA 1-4R; 120; CANR 1, 17, 42; DLB 28
Cohen, Leonard (Norman) 1934- **CLC 3, 38; DAC;**
    DAM MST
    See also CA 21-24R; CANR 14, 69; DLB 53;
    MTCW 1
Cohen, Matt 1942- .... **CLC 19; DAC**
    See also CA 61-64; CAAS 18; CANR 40; DLB 53
Cohen-Solal, Annie 19(?)- .... **CLC 50**
Colegate, Isabel 1931- .... **CLC 36**
    See also CA 17-20R; CANR 8, 22, 74; DLB 14;
    INT CANR-22; MTCW 1
Coleman, Emmett
    See Reed, Ishmael
Coleridge, M. E.
    See Coleridge, Mary E(lizabeth)
Coleridge, Mary E(lizabeth) 1861-1907 **TCLC 73**
    See also CA 116; 166; DLB 19, 98
Coleridge, Samuel Taylor 1772-1834 **NCLC 9, 54;**
    DA; DAB; DAC; DAM MST, POET; PC 11;
    WLC
    See also CDBLB 1789-1832; DLB 93, 107
Coleridge, Sara 1802-1852 .... **NCLC 31**
    See also DLB 199
Coles, Don 1928- .... **CLC 46**
    See also CA 115; CANR 38
Coles, Robert (Martin) 1929- .... **CLC 108**
    See also CA 45-48; CANR 3, 32, 66, 70; INT
    CANR-32; SATA 23
Colette, (Sidonie-Gabrielle) 1873-1954 **TCLC 1, 5,**
    16; DAM NOV; SSC 10
    See also CA 104; 131; DLB 65; MTCW 1, 2
Collett, (Jacobine) Camilla (Wergeland) 1813-1895
    NCLC 22
Collier, Christopher 1930- .... **CLC 30**
    See also AAYA 13; CA 33-36R; CANR 13, 33;
    JRDA; MAICYA; SATA 16, 70
Collier, James L(incoln) 1928- ... **CLC 30; DAM**
    POP
    See also AAYA 13; CA 9-12R; CANR 4, 33, 60;
    CLR 3; JRDA; MAICYA; SAAS 21; SATA 8,
    70
Collier, Jeremy 1650-1726 .... **LC 6**
Collier, John 1901-1980 .... **SSC 19**
    See also CA 65-68; 97-100; CANR 10; DLB 77
Collingwood, R(obin) G(eorge) 1889(?)-1943
    TCLC 67
    See also CA 117; 155
Collins, Hunt
    See Hunter, Evan
Collins, Linda 1931- .... **CLC 44**
    See also CA 125
Collins, (William) Wilkie 1824-1889 **NCLC 1, 18**
    See also CDBLB 1832-1890; DLB 18, 70, 159
Collins, William 1721-1759 **LC 4, 40; DAM POET**
    . See also DLB 109
Collodi, Carlo 1826-1890 .... **NCLC 54**
    See also Lorenzini, Carlo
    See also CLR 5
Colman, George 1732-1794
    See Glassco, John
Colt, Winchester Remington
    See Hubbard, L(afayette) Ron(ald)
Colter, Cyrus 1910- .... **CLC 58**

See also BW 1; CA 65-68; CANR 10, 66; DLB
    33
Colton, James
    See Hansen, Joseph
Colum, Padraic 1881-1972 .... **CLC 28**
    See also CA 73-76; 33-36R; CANR 35; CLR 36;
    MAICYA; MTCW 1; SATA 15
Colvin, James
    See Moorcock, Michael (John)
Colwin, Laurie (E.) 1944-1992 **CLC 5, 13, 23, 84**
    See also CA 89-92; 139; CANR 20, 46; DLBY 80;
    MTCW 1
Comfort, Alex(ander) 1920- . **CLC 7; DAM POP**
    See also CA 1-4R; CANR 1, 45; MTCW 1
Comfort, Montgomery
    See Campbell, (John) Ramsey
Compton-Burnett, I(vy) 1884(?)-1969 .. **CLC 1, 3,**
    10, 15, 34; DAM NOV
    See also CA 1-4R; 25-28R; CANR 4; DLB 36;
    MTCW 1
Comstock, Anthony 1844-1915 .... **TCLC 13**
    See also CA 110; 169
Comte, Auguste 1798-1857 .... **NCLC 54**
Conan Doyle, Arthur
    See Doyle, Arthur Conan
Conde, Maryse 1937- **CLC 52, 92; BLCS; DAM**
    MULT
    See also Boucolon, Maryse
    See also BW 2; MTCW 1
Condillac, Etienne Bonnot de 1714-1780 . **LC 26**
Condon, Richard (Thomas) 1915-1996 **CLC 4, 6, 8,**
    10, 45, 100; DAM NOV
    See also BEST 90:3; CA 1-4R; 151; CAAS 1;
    CANR 2, 23; INT CANR-23; MTCW 1, 2
Confucius 551B.C.-479B.C. **CMLC 19; DA; DAB;**
    DAC; DAM MST; WLCS
Congreve, William 1670-1729 **LC 5, 21; DA; DAB;**
    DAC; DAM DRAM, MST, POET; DC 2; WLC
    See also CDBLB 1660-1789; DLB 39, 84
Connell, Evan S(helby), Jr. 1924- **CLC 4, 6, 45;**
    DAM NOV
    See also AAYA 7; CA 1-4R; CAAS 2; CANR 2,
    39, 76; DLB 2; DLBY 81; MTCW 1, 2
Connelly, Marc(us Cook) 1890-1980 .... **CLC 7**
    See also CA 85-88; 102; CANR 30; DLB 7; DLBY
    80; SATA-Obit 25
Connor, Ralph .... **TCLC 31**
    See also Gordon, Charles William
    See also DLB 92
Conrad, Joseph 1857-1924 **TCLC 1, 6, 13, 25, 43,**
    57; DA; DAB; DAC; DAM MST, NOV; SSC
    9; WLC
    See also AAYA 26; CA 104; 131; CANR 60;
    CDBLB 1890-1914; DLB 10, 34, 98, 156; MTCW
    1, 2; SATA 27
Conrad, Robert Arnold
    See Hart, Moss
Conroy, Pat
    See Conroy, (Donald) Pat(rick)
    See also MTCW 2
Conroy, (Donald) Pat(rick) 1945- .. **CLC 30, 74;**
    DAM NOV, POP
    See also Conroy, Pat
    See also AAYA 8; AITN 1; CA 85-88; CANR 24,
    53; DLB 6; MTCW 1
Constant (de Rebecque), (Henri) Benjamin 1767-
    1830 .... **NCLC 6**
    See also DLB 119
Conybeare, Charles Augustus
    See Eliot, T(homas) S(tearns)
Cook, Michael 1933- .... **CLC 58**
    See also CA 93-96; CANR 68; DLB 53
Cook, Robin 1940- .... **CLC 14; DAM POP**
    See also BEST 90:2; CA 108; 111; CANR 41; INT
    111
Cook, Roy
    See Silverberg, Robert

Crowley, Edward Alexander 1875-1947
  See Crowley, Aleister
  See also CA 104
Crowley, John 1942- .... **CLC 57**
  See also CA 61-64; CANR 43; DLBY 82; SATA
  65
Crud
  See Crumb, R(obert)
Crumarums
  See Crumb, R(obert)
Crumb, R(obert) 1943- .... **CLC 17**
  See also CA 106
Crumbum
  See Crumb, R(obert)
Crumski
  See Crumb, R(obert)
Crum the Bum
  See Crumb, R(obert)
Crunk
  See Crumb, R(obert)
Crustt
  See Crumb, R(obert)
Cryer, Gretchen (Kiger) 1935- .... **CLC 21**
  See also CA 114; 123
Csath, Geza 1887-1919 .... **TCLC 13**
  See also CA 111
Cudlip, David R(ockwell) 1933- .... **CLC 34**
  See also CA 177
Cullen, Countee 1903-1946 **TCLC 4, 37; BLC 1;**
  DA; DAC; DAM MST, MULT, POET; PC 20;
  WLCS
  See also BW 1; CA 108; 124; CDALB 1917-1929;
  DLB 4, 48, 51; MTCW 1, 2; SATA 18
Cum, R.
  See Crumb, R(obert)
Cummings, Bruce F(rederick) 1889-1919
  See Barbellion, W. N. P.
  See also CA 123
Cummings, E(dward) E(stlin) 1894-1962**CLC 1, 3,**
  8, 12, 15, 68; DA; DAB; DAC; DAM MST,
  POET; PC 5; WLC
  See also CA 73-76; CANR 31; CDALB 1929-1941;
  DLB 4, 48; MTCW 1, 2
Cunha, Euclides (Rodrigues Pimenta) da 1866-1909
  TCLC 24
  See also CA 123
Cunningham, E. V.
  See Fast, Howard (Melvin)
Cunningham, J(ames) V(incent) 1911-1985 **C L C**
  3, 31
  See also CA 1-4R; 115; CANR 1, 72; DLB 5
Cunningham, Julia (Woolfolk) 1916- .. **CLC 12**
  See also CA 9-12R; CANR 4, 19, 36; JRDA;
  MAICYA; SAAS 2; SATA 1, 26
Cunningham, Michael 1952- .... **CLC 34**
  See also CA 136
Cunninghame Graham, R(obert) B(ontine) 1852-
  1936 .... **TCLC 19**
  See also Graham, R(obert) B(ontine)
  Cunninghame
  See also CA 119; DLB 98
Currie, Ellen 19(?)- .... **CLC 44**
Curtin, Philip
  See Lowndes, Marie Adelaide (Belloc)
Curtis, Price
  See Ellison, Harlan (Jay)
Cutrate, Joe
  See Spiegelman, Art
Cynewulf c. 770-c. 840 .... **CMLC 23**
Czaczkes, Shmuel Yosef
  See Agnon, S(hmuel) Y(osef Halevi)
Dabrowska, Maria (Szumska) 1889-1965**CLC 15**
  See also CA 106
Dabydeen, David 1955- .... **CLC 34**
  See also BW 1; CA 125; CANR 56
Dacey, Philip 1939- .... **CLC 51**
  See also CA 37-40R; CAAS 17; CANR 14, 32, 64;

DLB 105
Dagerman, Stig (Halvard) 1923-1954 **T C L C**
  17
  See also CA 117; 155
Dahl, Roald 1916-1990 ..**CLC 1, 6, 18, 79; DAB;**
  DAC; DAM MST, NOV, POP
  See also AAYA 15; CA 1-4R; 133; CANR 6, 32,
  37, 62; CLR 1, 7, 41; DLB 139; JRDA;
  MAICYA; MTCW 1, 2; SATA 1, 26, 73; SATA-
  Obit 65
Dahlberg, Edward 1900-1977 .... **CLC 1, 7, 14**
  See also CA 9-12R; 69-72; CANR 31, 62; DLB 48;
  MTCW 1
Daitch, Susan 1954- .... **CLC 103**
  See also CA 161
Dale, Colin .... **TCLC 18**
  See also Lawrence, T(homas) E(dward)
Dale, George E.
  See Asimov, Isaac
Daly, Elizabeth 1878-1967 .... **CLC 52**
  See also CA 23-24; 25-28R; CANR 60; CAP 2
Daly, Maureen 1921- .... **CLC 17**
  See also AAYA 5; CANR 37; JRDA; MAICYA;
  SAAS 1; SATA 2
Damas, Leon-Gontran 1912-1978 .... **CLC 84**
  See also BW 1; CA 125; 73-76
Dana, Richard Henry Sr. 1787-1879 ... **NCLC 53**
Daniel, Samuel 1562(?)-1619 .... **LC 24**
  See also DLB 62
Daniels, Brett
  See Adler, Renata
Dannay, Frederic 1905-1982 **CLC 11; DAM POP**
  See also Queen, Ellery
  See also CA 1-4R; 107; CANR 1, 39; DLB 137;
  MTCW 1
D'Annunzio, Gabriele 1863-1938 .... **TCLC 6, 40**
  See also CA 104; 155
Danois, N. le
  See Gourmont, Remy (-Marie-Charles) de
Dante 1265-1321 **CMLC 3, 18; DA; DAB; DAC;**
  DAM MST, POET; PC 21; WLCS
d'Antibes, Germain
  See Simenon, Georges (Jacques Christian)
Danticat, Edwidge 1969- .... **CLC 94**
  See also AAYA 29; CA 152; CANR 73; MTCW 1
Danvers, Dennis 1947- .... **CLC 70**
Danziger, Paula 1944- .... **CLC 21**
  See also AAYA 4; CA 112; 115; CANR 37; CLR
  20; JRDA; MAICYA; SATA 36, 63, 102;
  SATA-Brief 30
Da Ponte, Lorenzo 1749-1838 .... **NCLC 50**
Dario, Ruben 1867-1916 . **TCLC 4; DAM MULT;**
  HLC; PC 15
  See also CA 131; CANR 81; HW 1; MTCW 1,
  2
Darley, George 1795-1846 .... **NCLC 2**
  See also DLB 96
Darrow, Clarence (Seward) 1857-1938 **TCLC 81**
  See also CA 164
Darwin, Charles 1809-1882 .... **NCLC 57**
  See also DLB 57, 166
Daryush, Elizabeth 1887-1977 .... **CLC 6, 19**
  See also CA 49-52; CANR 3, 81; DLB 20
Dasgupta, Surendranath 1887-1952 ... **TCLC 81**
  See also CA 157
Dashwood, Edmee Elizabeth Monica de la Pasture
  1890-1943
  See Delafield, E. M.
  See also CA 119; 154
Daudet, (Louis Marie) Alphonse 1840-1897**NCLC**
  1
  See also DLB 123
Daumal, Rene 1908-1944 .... **TCLC 14**
  See also CA 114
Davenant, William 1606-1668 .... **LC 13**
  See also DLB 58, 126
Davenport, Guy (Mattison, Jr.) 1927- **CLC 6, 14,**

38; SSC 16
  See also CA 33-36R; CANR 23, 73; DLB 130
Davidson, Avram (James) 1923-1993
  See Queen, Ellery
  See also CA 101; 171; CANR 26; DLB 8
Davidson, Donald (Grady) 1893-1968 **CLC 2, 13,**
  19
  See also CA 5-8R; 25-28R; CANR 4; DLB 45
Davidson, Hugh
  See Hamilton, Edmond
Davidson, John 1857-1909 .... **TCLC 24**
  See also CA 118; DLB 19
Davidson, Sara 1943- .... **CLC 9**
  See also CA 81-84; CANR 44, 68; DLB 185
Davie, Donald (Alfred) 1922-1995**CLC 5, 8, 10, 31**
  See also CA 1-4R; 149; CAAS 3; CANR 1, 44;
  DLB 27; MTCW 1
Davies, Ray(mond Douglas) 1944- .... **CLC 21**
  See also CA 116; 146
Davies, Rhys 1901-1978 .... **CLC 23**
  See also CA 9-12R; 81-84; CANR 4; DLB 139,
  191
Davies, (William) Robertson 1913-1995**CLC 2, 7,**
  13, 25, 42, 75, 91; DA; DAB; DAC; DAM
  MST, NOV, POP; WLC
  See also BEST 89:2; CA 33-36R; 150; CANR 17,
  42; DLB 68; INT CANR-17; MTCW 1, 2
Davies, W(illiam) H(enry) 1871-1940 ... **TCLC 5**
  See also CA 104; DLB 19, 174
Davies, Walter C.
  See Kornbluth, C(yril) M.
Davis, Angela (Yvonne) 1944- ..... **CLC 77; DAM**
  MULT
  See also BW 2, 3; CA 57-60; CANR 10, 81
Davis, B. Lynch
  See Bioy Casares, Adolfo; Borges, Jorge Luis
Davis, B. Lynch
  See Bioy Casares, Adolfo
Davis, Harold Lenoir 1894-1960 .... **CLC 49**
  See also CA 89-92; DLB 9, 206
Davis, Rebecca (Blaine) Harding 1831-1910
  TCLC 6
  See also CA 104; DLB 74
Davis, Richard Harding 1864-1916 ..... **TCLC 24**
  See also CA 114; DLB 12, 23, 78, 79, 189; DLBD
  13
Davison, Frank Dalby 1893-1970 .... **CLC 15**
  See also CA 116
Davison, Lawrence H.
  See Lawrence, D(avid) H(erbert Richards)
Davison, Peter (Hubert) 1928- .... **CLC 28**
  See also CA 9-12R; CAAS 4; CANR 3, 43; DLB 5
Davys, Mary 1674-1732 .... **LC 1, 46**
  See also DLB 39
Dawson, Fielding 1930- .... **CLC 6**
  See also CA 85-88; DLB 130
Dawson, Peter
  See Faust, Frederick (Schiller)
Day, Clarence (Shepard, Jr.) 1874-1935**TCLC 25**
  See also CA 108; DLB 11
Day, Thomas 1748-1789 .... **LC 1**
  See also DLB 39; YABC 1
Day Lewis, C(ecil) 1904-1972**CLC 1, 6, 10; DAM**
  POET; PC 11
  See also Blake, Nicholas
  See also CA 13-16; 33-36R; CANR 34; CAP 1;
  DLB 15, 20; MTCW 1, 2
Dazai Osamu 1909-1948 .... **TCLC 11**
  See also Tsushima, Shuji
  See also CA 164; DLB 182
de Andrade, Carlos Drummond 1892-1945
  See Drummond de Andrade, Carlos
Deane, Norman
  See Creasey, John
de Beauvoir, Simone (Lucie Ernestine Marie
  Bertrand)
  See Beauvoir, Simone (Lucie Ernestine Marie

CDALB 1968-1988; DLB 2, 173, 185; DLBY 81, 86; MTCW 1, 2

Dietrich, Robert
See Hunt, E(verette) Howard, (Jr.)

Difusa, Pati
See Almodovar, Pedro

Dillard, Annie 1945-CLC **9, 60, 115; DAM NOV**
See also AAYA 6; CA 49-52; CANR 3, 43, 62; DLBY 80; MTCW 1, 2; SATA 10

Dillard, R(ichard) H(enry) W(ilde) 1937- CLC **5**
See also CA 21-24R; CAAS 7; CANR 10; DLB 5

Dillon, Eilis 1920-1994 .... **CLC 17**
See also CA 9-12R; 147; CAAS 3; CANR 4, 38, 78; CLR 26; MAICYA; SATA 2, 74; SATA-Essay 105; SATA-Obit 83

Dimont, Penelope
See Mortimer, Penelope (Ruth)

Dinesen, Isak .... CLC **10, 29, 95; SSC 7**
See also Blixen, Karen (Christentze Dinesen)
See also MTCW 1

Ding Ling .... **CLC 68**
See also Chiang, Pin-chin

Diphusa, Patty
See Almodovar, Pedro

Disch, Thomas M(ichael) 1940- .... CLC **7, 36**
See also AAYA 17; CA 21-24R; CAAS 4; CANR 17, 36, 54; CLR 18; DLB 8; MAICYA; MTCW 1, 2; SAAS 15; SATA 92

Disch, Tom
See Disch, Thomas M(ichael)

d'Isly, Georges
See Simenon, Georges (Jacques Christian)

Disraeli, Benjamin 1804-1881 . NCLC **2, 39, 79**
See also DLB 21, 55

Ditcum, Steve
See Crumb, R(obert)

Dixon, Paige
See Corcoran, Barbara

Dixon, Stephen 1936- .... CLC **52; SSC 16**
See also CA 89-92; CANR 17, 40, 54; DLB 130

Doak, Annie
See Dillard, Annie

Dobell, Sydney Thompson 1824-1874 .. NCLC **43**
See also DLB 32

Doblin, Alfred .... TCLC **13**
See also Doeblin, Alfred

Dobrolyubov, Nikolai Alexandrovich 1836-1861
NCLC **5**

Dobson, Austin 1840-1921 .... TCLC **79**
See also DLB 35; 144

Dobyns, Stephen 1941- .... CLC **37**
See also CA 45-48; CANR 2, 18

Doctorow, E(dgar) L(aurence) 1931-. CLC **6, 11, 15, 18, 37, 44, 65, 113; DAM NOV, POP**
See also AAYA 22; AITN 2; BEST 89:3; CA 45-48; CANR 2, 33, 51, 76; CDALB 1968-1988; DLB 2, 28, 173; DLBY 80; MTCW 1, 2

Dodgson, Charles Lutwidge 1832-1898
See Carroll, Lewis
See also CLR 2; DA; DAB; DAC; DAM MST, NOV, POET; MAICYA; SATA 100; YABC 2

Dodson, Owen (Vincent) 1914-1983CLC **79; BLC 1; DAM MULT**
See also BW 1; CA 65-68; 110; CANR 24; DLB 76

Doeblin, Alfred 1878-1957 .... TCLC **13**
See also Doblin, Alfred
See also CA 110; 141; DLB 66

Doerr, Harriet 1910- .... CLC **34**
See also CA 117; 122; CANR 47; INT 122

Domecq, H(onorio Bustos)
See Bioy Casares, Adolfo

Domecq, H(onorio) Bustos
See Bioy Casares, Adolfo; Borges, Jorge Luis

Domini, Rey
See Lorde, Audre (Geraldine)

Dominique

See Proust, (Valentin-Louis-George-Eugene-) Marcel

Don, A
See Stephen, Sir Leslie

Donaldson, Stephen R. 1947-CLC **46; DAM POP**
See also CA 89-92; CANR 13, 55; INT CANR-13

Donleavy, J(ames) P(atrick) 1926- . CLC **1, 4, 6, 10, 45**
See also AITN 2; CA 9-12R; CANR 24, 49, 62, 80; DLB 6, 173; INT CANR-24; MTCW 1, 2

Donne, John 1572-1631 .... LC **10, 24; DA; DAB; DAC; DAM MST, POET; PC 1; WLC**
See also CDBLB Before 1660; DLB 121, 151

Donnell, David 1939(?)- .... **CLC 34**

Donoghue, P. S.
See Hunt, E(verette) Howard, (Jr.)

Donoso (Yanez), Jose 1924-1996CLC **4, 8, 11, 32, 99; DAM MULT; HLC; SSC 34**
See also CA 81-84; 155; CANR 32, 73; DLB 113; HW 1, 2; MTCW 1, 2

Donovan, John 1928-1992 .... **CLC 35**
See also AAYA 20; CA 97-100; 137; CLR 3; MAICYA; SATA 72; SATA-Brief 29

Don Roberto
See Cunninghame Graham, R(obert) B(ontine)

Doolittle, Hilda 1886-1961CLC **3, 8, 14, 31, 34, 73; DA; DAC; DAM MST, POET; PC 5; WLC**
See also H. D.
See also CA 97-100; CANR 35; DLB 4, 45; MTCW 1, 2

Dorfman, Ariel 1942- CLC **48, 77; DAM MULT; HLC**
See also CA 124; 130; CANR 67, 70; HW 1, 2; INT 130

Dorn, Edward (Merton) 1929- .... CLC **10, 18**
See also CA 93-96; CANR 42, 79; DLB 5; INT 93-96

Dorris, Michael (Anthony) 1945-1997 CLC **109; DAM MULT, NOV**
See also AAYA 20; BEST 90:1; CA 102; 157; CANR 19, 46, 75; CLR 58; DLB 175; MTCW 2; NNAL; SATA 75; SATA-Obit 94

Dorris, Michael A.
See Dorris, Michael (Anthony)

Dorsan, Luc
See Simenon, Georges (Jacques Christian)

Dorsange, Jean
See Simenon, Georges (Jacques Christian)

Dos Passos, John (Roderigo) 1896-1970CLC **1, 4, 8, 11, 15, 25, 34, 82; DA; DAB; DAC; DAM MST, NOV; WLC**
See also CA 1-4R; 29-32R; CANR 3; CDALB 1929-1941; DLB 4, 9; DLBD 1, 15; DLBY 96; MTCW 1, 2

Dossage, Jean
See Simenon, Georges (Jacques Christian)

Dostoevsky, Fedor Mikhailovich 1821-1881NCLC **2, 7, 21, 33, 43; DA; DAB; DAC; DAM MST, NOV; SSC 2, 33; WLC**

Doughty, Charles M(ontagu) 1843-1926TCLC **27**
See also CA 115; DLB 19, 57, 174

Douglas, Ellen .... **CLC 73**
See also Haxton, Josephine Ayres; Williamson, Ellen Douglas

Douglas, Gavin 1475(?)-1522 .... **LC 20**
See also DLB 132

Douglas, George
See Brown, George Douglas

Douglas, Keith (Castellain) 1920-1944 TCLC **40**
See also CA 160; DLB 27

Douglas, Leonard
See Bradbury, Ray (Douglas)

Douglas, Michael
See Crichton, (John) Michael

Douglas, (George) Norman 1868-1952 TCLC **68**
See also CA 119; 157; DLB 34, 195

Douglas, William

See Brown, George Douglas

Douglass, Frederick 1817(?)-1895 .NCLC **7, 55; BLC 1; DA; DAC; DAM MST, MULT; WLC**
See also CDALB 1640-1865; DLB 1, 43, 50, 79; SATA 29

Dourado, (Waldomiro Freitas) Autran 1926-CLC **23, 60**
See also CA 25-28R; CANR 34, 81; DLB 145; HW 2

Dourado, Waldomiro Autran
See Dourado, (Waldomiro Freitas) Autran

Dove, Rita (Frances) 1952- . CLC **50, 81; BLCS; DAM MULT, POET; PC 6**
See also BW 2; CA 109; CAAS 19; CANR 27, 42, 68, 76; CDALBS; DLB 120; MTCW 1

Doveglion
See Villa, Jose Garcia

Dowell, Coleman 1925-1985 .... CLC **60**
See also CA 25-28R; 117; CANR 10; DLB 130

Dowson, Ernest (Christopher) 1867-1900TCLC **4**
See also CA 105; 150; DLB 19, 135

Doyle, A. Conan
See Doyle, Arthur Conan

Doyle, Arthur Conan 1859-1930 .. TCLC **7; DA; DAB; DAC; DAM MST, NOV; SSC 12; WLC**
See also AAYA 14; CA 104; 122; CDBLB 1890-1914; DLB 18, 70, 156, 178; MTCW 1, 2; SATA 24

Doyle, Conan
See Doyle, Arthur Conan

Doyle, John
See Graves, Robert (von Ranke)

Doyle, Roddy 1958(?)- .... CLC **81**
See also AAYA 14; CA 143; CANR 73; DLB 194

Doyle, Sir A. Conan
See Doyle, Arthur Conan

Doyle, Sir Arthur Conan
See Doyle, Arthur Conan

Dr. A
See Asimov, Isaac; Silverstein, Alvin

Drabble, Margaret 1939- CLC **2, 3, 5, 8, 10, 22, 53; DAB; DAC; DAM MST, NOV, POP**
See also CA 13-16R; CANR 18, 35, 63; CDBLB 1960 to Present; DLB 14, 155; MTCW 1, 2; SATA 48

Drapier, M. B.
See Swift, Jonathan

Drayham, James
See Mencken, H(enry) L(ouis)

Drayton, Michael 1563-1631 LC **8; DAM POET**
See also DLB 121

Dreadstone, Carl
See Campbell, (John) Ramsey

Dreiser, Theodore (Herman Albert) 1871-1945
TCLC **10, 18, 35, 83; DA; DAC; DAM MST, NOV; SSC 30; WLC**
See also CA 106; 132; CDALB 1865-1917; DLB 9, 12, 102, 137; DLBD 1; MTCW 1, 2

Drexler, Rosalyn 1926- .... CLC **2, 6**
See also CA 81-84; CANR 68

Dreyer, Carl Theodor 1889-1968 .... CLC **16**
See also CA 116

Drieu la Rochelle, Pierre(-Eugene) 1893-1945
TCLC **21**
See also CA 117; DLB 72

Drinkwater, John 1882-1937 .... TCLC **57**
See also CA 109; 149; DLB 10, 19, 149

Drop Shot
See Cable, George Washington

Droste-Hulshoff, Annette Freiin von 1797-1848
NCLC **3**
See also DLB 133

Drummond, Walter
See Silverberg, Robert

Drummond, William Henry 1854-1907 TCLC **25**
See also CA 160; DLB 92

Drummond de Andrade, Carlos 1902-1987
CLC 18
See also Andrade, Carlos Drummond de
See also CA 132; 123

Drury, Allen (Stuart) 1918-1998 .... **CLC 37**
See also CA 57-60; 170; CANR 18, 52; INT
CANR-18

Dryden, John 1631-1700 .... **LC 3, 21; DA; DAB;
DAC; DAM DRAM, MST, POET; DC 3; PC
25; WLC**
See also CDBLB 1660-1789; DLB 80, 101, 131

Duberman, Martin (Bauml) 1930- .... **CLC 8**
See also CA 1-4R; CANR 2, 63

Dubie, Norman (Evans) 1945- .... **CLC 36**
See also CA 69-72; CANR 12; DLB 120

Du Bois, W(illiam) E(dward) B(urghardt) 1868-
1963 **CLC 1, 2, 13, 64, 96; BLC 1; DA; DAC;
DAM MST, MULT, NOV; WLC**
See also BW 1, 3; CA 85-88; CANR 34; CDALB
1865-1917; DLB 47, 50, 91; MTCW 1, 2; SATA
42

Dubus, Andre 1936-1999 **CLC 13, 36, 97; SSC 15**
See also CA 21-24R; 177; CANR 17; DLB 130;
INT CANR-17

Duca Minimo
See D'Annunzio, Gabriele

Ducharme, Rejean 1941- .... **CLC 74**
See also CA 165; DLB 60

Duclos, Charles Pinot 1704-1772 .... **LC 1**

Dudek, Louis 1918- .... **CLC 11, 19**
See also CA 45-48; CAAS 14; CANR 1; DLB 88

Duerrenmatt, Friedrich 1921-1990 . **CLC 1, 4, 8,
11, 15, 43, 102; DAM DRAM**
See also CA 17-20R; CANR 33; DLB 69, 124;
MTCW 1, 2

Duffy, Bruce 1953(?)- .... **CLC 50**
See also CA 172

Duffy, Maureen 1933- .... **CLC 37**
See also CA 25-28R; CANR 33, 68; DLB 14;
MTCW 1

Dugan, Alan 1923- .... **CLC 2, 6**
See also CA 81-84; DLB 5

du Gard, Roger Martin
See Martin du Gard, Roger

Duhamel, Georges 1884-1966 .... **CLC 8**
See also CA 81-84; 25-28R; CANR 35; DLB 65;
MTCW 1

Dujardin, Edouard (Emile Louis) 1861-1949
TCLC 13
See also CA 109; DLB 123

Dulles, John Foster 1888-1959 .... **TCLC 72**
See also CA 115; 149

Dumas, Alexandre (pere)
See Dumas, Alexandre (Davy de la Pailleterie)

Dumas, Alexandre (Davy de la Pailleterie) 1802-
1870 **NCLC 11; DA; DAB; DAC; DAM MST,
NOV; WLC**
See also DLB 119, 192; SATA 18

Dumas, Alexandre (fils) 1824-1895 **NCLC 71; DC
1**
See also AAYA 22; DLB 192

Dumas, Claudine
See Malzberg, Barry N(athaniel)

Dumas, Henry L. 1934-1968 .... **CLC 6, 62**
See also BW 1; CA 85-88; DLB 41

du Maurier, Daphne 1907-1989 .. **CLC 6, 11, 59;
DAB; DAC; DAM MST, POP; SSC 18**
See also CA 5-8R; 128; CANR 6, 55; DLB 191;
MTCW 1, 2; SATA 27; SATA-Obit 60

Dunbar, Paul Laurence 1872-1906 . **TCLC 2, 12;
BLC 1; DA; DAC; DAM MST, MULT, POET;
PC 5; SSC 8; WLC**
See also BW 1, 3; CA 104; 124; CANR 79; CDALB
1865-1917; DLB 50, 54, 78; SATA 34

Dunbar, William 1460(?)-1530(?) .... **LC 20**
See also DLB 132, 146

Duncan, Dora Angela

See Duncan, Isadora

Duncan, Isadora 1877(?)-1927 .... **TCLC 68**
See also CA 118; 149

Duncan, Lois 1934- .... **CLC 26**
See also AAYA 4; CA 1-4R; CANR 2, 23, 36;
CLR 29; JRDA; MAICYA; SAAS 2; SATA 1,
36, 75

Duncan, Robert (Edward) 1919-1988 **CLC 1, 2, 4,
7, 15, 41, 55; DAM POET; PC 2**
See also CA 9-12R; 124; CANR 28, 62; DLB 5, 16,
193; MTCW 1, 2

Duncan, Sara Jeannette 1861-1922 .... **TCLC 60**
See also CA 157; DLB 92

Dunlap, William 1766-1839 .... **NCLC 2**
See also DLB 30, 37, 59

Dunn, Douglas (Eaglesham) 1942- ... **CLC 6, 40**
See also CA 45-48; CANR 2, 33; DLB 40; MTCW
1

Dunn, Katherine (Karen) 1945- .... **CLC 71**
See also CA 33-36R; CANR 72; MTCW 1

Dunn, Stephen 1939- .... **CLC 36**
See also CA 33-36R; CANR 12, 48, 53; DLB 105

Dunne, Finley Peter 1867-1936 .... **TCLC 28**
See also CA 108; DLB 11, 23

Dunne, John Gregory 1932- .... **CLC 28**
See also CA 25-28R; CANR 14, 50; DLB Y 80

Dunsany, Edward John Moreton Drax Plunkett
1878-1957
See Dunsany, Lord
See also CA 104; 148; DLB 10; MTCW 1

Dunsany, Lord .... **TCLC 2, 59**
See also Dunsany, Edward John Moreton Drax
Plunkett
See also DLB 77, 153, 156

du Perry, Jean
See Simenon, Georges (Jacques Christian)

Durang, Christopher (Ferdinand) 1949- **CLC 27,
38**
See also CA 105; CANR 50, 76; MTCW 1

Duras, Marguerite 1914-1996 **CLC 3, 6, 11, 20, 34,
40, 68, 100**
See also CA 25-28R; 151; CANR 50; DLB 83;
MTCW 1, 2

Durban, (Rosa) Pam 1947- .... **CLC 39**
See also CA 123

Durcan, Paul 1944- ... **CLC 43, 70; DAM POET**
See also CA 134

Durkheim, Emile 1858-1917 .... **TCLC 55**

Durrell, Lawrence (George) 1912-1990 **CLC 1, 4,
6, 8, 13, 27, 41; DAM NOV**
See also CA 9-12R; 132; CANR 40, 77; CDBLB
1945-1960; DLB 15, 27, 204; DLBY 90; MTCW
1, 2

Durrenmatt, Friedrich
See Duerrenmatt, Friedrich

Dutt, Toru 1856-1877 .... **NCLC 29**

Dwight, Timothy 1752-1817 .... **NCLC 13**
See also DLB 37

Dworkin, Andrea 1946- .... **CLC 43**
See also CA 77-80; CAAS 21; CANR 16, 39, 76;
INT CANR-16; MTCW 1, 2

Dwyer, Deanna
See Koontz, Dean R(ay)

Dwyer, K. R.
See Koontz, Dean R(ay)

Dwyer, Thomas A. 1923- ....**CLC 114**
See also CA 115

Dye, Richard
See De Voto, Bernard (Augustine)

Dylan, Bob 1941- .... **CLC 3, 4, 6, 12, 77**
See also CA 41-44R; DLB 16

E. V. L.
See Lucas, E(dward) V(errall)

Eagleton, Terence (Francis) 1943-
See Eagleton, Terry
See also CA 57-60; CANR 7, 23, 68; MTCW 1, 2

Eagleton, Terry .... **CLC 63**

See also Eagleton, Terence (Francis)
See also MTCW 1

Early, Jack
See Scoppettone, Sandra

East, Michael
See West, Morris L(anglo)

Eastaway, Edward
See Thomas, (Philip) Edward

Eastlake, William (Derry) 1917-1997 ..... **CLC 8**
See also CA 5-8R; 158; CAAS 1; CANR 5, 63;
DLB 6, 206; INT CANR-5

Eastman, Charles A(lexander) 1858-1939 **TCLC
55; DAM MULT**
See also DLB 175; NNAL; YABC 1

Eberhart, Richard (Ghormley) 1904- **CLC 3, 11,
19, 56; DAM POET**
See also CA 1-4R; CANR 2; CDALB 1941-1968;
DLB 48; MTCW 1

Eberstadt, Fernanda 1960- .... **CLC 39**
See also CA 136; CANR 69

Echegaray (y Eizaguirre), Jose (Maria Waldo)
1832-1916 .... **TCLC 4; HLCS 1**
See also CA 104; CANR 32; HW 1; MTCW 1

Echeverria, (Jose) Esteban (Antonino) 1805-1851
NCLC 18

Echo
See Proust, (Valentin-Louis-George-Eugene-)
Marcel

Eckert, Allan W. 1931- .... **CLC 17**
See also AAYA 18; CA 13-16R; CANR 14, 45;
INT CANR-14; SAAS 21; SATA 29, 91; SATA-
Brief 27

Eckhart, Meister 1260(?)-1328(?) .... **CMLC 9**
See also DLB 115

Eckmar, F. R.
See de Hartog, Jan

Eco, Umberto 1932- **CLC 28, 60; DAM NOV, POP**
See also BEST 90:1; CA 77-80; CANR 12, 33, 55;
DLB 196; MTCW 1, 2

Eddison, E(ric) R(ucker) 1882-1945 .... **TCLC 15**
See also CA 109; 156

Eddy, Mary (Ann Morse) Baker 1821-1910 **TCLC
71**
See also CA 113; 174

Edel, (Joseph) Leon 1907-1997 .... **CLC 29, 34**
See also CA 1-4R; 161; CANR 1, 22; DLB 103;
INT CANR-22

Eden, Emily 1797-1869 .... **NCLC 10**

Edgar, David 1948- .... **CLC 42; DAM DRAM**
See also CA 57-60; CANR 12, 61; DLB 13;
MTCW 1

Edgerton, Clyde (Carlyle) 1944- .... **CLC 39**
See also AAYA 17; CA 118; 134; CANR 64; INT
134

Edgeworth, Maria 1768-1849 .... **NCLC 1, 51**
See also DLB 116, 159, 163; SATA 21

Edmonds, Paul
See Kuttner, Henry

Edmonds, Walter D(umaux) 1903-1998 . **CLC 35**
See also CA 5-8R; CANR 2; DLB 9; MAICYA;
SAAS 4; SATA 1, 27; SATA-Obit 99

Edmondson, Wallace
See Ellison, Harlan (Jay)

Edson, Russell .... **CLC 13**
See also CA 33-36R

Edwards, Bronwen Elizabeth
See Rose, Wendy

Edwards, G(erald) B(asil) 1899-1976 ..... **CLC 25**
See also CA 110

Edwards, Gus 1939- .... **CLC 43**
See also CA 108; INT 108

Edwards, Jonathan 1703-1758 . **LC 7; DA; DAC;
DAM MST**
See also DLB 24

Efron, Marina Ivanovna Tsvetaeva
See Tsvetaeva (Efron), Marina (Ivanovna)

Ehle, John (Marsden, Jr.) 1925- .... **CLC 27**

See also DLB 95

Finch, Robert (Duer Claydon) 1900- .... **CLC 18**
See also CA 57-60; CANR 9, 24, 49; DLB 88

Findley, Timothy 1930-**CLC 27, 102; DAC; DAM MST**
See also CA 25-28R; CANR 12, 42, 69; DLB 53

Fink, William
See Mencken, H(enry) L(ouis)

Firbank, Louis 1942-
See Reed, Lou
See also CA 117

Firbank, (Arthur Annesley) Ronald 1886-1926 **TCLC 1**
See also CA 104; 177; DLB 36

Fisher, Dorothy (Frances) Canfield 1879-1958 **TCLC 87**
See also CA 114; 136; CANR 80; DLB 9, 102; MAICYA; YABC 1

Fisher, M(ary) F(rances) K(ennedy) 1908-1992 **CLC 76, 87**
See also CA 77-80; 138; CANR 44; MTCW 1

Fisher, Roy 1930- .... **CLC 25**
See also CA 81-84; CAAS 10; CANR 16; DLB 40

Fisher, Rudolph 1897-1934**TCLC 11; BLC 2; DAM MULT; SSC 25**
See also BW 1, 3; CA 107; 124; CANR 80; DLB 51, 102

Fisher, Vardis (Alvero) 1895-1968 .... **CLC 7**
See also CA 5-8R; 25-28R; CANR 68; DLB 9, 206

Fiske, Tarleton
See Bloch, Robert (Albert)

Fitch, Clarke
See Sinclair, Upton (Beall)

Fitch, John IV
See Cormier, Robert (Edmund)

Fitzgerald, Captain Hugh
See Baum, L(yman) Frank

FitzGerald, Edward 1809-1883 .... **NCLC 9**
See also DLB 32

Fitzgerald, F(rancis) Scott (Key) 1896-1940 **TCLC 1, 6, 14, 28, 55; DA; DAB; DAC; DAM MST, NOV; SSC 6, 31; WLC**
See also AAYA 24; AITN 1; CA 110; 123; CDALB 1917-1929; DLB 4, 9, 86; DLBD 1, 15, 16; DLBY 81, 96; MTCW 1, 2

Fitzgerald, Penelope 1916- .... **CLC 19, 51, 61**
See also CA 85-88; CAAS 10; CANR 56; DLB 14, 194; MTCW 2

Fitzgerald, Robert (Stuart) 1910-1985 .. **CLC 39**
See also CA 1-4R; 114; CANR 1; DLBY 80

FitzGerald, Robert D(avid) 1902-1987 ... **CLC 19**
See also CA 17-20R

Fitzgerald, Zelda (Sayre) 1900-1948 ... **TCLC 52**
See also CA 117; 126; DLBY 84

Flanagan, Thomas (James Bonner) 1923- .. **C L C 25, 52**
See also CA 108; CANR 55; DLBY 80; INT 108; MTCW 1

Flaubert, Gustave 1821-1880**NCLC 2, 10, 19, 62, 66; DA; DAB; DAC; DAM MST, NOV; SSC 11; WLC**
See also DLB 119

Flecker, Herman Elroy
See Flecker, (Herman) James Elroy

Flecker, (Herman) James Elroy 1884-1915**TCLC 43**
See also CA 109; 150; DLB 10, 19

Fleming, Ian (Lancaster) 1908-1964 **CLC 3, 30; DAM POP**
See also AAYA 26; CA 5-8R; CANR 59; CDBLB 1945-1960; DLB 87, 201; MTCW 1, 2; SATA 9

Fleming, Thomas (James) 1927- .... **CLC 37**
See also CA 5-8R; CANR 10; INT CANR-10; SATA 8

Fletcher, John 1579-1625 .... **LC 33; DC 6**
See also CDBLB Before 1660; DLB 58

Fletcher, John Gould 1886-1950 .... **TCLC 35**
See also CA 107; 167; DLB 4, 45

Fleur, Paul
See Pohl, Frederik

Flooglebuckle, Al
See Spiegelman, Art

Flying Officer X
See Bates, H(erbert) E(rnest)

Fo, Dario 1926-**CLC 32, 109; DAM DRAM; DC 10**
See also CA 116; 128; CANR 68; DLBY 97; MTCW 1, 2

Fogarty, Jonathan Titulescu Esq.
See Farrell, James T(homas)

Folke, Will
See Bloch, Robert (Albert)

Follett, Ken(neth Martin) 1949- .. **CLC 18; DAM NOV, POP**
See also AAYA 6; BEST 89:4; CA 81-84; CANR 13, 33, 54; DLB 87; DLBY 81; INT CANR-33; MTCW 1

Fontane, Theodor 1819-1898 .... **NCLC 26**
See also DLB 129

Foote, Horton 1916- .. **CLC 51, 91; DAM DRAM**
See also CA 73-76; CANR 34, 51; DLB 26; INT CANR-34

Foote, Shelby 1916- .. **CLC 75; DAM NOV, POP**
See also CA 5-8R; CANR 3, 45, 74; DLB 2, 17; MTCW 2

Forbes, Esther 1891-1967 .... **CLC 12**
See also AAYA 17; CA 13-14; 25-28R; CAP 1; CLR 27; DLB 22; JRDA; MAICYA; SATA 2, 100

Forche, Carolyn (Louise) 1950- **CLC 25, 83, 86; DAM POET; PC 10**
See also CA 109; 117; CANR 50, 74; DLB 5, 193; INT 117; MTCW 1

Ford, Elbur
See Hibbert, Eleanor Alice Burford

Ford, Ford Madox 1873-1939**TCLC 1, 15, 39, 57; DAM NOV**
See also CA 104; 132; CANR 74; CDBLB 1914-1945; DLB 162; MTCW 1, 2

Ford, Henry 1863-1947 .... **TCLC 73**
See also CA 115; 148

Ford, John 1586-(?) .... **DC 8**
See also CDBLB Before 1660; DAM DRAM; DLB 58

Ford, John 1895-1973 .... **CLC 16**
See also CA 45-48

Ford, Richard 1944- .... **CLC 46, 99**
See also CA 69-72; CANR 11, 47; MTCW 1

Ford, Webster
See Masters, Edgar Lee

Foreman, Richard 1937- .... **CLC 50**
See also CA 65-68; CANR 32, 63

Forester, C(ecil) S(cott) 1899-1966 .... **CLC 35**
See also CA 73-76; 25-28R; DLB 191; SATA 13

Forez
See Mauriac, Francois (Charles)

Forman, James Douglas 1932- .... **CLC 21**
See also AAYA 17; CA 9-12R; CANR 4, 19, 42; JRDA; MAICYA; SATA 8, 70

Fornes, Maria Irene 1930- **CLC 39, 61; DC 10; HLCS 1**
See also CA 25-28R; CANR 28, 81; DLB 7; HW 1, 2; INT CANR-28; MTCW 1

Forrest, Leon (Richard) 1937-1997**CLC 4; BLCS**
See also BW 2; CA 89-92; 162; CAAS 7; CANR 25, 52; DLB 33

Forster, E(dward) M(organ) 1879-1970 **CLC 1, 2, 3, 4, 9, 10, 13, 15, 22, 45, 77; DA; DAB; DAC; DAM MST, NOV; SSC 27; WLC**
See also AAYA 2; CA 13-14; 25-28R; CANR 45; CAP 1; CDBLB 1914-1945; DLB 34, 98, 162, 178, 195; DLBD 10; MTCW 1, 2; SATA 57

Forster, John 1812-1876 .... **NCLC 11**
See also DLB 144, 184

Forsyth, Frederick 1938-**CLC 2, 5, 36; DAM NOV, POP**
See also BEST 89:4; CA 85-88; CANR 38, 62; DLB 87; MTCW 1, 2

Forten, Charlotte L. .... **TCLC 16; BLC 2**
See also Grimke, Charlotte L(ottie) Forten
See also DLB 50

Foscolo, Ugo 1778-1827 .... **NCLC 8**

Fosse, Bob .... **CLC 20**
See also Fosse, Robert Louis

Fosse, Robert Louis 1927-1987
See Fosse, Bob
See also CA 110; 123

Foster, Stephen Collins 1826-1864 ..... **NCLC 26**

Foucault, Michel 1926-1984 ...... **CLC 31, 34, 69**
See also CA 105; 113; CANR 34; MTCW 1, 2

Fouque, Friedrich (Heinrich Karl) de la Motte 1777-1843 .... **NCLC 2**
See also DLB 90

Fourier, Charles 1772-1837 .... **NCLC 51**

Fournier, Henri Alban 1886-1914
See Alain-Fournier
See also CA 104

Fournier, Pierre 1916- .... **CLC 11**
See also Gascar, Pierre
See also CA 89-92; CANR 16, 40

Fowles, John (Philip) 1926-**CLC 1, 2, 3, 4, 6, 9, 10, 15, 33, 87; DAB; DAC; DAM MST; SSC 33**
See also CA 5-8R; CANR 25, 71; CDBLB 1960 to Present; DLB 14, 139, 207; MTCW 1, 2; SATA 22

Fox, Paula 1923- .... **CLC 2, 8, 121**
See also AAYA 3; CA 73-76; CANR 20, 36, 62; CLR 1, 44; DLB 52; JRDA; MAICYA; MTCW 1; SATA 17, 60

Fox, William Price (Jr.) 1926- .... **CLC 22**
See also CA 17-20R; CAAS 19; CANR 11; DLB 2; DLBY 81

Foxe, John 1516(?)-1587 .... **LC 14**
See also DLB 132

Frame, Janet 1924-**CLC 2, 3, 6, 22, 66, 96; SSC 29**
See also Clutha, Janet Paterson Frame

France, Anatole .... **TCLC 9**
See also Thibault, Jacques Anatole Francois
See also DLB 123; MTCW 1

Francis, Claude 19(?)- ....:.. **CLC 50**

Francis, Dick 1920- . **CLC 2, 22, 42, 102; DAM POP**
See also AAYA 5, 21; BEST 89:3; CA 5-8R; CANR 9, 42, 68; CDBLB 1960 to Present; DLB 87; INT CANR-9; MTCW 1, 2

Francis, Robert (Churchill) 1901-1987 **CLC 15**
See also CA 1-4R; 123; CANR 1

Frank, Anne(lies Marie) 1929-1945**TCLC 17; DA; DAB; DAC; DAM MST; WLC**
See also AAYA 12; CA 113; 133; CANR 68; MTCW 1, 2; SATA 87; SATA-Brief 42

Frank, Bruno 1887-1945 .... **TCLC 81**
See also DLB 118

Frank, Elizabeth 1945- .... **CLC 39**
See also CA 121; 126; CANR 78; INT 126

Frankl, Viktor E(mil) 1905-1997 .... **CLC 93**
See also CA 65-68; 161

Franklin, Benjamin
See Hasek, Jaroslav (Matej Frantisek)

Franklin, Benjamin 1706-1790**LC 25; DA; DAB; DAC; DAM MST; WLCS**
See also CDALB 1640-1865; DLB 24, 43, 73

Franklin, (Stella Maria Sarah) Miles (Lampe) 1879-1954 .... **TCLC 7**
See also CA 104; 164

Fraser, (Lady) Antonia (Pakenham) 1932- . **C L C 32, 107**
See also CA 85-88; CANR 44, 65; MTCW 1, 2; SATA-Brief 32

Fraser, George MacDonald 1925- .... **CLC 7**

See Kuttner, Henry

Gardons, S. S.
See Snodgrass, W(illiam) D(e Witt)

Garfield, Leon 1921-1996 .... **CLC 12**
See also AAYA 8; CA 17-20R; 152; CANR 38, 41, 78; CLR 21; DLB 161; JRDA; MAICYA; SATA 1, 32, 76; SATA-Obit 90

Garland, (Hannibal) Hamlin 1860-1940 **TCLC 3; SSC 18**
See also CA 104; DLB 12, 71, 78, 186

Garneau, (Hector de) Saint-Denys 1912-1943 **TCLC 13**
See also CA 111; DLB 88

Garner, Alan 1934- .. **CLC 17; DAB; DAM POP**
See also AAYA 18; CA 73-76; CANR 15, 64; CLR 20; DLB 161; MAICYA; MTCW 1, 2; SATA 18, 69; SATA-Essay 108

Garner, Hugh 1913-1979 .... **CLC 13**
See also CA 69-72; CANR 31; DLB 68

Garnett, David 1892-1981 .... **CLC 3**
See also CA 5-8R; 103; CANR 17, 79; DLB 34; MTCW 2

Garos, Stephanie
See Katz, Steve

Garrett, George (Palmer) 1929- **CLC 3, 11, 51; SSC 30**
See also CA 1-4R; CAAS 5; CANR 1, 42, 67; DLB 2, 5, 130, 152; DLBY 83

Garrick, David 1717-1779 . **LC 15; DAM DRAM**
See also DLB 84

Garrigue, Jean 1914-1972 .... **CLC 2, 8**
See also CA 5-8R; 37-40R; CANR 20

Garrison, Frederick
See Sinclair, Upton (Beall)

Garth, Will
See Hamilton, Edmond; Kuttner, Henry

Garvey, Marcus (Moziah, Jr.) 1887-1940 . **TCLC 41; BLC 2; DAM MULT**
See also BW 1; CA 120; 124; CANR 79

Gary, Romain .... **CLC 25**
See Kacew, Romain
See also DLB 83

Gascar, Pierre .... **CLC 11**
See also Fournier, Pierre

Gascoyne, David (Emery) 1916- .... **CLC 45**
See also CA 65-68; CANR 10, 28, 54; DLB 20; MTCW 1

Gaskell, Elizabeth Cleghorn 1810-1865**NCLC 70; DAB; DAM MST; SSC 25**
See also CDBLB 1832-1890; DLB 21, 144, 159

Gass, William H(oward) 1924-**CLC 1, 2, 8, 11, 15, 39; SSC 12**
See also CA 17-20R; CANR 30, 71; DLB 2; MTCW 1, 2

Gasset, Jose Ortega y
See Ortega y Gasset, Jose

Gates, Henry Louis, Jr. 1950- ..**CLC 65; BLCS; DAM MULT**
See also BW 2, 3; CA 109; CANR 25, 53, 75; DLB 67; MTCW 1

Gautier, Theophile 1811-1872**NCLC 1, 59; DAM POET; PC 18; SSC 20**
See also DLB 119

Gawsworth, John
See Bates, H(erbert) E(rnest)

Gay, John 1685-1732 .... **LC 49; DAM DRAM**
See also DLB 84, 95

Gay, Oliver
See Gogarty, Oliver St. John

Gaye, Marvin (Penze) 1939-1984 .... **CLC 26**
See also CA 112

Gebler, Carlo (Ernest) 1954- .... **CLC 39**
See also CA 119; 133

Gee, Maggie (Mary) 1948- .... **CLC 57**
See also CA 130; DLB 207

Gee, Maurice (Gough) 1931- .... **CLC 29**
See also CA 97-100; CANR 67; CLR 56; SATA

46, 101

Gelbart, Larry (Simon) 1923- .... **CLC 21, 61**
See also CA 73-76; CANR 45

Gelber, Jack 1932- .... **CLC 1, 6, 14, 79**
See also CA 1-4R; CANR 2; DLB 7

Gellhorn, Martha (Ellis) 1908-1998 **CLC 14, 60**
See also CA 77-80; 164; CANR 44; DLBY 82, 98

Genet, Jean 1910-1986**CLC 1, 2, 5, 10, 14, 44, 46; DAM DRAM**
See also CA 13-16R; CANR 18; DLB 72; DLBY 86; MTCW 1, 2

Gent, Peter 1942- .... **CLC 29**
See also AITN 1; CA 89-92; DLBY 82

Gentlewoman in New England, A
See Bradstreet, Anne

Gentlewoman in Those Parts, A
See Bradstreet, Anne

George, Jean Craighead 1919- .... **CLC 35**
See also AAYA 8; CA 5-8R; CANR 25; CLR 1; DLB 52; JRDA; MAICYA; SATA 2, 68

George, Stefan (Anton) 1868-1933 .. **TCLC 2, 14**
See also CA 104

Georges, Georges Martin
See Simenon, Georges (Jacques Christian)

Gerhardi, William Alexander
See Gerhardie, William Alexander

Gerhardie, William Alexander 1895-1977**CLC 5**
See also CA 25-28R; 73-76; CANR 18; DLB 36

Gerstler, Amy 1956- .... **CLC 70**
See also CA 146

Gertler, T. .... **CLC 34**
See also CA 116; 121; INT 121

Ghalib .... **NCLC 39, 78**
See also Ghalib, Hsadullah Khan

Ghalib, Hsadullah Khan 1797-1869
See Ghalib
See also DAM POET

Ghelderode, Michel de 1898-1962**CLC 6, 11; DAM DRAM**
See also CA 85-88; CANR 40, 77

Ghiselin, Brewster 1903- .... **CLC 23**
See also CA 13-16R; CAAS 10; CANR 13

Ghose, Aurabinda 1872-1950 .... **TCLC 63**
See also CA 163

Ghose, Zulfikar 1935- .... **CLC 42**
See also CA 65-68; CANR 67

Ghosh, Amitav 1956- .... **CLC 44**
See also CA 147; CANR 80

Giacosa, Giuseppe 1847-1906 .... **TCLC 7**
See also CA 104

Gibb, Lee
See Waterhouse, Keith (Spencer)

Gibbon, Lewis Grassic .... **TCLC 4**
See also Mitchell, James Leslie

Gibbons, Kaye 1960- ..... **CLC 50, 88; DAM POP**
See also CA 151; CANR 75; MTCW 1

Gibran, Kahlil 1883-1931**TCLC 1, 9; DAM POET, POP; PC 9**
See also CA 104; 150; MTCW 2

Gibran, Khalil
See Gibran, Kahlil

Gibson, William 1914-**CLC 23; DA; DAB; DAC; DAM DRAM, MST**
See also CA 9-12R; CANR 9, 42, 75; DLB 7; MTCW 1; SATA 66

Gibson, William (Ford) 1948-**CLC 39, 63; DAM POP**
See also AAYA 12; CA 126; 133; CANR 52; MTCW 1

Gide, Andre (Paul Guillaume) 1869-1951**TCLC 5, 12, 36; DA; DAB; DAC; DAM MST, NOV; SSC 13; WLC**
See also CA 104; 124; DLB 65; MTCW 1, 2

Gifford, Barry (Colby) 1946- .... **CLC 34**
See also CA 65-68; CANR 9, 30, 40

Gilbert, Frank

See De Voto, Bernard (Augustine)

Gilbert, W(illiam) S(chwenck) 1836-1911 **TCLC 3; DAM DRAM, POET**
See also CA 104; 173; SATA 36

Gilbreth, Frank B., Jr. 1911- .... **CLC 17**
See also CA 9-12R; SATA 2

Gilchrist, Ellen 1935- . **CLC 34, 48; DAM POP; SSC 14**
See also CA 113; 116; CANR 41, 61; DLB 130; MTCW 1, 2

Giles, Molly 1942- .... **CLC 39**
See also CA 126

Gill, Eric 1882-1940 .... **TCLC 85**

Gill, Patrick
See Creasey, John

Gilliam, Terry (Vance) 1940- .... **CLC 21**
See also Monty Python
See also AAYA 19; CA 108; 113; CANR 35; INT 113

Gillian, Jerry
See Gilliam, Terry (Vance)

Gilliatt, Penelope (Ann Douglass) 1932-1993**CLC 2, 10, 13, 53**
See also AITN 2; CA 13-16R; 141; CANR 49; DLB 14

Gilman, Charlotte (Anna) Perkins (Stetson) 1860-1935 .... **TCLC 9, 37; SSC 13**
See also CA 106; 150; MTCW 1

Gilmour, David 1949- .... **CLC 35**
See also CA 138, 147

Gilpin, William 1724-1804 .... **NCLC 30**

Gilray, J. D.
See Mencken, H(enry) L(ouis)

Gilroy, Frank D(aniel) 1925- .... **CLC 2**
See also CA 81-84; CANR 32, 64; DLB 7

Gilstrap, John 1957(?)- .... **CLC 99**
See also CA 160

Ginsberg, Allen 1926-1997 **CLC 1, 2, 3, 4, 6, 13, 36, 69, 109; DA; DAB; DAC; DAM MST, POET; PC 4; WLC**
See also AITN 1; CA 1-4R; 157; CANR 2, 41, 63; CDALB 1941-1968; DLB 5, 16, 169; MTCW 1, 2

Ginzburg, Natalia 1916-1991 . **CLC 5, 11, 54, 70**
See also CA 85-88; 135; CANR 33; DLB 177; MTCW 1, 2

Giono, Jean 1895-1970 .... **CLC 4, 11**
See also CA 45-48; 29-32R; CANR 2, 35; DLB 72; MTCW 1

Giovanni, Nikki 1943-**CLC 2, 4, 19, 64, 117; BLC 2; DA; DAB; DAC; DAM MST, MULT, POET; PC 19; WLCS**
See also AAYA 22; AITN 1; BW 2, 3; CA 29-32R; CAAS 6; CANR 18, 41, 60; CDALBS; CLR 6; DLB 5, 41; INT CANR-18; MAICYA; MTCW 1, 2; SATA 24, 107

Giovene, Andrea 1904- .... **CLC 7**
See also CA 85-88

Gippius, Zinaida (Nikolayevna) 1869-1945
See Hippius, Zinaida
See also CA 106

Giraudoux, (Hippolyte) Jean 1882-1944**TCLC 2, 7; DAM DRAM**
See also CA 104; DLB 65

Gironella, Jose Maria 1917- .... **CLC 11**
See also CA 101

Gissing, George (Robert) 1857-1903**TCLC 3, 24, 47**
See also CA 105; 167; DLB 18, 135, 184

Giurlani, Aldo
See Palazzeschi, Aldo

Gladkov, Fyodor (Vasilyevich) 1883-1958**TCLC 27**
See also CA 170

Glanville, Brian (Lester) 1931- .... **CLC 6**
See also CA 5-8R; CAAS 9; CANR 3, 70; DLB 15, 139; SATA 42

Glasgow, Ellen (Anderson Gholson) 1873-1945

TCLC 2, 7; SSC 34
See also CA 104; 164; DLB 9, 12; MTCW 2
Glaspell, Susan 1882(?)-1948. **TCLC 55; DC 10**
See also CA 110; 154; DLB 7, 9, 78; YABC 2
Glassco, John 1909-1981 .... **CLC 9**
See also CA 13-16R; 102; CANR 15; DLB 68
Glasscock, Amnesia
See Steinbeck, John (Ernst)
Glasser, Ronald J. 1940(?)- .... **CLC 37**
Glassman, Joyce
See Johnson, Joyce
Glendinning, Victoria 1937- .... **CLC 50**
See also CA 120; 127; CANR 59; DLB 155
Glissant, Edouard 1928-**CLC 10, 68; DAM MULT**
See also CA 153
Gloag, Julian 1930- .... **CLC 40**
See also AITN 1; CA 65-68; CANR 10, 70
Glowacki, Aleksander
See Prus, Boleslaw
Gluck, Louise (Elisabeth) 1943-**CLC 7, 22, 44, 81; DAM POET; PC 16**
See also CA 33-36R; CANR 40, 69; DLB 5; MTCW 2
Glyn, Elinor 1864-1943 .... **TCLC 72**
See also DLB 153
Gobineau, Joseph Arthur (Comte) de 1816-1882 **NCLC 17**
See also DLB 123
Godard, Jean-Luc 1930- .... **CLC 20**
See also CA 93-96
Godden, (Margaret) Rumer 1907-1998 . **CLC 53**
See also AAYA 6; CA 5-8R; 172; CANR 4, 27, 36, 55, 80; CLR 20; DLB 161; MAICYA; SAAS 12; SATA 3, 36; SATA-Obit 109
Godoy Alcayaga, Lucila 1889-1957
See Mistral, Gabriela
See also BW 2; CA 104; 131; CANR 81; DAM MULT; HW 1, 2; MTCW 1, 2
Godwin, Gail (Kathleen) 1937- **CLC 5, 8, 22, 31, 69; DAM POP**
See also CA 29-32R; CANR 15, 43, 69; DLB 6; INT CANR-15; MTCW 1, 2
Godwin, William 1756-1836 .... **NCLC 14**
See also CDBLB 1789-1832; DLB 39, 104, 142, 158, 163
Goebbels, Josef
See Goebbels, (Paul) Joseph
Goebbels, (Paul) Joseph 1897-1945 ..... **TCLC 68**
See also CA 115; 148
Goebbels, Joseph Paul
See Goebbels, (Paul) Joseph
Goethe, Johann Wolfgang von 1749-1832**NCLC 4, 22, 34; DA; DAB; DAC; DAM DRAM, MST, POET; PC 5; WLC**
See also DLB 94
Gogarty, Oliver St. John 1878-1957 .... **TCLC 15**
See also CA 109; 150; DLB 15, 19
Gogol, Nikolai (Vasilyevich) 1809-1852**NCLC 5, 15, 31; DA; DAB; DAC; DAM DRAM, MST, DC 1; SSC 4, 29; WLC**
See also DLB 198
Goines, Donald 1937(?)-1974 ... **CLC 80; BLC 2; DAM MULT, POP**
See also AITN 1; BW 1, 3; CA 124; 114; DLB 33
Gold, Herbert 1924- .... **CLC 4, 7, 14, 42**
See also CA 9-12R; CANR 17, 45; DLB 2; DLBY 81
Goldbarth, Albert 1948- .... **CLC 5, 38**
See also CA 53-56; CANR 6, 40; DLB 120
Goldberg, Anatol 1910-1982 .... **CLC 34**
See also CA 131; 117
Goldemberg, Isaac 1945- .... **CLC 52**
See also CA 69-72; CAAS 12; CANR 11, 32; HW 1
Golding, William (Gerald) 1911-1993**CLC 1, 2, 3, 8, 10, 17, 27, 58, 81; DA; DAB; DAC; DAM MST, NOV; WLC**

See also AAYA 5; CA 5-8R; 141; CANR 13, 33, 54; CDBLB 1945-1960; DLB 15, 100; MTCW 1, 2
Goldman, Emma 1869-1940 .... **TCLC 13**
See also CA 110; 150
Goldman, Francisco 1954- .... **CLC 76**
See also CA 162
Goldman, William (W.) 1931- .... **CLC 1, 48**
See also CA 9-12R; CANR 29, 69; DLB 44
Goldmann, Lucien 1913-1970 .... **CLC 24**
See also CA 25-28; CAP 2
Goldoni, Carlo 1707-1793 .... **LC 4; DAM DRAM**
Goldsberry, Steven 1949- .... **CLC 34**
See also CA 131
Goldsmith, Oliver 1728-1774**LC 2, 48; DA; DAB; DAC; DAM DRAM, MST, NOV, POET; DC 8; WLC**
See also CDBLB 1660-1789; DLB 39, 89, 104, 109, 142; SATA 26
Goldsmith, Peter
See Priestley, J(ohn) B(oynton)
Gombrowicz, Witold 1904-1969**CLC 4, 7, 11, 49; DAM DRAM**
See also CA 19-20; 25-28R; CAP 2
Gomez de la Serna, Ramon 1888-1963 .... **CLC 9**
See also CA 153; 116; CANR 79; HW 1, 2
Goncharov, Ivan Alexandrovich 1812-1891**NCLC 1, 63**
Goncourt, Edmond (Louis Antoine Huot) de 1822-1896 .... **NCLC 7**
See also DLB 123
Goncourt, Jules (Alfred Huot) de 1830-1870 **NCLC 7**
See also DLB 123
Gontier, Fernande 19(?)- .... **CLC 50**
Gonzalez Martinez, Enrique 1871-1952**TCLC 72**
See also CA 166; CANR 81; HW 1
Goodman, Paul 1911-1972 .... **CLC 1, 2, 4, 7**
See also CA 19-20; 37-40R; CANR 34; CAP 2; DLB 130; MTCW 1
Gordimer, Nadine 1923- **CLC 3, 5, 7, 10, 18, 33, 51, 70; DA; DAB; DAC; DAM MST, NOV; SSC 17; WLCS**
See also CA 5-8R; CANR 3, 28, 56; INT CANR-28; MTCW 1, 2
Gordon, Adam Lindsay 1833-1870 ...... **NCLC 21**
Gordon, Caroline 1895-1981 **CLC 6, 13, 29, 83; SSC 15**
See also CA 11-12; 103; CANR 36; CAP 1; DLB 4, 9, 102; DLBD 17; DLBY 81; MTCW 1, 2
Gordon, Charles William 1860-1937
See Connor, Ralph
See also CA 109
Gordon, Mary (Catherine) 1949- .... **CLC 13, 22**
See also CA 102; CANR 44; DLB 6; DLBY 81; INT 102; MTCW 1
Gordon, N. J.
See Bosman, Herman Charles
Gordon, Sol 1923- .... **CLC 26**
See also CA 53-56; CANR 4; SATA 11
Gordone, Charles 1925-1995 .... **CLC 1, 4; DAM DRAM; DC 8**
See also BW 1, 3; CA 93-96; 150; CANR 55; DLB 7; INT 93-96; MTCW 1
Gore, Catherine 1800-1861 .... **NCLC 65**
See also DLB 116
Gorenko, Anna Andreevna
See Akhmatova, Anna
Gorky, Maxim 1868-1936**TCLC 8; DAB; SSC 28; WLC**
See also Peshkov, Alexei Maximovich
See also MTCW 2
Goryan, Sirak
See Saroyan, William
Gosse, Edmund (William) 1849-1928 .. **TCLC 28**
See also CA 117; DLB 57, 144, 184
Gotlieb, Phyllis Fay (Bloom) 1926- .... **CLC 18**

See also CA 13-16R; CANR 7; DLB 88
Gottesman, S. D.
See Kornbluth, C(yril) M.; Pohl, Frederik
Gottfried von Strassburg fl. c. 1210- . **CMLC 10**
See also DLB 138
Gould, Lois .... **CLC 4, 10**
See also CA 77-80; CANR 29; MTCW 1
Gourmont, Remy (-Marie-Charles) de 1858-1915 .... **TCLC 17**
See also CA 109; 150; MTCW 2
Govier, Katherine 1948- .... **CLC 51**
See also CA 101; CANR 18, 40
Goyen, (Charles) William 1915-1983 . **CLC 5, 8, 14, 40**
See also AITN 2; CA 5-8R; 110; CANR 6, 71; DLB 2; DLBY 83; INT CANR-6
Goytisolo, Juan 1931-**CLC 5, 10, 23; DAM MULT; HLC**
See also CA 85-88; CANR 32, 61; HW 1, 2; MTCW 1, 2
Gozzano, Guido 1883-1916 .... **PC 10**
See also CA 154; DLB 114
Gozzi, (Conte) Carlo 1720-1806 .... **NCLC 23**
Grabbe, Christian Dietrich 1801-1836 . **NCLC 2**
See also DLB 133
Grace, Patricia Frances 1937- .... **CLC 56**
See also CA 176
Gracian y Morales, Baltasar 1601-1658 .. **LC 15**
Gracq, Julien .... **CLC 11, 48**
See also Poirier, Louis
See also DLB 83
Grade, Chaim 1910-1982 .... **CLC 10**
See also CA 93-96; 107
Graduate of Oxford, A
See Ruskin, John
Grafton, Garth
See Duncan, Sara Jeannette
Graham, John
See Phillips, David Graham
Graham, Jorie 1951- .... **CLC 48, 118**
See also CA 111; CANR 63; DLB 120
Graham, R(obert) B(ontine) Cunninghame
See Cunninghame Graham, R(obert) B(ontine)
See also DLB 98, 135, 174
Graham, Robert
See Haldeman, Joe (William)
Graham, Tom
See Lewis, (Harry) Sinclair
Graham, W(illiam) S(ydney) 1918-1986 **CLC 29**
See also CA 73-76; 118; DLB 20
Graham, Winston (Mawdsley) 1910- .... **CLC 23**
See also CA 49-52; CANR 2, 22, 45, 66; DLB 77
Grahame, Kenneth 1859-1932 ... **TCLC 64; DAB**
See also CA 108; 136; CANR 80; CLR 5; DLB 34, 141, 178; MAICYA; MTCW 2; SATA 100; YABC 1
Granovsky, Timofei Nikolaevich 1813-1855 **NCLC 75**
See also DLB 198
Grant, Skeeter
See Spiegelman, Art
Granville-Barker, Harley 1877-1946 ... **TCLC 2; DAM DRAM**
See also Barker, Harley Granville
See also CA 104
Grass, Guenter (Wilhelm) 1927- **CLC 1, 2, 4, 6, 11, 15, 22, 32, 49, 88; DA; DAB; DAC; DAM MST, NOV; WLC**
See also CA 13-16R; CANR 20, 75; DLB 75, 124; MTCW 1, 2
Gratton, Thomas
See Hulme, T(homas) E(rnest)
Grau, Shirley Ann 1929- .... **CLC 4, 9; SSC 15**
See also CA 89-92; CANR 22, 69; DLB 2; INT CANR-22; MTCW 1
Gravel, Fern
See Hall, James Norman

Graver, Elizabeth 1964- .... **CLC 70**
See also CA 135; CANR 71
Graves, Richard Perceval 1945- .... **CLC 44**
See also CA 65-68; CANR 9, 26, 51
Graves, Robert (von Ranke) 1895-1985 **CLC 1, 2, 6, 11, 39, 44, 45; DAB; DAC; DAM MST, POET; PC 6**
See also CA 5-8R; 117; CANR 5, 36; CDBLB 1914-1945; DLB 20, 100, 191; DLBD 18; DLBY 85; MTCW 1, 2; SATA 45
Graves, Valerie
See Bradley, Marion Zimmer
Gray, Alasdair (James) 1934- .... **CLC 41**
See also CA 126; CANR 47, 69; DLB 194; INT 126; MTCW 1, 2
Gray, Amlin 1946- .... **CLC 29**
See also CA 138
Gray, Francine du Plessix 1930- . **CLC 22; DAM NOV**
See also BEST 90:3; CA 61-64; CAAS 2; CANR 11, 33, 75, 81; INT CANR-11; MTCW 1, 2
Gray, John (Henry) 1866-1934 .... **TCLC 19**
See also CA 119; 162
Gray, Simon (James Holliday) 1936- **CLC 9, 14, 36**
See also AITN 1; CA 21-24R; CAAS 3; CANR 32, 69; DLB 13; MTCW 1
Gray, Spalding 1941- **CLC 49, 112; DAM POP; DC 7**
See also CA 128; CANR 74; MTCW 2
Gray, Thomas 1716-1771 ... **LC 4, 40; DA; DAB; DAC; DAM MST; PC 2; WLC**
See also CDBLB 1660-1789; DLB 109
Grayson, David
See Baker, Ray Stannard
Grayson, Richard (A.) 1951- .... **CLC 38**
See also CA 85-88; CANR 14, 31, 57
Greeley, Andrew M(oran) 1928- . **CLC 28; DAM POP**
See also CA 5-8R; CAAS 7; CANR 7, 43, 69; MTCW 1, 2
Green, Anna Katharine 1846-1935 ..... **TCLC 63**
See also CA 112; 159; DLB 202
Green, Brian
See Card, Orson Scott
Green, Hannah
See Greenberg, Joanne (Goldenberg)
Green, Hannah 1927(?)-1996 .... **CLC 3**
See also CA 73-76; CANR 59
Green, Henry 1905-1973 .... **CLC 2, 13, 97**
See also Yorke, Henry Vincent
See also CA 175; DLB 15
Green, Julian (Hartridge) 1900-1998
See Green, Julien
See also CA 21-24R; 169; CANR 33; DLB 4, 72; MTCW 1
Green, Julien .... **CLC 3, 11, 77**
See also Green, Julian (Hartridge)
See also MTCW 2
Green, Paul (Eliot) 1894-1981 ..... **CLC 25; DAM DRAM**
See also AITN 1; CA 5-8R; 103; CANR 3; DLB 7, 9; DLBY 81
Greenberg, Ivan 1908-1973
See Rahv, Philip
See also CA 85-88
Greenberg, Joanne (Goldenberg) 1932- . **CLC 7, 30**
See also AAYA 12; CA 5-8R; CANR 14, 32, 69; SATA 25
Greenberg, Richard 1959(?)- .... **CLC 57**
See also CA 138
Greene, Bette 1934- .... **CLC 30**
See also AAYA 7; CA 53-56; CANR 4; CLR 2; JRDA; MAICYA; SAAS 16; SATA 8, 102
Greene, Gael .... **CLC 8**
See also CA 13-16R; CANR 10

Greene, Graham (Henry) 1904-1991 **CLC 1, 3, 6, 9, 14, 18, 27, 37, 70, 72; DA; DAB; DAC; DAM MST, NOV; SSC 29; WLC**
See also AITN 2; CA 13-16R; 133; CANR 35, 61; CDBLB 1945-1960; DLB 13, 15, 77, 100, 162, 201, 204; DLBY 91; MTCW 1, 2; SATA 20
Greene, Robert 1558-1592 .... **LC 41**
See also DLB 62, 167
Greer, Richard
See Silverberg, Robert
Gregor, Arthur 1923- .... **CLC 9**
See also CA 25-28R; CAAS 10; CANR 11; SATA 36
Gregor, Lee
See Pohl, Frederik
Gregory, Isabella Augusta (Persse) 1852-1932 **TCLC 1**
See also CA 104; DLB 10
Gregory, J. Dennis
See Williams, John A(lfred)
Grendon, Stephen
See Derleth, August (William)
Grenville, Kate 1950- .... **CLC 61**
See also CA 118; CANR 53
Grenville, Pelham
See Wodehouse, P(elham) G(renville)
Greve, Felix Paul (Berthold Friedrich) 1879-1948
See Grove, Frederick Philip
See also CA 104; 141, 175; CANR 79; DAC; DAM MST
Grey, Zane 1872-1939 .... **TCLC 6; DAM POP**
See also CA 104; 132; DLB 212; MTCW 1, 2
Grieg, (Johan) Nordahl (Brun) 1902-1943 **TCLC 10**
See also CA 107
Grieve, C(hristopher) M(urray) 1892-1978 **CLC 11, 19; DAM POET**
See also MacDiarmid, Hugh; Pteleon
See also CA 5-8R; 85-88; CANR 33; MTCW 1
Griffin, Gerald 1803-1840 .... **NCLC 7**
See also DLB 159
Griffin, John Howard 1920-1980 .... **CLC 68**
See also AITN 1; CA 1-4R; 101; CANR 2
Griffin, Peter 1942- .... **CLC 39**
See also CA 136
Griffith, D(avid Lewelyn) W(ark) 1875(?)-1948 **TCLC 68**
See also CA 119; 150; CANR 80
Griffith, Lawrence
See Griffith, D(avid Lewelyn) W(ark)
Griffiths, Trevor 1935- .... **CLC 13, 52**
See also CA 97-100; CANR 45; DLB 13
Griggs, Sutton Elbert 1872-1930(?) .... **TCLC 77**
See also CA 123; DLB 50
Grigson, Geoffrey (Edward Harvey) 1905-1985 **CLC 7, 39**
See also CA 25-28R; 118; CANR 20, 33; DLB 27; MTCW 1, 2
Grillparzer, Franz 1791-1872 .... **NCLC 1**
See also DLB 133
Grimble, Reverend Charles James
See Eliot, T(homas) S(tearns)
Grimke, Charlotte L(ottie) Forten 1837(?)-1914
See Forten, Charlotte L.
See also BW 1; CA 117; 124; DAM MULT, POET
Grimm, Jacob Ludwig Karl 1785-1863 **NCLC 3, 77**
See also DLB 90; MAICYA; SATA 22
Grimm, Wilhelm Karl 1786-1859 ... **NCLC 3, 77**
See also DLB 90; MAICYA; SATA 22
Grimmelshausen, Johann Jakob Christoffel von 1621-1676 .... **LC 6**
See also DLB 168
Grindel, Eugene 1895-1952
See Eluard, Paul
See also CA 104
Grisham, John 1955- .... **CLC 84; DAM POP**
See also AAYA 14; CA 138; CANR 47, 69; MTCW

2
Grossman, David 1954- .... **CLC 67**
See also CA 138
Grossman, Vasily (Semenovich) 1905-1964 **C L C 41**
See also CA 124; 130; MTCW 1
Grove, Frederick Philip .... **TCLC 4**
See also Greve, Felix Paul (Berthold Friedrich)
See also DLB 92
Grubb
See Crumb, R(obert)
Grumbach, Doris (Isaac) 1918- . **CLC 13, 22, 64**
See also CA 5-8R; CAAS 2; CANR 9, 42, 70; INT CANR-9; MTCW 2
Grundtvig, Nicolai Frederik Severin 1783-1872 **NCLC 1**
Grunge
See Crumb, R(obert)
Grunwald, Lisa 1959- .... **CLC 44**
See also CA 120
Guare, John 1938- **CLC 8, 14, 29, 67; DAM DRAM**
See also CA 73-76; CANR 21, 69; DLB 7; MTCW 1, 2
Gudjonsson, Halldor Kiljan 1902-1998
See Laxness, Halldor
See also CA 103; 164
Guenter, Erich
See Eich, Guenter
Guest, Barbara 1920- .... **CLC 34**
See also CA 25-28R; CANR 11, 44; DLB 5, 193
Guest, Edgar A(lbert) 1881-1959 .... **TCLC 95**
See also CA 112; 168
Guest, Judith (Ann) 1936- **CLC 8, 30; DAM NOV, POP**
See also AAYA 7; CA 77-80; CANR 15, 75; INT CANR-15; MTCW 1, 2
Guevara, Che .... **CLC 87; HLC**
See also Guevara (Serna), Ernesto
Guevara (Serna), Ernesto 1928-1967
See Guevara, Che
See also CA 127; 111; CANR 56; DAM MULT; HW 1
Guicciardini, Francesco 1483-1540 .... **LC 49**
Guild, Nicholas M. 1944- .... **CLC 33**
See also CA 93-96
Guillemin, Jacques
See Sartre, Jean-Paul
Guillen, Jorge 1893-1984 **CLC 11; DAM MULT, POET; HLCS 1**
See also CA 89-92; 112; DLB 108; HW 1
Guillen, Nicolas (Cristobal) 1902-1989 **CLC 48, 79; BLC 2; DAM MST, MULT, POET; HLC; PC 23**
See also BW 2; CA 116; 125; 129; HW 1
Guillevic, (Eugene) 1907- .... **CLC 33**
See also CA 93-96
Guillois
See Desnos, Robert
Guillois, Valentin
See Desnos, Robert
Guiney, Louise Imogen 1861-1920 ...... **TCLC 41**
See also CA 160; DLB 54
Guiraldes, Ricardo (Guillermo) 1886-1927 **TCLC 39**
See also CA 131; HW 1; MTCW 1
Gumilev, Nikolai (Stepanovich) 1886-1921 **TCLC 60**
See also CA 165
Gunesekera, Romesh 1954- .... **CLC 91**
See also CA 159
Gunn, Bill .... **CLC 5**
See also Gunn, William Harrison
See also DLB 38
Gunn, Thom(son William) 1929- **CLC 3, 6, 18, 32, 81; DAM POET; PC 26**
See also CA 17-20R; CANR 9, 33; CDBLB 1960 to Present; DLB 27; INT CANR-33; MTCW 1

See also CA 5-8R; CANR 6; CLR 47; DLB 88;
JRDA; MAICYA; SAAS 10; SATA 6, 74

Harris, Frank 1856-1931 .... **TCLC 24**
See also CA 109; 150; CANR 80; DLB 156, 197
Harris, George Washington 1814-1869**NCLC 23**
See also DLB 3, 11
Harris, Joel Chandler 1848-1908**TCLC 2; SSC 19**
See also CA 104; 137; CANR 80; CLR 49; DLB
11, 23, 42, 78, 91; MAICYA; SATA 100;
YABC 1
Harris, John (Wyndham Parkes Lucas) Beynon
1903-1969
See Wyndham, John
See also CA 102; 89-92
Harris, MacDonald .... **CLC 9**
See also Heiney, Donald (William)
Harris, Mark 1922- .... **CLC 19**
See also CA 5-8R; CAAS 3; CANR 2, 55; DLB 2;
DLBY 80
Harris, (Theodore) Wilson 1921- .... **CLC 25**
See also BW 2, 3; CA 65-68; CAAS 16; CANR
11, 27, 69; DLB 117; MTCW 1
Harrison, Elizabeth Cavanna 1909-
See Cavanna, Betty
See also CA 9-12R; CANR 6, 27
Harrison, Harry (Max) 1925- .... **CLC 42**
See also CA 1-4R; CANR 5, 21; DLB 8; SATA 4
Harrison, James (Thomas) 1937-**CLC 6, 14, 33,
66; SSC 19**
See also CA 13-16R; CANR 8, 51, 79; DLBY 82;
INT CANR-8
Harrison, Jim
See Harrison, James (Thomas)
Harrison, Kathryn 1961- .... **CLC 70**
See also CA 144; CANR 68
Harrison, Tony 1937- .... **CLC 43**
See also CA 65-68; CANR 44; DLB 40; MTCW 1
Harriss, Will(ard Irvin) 1922- .... **CLC 34**
See also CA 111
Harson, Sley
See Ellison, Harlan (Jay)
Hart, Ellis
See Ellison, Harlan (Jay)
Hart, Josephine 1942(?)- .... **CLC 70; DAM POP**
See also CA 138; CANR 70
Hart, Moss 1904-1961 ..... **CLC 66; DAM DRAM**
See also CA 109; 89-92; DLB 7
Harte, (Francis) Bret(t) 1836(?)-1902**TCLC 1, 25;
DA; DAC; DAM MST; SSC 8; WLC**
See also CA 104; 140; CANR 80; CDALB 1865-
1917; DLB 12, 64, 74, 79, 186; SATA 26
Hartley, L(eslie) P(oles) 1895-1972 ... **CLC 2, 22**
See also CA 45-48; 37-40R; CANR 33; DLB 15,
139; MTCW 1, 2
Hartman, Geoffrey H. 1929- .... **CLC 27**
See also CA 117; 125; CANR 79; DLB 67
Hartmann, Sadakichi 1867-1944 .... **TCLC 73**
See also CA 157; DLB 54
Hartmann von Aue c. 1160-c. 1205 ..... **CMLC 15**
See also DLB 138
Hartmann von Aue 1170-1210 .... **CMLC 15**
Haruf, Kent 1943- .... **CLC 34**
See also CA 149
Harwood, Ronald 1934- .. **CLC 32; DAM DRAM,
MST**
See also CA 1-4R; CANR 4, 55; DLB 13
Hasegawa Tatsunosuke
See Futabatei, Shimei
Hasek, Jaroslav (Matej Frantisek) 1883-1923
TCLC 4
See also CA 104; 129; MTCW 1, 2
Hass, Robert 1941- .... **CLC 18, 39, 99; PC 16**
See also CA 111; CANR 30, 50, 71; DLB 105, 206;
SATA 94
Hastings, Hudson
See Kuttner, Henry
Hastings, Selina .... **CLC 44**

Hathorne, John 1641-1717 .... **LC 38**
Hatteras, Amelia
See Mencken, H(enry) L(ouis)
Hatteras, Owen .... **TCLC 18**
See also Mencken, H(enry) L(ouis); Nathan,
George Jean
Hauptmann, Gerhart (Johann Robert) 1862-1946
TCLC 4; DAM DRAM
See also CA 104; 153; DLB 66, 118
Havel, Vaclav 1936-**CLC 25, 58, 65; DAM DRAM;
DC 6**
See also CA 104; CANR 36, 63; MTCW 1, 2
Haviaras, Stratis .... **CLC 33**
See also Chaviaras, Strates
Hawes, Stephen 1475(?)-1523(?) .... **LC 17**
See also DLB 132
Hawkes, John (Clendennin Burne, Jr.) 1925-1998
CLC 1, 2, 3, 4, 7, 9, 14, 15, 27, 49
See also CA 1-4R; 167; CANR 2, 47, 64; DLB 2, 7;
DLBY 80, 98; MTCW 1, 2
Hawking, S. W.
See Hawking, Stephen W(illiam)
Hawking, Stephen W(illiam) 1942-**CLC 63, 105**
See also AAYA 13; BEST 89:1; CA 126; 129;
CANR 48; MTCW 2
Hawkins, Anthony Hope
See Hope, Anthony
Hawthorne, Julian 1846-1934 .... **TCLC 25**
See also CA 165
Hawthorne, Nathaniel 1804-1864 **NCLC 39; DA;
DAB; DAC; DAM MST, NOV; SSC 3, 29;
WLC**
See also AAYA 18; CDALB 1640-1865; DLB 1,
74; YABC 2
Haxton, Josephine Ayres 1921-
See Douglas, Ellen
See also CA 115; CANR 41
Hayaseca y Eizaguirre, Jorge
See Echegaray (y Eizaguirre), Jose (Maria
Waldo)
Hayashi, Fumiko 1904-1951 .... **TCLC 27**
See also CA 161; DLB 180
Haycraft, Anna
See Ellis, Alice Thomas
See also CA 122; MTCW 2
Hayden, Robert E(arl) 1913-1980**CLC 5, 9, 14, 37;
BLC 2; DA; DAC; DAM MST, MULT, POET;
PC 6**
See also BW 1, 3; CA 69-72; 97-100; CABS 2;
CANR 24, 75; CDALB 1941-1968; DLB 5, 76;
MTCW 1, 2; SATA 19; SATA-Obit 26
Hayford, J(oseph) E(phraim) Casely
See Casely-Hayford, J(oseph) E(phraim)
Hayman, Ronald 1932- .... **CLC 44**
See also CA 25-28R; CANR 18, 50; DLB 155
Haywood, Eliza (Fowler) 1693(?)-1756 . **LC 1, 44**
See also DLB 39
Hazlitt, William 1778-1830 .... **NCLC 29**
See also DLB 110, 158
Hazzard, Shirley 1931- .... **CLC 18**
See also CA 9-12R; CANR 4, 70; DLBY 82;
MTCW 1
Head, Bessie 1937-1986**CLC 25, 67; BLC 2; DAM
MULT**
See also BW 2, 3; CA 29-32R; 119; CANR 25;
DLB 117; MTCW 1, 2
Headon, (Nicky) Topper 1956(?)- .... **CLC 30**
Heaney, Seamus (Justin) 1939-**CLC 5, 7, 14, 25,
37, 74, 91; DAB; DAM POET; PC 18; WLCS**
See also CA 85-88; CANR 25, 48, 75; CDBLB
1960 to Present; DLB 40; DLBY 95; MTCW 1,
2
Hearn, (Patricio) Lafcadio (Tessima Carlos) 1850-
1904 .... **TCLC 9**
See also CA 105; 166; DLB 12, 78, 189
Hearne, Vicki 1946- .... **CLC 56**
See also CA 139

Hearon, Shelby 1931- .... **CLC 63**
See also AITN 2; CA 25-28R; CANR 18, 48
Heat-Moon, William Least .... **CLC 29**
See also Trogdon, William (Lewis)
See also AAYA 9
Hebbel, Friedrich 1813-1863 .... **NCLC 43; DAM
DRAM**
See also DLB 129
Hebert, Anne 1916-**CLC 4, 13, 29; DAC; DAM
MST, POET**
See also CA 85-88; CANR 69; DLB 68; MTCW 1,
2
Hecht, Anthony (Evan) 1923-**CLC 8, 13, 19; DAM
POET**
See also CA 9-12R; CANR 6; DLB 5, 169
Hecht, Ben 1894-1964 .... **CLC 8**
See also CA 85-88; DLB 7, 9, 25, 26, 28, 86
Hedayat, Sadeq 1903-1951 .... **TCLC 21**
See also CA 120
Hegel, Georg Wilhelm Friedrich 1770-1831
NCLC 46
See also DLB 90
Heidegger, Martin 1889-1976 .... **CLC 24**
See also CA 81-84; 65-68; CANR 34; MTCW 1, 2
Heidenstam, (Carl Gustaf) Verner von 1859-1940
TCLC 5
See also CA 104
Heifner, Jack 1946- .... **CLC 11**
See also CA 105; CANR 47
Heijermans, Herman 1864-1924 .... **TCLC 24**
See also CA 123
Heilbrun, Carolyn G(old) 1926- .... **CLC 25**
See also CA 45-48; CANR 1, 28, 58
Heine, Heinrich 1797-1856 . **NCLC 4, 54; PC 25**
See also DLB 90
Heinemann, Larry (Curtiss) 1944- .... **CLC 50**
See also CA 110; CAAS 21; CANR 31, 81; DLBD
9; INT CANR-31
Heiney, Donald (William) 1921-1993
See Harris, MacDonald
See also CA 1-4R; 142; CANR 3, 58
Heinlein, Robert A(nson) 1907-1988**CLC 1, 3, 8,
14, 26, 55; DAM POP**
See also AAYA 17; CA 1-4R; 125; CANR 1, 20,
53; DLB 8; JRDA; MAICYA; MTCW 1, 2;
SATA 9, 69; SATA-Obit 56
Helforth, John
See Doolittle, Hilda
Hellenhofferu, Vojtech Kapristian z
See Hasek, Jaroslav (Matej Frantisek)
Heller, Joseph 1923- **CLC 1, 3, 5, 8, 11, 36, 63;
DA; DAB; DAC; DAM MST, NOV, POP;
WLC**
See also AAYA 24; AITN 1; CA 5-8R; CABS 1;
CANR 8, 42, 66; DLB 2, 28; DLBY 80; INT
CANR-8; MTCW 1, 2
Hellman, Lillian (Florence) 1906-1984**CLC 2, 4,
8, 14, 18, 34, 44, 52; DAM DRAM; DC 1**
See also AITN 1, 2; CA 13-16R; 112; CANR 33;
DLB 7; DLBY 84; MTCW 1, 2
Helprin, Mark 1947- .. **CLC 7, 10, 22, 32; DAM
NOV, POP**
See also CA 81-84; CANR 47, 64; CDALBS;
DLBY 85; MTCW 1, 2
Helvetius, Claude-Adrien 1715-1771 .... **LC 26**
Helyar, Jane Penelope Josephine 1933-
See Poole, Josephine
See also CA 21-24R; CANR 10, 26; SATA 82
Hemans, Felicia 1793-1835 .... **NCLC 71**
See also DLB 96
Hemingway, Ernest (Miller) 1899-1961**CLC 1, 3,
6, 8, 10, 13, 19, 30, 34, 39, 41, 44, 50, 61, 80;
DA; DAB; DAC; DAM MST, NOV; SSC 1,
25; WLC**
See also AAYA 19; CA 77-80; CANR 34; CDALB
1917-1929; DLB 4, 9, 102, 210; DLBD 1, 15, 16;
DLBY 81, 87, 96, 98; MTCW 1, 2

See also CA 111; 164; DLB 70, 153, 156, 178; MTCW 2

Hoeg, Peter 1957- .... **CLC 95**
See also CA 151; CANR 75; MTCW 2

Hoffman, Alice 1952- .... **CLC 51; DAM NOV**
See also CA 77-80; CANR 34, 66; MTCW 1, 2

Hoffman, Daniel (Gerard) 1923- . **CLC 6, 13, 23**
See also CA 1-4R; CANR 4; DLB 5

Hoffman, Stanley 1944- .... **CLC 5**
See also CA 77-80

Hoffman, William M(oses) 1939- .... **CLC 40**
See also CA 57-60; CANR 11, 71

Hoffmann, E(rnst) T(heodor) A(madeus) 1776-1822
NCLC 2; SSC 13
See also DLB 90; SATA 27

Hofmann, Gert 1931- .... **CLC 54**
See also CA 128

Hofmannsthal, Hugo von 1874-1929 ... **TCLC 11; DAM DRAM; DC 4**
See also CA 106; 153; DLB 81, 118

Hogan, Linda 1947- .... **CLC 73; DAM MULT**
See also CA 120; CANR 45, 73; DLB 175; NNAL

Hogarth, Charles
See Creasey, John

Hogarth, Emmett
See Polonsky, Abraham (Lincoln)

Hogg, James 1770-1835 .... **NCLC 4**
See also DLB 93, 116, 159

Holbach, Paul Henri Thiry Baron 1723-1789 **L C 14**

Holberg, Ludvig 1684-1754 .... **LC 6**

Holden, Ursula 1921- .... **CLC 18**
See also CA 101; CAAS 8; CANR 22

Holderlin, (Johann Christian) Friedrich 1770-1843
NCLC 16; PC 4

Holdstock, Robert
See Holdstock, Robert P.

Holdstock, Robert P. 1948- .... **CLC 39**
See also CA 131; CANR 81

Holland, Isabelle 1920- .... **CLC 21**
See also AAYA 11; CA 21-24R; CANR 10, 25, 47; CLR 57; JRDA; MAICYA; SATA 8, 70; SATA-Essay 103

Holland, Marcus
See Caldwell, (Janet Miriam) Taylor (Holland)

Hollander, John 1929- .... **CLC 2, 5, 8, 14**
See also CA 1-4R; CANR 1, 52; DLB 5; SATA 13

Hollander, Paul
See Silverberg, Robert

Holleran, Andrew 1943(?)- .... **CLC 38**
See also CA 144

Hollinghurst, Alan 1954- .... **CLC 55, 91**
See also CA 114; DLB 207

Hollis, Jim
See Summers, Hollis (Spurgeon, Jr.)

Holly, Buddy 1936-1959 .... **TCLC 65**

Holmes, Gordon
See Shiel, M(atthew) P(hipps)

Holmes, John
See Souster, (Holmes) Raymond

Holmes, John Clellon 1926-1988 .... **CLC 56**
See also CA 9-12R; 125; CANR 4; DLB 16

Holmes, Oliver Wendell, Jr. 1841-1935 **TCLC 77**
See also CA 114

Holmes, Oliver Wendell 1809-1894 .... **NCLC 14**
See also CDALB 1640-1865; DLB 1, 189; SATA 34

Holmes, Raymond
See Souster, (Holmes) Raymond

Holt, Victoria
See Hibbert, Eleanor Alice Burford

Holub, Miroslav 1923-1998 .... **CLC 4**
See also CA 21-24R; 169; CANR 10

Homer c. 8th cent. B.C.- **CMLC 1, 16; DA; DAB; DAC; DAM MST, POET; PC 23; WLCS**
See also DLB 176

Hongo, Garrett Kaoru 1951- .... **PC 23**

See also CA 133; CAAS 22; DLB 120

Honig, Edwin 1919- .... **CLC 33**
See also CA 5-8R; CAAS 8; CANR 4, 45; DLB 5

Hood, Hugh (John Blagdon) 1928- .. **CLC 15, 28**
See also CA 49-52; CAAS 17; CANR 1, 33; DLB 53

Hood, Thomas 1799-1845 .... **NCLC 16**
See also DLB 96

Hooker, (Peter) Jeremy 1941- .... **CLC 43**
See also CA 77-80; CANR 22; DLB 40

hooks, bell .... **CLC 94; BLCS**
See also Watkins, Gloria
See also MTCW 2

Hope, A(lec) D(erwent) 1907- .... **CLC 3, 51**
See also CA 21-24R; CANR 33, 74; MTCW 1, 2

Hope, Anthony 1863-1933 .... **TCLC 83**
See also CA 157; DLB 153, 156

Hope, Brian
See Creasey, John

Hope, Christopher (David Tully) 1944- . **CLC 52**
See also CA 106; CANR 47; SATA 62

Hopkins, Gerard Manley 1844-1889 . **NCLC 17; DA; DAB; DAC; DAM MST, POET; PC 15; WLC**
See also CDBLB 1890-1914; DLB 35, 57

Hopkins, John (Richard) 1931-1998 .... **CLC 4**
See also CA 85-88; 169

Hopkins, Pauline Elizabeth 1859-1930 **TCLC 28; BLC 2; DAM MULT**
See also BW 2, 3; CA 141; DLB 50

Hopkinson, Francis 1737-1791 .... **LC 25**
See also DLB 31

Hopley-Woolrich, Cornell George 1903-1968
See Woolrich, Cornell
See also CA 13-14; CANR 58; CAP 1; MTCW 2

Horatio
See Proust, (Valentin-Louis-George-Eugene-)
Marcel

Horgan, Paul (George Vincent O'Shaughnessy)
1903-1995 .... **CLC 9, 53; DAM NOV**
See also CA 13-16R; 147; CANR 9, 35; DLB 212; DLBY 85; INT CANR-9; MTCW 1, 2; SATA 13; SATA-Obit 84

Horn, Peter
See Kuttner, Henry

Hornem, Horace Esq.
See Byron, George Gordon (Noel)

Horney, Karen (Clementine Theodore Danielsen)
1885-1952 .... **TCLC 71**
See also CA 114; 165

Hornung, E(rnest) W(illiam) 1866-1921 **TCLC 59**
See also CA 108; 160; DLB 70

Horovitz, Israel (Arthur) 1939- .. **CLC 56; DAM DRAM**
See also CA 33-36R; CANR 46, 59; DLB 7

Horvath, Odon von
See Horvath, Oedoen von
See also DLB 85, 124

Horvath, Oedoen von 1901-1938 .... **TCLC 45**
See also Horvath, Odon von
See also CA 118

Horwitz, Julius 1920-1986 .... **CLC 14**
See also CA 9-12R; 119; CANR 12

Hospital, Janette Turner 1942- .... **CLC 42**
See also CA 108; CANR 48

Hostos, E. M. de
See Hostos (y Bonilla), Eugenio Maria de

Hostos, Eugenio M. de
See Hostos (y Bonilla), Eugenio Maria de

Hostos, Eugenio Maria
See Hostos (y Bonilla), Eugenio Maria de

Hostos (y Bonilla), Eugenio Maria de 1839-1903
TCLC 24
See also CA 123; 131; HW 1

Houdini
See Lovecraft, H(oward) P(hillips)

Hougan, Carolyn 1943- .... **CLC 34**

See also CA 139

Household, Geoffrey (Edward West) 1900-1988
CLC 11
See also CA 77-80; 126; CANR 58; DLB 87; SATA 14; SATA-Obit 59

Housman, A(lfred) E(dward) 1859-1936 **TCLC 1, 10; DA; DAB; DAC; DAM MST, POET; PC 2; WLCS**
See also CA 104; 125; DLB 19; MTCW 1, 2

Housman, Laurence 1865-1959 .... **TCLC 7**
See also CA 106; 155; DLB 10; SATA 25

Howard, Elizabeth Jane 1923- .... **CLC 7, 29**
See also CA 5-8R; CANR 8, 62

Howard, Maureen 1930- .... **CLC 5, 14, 46**
See also CA 53-56; CANR 31, 75; DLBY 83; INT CANR-31; MTCW 1, 2

Howard, Richard 1929- .... **CLC 7, 10, 47**
See also AITN 1; CA 85-88; CANR 25, 80; DLB 5; INT CANR-25

Howard, Robert E(rvin) 1906-1936 .... **TCLC 8**
See also CA 105; 157

Howard, Warren F.
See Pohl, Frederik

Howe, Fanny (Quincy) 1940- .... **CLC 47**
See also CA 117; CAAS 27; CANR 70; SATA-Brief 52

Howe, Irving 1920-1993 .... **CLC 85**
See also CA 9-12R; 141; CANR 21, 50; DLB 67; MTCW 1, 2

Howe, Julia Ward 1819-1910 .... **TCLC 21**
See also CA 117; DLB 1, 189

Howe, Susan 1937- .... **CLC 72**
See also CA 160; DLB 120

Howe, Tina 1937- .... **CLC 48**
See also CA 109

Howell, James 1594(?)-1666 .... **LC 13**
See also DLB 151

Howells, W. D.
See Howells, William Dean

Howells, William D.
See Howells, William Dean

Howells, William Dean 1837-1920 **TCLC 7, 17, 41**
See also CA 104; 134; CDALB 1865-1917; DLB 12, 64, 74, 79, 189; MTCW 2

Howes, Barbara 1914-1996 .... **CLC 15**
See also CA 9-12R; 151; CAAS 3; CANR 53; SATA 5

Hrabal, Bohumil 1914-1997 .... **CLC 13, 67**
See also CA 106; 156; CAAS 12; CANR 57

Hroswitha of Gandersheim c. 935-c. 1002 **CMLC 29**
See also DLB 148

Hsun, Lu
See Lu Hsun

Hubbard, L(afayette) Ron(ald) 1911-1986 **CLC 43; DAM POP**
See also CA 77-80; 118; CANR 52; MTCW 2

Huch, Ricarda (Octavia) 1864-1947 .... **TCLC 13**
See also CA 111; DLB 66

Huddle, David 1942- .... **CLC 49**
See also CA 57-60; CAAS 20; DLB 130

Hudson, Jeffrey
See Crichton, (John) Michael

Hudson, W(illiam) H(enry) 1841-1922 **TCLC 29**
See also CA 115; DLB 98, 153, 174; SATA 35

Hueffer, Ford Madox
See Ford, Ford Madox

Hughart, Barry 1934- .... **CLC 39**
See also CA 137

Hughes, Colin
See Creasey, John

Hughes, David (John) 1930- .... **CLC 48**
See also CA 116; 129; DLB 14

Hughes, Edward James
See Hughes, Ted
See also DAM MST, POET

Hughes, (James) Langston 1902-1967 **CLC 1, 5,**

10, 15, 35, 44, 108; BLC 2; DA; DAB;
DAC; DAM DRAM, MST, MULT, POET;
DC 3; PC 1; SSC 6; WLC
See also AAYA 12; BW 1, 3; CA 1-4R; 25-28R;
CANR 1, 34; CDALB 1929-1941; CLR 17; DLB
4, 7, 48, 51, 86; JRDA; MAICYA; MTCW 1, 2;
SATA 4, 33

Hughes, Richard (Arthur Warren) 1900-1976
CLC 1, 11; DAM NOV
See also CA 5-8R; 65-68; CANR 4; DLB 15,
161; MTCW 1; SATA 8; SATA-Obit 25

Hughes, Ted 1930-1998 **CLC 2, 4, 9, 14, 37, 119;
DAB; DAC; PC 7**
See also Hughes, Edward James
See also CA 1-4R; 171; CANR 1, 33, 66; CLR 3;
DLB 40, 161; MAICYA; MTCW 1, 2; SATA
49; SATA-Brief 27; SATA-Obit 107

Hugo, Richard F(ranklin) 1923-1982 **CLC 6, 18,
32; DAM POET**
See also CA 49-52; 108; CANR 3; DLB 5, 206

Hugo, Victor (Marie) 1802-1885**NCLC 3, 10, 21;
DA; DAB; DAC; DAM DRAM, MST, NOV,
POET; PC 17; WLC**
See also AAYA 28; DLB 119, 192; SATA 47

Huidobro, Vicente
See Huidobro Fernandez, Vicente Garcia

Huidobro Fernandez, Vicente Garcia 1893-1948
TCLC 31
See also CA 131; HW 1

Hulme, Keri 1947- .... **CLC 39**
See also CA 125; CANR 69; INT 125

Hulme, T(homas) E(rnest) 1883-1917 . **TCLC 21**
See also CA 117; DLB 19

Hume, David 1711-1776 .... **LC 7**
See also DLB 104

Humphrey, William 1924-1997 .... **CLC 45**
See also CA 77-80; 160; CANR 68; DLB 212

Humphreys, Emyr Owen 1919- .... **CLC 47**
See also CA 5-8R; CANR 3, 24; DLB 15

Humphreys, Josephine 1945- .... **CLC 34, 57**
See also CA 121; 127; INT 127

Huneker, James Gibbons 1857-1921 ... **TCLC 65**
See also DLB 71

Hungerford, Pixie
See Brinsmead, H(esba) F(ay)

Hunt, E(verette) Howard, (Jr.) 1918- .... **CLC 3**
See also AITN 1; CA 45-48; CANR 2, 47

Hunt, Kyle
See Creasey, John

Hunt, (James Henry) Leigh 1784-1859 **NCLC 1,
70; DAM POET**
See also DLB 96, 110, 144

Hunt, Marsha 1946- .... **CLC 70**
See also BW 2, 3; CA 143; CANR 79

Hunt, Violet 1866(?)-1942 .... **TCLC 53**
See also DLB 162, 197

Hunter, E. Waldo
See Sturgeon, Theodore (Hamilton)

Hunter, Evan 1926- .... **CLC 11, 31; DAM POP**
See also CA 5-8R; CANR 5, 38, 62; DLBY 82;
INT CANR-5; MTCW 1; SATA 25

Hunter, Kristin (Eggleston) 1931- .... **CLC 35**
See also AITN 1; BW 1; CA 13-16R; CANR 13;
CLR 3; DLB 33; INT CANR-13; MAICYA;
SAAS 10; SATA 12

Hunter, Mollie 1922- .... **CLC 21**
See also McIlwraith, Maureen Mollie Hunter
See also AAYA 13; CANR 37, 78; CLR 25; DLB
161; JRDA; MAICYA; SAAS 7; SATA 54, 106

Hunter, Robert (?)-1734 .... **LC 7**

Hurston, Zora Neale 1903-1960 . **CLC 7, 30, 61;
BLC 2; DA; DAC; DAM MST, MULT, NOV;
SSC 4; WLCS**
See also AAYA 15; BW 1, 3; CA 85-88; CANR
61; CDALBS; DLB 51, 86; MTCW 1, 2

Huston, John (Marcellus) 1906-1987 .... **CLC 20**
See also CA 73-76; 123; CANR 34; DLB 26

Hustvedt, Siri 1955- .... **CLC 76**
See also CA 137

Hutten, Ulrich von 1488-1523 .... **LC 16**
See also DLB 179

Huxley, Aldous (Leonard) 1894-1963**CLC 1, 3, 4,
5, 8, 11, 18, 35, 79; DA; DAB; DAC; DAM
MST, NOV; WLC**
See also AAYA 11; CA 85-88; CANR 44; CDBLB
1914-1945; DLB 36, 100, 162, 195; MTCW
1, 2; SATA 63

Huxley, T(homas) H(enry) 1825-1895 **N C L C
67**
See also DLB 57

Huysmans, Joris-Karl 1848-1907 ... **TCLC 7, 69**
See also CA 104; 165; DLB 123

Hwang, David Henry 1957-**CLC 55; DAM DRAM;
DC 4**
See also CA 127; 132; CANR 76; DLB 212; INT
132; MTCW 2

Hyde, Anthony 1946- .... **CLC 42**
See also CA 136

Hyde, Margaret O(ldroyd) 1917- .... **CLC 21**
See also CA 1-4R; CANR 1, 36; CLR 23; JRDA;
MAICYA; SAAS 8; SATA 1, 42, 76

Hynes, James 1956(?)- .... **CLC 65**
See also CA 164

Ian, Janis 1951- .... **CLC 21**
See also CA 105

Ibanez, Vicente Blasco
See Blasco Ibanez, Vicente

Ibarguengoitia, Jorge 1928-1983 .... **CLC 37**
See also CA 124; 113; HW 1

Ibsen, Henrik (Johan) 1828-1906 **TCLC 2, 8, 16,
37, 52; DA; DAB; DAC; DAM DRAM, MST;
DC 2; WLC**
See also CA 104; 141

Ibuse, Masuji 1898-1993 .... **CLC 22**
See also CA 127; 141; DLB 180

Ichikawa, Kon 1915- .... **CLC 20**
See also CA 121

Idle, Eric 1943- .... **CLC 21**
See also Monty Python
See also CA 116; CANR 35

Ignatow, David 1914-1997 .... **CLC 4, 7, 14, 40**
See also CA 9-12R; 162; CAAS 3; CANR 31, 57;
DLB 5

Ihimaera, Witi 1944- .... **CLC 46**
See also CA 77-80

Ilf, Ilya .... **TCLC 21**
See also Fainzilberg, Ilya Arnoldovich

Illyes, Gyula 1902-1983 .... **PC 16**
See also CA 114; 109

Immermann, Karl (Lebrecht) 1796-1840**NCLC 4,
49**
See also DLB 133

Ince, Thomas H. 1882-1924 .... **TCLC 89**

Inchbald, Elizabeth 1753-1821 .... **NCLC 62**
See also DLB 39, 89

Inclan, Ramon (Maria) del Valle
See Valle-Inclan, Ramon (Maria) del

Infante, G(uillermo) Cabrera
See Cabrera Infante, G(uillermo)

Ingalls, Rachel (Holmes) 1940- .... **CLC 42**
See also CA 123; 127

Ingamells, Reginald Charles
See Ingamells, Rex

Ingamells, Rex 1913-1955 .... **TCLC 35**
See also CA 167

Inge, William (Motter) 1913-1973 **CLC 1, 8, 19;
DAM DRAM**
See also CA 9-12R; CDALB 1941-1968; DLB 7;
MTCW 1, 2

Ingelow, Jean 1820-1897 .... **NCLC 39**
See also DLB 35, 163; SATA 33

Ingram, Willis J.
See Harris, Mark

Innaurato, Albert (F.) 1948(?)- .... **CLC 21, 60**

See also CA 115; 122; CANR 78; INT 122

Innes, Michael
See Stewart, J(ohn) I(nnes) M(ackintosh)

Innis, Harold Adams 1894-1952 .... **TCLC 77**
See also DLB 88

Ionesco, Eugene 1909-1994**CLC 1, 4, 6, 9, 11, 15,
41, 86; DA; DAB; DAC; DAM DRAM, MST;
WLC**
See also CA 9-12R; 144; CANR 55; MTCW 1, 2;
SATA 7; SATA-Obit 79

Iqbal, Muhammad 1873-1938 .... **TCLC 28**

Ireland, Patrick
See O'Doherty, Brian

Iron, Ralph
See Schreiner, Olive (Emilie Albertina)

Irving, John (Winslow) 1942- .. **CLC 13, 23, 38,
. 112; DAM NOV, POP**
See also AAYA 8; BEST 89:3; CA 25-28R; CANR
28, 73; DLB 6; DLBY 82; MTCW 1, 2

Irving, Washington 1783-1859 **NCLC 2, 19; DA;
DAB; DAC; DAM MST; SSC 2; WLC**
See also CDALB 1640-1865; DLB 3, 11, 30, 59, 73,
74, 186; YABC 2

Irwin, P. K.
See Page, P(atricia) K(athleen)

Isaacs, Jorge Ricardo 1837-1895 .... **NCLC 70**

Isaacs, Susan 1943- .... **CLC 32; DAM POP**
See also BEST 89:1; CA 89-92; CANR 20, 41, 65;
INT CANR-20; MTCW 1, 2

Isherwood, Christopher (William Bradshaw) 1904-
1986**CLC 1, 9, 11, 14, 44; DAM DRAM, NOV**
See also CA 13-16R; 117; CANR 35; DLB 15, 195;
DLBY 86; MTCW 1, 2

Ishiguro, Kazuo 1954-**CLC 27, 56, 59, 110; DAM
NOV**
See also BEST 90:2; CA 120; CANR 49; DLB 194;
MTCW 1, 2

Ishikawa, Hakuhin
See Ishikawa, Takuboku

Ishikawa, Takuboku 1886(?)-1912**TCLC 15; DAM
POET; PC 10**
See also CA 113; 153

Iskander, Fazil 1929- .... **CLC 47**
See also CA 102

Isler, Alan (David) 1934- .... **CLC 91**
See also CA 156

Ivan IV 1530-1584 .... **LC 17**

Ivanov, Vyacheslav Ivanovich 1866-1949**TCLC 33**
See also CA 122

Ivask, Ivar Vidrik 1927-1992 .... **CLC 14**
See also CA 37-40R; 139; CANR 24

Ives, Morgan
See Bradley, Marion Zimmer

Izumi Shikibu c. 973-c. 1034 .... **CMLC 33**

J. R. S.
See Gogarty, Oliver St. John

Jabran, Kahlil
See Gibran, Kahlil

Jabran, Khalil
See Gibran, Kahlil

Jackson, Daniel
See Wingrove, David (John)

Jackson, Jesse 1908-1983 .... **CLC 12**
See also BW 1; CA 25-28R; 109; CANR 27; CLR
28; MAICYA; SATA 2, 29; SATA-Obit 48

Jackson, Laura (Riding) 1901-1991
See Riding, Laura
See also CA 65-68; 135; CANR 28; DLB 48

Jackson, Sam
See Trumbo, Dalton

Jackson, Sara
See Wingrove, David (John)

Jackson, Shirley 1919-1965**CLC 11, 60, 87; DA;
DAC; DAM MST; SSC 9; WLC**
See also AAYA 9; CA 1-4R; 25-28R; CANR 4,
52; CDALB 1941-1968; DLB 6; MTCW 2;
SATA 2

See also CA 97-100; CAAS 22; CANR 19, 43
Kelman, James 1946- .... **CLC 58, 86**
See also CA 148; DLB 194
Kemal, Yashar 1923- .... **CLC 14, 29**
See also CA 89-92; CANR 44
Kemble, Fanny 1809-1893 .... **NCLC 18**
See also DLB 32
Kemelman, Harry 1908-1996 .... **CLC 2**
See also AITN 1; CA 9-12R; 155; CANR 6, 71; DLB 28
Kempe, Margery 1373(?)-1440(?) .... **LC 6**
See also DLB 146
Kempis, Thomas a 1380-1471 .... **LC 11**
Kendall, Henry 1839-1882 .... **NCLC 12**
Keneally, Thomas (Michael) 1935- **CLC 5, 8, 10, 14, 19, 27, 43, 117; DAM NOV**
See also CA 85-88; CANR 10, 50, 74; MTCW 1, 2
Kennedy, Adrienne (Lita) 1931- **CLC 66; BLC 2; DAM MULT; DC 5**
See also BW 2, 3; CA 103; CAAS 20; CABS 3; CANR 26, 53; DLB 38
Kennedy, John Pendleton 1795-1870 ..... **NCLC 2**
See also DLB 3
Kennedy, Joseph Charles 1929-
See Kennedy, X. J.
See also CA 1-4R; CANR 4, 30, 40; SATA 14, 86
Kennedy, William 1928- **CLC 6, 28, 34, 53; DAM NOV**
See also AAYA 1; CA 85-88; CANR 14, 31, 76; DLB 143; DLBY 85; INT CANR-31; MTCW 1, 2; SATA 57
Kennedy, X. J. .... **CLC 8, 42**
See also Kennedy, Joseph Charles
See also CAAS 9; CLR 27; DLB 5; SAAS 22
Kenny, Maurice (Francis) 1929- . **CLC 87; DAM MULT**
See also CA 144; CAAS 22; DLB 175; NNAL
Kent, Kelvin
See Kuttner, Henry
Kenton, Maxwell
See Southern, Terry
Kenyon, Robert O.
See Kuttner, Henry
Kepler, Johannes 1571-1630 .... **LC 45**
Kerouac, Jack .... **CLC 1, 2, 3, 5, 14, 29, 61**
See also Kerouac, Jean-Louis Lebris de
See also AAYA 25; CDALB 1941-1968; DLB 2, 16; DLBD 3; DLBY 95; MTCW 2
Kerouac, Jean-Louis Lebris de 1922-1969
See Kerouac, Jack
See also AITN 1; CA 5-8R; 25-28R; CANR 26, 54; DA; DAB; DAC; DAM MST, NOV, POET, POP; MTCW 1, 2; WLC
Kerr, Jean 1923- .... **CLC 22**
See also CA 5-8R; CANR 7; INT CANR-7
Kerr, M. E. .... **CLC 12, 35**
See also Meaker, Marijane (Agnes)
See also AAYA 2, 23; CLR 29; SAAS 1
Kerr, Robert .... **CLC 55**
Kerrigan, (Thomas) Anthony 1918- .... **CLC 4, 6**
See also CA 49-52; CAAS 11; CANR 4
Kerry, Lois
See Duncan, Lois
Kesey, Ken (Elton) 1935- **CLC 1, 3, 6, 11, 46, 64; DA; DAB; DAC; DAM MST, NOV, POP; WLC**
See also AAYA 25; CA 1-4R; CANR 22, 38, 66; CDALB 1968-1988; DLB 2, 16, 206; MTCW 1, 2; SATA 66
Kesselring, Joseph (Otto) 1902-1967 .. **CLC 45; DAM DRAM, MST**
See also CA 150
Kessler, Jascha (Frederick) 1929- ,........ **CLC 4**
See also CA 17-20R; CANR 8, 48
Kettelkamp, Larry (Dale) 1933- .... **CLC 12**
See also CA 29-32R; CANR 16; SAAS 3; SATA 2
Key, Ellen 1849-1926 .... **TCLC 65**

Keyber, Conny
See Fielding, Henry
Keyes, Daniel 1927- .. **CLC 80; DA; DAC; DAM MST, NOV**
See also AAYA 23; CA 17-20R; CANR 10, 26, 54, 74; MTCW 2; SATA 37
Keynes, John Maynard 1883-1946 ...... **TCLC 64**
See also CA 114; 162, 163; DLBD 10; MTCW 2
Khanshendel, Chiron
See Rose, Wendy
Khayyam, Omar 1048-1131 **CMLC 11; DAM POET; PC 8**
Kherdian, David 1931- .... **CLC 6, 9**
See also CA 21-24R; CAAS 2; CANR 39, 78; CLR 24; JRDA; MAICYA; SATA 16, 74
Khlebnikov, Velimir .... **TCLC 20**
See also Khlebnikov, Viktor Vladimirovich
Khlebnikov, Viktor Vladimirovich 1885-1922
See Khlebnikov, Velimir
See also CA 117
Khodasevich, Vladislav (Felitsianovich) 1886-1939 **TCLC 15**
See also CA 115
Kielland, Alexander Lange 1849-1906 .. **TCLC 5**
See also CA 104
Kiely, Benedict 1919- .... **CLC 23, 43**
See also CA 1-4R; CANR 2; DLB 15
Kienzle, William X(avier) 1928- . **CLC 25; DAM POP**
See also CA 93-96; CAAS 1; CANR 9, 31, 59; INT CANR-31; MTCW 1, 2
Kierkegaard, Soren 1813-1855 ..... **NCLC 34, 78**
Kieslowski, Krzysztof 1941-1996 .... **CLC 120**
See also CA 147; 151
Killens, John Oliver 1916-1987 .... **CLC 10**
See also BW 2; CA 77-80; 123; CAAS 2; CANR 26; DLB 33
Killigrew, Anne 1660-1685 .... **LC 4**
See also DLB 131
Kim
See Simenon, Georges (Jacques Christian)
Kincaid, Jamaica 1949- **CLC 43, 68; BLC 2; DAM MULT, NOV**
See also AAYA 13; BW 2, 3; CA 125; CANR 47, 59; CDALBS; DLB 157; MTCW 2
King, Francis (Henry) 1923- .. **CLC 8, 53; DAM NOV**
See also CA 1-4R; CANR 1, 33; DLB 15, 139; MTCW 1
King, Kennedy
See Brown, George Douglas
King, Martin Luther, Jr. 1929-1968 **CLC 83; BLC 2; DA; DAB; DAC; DAM MST, MULT; WLCS**
See also BW 2, 3; CA 25-28; CANR 27, 44; CAP 2; MTCW 1, 2; SATA 14
King, Stephen (Edwin) 1947- **CLC 12, 26, 37, 61, 113; DAM NOV, POP; SSC 17**
See also AAYA 1, 17; BEST 90:1; CA 61-64; CANR 1, 30, 52, 76; DLB 143; DLBY 80; JRDA; MTCW 1, 2; SATA 9, 55
King, Steve
See King, Stephen (Edwin)
King, Thomas 1943- **CLC 89; DAC; DAM MULT**
See also CA 144; DLB 175; NNAL; SATA 96
Kingman, Lee .... **CLC 17**
See also Natti, (Mary) Lee
See also SAAS 3; SATA 1, 67
Kingsley, Charles 1819-1875 .... **NCLC 35**
See also DLB 21, 32, 163, 190; YABC 2
Kingsley, Sidney 1906-1995 .... **CLC 44**
See also CA 85-88; 147; DLB 7
Kingsolver, Barbara 1955- **CLC 55, 81; DAM POP**
See also AAYA 15; CA 129; 134; CANR 60; CDALBS; DLB 206; INT 134; MTCW 2
Kingston, Maxine (Ting Ting) Hong 1940- **C L C 12, 19, 58, 121; DAM MULT, NOV; WLCS**

See also AAYA 8; CA 69-72; CANR 13, 38, 74; CDALBS; DLB 173, 212; DLBY 80; INT CANR-13; MTCW 1, 2; SATA 53
Kinnell, Galway 1927- **CLC 1, 2, 3, 5, 13, 29; PC 26**
See also CA 9-12R; CANR 10, 34, 66; DLB 5; DLBY 87; INT CANR-34; MTCW 1, 2
Kinsella, Thomas 1928- .... **CLC 4, 19**
See also CA 17-20R; CANR 15; DLB 27; MTCW 1, 2
Kinsella, W(illiam) P(atrick) 1935- . **CLC 27, 43; DAC; DAM NOV, POP**
See also AAYA 7; CA 97-100; CAAS 7; CANR 21, 35, 66, 75; INT CANR-21; MTCW 1, 2
Kinsey, Alfred C(harles) 1894-1956 ... **TCLC 91**
See also CA 115; 170; MTCW 2
Kipling, (Joseph) Rudyard 1865-1936 **TCLC 8, 17; DA; DAB; DAC; DAM MST, POET; PC 3; SSC 5; WLC**
See also CA 105; 120; CANR 33; CDBLB 1890-1914; CLR 39; DLB 19, 34, 141, 156; MAICYA; MTCW 1, 2; SATA 100; YABC 2
Kirkup, James 1918- .... **CLC 1**
See also CA 1-4R; CAAS 4; CANR 2; DLB 27; SATA 12
Kirkwood, James 1930(?)-1989 .... **CLC 9**
See also AITN 2; CA 1-4R; 128; CANR 6, 40
Kirshner, Sidney
See Kingsley, Sidney
Kis, Danilo 1935-1989 .... **CLC 57**
See also CA 109; 118; 129; CANR 61; DLB 181; MTCW 1
Kivi, Aleksis 1834-1872 .... **NCLC 30**
Kizer, Carolyn (Ashley) 1925- . **CLC 15, 39, 80; DAM POET**
See also CA 65-68; CAAS 5; CANR 24, 70; DLB 5, 169; MTCW 2
Klabund 1890-1928 .... **TCLC 44**
See also CA 162; DLB 66
Klappert, Peter 1942- .... **CLC 57**
See also CA 33-36R; DLB 5
Klein, A(braham) M(oses) 1909-1972 .. **CLC 19; DAB; DAC; DAM MST**
See also CA 101; 37-40R; DLB 68
Klein, Norma 1938-1989 .... **CLC 30**
See also AAYA 2; CA 41-44R; 128; CANR 15, 37; CLR 2, 19; INT CANR-15; JRDA; MAICYA; SAAS 1; SATA 7, 57
Klein, T(heodore) E(ibon) D(onald) 1947- **CLC 34**
See also CA 119; CANR 44, 75
Kleist, Heinrich von 1777-1811 **NCLC 2, 37; DAM DRAM; SSC 22**
See also DLB 90
Klima, Ivan 1931- .... **CLC 56; DAM NOV**
See also CA 25-28R; CANR 17, 50
Klimentov, Andrei Platonovich 1899-1951
See Platonov, Andrei
See also CA 108
Klinger, Friedrich Maximilian von 1752-1831 **NCLC 1**
See also DLB 94
Klingsor the Magician
See Hartmann, Sadakichi
Klopstock, Friedrich Gottlieb 1724-1803 **NCLC 11**
See also DLB 97
Knapp, Caroline 1959- .... **CLC 99**
See also CA 154
Knebel, Fletcher 1911-1993 .... **CLC 14**
See also AITN 1; CA 1-4R; 140; CAAS 3; CANR 1, 36; SATA 36; SATA-Obit 75
Knickerbocker, Diedrich
See Irving, Washington
Knight, Etheridge 1931-1991 ... **CLC 40; BLC 2; DAM POET; PC 14**
See also BW 1, 3; CA 21-24R; 133; CANR 23; DLB 41; MTCW 2
Knight, Sarah Kemble 1666-1727 .... **LC 7**

See also CA 73-76; 29-32R

Lieber, Stanley Martin
See Lee, Stan

Lieberman, Laurence (James) 1935- **CLC 4, 36**
See also CA 17-20R; CANR 8, 36

Lieh Tzu fl. 7th cent. B.C.-5th cent. B.C.**CMLC 27**

Lieksman, Anders
See Haavikko, Paavo Juhani

Li Fei-kan 1904-
See Pa Chin
See also CA 105

Lifton, Robert Jay 1926- .... **CLC 67**
See also CA 17-20R; CANR 27, 78; INT
CANR-27; SATA 66

Lightfoot, Gordon 1938- .... **CLC 26**
See also CA 109

Lightman, Alan P(aige) 1948- .... **CLC 81**
See also CA 141; CANR 63

Ligotti, Thomas (Robert) 1953-**CLC 44; SSC 16**
See also CA 123; CANR 49

Li Ho 791-817 .... **PC 13**

Liliencron, (Friedrich Adolf Axel) Detlev von 1844-
1909 .... **TCLC 18**
See also CA 117

Lilly, William 1602-1681 .... **LC 27**

Lima, Jose Lezama
See Lezama Lima, Jose

Lima Barreto, Afonso Henrique de 1881-1922
TCLC 23
See also CA 117

Limonov, Edward 1944- .... **CLC 67**
See also CA 137

Lin, Frank
See Atherton, Gertrude (Franklin Horn)

Lincoln, Abraham 1809-1865 .... **NCLC 18**

Lind, Jakov .... **CLC 1, 2, 4, 27, 82**
See also Landwirth, Heinz
See also CAAS 4

Lindbergh, Anne (Spencer) Morrow 1906- **C L C
82; DAM NOV**
See also CA 17-20R; CANR 16, 73; MTCW 1, 2;
SATA 33

Lindsay, David 1878-1945 .... **TCLC 15**
See also CA 113

Lindsay, (Nicholas) Vachel 1879-1931 **TCLC 17;
DA; DAC; DAM MST, POET; PC 23; WLC**
See also CA 114; 135; CANR 79; CDALB 1865-
1917; DLB 54; SATA 40

Linke-Poot
See Doeblin, Alfred

Linney, Romulus 1930- .... **CLC 51**
See also CA 1-4R; CANR 40, 44, 79

Linton, Eliza Lynn 1822-1898 .... **NCLC 41**
See also DLB 18

Li Po 701-763 .... **CMLC 2**

Lipsius, Justus 1547-1606 .... **LC 16**

Lipsyte, Robert (Michael) 1938- ... **CLC 21; DA;
DAC; DAM MST, NOV**
See also AAYA 7; CA 17-20R; CANR 8, 57; CLR
23; JRDA; MAICYA; SATA 5, 68

Lish, Gordon (Jay) 1934- .... **CLC 45; SSC 18**
See also CA 113; 117; CANR 79; DLB 130; INT
117

Lispector, Clarice 1925(?)-1977**CLC 43; HLCS 2;
SSC 34**
See also CA 139; 116; CANR 71; DLB 113; HW 2

Littell, Robert 1935(?)- .... **CLC 42**
See also CA 109; 112; CANR 64

Little, Malcolm 1925-1965
See Malcolm X
See also BW 1, 3; CA 125; 111; DA; DAB; DAC;
DAM MST, MULT; MTCW 1, 2

Littlewit, Humphrey Gent.
See Lovecraft, H(oward) P(hillips)

Litwos
See Sienkiewicz, Henryk (Adam Alexander Pius)

Liu, E 1857-1909 .... **TCLC 15**

See also CA 115

Lively, Penelope (Margaret) 1933- **CLC 32, 50;
DAM NOV**
See also CA 41-44R; CANR 29, 67, 79; CLR 7;
DLB 14, 161, 207; JRDA; MAICYA; MTCW
1, 2; SATA 7, 60, 101

Livesay, Dorothy (Kathleen) 1909-**CLC 4, 15, 79;
DAC; DAM MST, POET**
See also AITN 2; CA 25-28R; CAAS 8; CANR
36, 67; DLB 68; MTCW 1

Livy c. 59B.C.-c. 17 .... **CMLC 11**
See also DLB 211

Lizardi, Jose Joaquin Fernandez de 1776-1827
NCLC 30

Llewellyn, Richard
See Llewellyn Lloyd, Richard Dafydd Vivian
See also DLB 15

Llewellyn Lloyd, Richard Dafydd Vivian 1906-1983
CLC 7, 80
See also Llewellyn, Richard
See also CA 53-56; 111; CANR 7, 71; SATA 11;
SATA-Obit 37

Llosa, (Jorge) Mario (Pedro) Vargas
See Vargas Llosa, (Jorge) Mario (Pedro)

Lloyd, Manda
See Mander, (Mary) Jane

Lloyd Webber, Andrew 1948-
See Webber, Andrew Lloyd
See also AAYA 1; CA 116; 149; DAM DRAM;
SATA 56

Llull, Ramon c. 1235-c. 1316 .... **CMLC 12**

Lobb, Ebenezer
See Upward, Allen

Locke, Alain (Le Roy) 1886-1954**TCLC 43; BLCS**
See also BW 1, 3; CA 106; 124; CANR 79; DLB
51

Locke, John 1632-1704 .... **LC 7, 35**
See also DLB 101

Locke-Elliott, Sumner
See Elliott, Sumner Locke

Lockhart, John Gibson 1794-1854 .... **NCLC 6**
See also DLB 110, 116, 144

Lodge, David (John) 1935- .. **CLC 36; DAM POP**
See also BEST 90:1; CA 17-20R; CANR 19, 53;
DLB 14, 194; INT CANR-19; MTCW 1, 2

Lodge, Thomas 1558-1625 .... **LC 41**

Lodge, Thomas 1558-1625 .... **LC 41**
See also DLB 172

Loennbohm, Armas Eino Leopold 1878-1926
See Leino, Eino
See also CA 123

Loewinsohn, Ron(ald William) 1937- ... **CLC 52**
See also CA 25-28R; CANR 71

Logan, Jake
See Smith, Martin Cruz

Logan, John (Burton) 1923-1987 .... **CLC 5**
See also CA 77-80; 124; CANR 45; DLB 5

Lo Kuan-chung 1330(?)-1400(?) .... **LC 12**

Lombard, Nap
See Johnson, Pamela Hansford

London, Jack ...... **TCLC 9, 15, 39; SSC 4; WLC**
See also London, John Griffith
See also AAYA 13; AITN 2; CDALB 1865-1917;
DLB 8, 12, 78, 212; SATA 18

London, John Griffith 1876-1916
See London, Jack
See also CA 110; 119; CANR 73; DA; DAB;
DAC; DAM MST, NOV; JRDA; MAICYA;
MTCW 1, 2

Long, Emmett
See Leonard, Elmore (John, Jr.)

Longbaugh, Harry
See Goldman, William (W.)

Longfellow, Henry Wadsworth 1807-1882 **N C L C
2, 45; DA; DAB; DAC; DAM MST, POET;
WLCS**
See also CDALB 1640-1865; DLB 1, 59; SATA 19

Longinus c. 1st cent. - .... **CMLC 27**
See also DLB 176

Longley, Michael 1939- ......,............ **CLC 29**
See also CA 102; DLB 40

Longus fl. c. 2nd cent. - .... **CMLC 7**

Longway, A. Hugh
See Lang, Andrew

Lonnrot, Elias 1802-1884 .... **NCLC 53**

Lopate, Phillip 1943- .... **CLC 29**
See also CA 97-100; DLBY 80; INT 97-100

Lopez Portillo (y Pacheco), Jose 1920-. **C L C
46**
See also CA 129; HW 1

Lopez y Fuentes, Gregorio 1897(?)-1966**CLC 32**
See also CA 131; HW 1

Lorca, Federico Garcia
See Garcia Lorca, Federico

Lord, Bette Bao 1938- .... **CLC 23**
See also BEST 90:3; CA 107; CANR 41, 79; INT
107; SATA 58

Lord Auch
See Bataille, Georges

Lord Byron
See Byron, George Gordon (Noel)

Lorde, Audre (Geraldine) 1934-1992**CLC 18, 71;
BLC 2; DAM MULT; POET; PC 12**
See also BW 1, 3; CA 25-28R; 142; CANR 16, 26,
46; DLB 41; MTCW 1, 2

Lord Houghton
See Milnes, Richard Monckton

Lord Jeffrey
See Jeffrey, Francis

Lorenzini, Carlo 1826-1890
See Collodi, Carlo
See also MAICYA; SATA 29, 100

Lorenzo, Heberto Padilla
See Padilla (Lorenzo), Heberto

Loris
See Hofmannsthal, Hugo von

Loti, Pierre .... **TCLC 11**
See also Viaud, (Louis Marie) Julien
See also DLB 123

Louie, David Wong 1954- .... **CLC 70**
See also CA 139

Louis, Father M.
See Merton, Thomas

Lovecraft, H(oward) P(hillips) 1890-1937**TCLC 4,
22; DAM POP; SSC 3**
See also AAYA 14; CA 104; 133; MTCW 1, 2

Lovelace, Earl 1935- .... **CLC 51**
See also BW 2; CA 77-80; CANR 41, 72; DLB
125; MTCW 1

Lovelace, Richard 1618-1657 .... **LC 24**
See also DLB 131

Lowell, Amy 1874-1925 **TCLC 1, 8; DAM POET;
PC 13**
See also CA 104; 151; DLB 54, 140; MTCW 2

Lowell, James Russell 1819-1891 .... **NCLC 2**
See also CDALB 1640-1865; DLB 1, 11, 64, 79,
189

Lowell, Robert (Traill Spence, Jr.) 1917-1977
**CLC 1, 2, 3, 4, 5, 8, 9, 11, 15, 37; DA; DAB;
DAC; DAM MST, NOV; PC 3; WLC**
See also CA 9-12R; 73-76; CABS 2; CANR 26,
60; CDALBS; DLB 5, 169; MTCW 1, 2

Lowenthal, Michael (Francis) 1969- .... **CLC 119**
See also CA 150

Lowndes, Marie Adelaide (Belloc) 1868-1947
TCLC 12
See also CA 107; DLB 70

Lowry, (Clarence) Malcolm 1909-1957 **TCLC 6,
40; SSC 31**
See also CA 105; 131; CANR 62; CDBLB 1945-
1960; DLB 15; MTCW 1, 2

Lowry, Mina Gertrude 1882-1966
See Loy, Mina
See also CA 113

Martines, Julia
See O'Faolain, Julia
Martinez, Enrique Gonzalez
See Gonzalez Martinez, Enrique
Martinez, Jacinto Benavente y
See Benavente (y Martinez), Jacinto
Martinez Ruiz, Jose 1873-1967
See Azorin; Ruiz, Jose Martinez
See also CA 93-96; HW 1
Martinez Sierra, Gregorio 1881-1947 .. **TCLC 6**
See also CA 115
Martinez Sierra, Maria (de la O'LeJarraga) 1874-
1974 .... **TCLC 6**
See also CA 115
Martinsen, Martin
See Follett, Ken(neth Martin)
Martinson, Harry (Edmund) 1904-1978 **CLC 14**
See also CA 77-80; CANR 34
Marut, Ret
See Traven, B.
Marut, Robert
See Traven, B.
Marvell, Andrew 1621-1678 **LC 4, 43; DA; DAB;**
DAC; DAM MST, POET; PC 10; WLC
See also CDBLB 1660-1789; DLB 131
Marx, Karl (Heinrich) 1818-1883 .... **NCLC 17**
See also DLB 129
Masaoka Shiki .... **TCLC 18**
See also Masaoka Tsunenori
Masaoka Tsunenori 1867-1902
See Masaoka Shiki
See also CA 117
Masefield, John (Edward) 1878-1967 **CLC 11, 47;**
DAM POET
See also CA 19-20; 25-28R; CANR 33; CAP 2;
CDBLB 1890-1914; DLB 10, 19, 153, 160;
MTCW 1, 2; SATA 19
Maso, Carole 19(?)- .... **CLC 44**
See also CA 170
Mason, Bobbie Ann 1940-**CLC 28, 43, 82; SSC 4**
See also AAYA 5; CA 53-56; CANR 11, 31, 58;
CDALBS; DLB 173; DLBY 87; INT CANR-31;
MTCW 1, 2
Mason, Ernst
See Pohl, Frederik
Mason, Lee W.
See Malzberg, Barry N(athaniel)
Mason, Nick 1945- .... **CLC 35**
Mason, Tally
See Derleth, August (William)
Mass, William
See Gibson, William
Master Lao
See Lao Tzu
Masters, Edgar Lee 1868-1950 **TCLC 2, 25; DA;**
DAC; DAM MST, POET; PC 1; WLCS
See also CA 104; 133; CDALB 1865-1917; DLB
54; MTCW 1, 2
Masters, Hilary 1928- .... **CLC 48**
See also CA 25-28R; CANR 13, 47
Mastrosimone, William 19(?)- .... **CLC 36**
Mathe, Albert
See Camus, Albert
Mather, Cotton 1663-1728 .... **LC 38**
See also CDALB 1640-1865; DLB 24, 30, 140
Mather, Increase 1639-1723 .... **LC 38**
See also DLB 24
Matheson, Richard Burton 1926- .... **CLC 37**
See also CA 97-100; DLB 8, 44; INT 97-100
Mathews, Harry 1930- .... **CLC 6, 52**
See also CA 21-24R; CAAS 6; CANR 18, 40
Mathews, John Joseph 1894-1979 **CLC 84; DAM**
MULT
See also CA 19-20; 142; CANR 45; CAP 2; DLB
175; NNAL
Mathias, Roland (Glyn) 1915- .... **CLC 45**
See also CA 97-100; CANR 19, 41; DLB 27

Matsuo Basho 1644-1694 .... **PC 3**
See also DAM POET
Mattheson, Rodney
See Creasey, John
Matthews, Brander 1852-1929 .... **TCLC 95**
See also DLB 71, 78; DLBD 13
Matthews, Greg 1949- .... **CLC 45**
See also CA 135
Matthews, William (Procter, III) 1942-1997 **C L C**
40
See also CA 29-32R; 162; CAAS 18; CANR 12,
57; DLB 5
Matthias, John (Edward) 1941- .... **CLC 9**
See also CA 33-36R; CANR 56
Matthiessen, Peter 1927-**CLC 5, 7, 11, 32, 64;**
DAM NOV
See also AAYA 6; BEST 90:4; CA 9-12R; CANR
21, 50, 73; DLB 6, 173; MTCW 1, 2; SATA 27
Maturin, Charles Robert 1780(?)-1824 **NCLC 6**
See also DLB 178
Matute (Ausejo), Ana Maria 1925- .... **CLC 11**
See also CA 89-92; MTCW 1
Maugham, W. S.
See Maugham, W(illiam) Somerset
Maugham, W(illiam) Somerset 1874-1965**CLC 1,**
11, 15, 67, 93; DA; DAB; DAC; DAM DRAM,
MST, NOV; SSC 8; WLC
See also CA 5-8R; 25-28R; CANR 40; CDBLB
1914-1945; DLB 10, 36, 77, 100, 162, 195;
MTCW 1, 2; SATA 54
Maugham, William Somerset
See Maugham, W(illiam) Somerset
Maupassant, (Henri Rene Albert) Guy de 1850-
1893 .. **NCLC 1, 42; DA; DAB; DAC; DAM**
MST; SSC 1; WLC
See also DLB 123
Maupin, Armistead 1944- ... **CLC 95; DAM POP**
See also CA 125; 130; CANR 58; INT 130; MTCW
2
Maurhut, Richard
See Traven, B.
Mauriac, Claude 1914-1996 .... **CLC 9**
See also CA 89-92; 152; DLB 83
Mauriac, Francois (Charles) 1885-1970**CLC 4, 9,**
56; SSC 24
See also CA 25-28; CAP 2; DLB 65; MTCW 1, 2
Mavor, Osborne Henry 1888-1951
See Bridie, James
See also CA 104
Maxwell, William (Keepers, Jr.) 1908- **CLC 19**
See also CA 93-96; CANR 54; DLBY 80; INT 93-
96
May, Elaine 1932- .... **CLC 16**
See also CA 124; 142; DLB 44
Mayakovski, Vladimir (Vladimirovich) 1893-1930
TCLC 4, 18
See also CA 104; 158; MTCW 2
Mayhew, Henry 1812-1887 .... **NCLC 31**
See also DLB 18, 55, 190
Mayle, Peter 1939(?)- .... **CLC 89**
See also CA 139; CANR 64
Maynard, Joyce 1953- .... **CLC 23**
See also CA 111; 129; CANR 64
Mayne, William (James Carter) 1928- **CLC 12**
See also AAYA 20; CA 9-12R; CANR 37, 80; CLR
25; JRDA; MAICYA; SAAS 11; SATA 6, 68
Mayo, Jim
See L'Amour, Louis (Dearborn)
Maysles, Albert 1926- .... **CLC 16**
See also CA 29-32R
Maysles, David 1932- .... **CLC 16**
Mazer, Norma Fox 1931- .... **CLC 26**
See also AAYA 5; CA 69-72; CANR 12, 32, 66;
CLR 23; JRDA; MAICYA; SAAS 1; SATA 24,
67, 105
Mazzini, Guiseppe 1805-1872 .... **NCLC 34**
McAuley, James Phillip 1917-1976 .... **CLC 45**

See also CA 97-100
McBain, Ed
See Hunter, Evan
McBrien, William Augustine 1930- ..... **CLC 44**
See also CA 107
McCaffrey, Anne (Inez) 1926- ..... **CLC 17; DAM**
NOV, POP
See also AAYA 6; AITN 2; BEST 89:2; CA 25-
28R; CANR 15, 35, 55; CLR 49; DLB 8; JRDA;
MAICYA; MTCW 1, 2; SAAS 11; SATA 8, 70
McCall, Nathan 1955(?)- .... **CLC 86**
See also BW 3; CA 146
McCann, Arthur
See Campbell, John W(ood, Jr.)
McCann, Edson
See Pohl, Frederik
McCarthy, Charles, Jr. 1933-
See McCarthy, Cormac
See also CANR 42, 69; DAM POP; MTCW 2
McCarthy, Cormac 1933- .... **CLC 4, 57, 59, 101**
See also McCarthy, Charles, Jr.
See also DLB 6, 143; MTCW 2
McCarthy, Mary (Therese) 1912-1989**CLC 1, 3, 5,**
14, 24, 39, 59; SSC 24
See also CA 5-8R; 129; CANR 16, 50, 64; DLB 2;
DLBY 81; INT CANR-16; MTCW 1, 2
McCartney, (James) Paul 1942- ..... **CLC 12, 35**
See also CA 146
McCauley, Stephen (D.) 1955- .... **CLC 50**
See also CA 141
McClure, Michael (Thomas) 1932- ... **CLC 6, 10**
See also CA 21-24R; CANR 17, 46, 77; DLB 16
McCorkle, Jill (Collins) 1958- .... **CLC 51**
See also CA 121; DLBY 87
McCourt, Frank 1930- .... **CLC 109**
See also CA 157
McCourt, James 1941- .... **CLC 5**
See also CA 57-60
McCourt, Malachy 1932- .... **CLC 119**
McCoy, Horace (Stanley) 1897-1955 ... **TCLC 28**
See also CA 108; 155; DLB 9
McCrae, John 1872-1918 .... **TCLC 12**
See also CA 109; DLB 92
McCreigh, James
See Pohl, Frederik
McCullers, (Lula) Carson (Smith) 1917-1967
CLC 1, 4, 10, 12, 48, 100; DA; DAB; DAC;
DAM MST, NOV; SSC 9, 24; WLC
See also AAYA 21; CA 5-8R; 25-28R; CABS 1, 3;
CANR 18; CDALB 1941-1968; DLB 2, 7, 173;
MTCW 1, 2; SATA 27
McCulloch, John Tyler
See Burroughs, Edgar Rice
McCullough, Colleen 1938(?)-**CLC 27, 107; DAM**
NOV, POP
See also CA 81-84; CANR 17, 46, 67; MTCW 1, 2
McDermott, Alice 1953- .... **CLC 90**
See also CA 109; CANR 40
McElroy, Joseph 1930- .... **CLC 5, 47**
See also CA 17-20R
McEwan, Ian (Russell) 1948- **CLC 13, 66; DAM**
NOV
See also BEST 90:4; CA 61-64; CANR 14, 41, 69;
DLB 14, 194; MTCW 1, 2
McFadden, David 1940- .... **CLC 48**
See also CA 104; DLB 60; INT 104
McFarland, Dennis 1950- .... **CLC 65**
See also CA 165
McGahern, John 1934- .... **CLC 5, 9, 48; SSC 17**
See also CA 17-20R; CANR 29, 68; DLB 14;
MTCW 1
McGinley, Patrick (Anthony) 1937- ..... **CLC 41**
See also CA 120; 127; CANR 56; INT 127
McGinley, Phyllis 1905-1978 .... **CLC 14**
See also CA 9-12R; 77-80; CANR 19; DLB 11, 48;
SATA 2, 44; SATA-Obit 24
McGinniss, Joe 1942- .... **CLC 32**

WLCS
See also CA 104; 130; CDALB 1917-1929; DLB 45; MTCW 1, 2
Miller, Arthur 1915-CLC 1, 2, 6, 10, 15, 26, 47, 78; DA; DAB; DAC; DAM DRAM, MST; DC 1; WLC
See also AAYA 15; AITN 1; CA 1-4R; CABS 3; CANR 2, 30, 54, 76; CDALB 1941-1968; DLB 7; MTCW 1, 2
Miller, Henry (Valentine) 1891-1980CLC 1, 2, 4, 9, 14, 43, 84; DA; DAB; DAC; DAM MST, NOV; WLC
See also CA 9-12R; 97-100; CANR 33, 64; CDALB 1929-1941; DLB 4, 9; DLBY 80; MTCW 1, 2
Miller, Jason 1939(?)- .... CLC 2
See also AITN 1; CA 73-76; DLB 7
Miller, Sue 1943- .... CLC 44; DAM POP
See also BEST 90:3; CA 139; CANR 59; DLB 143
Miller, Walter M(ichael, Jr.) 1923-CLC 4, 30
See also CA 85-88; DLB 8
Millett, Kate 1934- .... CLC 67
See also AITN 1; CA 73-76; CANR 32, 53, 76; MTCW 1, 2
Millhauser, Steven (Lewis) 1943-CLC 21, 54, 109
See also CA 110; 111; CANR 63; DLB 2; INT 111; MTCW 2
Millin, Sarah Gertrude 1889-1968 .... CLC 49
See also CA 102; 93-96
Milne, A(lan) A(lexander) 1882-1956TCLC 6, 88; DAB; DAC; DAM MST
See also CA 104; 133; CLR 1, 26; DLB 10, 77, 100, 160; MAICYA; MTCW 1, 2; SATA 100; YABC 1
Milner, Ron(ald) 1938- .. CLC 56; BLC 3; DAM MULT
See also AITN 1; BW 1; CA 73-76; CANR 24, 81; DLB 38; MTCW 1
Milnes, Richard Monckton 1809-1885 NCLC 61
See also DLB 32, 184
Milosz, Czeslaw 1911-CLC 5, 11, 22, 31, 56, 82; DAM MST, POET; PC 8; WLCS
See also CA 81-84; CANR 23, 51; MTCW 1, 2
Milton, John 1608-1674LC 9, 43; DA; DAB; DAC; DAM MST, POET; PC 19; WLC
See also CDBLB 1660-1789; DLB 131, 151
Min, Anchee 1957- .... CLC 86
See also CA 146
Minehaha, Cornelius
See Wedekind, (Benjamin) Frank(lin)
Miner, Valerie 1947- .... CLC 40
See also CA 97-100; CANR 59
Minimo, Duca
See D'Annunzio, Gabriele
Minot, Susan 1956- .... CLC 44
See also CA 134
Minus, Ed 1938- .... CLC 39
Miranda, Javier
See Bioy Casares, Adolfo
Miranda, Javier
See Bioy Casares, Adolfo
Mirbeau, Octave 1848-1917 .... TCLC 55
See also DLB 123, 192
Miro (Ferrer), Gabriel (Francisco Victor) 1879-1930 .... TCLC 5
See also CA 104
Mishima, Yukio 1925-1970CLC 2, 4, 6, 9, 27; DC 1; SSC 4
See Hiraoka, Kimitake
See also DLB 182; MTCW 2
Mistral, Frederic 1830-1914 .... TCLC 51
See also CA 122
Mistral, Gabriela .... TCLC 2; HLC
See also Godoy Alcayaga, Lucila
See also MTCW 2
Mistry, Rohinton 1952- .... CLC 71; DAC
See also CA 141

Mitchell, Clyde
See Ellison, Harlan (Jay); Silverberg, Robert
Mitchell, James Leslie 1901-1935
See Gibbon, Lewis Grassic
See also CA 104; DLB 15
Mitchell, Joni 1943- .... CLC 12
See also CA 112
Mitchell, Joseph (Quincy) 1908-1996 ... CLC 98
See also CA 77-80; 152; CANR 69; DLB 185; DLBY 96
Mitchell, Margaret (Munnerlyn) 1900-1949 TCLC 11; DAM NOV, POP
See also AAYA 23; CA 109; 125; CANR 55; CDALBS; DLB 9; MTCW 1, 2
Mitchell, Peggy
See Mitchell, Margaret (Munnerlyn)
Mitchell, S(ilas) Weir 1829-1914 ... TCLC 36
See also CA 165; DLB 202
Mitchell, W(illiam) O(rmond) 1914-1998CLC 25; DAC; DAM MST
See also CA 77-80; 165; CANR 15, 43; DLB 88
Mitchell, William 1879-1936 .... TCLC 81
Mitford, Mary Russell 1787-1855 .... NCLC 4
See also DLB 110, 116
Mitford, Nancy 1904-1973 .... CLC 44
See also CA 9-12R; DLB 191
Miyamoto, (Chujo) Yuriko 1899-1951 . TCLC 37
See also CA 170, 174; DLB 180
Miyazawa, Kenji 1896-1933 .... TCLC 76
See also CA 157
Mizoguchi, Kenji 1898-1956 .... TCLC 72
See also CA 167
Mo, Timothy (Peter) 1950(?)- .... CLC 46
See also CA 117; DLB 194; MTCW 1
Modarressi, Taghi (M.) 1931- .... CLC 44
See also CA 121; 134; INT 134
Modiano, Patrick (Jean) 1945- .... CLC 18
See also CA 85-88; CANR 17, 40; DLB 83
Moerck, Paal
See Roelvaag, O(le) E(dvart)
Mofolo, Thomas (Mokopu) 1875(?)-1948TCLC 22; BLC 3; DAM MULT
See also CA 121; 153; MTCW 2
Mohr, Nicholasa 1938-CLC 12; DAM MULT; HLC
See also AAYA 8; CA 49-52; CANR 1, 32, 64; CLR 22; DLB 145; HW 1, 2; JRDA; SAAS 8; SATA 8, 97
Mojtabai, A(nn) G(race) 1938- CLC 5, 9, 15, 29
See also CA 85-88
Moliere 1622-1673 LC 10, 28; DA; DAB; DAC; DAM DRAM, MST; WLC
Molin, Charles
See Mayne, William (James Carter)
Molnar, Ferenc 1878-1952TCLC 20; DAM DRAM
See also CA 109; 153
Momaday, N(avarre) Scott 1934- CLC 2, 19, 85, 95; DA; DAB; DAC; DAM MST, MULT, NOV, POP; PC 25; WLCS
See also AAYA 11; CA 25-28R; CANR 14, 34, 68; CDALBS; DLB 143, 175; INT CANR-14; MTCW 1, 2; NNAL; SATA 48; SATA-Brief 30
Monette, Paul 1945-1995 .... CLC 82
See also CA 139; 147
Monroe, Harriet 1860-1936 .... TCLC 12
See also CA 109; DLB 54, 91
Monroe, Lyle
See Heinlein, Robert A(nson)
Montagu, Elizabeth 1720-1800 .... NCLC 7
Montagu, Mary (Pierrepont) Wortley 1689-1762 LC 9; PC 16
See also DLB 95, 101
Montagu, W. H.
See Coleridge, Samuel Taylor
Montague, John (Patrick) 1929- ..... CLC 13, 46
See also CA 9-12R; CANR 9, 69; DLB 40; MTCW 1
Montaigne, Michel (Eyquem) de 1533-1592LC 8;

DA; DAB; DAC; DAM MST; WLC
Montale, Eugenio 1896-1981CLC 7, 9, 18; PC 13
See also CA 17-20R; 104; CANR 30; DLB 114; MTCW 1
Montesquieu, Charles-Louis de Secondat 1689-1755 .... LC 7
Montgomery, (Robert) Bruce 1921-1978
See Crispin, Edmund
See also CA 104
Montgomery, L(ucy) M(aud) 1874-1942TCLC 51; DAC; DAM MST
See also AAYA 12; CA 108; 137; CLR 8; DLB 92; DLBD 14; JRDA; MAICYA; MTCW 2; SATA 100; YABC 1
Montgomery, Marion H., Jr. 1925- .... CLC 7
See also AITN 1; CA 1-4R; CANR 3, 48; DLB 6
Montgomery, Max
See Davenport, Guy (Mattison, Jr.)
Montherlant, Henry (Milon) de 1896-1972CLC 8, 19; DAM DRAM
See also CA 85-88; 37-40R; DLB 72; MTCW 1
Monty Python
See Chapman, Graham; Cleese, John (Marwood); Gilliam, Terry (Vance); Idle, Eric; Jones, Terence Graham Parry; Palin, Michael (Edward)
See also AAYA 7
Moodie, Susanna (Strickland) 1803-1885 NCLC 14
See also DLB 99
Mooney, Edward 1951-
See Mooney, Ted
See also CA 130
Mooney, Ted .... CLC 25
See also Mooney, Edward
Moorcock, Michael (John) 1939- CLC 5, 27, 58
See also Bradbury, Edward P.
See also AAYA 26; CA 45-48; CAAS 5; CANR 2, 17, 38, 64; DLB 14; MTCW 1, 2; SATA 93
Moore, Brian 1921-1999CLC 1, 3, 5, 7, 8, 19, 32, 90; DAB; DAC; DAM MST
See also CA 1-4R; 174; CANR 1, 25, 42, 63; MTCW 1, 2
Moore, Edward
See Muir, Edwin
Moore, G. E. 1873-1958 .... TCLC 89
Moore, George Augustus 1852-1933TCLC 7; SSC 19
See also CA 104; 177; DLB 10, 18, 57, 135
Moore, Lorrie .... CLC 39, 45, 68
See also Moore, Marie Lorena
Moore, Marianne (Craig) 1887-1972CLC 1, 2, 4, 8, 10, 13, 19, 47; DA; DAB; DAC; DAM MST, POET; PC 4; WLCS
See also CA 1-4R; 33-36R; CANR 3, 61; CDALB 1929-1941; DLB 45; DLBD 7; MTCW 1, 2; SATA 20
Moore, Marie Lorena 1957-
See Moore, Lorrie
See also CA 116; CANR 39
Moore, Thomas 1779-1852 .... NCLC 6
See also DLB 96, 144
Morand, Paul 1888-1976 .... CLC 41; SSC 22
See also CA 69-72; DLB 65
Morante, Elsa 1918-1985 .... CLC 8, 47
See also CA 85-88; 117; CANR 35; DLB 177; MTCW 1, 2
Moravia, Alberto 1907-1990CLC 2, 7, 11, 27, 46; SSC 26
See also Pincherle, Alberto
See also DLB 177; MTCW 2
More, Hannah 1745-1833 .... NCLC 27
See also DLB 107, 109, 116, 158
More, Henry 1614-1687 .... LC 9
See also DLB 126
More, Sir Thomas 1478-1535 .... LC 10, 32
Moreas, Jean .... TCLC 18

See also Papadiamantopoulos, Johannes

Morgan, Berry 1919- .... **CLC 6**
See also CA 49-52; DLB 6

Morgan, Claire
See Highsmith, (Mary) Patricia

Morgan, Edwin (George) 1920- .... **CLC 31**
See also CA 5-8R; CANR 3, 43; DLB 27

Morgan, (George) Frederick 1922- ...... **CLC 23**
See also CA 17-20R; CANR 21

Morgan, Harriet
See Mencken, H(enry) L(ouis)

Morgan, Jane
See Cooper, James Fenimore

Morgan, Janet 1945- .... **CLC 39**
See also CA 65-68

Morgan, Lady 1776(?)-1859 .... **NCLC 29**
See also DLB 116, 158

Morgan, Robin (Evonne) 1941- .... **CLC 2**
See also CA 69-72; CANR 29, 68; MTCW 1;
SATA 80

Morgan, Scott
See Kuttner, Henry

Morgan, Seth 1949(?)-1990 .... **CLC 65**
See also CA 132

Morgenstern, Christian 1871-1914 ...... **TCLC 8**
See also CA 105

Morgenstern, S.
See Goldman, William (W.)

Moricz, Zsigmond 1879-1942 .... **TCLC 33**
<indeSee also CA 165

Morike, Eduard (Friedrich) 1804-1875 **NCLC 10**
See also DLB 133

Moritz, Karl Philipp 1756-1793 .... **LC 2**
See also DLB 94

Morland, Peter Henry
See Faust, Frederick (Schiller)

Morley, Christopher (Darlington) 1890-1957
TCLC 87
See also CA 112; DLB 9

Morren, Theophil
See Hofmannsthal, Hugo von

Morris, Bill 1952- .... **CLC 76**

Morris, Julian
See West, Morris L(anglo)

Morris, Steveland Judkins 1950(?)-
See Wonder, Stevie
See also CA 111

Morris, William 1834-1896 .... **NCLC 4**
See also CDBLB 1832-1890; DLB 18, 35, 57, 156,
178, 184

Morris, Wright 1910-1998 .. **CLC 1, 3, 7, 18, 37**
See also CA 9-12R; 167; CANR 21, 81; DLB 2,
206; DLBY 81; MTCW 1, 2

Morrison, Arthur 1863-1945 .... **TCLC 72**
See also CA 120; 157; DLB 70, 135, 197

Morrison, Chloe Anthony Wofford
See Morrison, Toni

Morrison, James Douglas 1943-1971
See Morrison, Jim
See also CA 73-76; CANR 40

Morrison, Jim .... **CLC 17**
See also Morrison, James Douglas

Morrison, Toni 1931- **CLC 4, 10, 22, 55, 81, 87;**
BLC 3; DA; DAB; DAC; DAM MST, MULT,
NOV, POP
See also AAYA 1, 22; BW 2, 3; CA 29-32R;
CANR 27, 42, 67; CDALB 1968-1988; DLB 6,
33, 143; DLBY 81; MTCW 1, 2; SATA 57

Morrison, Van 1945- .... **CLC 21**
See also CA 116; 168

Morrissy, Mary 1958- .... **CLC 99**

Mortimer, John (Clifford) 1923- .... **CLC 28, 43;**
DAM DRAM, POP
See also CA 13-16R; CANR 21, 69; CDBLB 1960
to Present; DLB 13; INT CANR-21; MTCW 1,
2

Mortimer, Penelope (Ruth) 1918- .... **CLC 5**

See also CA 57-60; CANR 45

Morton, Anthony
See Creasey, John

Mosca, Gaetano 1858-1941 .... **TCLC 75**

Mosher, Howard Frank 1943- .... **CLC 62**
See also CA 139; CANR 65

Mosley, Nicholas 1923- .... **CLC 43, 70**
See also CA 69-72; CANR 41, 60; DLB 14, 207

Mosley, Walter 1952- ..... **CLC 97; BLCS; DAM**
MULT, POP
See also AAYA 17; BW 2; CA 142; CANR 57;
MTCW 2

Moss, Howard 1922-1987 **CLC 7, 14, 45, 50; DAM**
POET
See also CA 1-4R; 123; CANR 1, 44; DLB 5

Mossgiel, Rab
See Burns, Robert

Motion, Andrew (Peter) 1952- .... **CLC 47**
See also CA 146; DLB 40

Motley, Willard (Francis) 1909-1965 .... **CLC 18**
See also BW 1; CA 117; 106; DLB 76, 143

Motoori, Norinaga 1730-1801 .... **NCLC 45**

Mott, Michael (Charles Alston) 1930- **CLC 15, 34**
See also CA 5-8R; CAAS 7; CANR 7, 29

Mountain Wolf Woman 1884-1960 .... **CLC 92**
See also CA 144; NNAL

Moure, Erin 1955- .... **CLC 88**
See also CA 113; DLB 60

Mowat, Farley (McGill) 1921- .... **CLC 26; DAC;**
DAM MST
See also AAYA 1; CA 1-4R; CANR 4, 24, 42, 68;
CLR 20; DLB 68; INT CANR-24; JRDA;
MAICYA; MTCW 1, 2; SATA 3, 55

Mowatt, Anna Cora 1819-1870 .... **NCLC 74**

Moyers, Bill 1934- .... **CLC 74**
See also AITN 2; CA 61-64; CANR 31, 52

Mphahlele, Es'kia
See Mphahlele, Ezekiel
See also DLB 125

Mphahlele, Ezekiel 1919- **CLC 25; BLC 3; DAM**
MULT
See also Mphahlele, Es'kia
See also BW 2, 3; CA 81-84; CANR 26, 76;
MTCW 2

Mqhayi, S(amuel) E(dward) K(rune Loliwe) 1875-
1945 .... **TCLC 25; BLC 3; DAM MULT**
See also CA 153

Mrozek, Slawomir 1930- .... **CLC 3, 13**
See also CA 13-16R; CAAS 10; CANR 29; MTCW
1

Mrs. Belloc-Lowndes
See Lowndes, Marie Adelaide (Belloc)

Mtwa, Percy (?)- .... **CLC 47**

Mueller, Lisel 1924- .... **CLC 13, 51**
See also CA 93-96; DLB 105

Muir, Edwin 1887-1959 .... **TCLC 2, 87**
See also CA 104; DLB 20, 100, 191

Muir, John 1838-1914 .... **TCLC 28**
See also CA 165; DLB 186

Mujica Lainez, Manuel 1910-1984 .... **CLC 31**
See also Lainez, Manuel Mujica
See also CA 81-84; 112; CANR 32; HW 1

Mukherjee, Bharati 1940- . **CLC 53, 115; DAM**
NOV
See also BEST 89:2; CA 107; CANR 45, 72; DLB
60; MTCW 1, 2

Muldoon, Paul 1951- . **CLC 32, 72; DAM POET**
See also CA 113; 129; CANR 52; DLB 40; INT
129

Mulisch, Harry 1927- .... **CLC 42**
See also CA 9-12R; CANR 6, 26, 56

Mull, Martin 1943- .... **CLC 17**
See also CA 105

Muller, Wilhelm .... **NCLC 73**

Mulock, Dinah Maria
See Craik, Dinah Maria (Mulock)

Munford, Robert 1737(?)-1783 .... **LC 5**

See also DLB 31

Mungo, Raymond 1946- .... **CLC 72**
See also CA 49-52; CANR 2

Munro, Alice 1931- **CLC 6, 10, 19, 50, 95; DAC;**
DAM MST, NOV; SSC 3; WLCS
See also AITN 2; CA 33-36R; CANR 33, 53, 75;
DLB 53; MTCW 1, 2; SATA 29

Munro, H(ector) H(ugh) 1870-1916
See Saki
See also CA 104; 130; CDBLB 1890-1914; DA;
DAB; DAC; DAM MST, NOV; DLB 34, 162;
MTCW 1, 2; WLC

Murdoch, (Jean) Iris 1919- **CLC 1, 2, 3, 4, 6, 8, 11,**
15, 22, 31, 51; DAB; DAC; DAM MST, NOV
See also CA 13-16R; CANR 8, 43, 68; CDBLB
1960 to Present; DLB 14, 194; INT CANR-8;
MTCW 1, 2

Murfree, Mary Noailles 1850-1922 ... **SSC 22**
See also CA 122; 176; DLB 12, 74

Murnau, Friedrich Wilhelm
See Plumpe, Friedrich Wilhelm

Murphy, Richard 1927- .... **CLC 41**
See also CA 29-32R; DLB 40

Murphy, Sylvia 1937- .... **CLC 34**
See also CA 121

Murphy, Thomas (Bernard) 1935- .... **CLC 51**
See also CA 101

Murray, Albert L. 1916- .... **CLC 73**
See also BW 2; CA 49-52; CANR 26, 52, 78; DLB
38

Murray, Judith Sargent 1751-1820 ..... **NCLC 63**
See also DLB 37, 200

Murray, Les(lie) A(llan) 1938- .... **CLC 40; DAM**
POET
See also CA 21-24R; CANR 11, 27, 56

Murry, J. Middleton
See Murry, John Middleton

Murry, John Middleton 1889-1957 ...... **TCLC 16**
See also CA 118; DLB 149

Musgrave, Susan 1951- .... **CLC 13, 54**
See also CA 69-72; CANR 45

Musil, Robert (Edler von) 1880-1942 **TCLC 12, 68;**
SSC 18
See also CA 109; CANR 55; DLB 81, 124; MTCW
2

Muske, Carol 1945- .... **CLC 90**
See also Muske-Dukes, Carol (Anne)

Muske-Dukes, Carol (Anne) 1945-
See Muske, Carol
See also CA 65-68; CANR 32, 70

Musset, (Louis Charles) Alfred de 1810-1857
NCLC 7
See also DLB 192

My Brother's Brother
See Chekhov, Anton (Pavlovich)

Myers, L(eopold) H(amilton) 1881-1944 **TCLC 59**
See also CA 157; DLB 15

Myers, Walter Dean 1937- **CLC 35; BLC 3; DAM**
MULT, NOV
See also AAYA 4, 23; BW 2, 3; CA 33-36R;
CANR 20, 42, 67; CLR 4, 16, 35; DLB 33; INT
CANR-20; JRDA; MAICYA; MTCW 2; SAAS
2; SATA 41, 71, 109; SATA-Brief 27

Myers, Walter M.
See Myers, Walter Dean

Myles, Symon
See Follett, Ken(neth Martin)

Nabokov, Vladimir (Vladimirovich) 1899-1977
CLC 1, 2, 3, 6, 8, 11, 15, 23, 44, 46, 64; DA;
DAB; DAC; DAM MST, NOV; SSC 11; WLC
See also CA 5-8R; 69-72; CANR 20; CDALB 1941-
1968; DLB 2; DLBD 3; DLBY 80, 91; MTCW 1,
2

Nagai Kafu 1879-1959 .... **TCLC 51**
See also Nagai Sokichi
See also DLB 180

Nagai Sokichi 1879-1959

See also CA 140

Ouida .... **TCLC 43**
See also De La Ramee, (Marie) Louise
See also DLB 18, 156

Ousmane, Sembene 1923- .... **CLC 66; BLC 3**
See also BW 1, 3; CA 117; 125; CANR 81; MTCW
1

Ovid 43B.C.-17 ...... **CMLC 7; DAM POET; PC 2**
See also DLB 211

Owen, Hugh
See Faust, Frederick (Schiller)

Owen, Wilfred (Edward Salter) 1893-1918 **T C L C
5, 27; DA; DAB; DAC; DAM MST, POET;
PC 19; WLC**
See also CA 104; 141; CDBLB 1914-1945; DLB
20; MTCW 2

Owens, Rochelle 1936- .... **CLC 8**
See also CA 17-20R; CAAS 2; CANR 39

Oz, Amos 1939-**CLC 5, 8, 11, 27, 33, 54; DAM
NOV**
See also CA 53-56; CANR 27, 47, 65; MTCW 1, 2

Ozick, Cynthia 1928-**CLC 3, 7, 28, 62; DAM NOV,
POP; SSC 15**
See also BEST 90:1; CA 17-20R; CANR 23, 58;
DLB 28, 152; DLBY 82; INT CANR-23; MTCW
1, 2

Ozu, Yasujiro 1903-1963 .... **CLC 16**
See also CA 112

Pacheco, C.
See Pessoa, Fernando (Antonio Nogueira)

Pa Chin .... **CLC 18**
See also Li Fei-kan

Pack, Robert 1929- .... **CLC 13**
See also CA 1-4R; CANR 3, 44; DLB 5

Padgett, Lewis
See Kuttner, Henry

Padilla (Lorenzo), Heberto 1932- .... **CLC 38**
See also AITN 1; CA 123; 131; HW 1

Page, Jimmy 1944- .... **CLC 12**

Page, Louise 1955- .... **CLC 40**
See also CA 140; CANR 76

Page, P(atricia) K(athleen) 1916- .... **CLC 7, 18;
DAC; DAM MST; PC 12**
See also CA 53-56; CANR 4, 22, 65; DLB 68;
MTCW 1

Page, Thomas Nelson 1853-1922 .... **SSC 23**
See also CA 118; 177; DLB 12, 78; DLBD 13

Pagels, Elaine Hiesey 1943- .... **CLC 104**
See also CA 45-48; CANR 2, 24, 51

Paget, Violet 1856-1935
See Lee, Vernon
See also CA 104; 166

Paget-Lowe, Henry
See Lovecraft, H(oward) P(hillips)

Paglia, Camille (Anna) 1947- .... **CLC 68**
See also CA 140; CANR 72; MTCW 2

Paige, Richard
See Koontz, Dean R(ay)

Paine, Thomas 1737-1809 .... **NCLC 62**
See also CDALB 1640-1865; DLB 31, 43, 73, 158

Pakenham, Antonia
See Fraser, (Lady) Antonia (Pakenham)

Palamas, Kostes 1859-1943 .... **TCLC 5**
See also CA 105

Palazzeschi, Aldo 1885-1974 .... **CLC 11**
See also CA 89-92; 53-56; DLB 114

Paley, Grace 1922-**CLC 4, 6, 37; DAM POP; SSC
8**
See also CA 25-28R; CANR 13, 46, 74; DLB 28;
INT CANR-13; MTCW 1, 2

Palin, Michael (Edward) 1943- .... **CLC 21**
See also Monty Python
See also CA 107; CANR 35; SATA 67

Palliser, Charles 1947- .... **CLC 65**
See also CA 136; CANR 76

Palma, Ricardo 1833-1919 .... **TCLC 29**
See also CA 168

Pancake, Breece Dexter 1952-1979
See Pancake, Breece D'J
See also CA 123; 109

Pancake, Breece D'J .... **CLC 29**
See also Pancake, Breece Dexter
See also DLB 130

Panko, Rudy
See Gogol, Nikolai (Vasilyevich)

Papadiamantis, Alexandros 1851-1911 **TCLC 29**
See also CA 168

Papadiamantopoulos, Johannes 1856-1910
See Moreas, Jean
See also CA 117

Papini, Giovanni 1881-1956 .... **TCLC 22**
See also CA 121

Paracelsus 1493-1541 .... **LC 14**
See also DLB 179

Parasol, Peter
See Stevens, Wallace

Pardo Bazan, Emilia 1851-1921 .... **SSC 30**

Pareto, Vilfredo 1848-1923 .... **TCLC 69**
See also CA 175

Parfenie, Maria
See Codrescu, Andrei

Parini, Jay (Lee) 1948- .... **CLC 54**
See also CA 97-100; CAAS 16; CANR 32

Park, Jordan
See Kornbluth, C(yril) M.; Pohl, Frederik

Park, Robert E(zra) 1864-1944 .... **TCLC 73**
See also CA 122; 165

Parker, Bert
See Ellison, Harlan (Jay)

Parker, Dorothy (Rothschild) 1893-1967**CLC 15,
68; DAM POET; SSC 2**
See also CA 19-20; 25-28R; CAP 2; DLB 11, 45,
86; MTCW 1, 2

Parker, Robert B(rown) 1932- .... **CLC 27; DAM
NOV, POP**
See also AAYA 28; BEST 89:4; CA 49-52; CANR
1, 26, 52; INT CANR-26; MTCW 1

Parkin, Frank 1940- .... **CLC 43**
See also CA 147

Parkman, Francis, Jr. 1823-1893 .... **NCLC 12**
See also DLB 1, 30, 186

Parks, Gordon (Alexander Buchanan) 1912-**CLC
1, 16; BLC 3; DAM MULT**
See also AITN 2; BW 2, 3; CA 41-44R; CANR 26,
66; DLB 33; MTCW 2; SATA 8, 108

Parmenides c. 515B.C.-c. 450B.C. ...... **CMLC 22**
See also DLB 176

Parnell, Thomas 1679-1718 .... **LC 3**
See also DLB 94

Parra, Nicanor 1914- **CLC 2, 102; DAM MULT;
HLC**
See also CA 85-88; CANR 32; HW 1; MTCW 1

Parrish, Mary Frances
See Fisher, M(ary) F(rances) K(ennedy)

Parson
See Coleridge, Samuel Taylor

Parson Lot
See Kingsley, Charles

Partridge, Anthony
See Oppenheim, E(dward) Phillips

Pascal, Blaise 1623-1662 .... **LC 35**

Pascoli, Giovanni 1855-1912 .... **TCLC 45**
See also CA 170

Pasolini, Pier Paolo 1922-1975**CLC 20, 37, 106;
PC 17**
See also CA 93-96; 61-64; CANR 63; DLB 128,
177; MTCW 1

Pasquini
See Silone, Ignazio

Pastan, Linda (Olenik) 1932- ..... **CLC 27; DAM
POET**
See also CA 61-64; CANR 18, 40, 61; DLB 5

Pasternak, Boris (Leonidovich) 1890-1960 **C L C
7, 10, 18, 63; DA; DAB; DAC; DAM MST,**

NOV, POET; PC 6; SSC 31; WLC
See also CA 127; 116; MTCW 1, 2

Patchen, Kenneth 1911-1972**CLC 1, 2, 18; DAM
POET**
See also CA 1-4R; 33-36R; CANR 3, 35; DLB 16,
48; MTCW 1

Pater, Walter (Horatio) 1839-1894 .... **NCLC 7**
See also CDBLB 1832-1890; DLB 57, 156

Paterson, A(ndrew) B(arton) 1864-1941**TCLC 32**
See also CA 155; SATA 97

Paterson, Katherine (Womeldorf) 1932-**CLC 12,
30**
See also AAYA 1; CA 21-24R; CANR 28, 59; CLR
7, 50; DLB 52; JRDA; MAICYA; MTCW 1;
SATA 13, 53, 92

Patmore, Coventry Kersey Dighton 1823-1896
NCLC 9
See also DLB 35, 98

Paton, Alan (Stewart) 1903-1988 **CLC 4, 10,
25, 55, 106; DA; DAB; DAC; DAM MST,
NOV; WLC**
See also AAYA 26; CA 13-16; 125; CANR 22;
CAP 1; DLBD 17; MTCW 1, 2; SATA 11;
SATA-Obit 56

Paton Walsh, Gillian 1937-
See Walsh, Jill Paton
See also CANR 38; JRDA; MAICYA; SAAS 3;
SATA 4, 72, 109

Patton, George S. 1885-1945 .... **TCLC 79**

Paulding, James Kirke 1778-1860 .... **NCLC 2**
See also DLB 3, 59, 74

Paulin, Thomas Neilson 1949-
See Paulin, Tom
See also CA 123; 128

Paulin, Tom .... **CLC 37**
See also Paulin, Thomas Neilson
See also DLB 40

Paustovsky, Konstantin (Georgievich) 1892-1968
CLC 40
See also CA 93-96; 25-28R

Pavese, Cesare 1908-1950**TCLC 3; PC 13; SSC 19**
See also CA 104; 169; DLB 128, 177

Pavic, Milorad 1929- .... **CLC 60**
See also CA 136; DLB 181

Pavlov, Ivan Petrovich 1849-1936 .... **TCLC 91**
See also CA 118

Payne, Alan
See Jakes, John (William)

Paz, Gil
See Lugones, Leopoldo

Paz, Octavio 1914-1998**CLC 3, 4, 6, 10, 19, 51, 65,
119; DA; DAB; DAC; DAM MST, MULT,
POET; HLC; PC 1; WLC**
See also CA 73-76; 165; CANR 32, 65; DLBY 90,
98; HW 1, 2; MTCW 1, 2

p'Bitek, Okot 1931-1982 **CLC 96; BLC 3; DAM
MULT**
See also BW 2, 3; CA 124; 107; DLB 125; MTCW
1, 2

Peacock, Molly 1947- .... **CLC 60**
See also CA 103; CAAS 21; CANR 52; DLB 120

Peacock, Thomas Love 1785-1866 ...... **NCLC 22**
See also DLB 96, 116

Peake, Mervyn 1911-1968 .... **CLC 7, 54**
See also CA 5-8R; 25-28R; CANR 3; DLB 15, 160;
MTCW 1; SATA 23

Pearce, Philippa .... **CLC 21**
See also Christie, (Ann) Philippa
See also CLR 9; DLB 161; MAICYA; SATA 1, 67

Pearl, Eric
See Elman, Richard (Martin)

Pearson, T(homas) R(eid) 1956- .... **CLC 39**
See also CA 120; 130; INT 130

Peck, Dale 1967- .... **CLC 81**
See also CA 146; CANR 72

Peck, John 1941- .... **CLC 3**
See also CA 49-52; CANR 3

Putnam, Arthur Lee
  See Alger, Horatio, Jr.
Puzo, Mario 1920-1999CLC 1, 2, 6, 36, 107; DAM
  NOV, POP
  See also CA 65-68; CANR 4, 42, 65; DLB 6;
  MTCW 1, 2
Pygge, Edward
  See Barnes, Julian (Patrick)
Pyle, Ernest Taylor 1900-1945
  See Pyle, Ernie
  See also CA 115; 160
Pyle, Ernie 1900-1945 .... TCLC 75
  See also Pyle, Ernest Taylor
  See also DLB 29; MTCW 2
Pyle, Howard 1853-1911 .... TCLC 81
  See also CA 109; 137; CLR 22; DLB 42, 188;
  DLBD 13; MAICYA; SATA 16, 100
Pym, Barbara (Mary Crampton) 1913-1980 C L C
  13, 19, 37, 111
  See also CA 13-14; 97-100; CANR 13, 34; CAP
  1; DLB 14, 207; DLBY 87; MTCW 1, 2
Pynchon, Thomas (Ruggles, Jr.) 1937-CLC 2,
  3, 6, 9, 11, 18, 33, 62, 72; DA; DAB; DAC;
  DAM MST, NOV, POP; SSC 14; WLC
  See also BEST 90:2; CA 17-20R; CANR 22, 46,
  73; DLB 2, 173; MTCW 1, 2
Pythagoras c. 570B.C.-c. 500B.C. .... CMLC 22
  See also DLB 176
Q
  See Quiller-Couch, SirArthur (Thomas)
Qian Zhongshu
  See Ch'ien Chung-shu
Qroll
  See Dagerman, Stig (Halvard)
Quarrington, Paul (Lewis) 1953- .... CLC 65
  See also CA 129; CANR 62
Quasimodo, Salvatore 1901-1968 .... CLC 10
  See also CA 13-16; 25-28R; CAP 1; DLB 114;
  MTCW 1
Quay, Stephen 1947- .... CLC 95
Quay, Timothy 1947- .... CLC 95
Queen, Ellery .... CLC 3, 11
  See also Dannay, Frederic; Davidson, Avram
  (James); Lee, Manfred B(ennington);
  Marlowe, Stephen; Sturgeon, Theodore
  (Hamilton); Vance, John Holbrook
Queen, Ellery, Jr.
  See Dannay, Frederic; Lee, Manfred
  B(ennington)
Queneau, Raymond 1903-1976 CLC 2, 5, 10, 42
  See also CA 77-80; 69-72; CANR 32; DLB 72;
  MTCW 1, 2
Quevedo, Francisco de 1580-1645 .... LC 23
Quiller-Couch, SirArthur (Thomas) 1863-1944
  TCLC 53
  See also CA 118; 166; DLB 135, 153, 190
Quin, Ann (Marie) 1936-1973 .... CLC 6
  See also CA 9-12R; 45-48; DLB 14
Quinn, Martin
  See Smith, Martin Cruz
Quinn, Peter 1947- .... CLC 91
Quinn, Simon
  See Smith, Martin Cruz
Quiroga, Horacio (Sylvestre) 1878-1937 . T C L C
  20; DAM MULT; HLC
  See also CA 117; 131; HW 1; MTCW 1
Quoirez, Francoise 1935- .... CLC 9
  See also Sagan, Francoise
  See also CA 49-52; CANR 6, 39, 73; MTCW 1, 2
Raabe, Wilhelm (Karl) 1831-1910 ...... TCLC 45
  See also CA 167; DLB 129
Rabe, David (William) 1940-CLC 4, 8, 33; DAM
  DRAM
  See also CA 85-88; CABS 3; CANR 59; DLB 7
Rabelais, Francois 1483-1553 . LC 5; DA; DAB;
  DAC; DAM MST; WLC
Rabinovitch, Sholem 1859-1916

See Aleichem, Sholom
  See also CA 104
Rabinyan, Dorit 1972- .... CLC 119
  See also CA 170
Rachilde 1860-1953 .... TCLC 67
  See also DLB 123, 192
Racine, Jean 1639-1699LC 28; DAB; DAM MST
Radcliffe, Ann (Ward) 1764-1823 .... NCLC 6, 55
  See also DLB 39, 178
Radiguet, Raymond 1903-1923 .... TCLC 29
  See also CA 162; DLB 65
Radnoti, Miklos 1909-1944 .... TCLC 16
  See also CA 118
Rado, James 1939- .... CLC 17
  See also CA 105
Radvanyi, Netty 1900-1983
  See Seghers, Anna
  See also CA 85-88; 110
Rae, Ben
  See Griffiths, Trevor
Raeburn, John (Hay) 1941- .... CLC 34
  See also CA 57-60
Ragni, Gerome 1942-1991 .... CLC 17
  See also CA 105; 134
Rahv, Philip 1908-1973 .... CLC 24
  See also Greenberg, Ivan
  See also DLB 137
Raimund, Ferdinand Jakob 1790-1836 NCLC 69
  See also DLB 90
Raine, Craig 1944- .... CLC 32, 103
  See also CA 108; CANR 29, 51; DLB 40
Raine, Kathleen (Jessie) 1908- .... CLC 7, 45
  See also CA 85-88; CANR 46; DLB 20; MTCW 1
Rainis, Janis 1865-1929 .... TCLC 29
  See also CA 170
Rakosi, Carl 1903- .... CLC 47
  See also Rawley, Callman
  See also CAAS 5; DLB 193
Raleigh, Richard
  See Lovecraft, H(oward) P(hillips)
Raleigh, Sir Walter 1554(?)-1618 ...... LC 31, 39
  See also CDBLB Before 1660; DLB 172
Rallentando, H. P.
  See Sayers, Dorothy L(eigh)
Ramal, Walter
  See de la Mare, Walter (John)
Ramana Maharshi 1879-1950 .... TCLC 84
Ramoacn y Cajal, Santiago 1852-1934 TCLC 93
Ramon, Juan
  See Jimenez (Mantecon), Juan Ramon
Ramos, Graciliano 1892-1953 .... TCLC 32
  See also CA 167; HW 2
Rampersad, Arnold 1941- .... CLC 44
  See also BW 2, 3; CA 127; 133; CANR 81; DLB
  111; INT 133
Rampling, Anne
  See Rice, Anne
Ramsay, Allan 1684(?)-1758 .... LC 29
  See also DLB 95
Ramuz, Charles-Ferdinand 1878-1947 TCLC 33
  See also CA 165
Rand, Ayn 1905-1982CLC 3, 30, 44, 79; DA; DAC;
  DAM MST, NOV, POP; WLC
  See also AAYA 10; CA 13-16R; 105; CANR 27,
  73; CDALBS; MTCW 1, 2
Randall, Dudley (Felker) 1914- CLC 1; BLC 3;
  DAM MULT
  See also BW 1, 3; CA 25-28R; CANR 23; DLB 41
Randall, Robert
  See Silverberg, Robert
Ranger, Ken
  See Creasey, John
Ransom, John Crowe 1888-1974 CLC 2, 4, 5, 11,
  24; DAM POET
  See also CA 5-8R; 49-52; CANR 6, 34; CDALBS;
  DLB 45, 63; MTCW 1, 2
Rao, Raja 1909- .... CLC 25, 56; DAM NOV

See also CA 73-76; CANR 51; MTCW 1, 2
Raphael, Frederic (Michael) 1931- ... CLC 2, 14
  See also CA 1-4R; CANR 1; DLB 14
Ratcliffe, James P.
  See Mencken, H(enry) L(ouis)
Rathbone, Julian 1935- .... CLC 41
  See also CA 101; CANR 34, 73
Rattigan, Terence (Mervyn) 1911-1977 .. CLC 7;
  DAM DRAM
  See also CA 85-88; 73-76; CDBLB 1945-1960;
  DLB 13; MTCW 1, 2
Ratushinskaya, Irina 1954- .... CLC 54
  See also CA 129; CANR 68
Raven, Simon (Arthur Noel) 1927- .... CLC 14
  See also CA 81-84
Ravenna, Michael
  See Welty, Eudora
Rawley, Callman 1903-
  See Rakosi, Carl
  See also CA 21-24R; CANR 12, 32
Rawlings, Marjorie Kinnan 1896-1953T C L C
  4
  See also AAYA 20; CA 104; 137; CANR 74;
  DLB 9, 22, 102; DLBD 17; JRDA; MAICYA;
  MTCW 2; SATA 100; YABC 1
Ray, Satyajit 1921-1992CLC 16, 76; DAM MULT
  See also CA 114; 137
Read, Herbert Edward 1893-1968 .... CLC 4
  See also CA 85-88; 25-28R; DLB 20, 149
Read, Piers Paul 1941- .... CLC 4, 10, 25
  See also CA 21-24R; CANR 38; DLB 14; SATA
  21
Reade, Charles 1814-1884 .... NCLC 2, 74
  See also DLB 21
Reade, Hamish
  See Gray, Simon (James Holliday)
Reading, Peter 1946- .... CLC 47
  See also CA 103; CANR 46; DLB 40
Reaney, James 1926- CLC 13; DAC; DAM MST
  See also CA 41-44R; CAAS 15; CANR 42; DLB
  68; SATA 43
Rebreanu, Liviu 1885-1944 .... TCLC 28
  See also CA 165
Rechy, John (Francisco) 1934-CLC 1, 7, 14, 18,
  107; DAM MULT; HLC
  See also CA 5-8R; CAAS 4; CANR 6, 32, 64;
  DLB 122; DLBY 82; HW 1, 2; INT CANR-6
Redcam, Tom 1870-1933 .... TCLC 25
Reddin, Keith .... CLC 67
Redgrove, Peter (William) 1932- ...... CLC 6, 41
  See also CA 1-4R; CANR 3, 39, 77; DLB 40
Redmon, Anne .... CLC 22
  See also Nightingale, Anne Redmon
  See also DLBY 86
Reed, Eliot
  See Ambler, Eric
Reed, Ishmael 1938- . CLC 2, 3, 5, 6, 13, 32, 60;
  BLC 3; DAM MULT
  See also BW 2, 3; CA 21-24R; CANR 25, 48, 74;
  DLB 2, 5, 33, 169; DLBD 8; MTCW 1, 2
Reed, John (Silas) 1887-1920 .... TCLC 9
  See also CA 106
Reed, Lou .... CLC 21
  See also Firbank, Louis
Reeve, Clara 1729-1807 .... NCLC 19
  See also DLB 39
Reich, Wilhelm 1897-1957 .... TCLC 57
Reid, Christopher (John) 1949- .... CLC 33
  See also CA 140; DLB 40
Reid, Desmond
  See Moorcock, Michael (John)
Reid Banks, Lynne 1929-
  See Banks, Lynne Reid
  See also CA 1-4R; CANR 6, 22, 38; CLR 24; JRDA;
  MAICYA; SATA 22, 75
Reilly, William K.
  See Creasey, John

Robinson, Lloyd
See Silverberg, Robert
Robinson, Marilynne 1944- .... **CLC 25**
See also CA 116; CANR 80; DLB 206
Robinson, Smokey .... **CLC 21**
See also Robinson, William, Jr.
Robinson, William, Jr. 1940-
See Robinson, Smokey
See also CA 116
Robison, Mary 1949- .... **CLC 42, 98**
See also CA 113; 116; DLB 130; INT 116
Rod, Edouard 1857-1910 .... **TCLC 52**
Roddenberry, Eugene Wesley 1921-1991
See Roddenberry, Gene
See also CA 110; 135; CANR 37; SATA 45;
SATA-Obit 69
Roddenberry, Gene .... **CLC 17**
See also Roddenberry, Eugene Wesley
See also AAYA 5; SATA-Obit 69
Rodgers, Mary 1931- .... **CLC 12**
See also CA 49-52; CANR 8, 55; CLR 20; INT
CANR-8; JRDA; MAICYA; SATA 8
Rodgers, W(illiam) R(obert) 1909-1969 . **CLC 7**
See also CA 85-88; DLB 20
Rodman, Eric
See Silverberg, Robert
<indexbody>**Rodman, Howard** 1920(?)-1985
CLC 65
See also CA 118
Rodman, Maia
See Wojciechowska, Maia (Teresa)
Rodriguez, Claudio 1934- .... **CLC 10**
See also DLB 134
Roelvaag, O(le) E(dvart) 1876-1931 ..... **TCLC 17**
See also CA 117; 171; DLB 9
Roethke, Theodore (Huebner) 1908-1963 **CLC 1,
3, 8, 11, 19, 46, 101; DAM POET; PC 15**
See also CA 81-84; CABS 2; CDALB 1941-1968;
DLB 5, 206; MTCW 1, 2
Rogers, Samuel 1763-1855 .... **NCLC 69**
See also DLB 93
Rogers, Thomas Hunton 1927- .... **CLC 57**
See also CA 89-92; INT 89-92
Rogers, Will(iam Penn Adair) 1879-1935 **T C L C
8, 71; DAM MULT**
See also CA 105; 144; DLB 11; MTCW 2; NNAL
Rogin, Gilbert 1929- .... **CLC 18**
See also CA 65-68; CANR 15
Rohan, Koda .... **TCLC 22**
See also Koda Shigeyuki
Rohlfs, Anna Katharine Green
See Green, Anna Katharine
Rohmer, Eric .... **CLC 16**
See also Scherer, Jean-Marie Maurice
Rohmer, Sax .... **TCLC 28**
See also Ward, Arthur Henry Sarsfield
See also DLB 70
Roiphe, Anne (Richardson) 1935- .... **CLC 3, 9**
See also CA 89-92; CANR 45, 73; DLBY 80; INT
89-92
Rojas, Fernando de 1465-1541 .. **LC 23; HLCS 1**
**Rolfe, Frederick (William Serafino Austin Lewis
Mary)** 1860-1913 .... **TCLC 12**
See also CA 107; DLB 34, 156
Rolland, Romain 1866-1944 .... **TCLC 23**
See also CA 118; DLB 65
Rolle, Richard c. 1300-c. 1349 .... **CMLC 21**
See also DLB 146
Rolvaag, O(le) E(dvart)
See Roelvaag, O(le) E(dvart)
Romain Arnaud, Saint
See Aragon, Louis
Romains, Jules 1885-1972 ...., **CLC 7**
See also CA 85-88; CANR 34; DLB 65; MTCW 1
Romero, Jose Ruben 1890-1952 .... **TCLC 14**
See also CA 114; 131; HW 1
Ronsard, Pierre de 1524-1585 .... **LC 6; PC 11**

Rooke, Leon 1934- .. **CLC 25, 34; DAM POP**
See also CA 25-28R; CANR 23, 53
Roosevelt, Franklin Delano 1882-1945 **TCLC 93**
See also CA 116; 173
Roosevelt, Theodore 1858-1919 .... **TCLC 69**
See also CA 115; 170; DLB 47, 186
Roper, William 1498-1578 .... **LC 10**
Roquelaure, A. N.
See Rice, Anne
Rosa, Joao Guimaraes 1908-1967**CLC 23; HLCS
1**
See also CA 89-92; DLB 113
Rose, Wendy 1948-**CLC 85; DAM MULT; PC 13**
See also CA 53-56; CANR 5, 51; DLB 175; NNAL;
SATA 12
Rosen, R. D.
See Rosen, Richard (Dean)
Rosen, Richard (Dean) 1949- .... **CLC 39**
See also CA 77-80; CANR 62; INT CANR-30
Rosenberg, Isaac 1890-1918 .... **TCLC 12**
See also CA 107; DLB 20
Rosenblatt, Joe .... **CLC 15**
See also Rosenblatt, Joseph
Rosenblatt, Joseph 1933-
See Rosenblatt, Joe
See also CA 89-92; INT 89-92
Rosenfeld, Samuel
See Tzara, Tristan
Rosenstock, Sami
See Tzara, Tristan
Rosenstock, Samuel
See Tzara, Tristan
Rosenthal, M(acha) L(ouis) 1917-1996 . **CLC 28**
See also CA 1-4R; 152; CAAS 6; CANR 4, 51;
DLB 5; SATA 59
Ross, Barnaby
See Dannay, Frederic
Ross, Bernard L.
See Follett, Ken(neth Martin)
Ross, J. H.
See Lawrence, T(homas) E(dward)
Ross, John Hume
See Lawrence, T(homas) E(dward)
Ross, Martin
See Martin, Violet Florence
See also DLB 135
Ross, (James) Sinclair 1908-1996**CLC 13; DAC;
DAM MST; SSC 24**
See also CA 73-76; CANR 81; DLB 88
Rossetti, Christina (Georgina) 1830-1894**N C L C
2, 50, 66; DA; DAB; DAC; DAM MST, POET;
PC 7; WLC**
See also DLB 35, 163; MAICYA; SATA 20
Rossetti, Dante Gabriel 1828-1882 **NCLC 4, 77;
DA; DAB; DAC; DAM MST, POET; WLC**
See also CDBLB 1832-1890; DLB 35
Rossner, Judith (Perelman) 1935- . **CLC 6, 9, 29**
See also AITN 2; BEST 90:3; CA 17-20R; CANR
18, 51, 73; DLB 6; INT CANR-18; MTCW 1, 2
Rostand, Edmond (Eugene Alexis) 1868-1918
**TCLC 6, 37; DA; DAB; DAC; DAM DRAM,
MST; DC 10**
See also CA 104; 126; DLB 192; MTCW 1
Roth, Henry 1906-1995 .... **CLC 2, 6, 11, 104**
See also CA 11-12; 149; CANR 38, 63; CAP 1;
DLB 28; MTCW 1, 2
Roth, Philip (Milton) 1933-**CLC 1, 2, 3, 4, 6, 9, 15,
22, 31, 47, 66, 86, 119; DA; DAB; DAC; DAM
MST, NOV, POP; SSC 26; WLC**
See also BEST 90:3; CA 1-4R; CANR 1, 22, 36,
55; CDALB 1968-1988; DLB 2, 28, 173; DLBY
82; MTCW 1, 2
Rothenberg, Jerome 1931- .... **CLC 6, 57**
See also CA 45-48; CANR 1; DLB 5, 193
Roumain, Jacques (Jean Baptiste) 1907-1944
TCLC 19; BLC 3; DAM MULT
See also BW 1; CA 117; 125

Rourke, Constance (Mayfield) 1885-1941
TCLC 12
See also CA 107; YABC 1
Rousseau, Jean-Baptiste 1671-1741 .... **LC 9**
Rousseau, Jean-Jacques 1712-1778 . **LC 14, 36;
DA; DAB; DAC; DAM MST; WLC**
Roussel, Raymond 1877-1933 .... **TCLC 20**
See also CA 117
Rovit, Earl (Herbert) 1927- .... **CLC 7**
See also CA 5-8R; CANR 12
Rowe, Elizabeth Singer 1674-1737 .... **LC 44**
See also DLB 39, 95
Rowe, Nicholas 1674-1718 .... **LC 8**
See also DLB 84
Rowley, Ames Dorrance
See Lovecraft, H(oward) P(hillips)
Rowson, Susanna Haswell 1762(?)-1824**NCLC 5,
69**
See also DLB 37, 200
Roy, Arundhati 1960(?)- .... **CLC 109**
See also CA 163; DLBY 97
Roy, Gabrielle 1909-1983 **CLC 10, 14; DAB;
DAC; DAM MST**
See also CA 53-56; 110; CANR 5, 61; DLB 68;
MTCW 1; SATA 104
Royko, Mike 1932-1997 .... **CLC 109**
See also CA 89-92; 157; CANR 26
Rozewicz, Tadeusz 1921-**CLC 9, 23; DAM POET**
See also CA 108; CANR 36, 66; MTCW 1, 2
Ruark, Gibbons 1941- .... **CLC 3**
See also CA 33-36R; CAAS 23; CANR 14, 31, 57;
DLB 120
Rubens, Bernice (Ruth) 1923- .... **CLC 19, 31**
See also CA 25-28R; CANR 33, 65; DLB 14, 207;
MTCW 1
Rubin, Harold
See Robbins, Harold
Rudkin, (James) David 1936- .... **CLC 14**
See also CA 89-92; DLB 13
Rudnik, Raphael 1933- .... **CLC 7**
See also CA 29-32R
Ruffian, M.
See Hasek, Jaroslav (Matej Frantisek)
Ruiz, Jose Martinez .... **CLC 11**
See also Martinez Ruiz, Jose
Rukeyser, Muriel 1913-1980 **CLC 6, 10, 15, 27;
DAM POET; PC 12**
See also CA 5-8R; 93-96; CANR 26, 60; DLB 48;
MTCW 1, 2; SATA-Obit 22
Rule, Jane (Vance) 1931- .... **CLC 27**
See also CA 25-28R; CAAS 18; CANR 12; DLB
60
Rulfo, Juan 1918-1986 **CLC 8, 80; DAM MULT;
HLC; SSC 25**
See also CA 85-88; 118; CANR 26; DLB 113; HW
1, 2; MTCW 1, 2
Rumi, Jalal al-Din 1297-1373 .... **CMLC 20**
Runeberg, Johan 1804-1877 .... **NCLC 41**
Runyon, (Alfred) Damon 1884(?)-1946 **TCLC 10**
See also CA 107; 165; DLB 11, 86, 171; MTCW 2
Rush, Norman 1933- .... **CLC 44**
See also CA 121; 126; INT 126
Rushdie, (Ahmed) Salman 1947-**CLC 23, 31, 55,
100; DAB; DAC; DAM MST, NOV, POP;
WLCS**
See also BEST 89:3; CA 108; 111; CANR 33, 56;
DLB 194; INT 111; MTCW 1, 2
Rushforth, Peter (Scott) 1945- .... **CLC 19**
See also CA 101
Ruskin, John 1819-1900 .... **TCLC 63**
See also CA 114; 129; CDBLB 1832-1890; DLB
55, 163, 190; SATA 24
Russ, Joanna 1937- .... **CLC 15**
See also CANR 11, 31, 65; DLB 8; MTCW 1
Russell, George William 1867-1935
See Baker, Jean H.
See also CA 104; 153; CDBLB 1890-1914; DAM

Silkin, Jon 1930- .... **CLC 2, 6, 43**
See also CA 5-8R; CAAS 5; DLB 27

Silko, Leslie (Marmon) 1948- **CLC 23, 74, 114;**
DA; DAC; DAM MST, MULT, POP; WLCS
See also AAYA 14; CA 115; 122; CANR 45, 65;
DLB 143, 175; MTCW 2; NNAL

Sillanpaa, Frans Eemil 1888-1964 .... **CLC 19**
See also CA 129; 93-96; MTCW 1

Sillitoe, Alan 1928- .... **CLC 1, 3, 6, 10, 19, 57**
See also AITN 1; CA 9-12R; CAAS 2; CANR 8,
26, 55; CDBLB 1960 to Present; DLB 14, 139;
MTCW 1, 2; SATA 61

Silone, Ignazio 1900-1978 .... **CLC 4**
See also CA 25-28; 81-84; CANR 34; CAP 2;
MTCW 1

Silver, Joan Micklin 1935- .... **CLC 20**
See also CA 114; 121; INT 121

Silver, Nicholas
See Faust, Frederick (Schiller)

Silverberg, Robert 1935- ...... **CLC 7; DAM POP**
See also AAYA 24; CA 1-4R; CAAS 3; CANR 1,
20, 36; CLR 59; DLB 8; INT CANR-20;
MAICYA; MTCW 1, 2; SATA 13, 91; SATA-
Essay 104

Silverstein, Alvin 1933- .... **CLC 17**
See also CA 49-52; CANR 2; CLR 25; JRDA;
MAICYA; SATA 8, 69

Silverstein, Virginia B(arbara Opshelor) 1937-
CLC 17
See also CA 49-52; CANR 2; CLR 25; JRDA;
MAICYA; SATA 8, 69

Sim, Georges
See Simenon, Georges (Jacques Christian)

Simak, Clifford D(onald) 1904-1988 . **CLC 1, 55**
See also CA 1-4R; 125; CANR 1, 35; DLB 8;
MTCW 1; SATA-Obit 56

Simenon, Georges (Jacques Christian) 1903-1989
CLC 1, 2, 3, 8, 18, 47; DAM POP
See also CA 85-88; 129; CANR 35; DLB 72; DLB Y
89; MTCW 1, 2

Simic, Charles 1938- **CLC 6, 9, 22, 49, 68; DAM**
POET
See also CA 29-32R; CAAS 4; CANR 12, 33, 52,
61; DLB 105; MTCW 2

Simmel, Georg 1858-1918 .... **TCLC 64**
See also CA 157

Simmons, Charles (Paul) 1924- .... **CLC 57**
See also CA 89-92; INT 89-92

Simmons, Dan 1948- .... **CLC 44; DAM POP**
See also AAYA 16; CA 138; CANR 53, 81

Simmons, James (Stewart Alexander) 1933-**CLC**
43
See also CA 105; CAAS 21; DLB 40

Simms, William Gilmore 1806-1870 .... **NCLC 3**
See also DLB 3, 30, 59, 73

Simon, Carly 1945- .... **CLC 26**
See also CA 105

Simon, Claude 1913-1984**CLC 4, 9, 15, 39; DAM**
NOV
See also CA 89-92; CANR 33; DLB 83; MTCW 1

Simon, (Marvin) Neil 1927-**CLC 6, 11, 31, 39, 70;**
DAM DRAM
See also AITN 1; CA 21-24R; CANR 26, 54; DLB
7; MTCW 1, 2

Simon, Paul (Frederick) 1941(?)- .... **CLC 17**
See also CA 116; 153

Simonon, Paul 1956(?)- .... **CLC 30**

Simpson, Harriette
See Arnow, Harriette (Louisa) Simpson

Simpson, Louis (Aston Marantz) 1923-**CLC 4, 7,**
9, 32; DAM POET
See also CA 1-4R; CAAS 4; CANR 1, 61; DLB 5;
MTCW 1, 2

Simpson, Mona (Elizabeth) 1957- .... **CLC 44**
See also CA 122; 135; CANR 68

Simpson, N(orman) F(rederick) 1919- . **CLC 29**
See also CA 13-16R; DLB 13

Sinclair, Andrew (Annandale) 1935-. **CLC 2,**
14
See also CA 9-12R; CAAS 5; CANR 14, 38;
DLB 14; MTCW 1

Sinclair, Emil
See Hesse, Hermann

Sinclair, Iain 1943- .... **CLC 76**
See also CA 132; CANR 81

Sinclair, Iain MacGregor
See Sinclair, Iain

Sinclair, Irene
See Griffith, D(avid Lewelyn) W(ark)

Sinclair, Mary Amelia St. Clair 1865(?)-1946
See Sinclair, May
See also CA 104

Sinclair, May 1863-1946 .... **TCLC 3, 11**
See also Sinclair, Mary Amelia St. Clair
See also CA 166; DLB 36, 135

Sinclair, Roy
See Griffith, D(avid Lewelyn) W(ark)

Sinclair, Upton (Beall) 1878-1968**CLC 1, 11, 15,**
63; DA; DAB; DAC; DAM MST, NOV; WLC
See also CA 5-8R; 25-28R; CANR 7; CDALB 1929-
1941; DLB 9; INT CANR-7; MTCW 1, 2;
SATA 9

Singer, Isaac
See Singer, Isaac Bashevis

Singer, Isaac Bashevis 1904-1991**CLC 1, 3, 6, 9,**
11, 15, 23, 38, 69, 111; DA; DAB; DAC; DAM
MST, NOV; SSC 3; WLC
See also AITN 1, 2; CA 1-4R; 134; CANR 1, 39;
CDALB 1941-1968; CLR 1; DLB 6, 28, 52;
DLBY 91; JRDA; MAICYA; MTCW 1, 2;
SATA 3, 27; SATA-Obit 68

Singer, Israel Joshua 1893-1944 .... **TCLC 33**
See also CA 169

Singh, Khushwant 1915- .... **CLC 11**
See also CA 9-12R; CAAS 9; CANR 6

Singleton, Ann
See Benedict, Ruth (Fulton)

Sinjohn, John
See Galsworthy, John

Sinyavsky, Andrei (Donatevich) 1925-1997**CLC 8**
See also CA 85-88; 159

Sirin, V.
See Nabokov, Vladimir (Vladimirovich)

Sissman, L(ouis) E(dward) 1928-1976 **CLC 9, 18**
See also CA 21-24R; 65-68; CANR 13; DLB 5

Sisson, C(harles) H(ubert) 1914- .... **CLC 8**
See also CA 1-4R; CAAS 3; CANR 3, 48; DLB 27

Sitwell, Dame Edith 1887-1964**CLC 2, 9, 67; DAM**
POET; PC 3
See also CA 9-12R; CANR 35; CDBLB 1945-1960;
DLB 20; MTCW 1, 2

Siwaarmill, H. P.
See Sharp, William

Sjoewall, Maj 1935- .... **CLC 7**
See also CA 65-68; CANR 73

Sjowall, Maj
See Sjoewall, Maj

Skelton, John 1463-1529 .... **PC 25**

Skelton, Robin 1925-1997 .... **CLC 13**
See also AITN 2; CA 5-8R; 160; CAAS 5; CANR
28; DLB 27, 53

Skolimowski, Jerzy 1938- .... **CLC 20**
See also CA 128

Skram, Amalie (Bertha) 1847-1905 .... **TCLC 25**
See also CA 165

Skvorecky, Josef (Vaclav) 1924-**CLC 15, 39, 69;**
DAC; DAM NOV
See also CA 61-64; CAAS 1; CANR 10, 34, 63;
MTCW 1, 2

Slade, Bernard .... **CLC 11, 46**
See also Newbound, Bernard Slade
See also CAAS 9; DLB 53

Slaughter, Carolyn 1946- .... **CLC 56**
See also CA 85-88

Slaughter, Frank G(ill) 1908- .... **CLC 29**
See also AITN 2; CA 5-8R; CANR 5; INT
CANR-5

Slavitt, David R(ytman) 1935- .... **CLC 5, 14**
See also CA 21-24R; CAAS 3; CANR 41; DLB 5,
6

Slesinger, Tess 1905-1945 .... **TCLC 10**
See also CA 107; DLB 102

Slessor, Kenneth 1901-1971 .... **CLC 14**
See also CA 102; 89-92

Slowacki, Juliusz 1809-1849 .... **NCLC 15**

Smart, Christopher 1722-1771**LC 3; DAM POET;**
PC 13
See also DLB 109

Smart, Elizabeth 1913-1986 .... **CLC 54**
See also CA 81-84; 118; DLB 88

Smiley, Jane (Graves) 1949- **CLC 53, 76; DAM**
POP
See also CA 104; CANR 30, 50, 74; INT CANR-
30

Smith, A(rthur) J(ames) M(arshall) 1902-1980
CLC 15; DAC
See also CA 1-4R; 102; CANR 4; DLB 88

Smith, Adam 1723-1790 .... **LC 36**
See also DLB 104

Smith, Alexander 1829-1867 .... **NCLC 59**
See also DLB 32, 55

Smith, Anna Deavere 1950- .... **CLC 86**
See also CA 133

Smith, Betty (Wehner) 1896-1972 .... **CLC 19**
See also CA 5-8R; 33-36R; DLBY 82; SATA 6

Smith, Charlotte (Turner) 1749-1806 . **NCLC 23**
See also DLB 39, 109

Smith, Clark Ashton 1893-1961 .... **CLC 43**
See also CA 143; CANR 81; MTCW 2

Smith, Dave .... **CLC 22, 42**
See also Smith, David (Jeddie)
See also CAAS 7; DLB 5

Smith, David (Jeddie) 1942-
See Smith, Dave
See also CA 49-52; CANR 1, 59; DAM POET

Smith, Florence Margaret 1902-1971
See Smith, Stevie
See also CA 17-18; 29-32R; CANR 35; CAP 2;
DAM POET; MTCW 1, 2

Smith, Iain Crichton 1928-1998 .... **CLC 64**
See also CA 21-24R; 171; DLB 40, 139

Smith, John 1580(?)-1631 .... **LC 9**
See also DLB 24, 30

Smith, Johnston
See Crane, Stephen (Townley)

Smith, Joseph, Jr. 1805-1844 .... **NCLC 53**

Smith, Lee 1944- .... **CLC 25, 73**
See also CA 114; 119; CANR 46; DLB 143; DLBY
83; INT 119

Smith, Martin
See Smith, Martin Cruz

Smith, Martin Cruz 1942-**CLC 25; DAM MULT,**
POP
See also BEST 89:4; CA 85-88; CANR 6, 23, 43,
65; INT CANR-23; MTCW 2; NNAL

Smith, Mary-Ann Tirone 1944- .... **CLC 39**
See also CA 118; 136

Smith, Patti 1946- .... **CLC 12**
See also CA 93-96; CANR 63

Smith, Pauline (Urmson) 1882-1959 ... **TCLC 25**

Smith, Rosamond
See Oates, Joyce Carol

Smith, Sheila Kaye
See Kaye-Smith, Sheila

Smith, Stevie .... **CLC 3, 8, 25, 44; PC 12**
See also Smith, Florence Margaret
See also DLB 20; MTCW 2

Smith, Wilbur (Addison) 1933- .... **CLC 33**
See also CA 13-16R; CANR 7, 46, 66; MTCW 1, 2

Smith, William Jay 1918- .... **CLC 6**
See also CA 5-8R; CANR 44; DLB 5; MAICYA;

NOV; WLC
See also CDBLB 1832-1890; DLB 21, 55, 159, 163; SATA 23

Thakura, Ravindranatha
See Tagore, Rabindranath

Tharoor, Shashi 1956- .... **CLC 70**
See also CA 141

Thelwell, Michael Miles 1939- .... **CLC 22**
See also BW 2; CA 101

Theobald, Lewis, Jr.
See Lovecraft, H(oward) P(hillips)

Theodorescu, Ion N. 1880-1967
See Arghezi, Tudor
See also CA 116

Theriault, Yves 1915-1983 **CLC 79; DAC; DAM MST**
See also CA 102; DLB 88

Theroux, Alexander (Louis) 1939- .... **CLC 2, 25**
See also CA 85-88; CANR 20, 63

Theroux, Paul (Edward) 1941- **CLC 5, 8, 11, 15, 28, 46; DAM POP**
See also AAYA 28; BEST 89:4; CA 33-36R; CANR 20, 45, 74; CDALBS; DLB 2; MTCW 1, 2; SATA 44, 109

Thesen, Sharon 1946- .... **CLC 56**
See also CA 163

Thevenin, Denis
See Duhamel, Georges

Thibault, Jacques Anatole Francois 1844-1924
See France, Anatole
See also CA 106; 127; DAM NOV; MTCW 1, 2

Thiele, Colin (Milton) 1920- .... **CLC 17**
See also CA 29-32R; CANR 12, 28, 53; CLR 27; MAICYA; SAAS 2; SATA 14, 72

Thomas, Audrey (Callahan) 1935- **CLC 7, 13, 37, 107; SSC 20**
See also AITN 2; CA 21-24R; CAAS 19; CANR 36, 58; DLB 60; MTCW 1

Thomas, D(onald) M(ichael) 1935- **CLC 13, 22, 31**
See also CA 61-64; CAAS 11; CANR 17, 45, 75; CDBLB 1960 to Present; DLB 40, 207; INT CANR-17; MTCW 1, 2

Thomas, Dylan (Marlais) 1914-1953 **TCLC 1, 8, 45; DA; DAB; DAC; DAM DRAM, MST, POET; PC 2; SSC 3; WLC**
See also CA 104; 120; CANR 65; CDBLB 1945-1960; DLB 13, 20, 139; MTCW 1, 2; SATA 60

Thomas, (Philip) Edward 1878-1917 ... **TCLC 10; DAM POET**
See also CA 106; 153; DLB 98

Thomas, Joyce Carol 1938- .... **CLC 35**
See also AAYA 12; BW 2, 3; CA 113; 116; CANR 48; CLR 19; DLB 33; INT 116; JRDA; MAICYA; MTCW 1, 2; SAAS 7; SATA 40, 78

Thomas, Lewis 1913-1993 .... **CLC 35**
See also CA 85-88; 143; CANR 38, 60; MTCW 1, 2

Thomas, M. Carey 1857-1935 .... **TCLC 89**

Thomas, Paul
See Mann, (Paul) Thomas

Thomas, Piri 1928- .... **CLC 17; HLCS 2**
See also CA 73-76; HW 1

Thomas, R(onald) S(tuart) 1913- **CLC 6, 13, 48; DAB; DAM POET**
See also CA 89-92; CAAS 4; CANR 30; CDBLB 1960 to Present; DLB 27; MTCW 1

Thomas, Ross (Elmore) 1926-1995 .... **CLC 39**
See also CA 33-36R; 150; CANR 22, 63

Thompson, Francis Clegg
See Mencken, H(enry) L(ouis)

Thompson, Francis Joseph 1859-1907 .. **TCLC 4**
See also CA 104; CDBLB 1890-1914; DLB 19

Thompson, Hunter S(tockton) 1939- **CLC 9, 17, 40, 104; DAM POP**
See also BEST 89:1; CA 17-20R; CANR 23, 46, 74, 77; DLB 185; MTCW 1, 2

Thompson, James Myers

Thompson, Jim (Myers)
See Thompson, Jim (Myers)

Thompson, Jim (Myers) 1906-1977(?) .. **CLC 69**
See also CA 140

Thompson, Judith .... **CLC 39**

Thomson, James 1700-1748 **LC 16, 29, 40; DAM POET**
See also DLB 95

Thomson, James 1834-1882 **NCLC 18; DAM POET**
See also DLB 35

Thoreau, Henry David 1817-1862 **NCLC 7, 21, 61; DA; DAB; DAC; DAM MST; WLC**
See also CDALB 1640-1865; DLB 1

Thornton, Hall
See Silverberg, Robert

Thucydides c. 455B.C.-399B.C. .... **CMLC 17**
See also DLB 176

Thurber, James (Grover) 1894-1961 . **CLC 5, 11, 25; DA; DAB; DAC; DAM DRAM, MST, NOV; SSC 1**
See also CA 73-76; CANR 17, 39; CDALB 1929-1941; DLB 4, 11, 22, 102; MAICYA; MTCW 1, 2; SATA 13

Thurman, Wallace (Henry) 1902-1934. **TCLC 6; BLC 3; DAM MULT**
See also BW 1, 3; CA 104; 124; CANR 81; DLB 51

Ticheburn, Cheviot
See Ainsworth, William Harrison

Tieck, (Johann) Ludwig 1773-1853 **NCLC 5, 46; SSC 31**
See also DLB 90

Tiger, Derry
See Ellison, Harlan (Jay)

Tilghman, Christopher 1948(?)- .... **CLC 65**
See also CA 159

Tillinghast, Richard (Williford) 1940- **CLC 29**
See also CA 29-32R; CAAS 23; CANR 26, 51

Timrod, Henry 1828-1867 .... **NCLC 25**
See also DLB 3

Tindall, Gillian (Elizabeth) 1938- .... **CLC 7**
See also CA 21-24R; CANR 11, 65

Tiptree, James, Jr. .... **CLC 48, 50**
See also Sheldon, Alice Hastings Bradley
See also DLB 8

Titmarsh, Michael Angelo
See Thackeray, William Makepeace

Tocqueville, Alexis (Charles Henri Maurice Clerel, Comte) de 1805-1859 .... **NCLC 7, 63**

Tolkien, J(ohn) R(onald) R(euel) 1892-1973 **C L C 1, 2, 3, 8, 12, 38; DA; DAB; DAC; DAM MST, NOV, POP; WLC**
See also AAYA 10; AITN 1; CA 17-18; 45-48; CANR 36; CAP 2; CDBLB 1914-1945; CLR 56; DLB 15, 160; JRDA; MAICYA; MTCW 1, 2; SATA 2, 32, 100; SATA-Obit 24

Toller, Ernst 1893-1939 .... **TCLC 10**
See also CA 107; DLB 124

Tolson, M. B.
See Tolson, Melvin B(eaunorus)

Tolson, Melvin B(eaunorus) 1898(?)-1966 .. **C L C 36, 105; BLC 3; DAM MULT, POET**
See also BW 1, 3; CA 124; 89-92; CANR 80; DLB 48, 76

Tolstoi, Aleksei Nikolaevich
See Tolstoy, Alexey Nikolaevich

Tolstoy, Alexey Nikolaevich 1882-1945 **TCLC 18**
See also CA 107; 158

Tolstoy, Count Leo
. See Tolstoy, Leo (Nikolaevich)

Tolstoy, Leo (Nikolaevich) 1828-1910 **TCLC 4, 11, 17, 28, 44, 79; DA; DAB; DAC; DAM MST, NOV; SSC 9, 30; WLC**
See also CA 104; 123; SATA 26

Tomasi di Lampedusa, Giuseppe 1896-1957
See Lampedusa, Giuseppe (Tomasi) di
See also CA 111

Tomlin, Lily .... **CLC 17**

See also Tomlin, Mary Jean

Tomlin, Mary Jean 1939(?)-
See Tomlin, Lily
See also CA 117

Tomlinson, (Alfred) Charles 1927- **CLC 2, 4, 6, 13, 45; DAM POET; PC 17**
See also CA 5-8R; CANR 33; DLB 40

Tomlinson, H(enry) M(ajor) 1873-1958 **TCLC 71**
See also CA 118; 161; DLB 36, 100, 195

Tonson, Jacob
See Bennett, (Enoch) Arnold

Toole, John Kennedy 1937-1969 ...... **CLC 19, 64**
See also CA 104; DLBY 81; MTCW 2

Toomer, Jean 1894-1967 **CLC 1, 4, 13, 22; BLC 3; DAM MULT; PC 7; SSC 1; WLCS**
See also BW 1; CA 85-88; CDALB 1917-1929; DLB 45, 51; MTCW 1, 2

Torley, Luke
See Blish, James (Benjamin)

Tornimparte, Alessandra
See Ginzburg, Natalia

Torre, Raoul della
See Mencken, H(enry) L(ouis)

Torrey, E(dwin) Fuller 1937- .... **CLC 34**
See also CA 119; CANR 71

Torsvan, Ben Traven
See Traven, B.

Torsvan, Benno Traven
See Traven, B.

Torsvan, Berick Traven
See Traven, B.

Torsvan, Berwick Traven
See Traven, B.

Torsvan, Bruno Traven
See Traven, B.

Torsvan, Traven
See Traven, B.

Tournier, Michel (Edouard) 1924- **CLC 6, 23, 36, 95**
See also CA 49-52; CANR 3, 36, 74; DLB 83; MTCW 1, 2; SATA 23

Tournimparte, Alessandra
See Ginzburg, Natalia

Towers, Ivar
See Kornbluth, C(yril) M.

Towne, Robert (Burton) 1936(?)- .... **CLC 87**
See also CA 108; DLB 44

Townsend, Sue .... **CLC 61**
See also Townsend, Susan Elaine
See also AAYA 28; SATA 55, 93; SATA-Brief 48

Townsend, Susan Elaine 1946-
See Townsend, Sue
See also CA 119; 127; CANR 65; DAB; DAC; DAM MST

Townshend, Peter (Dennis Blandford) 1945- **CLC 17, 42**
See also CA 107

Tozzi, Federigo 1883-1920 .... **TCLC 31**
See also CA 160

Traill, Catharine Parr 1802-1899 .... **NCLC 31**
See also DLB 99

Trakl, Georg 1887-1914 .... **TCLC 5; PC 20**
See also CA 104; 165; MTCW 2

Transtroemer, Tomas (Goesta) 1931- **CLC 52, 65; DAM POET**
See also CA 117; 129; CAAS 17

Transtromer, Tomas Gosta
See Transtroemer, Tomas (Goesta)

Traven, B. (?)-1969 .... **CLC 8, 11**
See also CA 19-20; 25-28R; CAP 2; DLB 9, 56; MTCW 1

Treitel, Jonathan 1959- .... **CLC 70**

Tremain, Rose 1943- .... **CLC 42**
See also CA 97-100; CANR 44; DLB 14

Tremblay, Michel 1942- **CLC 29, 102; DAC; DAM MST**
See also CA 116; 128; DLB 60; MTCW 1, 2

Van Doren, Mark 1894-1972 .... **CLC 6, 10**
    See also CA 1-4R; 37-40R; CANR 3; DLB 45;
        MTCW 1, 2
Van Druten, John (William) 1901-1957 **TCLC 2**
    See also CA 104; 161; DLB 10
Van Duyn, Mona (Jane) 1921-**CLC 3, 7, 63, 116;**
    DAM POET
    See also CA 9-12R; CANR 7, 38, 60; DLB 5
Van Dyne, Edith
    See Baum, L(yman) Frank
van Itallie, Jean-Claude 1936- .... **CLC 3**
    See also CA 45-48; CAAS 2; CANR 1, 48; DLB 7
van Ostaijen, Paul 1896-1928 .... **TCLC 33**
    See also CA 163
Van Peebles, Melvin 1932-**CLC 2, 20; DAM MULT**
    See also BW 2, 3; CA 85-88; CANR 27, 67
Vansittart, Peter 1920- .... **CLC 42**
    See also CA 1-4R; CANR 3, 49
Van Vechten, Carl 1880-1964 .... **CLC 33**
    See also CA 89-92; DLB 4, 9, 51
Van Vogt, A(lfred) E(lton) 1912- .... **CLC 1**
    See also CA 21-24R; CANR 28; DLB 8; SATA 14
Varda, Agnes 1928- .... **CLC 16**
    See also CA 116; 122
Vargas Llosa, (Jorge) Mario (Pedro) 1936- **C L C**
    3, 6, 9, 10, 15, 31, 42, 85; DA; DAB; DAC;
    DAM MST, MULT, NOV; HLC
    See also CA 73-76; CANR 18, 32, 42, 67; DLB
        145; HW 1, 2; MTCW 1, 2
Vasiliu, Gheorghe 1881-1957.
    See Bacovia, George
    See also CA 123
Vassa, Gustavus
    See Equiano, Olaudah
Vassilikos, Vassilis 1933- .... **CLC 4, 8**
    See also CA 81-84; CANR 75
Vaughan, Henry 1621-1695 .... **LC 27**
    See also DLB 131
Vaughn, Stephanie .... **CLC 62**
Vazov, Ivan (Minchov) 1850-1921 .... **TCLC 25**
    See also CA 121; 167; DLB 147
Veblen, Thorstein B(unde) 1857-1929 **TCLC 31**
    See also CA 115; 165
Vega, Lope de 1562-1635 .... **LC 23; HLCS 2**
Venison, Alfred
    See Pound, Ezra (Weston Loomis)
Verdi, Marie de
    See Mencken, H(enry) L(ouis)
Verdu, Matilde
    See Cela, Camilo Jose
Verga, Giovanni (Carmelo) 1840-1922 . **TCLC 3;**
    SSC 21
    See also CA 104; 123
Vergil 70B.C.-19B.C. **CMLC 9; DA; DAB; DAC;**
    DAM MST, POET; PC 12; WLCS
    See also Virgil
Verhaeren, Emile (Adolphe Gustave) 1855-1916
    TCLC 12
    See also CA 109
Verlaine, Paul (Marie) 1844-1896 ..**NCLC 2, 51;**
    DAM POET; PC 2
Verne, Jules (Gabriel) 1828-1905 ... **TCLC 6, 52**
    See also AAYA 16; CA 110; 131; DLB 123; JRDA;
        MAICYA; SATA 21
Very, Jones 1813-1880 .... **NCLC 9**
    See also DLB 1
Vesaas, Tarjei 1897-1970 .... **CLC 48**
    See also CA 29-32R
Vialis, Gaston
    See Simenon, Georges (Jacques Christian)
Vian, Boris 1920-1959 .... **TCLC 9**
    See also CA 106; 164; DLB 72; MTCW 2
Viaud, (Louis Marie) Julien 1850-1923
    See Loti, Pierre
    See also CA 107
Vicar, Henry
    See Felsen, Henry Gregor

Vicker, Angus
    See Felsen, Henry Gregor
Vidal, Gore 1925- **CLC 2, 4, 6, 8, 10, 22, 33, 72;**
    DAM NOV, POP
    See also AITN 1; BEST 90:2; CA 5-8R; CANR
        13, 45, 65; CDALBS; DLB 6, 152; INT CANR-
        13; MTCW 1, 2
Viereck, Peter (Robert Edwin) 1916- ..... **CLC 4**
    See also CA 1-4R; CANR 1, 47; DLB 5
Vigny, Alfred (Victor) de 1797-1863 ....**NCLC 7;**
    DAM POET; PC 26
    See also DLB 119, 192
Vilakazi, Benedict Wallet 1906-1947 . **TCLC 37**
    See also CA 168
Villa, Jose Garcia 1904-1997 .... **PC 22**
    See also CA 25-28R; CANR 12
Villaurrutia, Xavier 1903-1950 .... **TCLC 80**
    See also HW 1
Villiers de l'Isle Adam, Jean Marie Mathias
    Philippe Auguste, Comte de 1838-1889
    NCLC 3; SSC 14
    See also DLB 123
Villon, Francois 1431-1463(?) .... **PC 13**
    See also DLB 208
Vinci, Leonardo da 1452-1519 .... **LC 12**
Vine, Barbara .... **CLC 50**
    See also Rendell, Ruth (Barbara)
    See also BEST 90:4
Vinge, Joan (Carol) D(ennison) 1948- **CLC 30;**
    SSC 24
    See also CA 93-96; CANR 72; SATA 36
Violis, G.
    See Simenon, Georges (Jacques Christian)
Virgil 70B.C.-19B.C.
    See Vergil
    See also DLB 211
Visconti, Luchino 1906-1976 .... **CLC 16**
    See also CA 81-84; 65-68; CANR 39
Vittorini, Elio 1908-1966 .... **CLC 6, 9, 14**
    See also CA 133; 25-28R
Vivekananda, Swami 1863-1902 .... **TCLC 88**
Vizenor, Gerald Robert 1934- .. **CLC 103; DAM**
    MULT
    See also CA 13-16R; CAAS 22; CANR 5, 21, 44,
        67; DLB 175; MTCW 2; NNAL
Vizinczey, Stephen 1933- .... **CLC 40**
    See also CA 128; INT 128
Vliet, R(ussell) G(ordon) 1929-1984 ..... **CLC 22**
    See also CA 37-40R; 112; CANR 18
Vogau, Boris Andreyevich 1894-1937(?)
    See Pilnyak, Boris
    See also CA 123
Vogel, Paula A(nne) 1951- .... **CLC 76**
    See also CA 108
Voigt, Cynthia 1942- .... **CLC 30**
    See also AAYA 3, 30; CA 106; CANR 18, 37, 40;
        CLR 13, 48; INT CANR-18; JRDA; MAICYA;
        SATA 48, 79; SATA-Brief 33
Voigt, Ellen Bryant 1943- .... **CLC 54**
    See also CA 69-72; CANR 11, 29, 55; DLB 120
Voinovich, Vladimir (Nikolaevich) 1932-**CLC 10,**
    49
    See also CA 81-84; CAAS 12; CANR 33, 67;
        MTCW 1
Vollmann, William T. 1959-**CLC 89; DAM NOV,**
    POP
    See also CA 134; CANR 67; MTCW 2
Voloshinov, V. N.
    . See Bakhtin, Mikhail Mikhailovich
Voltaire 1694-1778**LC 14; DA; DAB; DAC; DAM**
    DRAM, MST; SSC 12; WLC
von Aschendrof, BaronIgnatz
    See Ford, Ford Madox
von Daeniken, Erich 1935- .... **CLC 30**
    See also AITN 1; CA 37-40R; CANR 17, 44
von Daniken, Erich
    See von Daeniken, Erich

von Heidenstam, (Carl Gustaf) Verner
    See Heidenstam, (Carl Gustaf) Verner von
von Heyse, Paul (Johann Ludwig)
    See Heyse, Paul (Johann Ludwig von)
von Hofmannsthal, Hugo
    See Hofmannsthal, Hugo von
von Horvath, Odon
    See Horvath, Oedoen von
von Horvath, Oedoen
    See Horvath, Oedoen von
von Liliencron, (Friedrich Adolf Axel) Detlev
    See Liliencron, (Friedrich Adolf Axel) Detlev von
Vonnegut, Kurt, Jr. 1922-**CLC 1, 2, 3, 4, 5, 8, 12,**
    22, 40, 60, 111; DA; DAB; DAC; DAM MST,
    NOV, POP; SSC 8; WLC
    See also AAYA 6; AITN 1; BEST 90:4; CA 1-4R;
        CANR 1, 25, 49, 75; CDALB 1968-1988; DLB
        2, 8, 152; DLBD 3; DLBY 80; MTCW 1, 2
Von Rachen, Kurt
    See Hubbard, L(afayette) Ron(ald)
von Rezzori (d'Arezzo), Gregor
    See Rezzori (d'Arezzo), Gregor von
von Sternberg, Josef
    See Sternberg, Josef von
Vorster, Gordon 1924- .... **CLC 34**
    See also CA 133
Vosce, Trudie
    See Ozick, Cynthia
Voznesensky, Andrei (Andreievich) 1933-**CLC 1,**
    15, 57; DAM POET
    See also CA 89-92; CANR 37; MTCW 1
Waddington, Miriam 1917- .... **CLC 28**
    See also CA 21-24R; CANR 12, 30; DLB 68
Wagman, Fredrica 1937- .... **CLC 7**
    See also CA 97-100; INT 97-100
Wagner, Linda W.
    See Wagner-Martin, Linda (C.)
Wagner, Linda Welshimer
    See Wagner-Martin, Linda (C.)
Wagner, Richard 1813-1883 .... **NCLC 9**
    See also DLB 129
Wagner-Martin, Linda (C.) 1936- .... **CLC 50**
    See also CA 159
Wagoner, David (Russell) 1926- ....**CLC 3, 5, 15**
    See also CA 1-4R; CAAS 3; CANR 2, 71; DLB 5;
        SATA 14
Wah, Fred(erick James) 1939- .... **CLC 44**
    See also CA 107; 141; DLB 60
Wahloo, Per 1926-1975 .... **CLC 7**
    See also CA 61-64; CANR 73
Wahloo, Peter
    See Wahloo, Per
Wain, John (Barrington) 1925-1994 . **CLC 2, 11,**
    15, 46
    See also CA 5-8R; 145; CAAS 4; CANR 23, 54;
        CDBLB 1960 to Present; DLB 15, 27, 139, 155;
        MTCW 1, 2
Wajda, Andrzej 1926- .... **CLC 16**
    See also CA 102
Wakefield, Dan 1932- .... **CLC 7**
    See also CA 21-24R; CAAS 7
Wakoski, Diane 1937-**CLC 2, 4, 7, 9, 11, 40; DAM**
    POET; PC 15
    See also CA 13-16R; CAAS 1; CANR 9, 60; DLB
        5; INT CANR-9; MTCW 2
Wakoski-Sherbell, Diane
    See Wakoski, Diane
Walcott, Derek (Alton) 1930-**CLC 2, 4, 9, 14, 25,**
    42, 67, 76; BLC 3; DAB; DAC; DAM MST,
    MULT, POET; DC 7
    See also BW 2; CA 89-92; CANR 26, 47, 75, 80;
        DLB 117; DLBY 81; MTCW 1, 2
Waldman, Anne (Lesley) 1945- .... **CLC 7**
    See also CA 37-40R; CAAS 17; CANR 34, 69;
        DLB 16
Waldo, E. Hunter
    See Sturgeon, Theodore (Hamilton)

Williams, Ben Ames 1889-1953 ..... TCLC 89
See also DLB 102
Williams, C(harles) K(enneth) 1936-CLC 33, 56;
DAM POET
See also CA 37-40R; CAAS 26; CANR 57; DLB 5
Williams, Charles
See Collier, James L(incoln)
Williams, Charles (Walter Stansby) 1886-1945
TCLC 1, 11
See also CA 104; 163; DLB 100, 153
Williams, (George) Emlyn 1905-1987 .. CLC 15;
DAM DRAM
See also CA 104; 123; CANR 36; DLB 10, 77;
MTCW 1
Williams, Hank 1923-1953 .... TCLC 81
Williams, Hugo 1942- .... CLC 42
See also CA 17-20R; CANR 45; DLB 40
Williams, J. Walker
See Wodehouse, P(elham) G(renville)
Williams, John A(lfred) 1925-CLC 5, 13; BLC 3;
DAM MULT
See also BW 2, 3; CA 53-56; CAAS 3; CANR 6,
26, 51; DLB 2, 33; INT CANR-6
Williams, Jonathan (Chamberlain) 1929-CLC 13
See also CA 9-12R; CAAS 12; CANR 8; DLB 5
Williams, Joy 1944- .... CLC 31
See also CA 41-44R; CANR 22, 48
Williams, Norman 1952- .... CLC 39
See also CA 118
Williams, Sherley Anne 1944- CLC 89; BLC 3;
DAM MULT, POET
See also BW 2, 3; CA 73-76; CANR 25; DLB 41;
INT CANR-25; SATA 78
Williams, Shirley
See Williams, Sherley Anne
Williams, Tennessee 1911-1983CLC 1, 2, 5, 7, 8,
11, 15, 19, 30, 39, 45, 71, 111; DA; DAB;
DAC; DAM DRAM, MST, DC 4; WLC
See also AITN 1, 2; CA 5-8R; 108; CABS 3;
CANR 31; CDALB 1941-1968; DLB 7; DLBD
4; DLBY 83; MTCW 1, 2
Williams, Thomas (Alonzo) 1926-1990 . CLC 14
See also CA 1-4R; 132; CANR 2
Williams, William C.
See Williams, William Carlos
Williams, William Carlos 1883-1963CLC 1, 2, 5,
9, 13, 22, 42, 67; DA; DAB; DAC; DAM MST,
POET; PC 7; SSC 31
See also CA 89-92; CANR 34; CDALB 1917-1929;
DLB 4, 16, 54, 86; MTCW 1, 2
Williamson, David (Keith) 1942- .... CLC 56
See also CA 103; CANR 41
Williamson, Ellen Douglas 1905-1984
See Douglas, Ellen
See also CA 17-20R; 114; CANR 39
Williamson, Jack .... CLC 29
See also Williamson, John Stewart
See also CAAS 8; DLB 8
Williamson, John Stewart 1908-
See Williamson, Jack
See also CA 17-20R; CANR 23, 70
Willie, Frederick
See Lovecraft, H(oward) P(hillips)
Willingham, Calder (Baynard, Jr.) 1922-1995
CLC 5, 51
See also CA 5-8R; 147; CANR 3; DLB 2, 44;
MTCW 1
Willis, Charles
See Clarke, Arthur C(harles)
Willis, Fingal O'Flahertie
See Wilde, Oscar
Willy
See Colette, (Sidonie-Gabrielle)
Willy, Colette
See Colette, (Sidonie-Gabrielle)
Wilson, A(ndrew) N(orman) 1950- .... CLC 33
See also CA 112; 122; DLB 14, 155, 194; MTCW

2
Wilson, Angus (Frank Johnstone) 1913-1991
CLC 2, 3, 5, 25, 34; SSC 21
See also CA 5-8R; 134; CANR 21; DLB 15, 139,
155; MTCW 1, 2
Wilson, August 1945-CLC 39, 50, 63, 118; BLC
3; DA; DAB; DAC; DAM DRAM, MST,
MULT; DC 2; WLCS
See also AAYA 16; BW 2, 3; CA 115; 122; CANR
42, 54, 76; MTCW 1, 2
Wilson, Brian 1942- .... CLC 12
Wilson, Colin 1931- .... CLC 3, 14
See also CA 1-4R; CAAS 5; CANR 1, 22, 33, 77;
DLB 14, 194; MTCW 1
Wilson, Dirk
See Pohl, Frederik
Wilson, Edmund 1895-1972 ... CLC 1, 2, 3, 8, 24
See also CA 1-4R; 37-40R; CANR 1, 46; DLB 63;
MTCW 1, 2
Wilson, Ethel Davis (Bryant) 1888(?)-1980 C L C
13; DAC; DAM POET
See also CA 102; DLB 68; MTCW 1
Wilson, John 1785-1854 .... NCLC 5
Wilson, John (Anthony) Burgess 1917-1993
See Burgess, Anthony
See also CA 1-4R; 143; CANR 2, 46; DAC; DAM
NOV; MTCW 1, 2
Wilson, Lanford 1937- CLC 7, 14, 36; DAM
DRAM
See also CA 17-20R; CABS 3; CANR 45; DLB 7
Wilson, Robert M. 1944- .... CLC 7, 9
See also CA 49-52; CANR 2, 41; MTCW 1
Wilson, Robert McLiam 1964- .... CLC 59
See also CA 132
Wilson, Sloan 1920- .... CLC 32
See also CA 1-4R; CANR 1, 44
Wilson, Snoo 1948- .... CLC 33
See also CA 69-72
Wilson, William S(mith) 1932- .... CLC 49
See also CA 81-84
Wilson, (Thomas) Woodrow 1856-1924TCLC 79
See also CA 166; DLB 47
Winchilsea, Anne (Kingsmill) Finch Counte 1661-
1720
See Finch, Anne
Windham, Basil
See Wodehouse, P(elham) G(renville)
Wingrove, David (John) 1954- .... CLC 68
See also CA 133
Winnemucca, Sarah 1844-1891 .... NCLC 79
Wintergreen, Jane
See Duncan, Sara Jeannette
Winters, Janet Lewis .... CLC 41
See also Lewis, Janet
See also DLBY 87
Winters, (Arthur) Yvor 1900-1968 . CLC 4, 8, 32
See also CA 11-12; 25-28R; CAP 1; DLB 48;
MTCW 1
Winterson, Jeanette 1959-. CLC 64; DAM POP
See also CA 136; CANR 58; DLB 207; MTCW 2
Winthrop, John 1588-1649 .... LC 31
See also DLB 24, 30
Wirth, Louis 1897-1952 .... TCLC 92
Wiseman, Frederick 1930- .... CLC 20
See also CA 159
Wister, Owen 1860-1938 .... TCLC 21
See also CA 108; 162; DLB 9, 78, 186; SATA 62
Witkacy
See Witkiewicz, Stanislaw Ignacy
Witkiewicz, Stanislaw Ignacy 1885-1939TCLC 8
See also CA 105; 162
Wittgenstein, Ludwig (Josef Johann) 1889-1951
TCLC 59
See also CA 113; 164; MTCW 2
Wittig, Monique 1935(?)- .... CLC 22
See also CA 116; 135; DLB 83
Wittlin, Jozef 1896-1976 .... CLC 25

See also CA 49-52; 65-68; CANR 3
Wodehouse, P(elham) G(renville) 1881-1975CLC
1, 2, 5, 10, 22; DAB; DAC; DAM NOV; SSC
2
See also AITN 2; CA 45-48; 57-60; CANR 3, 33;
CDBLB 1914-1945; DLB 34, 162; MTCW 1, 2;
SATA 22
Woiwode, L.
See Woiwode, Larry (Alfred)
Woiwode, Larry (Alfred) 1941- .... CLC 6, 10
See also CA 73-76; CANR 16; DLB 6; INT CANR-
16
Wojciechowska, Maia (Teresa) 1927- .. CLC 26
See also AAYA 8; CA 9-12R; CANR 4, 41; CLR
1; JRDA; MAICYA; SAAS 1; SATA 1, 28, 83;
SATA-Essay 104
Wolf, Christa 1929- .... CLC 14, 29, 58
See also CA 85-88; CANR 45; DLB 75; MTCW 1
Wolfe, Gene (Rodman) 1931-CLC 25; DAM POP
See also CA 57-60; CAAS 9; CANR 6, 32, 60;
DLB 8; MTCW 2
Wolfe, George C. 1954- .... CLC 49; BLCS
See also CA 149
Wolfe, Thomas (Clayton) 1900-1938TCLC 4, 13,
29, 61; DA; DAB; DAC; DAM MST, NOV;
SSC 33; WLC
See also CA 104; 132; CDALB 1929-1941;
DLB 9, 102; DLBD 2, 16; DLBY 85, 97;
MTCW 1, 2
Wolfe, Thomas Kennerly, Jr. 1930-
See Wolfe, Tom
See also CA 13-16R; CANR 9, 33, 70; DAM POP;
DLB 185; INT CANR-9; MTCW 1, 2
Wolfe, Tom .... CLC 1, 2, 9, 15, 35, 51
See also Wolfe, Thomas Kennerly, Jr.
See also AAYA 8; AITN 2; BEST 89:1; DLB 152
Wolff, Geoffrey (Ansell) 1937- .... CLC 41
See also CA 29-32R; CANR 29, 43, 78
Wolff, Sonia
See Levitin, Sonia (Wolff)
Wolff, Tobias (Jonathan Ansell) 1945-CLC 39, 64
See also AAYA 16; BEST 90:2; CA 114; 117;
CAAS 22; CANR 54, 76; DLB 130; INT 117;
MTCW 2
Wolfram von Eschenbach c. 1170-c. 1220CMLC 5
See also DLB 138
Wolitzer, Hilma 1930- .... CLC 17
See also CA 65-68; CANR 18, 40; INT CANR-18;
SATA 31
Wollstonecraft, Mary 1759-1797 .... LC 5, 50
See also CDBLB 1789-1832; DLB 39, 104, 158
Wonder, Stevie .... CLC 12
See also Morris, Steveland Judkins
Wong, Jade Snow 1922- .... CLC 17
See also CA 109
Woodberry, George Edward 1855-1930 TCLC 73
See also CA 165; DLB 71, 103
Woodcott, Keith
See Brunner, John (Kilian Houston)
Woodruff, Robert W.
See Mencken, H(enry) L(ouis)
Woolf, (Adeline) Virginia 1882-1941 TCLC 1, 5,
20, 43, 56; DA; DAB; DAC; DAM MST,
NOV; SSC 7; WLC
See also Woolf, Virginia Adeline
See also CA 104; 130; CANR 64; CDBLB 1914-
1945; DLB 36, 100, 162; DLBD 10; MTCW 1
Woolf, Virginia Adeline
See Woolf, (Adeline) Virginia
See also MTCW 2
Woollcott, Alexander (Humphreys) 1887-1943
TCLC 5
See also CA 105; 161; DLB 29
Woolrich, Cornell 1903-1968 .... CLC 77
See also Hopley-Woolrich, Cornell George
Wordsworth, Dorothy 1771-1855 .... NCLC 25
See also DLB 107

Literary Criticism Series
Cumulative Topic Index

This index lists all topic entries in Gale's *Classical and Medieval Literature Criticism, Contemporary Literary Criticism, Literature Criticism from 1400 to 1800, Nineteenth-Century Literature Criticism,* and *Twentieth-Century Literary Criticism.*

Topic Index

Twentieth-Century Literary Criticism
Cumulative Nationality Index

Nationality Index

Weber, Max **69**
Wedekind, (Benjamin) Frank(lin) **7**
Wiene, Robert **56**

GHANIAN
Casely-Hayford, J(oseph) E(phraim) **24**

GREEK
Cavafy, C(onstantine) P(eter) · **2, 7**
Kazantzakis, Nikos **2, 5, 33**
Palamas, Kostes **5**
Papadiamantis, Alexandros **29**
Sikelianos, Angelos **39**

HAITIAN
Roumain, Jacques (Jean Baptiste) **19**

HUNGARIAN
Ady, Endre **11**
Babits, Mihaly **14**
Csath, Geza **13**
Herzl, Theodor **36**
Horvath, Oedoen von **45**
Jozsef, Attila **22**
Karinthy, Frigyes **47**
Mikszath, Kalman **31**
Molnar, Ferenc **20**
Moricz, Zsigmond **33**
Radnoti, Miklos **16**

ICELANDIC
Sigurjonsson, Johann **27**

INDIAN
Chatterji, Saratchandra **13**
Dasgupta, Surendranath **81**
Gandhi, Mohandas Karamchand **59**
Ghose, Aurabinda **63**
Iqbal, Muhammad **28**
Naidu, Sarojini **80**
Premchand **21**
Ramana Maharshi **84**
Tagore, Rabindranath **3, 53**
Vivekananda, Swami **88**

INDONESIAN
Anwar, Chairil **22**

IRANIAN
Hedayat, Sadeq **21**

IRISH
A.E. **3, 10**
Baker, Jean H. **3, 10**
Cary, (Arthur) Joyce (Lunel) **1, 29**
Dunsany, Lord **2, 59**
Gogarty, Oliver St. John **15**
Gregory, Isabella Augusta (Persse) **1**
Harris, Frank **24**
Joyce, James (Augustine Aloysius) **3, 8, 16, 35, 52**
Ledwidge, Francis **23**
Martin, Violet Florence **51**
Moore, George Augustus **7**
O'Grady, Standish (James) **5**
Shaw, Bernard **45**
Shaw, George Bernard **3, 9, 21**
Somerville, Edith **51**
Stephens, James **4**
Stoker, Bram **8**
Synge, (Edmund) J(ohn) M(illington) **6, 37**
Tynan, Katharine **3**
Wilde, Oscar **1, 8, 23, 41**

Yeats, William Butler **1, 11, 18, 31, 93**

ITALIAN
Alvaro, Corrado **60**
Betti, Ugo **5**
Brancati, Vitaliano **12**
Campana, Dino **20**
Carducci, Giosue (Alessandro Giuseppe) **32**
Croce, Benedetto **37**
D'Annunzio, Gabriele **6, 40**
Deledda, Grazia (Cosima) **23**
Giacosa, Giuseppe **7**
Jovine, Francesco **79**
Lampedusa, Giuseppe (Tomasi) di **13**
Malaparte, Curzio **52**
Marinetti, Filippo Tommaso **10**
Mosca, Gaetano **75**
Papini, Giovanni **22**
Pareto, Vilfredo **69**
Pascoli, Giovanni **45**
Pavese, Cesare **3**
Pirandello, Luigi **4, 29**
Saba, Umberto **33**
Svevo, Italo **2, 35**
Tozzi, Federigo **31**
Verga, Giovanni (Carmelo) **3**

·JAMAICAN
De Lisser, H(erbert) G(eorge) **12**
Garvey, Marcus (Moziah Jr.) **41**
Mais, Roger **8**
McKay, Claude **7, 41**
Redcam, Tom **25**

JAPANESE
Akutagawa, Ryunosuke **16**
Dazai Osamu **11**
Futabatei, Shimei **44**
Hagiwara Sakutaro **60**
Hayashi, Fumiko **27**
Ishikawa, Takuboku **15**
Masaoka Shiki **18**
Miyamoto, (Chujo) Yuriko **37**
Miyazawa, Kenji **76**
Mizoguchi, Kenji **72**
Nagai Kafu **51**
Natsume, Soseki **2, 10**
Nishida, Kitaro **83**
Noguchi, Yone **80**
Rohan, Koda **22**
Santoka, Taneda **72**
Shimazaki Toson **5**
Yokomitsu Riichi **47**
Yosano Akiko **59**

LATVIAN
Rainis, Janis **29**

LEBANESE
Gibran, Kahlil **1, 9**

LESOTHAN
Mofolo, Thomas (Mokopu) **22**

LITHUANIAN
Kreve (Mickevicius), Vincas **27**

MEXICAN
Azuela, Mariano **3**
Gamboa, Federico **36**
Gonzalez Martinez, Enrique **72**
Nervo, (Jose) Amado (Ruiz de) **11**
Reyes, Alfonso **33**

Romero, Jose Ruben **14**
Villaurrutia, Xavier **80**

NEPALI
Devkota, Laxmiprasad **23**

NEW ZEALANDER
Mander, (Mary) Jane **31**
Mansfield, Katherine **2, 8, 39**

NICARAGUAN
Dario, Ruben **4**

NORWEGIAN
Bjoernson, Bjoernstjerne (Martinius) **7, 37**
Bojer, Johan **64**
Grieg, (Johan) Nordahl (Brun) **10**
Hamsun, Knut **2, 14, 49**
Ibsen, Henrik (Johan) **2, 8, 16, 37, 52**
Kielland, Alexander Lange **5**
Lie, Jonas (Lauritz Idemil) **5**
Obstfelder, Sigbjoern **23**
Skram, Amalie (Bertha) **25**
Undset, Sigrid **3**

PAKISTANI
Iqbal, Muhammad **28**

PERUVIAN
Palma, Ricardo **29**
Vallejo, Cesar (Abraham) **3, 56**

POLISH
Asch, Sholem **3**
Borowski, Tadeusz **9**
Conrad, Joseph **1, 6, 13, 25, 43, 57**
Peretz, Isaac Loeb **16**
Prus, Boleslaw **48**
Przybyszewski, Stanislaw **36**
Reymont, Wladyslaw (Stanislaw) **5**
Schulz, Bruno **5, 51**
Sienkiewicz, Henryk (Adam Alexander Pius) **3**
Singer, Israel Joshua **33**
Witkiewicz, Stanislaw Ignacy **8**

PORTUGUESE
Pessoa, Fernando (Antonio Nogueira) **27**
Sa-Carniero, Mario de **83**

PUERTO RICAN
Hostos (y Bonilla), Eugenio Maria de **24**

ROMANIAN
Bacovia, George **24**
Caragiale, Ion Luca **76**
Rebreanu, Liviu **28**

RUSSIAN
Aldanov, Mark (Alexandrovich) **23**
Andreyev, Leonid (Nikolaevich) **3**
Annensky, Innokenty (Fyodorovich) **14**
Artsybashev, Mikhail (Petrovich) **31**
Babel, Isaak (Emmanuilovich) **2, 13**
Bagritsky, Eduard **60**
Balmont, Konstantin (Dmitriyevich) **11**
Bely, Andrey **7**
Berdyaev, Nikolai (Aleksandrovich) **67**
Bergelson, David **81**
Blok, Alexander (Alexandrovich) **5**
Bryusov, Valery Yakovlevich **10**
Bulgakov, Mikhail (Afanas'evich) **2, 16**
Bulgya, Alexander Alexandrovich **53**
Bunin, Ivan Alexeyevich **6**

Nationality Index

TCLC-92 Title Index